CINEMA: A Critical Dictionary

Volume Two

KINUGASA to ZANUSSI

CINEMA
A Critical Dictionary

The Major Film-makers

Volume Two

KINUGASA to ZANUSSI

Edited by **Richard Roud**

The Viking Press
New York

© Martin Secker & Warburg 1980
Published in England by Martin Secker & Warburg Ltd
Published in the USA and Canada by The Viking Press

Printed in Great Britain

Filmset in Monophoto Plantin

Library of Congress Cataloging in Publication Data
Main entry under title:
Cinema: a critical dictionary
includes index.
1. Moving-pictures—Dictionaries.—1. Roud, Richard.
PN1993.45.C5   791.43′03   79–21892
ISBN 0–670 22257–7 (v2)

TEINOSUKE KINUGASA

John Gillett

Teinosuke Kinugasa (born 1896) has made over 100 films, most of which are completely unknown in the West. He began as an actor and female impersonator at a time when the Japanese cinema did not employ actresses. He started directing in 1922, and the two examples of his silent work known outside Japan (together with a few other examples by his contemporaries) suggest that the Japanese film of the 20s was, in some respects, far in advance of the West. *Kurutta Ippeiji* (*A Page of Madness*, 1926) and *Jujiro* (*Crossways*, 1928) are both dark, claustrophobic works depicting mental anguish and a kind of European *Angst*—although Kinugasa is said not to have seen any German expressionist films at this time. Both display an immense flair for atmosphere and psychological truth achieved through richly textured imagery and a camera which moves with effortless precision. In the former film, the depiction of the insane asylum often takes on a startling, surrealist quality, and the bawdy, violent streets of the Yoshiwara district in *Crossways* have a Sternberg-like shine and richness. After a visit to Russia (where he met Eisenstein) and Germany, Kinugasa returned to a busy career, as writer and director, in the Japanese sound cinema. In 1953 he made *Jigokumon* (*Gate of Hell*), basically a rather routine period piece, but remarkable as one of the earliest Japanese colour films. The few later films seen appear somewhat conventional and sentimentalized; but this report has, of necessity, to be an interim one until his long career can be seen in clearer perspective. One suspects that Kinugasa's major work may then stand alongside the best of Ozu, Mizoguchi, Gosho, Toyoda, Naruse, Ito and Uchida as representing the first generation of Japanese film-makers, all of whom helped give the Japanese cinema its distinctive tone and signature in its formative years.

I do not share Gillett's and many others' enthusiasm for what little of Kinugasa's work I have seen. And I find it hard to believe that Kinugasa had not seen any German expressionist films before making his in any case overrated curiosity *A Page of Madness*.

DIMITRI KIRSANOFF

P. Adams Sitney

The histories of the cinema have so far been economic in emphasis. We continue to consider the development of the star system, the emergence of the feature film and the characteristics of national schools as the important aspects of cinema history. When the formal histories of cinema are written, and they will be, many of the luminaries of our present chronicles will fade away, and other, now obscure, innovators will assume new magnitude. One such figure, now relegated to the footnotes of history because he was never a commercial success, and did not fit into any of the standard categories, is Dimitri Kirsanoff.

He came to Paris after the Russian Revolution as a musician. Independently, he produced several silent films. With modest support he made *Rapt* (1933), one of the most inventive sound films of the early 30s. Then, defeated by the economic pitfalls of his métier, he continued to produce a string of mediocre commercial films and an occasional brilliant short. Unlike Lang, L'Herbier or Murnau, Kirsanoff was unable to find a middle way between his vision and the commercial market. We must dismiss everything he did for money; and we must value what he made as art: *Ménilmontant* (1924), his masterpiece, *Brumes d'Automne* (1928), *Rapt*, *Deux Amis* (1946) and *Arrière-Saison* (1951).

Kirsanoff opens up a tradition in the French narrative film which culminates in the work of Bresson and Hanoun today. They are all artists who simultaneously dissect the rhetoric of cinematic story-telling and elliptically propel their stories forward. Their tradition coincides with an older and even stronger tradition in French literature which began in 1852 when Gustave Flaubert wrote to Louise Collet: 'What seems beautiful to me, what I should like to write, is a book about nothing, a book dependent on nothing external, which would be held together by the strength of its style, just as the earth, suspended in the void, depends on nothing external for its support; a book which would have almost no subject, or at least in which

Nadia Sibirskaya in *Ménilmontant*: 'there is not a moment in the film when metaphor does not merge with narrative'.

the subject would be almost invisible, if such a thing is possible.'

Ménilmontant combines several styles without seeming disjointed: elliptical montage, stream of consciousness and naturalistic mimesis. The incessant use of ellipsis, synecdoche and *hysteron proteron* makes the film both difficult to follow on first viewing and rewarding to return to. No other narrative, before or since, has equalled its opening in ambiguity and immediate horror. A doorknob turns vigorously; the door curtain is ripped as two people rush from the house, followed by a man who spots an axe and brutally chops them to death. The murder occurs in a few seconds: primarily in close-ups with dramatic use of offscreen space. We never learn the murderer's identity or his motive. The montage rests first on the thrown-away axe; then on the hearth continuing to burn. A series of shots, moving closer to the eyes of the heroine, makes it clear to us that she is one of the two daughters of the murdered couple, and only through her reaction do we share her horror at finding a crowd

around her slain parents.

Time passes unevenly in *Ménilmontant*. Events occur in ultra-rapid montage, as at the opening, or slowly, through actionless dissolves, as in the next sequence, where we see the two daughters mourning at their parents' grave, as weeds grow and eventually the monument crumbles. The camera alternates between static compositions and dynamic movements. The fixed shot of the girls, dissolving in stages on their walk down the road, reminiscent of the end of so many of Chaplin's short films, is immediately followed by a moving camera view, with layers of superimpositions of Paris. Typically, Kirsanoff does two things with his introduction of Paris. He shows us where the girls have gone, but he also jumps ahead in time, so that we do not see their arrival, but a typical day as they leave work at noon. The wildness of the movement, the sounds suggested by clocks striking noon and the wheels and horns of cars, create the impression of Paris for provincial girls newly arrived in the city; but the end of the sequence makes us realize that they have already been assimilated to Parisian life. Kirsanoff likes to keep the spectator behind the action. One of his favourite cinematic tropes is to present a sequence which we experience first in one way; then, because of the way it ends, we re-experience it retrospectively as a completely different scene or as in a different time. It has the effect of suddenly jolting our sense of what is present and what is past.

The most effective employment of this occurs just after the heroine is seduced for the first time. We see her walking along the Seine, apparently at dawn after having left her lover's room. She seems to be considering suicide, but soon we realize that a time interval has elapsed and her melancholy is a result of her waiting in vain for her lover to keep a subsequent rendezvous.

There is not a moment in the entire film when metaphor does not merge with narrative, when montage, superimposition or dissolves do not reflect the thoughts of the protagonists, at the same time recording their action. Most indirect, yet most effective of all is the montage of associations at the point at which the heroine considers suicide. The images flash back to her childhood as she plays in the woods. But the clothes she wears, the same as those she wore on the day of her parents' murder, evoke that bloody memory throughout this idyllic scene. No one went further than Kirsanoff in the silent period towards defining the relation between montage and the human mind.

The sparest of Kirsanoff's narratives, *Brumes d'Automne*, elaborates a single metaphor which compares the foggy, rainy weather of autumn with the mind of a young woman. From the shadow of a man leaving her door and a scene of burning letters we surmise that he has just terminated their romance, yet all explicit details are absent. In fact, his tolerance of ambiguity was central to Kirsanoff's cinematic sense; all his serious films derive a tension from the interaction between explicit action and the uncertainty of motivation, the past and the future.

Even *Rapt*, his most novelistic film, deriving from Benjamin Fondane's screen adaptation of Ramuz's *La Séparation des Races*, leaves unclear the attitude of the central character. The particular distinction of *Rapt* lies in its soundtrack. Collaborating with Honegger and Hoerée, Kirsanoff established musical motifs as counterparts to the visual rhythms and themes. Particularly interesting are the moments in which natural and artificial sounds merge: as when the sounds of the townswomen at their washing in the stream blend with a series of piano chords. Bits of sound from an actual storm are repeated, fragmented and even played backwards on the soundtrack to create an abstracted and artificial storm. Like Alban Berg in *Wozzeck*, Honegger chose to emphasize a number of narrative units in the film by using different classical forms with each scene: a fugue with the chase of a goat and dog, or a chorale during the abduction of the heroine. Numerous experiments were open to musicians only through film, since magnetic tape was not yet available.

The very beautiful *Deux Amis* and *Arrière-Saison*, films in which Kirsanoff turned to the ambience of provincial life, as Jean Epstein eventually turned to Brittany, are disappointing after the brilliant triumphs of *Ménilmontant* and *Rapt*. *Deux Amis* draws upon Kirsanoff's gift as a mimetic artist, elaborating the duel of two friends, based upon a story by Maupassant. *Arrière-Saison* distinguishes itself with the film-maker's even greater gift for analytical mimesis. In this, his last serious work, he returned to a theme which was crucial to the cinema of his origins: the Bovaryesque meditation as the basis for cinematic subjectivity had also been the theme of Germaine Dulac's two best films, *La Souriante Madame Beudet* and *Invitation au Voyage*.

Born in 1899, Kirsanoff died in 1957, having long outlived the period of his greatness. Ironically, his last film was a dud called *Miss Catastrophe* (1956).

GRIGORI KOZINTSEV AND LEONID TRAUBERG
David Robinson

Grigori Mikhailovich Kozintsev (1905–73) and Leonid Zakharovich Trauberg (born 1902) were *par excellence* children of the Soviet Revolution. Kozintsev's autobiography recalls movingly the strange and heady atmosphere of his schooldays in Kiev during the Civil War. 'Our teachers de-

scribed the flora and fauna of Africa, explained the conjugation of Latin verbs; and
meanwhile machine-guns chattered in the
suburbs.' Corpses lay in the ditches; troops
of both sides galloped through the city; black
marketeers were pilloried; by night, bandits
roamed, trying to break down the doors of
houses. The boy Kozintsev absorbed these
impressions at the same time as he was
discovering Gogol and Dumas, Mayakovsky
and Stravinsky, and the revolutions that were
taking place in the plastic arts.

In these confused but stirring times he
began to draw and paint and write. After
school he went to evening classes given by
Alexandra Exter. He was taken on by an agit-
train, and was allowed to decorate a wagon
and mount an agit-play all by himself at the
age of fifteen. He became assistant to the
stage designer, Isaac Rubinovitch, but was
soon himself designing in collaboration with
a slightly older boy, Sergei Yutkevitch. 'The
revolution had made way for the young,'
recalled Yutkevitch; 'an entire generation
had disappeared. Our elders had been
dispersed throughout the country, had perished in the Civil War, or had left Russia.
Hence the Republic lacked a clear organization, lacked people, and our way in was
easy—the country wanted us to work, the
country needed people in every department
of culture.' In next to no time Kozintsev and
Yutkevitch had been given a theatre and
had recruited other youthful collaborators.
Influenced above all by the god of those
times, Vladimir Mayakovsky, they launched
themselves into every kind of extravagance in
their productions, introducing haphazardly
into their theatre elements of circus, music hall,
puppet stage and even cinema—anything
so long as the old and the traditional
and the accepted might be overthrown.

Around 1921 Kozintsev arrived in Petrograd. 'My only baggage was a pillow-case,
containing a shirt, a book of Mayakovsky
poems and a series of reproductions of
Picasso paintings.' The city was in the grip of
famine and of an intense, unprecedented
intellectual excitement. 'No one bothered
about cold or hunger. Life seemed marvellously interesting, and there was no doubt at
all that this moment marked the coming of a
new era, the era of art ... as bold as the
workers' power itself, as pitiless towards the

past as the Revolution.' For a while he
worked in Nathan Altman's studio, before
joining up with Trauberg, the director Georgii Kryjitski, Alexei Kapler and Yutkevitch
(who had meanwhile been in Moscow) to
form FEX—'The Factory of the Eccentric
Actor'. The notion of a 'factory' rather than a
theatre was very much of the times; while 'the
word "Eccentric" seemed to us peculiarly
expressive'. The Factory presented a
few extravagantly experimental stage productions. Kozintsev and Yutkevitch exhibited
their collages at the celebrated Left Stream
Exhibition of 1922. Then the group
broke up. 'Trauberg and myself went from
bad to worse till we landed up in the cinema
... Ultimately it was clear that all our tendencies and our instincts drew us to this art.'

The two youngsters had a scenario accepted by Sevzapkino. Kozintsev describes
the scenario of *Pokhozdeniya Oktyabrini* (*The
Adventures of Oktyabrina*, 1924), which has
all the hallmarks of Eccentricism: 'a sort of
propaganda film-poster: the influence of the
propaganda plays and the Rosta windows
shows clearly in every moment of the film.
The capitalistic shark has been introduced to
Petrograd and demands repayment of the
Tsarist debts by the peasants and workers.
The shark wore a silk hat; he was played by
Sergei Martinson (whose first role it was)
with no make-up apart from enormous black
velvet eyebrows. Hearing of the arrival of
Coolidge Curzonovitch Poincaré (the name
of the shark), the NEP-man, in a fashionable
check suit, lets himself go. The plots of this
duo are foiled by the young komsomol girl
Oktyabrina (played by the dancer Z. Tarakhovskaia). The young girl, wearing a felt hat
with a Red Army star, puts things to rights,
and continues the struggle against survivals
of the past. All these characters seemed directly descended from the propaganda lorry
which entertained the populace at the May
Day parade. It was all rather disconnected,
but galloped along on the screen, full of dizzying abridgements of the story and shock
cuts. And when the narrative got stuck, letters would appear on the screen: dancing
about in the manner of cartoon films, they
would group themselves into words, forming
slogans that were then familiar.'

The young directors were undeterred by
technical limitations. They had only one old

and unreliable Pathé camera; but 'this prehistoric beast seemed to us a miracle. We could hoist its three feet to the highest point in the town and bend its glass eye downwards. We could bury it or stride over it. The handle could turn faster or slower; we could back the film and superimpose one, two (five, ten) other images. The discomfort of the places in which we chose to shoot was to play an important part in our destiny. The director assigned to the film, [B. V.] Tchaikovski, listened sympathetically to our ideas but when he discovered that the first shot was to be made on the sloping roof of a very tall building, he declined to be present at the start of shooting. As our next viewpoint was the spire of the Admiralty building, shooting from just below the weather-vane, we found ourselves working alone, without supervision.'

Like *The Adventures of Oktyabrina*, the team's second effort, *Mishki protiv Yudenicha* (*Mishka against Yudenich*, 1925) has long been unavailable; and again we have only the eye-witness recollections of a contemporary, Sergei Gerassimov, who played in the film: '*Mishka against Yudenich* was an improbable sort of muddle in which it was impossible to know what was what. The whole scenario was written on a little scrap of paper; everything had to be improvised in the course of shooting, and we might—had to—do anything that came into our heads. This adventure passed all imagining, and, when I think back to it, I tell myself that only our robust good health saved us from certain death. Regardless of the weather, we performed clad only in football shorts. We leapt from signals on to moving trains; we galloped along railway tracks, breaking the legs of the horses—and our own. It was an accumulation of the most audacious tricks, dizzy falls, the maddest inventions. The film was presented in a very small theatre, before a public that was utterly dumbfounded. Since then no one has looked at it again.'

By this time Trauberg was twenty-three, Kozintsev just twenty, Gerassimov nineteen. Apart from filming they were organizing classes and exercises in their studio. The group was absorbing the oddly assorted influences of American adventure and comedy films and the theatrical discoveries of Meyerhold, an incalculable influence upon the Soviet cinema of the period. *Chyortovo*

Koleso (*The Devil's Wheel*, 1926), from all accounts, demonstrated that they had also absorbed fully the lessons to be learnt from the first, and in every sense revolutionary, films of Eisenstein: *Strike* and *The Battleship Potemkin*. The story tells of a sailor from the *Aurora* who lingers too long ashore with his girl in a fairground and so becomes an unwitting deserter, but vindicates himself by routing a gang of criminals. There are odd anticipations of Hitchcock in the scenes set in the fairground, and in the memory man who turns out to be associated with the gang.

Kozintsev and Trauberg were by this time associated with the cameraman Andrei Moskvin, who was to photograph all their work. (In later years he worked with Eisenstein on *Ivan the Terrible* and Joseph Heifets on *The Lady with the Little Dog*.) Moskvin's dramatic photography, evidently inspired by German Expressionism, came into its own in the group's next film, *Shinel* (*The Overcoat*, also known as *The Cloak*, 1926). Gogol's grotesques were ideally suited to the FEX taste for Eccentricism (the film was based on two stories: *Nevsky Prospect* and *The Overcoat*). The historian Jay Leyda tells us: 'Andrei Moskvin's photography, as romantic or grotesque as the scenes call upon it to be, maintains the cloak's character as a fetish, observing the clerk with heroic and powerful camera-angles so long as he is wrapped in it, and photographing him mercilessly from above after it is taken from him . . . The co-ordinated effort of all participants achieves a unity that reminds one of the more perfect results of the collaboration of Mayer, Murnau, Freund, Herlth-Rohrig and Jannings in *Der letzte Mann* [*The Last Laugh*], perhaps a model that FEX followed here.' The film's designer, Yevgeni Enei, was to work with Kozintsev right to his last film, *King Lear*; over the years they pursued experiments begun in *The Overcoat* in re-creating past periods from the inside, in reaction to the upholstered fancy-dress re-creation which characterized pre-Soviet Russian cinema, where the past provided a comparative refuge from the attention of the severe Tsarist censorship. They returned to these preoccupations (following a contemporary comedy, *Bratishka* [*Little Brother*, 1927], about the love of a driver and a girl bus conductor) in *SVD* (*The Club of the Great Deed* or *The*

Club of the Big Deed, 1927) and *Novyi Vavilon* (*The New Babylon*, 1929).

SVD was (in the way of Soviet film commemorations) a rather belated celebration of the centenary of the Decembrist Revolt of 1825. Still photographs from the film indicate the imaginative splendour of the design and the dramatic expressiveness of Moskvin's chiaroscuro camerawork. *The New Babylon* remains the climax of Kozintsev and Trauberg's achievement in the silent period. The visual glamour and glitter are important elements in a study of social collapse under the threat of the German advance on Paris in 1871. The heroine, Louise Perrier, employed in the great department store 'The New Babylon', is a 'synthetic' heroine of the Commune, her social situation enabling her to link disparate elements—the workers with whom she lives, the rich whom she serves. The film's climax is the collapse of the Commune, though an element of optimism is provided by the social awareness which Louise's boy-friend discovers in the event. The musical accompaniment for *The New Babylon* was one of the earliest works of the young Dmitri Shostakovitch. Richly inventive in its use of sound and silence, it was a considerable embarrassment to the managers of provincial theatres, who had to deal with nightly complaints that the conductor of the theatre orchestra must be inebriated.

Shostakovitch provided the score of the first sound film of Kozintsev and Trauberg, *Odna* (*Alone*, 1931), actually completed in 1930 as a silent film but subsequently given a synchronized soundtrack. The story—a recurrent and important theme in Soviet cinema—concerned the difficulties of a young girl graduate from a Leningrad teachers' training college in tackling a new job in the wilds of the Altai. Jay Leyda's recollection of the film is that the dramatic contrasts were over-emphatic, but that 'the slow, tense, subtle and almost insinuating presentation of the film story seems more important now than its faults'.

Throughout the rest of the 30s, the team was occupied with the outstanding work of their collaboration, the *Maxim* trilogy (*Yunost Maksima* [*The Youth of Maxim*], 1935; *Vozvrashcheniye Maksima* [*The Return of Maxim*], 1937; *Vyborgskaya Storona* [U.K.:

The Vyborg Side or *The Vyborg District*, U.S.: *New Horizons*], 1939). As in *The New Babylon* they created a synthetic hero, this time an archetypal figure of the Soviet Revolution. At a moment when cinema, along with other Soviet arts, had been largely drained of humanity by the influence of the Stalinist concept of 'Socialist Realism', Kozintsev and Trauberg created one of the most human of all revolutionary films, the study of an individual—of no uncommon gifts or character—caught up in the revolutionary struggle, at first unwillingly, later with intense personal ardour. Their hero, Maxim, outgrew the films to become a permanent folk hero; the actor Boris Chirkov was called on to play and replay the same role in other films by other directors. His theme tune on the accordion remains to this day a popular favourite in Russia. The character of Maxim to an extent also outlived the inherent vitality of the film series. The liveliness of the episodic structure, the spicing of comedy in the first film of the trilogy, tends to fade somewhat in the second and third parts, where political history takes over. As political commissar in charge of the State Bank, Maxim himself is inevitably less fun than the jolly, impulsive and impressionable youngster of *The Youth of Maxim*. The overall achievement remains.

Apart from a brief film joke inserted in one of a series of compilation *Fighting Film Albums* issued in the early war period, Kozintsev and Trauberg seem to have been taken up with administrative tasks during the war; and not until 1945 did they undertake one more film together, *Prostiye lyudi* (*Plain People*), the first production completed in the Lenfilm Studios after the return from wartime evacuation. The film dealt with the evacuation of a factory, and showed in realistic terms the human problems produced by the migration. These were the most difficult times in Stalin's Russia; and realism (apart from the evasions of 'Socialist Realism') was not welcomed. *Plain People* was banned as unsuccessful, faulty and erroneous. It was finally released (no one knows to what extent it was cut or revised) in the 'thaw' year of 1956.

Along with many other careers at the time, those of Kozintsev and Trauberg were shadowed as a result of the *Plain People* affair. Personal relationships were often

Boris Chirkov in *The Youth of Maxim*: 'one of the most human of all revolutionary films, the study of an individual—of no uncommon gifts or character—caught up in the revolutionary struggle'.

affected by extreme political pressures. Whether or not this was the case with Kozintsev and Trauberg, the partnership came to an end; and from this time on the two directors worked independently. Trauberg's career never really recovered, though he continued to write and directed a few films (*Shli Soldati* [*Soldiers on the March* or *The Soldiers Marched*], 1958; *Mortviye Dushi* [*Dead Souls*], 1960; *Volnii Veter* [*Free Wind*], 1961). Kozintsev was to enjoy a total rejuvenation and three of his greatest triumphs.

For a while, following the *Plain People* affair, Kozintsev concentrated on writing, and directing in the theatre. He directed two historical biographies of the sort that flourished in the later Stalinist period, offering as they did less risk of offence than contemporary themes. Kozintsev's contributions to the genre were *Pirogov* (1947) and *Belinsky* (1953), which were hardly seen outside the Soviet Union and seem to have been forgotten as rapidly as most Soviet films of the era. The final period of Kozintsev's life was devoted to a trilogy which represents an outstanding achievement in the adaptation of classical literature to the screen. In 1957 he analysed the huge and spreading mass of *Don Quixote* into a taut and structured study of the doomed quest for the ideal. His leading actor was Nikolai Cherkassov, who had (like Chaliapin, with whom his early career had been associated) returned with irresistible fascination, again and again, to the character of the Don. With a vulnerably human Sancho (Tolubayev), a wholly credible re-creation of a parched and dusty Spain and of a distant age, and a use of colour exceptional in the period for its sophistication and restraint, the film remains arguably the best of all the many screen adaptations of Cervantes.

The film *Gamlet* (*Hamlet*, 1964) had been a life-long ambition; and much of the next ten years was taken up in its preparation. Kozintsev wrote and published extensive critical studies of Shakespeare and this play in particular, all directed ultimately towards the problems of translation into another language and another medium. He took his lead from Boris Pasternak's translations, always seeking valid equivalents rather than approximations or imitations of the original literary forms. Pasternak's versions of Shakespeare eschew literary archaism, seeking direct interpretation of the thought through strong, practical modern Russian speech. Kozintsev's adaptations in the same way look always to the interior qualities of the characters and to visual interpretation of the verbal imagery.

Above all (as he wrote constantly) Kozintsev saw Shakespeare as our contemporary, and interpreted the characters in wholly contemporary terms. His Hamlet owes nothing to any stage tradition of a moody and poetic hero doomed by indecision: as played by Innokenti Smoktunovski he is nervous, virile, positive, his tragedy being to find himself a man in an alien society, which he will fight and defy, and yet which must ultimately destroy him. It was a tribute to the breadth and universality of Kozintsev's view that this interpretation did not invite merely a narrow reading in the context of contemporary Soviet society. Yevgeni Yenei designed the film, as he was to design *Korolj Lir* (*King Lear*, 1971); and the plastic form of Kozintsev's Hamlet always reflects the verbal image of 'Denmark's a prison,' from the looming blind walls of the marooned castle to the dreadful iron corselet in which the soft body of Ophelia is strapped.

Lear was another long-cherished ambition. This time the preparation period was shorter, though the production seems to have been unnervingly drawn out by practical difficulties. In the West the film's reception was less warm than *Hamlet*'s, though in retrospect his last film may well seem the culmination of Kozintsev's creative career. Speaking of his interpretation he said that he saw the play not as Theatre of Cruelty but as Theatre of Mercy, a tragedy of reclamation rather than retribution. Humiliated, cast out, tormented into madness and death, Kozintsev's Lear nevertheless grows larger in human stature. The tyrant becomes a philosopher. Our first sight of him is as an irascible, autocratic old fool, tittering with his jester while consigning his realm to chaos. Later the sharp spare face of the Estonian actor Yuri Yarvet, with its pale, dry eyes ('I will not weep'), has the cast of a Voltaire.

Lear's moment of recognition, 'Oh I have ta'en too little care of this,' acquires new significance in Kozintsev's version, because the place is not the traditional lonely shelter but a doss house, crammed with naked wretches that 'bide the pelting of this pitiless storm'. The wanderings of Lear and Edgar, indeed, are never solitary; they are part of a Breughel-like caravan of vagabonds and idiots and victims of a merciless feudal world. From start to finish, indeed, *Lear* is seen not as an individual and private tragedy, a tale of filial ingratitude, but in a large social context ('Our present business is general woe'). From the opening, with a vast multitude of ragged, sad and silent people waiting on a hillside to hear the King's decree, to the end, where these same people are seen as the victims of the holocaust that the King's caprices have wrought, the screen seems always full of people. The main point, then, of Kozintsev's interpretation is that the King shares the very sufferings he has bequeathed to his subjects, and in sharing their sufferings becomes one with them, a man and a human being. It is an interpretation which succeeds in imposing a dynamic inevitability upon a notoriously difficult, elusive and apparently diffuse play. Even the side-tracks and sub-plots now are perceived as integral, impelling rather than retarding the movement.

Again, as in *Hamlet*, wherever the visual image can be more eloquent—a more faithful translation of the original than words can provide—Kozintsev dispenses with the text. Elsewhere the image reinforces the words. As every image of Hamlet sustained the notion of the prison-Denmark, the landscapes of *Lear*—wild, bleak plains with rocks and starved trees—play a dominant part in the drama. Yet the climax of the tragedy is less the storm scene—a virtuoso sequence of racing clouds and shattered landscapes buffeted by the eerie chords of Shostakovitch's score —than the sudden quiet which follows it, a sea of waving grass through which suddenly pokes the old King's bewildered face ('singing aloud, Crown'd with rank fumiter'). Kozintsev's Shakespeare is often as unexpected as this. The great passions that in the theatre are by tradition howled are here often simply murmurs. Lear's curse on Goneril is a hissed aside as he mounts his coach to move off in the bizarre cortège of his

The funeral procession from *Hamlet*: Kozintsev's life-long ambition, and a film ten years in preparation.

hundred knights, with hawks in cages, Cerberus dogs, a great mysterious strong-box, and the Fool, crouching on the back of the King's coach. Convention and cliché are thrown out of the window. Kozintsev's is a total reinterpretation; and all his characters are as unforeseen and as right as the King himself, not a towering majestic figure but a quick and wiry little man. The point is that all the characters have been chosen, and are made to work, in recognizable human terms.

Apart from their other qualities, these last films of Kozintsev's maturity are striking in their youthfulness; they are in no way the films of an old man. In a lengthy and perceptive study of *King Lear*, his old collaborator Sergei Yutkevitch convincingly traced the creative continuity of Kozintsev's career from its teenage beginnings to this majestic finale. This youthfulness was a quality in the man himself (and it was notable in other comrades of his early days). At the time of his death (in 1973) he seemed generations younger than his sixty-seven years, still gifted with the curiosity and excitement in

art of the days of FEX and the Left Stream. The 'Heroic Period' of Soviet art, it was clear, had truly been an enchanted age.

See also the article on Kuleshov. There are two works in French which deal with Kozintsev and Trauberg: *La Feks* by Mario Verdone and Barthelemy Amengual (1970), and a monograph by Marcel Oms on *Kozintsev* (1976). See also, of course, Jay Leyda's *Kino* (1960).

ROBERT KRAMER

Richard Roud

Born in 1940, Robert Kramer is, with Shirley Clarke, the most important of the American independent narrative film-makers, and the only one whose films are exclusively political in content. His first ambition was to be a writer, but he got mixed up in films working with Norm Fruchter and Robert Machover on their Newark film *Troublemakers* (1966). Shortly after, he made his own first two features *In the Country* (1967) and *The Edge*

(1968). But he was only to achieve widespread critical acclaim with his third film, *Ice* (1970), collectively produced by the Newsreel Group. Set in the future during a war with Mexico (presumably Kramer's guess as to the successor to Vietnam in the series of American colonial enterprises), it was described by Penelope Houston as 'a view from the New York Jewish Intelligentsia of America's *Alphaville*'. And that view was more than a little frightening. Concentrating on the 'native resistance' movement, the partisans whose battles with the security police and the government-controlled media are occasionally successful but more often end in violent death, the film seems to skirt the edges of paranoia. But as the world it portrays is that of its creators, one could not object: this was their view of American society in 1970, and considering what everyone now knows about what went on during the Nixon years, they were not so far off the mark. It was not in intention a realistic film, but one could not help being impressed by the accuracy of the dialogue and the rightness of the actors—none of whom was a professional.

Kramer's next film, co-directed with John Douglas (who also acted as its cameraman) was *Milestones* (1975), and with a few exceptions the cast was again non-professional. But the scope and range of the film are much greater than those of *Ice*: lasting well over three hours, *Milestones* ranged all over the United States in providing an almost Dos Passos-like view of what has happened to the radical generation of the 60s. The cast of characters is huge, but after the first half hour or so they begin to mesh, to interact, and at that point the film takes off and stays aloft for its whole course— culminating in the birth of a child. For rebirth is the subtext of the film: the beginnings of a new life for a political prisoner who has just been released from jail and whose father can't understand why he, an educated boy, wants to work in a box factory; the couples who break up and re-form; the father who tries to regain a place in his little boy's life. Paradoxically, one of the problems the film encountered with some viewers was that they thought it was a documentary and felt cheated when they discovered it was not. While it is not a documentary, it does employ its 'actors' in such a way as to achieve a kind of documentary truth which is all the more powerful for being so personal. Whether one likes it or not (and I do) it is a monument.

The presence of Robert Kramer and the absence of Stanley Kramer from this Dictionary are not accidental.

STANLEY KUBRICK
Robin Wood

In theory—if, that is to say, one abstracts the apparent ambitions, the sense of the kind of artist he would like to be, from the actual concrete realization and achievement— Stanley Kubrick (born 1928) demands sympathetic attention. The ambitions are there all right, expressed not only in the choice of subjects but in the pervasive insistence and assertiveness of style; and they are of a kind to elicit the enthusiastic approval of (leaving aside a very large number of critics) Orson Welles, who *is*, indisputably, an artist, if a seriously flawed one: 'Among those whom I would call "younger generation", Kubrick appears to me to be a giant.' Welles was speaking in 1965, and so hadn't witnessed the full flowering of Kubrick's creative personality in *2001: A Space Odyssey* (1968) and *A Clockwork Orange* (1971). But one can see that the stylistic idiosyncrasies even of so early a work as *Killer's Kiss* (1955)—the deliberate assertion of personality within a genre framework—would appeal to the creator of *Lady from Shanghai*. One sees why Welles would be attracted in general to Kubrick's work: both directors have (despite occasional flirtations like *The Stranger* and *Spartacus* [1960]), resolutely detached themselves from the Hollywood mainstream; both have striven consistently to assert themselves as artists in a sense in which artists like Ford and Hawks have not; both have cultivated personal style as the means of this self-assertion.

If a 'personal style' is sufficiently defined by certain consciously applied recurrent traits, Kubrick's work reveals personal style. The outward tokens are very easy to recognize and identify. One might instance his use of music: the 'Romantic piano concerto' pastiche for *Lolita* (1962), Vera Lynn singing 'We'll Meet Again' as the bombs explode at the end of *Dr Strangelove, or, How I*

Jamie Smith caught by Frank Silvera (left) in a warehouse full of shop-window dummies: *Killer's Kiss*.

Learned to Stop Worrying and Love the Bomb (1964), the 'Blue Danube' waltz of the spaceships in *2001*, Gene Kelly's 'Singin' in the Rain' to close *A Clockwork Orange*. Certain critics discern here profound wit and irony: I see childish facetiousness. The level of Kubrick's 'wit' can be sufficiently indicated by pointing to the speeded-up-motion copulation to the *William Tell* Overture and the false teeth in the glass of *A Clockwork Orange*, almost worthy of Gerald Thomas and the *Carry On* movies.

Kubrick's work reveals deeper evidence of the personal involvement which distinguishes the true *auteur*. His development has been remarkably consistent through an apparently heterogeneous range of projects, and each film's meaning becomes more confidently definable when one places it in relation to its fellows. As Peter Wollen once remarked, Kubrick, after expressing his contempt for humanity in his early films, annihilated it in *Dr Strangelove* and moved off into

outer space in *2001*—where he found, one is now forced to add, nothing better to do than come back and make *A Clockwork Orange*.

The formulation needs refining, of course, especially as a number of Kubrick's movies before *Strangelove* are explicitly 'humanitarian', consciously dedicated to protest against inhumanity, and *Strangelove* itself has been read similarly. That there *is* an impulse of this kind providing part of the motivating energy within the earlier works seems indisputable; *Paths of Glory* (1957) has considerable force, and the scenes in the gladiatorial training-school of *Spartacus* are among the most completely acceptable things Kubrick has done, with sufficient relevance to his other work to make any reflections that there he had less freedom than usual unduly cynical. But—with the exception, perhaps, of the *Spartacus* sequences—the effect is always equivocal. *Paths of Glory* is made with a passion in which anger takes precedence over compassion to the extent that the latter quality seems all but obliterated. The impulse to affirmation (embodied in the Kirk Douglas character) is in constant danger of being overwhelmed by a pervasive sense that humanity can be divided fairly neatly into fools and knaves. The striking and memorable features of the film are characterized primarily by Kubrick's sense of the grotesque, whether in the corrupt exploiters (Adolphe Menjou and George Macready) or their victims (Timothy Carey). Similarly, in the later stretches of *Spartacus*, it is the corruption of Rome rather than the nobility of the slaves' rebellion that really engages Kubrick: the nobility, in fact, is a matter of empty rhetoric, at its worst in the aftermath of the battle with the camera passing over carefully arranged 'peasant' stereotypes to elicit the simplest of stock responses. Against the affirmation centred in the integrity of the Kirk Douglas characters in both these films (an affirmation further undermined by the actor's apparent tendency to hysterical masochism), one has to set not only the conniving generals of *Paths of Glory* and the Romans of *Spartacus*, but, more sinister and equally typical, Kubrick's treatment of the Elisha Cook–Marie Windsor relationship in *The Killing* (1956), with its open invitation to cruel, derisive laughter.

The Killing attracted much attention when it came out. It is the sort of intellectually ambitious yet apparently unassuming 'B' feature that critics love to discover, and people who have become generally disenchanted with Kubrick's development continue to look back on it with nostalgic respect. The film appears to have two chief claims to fame: 'sharp' characterizations, and a complicated treatment of time. The characterizations, with such reliable players as Jay C. Flippen, Elisha Cook Jr and Timothy Carey, are memorable enough but scarcely profound: Kubrick's interest in his characters stops too far short of really sympathetic or imaginative involvement for profundity to be possible. The time-scheme—the film repeatedly doubling back over itself to analyse the various simultaneous operations involved in the execution of a race-track robbery—is certainly striking if obtrusive, but somewhat hard to justify in terms of function. Its chief effect is the sacrifice of suspense: one's reaction to being forced back

over the same period of time from another viewpoint tends to be mere frustration rather than increased tension. The sacrifice could of course be justified by the achievement of results incompatible with suspense: one might be tempted to enlist Brecht and talk of 'alienation' in the interests of analytical clarity. Yet the action so laboriously analysed seems somewhat lacking in rewards of interest or significance. What the sequences in question indicate most revealingly is Kubrick's fascination with mechanisms—with how something works, be it a race-track robbery or a spacecraft. The much more polished working of *Dr Strangelove*—which follows a strict scheme in which real time and cinematic time coincide, analysing an intricate network of interconnecting operations without recourse to doubling back—perhaps indicates Kubrick's own retrospective dissatisfaction with the time-scheme of *The Killing*.

It can of course be plausibly argued—particularly with *Dr Strangelove* in mind—that we live in a world in which affirmation has become impossible, or accessible only to the chronically self-deluding; but that is to miss my point. No one asks for easy, or even difficult, optimism. Yet human creativity is intimately bound up with the striving towards affirmation, the seeking out of that which may be honestly affirmed, and when that impulse is lost or stunted, creativity becomes something other, turning sour and destructive, losing its true vitality. In Kubrick's development, by the time one reaches *A Clockwork Orange*, creative vitality has become merely the will to egoistic self-assertion, at the expense of both characters and audience.

The crucial film is *2001*: an 'affirmative' movie if ever there was one. I think it is illuminating (risible as the comparison will seem to some, especially those who number Kubrick's film among the greatest ever made) to set beside it what remains the finest science-fiction movie I have seen, Howard Hawks' *The Thing* (nominally directed by Christian Nyby, but supervised by Hawks at every stage). The two films represent, with satisfying completeness, polar opposites in every respect—subject-matter, style and values. *The Thing*, entirely modest and unpretentious, makes minimal use of cinematic technology: within the science-fiction genre, its rejection of 'special effects', super-

Timothy Carey and Sterling Hayden behind some pistol-practice cut-out dummies: *The Killing*.

impositions, back-projection, model shots, etc. is very striking. The impact of *2001*, on the other hand, is inseparable from its impressive deployment of technology. The values of *The Thing* are centred in the lively give-and-take of human intercourse and affection; the human characters of *2001* are presented quite deliberately as dehumanized zombies —human relationships have become dead and superfluous, and the values of the film are accordingly centred in the machines, and in the notion of man's progress towards some non-'human' (in any meaningful sense) rebirth.

The 'Thing' of Hawks' film is an extra-terrestrial humanoid vegetable of immense intellectual development, from whose make-up emotion is totally absent; it is also devoid of sexuality, reproducing itself by dropping seeds from the palms of its hands. Its food is human blood, and it treats men as we treat cattle. The revelation of its nature is greeted by the leader of the film's scientific expedition with admiration and enthusiasm ('No

pleasure, no pain, no emotions ... Our superior in every way'). For Hawks, the Thing is the supreme villain; against it is set man's empirical human resourcefulness and capacity for spontaneous affection. It seems fair to say that if Kubrick were to re-make Hawks' film, the Thing would automatically emerge as the hero: as the scientists' anti-human ideal, it embodies most of the values affirmed in *2001*.

In *2001* Kubrick accepts man's dehumanization within a universe dominated by technology. The style of the film—its famous visual splendours—expresses this as clearly as its thematic progress, and again Hawks' film provides a revealing touchstone. *The Thing* (like Hawks' work generally) is devoid of 'visual beauty', in the sense in which *2001* might be felt to offer little else. The beauty of *The Thing* derives from its meaning and its essential values; that of *2001*, associated almost exclusively with its deployment of machines or with elaborate special effects, is a matter of technological display.

There seems no general agreement as to precisely what the ending of *2001* means, but its main lines seem clear enough: man, guided by the mysterious monoliths (a more dehumanized expression of the concept of a higher 'supernatural' agency would be impossible), achieves some form of rebirth (as universal spirit?). The concluding triumphal image of the luminous babe conveys, with undeniable effect, an immediate sense of awe, but conceptually it is too lacking in definition to offer real emotional or intellectual satisfaction. All it suggests at all clearly is a Being potentially very powerful surveying the universe (*its* universe?) from a position of total isolation. This apotheosis is reached, the film suggests, through man's casting-off of all his old-fashioned humanity (outgoing emotions, the capacity for human relationships) and the development of his intellect— intellect conceived as expressing itself exclusively through science and technology. It has often been noted that the most human character in the film is HAL, the ambitious computer (if only because it dies singing 'Daisy, Daisy'): an example of the glib and ultimately meaningless paradox to which Kubrick is prone. The final rebirth, or transformation, seems in human terms—in terms, that is, of any values by which we might order our lives—useless in its vague pretentiousness. The film's ambition challenges one to see it as a great work or as nothing; for me, the choice is easy.

If *2001* represents Kubrick's notion of affirmation, *A Clockwork Orange* can be seen as its logical counterpart and complement in rejection. The relationship between the two films again strikes me as glibly paradoxical: in the one, man moves forward, through technological development, to mystical rebirth; in the other, man lives in a technological-mechanistic world in which all human values appear finally degraded. The seeming opposition of optimism and pessimism is of course illusory as immediately becomes apparent if one ceases to regard the two films as literal prophecies about the future and takes them instead as fantasies, the projection of inner landscapes.

Many critics—though none, I think, for whose judgement I have much respect—have praised *A Clockwork Orange* for its 'visual brilliance', its technique. Chiefly, perhaps, one can take such a reaction as demonstrating once again that the majority of journalist-critics don't notice 'technique' unless they are hit over the head with it. The word 'technique' carries a certain ambiguity: at one end of the spectrum it becomes almost synonymous with 'style', at the other it signifies merely the deployment of cinematic technology. The two cannot of course be separated, but, equally clearly, to talk of the technique of *La Règle du Jeu* means something rather different from applying the word to *A Clockwork Orange*. There are two main things to be said about the technique of the latter: one, that it is very insistent; two, that it is mostly, like the generally grotesque acting, very crude on any but a mechanical level (the camera tracks smoothly, etc.); it is easy to achieve visual impact by means of the fish-eye or wide-angle lens. Similarly, it appears to serve two functions: one, to intensify our sense of the ugliness and brutality of the characters, two, to express the director's sense of his own superiority to the humanity the film depicts.

Much has been made, in defence of the film (and particularly its violence), of the way the stylization distances us from the action: the violence is to be considered less 'dangerous' than that of *Straw Dogs* because we are not drawn into it. Such an argument seems to me specious, its plausibility breaking down as soon as the nature and function of the stylization are defined more precisely. In *Straw Dogs*, certainly, we are drawn into the violence: spectators find themselves empathizing physically, the film drawing out their latent aggression. Such involvement has its dangers, but it is also what makes the film so disturbing: if there is a sense in which we enjoy the violence, we certainly are not allowed to do so with complacency. And complacency seems to me exactly what the 'distancing' of *A Clockwork Orange* induces: we get the kicks without the guilt. We are not encouraged (by the style or the acting) to feel superior to the characters of *Straw Dogs*: Peckinpah's Cornishmen, whether or not they are 'authentic' (which is beside the point), have a brutal, earthy energy that makes them formidable and half-attractive. The characters of *A Clockwork Orange* are presented as grotesque, stupid, ugly, despic-

'The dehumanized zombies' from *2001*.

able; the beating-up in time with 'Singin' in the Rain' can consequently be enjoyed as smart and funny.

The assertion of superiority at the expense of the characters seems to me the chief function of style in *A Clockwork Orange*. The 'technical brilliance' is unremittingly self-conscious and self-assertive: it seems to say, 'Humanity is debased and disgusting, but look at *this* for a piece of film-making.' In fact, a film made exclusively out of hatred and contempt can only be hateful and contemptible, and *A Clockwork Orange* seems to me probably the ugliest film I have ever seen.

It seems only fair to say that Robin Wood's view of Kubrick is a minority one; I should add that I share his view. With the release of *Barry Lyndon* (1976) many (not all) of Kubrick's admirers have begun to have doubts. It was about time. The standard works on Kubrick are Alexander Walker's *Stanley Kubrick Directs* (1971) and Norman Kazan's *The Cinema of Stanley Kubrick* (1976).

LEV KULESHOV

Tom Milne

'No one bothered about cold or hunger. Life seemed marvellously interesting, and there was no doubt at all that this moment marked the coming of a new era, the era of art. This art had to be as bold as the workers' power itself, as pitiless towards the past as the Revolution . . . The extent to which we were crazed about art in those difficult years now seems quite astonishing. Exhibitions would open in half-ruined rooms; in public debates passions ran high. Poets of different (and numberless) tendencies read their verses; new names appeared constantly, and people whose names already seemed legendary continued to write . . . Young hotheads enthusiastically greeted every word of the new order. All were ready, at once and with no reckoning the cost, to carry out the "Order to the Army of Art" given by Mayakovsky.'

Kozintsev's description of what it was like to be in Petrograd in 1920, in the first glorious flush of the Russian Revolution, seems a little forlorn when measured against the staid conformism of Russian art over the past half-century. But for a few bright years, before all the great innovators, from Mayakovsky and Meyerhold to Eisenstein and Dovzhenko, fell prey to accusations of formalism, the new U.S.S.R. was a ferment of artistic exploration. In those days of propaganda trains and puppet shows in the streets, of endless manifestos and aesthetic quarrels, of mushrooming little theatres and experimental workshops—so well described by both Yutkevitch and Kozintsev in their memoirs—all the 'isms' from futurism to constructivism were given their fling, in tandem with a determined populism derived on the one hand from the circus, pantomime and music-hall, and on the other from American slapstick, detective thrillers and serials. Out of this feverish activity, in which the most vital elements soon gravitated to the cinema, two figures emerged with international reputations so distinctive that the name of Eisenstein has become indissolubly linked with the concept of film montage, and Pudovkin has frequently been forced to deny authorship of the famous montage experiment involving the actor Ivan Mozhukhin. (To demonstrate that montage could create an illusion of emotional expression, Kuleshov intercut the same close-up of Mozhukhin's face with three different scenes: to an audience, it seemed that Mozhukhin was expressing in turn hunger, fear and pleasure.)

Yet Lev Kuleshov (1899–1970) could claim, with complete justification: 'I was the first in Russia to speak the word "montage", to speak of the action, of the dynamic of the cinema, of realism in the art of the film.' As teacher and theorist, he could also claim that he numbered among his pupils not only Eisenstein and Pudovkin, but about one-third of all Soviet film-makers to date. In this role, at least, he has been restored to his rightful position as a pioneer; but as a film-maker he remains neglected, partly because his best work was done in the silent period (inevitably he encountered problems as a formalist and was increasingly required to toe the party line), and partly because so few of his films have filtered through to the West.

The first thing that astonishes about Kuleshov's work, quite apart from the fact that it needs no excuses—*Neobychainiye Prikluchen-iya Mistera Vesta v Stranye Bolshevikov* (*The Extraordinary Adventures of Mr West in the Land of the Bolsheviks*, 1924) remains brilliantly fresh and funny in its satiric invention, and *Dura Lex* (*By the Law*, 1926) is a masterpiece by any standards—is that it so persistently prefigures the concerns of contemporary cinema. With *Dura Lex*, for instance, one is already three-quarters of the way into the pared down, ascetic poetry of interiority of Bresson; with *Velikii Uteshitel* (U.K.: *The Great Consoler*, 1933) one is already edging, albeit clumsily, towards the confrontation between illusion and reality with which Godard revolutionized cinema. It comes as no surprise to find that in his earliest articles, published in 1917, Kuleshov was already talking about 'painting with objects, walls and lights' (though in discussing the work of the designer rather than the cameraman), and was formulating an *auteur* theory *avant la lettre* in arguing that since cinema is a visual medium, the first sketch (the scenario) should ideally be written on celluloid, and that the scriptwriter can therefore really only be the director.

When once asked who should be credited with the discovery of montage, himself or D. W. Griffith, Kuleshov replied: 'Historically, I think it was Griffith. But the credit for the first theoretical studies on montage must perhaps go to me.' Arguably, a fair share of the credit should also go to Dziga Vertov; but limited by his Kino-Eye principles and his adherence to the actuality film, his theory and practice were perhaps less central to the cinematic explosion represented by the work of Eisenstein, Pudovkin, Kozintsev and Trauberg, and Dovzhenko. Kuleshov, at any rate, was the only one of the major Soviet directors to enter the cinema in the pre-Revolutionary period (in 1916); and it was during the shooting of his first film, *Proyekt Inzhenera Praita* (*The Project of Engineer Prite*, 1918), that chance sparked off his speculations about the possibilities of montage. Having neglected to film some necessary shots of his cast looking at electrical pylons, Kuleshov realized that he could simply marry shots of the actors and of the pylons taken separately and at different places. This discovery that the cinema could create a non-existent reality was at the basis of his experiments when, having been instrumental in the founding of the State Film School (VGIK), he was given his own workshop there: the Mozhukhin demonstration already mentioned; a sequence in which two people catch sight of each other, meet and shake hands in a Moscow whose geography has been reconstituted and incorporates the White House from Washington; and a scene of a woman sitting before a mirror doing her hair, attending to her make-up, putting on her shoes and stockings and completing her toilet, in which the woman was actually a composite of several different women who supplied the eyes, legs, hair, lips and so on.

At the same time, *The Project of Engineer Prite* (of which only two reels have survived) and *Na Krasnom Fronte* (*On the Red Front*, a fiction film, now lost, in which Kuleshov incorporated footage he shot on the Western front of the Polish war in 1920), both point to a radical departure, crucial in the formative years of the Soviet cinema. They both have vaguely agit-prop themes (the theft of an important invention in the first, and a secret dispatch in the second, by scheming foreign powers) which were resolved by extended chase sequences. American films, with their emphasis on action whether for comedy or thrills, had long been popular in Russia, but the pre-Soviet cinema specialized in bourgeois melodramas whose emotional subjectivism and implied ivory-towerism were rendered obsolete by the need for positive, collective action. Hence the astonishing proliferation, alongside the borrowings from circus and music-hall, of American and allied influences in the stage and theatre work of the Soviet experimentalists: Griffith, Jack London, O. Henry, serials, slapstick, technology, urbanism. And hence, too, in the training and direction of actors by Eisenstein and the FEX group as well as by Kuleshov, the emphasis on acrobatics, pantomime, pratfalls and pugilism rather than on 'building a character'. Stanislavsky, in other words, was out; and if one has any lingering doubts as to the necessity of this development during these formative years, one only has to compare the electricity generated by Kuleshov's students in *The Extraordinary*

Adventures of Mr West, or by the cast of Eisenstein's *Strike*, with the flabby melodramatics produced by the Moscow Art Theatre players when they were invited to apply their 'old style' to Dreyer's *Love One Another* (1921) and Wiene's *Raskolnikov* (1923), effectively ruining both films.

The weakness of the FEX approach, as evidenced by the first Kozintsev and Trauberg film, *The Adventures of Oktyabrina* (1924; a weakness corrected by the time of *The New Babylon* five years later)—and possibly also of Eisenstein's early stage work, though not of *Strike*—was that the 'eccentricism' of the actor was an end in itself, a new broom whose only purpose was to sweep away the old litter. Kuleshov, however, was training his actors with the montage principle in mind. If a film was to be a series of fragmented scenes in which the 'reality' would be created by montage, then the actor had no reality in himself: he was a puppet, a system of signs of absolute precision to be manipulated and incorporated to complete the montage. The object of all Kuleshov's work with his actors, which for a time featured scenarios 'staged' rather than filmed because raw stock was in such short supply, with drop-curtains and screens indicating the 'montage', was to chart a survey of the possibilities of the human body, extracting the essence from movements and gestures so that their emotional content could be harnessed as a motive force. In *Dura Lex*, for instance, three people are immured in a snow-bound cabin with the knowledge that when the spring eventually gives them their freedom, two of them must bring the third to judgement and execution: the tension of the situation is expressed by the rigidity of the postures (the half-frozen prisoner sitting bolt upright on his bunk with legs stretched stiffly out, a mathematical *reductio ad absurdum* as rectilinear as the log cabin set squarely in the middle of nowhere), and the wavering hysteria by Alexandra Khokhlova's angular arms, echoing in their awkward, uncontrollable agitation the windblown branches of the solitary blasted tree from which the prisoner will eventually be hanged.

The Extraordinary Adventures of Mr West in the Land of the Bolsheviks, the first film in which Kuleshov put his researches to practical use, and still not only a delightful satire but very relevant to contemporary Cold War attitudes, is in many ways a model of cinematographic story-telling. It opens, for instance, with the title 'Leaving for Russia' and a rapid mosaic of brief, impressionistic scenes: an unseen hand throwing a battery of suitcases to a porter on screen; a suitcase helpfully labelled 'J. WEST'; two doves being loosed; a gunslinger using bottles for target practice; the arrival of a letter. Mr West, we learn, is the president of the Y.M.C.A. about to leave America on a good-will tour of Soviet Russia; he will be accompanied by his cowboy aide, Jed; and Mrs West, tearfully seeing her husband off, has dire forebodings inspired by a magazine article illustrated with photographs of the leering, evil-hearted Bolshevik types who infest Moscow. Nevertheless, clutching an American flag and a talismanic photograph of his wife, Mr West sets off, the image of Harold Lloyd in horn-rims and Stars and Stripes socks. A trivial incident involving a stolen briefcase soon swells, thanks to Mr West's naïve imaginings, into a labyrinthine Bolshevik plot which is finally resolved, not by Jed's equally naïve recourse to traditional Western heroics, but by a kindly Soviet cop who introduces him to the real Russia after explaining how a gang of petty criminals have exploited his prejudices to bamboozle him.

Irresistibly inventive in its good-humoured satire, the film contains some magnificent conceits, such as the sequence in which Jed, complete with Stetson and woolly leggings, leaps to the top of a Moscow taxi-cab to pursue what he presumes to be the villains, firing away with his six-guns and roping motor-cyclists like steers. The proliferating gags, too, bear witness to the close and profitable study Kuleshov must have made of the principles of American comedy. As one example among many, one might cite the perfectly executed Keaton gag in which Jed escapes from the police by climbing along a rope stretched high up between two buildings which eventually snaps, swinging him like Tarzan down through a window to set a vase rocking perilously on its pedestal. Almost immediately he is involved in a fight with two men, cheered on by a third who watches from a ladder until dislodged by the battle, and the vase finally satisfies expectations by breaking.

The real innovation of the film, however, lies in its iconographic use of the actors. They are all typed, of course (in the Eisenstein sense of 'typage'), but Kuleshov pushes further than this, using caricatural poses and gestures to suggest a confusion between illusion and reality. When Jed lassoes the driver of a droshky and proceeds to tie him up with the lariat, a bourgeois lady in a fur-coat who happens to be passing clutches a lamp-post in terror and slithers down it in abject collapse as her legs give way. Still sitting there when Jed begins blazing away with his guns, she suddenly and disorientatingly executes a perfect back somersault out of danger. Engagingly, the villains exist on a sort of sliding scale which starts with drab reality (the hungry sneak-thief snatching the briefcase in the street), moves into the domain of serial fiction ('The Dandy' and 'The Countess'), and ends in wild imaginings (the one-eyed desperado with black eye-patch, crutches and a white mouse inexplicably perched on his shoulder). Stripped down to their figurative essence—a tier of three evil faces peering through a crack in a doorway, a series of alarmingly seductive poses by the vampiric Countess—they begin to assume a nightmare semblance of reality.

Luch Smerti (*The Death Ray*, 1925), loosely inspired by the Feuillade serials and repeating the plot about the stolen invention, is often visually striking with its proliferation of masked intruders, mysterious ladies brandishing guns in both fists, and sinister figures in black tights prowling the rooftops or climbing hand over hand from wires suspended high above the streets. It adds very little to the invention in *Mr West*, however, and looks exactly like what it is: an anthology of tricks and technical expertise designed to prove that the unit should be allowed to make more films. But with *Dura Lex*, based on Jack London's story *The Unexpected*, Kuleshov found a subject which could be performed in the 'eccentric' manner, but where effective treatment was dependent on stripping away rather than elaborating. And with it, as Bresson was to do later, he demonstrated that the cinema, in addition to creating a non-existent reality, could create an emotion which was also non-existent as far as the actors' performances were concerned.

The emotional depths of *Dura Lex*, weaving strange patterns of guilt and retribution and the exchange of roles between them, are so intense that one tends in retrospect to remember the bulk of the action as having taken place within the tormenting vortex of the cabin in which the three protagonists are imprisoned. In fact, much of the action takes place outside, with the film divided into five 'acts' (of unequal length) skilfully designed to lay a groundwork of facts and character notations which, though eclipsed by the stark ferocity of the central plot mechanism, are an essential factor in the emotional truth of its resolution. The first act begins in tranquil, measured calm with shots of water, a single tree on the bank, a lone tent, four people asleep. They are prospecting for gold in the Yukon, and they are paired: Edith Nelson and her husband Hans, a Russian prospector with a German. The fifth person, the Irishman Jack, wanders down to the water's edge and, worriedly watched by his dog—while Edith gets up and begins to comb her hair, Bible in hand—pulls out a flute and begins to dance by himself. It is this outsider (he is employed by the other four and has no stake in the claim), this untutored innocent (the pipe of Pan, the kinship with animals) who, to general rejoicing, accidentally strikes gold.

Act Two opens with an ominously wintry landscape. The prospectors are now installed in a log cabin. The water motif from the opening returns in two different guises, with Jack increasingly resentful of his position as he slaves over the laundry surrounded by buckets, and Edith's smiling face reflected in a pan of clear water as she sifts for gold. When Jack goes berserk and shoots the Russian and the German—and an hysterical Edith contrives to prevent her husband from exacting instant retribution—Kuleshov ends the moment of frenzy with a shot of the stain spreading from an overturned cup on the table. And Edith takes the gun from her husband: 'He should be delivered to justice; it must be done by the law.'

Act Three begins with Jack bound hand and foot, fiercely struggling to free himself and swearing to kill his captors, while Hans and Edith prepare to bury their two dead comrades. In a veritable deluge of emotion, both literal (the rain begins lashing down in torrents) and figurative (the extraordinary,

twisted attitudes of despair), they battle against the wind and ice to move the heavy sledges and to wrestle the corpses free of the water that threatens to engulf the graves. There is a curious and terrible sense of shared exaltation as they drive on against the elements, while inside, the veins standing out on his neck, Jack struggles over to the window to watch them and desperately tries to free his wrists from their bonds. With the elemental storms raging in and around this cabin where the rooftree is literally the trunk of a living tree, what one can only describe as a process of purification is completed by fire when Jack contrives to set his bunk alight with a candle, and Edith, for the last time, has to intervene to prevent her infuriated husband from executing their captive.

Act Four takes place entirely within the cabin, now flooded by water and with the three protagonists marooned, apart from each other, like islands in a great sea. A strange sense of reconciliation prevails with the coming of spring, and it is confirmed by the extraordinary sequence of Edith's birthday party, in honour of which Jack is shaved, offers his watch as a gift and is allowed to rejoin the human circle at the table. The memory of all the hieratic, anguished gestures is wiped out by the gentle, questing hesitancy with which Jack, his hands momentarily freed for the occasion, reaches out to restore a fallen candle to its place. Yet on the table, together, are a Bible and a gun.

The last act is a curiously tranquil yet somehow tormented marriage between compassion and duty, with Jack recognizing that there is no forgiveness for what he has done, and Hans and Edith—though riven by an awareness of Edith's growing involvement with Jack—forgiving him. The moral ambiguities, however, are subjected by mutual agreement to the process of the law. A portrait of Queen Victoria is nailed to the wall. A trial takes place. And with stark simplicity, Jack is found guilty, accepts his sentence and is hanged from the solitary tree waiting on the horizon. In a bizarre finale—real or phantasmic?—the ironies and ambiguities come flooding back as Jack returns to the cabin, takes the gold from the table and leaves in exchange the frayed rope from his neck: 'They say a rope that has hanged a man brings happiness. So take it . . .'

By the Law: 'The last act: Jack is found guilty, accepts his sentence, and is hanged from the solitary tree waiting on the horizon.'

With its metronomically exact montage alchemically fused by the enigmatic emotions latent in its outlandish movements and gestures, *Dura Lex* is an impossible film to describe in any way accurately, but it is an unquestionable masterpiece. After it, Kuleshov was not only hounded by accusations of formalism, but forced to work without Alexandra Khokhlova (his wife, lifelong collaborator, and surely one of the screen's great actresses), whose weird Goyaesque beauty and ungainly grace were deemed 'not suitable'. Few of his subsequent films were exported, and most of them are reported to be disappointingly routine. *The Great Consoler* uses the disparity between real-life facts and O. Henry's manipulation of them in his stories, and the spuriously consoling effect of the latter on an unhappy young woman

reader, to speculate intriguingly about the interplay of illusion and reality and the role of truth in fiction. But here the various levels are carefully spelled out by turns, instead of being simultaneously superimposed as they were in *Mr West* and *Dura Lex*. When formalism was cast out of Kuleshov's work, the heart went with it.

See also entries on Kozintsev and Trauberg and on Dziga Vertov. *Film Culture* published a fascinating issue (Spring 1967) largely devoted to Kuleshov, and there is also a monograph (in French) by Eric Schmulevitch (1974). See also Jay Leyda's *Kino* (1960) and Jean and Luda Schnitzer's *Cinema and Revolution* (1973).

In 1975 the collected writings of Kuleshov were published in English under the title *Kuleshov on Film*, edited by Ronald Levaco.

AKIRA KUROSAWA

Noël Burch

For the Western analyst, close scrutiny of the work of almost any Japanese film-maker in so far as he refuses to ape that cosmopolitan 'transparency' which I have attempted to define in my article on Fritz Lang (on p. 583), raises problems which are not explicitly encountered elsewhere. A time-worn critical ploy when dealing with Japanese films is to plead probable (and of course excusable) fallibility on the grounds of an insuperable 'cultural gap', and, notwithstanding, to propose with all due humility a reading 'through Western eyes' which can only leave the recipient with a diffuse feeling of frustration.

As a palliative to this avowed handicap, a few specialists have tried to scan the mainstream of Japanese cinema through the periscope of comparative cultural criticism, predicating most of their analyses and judgements on an assessment of 'Japanese values', their familiarity with which apparently constitutes the bulk of their credentials. Whether applied separately or in pragmatic combination, both these approaches seem to me to have proved hopelessly inadequate. The first fails, not so much because of the Western eye's incapacity to grasp, without comprehensive cultural and linguistic mediation, the actual work accomplished in Japanese films—indeed, it is precisely this Westerner's ambition to shed light here on some of the working realities in Kurosawa's films—but rather because there are in fact several 'Western eyes' and the one which ninety-nine per cent of our professional critics avail themselves of is irremediably unsuited to embracing the aesthetic and structural complexities of important Japanese films.

The second approach, though undeniably right-thinking as far as it goes, has thus far only served to obscure the issues. For in contrast to those contemporary scholars (Barthes, Brower and Miner, Keene, Roubaud) who have probed the traditional arts and literature of Japan in terms of modern Western thought, the handful of specialists who ought to be their cinematic counterparts are reading Japanese culture and traditional arts through an idealistic, impressionistic grille, inherited from nineteenth-century liberal humanism, which certainly cannot afford these specialists so much as a glimpse of the *inbred concern with abstract form, regarded as a primary cultural value on every level of social activity*, which is one of the essential traits of Japanese society, and which has, in my view, given the advanced core of Japanese films since the late 20s its unique impetus.

Briefly, my contention is this: Japanese painting, theatre, dance, music and poetry had completely ceased to develop by the end of the nineteenth century, i.e. by the time that sustained cultural and economic intercourse had been established with the West. However, the definitive 'opening' of Japan to the West coincided almost exactly with our own invention of the cinema and its immediate introduction into Japan (1897). Now, just as Japan's living artistic and literary practice rapidly became a mere extension of Western culture, leaving the traditional performing arts, in particular, in a museum-like stasis disturbed only superficially by occasional retouchings brought to an otherwise frozen repertoire, so too the Japanese film, from its earliest manifestations until the late 20s, seems to have followed the pattern of Western development, with an assimilation lag of several years.

Already, however, in ancient times, Chinese poetry and music had been imported and slavishly imitated for decades before the process of transmutation could begin. And this pattern was about to be repeated: Kinugasa's famous *Jujiro* (*Crossways* or *Crossroads*, 1928), one of the first Japanese films to win acclaim in Europe, was little more than a rehash of the purely dramaturgical elements in German *Kammerspiel* and 'expressionism', at a time when Western cinema had already achieved the complexity of *October*, *L'Argent* and *Spione*. Yet during those same years Ozu, Mizoguchi and Naruse were preparing to pursue the task begun by Eisenstein, Dreyer and Lang when the latter were obliged to abandon essential aspects of their research. Of course, the degree to which this 'transmission of a task' involved conscious or even unconscious influence is impossible to ascertain. What is important is that in Japan cinema became a fertile field in which the vital principles of all the terminated Japanese art-forms could, after a long purgatory, flower again 'by proxy' in a kind of posthumous symbiosis. Eisenstein pointed out the proto-cinematic importance of *framing* in Japanese painting (the artist filling in a *pre-determined* outline) as against the classical Western method of choosing an unframed canvas or sheet of paper of proportions suitable to the subject, centring the still-life, portrait or genre scene on that surface and finally adding the ornate frame (non-existent in Japanese tradition) only at the end of the process to 'set off' a picture whose composition is essentially centripetal. (This practice was no longer quite so general after Degas, whose discovery of Utamaro in the late 1850s may be regarded as a turning point in the history of Western art.) And Eisenstein's famous plea to the Japanese to develop their own art of the film on the basis of principles to be found in their traditional arts (he wrote of the montage principles in Kabuki, in scroll paintings and in ideograms) and to stop imitating European films got an almost immediate response, as it were, from the above-named masters at exactly the same period when the Western cinema, under economic and political pressures, had to all but relinquish its grasp of the formal values which the silent films of Eisenstein and a few others had embodied.

Contemporary scholars of various persuasions and various disciplines have since shed light on other aspects of Japanese culture which can also be seen as underlying sources of the then unprecedented *dialectical symbiosis* of abstraction and narrative achieved by Ozu and his great contemporaries. In this context it should be pointed out that, so far as one can gather from the bits and pieces of native Japanese film criticism available in translation, the films of Ozu's middle period (1935–45) were either criticized as 'overly formalistic' or praised for their ethical and social 'content' and for their 'style'. Thus, while the great film-makers were establishing a whole new mode of existence for films and at the same time giving new life to aesthetic values which had actually died, the critics, their contemporaries, were merely furthering the process of cultural colonization, applying to films (which actually challenged them in almost every way) the aesthetic values of Western mass ideology: the film as a 'window

on the world'; 'content' as a fantasy projection of ideological values; form and structure as secret, hidden, all but shameful recipes ('the mechanics and techniques of cinema') to achieve the illusion of reality and convey intangible 'human' messages. Unfortunately, the first comprehensive Western surveys of Japanese cinema, though recent enough to have benefited from the ideological insights of modern Western aesthetic theory, experimental psychology and structural analysis, have merely re-enacted this elementary error, as may be illustrated by two quotations from Joseph L. Anderson and Donald Richie's *The Japanese Film* (a book, I hasten to add, whose documentary value is none the less immense):

Camera movement was another way through which Mizoguchi suggested atmosphere. The final scene of *Ugetsu* is a very fine example. The child places food on his mother's grave and then, with the gentlest of movements, the camera begins to climb until finally the entire little settlement on the shores of the lake is seen in a shot which matches the opening of the film with its slow pan from lake to houses. In fact, almost any Mizoguchi film can be reduced to a catalogue of beautifully calculated effects which create the atmosphere of his film world. (pp. 352–53)

In contrast to the artless simplicity of the average Japanese picture, Kurosawa's films are heavily calculated and enormously artful. His interest in technique may call occasional attention to itself, as in the huge close-ups of *Shichinin no Samurai* [*Seven Samurai*, U.S. alternative title: *The Magnificent Seven*, 1954], or the perfectly balanced composition of set-ups in *Donzoko* [*The Lower Depths*, 1957] but more often than not the mechanics and techniques of cinema are used entirely for psychological effect. (p. 377)

The constant basic options to be found in the films of Kurosawa, considered together, demonstrate, I believe, how he alone kept alive for over ten years (1950–62) the essential heritage of Ozu, Mizoguchi and their generation when his elders and contemporaries had all but unanimously rallied to the dominant Western concept of 'form as the doting servant of content'.

Kurosawa (born 1910) may be regarded as the direct heir of Eisenstein in so far as he returned the shot-change to its true function as a *visible, avowed parameter* of filmic discourse and was the first to apply consistently the Russian master's principle of montage units, with its dialectics of 'correct' and 'incorrect' matches. This assertion of direct affiliation is, however, something of an over-simplification in that several Japanese masters (Ozu and Naruse in particular) whose careers began a good decade prior to Kurosawa's, displayed almost from the outset a keen awareness of the necessity for the 'intra-sequential' shot-changes being *seen*, both as an essential part of the film's abstract texture and as a contrapuntal component of its dramaturgy.

Now in Ozu's and Naruse's pre-war films, the anti-illusionist attitude which holds that there is nothing wrong about a shot-change being seen is especially noticeable in their almost total disregard for eyeline matching. Nearly every reverse-field set-up in the films which Ozu made during the middle 30s was 'wrong' from the normative standpoint of Western motion pictures, which by then had established very strict rules governing eyeline-direction and screen-position matching. The argument that this anomaly is merely Japanese naïveté, an aftermath of that historical lag observed during the previous period, is quite explicitly rebutted by the fact that Ozu's early comedies, up to about the time of *Tokyo no Gassho* (*Chorus of Tokyo*, 1931), contain a far greater proportion of 'correct' (invisible) continuity matches than the films of the 30s and early 40s in which the director scarcely ever misses an opportunity for a 'bad' match. These mismatched eyelines are part of a whole context of discontinuity in which 'illogical' reversals of screen direction, startling ellipses and a disruptive type of cutting of movement also abound.

Kurosawa's partial acceptance of his elders' attitude towards matching was undeniably a *choice*, essential to his mature formal conception, occurring as it did when he had been directing for nearly a decade. Indeed, during his first period (1942–51), Kurosawa ascribed far more importance to continuity than those elders had ever done, throughout a series of films which, though not always 'transparent' (i.e., devoid of formal preoccupations, reducible to plot and dramaturgy), were undeniably illustrative, both ethically and aesthetically, of the then worldwide concern with 'social realism' as exemplified by the notoriously transparent school of post-war Italy.

It was not until *Rashomon* (1950) and above all *Ikiru* (U.K.: *Living*; U.S.: *To Live*, 1952), that a resolutely 'brutal' approach to the shot-change became a permanent, fundamental option in Kurosawa's work. However, while he employs many devices to emphasize and *use* the discontinuous nature of the shot-change, attributing a 'rhythmic', i.e. *structural* role to the varying degrees of impact produced upon the spectator's perceptual system by those artificial caesuras in the continuity of the 'action', there is one important respect in which he diverges from Ozu and early Naruse. For, while he often skilfully violates the 'screen-positions rule' (and therefore incidentally the eyeline rule) when cutting from two-shot to two-shot in reverse-field set-ups, he never allows himself a 'bad' eyeline match when one or the other of his characters is alone in his or her respective shots. The basic difference between these two kinds of 'error' is that the one produces an open, unresolved, 'monolithic' disorientation, and the other is more richly dialectical in that it offers both an immediate contradiction and its *de facto* resolution through the patently visible reversal of positions. We may surmise that Kurosawa's rejection of the 'incorrect' eyeline match—in the case, for example, of successive close-ups—is motivated by an awareness that within a context of continuity, even if only partially *assumed*, such a device is not productive of dynamic structure.

Probably the first film in which Kurosawa harks back to Eisenstein's all but forgotten principle of montage units is *Ikiru*. Two of the film's key tête-à-tête scenes—the condemned Watanabe's meeting with the writer in the drinking stall, and his restaurant dinner with the girl Toyo—are built on what might be called a mixture of two montage units. Now if these scenes were simply alternations of mismatched field and reverse-field—as was the case in the early films of Naruse and in Ozu's films—it would be stretching a point to refer to them as being structured. At best, they would be merely

Toshiro Mifune and Machiko Kyo in *Rashomon*: 'One could also point out Kurosawa's extraordinary direction of actors—not only his favourite Toshiro Mifune, who has contributed much to his films, but all the others.'

paled over with an even cast of discontinuousness. However, each sequence also contains 'correctly' matched reversals as an integral part of the system of field-reversal running through the sequence. Interestingly enough, in the scene with the writer, it is the first pair of shots (in which Watanabe and the writer are separated: it is the moment when the dying man offers the other his sleeping pills) which matches, and in the scene with Toyo it is the initial and concluding pairs that do so. In both cases these correct matches seem to serve as reference points.

Now it is perfectly legitimate to put a dramaturgical interpretation on the morphology of these sequences, asserting that the second, bracketed as it is by 'correct' matches, has a 'closed' quality about it which metaphorically reflects the fact that Toyo has no intention of seeing Watanabe again (as indeed we discover in the subsequent scene outside the toy factory). Similarly, the fact that the scene with the writer involves only one such match (at the beginning) may be regarded as leaving the scene 'open' for Watanabe's pathetic night on the town, to which it is the prelude. Invariably, this kind of *correspondence* between narrative organization and the material options of set-up and editing will be encountered in any organically structured film—such symbiotic relationships abound in Ozu, Naruse and Mizoguchi—since an artist evolving a work with two or more structured levels will always tend to interweave them. The important thing is to guard against reducing the one to the other, against regarding as most important the level which superficially seems to communicate directly with our daily experience.

For the notion that structure is by definition a *code*, a configuration of signs which stand for 'something else', be it 'metaphysical', psychological, or merely behavioural, seems very much open to question today. It would, for example, lead to the dubious conclusion that this or that piece of scoring in a Wagner opera is predicated on purely dramaturgical considerations, whereas even if we are dealing with a leitmotiv which does, melodically analysed, have definite, codifiable bearings upon the libretto, the *totality* of the co-ordinates assigned to it (tonal, harmonic, rhythmic, instrumentational, etc.) sets up relationships with the overall formal conception of the work which are at least as important as its participation in the narrative discourse. And to take an even more familiar example, this same notion has also led to the kind of secondary school 'close reading' of English Romantic poetry which reduces form to a series of dramaturgical, 'expressive'

effects, always in the name of the 'higher' human values.

Thus, in *Ikiru*, the organization of these two sequences, while incontrovertibly 'attuned' to the film's narrative dimension, is to at least an equal extent involved in the total formal scheme (which in this case is essentially based on narrative modes!). It is also closely related to the general demand for what I can only call 'textural awareness' which all Kurosawa's major works place upon their audience, through the emphasis on shot-change *per se*. The difficulty with motion pictures, as Kurosawa and a few others have directed them, is that they are implicitly asking us to cope simultaneously with statements of several different species: we are being told a story and, at the same time, we are witnessing a kind of re-working of that space-time continuum which is occupied ideally (i.e., in our 'mind's eye') by that story. The re-working is as much a statement as the story itself; however, the simultaneous perception of both demands what the specialists call a 'good *Gestalt*'; in films this means a parallel awareness of both correspondences and variances, of likenesses and contrasts. In the present instance, it means recognizing these sequences as, indeed, 'open' and 'closed' in terms of the script movement, but also seeing them as structurally related in one respect (the repetition of the right–left reversals inherent in 'bad' matches), unrelated in others (the cutaway to the stray dog in the first, the presence, in the second, of a second 'correct' match).

Let us now examine the other ways in which Kurosawa 'drives home' the shot-change; for, taken together with the Eisensteinian 'mismatching' just discussed, they constitute in themselves a kind of vast, single variation form running through all his mature films, with the emphasis laid now on one mode, now on another. In *Rashomon* the emphasis is on radical oppositions between long-shot and extreme close-up; concomitantly, the 180-degree reversals, in which the film abounds, involve great 'depth of field' (actually exaggerated perspectives through the use of wide-angle lenses). Another, more general strategy, though closely related to the 180-degree reversals and to their corollary, mis-matched screen-positions, consists of broad displacements, from one shot to the next, of the main object of screen-attention, generally from one edge of the frame to the opposite. This is, of course, especially remarkable in the wide-screen films, starting with *Kakushi Toride no San Akunin* (*The Hidden Fortress*, 1958), and culminating in the masterful *Tengoku to Jigoku* (*High and Low*, U.S. alternative title: *The Ransom*, 1963). Here, the whole first half of the film, shot in the living room of a wealthy shoe manufacturer whose chauffeur's son has been mistaken by a kidnapper for the industrialist's own boy, is built upon whole-sale permutations and reversals of the characters on the screen (at times as many as seven or eight) from one shot to the next, and constitutes one of the most highly developed variation structures in Kurosawa's work.

It is interesting to note, in connection with this remarkable 'cloistered' section, that the film in which the editing is most 'brutal', in which the shot-changes ring out like so many pistol-shots in the mind's ear, is also the most claustrophobic of them all: *The Lower Depths*, drawn from the Gorky play. Over half the film takes place in one large room, and there is a heavy preponderance of 180-degree reversals among the shot-changes. Here, moreover, the limited range of shot-sizes allowed by the room makes these 'jarring' shot-changes all the more dissonant, as opposed to the emphatic size-oppositions in *Rashomon*, which had a more conventionally 'satisfying', resolved quality about them.

There is an interesting extension of Kurosawa's tendency to lay bare the reality of the shot-change: his use of hard-edge wipes in preference to dissolves. His one great 'samurai' film, *Kumonosu-jo* (*Throne of Blood*, 1957), based on *Macbeth*, is particularly rich in examples of this, the least transparent of all 'punctuation devices'. It is no doubt just this quality, moreover, which caused it to be so quickly abandoned, after the orgy of ornamental use to which it was put following its invention in the early 30s: the 'sophisticated' directors of the 40s saw only too well that this key, *par excellence*, to the essential artifice of films—the frameline itself crossing the spectator's effective field of vision and acting, besides, as a material embodiment of the shot-change—could unravel the illusionist tissue and give the whole game away. And it is in this light that Kurosawa's use of the wipe seems to me highly significant.

Aside from this basic emphasis on shot-change and the modal variation associated with it (differing degrees of obviousness, different ways of achieving it), there are other essential orientations which inform the works of Kurosawa. One of these is the idea of singularizing a certain figure or type of material. The long sequence-shot in *The Lower Depths* contrasting sharply with the fragmented texture of the rest of the film, making the most of the compositional possibilities afforded by the first really 'open-air' shot in the film and constituting a pivot and a breathing space on which the whole film may be said to rest, is one good example of this principle. Another is the pair of colour shots (showing the pink smoke which rises when the kidnapper burns the ransom brief-case) which intrudes stunningly upon the otherwise black-and-white context of *High and Low* and which also acts as a pivot: the film suddenly swings from the last of the long, static waiting scenes in the tycoon's lounge to the frantic chase across Tokyo with which all the rest of the film is concerned.

Different in substance and function, but related to the same attitude, are the three widely spaced interventions in *Ikiru* of an off-screen narrator, each shorter than the last, which break off entirely two-thirds of the way through the film on the words 'Five months later the hero of our story died.' Aside from their rarity, these passages are singularized in another way: all are associated with the heavily satirical setting of Watanabe's office in the city hall (they serve, in this context, to create a chastening 'distance' effect); and in this connection, one may further observe that the first line of the initial intervention (which is divided into several subsections) is spoken over the X-ray negative of Watanabe's stomach, an even more radical 'distance' device which destroys all conventional suspense and, at the same time, links this shot to the single other close-up of the X-ray, in the hospital consultation room.

Less significant perhaps, but nevertheless attesting to Kurosawa's sensitivity to the importance of this strategy, are the two slow-motion shots near the beginning of *Seven Samurai*, and the soundtrack cut near the end of *Tsubaki Sanjuro* (*Sanjuro*, 1962) as the two antagonists face each other before the final draw. This last scene, in which the interminably tense wait ends explosively in a single, lightning sword-stroke and a three-foot fountain of gushing blood, may be said to epitomize the last general construction principle which I should like to point out in Kurosawa's work: a systematic opposition between paroxysmic violence and protracted, sometimes lyrical, sometimes static scenes, from which narrative is momentarily evacuated but in which the tension builds.

It is in *Throne of Blood*, one of Kurosawa's most perfect achievements, that this principle is most meaningfully systematized. Its overall plan—which refers recognizably to the five acts of *Macbeth*—alternates with almost pendulum-like regularity between scenes of protracted lyrical (rather than expository) agitation—the dashing messengers, the first headlong ride through the storm-swept forest, the confused gallopings which *signify* rather than depict the battle that follows the first murder, the portentous panic of Miki's horse, the ominous invasion of the throne-room by a flock of birds—and similarly protracted moments of tense stasis, generally implying scenes of violence or momentous dramatic impact taking place *off-screen*: Asaji ('Lady Macbeth') waiting for her husband to return after murdering their lord, the funeral procession endlessly advancing towards the castle gates (a scene in which time and space are dilated with blatant artificiality), the long, tense introduction to the ghost scene. Constituting a kind of half-way house of subdued agitation between these two poles is the beautiful sequence early in the film depicting Washuzi's and Miki's blind wanderings through the mist-shrouded forest after their encounter with the witch: twelve times the horsemen come towards the camera, turn and ride away, in twelve shots materially separate but identical as to the space they frame—grey, misty, almost entirely abstract (not until the last shot do we realize this is a forest) ... and at this level, of course, the scene is acutely reminiscent of the strategies of Oriental theatre in general, with its boldly artificial representations of long journeys in the avowedly limited and concrete here-and-now of scenic space.

However, Kurosawa develops this scene into one of the most stunningly compact and sustained variation structures in all cinema, combining in never repeated order three or four well-defined stages chosen from the 'scales' provided by each of the following aspects of the action: the distance from the camera at which the approaching horses pause, the duration of their turn and the radius of the arc described, and their distance from the camera when the shot changes (at times they may ride into view out of the mist or disappear into it, at others the shot may begin when they are already in sight or end before they have vanished). From the eighth to the eleventh shot a shift occurs. The process grows increasingly complex; the riders reverse direction as they ride laterally to the (invisibly) panning camera, become separated as one rides out of the shot, join up again, ride out together leaving an empty shot, re-enter unexpectedly in close-up, etc. The last shot, which shows a landscape emerging from the rising mist, constitutes a finalizing return to the original cell: the horsemen ride towards the camera as in the beginning, but at a perceptibly slower pace than the steady trot which marked the rest of the sequence, then pull up in a medium shot: 'At last we're out of that forest,' says Washuzi, speaking the first words of a sequence in which the only sounds have been the hooves and whinnying of the horses, and an unobtrusive, very simple, sustained line of wood-wind music. The sequence is actually brought to its close by a thirteenth shot of Washuzi and Miki sitting at opposite sides of the frame, their battle pennants flying in the wind, calmly, amicably discussing the witch's prediction, but already separated symbolically by the castle (the seat of the power they will dispute) looming in the distance between them. Beyond this dramaturgical function of the shot, however, and its musical, coda-like bearing on what precedes, it is part of a larger, more fundamental option which underlies the entire film: that of rigorous symmetry, both in shot-composition—as here—and in the organization of the set-up–editing relationship (*découpage*), such as in the magnificent banquet sequence.

It is rare that a single *trouvaille* should inform an entire film, yet this is the case with

Toshiro Mifune and Minoru Chiaki (Macbeth and Banquo) contemplate the crown in *Throne of Blood*, 'one of Kurosawa's most perfect achievements'—and, incidentally, T. S. Eliot's favourite film.

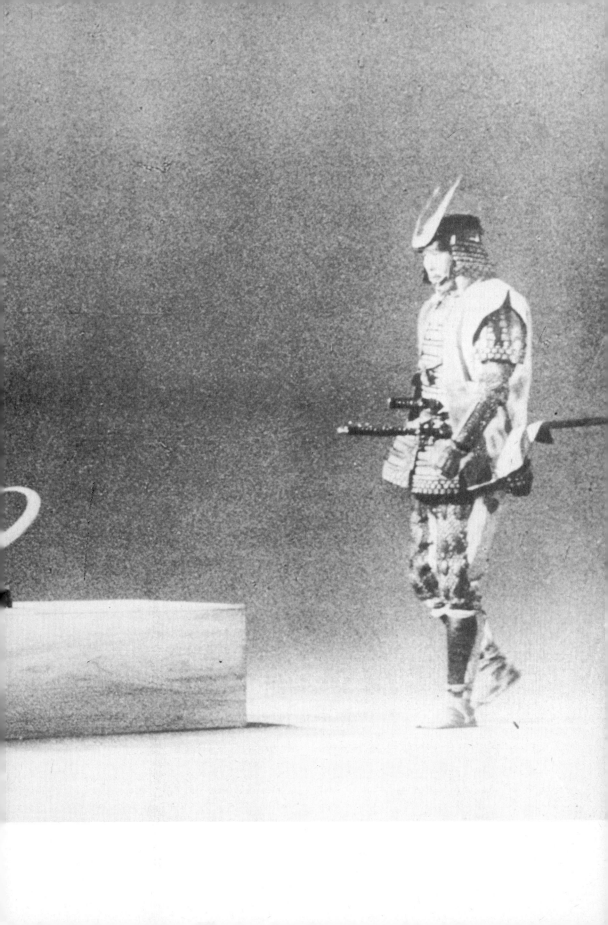

the final sequence in which Washuzi is pursued about the terraces of his castle by an unerring rain of whistling arrows shot at him by his own archers. This amazing piece of bravura, usually regarded by Western critics as either grotesque *and* gratuitous or brilliant *but* gratuitous, appears to me, on the contrary, as the very keystone of the film's formal organization: here at last the dialectically intense, horizontal relationship between scenes of 'empty' frenzy and scenes which are dramatically charged but *actionless* resolves itself in a *vertical* orgasm of protracted on-screen violence *and* dramaturgy combined at last on the screen, involving a complete—and unique—break in tone and style, the symmetrical principle, in particular, being almost totally abandoned here. The principle does, however, return in the postlude, in so far as it is a near-repeat of the opening sequence: the foggy landscape, the chanting chorus, Washuzi's tomb. I might add that this symmetrical principle, so shocking to many 'sophisticated' Western viewers, no doubt produces this effect precisely because of its anti-illusionist weight: *nothing discloses the manipulator's hand so much as symmetry*; and we need only compare the Western marionette with its invisible strings and hidden masters, and the *bunraku* puppet with its trio of exposed human servants, to understand how Kurosawa's approach, in this film as in many others, is related to the Japanese need to be aware of artistic *process*, their instinctive rejection of 'identification'. In contrast, one would be hard put indeed to find such consistent use of symmetry in any Western film since the 20s.

Throne of Blood is perhaps the ultimate in Kurosawa's work in this specific direction, but isolated instances of a comparable use of 'disrupting paroxysms' are to be found even in his early work: the incredibly long, silent, motionless confrontation of the lovers in a darkened office in *Waga Seishun ni Kuinashi* (*No Regrets for Our Youth*, 1946) and the wild paint-can battle at the end of *Yoidore Tenshi* (*Drunken Angel*, 1948) directly prefigure the two poles of this principle as it was developed in *Throne of Blood* (also, to a lesser extent, in *Rashomon*, *Akahige* [*Red Beard*, 1957] and, in the contrast between its two main parts, *High and Low*); while the all but unbearably protracted crying scene between the young doctor and the maid in *Shizukanaru Ketto* (*The Quiet Duel*, or *The Silent Duel*, 1949) prefigures Watanabe's harrowingly methodical rendition of 'his' song in the little honkey-tonk bar in *Ikiru*. Needless to say, long, 'empty' shots occur throughout the early works of Ozu, while extreme violence is a constant in much Japanese cinema. But Kurosawa's specifically dialectical use of the ambivalent contrast/identity between them must be regarded as unique.

Akira Kurosawa has made some twenty-four films to date. Even if we confined ourselves to the half-dozen masterpieces made between 1952 and 1963, there would be no room to analyse them all here. I have tried to give glimpses of the formal preoccupations of a few films from that period and to analyse one or two aspects of the complex *Throne of Blood*. Now I should like to outline a more comprehensive analysis of one of Kurosawa's best known films, *Ikiru*, to which I have already provided a few clues.

The basic formal idea, the conceptual cell which gives birth to the film as a complex whole, may be expressed as follows: the first two-thirds of the film will show the steps which lead from Watanabe's discovery that he has cancer (figured, as we have seen, in the film's very first image, even though the story begins earlier), to his realization that he can still do something with his life, whereas the last third will show the funeral ceremony at which he is eulogized, more or less hypocritically, by his fellow civil servants, who fill in, through flashbacks, the gap in the narrative, i.e. what Watanabe's actual accomplishment was: transforming an insanitary vacant lot into a children's playground. These two parts of the film are systematically antithetical in certain ways, parallel in others. The chief disparity between them is the extreme discontinuity of the first part, which stretches over some two and a half weeks of narrative time, contains countless ellipses and makes recurrent use of the 'montage' technique (or chain of ellipses) inherited from the 30s, as against the apparently absolute unity of time and place in the second part. The parallelism of the two sections is only slightly less obvious: first, both contain flashbacks (those in the first part being Watanabe's solitary recollections of his son's childhood and adolescence); moreover, it can be observed that the flashbacks in the first part (five in all) follow a pattern which is in fact a *diminished retrogradation* of the flashbacks in the second part of the film, at least in so far as their grouping and inter-relationships are concerned. In the first part, we move from two isolated flashbacks (the father and son riding in the back of a car behind the mother's hearse; Watanabe discussing his future with his brother) to two related flashbacks separated by a cutaway but linked by 'rhyming' movements (Watanabe watching his son play baseball from the bleachers: elation/back in the 'present' Watanabe sits down/in the bleachers: deflated, Watanabe sits down), then to two narratively unrelated but directly abutted flashbacks (the boy's appendectomy; his departure for the war). In the second part, the symmetrical series begins with two groups of two unrelated but directly abutted flashbacks, continues with a pair of related flashbacks separated by an ellipsis, and then proceeds to develop a succession of nine isolated flashbacks.

On the other hand, the mode of flashback employed in the first part is based solely on the 'rhyme' in various forms which here embody Watanabe's mental associations: his dead wife's photo recalls the hearse; the baseball bat which he uses to bar the door conjures up his son's hapless game; then comes the double sitting-down movement which, in turn, leads to the upward movement of the hospital elevator (perceptually, a downward movement, since the camera is in the elevator), then Watanabe's farewell to his son entering the operating room evokes another farewell—his son's going off to war. In the funeral, on the contrary, there is absolutely no rhyming: the flashbacks are directly narrative, they replace almost literally certain fragments of the mourners' evocations, and the temporal equivalence is such that the illusion of a continuous time flow during this part of the film is remarkably convincing. Also, of course, the flashbacks in the second part are spread out over the last half-hour of the film, whereas in the first they are concentrated in a single ten-minute sequence (and are related, moreover, to the three 'montage' sequences which precede and follow it).

Perhaps the most remarkable formal option attached to the funeral flashbacks, however, is that these brief scenes, designed though they are to fill a five-month gap in the narration, in fact show nothing of the actual stages which enabled Watanabe to achieve his goal. We see him doggedly, mutely putting pressure on a colleague through his presence alone, pleading in a choked voice with the deputy mayor, making his way painfully down a hall to that august functionary's office, silently resisting the intimidation of thugs, or suddenly noticing a sunset; but at no time do we see any decisive papers being stamped, any official throwing up his hands in surrender, or any other crucial stage of the action. We do not even see Watanabe's death, only the song on the swing which preceded it. In short, the narrative gap is bridged with moments which are merely bridges in themselves. It is not, in a sense, filled at all: the decisive moments of the narrative proper are 'left to the imagination', in a strange kind of mirrors-within-mirrors structure which provides one of the film's essential sources of unity.

The first part of the film is quite free in its form, even though a number of figures and leitmotivs are used to link separate sequences. We should add the cutaways to Watanabe's fallen coat in the X-ray room, whose function rhymes with a similar set of cutaways (to the black dog) in the drinking stall with the writer; the two shots of Watanabe starting to climb the staircase to his son's rooms on the first floor of his own house and stopping each time midway; plus two more developed motifs which also extend into the second part: Watanabe's new hat, which comes in four times in the first part, is evoked by his former underlings during the funeral narration, and is brought back by the policeman near the end of the film; and, of course, there is the song 'Life Is So Short'. The second part, on the other hand, is as rigorous in its overall construction as the first is free. Starting with a preponderance of wide, fixed shots of the rows of mourners, it gradually moves towards tighter and tighter shots, finally breaking down into a series of accompanying pan-shots as the drunken mourners lose all dignity and start crawling towards each other across the floor.

There remains to be made a very general remark about the themes which characterize

Kurosawa's films and the formal implications of these themes. It is a commonplace to point out that almost all his films are grounded in melodrama, that he has a miraculous gift for ennobling the melodramatic mood, for pulling off situations in which anyone else would have foundered on the shoals of ridicule. Indeed, who but Kurosawa could have 'got away' with the sequence in *Subarashiki Nichiyobi* (*One Wonderful Sunday*, 1947) in which the young man, alone at night with his girlfriend in an empty open-air concert hall, draws forth with a conductor's gestures the sounds of a full symphony orchestra playing Schubert's 'Unfinished Symphony'? And yet I am convinced that there is no miracle here: it is Kurosawa's formal organization—either confined to the dimensions of a sequence, as in the early film just cited, or embracing the entire film, as in *Throne of Blood*, *Ikiru* and the other masterpieces—that achieves the transmutation of narrative material which, as 'literature', would scarcely hold our attention. And this is simply one more reason why Kurosawa's work can scarcely be said even to exist without the double reading proposed earlier.

However, there is another dramatic factor, common to many of Kurosawa's most important films, which bears a direct, material relationship to their formal development. I refer to the obsessive, obstinate behaviour of so many of his main characters: the alcoholic doctor's stubborn insistence on treating the tubercular gangster in *Drunken Angel*; the young surgeon's absurdly tenacious refusal to tell his spurned and frustrated fiancée that he has contracted syphilis during the war in *The Quiet Duel*; the young detective's pig-headed determination to recover his revolver in *Nora Inu* (*Stray Dog*, 1949). Then, moving on to the more significant films: Watanabe's determination to build his park in *Ikiru*; the old patriarch's obsessive fear of nuclear warfare in the magnificent *Ikimono No Kiroku* (*I Live in Fear*, or *Record of a Living Being*, 1955); the complex guilt and power obsessions of *Throne of Blood*; the fascination with a mythical treasure in *The Hidden Fortress*. As for *Dodes'ka-den* (1970), it is a veritable catalogue of obsessions, most of them beyond the fringe of madness: the old man and the boy building an imaginary dream-house, the silent man obsessed by the idea of his wife's betrayal, the mentally retarded adolescent obsessed with tramways.

Now it seems clear to me that these obsessional themes, implying as they do in their very essence elements of both repetition and variation, serve as springboards for the complex formal elaboration of the films as totalities. Looking back over the film we have just examined, *Ikiru*, this would certainly seem to be true: Watanabe's obsessions, first with death, then with his self-appointed mission, serve as a *basso ostinato* principle underlying the two main sections of the film, contrapuntally in the first, then becoming the direct motor of the film's movement in the second. And I suspect that a similar demonstration could be made regarding some of the other films of that period. If so, it would tend to corroborate the opinion shared by Jean Ricardou and other contemporary theoreticians that while 'every director, really any creator, has a favourite myth', as Donald Richie puts it, its function is not to provide some kind of ideal unity of content, as generations of thematic critics have tried to teach us, but rather, in the case of a creator of Kurosawa's stature, to complete that combination of unity and diversity which is form . . . which is, indeed, the work itself.

Other views on Kurosawa exist, of course, and had not Donald Richie already written his *The Films of Akira Kurosawa* (1965), which takes a different approach, one might have included another piece on Kurosawa which could point out that formal values can co-exist with what Burch calls 'human values.' One could also point out Kurosawa's extraordinary direction of actors—not only his favourite Toshiro Mifune, who has contributed much to his films, but all the others. And that list would have to include the star of *Dersu Uzala* (1975), Maxim Munzuk. Shot in 70-mm and six-track stereophonic sound, it has been called Kurosawa's most Fordian film since *Yojimbo* (1961). What might so easily have been a cinematic version of that *Reader's Digest* series 'The Most Unforgettable Character I Ever Met' is transformed into an (unfashionable) hymn to the human spirit—precisely because of Kurosawa's formal genius. A genius which Burch has probably been the first really to analyse in his book *To the Distant Observer: Form and Meaning in the Japanese Cinema* (1979).

GREGORY LA CAVA

John Gillett

Gregory La Cava (1892–1952) is the missing link in the long line of American social satirists extending from DeMille, Lubitsch and Monta Bell to Hawks, Cukor, McCarey, Capra, Leisen, Stevens, Wilder and Sturges. Missing because, until recently, not enough of his work had been seen to make any critical reassessment possible, and even now many of his early films remain hard to come by, like the much-praised political fantasy *Gabriel Over the White House* (1933). La Cava's early training as a magazine caricaturist and a film animator with Walter Lantz can be seen in his ability to punch a gag swiftly home, and in the rapier thrusts of dialogue and narration which characterize his later features. His 'crazy' world is first seen in the silent comedies with W. C. Fields— *So's Your Old Man* (1926), *Running Wild* (1927)—and with Bebe Daniels (*Feel My Pulse*, 1928), in which running gags are built up to hysterical climaxes including, in the last named, a witty slow-motion sequence. La Cava's work in the 30s and 40s introduced his favourite theme of a group of disparate characters brought together in a family setting (or a boarding house or hotel) to be used as a springboard for satirical contrasts between the claims of rich and poor, based essentially on the polemics of the Depression and New Deal eras. Like other American directors of the time, La Cava seemed often to be making a left-wing statement while keeping one foot in the right-wing camp, but this political ambivalence does not seriously undermine the sharpness and relevance of his characters, rejoicing in their Park Avenue riches while the realities of the time gradually intrude on their lives.

Lee Tracy's con-man in *The Half-Naked Truth* (1932), the more seriously viewed mental patients of *Private Worlds* (1935), the wacky, argumentative families of *My Man Godfrey* (1936), *Fifth Avenue Girl* (1939), *Living in a Big Way* (1947) and, most famous of all, the beautifully delineated actresses' hostel in *Stage Door* (1937), find La Cava in his most lively and mordant mood. La Cava (who was often his own scriptwriter) imposed his own view on a variety of subjects and combined a surface brilliance with a subversively bitter view of American society, which makes him, in his best work, at least the equal of his better-known contemporaries. Although not a major visual stylist, he used his camera fluently and economically, with a fondness for gentle tracking shots, following characters around enclosed settings; and, like Capra, he was a brilliant director of ensemble scenes. Actresses such as Irene Dunne, Claudette Colbert (notably in *She Married Her Boss*, 1935), Carole Lombard, Ginger Rogers and Katharine Hepburn gave some of their most assured performances in La Cava's films.

Stage Door (1937), reseen recently, has gained rather than lost with the passage of time; Andrea Leeds remains embarrassing, but everyone else is fresh and lively, and the dialogue is as fast and witty as it is in *His Girl Friday* and almost as overlapping as in the films of Robert Altman. I would even put in a word for *Primrose Path* (1940); with its location shooting in one of the seedier fishing ports of California, it looks almost like an Italian neo-realist film. Andrew Sarris, who puts La Cava on 'The Far Side of Paradise', quotes W. C. Fields as having said that, next to himself of course, La Cava had 'the best comedy mind in Hollywood'.

FRITZ LANG: GERMAN PERIOD

Noël Burch

Lang's career and the body of writing that has grown up around it, in France especially, present a double paradox. From 1920 to 1932, along with Eisenstein and Dreyer, Lang (1890–1976) was one of the principal architects of that *langage sans langue* (language without speech) which, according to Christian Metz, is cinema. From 1933 onwards, exiled from Nazi Germany and settling shortly thereafter in the United States, he seemingly accepted all the (essentially regressive) inferences which the American sound film had drawn in particular from his best work in Germany; whether consciously or not, he identified himself with that anonymous being who was always much of a muchness, the all-purpose Hollywood director who turned out practically all of its product . . . whether made in California or elsewhere.

Since around 1950, however, a sizeable fraternity of (mostly French) critics and cinephiles, restricting themselves to an essentially thematic reading, have claimed to see no break between Lang's German and his American work, and argue either an exact parity between the two (*Moonfleet* = *Die Spinnen*, *The Big Heat* = *Mabuse*) or even the superiority of the American over the German films.

My purpose here is only incidentally polemical, and I shall not waste time demonstrating how and why *M* is not merely superior to *Fury* but belongs to an altogether different dimension. Instead, concentrating on the major works from Lang's German period, I shall attempt to define the nature of a series of achievements that match the history of the cinema's crestline of discovery stage by stage.

First Stage: Mastering a System

Though dating from 1922, the two-part film *Doktor Mabuse, der Spieler* (*Dr Mabuse, the Gambler*) already marks, in my opinion, a zenith in the gestation of a *literary genre within the cinema*. Its zenith, but also its terminal point: a whole line of similarly (but never quite so exemplarily) *transparent* cinema, including all the films Lang himself made after his departure from Germany, is rendered totally superfluous by this film. At the same time, however, *Doktor Mabuse, der Spieler* implicitly challenges this idea of 'transparency', for it is also an initial affirmation that articulations (here, changes from sequence to sequence, as opposed to 'matching' shot changes) can rate as entities in their own right, can be the components of an 'abstract' phenomenological discourse that may be read independently of the purely narrative discourse. This film, in other words, seems to me to be the precise point at which the cinema that reproduced the nineteenth-century novelistic discourse—and which postulated the essence of cinema, its vocation, as *being this reproduction*—defined its own limits and prepared to give way to that other complex, composite cinema which was both figurative and non-figurative, both artifice and reality, and whose first manifestation had probably been *Das Kabinett des Doktor Caligari* (*The Cabinet of Dr Caligari*, 1919), a film on which Lang had worked in its early stages.

My assertion that *Mabuse* tends essentially to reproduce the literary discourse may seem presumptuous, so I shall try to define this reproduction. The film is of course based on a serial by Norbert Jacques. But there are, after all, quite a number of cases where literary works have served as raw material for the elaboration of a cinematic form within which the 'literary' discourse as such does indeed still hold a real place, but no longer the one it held in the traditional novel, having become one code among several. For this reason I think an examination of the way this film *solicits the spectator's perception* would be more conclusive.

The reading of a novel in the manner of Balzac or Zola involves 'forgetting' the reality of the printed letters as well as the functions of grammar and syntax: we are invited to share in the illusion, not that what we are reading is literally 'true', but that the characters in the novel are 'true to life'. We are, in other words, expected to maintain the same sort of relationship with them *as we do with the people around us*, being sorry for them, admiring them, being afraid of or for them, hating them, mourning their deaths and so on. The author's voice is of course often heard, explicitly or implicitly, but his comments almost invariably serve to enhance the 'credibility' of the characters through an expedient which consists in suggesting that the author maintains precisely the same relationship with his characters that he is trying to induce in the reader. The same is true of the cinema represented, in this respect, by *Mabuse*. Fifty years after being committed to celluloid, the portraits of Mabuse, the Countess Told, Attorney Wenk and Cara Carozza are still as 'alive' and as captivating as they were in 1922.

It is in this sense that *Mabuse* was a consummation. For of course, long before *Mabuse*, this had been the ambition of practically every film made. But prior to Lang's first masterpieces, the cinema remained deficient in this area of novelistic credibility. Ince, Griffith, Perret and Feuillade all failed to endow their characters with the *density* that is the mark of their counterparts in novels; and all Lang's earlier films, including the very Feuillade-ish *Die Spinnen* (*The Spiders*, 1919), are tainted with this same deficiency (which is of course a deficiency only from the standpoint of cinema as a literary genre).

How does this deficiency actually manifest

itself . . . and how is it finally overcome in *Mabuse*? I have suggested that the reader's relationship with the traditional novelistic discourse is based on non-perception, on the 'invisibility' of the material articulations sustaining this discourse: in other words, syntax, grammar, and the perceptual form of words and symbols. In the cinema, this non-perception corresponds to a reading which 'sees' neither the edges of the frame nor the changes of shot—the two materialities which in fact tend to challenge the illusion of *continuity* that, as Robbe-Grillet has very rightly pointed out, underlies the credibility both of the traditional novel and of the cinema which has adopted the same specifications.

For these two material realities to become 'invisible' in the same way as syntax and printed characters, however, a major obstacle had first to be surmounted. *Through artifice, what was not 'naturally' invisible had to be so rendered.* In particular, the spectator had to be persuaded that the pro-filmic space (which for a time was the same as the theatrical proscenium) could be fragmented, and that these fragments, passing successively before him in a space that remained constant (the 'window' of the screen), could constitute a *mentally continuous* space. For it was hardly more complicated than that: to achieve novelistic credibility, one had to be able to film objects or characters close up—to isolate a face, a hand, some prop, just as the novelistic discourse does—without disorienting the spectator in his 'reasoned' or instinctive analysis, of the spatial continuum involved at that moment, and also without drawing his attention to the artifices whereby this illusion of continuity was achieved.

During the cinema's very early days, of course, the idea of switching angles or bringing the camera in closer during the course of a scene—that is, introducing a discontinuity of viewpoint into the continuity of a scene—was literally inconceivable. At the same time, however, as *The Great Train Robbery* (1903) shows, the single fixed shot kept audiences too distant from the characters for them to acquire an individualized presence, and therefore any novelistic density. In Porter's film, the characters are so dwarfed within the frame that one cannot distinguish between them, and they remain anonymous. Such was the prestige of this novelistic density, how-

ever, that the obstacles preventing the cinema from attaining it had to be removed if wider audiences were to be attracted; and as a first priority, the camera had to be able to move in to show details of a scene once the overall view had been established.

This was the impulse that was to lead to the discovery of the basic principles of continuity articulations, following on the gradual realization that shots present themselves to the eye like the successive images in a comic strip, and that they can be linked to each other by specifically orientative elements (eyeline matching between people looking at each other, matching screen direction when someone leaves one frame to enter the next). Gradually, between 1907 and 1917, it became possible to maintain the illusion of continuity while resorting to fragmentation (to *découpage*), and to impose the illusion so strongly that the very *existence* of shot changes, like the edges of the frame, became totally obscured.

By 1922, every practising film-maker was more or less familiar with this system of orientation, though few of them so thoroughly as Fritz Lang. At the very beginning of *Der Spieler: Ein Bild der Zeit* (the first part of *Mabuse*), he films a dialogue between Dr Mabuse and his secretary—who is behind him—in a series of cross-cut close shots which isolate each of the men in turn *in a setting we do not see*. As an opening gambit this was a dangerous move at the time; yet thanks to the perfect angular articulation between the direction of the secretary's eyes and of the glances Mabuse casts at him over his shoulder, the spectator can be in no doubt as to the relative position of the two men in the surrounding—and as yet hypothetical—space of Mabuse's salon. Dramaturgically, this opening sequence is exemplary, both in this perfect articulation which permits a close scrutiny of the characters from the outset, and in the striking concision with which the opening titles exactly pin down the two personalities and their relationship: Mabuse: 'You've been taking cocaine again'; Secretary: 'If you fire me, I'll kill myself.'

This demonstration of narrative mastery continues right through the celebrated second sequence of the film, with members of Mabuse's gang going about their business in alternating montage (one in a train, one up a telegraph pole, etc.), the continuity between all these shots in different settings being assured by close-ups of synchronized watches. Technically, this complex narrative, unprecedented in its virtuosity, was at least as effective as one of Gaston Leroux or Maurice Leblanc's best chapters. Let there be no misunderstanding, however: although the effect achieved would have been very much the same had this scene appeared in a novel by one of the best thriller writers of the day, the *means* employed by Lang are quite clearly *different* from those used in literature. Hence my conviction that in the cinema this process constitutes a *separate literary genre*, as autonomous in relation to the novel and the theatre as these two genres are in relation to each other. And it is this specificity in the dramaturgic cinema's means that reveals the germ of a cinema which would one day finally break free from the traditional novel.

One important aspect of this specificity is the immediate and total materialization of discontinuity whenever indication of this discontinuity answers a dramatic need. In other words, moving from one décor to another in a 'classic' novel usually involves a gradual process—describing the new setting, situating the new characters in it, and finally getting the new action under way—with the hiatus in reading introduced by a new paragraph or chapter contributing to the fact that these transitions are generally smoothed over. This is obviously not so in the cinema, especially if the use of what have come to be known as punctuating devices (the dissolve, iris in or out, fade in or out, designed precisely to soften such transitions in the manner of the novel and theatre) is as restricted as it is in *Mabuse*; for in the cinema, when these transitions take the form of simple shot changes, they are instantly perceived as radical breaks, as elements of extreme discontinuity.

This, of course, had always been so. But Lang was, I think, the first to exploit fully the dialectical possibilities in this introduction of an element of discontinuity within the narrative continuity. In Griffith's celebrated parallel montage for the final sequences of *Birth of a Nation* and *Intolerance*, the way the 'shot change' phenomenon functions in the succession of shots is usually purely arbi-

trary: the change of scene could easily have taken place a few seconds earlier or later, and one even feels that often these segments from scenes could be permutated without making much difference, for never at any moment in Griffith's use of this kind of montage does one sequence relate to the next other than through the shot change at the precise moment when it occurs. Directly on the level of perception there is consequently a total rupture, the only factor of continuity being one furnished purely by memory: the continuity linking together the characters and their acts in the context of the film as a whole. The result, to my mind, is a complete lack of tension and considerable uncertainty in the progress of the narrative, despite the supposedly 'rhythmic' (but can there be rhythm without directional movement and without tension-relaxation?) rapid succession of shots.

In *Mabuse*, on the other hand, where the basic organizing principle (first set forth in the sequence concerning the theft of the documents from the train) is in fact alternate montage, Lang always establishes precise relationships between the end (or the suspension) of one scene and the initiation (or resumption) of another. This connection sometimes assumes the rather crude form of a question and answer ('Who can be behind all this?' asks a shot of Attorney von Wenk; 'Him!' answers a shot of Mabuse disguising himself); sometimes a rather more subtly cerebral counterpoint, when the thoughts or acts of one of the participants in this emotional quadrille worthy of Corneille (La Carozza loves Mabuse, who loves Countess Told, who loves no one, not even her discreet admirer von Wenk) leads quite naturally to the appearance of one of his partners. In a more general way, and no matter what its function, each sequence change takes over the relay, makes the necessary transmission of *narrative movement* (in the sense that one talks of the movement of a clock). It should be stressed that all these transitions are purely dramaturgic: the 'visual rhymes' of *Das Testament des Doktor Mabuse* (*The Testament of Dr Mabuse*; also known as *The Last Will of Dr Mabuse* and *The Crimes of Dr Mabuse*, 1933) were still to come. But they weave *specific* links across each sequence change, maintaining a constant presence (that of the narrative's movement *forward*, as

M: 'One of the three "insert" sequence-shots: a police notice against which Elsie Beckmann bounces her ball and on which the killer's shadow falls.'

opposed to Griffith's hesitations) in face of the violent rupture caused by the shot change in itself; hence the dialectical tension produced by each change of scene in the film, which on this level prefigures Eisenstein's dialectic. It is through the disposition of these privileged moments—as the scene articulations become here—that Lang organizes the 'respiration', the rhythmics of his narrative (and perhaps for the first time in the history of the cinema one can talk of a completely controlled rhythm).

Although what we are dealing with here is primarily a novelistic form (the main function of the structure and rhythm being to carry, to 'deliver' the narrative), a new and more strictly cinematic form—closer to opera than to literature—can be seen outlined in Lang's awareness of the dialectic potential of these ruptures in film, an awareness which was to become explicit in the trio of masterpieces to come: *Spione* (*Spies*, 1928), *M* (1931) and *The Testament of Dr Mabuse*.

Second Stage: Dissolution of the Code: Towards Montage

If the first *Mabuse* can thus be considered an end-stage not only in Fritz Lang's career but in the course of the cinema, *Metropolis* (1926) is undoubtedly a transitional work. It is also a fundamentally ambivalent film, in both style and ideology. Siegfried Kracauer and others have already demonstrated the ways in which this film is linked to the 'social criticism' peculiar to budding Fascism: the idealistic reconciliation of capital and labour, the deliberately derisory representation of the revolutionary act, the careful avoidance of any direct repression of man by man ('It's the Machine that has enslaved us; let's go back to real values . . .'). At the same time, however, the evident desire to denounce capitalist alienation has led some rather ingenuous critics, including Francis Courtade, to see *Metropolis* as 'first and foremost a social film, dealing with the class struggle' and showing 'what the life of the working classes would be under the Nazi régime'. At all events, as Theodor Adorno has demonstrated with reference to Wagner, an accomplished work of art can very well carry progressive and reactionary elements at one and the same time: it can be a faithful reflection of the ideology of the ruling class while offering forms, structures and aesthetic effects which are not only progressive or indeed revolutionary as far as the organic history of the particular art form is concerned, but also contain an implicit critique of the prevailing ideology, even prefiguring the advent of its antithesis.

I tried to stress earlier that the consequence, the *raison d'être*, of the orientation code mastered by Lang in *Mabuse* was to obscure the reality of the shot change in conditions of continuity (within a sequence). It was quite a different matter in *Metropolis*. Here, in the wake of the first French avant-garde (Gance, L'Herbier), Lang sets out to conquer Montage. The tripartite alternative—sequence shot, reverse angle, axial match—that defines the limits of the 'intra-sequential' style of *Mabuse* here loses its mandatory quality. Apparent instead is a desire *not* to conceal the shot change behind the 'natural' movement of the scene (bringing the camera in closer when the spectator is likely to want a closer look, turning it round so that he can see what is happening 'opposite') but to make it play a more positively *expressive* role. Here again, of course, we remain purely in the dramaturgical domain: montage, with Lang, is designed to stress the pathos of the action.

As an illustration one might cite the extremely effective sequence in which, trying to escape from Rotwang's clutches, Maria grabs the bars of a skylight and is filmed from various different angles in rapid succession. But another example, the meeting between Maria and Freder in front of the altar in the catacombs, will also indicate another important point. Their embrace is filmed from a series of opposing angles, edited in a 'breathless' tempo. Here the shot changes are anything but invisible, all the more so in that Lang, apparently oblivious of the rules he had contributed so much towards consecrating, perpetrates some particularly glaring bad matches: almost systematically crossing the median line, he shows the actors from angles which mean that their respective positions on the screen are constantly reversed. Although these bad eyeline matches might at a pinch be said to enhance the desired effect, others—notably in the first scene between Fredersen and his son in the former's office—incontestably weaken it. Not even an involuntary echo of Eisenstein's dialectical use of good and bad matches in *Strike*, they seem simply to be inexplicable lapses; and they were to disappear almost completely when Lang more or less definitively abandoned the pursuit of Montage in his very next film (Montage in the cruder sense implied by the capital letter) to return to the problems of scene articulation (which is merely another aspect of montage in the wider sense). *Metropolis* is in fact at its most effective whenever montage, instead of attempting to assume an 'expressive' role within sequences (a simplistic interpretation of the Expressionist doctrine?), confines itself to the task of providing narrative rhythm: for instance our first introduction to the Hall of Machines, seen in parallel montage with a scene in Fredersen's office, or the flash of Maria retreating before Rotwang along a wall, a shot inserted into a scene depicting the tribulations of Fredersen's son in the subterranean world. And after *Spione*, this was the track to which Lang was to return.

Third Stage: Considering the Ellipse . . . and Imposing It

Often neglected because of the stereotyped banality of its plot, *Spione* nevertheless denotes a peak in the first great period of cinematic discoveries. Despite certain parallels with the first *Mabuse*, the area investigated here is essentially different. The film's metabolism is established through a systematic alternation of serenely discursive passages scrupulously respecting 'real time' with other moments so audaciously elliptical that they may have presented genuine difficulties to audiences of the period.

The ellipse and its evolution play a central role in the history of cinematic style. So that Lang's achievement in *Spione* may be seen in its proper perspective, it may be helpful to recall some basic concepts.

In language, properly speaking, an ellipse can be defined as the syntactic or stylistic omission of one or more words which the mind supplies more or less spontaneously . . . By extension: the art of abridgement or implication. In phrases like 'Each in turn' ('Each *must act* in turn'), usage has completely obscured our perception of the ellipse, and the elliptical form has substituted itself for the fuller version; at the other end of the scale, poetic ellipse (e.g. Mallarmé) sometimes leaves one unable to supply the missing words spontaneously.

The many gradations between perceived and non-perceived ellipse are also found in the cinema. In its cinematic sense, borrowed fairly freely from the literary definition, 'ellipse' has come to mean primarily 'a temporal abridgement'. One could of course call it the omission of one or more acts or events which the mind supplies more or less spontaneously. Cinematic practice suggests a more precise formulation, however: each time the circumstances of a shot change are such that, while establishing a chronological relationship between the two successive shots, it also—and by whatever means—suggests a time lapse between the end of one shot and the beginning of the next, then there has been an ellipse. This might be described as a strict definition. However, as we shall see later in examining the various manifestations of the 'elliptical effect' in *Spione*, the ellipse is often used in conjunction with another trope—synecdoche—whereby 'the detail signifies the whole'.

Now, in the development of the dramaturgic expedients already discussed, the ellipse played a major role, notably with a view to perpetuating the priorities presented by the traditional novelistic narrative.

We have seen how, since the primitives presented each shot as an autonomous tableau, the shot change was therefore always a break in temporal continuity, and consequently always an ellipse; but one can also say that it was almost invariably the same kind of ellipse, essentially indeterminate in its time value, and syntactically equivalent to the inter-title 'Some time later' (in which it later came to be embodied). It was only with the introduction (notably by Griffith) of a sense of real continuity artificially created between shots by montage that the ellipse was to assume an entirely specific and diversified character in the face of this newly affirmed continuity.

Nevertheless even in Porter's films, despite the absence of this crucial element provided by the impression of perfect continuity, one can already see a rudimentary distinction in the respective time values of certain ellipses.

It is difficult in the present state of film research to trace precisely the steps whereby the progressive film-makers attained a genuine mastery, not of the ellipse as a stock figure of speech (this 'transparent' use was developed hand in hand with the code of orientation), but of a systematic manipulation of greater or lesser invisibility in the ellipse considered as an essential parameter in constructing a *découpage*. Even so it seems certain that, among the silent film-makers, Fritz Lang ventured furthest along this path with *Spione*.

The rapid series of shots with which *Spione* opens immediately places the film under the sign of the ellipse: gloved hands opening a safe/the hands placing documents in an envelope/a leather-clad figure riding on a motorcycle/radio antennae: waves radiating/a newspaper headline announcing the theft of secret documents/an official on the phone/a car on the road with chauffeur and passenger; another car overtaking it; a shot/the passenger crumpling up, a hand takes a briefcase from him/an official on the phone/another headline. For the space of a few shots the action then becomes less disjointed, though no less swift: reverse editing between harassed officials in the confusion of their office. Then the choppy movement starts again: another headline/two officials tele-phoning back and forth/a diplomat standing behind his desk/insert of a letter he is reading/a car stopping before an official build-ing, a leather-clad man running up the steps and/going inside/erupting into the diplomat's office/title: 'I saw the man who . . .'/close-up of a bullet piercing a window/the leather-clad man falling/the furious diplomat exclaiming/ title: 'Who can . .'/'. . . be behind all this?'/ close shot of Haghi (Rudolph Klein-Rogge), then/a huge title: 'ME'.

From the outset here a sort of panorama of the field of elliptical modalities may be discerned. The two extremes already defined take precedence, of course, though not with-out frequent nuances which induce a movement in tight counterpoint to that of the narrative. To start from the beginning: the first two shots define an ellipse relatively con-crete in duration; linked by the gloved hands, they are obviously separated from each other only by a few moments within the 'virtual' narrative time. The third shot introduces an ellipse of a quite different order: is this the same man, and the action therefore a contin-uation? His costume might suggest so, but this is mere assumption; the ellipse is there-fore on the borderline between what I have described in my *Theory of Film Practice* as the 'small measurable ellipse' and the 'large indefinite ellipse', since the action in this shot could very well simply be occurring parallel to the first action, or even have no definite connection with it. But the following ellipse falls unmistakably into the second category: the radio waves are linked to what has gone

before only by a relationship of causality (dif-fering from the 'causal match' in that there is no illusion even of temporal continuity). Next come three similarly indefinite ellipses, then the murder on the highway introduces the first continuity cut; two more 'large el-lipses', then the short reverse field sequence, two more indefinite ellipses, then an example of what one might describe with some justifi-cation as a 'spatial ellipse', because the alter-nate montage of a telephone conversation presents the temporal continuity and spatial discontinuity which in this stylistic context may be seen as symmetrically equivalent to the characteristics of the temporal ellipse. The sub-sequence that follows introduces what I consider to be the third main type of strictly temporal ellipse: although the match cut which takes us from the diplomat to the insert of the letter he is reading is decidedly in continuity, the next one *seems* at first to belong to the type of 'indefinite ellipse'. The entry into the building of the character (whose costume refers to the motorcyclist at the beginning) is accomplished through a match with a 90° angle change; then an in-visible ellipse takes us into the preceding character's office, retroactively modifying our understanding of the previous articulation which, instead of 'large indefinite' becomes 'small measurable'. As we shall see, this type of ellipse, which I have described as 'defer-red', plays an important role in *Spione*. Finally, there is the close-up of the window pierced by a bullet: although we tend now, conditioned by fifty years of sound cinema, to see it chiefly as a substitute for sound ef-fects, in a silent context it also plays the el-liptical role of synecdoche.

Although an overall analysis of the film is impossible here, attention should be drawn to what seems to me to be one of its key-stones: the crucial stages in the first three-quarters of the main story (the love affair between Sonja and Tremaine, interrupted midway and relayed, as it were, by the short and tragic love of Matsumoto and Kitty) are marked by three 'cascades' of ellipses which are like so many echoes of the one used to open the film. As one might expect from the principle of variation adopted by Lang, these cascades are very different in kind. The first comes in Tremaine's apartment, after his encounter while disguised as a tramp with

Sonja, who tells him she has just killed a man. Once the police have gone, Tremaine takes a long look at himself in a mirror, and decides to spruce himself up before confronting the lovely lady hiding in his bedroom. There follows a series of almost crudely elliptical shots, in which reappears not only the idea of the synecdoche, but also of the 'expressive' ellipse-articulation (litotes): (1) a running tap; (2) a cake of soap being placed on a soap-dish; (3) a towel being placed on a towel-rail; (4) a bath-thermometer being inserted into the water. The bath itself and the dressing afterwards take place off-screen, behind two shots in which Sonja searches the room into which Tremaine had shut her, and a third shot of the manservant watching the door (another form of ellipse by insert, where the temporal abridgement occurs under cover of a 'third' shot; in this case the process is a dual one, Tremaine's ablutions being abridged in favour of Sonja's search, and the search being abridged in favour of the shot of the manservant).

But the most splendid cascade of ellipses of this type is probably the second in this 'series'. Under coercion from Haghi, Sonja writes and seals a letter for Tremaine which she addresses thus (close-up): 'Hotel Olympic Room 119/120' (dissolve)/close-up of the number on the door of Room 120/close-up of the letter held down by a statuette in Tremaine's room (we saw this statuette several times during Sonja's search) dissolve)/close-up of the letter as presumably Tremaine reads it/close-up: Tremaine's hand turns the letter over (at the foot of the statuette) and we read: 24 Park Street/dissolve: in front of No. 24 a man arrives, back to camera—but it is not Tremaine, it is a 'Japanese' who furtively takes an impression of the lock under the eyes of a lookout linked telephonically (two inserted shots) to Matsumoto himself; and it is only after this interpolation that Tremaine himself arrives in front of the house in a taxi, with the 'Japanese' humbly opening the car door for him before moving away. Lang here displaces the 'logical' outcome of his abridgement, cheating our expectations by making the final ellipse at first definite (apparently it bridges the time lapse between Tremaine's reading of the letter and his arrival at the house), then indefinite (it is not Tremaine in front of the

house, so this shot has no temporal relation to the preceding one, but was merely an associative link, a rhyme such as Lang often uses), and finally reversing this again to show that we were right all along: it was a definite ellipse, only we were a few seconds ahead of Tremaine.

The third cascade preludes the other great sentimental encounter in the film, between Dr Matsumoto and Kitty, the treacherous ingénue sent by Haghi to seduce the Japanese. Matsumoto, who has just comforted Tremaine over Sonja's disappearance by revealing that she is a spy, remains alone on the pavement after Tremaine leaves. (1) a close-up of newspapers blowing in the wind; (2) repeat of the shot of Matsumoto; he holds out his hand; (3) close-up of a drop of rain falling on the hand; (4) repeat of the shot of Matsumoto; he starts walking; (5) close-up of posters torn by gusts of wind; (6) rain pelting down; Matsumoto enters the frame and passes Kitty, who is huddled in a doorway, her slender figure moulded by her soaked garment; (7) close-up as Matsumoto does a double-take and turns to the 'poor waif'. The configuration here is a novel one, for although only two of these shot changes (4–5 and 5–6) are strictly speaking elliptical, the two earlier close-ups (the newspapers blowing, the drop of rain on the hand) have some of the characteristics of what one might call an elliptical movement, accelerating in pace and displaying in epitome the 'natural' stages of a storm-burst.

There is space enough here only to allude to the other aspect of the film: the many passages where, in striking opposition to the elliptical ones, time draws out, gets bogged down, where camera and montage linger lovingly over gestures, attitudes, faces ... almost as though only the narrowest possible area were to be allocated to the meagre prose of the story, the better to allow it to expand between a pyrotechnic poetry, often obscure, often built on elements superfluous to the narrative, and the languorous poetry of 'undue' gestures, of 'excessively long' shots, a poetry of time beguiled. Here we have an absolutely original dialectic that warrants more detailed examination.

Fourth Stage: Development of Rhyme

It is necessary for the coherence of this study to reverse chronology in the two last stages of Lang's German career. For despite the virtuosity it displays, *The Testament of Dr Mabuse* is far from achieving the same faultless mastery as *M*, made the year before.

On one very precise point, however, Lang's last German film makes a considerable contribution. I noted earlier of the first *Mabuse* that no matter how purely narrative their function, the articulations between sequences clearly heralded a cinema which would reject systematically transparent illusionism in that they revealed the continuous-discontinuous (dialectic) potential of spatio-temporal rupture in the cinema. And one can say that this sequel which Lang and Harbou decided to append to the narrative of their first masterpiece was also to be a continuation—and more particularly a development—of the formal approach inaugurated by it. Of course one finds the same type of articulations in *The Testament of Dr Mabuse*—by question and answer, by mental association, or simply by cause and effect—but one also finds a number of others not reducible in this way to the substance of the plot but which at the same time do reveal, through the close links they maintain with the 'narrative' articulations, the existence of a much more general category of articulations between shots completely discontinuous spatially (in other words, between sequences).

This category I call 'rhyme'. And in *The Testament* Lang has subjected rhyme to a process of variation at least as rich as that undergone by ellipse in *Spione*. In order to gather some of the elements for a pragmatic definition of this protean and rather elusive figure, some of the aspects assumed by rhyme in *The Testament* should perhaps be listed. Some samples will, I think, also help to demonstrate that the distinction between narrative and 'plastic' rhymes, which may seem palpable when one passes from an examination of the first *Mabuse* to the second, is in fact probably a delusion, and that in the context of a dialectical analysis of a *composite* cinema (abstract-concrete, formal-narrative) only the general notion of rhyme has any real bearing.

Not surprisingly, the new dimension of sound greatly aided Lang in his task of extending this concept of rhyme. The passage from the first to the second sequence, for instance, involves a musical rhyme: the deafening throbbing of some mysterious machinery,

the only sound accompanying the scene in which the ex-policeman Hofmeister is spotted by two of the counterfeiters, 'changes into' the roar of a lorry starting up at the very moment when Hofmeister, thinking he has had a narrow escape, emerges from the warehouse-hideout. Here these two sounds 'rhyme' through their timbre and their sustained character, while the second differs from the first in pitch and volume (being sharper and weaker). And as we shall see, one of the essential characteristics of these rhymed articulations is in fact that the rhyme always (apart from exceptional cases, instanced later) reproduces the continuous-discontinuous phenomenon already described, but in the form of a 'resemblance-dissemblance' phenomenon. A few moments later, for instance, the crooks hurl a metal drum at Hofmeister which explodes in flames, and in the darkness that follows we hear a voice (talking about a cremation) use the word 'pyre'; then we discover the speaker, Inspector Lohmann, in his office preparing to go on leave. Here the rhyme is in the nature of a pun—whose generic essence is precisely an opposition between resemblance and dissemblance—but no matter how different in *substance* this rhyme is from the first example, the method of 'transmission' remains the same.

Further on in the film comes a remarkable succession of sequences, rich in rhymes of every kind, which will give some indication of the range Lang felt this device could cover. When the hero Kent and his girl are imprisoned in the 'curtained room' and hear the faint but unmistakable ticking of a hidden time-bomb, Lang turns to the last of a series of scenes depicting the quaintly bourgeois way of life of the members of the gang; here the irregular tapping of a spoon on a boiled egg echoes the regular ticking of the bomb. A few moments later, with the police already laying siege to the gang's apartment, a brief alternating montage is sketched between the gang's absurd attempt to escape by knocking a hole in the ceiling, and Kent's equally futile efforts to make some impression on the walls of his prison with a fragile penknife. Then, at the moment of surrender, the toughest gang member puts a bullet into his own brain; the police rush in; in close-up the hand holding the gun falls to the ground, and another hand enters the frame to seize the gun. Next comes another close-up with the gun in the same hand as though it were being examined. We then realize that we are in Inspector Lohmann's office, and that we have just witnessed a sort of rhymed ellipse, *retroactively perceived* (which in fact happens where both elements of the rhyme are identical, and where the rhyme can therefore only be perceived retroactively at the same time as the ellipse that divides it, because at the moment of articulation the conditions required to produce rhyme—spatio-temporal discontinuity—did not appear to be fulfilled). The scene continues with Lohmann, questioning one of the gang in his office, talking about 'the man who pulls the strings', and we are taken back again to the curtained room where Kent and the girl, having cut through a pipe, are anxiously watching the water level rise; but the first image that follows Lohmann's remark shows only the wooden cut-out figure used by the mysterious gang-member to sustain the illusion of his presence behind the curtain. With this single but fragmented scene alternating with a number of 'outside' scenes boldly and brilliantly dovetailed into it, we hear Lohmann mention for the first time the name of Dr Baum, the man whom Mabuse has posthumously turned into his slave; back in the room, we see, floating on the rising water and entering the empty frame, the loudspeaker through which Baum, as the shadowy gang leader, used to address his henchmen. When Lohmann rubs his hands and exclaims 'Things are hotting up!' after telephoning Baum to lay a trap for him, our return to the room is followed almost immediately (the slight delay merely accentuating the rhyme) by the long-dreaded explosion ... which, muffled by the mass of water, in fact frees the two lovers (in a way this rhyme is an inversion of the 'pyre' one at the beginning of the film). 'We're free!' cries Kent ... 'Let me out of this cage!' echoes one of the gang members back at the police station, where Lohmann is arranging a confrontation with Dr Baum.

One can see quite clearly here how Lang runs the whole gamut in order to bridge the disjunction between sequence articulations with links that are as diversified as possible; hence the sense of a mechanism whose workings are as inexorable as they are constantly varied. Since *The Testament of Dr Mabuse*, these rhyming methods have been much used, and mostly abused, generally to titivate an articulation here and there. This is why they seem so gratuitous nowadays ... and generally are inasmuch as they are not used with the same methodical variation as in Lang's film, which therefore offers a lesson still valid today, if not always through the excellence of its rhymes, at least in the attitude which governs their organization.

Fifth Stage: Large Scale Form

Unquestionably Lang's masterpiece, *M* provides us with one of the very first examples, along with *Battleship Potemkin* and *Vampyr*, of a composite form, simultaneously incorporating every aspect of a group of cinematic parameters and every moment of the film within a totally coherent combination.

The film can be seen as divided into nine clearly distinguished parts, each one having its own manner of functioning, obeying, one might almost say, its own laws. A certain number of general guiding principles circulate through the film as a whole, however, with those which govern the functioning of each part appearing in others, but according to a different prescription and with a different field of application. It is the very complex interaction between these principles which governs the form, or in other words 'the mode of existence of a work which, while ensuring its unity, tends towards the greatest possible diversity' (André Hodeir).

The nine parts of the film can be defined as follows: (1) the murder of Elsie Beckmann; (2) fear of the child-murderer spreads in the city; (3) police procedures and their inefficacy; (4) the underworld and the police pull together ... each in its own way; (5) the two searches get under way; (6) the searches end; (7) M at bay—the building torn apart—M captured; (8) the police pick up M's trail; (9) the two trials.

As in all Lang's major films—with the exception already noted of *Metropolis*—the parameters productive of structures are essentially those relating to sequence changes (the same as changes of place in my analysis). It is through the arrangement of the frequency and 'degree of discontinuity' of those articulations, as well as the way in which their constituent element of *continuity* functions, that these nine parts are organized,

M: 'Fear spreads in the city: a police notice is read aloud from a newspaper in a café.'

both internally and in relation to each other.

Furthermore, the film is traversed by two broader movements which are, in a sense, independent of the division into parts. One of them, more or less constant, carries the film as a whole from the discontinuous towards the continuous. The other, which one might describe as recurrent, consists of a gradual 'unveiling' of the central character: it makes its appearance on seven occasions, always in a different tempo and aspect, but its overall progression through the film to the final 'nakedness' is constant.

These two broader movements, whose constituent elements naturally contribute to the particular style of the film, nevertheless derive directly from the terms of the theme that serves as a point of departure: an *unknown* murderer, *unseen*, making *intermittent appearances*, sows terror *on all sides* and *among all classes*; he is *progressively tracked down* and finally forced into a *sustained confrontation*. Nothing would be more misleading, however, than any attempt to reduce the form of the film or its style to a simple substantiation of this plot. As I hope to demonstrate, what we have here is a fully composite work, in which the structures retain their autonomous, 'abstract' function, but in sym-

biosis with the plot which they both support and challenge.

1—*The murder of Elsie Beckmann*

The film opens with a series of shots in three different settings which are nevertheless shown to be contiguous (the courtyard of a block of flats where children are singing 'The Killer's Song'; the landing where the housewife who has just told off the children stops to speak to Frau Beckmann; and the latter's kitchen) and which provide from the outset a sort of surety for the continuity so often to be abandoned or subsequently challenged. Immediately after this, in fact, begins the first and one of the most subtle of the succession of alternate montage sequences ranged throughout the film and constituting one of its basic principles. Here, alternating with scenes showing Frau Beckmann going about her household chores and worrying about her little girl being late in coming home, we find two series of three 'insert' shots: the first sketches a very condensed account of the little girl's journey to her death (leaving school; a police notice against which she bounces her ball and on which the killer's shadow falls; the purchase of the toy balloon), while the second comprises 'empty' shots emphasizing the little girl's absence and accompanied by the mother's shrill cries (an angled shot down the empty staircase; the deserted attic with some clothes drying; Elsie's vacant chair). This second series, however, is heralded even before the end of the first, when this same shot of the empty staircase makes two anticipatory appearances, cut in to shots of Frau Beckmann leaning over the banister. Furthermore, if this second series is 'clinched' by a shot (the empty chair) deriving both from the kitchen series and the 'cut in' series, this whole first part is similarly clinched by the pair of shots which, signifying through synecdoche the death of the little girl (the ball rolling on the ground, the balloon catching in the telegraph wires), also refer to the only two shots in the first series in which the killer was present (the poster, the balloon-vendor); the continuity between these new, isolated shots and the earlier series is ensured by Frau Beckmann's voice calling Elsie.

This part of the film also contains the first of the seven different and more or less progressive 'unveilings' through which we gradually move towards acquaintance with the killer, and which, taken together, compose a movement of approach essential to the general metabolism of the film. Here, from an off-screen presence (first appearance of the whistled tune) becoming a shadow on screen, the murderer gets as far as being seen in back view (the shot with the balloon-vendor); then the process is suspended, with the unveiling of the face not coming until much later, in successive stages.

2—*Fear spreads in the city*

Essentially, this part of the film comprises four comparatively elaborate sequences showing the effects of this fear on the average citizen. Although radically disjunctive as regards both characters (who appear only in this context) and settings (completely isolated from each other and never seen again), this series is tightly fused by way of various rhymes, a device which reappears in amplified form later in the film. A man reads aloud a police notice before which a crowd is assembled; the same text continues first in the form of a radio broadcast, then read aloud from a newspaper in the café which serves as a setting for the following sequence

... and where the excited customers end by coming to blows, with the victim accusing his assailant of 'slandering reputations'. These words, on which the scene ends, rhyme with the 'What a slander!' uttered by a man whose apartment is being searched by the police on the strength of an anonymous letter. Finally, when this man, wrongfully suspected, says that the killer 'might be absolutely anybody in the street', these words instantly introduce the fourth episode of the series: a man is manhandled by the crowd as the result of a tragic-comic misunderstanding.

But just as important as this continuous-discontinuous movement are the three shots which *precede* this series: the first two, in which newsvendors raise the cry about the murder, recapitulate but also anticipate, since their cry is 'Who is the killer?' and the next shot (another example of the question-answer device) shows us the killer himself, sitting with his back to camera, writing a letter to the newspapers (one can barely see him; this is the first piece in a schematic unveiling completed only in Part 3). This shot also refers to Part 1, since we hear the whistled tune for the second time; and the next shot, introducing the series of four sequences, refers to the only other shot in the first part in which the killer 'appeared', since the poster in front of which the crowd is assembled begins with the same words as the one we saw earlier—'10,000 Marks reward: who is the murderer?'—with the typography ensuring that only these words are legible.

One can thus see how careful Lang is to weave a complex network of affiliations between the first two parts of the film, before embarking on this series of four comical sketches which involve not only a complete break in tone but a different narrative method.

3—*Police procedures and their inefficacy*

This part offers two subdivisions radically opposed in every respect. The first is one of the most discontinuous passages in the film: over the phone, the commissioner of police informs his minister of the extensive measures taken by his men, while we see his remarks illustrated by series of very short and totally disjointed sequences. The other comprises the first (and for a considerable time, the only) long continuous sequence: a raid on one of the city's big whorehouses. It should be noted, however, that the continuous mode has already been introduced into the commissioner's illustrated report during the little comic sketch in which two eye-witnesses quarrel about what they saw; and that the portion of the long, two-part final sequence that takes place in the streets is introduced by overlapping of the commissioner's voice off screen ('But these measures have proved as ineffective as the nocturnal raids on underworld haunts') as though the illustrations were simply to continue. It is only when preparations for the raid are fairly advanced that we realize the narrative mode has changed yet again (and retroactive articulations of this type play a similarly privileged role throughout the film). It is also worth noting how this illustrated report is divided into several segments framed (asymmetrically) by shots of the commissioner and of the minister. Particularly striking here, however, is the insert of a close-up of the killer in his room, making hideous faces at himself in a mirror: a shot it seems legitimate to take as the conclusion of the second 'unveiling' movement, which also started in the killer's room (these are in fact the only two shots in which we see him at home) in the shot showing him writing his letter at the beginning of Part 2; here again, though, given the facial distortions, his features are not completely unveiled.

4—*The underworld and the police pull together*

Simplistic in appearance, the structure here is perhaps the most complex in the film. After a purely narrative (transparent) and entirely continuous preamble (representatives from the various underworld organizations meet to discuss measures for dealing with the inconvenience indirectly caused them by the child-murderer), we embark on another (and very long) alternate montage series which takes up the rest of Part 4. At first sight the simple alternation—between a meeting of police officials trying to decide on more efficient measures, and the underworld conference which will result in a 'parallel action'—may seem platitudinous, not to say facile. But at a closer look one realizes that Lang has incorporated an extemely subtle variational principle which brings a whole range of oral rhymes into play.

The first rhyme is achieved through the completion of a sentence: addressing his colleagues, Schränker, the notorious crook presiding over the underworld meeting, says 'I am asking you ...'/' ... for your advice' finishes the police commissioner in the next shot. This first sequence involving the police ends on a very different rhyme, a sort of tit-for-tat retort: 'What we need,' a police officer says, 'is more and more frequent and tougher and tougher raids,' then he sits down/the racketeer immediately gets up to address the crooks: 'Informers! What we need is informers planted among the police so that we are warned about new measures in time.' A few moments later the Hustler maintains that 'the police ought to be looking elsewhere ... because the man they want isn't a crook' /'Except during one of his fits, he's a man who probably looks like a respectable citizen,' an elderly police inspector continues, completing a rhyme that might be described as 'corroborative'. The passage which follows is the longest involving the police: uniquely, it ends in a cul-de-sac, with no liaison whatsoever to the next scene at the crooks' conference. As though to accentuate this break, the scene begins with a long silence in the smoky atmosphere. Finally the Pickpocket interjects a suggestion so completely harebrained that/a police officer cuts him off in mid-sentence with a 'contradictory' rhyme (and overlapping sound). But the officer's remarks are no more convincing, and an inspector says angrily, 'All this is getting us nowhere'/'That's no use,' echoes the Hustler (rhyme through reiteration). As for the two articulations that follow, they are in perfect 'assonance', in the sense that the discourse passes from one setting to the other without any break in continuity, forming a perfectly unified whole. Then the Hustler acknowledges defeat: 'Well, what then?'/the police remain silent/ so do the crooks/still the police are silent/and so are the crooks ... until Schränker finally has an idea: 'We must catch him ourselves'/And Inspector Lohmann, 'facing' him, echoes: 'There may perhaps still be a way ...' Finally, in the last shot of the series, Schränker explains that the city's beggars must be mobilized (here the rhyme is no longer between two lines of dialogue, but has expanded to cover both sequences in their entirety).

M: 'A close-up of the killer (Peter Lorre) in his room, making hideous faces at himself in a mirror
. . . given the facial distortions, however, his features are not completely unveiled.'

It should be added that the spatial organization of the *découpage* here (the sequence of camera angles and distances) contributes to the creation of a sort of semi-illusion of continuity between the two settings, so that certain rhymes are further complicated by a slight delay in perception of the change in setting.

5—*The two searches get under way*

Essential though it may be, this part is very simple in style. Initially connected with what preceded it by Schränker's last words ('the beggars')—just as Part 4 was connected to Part 3 by the Pickpocket seeing the police wagons passing the window after the raid—it begins with sequences that are continuous and firmly linked to each other (all take place in the same building: the beggars' 'market'). In addition to the apparent purpose here of starting each of the main subdivisions with an affirmation of continuity, one finds from now on a progressive expansion of this sense

of continuity up to the great final *séquence-fleuve*.

Next we move, bridged by the sound of a barrel-organ, to a shot which shows the beggar-musician watching over the children playing in a courtyard (an echo of the first shot in the film), and which is followed by three other similar tableaux. When we come after this to the corresponding police operations, they are set out not in this linear and directly elliptical manner, but by way of another alternate montage which reintroduces the killer, after his longest absence yet, in the most gradual of the seven unveilings. The first shot of the second series shows the killer leaving home furtively, huddled into his overcoat, hat pulled down over his eyes; we hardly have time to recognize him before he goes out of frame right. Almost immediately one of Lohmann's men enters left and goes inside the building. After this shot which introduces its two protagonists, the alternate montage begins: while the policeman gains admittance to Herr Beckert's room and submits it to a routine search, the killer buys an apple (partially masked by the pile of fruit), stares hypnotized at a window-display of cutlery (close-up of the face . . . but blurred by glittering reflections in the glass), finds his eyes drawn to a little girl whom he is about to follow; we hear his whistling off . . . but the little girl is rejoined by her mother and the killer hides in the doorway of a bookshop . . . then hurries (back to camera) to the terrace of a café where, almost entirely hidden by a screen of ivy, he has a cognac to calm himself.

The final sequence in this series, which interrupts the alternate montage's to-and-fro, might perhaps be considered as a pendant to the two sequences at the beginning in which the policeman, after an exchange on the landing with the deaf landlady, finds himself alone in Beckert's room. What is incontestable, however, is the psychological movement here: the character retreating back into the shadows the moment his impulse is frustrated.

6—The searches end

The simplest of the nine parts, this one works basically through pairs of alternating sequences, if one excludes the first in which the policeman makes a routine report to Lohmann about Beckert (although this sequence can be taken as pairing with the last, in which the police move in to Beckert's room, to wait in vain for his return).

7—M at bay—the building torn apart—M captured

This part is the freest in the entire film. In a sort of fantasy on the theme of departure, each aspect of the film is reproduced, but on a reduced scale: the fourth unveiling is repeated (when the camera discovers M emerging from the shadows in the attic after the nightwatchman passes), as well as the principle of alternate montage, carried to climactic lengths but at the same time tailored to the 'recognizable' geography of the building, thus considerably attenuating its disjointed quality both spatially and temporally. On the other hand, it is here that one really finds oneself confronted by the killer for the first time—physically, that is; the verbal confrontation will not come till the end—

while watching in close-up his desperate efforts to escape from his attic prison. And lastly, as already suggested, this part marks a great stride towards the absolute continuity of the final trial, in so far as alternate montage, restricted by the mental space-time, makes the ellipses much less obvious. Towards the end of this part, moreover, this sense of relative continuity is reinforced, contrariwise, by the only shot that violates it spatially: the teleprinter at the police station receiving the alarm signal when the nightwatchman manages to trigger it . . . which has the effect of accelerating the movement ending in the sixth unveiling when M is discovered and again emerges from the shadows of the lumber-room (duplicating almost exactly the fifth unveiling, but 'in front of witnesses').

8—The police pick up M's trail

This extremely curious part is the only one whose exact beginning is in effect obfuscated. When the Burglar calls up for a ladder, filmed from above through the hole he has dug in the bank's ceiling, one might think— as he does—that some of his comrades are waiting for him up there; but when he emerges from the hole, he finds the police (off). Unknown to us, an ellipse had therefore separated this shot from the one preceding it; the other crooks left a good while earlier . . . and Part 8, presided over by the police, had already begun.

This eighth part is doubly (even triply) recapitulatory. The file which Lohmann is shown by his colleague Groeber not only resurrects the essence of the previous sequence (photographs showing the now deserted building where the action took place); this series of disjointed images commented by a voice off is also a distinct reminder of the form of Part 3. One might even hazard that the lengthy interrogations of the Burglar (used to frame his re-exposition) recall the gambling den sequence, both in their continuity and in the sort of relationships established between police and crooks. But at all events they undoubtedly form the penultimate stage in the film's takeover by the principle of continuity, which achieves absolute control during the climactic trial. Yet discontinuity is still present in three different ways: through the insert showing the famous hole in the ceiling when the Burglar protests that damage to property was all that happened; through the insert of the nightwatchman stuffing himself with sausages (a shot giving the lie to Lohmann's ploy of making the Burglar think one of his colleagues 'hit too hard'); and through the unexpected shot of Lohmann splashing water on his face in the lavatory where he has fled to recover from the excitement of what his prisoner has just revealed. Eventually this sequence ends on what seems to be a 'mental flash', apparently functioning like the inserts of the hole in the ceiling and the nightwatchman, and showing the exterior of the factory which the Burglar indicates as the place where the killer is being held. But as the next shot brings us closer to the factory, and a third takes us inside (inaugurating Part 9), the role of this 'flash' is retroactively modified, and rather than 'subjective' is seen to be 'objective' (the same device occurred in Part 6: in Lohmann's office, the officer who searched Beckert's room suddenly remembers the window-ledge/a close-up of the ledge, apparently 'mental' but in fact describing an ellipse, retroactively perceived when a policeman's hand holding a magnifying-glass enters the frame).

9—The two trials

The first is of course the famous virtuoso passage in which Peter Lorre as Franz Beckert/M confronts his accusers. This sequence is characterized essentially by an illusory continuity (a continuity imposed through the editing, in other words, rather than through actual continuity in the images) which is absolute and unblemished: no matter how closely one examines it, the duration of the action appears to correspond exactly to its screen time. Another important characteristic is that M *talks* for the first time. Hitherto he has uttered barely half-a-dozen completely non-committal phrases, and in the only scenes in which we had really been close to him (in the attic) he was silent apart from a few oaths.

We now come to the final, brilliant blending of these two movements that have run through the film: the movements towards continuity and towards the unveiling of M (the last stage visually in this unveiling being of course the moment when M himself tears off the coat covering his head to face his per-

secutors). In the context of this twin fulfilment, tokens of recall like the balloon floating in the air or the photographs of the murdered children are completely assimilated into the emotional movement, which naturally dominates here. This sequence stands alone, cut off from everything else. The concern for continuity, for unity, is such that when the police invade the factory, we do not see them—looking off-screen, the crooks slowly put their hands up—because any intrusion on screen by characters whose real (formal) role was completed in Part 8 would certainly have undermined the privileged autonomy of this sequence.

The film ends with the second, derisory trial: a shot of a court bench where the judge begins reading a verdict we do not even hear—a shot which, because of its total isolation in space-time, and especially because of its extreme brevity, even further accentuates the solemn finality of the preceding sequence while at the same time acting as a coda. But the final 'articulation' is the shot of Frau Beckmann which brings us right back to the beginning of the film: 'That won't bring back our children. They should be better looked after' (a line memorable for its formal role rather than for its curiously moralizing tone).

Another masterpiece, already mentioned—*The Testament of Dr Mabuse*—and that was the end: a silence lasting some thirty films.

Translated by Tom Milne

See the article immediately below for a different view of Lang's American films and for bibliographical information about Lang.

FRITZ LANG: 1936–60

Robin Wood

With Fritz Lang one may begin at the end. The formal symmetry so characteristic of his individual movies is satisfyingly reflected in the overall symmetry of his career, at the close of which he returned to Germany to make the two Indian adventure films scripted by Thea von Harbou that he was to have directed in 1920 (and which were made, in the event, by the producer Joe May), following these with his last farewell to the character so particularly associated with him, and also his farewell to the screen, *Die Tausend*

Augen des Dr Mabuse (*The Thousand Eyes of Dr Mabuse*, 1960).

The pair of films that make up *The Tiger of Eschnapur—Der Tiger von Eschnapur, Das Indische Grabmal*—(U.K.: *Tigress of Bengal*; U.S.: *Journey to a Lost City*, 1959) offer a convenient starting point, because they contain so many characteristic motifs in a form purified of the half-enriching, half-concealing complications of Hollywood's psychological realism and expressed through a correspondingly pure style. They are what one might deduce from their date and history: the thematic patterns of Lang's German period (to which he has always been, if somewhat deviously, faithful) executed with the purity of line and economy of means learned in Hollywood. The films are extraordinarily beautiful, the beauty deriving more from their stylistic rigour than from their exoticism. Lang uses real Indian locations to create a world at once fabulous and authentic. The subject matter and narrative method continually evoke the silent serials, and perhaps the films with which *The Tiger* should be compared are those of Feuillade. We are always aware of the 'comic strip' nature of the material, but nowhere does one sense that it is being 'sent up': Lang's scrupulous avoidance of anything in the nature of 'camp' is one of the many tokens of the moral purity of his art. In one scene the escaping lovers hide in a cave and, as their pursuers approach, a spider (directed, it is hinted, by a benevolent deity) spins its web over the entrance; their pursuers, seeing the web unbroken, assume that no one has passed inside. Staged and acted with characteristic simplicity, with a refusal of all affectation and ostentatious 'magical' effects, the scene has the authentic magic of fairy-tale.

Perhaps because (not necessarily to its discredit) the content provides relatively few distractions, the qualities of Lang's style can be perceived in the *Tiger* films with particular clarity. Those qualities are, of course, not really separable, but one can for convenience attempt a list, moving back freely through the American films to illustrate it.

Economy: arguably the supreme virtue of Lang's *mise en scène*, obscured during the German period by the 'spectacular' Expressionist trappings, practically encouraged by the low budgets of many of his Hollywood

movies, emerging as a central creative principle in the late films. Everything is stripped to essentials, and this principle is applied to every aspect of film-making: décor, camera style, acting. Lang spends scarcely more time dwelling on the beauties of the Indian palaces and locations of the *Tiger* films than he does on the undistinguished functional sets of *Beyond a Reasonable Doubt* (1956). This doesn't mean that he is insensitive to their beauty (every shot is composed and framed with the utmost elegance); simply that he refuses to be distracted by it or to allow it to become an end in itself. Similarly, one wouldn't go to Lang's movies for great acting performances: that isn't what they're all about. The acting in his films is in fact uniformly admirable (it is difficult to think of an inadequate performance), but it is pared down to the necessary gesture, the necessary expression. Again, although Lang developed as an artist during the Expressionist movement, what one thinks of as 'Expressionist' acting (see, for instance, *Metropolis*, 1926) was quite alien to his true nature and swiftly discarded. If one had to suggest the ideal Lang interpreter, one might fasten upon Dana Andrews, and his performances in Lang's last two American pictures.

Functional precision: economy is a somewhat negative virtue; this is its positive side. So long as the description is not taken to exclude humanity and flexibility, one might say that a Lang film has something of the perfection of a polished mechanism. This is the quality that, in Lang's achieved works, fuses scenario and *mise en scène*, the rigorous logic of the former realized in the dynamic movement of the latter, in which one frequently has the sense that every shot is necessitated by its predecessor. As in a perfect machine, every shot, and every detail, gesture, movement within the shot, has a precise function in relation to the working of the whole. In the films of (for example) Renoir, there is often a rich profusion of detail delighted in for its own sake; in another sense, one could argue that this delight in existence, in the idiosyncratic and superfluous, is an essential part of what Renoir's films are about. In either case, Renoir's attitude to his raw material, to its ostensible subject, is radically different from Lang's.

A comparison of Lang's two remakes of

Renoir movies (*Scarlet Street*, 1945, and *Human Desire*, 1954) with their originals (*La Chienne*, 1931, and *La Bête Humaine*, 1938) is a most instructive exercise in defining the style and method of these two great artists and, through that, their contrasting metaphysics. The conventional description, that Lang's versions are 'harsher', 'colder' than Renoir's, won't really do; one can see well enough in general terms how such an impression can be received from the films, but one needs a more precise and demonstrable formulation. What *can* be demonstrated is that Renoir, in *La Chienne*, continually invites us to enjoy the human oddities and particularities of his people in a way in which Lang in *Scarlet Street* does not: Lang is interested in the tragic process, and refuses to allow himself to be distracted from it. Not only the tone differs, but the fundamental movement: a Renoir shot has about it an air of improvisation, of inventing bits of business, of drawing spontaneously on the particular gifts and attributes of the players; a Lang shot functions strictly in relation to the one that preceded it and the one that follows it—everything irrelevant to the film's forward movement, to the demonstration of pattern and the unfolding of process, is rigorously rejected. One could point, as specific evidence, to the performances of Michel Simon and Edward G. Robinson: two masterly performances in fundamentally different traditions, the one generously inventive, the other pared down and disciplined to the precise expression of the essential. Or one could point to the camera style characteristic of the two directors. Both Lang's and Renoir's camera movements could be described as 'functional' in that neither is interested in decorativeness or the rhetoric of 'angles'; yet the function is quite different in each case. Renoir's camera is habitually at the service of the actors, Lang's at the service of the precise and rigorous expression of an idea.

Detachment: my description so far would do almost as well for Hitchcock as for Lang; the fundamental distinguishing feature is the detachment with which the action in Lang's films is presented. This is less a matter of the relationship of the director to his material than of the relationship he sets up between the action and the spectator. Neither director shows that obvious personal involvement (verging on identification) with his characters that one senses in the films of (for example) Bergman, Fellini and Welles; though the fact that one can speak meaningfully of 'the Lang hero', 'the Hitchcock protagonist'—the recurrence of types, predicaments, motifs—reveals a close involvement beneath the 'impersonal' surface. The difference is one of method, and, through method, of spectator experience.

It is curious that, at certain points in the Peter Bogdanovich interview book *Fritz Lang in America*, Lang speaks of this aspect of his films in a way that might almost be mistaken for Hitchcock: '... you show the protagonist so that the audience can put themselves under the skin of the man. First of all, I use my camera in such a way as to show things, wherever possible, from the viewpoint of the protagonist; in that way my audience identifies itself with the character on the screen and thinks with him ...'

This is taken up later when Lang describes the construction of a sequence in *The Big Heat* (1953): '... Glenn Ford sits and plays with his child; the wife goes out to put the car in the garage. Explosion. By not showing it, you first have the shock. What was that? Ford runs out. He cannot even open the car. He sees only catastrophe. Immediately (because they see it through his eyes), the audience feels with him.'

When Lang talks about using his camera 'to show things, wherever possible, from the viewpoint of the protagonist', and about seeing the catastrophe 'through his eyes', it is clear that he is speaking figuratively, whereas with Hitchcock such a description could be literal. There *are* subjective shots in Lang, but they don't characterize his cinema as they do Hitchcock's: they are a part of a complex narrative method rather than a central principle. In the sequence Lang specifies, Glenn Ford's is indisputably the consciousness we share: we know only what *he* knows, we are kept in the room while he tells his daughter bedtime rhymes, we hear the explosion with him, leave the house only when he leaves it. On the other hand, our attention throughout the sequence is visually directed towards *him*. His anguish is communicated not by our being placed physically in his position by means of the subjective camera, but by our being made to study his reactions. The moment of strongest empathy is perhaps when he pulls at the shattered, splintering glass of the car window with his bare hands: the physical sensation communicated is vividly expressive of his frenzy, emotional pain and helplessness.

One can see that Lang wants us to identify with his heroes; the complexity of his American films can be suggested by the impression that they are also on trial, and we are judging them. There is a strong pull in Lang's style against the subjective, identifying tendency: one can isolate it in his fondness for moving back from an action to long-shot. There is a good—and representative—example in that supremely Langian film *Beyond a Reasonable Doubt*. As part of a newspaper campaign against capital punishment, Tom (Dana Andrews) agrees to incriminate himself in a murder case. He and his editor (Sidney Blackmer) drive out to the scene of the crime to 'plant' the lighter Tom was given by his fiancée. Tom poses smugly for the photographs that will eventually prove his innocence. As the two men walk away, Lang suddenly cuts back to a high-angled long-shot. Tom, who thinks he is controlling the game, is suddenly a pawn in it. The effect is ambiguous, and the ambiguity is central to Lang's cinema: we can feel ourselves placed above and at a distance, as judges; or we can interpret the long-shot as a sudden intimation of Tom's subjection to a destiny that, unknown to him, is working itself out.

If one sets beside these characteristics of style certain recurrent motifs which are closely related to them, a coherent portrait of Lang as an artist begins to emerge. Again, one can take the *Tiger* movies as starting point, and look back from them over the American films.

The trap: a motif epitomized in the first part of *The Tiger of Eschnapur*. The hero is escaping from the palace, where his life is in jeopardy. In every room or corridor he enters, all doors are locked but one. He believes that each exit he takes is leading him nearer to freedom and safety. He runs through the last door and, as it closes behind him, finds himself in the tiger-pit, the Rajah and his guards looking down on him from the sides. He imagined himself to be using his free intelligence; in fact, his every choice was

predetermined, every movement guided.

This, in the distilled, 'comic strip' mode of the *Tiger* films, is a particularly pure example of an obsession that runs through Lang's work, from the German Expressionist period to *The Thousand Eyes of Dr Mabuse*. It takes many forms, literal and metaphorical, ranging from quasi-diabolical machinations to traps laid for the protagonist by himself, formed within the workings of his own psychology. Sometimes the hero traps himself inadvertently, through a slip that could be taken to express his own subconscious desire for retribution: in *The Woman in the Window* (1944), Edward G. Robinson, invited by a friendly police detective to assist in an investigation of the murder he himself committed, forgets his supposed ignorance of the circumstances so far as to walk on ahead through the trees towards the spot where the body was found; in *Beyond a Reasonable Doubt*, Dana Andrews reveals his guilt to his fiancée by referring to the girl he murdered by her real name, which he is not supposed to know. The 'trap' motif points on the one hand towards the paranoia that so pervades Lang's world, and on the other to the sense of fate that ultimately determines it.

Two of Lang's finest 'trap' movies, *You Only Live Once* (1937) and *Scarlet Street*, provide extended variations on the motif sufficiently dissimilar to suggest its potential range and complexity. In both films, the protagonist's entrapment is determined by an interaction of external and internal forces—of an impersonal destiny and the promptings of inner psychological drives. The central thrust of Lang's development in his American period is suggested by the very different ratio in these films between destiny and personal responsibility. The sense of fate (but perhaps 'doom' better suggests the atmosphere) is central to German Expressionism and the primary motive power behind most of Lang's German movies. In *You Only Live Once*, his second American film, Eddie (Henry Fonda), the ex-convict trying to make an honest life for himself and his wife, is throughout the almost helpless victim of chance and social pressures, driven to a position where his only escape appears to lie through violence and criminality, finally damning himself irremediably by shooting a priest (albeit inadvertently). He acts hastily and makes wrong decisions, but the degree of blame we can attach to him is slight. The fate of Chris (Edward G. Robinson) in *Scarlet Street*, on the other hand, is to a much greater degree explainable in terms of the character's personal blindnesses and limitations. The instinctive, 'primitive' talent that makes him a 'Sunday painter', a kind of American Douanier Rousseau, is an aspect of the urge that drives him into the affair with Kitty (Joan Bennett); the innocence—or unawareness—that accompanies this makes him unable both to cope with the petty tyranny of his wife and to grasp that Kitty is exploiting him mercilessly.

The inner movement of both films is a relentless working out of the process whereby the trap closes on the protagonist. The endings, as in many of Lang's films, have the feeling of inevitability associated with Greek tragedy. Yet such an effect is necessarily achieved through style and tone as much as through the logic of the action: indeed, one can question whether the action of a fiction *has* a logic independent of the drives of its creator or realizer. The particular quality of Lang's American films derives from the interaction of his German Expressionist background, its characteristics of doom and repression, with the American belief in freedom and individualism. The concept of 'fate' has increasingly to take the form of psychological determinism.

The suppressed underworld: in *The Tiger of Eschnapur* this motif is literally embodied in the leper colony imprisoned beneath the palace. One's first association may well be with the underground world of slaves in *Metropolis* (made seven years after the *Tiger* films were first planned). But the secret, buried world of the lepers provides an apt symbol for certain potent forces in Lang's universe. Again, what is overtly 'Expressionist' (or symbolic) in the German movies is forced into 'naturalistic' (or psychological) form in the American movies, and becomes subtler and more complex in the process. The sense of repressed but powerful drives in Lang's characters is very strong, from Joe (Spencer Tracy) in *Fury* (1936) to Tom Garrett in *Beyond a Reasonable Doubt*, and either the main action of the film or its climax frequently depends on their release. Logically, this motif associates with that of

the 'trap', the connection brought out in the later Hollywood films by the identification of destiny with personal psychology. Thus Chris, in *Scarlet Street*, is driven first to adultery, then to murder, by powerful suppressed forces which he can't control because he never sufficiently understands them; eventually, his guilt at the execution of an 'innocent' man (who is morally far guiltier than he) for the murder he committed, drives him to despair, ruin and near-insanity. The pattern is essentially that of the revolt, overthrow and destruction of the underground leper colony, translated into psychological terms.

In this connection, Lang's psychopaths become particularly interesting, for they represent the most extreme extension of men driven by 'buried', hence uncontrollable, forces. The most striking realization of a psychopath in Lang's work is of course Peter Lorre's child-murderer in *M* (1931); but that character is echoed many years later in John Barrymore Jr's obsessive sex murderer in *While the City Sleeps* (1956) and, more equivocally, in the Michael Redgrave character of *Secret Beyond the Door* (1948) who 'collects' famous crimes in his house. Beyond these overtly psychotic characters, Lang's American period is rich in near- or potential psychopaths, of whom Lee Marvin in *The Big Heat* and Broderick Crawford in *Human Desire* are only the two most obvious. What most clearly relates the murderers of *M* and *While the City Sleeps* to the Expressionist motif of the underground race is the way Lang locates them as (literally and metaphorically) at the heart of the city, as if they represent, in human terms, the price civilization must pay for existing, the suppressions it must enforce.

Revenge: Lang was very fond of (and fond of quoting) the 'Ballad of Chuck-a-Luck', which begins and ends *Rancho Notorious* (1952)—a tale of 'Hate, Murder, and Revenge'. The drive to revenge is a recurring motivation in his films, from *Die Nibelungen* (1924) right through to *The Tiger of Eschnapur*, and it is very complexly and ambiguously treated. If it never (with perhaps one exception) has Lang's full approval, it is never presented entirely without respect; it motivates 'good' and 'evil' characters alike, and may be directed against the evil (*The Big Heat*) or the

Sylvia Sidney and Henry Fonda in *You Only Live Once*, 'one of Lang's finest "trap" movies'. Note the characteristic use of both peep-hole (like the television screens in *The Thousand Eyes of Dr Mabuse*) and the overhead mirror.

good (*The Tiger of Eschnapur*). In his post-1935 work, there are two films in which revenge is undertaken but finally repudiated (*Fury* and *The Tiger of Eschnapur*), with the repudiation seen as the hero's move towards salvation; and two in which it is accomplished, with the execution seen as a necessary if equivocal purgation (*Rancho Notorious* and *The Big Heat*).

The ambivalence of Lang's attitude to revenge is partly explained by his identification of it (in the Bogdanovich interview book, pages 85–6) with 'the fight against fate', which he himself sees as central to his work. For the heroes of *Rancho Notorious* and *The Big Heat*, 'fate' descends, irrevocably, near the beginning of the movies, with the deaths of (respectively) fiancée and wife (the latter death provoked partly by the hero's own actions). Revenge therefore becomes the protagonist's only possible expression of protest and defiance, the nearest he can come to denying the destiny that has overtaken him. In both films he acts from wholly justifiable moral outrage. Yet the relentless and fanatical pursuit of revenge increasingly dehumanizes him. He loses his responsiveness to other people; living only for the sterile objective of revenge, his life has little meaning when his mission is accomplished.

The ambivalence with which Lang views these two 'revenge' heroes is reflected in the effect they have on the morally impure but sympathetically presented women with whom they come into contact (Marlene Dietrich in *Rancho Notorious*, Gloria Grahame in *The Big Heat*). The most touching aspect of both films is the woman's movement towards awareness—a movement provoked in each case by the hero's sense of moral outrage and the terrible purity of his own drives. But if each woman is saved by contact with the hero, she is also ultimately destroyed by it. Her involvement costs her her life, and the sacrifice brings little reward. Only when he knows that Debbie (Gloria Grahame) is dying, at the end of *The Big Heat*, can Bannion (Glenn Ford) afford to show her any tenderness. The tension and discomfort we feel at the morally pure hero's treatment of her is evidence of the subtle complexity of Lang's moral sense.

If *The Big Heat* is among Lang's finest films, this is partly attributable to the fact that its 'revenge' theme is intensified and deepened by its combination with another characteristic Lang motif, which again goes back to his early German period and is partly explainable in terms of the coincidence of his development with the rise of the Nazis. The dread of the criminal empire—of the takeover and abuse of power by an exploitative tyrant-figure—in fact antedates the Hitler era by many years: it is there in the first *Mabuse* film (*Dr Mabuse, der Spieler—Ein Bild der Zeit*, 1922) and in *Spione* (U.K.: *The Spy*; U.S.: *Spies*, 1928). *The Big Heat* follows the general pattern of Lang's American period by finding a rationalized, 'naturalistic' form for the early fantasy; but between came the experience of Hitler. Bannion's revenge mission acquires a heroic stature quite beyond that of the hero of *Rancho Notorious* because Bannion (from the outset, before the death of his wife) is a Siegfried defying the totalitarian dragon. Of all Lang's revenge heroes, he is the most completely validated by results; much of the film's tension derives from our sense of the cost, in terms of his humanity. The film is also particularly rich in its portrayals of the guilty-innocent: the unaware, like Debbie, with no aim beyond a good time, who don't grasp until it's too late what they're a part of; the frightened, like Atkins (Dan Seymour), who pretend not to grasp it because of the dangers awareness involves; the crippled woman (Edith Evanson) who, timidly and gallantly, gives Bannion crucial information through the wire fence before limping back to her prison.

The pervasive Langian paranoia is closely related to this motif. It is still there at the end, in *The Thousand Eyes of Dr Mabuse*, in the revelation that all the mirrors of the hotel are television 'eyes' continually watching everyone's movements. In certain of the American films it takes subtler forms, spreading through the texture of 'normal' life. *While the City Sleeps* is built partly on the notion that everyone is watching everyone else and that this is an inherent feature of the competitive world of American capitalism. The theme finds repeated visual expression in the newspaper office scenes, with the characters separated from each other by glass partitions through which, each in his own cage, they study each other's movements

Gloria Grahame and Glenn Ford in his hotel room in *The Big Heat*: 'I like it,' she says, 'Early Nothing.'

in simultaneous fear and greed.

Lang is one of the cinema's sternest moralists: we have the sense, encouraged by the rigour and purity of his *mise en scène*, that his characters are not allowed to get away with anything, that every sin or weakness is scrutinized and judged. Yet the morality is far from simple, and there are features that strongly qualify any sense of the puritanical.

The central characterizing tension of Lang's cinema—which is one built on tensions, his films achieving at their best the purity of dialectic—is that between morality and fate. The strictness and consciousness of the moral sense his films convey set them apart from those of other directors obsessed by the notion of destiny. They can be contrasted, for example, with those of the other great artist whose development was rooted in German Expressionism (and took the form,

like Lang's, of a struggle to escape from or transcend its limitations): F. W. Murnau. If Lang's is above all a cinema of clarity, Murnau's is a cinema of (in several senses, including the literal one) obscurity. Lang's heroes may be driven by dark inner forces which they don't understand and can't control, but we always have the sense that these forces are understood by Lang, we are always distanced from the hero's struggle. In the films of Murnau such forces remain to a great degree dark and incomprehensible. In *Nosferatu*, through a series of remarkable 'mirror' images, the vampire is revealed as the hero's *alter ego*, or as an uncontrollable *inner* force that, once released, spreads like a blight over the universe. The moral issue in *Sunrise* is too obvious to be important. The film derives its power from its sense of potent and mysterious forces against which moral struggle is virtually impossible: they are defeated, not by the exertion of rationality, but by the equally unpredictable and mysterious forces of nature. In Murnau the 'fight against fate' is less a matter of conscious decision and force of will than of a cosmic conflict for which the human being is merely the battle-ground. This is as true of his *City Girl* and *Tabu* as of *Sunrise*; Hollywood gave Murnau new conventions, but he informed them with his own obsessions and then fled to the South Seas. His characters are beyond moral judge-ment; they are powerless morally to oppose the forces that drive them, be they internal or external.

In Lang's films, on the other hand, one is confronted with continuous paradox: his characters are regarded as doomed, yet responsible. He carried strong Expressionist elements over into his first American films (especially *You Only Live Once*, with its strong sense of fate and its unifying imagery of prison bars and their shadows), but these already seemed qualified by a possible (and not merely 'Hollywood') optimism. If one compares *You Only Live Once* with *Tabu*—two films centred on young couples on the run, pursued by an inexorable fate—one is struck by the absence in Lang's film of any-thing corresponding to the figure of the old man Hitu and the forces he represents: forces, characteristically, that go beyond rational explanation. There is no equivalent in the Lang for Murnau's 'doom' images of the ship mysteriously intruding into the frame, or the old man's shadow falling across the lovers as he emerges Nosferatu-like from the night. For Lang, Fate is a mechanism capable of explanation rather than a Dark Force; and if the mechanism can be ex-plained, there is always the possibility that it can, with awareness (the sort of awareness both exemplified and encouraged by Lang's style), be overcome or evaded.

The sense of the power of destiny counter-balances the strictness of Lang's moral judge-ment with compassion. This helps, perhaps, to explain another paradox of his moral sense which further undercuts any effect of the puritanical—that it is repeatedly turned against the morally pure. Lang never allows us to indulge any of our vices vicariously, but for him the ultimate vice is righteousness without compassion. I have already sug-gested how, in the revenge movies, the

fanaticism of the hero is criticized through the growing commitment of a woman he rejects on moral grounds. Similarly, at the end of *Human Desire* Lang plays ironically with our expectation of a conventional 'happy ending', at once fulfilling and criticizing it: the hero's wholly unearned complacency tips the balance of our sympathy towards the two 'impure' characters (Broderick Crawford and Gloria Grahame), so that our final involve-ment is with the bitterness of their tragedy rather than with the hero's satisfaction at having extricated himself. The same effect is achieved at the end of *Beyond a Reasonable Doubt*.

This movie is one of the cinema's great audience traps. Through the first part of the film, Tom Garrett is heroically framing him-self for a crime he didn't commit, in order to build up a case against capital punishment. Part of his strategy involves courting a dan-cer from a strip-joint, a friend of the girl who was murdered. The critical distance main-tained throughout (this is the most severely 'objective' in *mise en scène* of all Lang's films) allows us to balance conflicting attitudes: Tom is a hero campaigning for a cause, and the behaviour of his fiancée Susan (Joan Fontaine) strikes us as lacking in trust and understanding; on the other hand, Tom is irritatingly cool, even complacent, curiously unperturbed at losing her, too confident that it will all come right when the reasons for his actions are known. When the trap is sprung on him—the only man who can exonerate him dies in a motor accident—we are half glad to watch him squirm a bit. But our satis-faction depends on *our* confidence that it will 'all come right'; and it is Susan, rallying, who begins to fight for the truth, becoming the trusting, devoted heroine we wanted her to be. By the time Tom's acquittal is won, we are satisfied that he has suffered enough, are glad to sit back and welcome the happy end-ing. Then the trap is sprung on *us*—he is guilty after all, and Susan is faced with the dilemma of whether or not to reveal the fact. She betrays him, and he becomes the victim of the capital punishment he was campaign-ing against. We see that his commitment to his cause had every reason to be sincere: he knows, all too well, how easy it is to commit murder. The moral tension of the ending is supremely Langian. Tom gets precisely the poetic justice he deserves (because of the way he challenged destiny, and because of the arrogance with which he took a human life) yet doesn't deserve (because no human being deserves it). Susan is morally impeccable in her decision yet (as Peter Bogdanovich says) 'more reprehensible' than Tom: a destiny can be deserved without exonerating the person who wittingly betrays one to it. Lang tentatively defends Susan against Bogdanovich's strictures (in a characteristically compassionate way—'She is just a human being': even the uncompassionate righteous must be forgiven if we are to avoid the same pitfall). Yet his dislike of the character—given that she is ostensibly the heroine of a genre movie—seems to me evident throughout the film, expressed even in the way Joan Fontaine is dressed and coiffed (which accentuates her stiffness, in striking contrast with the sensitive tenderness one usually associates with this actress). She is the antithesis of Lang's feminine ideal.

That ideal is not likely to recommend itself in these days of Women's Liberation, and it would not be difficult to argue that it points to a retrograde element in Lang's work, rooted still in German Romanticism. Nevertheless, it receives several touching embodiments. Its perfect representative is surely Sylvia Sidney, star of Lang's first three American films (*Fury, You Only Live Once, You and Me*, 1938). In the first and third she becomes the film's moral spokeswoman, diverting the hero from revenge in *Fury*, and in *You and Me* delivering a Brechtian lesson in social conformity (one of the cinema's most curious anomalies!). In all three films she is morally stronger than the hero yet has her meaning only in relation to him. Her selfless commitment (reminiscent of William Blake's 'clod of clay/Trodden with the cattle's feet') provides *You Only Live Once* with its moral centre; hunted outcasts, the couple preserve their essential integrity through their devotion to each other—literally, to the death.

This devotion is echoed later, but one-sidedly, in the Gloria Grahame character of *The Big Heat* and, especially, Joan Bennett's 'little streetwalker' of *Man Hunt* (1941), a character (she is not in the original Geoffrey Household novel) who, Lang says, 'I must admit had all my heart.' She motivates the

one revenge in Lang that appears to have the director's unequivocal approval—linked as it is, once more, with the struggle against Fascism. Walter Pidgeon, hiding in a narrow cave, is tracked down by Gestapo chief George Sanders, who passes into the cave Joan Bennett's arrow-shaped hatpin as a token that she has been tortured and killed. Pidgeon keeps him talking while he improvises a makeshift bow, fits the hatpin to a stick, and shoots Sanders in the head with it: a marvellous example of Lang's poetic justice. An outrage is avenged, and Siegfried slays the dragon.

Finally, the purity of Lang's moral sense is epitomized in his presentation of violence. The whole issue of violence on the screen is obviously complex, and Lang's is not the only valid solution. It is, none the less, an impressive and admirable one. If violence is an integral part of the action, the director who scrupulously avoids showing it risks being accused of dishonesty; the director who spares us none of its detail, of sadistic relish. Lang avoids either extreme without any sense of compromise. He is concerned always with pain rather than with outward appearance—at the opposite extreme from Sam Peckinpah, whose work (especially *The Wild Bunch*) testifies to the fact that elaborate displays of carnage do not necessarily communicate physical sensation. Part of Lang's method is simply to show—without the visual emphasis of close-up—the object by which pain is or may be inflicted, and let our imagination work: the torn tin mug of *You Only Live Once*, the open razor of *Rancho Notorious*, the scalding coffee of *The Big Heat*. Another incident in this last film is also characteristically treated: that in which Lee Marvin deliberately burns a woman's hand with a cigarette. The whole action is filmed in long-shot, with no cut in to close-up; the camera neither flinches nor goes to stare. The sense of pain is acute precisely because we are not distracted by visually horrifying detail; at the same time, the scene's integrity is not interrupted, the physical cruelty is kept in its place as but one detail of an action involving a number of people, with complex implications.

Lang's other method is to keep the actual violence off-screen but only just: the scalding of Gloria Grahame in *The Big Heat* is the classic instance. The incident (it is one of the moments in the cinema when I most want to look away, despite the fact that I know there is nothing visual to flinch from) gains its extraordinary force partly from the economy and precision of the *mise en scène*, the speed and abruptness with which it happens; partly from our being given all the necessary information but having the act itself (not its aftermath) left to our imagination. The combination of tact and intensity—no one could accuse Lang of softening the violence by not showing it, but equally there is no morbid lingering—is typical of Lang, and very rare outside his work. The closest parallels are in the work of Mizoguchi—the brandings in *Sansho the Bailiff*, and the laming of Tamaki in the same film. There is no higher compliment.

Lotte Eisner's long-awaited full-length study, *Fritz Lang*, was finally published in 1976. But her *Haunted Screen* (1969) also offers valuable insights on Lang's German films. For the later films, the most important book is the one from which Wood has quoted, Peter Bogdanovich's *Fritz Lang in America* (1968). In French there is Luc Moullet's *Lang* (1963).

Fritz Lang died in 1976, fifteen years after he made his last film. Or, as Burch would say, over forty years after he made his last 'good' film. My own position is somewhat ambivalent. Although I cannot share Wood's admiration for the *Tiger* films, *The Thousand Eyes of Dr Mabuse*, or many of the American films, it seems to me that *Beyond a Reasonable Doubt* is indeed all that Wood (and Jacques Rivette) claim it to be. I would also put in a word for one American film Wood doesn't mention: *Clash by Night* (1952), with its fascinating mixture of Odetsian dramatics and the harsh, realistic background of a cannery town, and also, in Barbara Stanwyck's brilliant performance, one of Lang's best women's roles. *Moonfleet* (1955) also has many admirers, especially in France.

HARRY LANGDON

Richard Koszarski

That Harry Langdon could do so much within the relative straitjacket of his baby-face character was a feat unparalleled among the great silent clowns; certainly none of his rivals could do as much with so limited a bag of tricks, and we may wonder less at Langdon's fall than at the tremendous success he managed to achieve in the first place. Born in Council Bluffs, Iowa, on 15 June 1884, Langdon was on stage from boyhood, gradually achieving a considerable vaudeville success in the years following the First World War. In his stage act he developed the basic character and situations that he would later utilize in his great screen comedies. Mack Sennett was the first to put him into films (1924), in a series of shorts which were often ill-suited to his already developed comic character, but as soon as he gained some self-assurance and screen popularity Langdon began to take firmer control of his projects. Working with Harry Edwards and Frank Capra, he suddenly seemed to critics a new Chaplin (it should be remembered that the Master released no new films between 1925 and 1928, Langdon's brief period of ascendancy). But while Chaplin and Langdon did share a knack for pantomime, the excessively passive nature of Langdon's screen character was basically opposed to the assertiveness of Chaplin's tramp.

With his collaborators, Langdon broke from Sennett and produced independently *Tramp, Tramp, Tramp* (1926), *The Strong Man* (1926) and *Long Pants* (1927), his greatest successes—then dismissed Edwards and Capra and attempted to continue alone. This proved to be a mistake both artistically and financially, since Langdon lacked commercial sense, and the intensely personal comic vision displayed in the films he himself directed was alternately too maudlin (*Three's a Crowd*, 1927) or too dark (*The Chaser*, 1928) for any wide public acceptance. Care should be taken in accepting Frank Capra's recent self-serving account of Langdon's fall; on the other hand, there seems some evidence of deliberate distributor sabotage on the part of First National. The approach of old age sealed the fate of Langdon's screen character even more firmly than the arrival of sound, and although he continued to work as a writer (and to appear in shorts and in supporting roles in minor features), he never recaptured the spectacular success of his first features. He died in Hollywood on 22 December 1944. Sporadic attempts to revive his reputation by James Agee, Walter Kerr and a handful of others have won Langdon a small but loyal cult following in recent years, but a major critical study (and widespread popular acclaim) is still to come.

See also the articles on Capra and Sennett. Kevin Brownlow (in *The Parade's Gone By*, 1968) has some interesting things to say on Langdon, as do James Agee (*Agee on Film*, Vol. 1, 1958) and Walter Kerr (*The Silent Clowns*, 1975).

ALBERTO LATTUADA
Edgardo Cozarinsky

Lattuada's eclecticism has obstructed an evaluation of his unusual achievement. Born in 1914, for over thirty years he has turned out films of considerable interest which belong to the cultural and industrial context of their period without surrendering to opportunism. This would not be amazing in a Hollywood practitioner of the older generation, but (with Renoir as the notable exception) prolific European film-makers usually exhaust their professional abilities in a shorter time. Lattuada's early literate, 'calligraphic' films were overshadowed by the immediate emergence of neo-realism. But, characteristically, his best film in that key was *Il Delitto di Giovanni Episcopo (Flesh Will Surrender)*, made in 1947, when he had already approached the style in fashion with *Il Bandito* (U.S.: *The Bandit*, 1946), and just before *Senza Pietà (Without Pity*, 1948)—films that have aged better than most contemporary observations of post-war life (and now reveal an unsuspected kinship to American *film noir*). On the other hand, *Il Capotto (The Overcoat*, 1952), after Gogol, builds a system of absurd fantasy very much as its literary source did—through an accumulation of minutely rendered debris of lifelikeness: an unintentional parody of the neo-realist method. Most of Lattuada's minor films look considerably better years after they were made—*La Spiaggia* (U.K.: *The Beach*, 1954), *Guendalina* (1957) and *Lettere di una Novizia* (1961) are obvious examples, but there is also *Don Giovanni in Sicilia* (1967) and *Venga a Prendere il Caffè da Noi* (1970), which now look much more penetrating than other sex farces about

indefatigable males, and *Fräulein Doktor* (1969), with its full atemporal nonsense. The capacity to work with given materials and achieve something else, in quality and tone, has been one of Lattuada's elusive talents; very much isolated in the Italian cinema of the 70s, his solid, unadventurous films often prove more biting, more complex even than the flashy concoctions of most 'new' Italian directors.

Since this was written, Lattuada has made, after Mikhail Bulgakov's novel *Heart of a Dog*, *Cuore di Cane* (1975); alas, unlike his earlier 'Russian' film *The Overcoat*, the new film shows signs that Lattuada has finally 'surrendered to opportunism' and that his professional abilities have now become exhausted. But this may be only a temporary lapse.

CHARLES LAUGHTON
Robin Wood

Charles Laughton (1899–1962) directed only one film, but it deserves lasting recognition as one of the classics of the American cinema. *Night of the Hunter* (1955) is at once a strikingly individual work and the product of more than one talent. James Agee's script follows the outline of Davis Grubb's novel faithfully but eschews any temptation to reproduce or find a visual equivalent for its lush, self-indulgent style. Laughton, in turn, faithfully follows the script, which is extremely detailed and 'cinematic'. Many of the film's brilliant stylistic inventions—such as the electrifying helicopter shots that accompany Preacher's cross-country drive near the beginning—are Agee's, though Laughton frequently refines them: the iris-out that reduces the image to the tiny area where the children's faces peer from the cellar window replaces Agee's simple dissolve.

This last suggests something of the film's stylistic idiosyncrasy, the iris being an archaic device associated with the silent cinema (until Godard and Truffaut reinstated it). The film's ancestry seems mixed: it recalls at times the simplicity of the American silent cinema (the casting of Lillian Gish in a leading role was surely no coincidence), at others the elaboration of German Expressionism—as if Laughton were uniting the Griffith of *Way Down East* with the Murnau of *Sunrise*. Certain images (especially during the children's river journey, where their boat drifts in long-shot while the foreground is dominated by animals—toad, rabbit, spider—made huge by close-up) evoke the American 'primitive' painters, or illustrations from a child's story-book. The total effect is neither primitive nor eclectic. Apparently naïve devices and effects are used in a sophisticated, deliberate way that never becomes precious or suggests affectation. The film is centred on the children, yet the audience never becomes simply identified with their experiences. The deliberate naïveté thus has a direct appropriateness, but, because we are aware that it *is* deliberate, acts also as a distancing device.

Full of artifice, the film is also one of the most moving the American cinema has given us. Its power lies partly in the rich, passionate performances Laughton obtained from his actors (Robert Mitchum, Gish and Shelley Winters are all extraordinary) and partly in the intensity of certain isolated images and moments. But both of these are dependent on the cumulative effect of the whole, on unity and progression achieved by means of recurrent motifs that accumulate complex resonances. One of these is Preacher's song, 'Leaning on the Everlasting Arm', associated with his hypocrisy and with the narrow, repressive Revivalism that is part of the action's context, but juxtaposed also with the unforgettable dream-like image of the murdered Willa in the car under water, her hair streaming out like water-weeds; and finally taken up by Lillian Gish, in one of the film's great moments, as she guards the children at night from the prowling Preacher. Another motif is that of apples, which acquire as the film progresses the dual significance of the sin of Eve and the richness of natural fertility. The film's fitting climax is the boy's gift of an apple as Christmas present to Lillian Gish, and her acceptance of it—the action summing up an implied view of life more complex than the film's deceptively 'naïve' imagery might at first glance suggest.

See *Charles Laughton: An Intimate Biography* (1976) by Charles Higham. Andrew Sarris has pointed out that a comparison of three James Agee scripts—*The Night of the Hunter, The African Queen* and *The Bride Comes to Yellow Sky*—with the three films made from these scripts by Laughton, Huston and Windust respectively, proves conclusively that 'directors, not writers, are the ultimate *auteurs* of the cinema'.

LAUREL AND HARDY
David Robinson

Laurel and Hardy were the last arrivals in the Golden Age of screen comedy. Although they had been in films respectively since 1917 and 1913—before Langdon, before Keaton, before the great flowering of the 20s—they did not team together officially until 1927, when the Golden Age was passing, and many of its stars had already vanished. By that time Laurel was already thirty-seven, Hardy thirty-five.

Laurel was English, born Arthur Stanley Jefferson in Ulverston, Lancashire, in 1890. His father, a well-known theatrical manager in the north of England, tried to educate him formally, or at least interest him in the white-collar side of the business rather than its red-nose department; but Stanley had a vocation, and made his debut as a boy comedian in 1906. Soon afterwards he joined Fred Karno's legendary comedy sketch company. In the celebrated *Mumming Birds* act—a knockabout set in a stage-within-the-stage music hall—he understudied Charles Chaplin as 'The Drunk'; and he later asserted that Chaplin pinched the plum title role of *Jimmy the Fearless* after he, Stanley Jefferson, had already successfully built up the character.

Laurel left the Karno company in the course of an ill-planned and exhausting tour of the United States in 1910, and went into partnership with Arthur Dandoe in a sketch called *The Rum'uns from Rome*. After ups and downs with other partners and other acts, Jefferson (as he still was) rejoined Karno in 1913 for another American tour, which collapsed when Chaplin, by this time the star of the company, deserted to the movies. Jefferson thereupon tried his luck in American vaudeville with other partners and in various acts: The Three Comiques; Hurley, Stan and Wren; The Keystone Trio (Sennett's comedies were already famous); The Stan

Jefferson Trio; and finally, settling on a shorter surname for ease of marquee billing, Stan and Mae Laurel (Mae was an Australian singer who has passed into historical oblivion).

He was successful enough to be enticed into movies; the title of his first film, *Nuts in May* (1917), has the Laurel ring to it, though the frenetic slapstick character he appears to have played had little relationship with the trundling little clown of later days. He moved to Universal, but after a few films as a character called Hickory Hiram, went back to vaudeville. The next year he tried films again, summoned by Hal Roach to make a series of two-reelers. But Harold Lloyd was the established star of the Roach studio and no effort was made to keep Laurel; he went on to play supporting roles in the films of Larry Semon, that Pierrot Lunaire of slapstick comedy. When Semon became jealous of Laurel's comedy gifts (so the story goes), Laurel was released and went back again to vaudeville. In 1919–20 he returned to the screen in a series of parodies of celebrated screen successes of the time, produced by 'Bronco Billy' Anderson. Roach hired him again; let him go again to make a series of two-reelers for Joe Rock; and only finally signed him up in 1926 to what was to be a long-standing and eventful contract. Laurel was hired as a writer and gagman. He had finally decided that work before the cameras was not for him.

His eventual partner, Oliver Hardy, was born in 1892 in Harlem, Georgia, to a middle-class family. His father died when he was a boy, and he legally added the senior Hardy's first name, Oliver, to his own given name of Norvell. In their films together Laurel and Hardy use their own names; and when Hardy wanted to be particularly impressive he always introduced himself in full, as 'Mr Oliver Norvell Hardy'. He was sent to Georgia Military College, but did not like it; and later to the Atlanta Conservatory of Music, from which he played truant to sing in a movie-theatre quartet. Earlier, at eight years old, he had run away from home for a brief spell as boy soprano in a minstrel show. According to his own account he thought at one time of being a lawyer, and spent a short period at the University of Georgia. When he was eighteen he opened the first movie theatre in Milledgeville, Georgia;

but in 1913 gave it up to go into film-making, and joined the Lubin Company in Jacksonville, Florida. Already a very tall and stout man he was a useful character player, either for knockabout or for moustachioed villains (he was proud of his leer). Comedy, however, proved his forte. After three years with Lubin he worked for Vim comedies, went on to play comic heavy for Billy West (a Chaplin impersonator), Earl Williams and Jimmy Aubrey; and eventually became, like Laurel, an effective foil for Larry Semon. By the middle 20s he was working as a useful supporting player at the Hal Roach Studios.

At the end of their careers, Laurel and Hardy presented a charming stage act, which began with the two of them intent on an assignation, but forever walking in and out of three doors in the stage flat, always missing meeting each other by a teasing hair's breadth. The circumstances of their early careers, the decade in which, unknowingly, they were drifting together, were much the same. In 1917 Hardy had appeared in a supporting role in a Stan Laurel two-reeler called *A Lucky Dog*, directed by Jess Robbins. They just missed each other while working in Semon's company. In 1926 Laurel, congratulating himself that his acting days were behind him, was directing Harry Myers in *Get 'Em Young* when the actor playing the comic butler scalded himself with boiling fat (being an enthusiastic cook and gourmet). Laurel was obliged to take over the role, though the actor returned before the end of the shooting to play opposite him. The injured player was Hardy. In a further film, *Slipping Wives* (1927), Laurel was again persuaded to play the comic support opposite Hardy; and the team was born, though it took ten more pictures and several months before they actually starred together in Roach Comedy All Stars shorts.

The first Laurel and Hardy film proper, *Putting Pants on Philip* (1927), was not yet typical: the relationship had not crystallized. Yet the very plot seems like an announcement of the new partnership. Laurel (as Philip) arrives off the boat from England to join his uncle, Hardy, who is much distressed by his relation's embarrassing Scots kilt. The mishaps which provide the comedy for the rest of the film arise from efforts to trouser Philip decently. Already Hardy is pompous and expansive, with the grand gestures and fine manners of a Southern gentleman. Already most of his misfortunes arise from his mistaken assurance that he is smarter than his foolish partner. Already gestures later to be familiar, like Laurel's crumpled-face crying, are evident; already in moments of special anguish Hardy turns his face in mute, exasperated appeal to the camera.

After this the team were quickly in their stride. The record of their early films is far from clear, but they made at least three more shorts in 1927, including *The Battle of the Century*, which climaxes in the biggest and most extravagant custard-pie battle in the history of slapstick. Ten films in 1928 included *Leave 'Em Laughing*, in which the effects of laughing gas cause them to bring California traffic to a crashing stop; *From Soup to Nuts*, in which they are the outstandingly inept help at a society dinner; and *Two Tars*, which has a sustained sequence in a traffic jam which remains one of their classic scenes of orgiastic destruction of property. 1929 brought thirteen films, including at least one unqualified comic masterpiece, *Big Business*, in which they appeared with James Finlayson of the tormented face, a Scottish comic to whom Laurel had at one period played in supporting roles, and who was in turn to provide support in many Laurel and Hardy starring vehicles. A trifling exchange of words over a Christmas tree which Finlayson prefers not to purchase from them, it being midsummer, leads to an escalating contest of mutual, destructive revenge. Each party takes turns to inflict ever worse vandalism on the property of the other. Piece by piece Finlayson destroys their car while they wreck his house—each party, with exquisite courtesy, standing back to let the other take his turn before exacting his next tribute of revenge. When all is over, and the whole locality reduced to tears, Laurel and Hardy suddenly leave off their remorseful crying to burst into reprehensibly shocking laughter.

In the same year they surmounted the problems of sound films, which had been the artistic death of many of their compeers. Their success lay in their determination not to change their style, characters or pace. They simply accepted sound, without compromise, taking advantage of dialogue possibilities (their voices were as complementary

as their shapes—Oliver's a resonant Southern tenor; Stanley's a quaint little music-hall cheep, with an accent that derived from some mysterious vaudeville region between Lancashire and Hollywood). They made sound effects—the dyspeptic jangle of the innards of a piano they are moving in *The Music Box* (1932), or the terrible bangs and thumps offscreen as Stanley gazes in painful sympathy from the head of a stairwell down which his large partner has fallen. In 1930 they completed eight shorts; in 1931, seven, including *Laughing Gravy* about the perils of concealing a dog in lodgings; in 1932, six, including their Academy Award winner, *The Music Box*. This film has the simplicity of a true classic. Throughout its two reels they struggle to get a piano up a tremendous flight of stone steps. After terrible struggles and endless returns to the bottom of the steps in pursuit of the wayward instrument, they finally reach the top, where a postman tells them it would have been easier for them to drive it up the back way. Gratefully they thank him and toil back down the stairs to bring the piano up the easy way.

For three years more they continued to make shorts: six in 1933, four in 1934, and three—their last—in 1935. While the market for short comedies of the sort they made was declining with the competition of the Walt Disney cartoons, Laurel and Hardy had surmounted the second crisis of their professional career, the move to feature comedies. Their first feature films—*Pardon Us* (U.K.: *Jailbirds*, 1931) and *Pack Up Your Troubles* (1932)—were tentative, mere assemblies of two-reel subjects. In other films their comedy was packaged, with greater or less success, with operetta subjects—*Fra Diavolo* (1933), *Babes in Toyland* (1934) and *The Bohemian Girl* (1936). But their best features contain some of their most accomplished and sustained comedy, and bear comparison with any feature-length comedies of the period: *Our Relations* (1936); *Way Out West* (1937), with its inspired dialogue and enchanting dance number; *Swiss Miss* (1938), which contains the surreal moment recalled by James Agee, 'simple and real . . . as a nightmare. Laurel and Hardy are trying to move a piano across a narrow suspension bridge. The bridge is strung over a sickening chasm, between a couple of Alps. Midway they meet a gorilla.' Hal Roach produced three more features with them, of which the best was *Block-Heads* (1938), a tale of beautiful idiocy which opens with Stanley as the soldier who was left behind on the Western Front in 1918 and in 1938 still sits beside a growing mountain of empty bean-cans, unaware that the war has ended. The rest of the story is of the inevitable disasters that disrupt the home life and marriage of his old buddy, Oliver, when he adopts him into his home.

The years between 1927 and 1938 represent the sustained peak of a career that was to be prolonged for as long again. During this period they had a variety of directors—Clyde Bruckman, James Parrott, Leo McCarey, James Horne, their occasional co-star Edgar Kennedy, Lewis Foster, George Marshall, Lloyd French, Charles Rogers, John G. Blystone—some of whom reappear in their credits at intervals throughout their whole career. But the consistency of the style, the invention, the acute sense of gag *mise en scène*, the appreciation of the characters and their relationship are clear evidence of a single authorship. Stan Laurel brought from his music-hall days and the Karno company a gift and a passion for devising and staging comic business. In the film-making he always took a forceful hand in the direction, and it appears that the so-called director, particularly in the early days, was principally required to stand behind the camera while Stan himself was in a scene. His concern extended from the first conception to the cutting room. Hardy, a man of quite different temperament, liked to play his scenes and get off to the golf links (one of his occasional opponents was W. C. Fields), admiringly leaving the creation of the pictures to his partner.

In an interview with me in 1954 Laurel gave his opinion that it was not possible to make a slapstick comedy by the usual method of discontinuous shooting. Therefore the films for Roach were generally shot in continuity—which must have been a costly method. The team went on the set with a basic idea and an outline of the business they were to introduce; but the main work of creation was done on the set. The actual business and its timing were worked out in accordance with the reactions of the informal audience of technicians and the like who were on the set.

There were hazards to this sort of improvisational shooting: 'We had a scene where we're together on a bed. We went on the lot the first day, got up on the bed and started laughing. We laughed so much we couldn't stop. So we weren't able to shoot anything that day. Next day we went back, got up on the bed, and the same thing happened again. So we weren't able to shoot anything that day either.'

Laurel had his own editing technique, which was made possible by the method of shooting in continuity. The film was fairly finely cut as it was shot; so that at every stage Laurel and Hardy could see an approximation of the final version, up to the point they had reached in shooting. The timing and cutting of the final version were reached, however, only after the reactions of preview audiences had been carefully studied. Laurel's film technique, in fact, seems to have been to approximate the conditions of comedy creation as near as possible to those of the live theatre. The creative autonomy he was able to exercise in the twelve years of the team's major creations was much the same as that which was necessary to the other great comedians, Chaplin, Keaton and Harold Lloyd. Keaton's career, for instance, came to a virtual end the moment he became subject to the control of studio supervisors. In sound films, Mae West and W. C. Fields retained the integrity of their comic personas by demanding working situations in which they were able to write and control their own material.

Roach recognized the eventual economy of giving Laurel and Hardy the degree of freedom demanded by such methods; but in the big studios—at RKO, Fox and MGM, between which they wandered like nomads in the later years—they were frustrated. With writers and directors haphazardly delegated to their films, without regard to their suitability or sympathy, decline was inevitable. They made nine more films, all best forgotten, after finally leaving Roach. In America their last appearance was in *The Bullfighters* (1945), directed by a once great director of comedy, Mal St Clair, now fallen on evil days. Their last film was bizarrely made in France, with a French cast. Laurel and Hardy were horrified by the dilatory methods of production; Laurel was seriously ill during most of the time it was being made. Without

Laurel and Hardy (and Laurel and Hardy) in *Brats*, directed by James Parrott and produced by Hal Roach in 1930.

exaggeration Laurel called *Atoll K* (U.K.: *Robinson Crusoeland*; U.S.: *Utopia*, 1951) 'a catastrophe'. In their last years they made a few music hall tours, and passed into retirement, battling with ill-health, living on modest means while watching other men grow rich by the sales of their old films to television. From time to time there were rumours of returns to the screen. Hardy died in 1957; Laurel in 1965.

The full appreciation of their comedy creation has only come since their departure from the screen and from life. Perhaps, as with W. C. Fields, the essential anarchy of their assault upon Establishment values strikes us today with a new validity. Charles Barr, in his fine study of their comic style, wrote: 'They are supreme liberators from bourgeois inhibitions, yet essentially they are, or aspire to be, respectable bourgeois citizens.' Their very dress proclaims their bourgeois aspir-

ations—their bowlers, wing collars and bow ties, their slightly rumpled suits, Stanley's conservative, Oliver's slightly bolder in cut. Whatever the results, their motives are generally exemplary, and they show (most of the time) due deference to authority and—at least when they are in sight—the virago wives who generally watch over them like angry governesses. However patronizing he is to Stanley, Ollie is unfailingly courteous and polite to strangers and policemen. Of course they are fated, by destiny as well as their own obtuseness: inevitably they will be the causes of an orgy of destruction; and inevitably there will come a point when their bourgeois delight in propriety and order will break down and they will be released (as in that laughing scene at the end of *Big Business*) into the ecstatic pleasure of chaos and destruction.

There are more fundamental and eternal

fountains of comedy in their teaming. Their contrast is itself a cause of laughter. It is the old joke of Falstaff and his page ('the sow that hath overwhelmed all her litter but one'), of Belch and Aguecheek, the Walrus and the Carpenter. And besides the fun inherent in their teaming there is a constant striving after the grotesque—in their costumes, their funny wigs, the donkeys they ride in *Fra Diavolo*, the pony sled in *Way Out West* on which the mountainous Ollie is drawn by Stan and a minute donkey. Their contrast has been described as 'the battle . . . of Dither versus Dignity'; but the association is too complementary ever to be accurately seen as a battle.

Hardy, whose basic costume and make-up were originally based on a cartoon character, 'Helpful Henry', always proposes and leads every enterprise. (It is interesting that the form of most of their films is the proposition of an enterprise, the progressive frustration of its execution and its final catastrophic abortion which leaves them where they were at the beginning, or more likely one step back.) Oliver always gives the orders, explaining each step with a much-tried patience. He always knows best ('Well, I'm *bigger* than he is, so I think I should know best,' he explained in an interview with me). As the 'brains' of the partnership, he generally delegates the dirty work to Stan. Yet finally, sadly and inevitably, the misfortunes and ruin fall upon Oliver, leaving Stanley standing by unharmed, looking with helpless amazement at the havoc of which he is most likely the innocent cause.

In contrast to Stanley's shamblings, Oliver is all elephantine elegance. His walk is assured, head in the air (with the predictable consequences of that attitude). His huge hands affect an elegant grace; a simple act like ringing a doorbell will be preceded by a whole series of elaborate gesticulations and gyrations. Most of his misfortunes are due to his inability to bend to circumstances. Instead he faces them full square and usually falls flat on his back as a result. He remains magnificently unaltered in any situation. Up to his neck in water in *Way Out West*, he folds his arms in a characteristic gesture of irritation.

Stanley is the extreme of clownish humility. He is the pure simpleton, to all appearances utterly vacuous. Well aware of his own limitations, he is content most of the time to teeter along behind his big companion and to repeat and accept all his instructions. His moments of enlightenment and revolt surprise him as much as they surprise Oliver. He is not perhaps so much a fool as a child. (In *Be Big*, 1930, his preparations for a day in Atlantic City consist of packing his toy yacht.) The child's innocence is a quality which Hardy shares with him and which is perhaps the distinctive quality of their comedy work. They are the most innocent of all the clowns; more innocent than Keaton's single-minded heroes, than Raymond Griffith or Lloyd, certainly more innocent than Harry Langdon in his slightly improper moments. The motives which impel them have a childish logic; their jealousies and meannesses (sometimes they will deceive each other) are simple babyishness. When Stan drinks (it is always he who drinks) it is about as vicious as a cigarette in the lavatory. In their films they often have wives; but to them a wife is no more than a kind of starchy governess, to be deceived (in simple matters only), outwitted and escaped for the afternoon. They are always recaptured. Extra-marital interests are on the erotic level of an apple for the lady teacher.

Their innocence is no protection. 'In this case the meek are not blessed. They do not inherit the earth.They inherit chaos. Chaos most active and violent and diabolical takes advantage of their inhibitions' (John Grierson). Tacks are there to be trodden on; banana skins to be slipped on; roofs to be fallen off; trousers to tear; beds to collapse; pianos to fall downstairs; windows and doors to be trapped in. Again and again Oliver will turn up his face from the mud or tar in which he has fallen to gaze his pathetic appeal to the camera; again and again he will accuse poor Stanley: 'That's another fine mess you've gotten me into'; again and again Stanley will screw up his face and cry. It is not of their choice. 'They are perhaps the Civil Servants of comedy. Nothing on earth would please them more than a quiet permanence in all things.' But that was not their comic destiny.

Apart from the study by Charles Barr quoted by Robinson (*Laurel and Hardy*, 1967), there are four other books devoted to

Laurel and Hardy: William Everson's *The Films of Laurel and Hardy* (1967), *Mr Laurel and Mr Hardy* by John McCabe (1961), as well as McCabe's *The Comedy World of Stan Laurel* (1974), and finally *The Laurel and Hardy Book*, edited by Leonard Maltin (1975).

DAVID LEAN, see p. 831

MITCHELL LEISEN

John Gillett

Now recognized as one of Hollywood's most civilized talents, Mitchell Leisen (1897–1972) had a visual elegance which can be attributed to his early years as art director for Cecil B. DeMille and as costume designer for such distinguished silent films as *Robin Hood* (1922) and *The Thief of Bagdad* (1924). His own directorial career started in 1933; it is most notable for the series of suave, sophisticated comedy romances dealing with perennial American themes like the search for money and respectability (or conversely the relinquishing of money for love), often set in an 'upper-crust' milieu and viewed with the kind of worldly irony usually associated with Lubitsch and Preston Sturges. The latter, in fact, as well as Brackett and Wilder, provided Leisen with some of his wittiest and most probing scripts of the 30s and 40s for such films as *Easy Living* (1937), *Remember the Night* (1940) and *Midnight* (1939) which, together with *Hands Across the Table* (1935), comprise his most distinctive work in this vein. Leisen worked best when surrounded by the finest writing and technical talents, moulding them together into a seamless whole and never apparently obtruding his own personality; yet the films' very precision and economy testify to the effectiveness of his 'invisible' direction.

Like Cukor, he was particularly successful in drawing out the best from his players— Jean Arthur, Carole Lombard, Claudette Colbert, Barbara Stanwyck and Paulette Goddard rarely surpassed their performances for Leisen, and he helped actors like Fred MacMurray and John Barrymore (in *Midnight*) to shade their playing into filmic terms. After *Kitty* (1945), with its lavishly realized English period settings, his career declined, probably because his kind of fastidiousness and taste was passing out of fashion.

There is a full-length study of Leisen's work: *Hollywood Director: The Career of Mitchell Leisen* by David Chierichetti (1973). Some critics have seen Leisen's tear-jerking melodramas of the mid-40s as the ancestors of Douglas Sirk's films of the 50s; and I do remember with a certain affection such soulful studies as *Hold Back the Dawn* (1941) and *To Each His Own* (1946). One film not mentioned by Gillett is *Arise My Love* (1940), the first half of which, at least, is as brilliant and sparkling as anything by Leisen. Andrew Sarris attributes the decline of Leisen to the 'promotion of Preston Sturges and Billy Wilder from writers' cubicles to directors' chairs'. With his best scriptwriters directing their own scripts, Leisen found himself, says Sarris, in the 'unenviable position of an expert diamond cutter working with lumpy coal'.

PAUL LENI

Carlos Clarens

Unusually modest, Paul Leni (1885–1929) kept designing sets for directors lesser than himself (e.g., Arthur Robison) even after creating in *Das Wachsfigurenkabinett* (*Waxworks*, 1924) one of the classic German films of the 20s. Brought to California by Carl Laemmle, he directed four pictures at Universal, long regarded as commercial compromises, but one of which, *The Man Who Laughs* (1928), stands today as the most relentlessly Germanic film to come out of Hollywood. In fact, like Lubitsch before and Lang after, Leni was shrewd enough to redefine Expressionism in American terms, and thereafter found himself ensconced in a horror genre he created almost singlehandedly. In Berlin, Leni's sets had been as integral a part of *Hintertreppe* (*Backstairs*, 1921) as the gnarled body language of Fritz Kortner, and he deservedly shares the credit with stage director Leopold Jessner. But in America he relinquished actual designing to the Universal art department to concentrate on absolute *mise en scène*. Laura La Plante and Creighton Hale are hardly performers in the Max Reinhardt tradition, yet Leni manoeuvred them as superb props in *The Cat and the Canary* (1927); and supporting Conrad Veidt in *The Man Who Laughs* there is a cast of Hollywood reliables who look and behave like so many Dieterles and Janningses. Succeeding where Griffith and others failed, Leni established an archetypal mixture of grotesquerie and menace for Whale, Browning and Polanski to follow. For all the comedy relief—the *Caligari* parody in *The Cat and the Canary* is symptomatic—there is a real if intangible evil lurking in the Gothic recesses of Leni's abandoned mansions and theatres, a core of metaphysical *Angst* retained in the context of summer stock material like *The Last Warning* (1929).

There is a monograph, in French, devoted to Leni by Freddy Buache (1968). Otherwise there remains, for the German films, the invaluable (and inevitable) *The Haunted Screen* by Lotte Eisner (1969).

SERGIO LEONE

Richard Corliss

In the mid-60s, about the time the American Western was either waxing elegiac or waning arthritic (depending on your sympathies), an unlikely challenger rode into the genre from the far-off plains of Cinecittà. At first, critics chose to ignore or deplore these 'spaghetti Westerns', with their pseudonymous directors, their has-been or never-was American stars, their spasms of violence and their purloined plots. (Wasn't the progenitor of the cycle, the 1964 *Per un Pugno di Dollari* [*A Fistful of Dollars*], simply a clinical and cynical rip-off of Kurosawa's 'Eastern Western' *Yojimbo*?) If Ford, Hawks, Walsh, Anthony Mann *et al.* were seen serving the genre as honourable, authentic Men of the West, then the Italians were little more than alien interlopers—mercenaries—plundering the old homestead and leaving nothing in their wake but a bloody trail of Chianti and tomato sauce.

Critics who focused, myopically, on this scurvy class portrait overlooked the star student in the middle: director Sergio Leone, most likely to succeed. And succeed he did. With each of his films after *A Fistful of Dollars* (*Per Qualche Dollari in più* [*For a Few Dollars More*, 1965]; *Il Buono, il Brutto, il Cattivo* [*The Good, the Bad and the Ugly*, 1966]; *C'era una Volta il West* [*Once upon a Time in the West*, 1968]; and *Giù la Testa* [U.K.: *A Fistful of Dynamite*; U.S.: *Duck, You Sucker!*, 1971]) Leone's imagery became more aptly voluptuous, his reverberations of Western ritual more resonant, his outsize characters at once more magisterial and more mysterious. And Leone's own artistic lineage became clearer: he was not only a delirious descendant of *both* John Fords, but a spiritual brother of such 'operatic' Italians as Visconti, Bertolucci (who worked on the screenplay of *Once upon a Time in the West*), Minnelli and Coppola—a natural film-maker whose love of the medium and the genre is joyously evident, and infectious, in every frame he shoots.

The Leone universe is a blend of seamless contradictions: labyrinthine plots and elemental themes, nihilistic heroes with romantic obsessions, microscopic close-ups and macrocosmic vistas, circular camerawork and triangular shoot-outs, a sense of Americana and a European sensibility, playful parody and profound homage. In a desertscape too desolate for ranchers or cowboys—or, for that matter, Indians—Leone's hero (Clint Eastwood or Charles Bronson) will stand stoic and squinty-eyed, and wait a lifetime to taste the cold dish of revenge, testing his own will and his adversary's patience in the interim. And Leone's villain (Lee 'Angel Eyes' Van Cleef or Henry 'Blue Eyes' Fonda) will keep gunning down men, women and children—but with style, always with style. Inevitably, the final gunfight will be heralded by a reel of intricate foreplay, with the protagonists describing impossible geometric figures—moving simultaneously forward and in circles, and suggesting both a Calvary march and the mating dance of deadly enemies—until the villain discovers his original sin and, in a split-second of gunfire, receives his penance and absolution. (All this religious symbolism is indeed in the films: Eastwood is very much the grizzled Christ figure; Bronson seems a superhuman apparition; and Eli Wallach, in *The Good, the Bad and the Ugly*, endures a hilarious hanging-crucifixion. But it's not meant to be taken any more solemnly than Leone's other cross-cultural references.)

If the wide-screen, big-budget, all-star, Western epic had not existed, Leone would have invented it—and, in *Once upon a Time in the West* he did, stunningly summarizing the formal and thematic preoccupations of his early work, and in the process creating a very personal fresco of surpassing scope and grandeur. (Predictably, it just about cost him his career.) The film is Leone's masterpiece, from the opening sequence of Woody Strode and Jack Elam waiting for a showdown like two archbishops preparing for the most sacred of black masses, to the final, four-minute tracking shot that follows Claudia Cardinale as she carries civilization to the West on her beautiful broad shoulders. In this shot, Cardinale walks out of her hard-won home to greet the men laying tracks for the first transcontinental railway; and Leone obviously means us to associate these tracks with those upon which his camera is gliding. For a moment, train and camera travel on the same track; in a breathtaking synthesis that resolves the narrative even as it enters the realm of 'pure cinema'.

As either cinema or opera, Leone's films are significantly enriched by the work of cinematographer Tonino Delli Colli, and even more by composer Ennio Morricone. Morricone's prodigally melodious score for *Once upon a Time in the West* includes a separate and haunting motif for each of the six major characters and, as the main theme, a lush rephrasing of Victor Herbert's 'Ah, Sweet Mystery of Life'. It remained for Sergio Leone to apotheosize, in this and all his films, the bitter-sweet mystery of death.

It would seem that the 'spaghetti Western' has gone into a decline. Leone has not been active of late (except as producer), and the *Trinità* series gets more mediocre with each film. A temporary eclipse of the genre, or is it played out? I'd plump for the latter explanation, but we shall see.

MERVYN LEROY

Tony Rayns

The appearance of Mervyn LeRoy's name as director on some seventy features threatens to obscure the fact that his professional skills more closely resemble the traditional attrib-utes of a producer. His strengths are shrewdness and adaptability rather than individuality; his major successes look like 'anonymous' summations of his studio's house style (mainly Warners in the 30s, and MGM in the 40s and early 50s). His knack of making his 'common touch' synonymous with front-office interests finds its perfect cypher in his marriage into the Warner family.

The shrewdness admitted an occasional innovation in his early career. *Five Star Final* (1931) and *I Am a Fugitive from a Chain Gang* (1932) invest standard melodramas with a suggestion of social criticism, establishing a punchy, journalistic tone which Warners made its own; *Little Caesar* (1931), tame as it looks today, did more to define the emerging gangster genre than Sternberg's *Underworld* had done. At the same time, it is its sheer ingenuousness that makes a modest programmer like *Two Seconds* (1932) (a virtual blueprint for Raoul Walsh's *Manpower*, incidentally) one of the starkest outbursts of misogyny of its day. LeRoy (born 1900) comes nearest to a distinctive voice in his treatment of the Depression: the linking material in *Gold Diggers of 1933* (1933; with an acid Ginger Rogers) and the entirety of his best film *Hard to Handle* (1933; with an ultra-cynical Cagney as a con-man) are untypically abrasive in their flippancy. It took less than four years for this energy to mellow into complacency. *They Won't Forget* (1937), least soft-centred of all the Warner exposés, finds LeRoy's attention fixed chiefly on the bounce of his discovery: Lana Turner's breasts. His MGM work is, naturally, even softer. *Waterloo Bridge* (1940) and *Random Harvest* (1942) all but melt in the mind; *Madame Curie* (1943) was a tearful riposte to the Warner/Paul Muni bio-pics, and the musicals *Million Dollar Mermaid* (1952) and *Rose Marie* (1954) stake everything on their Busby Berkeley choreography.

The inevitable corollary of LeRoy's ease within the studio system was that Hollywood's decline brought him down too. His last films, many of them would-be blockbusters, are scattered and uncertain, as if he was shadow-boxing with the tastes of an audience he no longer knew how to exploit. The closing chapters of his bland autobiography *Take One* bristle with dislike and resentment of the 'new' Hollywood.

LeRoy's autobiography has appeared as *Take One*, by Mervyn LeRoy, as told to Dick Kleiner (1974). With time, 'hard-hitting' films like *They Won't Forget* and *I Am a Fugitive from a Chain Gang* now seem pretty tame, whereas the more light-weight films stand up better. As Rayns points out, the change in LeRoy's style after his move from Warners to MGM is a striking proof of the importance of the studios. (See pp. 13–14 in my Introduction to the Dictionary. There is also an extended essay on Leroy by Kingsley Canham in *The Hollywood Professionals*, vol. 5 (1976), edited by Clive Denton.

RICHARD LESTER

Richard Corliss

With *A Hard Day's Night* (1964), Richard Lester (born 1932) became a prime beneficiary—as he was later to be a signal casualty —of the Swinging London image of the mid-60s. The mystique may have been manufactured, but the enthusiasm this lyrical-satirical-musical-documentary conveyed and evoked was genuine enough to nominate Lester as the decade's *Zeitgeist* director (perhaps *ex aequo* with Godard). Seen today, this first Beatles film retains its vigour, its good humour, its North Country courtliness and easy grace, and especially its distillation of a moment when, maybe for the last time, it felt good to be young. Already, in its successor, *Help!* (1965), one could hear a minor key of cynicism in the group's music and sense a change in Lester's role: from older brother to Big Brother, portraying his stars as passive Alices in a Bondian Wonderland.

North American-born, like several other notable contributors to what is thought of as the indigenous eccentricity in post-war British film (writers William Rose and Frederic Raphael, directors Alexander Mackendrick and Joseph Losey), Lester developed a penchant for the colloquial into an incapacitating obsession until, with *How I Won the War* (1967) and *The Bed Sitting Room* (1969), any moviegoer not born within the sound of Bow Bells needed a set of Received Standard English subtitles to understand the dialogue. This tactic combined with a tendency towards helter-skelter, TV-commercial montage and a 'sprung-rhythm' tempo (in which the comic pace is broken by a lingering shot of a bemused or humiliated bit player) to create a distancing effect that was all too effective: viewers kept their distance from theatres where his films were playing, and producers put him in cold storage along with their Nehru jackets and Liverpudlian slang.

The burial was premature, though interment lasted for almost five years. Earlier on, Lester had twice forgotten about trying to be both Swift and Juvenal, and had shown a gift for translating, maybe transcending, material from other media: the Broadway burlesque of *A Funny Thing Happened on the Way to the Forum* (1966), the mod soap-operatics of *Petulia* (1968). He set *Forum* in the festering epic ruins of an old Samuel Bronston set, and the movie as a whole has an agreeably seedy pungency, the perfect aura and aroma for Zero Mostel and his band of raunchy sexagenarians. *Petulia* plays its 30s-style quadrangular love story against the backdrop of a San Francisco which uneasily accommodates both Nob Hill and Haight-Ashbury, but Lester is less interested here in local colour than in the off-black shades of despair, flakiness, impatience and perseverance in post-Hollywood romance. The film reveals Lester at his most audacious: trusting his audience instead of lecturing and hectoring; working with emotions instead of playing with ideas; finding humour in the everyday instead of slapstick in World Wars II and III; gauging human complexities instead of political theorems. His characters (and actors) are more than witty marionettes; his *mise en scène* is more than the sum of its shots. The restraint, control and compassion of *Petulia* marked Lester's rite of passage from boy scientist to adult film-maker— which was followed by another painful transition: to unemployed director.

Lester's years in exile taught him to take what he could get, and make of it what he could. At least twice, he has made something very good indeed: with *Juggernaut* (1974), a beautifully crafted (if machine-tooled) melodrama in which Hawksian ideals are treated with serious affection; and with *The Four Musketeers* (1974), a darkly passionate gloss on Dumas *père*. Lester seems resigned to applying his *Goon Show* humour ever-so-lightly to traditional genres, as a modern-day hybrid of Curtiz and Sturges. But this very resignation should be cause for hope. Lester has proved as susceptible as any intelligent artist to the lure of the Grand Statement; but when he curbs his dogmatism and hires himself out, he can do handiwork as rich and satisfying as any in contemporary cinema.

Lester's career has indeed had its ups and downs; for me, one of the upper 'ups' was *The Knack* (1965), a brilliant adaptation of Ann Jellicoe's play. And two of the lower 'downs' were his adaptation of Terence McNally's play *The Ritz* (1976) and, for me, the turgid *Robin and Marion* (1977).

MARCEL L'HERBIER

Noël Burch

To write today in a manner neither contemptuous nor archaeological about Marcel L'Herbier (born 1890) is necessarily to assume the mantle of rehabilitator. At least this is so in Paris, the only place where his films are still likely to be seen.

Elsewhere, however, the masking, vignettes and other technical devices of *Rose-France* (1918), the distorting lenses, selective *flous* and multiple superimpositions of *El Dorado* (1921), the accelerated montage of *L'Inhumaine* (1924) might well be *recognized* by the underground generations; for they, at least, have deconsecrated the cinematographic image, so long held sacred under the reign of men like Bazin and Rossellini, and they care nothing for the peculiarly Parisian terrorism exercised by the disciples of André Breton, who are still busy paying off old scores, calling Germaine Dulac to account for *La Coquille et le Clergyman* and L'Herbier for his 'decadent' aestheticism.

A decadent aesthete the young L'Herbier undoubtedly was just after the First World War. As a man of letters, his gods were Claudel and Wilde (but also Villiers de l'Isle Adam and Proust); as a musician, his master was Debussy. As one might expect, he despised the cinema—until the day he suffered, like the rest of the Parisian intelligentsia, the shock of DeMille's *The Cheat* (1915). Paradoxically, this first glimpse offered to Paris of a new cinematic dramaturgy—with a supple, quasi-invisible *découpage* or shot-structure which at last succeeded in fragmenting the screen space without shattering it—was to set L'Herbier, Gance and Epstein on a course which would lead them to the antipodes of the academic pole it actually signposted. In fact, only Delluc learned a direct lesson from this film. For the rest, including L'Herbier, it was the point of departure for an impassioned quest: the quest for that famous specific nature of cinema.

First stage: *Rose-France* (1918), 'a slim volume of verses published at the author's expense'. But although rooted in a literary-economic tradition derived from the nineteenth century, nothing could be further from the drawing-room aesthetics of *The Cheat* than this curious collage which mingles pretty postcards of pure 1914–18 camp with title cards copiously laden with verses culled from Charles d'Orléans and Péguy, the whole being packaged in an orgy of maskings, superimpositions and process shots which provoked Delluc to remark that 'L'Herbier is the finest photographer in France' ('perhaps to finish me for good', comments L'Herbier). This genuinely experimental film, which almost ruined L'Herbier, embodies an idea which casts even further than the major works to come: the idea of narrative as plastic by vocation. Here there is no dramaturgy, virtually no story, only a succession of symbolic actions articulating an 'impressionist' evocation through the indeterminately placed titles and inserts. But although this technique derives from *fin de siècle* conventions, it looks forward to our own times, to our concern with discontinuity, heterogeneous materials, irrational narratives. And beyond the frenzied patriotism it expounds so faithfully, *Rose-France* emerges today as the 'visual music' dreamed of by L'Herbier, Gance and Dulac, and which three generations of critics and historians, preoccupied (quite justifiably, admittedly) by another approach to literature, were unable to hear.

A defeat for poetry, therefore, and an enforced return to *The Cheat*: to dramaturgy, in other words. First came the hack work designed to secure his position with Gaumont and to teach him more acceptable techniques (*Le Bercail*, 1919, *Le Carnaval des Vérités*, 1919), and then *L'Homme du Large* (1920), based on Balzac's *Un Drame au*

Bord de la Mer. This time artifice made a reappearance (masks, superimposition, stylized lighting and framing), with the result that the natural landscapes inherited from the Swedish cinema are transformed into magnificent studio décors, nowadays unmistakably giving the lie to the naturalistic label that has stuck to this film for so long. Of crucial importance, too, is the idea adumbrated in the film that, through the mediation of the *découpage*, the shot-structure, dramaturgical methods can *also* be structure (music, according to the ideology of the time). For instance, a confrontation scene starting with comparatively brief shots and ending with a slow dissolve between the last shot and reverse angle, followed by an iris out, will inevitably bestow a double function on the *découpage*, appealing to the spectator in double guise: as narrative medium and as pure structure (rhythm), because this doubly 'cushioned' fall, in opposition to the previous progression along a series of peaks, carries the narrative, but at the same time asserts its abstraction. Thus the sequence where the father and son confront each other with the titles superimposed on the images (Henri Langlois compared these shots to ideograms) closely blends the visual and narrative functions.

It is easy to view the histrionics of Jaque Catelain, Roger Karl, Marcelle Pradot and the young Charles Boyer as grotesque; and it is true that with a very few exceptions the French actors of the day did not adapt too well to the screen (which may be why Renoir looked to Germany for his *Nana*, just as L'Herbier did for his Baroness Sandorff— Brigitte Helm—in *L'Argent*).

Actually, Eve Francis and Philippe Hériat—playing what are in effect the leads in *El Dorado* (1921)—are among the handful of French actors from the period who are still watchable today. But irrespective of these questions of taste and fashion, the sequence-shot in which Eve Francis, racked by grief, falters slowly down a flight of steps after being thrown out of the villa belonging to her seducer's father—like the one in which she walks interminably along a huge white wall from long shot into close-up—prefigures the 'infernal *longueurs*' of Godard or Garrel. A first (provisional) landfall along L'Herbier's route, *El Dorado* contains on the one hand

some spectacular *trouvailles* which have kept historians happy and can still excite the imagination today since they have never been followed up, and on the other, more importantly, scenes structured with a spatio-temporal freedom far in advance of the period which foreshadow the birth of modern *découpage* in *L'Argent* (1928). Among the isolated *trouvailles* may be cited the shot where Eve Francis, day-dreaming on a bench before going on stage at the cabaret, is seen as a blur while the other dancers sitting on either side of her remain perfectly in focus; the arrival of Eve Francis in the Alhambra gardens against a background twice transformed by means of enigmatic dissolves which do not seem to affect her movement in any way; the 'Cubist' split-screen in which the upper half of the image contains a shot of water filmed vertically from above, while in the lower half Jaque Catelain crosses the screen in long shot, presumably passing this same pool of water. Among the sustained *découpages* must be mentioned the two sequences in the cabaret which open and close the film: the first handles the cut-in/cut-back mode of matching with unprecedented freedom, and the second is distinguished by a very skilful use of cross-cutting, with shadows from both stage and auditorium projected on to the backcloth behind which Eve Francis kills herself. Particularly remarkable, however, is the scene in the Alhambra in which Eve Francis secretly watches her seducer's movements among the pillars with his new mistress. Here the diversification of angles and distances, the contrasts between foregrounds and backgrounds, the use made of entries and exits from the frame, are an already remarkably assured affirmation of an attitude which would lead progressively to a rejection—from within the dramaturgical cinema itself—of *mise en scène* in favour of *mise en forme*.

These few references to the plot suffice to indicate that *El Dorado* is, in the figurative sense, a melodrama. But it is also a melodrama in the literal sense: the film, for the first time in the history of the cinema—and such incontestable 'firsts' are rare—was accompanied by a musical score composed with reference to the images and intended to be performed in constant synchronism with them.

Next come L'Herbier's two most celebrated films: *L'Inhumaine*, considered as the height of absurdity by his detractors, and *Feu Mathias Pascal* (U.K.: *The Late Mathias Pascal*; U.S.: *The Living Dead Man*, 1925), which the same detractors and the average historian are agreed in finding, all things considered, the best thing he has done. Today, while *L'Inhumaine* hardly seems to warrant such excessive severity, the slightly condescending accolade (second class) given to *Feu Mathias Pascal* totally falsifies historical perspective.

Curiously enough, both films have a feature which distinguishes them from the rest, although this trait has been very loosely attributed to L'Herbier's work as a whole: the mixture of styles. It is worth noting, first of all, that the generally high opinion enjoyed by *Feu Mathias Pascal* is bound up with a 'psychological' and dramaturgical justification of this anomalous element, while the opprobrium invariably encountered by *L'Inhumaine*—except among the more extreme devotees of camp—is primarily due to the fact that the admixture in this case is *pure artifice*.

L'Inhumaine was in fact a commissioned film, partly financed by its star, the singer Georgette Leblanc (who had almost been Debussy's original Mélisande in 1901) and intended as a showcase offering Americans examples of contemporary French art: painting, music, design, architecture, fashion, dance and, presumably, cinema. Each set was created by a different designer (Cavalcanti, Autant-Lara, Léger, Mallet-Stevens), and it is evident that L'Herbier deliberately attempted to mould the tone and development of each sequence in terms of the décor. Even the sequences shot in real interiors (the Ballets Suédois at the Théâtre des Champs-Elysées) or on location (the hallucinatory car races) seem to be governed by this principle, which is, moreover, in no way aberrant in itself: now that the essentially composite character of cinema has begun to be recognized, one can say that a film subscribing wholly to it would not be running counter to the specific nature of cinema. In the final analysis, *L'Inhumaine* falls apart into a series of bravura pieces, some of them quite remarkable, but which can only be considered in isolation. To my mind the lack of any underlying unity is due less

to the framework provided by the script—admittedly weak by literary standards but nevertheless lending itself quite well to the discontinuity principle that conditions the film (L'Herbier says of this script that it was a 'figured base' on which to build 'plastic harmonies')—than to the inconsistency of the actors, who are after all the only elements of continuity in the film. Georgette Leblanc may have been too old for her role as a man-eating blue-stocking, and her acting is even more disastrous; and Jaque Catelain, who had a certain naïve charm in *Rose-France* and *L'Homme du Large*, is horribly miscast in the role of a passionate and worldly young scholar. Only the remarkable Philippe Hériat manages to bring conviction to his musical comedy role as a Rajah, and in some of the sequences in which he appears, no matter how divergent the styles, he contrives a semblance of unity which is entirely lacking elsewhere. It is possible that Darius Milhaud's score may have been a factor in lending overall unity; this, unfortunately, is something that cannot at present be verified.

Several sequences may be cited, however, to show how L'Herbier was continuing the experiments he had been conducting with exemplary persistence from the outset of his singular career. The artiste juggling a black and white painted cube on the balls of his feet is *encompassed* from every angle and distance, and the montage of this passage from the first sequence anticipates Eisenstein's analogous experiments by several years. Georgette Leblanc, venturing into the young scholar's bizarre house to pay her last respects to what she believes to be his corpse, is 'tracked' through a vast, bare set by a camera concerned to exploit to a maximum the possibilities of creating a new space by restructuring angles and by isolating the fields of vision from each other. Here again the *découpage* is both dramaturgy—the hallucinatory tension of this scene still works perfectly today—and a structural progression in itself. When the Maharajah, having substituted himself for Georgette Leblanc's chauffeur, races along the *corniche* with the '*inhumaine*' agonizing in the back seat of the car—victim of a poisonous snake hidden in a bouquet of flowers by the Maharajah himself—this extremely Feuillade-esque sequence is treated on the principle of a cyclical montage of variations, with the same shots recurring in a different order each time.

As for the famous accelerated montage of the long resuscitation sequence which climaxes the film, however—in a laboratory designed by Léger and staffed by dancers from the Ballets Suédois—it looks for once as though all L'Herbier has done is to take over one of the *idées fixes* of French film-makers at that time: to express movement, to create 'visual rhythms' by an essentially musical organization of extremely brief shots representing *inanimate* objects—a procedure based, it would seem, on the intuition that a static shot becomes pure duration and is therefore comparable to a *note value* in music. This (false) intuition had already inspired the sequences that today seem most debatable in that masterpiece *La Roue*. Not until the Russians would 'rapid montage' acquire a meaning, through the organic articulation of organic movements. The mechanical rigidity (even in movement) of the shots treated in this way in *La Roue* and *L'Inhumaine* results, despite frenzied accelerations, in a stilted static effect that is almost unwatchable today. There is confirmation here of a truth revealed to be fundamental: although there is an effective reality behind the cinema-music analogy, any mechanistic attempt to pattern a composite art on a homogeneous art is an error.

In this same sequence of *L'Inhumaine*, however, there is an experiment much more significant today (because it in fact draws attention to this composite nature): the insertion (in a tinted context: like most films of the period, it was tinted throughout) of very brief flashes of pure white and red which caused a contemporary critic to exclaim, 'Tristan's cry comes true: I hear the Light!' (The word 'psychedelic' hadn't been invented yet.)

Unlike *L'Inhumaine*, the subject of *Feu Mathias Pascal* had an unassailable pedigree: no less than a novel by Pirandello. L'Herbier offered the part of Mathias to the excellent Russian émigré actor Ivan Mozhukhin (or Mosjoukine as he was known in France), and the project became a co-production with Alexandre Kamenka's famous Albatros company. It must be admitted that the dominant factor here is not the rigour of L'Herbier at his best, but the very free 'Albatros style' (e.g., Mozhukhin's *Le Brasier Ardent*, Epstein's *Le Lion des Mogols*, Volkoff's *Kean*): 'witty' camera angles and tricks, dream sequences shot against a black background, and so on. The film is made with great virtuosity, passing easily from rural *Kammerspiel* to comic fantasy by way of an excursion into expressionist comedy of manners. At the same time, everything here contributes towards the creation of that unity in diversity which was missing in *L'Inhumaine*: outstanding performances, beautiful photography, fine sets, a 'strong' plot. Yet the film is a retrograde step both in the history of the cinema and in L'Herbier's work. It takes us back to the notion of *mise en scène* as being solely *at the service of a story*: it is *The Cheat* revised and corrected according to the Parisian-Russian aesthetic. The double function of the *découpage* which L'Herbier had already outlined in three of his films seems to be entirely missing here: each shot simply invents a new trick designed to display the Mathias–Mozhukhin character, and each sequence a new style which will 'reflect' the next stage in the story. But since cinematographic form was thought of precisely in these terms and no others for years, it is hardly surprising that where official history is concerned, *Feu Mathias Pascal* passes for L'Herbier's masterpiece.

His real masterpiece was to come very soon. In 1925, to offset the losses sustained by his own production company, L'Herbier made two commercial chores: *Le Vertige* and *Le Diable au Coeur*. When Jean Dréville, then a young admirer, taxed him with commercialism, L'Herbier replied that perhaps the period of experimentation was over; in his opinion 'the first avant-garde' (as it was subsequently named to distinguish it from the second: Man Ray, Chomette, etc.) had lived out its life: it was time to pass on to serious matters. Dréville felt that this was a final abdication. And the project L'Herbier then had on hand might well have confirmed his fears: a Franco-German co-production with a bigger budget than the French cinema had ever known.

L'Argent undoubtedly marks the end of the period of experimentation, since it is itself the culmination of all these experiments—not just L'Herbier's, but those of the first avant-garde and even, to a certain extent, of the entire Western cinema (with the exception of the Russians). I shall therefore attempt a closer analysis of this masterpiece.

My earlier statement that *L'Argent* gave birth to 'modern *découpage*' is based on the conviction that here, for the first time, the *style* (framing, camera placement and movement, positioning of actors, entries or exits from the frame, shot changes) systematically assumes a double role, dramaturgic and plastic, and that the interpenetration of these two functions creates an authentic cinematic dialectic, distinct equally from novelistic and musical dialectic, yet partaking of both.

The success of L'Herbier's undertaking was conditioned initially by seminal options in all departments: on the one hand, a novel by Zola in a tightly structured modern adaptation very different from the usual digest (the film runs for about three hours), and an international cast contrasting sharply with the actors in most French films not only by their physical presence but by their sober conviction (among the victims: Mary Glory, Henry Victor) or their controlled virtuosity (among the tormentors: Brigitte Helm, Alcover, Alfred Abel); and on the other, sets fantastic in size but extremely stark, with luminous photography accentuating this process of purification, and an absolutely unprecedented camera mobility.

L'Herbier claims that he made *L'Argent* because he hated money; and it is certainly true that the film, like the novel, is a sharp indictment of the cynicism of big business. At the same time, however, it was the enormous budget which not only determined the film's dramatic scope but made its formal ambitions possible (costly settings, camera movements necessitating the development of new techniques).

How does the dialectic that links these two axes of gestation function? One of L'Herbier's great achievements in this film is that he was not only the first to solve the tricky problem of the relationship between camera movements and shot changes, but that he did so more effectively than anyone else until the Welles–Kurosawa generation.

In *L'Argent*, as in all cinema 'descended' from *The Cheat*, the sequence of shots is at each moment a narrative vehicle. The camera movements, however, *inform* these shot changes on another level, establishing them as rhythmic or plastic elements. There are, for instance, a number of transition scenes set in the vast corridor of the bank where the characters keep a wary eye on each other as they pass under the white marble pillars; but although the look 'off' calls for a shot change according to traditional dramatic principles, the tracking shots which pursue or encircle the characters mean that these shot changes are seen to be obeying a double need: they indicate both a narrative movement (revealing what is seen, introducing new characters or new doorways) and a *formal* movement. For, although the camera movements themselves are never completely independent of the evolutions of the characters (and therefore participate in the dramaturgy precisely to the extent that they are subordinate), they do establish evidence of a frame in *constant and spectacular evolution* (owing to the expansiveness of both the movements and the sets which make them possible). Withdrawing to make disclosures, drawing closer to avoid them, gliding about in permutation and recomposition, these movements are completely devoid of the mentalistic function that has commonly been assigned to them since the introduction of the crane and dolly, for the *effect* they produce is unmistakably plastic. This is true not only of images in motion taken individually, but also of the totality of movements a sequence may comprise. At the same time the articulation of these movements, their 'broken continuity' spanning the cutaways which are dramatic in purpose *but which structure them*—like the flexible subordination of camera movements to character movements already mentioned—results in a crucial symbiosis: the dramaturgic and plastic functions are at once distinct and indissoluble.

Another manifestation of the same bivalence: the movement of characters within a fixed angle. In the long sequence in the Stock Exchange restaurant where Saccard moves from table to table being introduced to all the characters who are to represent the power of money, the changes of shot and framing, whether static or in motion, are so tightly bound up with the unfolding of the plot that their functioning may at first glance seem to be univalent throughout. This is not

Brigitte Helm in *L'Argent*.

so; it is merely that the instrument which animates them is no longer the same. Here this role is taken over by the entrances and exits from frame of the crowd of extras. Instead of being studiously 'realistic', and therefore invisible, as prescribed in studio-based films predicated upon the dialogue and the attitudes of the protagonists, these elements are stylized through acceleration or proliferation, and above all through a more or less precisely calculated spatio-temporal relationship to the elements of the *découpage* proper (changes of shot and camera movements), so that over and above their continuing dramatic function, the latter contribute to what one might call 'a superior rhythm'.

Sometimes the elements of the dichotomy appear horizontally rather than vertically. At the climax of the film, the confrontation between Mme Hamelin and Saccard introduces a series of cross-cut shots in close-up, interspersed with titles, which temporarily excludes any idea of a double discourse. But this series is then cut into by a brief track forward so that the frame is almost entirely blocked by the actor Alcover's elephantine bulk: a very striking visual effect, but one that is absolutely gratuitous by any direct dramatic principles, especially those established by what has gone before. The scene finally closes on a less tight shot of Mary Glory in which she is almost entirely hidden by a plaster bust in the foreground, while Alcover, very much in evidence, attempts to browbeat her: a dialectical situation created by the *découpage* which in a sense resumes the two preceding ones.

Fourthly and finally, let us examine a dialectical process which has been described —erroneously, to my mind—as metaphorical. When the aviator Jacques Hamelin takes off on the Atlantic crossing attempt that is to demonstrate the value of a new fuel on which the Stock Exchange is speculating, L'Herbier combines the two actions in a parallel montage, and *assimilates* them on the *découpage* level either by visual 'rhymes' (the propeller turning before take-off, followed by the rotation of the tiny central enclosure at the Stock Exchange under a camera diving vertically from a rope) or more particularly by a device arising from the 'subjective camera' principle (shots in which the camera skims over the Stock Exchange, cross-cut with shots of the aircraft flying over the aerodrome before departure). This sequence has been compared to the one in Gance's *Napoléon* where shots of the hero sailing stormy seas are intercut with, and then superimposed on, shots of the equally stormy Convention; the double structuring of this sequence—both metaphorical and plastic—is certainly superb, but it does not involve the dramaturgic dimension (in the material sense implied here): at this point in the film, only destiny links Napoleon to the Convention. What we have here is akin to the 'montage of attractions' as demonstrated in *Potemkin* (the stone lions) or *October* (Kerensky's bronze peacock), where the organic unity of the discourse is ultimately sacrificed to the metaphorical message (whatever the considerable interest in other respects of these devices in both Gance and the Soviet film-makers). Moreover, when Gance's camera swings like a pendulum over the delegates' heads in the Convention, no spatial orientation is established between the two actions. In *L'Argent*, on the other hand, the cross-cutting situates the aircraft 'above' the Stock Exchange in a continuum which may be imaginary but is none the less material. Furthermore, consistent with the principle that underlies the whole film, the texture here too is dramatic materiality, with no verbal metaphor intervening (it is this very aircraft that is the object of concern to the Stock Exchange). This sequence also throws new light on the film as a whole, particularly when considered in relation to the other three sequences described: for we are confronted here, in a radicalized form, with the opposition between an idea of continuity which bridges shot changes, and an idea of discontinuity introduced on another level by these shot changes. This dialectic, which is the very essence of all cinema, manifests itself throughout *L'Argent*, notably through the parameters cited above; but it is in this sequence that its presence makes itself felt most sharply, for although the aircraft and the Stock Exchange become increasingly *present* in relation to each other as the sequence builds ('imaginary' continuity), there can be no doubt as to the discontinuity between these shots in terms of narrative space. The structure of this sequence was further stressed by one of the first attempts to provide sound effects for a film. When *L'Argent* was first shown, it was accompanied by gramophone records alternating the sound of an aircraft in flight with the noise of the Stock Exchange.

For over forty years established film historians, parroting the contemporary view, have described *L'Argent* as a ponderously boring white elephant. It is only recently that the evolution of cinematographic language has enabled us to *see* a film which must have remained totally *invisible* at the time. Such purgatories are not uncommon in art. To be understood, Bach had to wait for Mendelssohn and Liszt.

Of all the many preconceptions about L'Herbier's work, the least erroneous is probably the idea that his career really ended with the coming of sound, even though he made twice as many sound films as he did silents. At least one remarkable effort from the early sound period deserves to be noted, however: *Le Parfum de la Dame en Noir* (1931), a film totally forgotten today. Distinguished by its disorienting effects (mirror images, spatially elusive sets, fragmented *découpage*) and by some wonderfully inventive sound (the mysterious noises which silence the hallucinatory hubbub at the sinister dinner), this very personal adaptation of Gaston Leroux's novel seemed to herald a career in sound films as brilliant as his silent days had been. After two years of voluntary inactivity, however, during which he turned down numerous offers, L'Herbier finally agreed to film a successful 'boulevard' play, *L'Epervier* (U.K.: *Bird of Prey*, 1933), followed by two more of the same, *Le Scandale* (1934) and *L'Aventurier* (1934).

What had happened? L'Herbier himself has explained with remarkable lucidity: 'It is sometimes hard to know yourself what you did or what you didn't do. What is certain, however, is that when sound came, conditions of work became very difficult for a filmmaker like me. For economic reasons, you couldn't consider making sound films like the ones we had done in the silent days, sometimes even at our own expense. You had to exercise a good deal of auto-censorship, and, as far as I was concerned, even accept forms of cinema which were the very ones I'd always avoided. Because of the dialogue, we were suddenly obliged simply to can plays . . .'

Raoul Walsh claims that his master, Griffith, simply didn't know how to adapt to the 'new language'. Maybe. But it is curious to note the number of great film-makers who, like L'Herbier, made one or two very fine and very important films *after* the coming of sound, only to lapse subsequently into distressing conformity. It was between 1928 and 1931 that Epstein, Lang and Sternberg made their masterpieces, reaching heights they were never again to attain. After completing nine films between 1920 and 1929, and then his masterpiece, *Vampyr*, in the early years of sound, Dreyer had to content himself with one film every ten years for the rest of his life. Let there be no misunderstanding, however: L'Herbier's career needs no excuses. *L'Argent* earns him his place among the masters.

Translated by Tom Milne

Noël Burch has written, in French, a full-length study, *Marcel L'Herbier*, published in Paris in 1973. In English, there is only Jacques Brunius' piece included in Roger Manvell's anthology *Experiment in Cinema* (1949). A screening of *L'Argent* at the sixth New York Film Festival (1968) convinced many that L'Herbier is indeed—at least in this film—the master that Burch claims him to be. See the entry on Mozhukhin.

PER LINDBERG

Edgardo Cozarinsky

Lindberg's name is not to be found in most film histories. In Scandinavia he is mainly remembered as a stage director, an innovator after Max Reinhardt. His film work has been inaccessible for a long time, even in Sweden, where his two silent films of 1923 were considered lost. Between 1937 and 1941 Lindberg directed seven sound films, never indifferent, often astonishing, which can be appraised on their own. *Gläd dig i din ungdom* (*Rejoice in Your Youth*, 1939), a pastoral about a future writer's youth, belongs to that same national vein to which Widerberg and Troell would later contribute; but its opening shot-by-shot interplay between radiant youth recalled and adult drabness today seems to announce not only Bergman's *Sommarlek* but also, most unexpectedly, Resnais' *Hiroshima Mon Amour*. Lindberg's talent, however, is not merely that of a pioneer whose finds remained unpublished, himself wrapped in the glamour of an *auteur maudit*. His less striking films are most telling of his approach—*Juninatten* (*June Night*, 1940), a vehicle for Ingrid Bergman of a delicacy far superior to even Molander's most tasteful contemporary confections, builds its narrative around a series of variations on a musical motif; *Gubben kommer* (*The Old Man Arrives*, 1938), the adaptation of a novel into a 'well-made play', heightens its inherent theatricality until mechanical contrivances become an absorbing counterpoint of dramatic devices. Lindberg's preoccupation with the overall rhythmical structure of his films, beyond camera set-ups and editing, led him to relate sequences, to have episodes 'rhyme' and counterbalance each other. This is less happily realized in an ambitious project—*Stål—En Film om Svensk Arbete* (*Steel—A Film about Swedish Work*, 1939), a two-level, Elizabethan-inspired dramatic structure about power struggle and workers' unrest at a steel plant; and it sadly misfires in his only attempt at a real musical—*I Paradis* (*In Paradise*, 1941). *Det sägs på stan* (*The Talk of the Town*, 1941), however, is an incomparable achievement in spite of obvious technical limitations. Lindberg turns a story about anonymous letters in a small town (one year before Clouzot's *Le Corbeau*) not just, as he intended, into a parable about fascism; camera movements and sound mixing (long before magnetic tape made it easily manageable) approach, prowl round and prey on the dramatic material as gossip would on ambiguous appearances, attaining a gruesome *reproduction* of collective hysteria. Made the same year as *Citizen Kane*, this ignored or unknown feat is also rich in the heritage of expressionism, and now looks pregnant with future developments.

Lindberg cannot even be said to be a 'subject for further research', because, as far as I know, very few people have seen *any* of his films. He is the only director in this Dictionary about whom this could be said. Is Cozarinsky right? Perhaps we shall find out one day; meanwhile, Lindberg has his place in this Dictionary as a salutary example of *terra incognita* in film history and criticism.

HAROLD LLOYD

Jean-André Fieschi

In the beginning, inevitably, comic characterizations—the types, the individuals—were developed in relation to Chaplin. With Chaplin, the tribal spirit was finally abandoned, and the destructive frenzy of the group (Durand, Sennett) superseded: from now on, laughter and emotion would be centred on a single person. The importunate Little Fellow had opened the floodgates to identification.

In his early days, Harold Lloyd (1893–1971) therefore called himself Lonesome Luke in a characterization developed, as he himself freely admitted, from Chaplin's. Instead of the immortal tramp's baggy costume, he wore clothes that were too tight. The transposition deceived no one, Lloyd himself least of all. He still had far to go.

What became of him is history, as is the paradox on which Lloyd was to build his reputation. It was his amazing ordinariness that made him stand out from the crowd, and it was by looking like Mr Average that he asserted his difference. As he revealed later, it was the character of a clergyman in some forgotten film that inspired his definitive characterization. Suddenly casting aside his professional dignity to deal with the villain who had abducted the girl, the clergyman erupted into a burst of amazing athletic feats totally at odds with his appearance. Above all, Lloyd said, this clergyman wore glasses as a sign of his usual placidity. Hence, as he defined it in 1928, his characterization as 'quiet, normal, boyish, clean, sympathetic, not insensible to romance'. An average American with none of the extremes of elegance (Keaton), obscenity (Arbuckle), pathos (Chaplin), poetry (Langdon) with which one won admission to (or exclusion from) the Dynasty.

The straw hat, tight suit and horn-rims contribute notably to the creation of a pale-faced, slightly gawky, rather circumscribed figure having, it would seem, no ghosts and no truck with the imaginary. So it would seem, because it is as though despite himself that Lloyd wanders into areas set with traps. But given the terrifying power of obsessions—those repeated ascents of a sky-scraper, for instance, from *Safety Last* (1923) to *Feet First* (1930): vertiginous variations on the falling nightmare—Lloyd, despite appearances, is not *secure* (from violence, menace, fear: he passes through them, always arriving intact). He is in fact probably alone among the great silent comedians in being a placid conquering hero, magnificent and prosaic, who enshrines some part of the collective dream of social success. Love and money are always the reward for his ventures. Harold is a winner.

The physical exploits he is capable of, the ingenuity he exhibits, even his simulated clumsiness, reveal a very ordinary extraordinariness, as well as an artful dodging with reality in which peril and precision both play their part. Astonishing as it may seem, he really did climb those skyscrapers ('I must have been mad in those days'). He even got hurt when the nozzle of a fire-hose hit his head instead of vanishing into space. Lloyd fainted. But the scene was not used in the film because 'you can't show real injuries. The audience wouldn't laugh.' There could be no better instance of the lure essential to cinema, or of the price that must be paid for it.

Lloyd, it seems, even managed to be happy. Or at any rate, fabulously wealthy: idealism and realism mesh, in the man with the horn-rimmed glasses, like the workings of an automaton.

Translated by Tom Milne

Lloyd's five sound films are seldom mentioned, yet most of them are very funny indeed, especially *The Milky Way* (directed by Leo McCarey in 1936) and Preston Sturges' *The Sin of Harold Diddlebock* (1947, re-released in 1950 as *Mad Wednesday*). This, Lloyd's last film, included the great sequence from *The Freshman*. Perhaps, as Andrew Sarris has suggested, the lack of success of Lloyd's sound films was not so much a failure of inspiration on his part but more that 'his comic type had become obsolete after the Crash of 1929. The aggressive values he had embodied in the giddy 20s seemed downright irresponsible in the hung-over 30s.' The younger generation rediscovered him thanks to his compilation films, *Harold Lloyd's World of Comedy* (1962) and *Harold Lloyd's Funny Side of Life* (1964).

For further reading see his autobiographical *Harold Lloyd's World of Comedy*

(1964) and the relevant sections in Kevin Brownlow's *The Parade's Gone By* (1968), *Agee on Film*, Vol. 1 (1958), and Walter Kerr's *The Silent Clowns* (1975).

KENNETH LOACH

James Monaco

Born in Warwickshire in 1936, Kenneth Loach studied law at Oxford before joining the BBC as a director in the early 60s. Since 1965, working most often with producer Tony Garnett with whom he collaborates closely, Loach has completed three feature films (*Poor Cow*, 1967; *Kes*, 1969; *Family Life* [U.S.: *Wednesday's Child*, 1972]) as well as nine individual television films and one major TV series. In the process he has worked out a subtle cinematic language which merges elements of the documentary and fictional traditions to produce what may be a third basic narrative style situated halfway between story-telling and reportage. Like those of his contemporaries Maurice Hatton and Barney Platts-Mills, Loach's films are also strongly rooted in politics— specifically working-class politics—a factor which has sometimes made it difficult for the films to get wide distribution.

Based on the novel by Nell Dunn, *Poor Cow* offers a portrait of a working-class couple (Carol White and Terence Stamp) which is both sympathetic and distanced: an essay on distorted working-class sex roles and the oppressive conditions which create them. Like all Loach's films one of its prime attractions is that it arrives at its politics deductively rather than inductively. That is, the political force of the film grows out of the very real characters Loach has created with Dunn and the actors rather than being imposed upon them. *Kes*, which quietly describes the desperation of a young Yorkshire boy who rebels against a rigid school system and finds some measure of selfhood training a kestrel hawk, is likewise a film marked by respect for the people it is about and by a rare restraint. Both *Kes* and *Poor Cow* are generalized films; *Family Life*, on the contrary, is specific, a thesis film which sets up a crude dialectic between behavioural psychiatry and the more humane methods pioneered by R. D. Laing. It never develops this dialectic, nor does it treat these complex competing theories with any degree of sophistication, and the result is that, alone among Ken Loach's films, *Family Life* is tendentious and at times seems to oppress its central character, a schizophrenic young woman (Sandy Ratcliff), almost as much as the behavioural villain of the piece who *also* desperately wants this human being to fit a theory.

Possibly Loach's best work has been done for television and consequently not widely seen outside Great Britain. *Cathy Come Home* (1966), also with Carol White, was a harrowing analysis of the absurd and constricting system of housing which confronts a young working-class mother and nearly destroys her. The film led eventually to changes in the housing laws. *The Golden Vision* (1968) was a semi-documentary about football and the phenomenon of fans which was widely discussed for its unique mixture of fact and fiction. *In Two Minds* (1966) was the original David Mercer play upon which *Family Life* was later based. *The Big Flame* (1968) dealt with a revolt on the Liverpool docks and raised issues of occupation strategies and workers' control, as did *The Rank and File* (1971), one of Loach's best films, which gave us the story of a strike at a glassworks, closely modelled on an actual series of events in the Lancashire town of St Helens. *The Rank and File* sharply described the bankruptcy of the establishmentarian leadership of the trades union movement and discussed ways in which the rank and file may regain control of their destinies. The film foreshadowed actual events as well as capturing the acute discontent among the rank and file.

Possibly Loach's most accomplished television film was *After a Lifetime* (1969), a quiet, absorbing and at times quite witty fiction about the period between a man's death and his funeral. His two sons find out more about him now he is dead than they knew when he was alive and in the process begin to develop a consciousness of the history of the working class, of which they are a part. The images are simple, restrained, the dialogue is muted, but the people of this film and Liverpool's working class come vividly alive.

Loach's most ambitious effort is a multi-part series called *Days of Hope* (1975) which traces the development of a working-class family in England from 1914 and the outbreak of the First World War to the General Strike of 1926: a realization, as it were, of the memories expressed in *After a Lifetime*. Loach's other television films include *Up the Junction* (1965), *The Coming-Out Party* (1965) and *The End of Arthur's Marriage* (1965).

In almost any other country besides Britain, Loach would have had many more than three feature films to his credit by now. *Black Jack* (1979), his first theatrical film since 1972, confirmed his stature as the finest younger talent in Britain.

JOSEPH LOSEY

Edgardo Cozarinsky

Among film-makers with a distinguished stage record, Joseph Losey is one of the few who have developed an original method in the new medium. While Kazan or Visconti, no matter how accomplished some of their films, seem to have found in them the occasion for a larger and more complex exploration of possibilities which their stage work could approach only timidly, Losey, like Bergman, has made films where the extent and quality of his theatrical experience are apparent but which, at the same time, have unmistakably enriched film language.

Losey (born 1909) made his first feature film comparatively late, at the age of thirty-nine, after eighteen years of theatre work and almost ten years of intermittent film-making of a kind most unfamiliar to Hollywood. Somewhere between such apparent extremes as the Radio City Music Hall on the one hand and, on the other, his close and influential association with Brecht, which extended far beyond the famous stage production of *Galileo Galilei*, his experience included a study tour of Scandinavia and a sojourn in the Soviet Union, where he became acquainted with Piscator's theory and Meyerhold's practice, and a characteristic New Deal experience in *The Living Newspaper*, where he first used filmed materials. His early film work was done in the educational

field, on projects sponsored by the government or by foundations. The later *A Gun in
His Hand*, a short in MGM's *Crime Doesn't
Pay* series, for which he won an Oscar
nomination in 1945, was the closest he got to
the Hollywood production system.

Losey has described his upbringing as
Puritanical and middle-class, but the illuminating fact about it is his emergence into
adulthood and professional life in the intellectual climate of the Depression and the
New Deal years. Without yielding to the
facile temptations of biographical criticism,
we may better understand many of the
ideological and compositional tensions in
Losey's work if we look at them in the light
of the clash between a Left-wing commitment to denounce the injustice of the bourgeois social order, its corruption of a perfect-
ible humanity, and the timeless struggle of
Good and Evil which permeates and colours
with its own spectral light his strongly mate-
rialistic outlook. Like Hawthorne, in the
Introduction to *The Scarlet Letter*, imagining
the outraged comments of his elders on his
choice of writing as a profession, Losey
perhaps might also conclude: 'And yet, let
them scorn me as they will, strong traits of
their nature have intertwined themselves
with mine.' At least, explaining the background of *Eve* (1962) for a French audience, he remarked: 'This Biblical influence of
the "Bible Belt", this terrible Puritanism . . .
against which people spend their entire lives
trying to revolt without success—this is what
psychiatrists live on.'

It may be frivolous to wonder just how
tight the Bible Belt was around La Crosse,
Wisconsin, Losey's home town (also, two
years later, that of Nicholas Ray, and in the
same state where, in Kenosha, Orson Welles
was born six years later). But at a mature
moment in his own career, Losey was to
recall that Brecht had 'the drive of a Puritan
without the self-penalizing guilt. (How he
escaped the latter I will never know.)' This
admiration for the way Brecht solved a conflict which he may never have experienced as
such, or perhaps only in completely different
terms, points to one of the unresolved tensions preserved in Losey's own work.

One of its forms is the opposition between
an allegorical bent and the need to give that
bent a fresh intellectual validation. The link

between Puritan thought and allegory needs
no illustration. But, as regards the film-
making craft of Joseph Losey, some remarks
on literary allegory may shed a useful light.
'An allegory starts from the writer's need
to create a specific world of fictional
reality. His reality comes into existence and
comes to mean something at the same time.
. . . The double purpose of making a reality
and making it *mean* something is peculiar to
allegory and its directive language' (Edwin
Honig in *Dark Conceit*, 1959). While Cole-
ridge impugned allegory in the name of symbolism, in nineteenth-century America Henry
James conducted the struggle in the name of
French realism; however, James' own stories
about artists and writers show how far allegorical devices may be put to unforeseen
ends.

Given a new concept of realism (Brecht's,
in this case), further work with allegory-
trained instruments may yield different
results. Already in Losey's first feature, *The
Boy with Green Hair* (1949), there is a visible
attempt to wash the allegorical practice clean
of Puritan references and to make it work in
another ideological space. In this particular
instance the attempt failed—the film was
supposed to be pro-peace, but it had a plot
better suited to an anti-racist plea, and the
different levels of convention invoked,
instead of enriching each other, created a disruptive, centrifugal clash—studio sets
designed to convey 'fantasy' in a Technicolor
Hollywood film of the 40s, where 'reality'
was only a few degrees less stylized; Broadway, Irish music-hall and didactic theatre, a
mixture that, nevertheless, had sustained a
stage success like *Finian's Rainbow* the
previous year. (A musical, incidentally,
which featured designer John Hubley and
entertainer Albert Sharpe, both considered
for Losey's film, though only Hubley finally
worked on it.)

Each in its own key, films like *The Boy
with Green Hair*, *The Damned* (U.S.: *These
Are the Damned*, 1962), *Boom!* (1968),
Figures in a Landscape (1970) and *Mr Klein*
(1976) all seem hesitantly perched between
fable and allegory. Less obviously, an allegorical approach can be recognized in
straight dramatic films. The choice of
enclosed communities, for instance, allows a
minute study of patterns in social relation-

Jeanne Moreau in *Eve*: a link between Puritanical thought and allegory?

ships—the island in *Boom!*, the foreign countryside in *Figures in a Landscape* are stark realizations of a principle also at work on the country estate of *The Go-Between* (1971), in the prison of *The Criminal* (U.S.: *The Concrete Jungle*, 1960) and the barracks of *King and Country* (1964), in the film studio of *The Intimate Stranger* (U.S.: *Finger of Guilt*, 1956) and the Chelsea house of *The Servant* (1963), in the Oxford of *Accident* (1967) and, most extremely, in *The Assassination of Trotsky* (1972), where the fortress-home in the exile of Mexico City works as an 'island within an island', and in the Nazi-occupied, segregated Paris of *Mr Klein*.

Games and ballads also contribute to shape dramatic action in meaningful patterns. Games as formalized releases of tension from formalized intercourse can be coarsely brutal like the pig grabbing in *The Gypsy and the Gentleman* (1958), civilizedly brutal like the indoor rugby in *Accident*, or mythically brutal like the bull-fighting in *The Assassination of Trotsky*; sinister like the cat-and-mouse hide-and-seek in *The Servant* or subtle re-enactments of the social comedy like the cricket match in *The Go-Between* (where the low-born farmer is able to beat the gentlemen bowlers because he can afford *not* to bat 'stylishly', but is caught out by the same little boy who, outside the game, catches him on a haystack with the well-born girl). In *Mr Klein* the 1943 round-up of the Paris Jews is the culminating sequence, but its preparations (official meetings under a large, lighted map of the city; neutral voices enunciating how many minutes are needed to reach one vital point of the city from another; the Vel d'Hiv' being made ready for its unwilling guests) break the narrative at regular intervals, often in the form of one-shot caesuras.

These games play a part not unlike the play-within-a-play (dreams, films, cartoons, ballads, straight plays) in many Bergman films: concise, intensified summing-up of what lies between the lines of dramatic action. Not coincidentally, Bergman is one of the few 'authors' whose work may relevantly elicit the question of allegory, and one whom, rather surprisingly, Losey has mentioned (in connection with *The Virgin Spring*!) as an example of Brechtian form adapted to film language.

Ballads are a more explicit device. 'Nature Boy' in *The Boy with Green Hair* and 'Baby' in *The Prowler* (1951) already commented on the action, as Cleo Laine would do from the soundtrack of *The Criminal* and *The Servant*; while Billie Holiday in *Eve* enters into a complex play of relationships—her singing voice punctuates the film, her myth is a larger-than-life projection of the heroine, who reads *Lady Sings the Blues* as a clue to her own character and in ironical contrast to the clean, bourgeois business girl, who displays a copy of a book by T. S. Eliot. The intricacy of connotation is further involved by Losey's frequent use of 'objective correlatives' which do not work any less intellectually for being visual—the Royal Artillery War Memorial behind the credits in *King and Country*, the Elisabeth Frink sculptures in *The Damned*, op art and comics in *Modesty Blaise* (1966), 'revolutionary' murals in *The Assassination of Trotsky*, even towns: Venice, in *Eve*, with the fascinating, unending decadence of its commerce-based splendour; Weymouth in *The Damned*, its late-Victorian staleness disrupted by bursts of rock and roll and motor-cycling leather jackets; Baden-Baden as the appropriately literary hide-out where *The Romantic Englishwoman* (1975) may meet her novelettish dreams, half come true. *Secret Ceremony* (1968), where the uneasy relationship between a formidable house and its inadequate inhabitants is even sharper than in *The Servant*, may be the most convoluted instance—this story of isolated, inbred English Catholics is rich with Pre-Raphaelite echoes in its interior decoration, and its central character is a willow-haired ambiguous nymphet named Cenci...

This method must be clearly distinguished from, say, Godard's way of relating cultural references by a Burroughs-like sort of 'cut out' and 'fold in' composition—a 'serial' procedure, different from though not necessarily opposed to Losey's 'structural' one. Although the wealth of allusion and connotation in most Losey films is perfectly controlled, its richness occasionally threatens to achieve a palimpsest-like effect. The paradox is that, in trying to make clear and eloquent the many significant layers in a piece of drama or narrative, Losey may articulate an interplay of relationships which is baffling in its sheer intricacy. But then, this would only add a further conflict to works sustained by the vivacity of their unresolved tensions: between intellectual brilliance and ideological simplicity, between manneristic variations and the stark dramatic clashes that provide them with an original motif. In terms of story-telling, this means making the most out of the shifting distance between plot and story.

The cross-cutting in *Accident* between sequences which, in story development, are neither simultaneous nor associated by flashback but plainly contiguous, as well as the use of non-synchronized dialogue; the intrusion into a period narrative in *The Go-Between* of present-day glimpses, which gradually develop until they absorb the past action, turning its 'historical present' into a 'past participle': these are only the boldest of the many devices used by Losey to expose his story-telling as a perfectly disingenuous, contrived procedure, whether directly as an intellectual experience or working at it in terms of almost musical composition. His method, however, finally reabsorbs every element on the intellectual level. The overwrought decoration, the emotional outbursts, the heightened effects of *mise en scène*, from actors' gestures to camera movements, are all there as if between quotation marks: they illustrate something else, just as Brecht asked of actors that they should not seem to feel but to quote.

'I've made this film because the story is so commonplace, so classical in its own way, that there was no need to tell the audience: this is the story, this is what happens—they already know it. In this way it becomes possible to stand apart from it and, using it as a frame, to tell another story . . .' Thus Losey on *Eve*, but also on his approach to filmmaking. He has often gone on record as recognizing *The Prowler* as his first 'satisfying' film. It is, too, the first one in which he works inside recognizable genre references, if not conventions: those of the thriller, the ripe *film noir* of 1950. The advantages of this policy are not only those of an easier processing through the established channels of film production and merchandizing, which even Orson Welles accepted at the time (*The Lady from Shanghai* was a thriller; the Shakespeare films, patent quality products). The wider audience to be reached by those channels is

one which would be repelled by the frankly off-beat but can be occasionally sensitive to richer shades of observation, if these are worked into genre films.

This approach was developed by Losey into a consistent method, which operates constantly on a second level of narrative and language. The story becomes something 'given', a 'found' object which the film expounds only to be able to work upon it, setting off some aspects, gliding perfunctorily over others. (This is closely related to Losey's fondness for 'pre-designing', on which he worked in the United States with John Hubley and in Europe with Richard MacDonald. Halfway between art direction and story-board, this method goes far beyond both, and Losey has called it a pinpointing of 'useful movement of actors, useful movement of camera'.)

Eventually the idea of *mise en scène*, which at its simplest implies the choice of camera angle, of actors' movements in and out of frame, a certain relationship of light and décor, takes over every aspect of the film, reaching those finer shades which may be brought out by a thorough story development, working with the most musical aspects of construction—what to leave out, where to linger, when to sustain a tone or break it: a rewriting and editing of a nevertheless still visible first draft. Consequently, Losey's intellectual attitudes come off better when minutely worked into the texture of such wild melodramas as *Blind Date* (U.S.: *Chance Meeting*, 1959) or *Secret Ceremony* than when directly confronted with a naked issue, as in *King and Country* or *A Doll's House* (1973). In recent years he has developed, as a further refinement, a way of dealing even with documents, as in *The Assassination of Trotsky*, which leaves him free to manipulate facts like the basic stuff of a historical play by Shakespeare.

The three films on which Losey collaborated with Harold Pinter have played an essential part in this development. For a large audience, of course, *The Servant*, *Accident* and *The Go-Between* were stages in Losey's breakthrough from obscurity (or from the deceptive light of a cult following) into international eminence. Having found such a congenial scriptwriter, though, the resulting films achieved a perfection which deprives them of that unresolved tension between the

Delphine Seyrig and Dirk Bogarde through the window of Nick's Diner in *Accident*: '*The Servant*, *Accident* and *The Go-Between* were stages in Losey's breakthrough from obscurity into international eminence.'

director's will and the variably docile materials he is shaping. *Accident*, for instance, is what may be called a very intelligent film, while *The Criminal* and even *Boom!* are films where the intelligence of the film-maker may be observed making its own difficult, unremitting way. This partnership of Losey and Pinter is a complex, undeniably a fruitful one. A remark by Richard Roud may be relevant in this connection—the comment that both partners are, in different ways, outsiders to the social milieux their films prefer to investigate.

For Losey, of course, this relates to the larger question of being 'at home' in feeling 'foreign'. 'Even in the Middle West, where I was born and brought up, I always felt alien. I *was* very much part of it, but I *was* a foreigner in that I was not a part of it in the sense of being willing to belong and be put in a package. And in England, I don't feel at home either. In Italy, I don't feel at home either, but I feel at home everywhere in a sense, so that I am everywhere at home.' In the same way that foreigners may grasp the particular quality of a place, overlooked by its inhabitants, so social distance, like a sidelight, brings out volume and relief more eloquently than the plain, frontal light of familiarity. And Losey's method, as described, is but a reading of pre-existent texts—whether a narrative, a set of social allegiances, a certain balance (or imbalance) of power between economic or sexual forces.

This wilful alienation of point of view can be worked into the films themselves, objectified as it were in the fictional material—the 'foreigner' intrudes on a social body, bringing into sharp focus emotional ties and economic motives, redefined for the occasion. *The Boy with Green Hair* is, of course, a clear-cut allegorical instance, but it set the pattern for such characters as the Mexican boy in *The Lawless* (U.K.: *The Dividing Line*, 1950), the child murderer in *M* (1951), the policeman in *The Prowler*, the men on the run in *The Big Night* (1951), *Imbarco a Mezzanotte* (*Stranger on the Prowl*, 1952) and *Figures in a Landscape*, the psychopath in *The Sleeping Tiger* (1954), the American in *The Intimate Stranger*, the alcoholic in *Time Without Pity* (1957), the gypsies in *The Gypsy and the Gentleman*, the Dutch artist in *Blind Date*, the American tourist and the woman sculptor in

The Damned, the unwitting deserter in *King and Country*, the young students in *Accident*, the uninvited poet in *Boom!* and *The Romantic Englishwoman*, the motherly whore in *Secret Ceremony*, the middle-class boy and the plebeian farmer in *The Go-Between*, and the supremely involved international sets of exiles in *The Assassination of Trotsky* and of hangers-on in *Eve* (where the original—later massacred—soundtrack included a variety of languages and accents).

Films like *The Prowler, Blind Date, The Servant, King and Country, Accident* and *The Go-Between* work with social distance as a device for the mutual definition of interrelated terms, each class or hierarchy being what the other makes it. In *Mr Klein*, a minute dissection of the French bourgeoisie under the Nazi occupation is performed in the margin, as the film traces the title character's progress—a presumed Aryan's search for an elusive, perhaps non-existent Jewish namesake, with the purpose of insuring his own faultless origins, and becoming in the process, for all structural purposes, *the* Jewish Mr Klein.

This, up to a point, is also valid for the personal oppositions at the centre of most Losey films. The French (or Canadian?) Mornard (or Jacson?) in the Trotsky film has his first moment of relaxation in the final close-up, when he can demonstrate some kind of identity—that of being Trotsky's murderer. His previous actions tended less to hide than to blur all possible clues as to his origin and motives. In an unexpectedly stark moment, he leans overboard during a Sunday outing to meet his reflection with Stalin's features; his other reflections, in a mirror while shaving, are either partial or double. Trotsky, by contrast, appears confronted with his own recorded voice, a duplicate which is also a reminder of his historical persona, in between scenes of very English-looking garden life, preserved by high walls, electric wires and supervising guards which make clear the very peculiar nature of his exile—an unwelcome revolutionary in a country ruled by a self-styled 'Partido Revolucionario Institucionalizado' . . .

The Assassination of Trotsky (whose scriptwriter was Nicholas Mosley, author of the novel on which *Accident* was based) is, of course, an extreme example, but Losey tends to build most dramatic relationships as highly charged love–hate duets. Almost erotic in their repressed violence, which may be released through extremely formalized murder, they often adopt the form of a protracted, often interrupted duel. Master and servant in *The Servant*, Aryan profiteer and (unseen) Jewish *Doppelgänger* in *Mr Klein*, captain and private in *King and Country*, scientist and thug in *The Damned*, lover and (also unseen) husband in *The Prowler*, the man who wants the innocent saved and the man who wants the innocent hanged in *Time Without Pity*, fake mother and fake daughter in *Secret Ceremony*—these are obvious examples. But the uneasy friendship of detective and suspect in *Blind Date* is of the same kind, and they finally realize that they are both outsiders; the strip-cartoon master spies of *Modesty Blaise* are bound by enduring hate; and by the end of *The Gypsy and the Gentleman* the lover turns his rescue of an unloving mistress into murder, pulling her down into the water with his embrace until they both drown.

In all these instances, it is not the fictional frame or the psychological motives that Losey plays up but the mechanics of these disturbed relationships: very much as Brecht, in his early play *In the Jungle of Cities*, asked the audience not to enquire into the reasons of the unexplained business war he depicted but to pay attention to its development, its petty ambushes and false truces. (*Figures in a Landscape* starts from a related premise— nothing is to be known about the crimes committed by the escaping prisoners, the scenery is to be just a 'foreign' landscape; inevitably, the strategies of a magnified hide-and-seek occupy the foreground.)

Losey declared in 1960 that 'for almost twenty-five years, Brecht has inspired my life and my work', and in a list of aspects in which the master's method may have influenced his own, he mentioned first 'the stripping of reality and its precise reconstruction through selection'. Among filmmakers working in the tradition of narrative cinema, his work is unique in that it is not structured around 'themes', like Bergman's, nor does it try for a certain 'tone', like Truffaut's. It is, in the first place, a practice, the perfecting and exercising of a method which can be applied to widely different subjects and genres. It cuts across 'reality' in precise and eloquent patterns which are as telling as to its own functioning as about the functioning of that 'reality' upon which it exerts itself.

Losey has always been a controversial director. There are those who believe that his best films were made in America (see Pierre Rissient's *Losey* [Paris, 1966]); there are others who believe, on the contrary, that his best films are the collaborations with Harold Pinter. His reputation with critics has always been at its highest in France, where he is considered (to my mind, rightly) as one of the most important directors of all time. But his position in England and America has been more problematical, to say the least.

He is, however, supremely the director's director, and film-makers as far apart as Alain Resnais and Bernardo Bertolucci recognize him as a master of the art. To them, it matters little that he has often been obliged to work with unsuitable or unworthy material. His direction of actors, his handling of the camera—his *mise en scène*, in short—have triumphed over many a weak script.

Alas, *Les Routes du Sud* (1978) had a weak script by Jorge Semprun, and Losey did not manage to triumph over it. For one thing, apart from Yves Montand (adequate), the rest of the cast was not very good. And Losey seems to have felt the need to paper over the cracks in the film with an almost non-stop 'symphonic jazz' score by Michel Legrand. As usual, it works against the film. Although Losey is much admired in France, his work there seems to me to show a temporary falling-off.

In English, one can consult Tom Milne's interview book *Losey on Losey* (1967) and James Leahy's *The Cinema of Joseph Losey* (1967). Apart from Rissient's rather grotesque study, cited above, there is also, in French, Christian Ledieu's *Joseph Losey* (1963) and *Joseph Losey—Entretiens avec Michel Ciment* (1979).

ERNST LUBITSCH: GERMAN PERIOD

Enno Patalas

Ernst Lubitsch (born 28 January 1892), the son of a Berlin draper, was an actor with Max Reinhardt at nineteen and came to films at

twenty. He called himself Meyer in most of
the shorts in which he played leading parts
during the following years: a little Jew from
Berlin whose talent for improvisation is put to
the test in difficult situations (in the mountains, in the army). 'What does little Meyer
do in the Himalayas?' was a verse from a
popular song of the period in Berlin.

All this reminds one of his almost exact
contemporary Chaplin and his career during
the same years. Reminiscent of the Charlie
in the Essanay and Mutual two-reelers is
also Meyer–Lubitsch's acting, his *nebbish* gestures, his Don Juanism and upstart behaviour. Like Charlie in *The Immigrant*, who
comes to New York by boat, so Ernst Lubitsch as Siegmund Lachmann in *Der Stolz
der Firma* (*The Pride of the Firm*, 1914)
arrives in Berlin from Ravitsch, a god-for-
saken place in the Prussian province of Poz-
nan. Like Charlie he is hungry, counts his
pennies and chats up the ladies. The roots
in popular art, the slapstick origins in
vaudeville films, remained alive in Lubitsch's
later films, too, as they did with Chaplin,
Keaton, the Marx Brothers and Jerry Lewis.

The films Lubitsch made from the end of
the First World War until he left Germany in
1922—twelve features in five years, apart
from a number of shorts, an achievement
even in those days—constitute a unique and
explosive wealth of subjects and forms.
These five German years were to the twenty-
five American years which followed what a
crazy fast-motion shot is to a normal shot.

Lubitsch's German films are doubly tied
up with the inflation period. On the one
hand, they could not have been made at
any other time. In those days, owing to the
devaluation of the Reichsmark, the profits
made by one film in Switzerland or Holland
were sufficient to pay off production costs.
This made possible all kinds of experiments.
Lubitsch's films are 'inflation films' in
another sense, in that they reflect the destruction of conventional values. In ever new
variations, these films show how something is
used up, worn out, wasted. Something is
consumed, something else appears in its
stead, is consumed too, and so on. Often the
films are themselves built on this principle.

'It's a wonderful *tour de force*, but it will
get the cinema nowhere. One can't learn

from it—it's too individual a style of expression.' This was, according to Herman G.
Weinberg, Lubitsch's judgement of Dreyer's
La Passion de Jeanne d'Arc. Like Sternberg
and Hitchcock, Lubitsch did not consider
himself an original genius but a servant of the
medium; it is not the author but the cinema
itself which has to be given expression and to
be developed. He never intended to make
author's films, personal art. Instead of delv-
ing into the depths of his soul he looked for
truth in matter: he was an architect. Bourgeois prejudice accused him of having been a
manufacturer of ready-made goods. 'Silks,
velvets, and decorations enchanted the clever
eyes of the former rag-trade clerk.' Sternberg's films, too, profited from an apprenticeship in a lace-shop. The letter written by
Lubitsch on 10 July 1947, four and a half
months before his death, to Herman G.
Weinberg demonstrates through the example
of his early German career what he meant by
developing films, by learning through filming
and by making films from which one can
learn for other films and for life. He sees
progress in film as a permanent interaction
with already existing works.

The young Lubitsch did not feel called to
the career of writer and director. It was
necessity that made him undertake it, when
the Berlin film producers had no more parts
for him to play. 'If my acting career had pro-
gressed more smoothly I wonder if I ever
would have become a director.' So he wrote
and directed the parts himself, following
the existing models. Salomon Pinkus, whom
he played, directed by himself, in 1916
in *Schuhpalast Pinkus* (alternative title
Schuhsalon Pinkus; *Shoe Salon Pinkus* or
Shoestore Pinkus) is no different from
Siegmund Lachmann, the son of another
Salomon, in the film of 1914 whose director
was a certain Carl Wilhelm. Lubitsch had to
be urged, too, to make the feature films
which won him his world reputation.

The chronological sequence of Lubitsch's
German films is characterized by changing
reactions: in response to the Italian history
films of 1912 to 1916 he made his own,
Madame Dubarry (U.S.: *Passion*, 1919),
Anna Boleyn (U.S.: *Deception*, 1920) and *Das
Weib des Pharao* (*The Loves of Pharaoh* or
The Wife of Pharaoh, 1922): 'I tried to de-
operatize my pictures and to humanize my

historical characters. I treated the intimate nuances just as importantly as the mass movements and tried to blend them both together.' The 'antidote', as he called it, to the feature films he supplied himself in the form of discreet *Kammerspiel: Rausch* (*Intoxication*, 1919) and *Die Flamme* (*The Flame* or *Montmartre*, 1923). In between he had the comedies and grotesques, *Die Austernprinzessin* (*The Oyster Princess*, 1919), *Die Puppe* (*The Doll*, 1919), *Kohlhiesels Töchter* (*Kohlhiesel's Daughters*, 1920) and *Die Bergkatze* (*The Mountain Cat* or *The Wild Cat*, 1921). No two of these films are alike. *Die Puppe* was shot in completely artificial sets, *Kohlhiesels Töchter* on location in the Bavarian Alps, yet the mountains are without a trace of the eternal and fateful aspects with which the German mountain films of the 20s invested them, and look as if they were waiting to be demolished.

To learn for Lubitsch meant to react against the familiar, to make something different, to try out new possibilities. He followed this rule by leaving Germany and by using the following motto to introduce himself in Hollywood: 'Goodbye slapstick—hello nonchalance!' To try out a number of different possibilities, to eliminate one after the other, to find a possibility that had not yet been tried—that was the fundamental pattern of his career and of many of his films. It is expressed in the scene from *Die Austernprinzessin* which he remembered when he recalled the film after twenty-eight years: Prince Nucki's emissary hops along the lines of the star ornament on the floor, while he waits for the oyster king, until he has exhausted all the possibilities. Lubitsch's aim is not the unique, unmistakable 'work' with firmly delineated borders but the series which is not meant to have an end but to progress by ever new variations.

In the first scene of Lubitsch's we have, at the beginning of *Der Stolz der Firma*, he is sacked by his employer, sheds bitter tears and intends to drown himself. But then he decides (title) 'I'll have supper first.' For Lubitsch's characters it is always immensely important to eat. In *Die Austernprinzessin* the bride, Ossi Oswalda, says after the wedding feast to Julius Falkenstein, the bridegroom: 'I haven't eaten as well as this for a long time!' And this is not merely an incongruous comic statement in the context of the film; we have seen that Falkenstein has eaten his fill for the first time in ages at his rich father-in-law's table. The German audiences of 1919 must have understood this. The father-in-law is called Mr Quaker.

There is much eating and good eating in Lubitsch's German films, mostly of typical German food: dumplings, sausages and pig's trotters. In Lubitsch the senses of taste, smell and touch are at least as important as the artistic and cultural aspects generally favoured by bourgeois taste. Never again in Germany would anyone make such plebeian films. For the wedding feast in *Die Austernprinzessin* Lubitsch hired 300 real waiters. Behind every guest stands a waiter at each course of the meal. After every course, there is a clear-out—of plates and of waiters—and the next line steps forward. The presentation of consumption is always liberating and entertaining with Lubitsch. Brecht: 'The house is filled with joy by the eater: he empties it' (*Ballad of Poor B.B.*). Or take the way in which Henry VIII loves women in *Anna Boleyn*. Emil Jannings as Henry VIII, the ladykiller, is the massive embodiment of sensuousness which devours its object whole and demands constant change. Henry gets rid of Katharine and takes Anne Boleyn, then takes Jane Seymour and executes Anne. By strictly following the pleasure principle, he destroys age-old traditions (breaking with the Pope and ignoring the law). Lubitsch, the film-maker of the German inflation, confronted his cinema of consumption, waste, luxury and sensuousness with a culture directed towards conserving and accumulating spirituality and pretentious meaning.

In his historical films of 1919 and 1920 Lubitsch shows how closely power and the strivings of libido relate. Before *Anna Boleyn*, the film about absolutism, there had been *Madame Dubarry*, a film about society in change, the decline of the aristocracy, the bourgeois money economy and the exploitation of the third estate. The king and Jeanne, the girl from the people, are both puppets in the theatrical show staged by the powers of finance. After having seduced Jeanne by tempting her with a valuable necklace, the banker Dubarry leaves her to the king in order to get him to agree to a loan. The scene

Pola Negri, Paul Wegener and Jenny Hasselquist in *Sumurun* (U.S. title: *One Arabian Night*). As early as 1920, one of Lubitsch's characteristic triangle situations (and shots).

in which Dubarry (Eduard von Winterstein) seduces Jeanne (Pola Negri) is very effective. Jeanne looks at the jewellery with the same loving expression with which she had previously looked at her lover, whom she has forgotten for the moment. Something in Lubitsch's characters makes them accomplices of pearls, precious metals and paper money. Lubitsch leaves no doubt that desire is not directed at a person but feeds on attributes, characteristics, abilities. With him, love always has traits of fetishism. If the partner is able to make one happy, one has reason to love him. In *Kohlhiesels Töchter* two couples are in a muddle because two of them love crosswise—until there is an exchange of kisses. Happy surprise. Liese: 'He can kiss.' Peter: 'Her kisses are much hotter than Grete's.' The way they learn to like making love by trial and error is analogous to what happens to the young romantic musician in *Die Flamme*. He has discovered that the

adored Pola Negri is a high-class whore and comes home completely broken. His mother serves him coffee and biscuits. Lost in thought he takes a sip, then he has a biscuit—not bad at all—and soon he is feeling much better. Or the end of *Romeo und Julia im Schnee* (*Romeo and Juliet in the Snow*, 1920): sadly, Romeo takes the poison vial, sips once, twice, it doesn't taste bitter at all but quite sweet (the pharmacist has put sugar water into it), until Juliet has to take the bottle away from him because he might finish it off by himself.

With Lubitsch love is never exclusive, no special distinction for certain individuals; it is something very general. It favours those who least deserve it. The successful lovers in *Die Austernprinzessin*, *Schuhpalast Pinkus*, *Die Puppe* and *Die Bergkatze* are usually gigolos, cheats, bankrupts and cheeky apprentices. In *Kohlhiesels Töchter* Peter, now happy with his Liese, sends Grete, his former sweetheart, a note that he cannot keep his date with her; the same message is sent to him by Grete, who has meanwhile found her Paul. The messengers, a boy and a girl, meet at the appointed place—and immediately give each other loving looks. The date is kept, after all; only the cast has changed. All is interchangeable; what remains is the pattern which love follows.

This explains the function of machines in Lubitsch's films, right from the start. Machines throw light on his characters. *Die Puppe* anticipates a motif from *Design for Living*. The later film uses a Remington typewriter as an image for a love relationship. Fredric March has given it to Miriam Hopkins to look after; she is now involved with Gary Cooper and has forgotten to oil it; it has grown rusty, the keys are broken, 'but it still rings!' In *Die Puppe* the owner is advised to oil it twice weekly. Lubitsch's obscenities are sometimes discreet (he knew his censors), sometimes of disarming frankness (particularly before the *Reichslichtspielgesetz* [Reich Cinema Law] ended the censorless state of affairs). He is never inhibited. He exposes the mechanisms which guide individual human behaviour.

The masses in Lubitsch's German films are made up of many identical people. The principle of the series which governs his films—no ending, no limits, openness—also manifests itself there. For instance, the army of typists to whom Mr Quaker, the oyster king, dictates are all writing the same thing. Again a senseless activity which misses its target, wastes capital. Anonymity, similarity are not frightening in Lubitsch. In this he was an American even before he went to Hollywood.

Translated by Gertrud Mander

No one would claim that Lubitsch's German films were more important than his American ones (cf. Fritz Lang). So the decision to have two articles on Lubitsch was made for the sake of convenience, and because it seemed important to have a German writer put the early Lubitsch into its historical and economic context.

ERNST LUBITSCH: AMERICAN PERIOD
Andrew Sarris

In the well-mannered, good-natured world of Ernst Lubitsch, the most gracious civility transcends man's falls and pratfalls. *To Be or Not to Be* (1942), widely criticized as an inappropriately farcical treatment of Nazi terror, bridges the abyss between laughter and horror. For Lubitsch it was sufficient to say that Hitler had bad manners, and no evil was then inconceivable. What are manners, after all, but the limits to man's presumption, a recognition that we all eventually lose the game of life, but that we should still play the game according to the rules? A poignant sadness infiltrates the director's gayest moments, and it is this counterpoint between sadness and gaiety that represents the Lubitsch touch, and not the leering humour of closed doors. Thus, describing Lubitsch as the Continental sophisticate is as inadequate as describing Hitchcock as the master of suspense. Garbo's pixilated speech in *Ninotchka* (1939) is pitched delicately between the comic and the cosmic, and in one breathtaking moment, Garbo and Lubitsch sway on the tightrope in their attempt to balance mere giddiness with emotional ecstasy.

Lubitsch's German period lasted from 1914 to 1922, his American period from 1923 until his death in 1947, or three times as long. Unlike Lang and Murnau, therefore, Lubitsch is much more an American director than a German director, and must be evaluated accordingly, particularly after 1933 for such neglected masterpieces as *Design for Living* (1933), *The Merry Widow* (1934), *Angel* (1937), *The Shop Around the Corner* (1940), *To Be or Not to Be*, *Heaven Can Wait* (1943) and *Cluny Brown* (1946)—all in all, a dazzling display of the power of stylistic unity to transcend the most varied source materials. The most influential reviewers of the period decreed that Gary Cooper and Fredric March were miscast for *Design for Living*, that Chevalier was too old for *The Merry Widow*, that Marlene Dietrich was too stiff for *Angel*, that James Stewart and Margaret Sullavan were too brash for *The Shop Around the Corner*, that Carole Lombard and Jack Benny were too discordant for *To*

Be or Not to Be, that Gene Tierney and Don Ameche were too guileless for *Heaven Can Wait*, and that Jennifer Jones and Charles Boyer were too strained for *Cluny Brown*. And that was supposed to be that.

Posthumous reappraisals of Lubitsch's *oeuvre* indicate, however, that the magical qualities of his style have survived the topical distractions of his detractors. If *Angel* evokes Pirandello as *The Shop Around the Corner* evokes Molnar, it is because Lubitsch taught the American cinema the importance of appearances for appearances' sake (Pirandello), and the indispensability of good manners (Molnar). Lubitsch was the last of the genuine Continentals let loose on the American continent, and his art is inimitable and irreplaceable because the world he celebrated had died—even before he did—everywhere except in his own memory.

It was with *Madame Dubarry* (U.S.: *Passion*), in 1919, that Lubitsch almost single-handedly lifted Germany into the forefront of film-producing nations. In contrast to the cumbersome Italian historical spectacles, and even to the cinematically dynamic but thematically sentimental epics of D. W. Griffith, Lubitsch's *Dubarry* featured a very modish debunking of historical personages. By presenting the spectacle of Pola Negri's Dubarry grappling grotesquely with Emil Jannings' Louis XV, Lubitsch was hailed far and wide as a 'humanizer of history'.

Lubitsch's contribution to the 'art' of the cinema is difficult to define in the formal textbooks because the wit of his cutting is completely wedded to the context of his narrative. His career overlapped those of Murnau, Lang and Pabst, but he left Germany a few years before the stylistic fruition of the Golden Age. Indeed, he was slightly outside the morbid mainstream of German cinematic subjectivity which Siegfried Kracauer condemns in *From Caligari to Hitler*. None the less, the end of his German period (1919–23) remains one of his richest, with such masterpieces as *Die Puppe* (*The Doll*, 1919), *Sumurun* (U.S.: *One Arabian Night*, 1920), *Anna Boleyn* (U.S.: *Deception*, 1920), *Das Weib des Pharao* (*The Loves of Pharaoh* or *The Wife of Pharaoh*, 1922) and *Die Flamme* (*The Flame* or *Montmartre*, 1923).

Still, at the peak of his prestige, Lubitsch chose to come to America to direct Mary Pickford in *Rosita* (1923), a project agreed upon after much wrangling. It is a sumptuously sentimental vehicle for Pickford, an oddity in Lubitsch's career, a mere entrée as it were to his next Golden Age, this time for a then small studio called Warner Brothers, for which he turned out between 1924 and 1926 *The Marriage Circle* (1924), *Three Women* (1924), *Forbidden Paradise* (1924), *Kiss Me Again* (1925), *Lady Windermere's Fan* (1925) and *So This Is Paris* (1926). After this burst of comic brilliance, Lubitsch went into a more sombre, more pretentious period with *The Student Prince* (1927), *The Patriot* (1928) and *Eternal Love* (1929). But his decline was checked abruptly by the coming of sound, that traumatic stumbling block for so many directors, but for Lubitsch his stylistic salvation. He had revolutionized the genre of drawing-room comedy with his distinctively impish humour, and had spawned a host of imitators. But he seemed to drift into 'serious' projects as if to repair his self-esteem. Like the comedian who wanted to play Hamlet, Lubitsch wanted to be taken seriously by the apostles of fusty realism. It is perhaps fortunate for the history of film that he never succeeded.

Lubitsch enjoyed a curious immunity in the 30s in that his reputation at the end of the decade was almost as high as it had been at the beginning. By contrast, Josef von Sternberg, King Vidor, Frank Borzage, René Clair, Rouben Mamoulian and Lewis Milestone had lost their early 30s pre-eminence by the 40s, whereas John Ford, Frank Capra, Leo McCarey, Alfred Hitchcock, Gregory La Cava and William Wyler seemed to come out of nowhere in the middle 30s to shape the last half of that decade. Lubitsch had his ups and downs certainly, but he never passed permanently out of fashion. *Monte Carlo* (1930) helped to usher in the decade with an artful blend of sound montage and visual music in Jeanette MacDonald's rendition of 'Beyond the Blue Horizon', and *Ninotchka* helped lower the curtain on the 30s in a grand manner with Greta Garbo's exquisite evocation of an ideological iceberg melting in mirth.

In between these two epiphanies of his delicate style, Lubitsch contributed distinctively personal sketches to two omnibus revues: *Paramount on Parade* (1930; the Chevalier/Frenchie numbers) and *If I Had a Million* (1932; the famous Laughton Razzberry). He also directed seven other films outright: *The Smiling Lieutenant* (1931), *Broken Lullaby*, originally *The Man I Killed* (1932), *Trouble in Paradise* (1932), *Design for Living*, *The Merry Widow*, *Angel* and *Bluebeard's Eighth Wife* (1938). *One Hour with You* (1932), was directed by George Cukor from a Lubitsch plan, and signed by Lubitsch, thus providing an interesting mix of Lubitsch snap and Cukor stretch. Similarly, the Lubitsch-produced and Borzage-directed *Desire* (1936) offered a stylistic conflict between the twinkle and the tear. All in all, a productive decade for a director who had survived the trip from Germany to America, the transition from silence to sound, the rise in power (if fall in glory) from director to producer–director at Paramount, and the changing tastes of the fickle public. Still, Lubitsch never won a competitive Oscar or a New York Film Critics Award, a symptom, perhaps, of an ultimate lack of respect for the 'mere' stylist and entertainer.

Indeed, there is a conventional attitude towards Lubitsch which often stands in the way of a clear-eyed appraisal of his career. This conventional attitude may be summed up in the phrase *The Lubitsch Touch*—which is also the title of Herman G. Weinberg's exhaustive critical study, itself a compendium of all the conventional wisdom on its subject. In these enlightened times, however, to speak of Lubitsch in terms of his 'touch' is to reduce feelings to flourishes. A complex directorial style is reduced to its most obvious effects, to its most transparent techniques; Lubitsch becomes a creature of closed doors and deadpan reaction shots, a sophisticated continental, a world-weary head waiter, a mouldy Molnar. In fact, even in the most affectionate tributes to Lubitsch there has always been a touch of social condescension. Both Lotte Eisner (in *The Haunted Screen*) and Herman G. Weinberg often seem obsessed by Lubitsch's Jewishness even though they themselves are Jewish. Even in his more refined American comedies, we are told by Madame Eisner, 'There always remained a little of the vainglory of the *nouveau-riche*.' Berlin is also blamed by Lotte Eisner for Lubitsch's lapses

into vulgarity. Indeed, she goes so far as to preface her chapter with Goethe's description of a musician friend named Zelter (from Eckermann's *Conversations*, 1827): 'At first sight he may appear a trifle rough, even vulgar. But you have to remember that he spent more than half a century in Berlin where there lives—as many a detail has made me realize—a species of the human race so bold that little can be gained by treating them with nicety; on the contrary, you have to bare your teeth and resolve to be brutal yourself if you don't want to go under . . .'

Ernst Lubitsch was a shopkeeper's son who began his movie career in the Berlin of 1913 by playing German Jewish *Dummkopf* roles; thus the critics and historians who 'knew him when' never allowed him to forget his humble origins. More important was the constricting critical context in which Lubitsch was ever after typed as the actor-comic type of director, virtually a panderer to the audience's funny-bone. And if the audience didn't laugh, then off with the head of the vulgar jester.

Weinberg's very informative book is saturated with noble quotations on the profundity of comedy, but the fact remains that comic talents are seldom taken as seriously as tragic or even merely sombre talents, especially in Hollywood. Consequently, the comic talents often overcompensate for their low estate by essaying completely humourless projects to prove their seriousness. (*Vide* Leo McCarey's discomfiture at getting an Oscar in 1937 for *The Awful Truth* rather than for *Make Way for Tomorrow*.) And so it was with Lubitsch in the 30s as he attempted to prove his seriousness (and even his pacifism) with *The Man I Killed*. Of all his films in this decade, *The Man I Killed* emerges today as Lubitsch's least inspired and most calculated effort, all surface effect, all ritualistic piety toward a 'noble' subject. The film died at the box-office, as much for the right reasons as for the wrong ones. None the less, the critics held Lubitsch's hand during the wake, castigated the public for its inattentiveness at intolerable sermons and, with a sigh (and a subconscious sense of relief), returned the repentant jester to his more frivolous pursuits.

By contrast, strikingly unconventional

comedies, more in the mellow manner of later Lubitsch, like *Design for Living*, *The Merry Widow* and *Angel*, have been dismissed by Weinberg and the other official film historians as unedifying failures. *Design for Living* was invidiously compared in its casting (Gary Cooper, Miriam Hopkins, Fredric March) to the stage original (Alfred Lunt, Lynn Fontanne, Noël Coward), not to mention the sacrilege of Ben Hecht's brassily romantic screenplay presuming to improve on Coward's gilded cynicism. *The Merry Widow* lacked—at any rate in Weinberg's eyes—Stroheim's scathing documentation of imperial decadence (in the 1925 version with John Gilbert and Mae Murray). Fortunately, Lubitsch lacked also Stroheim's snickering villainies and overstuffed ornamentation. As for *Angel*, it was simply misunderstood as failed bedroom farce *à la* Feydeau rather than as a rhyming exercise in Pirandellian role-playing. Far from being failures, these three films mark an evolution of Lubitsch's style away from the sparkling balancing acts of *The Marriage Circle* and *Trouble in Paradise* to the somewhat heavier, but richer, concoctions of the 40s—*The Shop Around the Corner*, *To Be or Not to Be*, *Heaven Can Wait* and *Cluny Brown*.

Of course, critics in the 30s could hardly have anticipated Lubitsch's last burst of stylistic development in the next decade, but they might have given him more credit as an innovator in his own right, rather than maligning him as a manipulative mimic of Chaplin and René Clair. Weinberg's book helps perpetuate the legend of Chaplin's *A Woman of Paris* (1923), as the brilliant precursor of Lubitsch's 20s Hollywood comedies, and Chaplin himself shrewdly contributed to this legend by withholding *A Woman of Paris* from vulgar view for some half a century. As Eric Bentley noted, writing eloquently about this forbidden classic in *Moviegoer*, Chaplin's genre is Victorian melodrama. What must have impressed Lubitsch was not Chaplin's style, rather stodgy and derivative even in comparison with *Die Puppe* and *Anna Boleyn* in 1919–20, but rather Chaplin's demonstration that American audiences were not entirely alien to European sophistication and cynicism about what Preston Sturges was later to designate (in *The Palm Beach Story*) as Topic A. To the

end of his career, Chaplin was never able to take casual carnality in his stride. Indeed, as Chaplin's films became more autobiographical, the wistful romanticism began to wither into nasty misogyny—whereas Lubitsch never lost his lilt even at death's door.

As for René Clair, it is difficult to believe how much superior to Lubitsch he was considered in the early 30s by critics who should have known better. Although Lubitsch long antedated Clair in cinema, Clair was generally considered the source from which all cinematic wit and whimsy had sprung. Even Chaplin was condemned (by Otis Ferguson) for lifting Clair's assembly line in *A Nous la Liberté* for use in *Modern Times*. Part of the problem with Lubitsch is that his powerful position at Paramount made him a spokesman for an unpopular industry. He was blamed for Sternberg's troubles at the studio. And he was criticized for stressing the need to please a mass audience. Look at Clair, the critics said. He doesn't care about audiences. He is concerned only with his own art. It was one thing for *New York Times* critic Frank S. Nugent (later John Ford's scenarist) to declare flatly that *The Informer* was thematically superior to Max Ophuls' *Liebelei*: a turgid allegory is always superior in some aesthetics to a tender love story. But that Lubitsch's talent should be considered spiritually inferior to such a more tinkly than tingly mechanical-doll talent as René Clair's is almost beyond understanding. On any ultimate scale of values, Lubitsch's only sin seems to have been his assuming power in a situation in which highbrows computed glory in inverse proportion to power and even potency. As a result, Lubitsch has never been credited for his undeniable influence on directors as disparate as Ophuls (*The Bartered Bride*), Hitchcock (*Waltzes from Vienna*), Bergman (*Smiles of a Summer Night*), Renoir (*La Règle du Jeu*), Mamoulian (*Love Me Tonight*), Chaplin (*The Countess from Hong Kong*), Hawks (*Paid to Love*), Sternberg (*The King Steps Out*), Lewis Milestone (*Paris in the Spring*), and more of Preston Sturges, Mitchell Leisen, Frank Tuttle and Billy Wilder than can be encompassed in a few film titles. Indeed, if 'influence' were the sole criterion of greatness, Lubitsch's name would be near the top of the list with D. W. Griffith and not too many more.

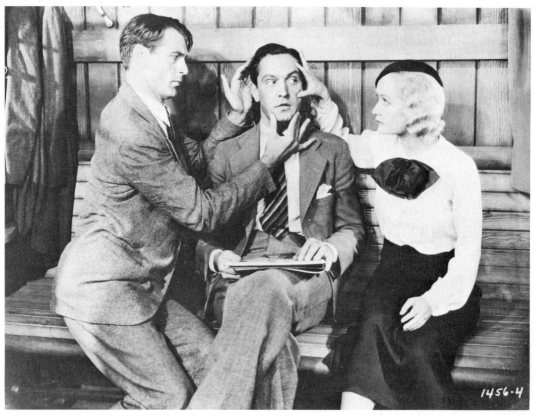

Fredric March torn between Gary Cooper and Miriam Hopkins in the ambiguous *Design for Living*.

Ernst Lubitsch presents problems for the film historian over and above the usual one of sifting the coarse sands of a collaborative art-form for the gold dust of an individual style. The writers alone would take a chapter. Samson Raphaelson (*The Smiling Lieutenant, The Man I Killed, One Hour with You, Trouble in Paradise, The Merry Widow, Angel*) was especially conspicuous as a collaborator during this decade. Other Lubitsch scriptwriters worthy of mention (and perhaps even analysis) are Ernest Vajda (*The Love Parade*, 1929, *Monte Carlo, The Smiling Lieutenant, The Man I Killed, The Merry Widow*), Charles Brackett and Billy Wilder (*Bluebeard's Eighth Wife, Ninotchka*), Ben Hecht (*Design For Living*) and Walter Reisch (*Ninotchka*). But even these highly talented and idiosyncratic screenwriters were usually mere middlemen between bits and pieces of theatre, fiction and anecdotal conversations on one side and Lubitsch's storyboard implemented by an army of technicians (generally from Paramount) on the other.

The important thing to remember is that Lubitsch was as much a force as he was a beacon. His influence on the Paramount Studio is thus comparable to Zanuck's at Fox, Thalberg's at Metro, Laemmle's at Universal, and all the brothers Warner put together. Chaplin remained his own producer and his own creator throughout his career, but in the 30s Chaplin was too inimitably individualistic and technologically reactionary to exercise much influence on other directors. Capra had *carte blanche* at Columbia for a time, but he never meddled with the overall mediocrity of Harry Cohn's commercial factory. Alone among the distinguished directors of the decade, Lubitsch looked beyond his own creative concerns to the evolution of public taste.

The dividing line was 1934. The resurgence of censorship, the delayed realization that breadlines and continental sophistication didn't mix, that a wink was no match for a wisecrack, and the pervasive humourlessness of both the Left and the Right, brought hard times for such stylistically playful directors as Sternberg, Milestone, Mamoulian and Clair, and an end to many genres—most notably the subjective gangster films, the rhymed-couplet musicals and the upper-class soap operas (goodbye, *East Lynne*, and hello, *Stella Dallas*).

What makes Lubitsch's films of the period especially fascinating today is their sense of strain between a director's sensibility within and a producer's sensitivity without. *The Smiling Lieutenant*, for example, is gravely flawed by the contradiction between the director's exquisitely flavoursome treatment of Claudette Colbert's demi-mondaine and the puritanical resolution of the plot to allow Miriam Hopkins' prissy princess to come out on top for the sake of the presumably sacred marriage contract. Indeed, the Colbert character must even contribute to her own romantic downfall by advising her rival how to snare the smiling but straying Lieutenant (Maurice Chevalier) with a song about sexy underwear, as if the Elective Affinities were merely consumer goods and textbook tactics. Still, Claudette Colbert's glowing performance in *The Smiling Lieutenant* is as much a testament to the winsome womanliness of her

Laura Hope Crews and Marlene Dietrich in *Angel*: Lubitsch was able even to suggest a high-class *maison de rendezvous* without the censor making a fuss. A flop at the time, *Angel* now seems to be one of his best films.

early 30s persona as her excruciatingly sadistic performance in *Bluebeard's Eighth Wife* reflects the horrible torture inflicted on sex comedy after censorship reared its ugly head.

By 1938 American audiences had regained their emotional adolescence in their quest for seriousness and significance. It was as if Lubitsch had never come to these shores with his expansive smile, his cigar and his gourmet tastes. And Lubitsch himself had to trim his sails after the colossal failure of *Angel*, one of his most anachronistically civilized works, released as it was at a time when Harry Brandt had decreed that Marlene Dietrich, Greta Garbo, Katharine Hepburn and Joan Crawford were all box-office poison. With *Bluebeard's Eighth Wife* and even *Ninotchka*, the Lubitsch champagne is beginning to be diluted with vinegar from the well-stocked cupboard of Billy Wilder. In the 40s, the sweetness of the Viennese tradition will be perpetuated by Lubitsch and Preston Sturges, but the sourness of that same tradition will pass on to Billy Wilder, especially after Charles Brackett has been succeeded by I. A. L. Diamond.

Even from the beginning of the sound era, however, Lubitsch seemed aware of the limited leeway he had with an increasingly impatient audience. His four musicals follow a pattern of progressive stylization and self-consciousness as audience resistance to the integrated poetics of rhythmic *mise en scène* increases. *The Love Parade* is relatively care-free and unforced at a moment in film history when sound seemed to be stifling movement. Its artfully raised eyebrows and its clever cutting between the royal couple and the watchful court made it seem like an unbroken link between the visual mellifluousness of the silent cinema and the verbal–musical dynamics of the talkies. (Otherwise, *The Love Parade* is merely a one-song musical, whose one melodious tune—Victor Schertzinger's 'Dream Lover'—popped up later on the Paramount lot in Billy Wilder's *The Major and the Minor* and Cecil B. DeMille's *The Greatest Show on Earth*.)

Monte Carlo came along at a time when the screen had been so saturated with musicals that producers saddled with musical properties were keeping the ridiculous plots and throwing out the redeeming songs. Jeanette MacDonald's acting had not improved appreciably since *The Love Parade*, and her new leading man (Jack Buchanan) lacked the charm and authority of Maurice Chevalier. But *Monte Carlo* succeeded none the less by virtue of Lubitsch's spectacular montage mounting of 'Beyond the Blue Horizon' (MacDonald/train/countryside/peasants)—a sequence so spectacular that few viewers could remember much else about the movie, fortunately for MacDonald and Buchanan.

Lubitsch regained Chevalier for *The Smiling Lieutenant*, but he sensed that the operetta style of love duets was going out of fashion, and so Chevalier was flanked by two straight actress-personalities, Claudette Colbert and Miriam Hopkins. *The Smiling Lieutenant* thus stands almost half-way between the lilting lyricism of *The Love Parade* and the tempered ironies of *Trouble in Paradise*. In fact, Lubitsch was so busy with *Trouble in Paradise* that he delegated most of the directorial drudgery of *One Hour with You* to George Cukor (designated by Herman G. Weinberg in *The Lubitsch Touch* as the 'dialogue director'). Without plunging into period memoirs over who did what and to whom, we can safely say that *One Hour with You* marks a discernible break stylistically with both previous and subsequent Lubitsch films. Cukor, like Preminger later, superimposed on a Lubitsch project an essentially theatrical *mise en scène*, lighter on the witty cut and heavier on the lyrically long take and sweeping camera movement.

Lubitsch's final fling with the musical (apart from his fatal misalliance with Betty Grable in *That Lady in Ermine* in 1947) reunited Maurice Chevalier and Jeanette MacDonald in that trusty warhorse of operettas, Franz Lehar's *The Merry Widow*. There is one beautiful song in *The Merry Widow* that cannot be bluffed or faked or kidded by a music-hall style: 'Vilia'. There are a few things in the world that are too beautiful to be burlesqued even by the most gifted clowns and the most charming straw-hat rascals. Lubitsch knew that Chevalier couldn't sing 'Vilia' himself with his jaunty *chansonnier*'s chirp, and yet the song was too good to be sacrificed. The solution? Maurice Chevalier's gawky country bumpkin orderly (Sterling Holloway) sings the song (dubbed of course by a straight tenor) with Chevalier standing behind him like a combination puppet-master and Cyrano, the sweetness tempered once more by the irony of a device breathtakingly ingenious in its audacious directness.

The evaluation of film musicals is sheer folly after a certain point. A song here, a dance there, performers at a peak or in a pique, can make all the difference between enchantment and ennui. Hence I would not argue too strenuously with the persuasive defenders of Rouben Mamoulian's *Love Me Tonight* as the best of the 'Lubitsch-like' musicals. None the less, I would not trade Lubitsch's daringly subdued and scintillatingly circular treatment of 'The Merry Widow Waltz' as a prison-cell *pas de deux* for all the slow motion and showy camera angles in *Love Me Tonight*. Lubitsch makes of *The Merry Widow* the last musical of a certain spirit and style to be made on this planet. And it is his intimation of a genre's mortality and the sad smile that goes with this intimation that make Lubitsch ultimately inimitable and ineffable.

In a sense, Lubitsch's reputation was trapped for ever in the socio-aesthetic perfection of *Trouble in Paradise* for 1932. This movie seemed to have everything: the grace and elegance of the 20s, the egalitarian conscience of the 30s, the visual wit of the silent cinema and the verbal wit of the talkies. The triangle formed by the jewel thieves of Herbert Marshall and Miriam Hopkins and the industrial heiress of Kay Francis was toyed with in a tantalizing fashion, but then resolved with both class logic and fair-minded sentiment. Also, the comedy relief routines of Charles Ruggles and Edward Everett Horton were still fresh and sparkling. Never again was Lubitsch to experience such rapport with his audience and his medium. As his films in the 40s became increasingly sombre and reflective, he was regarded as increasingly out of touch with the tastes of the times. Twice in the decade, he attempted remakes of previous successes in the silent era: *That Uncertain Feeling* (1941) from *Kiss Me Again,* and *A Royal Scandal* (1945) from *Forbidden Paradise.* In both instances, the severe censorship then in force reduced sexual intrigues to sexual innuendoes. *That Uncertain Feeling* suffered also from the glacial miscasting of Melvyn Douglas, Merle Oberon and Burgess Meredith in the form of

a triangle. And in the absence of dry wit, a desperate zaniness took possession of the film.

Ernst Lubitsch did not even do most of the shooting on *A Royal Scandal.* He fell ill, and Otto Preminger completed and signed the picture with a *mise en scène* more theatrical in its long takes and integral space than we have come to associate with Lubitsch. Preminger, like Cukor (*One Hour with You*), and unlike Lubitsch, came to the cinema after sound, and therefore thought of image and sound simultaneously rather than discretely.

But if Lubitsch was unable to recapture the past in the 40s, he was far more successful when he moved on to relatively new terrain with *The Shop Around the Corner* (working-class whimsy), *To Be or Not to Be* (anti-Nazi farce), *Heaven Can Wait* (manners versus instincts in a topsy-turvy world). He was especially fortunate in the emotional warmth provided his heroines by such affecting actresses as Margaret Sullavan (*Shop*), Carole Lombard (*To Be*), Gene Tierney (*Heaven*) and Jennifer Jones (*Cluny*).

Ernst Lubitsch died of a heart attack on 30 November 1947. His next project was to have been *That Lady in Ermine,* with Douglas Fairbanks, Jr and Betty Grable. He lived only long enough to shoot eight days of this otherwise ill-fated film, which Otto Preminger completed and signed.

Herman G. Weinberg's book *The Lubitsch Touch,* mentioned by Sarris, remains the only full-length study in English; it was published in 1968. Lubitsch's reputation is now on the upswing, as a younger generation of film-makers (improbable though it may sound, *Trouble in Paradise* is one of Jean-Marie Straub's favourite films) and critics see his work in Cinémathèques and film museums. Even *Angel* is now seen as the minor-key masterpiece it surely is: a 'Munich' (1938) film, if ever there was one. (For a different view of *Love Me Tonight,* see Milne's entry on Mamoulian.)

SIDNEY LUMET

Richard Combs

Unlike most of his confrères who went from television to the movies in the late 50s, came to the fore with the movement away from

Herbert Marshall torn between Kay Francis and Miriam Hopkins in *Trouble in Paradise*: 'this movie seemed to have everything: the grace and elegance of the 20s, the egalitarian conscience of the 30s, the visual wit of the silent cinema and the verbal wit of the talkies'.

Hollywood in the early 60s, but rather lost their way both artistically and commercially towards the end of the decade, Sidney Lumet (born 1924) has at least kept up the pressure of a prolific and varied output. The eclecticism of his subjects has done something to mitigate the jagged, theatrical heaviness of his style. But in retrospect, it is ironic that, as a New Yorker rejecting Hollywood, he should have been hailed as an innovator in the American cinema, for his films have remained locked into a TV-cum-theatrical style for staging conflicts and setting problems.

Within the jury-room setting, and the airtight dramatic conventions of Lumet's first film, *12 Angry Men* (1957), the stylized clash of social and political forces had a cerebral excitement. When dragged into the open air and yoked to contemporary issues, such tactics resulted in the uncomfortable 'tract' films of the mid-60s: *Fail Safe* (1964), *The Pawnbroker* (1965) and *The Hill* (1965). Subsequently abandoning the role of high-pressure salesman of big issues to become the creator of more elusive mood pieces, Lumet proved no less stiff and clumsy with the nostalgic regret of *Bye Bye Braverman* (1968), the ennui of modern love in *The Appointment* (1969) and the moral nihilism of espionage in *The Deadly Affair* (1967). His straight theatrical adaptations have meanwhile declined from the scrupulous reading and density of performance in *Vu du Pont* (*A View from the Bridge*, 1962) and *Long Day's Journey into Night* (1962) to the thematic pretensions and

behavioural frenzy of *The Offence* (1972) and
Child's Play (1972). With no message to
deliver in *Murder on the Orient Express*
(1974), Lumet simply directed straight into
the staginess of the piece and lent the performances a properly theatrical solidity and
resonance.

But the splintered rhythm, the heavy progression of Lumet's films in self-contained
scenes played out in measured close-up, may
have evolved in the 70s into an embryonic
epic form—a modern mosaic in which socio-
economic observations are assembled, not
into a message, but into a deterministic trap
which the hero wilfully enters. The method
is foreshadowed in *The Group* (1966), but
comes into its own with *The Anderson Tapes*
(1971) and *Serpico* (1973), both of which
feature a protagonist who follows his obsessions at the cost of either his life or his liberty. The formal dislocations of the movies
result in a prismatic presentation of character; heroes who are seen from different perspectives *within* the films. Lumet's approach
may never make for a graceful style, but it
retains an energy and complexity which have
drained from colleagues who seemed to make
an easier transition from one medium to the
other: Robert Mulligan has disappeared into
an ever more insubstantial romanticism;
John Frankenheimer seems frozen in the
pose of a Hollywood classicist.

**Lumet's upward swing continued with *Dog
Day Afternoon* (1975), arguably one of his
best films. Always very much at the mercy
of script and cast, his career has been spectacularly uneven. *That Kind of Woman*
(1959) brilliantly cross-cast Sophia Loren
and Tab Hunter; and Al Pacino and the
others helped make *Dog Day Afternoon* the
success it was. Ultimately, as Combs suggests, he is at his best when he tackles
relatively unambitious projects. *Network*
(1976), scripted by Paddy Chayefsky, was a
huge box-office success; but its vulgarity was
more pronounced than the television vulgarity it was supposed to be satirizing.**

LEO McCAREY
Robin Wood

Renoir said of Leo McCarey (1898–1969)
that he was one of the best American directors because he really understood people.
The apparently banal remark takes on
increasingly vivid and defined meaning as
one explores McCarey's films, and it makes a
useful starting point for a brief definition of
McCarey's limited, but deeply sympathetic
and engaging, art: an art that, simple, self-
effacing and drawing only minimally on the
resources of cinema, may withstand the test
of time and repetition better than that of
many more immediately striking and asser-
tively cinematic directors.

Both McCarey's excellence and his limitations can be suggested by juxtaposing his
work with Renoir's and noting the resem-
blances and the differences. One aspect of the
understanding of people in their films is the
understanding of actors: the work of both is
actor-centred. One might contrast the cinema of Renoir, McCarey and Hawks with
that of Hitchcock, Sternberg and Antonioni. Hitchcock denies that he said that actors
are cattle: he said they should be *treated* like
cattle. To Sternberg, actors are 'puppets';
and to Antonioni, in the words of Arthur
Penn, they are 'beautiful statuary'. To
Renoir, McCarey and Hawks they are
responsive human beings, with particular
gifts, particular limitations, particular reactions, out of which the film develops: that is
the foundation of their 'humanism'. Some of
the most delightful scenes in the American
cinema grew directly out of McCarey's
creative collaboration with his actors, even
out of his knowledge of their limitations.
Witness the famous scene in *Ruggles of Red
Gap* (1935) where Leila Hyams teaches
Roland Young to play the drums; or the
'Home on the Range' scene in *The Awful
Truth* (1937), improvised on the first day of
shooting when McCarey discovered that
Ralph Bellamy couldn't sing and Irene
Dunne was an inexpert pianist.

McCarey worked with most of Hollywood's great clowns, including W. C. Fields,
Harold Lloyd and Mae West. In particular,
he directed two of the finest Laurel and
Hardy shorts (*Liberty*, 1929, and *Wrong*

Charles Boyer and Irene Dunne in *Love Affair* (1939): far superior, to my mind, to the remake, *An Affair to Remember*. Kitsch? Maybe, but on this level, who cares?

Again, 1929) and indisputably the best Marx Brothers movie (*Duck Soup*, 1933). Though it is obvious that one scarcely presumes to 'direct' Laurel and Hardy or the Marx Brothers, I am increasingly disinclined to believe that this is mere coincidence. The outstanding quality of these films is their lack of inhibition, their audacity in carrying insane actions through with relentless and hilarious logic. *Duck Soup* is the one Marx Brothers film that dispenses entirely with extraneous plot, love interest, musical numbers (apart from songs involving the brothers). In *Wrong Again*, the action reaches the point where Laurel and Hardy, delivering a race-horse called Blue Boy to the owner of a missing painting called Blue Boy, are told by the

(off-screen) owner to 'put it on the piano'. Most directors would have been content to stop there. Not McCarey: the profoundly satisfying effect of the short depends on the visible evidence of a real race-horse on a real (and collapsing) grand piano.

From his work with comedians in the early 30s, McCarey carried over two tendencies into his later films. One was his affection for performers and performance, combined with his tact in leaving good things alone; again and again he would be content merely to place the camera in front of two actors and record their speech and behaviour in a single static take. The result is neither uncinematic nor unimaginative (one may recall, in any case, that Renoir agreed with his father that imagination is a most overrated quality): it is simply evidence of McCarey's wise and sympathetic awareness of what his players could give and what his audiences wanted to watch. There are magnificent sustained dialogues, for example, for Victor Moore and Beulah Bondi in *Make Way for Tomorrow* (1937), and for Cary Grant and Ginger Rogers in *Once Upon a Honeymoon* (1942).

The second tendency was the lack of inhibition already noted, though it often took forms other than comic exuberance. McCarey is often accused of sentimentality; I think the charge may be partly a defence against the embarrassingly direct and simple emotional appeal his films frequently make. How many directors would have allowed Beulah Bondi to recite an entire sentimental poem to her husband in the hotel restaurant in *Make Way for Tomorrow*? (But how many would have dared make that extraordinarily honest and desolating film at all?) The sentimentality, here, is in the poem, not the scene, the context of which places and comments on the sort of comfort the poem offers. The film, in fact, is as remarkable for its toughness as it is for the emotional generosity that some call 'sentimental'.

The standard two-shot of the Hollywood cinema, in which the characters are balanced within the frame on terms of perfect equality, has a general significance as an expression of democracy which takes on particular meaning in the work of McCarey, where it becomes an artistic principle. He and Renoir are, indeed, the cinema's ideal democrats. Rather as Renoir allows every point of view its expression, and will allow dominance within the action and within the image to pass continually from character to character, so McCarey will lavish equally loving care on each bit part player, building up a marvellously vivid characterization within a minute or so of screen time. In *Once Upon a Honeymoon* (a film whose theme is the democratic ideal, characteristically expressed in the exchange of ethnic jokes as Ginger Rogers tests Albert Dekker's genuineness of commitment) there are the Viennese maid, the Polish waiter, the French hotel proprietress—the last a human being created in little more than a single brief speech, as she tells Cary Grant that Ginger Rogers was crying when she left.

If Renoir must ultimately be judged the superior artist (though I feel for his films no greater affection than for McCarey's best work), the judgement must be founded on the fact that he achieves what McCarey does not, a visual style that in itself expresses a metaphysic, a personal view of life. The achievement of significant style is the manifestation of an artist's mastery of his material and his means; McCarey, in comparison, is much more at the mercy of scripts, casting and ideology. This is not, of course, to imply that McCarey's films lack personality; it is simply to say that Renoir is, in the last resort, more consciously an artist.

Not only was Renoir more consciously an artist, but his career did not take such a catastrophic turn as did McCarey's in the 40s. Renoir could never have made such appallingly sentimental films as *Going My Way* (1944) and *The Bells of St Mary's* (1945) or such a ridiculously tendentious one as *My Son John* (1952). McCarey's career never recovered, although there are many who think highly of *An Affair to Remember* (1957). But the original *Love Affair* of 1939, of which the later film was a remake, was to my mind far superior. Curiously enough, McCarey agreed, and he has been quoted as saying that Cary Grant's irony in the remake took away from the 'beauty' of the original.

NORMAN McLAREN

Jonathan Rosenbaum

Initially, one is tempted to call Norman McLaren (born 1914) the greatest doodler that the cinema has known—a filmic equivalent to Saul Steinberg—and simply leave it at that. Clearly the role played in his work by improvisation is central, implicitly linking his style to the jazzier suspensions of live-action narrative directors like Hawks, Welles, Godard, Rivette and Altman. But to see him divorced from the grand school of 'solo animation'—from Cohl, Fischinger and Lye (his acknowledged masters) to Breer, Smith and Belson—is merely to indulge in the sort of myopia that affects any spectator experiencing McLaren's work in isolation, without an adequate grasp of his relative position in a rich and varied tradition.

Reluctantly adopting this myopia as an alternative to misconstruing McLaren's context, I would nominate *Begone Dull Care* (1949) as the quintessential jazz film. Not because it contains the best jazz (Oscar Peterson is a dazzling piano virtuoso, but certainly not a distinctive stylist of the calibre of Waller, Tatum, Powell or Tristano), but because, virtually alone among jazz films, it works *with* the music rather than against it. Emblematic of all McLaren's best animation with music (e.g., *Fiddle De Dee*, 1947, with its screechy violin, *A Chairy Tale*, 1957, with Ravi Shankar), it reveals a response to melody and rhythm suggesting something closer to a duel or duet than a commentary—utilizing a tension wholly absent from *Fantasia*, where the visuals never pass beyond their illustrative function. It is as proper to say that in *Begone Dull Care*, Peterson illustrates McLaren; the relationship, in any case, is much more symbiotic (and it must be noted that if Peterson were a more considerable pianist, this 'balance of power' might have fatally shifted).

An amateur *par excellence* in the modesty of his tools and ambitions and the prolific range of his techniques, McLaren can count among his more endearing trademarks a solid grasp of syncopation and a penchant for integrating titles and credits into his graphic designs (both evident in *Blinkity Blank*, 1954), an imagination that flirts with abstraction without ever entirely succumbing to it (as in the dance-like *Le Merle*, 1958, or the 'animated painting' of *La Poulette Grise*, 1947), and a tendency to limit his visual patterns to bone essentials—such as the strips, squares and sprocket holes of *Synchromy* (1971)—and then do his witty best to make the most of them.

McLaren, although often thought of as Canadian, was actually born in Scotland, and his first films were made for Grierson and the GPO unit in London. Later, he went to the States and made some films for NBC; only when he was twenty-seven did he settle in Canada, where he has worked ever since. Mention should be made of one of his most beautiful films, *Pas de Deux* (1967), in which photographic images were used both stroboscopically and in stop-frame technique.

For further reading, see Maynard Collins' *Norman McLaren* (1976).

DUŠAN MAKAVEJEV
Robin Wood

Makavejev's films are among the most immediately striking and original of the post-New Wave generation. His particular contribution to the expressive potentialities of modern cinema has been the development of an increasingly complicated collage method: the juxtaposition of heterogeneous materials to produce complex ironies and ambiguities. The basic elements of his thematic were established fairly comprehensively in his first feature, made in 1966, *Covek Nije Tica* (*Man Is Not a Bird*), a film whose assurance may be partly attributable to the fact that Makavejev had been making shorts and documentaries, unfortunately inaccessible, since 1953; and confirmed in the closely related *Ljubavni Slucaj* or *Tragedija Sluzbenice P.T.T.* (U.K.: *The Switchboard Operator*, alternative title *The Tragedy of a Switchboard Operator*; U.S.: *Love Affair*, alternative titles *The Case of the Missing Switchboard Operator* and *An Affair of the Heart*, 1967): the exploration of tensions between the traditional and the progressive, restriction and emancipation, inhibition and liberation, on both the political and sexual levels, the two seen as parallel and interacting.

Makavejev (born in Belgrade in 1932) is often referred to as a follower of Godard, but his method is very different and seems to derive rather from a combination of Brecht and Surrealism. The effects he achieves have often more in common with Buñuel than with Godard: compare, for example, Makavejev's collage method with the intercutting of prayers and labour in *Viridiana*, or the use of the Beethoven Choral Symphony in *Man Is Not a Bird* with Buñuel's use of the Hallelujah Chorus to accompany the beggars' orgy—the effect is not one of simple point-making but of complex ironies and an interacting, two-way criticism. The fictional sequences of Makavejev's first two features are like Godard only in their seeming casualness, their improvisatory quality, their ability to make something out of almost nothing; unlike Godard, Makavejev at this stage seldom interferes with the audience's illusion of reality *during* a narrative scene—on the contrary, he carries 'naturalism' as far as any neo-realist. Distancing here arises not from our awareness of the actors as actors or of the scene as 'cinema', but from the surprising juxtaposition of 'straight' fictional episodes with various other materials—film-clips, documentaries, lectures—that are unconnected on the narrative plane and whose thematic relevance the spectator is left to work out for himself. Usually, the possible connections are themselves ambiguous or contradictory, so that the spectator is forced into an active participation, invited to supply his own synthesis to the dialectic of thesis and antithesis proposed by the film.

Makavejev's strategies can generally be explained in two ways: as motivated by the desire to keep the spectator mentally alert, and as the expression of his own uncertainties. One aspect of the structure of *Switchboard Operator* answers clearly to the former explanation: the decision to treat parts of the fictional story non-chronologically. We see the first meeting of Ahmed and Isabella in a crowded street; Makavejev cuts to a sequence of a girl's body being hauled up from a sewer-well. Later, the couple's first night together is followed by an apparently 'documentary' sequence of the body being examined and dissected in a morgue. It is only at the end of this sequence that we are given a decisive clue that the body is Isabella's; up to that point, Makavejev encourages speculation without offering more than the slightest of hints.

More importantly, collage is for Makavejev a complex medium for the definition of contemporary uncertainties—not so much for the resolution of our confusions, but for bringing them to full consciousness. The fictions of the first two films juxtapose and contrast characters who live by traditional values, ideals of permanence and stability in relationships, with 'modern', emancipated characters; neither side is endorsed by the films, the former becoming associated with possessiveness, jealousy, even with suicidal or homicidal tendencies, the latter with shallowness and triviality.

Both the method and the thematic are taken up and extended in Makavejev's fourth feature film, *WR—Misterije Organizma*

(*WR—Mysteries of the Organism*, 1971). There are several important differences, not all of which strike me as unequivocally propitious developments. The material drawn together for the collage is much more diverse, which at once multiplies the possibilities of meaning, irony and collision, and makes the effects much harder to control. Responses in *Switchboard Operator* are provoked by tensions, oppositions, ambiguities whose terms are very precisely defined by the film. Confronted by the great mass of heterogeneous material that makes up *WR*, the spectator is much freer to make his own patterns. It could be argued that this encourages a still more active participation; it is more likely to lead to vagueness, and may offer an explanation of *WR*'s popularity beyond the obvious one of 'sensational' content: it is easy to treat the whole thing as an amusing phantasmagoria.

This is further facilitated by the second major difference: in place of the meticulously detailed, sensitively observed 'realist' fictions of the first two films, *WR* offers a stylized, mostly comic charade which recapitulates their thematic while largely denying the audience the sympathetic involvement that (repeatedly interrupted and interrogated) generated such intensity of response. This in turn merges with the third difference: the balancing of 'traditional' and 'progressive' attitudes is in *WR* decisively tipped in favour of the latter (which doesn't mean that its heroine's 'emancipated', free-fucking morality is simply endorsed: on the contrary, it is presented satirically). The important thing here is that, if there *was* an imbalance in the earlier films, it was—in terms of sympathy if not of structure—on the other side: the 'emancipated' characters were presented externally and regarded as incapable of the emotional depth of those still trammelled by tradition. It is also significant that the most 'traditional' (and suffering) character in the films is always a man. For all that much of their material is drawn from outside sources, Makavejev's films have strong elements of the 'psychodrama': the tensions they repeatedly explore are clearly his own. One can argue, I think, that by reducing the 'traditionalist' side of himself to the parody-figure of the Stalinist ice-skater of *WR*, Makavejev is doing himself an injury, and that this is underlined by the transition to the mode of stylized caricature, a mode more easily dominated by the consciousness than that of exploratory 'realist' narrative.

Inevitably, too, this has repercussions on other aspects of the film. The treatment of Wilhelm Reich is very disturbing: his assertion of the need for sexual liberation is presented as though it were central to the film's impulses, yet Makavejev concentrates attention almost exclusively on the more ludicrous excesses of Reich's later years, so that the image which emerges is predominantly that of a charlatan or a 'crank' (certain Reichians in America quite understandably wanted the film suppressed as damagingly misleading). The tension produced here seems merely awkward and unprofitable, resting as it does on the trivialization of Reich's work. It is as if Makavejev were unconsciously undercutting his own apparent endorsement of 'liberation', rather than provoking a rational critique of it.

The last sequences of *WR*, however, generate a characteristic emotional intensity, the collision between repression and emancipation producing a catastrophe that, by suggesting the potential depth of human needs, calls both sides into question. And the final juxtaposition—the suddenly smiling severed head of Milena Dravic, followed by a photograph of a smiling Reich—is perhaps the most moving moment in Makavejev's films, with its expression of hope for future wholeness in the midst of the catastrophes and dislocations of the present.

Wood's doubts about Makavejev were dramatically confirmed in *Sweet Movie* (1974), a critical disaster, and a film which has hardly been seen anywhere. There has always been, to my mind, a streak of opportunist vulgarity in Makavejev and in *Sweet Movie* that streak, as it were, took over. Let us hope it was only a temporary lapse. There is an extended essay on Makavejev by Wood in *Second Wave*, edited by Ian Cameron, 1970.

LOUIS MALLE
James Monaco

Louis Malle (born 1932) appears to be the most eclectic of the New Wave directors who dominated French films in the 60s. In the mid-50s he served as assistant on films by both J.-Y. Cousteau and Robert Bresson. His first feature, *Ascenseur pour l'Echafaud* (U.K.: *Lift to the Scaffold*; U.S.: *Frantic*, 1958) was a straightforward *policier* distinguished by a Miles Davis score. *Les Amants* (*The Lovers*, 1958), a romantic bourgeois love story, gained him some international attention, partly because of a demure semi-nude love scene which caused censorship problems. *Zazie dans le Métro* (*Zazie*, 1960), his third film, was a frenetic, brash, breathless and colourful comedy about a twelve-year-old girl with a foul mouth. In the 60s Malle also completed *Vie Privée* (*A Very Private Affair*, 1962), with Brigitte Bardot and Marcello Mastroianni; *Le Feu Follet* (U.K.: *A Time to Live and a Time to Die*; U.S.: *The Fire Within*, 1963), about the last few days in the life of an alcoholic; *Viva Maria* (1965), a Western, of sorts, and a women's 'buddy' movie starring Bardot and Jeanne Moreau; *Le Voleur* (U.S.: *The Thief of Paris*, 1967), a romantic period piece; and *William Wilson*, a half-hour retelling of the Edgar Allan Poe story included in *Histoires Extraordinaires* (U.K.: *Tales of Mystery*; U.S.: *Spirits of the Dead*, 1968). In 1967 he spent six months in India filming a feature, *Calcutta* (1969), and a seven-part television series, *Phantom India* (1968). (He had already made two other documentaries: *Vive le Tour*, 1966, and *Bons Baisers de Bangkok*, 1964.) *Le Souffle au Coeur* (U.K.: *Dearest Love*; U.S.: *Murmur of the Heart*, 1970) is best described as a comedy about incest. *Humain, Trop Humain* (1973) is a curiously apolitical documentary about automobile assembly line work. *Lacombe, Lucien* (1974), probably Malle's most successful film, was a study of a country boy's insouciant yet vicious collaboration with the Gestapo during the Occupation—an essay on the banality of evil. This was followed in 1975 by *Black Moon*, a hyper-realistic fantasy almost without dialogue which Malle filmed in and around his own farmhouse near Limogne.

These sixteen films certainly display a remarkable variety of interests; and since Malle's directorial style is notable for restraint and objectivity—even diffidence— there seems to be little we can point to that unites the various elements. Malle finds the 'current emphasis on the *auteur* theory a little absurd', and suggests that the range of his career might be an unconscious reaction to it. Yet if the films do not share an obvious stylistic identity, there is nevertheless a coherent and uniform approach evident in each of Malle's projects. 'I'm always interested in *exposing* something,' he explains, 'a theme or character or situation which *seems* to be unacceptable. Then I try to make it work.'

Thus, having made *Le Souffle au Coeur* about an unacceptable facet of adolescent sex (incest), it was natural for him to recast these elements in terms of politics in *Lacombe, Lucien,* a film which makes Fascist collaboration seem understandable, almost normal. Likewise, *Black Moon* attempts with its hyper-realistic style to make the fantasy life of a young girl seem almost mundane. The identifying factor is the attitude of the filmmaker towards the materials. This is most evident in the quiet dialectic which Malle constructs between his subjects and the contrasting, objective, distanced style in which he films them. At their best, Malle's films rework and reconstruct established attitudes for his audience. It is not surprising, then, to discover that his central characters are often adolescents, who by definition have not yet fully formed their own sense of morality, politics or language. Finally, it must be said that in most of the films there remains a sense that, except for the element of contradiction, Malle's own ideas are still vague and formless. He never quite makes the quantum jump from experimentation to synthesis. His mastery of technique is admirable, his logic is intriguing, but to what end we don't yet know.

Malle has always oscillated between documentary and fiction; even before *Ascenseur pour l'Echafaud*, his first credit in the cinema was that of co-director (with Jacques-Yves Cousteau) of *Le Monde du Silence* (*The Silent World*, 1956). Part of his charm is in his unpredictability and his resistance to classification.

Pretty Baby (1978), indeed, was unpredictable, but in the wrong way: a period picture set in a brothel in New Orleans in 1917, it tells, none too compellingly, the story of a twelve-year-old girl, daughter of a prostitute, brought up in the brothel and her marriage with a rather catatonic photographer. It's lovely to look at (Sven Nykvist photography), but it lacks narrative drive (script by Polly Platt) and plot coherence. It is not a bad film, merely a forgettable one.

ROUBEN MAMOULIAN

Tom Milne

One of the more satisfactory Hollywood legends is that the only gangster movie of which Al Capone wholeheartedly approved was Rouben Mamoulian's *City Streets* (1931). The principal feature of the cycle sparked off by *Little Caesar* (1930) and *Public Enemy* (1931) was the rattle of machine-guns in the streets signalling yet another gang war or execution of a boss growing too big for his boots. But in *City Streets* not a single killing is shown on screen; and for Capone, who prided himself on his ability to conceal his *mains sales*, Mamoulian's portrayal of the racketeer as a respectable businessman with hirelings to take care of the dirty work was obviously more to the point than the two-gun mobster of *Scarface.*

It was not until the revival of the gangster movie in the late 60s and the 70s that the implied sophistication of Mamoulian's approach was taken up and fully developed in a series of films which demonstrated that, at least to all outward appearances, there was (and is) little difference between the syndicate gangster and the solid Wall Street citizen. One recognizes *The Godfather* in embryo in a scene in *City Streets* in which a contract to kill is drawn up in a single line of off-hand dialogue ('I'd be willing to do business with you—if anything happened to Blackie') and signed equally elliptically when the second party lights his cigar, looks at the match, and then pensively snuffs it out.

Though hired by Hollywood as an experienced stage director in the panic years after the coming of sound—he had just made his Broadway reputation with a highly successful production of *Porgy* in 1927—Mamoulian, ironically enough, never needed to rely on dialogue to make a point. The killing which follows this casual innuendo in *City Streets* is a brilliant example of pure cinematic technique which demonstrates that, even in his second film, Mamoulian had not only left his stage technique far behind on Broadway, but saw no reason why he should not make considerable demands on his audience's intelligence in fragmenting his narrative into a stylized pattern of dialogue, gesture and symbolism. Throughout the entire sequence, there is no direct reference either to the victim or to the fact that he is to die. Instead, Mamoulian focuses on a sinuous statuette of a white cat beside the telephone as the killer makes a phone call; a matching one of a black cat beside the victim's moll as she broods on revenge for a beating-up; then a swift, predatory cut between the two cats as the killer lights a cigar, casually remarks on how the ash builds up on the tip, and goes out leaving it burning in the ashtray. Only when, in the next shot, alarm bells ring and police converge on a street corner, does one realize not only that the murder has been committed, but that the phone call arranged a means of getting rid of the murder weapon, and that the cigar (given a gingerly puff by the moll so that the ash is undisturbed) will provide a watertight alibi for the killer when he returns to the apartment, claiming never to have left.

When Mamoulian (who was born in 1898) arrived at Paramount's Astoria Studios in New York to make his first film, *Applause* (1929), he didn't exactly deliver the goods he had been hired to produce. 'Here I had been recruited as a stage expert on dialogue,' he remarked in an interview with Andrew Sarris, 'and all I could think of was the marvellous things one could do with the camera and the exciting new potentials of sound recording.' *Applause* is based on a rather rickety novel by Beth Brown about an ageing burlesque queen who sacrifices herself for her daughter in the best tradition of mother-love and show-must-go-on melodramatics; but right from the very beginning Mamoulian insists on telling his story (a thing unheard of in those days of primitive sound cameras enclosed in booths) primarily through the mobility of his camera. First, a handful of shots establishing a shuttered shop-front,

an empty windblown street, a theatre poster advertising an appearance by the burlesque queen, a brass band introducing her triumphal progress in an open carriage through the crowds in the main street. Then, as the music changes to ragtime, the camera cuts inside the burlesque theatre, tracks steadily left past the musicians in the pit, pans up and tracks right along a row of plump, lackadaisically kicking legs, then pans up further still and tracks back again along the blowzy faces of the row of tired chorus girls as they perform their bumps and grinds.

Throughout the film, with the grimy, weary realism of its backstage atmosphere, the discreet use of expressionist shadows which were to become a trademark, and a magnificent performance from Helen Morgan as the burlesque dancer who chooses to commit suicide rather than shame her convent-bred daughter, Mamoulian managed to turn the conventions of the plot into touching tragedy. Nowhere more so than in a scene perilously fringing on bathos where, after the daughter has come home from the convent to discover the truth about her mother's profession (she sees the lascivious dance silhouetted and obscenely magnified on the stage backcloth), Helen Morgan tenderly sings the unhappy girl to sleep as she mutters a prayer and reaches for the crucifix under her pillow. Although Mamoulian's control of both emotional and expressionistic elements (neon lights flickering on and off from the street outside, the ominous shadow of the mother's no-good lover looming from the doorway to bring the sequence to an end) is still extremely effective and affecting, the technique employed in this sequence is nowadays in no way unusual; but in 1929 the complex soundtrack combined with a moving camera was revolutionary. As Mamoulian has commented, 'They said we couldn't record the two things—the song and the prayer—on one mike and one channel. So I said to the sound man, "Why not use two mikes and two channels and combine the two tracks in printing?"'

In his early films Mamoulian was a persistent iconoclast, insisting that none of the limitations imposed on the sound camera were really necessary, and many of his experiments have now become common film language. In *City Streets* he experimented with

Helen Morgan and Fuller Mellish Jr in Mamoulian's first and best film, *Applause*: 'the grimy, weary realism of its backstage atmosphere, and a magnificent performance from Helen Morgan as the burlesque dancer who chooses to commit suicide rather than shame her convent-bred daughter, turned the conventions of the plot into touching tragedy'.

subjective sound in a scene where Sylvia Sidney, having unsuccessfully tried to persuade Gary Cooper to get rich quick by becoming a bootlegger, is jailed because of her own connections with the racketeers. She is visited by Cooper, now resplendent in a fur-collared coat, who explains that he has joined the beer racket to raise the money to get her out of jail; and as the full irony of the situation hits her later in her cell, his voice returns to her with the operative word, 'Beer', repeated over and over again and becoming distorted in mockery. In *Dr Jekyll and Mr Hyde* (1931) Mamoulian used a subjective camera throughout the opening reel; so that our first view of Jekyll (apart from a glimpse of his reflection in a mirror), heralded by a sweeping 360-degree pan round the audience in the amphitheatre, is when he starts his

lecture on the possibility of separating the two natures of man. The result is not only to arouse curiosity about this man, but to stress his extraordinary arrogance—the man who sees himself as the centre of the universe and about to usurp God's role as creator.

Love Me Tonight (1932), apart from giving the Hollywood musical a much needed new choreographic flavour by extending and perfecting Lubitsch's technique of matching movements (of camera and actors) exactly to a pre-recorded score, also made witty use of non-realistic sound: an explosion when a precious vase crashes to the ground, canine yaps replacing the voices of three agitated maiden aunts. In *Queen Christina* (1933), the celebrated last shot, that seemingly endless close-up of Garbo standing expressionlessly on the prow of the ship taking her with her dead lover back to his homeland not only necessitated the invention of a special graduated lens to achieve the uninterrupted transition from long shot to close-up, but also applied Kuleshov's theory about the expressiveness of inexpression to create what is perhaps the quintessential Garbo moment. Mamoulian told her to make her mind and heart a complete blank: 'With a tragic ending like this, no matter what feelings are portrayed by the actress . . . some of the audience would disagree, find them wrong . . . If the face is blank . . . then every member of the audience inevitably will write in his own emotions.'

In 1935, finally, entrusted with the direction of the first feature in the new three-colour Technicolor process, Mamoulian (with his designer Robert Edmond Jones) made such delicately controlled use of the limited tones available to him that *Becky Sharp* still remains an exquisitely beautiful colour film. It also ranks as the only film until many years later to use colour dramatically rather than decoratively, most notably in the magnificent sequence of the Duchess of Richmond's eve of Waterloo ball. As the guns rumble in the distance, the dancers momentarily freeze (another innovation) on the ballroom floor. Curtains billow out, extinguishing the candles, and gunfire on the horizon illuminates the scene of panic as the guests leave; ladies first, draining the scene of colour as they rush out, followed by the gentlemen in their black tailcoats, until finally the screen is suffused in ominous, menacing red as the scarlet-cloaked officers assemble to prepare their departure for the holocaust of Waterloo.

After this film, Mamoulian's reputation as one of Hollywood's major talents went into a decline, not attended by any corresponding decline in his work. The movie tycoons were suspicious of his unpredictability and therefore reluctant to trust him as they trusted the comfortable studio hacks; and after duly praising the ingenuity of his early experiments, contemporary critics and historians, still confusing film with literary and dramatic aesthetics, began to take him to task for the 'triviality' of his subject matter. (The same accusations that they were wasting their time on comedies, musicals, costume extravaganzas and horror films were also levelled at the other great Hollywood stylists of the 30s: Josef von Sternberg, James Whale and George Cukor.) The fact remains that, by the time he had completed *Becky Sharp* and had finished inventing a cinematic vocabulary for himself, Mamoulian had established a wholly distinctive style which is as recognizable in his last musical, *Silk Stockings* (1957), as in his first, *Love Me Tonight* (1932).

This style is evolved, paradoxically enough, from the two main features of his stage work. First, the Stanislavsky naturalism (he had been a pupil of Vakhtangov at the Moscow Art Theatre) which characterized his first stage production in London in 1922 and thereafter remained a marked element in his staging even of musicals like *Oklahoma!* and *Lost in the Stars*. In the cinema, this bedrock of realism means that in the swashbuckling *The Mark of Zorro* (1940), for instance, the climactic duel between Tyrone Power and Basil Rathbone has a chillingly ferocious edge to it, and in the musical *High, Wide and Handsome* (1937), set in the Pennsylvania oilfields in 1859, the plot concerning the struggle for survival by poor farmer-prospectors against grasping railroad tycoons has an epic authenticity not usually associated with musicals. Second, there was Mamoulian's belief in, and development of, 'a theatre that would combine all the elements of movement, dancing, acting, music, singing, décor, lighting, colour and so on'—a theatre, in other words, that would 'integrate all theatrical elements into one stylized rhythmic pattern'.

The purest example of this amalgam, transposed almost exactly in *Love Me Tonight*, is the celebrated 'Symphony of Noises' which knocked Broadway on its ear when *Porgy* opened in New York at the Guild Theatre in 1927. As Mamoulian himself describes it, 'The curtain rose on Catfish Row in the early morning. All silent. Then you hear the Boom! of a street gang repairing the road. That is the first beat; then beat 2 is silent; beat 3 is a snore—zzz!—from a Negro who's asleep; beat 4 silent again. Then a woman starts sweeping the steps—Whish!—and she takes up beats 2 and 4, so you have:

Boom!—Whish!—zzz!—Whish!

and so on. A knife sharpener, a shoemaker, a

woman beating rugs and so on, all join in. Then the rhythm changes: 4:4 to 2:4; then to 6:8; and syncopated and Charleston rhythms. It all had to be conducted like an orchestra.'

With every action, gesture and line of dialogue thus conceived in terms of stylized rhythm, and sequences built as though to a musical pattern, Mamoulian's films are *choreographed* rather than directed, making them flow like musicals even when they are not. *The Mark of Zorro*, for instance, opens with a dozen brief shots of the young Zorro among two rows of cadets going through their paces on horseback at a Spanish riding academy and suddenly becoming, just for a moment, dancers in an elegant but ominous military quadrille. Using the same characteristically swift, elliptical setting of scene and mood, *We Live Again* (1934), an adaptation of Tolstoy's *Resurrection*, opens with a series of low-angled dissolves of fields and cows, sensuously framed by trees heavy with blossom in a brilliant pastiche of Dovzhenko, until suddenly, appearing in unison over the sky-line with the same burst of exhilaration as the three sailors in *On the Town*, come three horses and three ploughs. In *Queen Christina*, the emotional climax of the snow queen's brief experience of love comes in Garbo's tour of farewell to the room in which she discovered happiness, a caressing adagio of movement in which she slowly drifts round the room, stroking her hands gently along the surface of a sideboard, pausing at a mirror to smile at her lover's reflection, touching a box, a spinning-wheel, a wall, as though they had shared the secret with her, closing her eyes to remember, then continuing her journey, round the bed, across it to kiss the pillow, to run her fingers wonderingly over an icon on the wall, until her lover asks what she is doing, and her soft, husky voice explains: 'I have been memorizing this room. In the future, in my memory, I shall live a great deal in this room.' Exquisite in itself, this sequence ('The movement must be like a dance. Treat it the way you would do it to music,' Mamoulian told Garbo) is given its deep emotional sorcery by being designed as an interlude of rhythmic warmth between the frosty opening scenes of courtly elegance and the great elegiac rite, the absolute stasis, of the end.

Mamoulian's method, refined and purified from film to film, though some of his later assignments (notably *Golden Boy*, 1939, and *Rings on Her Fingers*, 1942) resisted him because the scripts were too verbose and plot-ridden, is seen at its best in his two last and most underrated films, *Summer Holiday* (1948) and *Silk Stockings*. The breezily elliptical opening sequences which set both pace and tone (in *Summer Holiday*, the 'It's Our Home Town' song which whisks us through the small town of Eugene O'Neill's nostalgic memory and introduces us in turn to all the members of his *Ah! Wilderness* family; in *Silk Stockings*, the close-ups of Fred Astaire's feet which joyously trace his journey from flat to stage door by way of lift, revolving door and taxi, taking in a leer at a pair of high heels on the way). The tinge of expressionism in his images (the predatory saloon-girl getting bigger and bigger and redder and redder as the adolescent boy finds her too much of a sexual fantasy in *Summer Holiday*; the draining away of colour to leave a drab wash of greys, browns and blues for the gloomy 'Red Blues' number in *Silk Stockings*). The foot kept firmly anchored in reality (by Walter Huston's doggy recitative, anticipating Rex Harrison's talking songs in *My Fair Lady*, of the opening song in *Summer Holiday*; by the genuine psychological and dramatic development carried in the Astaire–Charisse dances which chronicle their romance in *Silk Stockings*). And above all, the unerring sense of style and grace with which Mamoulian's camera simulates dance movements and musical rhythms round his characters so that when they do break into song and dance there is virtually no perceptible transition.

In *Summer Holiday*, with its glowing evocation of small-town America as a nostalgic memory of endless summer days filled with picnics and polkas and hayrides and the sweet pains of growing up, all swept up into a joyous celebration of time remembered, one is astonished to find that, despite some admirable steps created by Charles Walters, there are really no formal dance numbers. In *Silk Stockings*, which is predicated upon a series of formal dance solos and duets for Fred Astaire and Cyd Charisse, one is almost hoodwinked into believing that the many dialogue and comedy interludes are equally

Bette Davis, Thelma Ritter and Celeste Holm in *All About Eve*.

formally choregraphed. Movement, for Mamoulian, is the essence of cinema.

There is an excellent full-length study of Mamoulian's work by Tom Milne: *Rouben Mamoulian* (1969).

JOSEPH L. MANKIEWICZ

Richard Corliss

'I shall never understand the weird process by which a body with a voice suddenly fancies itself as a mind.' So speaks the handsome and famous young playwright in *All About Eve* (1950), and through him Joseph L. Mankiewicz (born 1909), the film's writer-director. The word 'author' might be appro-priate here. If film-makers can be classified by their preference for the word, the image, or the performance, Mankiewicz is certainly a proud resident of the first group: the 'screen playwrights' who see talking pictures as an extension of theatre, with the author controlling both the staging of his work and the movement of all those 'bodies with voices'.

During his peak years at mid-century, when he won consecutive writing and direct-ing Oscars for *A Letter to Three Wives* (1949) and *All About Eve*, Mankiewicz wrote gen-uine 'screen plays', full of resounding fury that always took care to Signify Something, whether the inequity of oil depletion allow-ances or the banality of radio drama. The cadences of his most characteristic films—*A*

Letter to Three Wives, All About Eve, The Barefoot Contessa (1954)—spring from the theatre (soliloquies) rather than from the movies (stichomythia). At its best, this tendency can produce the effect of a dazzling after-dinner conversation over some good port. At other times, it numbs viewers with the logorrheic rhythms of a long-winded orator. But, as Mankiewicz would say, 'People will talk.' And talk . . .

It took a twenty-year apprenticeship in Hollywood before Mankiewicz was allowed to seize control of his own films. Not that he was cast in the mould of his self-destructive elder brother Herman, whose fate it was to write *Citizen Kane* and a sheaf of I.O.U.s. Joe's demons (early in his career) were more mundane: Louis B. Mayer and his pride of MGM moguls. At twenty Joe was writing intertitles for the silent versions of sound films; at twenty-two he was nominated for an Academy Award; at twenty-seven he was the producer of *Fury* (1936). If Mankiewicz had been blessed with the soul of an accountant, he might have rejoiced at achieving an important administrative position. But he wasn't cut out to rewrite other people's scripts (even Scott Fitzgerald's); and although he contributed mightily to such MGM successes as *The Philadelphia Story* (1940) and *Woman of the Year* (1942), Mankiewicz refers to that seven-year tenure as his 'black years'.

Mankiewicz had to follow his mentor, Ernst Lubitsch, to Fox to be allowed to direct. After still more prentice work—this time as director of amiable Gothic romances of the order of *Dragonwyck* (1946) and *The Ghost and Mrs Muir* (1947)—he found his stride with the series of social satires for which he is most fondly remembered. For all their limitations as cinema, *A Letter to Three Wives* and *All About Eve* are quintessential Hollywood movies, with all the glamour and brittle sophistication of the best American high comedy. And *Five Fingers* (1952), for which he did not receive a writing credit, is something more: a graceful blending of political intrigue and sexual politics, with as mordant a tone as any of the black comedies it prefigured.

With his hot-house ironies, Mankiewicz was in full flower; but the bloom was fast fading from the Hollywood rose. The studio system was breaking down. Directors who had once glided from project to project, steered by a Hal Wallis or an Arthur Hornblow, Jr, now found themselves inexorably concerned with nuts-and-bolts production problems. Mankiewicz directed a dozen films in the eight years from *Dragonwyck* to *The Barefoot Contessa*; he has made only seven films since—another, more painful two decades of waiting for a break. He now inhabits that Leisure Valley of veteran *metteurs en scène* for hire, and in a final irony is now appreciated for his visual felicities. The body with a mind is suddenly fancied as having an eye.

More About All About Eve (1972) is a colloquy by Gary Carey with Mankiewicz; it also contains the screenplay of *All About Eve*. Mankiewicz's later films are not entirely negligible: there were pleasant moments in *The Honey Pot* (1967); among his early films one might also mention *The Late George Apley* (1947) and his uncharacteristically gloomy but still fascinating *House of Strangers* (1949).

In 1978, there appeared a definitive biography of Mankiewicz: called *Pictures will Talk*, and written by Kenneth L. Geist, it may tell one more than one wants to know about Mankiewicz, but it is none the less a fascinating study of how Hollywood worked, and why it does not in the same way any more.

ANTHONY MANN
Robin Wood

Anthony Mann's place in the American cinema is assured by the group of Westerns he made with James Stewart in the 50s, and their magnificent successor and summation, *Man of the West* (1958). One tends to honour his other films according to the degree to which they relate to these, finding considerable interest in *Men in War* (1957) because of its treatment of psychological tensions in and between men under stress, and some in the late *The Heroes of Telemark* (1966) because of its feeling for mountainous landscapes, the challenge they represent and the effort they demand. The great exception is *El Cid* (1961), whose thematic relationship to the Westerns is less obvious. But it is on the

Westerns that appreciation of Mann's achievement must centre.

When Mann died in 1967, at the age of sixty-one, he was planning a film called *The King*, a Western version of *King Lear*, with the daughters translated into sons—a long-cherished project. It is the choice of play that is significant, and what of it might have survived such a transposition: the plot rather than the poetry. Mann gravitated repeatedly towards family tensions, rivalry and hatred between brother and brother, father and son. Sometimes his antagonists are literally brothers: *Winchester 73* (1950), the first of the Stewart Westerns, in which a man seeks revenge on his own brother for the murder of their father, immediately established the archetypal Mann situation in its purest form. More usually, the characters are not related by blood, but become involved with each other in intense love–hate relationships characterized by mutual resentment and fascination, guilt and rivalry.

Retrospectively, one can see that Mann was already reaching towards *Lear* when he made the last of the Stewart series, *The Man from Laramie* (1955). Here the father (Donald Crisp) is, like Lear, preoccupied with the inheritance of his kingdom (the cattle range) and, like Gloucester, growing blind. The plot centres on the complex developing tensions between his real son (Alec Nicol), a vicious psychopath, his adopted son (Arthur Kennedy), a sympathetic figure of compromised integrity, and the 'pure' outsider (Stewart), bent on avenging the death of his own younger brother, who wins the old man's respect. Alerted in this way to look for possible transpositions, one cannot but see the scene in which the psychopathic son deliberately shoots Stewart's hand at point blank range while it is held still by 'servants' (the ranch cowboys) as Mann's rendering of the blinding of Gloucester: there is the same sense of moral outrage, of gratuitous excess, and the sequence ends with two of the 'servants', horrified at the action to which they have been a party, helping Stewart on to his horse. The sequence, with its sense of violation (the notion of castration is clearly implicit), its undertones of fraternal jealousy, and its disturbingly immediate rendering of violence and pain, can stand as representative of Mann's work at its most intense, though the

film as a whole is inferior to some of its predecessors, notably *Bend of the River* (U.K.: *Where the River Bends*, 1952) and *The Naked Spur* (1953).

There is another important aspect to the relationships between Mann's 'brother' figures: our sense of them as in certain respects mirror reflections of each other. At the outset of *Bend of the River* parallels are established between James Stewart and Arthur Kennedy: both are ex-gunfighters who have narrowly escaped hanging (Stewart bears the marks of the rope around his neck); both seek to reform and integrate themselves in civilization. From this common starting point the two men develop morally in opposite directions. The action moves inevitably towards their antagonism and confrontation, and the psychological implications of the conflicts in Mann's movies become clear: in destroying Kennedy, Stewart is violently suppressing a part of his own nature—an idea vividly expressed in the climactic fight, where the hero forces his *Doppelgänger*'s head down under the water of the tumultuous river in which they are struggling.

Personal tensions are always at the forefront of Mann's work, but the traditional themes of the Western—its historical/mythic concerns—incorporate them with ease. The struggle between primitive and civilized elements, the opposition of garden and wilderness, the suppression of lawlessness which may also be the suppression of natural vitality—in Mann's Westerns such tensions are dramatized in the conflicts between his 'familial' antagonists and, in the most powerful of his films, within the protagonists themselves. In *Man of the West*, Mann's greatest film and one of the half dozen or so 'essential' Westerns, all his major preoccupations are bound in a satisfying unity. The basis of Reginald Rose's screenplay is dangerously schematic in its allegorizing bent: the hero, 'Link' Jones (Gary Cooper)—the link between the old West and the new—is travelling from the new community of Good Hope to the established township of Fort Worth to hire a teacher for the newly built school. Link is a reformed gunfighter who used to ride with 'Dock' (the most tenacious of weeds) Tobin (Lee J. Cobb). During the journey the train is held up and robbed, and

Link, stranded in the wilderness with a showgirl and a gambler, returns to the gang's old hideout for shelter—to be welcomed back by Dock as a prodigal son. In effect, the strong, bold lines of the allegory provide Mann with an opportunity to develop with extraordinary force the tensions central to his art (together with his symbolic use of landscape, the progression from fertile valley to barren rock, from civilized community to ghost town, paralleling the development of the action). Link, having acquired civilization, is a convinced pacifist; step by step, he is forced into killing off the gang, member by member. The sense of violence as violation for both perpetrator and victim is pervasively present in the disturbing pain and messiness: the long, sustained public fight between Link and one of his 'brothers', as the rest of the gang look on, culminating in

Link's stripping the other man of his clothes, reveals a response to humiliation that evokes the Bergman of *Sawdust and Tinsel*. Fundamental to the pain is, of course, the sense that the gang members are at once Link's *alter ego*s and family, as well as civilization's dark, suppressed underside. The film's fusion of Freudian and Western mythology can be typified in a single image: the moment when the train stops for water, and the gang surge up from the darkness under the railroad.

Our sense of the necessity for Link's annihilation of the gang is qualified everywhere by an equally strong sense of betrayal. Link's opposite is Claude, the 'brother' who has stayed with the gang out of loyalty to the 'father', Dock. Yet Link is the favourite son, who broke Dock's heart once by leaving, and, in the inevitable final confrontation, will

'The long, sustained public fight between Link (Gary Cooper) and one of his "brothers", as the rest of the gang look on, culminating in Link's stripping the other man of his clothes, reveals a response to humiliation that evokes the Bergman of *Sawdust and Tinsel* (*The Naked Night*).'

gun him down. The intensity and grandeur of Cobb's performance, and the heightening effect of Mann's crude, but strong and eloquent, images, again evoke Shakespeare— or, rather, what Shakespeare means to Mann; the moral–emotional effect could be likened to a *Lear* which ended with Cordelia gunning down her father.

Jim Kitses (to whose magnificent essay in *Horizons West* anyone who thinks or writes about Mann's work must be indebted) suggests that Mann's 'over-reaching' led him logically to the epic. And indeed, *El Cid* is the most fully realized and satisfying of the 'period' epics with which Hollywood in the early 60s faced the challenge of television. It stands, however, partly to one side of Mann's achievement. Its central theme is the cost of heroism: the way in which the demands made on the heroic figure deprive him of his flexible, living humanity, until he ends as (literally) a rigid corpse strapped to a horse, leading his men to victory. The theme is powerfully rendered, but the film lacks the ultimate intensity of Mann's finest, and most disturbing, work because it lacks the fallible, divided protagonist to whom he naturally gravitated. The film is an impressive addendum to his achievement rather than its crown.

Another 'marginal' film by Mann that deserves mention is his early The Tall Target (1951), with its fascinating evocation of Lincoln's troubled progress to Washington for his first inauguration. Jim Kitses' Horizons West (1970), cited by Wood, is indeed the best source for further reading on Mann; there is also Philip Hardy's Aspects of the West (1969). In French, there is Jean-Claude Missiaen's Anthony Mann (1964).

CHRIS MARKER

Richard Roud

Chris Marker's life (he was born in 1921), like those of Godard and St Paul, can be divided into two parts. The first part was as a member—indeed the sage—of the group known as the Left Bank—which included Agnès Varda and Alain Resnais. The Left Bank: not so much an area, more a state of mind. It implies a high degree of involvement in literature and the plastic arts.

(And, indeed, before he made films Marker had gained some reputation as a novelist and editor at the Editions du Seuil.) It implies a fondness for a kind of Bohemian life and an impatience with the conformity of the Right Bank. A centre of the *avant-garde* and a cosmopolitan refuge since the turn of the century, it has also been traditionally frequented by the political Left. The Dôme was not only a rendezvous for Picasso, Joyce and Hemingway; Trotsky and Lenin were also *habitués*.

Marker's early work reflected the social and artistic climate of the neighbourhood; his work of recent years has been almost exclusively politically oriented. But he has always felt that personal problems and emotions should be seen in a social context, and his early films all dealt more or less directly (albeit in a highly individual manner) with political and social issues.

His first four films were *Dimanche à Pekin* (1956), *Lettre de Sibérie* (1958), *Description d'un Combat* (1960) and *Cuba Si!* (1961). 'I write to you from a far-off country,' begins the letter from Siberia, and each of these shorts was a letter, an essay, a declaration. More than any other director, Marker fulfilled Astruc's famous prophecy of the *caméra-stylo*, writing films as one writes a book. But the most remarkable thing about his film essays is that their fascinating, maddening, highly literary commentaries (Malraux + Giraudoux divided by X) seem neither to have preceded the shooting of the films nor to have followed it. Image, text and idea seem miraculously to have been created simultaneously. Although the commentaries have been published, they only take on real meaning when one has seen the films. The great episodes—like the parade in *Cuba Si!* which transforms itself into a jubilant conga line, or the parodies of communist–capitalist propaganda in *Lettre de Sibérie*—hardly come over on the printed page. And yet Marker was constantly accused of being over-literary and precious. But what wasn't he accused of! *Cuba Si!* was banned in France and Germany; *Les Statues Meurent Aussi* (1950–53), which he co-directed with Resnais, was available only in a truncated version for over a decade. And yet one felt that Marker made his films not so much as propaganda, not so much to convince others, as because he felt the need to express what he personally felt about China, Russia, Israel and Cuba. And if he had ever made his *L'Amérique Rêvé*, we would have seen realized his life-long obsession with America, including its comic strips—all part of his fascination with the image, in whatever form it appears: Mandrake or Miró. 'Images, portents, signs.' But Marker's calligraphy was also made up of music, animation, poetry, colour: every technique, every effect was conjugated and the result was a kind of one-man total cinema, a 1 to 1 : 33 Montaigne.

Le Joli Mai (1963) marked a break in his *oeuvre*, although this was not immediately apparent at the time. But one should have realized that the transfer of his attention from far-off lands to Paris was significant. Also, although in this film we still hear Marker's voice, we hear those of many other people as well. Superficially the film could be described as *cinéma-vérité*—a group of interviews with Parisians on their reactions to the events of May 1962—the Salan trial, the anti-O.A.S. riots, etc. And it is, extraordinarily, that. But the linking sequences show us Marker's Paris, now an ant-hill covered with bustling grubs, now (as in the funeral of the O.A.S. victims) a tragic stage worthy of Epidaurus. Nevertheless, this was a more objective film than any he had previously made.

The next three films were a return to the more personal manner: *La Jetée* (U.K.: *The Pier*, 1963), *Le Mystère Koumiko* (1965) and *Si J'avais Quatre Dromadaires* (*If I Had Four Dromedaries*, 1966). It is perhaps significant that two of these films were made up entirely of stills.

La Jetée runs only about half an hour, but many still feel it to be Marker's greatest achievement. It has been described by Robert Vas as 'an intellectual essay in style and feeling, about a childhood memory pursued through past and future, always lost and always growing. The film achieves its unity of form and content by the extraordinary way it uses still photographs, the split second pinned down for eternity ... this is more than just a pocket version of a Resnais subject; its evocation of horror (of a third world war which destroys Paris) is frightening and clinical, and finds a touching counterpart in its vision of love and beauty.'

Le Mystère Koumiko was less interesting,

perhaps because it concentrated entirely on the person of a rather uncommunicative Japanese girl, Koumiko. What the film had to say about her was never as interesting as what it had to say about Japan. The first period of Marker's work closed with the little-known *Si J'avais Quatre Dromadaires*. Or, as it could be called, especially since the Apollinaire reference is pretty obscure, Around the World in 800 Photographs with Chris Marker. And the film is in fact made up solely of 800 still photographs. But—and once again the Marker miracle was operative—commented on by three voices, punctuated by music and articulated by the master editor Marker, it became his most totally personal film. The commentary was unmistakably his: apropos the American pavilion at the Moscow Fair, he remarks, 'It was made to look as if Abraham Lincoln had married Marilyn Monroe, who then gave birth to lots of little refrigerators.'

It was in the year following this film that Marker underwent some kind of crisis in his life, one sufficiently important for him to decide to give up film-making as an individual and henceforth to work only as part of a group. This *crise de conscience* was not immediate, and it was also compounded by political events in France. But, as with Godard, it curiously foreshadowed the events of May 1968. Already in early 1967 Marker had organized a collective to make *Loin du Vietnam* (*Far from Vietnam*). The film's episodes were directed by Godard, Resnais, William Klein, Joris Ivens, Agnès Varda (her episode was dropped) and Claude Lelouch, but the organizer of the concept was Marker, and he supervised the editing. In order to produce the film, Marker formed a company, or rather an association, called SLON. After *Far from Vietnam*, SLON lay dormant until a few months before May 1968, when it produced a film called *A Bientôt j'espère* which dealt with the problems of workers at the Rhodiacéta factory near Lyon. This was followed by *Classe de Luttes* (1970), made by the SLON group but this time with the collaboration of the workers themselves. Then SLON went on to encourage workers to make their own films, and they achieved a surprising degree of success in this attempt.

At this point, I suppose, an article on

A surrealistic shot from Marker's most realistic film: *Le Joli Mai*.

Chris Marker should close; one can guess at the major contribution he made to some of the later SLON films like *Le Train en Marche* (U.K.: *The Train Rolls On*, 1971), which was made to introduce the feature *Happiness* by Medvedkin. But since Marker wants to preserve his anonymity, or rather to submerge his personality into a group effort, one should respect his wish. But this phase may not last for ever. Marker is trying to get enough money to produce a film of his own, *Le Fond de l'Air est Rouge*. This will be a montage film, using not only documentary material but also footage Marker has shot himself over the years. The third act begins?

The third act began a little ahead of schedule, not with *Le Fond de l'Air est Rouge* (1977), but with a documentary about Yves Montand, *La Solitude du Chanteur de Fond* (1975). Something of an *oeuvre de circonstance*, its interest is somewhat dependent on one's interest in Yves Montand.

Marker's 'screenplays' have been published in French under the title of *Commentaires*, Volumes I and II (1961 and 1967).

THE MARX BROTHERS

André Hodeir

Among other booms ended by the Depression in 1929 may be mentioned the essentially visual comedy of character and situation which contributed so much, through the films of Chaplin, Langdon, Keaton, and Laurel and Hardy, to the palmy days of the silent cinema. This type of comedy (surviving anachronistically into *Modern Times*, 1936) then gave way to a 'comedy of the absurd' which, after a period of gestation in the theatre, was to find its definitive form in the context of the sound cinema.

Flourishing over a very short period—to reappear only on rare occasions with successors like *Hellzapoppin'* (1942)—the comedy of the absurd was also confined to a very small number of films: some of the W. C. Fields comedies, and more particularly the Marx Brothers' Paramount series (1929–33), five films of variable quality but with the last, *Duck Soup* (1933), being one of the masterpieces of slapstick comedy.

Coinciding with the Depression, the Paramount series is the focal point of the Marx Brothers' career. Before it, these down-at-heel clowns had conquered Broadway during the good years of the 20s. After it, Irving Thalberg turned them into internationally famous stars whose comic routines were slotted after a fashion into big commercial musical productions, sometimes very successfully, as in *A Night at the Opera* (1935). Of the five Paramount films, two—*Cocoanuts* (1929) and *Animal Crackers* (1930)—are adaptations of hit musical comedies in which the Marx Brothers had appeared; the other three, *Monkey Business* (1931), *Horse Feathers* (1932) and *Duck Soup*, have no antecedents in the theatre. Each of them is constructed round the Marx Brothers as a group and in terms of the group, with the evident aim of enabling the group to achieve maximum comic effect. But it is only with the fifth film, *Duck Soup*, that this procedure is rigorously applied. *The Cocoanuts* is cluttered with the debris of musical comedy,

and so to a lesser degree is *Animal Crackers*; in *Horse Feathers* and *Monkey Business* the prominence given to a totally unnecessary juvenile lead, and a certain tendency for the plot to stray, detract from the purity of the comedy. Of course, certain sequences in these films attain a very high level of comic brilliance, just as marvellous routines still survive in the later ones; but the conjunction of greatest comic brilliance and purest script occurs in *Duck Soup*, which is also by far the best directed of the Marx Brothers' films (it was directed by Leo McCarey). *Duck Soup* therefore stands as a perfect synthesis of the art of the Marx Brothers; and it seems legitimate to limit a study of this art to an examination of its essential characteristics as revealed in this film.

The absurd being the fundamental principle of the world in which the Marx Brothers evolve, nothing could be more difficult than to conceive a coherent action or plot into which their corrosive counter-action could be inserted (for the Marx Brothers are demolitionists by vocation). Yet this is what the scriptwriters Harry Ruby and Bert Kalmar succeeded in doing, with the aid of dialogue-writers Arthur Sheekman and Nat Perrin and doubtless—though to what extent it is impossible to say—the Marx Brothers themselves. In *Duck Soup*, where the song and dance routines are annexed to the comedy, the time-honoured interludes featuring Chico the pianist and Harpo the harpist would be out of place: their surroundings are so perfectly adapted to them that they can develop their incongruities without resorting to these *temps morts* which slow down their other films so tiresomely. The action, as distinct from the comic process, exerts no pressure on the comedy, being almost a motif woven along the way by the gags themselves as they unfold and begin to accumulate.

1933: the year in which Hitler seized power. The economic crisis was at its height and would ultimately bring world war. A virulent political satire, *Duck Soup* begins with the crisis and ends in war.

Supporting the Marx Brothers are the regular inhabitants of their films: the wealthy, idealistic widow (invariably played by Margaret Dumont), ready to melt under the pressing gaze of King Leer-Groucho; the treacherous ambassador representing the enemy country; the alluring vamp who spies. The Marx Brothers themselves are divided into two pairs, initially on opposite sides but eventually joining forces. Groucho, the *arriviste arrivé* and a stranger to all proprieties, is accompanied by his secretary Zeppo (devoid of any comic talent, Zeppo, like his brother Gummo, soon abandoned the cinema; this was his last role). In a way this master–slave couple prefigures the Pozzo–Lucky relationship in *Waiting for Godot*; but Beckett was to give the slave more prominence. Equality, on the other hand, reigns in the Chico–Harpo pair, the general factotums who work for the ambassador as spies. The person they are spying on, of course, is Groucho, who has just been appointed leader of the government. But the conception held by Chico and Harpo of their profession as spies is not without analogy to Groucho's conception of statesmanship. The fatality

that governs the world of the absurd means that the other characters, though not without certain qualms, finally come to accept them in spite of their eccentricities. A brilliant twin exposition establishes the nature of this relationship right from the beginning of the film: appointed prime minister, Groucho makes a travesty of his office and annihilates his colleagues; visiting their employer, Chico and Harpo submit his person to a bizarre aggression. The latter scene, one of the craziest anyone has ever dared put on the screen, is a perfect précis of all the major Harpoisms: the scissors, the motor-horns, the blowlamp, the alarm clock, the rat trap, the mask with articulated eyes—all this paraphernalia is brought into play here with an effectiveness explained by the abruptness and very swift tempo of the scene.

That *Duck Soup* is so unusually effective is partly due to the fact that the tempo peculiar to each scene is so precisely calculated.

Harpo Marx and Edgar Kennedy as the peanut seller and the lemonade vendor in *Duck Soup*: 'the scene has a permutational structure which foreshadows the scene with the hats in *Waiting for Godot*'.

Margaret Dumont (for once made happy, if only temporarily, by the monstrous Groucho) in *Duck Soup*.

With the Marx Brothers, tempo is never systematic. The difference in tempo between the second introductory scene and the one in which Chico and Harpo, plying their trade as spies, are seen selling peanuts under Groucho's window, introduces an indispensable element of contrast since the two scenes are variations on the same theme, with Chico and Harpo now heaping indignities on an unfortunate lemonade vendor instead of the ambassador. The difference between the two scenes lies in the adoption for the second of a slow Laurel and Hardy tempo and a permutational structure which foreshadows the scene with the hats in *Waiting for Godot*. Each permutation is ritually punctuated by Harpo offering the vendor a 'leg-shake'. As the scene develops, so the tempo accelerates. Interestingly, there is a backwash to this scene a little later on in the film, in a sort of coda from which Chico is eliminated. Confronting the vengeful vendor alone, Harpo triumphantly puts an end to hostilities by taking a foot-bath in the lemonade. And towards the end of the film it is from another bath that Harpo emerges sounding the trump of war. The three sequences are thematically related, but the last two are treated antithetically: whereas Harpo's preparations for his foot-bath are explicitly shown, the only warning of his emergence from the bathtub full of water comes from the soundtrack. The comic situation is treated here with a remarkable economy of means.

The first introductory scene, during which Groucho slides down into the council-room by way of a fireman's pole—thus making his entry into frame from above—is one of the most cunning traps ever set for an audience. This trap derives, not from the situation as in some of Jean Genet's plays—in fact the situation has been quite scrupulously defined in a short prologue—but from the style of the film. Before Groucho's appearance, we are established in a musical comedy kingdom with due pomp and circumstance and fancy dress characters, and it looks as though we are about to embark on an operetta, with the chorus standing stolidly round in groups awaiting the arrival of the new prime minister. This very stagy and deliberately archaic scene is in fact an extremely subtle gag which introduces comic heterogeneity into a film that is absolutely unified in style. *Duck Soup* begins as another film: the film it isn't.

The meeting between the two pairs takes place comparatively late in the film. Groucho, bored in his premier's office, invites the peanut vendor Chico to come to see him. In this scene the dialogue attains the heights of absurdity, perhaps more quintessentially even than in the house scene in *Animal Crackers* because more revealing of the characters' subconscious. In this connection the importance of the dialogue in the Marx Brothers' films cannot be too highly stressed. For the first and perhaps the last time in the comic cinema, the explosive quality of the dialogue—over and above the puns and travesties that sustain it—matches that of the images. With Chico, exceptionally, Groucho abandons the bombast and the insults he showers on the other characters to talk to him as an equal. Then Harpo, the only great silent character in the talkies, tackles Groucho in his turn, and the interrupted dialogue reconstitutes itself on another level. The scene acquires a poetic, almost oneiric effect: the comic devices—like the glimpse of a live dog's head among the tattoos on Harpo's back: a rare Marx Brothers borrowing from the animation film—belong to the world of unreality. Harpo's scissors seem invested with a magic power, and are implicitly responsible for the marvellous off-screen gag which closes the scene: after Harpo leaves, Zeppo enters, doubtless having passed him in the lobby, and he is wearing one half of a straw hat on his head.

After this the plot comes to a head around the increasing animosity between Groucho and the ambassador, who are both suitors for the hand of the rich widow. In vain she attempts to reconcile them. Three times Groucho slaps the ambassador. 'This means war!' the latter finally declares. Meanwhile, Chico and Harpo are trying to effect a nocturnal entry into the villa where the national defence plan is hidden. Concealed behind a hedge, they wait for the butler to answer their ring and come out into the garden. When he finds no one there, they will slip inside. But since the first brother to get inside closes the door in the other's face, the one outside has to start the manoeuvre all over again. This time his brother opens the door and comes out into the garden where he finds no one there, and so on. The mechanism of the scene, whose mainspring is the permutation principle (echoed by the music), recalls the scene on the landing in Georges Feydeau's *Le Fil à la Patte*. But the comedy in Feydeau's farce is situation comedy (the man in his underpants can't get back to his own room), whereas in the hedge scene it is purely structural comedy.

Chico and Harpo have managed to get into the villa; Chico has contrived to lock Groucho in his bathroom; unknown to each other, both Chico and Harpo decide to disguise themselves as Groucho. And since Groucho eventually manages to get out, before long there are three identical Grouchos —moustache, glasses, cotton nightcap and long nightshirt—prowling round the villa, going into the wealthy widow's bedroom, sometimes meeting there, which means that one of them has to hide under the bed (a favourite Marx hiding-place, inherited from vaudeville). Harpo tries to open a safe, actually a radio set, which suddenly blares out a stentorian military march. Harpo reduces the radio to fragments, but with no effect on the noise, so he has to throw it out of the window. This scene is a preliminary sketch for the best musical number the Marx Brothers ever did: the destruction by Harpo, in *A Day at the Races* (1937), of a grand piano on which he plays, with the delicacy of a series of depth charges, Rachmaninoff's 'Prelude in C Sharp Minor'. In *Duck Soup*, the only instrumental number—happily very brief—takes place at the villa: inspired when a music box suddenly starts to play, Harpo plucks the strings of a piano and elicits from it a few chords . . . of harp music.

The sequence at the villa ends with the most brilliant moment in the film, the mirror scene. By breaking the big mirror in the salon, Harpo sets up the encounter between Groucho and Chico-disguised-as-Groucho; and the brothers go into a celebrated circus routine, here appreciably embellished, which was first filmed by Max Linder. From the outset Groucho is very well aware that Chico is not his reflection, and Chico knows that Groucho knows. Nevertheless, defiantly taking up the challenge, or maybe just for the hell of it, they launch into the mirror routine. Groucho tries to catch Chico out, only to have him reproduce the most unlikely

gestures and attitudes to perfection; and when Groucho suddenly spins round, catching Chico off-guard, the latter mimes the end of the movement. Here the audience can see more than the two adversaries; so when Groucho holds a white hat behind his back, we see that Chico has only managed to have a black hat in readiness—but when he claps the hat on his head a moment later, it is a white one, thus trumping not only Groucho but the audience. The scene takes on an unexpected new dimension when Chico drops his hat and Groucho courteously hands it to him, thus passing through the imaginary mirror. Then comes the marvellous gag in which, making a slow turning movement, they each take the other's place. This simple exchange carries us over the frontiers of the fantastic, and we are held spellbound until the charm is broken with the whirlwind arrival of the third Groucho (Harpo) to bring the scene to an end.

After this moment of high poetic intensity—the scene is silent: it contrasts vividly with the rest of the film, in which there is a great deal of dialogue—the film relapses into the commonplace with the trial sequence. In surroundings where the serenity of Justice is to be severely tried, before a tribunal composed of a splendid array of magistrates and grotesque military, Chico and Groucho confront each other. They toss riddles back and forth, offer odds on the verdict. But Groucho doesn't take long to cross the bar: taking his place by Chico's side in a symbolic gesture, he appoints himself counsel for the defence. The rapprochement between the two pairs is now complete: the Marx Brothers will henceforth present a united front against the world.

The trial is interrupted by the war. Patriotic fervour erupts in a picturesque ballet set in motion first by Harpo as a magnificent drum major, and then by the four brothers in a choral scene in which the borrowings from American folklore make the kinship between the imaginary country where the action takes place and the real one where it was conceived unequivocally clear. Unlike the other Marx Brothers films, the irruption of musical comedy here—loftily but antithetically motivated by the declaration of war—neither breaks the rhythm nor dilutes the style. The Marx Brothers remain in the foreground; it is simply another aspect of their comic genius that is revealed to us.

After Groucho, decidedly allergic to the ambassador (as he had been to Chandler in *Animal Crackers* and would be to Gottlieb in *A Night at the Opera*), has aborted a last attempt at reconciliation—the psychological mechanism of anger is displayed here with great comic subtlety—it only remains for battle to commence. As war descends on the land, Harpo rides like Paul Revere through the countryside on horseback to declare the state of mobilization. In the evening he finds lodgings with a girl, and the camera reveals Harpo's shoes, his landlady's slippers and his steed's four horseshoes ranged at the foot of the bed before showing us—supreme glorification of the Hays Code—the man and woman in bed separated by the horse. This analytical panning shot followed by an overall view of the scene is one of the finest comic effects made possible by cinematic vocabulary. It is, as a matter of fact, highly unlikely that a more mobile or more 'intelligent' camera could improve on the comic mastery of the scene. It is one which could only be realized on the cinema screen: what more can one ask of it?

Finally the war explodes, implacable and insane, with its onslaught of tanks, cross-country runners, baboons and porpoises, its sandwich-men parading on the battlefield, its shells entering one window at HQ and going out by the other until Groucho testily pulls down the blind. Leo McCarey very skilfully sets realistic details off against the extravagant fantasies of the Marx Brothers. Chico, the minister of war, checks in on the ministry timeclock like a metal-worker. Groucho fires on his own troops, and when Zeppo points this out, gives him five dollars to buy his silence, then takes them back to buy his own: the whole history of corruption is told in this single exchange, which lasts only a moment. The tempo accelerates, effects are left increasingly unstressed: unlike Laurel and Hardy's, Marxian comedy is based on the avoidance of excess.

The final sequence takes place in the villa. Having come to the rescue of the wealthy widow, the Marx Brothers find themselves surrounded by the ambassador's troops. Shut up by mistake in an ammunition dump, Harpo stages the fireworks scene from *Les Vacances de M. Hulot* twenty years before its time by blowing up the ammunition. Groucho is crowned by a jug which comes down over his ears: his spectacles and moustache are painted on it before it is blown off with dynamite (and he thus continues to reign over a kingdom growing smaller by the minute). Soon the first enemy soldiers appear: they are brained, classically. But the next person to appear is none other than the ambassador himself. Wedged in the doorway, he undergoes a terrible bombardment of baked apples. 'I surrender,' he cries. At these words, the widow launches into a full-throated song of victory. After a moment's hesitation, the Marx Brothers begin hurling their apples at her. Thus the closing gag of the closing sequence resolves the fundamental ambiguity of this deeply subversive film. Who is the real enemy? The ambassador? The answer is both the ambassador and the widow: bourgeois society.

And in fact, over and above the satire on political mores, it is bourgeois society that is under fire from all the Marx Brothers' films, but *Duck Soup* in particular. The position of 'respectable' people is under constant assault—from within by Groucho and from without by Chico and Harpo. Under pressure of ridicule, such people are forced into situations where they feel ill at ease. The cabinet meeting early on in *Duck Soup* is particularly significant in this respect, even more so than the various society receptions that are a notable feature of the Marx Brothers' films. Groucho's nonchalant way with the problems of government not only suggests, in an anarchist-style critique (of democratic principles? of dictatorship?), the futility of all decisions; it also tends to deny the ministers their importance, even their very existence. And unlike Chaplin or Keaton, the Groucho character never presents himself as a victim of society. On the contrary, he is an avenger, a ruler. Marx the Magnificent: the description could apply equally well to Chico or Harpo, although they come lower down on the social scale. The Marx Brothers are no losers; they rarely raise laughs at their own expense (one instance comes, however, when the momentarily victorious lemonade vendor empties the contents of a horn into Harpo's trousers; but a little later on Harpo burns the vendor's hat). They do not excite pity like

Keaton or Chaplin; they do not hold themselves up to ridicule like Laurel and Hardy.

With Groucho's painted moustache,
Chico's hat, Harpo's wig, they are out of the
ordinary run of men, on the fringes of the
world. As clowns, they can cheerfully acknowledge their baser instincts, display their
dishonesty without any loss of face. Whether
they are taking part in a society bridge party
as in *Animal Crackers*, or stealing a game of
chess from two unfortunate passengers in
Monkey Business, they reveal themselves to
be not only cheats (like W. C. Fields in *Tillie
and Gus*) but impostors. Harpo's hand contains thirteen aces of spades, and he plays
them calmly one after the other. Likewise, in
the scenes with the sidecar in *Duck Soup* (the
only example, to my knowledge, of a recurring gag in the Marx Brothers' films), the
vehicle always splits in two and it is always
the half containing Groucho that remains in
shot. In these cases the context is so charged
with nonsense that these bizarre events
provoke almost no reaction. The reign of im-
posture is absolute.

But the madness of the Marxes is not
always so sedate. There are chases in pursuit
of over-irresistible girls. There is the scene in
the customs shed in *Monkey Business* where
Harpo, clambering over a desk, wildly
stamps every bald head in sight with the official seals. Another moment of lyrical mania:
the celebrated cabin sequence in *A Night at
the Opera*, an expanded variation on one of
the best sequences in Buster Keaton's *The
Cameraman*. Sometimes it is the world that
goes mad around the Marxes, as in the scene
in *Animal Crackers* where, in a hall with two
doors, one opens on to a rainy landscape, the
other on brilliant sunshine: an extraordinary
suggestion that beyond the screen there lies a
world completely different from ours.

The Marx Brothers' style of comedy gave
birth to no successors worthy of consideration. Perhaps they only made one film, and
that film, oddly enough, had very little
success at the time: after *Duck Soup*, Paramount did not renew their contract. Yet this
film, unique in intention and in performance,
and in the density and profusion of the gags
that sustain it, should suffice to ensure an
imperishable glory for the Marx Brothers.

Translated by Tom Milne

A little necrology, first: Chico, born in 1887, died in 1961; Harpo, born in 1888, died in 1964. Groucho, born in 1890, died in 1977; before his death he occasionally appeared on television and in concert, never more memorably than at a memorial evening for T. S. Eliot in London during which he read a few of the *Old Possum* rhymes and some of his correspondence with Eliot. The later films, for the record, were: *A Night at the Opera*, *A Day at the Races*, *Room Service* (1938), *At the Circus* (1939), *Go West* (1940), *The Big Store* (1941), *A Night in Casablanca* (1946) and *Love Happy* (1950).

The bibliography is extensive, and in-cludes *The Marx Brothers* by Raymond Durgnat (1966); *The Marx Brothers: Their World of Comedy* by Allen Eyles (1969). Then there are the autobiographical works: *Groucho and Me* by Groucho Marx (1959), *Harpo Speaks* by Harpo Marx (1961) and finally *The Groucho Letters* by Groucho Marx (1967).

GEORGES MÉLIÈS

David Robinson

Georges Méliès, a nineteenth-century Paris magician and *prestidigitateur*, can properly claim the title of the cinema's first artist. Undoubtedly he is the earliest artist working in the medium whose films can still be revived, sixty and more years after the last of them was made, with pleasure and without apology, standing firmly on their own intended merits. This durability is not the less remarkable since in contrast to his con-temporaries Méliès was (and became increas-ingly in the course of his career) something of a reactionary. His contemporaries were es-sentially pioneers, developing a new inven-tion and techniques of the new century. Méliès, though he brought so much that was new to the cinema, was essentially exploiting it as an extension of existing theatrical forms. His cinema was the culmination and conver-gence of a number of nineteenth-century theatrical traditions.

Nevertheless, the very fact that Méliès

sought to link the cinema with older *theatrical* forms was in itself original, and the root of his most significant discovery— simple and obvious as it may now seem. It is difficult now to realize the very considerable delay before the first cinema showmen perceived the theatrical possibilities of the new medium. It was thought of as a scientific curiosity, a toy as amusing but no more useful than the zoetrope or the praxinoscope or the other elementary moving picture novelties of the Victorian nursery. It could equally be regarded as a novel adjunct to the magic lantern—an unusually elaborate form of lantern slide, in fact; but the magic lantern was only in a limited sense a theatrical entertainment. The repertory of the early film-makers was inspired by picture postcards and stereoscopic views rather than by the theatre: *High Seas at Brighton, Arrival of a Train, Demolition of a Wall.*

Méliès' discovery was that scenes could be *staged* for the camera in a theatrical way: the film-maker need not restrict himself to moving snapshots taken from life. This explains his pride, to the end of his life, in being the '*créateur du spectacle cinématographique*'.

He was born in Paris in 1861. His father was a well-to-do footwear manufacturer; and at seven Georges was sent to the Lycée Michelet at Vanves, near Paris, where he stayed till 1879 when he went to do his military service. In later years he was at pains to stress this 'literary formation', to refute, as he said, 'certain articles in which younger writers about the cinema have accused the pioneers of cinematography of being mere "primitives", illiterates incapable of producing anything artistic'. Writing about himself, rather quaintly in the third person, Méliès goes on to say, in his manuscript *Memoirs*, 'Méliès was driven by the demon of drawing; and was often punished for this artistic passion, which was sometimes stronger than himself . . . While he should have been ruminating on a French composition or a Latin verse, he would be scribbling portraits or caricatures of his teacher and school friends, when he was not creating palaces of fantasy and strange landscapes which already had a theatrical air about them . . . Before he was ten years old he was making puppets and pasteboard theatres . . . and getting beaten for them, too.'

To discourage his artistic ambitions, his father, who wanted him to go into the family business, sent him to London to perfect his English. From his father's point of view the results were disastrous. Méliès took the opportunity to absorb new theatrical impressions; and to avoid the strain which the regular spoken drama placed upon his small command of the language, he frequented those entertainments—of which London in the mid-80s offered plenty—where there was not much to listen to but plenty to see. He must have gone to the Royal Aquarium, to the Crystal Palace, to the Christmas pantomimes, to the Alhambra (which was then celebrating the restoration of its music-hall licence with the presentation of new and more elaborate ballet spectacles) and to the newly opened Empire which at the time of Méliès' London stay was showing a French musical play, *Chilbéric.*

'He went particularly,' he later recalled, 'to the Egyptian Hall, directed by Maskelyne and Cooke, a theatre devoted to prestidigitation, to fantasy plays and to big scenic illusions. This devotion to the Egyptian Hall made him a great enthusiast for magic. He began to work hard at it himself and added the art of illusion to his artistic baggage. On his return to Paris he started to go regularly to the Magic Theatre which had been founded by the great French magician Robert-Houdin.'

Completely hooked, Méliès became a magician himself. He appeared at the Musée Grévin and the Galerie Vivienne. When in 1888 the Théâtre Robert-Houdin itself came up for sale, Méliès, whose own considerable fortune had been augmented by a rich marriage, leased the theatre. He proved a worthy successor to its founder; he was elected president of the Chambre Syndicale des Artistes Illusionistes, and held the office for forty years.

Installed in his own theatre, he was not only proprietor and manager, but producer, actor, designer, author and conjuror. The entertainments he presented reveal the variety of his theatrical interests and anticipate the character of his films. Conjuring in the mystical and decorative manner of Robert-Houdin mingled with the new, more sceptical and pseudo-scientific style of Maskelyne and Cooke. The pantomime-spectacles of the

Eden and Châtelet theatres (from which Méliès was later to recruit his *corps de ballet*) met the more English manner of the Alhambra ballet and the English pantomime.

By the time of the historic first Lumière film show, in December 1895, Méliès had been in command of his own theatre for seven years. As he recalled it: 'In 1895, at the invitation of Louis Lumière, he attended the first cinema show, and was thrilled by the sight of the earliest moving photographs. He asked to buy a machine for his theatre, but Lumière *père* refused.' According to Méliès, Lumière's words were: 'Young man, you should be grateful that I refuse, since, although my invention is not for sale, it would undoubtedly ruin you. It can be exploited for a time as a scientific curiosity, but apart from that it has no commercial future whatsoever.'

Undeterred, Méliès discovered that R. W. Paul in England was marketing a rival invention, and he bought a projector from Paul. He acquired a crate of Eastman film stock and set himself to make his own camera. Initially he saw the moving picture as a novel addition to his repertory of spectacle and illusion. Soon it was to supplant his magic theatre as his primary interest. As a filmmaker Méliès delighted in his versatility. Just as in his theatre he had been all things, he was now producer, director, scenarist, designer, cameraman and generally actor (a good actor too: his performances remain valid in their easy relaxation while his contemporaries, even his collaborators, tend to look the most fearful hams). He designed and built the world's first true film studio, an outsize glass-house at Montreuil-sous-Bois. There, between 1896 and 1914, he made over a thousand films, ranging from three-minute conjuring tricks to twenty-minute stories and spectacles. His letter-heading indicates the range of his repertoire: '*Spécialité de Vues et Transformations, Trucs, Féeries, Apothéoses, Scènes Artistiques, Scènes Fantastiques, Sujets Comiques, Scènes de Guerre, Actualités, Fantaisies, Illusions, Etc.*'

Méliès remained a magician, however, and it was as a magician that he arrived at some of his most influential discoveries. Approaching the problems of film-making with the ingenuity of a professional illusionist, he worked out, long before anyone else, a whole tech-

nique of motion picture trickery. He claimed to have discovered the trick of substitution one day when the film stuck momentarily in his camera while he was shooting a Paris street scene. When the film was projected, a hearse seemed suddenly and comically to take the place of a bus. Whatever the truth of this, when he came to shoot his first trick film, *Escamotage d'une Dame chez Robert-Houdin* (*The Vanishing Lady*), in the autumn of 1896, he accomplished it not by the methods he would have used on the stage of his theatre, but by stopping the film and making the necessary substitutions.

He ingeniously adapted to the cinema such photographic tricks as multiple exposure. (Significantly, trick photography was included in Albert Hopkins' *Magic*, a well-known manual of the 90s with which Méliès was certainly familiar: a number of his film illusions, including *L'Homme à la Tête de Caoutchouc* [U.K.: *A Swelled Head*; U.S.: *The Man with the Rubber Head*, 1902], were suggested by illustrations in Hopkins.) No one has ever used multiple exposure with such elegance and virtuosity as Méliès in his masterpiece *Le Mélomane* (*The Melomaniac*, 1903). In this the hero—played of course by Méliès—is a diabolic music master. Each time he removes his own head it is replaced by another, so that he is able to throw a whole series of grimacing, chattering heads up on the telegraph wires where they perch as the musical notation of 'God Save the King'. In *The Man with the Rubber Head*, in which the hero (Méliès again) inflates his own head to massive size, double exposure is again used, along with the effect of magnification attained by tracking-in towards an object—a technique readily suggested by the then venerable device of the phantasmagoria magic lantern.

Méliès' enduring attraction lies deeper than ingenuity, however. His trick films have marvellous pace, rhythm and variety. Insects and butterflies metamorphose into voluptuous hour-glass beauties. Devils come and go in puffs of smoke. The magician produces from small and mysterious coffers the furnishings of a garret or a palace, or an entire Châtelet chorus-line. Often there is a dream or nightmare fantasy, which explains the enthusiastic discovery of Méliès by the surrealists of the 1920s.

In the *féeries* and fantasy films these same trick techniques are wedded to *mises en scène* conceived in the appealing Victorian baroque of the Châtelet or Alhambra ballets. Among the subjects—two versions of *Cendrillon* (*Cendrillon* [*Cinderella*, 1899] and *Cendrillon ou la Pantoufle Mystérieuse* [*Cinderella, or the Glass Slipper*, 1912]), *Le Royaume des Fées* (U.K.: *Wonders of the Deep*; U.S.: *Fairyland, or the Kingdom of the Fairies*, 1903), *Barbe-Bleue* (*Blue Beard*, 1901), *Le Palais des Milles et une Nuits* (*The Palace of the Arabian Nights*, 1905), *La Fée Carabosse ou le Poignard Fatal* (*The Witch*, 1906)—were several already familiar at those theatres. In the fantasies, *Le Voyage à travers l'Impossible* (U.K.: *Whirling the Worlds*; U.S.: *An Impossible Voyage*, 1904), *20,000 Lieues sous les Mers ou le Cauchemar d'un Pêcheur* (*Under the Seas*, 1907), *A la Conquête du Pole* (*Conquest of the Pole*, 1912) and the earliest, most famous and most beautiful, *Le Voyage dans la Lune* (*A Trip to the Moon*, 1902), the Châtelet style is irresistibly combined with Jules Verne. In at least one case Méliès was directly associated with a Châtelet production. In 1906 the theatre presented a fairy ballet by Victor de Cottens entitled *Les Quatre Cents Coups du Diable*; and Méliès was commissioned to make two film inserts which could be shown while the stage scene was being changed. Afterwards he was permitted to build a film of his own around the fragments; and *Les 400 Farces du Diable* (*The Merry Frolics of Satan*, 1906) includes some of his most inventive designs, including the haunting skeleton coach which careers through a sky of painted clouds and stars which beam with the faces of turn of the century beauties.

For present-day audiences one of the oddest and most charming aspects of Méliès' productions is his reconstructed actualities. Ambitiously he reconstituted the eruption of Mont Pelée and a visit to the submarine *Maine*, by means of models—the second subject being filmed entirely through a gold-fish tank. The climax of his career as a history-stager came in 1902 when the Warwick Film Company of London commissioned him to stage the coronation of Edward VII, which could not at that time have been filmed in the gloom of the Abbey, even if permission had been given. Méliès gamely constructed Westminster Abbey in his little studio, found a waiter who looked like the King and a Châtelet *danseuse* for the Queen, and delivered to his customers a film which had an excellent success in the British music halls and (it is said) gave great amusement to the King himself.

It is important to recognize that such reconstructions of actuality were in no way intended as deceptions. As the early film-maker saw them, they were the equivalent of the artists' impressions through which illustrated magazines had presented the events of the world to their readers before photographic reproduction became general.

Thus, in his little studio Méliès created a whole unique and peculiar universe. He made images of this world as well as of lands of fairies and witches and demons. He recreated the present. He recreated the past —in *Le Civilisation à travers les Ages* (*Humanity Through the Ages*), a 1908 anticipation of *Intolerance*. He created the future in *Le Tunnel sous la Manche ou le Cauchemar Franco-Anglais* (*Tunnelling the English Channel*, 1907) and *Le Voyage dans la Lune*. His world was self-contained and self-sufficient. He himself painted every house and every tree and every leaf. The extent of this self-sufficiency becomes apparent when in his second *Cendrillon* he shoots a couple of outdoor scenes; and the intrusion of the real world of hedges and trees and breezes is startling.

Ultimately, the claustrophobic self-sufficiency of his world, and his inability as time went on to change his methods, were the cause of his downfall. By the time of the First World War, audiences which had adored his *Voyage dans la Lune* had tired of Méliès. They already preferred Feuillade's thrillers and the new American slapstick comedies—films that took in a world wider than Méliès' 20-foot stage could comprehend. Costs of production had risen. Pirates had cut his profits. Already the cinema was the world of big businessmen rather than of the solitary artist. Méliès was forced to join the giant Pathé organization, and finally to give up production altogether. He turned his studio into a theatre where he struggled on for a few more years. In 1923, he recalled: 'Méliès, his daughter, son, son-in-law and his two little granddaughters, the youngest barely four months, left the family home for

Méliès did not only make fantasy and trick films: 'for present day audiences one of the oddest and most charming aspects of Méliès' production is his reconstructed actualities. The climax of his career as a history-stager came in 1902 when he was commissioned to stage *The Coronation of Edward VII*, which could not at that time have been filmed in the gloom of Westminster Abbey, even if the permission had been given. It is said that the film gave great amusement to the King himself.'

ever and with no hope of ever seeing it again. For this estate with its fine park was split up and sold off in lots. At the very same time the Théâtre Robert-Houdin was to vanish to make way for the Boulevard Haussmann, and Méliès was obliged to shift all his theatre equipment, as well as everything from his shop, which was also to be demolished. Fate pursued him. What could he do with all the crates containing the hundreds of negatives which were the work of years? He had nowhere to put them, and no money ever to resume his job as a film-maker. In a moment of anger and exasperation, he ordered the destruction of the whole lot.'

Late in the 20s Méliès was discovered keeping a little toy kiosk in the Gare Montparnasse. He became news, and was fêted with a special Méliès Gala at the Salle Pleyel. A whole new generation learned to marvel at his inventions. He was awarded the Cross of the Legion of Honour at the hands of Louis Lumière, who himself named Méliès '*Créateur du Spectacle Cinématographique*'. Ironically, it was another four years before anyone thought of rescuing Méliès from his little kiosk ('open to all the winds, in a courtyard, icy in winter, torrid in summer . . . martyrdom for a man already aged'). Finally in 1932 he was found a place in a home for cinema veterans at the Château d'Orly, where he spent his last years in some kind of comfort, with his second wife and former leading lady, Jehanne d'Alcy. He even appeared before the cameras again, in a couple of publicity films. He kept on drawing as he had always done, and at the very end of his life, in the hospital where he died on 21 January 1938, he was designing a film.

As more and more tinted prints of Méliès films have come to light and have been shown more widely, our opinion of him simply as a graphic artist has continued to rise. An exhibition put on by the Cinémathèque Française at the Museum of Decorative Arts in Paris a decade ago confirmed his talent as draughtsman and colourist.

There is one book in English on Méliès: Paul Hammond's *Marvellous Méliès* (1974); and several in French: Madeleine Malthète-Méliès' *Méliès, L'Enchanteur* (1973) and George Sadoul's monograph *Georges Méliès* (1961). See also the article in the Dictionary on French Cinema: Origins.

JEAN-PIERRE MELVILLE

Tom Milne

In 1966, after nearly twenty years as a film-maker, Jean-Pierre Melville achieved his first major box-office success with *Le Deuxième Souffle* (U.K.: *Second Breath*). A tough, brutal thriller about an ageing gangster who escapes from jail determined to prove that he is not yet finished, it not only established Melville's reputation as a brilliant refurbisher of the immemorial imagery of the genre—gleaming night streets, raincoats with bulging pockets, gunmen prowling in deserted stairways, cars hurtling along the highway—but also revealed a new, classical control in his style. The opening sequence of Gu Minda's jail-break, in particular, is handled with a sense of rigorous withdrawal which inevitably recalls *Un Condamné à Mort s'est Echappé*: the grey half-light before dawn; stark, angular concrete walls; warders prowling on their rounds; three men on the roof, waiting, tensing themselves for the moment of escape; and finally the sudden, joyous break for freedom. Here, and in the indefinable sense of grace—not God's perhaps, but humanity's—which hovers over Gu as he destroys himself in pursuit of his integrity, more than one critic saw the influence of Bresson. To which Melville, characteristically and as it happens not without justification, retorted: 'I'm sorry, but it's Bresson who has always been Melvillian.'

It is only one of several paradoxes that Melville, self-confessed Americanophile, Hollywood *aficionado*, and himself almost a movie-hero in his Texas-style Stetson and dark glasses, should make films which are invariably and unmistakably French, no matter how much inspiration they may draw from American models. Even when he went to America to make *Deux Hommes dans Manhattan* (1959), a thriller in which a French journalist and a news photographer pursue a story about a mysteriously vanished diplomat through a sleazy, neon-lit New York night of callgirls, night-clubs, lesbians, stage doors and recording studios, his dominant motif was a Cartesian concern for ethics: whether the photographer is justified in using brutality and deceit to secure the photograph which will clinch his scoop, and whether, contrariwise, when he is finally stirred in his conscience by a woman's tears and throws the photograph away, he is thereby betraying the code of absolute professionalism demanded by his job. In *Le Doulos* (U.S.: *Doulos—the Finger Man*, 1963), Melville copied one of his sets exactly from the police headquarters in Mamoulian's *City Streets*, and the bars, subway entrances and street lamps are all American; but the ambience of the film is otherwise entirely Parisian, so that the action seems to be taking place in a limbo of doubt which echoes the theme of duplicity. Again Melville is concerned less with the thriller mechanism than with the Pirandellian moral tangle (in which we never do reach a final truth) posed by an informer's divided loyalties to two friends, one a crook on the run and the other a police inspector. And *L'Ainé des Ferchaux* (1963) remains Melville's most persistently underrated film, probably because the plot is casually allowed to suspend itself at crucial moments such as the arrival of the two runaways in New York, when the camera embarks on a sentimental journey in search of the house where Frank Sinatra was born. Apart from one or two obligatory exteriors, the entire film was shot in France, and to make sense it must be seen primarily as a dream of America, the exploration of a fantasy, rather than as a thriller in a real landscape.

The second paradox is that like so many supposedly tough, cynical observers of a predominantly masculine milieu, underworld or otherwise—Hemingway is an obvious example—Melville is at heart a tender romantic. The sense of honour and absolute loyalty which motivates crooks like Bob Montagné in *Bob le Flambeur* (1956), Gu Minda in *Le Deuxième Souffle*, even Faugel and Silien in *Le Doulos*, is much more than a sentimental cap doffed in the direction of that cliché of the gangster film, the criminal code. One of Melville's most moving films is *L'Aîné des Ferchaux*, where the tragedy begins precisely because old Ferchaux (Charles Vanel) comes to rely totally and exclusively on the loyalty he assumes in the young strong-arm man (Jean-Paul Belmondo) he has hired and grown to love. In *Le Deuxième Souffle* there is a terrifying scene where Gu Minda, confronted in the police station with the colleague he has been tricked into betraying, goes literally berserk, thrusting his handcuffed wrists through a window-pane and hurling himself head first against a steel filing-cabinet, as though by destroying himself he could wipe out the memory of his one inadvertent lapse from grace. Yet this is the man who commits seven murders, more or less in cold blood, in planning and executing the robbery which will not only prove that he is still the man he always was, but allow him to retire in comfort. No attempt is made to whitewash him morally; yet in the context of the film it is difficult to quarrel with the epitaph he is given after he has died in pursuit of his self-imposed quest for perfection, and through it, the love and respect of the *milieu*: 'He is a danger to society, but he has preserved a sort of purity.'

A sort of purity: it is this that attends all Melville's heroes in their struggle to achieve the impossible. It is why the French girl in *Le Silence de la Mer* (1947) can return the German officer's love even when she cannot accept it. It is what Paul has and Elizabeth covets in *Les Enfants Terribles* (*The Strange Ones*, 1950); what Bob le Flambeur has but thinks he has discovered only at second-hand in the young couple he watches so tenderly as they sleep in his apartment; what the young priest has in his tactful appraisal of both Barney's love and her religious conversion in *Léon Morin, Prêtre* (U.K.: *Leon Morin, Priest*, 1961); what Maurice Faugel has in his cold rage when he thinks Silien has be-

trayed him in *Le Doulos*; and even, in an odd way through his blind faith in Michel Maudet, what the old banker in *L'Aîné des Ferchaux* has. It is, too, why the hired killer arranges his own death at the end of *Le Samourai* (U.K.: *The Samurai*; U.S.: *The Godson*, 1967), having fallen in love with the one flaw in his otherwise perfect armoury.

The third paradox is that Melville's first five films, from *Le Silence de la Mer* to *Deux Hommes dans Manhattan*, saw him enshrined as a sort of spiritual father to the *Nouvelle Vague*—an innovator in techniques of low-budget film-making—which enabled him to thumb his nose at the industry and to make his films exactly as he wanted without worrying about producers, circuits or middlemen. Then suddenly, almost in a spirit of contradiction, it seems, since the *Nouvelle Vague* was by then at flood tide, he announced with his sixth film, *Léon Morin, Prêtre* in 1961, that he was tired of being the darling of a handful of *cinéastes*; and his subsequent films saw him repudiated by the younger generation of film-makers as he set out deliberately to address a wider audience. Although the subject of *Léon Morin, Prêtre* gave initial cause for doubt—it was adapted from Béatrix Beck's novel about a girl who falls in love with a handsome young priest—in the event it turned out to be a sober psychological study, primarily concerned with the spiralling frustrations caused by the German Occupation and having little in common with the facile pietism of such films as *Monsieur Vincent*. Coming as it did after the easy, freewheeling charm of *Bob le Flambeur* and *Deux Hommes dans Manhattan*, films dominated by the sheer joy of film-making and by the location shooting which enabled Melville to write them as love-letters to Paris and New York, the very sobriety of his approach to this film disconcerted his admirers, obscuring the fact that *Léon Morin, Prêtre* was in fact, stylistically and thematically, a direct development from *Le Silence de la Mer*.

An entirely outlaw production, since Melville had no union card, no authorization to buy film stock, and no rights to Vercors' novel, *Le Silence de la Mer* was an act of defiance in more ways than one, and not least because Vercors' story was, as Melville remarked, essentially anti-cinematographic.

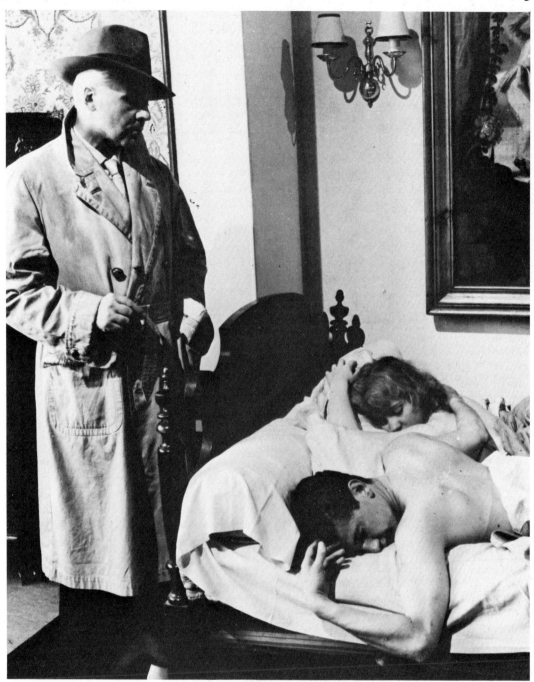

Bob le Flambeur: 'A sort of purity attends all Melville's heroes in their struggle to achieve the impossible; it is what Bob le Flambeur has but thinks he has discovered only at second-hand in the young couple he watches so tenderly as they sleep in his apartment.'

Dramatically, it is virtually a monologue by the German officer, a musician billeted on an old Frenchman and his niece, who have sworn never to address the invader; a monologue in which they listen, mute and unresponsive, as he pours out his feelings about music, his hopes for France and Germany, his gradual, despairing realization of the truth of the war; a monologue in which, mysteriously sparked by some tangential meeting between his words and her silence, a love is born. Melville's solution, which was later taken over and polished to perfection not only by Bresson but by Dreyer in *Gertrud*, was to use his images as notations to the presence of an unwritten melody: 'I wanted to attempt a language composed entirely of images and sounds, and from which movement and action would be more or less banished. So I conceived the film a little like an opera ...' *His* words which increasingly cry out for the right to be silent; *her* silence, increasingly crying out for the power of speech; the uncle's calm voice bridging the gap with a veiled, neutral commentary; the sense of absolute stasis in which the German's awaited arrival every night, simply to stand in the doorway and think aloud, explodes like a tidal wave of movement in the still, quiet sitting-room. In *Le Silence de la Mer*, everything happens beneath the surface.

There is a touch of Racine about *Le Silence de la Mer*, a tang of pure poetry which is unique in Melville's work, except perhaps for his second film, *Les Enfants Terribles*, which he directed at the request of Jean Cocteau, who wrote the novel. In this film Melville is again so entirely beneath the surface, so inside the characters and the mysterious forces they are unaware of being driven by, that the commentary spoken by Cocteau, such an integral part of his own *Orphée*, time and again here becomes tautological. This is particularly evident in the scene where the ball of poison arrives from Dargelos, and the camera's sudden hesitant, fascinated impulse towards the mysterious object shrouded in newspaper precisely expresses the attraction–repulsion of this symbol of death which Cocteau's voice duly records. But it is equally apparent in sequences like Paul's strange, restless prowl through the billiard-room dragging his blankets behind him,

part animal and part somnambulist, which preludes his retreat to a private lair; or the discovery of the 'strange gallery which leads nowhere', made magical by the fragment from Bach which *exactly* punctuates the journey of the characters across the hall and up the stairs until the moment of Elizabeth's invocation: '*Et maintenant, admirez!*'

'At that time,' Melville later remarked of *Le Silence de la Mer*, 'I wasn't afraid of poetry in the cinema. Now it terrifies me. I realized that poetry in the cinema is dangerous the day André Gide saw my film ... At the screening it was obvious that he wanted them to rush into each other's arms.' Joke or not, this remark perhaps explains Melville's subsequent practice of filtering his poetry through a thick, busy plot line, usually of thriller origin, which is firm enough to stand in its own right. *Bob le Flambeur*, for instance, is a brilliantly constructed *policier*, an ironic variation on *The Asphalt Jungle* in which a carefully planned robbery of a casino goes wrong—or possibly right—when the amiable gambler–mastermind breaks the bank before his gang can break into it, and may or may not be able to enjoy his legally gotten gains depending upon whether he can be proved technically innocent of intent to rob. Beyond this, however, the film is also a superbly evocative portrait of Montmartre in the hour of the wolf, of the people who live by night, the borderline between lawfulness and crime, the hospitably sleazy bars, the tired detritus of young girls and sailors and ageing gamblers vanishing at dawn with the water-cart. And beyond this again echoes the heart of the matter, Bob's morose self-reproach when he catches the glimpse of his ageing, unshaven face in a mirror—'*Belle gueule de voyou!*'—which provokes his despairing attempt to prove to himself that his life means, or at least has meant, something.

Melville's approach is perhaps best illustrated through *Le Samourai*, not only his most accomplished film but also by way of being a blueprint for all his later work (not excluding *L'Armée des Ombres*, 1969, in which the exploits of the Resistance in Occupied France have the stamp of the gangster on them). In the opening sequence, a man (Alain Delon) lies stretched out on a bed, almost invisible in the darkened room. He is Jeff Costello, a hired killer. There is a soft,

Alain Delon in *Le Samourai*: 'not only Melville's most accomplished film but also by way of being a blueprint for all his later work'.

squeaking noise which turns out to be a budgerigar in a cage, a faint glow which proves to be a burning cigarette; otherwise darkness as of the grave until one's eyes grow accustomed to the light and the man gets up, slowly and unhurriedly, and sets out to lay the groundwork for his next contract. Jeff is wholly self-contained, wholly ruthless and wholly efficient. He lives alone in the dingy, anonymous room with the budgerigar as his sole companion (and 'watchdog'), while the girl who loves him waits with resigned devotion in a luxurious apartment paid for by another lover, to serve him in the only way he asks, by helping to establish an unshake-able alibi. He executes his contract with clean, cold-blooded skill, strolling into a backstage office at a night-club, pulling the trigger, and walking evenly out again, paus-ing only to stare neutrally at a girl who happens to cross his path in the corridor. Taken

twice at a disadvantage by a hood sent to eliminate him, and again by a whole posse of police on his tail, he deals almost disdainfully with the opposition. Nobody, not even Hus-ton or Hawks, ever handled the mechanics of the thriller better than Melville does in such scenes, executed almost entirely without dialogue, as Jeff's theft of a car, un-hurriedly trying out ignition keys methodically detached one by one from a huge bunch on the seat beside him; the equally methodical preparations for his superbly ingenious three-part alibi; the encounter with the hood on a deserted railway bridge; or the fantastic tailing sequence in the Métro, a veritable manhunt with beaters to flush the game, trackers with communication devices to hold the trail, and guns waiting to seal every exit.

But Jeff Costello, as Melville pointed out, is already 'laid out in death' in the opening sequence. When he gets up from the bed, he is death set in motion. And the action of the film is the *hara-kiri* of the samurai who feels he has failed his code of honour. Traditionally, as in *Le Deuxième Souffle*, the world of the gangster film is a chiaroscuro one, bounded by night and the city, but this has largely gone by the board since colour became the rule rather than the exception in film-making. From its opening sequence, however, *Le Samourai* (only Melville's second film in colour, after *L'Aîné des Ferchaux*) might almost be a black-and-white film; then one notices that the packet of cigarettes, the banknotes, the labels on the bottles of Evian water in Jeff's room, have been drained of their colour to give them a listless, atonal quality echoing his livid, expressionless face and automaton movements. Throughout the film subsequently, colours are muted into a pearly range of soft blues and greys which is not merely an equivalent to Jeff's steely, passionless mind, but a mutation of the chiaroscuro of the city into something alien and unknown. Paris becomes a city of shadows, as silent and mysterious as Cocteau's *zone de la mort*; a place, in fact, where one is not in the least surprised to find Death herself waiting, beckoning the lonely samurai into her arms.

The girl from the corridor, a pianist in the night-club, haunts Jeff because he feels he should have killed her as the only witness to his crime, but didn't; and because she should logically have betrayed him to the police, but didn't. Beautiful and enigmatic, she tempts him into love. But when he returns to the night-club to see her, the barman's snide remark ('The murderer always returns to the scene of the crime, you might say') tells him that he has broken the first rule by which he lives and successfully exercises his profession: complete emotional anonymity. As in Cocteau's *Orphée*, the only meeting place for an impossible love is death; and whereas Orphée was called to the underworld by a beautiful white woman dressed in black, Jeff is summoned by his ravishing black pianist in a robe of dazzling white. But in Melville's world even fairytale romances are beset by betrayal and by the essential solitude of man. Jeff discovers that the pianist has inadvertently betrayed him, and that because she knows too much to be allowed to live, she has been assigned to him as his next contract. He carries out the commission calmly and faithfully, but with an empty gun, and is shot down by the police. It is a marvellous, indefinable moment: the *hara-kiri* of the samurai who has failed, the last gallant gesture of the knight errant, the helpless cry of despair of the man who wants to feel but cannot.

The impossibility of love, of friendship, of communication, of self-respect, of life itself: all the themes from Melville's work are gathered up in one tight ball in *Le Samourai*. Where you have two people, Melville says, one betrays. In his world, the only refuge from this betrayal is in solitude; but solitude, given man's instinctive need for human contact, leads back again in a vicious circle to betrayal. It is no accident that Melville's favourite film should be that classic of doom and double-cross, *The Asphalt Jungle*; or that—the fourth and final paradox—the work of this supremely and classically French filmmaker should hark back so insistently, in mood rather than style, to the dark, bleak despair of the *film noir* of the Hollywood 40s and what Robert Warshow called its 'dangerous and sad city of the imagination'.

Melville's last films after *L'Armée des Ombres* **were** *Le Cercle Rouge* **(U.K.:** *The Red Circle*, **1970) and** *Un Flic* **(U.K.:** *Dirty Money*, **1972). He died in 1973. Melville was not his real name; he had been born Jean-Pierre Grumbach in 1917, and it was the discovery of** *Moby Dick*, **which he read in Marseille during the Occupation, before he escaped to England, which made him change his name. With the exception of** *Le Samourai*, **I personally prefer the earlier films—everything up to** *Bob le Flambeur*, **not forgetting a little-known melodrama called** *Quand Tu Liras cette Lettre* **(1953). Melville makes a striking cameo appearance in Godard's first feature,** *A Bout de Souffle* **(***Breathless***, 1960).**

There is an excellent interview book, Rui Nogueira's *Melville on Melville* **(1971), which is packed with information about the director and his films.**

LEWIS MILESTONE

Richard T. Jameson

In the cinema of Lewis Milestone technique is mistakenly thrust forward as a substitute for style. Almost everywhere one looks, one finds evidence of an admirable cinematic intelligence, often capable of ingenious narrative invention. But far too frequently Milestone's penchant for theoretical experimentation derails rather than sustains the narrative, bending its course into academic *culs-de-sac* and, at worst, betraying the implicit logic of the director's topical intentions.

Milestone's strengths and weaknesses are both pointedly indexed in an oft-quoted sequence from *All Quiet on the Western Front* (1930), a universally honoured anti-war classic. One army defends its trenches as another charges across the empty waste of no-man's-land. The defenders spray the advancing enemy with machine-gun fire, and Milestone's camera tracks relentlessly across the attackers' path. As each enemy soldier is brought into camera range, he falls: it is as though the camera eye were synchronized with the mechanized pattern of gunfire, meting out death with an awful inevitability. And when, somehow, the attackers succeed in overrunning the trenches, drive out the defenders, and then become defenders themselves, with the first army counter-attacking to regain its own ground, Milestone repeats the visual device: another 'machine-gunning' camera chops down the soldiers on that side. The machinery of war devastates both armies with chilling impartiality, and Milestone's structure eloquently defines the tragic absurdity.

Or would have, if it hadn't been violated at midpoint. For as the enemy's second wave reaches the defenders' trenches, Milestone's camera performs yet another tracking manoeuvre, this time aimed down into the trenches as it moves along. And as the camera arrives at any given point on its course, so too does an attacker, leaping into the ditch and engaging in hand-to-hand combat with his opposite number. Technically, the device is impressive; conceptually, it is loathsome. Unlike the camera-as-machine-gun, there is no inherent logic in it. The co-ordination of the camera's arrival with that of an enemy trooper bespeaks no necessity beyond the director's design. A scene about the impersonal horror of war becomes a balletic speciality number.

It is biographically irrelevant but mythically appropriate that a director born near Odessa (in 1895) should have cleaved obsessively to an insistently montage-oriented style. Sadie Thompson's two entrances in *Rain* (1932)—her apparition in the door of her shipboard cabin and her painted restoration after temporary religious conversion—are abstracted into close-ups of gaudy high heels and jangling bracelets; when that Hecht-MacArthur 'bolt of lightning' strikes in *The Front Page* (1931), the weighted gallows grainsack drops right on to the lens in a shock cut; Murphy's and Bensinger's respective doses of 'slop on the hanging' are disposed in separate dead-air pockets rather than rendered in Hawksian depth-of-field living space; and Earl Williams' 're-enactment' of his crime escalates through intercutting with Hildy Johnson's 'farewell to the newspaper game'. The device is always conspicuous, the single narrative point is clear as of the first splice, but the completion of the editorial movement tends to increase one's sense of labour expended rather than of tension built.

But though Milestone entered movies as a cutter, his first pictorial experience came as a photographer's assistant, and from his earliest films he manifested a commendable concern for integral composition as well as shot juxtaposition. Foregrounds and backgrounds rarely go unfilled, and his frequently moving camera recedes or penetrates almost as often as it drifts laterally. He is at great pains to cinematize dramatic space even when, as in *The Front Page* or *Rain*, that space has been essentially ordained by a pre-existing theatrical text. When under less overt pressure to 'open up' an enclosed property his respect for whole space is even more persuasive: troops continue to move up outside doors and windows as his *All Quiet on the Western Front* recruits settle down for a breather, and a drought-blasted tree limb snaps off in the middle distance as his protagonists ride across the foreground of *Kangaroo* (1952). Such 'touches' may be no less flashy than razzle-dazzle montage but, by definition, the

Madeleine Carroll and Gary Cooper in *The General Died at Dawn*: 'the closest Milestone has come to suggesting an interesting narrative personality is, curiously, in the Sternbergian over-ripeness of *The General Died at Dawn*'.

very integrity of screen space makes a more lasting claim on the viewer's credence—which is to say that Milestone can be both efficient and effective as a straight action narrator.

The key films of Milestone's classic period (1928–45) accorded fortuitously with the prevailing critical desideratum of the time: that films should remain pre-eminently visual and mobile, resisting the tyranny of dialogue, while serving up redeeming social commentary. To an extent, Milestone's reputation as a serious film artist derived from the built-in topicality of Erich Maria Remarque's anti-war message in *All Quiet on the Western Front*; Hecht-MacArthur's professional insider's view and cynical political savvy in *The Front Page*; the inveterately suffering low-income societies of that baroque

cross-section of Depression survivalism, *Hallelujah, I'm a Bum* (U.K.: *Hallelujah, I'm a Tramp*, reissued as *Lazy Bones*, 1933), and that doomed romance of men and the land, John Steinbeck's *Of Mice and Men* (1940); and of course the cycle of wartime films: *Edge of Darkness* (1943), *North Star* (1943), *The Purple Heart* (1944) and *A Walk in the Sun* (1946). Only a commitment to competent craftsmanship distinguishes the director's job-of-work interludes, the routine comedies and adventure dramas which an authentically personal artisan like, say, Ford tended to make his own without half-trying.

Recent partisans of Milestone have suggested that his *auteur*ship is evident in a predilection for examining the dynamics of 'men in groups' in the style of Ford and Hawks—a dubious observation, since the dynamics of a Milestone group tend to be rhetorical above all, and in the last analysis any such 'predilection' seems to be a function of a general Hollywood concentration on male-dominated narrative plus directorial typecasting. The authorial excitement Milestone brought to his liveliest films is the excitement of technical exploration. Many of the devices of his early sound pictures seem dated and mannerist—bouncing-camera song accompaniment, dizzying 360-degree dollies which mostly prove only that 360-degree dollies were possible with blimped cameras if you worked at it hard enough—but they were honourable tries, good-sounding ideas that ultimately didn't work apart from the director's scrupulously employed storyboard, but absolutely had to be attempted, sometime, by someone. On the other hand, the swooping, rushing, craning, even (this was 1943) *zooming* coverage of action sequences in *Edge of Darkness* generated some of the most thrilling Second World War footage ever shot; and the brooding Earl Robinson ballad in *A Walk in the Sun*, laid over Russell Harlan's stunningly realistic photographic textures, pioneered a whole new approach to cinematic narration.

But the closest Milestone has come to suggesting an interesting narrative personality is, curiously, in the Sternbergian over-ripeness of *The General Died at Dawn* (1936) and the extravagant pseudo-orientalism of *The Purple Heart*, with its unlikely but quite exhilarating bursts of ritual samurai swordplay and face-saving assassination—as if Milestone had fictively glimpsed a life-style based on behavioural montage. If only Milestone, like Sternberg, had dealt with characters to whom form and style were the substance of life, his vigorous flamboyance might have led to lasting art rather than historically notable artefacts. Still, the vigour was always real. It is worth noting that, after years of interference and cancelled projects in the international film world of the 50s and 60s, Milestone's last work was done in the supremely technological medium of television: he wanted to see how it worked.

Seen today, *The Front Page*, in spite of Jameson's legitimate observations, does have a vigour and speed which were lacking in Billy Wilder's remake, even if it never approaches the genius of Hawks' switcheroo version, *His Girl Friday*. And *The Strange Love of Martha Ivers* (1946) remains one of the best of those woman-oriented *films noirs* that were so popular in the 40s. One third of *The Hollywood Professionals*, Vol. 2 (1974), by Clive Denton and others, is devoted to a study of Milestone.

VINCENTE MINNELLI AND THE 1940s MUSICAL

Gary Carey

Statistics support one of the oldest of Hollywood adages: the popularity of film musicals runs in cycles. The first craze for the genre died out in 1930, when the public became sated with the all-star, all-singing, all-dancing musical revue, a plethora of which had glutted the market in the first three years of sound. In September 1930 *Theatre Magazine* called these plotless extravaganzas 'rhapsodies in red', the colour referring to box-office accounts. Three years later *Forty-second Street* opened, Busby Berkeley and Fred Astaire came to town, and in their wake the musical regained its popularity.

By the end of the 30s, this second cycle of popularity was approaching its end. Berkeley had seen the palmiest of his Gold-Digging days and those on-again-off-again lovers, Astaire and Rogers, had finally called it a day, bidding farewell with *The Story of Vernon and Irene Castle* (1939), the least if not really the last (there was to be a brief reunion in the 1949 *Barkleys of Broadway*) of their musicals. The public was becoming increasingly bored with the endless variations these titans of the 30s musical wrought upon their respective formats. Variations were no longer enough to disguise what was all too frequently mere repetition. A whole new look was needed, and while it was aborning the film musical plodded along, cheerfully and tunefully enough, but without real distinction.

Berkeley was still around but he had exchanged his Manhattan babies for MGM's babes in arms, Judy Garland and Mickey Rooney, whom he directed in a series of teenage musicals (*Babes in Arms*, 1939, *Strike Up the Band*, 1940, *Babes on Broadway*, 1941), which have his peppy rhythm and his beloved backstage platitudes but little of his illustrative choreography with its invigorating use of space. Astaire was changing studios (MGM, Columbia, Paramount, back to RKO, finally roosting at MGM) as often as partners (Eleanor Powell, Paulette Goddard, Rita Hayworth, Marjorie Reynolds, Joan Leslie), but he never seemed quite at home either with his partners or with the story formats the studios devised for him.

The best of the early 40s musicals (finally achieving second place in the musical sweepstakes for the decade) were those made at 20th Century–Fox. These featured either the phlegmatic charm and plump figure of Alice Faye or the perky cheapness and dimpled knees of Betty Grable. Neither of these ladies was monumentally talented, but they were highly professional and appealing because of the aplomb with which they went through their limited paces. As ridiculously bedizened and cosmetically Technicolored as these films are, they are still charming today because of the ingenuous goodwill with which a lot of not so talented people threw together an instantly forgettable, pleasantly unpretentious entertainment.

There was a great deal of musical talent around Hollywood in the early 40s, some of it first-rate. Every studio had on its roster a number of musical performers. MGM was youth-oriented: it already had Garland and Rooney and soon imported from the New York stage Gene Kelly, June Allyson, Desi Arnaz, Nancy Walker and Vera-Ellen. Paramount added Betty Hutton, also from the Broadway stage, to such veterans of the 30s as Bing Crosby, Mary Martin, Bob Hope and Dorothy Lamour. Universal was content with easing Deanna Durbin through the uneasy stages of her late adolescence. RKO had little success in capturing the 78-rpm vocal magic of Frank Sinatra on celluloid (*Higher and Higher*, 1943, *Step Lively*, 1944), nor did they fare better with Anna Neagle in her bid for American stardom (*Irene*, 1940, *No, No, Nanette*, 1940, *Sunny*, 1941). Columbia had the dancing feet of Rita Hayworth and, in her support, Janet Blair, Lee Bowman and Larry Parks.

Much of the vitality of the early 40s musical came from its comedians—Eve Arden, Jack Oakie, Eric Blore, Frank Morgan, Charlotte Greenwood, Phil Silvers, Lucille Ball, Virginia O'Brien, Red Skelton and Billy De Wolfe—sometimes playing leads but usually adding colourful support for the (frequently) bland leads. It also gained a distinctive, campy flavour from the occasional appearances of such exotica as Oscar Levant, José Iturbi, Jerry Colonna, Carmen Miranda, Ethel Smith and Alexander Woollcott. 20th Century–Fox went on ice for Sonja Henie and MGM dived underwater for Esther Williams. Many films would include a supper-club scene, in which the heroine could sing with the big bands of Artie Shaw, Harry James, Tommy Dorsey or Xavier Cugat.

These slaphappy, slapdash musicals were constructed mainly around whatever talent happened to be loose and at liberty on the lot. Made up of a few gags, some songs and dances, and lots of colourful backgrounds (both nineteenth-century Americana and modern Latin America were popular settings), these films made little attempt to bind plot and musical values into a logical unit or to give them an overall unity of style.

The studios apparently thought of the musical as just another routine assignment in the overall yearly production schedule to be doled out to its regular contract directors, few of whom had any real affinity for the genre. Besides Berkeley, other exceptions were Mark Sandrich, the director of most of the Astaire–Rogers vehicles but whose other musicals show little individuality; and Victor Schertzinger, a former composer, who was more at home with old-fashioned operettas than with the livelier, more contemporary forms of the musical. The other main helmsmen of the early 40s musicals—Irving Cummings, Walter Lang, H. Bruce Humberstone (Fox); Roy Del Ruth, Charles Reisner, Norman Taurog (MGM); Claude Binyon, George Marshall, Mitchell Leisen (Paramount)—did their duties skilfully enough but with little distinctive personality. Several musicals of this period are signed by men whose directorial touch seems altogether too dark and dank for the insouciance and lightness needed for the genre: Michael Curtiz, Robert Florey, Edward Dmytryk.

One studio, or rather one studio head—Louis B. Mayer—was interested in the musical. MGM had had a great success in 1939 with *The Wizard of Oz* and, perhaps as a result, Mayer decided to start a musical production unit at the studio. To head it he chose Arthur Freed, a former vaudeville entertainer and song-writer, who had been associate producer on *The Wizard of Oz*. The unsung hero of the 40s–50s musical, Freed, with his production team at MGM, gave a new look and direction to the genre, recharging it with a host of young talents, many of whom he trained personally. All the great MGM musicals of the 40s and 50s were produced by Freed, and all the great musicals of this period were made at MGM. It is a prodigious record. Freed and his unit were, almost single-handedly, responsible for the second golden age of the movie musical.

Freed's first production was *Babes in Arms*, an adaptation of a Rodgers and Hart Broadway musical, directed by Busby Berkeley. For the next four years, Freed continued to work with Berkeley and lesser contract directors at MGM. Many of these early films are charming, none memorable, except perhaps for the soft-shoe charm with which Judy Garland and Gene Kelly (making his screen début) perform the best numbers in Berkeley's *For Me and My Gal* (1942). Certainly, none is innovative. Another musical of the same year, *Panama Hattie*, routinely directed by Norman McLeod, contains some strikingly designed musical numbers, the work of Vincente Minnelli.

Minnelli, born in 1913, had begun his career at the age of sixteen as a window decorator for a Chicago department store. Later, he designed costumes and settings for vaudeville, Radio City Music Hall and finally the Broadway stage. On Broadway, he graduated to direction. His theatrical design was noted for the influence of surrealism and other modern art, an influence he would carry over into his film work.

Minnelli came to Hollywood in 1940 at Freed's invitation. Under Freed's supervision, he worked for two years in various departments of picture-making. After this apprenticeship, Minnelli was given his first directorial assignment, *Cabin in the Sky* (1943). This musical fantasy—an injured black, lying near death, dreams that the forces of good and evil are struggling for the

possession of his soul—is typical of Minnelli's later work and the direction in which the MGM musical would travel. There is an obvious break with the backstage musical, moving song and dance logically into non-professional surroundings. (Because of Minnelli's commitment to fantasy, his musicals always have a rather rarefied, often recherché, atmosphere.)

The musical began to gain a whole new look. It was no longer a thin narrative thread used as the excuse to link together a number of solo turns, photographed in garish, haphazardly selected colours. Its book was intended to carry as much interest and weight as the songs and dances that grew out of it. Minnelli then approached the script in quest of, he has said, its 'appropriate style and mood', making the film a unified whole. Fantasy and the real are blended into a semi-real world, created through carefully chosen colour and highly stylized sets; the film becomes a logical setting for characters whose heightened emotions move them to express themselves through song and dance.

Minnelli's best film is his third, *Meet Me in St Louis* (1944). Aglow with nostalgia, the musical concerns the Smith family of St Louis during the year 1903. It is divided into four 'acts', one for each season of the year, all introduced by a tintype photograph from an old album which then springs to life. Minnelli here abandoned modern art to look back to Currier and Ives. Even the obligatory fantasy sequence, a young child's fearful visions on Halloween, have a charming, James Whitcomb Riley flavour. The style is absolutely right for the material, but it isn't all style, for the script is filled with a sweet humanity and an engaging vitality. These qualities supported Minnelli's pictorial bent and kept it from becoming affected.

It is possible to recognize Minnelli's importance to the 40s musical and still have reservations about the style he imposed on it. His acclaimed 'surrealism' and the painterly references he has strewn through his musicals can become, at worst, a low rendezvous with high art: often the actors look like overdressed mannequins who have come to life in a Fifth Avenue window display designed to impress as Chirico-esque. When a script allows the aesthete in Minnelli to reign unchecked, as in the more pretentious

Margaret O'Brien and Judy Garland in Minnelli's *Meet Me in St Louis*: 'aglow with nostalgia'.

segments of *Yolanda and the Thief* (1945), *The Ziegfeld Follies* (1946) and *The Pirate* (1948), the films become distressingly chi-chi and bloodless.

The best of Minnelli's later musicals is *The Band Wagon*, made in 1953. (The innovations introduced in the 40s film musical continued, with few variations and little advancement, well into the 50s.) *The Band Wagon*, alone among Minnelli's musicals, uses the tried-and-true backstage story, but with a difference. Scriptwriters Betty Comden and Adolph Green have admitted that *The Band Wagon* is a film *à clef*: the director, played in the film by Jack Buchanan, is undoubtedly based in part upon Minnelli. Specifically, his attempt to turn Goethe's *Faust* into a high-toned Broadway musical, complete with dazzling *Angst*-ridden sets, seems a good-natured spoof on Minnelli's own artsy-craftsy inclinations. When the

musicalized *Faust* flops out of town, not only is 'art' thrown out of the window but so is the story-line, and *The Band Wagon* follows suit: it becomes a glittering revue of boffo production numbers. The 'message' of *The Band Wagon* seems to be that the musical had over-refined itself; that, in its attempt to be taken seriously, it had become too serious, cutting itself off from its true *raison d'être*—the exhilaration that results when a gifted performer, for no particular reason, goes into a song and dance.

But whatever reservations one may have after the fact, it must be admitted that Minnelli's influence at the time was as beneficial as it was widespread. Other companies tried to copy his kind of musical (*vide* Columbia's *Cover Girl* in 1944) and certainly no one at MGM could ignore his example. George Sidney, whose career at MGM began at approximately the same time as Minnelli's, made a couple of undistinguished musicals before Minnelli provided him with a visual style he could emulate. His *Anchors Aweigh* (1945) uses an old-fashioned story and placement of musical numbers, but its overall look and staging have a bright, contemporary look. *The Harvey Girls* (1946) is a perfect imitation of a Minnelli musical, and its high-point, Judy Garland's rousing version of 'On The Atchison, Topeka and the Santa Fe', is almost a homage to Garland's singing of 'The Trolley Song' in *Meet Me in St Louis*. Sidney made several other highly entertaining, modish musicals, notably *Annie Get Your Gun* (1950), *Show Boat* (1951) and *Kiss Me, Kate* (1953), without ever evolving a style of his own.

Charles Walters and Stanley Donen to Hollywood from the New York stage. After a training programme similar to that which

Minnelli had pursued, these men became important additions to MGM's musical unit. Walters, a former dancer and dance director, worked on less expensive musicals than those generally assigned to Minnelli. Often they revert to old-fashioned conventions like the college musical—*Good News* (1947)—or the backstage story—*Easter Parade* (1948), *Summer Stock* (U.K.: *If You Feel Like Singing*, 1950)—consequently they are much more cavalier about the logical introduction of musical numbers into the plot. But for this very reason the musical numbers are more free and easy, more down-to-earth than those in Minnelli's films. Walters' musicals are buoyant, brash and brassy; in short, very American.

Stanley Donen, brought to Freed's attention by Gene Kelly, was also, like Walters, a dancer and dance director. Donen made his début as co-director with Gene Kelly on *On*

Cyd Charisse and Fred Astaire in 'the best of Minnelli's later musicals' *The Band Wagon*: 'the onslaught of ballet'.

Dan Dailey, Gene Kelly and Michael Kidd in *It's Always Fair Weather*, directed by Gene Kelly and Stanley Donen: 'the last of the important original screen musicals'.

the Town (1949) and they later collaborated on *Singin' in the Rain* (1952), arguably the best of all American film musicals. Both films have sparkling scripts by Comden and Green, who had ample opportunity to take satirical side-swipes at contemporary ephemera and showbiz folly, the mainstays of all these writers' best work. Kelly and Donen introduced a new look into the staging of musical numbers, since then overused and frequently ill-used: instead of keeping them in one specific area of space, they fragmented a song and dance routine, so that it was performed against a variety of different locales. (This technique is first used in the 'New York, New York' number at the beginning of *On the Town*.) Perhaps the most important aspect about these musicals is their emphasis on dance: these are all-dancing, some-singing musicals, and a song often seems no more than an introduction to a dance. Nor is

dance quite the proper term, here. This is choreography, with a nod occasionally to tap, soft-shoe or ballroom, but centring on balletic movement.

The ingratiating and lively Donen–Kelly musicals went astray only in their flat-footed courtship with ballet. Though Hollywood had been flirting with ballet for some time (George Balanchine had been re-imported to Hollywood to stage the dances for *Star-Spangled Rhythm* in 1942), it was not until the phenomenal success of *The Red Shoes* (1948) that its commercial potential was seriously considered. Not surprisingly, Minnelli was one of the first to act upon the possibilities. He ended *An American in Paris* (1951) with a big, pedestrianly choreographed and danced story ballet which literalized George Gershwin's symphonic jazz poem. With each of its scenes designed to evoke French artists of the Impressionist and post-

Impressionist era, the whole affair became a *beaux-arts* bon-bon with a hollow centre.

The onslaught of ballet continued. Big ballets became the *pièce de résistance* of *Singin' in the Rain* and *The Band Wagon*. The one in *Singin' in the Rain* starts promisingly enough as a take-off on a Busby Berkeley production number (the film is a spoof on the early sound days in Hollywood) but it goes soft when Cyd Charisse, draped in yards and yards of trailing tulle, goes *en pointe* and tiptoes through a Minnelli-esque fantasy setting. Henceforth, performers didn't go into their dance, they did a *jetée* into it, an effect Donen pushed to its limits in *Seven Brides for Seven Brothers* (1954). Kelly took it one step further in *Invitation to the Dance* (one episode of the film, *The Magic Lamp*, was

released separately in the U.K., 1956), a film that was all dance with no plot, no songs, no dialogue. *Seven Brides for Seven Brothers* was not the popular success MGM had expected; *Invitation to the Dance* was the total failure they had feared.

Kelly and Donen reunited with Comden and Green for *It's Always Fair Weather* (1955), a kind of extended epilogue to *On the Town*, and though it captures some of the vitality and infectious happiness of the earlier collaborations, it is, overall, rather calculated. It plays a bit too artfully with the wide screen, dividing it or reframing it through various masking devices. When Kelly attempts to recapture the ecstatic euphoria of the title number from *Singin' in the Rain*, he has to resort to roller skates as a varia-

Kay Thompson behind the desk, Fred Astaire coming through the door like St Veronica bearing the veil on which is imprinted the face of Audrey Hepburn in a scene from Stanley Donen's *Funny Face*. Carey calls it 'over-chic but pleasant'; I thought it was terrific. The 'Special Visual Consultant' was Richard Avedon—and it shows.

tion. It's the kind of variation that spells death.

It's Always Fair Weather is, in fact, the last of the important original screen musicals. The demise of the second golden age of the screen musical was hurried by the atrophy of the studio system of contract players and directors. The musical units of the studios fell apart and their talent wandered into other areas and directions. Minnelli made the over-dressed and *très* ooh-la-la *Gigi* (1958) and Stanley Donen the over-chic but pleasant *Funny Face* (1957), but both men worked mainly on non-musical projects, as did Kelly and Charles Walters.

There were fewer and fewer original musicals during the 50s and 60s. Instead there were the blockbuster embalmings of Broadway successes, the musical biography (*Love Me or Leave Me*, 1955), or essentially dramatic stories with musical interludes (George Cukor's *A Star Is Born*, 1954). Most of the film musicals of the 50s and 60s were directed by non-musical specialists, directors as diverse as Cukor, Joseph L. Mankiewicz, Robert Wise and William Wyler. Perhaps the film most representative of Hollywood's attitude towards the musical in this period was Billy Wilder's adaptation of *Irma La Douce* (1963), in which the songs weren't sung but reduced to background music.

By 1970, with the resounding thud of *Star!* (1968), *Paint Your Wagon* (1969), *Hello, Dolly!* (1969) and *Sweet Charity* (1969) shaking the very foundations of the studios that produced them, the film musical had once again become a rhapsody in red. Again, the fault lay less with a whimsical public than with the films themselves, which had shown no significant advance since the MGM musical of the 40s. If a new cycle of popularity is to appear in about five years, as Darryl F. Zanuck has predicted, it will need another Arthur Freed, and one with a radically new approach.

See also the articles on Dance in Film and Stanley Donen.
Carey's predictions about the return of the musical had already begun to be partially fulfilled thanks to Barbra Streisand, whose *Funny Girl* (1968) and *Funny Lady* (1975) (both romanticized versions of the life of Fanny Brice) were big hits, as was her *A Star Is Born* (1977). Minnelli's career bifur-

cated with intermittent success into comedy (*Designing Woman*, 1957) and drama (*The Bad and the Beautiful*, 1953, *The Cobweb*, 1955 and *Some Came Running*, 1959). The 60s saw his downfall with duds like *The Four Horsemen of the Apocalypse* (1962) and *The Sandpiper* (1965). Some critics defended *On a Clear Day You Can See Forever* (with Streisand and Yves Montand, 1970), but there were only a few to stand up for his return to the screen in 1976 (with his daughter Liza Minnelli) in *A Matter of Time*.
Minnelli has written his autobiography, *I Remember It Well* (1974), and there is a French study of his work by Marion Vidal, *Vincente Minnelli* (1973).

KENJI MIZOGUCHI
Donald Richie

Kenji Mizoguchi was born in Tokyo on 16 May 1898. After the early death of his mother—he was seventeen at the time—he left Tokyo for Kobe, where he designed advertisements for a living. He had been fond of drawing and painting since childhood and continued this interest all his life. He was not, however, truly interested in advertisements. Three years later, when he was twenty-one, he returned jobless to Tokyo. He did not at once succeed in finding work. Instead, he lived with, and off, an acquaintance who lived in Mukojima, the old section of Tokyo, across the Sumida River. This friend was a *samisen* teacher and often went to the Mukojima Studio of the Nikkatsu Motion Picture Company to give lessons and to act as an adviser on historical matters. Having nothing better to do, Mizoguchi would accompany him; he met several of the directors, and was eventually offered a job as an actor. There is no record of his ever appearing in that capacity and, in any event, he was shortly elevated to directorial assistant. Some thirty years later, during an interview, when a comment was made on the fact that he had totally forgotten some of his early films, Mizoguchi said: 'Yes, one does forget—at the same time, I will never forget my first day at work in the studio. I was nothing at all, but by the end of that day I knew that this was the work for me.'

There has long been disagreement about

just how many films Mizoguchi made between 1922 and 1956. Mizoguchi himself said he made 'only about seventy-five or so— not really very many'; but some researchers have put the number as high as ninety. There are several reasons for the confusion: studio records covering the earliest period were destroyed, either in the 1923 earthquake or during the 1945 fire raids on Tokyo; the press did not invariably review films during this period, nor were separate records kept of cast and credits; Mizoguchi's memory was not at all reliable and, in addition, he would disclaim films which he had actually made but disliked. Recent Japanese scholarship has put the total at ninety-three, but this figure is really no more trustworthy than the others.

In any event, when he began to make pictures the young director had little control over their content—though his very first, *Ai ni Yomigaeru Hi* (*The Day That Love Returned*, 1922), is surprisingly close, in story at any rate, to the much later *Chikamatsu Monogatari* (*The Crucified Woman* or *The Crucified Lovers*, 1954). His early films were based on popular stage successes, on light novels, on German novellas. He adapted the Cardillac story from *The Tales of Hoffmann*, did an Arsène Lupin adventure, made pictures based on newspaper cartoons and Eugene O'Neill alike. Later he was to say: 'I made my first film in 1921 [*sic*] and have been working at my craft for thirty years now. If I reflect on what I've done I see a long series of arguments and compromises with capitalists (they are called producers today) in an effort to make films which I myself might like. I've often been forced to accept work that I knew I wouldn't be successful with ... This has happened over and over again. I'm not telling you all this to excuse myself—the same thing happens to filmmakers all over the world.'

During the last decade of his life, Mizoguchi's studio, Daiei, was to offer him a freedom which was almost absolute, but in the early days he had to make so many films which did not in any way interest him that, as he himself said: 'It was only after *Naniwa Hikâ* (*An Osaka Elegy*, 1936) and *Gion no Shimai* (*Sisters of the Gion*, 1936) that I was able finally to learn how to show life as I see it.'

Life as he saw it resulted in the celebrated Mizoguchi 'style', one which was as eclectic

as it was beautiful and which remains, even now and for perhaps the majority of Western filmgoers, what the Japanese film is supposed to look like. Mizoguchi's identification with a purely Japanese way of seeing things began as early as 1927, when his 1926 film *Kyoren no Onna Shisho* (the French title, *L'Amour Fou d'une Maîtresse de Chant* well captures the feeling of the Japanese) was shown to French and German audiences, and was considerably reinforced by his later pictures, particularly *Ugetsu Monogatari* (1953). The Japanese, on the other hand, have never been so certain of the Japaneseness of Mizoguchi, reserving the title of most-Japanese for Yasujiro Ozu.

A director's style, of course, is not purely visual. It is both created and conditioned by what he makes most of his films about. In the work of Mizoguchi one finds that forty-six films out of an accepted total of ninety are either directly about women, or else are seen from the woman's point of view. At the same time one would hesitate to call him a 'woman's director', in any accepted sense of the term. Rather, in his finest pictures, and somewhat in the manner of George Cukor— another director commonly associated with the woman's film—Mizoguchi sees women as the best vehicle for the complaint he is making or the truth he is showing. He did not, therefore, make films for women, but about them.

It is interesting in this connection that Mizoguchi, who was later to create some of the cinema's most memorable women, first made pictures using only female impersonators. This was then the custom of Japanese cinema, which long remained under the influence of the stage—in acting styles, in the use of the *benshi* narrator, in the continued practice of men appearing in women's roles. There is even the story—never denied by Mizoguchi—that his roles, had he ever appeared as an actor, would have been female. (Teinosuke Kinugasa, who was thirty years later to become world-famous as the director of *Gate of Hell*, was a well-known female impersonator during his early years in film.) And it is ironical that Mizoguchi, who was to become known, however wrongly, as the 'woman's spokesman', should have entered films as something of a rear-guard apologist for the use of female impersonators.

That Mizoguchi's interest in women was not entirely due to their fitness for showing things in a more complicated and hence more subtle fashion is shown in what little is known of his private life—in particular what we shall have to call his love life. He was from an early age a great womanizer, had much experience and many affairs. During the early part of his career he lived with a young lady but never married her. There is a story that he was as fiery-tempered as he was passionate and took after her with a sword, after which they saw little of each other. Later, towards the end of the 20s, he married another woman, who in the middle 30s became unbalanced and was committed to a hospital. After this he adopted a younger relative of his wife and her two children, both girls, and they lived together until his death. Such details do not, perhaps, explain much about the man, but they do indicate that for him women were more than characters to express his thoughts; and, at the same time, his own experiences—as a look at a précis of his best films indicates—served as material for those scripts which he himself wrote.

It was through women, however, that Mizoguchi viewed, ordered and presented his world, and a partial listing of themes will illustrate this. The often destructive contrast between old and new is seen in *Samidare Soshi* (*A Chronicle of the Spring Rain*, 1924), *Kaminingyo Haru no Sasayaki* (*A Paper Doll's Whisper of Spring*, 1926), *Nihonbashi* (1929), *Gion Matsuri* (*Gion Festival*, 1933), *An Osaka Elegy*, *Sisters of the Gion*, *A Furusato* (*Hometown*, 1938), *Josei no Shorai* (*The Victory of Women*, 1946), *Yoru no Onnatachi* (*Women of the Night*, 1948), *Yuki Fujin Ezu* (*A Picture of Madame Yuki*, 1950), *Musashino Fujin* (*A Lady from Musashino*, 1951), *Gion Bayashi* (*Gion Music*, 1953), *Uwasa no Onna* (*A Talked About Woman*, 1954) and *Akasen Chitai* (*Street of Shame*, 1956). The limitations of a feudal society are seen in *Ningen* (*A Human Being*, 1925), *Tokyo Koshinkyoku* (*Tokyo March*, 1929), *Tokai Kokyogaku* (*The Symphony of a Great City*, 1929), *Shikamo Karera wa Yuku* (*And Yet They Go On*, 1931), *Aizotoge* (*The Pass Between Love and Hate*, 1934), *Aienkyo* (*The Straits of Love and Hate*, 1937), *Naniwa Onna* (*A Woman of Osaka*, 1940), *Joyu Sumako no Koi* (*The Love of Sumako, the*

Actress, 1947), *Waga Koi wa Moeru* (*My Love Is Burning*, 1949), *Saikaku Ichidai Onna* (*The Life of Oharu*, 1952), *Sansho Dayu* (*Sansho the Bailiff*, 1954) and *Chikamatsu Monogatari*. Love—a woman's love—as dignifying and giving meaning (if also death) is a theme seen in *Kiri no Minato* (*Foggy Harbour*, 1923), *Gendai no Jo* (*A Modern Queen*, 1924), *Jose wa Tsuyoshi* (*Women Are Strong*, 1924), *Nihombashi, Furusato* (*Hometown*, 1930), *Taki no Shiraito* (1933), *Gion Festival*, *Zangiku Monogatari* (*A Story of Late Chrysanthemums*, 1939), *Utamaro o Megura Gonin no Onna* (*Utamaro and His Five Women* or *Five Women Around Utamaro*, 1946), *Ugetsu Monogatari*, *Chikamatsu Monogatari* and *Yokihi* (*The Empress Yang Kwei Fei*, 1955). It will be seen that several of the themes overlap in the same picture, and it should be noted that a concern for such themes as these is not Mizoguchi's alone: many Japanese directors share it, but Mizoguchi used them more often and better.

Though this is only a partial listing of Mizoguchi's pictures, it becomes apparent that women—in his films as in his life—became what one might call the prime 'distancing effect' without which the artist has difficulty in realizing himself. Mizoguchi just as naturally put a woman in place of himself as John Ford put a man—Kinuyo Tanaka or Isuzu Yamada were as necessary to the Japanese director as John Wayne or Ward Bond were to the American. Mizoguchi—like the finest directors from Stroheim and Sternberg to Godard and Antonioni—always identified with his chosen actress to the point of being half in love. This, however, is a very special kind of love. It is a kind of possession, often very hard on the actress, which results in the director becoming whatever woman he is creating through the medium of the impersonator. This is difficult for anyone, and there are as many stories of Kinuyo Tanaka in tears in Japan as there are of a red-eyed Monica Vitti in Italy. And yet, from this came perfect performances.

Like Ozu, like Kurosawa, Mizoguchi was a perfectionist, which means that he was exacting, rarely satisfied, and even something of a martinet. He would hold up shooting and send the scenery back if it did not seem right to him. Kinuyo Tanaka remembers a terrible day on the *Ugetsu* set where he made her rehearse the same line—with full lights, in full costume—dozens of times, then filmed it an almost equal number of times, and finally stormed off not having got what he wanted.

Yet it is just this concern for detail, this insistence on what is right, this fidelity to vision, which makes a film great. When Stroheim, Murnau and Sjöström upset Hollywood with a like concern, it was thought reprehensible. In Japan, however, such methods were—for whatever reason—unquestioned; with the result that Mizoguchi's pictures very often became precisely what he intended them to be.

'You want me to speak about my art? That's impossible,' he once said. 'A film-maker has nothing to say which is worth saying.' Later he added: 'Let us say that a man like myself is always tempted by the climate of beauty.' Though he was speaking of a certain historical era of the time, that phrase—'climate of beauty'—seems peculiarly apt in describing Mizoguchi's films.

This is because in the Mizoguchi picture pictorial beauty is the second distancing effect that the director has both allowed himself and insisted upon.

Mizoguchi, like so many Japanese directors, had a definite appreciation of painting, collected pictures, could himself draw in an individual and professional manner, and continued to paint throughout his life. The pictorial beauty of the Mizoguchi picture stems originally from this interest, and some of the best remembered images from his films are almost painterly: the bridge sequence in *Taki no Shiraito*, the final hospital scene in *Sisters of the Gion*, the fog-filled last sequence of *A Picture of Madame Yuki*, the mother on the cliff in *Sansho the Bailiff*, the boat scenes from *Ugetsu* and *Chikamatsu Monogatari*, and many others.

In Mizoguchi's several colour films the painterly quality became even more evident. The Western (unrealized) ideal of naturalistic colour has never been that of Japan, and it is perhaps for this reason that foreign critics have been so surprised by and appreciative of Japanese colour, which is rarely used realistically and almost always contributes to the design or composition of the scene. In *Shin Heike Monogatari* (*New Tales of the Taira Clan*, 1955), Mizoguchi was able (for the first

time since *Chikamatsu Monogatari* to avail himself of Kazuo Miyagawa, one of the world's greatest cinematographers. Working closely together, they would decide which colour was to predominate in each scene. (Miyagawa, when working with Ozu, said that one must make a choice among colours, that only several in the spectrum could be captured as one would want them and that all the others change—one decides which shades are important.) In *The Empress Yang Kwei Fei* (photographed by Kohei Sugiyama, a cameraman much influenced by Miyagawa) a system of colours was worked out which were like leitmotivs in their implications. The concern was for pictorial values (sometimes for their own sake) and the result was a control of colour in which shade itself became drama.

Since Mizoguchi was not, however, a painter, this concern for pictorial values became something other than merely that. Since he was not himself a woman, the woman's point of view could be put to use; since he was not a painter, the painterly qualities of his images could be put to use. And the use was the same. Both allowed distance—that quality which ensures an attitude which is aloof, apparently uninvolved, objective, presumably impersonal, unemotional, reasoned: that attitude which once was the highest ideal of all art in all countries.

Mizoguchi himself thought of it somewhat differently. In speaking of the 1936 period, when 'I was able finally to learn how to show life as I see it,' he added, 'it was also from about that time that I developed a technique of shooting an entire sequence in a single cut, the camera always remaining at a certain distance from the action.'

Though such construction, apparently so similar to the one-cut one-scene days of the earliest cinema, would have bothered no one in the audience, by the 30s critics knew something of the theories of Eisenstein and were using expressions like 'spectator identification'. A psychology professor once told Mizoguchi that no spectator could properly identify with a scene shot in that manner. 'It appeared that ... they were bored with a scene lasting five minutes and photographed from a single point of view. But in shooting in this manner I certainly did not want to inhibit such identification. Rather, I tried to

A scene from *Shin Heike Monogatari* (*New Tales of the Taira Clan*), Mizoguchi's most beautiful colour film. The lady descending is Michiyo Kogure. 'Let us say that a man like myself is always tempted by the climate of beauty,' said Mizoguchi.

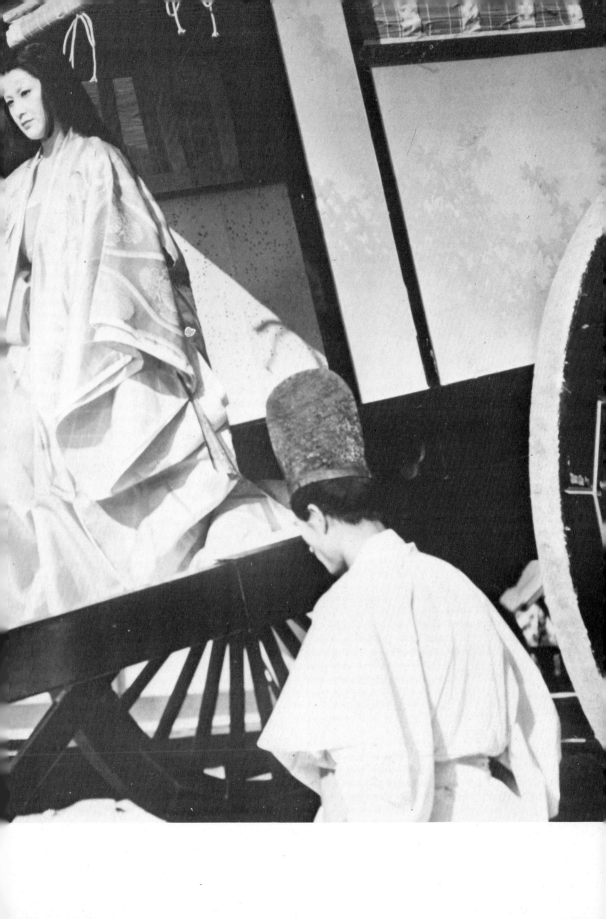

use it . . . at precisely the most intense psychological moments.' He went on to explain the reasons. 'During the course of filming a scene, if I feel that a kind of psychological sympathy has begun to develop, then I cannot without regret cut into this. Rather, I then try to intensify, to prolong the scene as long as possible.' Later he added: 'For a long time I found it difficult to avoid the style of the silent picture—but at the same time I did want to avoid the close-up, that over-used if classical method of psychological description.'

One remembers such scenes—they become a part of one's life: the beautifully composed final scene of *Sisters of the Gion*, the lovers in the boat in *Chikamatsu Monogatari*, the celebrated lawn-scene in *Ugetsu*. And one also knows that the psychology professor was wrong. Indeed, as Antonioni has sufficiently indicated, pulling away at psychological heights makes them the more impressive if only because the audience must then exert itself. And an absence of cuts within a single scene can—as André Bazin pointed out—heighten the probability and hence the truth of that scene.

For Mizoguchi these two techniques—action at a distance from the camera, action continued for a time without cut—defined a part of his style. Addressing a group of students, he once said that he believed films were mainly composed of atmosphere—it was to film, he said, as light was to painting, and he mentioned the pertinent example of Vermeer. One must learn, he said, to create this atmosphere, and the two main ways to create it were, it turned out, precisely those two techniques mentioned above: the long-held uncut scene, with the actors far from the camera. He also mentioned camera movement and gave as an example the opening and closing panoramas of *Ugetsu*.

These, it is remembered, contain or hold the body of the film. *Ugetsu* opens with a long panorama around a lake, a shot which begins on the far shore and then tilts down to reveal the village at the conclusion. It closes with the child and the father offering a bowl of rice at the mother's grave, in the proper ceremonial fashion, with the camera moving off into an upward tilting panorama which describes the movement of the opening and ends on a tableau of the far side of the lake.

Besides being apt rhetorical devices (suggesting a sameness, a spiral-like quality of experience itself), the panoramas visually complete a circular story. (A potter leaves his family and home and returns; he leaves one woman to be with another—a ghost—and then goes back to the first; both women have their own circular paths, coming and going, the wife to the city and back, the ghost from the land of the dead to which she returns.) And yet each of these encircling panoramas, so like brackets to the film, is separate but similar (as are the stories of the two women, separate yet inverted: the wife moves from life to death, the ghost from death to life; the wife discovers her identity by renouncing fleshly love, the ghost by attaining it, etc.). In this beautifully balanced film, perhaps Mizoguchi's masterpiece, even first and last scenes are thus precisely concerned with the illumination of the film as a whole. As Mizoguchi said, they 'do' something; and all camera movement must equally do something. It should not, cannot, exist for itself.

In this respect, perhaps, Mizoguchi differs most from Murnau and Ophuls, directors with whom the West often brackets him. There is in the major Mizoguchi films no effect which exists for its own sake. In *Taki no Shiraito* there is a sequence which opens with the autumn sky, the camera moving to a tree, panning down with the leaves as they fall. It watches them gather, and then moves smoothly to catch theatre posters being taken down, moves past this scene, on, inside the theatre, watches the packing, glides past, and then finally stops—and this is all one shot—to catch one of the characters saying what we have already seen, that this is the end, that the season is over. Again, in *Sisters of the Gion*, the opening scene—one long tracking shot—begins the story, illustrates the theme, and introduces the characters: we glide from the street (the milieu) into the shop (the theme: changing ways in 1936 Kyoto) and continue to the inner rooms, where we find the character already there, the story already begun.

Here we have, then, the major elements of Mizoguchi's style: scenes photographed—with moving camera or not—from a certain disengaging distance, which last for as long as the director considered commensurate with the emotional (or psychological) power of the scene itself; scenes moreover contrived with an economy and beauty which display or illustrate both the import of the action and the theme of the film.

Such aesthetic rigour, such successful story-telling are not—for reasons the director himself indicated—invariable in Mizoguchi's pictures, but they occur with a frequency and a power which together support his reputation, his importance, and his influence.

This last has been greater in Japan, understandably, than elsewhere. Unlike some directors (Yasujiro Shimazu, for example) Mizoguchi never had any pupils, and his assistant directors did not, with several exceptions, prove equal to displaying what they had perhaps learned. None the less, Mizoguchi's influence is seen strongly in the films of Tomotaka Tasaka, of Kimisaburo Yoshimura—who completed in perfect fashion the film upon which Mizoguchi had been working at the time of his death, *Osaka Monogatari* (*An Osaka Story*, 1956)—of Masahiro Shinoda, whose *Double Suicide* and *The Scandalous Adventures of Buraikan* are full of the Mizoguchi feeling, and—more surprisingly—of Akira Kurosawa, who has never disclaimed the great if not instantly apparent influence of Mizoguchi upon his works.

In Japan Mizoguchi is now considered a classic, which means that his films are more talked and written about than seen. He is also found to be a humanist, in the Japanese sense of the word, a believer that life is, generally, a worthwhile proposition. Mizoguchi himself was much more precise—certainly in his films, but even in his words—about what he believed and what he knew he was: 'Today,' (around 1954, two years before his death) 'and as always, I am interested in showing how a particular people live. Since I do not want my spectator to be driven to despair by the spectacle, however, I also want to make a sense of the new for him, so that he will not despair. And yet, I cannot altogether disregard the old. I love the past and I have but little hope for the future.' Then he spoke of his private and individual humanism, a belief apparent in most of his later films, which saw the world as a rapidly worsening place, and found a few people who should have been saved, and who—his art shows us—perhaps were.

There is no full-length study of Mizoguchi in English. And even in France, where he is considered one of the supremely great directors, there are only two: Michel Menil's *Kenji Mizogushi* (1965) and Ve-Ho's *Mizogushi* (1963). Of course, the problem is obvious: it is difficult to write a book about a man who made so many films, most of which are unavailable to Western viewers—and hard to see even in Japan, as Richie points out. As I mentioned in my Introduction, my own preferences go to Ozu rather than to Mizoguchi; but it is only fair to say that this is very much a minority view, and one which probably says more about me than about Ozu and Mizoguchi.

IVAN MOZHUKHIN
John Gillett

Ivan Mozhukhin (1889–1939) (or Mosjoukine as it is spelled in France) will be best remembered for his performances in several famous French silent films which used his strange, serio-comic personality (in repose, his long, deadpan face often took on the sad contemplative look of a Keaton) to good effect. After a considerable theatrical and film career in Russia, he left after the Revolution and settled in Paris together with a number of other film émigrés, including Volkoff, Tourjansky and Protazanov, in whose films he appeared. But it was his performance in L'Herbier's *Feu Mathias Pascal* (U.K.: *The Late Mathias Pascal*; U.S.: *The Living Dead Man*, 1925) which brought him international acclaim. The two films he directed himself make it regrettable that his directing career was so brief. The better known, *Le Brasier Ardent* (U.K.: *Infatuation*, 1923, supervised by Volkoff), is a beautifully constructed experimental essay, embodying a forward-looking use of various film devices like slow motion, superimposition, rapid montage and surrealist décor in a dream-like continuity, enlivened by Mozhukhin's own performance with its sharp bursts of bizarre, even prankish, humour. Many of his other films remain unseen, and his career faded with the coming of sound, possibly because of his thick accent. After a few minor films in the 30s, he died in Paris in 1939. His first wife, Nathalie Lissenko, was herself a considerable actress and played opposite him in both Russia and France.

Jean Mitry has published, in French, a monograph, *Ivan Mosjoukine* (1969). See also Noël Burch's entry on Marcel L'Herbier.

ROBERT MULLIGAN,
see p. 763

F. W. MURNAU

Jean-André Fieschi

Although Murnau (1889–1931) is the most generally admired film-maker in the entire silent period, along with Griffith and Eisenstein, he is probably also the least closely examined. It is as though mere recognition of his importance were enough, and made any further scrutiny unnecessary. At best, thematic forays establish the continuity of his work in Germany and Hollywood: beyond the contingencies, relegated to secondary importance, and beyond any disparities in skill, genres and styles, the same obsessional chain is traced from *Der Gang in die Nacht* (1920) to *Tabu* (1931). Where form is mentioned, it is to credit Murnau (in contrast to Griffith, Eisenstein or Stroheim, whose overall approach is more readily perceived) with qualities that are, if not contradictory, at least divergent and never systematic, and for which he is readily praised. Discussion of *Nosferatu* (1922) involves appraisal of *Stimmung* and plastic effects; of *Der letzte Mann* (*The Last Laugh*, 1924), the triumphant mobility of the camera, the acme of *Kammerspiel* perfection, the elimination of all titles; of *Tartüff* (*Tartuffe*, 1925), as a rule, what to say is something of a puzzlement; in *Faust* (1926), the painterly compositions are singled out, and the film-maker's culture; in *Sunrise* (1927), the dramaturgy; in *Tabu*, the transposition/transcendence of Expressionism and its tenets, that dazzling natural light in which half-naked bodies disport themselves.

Constantly recurring, however, are two points: Murnau's *oeuvre* emerges as both manifest (no one doubts its historical importance or—and the vacuous term is employed here with polemic intent—its beauty) and mysterious. Few positive reasons, one may say, are adduced in support of this manifest quality and this beauty.

So there remains the mystery. First of all in the taste for mystery revealed by the films themselves (*Nosferatu*) and remaining marked throughout his work. Then in the difficulty immediately apparent, once this has been said, of tracing any unity here other than a crudely and superficially thematic one (the Poet of Mortality, and suchlike evasions). Mysterious in its divergences, with *Nosferatu* and *The Last Laugh* as the two poles, rather too casually labelled 'fantastic' and 'realistic'. Mysterious, above all, in its constant and probably strategic refusal to let itself be defined by any particular aesthetic dogma—Expressionism, *Kammerspiel*, Realism—though borrowing from each in turn in its original integrity, each time in a manner that is entirely irreducible, or at any rate proof against schematization.

About Murnau's name, too, hangs a sort of legend, carefully nurtured, and to some extent sustained by the gaps extant in his work today: of the twenty-one films Murnau made in the ten years between 1919 and 1929, nine (including his first six films) remain unknown quantities today, while *Der brennende Acker* (1922) survives only in a fragmentary, much deteriorated print. And one of the American films, *City Girl* (1930), was mutilated by its producer.

The details of Murnau's life (assembled by Lotte H. Eisner in her invaluable book) add considerably to the perplexities aroused by the missing films, and much play is made of enigmatic and unspeakable hints, of anything attesting to parallels, or indeed a fusion, between the man and his work, which may thus be considered as the ghostly reflection of an anguished and unhealthy subjectivity, aristocratic and languishing in exile: 'I am at home nowhere, in no house and in no country.' (Letter written to his mother from Tahiti, quoted in *Murnau* by Lotte H. Eisner, 1973.)

Murnau's brother relates that he was struck by the revelation that during the seventeenth century two of his ancestors had been burned as witches. Et cetera. Anecdotes like this are eagerly seized upon, uncritically, in most critical studies.

Duly accorded undue prominence, a number of factors tend to make of Murnau's life a heady fiction, and of his films that fiction's fallout. Murnau's sudden death, for instance, in an automobile accident in California that has never really been explained, supposedly happened shortly after he ignored all warnings and defied Tahitian taboo by moving some sacred stones in the spot where he was building a set. To find critics subscribing to superstition like this may well seem surprising; it is in fact a symptom of manifest critical impotence, an anecdotal substitute. One cannot for a moment imagine that the people reporting stories like this are taken in by them, but it doubtless suits them to thicken the positive mystery seemingly inherent in Murnau's films by adding a biographical mystery; a comforting move, all things considered, in that, obviating any need for mediation, it painlessly transforms Murnau into one of his own characters, sharing something of Hutter, something of Faust, something of Matahi (in other words: foolhardy venturer, stealer of fire, Romantic Artist).

Once started on this track, other enigmas spread as though by contagion. There was, for instance, the somewhat shopworn mystery of who played Nosferatu. That fantastic make-up supposedly masked the features of an unidentified actor, of Murnau himself, or indeed of Nosferatu in person. Max Schreck really did exist, however, and Lotte Eisner notes that he played one of the conspirators in another Murnau film, *Die Finanzen des Grossherzogs* (1923).

Against such fantasies, as well as against facile criticism reducing the films to their thematic concerns, must be set a consideration of Murnau's real importance in the history of forms. Also, if such a thing is possible, of the articulation of these forms with an ideology (rather than a thematic) steeped in metaphysics and culturally over-determined. And finally, of Murnau's role in laying the foundations for a certain number of codes which, before the arrival of sound (but preparing for that moment), he more than any other film-maker helped to establish.

More generally, his status as a pioneer must be examined. When Murnau made his first films in 1919, it was under the impact of *The Cabinet of Dr Caligari*, a turning-point in cinema whose fundamental role should not be underestimated: the rehabilitation of a certain archaism in the use of frontal camera and flat perspectives (Méliès, the primitives), but by way of an extremely sophisticated theoretical deviation, which re-established contact with the old theatrical sources only the better to reject a certain realism which

was then thought to go essentially hand-in-glove with the motion picture camera, that 'machine for recording life', as Louis Delluc described it. On the contrary, as Kasimir Edschmid, one of the leading Expressionist theorists, peremptorily asserted, one must combat 'the bourgeois decalcomania of naturalism with its mania for recording mere facts, and its paltry aim of photographing nature or daily life. The world is there for all to see; it would be absurd to reproduce it purely and simply as it is.' (Quoted by Lotte H. Eisner in *The Haunted Screen*.)

But this influence is balanced by another, contradictory, one: the influence of the Swedish cinema—Sjöström, and above all Stiller—with its photogenic locations and brilliant natural luminosity. With Sjöström's *The Outlaw and His Wife* (1918) a 'masterly' new character was universally hailed: the landscape.

Murnau never really opted firmly for one or other of these aesthetic approaches, with the result that in his art a constant equilibrium is maintained between stylization and transparency, abstraction and incarnation. (The coexistence of Expressionist elements—the acting and make-up of Max Schreck and Alexander Granach as Renfield—and their reverse in the natural landscapes is particularly marked in *Nosferatu*. And of course the audacious admixture has a good deal to do with the film's still unimpaired poetic effect.)

For Murnau, the problem probably never presented itself, consciously or otherwise, in quite these textbook terms. Stills of him at work show him wearing a white overall, looking through the viewfinder, examining a set, giving some stage direction. Not the grey workman's overall affected by Feuillade, but the white overall of a surgeon, an engineer, a chemist. Laboratory, factory or work-bench, the cinema was then testing its materials, searching dimly for the laws governing them. How did Murnau, for his part, explore the possibilities he did more than simply envisage? First, by considering each film, separately, as an arena for formal experiment. Knowing, sensing that a film is a complex formal network, composite and polyphonic, Murnau rarely set out to explore isolated formal elements (as he did with the process shots in *Phantom*, and as the French avant-garde often did), but rather the foundation assumed by each element within the architecture of the whole.

In attempting to support the foregoing statements (and to be more specific about Murnau's contribution in various areas), I must undertake the rather thankless task of basing my analyses on prints that are sometimes suspect, while only too well aware of the contingencies and hazards that this involves. I shall concentrate chiefly on four films, in that the very differences between them pave the way for certain critical arguments which make no claim to be exhaustive, merely to draw attention to what seem to me to be key points. The four films are *Nosferatu, Tartüff, Faust* and *Sunrise*.

Despite the very real merits of *Der Gang in die Nacht*, and more particularly *Schloss Vogelöd* (1921), *Nosferatu, eine Symphonie des Grauens* is rightly considered to be Murnau's first work of maturity and one of his (or indeed the cinema's) least contestable masterpieces. As for *Sunrise*, made only five years later, it is generally agreed to be a summation, a point of perfection in the silent cinema and in Murnau's achievement. I shall try to demonstrate the justification for this point of view, and also how it may be taken as equivocal praise.

To begin with I shall be dealing chiefly with formal space, construction and dramaturgy, and then proceeding to a brief thematic recapitulation, since I feel that this can only be productive once the main lines of Murnau's concrete approach to the materials to be organized have been noted.

So in 1922 Murnau made *Nosferatu*. This was the year of *Dr Mabuse, der Spieler* (Lang), *La Femme de nulle part* (Delluc), *Orphans of the Storm* (Griffith), *Nanook of the North* (Flaherty). It was also the year of the first *Kino Pravda* (Dziga Vertov)—but there begins another story with different consequences.

Nosferatu was of course an adaptation of Bram Stoker's *Dracula* by Henrik Galeen (who himself directed a very fine version of *The Student of Prague* in 1926). For reasons of copyright, the names of the leading characters in the novel were changed: Jonathan Harker thus became Hutter; his wife Ellen, Nina; the vampire's associate Renfield, Knock; and Dracula himself became Count Orlock. (Since recent prints have restored the original names, for the sake of convenience I shall also use them here.) The adaptation is extremely ingenious in its pruning and alterations; and Murnau's own copy of the script, published in Lotte Eisner's book, reveals the active role he played in this transformation of the novel. What matters, however, is not the problem of adaptation, but the possibilities this literary material held for Murnau; this epistolary novel, predicated upon shifting viewpoints, incorporating a great deal of complementary material (diaries, press cuttings, ship's log, telegrams, etc.), justified a fragmentation of the univocal, linear narrative, and the construction instead of an imaginary space composed of intersections, collisions, analogies, repulsions which Murnau organized, with a skill even now unsurpassed, into a visual and narrative architecture that still astonishes.

These changes of viewpoint therefore support a formal single-voiced narrative, based on the articulation of extremely complex parallel montages. For this multiple narrative cannot be attributed either to an invisible narrator organizing the sequence of events from beginning to end, or to the 'subjectivity' of one of the characters involved in the story; on the contrary, it establishes itself in the 'spaces', the ellipses, the gaps between events brought into association with each other, events which compare or contrast a whole series of movements, attitudes, visual rhymes. At a time when specific orientation codes (eyeline matches, matching screen direction, continuity in movement and lighting) were established to support a 'flowing', 'realistic' texture, Murnau was undoubtedly one of the first to use this texture while at the same time perverting it to ensure a screen space no longer reassuring in its settled landmarks, but an imaginary (dynamic) space composed of modifications, metamorphoses, subsidences. The screen space here is a space with several 'inputs':

—narrative space (organizing the chain of events and its relay system of scenes);

—formal space (figuration and architecture of each shot, determining the set-up and movement within the frame);

—and lastly, imaginary space, produced by the circulation of signs within the narrative/ formal movement, and their implications; an imaginary space not reducible to the simple sum of its components, or simply to the successful management of some purely 'illustrative' technique: we are, I repeat, a long way here from the usual problems of adaptation, of fidelity, etc.

The first impulse to this narrative movement comes from the chronicle of the Great Death by the Bremen historian Johann Cavalus which accompanies the opening images and the first titles ('Nosferatu! The very name freezes my blood! Was it he who brought the plague to Bremen in 1838?' Then, 'I have long sought the causes of that terrible epidemic, and behind both its beginning and its end I have found the innocent figures of Jonathan Harker and his young wife, Ellen'). But very soon the titles, whether carrying dialogue or resuming the action, or indeed anticipating events (for instance the line so disturbing to Surrealist sensibilities at the time: 'And when he reached the other side of the bridge, the phantoms came to meet him'), begin to function with true autonomy in relation to this 'indirect' chronicle. Later, the *Book of Vampires* glanced at by Jonathan and then feverishly read by Ellen once again centres the fiction on a text: a text which reveals the law governing the narrative even as it unfolds, the law which presides over the destinies of the characters (Jonathan is sceptical, but Ellen follows the Book's direction to the letter) and suggests how the tragedy may be ended. Other graphic elements take over the relay, circulating from character to character or gathering information, amplifying it, disseminating it: Jonathan's letters to Ellen ('I have had some terrible dreams, but they were only dreams . . .'); the press cutting that tells Renfield of the plague epidemic and the imminent arrival of his Master; the log kept by the captain of the *Demeter* and found on board after his death ('We have passed Gibraltar. Panic on board. Three men are dead. The first mate has lost his reason. There are rats in the hold. PLAGUE? . . .').

Like a reducing gear, this system of graphic relays articulates sequences of images or events, engaging the potential narrative movement in often unexpected or intriguing ways. One axis, for instance, is the bestiary prosaically introduced by the kitten Ellen plays with on her balcony at the very beginning of the film, and which produces in turn a hyena, terrified horses, the flies and the spider in Renfield's cell, rats, the carnivorous plant and the polyp, and the cock that finally banishes the night and its parade of terrors.

There is the metaphysical axis, which of course reaches its peak in Professor Van Helsing's lecture at the very heart of the film, an 'aberrant' (non-narrative) episode whose function is to extend the principle of vampirism to the entire universe, first through a vegetable example, then an animal one. So while Nosferatu is aboard the *Demeter* on his way to Bremen, Harker is delirious in a hospital bed ('Coffins . . . coffins filled with earth'), Renfield in his cell is eating flies ('Blood . . . blood!') and attacks his warder, and Ellen remains frozen in highly romantic poses of anxious expectation ('Often Ellen was to be seen, alone on the dunes, watching the horizon, awaiting her husband's return'), Professor Van Helsing instructs his pupils in the secrets of nature. He tells them of (and shows them: a veritable 'collage' anticipating the celebrated inserts in *L'Age d'Or* and *Land Without Bread*) the existence of a carnivorous plant, 'vampire of the vegetable kingdom', then a polyp, 'translucent, without substance, almost like a phantom'. The narrative movement here, amplified, counterpointed for five voices, provides perhaps the most disturbing moments in the film.

Also gearing down the 'fluidity' of the narration, the series of process shots directly challenges the documentary nature of the images (in a way quite different from both *Caligari* and French avant-garde films like *El Dorado* or *Coeur Fidèle*): the passage projected in negative during the drive through the forest in the Count's carriage, where formal values are reversed in appearance; the speeded-up motion for the careering carriage, or for the scene as the Count prepares to leave the castle and feverishly piles up earth-filled coffins before climbing into the topmost one; and finally the various appearances and disappearances of the Vampire, either superimposed or vanishing through walls: all of them enrolling the Imaginary in support of its representation.

These are only some of the parameters whereby the dramaturgy of *Nosferatu* remains so effective today. Suffice it to say that such mastery in the organization of narrative signs, forms and techniques was unrivalled in 1922.

This diversification in the narrative relays (and graphic signals), this many-voiced narrative based on varied series of appurtenances (metaphors, process shots, etc.), is also supported by a cellular conception of the shot. Murnau was one of the first systematically to consider the shot—described as a 'tableau' by the early cameramen, and by their descendant Franju as 'a glass to be filled'—as dependent not only on its expressive content and its plastic composition, but as a space negotiable in every way, open to every menace, inviting the most unpredictable courses. Like a stage whose specific (variable) scale induces the precedence of gesture, movement, attitude over plot or décor. Murnau's discoveries on that score in *Nosferatu* were of great importance; here, liberation from the theatre was finally and decisively achieved. After this, instead of imposing its mark on the way scenes were structured, décor would be conceived—or fragmented—in terms of frame composition. (In *Faust*, for instance, the designer Robert Herlth tells us that Faust's study was not conceived as a single room— 'that would be like in the theatre', Murnau said—'but in accordance with the shots that had been decided on, in four separate parts, built one after the other'. And in *Tartuffe*, 'the hall consisted merely of a wall: its dimensions were suggested by the shape of Jannings walking up and down with his breviary in his hand . . .')

What else does this mean but that, in *this* cinema, the notion of *découpage* had taken command? During the 30s, with the arrival of sound, this advance was violently repulsed by the return in force of a shabby, highly regressive theatrical dramaturgy more or less tailored to the reigning fashion.

In most cases, of course, Murnau does not suppress from the scene the reference points which clarify the relationships of the characters to the décor and to each other. Usually (in this anticipating many academic gambits to come) he even takes care to provide a master shot in relation to which the closer shots will pose (in this respect at least) no problems of disorientation. And his construction of each scene even follows, fairly systematically, an almost invariable model: the opening shot

shows the décor as a whole; the following, closer shots are a succession of eyeline matches or matching screen directions; the shot ending the scene usually repeats the opening set-up. Murnau even reveals here a very marked taste for symmetry—principles which were to be pushed to extremes in *Tartuffe*.

So it is in his investment of the shot, in the interplay of camera set-ups and of actors' movements, that Murnau is at his most inventive. Here his efforts take an almost exhaustive turn: *Nosferatu* offers a veritable (and dramatically hierarchical) repertory of entries and exits from the frame, of trajectories where the screen space is often explored in extremely unexpected ways. Oblique, diagonal, semi-circular, zigzagging trajectories, coming out of the background or leading into it: retained here, systematically, and applied to different material (to a different aesthetic) is the dynamic lesson of *Caligari*.

Furthermore, it is as though each character in *Nosferatu* had his own rhythm of movement, his own personal (and habitual) way of occupying space, and turning his passage into a tangible trace of joy, terror or menace.

From his first appearance, when he emerges from a dark porchway, the Vampire moves primarily out of or into the background: his silhouette swells or fades away within the frame, disturbingly like an optical illusion; and as the narrative progresses, his presence tends to expand until it contaminates the entire surface of the film. His appropriation of the frame suggests the manoeuvres of some baleful insect, his movements weave spiders' webs between one shot and the next (or within a single shot). For instance, when the captain of the *Demeter*, her sole and terrified survivor, lashes himself to the wheel, suddenly a reverse angle picks out, against the sky, the ship's mast with its sails and rigging, and the hatchway of the hold. The Vampire appears at the edge of the screen left, slowly describes a semi-circle, and disappears along the right edge of the frame which, because of the angle chosen, he appears to climb.

In contrast to the impropriatory structure which has Nosferatu at its centre and as its emblem, Harker's movements, feverish or frightened, suggest an instinctive space, fragile and constantly threatened by imbalance. Whether rushing blindly towards Adventure at the beginning ('Wait, young man, you cannot escape destiny by running away,' Professor Van Helsing tells him; and Renfield, 'You will enjoy a marvellous voyage; what matter if it costs you a few drops of sweat . . . or even blood'); or whether later succumbing to increasingly specific hallucinatory terrors, Harker is the living token of an ambivalence (fear/pleasure) which makes him function as the spectator's imaginary surrogate (identification), and therefore simultaneously as one of the narrative's key motive agents. He is, in a sense, a strictly instrumental character.

All his movements suggest the incarnation of an attraction/repulsion system (attraction/repulsion by the Vampire, or more accurately by what the Vampire represents). So Harker reveals as much tendency to besiege the frame, frequently entering it like a bullet from a gun, as to desert it, often by means of ingenious cowerings. One scene reveals this dual attitude particularly clearly, summarizing it with perfect symmetry: the discovery of Nosferatu's body in the crypt at the castle. In the master shot of the crypt, Harker appears at the top of the steps, facing camera, crosses down left, and comes to a halt when he sees the coffin, partly masked by the left-hand edge of the frame, his back three-quarters to camera. Then he approaches the coffin quickly (back to camera) and peers down at it. Close-up of Nosferatu's face (tilt shot down) seen through the splintered planks, an eye wide open. The master shot is then repeated: Harker retreats in terror, comes to a halt, then rushes up to the coffin. A continuity cut: Harker suddenly lifts the lid of the coffin, discovering the Vampire lying there with his hands folded on his chest. He retreats again, back three-quarters to camera, again comes to a halt at the left-hand edge of the frame, then retreats backwards (so that he is now facing us) till he reaches the steps in the background and crouches down on them, staring at the coffin. Continuity cut to Harker at the foot of the staircase, walking up the stairs backwards until he exits from the frame, upper right.

This movement, of diagonals at cross purposes, is like a symbolic reduction of the drama. Another variant appears later when the *Demeter*'s mate goes down into the hold

to try to solve the mystery of the epidemic. His terrified flight after discovering the Vampire and his fall backwards off the bridge reiterates the underlying to-and-fro structure on which the aesthetic (the dynamic) of the film is partly based.

The other characters (Ellen, Renfield, etc.) are similarly invested with their individual motivating impulses, conceived in terms of their place in the narrative. For instance, the contortions, convulsive movements and 'gestural explosions' of Alexander Granach (Renfield) derive from a particularly intelligent assimilation of the Expressionist style of which this actor (along with the 'greats'—Jannings, Veidt and Krauss—all three of whom were used by Murnau) was a particularly effective but also moving exponent; because of this, Granach is able to make Renfield's dependence ('primal', 'animal': sexual) on the Master, whose clownish and pitiful counterpoint he is, *credible* without recourse to psychological clichés.

But while noting the derivation of these motivating impulses solely from the *logic* of the narrative, I would like to stress the principal factor underlying their organization. The narrative construction I have outlined, and the visual architecture (already so widely praised that its photogenic qualities need not be repeated here) sustain and are sustained by a particularly innovatory conception of *imaginary* space. What I mean by this is not simply that the film describes a phantasmagoria—which goes without saying—but that it imposes an operational logic which articulates a narrative space-time, then entirely new, in which the signs put into circulation refer back and forth to each other in a circulatory process connected on many levels of the story. An essentially poetic montage is established, comprising multiple attractions and reverberations. Fresh networks (networks of the wish, not of the 'real') are woven between the characters beyond the 'realism' of the space autonomous to each scene. What Murnau does here on the scale of the large narrative unit—following **Griffith**, but using the parallel montage principles of *Intolerance* to less obvious (and less moralizing) effects—is what Eisenstein was to experiment with, using more 'discrete' narrative units, in his equally metaphorical montage, though on different practical and ideological bases (specifically: the criticism and supplanting of the ideological assumptions of Griffith and Lang, if not of Murnau). 'The juxtaposition of two fragments of film looks more like their product than their sum,' Eisenstein wrote in 'Montage 1938'. There is no fragment of *Nosferatu*, entirely devoted to a calculated terror, that does not reach out both backwards and forwards, extracting the substance for some additional turn of the screw and to replenish its poetic energy.

A 'poetic' montage, therefore, supporting —in the wake of Griffith but before Eisenstein, Murnau being in a sense the connecting link—an innovatory notion of attraction. Murnau was probably the first to divert the eyeline match from its 'realistic' function as a liaison in order to articulate a mental or wishful space in this way. An example is the parallel montage between Harker's first night at the Vampire's castle and Ellen's fit of somnambulism at Bremen. While Harker huddles by his bed as the monster approaches towards the left of the frame, Nosferatu suddenly and unexpectedly turns *to the right*. Ellen, according to the (geographical) logic of the narrative, is at this moment in a quite different space; yet when she suddenly gets out of bed and holds out her arms to the left, it is towards . . . Nosferatu. Established here, ineluctably and disturbingly, is not only the premonition that warns Ellen of the danger her husband is facing, but also—as the narrative subsequently confirms—one of the keys to the sexual mechanism of the story: Ellen's secret attraction to the Vampire. Later, during another troubled night, the suggestion becomes more precise: 'He is coming. I must go to him.' 'He?' Harker or Nosferatu? The title confirms the ambiguity through the deliberate imprecision of the personal pronoun. Here the cinema, using its own specific materials, reveals itself even more than in *Caligari*, which was a forerunner in this area, to be the black ink which traces the dynamic, mutating figures of the unconscious on the dream screen.

Though these are characteristic examples, they have been deliberately isolated; and the overall functioning of the film corresponds to such figures. Similar links connect Renfield to his Master ('The Master is near! . . . The Master is here!', then, 'The Master is dead!'), and, if one looks more closely, bind all the characters together within a sweeping metaphorical statement whose emblem is the spider's web.

The genius of Murnau: *Nosferatu* marks the advent of a total cinema in which the plastic, rhythmic and narrative elements are no longer graduated in importance, but in strict interdependence upon each other. With this film the modern cinema was born, and all developments to come, notably those of the Soviet film-makers, became possible.

A few words on *The Last Laugh*. The important point is not so much that the thematic of *Nosferatu* is turned upside down, with the fantastic giving way to social drama, but that the inversion is total, incurring an extreme shift in the notion of movement: movement of the camera (the much-vaunted virtuoso mobility of Karl Freund's camera), movements within the shot.

By courtesy of Jannings, there is now also a monumental way of occupying and dealing with space. There is also a return to novelistic linearity after the complex atomization of *Nosferatu*. That the influence of Carl Mayer was decisive here is now well enough established to be in little doubt: a remarkable pioneer, he is undoubtedly the only man to have made films by proxy—and what proxies, or at any rate what films: *Caligari*; *Schloss Vogelöd, The Last Laugh, Tartuffe, Sunrise* (Murnau); *Hintertreppe* (Jessner); *Scherben, Sylvester* (Lupu Pick). And Murnau's sensitivity in his choice of collaborators (scriptwriters: Mayer, Hans Janowitz, Henrik Galeen, Thea von Harbou; cameramen: Carl Hoffmann, Karl Freund, Fritz Arno Wagner, Charles Rosher, Floyd Crosby; designers: Hermann Warm, Albin Grau, Robert Herlth, Walter Röhrig, Rochus Gliese; actors: Conrad Veidt, Werner Krauss, Jannings, Alfred Abel, Lil Dagover, Yvette Guilbert, Janet Gaynor) certainly reveals an acute strategic awareness of the cinema as collective art/personal expression. But the most astonishing thing is the flexibility of the man himself, his disregard for accepted categories, as if all his efforts had tended less towards mining deeper into his own work (towards his brand image, with all that implies of cliché and recurring obsessional patterns: Stroheim, Eisenstein, Welles, Bresson,

Jancsó, etc.) than to exploring the field of cinema itself with the data available at the time (1920–30) and place (Germany, then America). Murnau's work both completes and pushes beyond these data. Sometimes with a sort of frankly assumed cunning: *The Last Laugh*, a big UFA prestige production, was also a visiting card, a more or less discreet bid for American attention (as Lubitsch had made and Hitchcock was to make later), saying 'see what we can do'.

The Last Laugh contains about 150 shots fewer than *Nosferatu* (which has 540): here the conception of the *découpage* is radically transformed by modification of the plastic and dramaturgic parameters. Unlike Lang or Lubitsch, film-makers whose work then tended towards systematization, Murnau does not have *a* style but several, subjected to re-examination with each new film.

Such stylistic variations are intangible proof of a positive determination to experiment, and Murnau was the first to realize the fact that the experiments were primarily formal. Some notes dating from 1923, typed on paper with the Decla-Bioscop letterhead, bear this out: 'What I refer to is the fluid architecture of bodies with blood in their veins moving through mobile space; the interplay of lines rising, falling, disappearing; the encounter of surfaces, stimulation and its opposite, calm; construction and collapse ... the play of *pure movement*, vigorous and abundant.' (*Murnau* by Lotte H. Eisner.)

These lines might have been written by Germaine Dulac. But for Murnau this formal interplay is inseparable from a dramaturgy, even though contradictory elements in that dramaturgy may be given prominence from one film to the next. Thus the swing away from *Nosferatu* is radical in *The Last Laugh*: here everything is centred on Jannings (both as a character in the drama and as a massive physical presence), on the description of a milieu, on the laws of dramatic unity (time, place), on the decisive outcropping of psychology. I have noted the importance of the graphic elements in *Nosferatu*. By suppressing all inter-titles, *The Last Laugh* caused Robert Desnos a good deal of irritation: 'Inter-titles are one of the more pleasing preoccupations of the cinema today. Pleading purity, certain people would like to suppress them.' And: 'Everything that can be projected on the screen is part of cinema, letters just as much as faces.' (*Cinéma*, 1966.)

But in its intransigence—or arbitrariness—this suppression of titles reveals the provocative taste shared by Murnau and Mayer for adopting stances as productive elements. Murnau may not be a systematic film-maker in the development of his work, but he undoubtedly is within the context of each of his films, foreshadowing the attitude to filmic materials of 'modern' film-makers like Resnais and Oshima.

With *Tartuffe*, perhaps Murnau's masterpiece along with *Nosferatu*, the quest for a controlled, extremely rigorous texture is achieved, based on a very fragmented *découpage* (over 500 shots), favouring deliberately symmetrical series of shots within each sequence, the regular repetition of identical compositions, a meticulous system of variable shot sizes, and the frequent use of empty frames at the beginning or end of a shot, emphasizing a character's entry or exit, and more particularly the space off, which is often where the action is really taking place.

The undertaking here, the venture, was to transpose the original dramaturgy into a visual architecture yielding a sort of essence of pure theatricality; by which I mean that, as in *Nosferatu*, the determining factor is the idea of theatre, but a theatre *enacted* in each shot, in the sequence of these shots, in the numerous changes of viewpoint that govern them, and in the reiteration of empty frames imposing another stage (imaginary, virtual) either summoned, betokened or rejected by each separate shot. Thus the theatricality entirely banishes any notion of filmed theatre, substituting instead a constantly shifting and changing locus of representation. This is underlined by the very skilful 'placing in abyss' structure comprising the 'contemporary' prologue and epilogue, and the 'seventh-century' story they enclose.

To resume the argument of this double-entry story: an elderly and odious housekeeper is humouring (and slowly poisoning) an old man in the hope of inheriting his money. She keeps away from the house a potential trouble-maker, the old man's nephew, a young actor. The nephew arrives in disguise, however, proposing a home cinematograph show. The film shown is a strange version of *Tartuffe*, and tells how a pious hypocrite, formerly a convict, takes advantage of Orgon's credulity to swindle him and attempt to seduce his wife. Finally unmasked, the crook is thrown out. The epilogue unmasks the female Tartuffe in her turn, opening the foolish old man's eyes.

In general fairly mechanical, this plot serves Murnau as an opportunity to concentrate not on illustration, but on structures. A few of the effects may be noted.
—Method of articulating the two 'stories'. The two 'spectators' (the old man and the housekeeper) are framed full face, expectant, she dwarfing the frail old man with her bulk./The nephew blows out the candle lighting the scene and goes out to the right, moving backwards./Another candle, an enormous one, divides the screen into two equal halves: on the left, the two spectators in the same position as before. On the right, the nephew's face appears in frame. He blows out the second candle./Facing the couple, in the beam from the projector, he pulls the curtain, revealing the screen: empty white frame./A hand then enters the screen, lighting candlesticks./A match cut shows the candlesticks in front of a mirror, Elmire lighting the candles, then pausing in her toilette for a moment before turning round joyfully: the young wife awaiting Orgon's return. The connection at the end is achieved more abruptly by the blank screen again, then the nephew's entry into frame to address the spectators and draw the anticipated moral of the story.

This use of the (blank) screen as a base for the central fable has a distinctly modern look about it today, especially as other signs are addressed—directly—to the real audience; for instance when the nephew, the first time he is thrown out of the house, walks to camera (the edge of the stage, as it seems) to announce his intention of seeing justice done. An interchange is set up between theatricality and projection. Whether the transition is established by substitution (the candles in the prologue/the candlesticks in Elmire's room) or by rupture (the blank screen), the accent is on the methods of articulation: the articulation of a discontinuous chain (prologue/story) or Chinese box

narrative. What Murnau had realized was that the discontinuous nature of cinematic material meant that the dramaturgy must be entirely subjected to this basic discontinuity, and not vice versa. Subjected, but not discarded. Murnau's contribution is crucial in achieving this submission, in the modification of the narrative substance by the edges of the frame and by the shifting camera viewpoint. The method of articulating the two stories is thus only a particular example of the general articulation of filmic narrative.
—The empty frames. That the shot is the mother cell, the discrete unit from which dynamic space is assembled, modified, intensified, has already been suggested in connection with *Nosferatu*. In *Tartuffe*, this idea becomes a strategic basis for the formal mechanism, notably in the persistent use of the empty frame: a suspension of the scene, interrupting the drama, or despatching it either beyond or this side of the screen and inscribing it within an absence (and elsewhere) that functions quite differently from representation. A dramatic gain, undoubtedly; but also, and more importantly, the integration into cinematography of an expressive register reinvented by its importation from the theatrical stage to the fragmented scene of film-making: assuming a rhythmic, punctuating, respiratory, plastic function. Affirming the palpable importance of the signifier in the process of aesthetic and imaginative conquest.

It is in the second shot of the film (the shrewish housekeeper waking up) that a principle is established which is subjected to variations and used to very different ends throughout the film. The housekeeper gets up. She walks forward, then goes out of frame. Empty frame. Then just the arm reappears to reach for a jacket.

A demonstration, discreet at first but none the less compelling, that no matter how anodyne or how empty of emotion, no matter how little charged with interesting or exciting occurrences, a composition can suddenly be reinvested once its theme is apparently exhausted; here again in non-fantastic territory, is the effect of surprise or menace which in *Nosferatu* might have seemed occasioned by the fact that the main purpose of the exercise was the bizarre. Involved here is the idea of the filmic event itself. The event is what appears in frame, emerging to occupy a space with marked boundaries, irrespective of its intrinsic dramaturgic value, since its value is in fact given to it by the frame (and the camera axis and the relationships between frames).

In general, however, the empty frames in the prologue serve mostly to provide a rhythm, a pulsation, transforming *temps morts* or necessary transitions like the actors' exits and entrances into more or less unpredictable micro-events.

With the Tartuffe story this conception is maintained and even intensified to a point where it becomes one of the stylistic features of the film. But other, more urgent uses of this device make it more of an essential trait. For instance during Elmire's sobering reunion with Orgon. The setting is the top of the staircase with the vast curving banister whose dark arabesque is used for a number of visual effects. Above, to the left, is the door of Orgon's room. Elmire runs up towards her husband's room, opens the door and disappears inside. The frame remains empty for some seconds, long enough for one to feel uncomfortable, almost irritated. Finally the door reopens. Elmire reappears, upset, closes the door by letting her whole body sag against it, remains motionless for a moment, then with her back to camera slowly moves to the stairs.

So perfect are the composition, tempo and expressive quality here that this shot has the relative autonomy of a sequence. Elmire's movement, eager and graceful at first, then slow and heavy, a two-way traffic of unequal speeds and densities enclosing a dramatic expanse of suspension, of emptiness between the opening and closing of a door, retains intact its emotional power and its modernity. Furthermore, the same tactic is used elsewhere to different effect, becoming frankly comic instead of tragic. This time Tartuffe is standing in front of a table laden with food, facing the camera. In the background, on a slightly lower level, can be seen the dome of a summerhouse in the garden. Seated on the right in the foreground, Orgon gestures to his mentor and confessor to be seated. With an air of irritation Tartuffe declines the invitation, and after sticking his nose into his breviary, walks away with his back to camera (descending towards the lower edge of the

frame: a few steps, one imagines, lead down to the garden). Orgon immediately follows the reverend gentleman, though not without first producing his own breviary. One behind the other, identical automata, they go off left. Empty frame. Then Tartuffe reappears from the left in profile, nose in breviary and still followed of course by his faithful shadow. Both cross the screen laterally, and go off right. Another empty frame, then the same manoeuvre in reverse, until Tartuffe goes off left. As in the previous example, the empty frame takes all its weight from the contrasting movements, but functions as a gag (a token of comedy) rather than augmenting the pathos. Murnau excels in these ruptures in tone, all the more effective in that they derive from identical figures, though they are rarely used univocally.

—Constructions. Some of the construction methods used in *Tartuffe* are demonstrated by the scene—one among several—in which Elmire lays a trap for Tartuffe by inviting him to an intimate collation at which Orgon is to be present hidden behind the curtains.

Relatively simple in its dramatic intent, the sequence describes the stages of an unsuccessful plot imagined by the innocent girl to trap the impostor under the gull's very eyes. It takes Murnau some seventy shots to elaborate this scene. The opening is, literally, exposition: of Elmire's room. In the foreground, the tea-table is set. To the right, a window lights the scene. In the background, the door opens, Elmire enters, followed by Orgon. She indicates the curtain behind which he is to hide. In a few closer shots: the last protests of Orgon. Then comes the reprise, systematic throughout the film, of a shot that has already punctuated the narrative several times: the one of the top of the staircase, particularly associated with the first appearance of Tartuffe a few hundred shots earlier. Here he is once again, breviary in hand, standing still, then moving towards the stairs. The room again. The maid announces that 'he' is arriving, Orgon dithers, finally hides, and Tartuffe enters. Elmire, facing camera, arms held out against the curtain that hides Orgon, looks left: a slow pan turns away from Elmire, following what she is looking at, passes the fireplace, and finally discovers Tartuffe with his back to the door, facing the camera, eyes raised to heaven and book in hand. An exchange of glances in close-up, then an insert, an angled shot down on the table ready laid. A few shots later, on the table to the left, there is the enormous teapot. The frame is crossed diagonally by Elmire's white arm—towards a cup. Everything is set.

The sequence is exemplary both in its coherence and in the ways whereby it is linked to the overall fiction. The following points may be noted:

—The setting of the mechanism which, as so often with Murnau, permits a twofold division of the scene: at one pole the spectator's view (of the film), and at the other Orgon's (the voyeur)—not to mention the two spectators of the film-within-the-film. This structure is further complicated by the reverse angle shots of Elmire and Tartuffe: a space in constant destruction/reconstruction.

—The enclave principle has been mentioned earlier (the repetition of set-ups already used elsewhere). But the scene is also reinforced in specific ways: for instance, the seduction of Tartuffe by Elmire triggers a series of close-ups doubly privileged in that they exhibit erotic mobile objects (parts of the body: throat, arms, ankles, shoulders): loci of carnal provocation. The eroticism is not so much presented to view; rather it occupies the locus, transforms it: an eroticized space.

This would be little enough, but this scene does not function solely on these premises. It is additionally articulated, as it were, to an object which is perceived from the outset to be strictly functional, but whose role evolves throughout the scene, revealing its functions only at the end: the teapot.

At first, on the table, the teapot appears to be merely a prop, an object of no significance to the action. Then gradually another function, a visual one, begins to emerge: the teapot serves as a reference point for the changes of viewpoint between Elmire and Tartuffe, occupying varying positions in the different set-ups, sometimes in the foreground, sometimes dividing the frame in two, sometimes restored to its purely utilitarian role. Thus it becomes both the pivot on which the space is articulated, and the particular figurative element used as a shot gauge.

It is only at the end of the scene that a close-up adds a third significance, making up for the other two. For it is on the polished surface of the teapot, acting as a distorting mirror, that Tartuffe sees Orgon's reflection watching him from the other side of the room as he draws closer to Elmire.

Prop, visual reference, and finally dramatic object: in this evolution, in these different levels of meaning, one can see how Murnau works by down-gearing significances. Here again narrative space, plastic space and dramatic space do not express each other, but trigger a specifically cinematic system of forms and meanings whose components—all of them—are used dialectically.

Reputedly a mysterious, ineffable film-maker, surrounded by an almost religious aura (touched, in other words, by grace, which is the exact opposite of *work*), Murnau thus seems to me, if not exhaustible, at least legible. He is open, in other words, to textual analysis; and one may well wonder why it has taken so long for a start to be made.

A film like *Faust* alone would warrant a detailed critical approach (dramaturgy, plastic effects, *découpage*, ruptures in tone, etc.). Here again I shall merely note one or two features in the course of a brief analytical summary:

—The Prologue in heaven poses an abstract opposition, against a background of clouds, between Angel and Demon, White and Black, Heaven and Hell, and states the film's ambition (its metaphysical anchorage) from the outset.

—The little town, the Doctor's study, his researches and disappointments; the Plague spilling out from the Demon's mantle in a cloud of black smoke; at the fair, the mountebanks are struck down, and their acrobatics become the grimaces or contortions of death. A storm rises. The city is thronged by processions, of mourning and carousal, of a dying world.

Wonderful imagery full of pictorial references (Rembrandt, Altdorfer, Mantegna) is traced in the chiaroscuro of Carl Hoffmann's camerawork. Very different, of course, from the recreation of old master paintings that is so caricatural in Laurence Olivier's work, or even Cocteau or the Dreyer of *Day of Wrath*.

No sooner is it established than the pictorial quality is undermined, then reasserted by movement or sudden pauses. Fluctuations in depth and multifarious lateral sweeps de-

Camilla Horn (as Gretchen) in *Faust*: 'wonderful imagery is traced in the chiaroscuro of Carl Hoffmann's camerawork'.

scribe a non-static pictorial quality in which the lines, volumes and shades shift only to find new symmetries that are undermined in their turn: here again a plastic narrative redoubles the dramaturgy.

—The meeting between Faust and Mephistopheles in the night, the wonders, the circles of fire, the black trees writhing up towards the moon: this time it is classical romantic imagery (Caspar David Friedrich), taking over from the old Dutch, German and Italian masters, that achieves poetic conviction and a truly amazing power of suggestion.

—Then comes the Pact, and the extraordinary aerial voyage, a fabulous flight over models whose beauty still takes the breath away: the rooftops of the town, plains, palaces, mountains, grottoes, rivers and waterfalls, forests, and finally rocks, the sea, boats in the distance . . . Rarely has any effect been so in keeping with the myth; and the images here come close to the full stretch of their powers. Before this there had been the still somewhat lame phantasmagorias of Méliès. Afterwards, only animation could compete (Alexeiff, or the Kubrick of *2001: A Space Odyssey*).

—The second part is dominated from the outset by the counterpoint between Faust/Marguerite and Mephisto/Dame Marthe. The latter pair get the best of it, chiefly because of the *dimension* of the actors (Jannings and Yvette Guilbert): a comic ballet (even grotesque in the manner of Lubitsch, that 'Murnau of comedy' as Claude Ollier pleasingly describes him) defuses and amplifies the tragedy in a welter of face-pulling, obscene innuendo and parodic antics. A sudden reversal (and confirmation) of the poetic quality, an extremely audacious tragi-comic seesaw in which the pictorial splendours are keyed to the point of self-derision.

—After this the whole last part of the film is subjected to a new and distinctly progressive reversal: white begins to dominate settings and scenes (lighting, costumes, interiors) until the final sequences are enveloped in snow. A total purification of signs takes place until the obverse of Expressionism is achieved: a different sort of abstraction, no longer realized through a surcharge of signification, but through its depletion.

If the term 'exercise in style' had not currently acquired a pejorative (formalist) connotation, it might have been employed here with absolute confidence. *Faust* shows how Murnau uses (simultaneously subverting and perfecting it) a prestigious dramatic and symbolic prop (the myth, Marlowe, Goethe) in a series of formal metamorphoses; the utilization of a heteroclite plastic material (borrowings from various schools, countries and eras) justifies a course, a *voyage through forms* (and themes) in which the differences, divergences and contrasts tend to be grounded in a new coherence. In other words, here again a fundamental discontinuity is risked in order to establish the deceptive fact of cinematic flow.

Sunrise, according to Lotte Eisner, who echoes a widespread view, is 'Murnau's most powerful and advanced film'. In a *Cahiers du Cinéma* poll in 1958, it was voted 'the most beautiful film in the world'. And as we all know, along with Sjöström's *The Wind* and Vidor's *The Crowd*, *Sunrise* marked the summit (the end) of the silent period's achievements and was a portent of the cinema to come (the dominant cinema to come, one should perhaps specify). The question—as always when a point of rupture, of transformation, can be determined in retrospect so distinctly and so unanimously—is therefore: what was it, in the history of cinematic forms, that reached completion with *Sunrise*, and what was it that then began?

Here a historical and economic point opens the question up again (and is sometimes used to evade it). *Sunrise* is an American film. So there is a way the question can be posed in other terms: is *Sunrise* more American than German, or vice versa? A variant of this question: what did Murnau give up, or in what way did he use the Hollywood system to bring his work to fruition?

The same question might be asked of Lubitsch, and after him, of Lang and Hitchcock. But with Murnau the question does not simply involve the enrolment of a personal body of work, no matter how prestigious, into another production system (into another culture with different aims and means). It cuts across a critical moment: the imminent arrival of sound, with the many upheavals (economic, ideological, formal) that were to follow.

Here it should be stressed that the silent cinema (not the general run but its crestline: in no special order, Porter, Griffith, Feuillade, Jean Durand, Christensen, Gance, Epstein, *Caligari*, Lubitsch, Lang, Lupu Pick, Carl Mayer, the slapstick comedians, Kuleshov, Kozintsev, Eisenstein, Vertov, Renoir, Browning, Dreyer . . . and Murnau) was in no way handicapped—talking pictures without the dialogue, or something like that—but was a *different kind of cinema* which, technically and structurally prevented from being simply a filter or counterpart to reality, had achieved in its major films a considerable amount of work on the nature of representation between 1915 and the late 20s. With *Sunrise*, the conquest of narrative (novelistic) fluidity is achieved at the expense of abandoning the attainments specific to the silent period (in a sense, liquidating the tradition). Dramaturgy was now firmly in the driver's seat; and for decades cinema was chiefly to mean well-told stories. But could one so describe *Caligari*, *La Passion de Jeanne d'Arc*, *October*, *Nosferatu* or *Tartuffe*? The aim in preparing a shooting script now became transparency (with the articulations concealed, tending to create the illusion of spatio-temporal continuity); that transparency which can be seen as a dual symptom, ideological and formal, of Hollywood films from the 30s until the 60s. So *Sunrise*, universally praised, occupies a somewhat equivocal position. Today, to an extent shared by few other silent films, its story, *découpage* and imagery have an air of familiarity about them: one feels like saying that only sound is missing.

Sunrise was to create its own tradition in which the 'sentimental (and psychologizing) virus' would dominate. Of course *Sunrise* can in no way be reduced to these terms, nor can it be retrospectively discredited because of a bastard progeny. One might just as well hold Mahler responsible for Dimitri Tiomkin. What concerns us here is the reading of *Sunrise* which was to be disseminated through films into the cinema to come; what was retained by this reading, and what it omitted.

There is a frequently quoted shot in *Sunrise*: the scene in the marshes where the young peasant meets the city vamp. Marcel Carné, among the first to be bowled over by it, noted at the time in an article called 'The camera, a character in the drama': 'Here the mobile camera gives the impression that a second person was following the hero

through the fields.' I want to try to describe this shot, the thirty-third in the film.

On the right of the frame, seen from the back, the man moves forward ponderously. High up on the left, in the background, is the moon. Followed by the camera, the man walks towards a little bridge (the moon goes out of frame). He crosses the bridge, veers to the right—he is then in profile—towards some low branches—and again has his back to the camera. He ducks to pass under the branches, and the camera, avoiding the tree, veers left; the man comes through the branches, also towards the left, now in profile, up to a gate which he steps over, *facing the camera*. The camera comes to a halt; the man advances towards it, until he is in a waist shot. The camera then leaves him, turns obliquely left towards a dark, overgrown thicket and plunges rapidly into the foliage. There, on the right, seen in profile and wearing black, the woman is waiting. The moon is again visible, with its reflections in the water. The woman turns her head to the right, then resumes the profile position. Suddenly she looks left, checks her make-up, stands still again, smiles. Several seconds go by. Finally the man enters the frame *from the left*, and halts. She goes to him, and they embrace.

There is something here which cannot be reduced simply to an exercise in virtuosity, or even to the identification of the camera with some invisible pseudo-character. There is here, within this single take (and sequels to that were a long time in coming: Dreyer's *Vampyr*, Hitchcock's *Rope*, Skolimowski's *Walkover*, Rouch's *Gare du Nord*), a radical autonomization of the camera in relation to the scene; and at the same time, with the invention of a sort of ellipsis within the shot, there is also the creation of a literally impossible space, emerging from the interplay of movements, durations, and the autonomy of this camera seemingly endowed with its own momentum. The camera is no longer merely a filter (or an instrument of transmission); it no longer moves in imitation of the subject within the frame, following, preceding or indeed replacing the subject. It is one of the poles of the representation, a privileged pole; the point of view, within the narrative, of the narrative as it evolves, capable of decision and of anticipation, endowed with a motor function that is no longer merely functional but promotional: the selector-head of a space-time to be explored, realized, inventoried, which Murnau was again one of the first to survey.

The metaphysical residuum of *Sunrise*: the signification operates here on the basis of a series of pairs of opposites very strongly invested as fictional motors. Town/Country, Nature/Culture, Man/Woman, Night/Day, Earth/Water, Wish/Real, Good/Evil, etc. Murnau works within the framework of an ideology of duality, where the forms and structures are polarized and developed through a dynamic of opposites (fiction here is the dynamic product of the clash of opposites; in this respect Murnau, like the romantics and most of the Expressionists, virtually bathes in the fallout from classical German philosophy).

These opposite poles therefore organize the signifying chain: the difference between the sexes, the aberrations of the soul, the social distinctions, even the cycle of days and seasons seem to correlate to this metaphysical bipartition; and the whole film evolves from this matrix. Following these lines, one could probably arrive at a sort of seminal model for Murnau fictions, based on his philosophical (idealist) presuppositions.

What we know of his first films, now lost, tends to confirm the preponderance of some such generative mechanism. *Der Januskopf* (1920), for instance, adopted by Hans Janowitz from Stevenson's *Dr Jekyll and Mr Hyde*, apparently concerns a bust with two faces, one godlike, the other demonic. And like *Faust*, *Satanas* (1919) featured a celestial prologue in which, according to Lotte Eisner: 'Lucifer, the fallen angel, deplores his lost halo. God promises him salvation if he can find a single human being capable of bringing good out of evil.'

What happens in *Sunrise* is, on the basis of the same ideology, the deflection of metaphysics into psychology. The possibility of this step was of course hinted at by *The Last Laugh* and the *Kammerspiel* in general. But *The Last Laugh* adapted the metaphysics to social man in a fable about the Fall where, in the guise of a grotesque hall porter, the destiny of Man himself, torn between obscure and opposing forces that are beyond his understanding, seemed to be pressing its claims to

attention. Here the prologue to *Faust* serves as a veritable heraldic figure: in the heaven of ideas, where everything is devised and decided, Angel and Demon are in conflict over a soul. The second prologue to *Faust* (Goethe's version) probably offers the key by postulating less a rivalry between the Angel and the Demon than their former complicity: after all, it is this that makes the world go round, and these allegorical figures in fact emerge as two sides of the same coin, as a duality (positive and negative); contradictory and complementary figures, identical in their difference.

Basically, an ideological landscape like this would be little more than a cultural commonplace had Murnau—more or less intuitively? or if premeditated, to what extent?—not brought it into play, having extracted from it a whole series of formal inferences, as an immense potential reservoir of forms, images and narratives (through a dual process: formalization of the thematic, thematization of the forms and structures).

Mephistopheles, Tartuffe, Nosferatu, the Vamp in *Sunrise* and the priest in *Tabu* have in common, in their status as evil characters, that they are (like Lang's Mabuse) machinators, manipulators, *metteurs en scène*: they are the representatives, within the fiction, of its own laws. On them devolve the dangerous powers of expropriation, of possession (of sexuality). Around them are woven webs of attraction and repulsion, of wish and dread. They are those without whom no fiction could unfold: bringers of the law, of taboo, of retribution: they are the guardians, the guarantors of turbulence in the drama. Nosferatu, the Living Dead who feeds on life ('This blood ... this precious blood'), grotesque and terrifying form of the Wish towards whom Ellen feverishly holds out her white arms in the dark Bremen night, is the mythical epitome of this aesthetic. And the ideas (metaphysical, moral) are expressed in light and shadow, movement and repose, overture and withdrawal. The frame is the stage (the other, imaginary, stage) on which impulses are revealed, brought into play, represented.

All Murnau's films should be read primarily as voyages into the imaginary. Each time a point of transit is featured in the story, denoting the symbolic space where the

Janet Gaynor and George O'Brien in *Sunrise*, 'generally agreed to be a summation, a point of perfection in the silent cinema and in Murnau's achievement . . . but the conquest of narrative (novelistic) fluidity is achieved at the expense of abandoning the attainments specific to the silent period'.

fiction divides into two. The bridge in *Nosferatu*, the revolving door in *The Last Laugh*, the blank screen in *Tartuffe*, the circles of fire in *Faust*, the lake in *Sunrise*.

To retrace these journeys, examining their various stages and interconnecting their landmarks, is to consider the cinema in the course which turned it into a classical art—master of its means and its aims—and to consider also what remains seminal for the cinema of the future in the hazardous campaigns of an imagination cut short by death in 1931 and forever bearing a name that also belongs to the imagination: Friedrich Wilhelm Murnau.

Translated by Tom Milne

Lotte Eisner's *Murnau* (1973) is the definitive text on Murnau; however, as Miss Eisner herself points out in the introduction to that work, she has put the emphasis on those of Murnau's films she had not already discussed at some length in her earlier *The Haunted Screen* (1969); and since those films include *Nosferatu*, *The Last Laugh*, *Tartuffe* and *Faust*, the earlier work is equally valuable. One can also consult, in French, Eric Rohmer's *L'Espace Cinématographique dans l'univers de F. W. Murnau* (1978).

As I mentioned in my Introduction, Murnau is one of my blind spots—except for his American films and I should point out that in spite of the interference and 'mutilation' by the producer of *City Girl* that Fieschi mentions, it still remains an extraordinarily beautiful film. I think that America was good for Murnau (as it was for Lubitsch), and who knows what he might not have achieved there had it not been for his untimely death?

MIKIO NARUSE

Donald Richie

Born in Tokyo in 1905, Mikio Naruse was orphaned at an early age and began working when still quite young. Unable to attend a university, he attempted to educate himself in public libraries, and it was not until he was twenty-one that he took a full-time job, as an assistant at the Shochiku–Kamata film studios. Later, remembering this period, he said, 'From the earliest age I have thought that the world we live in betrays us. This thought still remains with me. My parents died when I was fifteen, and I immediately had to become adult. It was the darkest period of my life—but the darkness continued.'

Still, during the early days at the film studio, he made a few friends who were to last throughout his life, among them the directors Heinosuke Gosho and Yasujiro Ozu. It was the former who prevailed upon the company to give Naruse his first directorial assignment and who later helped him edit this first film.

Naruse's section in the company was that devoted to light comedy, obviously not a genre that suited him. Yet it was through such comedies (and he made many) that he was able to find his own subject. Japanese comedy is usually family comedy, and it was in the family that Naruse was to find his theme. One of the differences between his very early films and those which came later was that of intent. His first film was about the break-up of a marriage. Several of his finest later films—*Meshi* (*Repast*, 1951), *Tsuma* (*Wife*, 1953), *Yama no Oto* (*Sounds from the Mountains*, 1954)—were also about marital break-ups. Yet the first was what the Japanese still call 'nonsense-comedy' and the later films, if not tragedies, were detailed and serious studies. 'I often,' Naruse said, 'make films about this—and I will always continue. The problem, after all, continues.'

To be sure, all of Naruse's later films are problem-pictures, but the problem is so large as to render the phrase almost meaningless. It is not the impossibility of marriage, or finding a job, or discovering love—it is the impossibility of life itself. Naruse defined this quality when speaking of characters in his later pictures: 'If they try to move forward even a little, they quickly hit a wall.' Life consistently betrays Naruse's people, and all their often touching efforts come to nothing. We are in a floating world which has no meaning for us, and yet we hope. This theme of expectations invariably ending in disappointment continues throughout all the director's best and most typical films.

The family (his invariable setting) is held together by bonds so strong that no single member can break them; life is a daily round of fixed customs, and even ways of expressing emotions are formalized. With all dramatic elements gone, even the slightest personal emotional reaction has a major and usually unfortunate effect. Tragedy constantly hovers over the Naruse character, and he is never more vulnerable than when, for once, he decides upon a personal action.

In *Wife*, both husband and wife try and fail; in *Sounds from the Mountains*, the wife tries and fails; in *Arakure* (1957), a woman makes extraordinary efforts, but fails; in *Onna ga Kaidan o Agaru Toki* (*When a Woman Ascends the Stairs*, 1960), the heroine grasps at happiness, thinks she has caught it, but finds she has not; in *Ukigumo* (*Floating Clouds*, 1955), the lovers try and fail; in *Nagareru* (*Flowing*, 1956) the geishas think they have solved their problems, but the real problem is only beginning. Yet there is little solemnity and no moral earnestness in Naruse's films. If such a term as light tragedy did not sound so pejorative it might well indicate the quality of such sunny yet hopeless pictures as *Okasan* (*Mother*, 1952) or *Flowing*. Naruse's first craft was comedy and—as with Ozu before him—its lesson was never forgotten.

In speaking of his subject, the family, Naruse once said, 'I am not interested in simple, trite home dramas.' Rather, he was interested in richly detailed, meticulously honest home dramas, and it was through them that he both accurately reflected a major fact of Japanese life and defined his own pictorial style. In this, like Ozu, Naruse used such constriction to advantage. One knows the house in *Wife* architecturally, for emotionally we have spent an hour and a half in it. The atmosphere becomes palpable; the same kind of shot, from the same general angle, appears again and again. Monotony is successfully suggested, but one is kept from monotony through the interest one feels in character and story and, perhaps most important, in structure.

The structure of this film—and that of most of Naruse's pictures—is also purposely restricted. There is but a single theme: the petrifaction of a marriage. This single strand is enriched by using and re-using it as minor as well as major theme. Thus early in the film the troubles of the couple upstairs are a presage of what eventually occurs downstairs; later, another minor story is introduced—a woman has been abandoned by her husband—and this too, we understand, is a possibility the heroine must face. This canon-like structure—all themes being segments of the same theme—creates a number of parallels which both continue and intensify our interest. At the same time it lends an ironic flavour to the film. Narise forces us that step backwards towards objectivity which ensures interest yet thwarts our native sentimentality.

Naruse is extremely skilful with this kind of meaningful restriction. During the coda of *Flowing* there is a fascinating combination of restrictions. We leave the geisha house and move backwards, as it were, along the river, down to the sea—by showing us more Naruse has suddenly begun to show us less as the camera leaves behind those we know and care about. At the same time the tempo slows and finally stops. The film unravels as though its very restrictions can no longer hold it together—both spatially and temporally the picture dissolves into that great, final and only true restriction: nothingness.

Yet, as with Ozu, less always implies more in the films of Naruse. And while his style is eclectic to the degree that he does not, as does Ozu, define extreme limitations for camera, grammar and structure, yet he shares with Ozu—and with most Japanese craftsmen and artists—a profound respect for life and a transparent honesty in picturing it.

He lacks, to be sure, that hope which is the higher wisdom—and which animates the greatest art, including that of Ozu. And because of this his world remains a narrow one and his art is, by definition, not transcendental. At the same time, given Naruse's skill, devotion and honesty, the world he created on film remains both profoundly troubling and deeply moving.

Naruse is almost unknown in England and America. He is better known in France, where his *Mother* has almost the status of a classic and turns up at the Cinémathèque Française quite often. See also Richie's article on Ozu.

ERMANNO OLMI

Gavin Millar

There is an incident which recurs in at least three of Ermanno Olmi's films. The hero is driving by car along a country road when he is involved in an accident or a near-accident with a horse- or hand-cart. The transgressor in each case is the motor car, and it would not be unfair to say that Olmi's sympathies are with what is old-fashioned, or, more accurately, beyond fashion. The heroes of his near-documentary feature films are themselves a little old-fashioned: not smart, not witty, not especially intelligent, made remarkable only by the close attention Olmi pays them. For this reason he often works with non-professionals whose jobs and lives are as similar as possible to those in the film. He is a chronicler of men and women at work in ordinary jobs and he is unusual in that, while the documentary situation may be dramatized, yet the work is not merely a background to the drama, but also the milieu in which it is played and the action which provokes its development. Thus in *Il Tempo si è fermato* (*Time Stood Still*, 1959) the setting is a hydroelectric dam high in the Italian Alps, the characters an old watchman and a youthful helper newly arrived as a holiday replacement. The story is of the growth of respect and affection between them, the old man modifying his initial mistrust, the young man his brashness. The agent in this growth is the job itself: routine and yet demanding, revealing the two men's characters to each other and to the spectator. The physical conditions of their lives, even the climate—a storm provokes the dénouement—act as the cement in their relationship.

In *Il Posto* (U.K.: *The Job*; U.S.: *The Sound of Trumpets*, 1961), the film's title itself indicates that it is wholly concerned with a job. A boy from the outskirts of Milan is sent by his poor family to apply for a lowly position with a large company in the city. He is successful and eventually achieves a small promotion. But the film leaves us in no doubt about the stultifying and unnecessary routine that his future as a clerk promises. The demands of work separate the engaged couple of *I Fidanzati* (U.K.: *The Engagement*; U.S.: *The Fiancés*, 1963), much to the distress of the girl who fears that she and her Milanese steel-worker will drift apart when he is sent to Sicily to help open up a new factory. In the event the separation allows them to view their affair in a new light and refreshes their love for one another. *Un Certo Giorno* (U.K.: *One Fine Day*, 1969), catches a middle-aged business man at the

moment of an important promotion. One of the road accidents noted above, in which a farmworker dies, forces him to reconsider his responsibility to himself and others and the place his career has in it.

The title of *I Recuperanti* (*The Scavengers*, 1970) describes the work of the two principal characters, an old man who makes a living from unearthing relics of scrap-iron in First World War battlefields, and the young man who, for a while, is persuaded to take up the trade. When the young man finally quits, it is to start a job on a building site, and it seems appropriate that he should be involving himself with construction rather than with the relics of destruction. As in the other examples, their attitude to work defines the characters of the two men.

Though the conditions of work are rarely satisfying nor the type of work particularly rewarding in itself, yet Olmi's own attitude to work is not overtly political. He is not a doctrinaire socialist any more than he is a doctrinaire Catholic, and it is pointless to look for any identifiable social theory in his work. Bruno, the main figure in *One Fine Day*, is an obvious target for conventional left-wing criticism. He is the assistant managing director of the Italian branch of a large European advertising agency. When his superior suffers a heart attack and is forced to retire temporarily, it is Bruno who is in line for promotion. He uses his friendship with a rich food manufacturer to obtain an invaluable account for the agency and so consolidate his position. He is thereafter in charge of a campaign to persuade the public to buy a packaged food entitled 'Job Dinner', which may have a ring of greater charm to Italian ears than to ours, but which in any case Olmi clearly intends to be a product of no great allure. Despite being cast in the role of the traditional capitalist exploiter, Bruno suffers no easy political condemnation at Olmi's hands. He is viewed sympathetically as an individual and not as a function. He is anxious about his employees' welfare. Neither the agency nor the factory appears to be a hard-hearted employer. Bruno, though unfaithful, is tender and solicitous to his wife and family and genuinely concerned about the possible harm he may do his superior, Davoli, in superseding him. There is at the same time a figure in the film who might pass for the type of revolutionary socialist, a lowly artist in the design department who is also involved with the secretary with whom Bruno is having an affair. He is at the other end of the scale from Bruno. He lives in a damp and comfortless garret and even gives it up to friends who say they need it, though they appear to need it less than he does. Speculative and solitary, he has few possessions and he makes no claim on the girl. It would be easy to force some kind of political message out of a confrontation engineered between these two, but there is no confrontation and no such message. Olmi observes people as they are and not as he would wish them to be. He will not make them serve other purposes at the expense of their individuality. The character Bruno is played by Brunetto del Vita, a non-actor whose real-life job is almost exactly what it is in the film. Olmi has recorded that he rewrote dialogue and events based on conversations he had had with Brunetto del Vita about his own life. Signor del Vita complained at one point that the film seemed to be revealing too much about him, but in the end confessed that he had drawn great benefit from it.

At the same time Olmi does not underestimate the drudgery which the organization of modern industry can impose on the ordinary worker. It is the central thesis of *Il Posto*. He has said: 'Work is not a damnation for man. It is his chance to express himself, the average person's opportunity to be creative. But work as it is organized becomes a condemnation. It annuls man. I am certainly not against work; or even against work which produces the things that society demands today. I am against the relationship man has today with the world he works in. Man is conditioned but he is also guilty of letting himself be conditioned.' Hence, therefore, Olmi's refusal to blame man's condition on any one social system. The remedy lies within himself, and it is to the individual that Olmi addresses his attention and curiosity. In order to avoid inaccurate generalization he draws constantly on first-hand experience, as in the case of Brunetto del Vita, or indeed in his own case.

Much of Olmi's own experience is reflected in his films. For example, he was himself a clerk for ten years, so he says, though for at least part of that time he must have been making the documentary films for the Edison-Volta company in Milan which culminated in *Time Stood Still*. Born in Bergamo in 1931, he moved with his family to Milan to look for work. Both he and his mother (his father died during the war) got jobs at the Edison factory, and it was there that his interest in the cinema was born and was cultivated. As a young man Olmi's first experience of the cinema was the post-war flowering of neo-realism, and his own interests and the circumstances of his career led him in the same direction. He began to make short documentaries for Edison about the company's own affairs: its welfare services, its holiday camps and schools for employees, the problems of apprentices as well as of those approaching retirement. From the last subject grew one of his most discussed early documentaries, *Il Pensionato* (1958), and from a visit to the company's hydroelectric projects in the Alps and the Dolomites came the knowledge which enabled him to plan *Time Stood Still*.

But if the first influences on Olmi were neo-realist, he managed to absorb the least melodramatic qualities of this movement. There is no hint of the overt sentimentality, the faint condescension which sometimes mars the neo-realist discovery of the working class, and though Olmi finds plenty of humour in his situations it is never cruel nor at the expense of his characters. It may be that having worked with the situations as real problems to be solved, in his time at Edison, he cannot therefore simply treat them as amusing incidents in a script. There is an old man in *Il Posto* who comes and sits in the office day after day, and waits patiently for the bell to release him in the afternoon. He has retired months ago, but cannot shake the habits of a lifetime. Olmi will not dwell on him. The situation is not indulged, merely presented for what it is worth as an incident in the education of the boy, Domenico.

It is this respect for the individual and for his privacy, coupled with acuteness of observation, which gives Olmi's work its particular blend of reticent affection. In his mountain hut amidst the snows the old watchman of *Time Stood Still* is observed at his housework one morning: cheerfully cleaning, brushing, dusting, while the radio plays. Suddenly the announcer introduces a programme 'for housewives in the home' and at the implied slur on his masculinity the old man hurries to switch it off. When he sets the table for the first meal he has prepared since the youth arrived, we feel the tension of his efforts to impress the boy, although they have hardly exchanged a word. The youth's jacket, carelessly draped over a chair, pulls it to the floor, and in this slight way Olmi makes us feel the weight and clumsiness of the young man's intrusion. He brings the two together with great tact. When each of them goes out to the lavatory, the other sneaks a glance at the book he is reading, carefully replacing it to avoid betraying his curiosity. Besides lacking confidence, the old man is comparatively inarticulate and his thoughts must therefore be shown by gestures. He asks the boy if he wants to move his bed into the warm kitchen with him, disguising his knowledge that the boy is nervous by himself in the storm by pretending that the reason is simply to combat the cold. The only sign that this offer has cost the old man effort is his own nervous clinking of a spoon in the soup plate just before he speaks.

The characters of Olmi's films themselves pay great attention to gestures, and seem to rely on other people's gestures rather than their words as a more trustworthy guide to behaviour. Domenico, the boy in *Il Posto*, and Antonia, the girl he falls for while taking the company exam, slip into a bar for a coffee at lunchtime. They are not quite sure what to do with their empty cups. It might be too provincial to return them to the counter. On the other hand, it might seem cavalier simply to leave them on the table. At the next table an older woman finishes her coffee, casually pushes the cup away from her and leaves. With relief the young pair copy her gesture to the letter. Earlier a degree of intimacy between the two is struck, much to Domenico's delight, merely by their having to share a spoon. In the office wordless stories are told about the clerks whom Olmi no doubt had had time to study in former years: the warm, annoying clown who is forever throwing waste paper into other people's baskets and missing; the elderly and miserly dandy who carefully cuts his cigarette in half before inserting it in his holder; the owlish, secretive, shy one who is writing a novel in his bedsitter and whose death will create a

vacancy for Domenico to fill. The charm of apprenticeship and the sadness of retirement remain constant themes for Olmi, and behind them the grim fact that one man's failure creates another man's opportunity: the shy clerk's death here, the illness of Davoli in *One Fine Day*.

It is often carelessly said that very little happens in an Olmi film. One partial but adequate answer is to recommend a study of his soundtracks. Even when no action is taking place—Domenico and his superior, the postman, sitting listlessly at their desk in the corridor—the life of the building can be heard going on around them, its unseen bustle giving point to their immobility. Even at the quietest moments the building itself seems to have a life of its own. There is a quiet, non-human rhythmic breathing, perhaps the ventilation system, perhaps not, but something, anyway, which Olmi seems to use to indicate that silence is never absolute, that life never quite gives up. The same sound, oppressively lonely now, can be heard in the rather unfriendly hotel where Giovanni is put up by his firm on his first night in Sicily (*I Fidanzati*).

Much of the atmosphere in Olmi's best sequences is established by the soundtrack as much as by the picture. Two memorable dance-hall episodes, in *Il Posto* and *I Fidanzati*, depend for their success on the careful build-up of sound. When Domenico, eagerly expectant, hurries to the company's New Year Party, he is crushed by the tomb-like silence of the near-empty hall. He is among the first to arrive and the banal sounds of last-minute preparation and forced gaiety among the few guests are emphasized by isolation. The beginning of *I Fidanzati* is distinguished by a similar effect. Patrons are assembling silently in a dimly lit dance-hall. Such is the gloom and the hush that we might be attending a funeral service, and indeed the dancers, when they begin, go about their ritual in much the same grim way. Before the lights go up and the dance begins, in order to emphasize the sense of subdued purpose, Olmi has isolated trivial but significant sounds: the echoing of solitary footsteps across the floor, the scraping of the occasional chair, the odd cough.

This technical sureness of touch and tact towards his subject is notably absent in

The dance-hall sequence from *I Fidanzati*: 'Patrons are assembling silently in a dimly lit dance-hall. Such is the gloom that we might be attending a funeral service, and indeed, the dancers, when they begin, go about their ritual in much the same grim way.'

Olmi's only widely acknowledged failure, the dramatized study of the life of Pope John XXIII entitled *E Venne un Uomo* (U.K.: *A Man Named John*; U.S.: *And There Came a Man*, 1965). Here the actor Rod Steiger is partly identified with Pope John and partly used as an external commentator on the action, and neither he nor Olmi quite manages to make the split role work. There are very routine assemblages of newsreel footage alternating with dramatized sections in which Steiger is seen, in the guise of the Pope—though dressed soberly as Rod Steiger—spending ten years as the Apostolic Delegate to Bulgaria, or appearing as the Papal Delegate in Paris. Olmi himself confessed that he may have been intimidated or inhibited by his great respect and affection for Pope John. But then it is one of Olmi's strengths that he shows respect and affection for all his subjects and this hardly therefore seems a convincing reason. At any rate the virtue of the film is characteristic: that he has celebrated Pope John as an ordinary man. Olmi's particular gift, in the aftermath of neo-realism, is to have avoided making universal or romantic heroes out of the poor and the working class, and instead to have celebrated the ordinary man, not for his ordinariness, but for his singularity.

Olmi's next film after *The Scavengers* was *Durante l'Estate* (*In the Summertime*, 1971). Visually his most stunning film, it was also his most Chaplinesque in mood. Its hero (known only as the Professor) makes a modest living colouring maps; its heroine gives away free soap samples. During a summer in an all but deserted Milan, the two meet, as if on a desert island. But society separates them: the Professor's fondness for conferring nobility on everyone *he* thinks worthy (establishing genealogies is his sideline) turns out to be illegal. But this is not important: he has made of his girl a princess, and a princess she remains.

A shot from *The Tree of the Wooden Clogs*, the film that won the Grand Prize at the Cannes Film Festival in 1978, thus reminding the world that Olmi is one of the great directors, and that 'his particular gift is to celebrate the ordinary person, not for his ordinariness, but for his singularity'.

As usual, Olmi's film did not do very well commercially in Italy (or anywhere, for that matter), and it was not until 1974 that he was able to make his next film: *La Circonstanza* (*The Circumstance*). The milieu is upperclass Milanese; this time, without sacrificing any of his 'humanity' or his realistic approach, Olmi has moved on to a different plane of film-making. The organization of the film is richer, more complex; the editing more aggressive; the narration more elliptical, denser. He displays no complacency towards his characters: all have their weaknesses, none is wholly admirable and yet each is totally understandable.

The film takes place during the course of a summer; it ends with the end of summer, and the end of some illusions. The 'Circumstance', the incident—the witnessing by the mother of an automobile accident in which a young man is seriously hurt—is in no way the 'key' to the film, simply the incursion of a different reality into the mother's life, just as the 'Business Game' seminar the father is obliged to attend is an incursion into his life. By the end of the film, the father, though disgusted by the manipulations attendant on the Business Game, manages to hang on to his job, though perhaps only for a while: he now realizes the precariousness of his position. The mother, who had taken a great interest in the injured young man, suddenly finds that his parents have taken him from the hospital and she will never see him again: her life will go on as before.

All the characters (including the children of the family) are presented to us in brief glimpses, with lots of overlapping dialogue—either a conversation precedes a shot-change, or it continues after a shot-change. This makes the opening sections of the film a little confusing, but not for long. The influence of Resnais is perhaps the cause of the fragmentation of the scenario, but the influence (if influence there be) has been completely assimilated.

Once more, the film was a flop in Italy, and in Britain its only non-festival screening has been on television. It seems to me that Olmi is one of the most important directors of the 60s and 70s and yet his films are just not very widely appreciated, and for the life of me I can't figure out why. It's not as if they were hard to understand, or remote in their subject-matter. After *La Circonstanza* he was again idle for several years, and only in 1977 was a new project announced. One film every three years is not enough for a talent like his.

However, the new project was *L'Albero degli Zoccoli* (*The Tree of the Wooden Clogs*) and when it was shown in 1978 at the Cannes Film Festival (from which Olmi had been absent for fifteen years) it won the Grand Prize, thus bringing Olmi's name back to an international public which had largely forgotten his very existence.

It is not an easy film, either; running for three hours, it treats peasant life in the region of Bergamo in northern Italy at the end of the last century. It is, in a sense, a return to his roots, for the film is based on stories told him by his grandmother.

The film is realistic in the sense that Olmi insisted on direct sound (something very rare in the Italian cinema) and, what's more, the actors speak, not Italian, but Bergamasque. Actually, they are not actors, but peasants themselves, living, re-living a series of moments out of their collective history.

Olmi starts out from a realistic basis, but only in order immediately to transcend it: these stories told him by his grandmother are transformed into a magnificent fresco of the life of a group of share-croppers through the course of a year. A baby is born, a family is thrown off the farm by the landowner, two young people become engaged and get married (their honeymoon trip to Milan by barge is perhaps the most beautiful single sequence), a cow sickens, but responds miraculously to prayer, etc. Elegiac would be the best word to describe the sensual beauty of the film were it not for Olmi's essential toughness and spare simplicity. This is not a nostalgic evocation of the past; however tender and moving the relations between the characters, it is a film about a system which thankfully no longer exists. One comes out of the film feeling as if one had spent—not three hours but a lifetime in another world.

MARCEL OPHULS

David Wilson

At a time when documentary film-making has fragmented into a multitude of styles and methods, Marcel Ophuls (born 1927) has established a steady reputation for consistency. That reputation was founded on *Le Chagrin et la Pitié* (*The Sorrow and the Pity*, 1970), a marathon enquiry into what really happened during the German wartime occupation of France. Exploding the comfortable myth of the Resistance in its revelation of the extent of the French people's complicity in the occupation, this film ruffled not a few governmental feathers and sparked off a considerable debate in France and abroad. The frequently hostile reaction to the film in France simply confirmed Ophuls' conviction that politics and everyday life are indissoluble; a conviction which motivated a later film, *A Sense of Loss* (1972), about the continuing crisis in Northern Ireland, which turned its focus on the effect on the ordinary people of Ulster of political and sectarian murders.

Ophuls inherited none of the baroque style of his father, Max Ophuls. His films (all documentaries apart from a successful comedy, *Peau de Banane* [1963], a thriller, *Feu à Volonté* [1964] and a contribution to the multi-national *L'Amour à Vingt Ans* [*Love at Twenty*, 1962]) owe nothing to embellishment and everything to a meticulous working method, perhaps attributable to an apprenticeship in television journalism. Assiduously researched, they are films assembled in the cutting-room from the raw material of numerous interviews. Dispensing with commentary and relying on people's willingness to be revealing about themselves in front of a camera, Ophuls constructs a kind of impressionist fresco which speaks volumes about the relationship of people and politics. The method is vindicated by the response which his films provoke, although his choice of subject also usually carries a built-in guarantee of controversy.

The Memory of Justice (1975) was indeed controversial on every level. During its long period of gestation, the film was taken away from Ophuls to be re-edited (shades of *Lola Montès!*). Happily, after some intense fighting, Ophuls regained control of the film, and it is *his* version which was shown all over the world (except on German television). What was the controversy about? Simply that Ophuls in this film tried to compare German war crimes with what has happened since in other places in the world: places like Algeria and Vietnam. The idea of the film began as an examination of the validity of the Nuremberg trials, but Ophuls soon realized that the subject of war guilt and punishment could not be seen in isolation. And the film grew and grew until it reached its final length: 4 hours and 38 minutes.

Its very length also made the film controversial: in Britain it was shown during one evening on BBC television; in America it opened in a cinema, but commercially its length told against it. Nevertheless, it seems to me that the film is Ophuls' best to date; less tidy, perhaps, than *Le Chagrin et la Pitié*, it attempts to deal with questions that are more ambiguous and more controversial than the German occupation of France. And it succeeds brilliantly in holding an audience spellbound throughout its length. Thanks to Ophuls, documentary is no longer a dirty word.

MAX OPHULS

Jon Halliday

When Max Ophuls died in hospital in Hamburg in 1957, at the age of fifty-five, the book beside his bed was Goethe's *Faust*. And just as Goethe's *Faust* will probably remain beyond the reach of cinema, so the cinematic work of Max Ophuls will probably remain beyond the reach of words and verbal criticism for ever.

For no *description* can hope to capture the essence of Ophuls' cinema. A purely thematic or stylistic analysis would be worthlessly empty compared with the incredible richness of what Ophuls managed to put on film. It is probably easier to write about John Ford or Josef von Sternberg: much of Ford's most masterly work is done with a still camera; much of Sternberg's through the use of light. Most of Ophuls' greatest moments were achieved through highly complex camerawork: the ball sequence in *La Signora di Tutti* (1934), the dance-hall sequence at the beginning of *Le Plaisir* (1952), numerous moments in *Lola Montès* (U.K.: *The Fall of Lola Montes*, 1955). The intense emotion which Ophuls can conjure up as we follow the masked dancer, circling till he falls, in *Le Plaisir* may well never be surpassed in cinema.

Like Douglas Sirk, Ophuls paid a lot of attention to titles. And the trio of *Liebelei* (1932), *La Ronde* (1950) and *Le Plaisir* contains a possible outline (not a description) of the Ophulsian view of the world, and what elements make for drama and emotion.

Olga Tschechowa and Paul Otto in *Liebelei*, 'Ophuls' first big success'.

Martine Carol (in foreground) in a shot from *Lola Montès*, a film 'that shows one of the essential ingredients of Ophuls' world at its clearest: exploitation'.

Ophuls had worked for over a decade in the theatre, and had made his mark very early on as a prodigiously prolific and successful stage director, with over 200 productions to his credit. Like Sirk, who was also schooled in the tough commercial world of the theatre in Weimar Germany, Ophuls developed a healthy respect for audiences, and never meandered off into exoticism or 'artiness'. He believed in entertainment.

But, like all accomplished dramatists, Ophuls was well aware that not everything is interesting, and even less is dramatic. His chosen terrain was love. Not straightforward love, of course, but desire without love, pleasure without love, unrequited love (as, for example, in *Letter from an Unknown Woman*, 1948). Where true love does occur, as in *Liebelei*, it is blocked by social circumstances.

Liebelei, Ophuls' first big success, is a good film to start with, since it gathers together many of the elements in his picture-making. It has often been remarked that Ophuls was deeply concerned with the lost world of Habsburg Vienna. But, as Arthur Schnitzler, the author of the originals of both *Liebelei* and *La Ronde* (*Reigen*), well knew, Vienna in the years prior to the collapse of the Austro-Hungarian Empire was not the wonderful city of romance which it was often portrayed to be. Rather, it was a rotting but still hidebound nightmare, where class, formality and pretence were sure to win out over true love. If true love were ever to appear, it would probably be shot down—in this case in a horrible (off-screen) duel. People were simply not allowed by the society and its code to be happy and fall in love. In another way, both the successful concert pianist, Stefan Brand (Louis Jourdan), and Liza Berndl (Joan Fontaine) in *Letter from an Unknown Woman* are the creatures of the false world of old Vienna, and the pressures it generated. Stefan Brand belongs to the society which has made him in its own likeness: elegant, charming, thoughtless, shallow. Like Fritz Lobheimer (Wolfgang Liebeneiner) in *Liebelei*, Stefan Brand, too, is consigned by Ophuls to (presumably) death in a duel.

It is too easily forgotten, or ignored, that Ophuls' career in the theatre before he entered films in 1930 brought him into contact with a world of great political ferment. Most of the leading playwrights of his generation were highly political, and Ophuls—who was working mainly in Germany—was inevitably affected by this. After Ophuls fled from Germany at the time of the Nazi takeover, he was invited to go and work in the U.S.S.R. He went so far as to visit Russia and inspect working conditions there. Apparently, he found them unsatisfactory or uncongenial. But if one compares him with other romantics—Borzage or Rossellini—it is unimaginable that someone like Borzage would even have considered working in the Soviet Union in the 30s.

The aspect of social criticism certainly needs working into any analysis of Ophuls. All his characters are prisoners of social circumstances and of class. This is sometimes masked to some extent by wealth, which appears to mitigate suffering. But a closer look will reveal that wealth is no way out for Ophuls' characters. On the contrary: one can easily travel downwards, even with money (as in *La Signora di Tutti*). And the title of one of Ophuls' films, *Komedie om Geld* (1936), is a statement all on its own. *De Mayerling à Sarajevo* (U.K.: *Sarajevo*; U.S.: *Mayerling to Sarajevo*, 1940) likewise describes the trajectory of doom—this time for royalty.

Romanticism (not to be confused with romance) is one of the constants of Ophuls' picture-making. But Ophuls' type of romanticism is light-years away from Anglo-Saxon romanticism, and has been notoriously difficult for film critics in both the U.S.A. and Britain to grasp. The term 'bitter-sweet' is sometimes evoked in this connection. But Ophuls goes far beyond the whimsical scratchings of the classless bitter-sweet English playwrights and film directors. The world of money is evoked with great ruthlessness in his films, but never without style. Two examples are *La Signora di Tutti* and *Lola Montès*. The downfall of the rich businessman, Leonardo Nanni (Memo Benassi), who has squandered his money on the beautiful Gaby Doriot (Isa Miranda), is painted just as faithfully in *La Signora di Tutti* as is a parallel downfall in any American film about business. And both *La Signora di Tutti* and *Lola Montès* show one of the essential ingredients of Ophuls' world at its clearest: exploitation. Neither film is only about the relationship between show-business and the public. They are both about men exploiting women for show, and about men pushing women beyond the limits of their endurance—for money, essentially. For, although Ophuls (like Sternberg, Renoir and Sirk) often gives the more interesting parts in his films to women, who think more and better than the men, he is well aware of the structure of exploitation, particularly in the entertainment business, which he well knew to be in large part a business in which men pay women to entertain men.

But to talk about the spectacle and exploitation as 'pure' phenomena is to reduce Ophuls' artistry to something paltry and mean. For Ophuls knew that art has to mediate reality. The Anglo-Saxon utilitarian tradition finds it particularly hard to cope with this kind of vision. Richard Roud in his 1958 *Index* on Ophuls quotes Penelope Houston: 'He is a director who rarely moves out of a minor key, and who, within self-imposed limitations, has achieved a real personal style; his films may be unimportant, but they are never trivial.' This is a truly ludicrous statement. The whole concept of a film as 'important' is patently absurd. Ophuls' films are about some of the deepest—and most important—feelings and emotions in people's lives. How one feels about love, despair, social pressures, etc. is extremely important. But Houston's utilitarianism prevents her appreciating what Ophuls is all about. Perhaps this is part of the British disease of refusing to think seriously about films about wealth. But wealth may be more 'important' than poverty and it is frequently more interesting.

Not always, of course. In Weimar Germany Ophuls staged a number of plays with a definite proletarian content—e.g. Wolf's *Die Matrosen von Cattaro* (*The Sailors of Kotor*), about a mutiny in the Austro-Hungarian navy during the First World War. But whereas Ophuls was able to work consistently, more or less, on projects of his own choosing in Weimar Germany, where there was a vital left-wing culture particularly active in the theatre, once he left Germany he was obliged to work mainly in societies where left-wing culture was much weaker and where he had less freedom of choice over his projects. These situations have frequently led dramatic directors to steer away from the present. When confronted with the right story, Ophuls was perfectly able to deal with the present—as in *La Signora di Tutti*, *The Reckless Moment* (1949) or *Caught* (1949). And the one time he reached more than a hundred years back (*The Exile*, made in 1947), he seemed not entirely at home with the period. But the fact is that the majority of his films from 1933 onwards are set in the past. This is not just because, as Anton Walbrook says in *La Ronde*, 'the past is more restful than the present—and more sure than the future'. It may also be because there is a greater popular consensus on the past. It goes without saying that the past is just as good a subject for drama as is the present. Every playwright from Shakespeare downwards bears witness to that. But it is also true that, particularly in unsettled times, the past may collect a greater degree of mass agreement—and Ophuls was always after a mass audience. He realized that nothing dates like a 'topical' film.

Ophuls seized the mass acceptance of the past (an acceptance equally widespread on both sides of the Atlantic) to enchant and entice his audience. Many times he 'presented' his own film: for example, the barker at the beginning of *Komedie om Geld*, or Anton Walbrook at the opening of *La Ronde*. At other times, he used voice-over techniques (*Letter from an Unknown Woman*) or a combination of the two (*Lola Montès*) to lead his watchers complicitly into his own magical world—magic to them, too, because it was also their world, even if only the world of their dreams. But Ophuls, like Calderón and Shakespeare, knew that dreams are frequently more real and more powerful than so-called real life. As an entertainer, he knew that he had to snare the audience's attention, to dazzle their senses with fine costumes, the semblance of romance, wealth, beauty and the other ingredients of bourgeois dreams. He nearly always allowed himself a double seduction: having enchanted his audience into the world of his film, he would then lead them on to a performance at the opera, where his audience could participate with the film's cast in a spectacle, Mozart's *Die Entführung aus dem Serail*, for example. This apparently simple device would serve to deepen the audience's participation in the film (cf. Visconti's *Senso*). But, having made sure of his audience by these devices, Ophuls would often subtly move the film on to another level. With *Liebelei*, for example, the audience want to know that they are watching a drama, but at another level they would like what they are watching to be 'real'. And it is real. One is moved by Fritz's death, and—even more—by that of Christine Weiring (Magda Schneider). A director has to make people believe. And the past is better terrain for this 'make-believe' than the present. In its way, a film like *The Reckless Moment* is relentlessly 'realist': there is no evident 'make-believe'. Yet, at another level, the whole film is another version of 'make-believe', quite different from the illusions staged by Ophuls in, say, *De Mayerling à Sarajevo* or *La Ronde*.

More than any other director, except possibly Sternberg or Sirk, Ophuls has been criticized for his use of décor—in particular, staircases. It is clear from watching Ophuls' films that he, like Sternberg and Sirk, was thoroughly familiar with all the major theories of staging and representation which were current in his time. Bertolt Brecht, in particular (but not only he), had emphasized the importance of objects. The staircase had taken on a central role in the theatre of Leopold Jessner, one of the dominant figures in the German theatre during Ophuls' formative period. On stage, as in films, things can be as important as people. This goes not just for individual objects, such as a knife or a gun, but for the décor as a whole. People *become* their décor. People are heavily influenced by, say, the armchairs in their own sitting-rooms. Visitors to a house are frequently shown the house before the people. Acquaintances who meet may turn first to each other's clothes rather than to their persons. Ophuls uses the ritual of old Vienna to encase his characters: many of them are strapped into their uniforms, both military and mufti. One of the most stunning and elegant demonstrations of the power of décor is the end of *Liebelei*: after Christine has jumped to her death the camera takes us slowly round the empty flat, allowing us to relive the relationship between Christine and Franz. Joan Fontaine's return to the winding staircase in *Letter from an Unknown Woman* does more than simply allow her to relive *her* memories: it also makes the audience relive *their* memories.

Perhaps the most amazing demonstration of the 'Brechtian' theses about objects is *Madame de . . .* (U.S.: *The Earrings of Madame de . . .*, 1953). Here the central 'character' actually is an object—a pair of earrings. These are not just the attributes of human beings. They assume a power of their own; they greatly influence people's behaviour. The long take of Danielle Darrieux pacing from one closet to another in her luxurious bedroom is not just a *tour de force*: it is a further illustration of the sick relationship between allegedly thinking human beings and objects (possessions). Ophuls never lays this on too heavily. He does not have to. For the world he evokes is a total one, which he can convey with a swift, almost impressionistic touch. Like a work by Velazquez, the picture he presents is that of a world, for those who wish to look.

Ophuls' work suffered terribly in his own lifetime from producers, constant interruptions and forced inactivity: for six long years, he was out of work in Hollywood. His films were frequently mauled by stupid critics, and remain exceedingly hard to see, which in turn has affected appreciation of his *oeuvre*. It is time he was placed right at the top of the pantheon, where he belongs. This brief appreciation has not begun to touch on the enchanted sadness which Ophuls could bring to the screen: the magical camera movements, his mastery of music, his gift for epigram—and his ability to merge all these talents into a whole. No other director in the history of cinema, except perhaps Jean Renoir, had such extraordinary control over every aspect of film-making. Few were more shabbily treated in their time, or less adequately appreciated after their careers were over. Ophulsian cinema is best exemplified in the magnificent scene at the end of *Le Plaisir*. As the two men watch Jean (Daniel Gélin) wheel his crippled wife Josephine, whom he has married only out of sympathy, along the sands in a wonderfully gloomy light, one says to the other: 'How sad.' 'Yes,' comes the reply, 'but happiness isn't gay.'

Halliday's pointing up of the political significance and the material basis of Ophuls' world is a welcome counter-balance to most appreciations of Ophuls, which tend to con-

centrate on his more romantic side. These elements, however, are important. Halliday quotes from Penelope Houston in my own brief *Index* (1958); there are two longer studies of his work in French: Claude Beylie's *Max Ophuls* (1965) and Georges Annenkov's *Max Ophuls* (1962). Ophuls' own memoirs were published in book form in 1959 as *Max Ophuls par Max Ophuls*. Ophuls, as Andrew Sarris has pointed out, is 'more than the sum of his camera movements' and although his films are dominated by women, his view of men is almost as penetrating. This being said, one must add that the performances he drew from Isa Miranda and Danielle Darrieux rank high in the history of film acting.

I think, by the way, that Halliday has not grasped the irony intended in Penelope Houston's statement that 'his films may be unimportant'. At the time, Ophuls was incredibly under-rated and *Sight and Sound* and *Sequence* were his chief defenders outside France.

NAGISA OSHIMA AND JAPANESE CINEMA IN THE 60s

Noël Burch

There is much to be said for a division of Japanese film history into four broad periods of alternating poverty and richness: prior to 1930 or so, a long period of assimilation of the narrative techniques developed in Europe and America with, so far as we are able to judge today from the handful of surviving films, only an occasional vanguard work (Kinugasa's recently discovered *Kurutta Ippeiji* [*A Page of Madness*, 1926] is the most notable example) to herald the decisive refutation of the Hollywood ethos that was still to come; from 1930 to 1945 a period of sustained fertility, not only in the work of such undisputed masters as Yasujiro Ozu, Kenji Mizoguchi and Mikio Naruse, but also in the often forgotten accomplishments of men like Heinosuke Gosho, Tomotaka Tasaka, Sadao Yamanaka and Hiroshi Shimizu. The culturally repressive American occupation and the years that followed the peace treaty saw the rise of only one major figure, Akira Kurosawa, who bridged the gap between the pre-war masters and the young radicals, while around him an overwhelmingly predominant mercantile academicism marginally accommodated a form of social realism. I shall attempt to describe here the generation of film-makers who, in the 60s, once again put Japanese films among the vanguard of international cinema.

The best known and/or most significant directors of this period are, in the approximate order in which they came to be known in Europe, Hiroshi Teshigahara, Susumu Hani, Nagisa Oshima, and Yoshishige Yoshida. Briefly we might say that these directors have combined the salient features of each of the previous generations, features which they have tended to *radicalize* in both senses of the term. Rejecting the academic transparency of Tadashi Imai, Kajiro Yamamoto *et al.*, they none the less share these film-makers' sense of political commitment (as opposed to the purely social commitment of Mizoguchi, Ozu, Naruse and their generation), which they have radicalized in precisely the same degree that a whole generation of left-wing intellectuals, under pressure from the young, have moved to the left of the Communist Party. This political radicalization, moreover, has gone hand in hand with a rehabilitation, via the work of Kurosawa, of the aesthetic attitudes inherent in the work of the pre-war masters, a rehabilitation which is also a radicalization in that the ethos of transparency, rejected only partially by Ozu and Mizoguchi, has been radically disavowed by Oshima, Toshio Matsumoto, Yoshida, Shinsuke Ogawa and many of their contemporaries.

It is very difficult for a Westerner, even when he is sympathetic to or involved in the revolutionary movements of the West, to understand the complex attitudes of contemporary Japanese radicals. One has only to recall in this connection the traumatic effect which the novelist Yukio Mishima's spectacular suicide had on the bulk of young ultra-leftists, some of whom went so far as to perpetrate sickening atrocities on erring comrades, purportedly to prove that blood sacrifice was not a monopoly of the militarist caste. Although the young radicals reject the 'nationalist' paraphernalia of the extreme right (traditional dress, martial arts), they do tend to invoke a number of traditional moral and/or aesthetic values in their challenge to the cosmopolitan, U.S.-oriented class of technocrats who have controlled 'Japan Inc.' since the end of the war and whose unbridled liberalism has succeeded in constituting the world's second economic power at a speed which imperils not only the health of the nation but the very ecology of the islands themselves.

This 'traditionalist' view of the new Japanese left is no doubt superficial. For whatever it is worth, however, it does seem to find striking corroboration in the way in which these young film-makers have embodied the proposition that Japanese cinema at its best constitutes a 'reactivation' of Japan's fossilized traditional arts. The radically 'decentred' framing of Yoshida, Matsumoto's 'Brechtian' adaptation of a Kabuki drama, Wakamatsu's ritualization of violence, Ogawa's unending, spiral-like meditations on a single political struggle are merely the most obvious pieces of evidence that classical painting, theatre and the 'domestic arts' live again in the most advanced Japanese film-making.

Teshigahara, Hani, Yoshida and Oshima all began making films in the late 50s or early 60s. All started with the major companies and found it necessary, at one stage or another of their careers, to 'go independent', if only temporarily. Of the four, Teshigahara is perhaps the most ambitious, and to my mind the least rewarding. Even more easily than the other film-makers of his generation, he tends to become involved in heavily symbolic, intricate subjects, often drawn from post-war Japanese literature and intrinsically fated, it seems, to stimulate, at best, superficially brilliant stylistic revamping rather than any thorough-going textual reorganization in terms of specific cinematic parameters. His most interesting film to date still seems to me to be his first, *Otoshi Ana* or *Kashito Kodomo* (*Pitfall*, 1962), an odd mixture of virulent social satire—it deals with a rather caricatural labour conflict—and the traditional elements of the ghost film (*kwaidan eiga*), one of the most popular and widespread genres in Japanese mass cinema and the one which has traditionally offered the area of widest invention within a fixed framework, the elements of suspense and magic being subjected to endless variations as to their modes of presentation. Though Teshigahara was not completely successful in dialecticizing the conflicting modes of discourse which he chose to combine, that film certainly contained more exciting potentialities than the very slick, totally linear *Suna no Onna* (U.K.: *Woman of the Dunes*; U.S.: *Woman in the Dunes*, 1964), drawn from a neo-Kafka-esque novel by Koto Abe. Not only did this film establish Teshigahara's reputation on the international art cinema market, but it also seems to have determined once and for all his line of endeavour. Both *Tanin no Kao* (*The Face of Another*, 1966) and *Moetsukita Chizu* (U.K.: *Man Without a Map*; U.S.: *The Ruined Map*, 1968) were allegorical dramas literally far more 'sophisticated', by Western standards, than most Japanese films; but one feels precisely that Teshigahara is perhaps too attentive to Western standards of psychological complexity and metaphysical generalization as against the highly structured behaviour patterns which are concretely and peculiarly Japanese and which seem so much more conducive to the production of specifically cinematic 'texts'. However, I must insist that I regard none of the judgements offered in this article as definitive: Teshigahara, for example, has made fewer than half a dozen films, all of which are nothing if not courageously 'off the beaten track', and there is nothing to prove that a director as young as he still is will not evolve in a completely unforeseeable direction.

Susumu Hani, at least in his early films, chose far more modest, essentially intimist, tragi-comic subjects and developed them into his best work. More recently, however, he seems to have allowed his technical mastery to lead him into stylistic exercises involving overly ambitious, 'transcendental' treatments of modishly erotic themes; *Hatsukoi Ji-gokuhen* (*The Inferno of First Love*, 1968), contains some startlingly attractive scenes, in particular one in which the adolescent hero sexually 'assaults' a child in a park, but the rigorous developments to which Oshima has subjected material of this kind puts Hani's accomplishment into properly modest perspective. His best film to date is probably *Kanojo to Kare* (*She and He*, 1963), a delicate study in neo-Dostoevskian psychology: the character of the wife, as stunningly interpreted by Hani's own wife, may be regarded as a variant on Prince Mishkin, a woman continually bringing on minor domestic dramas through her compulsive urge to do good, to sacrifice herself for others. Stylistically, the film is constantly and rigorously inventive, in a way reminiscent of middle-period Antonioni: there is a concern with renewing the movement of the set-up/editing texture, and a skilful use of ellipsis. These qualities also recur in *Bwana Toshi no Uta* (*Bwana Toshi* or *The Song of Bwana Toshi*, 1965), a study of the serio-comic relationships between a Japanese employee come to an African village to prepare for the arrival of his firm there and the ... natives. Here, Hani's main effort at conceptualization was again devoted to the set-up/editing relationship, undeniably very original: unexpected ellipses and well-dosed passages of 'overcutting' give the film a pleasantly syncopated movement. Hani is practically the only Japanese film-maker to have made several films abroad. And though he has achieved some of his most satisfying results portraying

the relationships between Japanese and non-European cultures (*Bwana Toshi*, but also *Andes no Hanayome* [*Bride of the Andes*], 1966), his recent work (in Europe) has been less convincing. But it seems difficult to believe that the maker of *She and He* won't eventually find his way again.

The case of Yoshishige Yoshida is perhaps even more contradictory. His early films, made for a major company, were quite traditional, intimist dramas, in the manner of Ozu and Naruse, but on a level with, say, post-war Tasaka (i.e., respectable). Then, in 1969, he produced the film that made his small reputation in Europe: *Eros plus Gyakusatsu* (*Eros Plus Massacre*). This three-and-a-half-hour chronicle deals with the life and death of a famous Japanese anarchist, strangled by the political police along with his wife and child early in this century. The film combines scenes of present-day Japan—an adolescent couple evoke the memory of the martyr along with their own personal and ideological problems—with re-enactments of scenes from the anarchist's life and his relationships with three different women; and it also involves radically unrealistic, theatrical scenes in which the brutal execution and other symbolically crucial moments are staged with great lyrical intensity. Characters move back and forth between the two historical periods (a woman in period dress takes a modern train, gets out at a modern station, ultimately reaches a period house), and the treatment shifts from semi-realism to extreme stylization, in particular through radical decentring of the (CinemaScope) frame and skilful use of telephoto lenses. The culminating fantasy sequence of the imagined death of the martyr, toppling screen after screen in headlong, lurching flight, is one of the most splendid variations I know on histrionic death, an age-old theme of Japanese culture.

In subsequent films, Yoshida has tried to develop the various approaches which characterized *Eros Plus Massacre* and were so brilliantly combined in it. Unfortunately, *Rengoku Eroica* (*Heroic Purgatory*, 1970) seems to me little more than a brilliant exercise in editing decentred shots woven into a rather obscure politico-metaphysical discourse, while *Kokuhaku Teki Jogu Ron* (*Confession, Theories, Actresses*, 1971) is a stylistically rather flat attempt to build a vaguely Pirandellian edifice round the professional and personal problems of three film actresses. One senses, in all his recent films, that Yoshida is going through a serious crisis: it is impossible for him to go back to the safe ground he trod before *Eros Plus Massacre*, yet this film seems to have set him on paths which he may not be equipped to negotiate. Generally speaking, I feel that the need experienced by these three directors to 'reactivate' the overt stylization to be found in classics such as *A Page of Madness* or, closer at hand, *Rashomon* and *Throne of Blood*, has overshot its mark, so to speak, falling into a mechanistic aestheticism.

Of the four directors, only Nagisa Oshima, by far the most important Japanese filmmaker of his generation, has succeeded in avoiding this pitfall, at least in most of the films he has made since 1966. Oshima began his directing career with a major company (Shochiku) and specialized in 'youth films' (*seishin eiga*), which no doubt seem fairly undistinguished today but have a sequence here or there in which the director's resolutely experimental spirit can already be glimpsed. (I recall, in *Seishun Zankoku Monogatari* [*A Story of the Cruelty of Youth*, also known as *Cruel Stories of Youth* and *Naked Youth* (*A Story of Cruelty*), 1960] a strikingly long single-shot sequence in which the youthful hero slowly munches an apple.) The single-shot sequence and its dramaturgical and structural implications were to preoccupy Oshima for several years. What is generally regarded as his first 'personal' film—*Nihon no Yoru to Kiri* (*Night and Fog in Japan*, 1960)—took as its principal narrative figure long, methodically searching pan-shots picking out now one, now another of the participants in a heavily symbolic, theatrically staged wedding reception. The theme of the film is what Oshima's peer-group regard as the Japanese Communist Party's 'betrayal' at the end of the American occupation (many then felt and still feel that concerted extra-parliamentary action might have brought on a revolutionary situation), and the narrative otherwise consists of flashbacks from this gloomy reception to a students' dormitory in the early 50s filmed in the academically 'expressive', over-serious

style of the neo-realist films of that period, so that they smack a little of pastiche.

This eclecticism disappeared in Oshima's very next film, his first really substantial work; and while he has almost always been at great pains to stake out a completely new area of research with each film, nearly all of them, from *Shiiku* (*The Catch*, 1961) on, possess an extraordinarily rigorous internal system. It was in *The Catch* that he seems to have decided to come to grips with the problems of organizing the long take, employed here with Mizoguchi-like exclusiveness. The film is a relentlessly savage fable about a Japanese mountain village whose inhabitants accidentally capture a black American airman only a few weeks before the 1945 capitulation. The 'prisoner of war' acts as a catalyst, bringing out all the repressed aggressions and latent political conflicts beneath the tradition-girded surface of the community, until the villagers finally murder their prisoner, ostensibly to avoid having 'an extra mouth to feed' in those times of great scarcity. Oshima displays a very original approach to the organization of the single-shot sequence (and long takes in general), based on slow, brief reframings and subtle recompositions of an always fully articulated screen-surface, rather than indulging in the crane-powered acrobatics generally associated with long takes in the West (Wyler, Ophuls, Jancsó); in his use of frame-edge to achieve maximum dynamic change through minimum camera movement, he comes close to the spirit of certain periods of Japanese graphic art, emphasizing as he does depth of field and radical frame-distinctions within each shot.

Oshima's next two important films involved a complete reversal, typical of his restless intelligence: both *Hakuchu no Torima* (*Violence at Noon*, 1966) and *Ninja Bugeicha* (*Tales of the Ninja*, 1967) are radically disjunctive films, involving well over two thousand shots each! *Tales of the Ninja* is something of an oddity: it is made up entirely of panels from a popular comic strip, one which began the present craze for *manga* (comics for adults), violent, erotic and often extraordinarily sophisticated in their pseudo-cinematic layouts, a craze which is shared by men, women and children of all ages and all classes. The explosively fast cutting of *Tales of the Ninja*, whose stylized images are accompanied by naturalistic spoken dialogue and richly musical sound effects, producing a strange and often very striking vertical disjunction, is closely related to the structural texture of what I regard as one of Oshima's greatest films, *Violence at Noon*. This often deliberately obscure study of a sex criminal, taken from an actual case history, was perhaps the first film since *October* and *The General Line* systematically to employ Eisenstein's principle of the 'montage unit'. In a sense, Oshima may be said to have gone even further: cutting each sequence into what would normally be regarded as an inordinate number of shots, often radically contrasting in size, he 'crossed the line' so frequently that after a very short time the very notion of correctness or incorrectness in matching tends to blur, and one enters an entirely new relationship with pro-filmic space, whose only logic is that of the successive disjunctive images on the screen and our imagined notion of continuity. To what extent *Violence at Noon* goes beyond this experimental system, clearly perceivable on first viewing, to what extent it is informed as rigorously as the masterpieces of Dreyer and Eisenstein to which it is related, is difficult to say without closer analysis, quite impossible at the moment because of a conflict between Oshima and the production company regarding the film's distribution abroad (like most of Oshima's films, *Violence at Noon* had only the briefest of runs in Japan, where revivals are almost unknown, even in Tokyo; in fact, most Japanese films—prints and negatives—are actually destroyed soon after their commercial career—three or four years at best—is deemed to be over, which explains why a country which has been producing an average of four hundred to five hundred films a year for over fifty years has managed to preserve only a few hundred from its prestigious pre-war period, and why so many presumed masterpieces are probably lost for ever).

Apart from an apparent preoccupation with making each film as different from its predecessor as possible, I believe one may distinguish in Oshima's work, almost from its very inception, two main tendencies. On the one hand are films like *The Catch*, *Violence at Noon*, *Koshikei* (*Death by Hanging*, 1968), *Shinjuku Dorobo Nikki* (*The Diary of a Shinjuku Thief*, 1969) and *Tokyo Senso*

Sengo Hiwa (*The Man Who Left His Will on Film*, 1970), each of which in a characteristically different way tends to subvert the codes of narrative transparency, designating them as codes and *organizing* their parameters with the same movement that 'deconstructs' them. The other tendency, which has always alternated with the first, seems on the contrary to subsume those codes, more or less uncritically, and to centre the 'creative' effort on the narrative as such (acting). True, the fundamental *linearity* of such films as *Shonen* (*Boy*, 1969) and *Gishiki* (*The Ceremony*, 1971), two of Oshima's major successes in Europe and the United States, does not prevent them from being remarkable social and psychological studies, among the most sophisticated to have been made anywhere in the last decade; but to my mind, they are far less important than the anti-linear, dialectical films mentioned above, while neither *Nihon shunka-ko* (*Treatise on Japanese Bawdy Songs*, 1967), a rather recondite examination of how Japanese youth approaches the question, primordial to Oshima since that film, of what it means to be Japanese, nor above all *Natsu no Imoto* (*Dear Summer Sister*, 1972), his most academic film to date, produced on the occasion of Okinawa's return to Japan and involving an allegorically critical appraisal of Japan's role as a colonizing nation, can be regarded as worthy of the author of *Violence at Noon* or *Death by Hanging*.

It is this last film which first earned Oshima a reputation abroad. Among a generation of film-makers who have often been deeply and explicitly influenced by the concepts of Brecht, so intimately connected with their own traditional arts (as Brecht himself and, more recently, Roland Barthes have penetratingly demonstrated), it is *Death by Hanging* which perhaps best illustrates this intercultural encounter. Beginning like a documentary against the death penalty, it seems to develop into a black comedy when the 'condemned man's body refuses to die'. But this hitch in the legal process sets off another process—incidentally denouncing the absurdity of the death penalty, but primarily embodying the struggle to achieve political consciousness of an oppressed ethnic minority (the Koreans of Japan)—a process involving the deconstruction both of Japan-

A scene from Oshima's *Boy*, a 'remarkable social and psychological study'.

ese ruling-class ideology and of a certain approach to narrative linearity. As it becomes increasingly difficult for the jailers, caught up in their own ideological and pseudo-legalistic contradictions, to hang 'R', their victim, they gradually become involved in the re-enactment of his life story—actually 'R' is being tried all over again—and after a series of sequences in the course of which the original verisimilitude is completely undermined by theatricalization (at one point the jailers and officials spread newspapers around the walls and floor of the execution chamber and act out scenes from 'R' 's childhood), the film starts erupting on to ever higher levels of unreality: after well over an hour of film spent confined in the execution chamber, the entire cast suddenly rush out of the door . . . and we find them in the shantytown where 'R' was raised. There ensues a farcical chase across town to the school roof where 'R' committed his crimes (rape and murder) and where one of the jailers now re-enacts them with such abandon that he actually commits them again. Brought back to the ex-

ecution chamber, the girl's body comes to life again—as 'R' 's own sister! And it is she who finally raises him to a clear political consciousness—before the weight of the power structure has the last (ambiguous) word. Such specifically Brechtian (Godardian) devices as intertitles which comment on, explain or foretell the action, sudden breaks of tone and acting style, tend to make the film function remarkably like what Brecht the theoretician saw epic theatre to be, and what no theatrical performance, not even those of the Berliner Ensemble, ever seems to achieve. Possibly film possesses an intrinsically richer potential here, simply because illusionism is so much stronger in the cinema than in the theatre, so that the distance effect offers a more striking antithesis.

It is interesting to compare *Death by Hanging* with the films that immediately preceded and followed it, for each contains one of the basic components of the intervening film, yet is less successful for want of the other. *Muri Shinju: Nippon no Natsu (Japanese Summer: Double Suicide,* 1967) is an extravagant piece of political fiction in which the whole structure of Japanese society seems to be symbolically threatened by a 'foreigner' (an American) who has gone berserk with a rifle. However, the steadfast linearity of this film, and an emphatically 'expressive' style reminiscent of what was least original in *Night and Fog in Japan*, make a discourse meant to be didactic seem little more than bombast. Far more interesting is *The Diary of a Shinjuku Thief*, in which the stylistic sutures (intertitles intruding on the narrative, colour shots injected into a black-and-white context, improvised *cinéma-vérité* sequences alternating with both 'realistic' and 'theatrical' acting —the latter designated as such, with Brechtian 'songs', etc.) constitute an even more radically disjunctive system than in *Death by Hanging*. Here, however, what seems to be lacking is a politically rigorous reflection that would give this non-linearity a dialectical meaning: perhaps this is because Oshima was becoming overly involved with the neo-existentialist problems of the young bourgeoisie of Tokyo and elsewhere (the date —1969—of the film is significant and in fact it contains allusions to the 'events' of 1968 in France).

Boy is in almost every way at odds with the previous film, and indeed with all the previous films. Its stylistic 'classicism' is clearly meant to be exemplary, and the subject—a boy's parents have trained him to be knocked down by cars in order to blackmail the drivers—seems to have been chosen deliberately so as to impose an approach of what can only be described as horrified discretion. Still, there are two rather interesting exceptions to the principle of transparency: protracted shots involving soundtrack cut-offs (curiously reminiscent of Kurosawa's *Ikiru*) and sequences in which polychromaticism is *drained* out of the image in the course of a single shot, leaving only a pale dominant. What is most interesting about these devices is that they have absolutely no intellectual or dramaturgical 'justification', and seem only to serve as welcome reminders that linear transparency is only one face of a cinema conscious of its own production.

The Man Who Left His Will on Film is also unique in Oshima's work, his only attempt so far at a specifically 'serial' organization of narrative *per se*. Though at times somewhat mechanistic (the end of the film, repeating as it does the beginning from another viewpoint, is a bit too pat), the film none the less constitutes an interesting systematic echoing of its own central subject: contradictions within a group of young radical film-makers (who play themselves) embodied in the symbolic schizophrenia of one of their members.

Much has been written about Oshima's most celebrated film, *The Ceremony* (the title more properly translates as *Ceremonies*). It is certainly the film in which he has expressed most intensely his attitudes towards the Japanese family as a paradigm of the Japanese nation. However, it is precisely this 'expressive' project which makes this film seem fundamentally retrograde in comparison with such achievements as *Violence at Noon* or *Death by Hanging*, each of which represented a point of no return, the first a definitive break with the codes of orientation and continuity, the second with those of linear representation and illusionism. Or so they seem to me, though not, it would appear, to Oshima. Perhaps it was the relative lack of success of his earlier films that caused this neo-classical turning. Even in a film world as non-élitist as that of Japan, success can become a spiritual necessity. Of course, it is impossible to deny the dramaturgical power of such sequences as the brideless marriage ceremony and its extravagant aftermath in which the groom parodies the wedding night, forcibly taking his patriarchal grandfather as a stand-in for his bride. And yet twenty years after the death of Dziga Vertov, here is yet another return to what he described so aptly as a 'literary skeleton with a cinematic skin', by a film-maker who had shown himself to be one of the few to have understood the Soviet legacy. It is hard to believe, however, that one of the most rigorously dialectical film-makers of the 60s can have definitively fallen back on conformism. To be continued.

In 1971 Teshigahara made a very interesting and promising departure from his more metaphysical films: *Summer Soldiers* was a hard-hitting portrait of a G.I. deserter on the run in Japan and the bar-girls and radical leftists who try to help him. Even more surprising, coming from Teshigahara,

Kazuko Yashiyuki and Tatsuya Fuji as the doomed lovers in *Empire of the Passions*.

was the wit of the film when it showed the comic side of the culture clash between the grass-roots, corn-fed G.I. and his Japanese hosts.

In writing of Oshima's chequered career, Burch concludes with the words 'To be continued'. I don't know what he thinks of Oshima's most recent film, the Franco-Japanese *Ai No Corrida* (also known as *L'Empire des Sens*; U.K.; *Realm of the Senses*; U.S.: *In the Realm of the Senses*, 1976), but it certainly made Oshima's name known all over the world. For many people, it was a breakthrough in the serious and artistic treatment of explicit sex on the screen. Using the front-page story of a bizarre love affair between a gangster and a prostitute in the Japan of the 30s, Oshima blended tenderness and brutality, spontaneity and ritual, love and death into what many felt to be a savoury brew. It was, they said, that rare hard-core film which saw its characters as more than the sum of their parts, and perhaps the most ferocious film ever made about sexual obsession. That was not my view, nor that of most American critics. I found it boring, an

all-too-obvious attempt to exploit those ideas of the late Georges Bataille about the close connections between sex and death which had been explored far more interestingly in Bertolucci's *Last Tango in Paris*. Although the production was very stylish (ravishingly beautiful kimonos), I found the film somewhat phoney. But I have always found Oshima more than a little suspect, more than a little opportunist. Whereas Burch finds Oshima's endeavour to do something different in each film an admirable attempt at perpetual self-renewal, I am afraid I have always seen him as something of an imitator of the styles of other men: anything they can do I can do better, would seem to be his motto. None the less, it must be admitted that, with the single exception of Kurosawa, he is the most interesting Japanese director at work today.

In 1978 Oshima made, again as a Franco-Japanese co-production, *L'Empire des passions*. Again, his source was a true story, this time one that goes back to the turn of the century, and one set, not in Tokyo, but in a small country village. The subject-matter is somewhat similar: *l'amour fou*—but this time it is between a woman in her forties and a man twenty years younger. Together they murder her husband, but the past is not laid so easily, and his ghost and their remorse finally end up by trapping the lovers. But their love survives torture and, we are told, even death. A much more tender film, it is also sexually much less explicit than *In the Realm of the Senses*; I happen to think it is a finer work.

There is an essay on Oshima by Ian Cameron in *Second Wave*, edited by Cameron in 1970. See also Noël Burch's *To the Distant Observer: Form and Meaning in Japanese Cinema* (1979).

YASUJIRO OZU

Donald Richie

Yasujiro Ozu, the director the Japanese themselves find 'most Japanese', known in the West mainly for his 1953 *Tokyo Monogatari* (*Tokyo Story*), was born in Tokyo on 12 December 1903. When still young he was taken by his mother to live in Matsuzaka in Mie Prefecture, while his father stayed in Tokyo to manage the family business. All but actually fatherless, the young Ozu did badly at boarding school and was eventually expelled. This, and the fact that his mother was very indulgent with him, gave him more free time than was usual for schoolboys of his time. He used it to see movies. While in the final year at the Fourth Mie Prefectural Middle School, he was sent to Kobe to apply for admission to a higher school. This he did not do, and the reason was that *The Prisoner of Zenda* was playing in Kobe. Around this time he also saw Ince's *Civilization* and several Rex Ingram films. If he had not seen them, he was later to say, he might never have gone into the movies.

In 1923 he joined the Shochiku Studios at Kamata near Tokyo, through the influence of a friend of his father's, and started work as an assistant to Tadamoto Okubo, one of the first Japanese directors to specialize in light comedy. In the new company Ozu had opportunity enough to get ahead but 'the real truth is that I didn't want to. As an assistant I could drink all I wanted and spend my time talking. Still, my friends all told me to go and

try, and finally orders came through making me a full director.'

Though Ozu later became an almost notoriously hard-working director whose entire life was film, he also remained fond of talking and drinking—and in many important respects he remained the truant schoolboy. He lived with his mother all his life—and she outlived him by several years—and was always falling in love with his actresses. He had relatively few friends—among them the late Kogo Noda, with whom he wrote most of his finest films—but they were extremely close.

It was with Noda that he wrote his first picture, *Zange no Yaiba* (*The Sword of Penitence*, 1927); afterwards he turned to the light comedies which his company found more lucrative. It was not until his fifth film, he later commented, that he 'began to like being a director'. This was because 'I finally felt I knew what I was doing'. He was discovering his own personal style. This discovery of style—which is, at the same time, always a discovery of self—was an unusually slow process which can perhaps best be examined chronologically. The comedies of 1928–29 indicate that the basis of Ozu's style was his adaptation of the house-style of his company, Shochiku, to his own purposes.

It has a name in Japanese, Ofuna-*cho*—the reference being to the city of Ofuna where Shochiku moved its Kamata studios after the arrival of sound. We would now identify this house-style as naturalistic domestic drama. A little smile, a few tears, a full, warm feeling—these were what Shochiku rightly thought its public wanted. Ozu's contribution, from the beginning, was to make both smiles and tears natural, to make the full, warm feeling a genuine one. In our culture—and indeed in contemporary Japan as well—'domestic drama' is a pejorative term; but this was not always so, in either place. We, with our end-of-the-century disillusionment, find domestic drama sentimental, not often realizing that our own cynicism is but another form of sentimentality. And in any event what Ozu did with domestic drama is perhaps more important than the fact that the style of his films was so firmly grounded in it.

What he did, precisely, was to de-sentimentalize it. One of the ways he did this was to show strong emotions in so under-stated, so subtle a fashion that a charge of sentimentality can be made only by the captious. Another way was to insist upon humour. He began as a director of comedies, and the majority of his pictures—no matter how tragic their *dénouements*, though one hesitates to use so weighted a word about these films—are genuinely funny.

Yet another way was through his very personal adaptation of the *shomin-geki*. This was a genre devoted to the lives of that lower-middle-class majority which, until recently, was the economic backbone of Japan; the *shomin* were, in the Japanese phrase, 'people like you and me'. In the films of Ozu, Heinosuke Gosho, Yasujiro Shimazu, Kenji Mizoguchi—and later in those of Shiro Toyoda, Keisuke Kinoshita, Yasuke Chiba and Tadashi Imai—the genre achieved a long and honourable history, known and highly regarded for its honesty. It may have somewhat overplayed life's hardships, but at least it did not gloss over any of life's real difficulties. In Ozu's refusal to give either himself or his domestic-drama audience an easy sentimental way out, he discovered a natural form in the *shomin-geki*, though, unlike other directors, he refused to be circumscribed by the genre.

Japanese critics first saw Ozu's style in his first *shomin-geki*, *Kaishain Seikatsu* (*The Life of an Office-Worker*, 1929). The story is simple. Japanese films were never strong on plot, and with Noda (who again worked with him on this film) Ozu managed to reduce what few plot complications remained. The film was also a comedy. A man and his wife look forward to spending his annual bonus only to find that, because of the general depression, he is not going to get one—not perhaps a subject a Western director would have chosen for a comedy, but a choice indicating the direction in which Ozu was evolving.

Having limited what he was going to show—and Ozu's style, like that of all true creators, was evolved through limitation—the director also began to limit the means through which he showed it. The later Ozu picture, for example, is a series of scenes in which the camera is always at the same height, that of a person seated on the *tatami* matting of the Japanese room; the camera never pans and rarely dollies; the scenes are connected only by the simple cut.

By 1930, Ozu was already moving towards this severe and mature style. In *The Life of an Office-Worker*, he later remembered, 'I still used a few dissolves. A dissolve is a handy thing, but it's not interesting. Of course, it all depends on how you do it.' And he mentioned the only successful use of the dissolve he had ever seen, in Chaplin's *A Woman of Paris*. 'Most of the time it's a form of cheating.' A few years after this, he recalled, 'I gave up fade-in and fade-out. Generally overlaps and fades aren't part of cinematic grammar—they are only attributes of the camera.' Asked to explain, he did so in typical Ozu fashion: 'When I first got into the movie business, you had to carry the camera around from place to place. I was husky, so they made me do all the lugging. I carried that camera for so long that I knew all about it. The stuff it can do doesn't have anything to do with cinema.'

It is easy to see how Ozu's interest in his own family led him to his interest in *Ofunacho* domestic drama, and towards his major theme: the Japanese family, either directly or in its extensions—the school, the company; and how this, in turn, led him to an interest in society at large, though he always preferred to see this larger group reflected in the smaller. It is less easy to understand how he began to apply to himself restrictions which, though they are the hallmark of art, did not then occur to other Japanese directors and, in any event, were appearing at precisely the time when cinema was vastly enlarging its own vocabulary.

A possible explanation may lie in Ozu's extremely workmanlike approach to his craft. In this he was like the mason who knows how to work with the texture of his stone, the carpenter who knows how to work with the grain of his wood. This kind of craftsmanship—almost lost in the West and now rare even in Japan—led Ozu to understand the true nature of film. Film is marvellously capable of capturing surface reality—but that is all it is capable of: ostensible reality is the only reality in cinema. This is one of its most important, and most often forgotten, attributes. It is now again being remembered in the West—the theories of Bazin, *cinéma-vérité*, to name but two examples—but Ozu was convinced of it as early as 1930, and most of his fifty-one films are examples of its validity.

1930 also saw the first appearance of another attribute of the Ozu style—the actor Chishu Ryu. He had been in all the early films (and was to appear in all the later ones, except for *Bijin Aishu* [*Beauty's Sorrows*, 1931] and *Shukujo wa Nani o Wasuretaka* [*What Did the Lady Forget?*, 1937]) but now appeared for the first time in a leading role. The film was *Rakudai wa Shita Keredo* (*I Flunked, But* . . ., 1930), part of a series of awkwardly titled pictures, and also part of a series of films about a college life which Ozu had never enjoyed and whose lack he continued to feel. Ryu, then twenty-four, later became responsible for much of the Ozu-like feeling in the Ozu films. Several critics have maintained that this feeling would have been impossible without the actor playing what they called 'the Ozu role'.

Ryu himself soon became aware that he was playing Ozu's persona. 'Today,' he wrote in 1958, 'I cannot think of my own identity without thinking of him. I heard that Ozu once said: "Ryu is not a skilful actor— and that is why I use him." And that is very true.' The actor was not being modest. Without Ozu he can be, as he has often demonstrated, very bad indeed; yet with him, he is capable of performances—that of the father in *Chichi Ariki* (*There Was a Father*, 1942), for example—which rank among the best in Japanese cinema.

That Ozu, from 1930, began to need someone to play himself became clear only later on. It was not until 1970, after the publication of Tadao Sato's brilliant book on the director, that it became apparent how biographical many of the Ozu films are. This fact escaped general notice because, as Sato indicated, the biographical element can be correctly interpreted only if one's reading is as oblique as Ozu's.

Part of this indirection is seen in the man himself, in the apparently casual way he went about film-making, and in his various refusals. Ozu soon became known around the studio as the man who said no. He said no to becoming a full director; later he said no to a number of scripts the studio wanted to fob off on him; he was always saying no to his actors, making them work harder than

any other director had ever asked them to. Later, he would refuse to make talkies, for a time at any rate. He would eventually refuse to make more than one film a year. Still later, he would refuse colour, to succumb eventually, though he never had any good words about either widescreen or the various Scope formats ('I got fed up in the middle of *This Is Cinerama*'). Yet, at the same time, Ozu is also remembered as being an extraordinarily affable man—off the set at least—who liked to talk as much as the next, and to drink even a bit more.

Ozu's many films about college life might then be accounted for by the fact that the director had not had one; certainly, his later interest in fathers was due to a 'fatherless' childhood and the fact that his father died in 1934; and the full, warm family life which he so often portrayed may, likewise, be read as an indication that he had in fact not had one.

From 1931 what Ozu always called his 'darker side', and what we would call his mature style, began to emerge. *Tokyo no Gassho* (*Tokyo Chorus*, 1931) was a comedy about a man who loses his job and has to support his family by becoming a sandwich man. The film appeared during a general depression when other directors were crying for social and economic reform. Ozu, from the beginning, was uninterested in reform, but he was interested in the social unease within his country and how it affected his characters. Thus he did not blame the feudal family-system of Japan any more than he did capitalism—both prime targets of social critics—and was consequently long if wrongly criticized for a degree of passivity which he did not in fact possess.

Confusing the passiveness of the Ozu character with a passiveness on the part of the director, Japanese critics sometimes fail to understand what Ozu was doing. At least in these pre-war films, he was showing conditions in so faithful a manner that they indicted themselves. At the same time, even before the war he was quietly celebrating a character—a personal rather than a national attribute—who could remain brave in the face of family pressure, who could continue to hope in the teeth of an increasingly restrictive social order, and who could remain simple, naïve, strong enough to continue to have faith in himself. From this stuff of tragedy he fashioned some of his best comedies.

In 1932 Ozu made the first of his great films, *Umarete wa Mita Keredo* (*I Was Born, But . . .*), a picture about two little boys who question their father's subservience to his boss, never realizing that when they grow up they will probably be just like him. Ozu has said of it that 'while I had originally planned to make a fairly bright little story, it changed while I was working on it (with Akira Fushimi), and it came out very dark'. In it Ozu brought together in almost perfect form the various elements which comprise his style. The film was a *shomin-geki* and the rigidity of Japanese society was strongly implied; it was about a family unit but Ozu was more interested in the members than he was in the unit; it was, in part, about children and Ozu was often again to use their innocence to reflect the falseness of adult society; it was a domestic-drama comedy, though a serious one. In this film the director also presaged much that was to come: children reflecting society were seen again in many of his films: *Hitori Musuko* (*The Only Son*, 1936), *There Was a Father*, *Nagaya Shinshi Roku* (*The Record of a Tenement Gentleman*, 1947) and *Ohayo* (*Good Morning!*), that 1959 'remake' of *I Was Born, But . . . .*

In 1933 Ozu made another archetypal film, *Dekigokoro* (*Passing Fancy*). Here a boy and his widowed father live together, and when the latter becomes attracted to a young woman, the son is disappointed, fearful. This is a situation which was to appear again and again in Ozu's pictures. In reverse form (the child eventually marries) it is seen centrally in *Banshun* (*Late Spring*, 1949), in *Akibiyori* (*Late Autumn*, 1960), in the director's last film, *Samma no Aji* (*An Autumn Afternoon*, 1962), and in several others.

By the middle 30s almost all the themes which Ozu was to use throughout his career had already appeared. The life of the office-worker had appeared and would reappear at intervals, culminating in *Soshun* (*Early Spring*, 1956). The theme of the missing parent was first seen in *Haha o Kowazuya* (*A Mother Should Be Loved*, 1934), and reappeared in *Ukigusa Monogatari* (*A Story of Floating Weeds*, 1934), its 1959 'remake', *Ukigusa* (*Floating Weeds*), and *Tokyo Bosh-*

oku (*Tokyo Twilight*, 1957). The theme of the gap between young and old in the Japanese family had been seen, to an extent, in *I Was Born, But . . .* and continued in *Munakata Shimai* (*The Munakata Sisters*, 1950), *Tokyo Twilight* and *Higanbana* (*Equinox Flower*, 1958). The theme of the failed marriage was seen in both *Floating Weeds* pictures, in *What Did the Lady Forget?*, in *Kaze no Naka no Mendori* (*A Hen in the Wind*, 1948), and in *Ochazuke no Aji* (*The Flavour of Green Tea over Rice*, 1952). The theme of the Japanese family in all its complexity was seen in *Toda-ke no Kyodai* (*The Brothers and Sisters of the Toda Family*, 1941), in *Bakushu* (*Early Summer*, 1951), in *Kohayagawa-ke no Aki* (*The Autumn of the Kohayagawa Family*, also known as *The End of Summer* and *Early Autumn*, 1961), and in Ozu's masterpiece, *Tokyo Story*.

'In making films,' Ozu once said, 'the most difficult part is writing the script.' It began with an idea, usually though not invariably his own, and this he thought about until he was ready to talk about it. He always talked it over with his writer Kogo Noda, or the several others with whom he worked in his earlier films, and this was crucial. 'When a writer and a director work together, if their physical constitutions aren't alike they won't work very well. If one of them likes to stay up late and the other likes to go to bed early, then they'll both get tired out. With Noda and me, we are alike in staying up late and drinking. That is the most important thing.'

Ozu's method was always the same, to stay up late drinking until the ideas came. They came in various ways but one of the most important was through dialogue. Noda and he would try out various lines and see where they led. Often what the character said would lead them into the situation they wanted. 'On the scenarios that Noda and I do together, the dialogue is written by both of us. Though we never write down the details of the sets or the costumes, they are eventually identical in our minds. We think alike, down to the smallest word—it is amazing.' At the same time, and this is another way in which ideas came, both Ozu and Noda were working from models. 'It is impossible to write a script unless you know who is going to play the part, just as a painter cannot paint until he knows what colours he is going to use.' Thus casting itself was part of the creation. 'Name stars have never been of special interest to me. What is important is the character of the actor. It is not a matter of how skilled an actor is or is not. It is a matter of what he is as a human being. I mean, not the character he projects, but the man he actually is.'

Ozu's pictures are, thus, from their inception about character—what people say, what people are. In this he was different from most directors, who tend to think of plot or story or theme, and then create characters who are to carry the plot forward or illustrate the theme. Ozu's way was to be led by his characters to create a pattern—often a simple set of parallels, a pair of intersecting curves, or—more elaborately—an X-pattern, such as that of *Equinox Flower*. This pattern would then express the theme.

Not that Ozu ever thought of it in this way. His main concern was that characters be right, by which he meant real. The theme could be left to take care of itself. It always did, and Ozu's themes are similar to each other. Just as the titles of his films resemble each other, so do the ideas in his films. Actually, they are both facets of the central and unshown idea, which is the result of all Ozu's films—the result of Ozu the man himself.

Shimbi Iida, a senior Japanese film critic and long an admirer of Ozu, finds three major themes in his films. The first is that of the hero or heroine who is ready to give up at the hopelessness of the world but then finds strength to go on, compromising with the world as it is. The examples Iida chose to support this were *Tokyo Story* and *Tokyo Twilight*. The second theme is that of a group of people who live or work together, the story constituting 'a humorous portrayal of social life'. Here Iida's examples were *The Record of a Tenement Gentleman* and *Good Morning!* Finally, there is the theme of the central character who does not compromise with the hopelessness of the world but goes on and does what he wants or thinks best. Examples of this were *There Was a Father*, *Late Spring* and *Late Autumn*.

What Ozu and Noda, or the other writers, completed first was, therefore, a dialogue script—usually the last thing finished in the films of other directors. This they then filled in, deciding on place, time of day, season, etc. The finished script was then rewritten by Ozu and each scene was usually illustrated with a sketch showing the placement of the characters. The film was therefore finished before it was shot. The director had a complete blueprint, shot by shot, and could set about making the film, just as the master architect sets about making the house. One may continue the parallel. Just as the architect's task is simplified in that the traditional Japanese house is made of module units (the *tatami* are always the same size, as are the *fusuma* or *shoji* doors, etc.), so Ozu's task was simplified in that in his later films he had a number of such units as components of his style.

The beginning of the later Ozu film is almost invariable. We are moved, swiftly, from one milieu to another, the smaller illustrating the larger and (often) also illustrating the theme. For example, the beginning of *Late Spring*: the Kitakamakura railway station with its associations of travel (and the final trip the heroine will take); a further view of the station; a temple roof over the nearby trees; the inside of the temple, the tea ceremony (at which the as yet unmarried heroine appears) just beginning. *Late Autumn* (this film's 'remake') opens with a Tokyo tower with its associations of modernity; another shot of the tower further away; a temple nearby; inside the temple, the seven-year funeral anniversary ceremony (at which the heroine, eventually to go her own modern way, is present) just beginning.

Another unit in the later films is that joint (or pivot scene) which occurs between two sequences and usually, if not always, reverts to the distant view of the milieu, but is also somewhere in the environs of (outside) the locality of the next scene (inside). In *Early Spring*, for example, there are two pivot scenes, often repeated. Just before a sequence in the hero's house there is a small scene of the street outside; just before a sequence at his office there is a small scene of the outside of his office building. These scenes are unvaried but their appearance is by no means mechanical. For one thing, they are carefully composed still lives (usually devoid of people) which are a pleasure to look at; for another, they mark both a necessary

An uncharacteristic exterior shot from *Kohayagawa-ke no Aki* (*The Autumn of the Kohayagawa Family*, also, and confusingly, known both as *The End of Summer* and *Early Autumn*). If the shot is uncharacteristic, the film is not: 'the theme of the Japanese family in all its complexity'.

separation and an agreeable pause; for yet another, their number is not invariable: sometimes, if Ozu must move us further—from Kamakura to Tokyo, for example—there will be an entire short sequence made from these small, empty scenes.

Yet another unit is the sequence pattern itself. Tadao Sato in his book on Ozu has indicated its essentials. The sequence often begins with the scene empty or with only one person in it. Then another enters and dialogue begins. This dialogue is rarely shot with both people (or more) on the screen, though for groups of four or more Ozu will sometimes include them all. More common is one scene for each line of dialogue (no matter how short), and this scene not only contains the person speaking but almost always shows him speaking either directly into the camera or as though to someone directly beside it. This dialogue (only action is shown, rarely reaction) continues for a time, usually until—in the most naturalistic way—a story point is made and, at this point, where most directors would have turned off the camera, Ozu keeps his running. Talk will cease, or at the most there will be a comment about something as general as the weather, or phrases repeated from the previous conversation. And the characters will sit, at rest, serene.

Ozu's films are made of character and his observation of it, and he refuses to use character for purposes of story because, as he once said, 'to use character is to misuse it'. He did, indeed, use character to the extent that his films got made, but he would not have allowed a story-line to dictate his characters' actions to him. In the same way, he had no use for plot at all. 'Plot,' he said, 'bores me.' The reason, of course, is that plot ascribes motivations and creates actions which Ozu felt should come not from structure but from character itself. Having begun his film by creating characters he remained loyal to them.

One might mention many other units in the Ozu film. Music, for example. It always steals into the scene during these moments of repose, rises in volume and intensity through the intervening still-life scene, and often rather abruptly ends as the next sequence is beginning. Other module-like units occur even in the acting, in the form of characteristic movements. In the early *Tokyo Chorus* the

hero has a habit of ruefully rubbing his hip; in both *Late Spring* and *An Autumn Afternoon* the men rub their pipes (cigarette holders in the former) against their noses so that the oil there will form a patina on the burr.

Feeling as he does about character, Ozu works carefully with his actors. The character was almost invariably written with a certain actor in mind, but at the same time the actor must also satisfactorily portray the character, and here Ozu was not easy to satisfy. With each sequence broken into a mosaic of short one-line conversation scenes, the actor had no opportunity of building up a feeling for the part during the shooting, and in any event Ozu was not concerned with an actor feeling his role. In *Tokyo Story* there is a scene where Haruko Sugimura is on the telephone saying that she will go to the station to pick up the old folks. Ozu had her hold a fan and follow its outline with her eyes, making a complete semi-circle with her head which coincided with the end of the phrase. Sugimura, a very serious actress, was confounded. 'What am I supposed to be feeling?' she asked. 'You are not supposed to feel, you are supposed to do,' said Ozu.

While shooting, Ozu was always telling his actors to do this or that, entirely physical things, which may have seemed arbitrary but which resulted in the effect he wanted. Sometimes this became very hard work and Kinuyo Tanaka, a fine actress, remembered a day on the set of *Equinox Flower* when he took the same scene (a very short scene of her saying, 'Yes, that's so') several dozen times and was still not satisfied.

Just as he would move his actors about, so Ozu would rearrange his sets. The properties must, he felt, say something about his characters—and he often used furniture from his own home if he thought that it expressed their taste. The arrangement, however, had to express something more. It must, in a word, express Ozu's extreme sense of order, or beauty. He once said that the reason he photographed all scenes at right angles (one searches in vain for a diagonally shot scene in his later films) is that this is the only way to photograph the Japanese house. He also felt that the composition of the shot should be fitting, that is, ordered. To create this ordered beauty he purposely balanced his compositions (the startlingly beautiful opening shot of the 1959 *Floating Weeds*, for example) and would not hesitate to rebalance during shooting.

The director Masahiro Shinoda remembers that during the shooting of *Tokyo Twilight* (on which he was an assistant) Ozu, in the middle of a sequence, looking through the viewfinder, ordered all the objects on the table to be moved this far to the right, that far to the left. Shinoda objected, saying this would destroy the continuity. Ozu said that the continuity would take care of itself. And he was right. No one noticed, though they may have felt a fitness in the way the objects on the table were composed.

Usually, in shooting an Ozu scene, there was a rehearsal and then a take, followed by at least several more. In cutting, Ozu would choose from the various versions. Once during the cutting of *Late Spring* there were several versions of the moment when Haruko Sugimura cries (with pleasure) when she hears that Setsuko Hara has agreed to marry. Ozu's assistants had all agreed that one was wonderful, one was bad and the others were indifferent. When Ozu chose the bad one, they all complained, saying that the good one was Sugimura's best and her high point in the film. Ozu agreed and said that was why he was not including it. She had overacted, he said, and in any event he never wanted a 'high point' in his films or an actress who would distinguish herself at the expense of the ensemble acting that he wanted.

In splicing the dialogue scenes together, during the 30s, Ozu would often incorporate two seconds of silence between one line and the next. Later he said that the babbling of television had conditioned everyone to faster exchanges, and in *Tokyo Twilight* he left only half a second between lines. This did not, oddly, affect the tempo of the film, which, according to those who do not like it or who do not have patience, is too slow. Actually, if cutting ratio is an index of tempo then Ozu's films are faster than most. *Floating Weeds* has more cuts in it than many other Japanese films of that year. In the same way, the Ozu film has more sequences than is usual. What make his films appear slow to some are, of course, those scenes in which little or nothing happens: the Noh theatre sequence in *Late Spring*, the golf-practising scene in *An Autumn Afternoon*, etc.

Ozu, however, shares with Dreyer and Bresson—and several other directors—a concern for things as they are and a faith that he who looks will see. The Noh theatre sequence in *Late Spring*, about three minutes long, has twenty-six shots in it, and one action: Ryu bowing to the woman his daughter thinks he is going to marry, and her own reaction to it. The sequence has no dialogue, and shots of the principals are intercut with scenes on the Noh stage. There is no parallel in action but there is, as always in Ozu, a parallel in feeling. Nothing much happens, but those who think that something happening is the point of an Ozu sequence have missed the point. Ozu felt, rightly, that this is the most important sequence of the film. Consequently, he did not use dialogue; consequently, he did not shorten but rather lengthened the sequence. One must bring oneself to this sequence just as one must bring oneself to the Noh. The result is—and it is the aim of all Ozu's films—a richer understanding of character. This, one now sees, was as much a part of his earlier films as it is of his later.

The consistency of Ozu as a director has excited much comment both in Japan and abroad. Works of art so clearly facets of a central character are rare in this century. One thinks of Henry James or, perhaps better, Jane Austen—whose sense of irony Ozu shares; one remembers Erik Satie who, in a way, always wrote the same piece of music, and, in any event, shared with Ozu a schoolboy sense of fun; one finds a strong parallel with Giorgio Morandi, the Italian artist (who died only a year after Ozu), who painted the same things (vases, pots, etc.) with a dedication, a skill, an awareness which eventually transcended the objects themselves.

Ozu's films proceeded directly from the man himself and the man is his style. It is this which makes his films unique and it is to this the average Japanese refers when he calls Ozu the 'most Japanese' of all Japanese directors. This quality, so easy to discern, is difficult to describe, but once having seen an Ozu film one will not forget it.

Ozu's films are so completely his, and the growth of his style is so naturally organic, that he confounds those critics who prefer to think in periods and who consequently find middle preferable to late or the other way about. Such an arbitrary division is impossible with Ozu's work, but this has not prevented a number of French critics from discovering that he was somehow more imaginative filmically in earlier films (*The Only Son*) than in later films (*An Autumn Afternoon*), and that, indeed, the post-war films are something of a falling off. This is not so, though such arbitrary divisions would indeed make a major artist easier to comprehend. What does occur, of course, is that in the later films Ozu becomes more philosophical about life itself. The mother in the 1934 *Story of Floating Weeds* is truly bitter about her final abandonment; the mother in the 1959 version is more resigned; she knows that life is life. The difference between the pre-war and post-war films is largely one of attitude—the filmic imagination remains on its extraordinarily high level.

The Ozu shot, camera three feet from the floor, the picture taken from the level of a person seated in traditional fashion on the *tatami*—this is the essence of the Ozu film. The traditional view is the view in repose, commanding a very limited field of vision. It is the attitude for watching, for listening; it is the position from which one sees the Noh, from which one partakes of the tea ceremony. It is the aesthetic attitude, the passive attitude. It is the attitude of the *haiku* master who sits in silence and with an occasionally painful accuracy observes cause and effect, reaching essence through an extreme simplification.

As Richie indicates, there is a difference of opinion as to the value of Ozu's middle-period works as against his later films. My feeling is that the reason the French so prize the middle-period films is simply that they discovered him so late; and not wishing merely to echo received Anglo-Saxon opinion, they consciously or unconsciously opted for a different critical approach. Personally, I'm with Richie. Richie has written a full-length study, *Ozu* (1974); and there are also Paul Schrader's *Transcendental Style in Film: Ozu, Bresson and Dreyer* (1972) and Noël Burch's *To the Distant Observer: Form and Meaning in Japanese Cinema* (1979).

G. W. PABST

Edgardo Cozarinsky

G. W. Pabst (1885–1967) belongs (with René Clair, V. S. Pudovkin and, up to a point, Charles Chaplin) to a group of film-makers who attained a high point in critical esteem around 1930, and were duly consecrated in the first histories of film. These reputations saw them through, with minor accidents, until that period of closer second viewing and thinking that started in the middle 50s and has not stopped since. In the case of Pabst, the tide of critical fashion in the last two decades has witnessed a consistent downgrading of his work, parallel to the upgrading of Murnau's and the reaffirmation of Lang's. The fact that his ambiguous political behaviour during the Second World War had already estranged him from his staunchest supporters only added to the difficulty of assessing a body of work that is clearly both uneven and eclectic.

Pabst's talent may be said to be of an intensely mercurial kind. The *Zeitgeist*, if anything, speaks through his work and makes it refractory to any *politique des auteurs* approach. His personal tastes and sympathies can be watched, as they are shaped by the shifting cultural context of the Weimar republic, and in their turn contribute to it. Up to, say, 1932 Pabst's career seems to be kept going by those same contradictions and unresolved tensions that make for the elusive, gripping quality of his best films of the period. Whether dealing with 'content' or 'form', Pabst operated as a *metteur en scène*. He lacked a bold conception of film language, and was never the radical agitator some mistook him for. What he had was an unfailing gift for choosing, say, the right soft-focus low-key lighting for Louise Brooks, and the right black silk for her mourning dress as she paces up and down her just-inherited flat like an impatient, glossy panther, in a long shot placed immediately after her static close-up in the courtroom scene (*Die Büchse der Pandora* [*Pandora's Box*, 1929]); a gift for incorporating in his first sound film (*Westfront 1918* [*Comrades of 1918*, 1930]) the clash of French and German dialogue that is more telling than its intended pacifist message.

Pabst's art is one of *trouvailles* and of knowing how to orchestrate them. The corollary to these virtues is an outstanding sense of casting. It comes as a mild shock to recognize that this European director, with an intellectual reputation, really had a showman's flair worthy of Hollywood for matching parts and presence. He played Asta Nielsen against Greta Garbo in *Die Freudlose Gasse* (U.K.: *The Joyless Street*; U.S.: *Streets of Sorrow*, 1925) and made that confrontation bring out the best in each of them. He led the marble-like Brigitte Helm from angelic piety in *Die Liebe der Jeanne Ney* (U.K.: *Lusts of the Flesh*; U.S.: *The Love of Jeanne Ney*, 1927) through the neuroticism of *Abwege* (U.K.: *Crisis*, 1928) up to an ambiguous fusion of her two *Metropolis* roles in *Die Herrin von Atlantis* (1932). He found a way to use the weird talents of Valeska Gert. And, of course, there is Louise Brooks. Despite the second-rate surrealism she aroused in many French-language non-writers, with Pabst she attained full mythical star quality.

In retrospect, Pabst's first film, *Der Schatz* (1923), appears as an almost academic exercise. Modelled after Wegener's 1920 *Der Golem*, it shows how easily Pabst could appropriate, and use, all the elements of Expressionism and show none of his later traits of style. Architecture (a shapeless, womb-like house), lighting (fully contrasted, playing with shadows, silhouettes, furnace smoke and fire) and fable (cupidity and repressed lust have the house finally falling down, after the young lovers escape) are timeless; and, as Lotte Eisner points out, instead of the fluid editing that would make him famous Pabst just seems to wait for the shots to run out of action or information before replacing them. Even the erotic overtones of melted bronze, glowing as it flows heavily amid the silent characters, are closer to the occasional symbolism of Expressionism than to Pabst's more mercurial sense of desire at work. And yet it is a far from negligible, if belated, contribution to a by then already waning school.

In *Geheimnisse einer Seele* (*Secrets of the Soul*, 1926), on the other hand, Expressionism is only a set of available devices to illustrate the workings of the subconscious—the stage where one of the two parallel actions of the film takes place. The other one is a draw-ing-room drama of jealousy, impotence overcome and final marital bliss, explained and carried along by the first. The principle itself is rich in possibilities, but the film is outweighed by a sense of its own novelty—the 'surface' plot is not interesting, while the insights of the submerged plot are explanatory, and never take off from the allegorical ground towards sheer imagination, as the best Expressionist examples, however stagey their sets and lighting, often did. When episodes and dreams are told to the analyst, cut-out figures are seen on blank backgrounds to convey the process of verbalization which removes these experiences from their original context. This didactic stance, usually related to the New Objectivity (*Neue Sachlichkeit*), explains the non-fantastic use of fantastic imagery: ladders and barriers which beset the sleeping man, the drum-beating court, the train—with his smiling rival at the window—that bolts out of nowhere and threatens to run over him. If the mother cutting up her grown-up son's meat appears simply to illustrate regression, the opening sequence is full of menace—close-ups of a man shaving, razor in hand, then his clumsy cutting of a lock of his wife's hair, and the sudden eruption of an 'outside' world, where the latent violence has somehow been projected and allowed to break out (through an open window cries of 'Help!' are heard, and a man is seen running through the streets).

Die Freudlose Gasse was hailed in its time as the definitive change in German cinema from Expressionism to realism: an instance of the process, analysed by Roman Jakobson, through which every call to realism is in opposition to a previous convention, now sclerotic but in its time also supposed to have embodied some notion of realism. What now seems telling about the film is its adaptation of Expressionist motifs to a portrait of post-war Vienna and its decayed middle class. Pabst uses hard facts as a painted backdrop for melodrama, for starkly defined types and immediately recognizable situations, thus setting a pattern which would be that of his best films.

The street, that no-man's-stage of social conflicts explored by nineteenth-century novelists of urban life, is here a studio set where yesteryear's Expressionism can still be read, but where only the queue of women outside the butcher's shop produces the intended realistic connotation, coming as it does from a different set of conventions. The fat, oily butcher and his menacing dog are already endowed with the typicality that is proper to melodrama, whether bourgeois tear-jerker or socialist agit-prop. Between decayed, stagnant middle-class home and seething classless brothel, the agony of a social stratum that finds no place safe in a time of change is called upon to test the relevance of an old set of devices, finally proven apt for a new, poignant topicality. When Garbo's newly acquired fur coat hangs by the side of her worn-out woollen one, the implicit summing-up is less important than the fact that the camera lingers, however briefly, to impose a joint vision. Pabst's sensitivity is already in evidence—an ability to share the scepticism of the defeated, to acknowledge the harbingers of change, and to move in between, capturing a synthetic glamour of transience. In this aspect, and in spite of a *deus ex machina* in the guise of an American soldier, *Die Freudlose Gasse* is more rewarding than the better-balanced exercise in style of *Der Schatz*, more probing than the application of Freudian imagery in *Geheimnisse einer Seele*. It announces, however tentatively, a tone that would be, unmistakably, Pabst's major achievement in his best films of the period.

Die Büchse der Pandora derives from two plays by Frank Wedekind (*Erdgeist*, 1893, and *Die Büchse der Pandora*, 1904), while *Tagebuch einer Verlorenen* (*Diary of a Lost Girl*, 1929) adapts a cheap contemporary novel; both films, however, have much more in common than Louise Brooks' prodigious presence. In both cases, like an electric discharge she animates a series of episodes recording the ups and downs of a central figure on the scale of fortune and respectability; both films, also, are organized mostly in long sequences, which explore in detail those stages in social mobility. While in *Die Büchse der Pandora* sexual attraction is a driving force which keeps the heroine going, destroying most people around her and finally herself, *Tagebuch einer Verlorenen* uses sex as one more element in the social play of conventions which suddenly give way when money is at stake. Thus the feverish drive of *Die Büchse der Pandora*, its glimpses of backstage frenzy on opening night, of a dazzling floating casino or a derelict London street, advertise a certain flimsiness, the sheer connotative pregnancy of backdrops for a dream. In *Tagebuch einer Verlorenen*, pharmacy, reform school and brothel are simplified but eloquent, richly observed surfaces of daily social intercourse. Accordingly, the hectic somnambulism of action in the first film (rendered almost visible in the train sequence, where shaking corridors, doors opening and closing, produce a reduced scale stage for dissimulation and plotting) is replaced in the second by a straightforward, almost brutal series of plot reversals which lay bare both the mechanisms of melodrama and those of the bourgeoisie they deal with.

Each of the longer episodes in *Die Büchse der Pandora* is built round a situation where the basic action is opposed by a parallel activity, an 'undercurrent' which disrupts and threatens to dissolve it: not only the wedding reception, where the intrusion of Lulu's circus friends has the action shifting from kitchen to salon to bedroom, or the opening night at the theatre, where the two-character confrontation in a dressing-room is literally besieged by nervous stage-hands and passing pieces of décor; but even when the agitation is less obvious (in the opening visit of Lulu's low-life acquaintances to her newly acquired respectable surroundings, or in the final sequence, when Jack the Ripper's identity gives the sexual preliminaries an extra dimension), Pabst's cutting bites off each shot to achieve a continuity based on instability. In *Tagebuch* the mechanisms of economic fate work mostly between sequences; it is their consequences which the film explores. Camera set-ups, even occasional descriptive movements, are more important here—the camera pulling back from the reform school headmistress, as she strikes a gong, to the girls drinking their soup. Another scene in the same episode shows the headmistress making the girls march to the rhythm of her cane, beating ever more quickly until they are reduced to puppets and she achieves an orgasm of sorts; though famous for its cutting, it seems more striking as a textbook example of the relation between authoritarian and erotic patterns that Wilhelm Reich was studying at the time. The

Louise Brooks in *Die Büchse der Pandora*: 'like an electric discharge she animates a series of episodes recording the ups and downs of a central figure on the scale of fortune and respectability; sexual attraction is a driving force which keeps the heroine going, destroying most of the people around her and finally herself'.

stimulus of *Die Büchse der Pandora* is stronger on the imagination, while *Tagebuch einer Verlorenen* works on the intellect, with the recognition of a genre and of the coincident mechanics of genre and society.

Less pungent, more spectacular, *Die Liebe der Jeanne Ney* partakes of both kinds of approach. It was intended by UFA to be fashioned after Hollywood, i.e. as an expert dosage of romance, adventure and fast-changing locales, and Pabst found in the Ilya Ehrenburg novel a capacious plot for it all—revolution in the Crimea, exile in Paris, and a girl who loves the man who killed her father. The fact that the motives for killing are political lays bare one aspect of Pabst's illusionism—the topical issue that allows a cultivated audience to enjoy the obvious melodrama with a safe cultural conscience: a notion of 'radical chic' is essential for understanding both Pabst's appeal and his limitations. The early sequence of the White officers' orgy sets the approach —it is reflected in a high mirror, and it is that reflection which the camera records. Something is thrown at the mirror, it breaks, but one piece, large enough, keeps on reflecting the wild party for a camera that is kept steady, as it were, by the audience's voyeurism. Later on, there is the famous sequence in the Paris hotel room—the embarrassed lovers just stand by the window and watch a very bourgeois wedding on the other side of the street (itself a reflection of the way of life they have been cut off from, by history and passion); then the bride walks over to the window and weeps, hiding her distress from the guests, and in doing so reveals it to the lovers. Both examples titillate the spectator, mildly excite his appetite for discovery and finally fulfil it.

Pabst's technique of cutting on movement to achieve a smoother flow of action, with all its undialectical efficacity, attains in this film an intoxicating inevitability of fictitious cause and improbable effect, whether linking camera movements (the long, impetuous tracking shot that follows the lovers in the Parc Montsouris) or partial, slightly off-centre frame compositions which impose on the shots a sense of uncertainty and menace (as in the sequence where the Russian swindler strangles Jeanne's detective uncle near the safe where a just retrieved diamond has been kept—itself a tight knot of novelettish connotations). The basic appeal of melodrama is glamorized by a consciousness of impermanence, social and emotional, which the period between the wars coined as the only possible romanticism for modern times. This is the elusive quality which has kept *Die Liebe der Jeanne Ney*, and also *Die Büchse der Pandora* and *Tagebuch einer Verlorenen*, much more alive than the openly 'committed' films that followed, highly praised at the time but now appearing to a certain extent inadequate, even trivial.

'Radical chic', of course, plays a large part in any assessment of Pabst's critical fortune. The notion itself may be said to have been ruthlessly dissected from a Marxist viewpoint by Walter Benjamin, whose observations on Erich Kästner's poetry, written in 1931, perfectly fit Pabst's work up to that date, illuminating the reasons for its contemporary success as well as the long-term dissatisfaction with its claims to political relevance:

> Despite its appearance, this lyricism protects in the first place the status interests of an intermediate section—agents, journalists, heads of departments. Its proclaimed hatred towards the *petite bourgeoisie* had itself a very intimate *petit bourgeois* flavour. . . . Left-wing radical publicists like Kästner, Mehring and Tucholsky are the decayed bourgeoisie's mimicry of the proletariat. Their function is to foster in politics not parties but cliques, in literature not schools but fashions, in economics not producers but agents. And indeed, for the last fifteen years, this left-wing intelligentsia has not ceased to be an agent for every spiritual conjuncture, from Activism via Expressionism to the New Objectivity. Its political significance, however, exhausted itself in the transposition of those revolutionary reflexes, which, arising in the bourgeoisie, become therefore objects of distraction, of amusement, of consumption.

Westfront 1918, Kameradschaft (1931) and, in uneasy proximity, *Die Dreigroschenoper* (U.S.: *The Threepenny Opera*, 1931) stand as Pabst's more outspokenly 'committed' films. Since he had worked best with oblique comments, drawing conclusions from the exposure of social fictions and frictions, any frontal approach to an issue, however honest, offered a challenge to Pabst. A dialogue line in *Kameradschaft* establishes the link with *Westfront 1918*—'the miner has only two enemies, gas and war'. Reaching back to the previous film, the remark also uncovers the infirmity of both films in their grasp of the social and historical reality they intend to comment upon—war is 'naturalized' as yet another unpredictable disaster.

The novel behind *Westfront 1918* belongs to the wave of pacifist literature that was just reaching the screen with Milestone's version of Erich Maria Remarque's *All Quiet on the Western Front*. Built as a series of tableaux, the film depicts with almost exemplary neatness the *loci classici* of the genre. Pabst reviews a destroyed church turned hospital, the long-awaited leave that only discloses a deteriorated civilian life behind the lines, the trench inferno between explosions, offensive and defensive moves. From this 'Disasters of War'-like series, without a conventional narrative nexus, there occasionally emerge fuller figures and more developed episodes (a German student's brief liaison with a French canteen girl, another German soldier going back to his wife and finding her in bed with the village butcher). Isolated observations are meant to speak for a larger context (a carpenter indifferently making one wooden cross after another, a long line of women waiting for food as the soldier goes home to his unfaithful wife). Though not a central element of visual and narrative developments as in *Die Freudlose Gasse*, the queue exemplifies Pabst's way of commenting on a social and political issue: it is not the wife's counter-accusation of her husband (a soldier, a representative of war) that speaks for her but that previous glimpse of haggard women in the street.

In *Kameradschaft* there is a stronger collective drive, modelled on the Russian classics. The pacifist point is developed concentrically, from an opening dispute of children playing marbles in front of customs officers, through a ball sequence where French girls won't dance with German boys, up to the epic treatment of the disaster sequence. As *Westfront 1918* opposes elaborate compositions of corpses, barbed wire and upturned ground for its sequences on the front, with

comparatively plain set-ups for the sequences behind the lines, *Kameradschaft* alternates open-air sequences of location shooting with studio-built mine galleries that allow rich chiaroscuro effects. Its didacticism is most blatant in the use made of bars—those of the iron gates of the mine, guarded by the police against the crowd that wants to reach the miners; those which set the national frontier in the middle of a mine corridor, and which the German miners break through to rescue their French fellow-workers, only for them to be officially re-sealed in the last sequence, a sceptical counterpoint to the celebrations and speeches above ground. But Pabst's treatment is always one that enhances any element by placing it in a particular relationship: the miners' changing room has their clothes hanging from the ceiling as a nightmarish upper level for the everyday routine underneath; the lighting of the shower room makes it an eerie space of glistening bodies and shifting vapours; the shots of a crowd running in the streets are intercut with one of a shopkeeper watching as indifferently as the dummy in his shop window.

Both films are bilingual and show an eagerness to compose a soundtrack of 'natural' sounds—cries and moaning in the bombed church, silence broken by occasional faint sounds in the dark mine. Their ideological context is that of pacifist lyricism. If *All Quiet on the Western Front* ends with the soldier's hand immobilized just before touching a butterfly, *Westfront 1918* closes with a French soldier muttering 'I ... comrade ... not enemy' while clasping the hand of a dead German soldier. But, while the final question of Pabst is 'The end?', Milestone and Remarque venture as far as 'Why?' and their film was banned by German censorship, while Pabst's was accepted and even considered a homage to the courage of war veterans.

The film of Bertolt Brecht's *Die Dreigroschenoper* led to a lawsuit between Brecht and the producers, which the writer lost. It allowed him, though, to sustain his defence not on the grounds of 'author's rights' but of 'audience rights'—an interesting point derived from the equivocal nature of the play's success with the Berlin public. The romantic aura of the underworld, reinforced by parodic songs and teasing stage design, rediscovered for a

Left-wing bourgeoisie the 'poetry' of low-
life, while social satire acted as a cautionary
deposit allowing them to embark on a contemporary (tongue-in-cheek, brittle) sentimental and social delusionism. This is, of
course, the perennial appeal of the play; it
has survived, so far, even the most radical
production concepts and it is what made
Warner and Tobis interested in doing two
versions of it, with a French and a German
cast. Also, it is the aspect best suited to
Pabst's talents—the heady, decadent aura of
the film being barely questioned by the play's
ironic, disenchanted humour. Charm is the
main un-Brechtian achievement of Pabst,
even in the German-language version, with
its aggressive cast (matched in the French
version only by Margo Lion and Artaud).
What makes that achievement incomplete is
the lack of a sustained, properly cinematographic approach. With André Andreiev as
designer and Fritz-Arno Wagner as photographer, Pabst created an intricate play of
smoke, fog, steamy glass, transparent curtains, reflections in shop windows and variously filtered light which is fascinating in the
most ambiguous sense. The film is as full of
trouvailles as a fastidious stage production,
but lacks a recognizable attempt to evolve
some system out of, say, the fact that the
camera prowls tirelessly when there is no
sound to be recorded and stays put when a
song is due. Also, Pabst may have felt
shocked by Brecht's political realism. While
the play closes with the reinforcement of
capitalism, the film turns the beggars' parade
into an overture to revolt—a colourful dénouement that the original Berlin theatre
audience might have enjoyed and deemed
'revolutionary'.

Die Herrin von Atlantis, Pabst's last film
before the advent of National Socialism and
his second in both French and German versions, is a piece of stilted fantasy that no par-
ticle of verisimilitude contaminates. (It is
based on the same novel as Feyder's earlier
L'Atlantide.) Far from the shadows and
thwarted perspectives of the traditional
Expressionist approach, Pabst stages an
obsessive mechanism of desire in a dazzling
labyrinth of glistening pools and chalk-white
sand and architecture, where the statuesque
Brigitte Helm dispenses hypnotic fascination
and death. Its exoticism is sheer cliché, ren-

dered with such undeflecting relish that it
attains a hard, self-sufficient existence all its
own (lacking, for instance, in the intellectual
manipulation of similar material later attempted by Alain Robbe-Grillet).

Don Quichotte (*Don Quixote*, 1933), Pabst's
first film as an exile in France, illustrates the
opposite approach. As if conscious that no
adaptation could try to reproduce, however
transposed, the complexity and amplitude of
Cervantes, the film sets out to be a series of
variations, of commentaries almost, on
episodes from the novel, in the form of a
musical. The songs are placed in such
a way as to suggest that the successful *Die
Dreigroschenoper* served as a model; actually,
Cervantes' playing with dramatic illusion to
reinforce a basic realism makes him ideal for
a Brechtian reading. Such a possibility is
almost realized in the episode where the
knight receives his orders, transposed from
the courtyard of an inn to the makeshift stage
of a travelling company. Though dialogue by
Paul Morand and a score by Jacques Ibert
establish a tone of Parisian wit, one of Pabst's
great finds has the film ending on an unexpected high note—the knight's books are
being burned (is it possible to dissociate the
scene from the contemporary Berlin bon-
fires of 'degenerate literature'?) and, while
Chaliapin's voice delivers the best song in
the film, a long take in reverse movement
produces from the ashes a dance of flames
which slowly give way to paper until the title
page of Cervantes' *Don Quixote* triumphantly
emerges.

The rest of Pabst's work in the 30s is oddly
inconclusive. His major projects failed to
materialize. His American venture, whatever
the intrinsic achievement of *A Modern
Hero* (1934), was a traumatic experience,
as witness his bitter article about the
predicament of the director in Hollywood.
The most interesting of the other films of the
30s were *Mademoiselle Docteur* (U.S.: *Street
of Shadows*, 1936) and *Le Drame de Shangaï*
(1938). Emasculated by French censorship of
their intended political overtones, they stand
as intermittently absorbing spy stories and
rewarding star vehicles. The director's
inclination to approach the general through
the particular is more impressive when he
avoids obvious violence. In this context the
most remarkable scene is the knifing of

Louis Jouvet in *Le Drame de Shangaï*: 'an intermittently absorbing spy story and a rewarding star vehicle; in this period Pabst found his ideal director of photography in Eugen Schüfftan'.

Christl Mardayn in *Le Drame de Shangaï*, while she mingles with a street demonstration of Chinese workers: instead of falling, her dead body, eyes wide open, fixed on nothing, is carried along by the exulting crowd. In this period Pabst found his ideal director of photography in Eugen Schüfftan, whose intricate patterns of lighting, less stark than F.-A. Wagner's, trace zones of varying half-tones in every shot, inscribing actors and props alike among shadows or patterns of zebra-striped light filtered through shutters.

A biographical digression may be allowed to point to the fact that Pabst, film apostle of idealistic brotherhood between nations and a confirmed pacifist, was caught up by the outbreak of the First World War in France and by the outbreak of the Second in post-*Anschluss* Austria. In 1914 he had been sent to a French detention camp where he spent four years in confinement, and organized a theatrical group and produced regular

shows for German prisoners and French guards alike. In 1939, when Pabst recklessly returned to Vienna for family reasons, Goebbels repeated more curtly his standing invitation to work in Germany, to erase his leftist record. Pabst made three German films during the war—*Komödianten* (1941) in Munich, *Paracelsus* (1943) and the unfinished *Der Fall Molander* (1944) in Prague. The ironic symmetry of his fate has been ignored by many writers anxious to dismiss him as a collaborator, even if a very special one. After the war Pabst claimed rather naïvely that both completed films were historical and had no propaganda value. He was answered that such films played a precise role in the cultural policy of National Socialism. This is true, but in spite of the gruesome nature of Nazism and the banality of the films themselves, Pabst's part in this was no more scandalous than the record in adaptability of such admirable film-makers as Eisenstein and Rossellini.

If history caught up with Pabst, he seemed perpetually unable to catch up with it in his post-war work. The permeability to social and cultural change of his best work during the Weimar Republic runs together with an alertness to meet it on a choice arena and with fine instruments. With the possible exception of *Der Letzte Akt* (U.K.: *Ten Days to Die*; U.S.: *The Last Ten Days*, 1955), the last part of Pabst's career seems dominated by fatigue. Whatever contemporary realities left their imprint on it were occasional, undistinguished, and operated on bland, unresponding matter. Nor were they rejected by an air-tight obsessiveness such as Sternberg's or Buñuel's.

Even though it was a project of Pabst since the early 30s, *Der Prozess* (U.S.: *The Trial*), made in Austria in 1947, was an unfortunate choice of subject matter for a director who had worked in Germany during the war. The film, set in rural Hungary at the turn of the century, centres on a nationalist attempt to exploit a peasant girl's suicide to set off an anti-Semitic reaction. It proceeds as a series of clichés in characterization, narrative and self-righteous humanitarianism, heavy with ironical cross-cutting and laboured suspense effects. Whatever his intentions, film language, its assumptions and performance, are the same in *Der Prozess* as in *Paracelsus*; and the glossy photography and colourful period décors and wardrobe are those of UFA 'quality' productions. The general emphasis on plastic composition, though far from the boldness of Expressionism, is impossible to understand without that illustrious precedent. Supported by the misconception that stylization guarantees artistic effect, *Der Prozess* appears as a debased instance of that 'German predisposition towards Expressionism' (Lotte Eisner) which would survive in ever shabbier garb, whenever ambitious films were concerned, throughout post-war German cinema, until the emergence of Straub and Kluge in the middle 60s.

In post-war Vienna and in Italy during the 50s, Pabst tried his luck without success. Back in West Germany after 1954, he made five films in two years, saw important projects fall through, finally retired, and died in 1967. Of this last chapter of his career a few items deserve attention. The script he wrote with Paul May for the May-directed *Duell mit dem Tod* (1949), produced by Pabst's own Austrian company, proposes a contrived case of mistaken allegiances; *La Voce del silenzio* (U.K.: *The Voice of Silence*, 1953), based on original material by Zavattini but not intended to catch up with the by then already decaying neo-realism, shuffles 'representative' figures on a weekend of 'spiritual retreat' with a Grand Hotel or Orient Express device of private dramas strengthened by the shared, enclosed premises. Both films are supposed to be serious reflections on the muddled morals bequeathed by the war to heroes and victims alike. Both are unconvincing and uninteresting.

More telling are the two German films dealing with wartime Nazi history. *Es Geschah am 20 Juli* (U.K.: *Jackboot Mutiny*, 1955), a reconstruction of the 1944 attempt on Hitler's life by a group of army officers, echoed the trend launched by Hollywood with *The Desert Fox* and followed eagerly in West Germany by several films in the 1955–56 season. A very simple idea backs them all: inside the Third Reich, even in the highest ranks of the Army, some sort of opposition was possible; Hitler is the monster, the sick arch-villain, and those who submit to his will are the weak, the mean, the stupid who always thrive under oppression. Such dilution of history into morals, itself a feat of ideological legerdemain, can also be read into Pabst's taut assembling of would-be documentary fragments of action. Aiming to combine history and tragedy, he fails to suggest any larger forces at work.

The comparative success of *Der Letzte Akt* (1955) may derive from the way it invests the incredible facts of Hitler's last days with a *Götterdämmerung* treatment, instead of pretending to take myth for fact. The Führer himself for Pabst is a *metteur en scène*, whose last production cannot afford the grandiose Riefenstahl: the stage has been reduced to the stifling bunker; instead of mass choreography there is allegory, half-way between Dance of Death and Ship of Fools. The audience is acquainted with the situation by the arrival of a young officer; near the end of the film, he is killed for security reasons, his body propped up against a bar to simulate a drunkard, and the final dance orgy takes place around him. Throughout, Pabst's eye for detail is at his perverse best (half a sausage is casually produced from a tin box full of medals) as are his shifts of tone—a teenager brought by Goebbels for a decoration says the wrong words to the Führer; later, a party turns into orgy, the dancing into military steps, the wedding finds a fitting culmination in the burning of the newly-weds. Tilted shots and dizzying camera movements, consistently low-key lighting and flames flickering over close-ups do not overstate the enormous. Instead, they transpose the action into a combination of puppet-show and shadow play: a last and late instance of Expressionism revisited. The results are thin and, once again, fascinating, oddly pertinent and unmistakably dated—a deferred reflection of Pabst's most celebrated exploits in an alien, yet totally mastered context.

There are two monographs in French on Pabst: Barthelémy Amengual's *Georg-Wilhelm Pabst* (1966) and Freddy Buache's *Pabst* (1965). See also Kracauer's *From Caligari to Hitler* (1947) and Lotte Eisner's *The Haunted Screen* (1969).

MARCEL PAGNOL

Richard Roud

Like Guitry—and like Cukor in America—Marcel Pagnol was a director whose films were enormously popular, but have been held in low esteem by the more serious critics. Because Pagnol naïvely maintained that his films were simply reproductions of his plays, he was taken at his word. And yet most of his best films were imaginative adaptations of works by another writer, Jean Giono.

André Bazin was the first to attempt the rehabilitation of Pagnol, but others have since come to appreciate his best works at their true value. Like Guitry, however, Pagnol had a long and very uneven career; on occasion, as in *Angèle* (1934), he could attain a kind of classic sublimity; at other times, he fell into a merely Marseillais kind of boulevard comedy, full of folkloric complacency. Again like Guitry, he was obsessed with words, and his Mediterranean eloquence could be as tiresome as Guitry's Parisian chatter.

Marcel Pagnol was born near Marseille in 1895, and he began to write plays at the age

of fifteen. His first successful play was put on in Paris in 1925; but it was in 1928, with *Topaze*, and in 1929, with *Marius*, that he became famous. And it was about this time that the talking picture began to appear. Until then Pagnol had despised the cinema; for him it was simply a record on film of pantomimes, and he was not interested in mime. But now he suddenly saw his chance: finished those evenings of playing for 1,000 people, finished the tiresome provincial tours; now he could, he thought, *film* his plays and they could be seen by the millions.

But he wasn't quite ready to do the actual filming himself. He needed technical help, and he chose the young Alexander Korda to film his *Marius* (1931). It was clearly understood, however, that this was to be Pagnol's film—he had chosen the actors, he had directed them on the stage, and he was also the producer of the film. Korda's role was simply to record Pagnol's *mise en scène*. There were grave doubts as to whether the film would be a success, and many in France feared that even people from northern France would neither get it nor like it. As it turned out, of course, the film was a tremendous success not only in Lille, but in New York, London and Tokyo. A year later, Pagnol chose Marc Allégret to film the second part of the trilogy, *Fanny* (1932), and the results were even more successful. So, emboldened by success, Pagnol himself directed *César* (1936).

Up to this point, Pagnol had been faithful to his principles of what he rather quaintly called *cinématurgie*, and it had worked. Aestheticians could complain that these films weren't 'cinema', but they were and remain to this day living works. For Pagnol, all unknowing, had discovered intuitively what Bazin and the Nouvelle Vague were later to work out theoretically; i.e. that sacrosanct 'montage' was not necessarily the essence of the cinema. That what happened during a shot was just as important as the relationship between the shots. That *mise en scène* was first and foremost the choice and direction of actors—they were the true raw material of cinema. Or, to put it more timidly, that there was a different kind of cinema from that of either the German expressionists or the Russian formalists.

And the performances of—above all—Raimu and Orane Demazis were extraordin-

Raimu, Pierre Fresnay and Orane Demazis in *Fanny*, a quintessentially Pagnol film, even if it was directed by Marc Allégret (just as *Marius* had been directed by Alexander Korda). But Pagnol, in both cases, had chosen the actors, directed them on the stage, and was also the producer of the film. The 'director's' job was simply to record Pagnol's *mise en scène*.

ary: both were theatre actors, and yet their performances on film have seldom been surpassed. It is true that the famous trilogy is creaky in parts—particularly *César*, which was the least successful of the three as a play. But the test of time has been triumphantly passed: perhaps the three films weren't 'cinema', but they certainly were and are movies.

But Pagnol was not content to stop there. In 1934, he made *Angèle*, his most important achievement in historical terms. A year before *Toni*, Pagnol left the studios, went into the hill towns of Provence and made what we can consider the first neo-realist film, and with direct sound as well: the creaking of the windmills and the chirping of the crickets provide a continual background accompaniment to the dialogue.

This time, it was not a play of his own that he was filming, but rather an adaptation of a short story by that other Provençal, Jean Giono. The story is somewhat melodramatic, with Orane Demazis getting mixed up with a thoroughly bad chap in Marseilles, and bearing his illegitimate child. Fernandel, who has always loved her but whom she has disdained, finally succeeds in winning her over by offering to take her with the child. The Giono story is a lyrical poem about redemption through a return to the soil, but from these few pages Pagnol made a film which ran two and a half hours; it has its melodramatic moments, but the quality of the acting and the determining role of the landscape which Pagnol so beautifully evokes allow the film to transcend both its plot and Pagnol's occasional facilities. Of its kind, it is only equalled by *Toni*, which, let it not be forgotten, was produced by Pagnol.

Interestingly enough, Pagnol's three other best films were also adaptations of Jean Giono—*Jofroi* (1937), *Regain* (*Harvest*, 1937) and *La Femme du Boulanger* (*The Baker's Wife*, 1938). *Harvest* has lost some of its charm over the years, looking almost a little neo-Fascist these days with its celebration of soil and bread. But *The Baker's Wife* still works, and Raimu's performance as the unhappy baker is one of the monuments of screen acting. It, too, was largely shot on real locations without any post-synching. One more example of the paradoxical development of a man of the theatre who didn't believe in cinema and yet who ended up as a precursor of neo-realism. As André Bazin put it: 'In his best films at least, Pagnol demolished the formalist myth of Cinematographic Art. A heritage of silent cinema, this was the feeling that cinema should be pure, specific and unable to be reduced to its content; the cinema was to be an art of moving images and depended totally on the rhythm of its montage. Quietly but irrefutably, *Angèle* and *The Baker's Wife* disproved this idea. Not because, as Pagnol believed, his successes contradicted the existence of the cinema as a specific means of expression, but because his ignorance of those technical habits and customs current in professional circles led him unconsciously to the discovery of other, no less cinematographic values which only his turning to realism could reveal. Pagnol's *oeuvre* is there to negate not only those who believe that the cinema has only to do with framing, lighting or *découpage*; it also demonstrates the foolishness of Pagnol's own belief in the future of "filmed theatre". Alas, his failures, more numerous than his successes, are sufficient proof that a contempt for technique is an even more dangerous recipe than formalism.'

Alas, indeed: after *The Baker's Wife*, Pagnol's career declined until his death in 1974. Those few who saw *Manon des Sources* (U.K.: *Manon of the Springs*, 1952) in its original six-hour version, and projected in its original Roux-colour process, maintain that it had many fine qualities. But *La Fille du Puisatier* (*The Welldigger's Daughter*, 1940)

(with its opportunistic two endings: in the first, released during the Occupation, father and daughter are reconciled listening to a radio speech of Pétain; in the second, post-Liberation version, Pagnol simply changed Pétain's voice to that of de Gaulle!), the second *Topaze* (1951) and *Lettres de mon Moulin* (*Letters from My Windmill*, 1954) were unworthy of the pre-war Pagnol.

His place in film history is none the less secure, not only for his best films but for his exemplary technique of shooting. And just as it is not, I think, too fanciful to see in Guitry the precursor of an Eric Rohmer, so one could say (and in fact, André S. Labarthe predicted as much ten years ago) that without Pagnol's example a director like Jean Eustache could never have made *La Maman et la Putain*.

Pagnol wrote two autobiographical works: *The Days Were Too Short* (1960) and *The Time of Secrets* (1962). There is a monograph in French by Claude Beylie (1974), and both Bazin and Truffaut have written glowingly about him in *Cahiers du Cinéma*. In 1977, C. E. J. Caldicott published a study of Pagnol as both playwright and filmmaker, *Marcel Pagnol*.

ALAN J. PAKULA and ROBERT MULLIGAN
Robin Wood

Considered as a corpus, the films of Robert Mulligan (born 1925) reveal a likeable but somewhat ineffectual and undynamic artistic personality, with a tendency to fall back on charm to disarm criticism. Such a description, however, fails to account satisfactorily for his best work, which was produced by Alan J. Pakula (born 1928). One's guess that Pakula's role in the films was one of active creative participation is satisfyingly confirmed by the four films Pakula has directed since: three of them seem to me decisively superior to their nearest parallels in Mulligan; tougher, more complex, more assured, more strongly structured. And Mulligan's subsequent attempt at a 'strong' subject—without Pakula's support—proved quite disastrous (*The Other*, 1972). The most telling comparison is between *The Sterile Cuckoo* (U.K.: *Pookie*, 1969), directed by Pakula, and *Summer of '42* (1971), directed by Mulligan without Pakula. Both are concerned with the pains of adolescence, but where Mulligan easily indulges his characters (and, worse, the audience), exploiting their 'cuteness', inviting a response at once nostalgic and superior, Pakula indulges nobody and softens nothing: we are encouraged neither to chuckle condescendingly at his teenagers' quirks and inadequacies nor to wish we could 'live it all again'.

Themes and motifs interestingly connect the Mulligan/Pakula films with Pakula's own: the relationship of Gregory Peck to the mysterious Indian, the menace in the shadows, in *The Stalking Moon* (1969) anticipates the relationship of Donald Sutherland to the murderer in *Klute* (1971); Pakula's interest in psychological abnormality and in psychoanalysis as a formal structure as well as a practice is established from the first film he and Mulligan made, *Fear Strikes Out* (1957).

Klute—Pakula's richest film to date, described by Godard as 'casually Fascist', and often treated simplistically as a 'male chauvinist' tract—is a complex and disturbing work whose characters are related on two parallel continuums: the three call-girls (one dead before the film opens, one murdered during its course, one threatened but surviving) and the three men (the husband, dead after the pre-credit sequence, his friend and apparent counterpart who is in fact his murderer, and who dies during the film, and the detective, John Klute). Klute and the murderer are ambiguously compared and contrasted throughout the film: the murderer has had all his devious and pathological impulses released by the permissiveness of the call-girl ethos; Klute (whose very name suggests 'closure', by both its terseness and its etymology) lives by refusing to explore himself and remains an almost totally enigmatic figure. The two are placed in the role of spies and voyeurs, and are visually linked by being filmed through glass, their features blurred. The film's detractors are apparently unaware of how the 'happy ending' is undercut by its expressive and structural ambiguities.

Since *Klute*, Pakula has directed his one failure, *Love and Pain and the Whole Damn Thing* (1973) (which has an excellent first hour and the far from inestimable distinction of securing a disciplined and restrained performance from Maggie Smith in a role that would lend itself easily to caricature: Pakula is evidently an unerring director of actors), and the brilliant *The Parallax View* (1974); among the most uncompromising of all cinematic American nightmares, which develops the urban paranoia of *Klute* with characteristic control, a notable absence of hysteria, and a series of haunting and evocative images of the individual's isolation in a world of machines and machination. The film confirms the centrality to Pakula's view of things of the more disturbing implications of *Klute*.

Mulligan continued to decline (*The Nickel Ride*, 1974), while Pakula had his biggest hit with *All the President's Men* (1976). Its success was of course partially due to the topicality of its subject matter; it was also very finely conceived and executed even if, for me, it lacked the psychological complexity and emotional intensity of *Klute*. But given the subject, that was doubtless unavoidable.

PIER PAOLO PASOLINI
Oswald Stack

Pier Paolo Pasolini (1922–75) was the kind of romantic who disappeared in most of northern Europe with the industrial revolution, long before the cinema was invented. In the Anglo-Saxon world he came to prominence as the Marxist who made *Il Vangelo secondo Matteo* (*The Gospel According to St Matthew*, 1964). Basically, he was a pre-industrial poet, alive in the age of both Marxism and the cinema. In addition, being Italian, he had to operate in a context with special problems of language and religion.

Pasolini defined himself as a *pasticheur*, picking out items, themes, objects and even styles from here and there. This self-definition is a good starting point from which to locate him and his work at the level of both style and content—since he changed both several times: in style ranging all the way from post-neo-realist realism (*Accattone*, 1961) to surrealism (*La Terra vista dalla Luna*; episode in *Le Streghe*, 1966); and in content from pimps to Jesus Christ. But quite apart from this aspect of pastiche, the very range and remoteness of the components of his work (for example, Pascoli, Gramsci, Rossellini) have made it difficult for foreign critics to follow it as an ensemble. For this reason it is worth considering briefly the ambivalent heritage of Italian culture.

At an ideological level, the two main elements in contemporary Italian culture are Catholicism and Marxism: Pasolini's remark, 'All Italians are Marxists,' is paralleled, and preceded, by the observation by Italy's most famous (and highly idealist) philosopher, Benedetto Croce, that 'All Italians are Catholics.' Pasolini, like the culture as a whole, did not achieve a synthesis of these two elements—a synthesis which would, of course, be impossible anyway. More specifically, in the cinema the main post-war movement in Italy was what has been called neo-realism. This term was apparently originally coined by the Marxist critic Umberto Barbaro during the Fascist period, and embodies an unresolved contradiction. This can be seen from the actual films which are called 'neo-realist'. In Rossellini, for example, the two outstanding elements are realism *and* sentimentality: compare Rossellini's Anna Magnani film (*Roma, Città Aperta*) with Pasolini's Magnani film (*Mamma Roma*, 1962). Pasolini's films, at any rate up to around 1966 (*Uccellacci e Uccellini* [*The Hawks and the Sparrows*]), reproduce these contradictory traits. It is for his gifted representation of contradictions, not solutions, that Pasolini can lay some claim to attention as a director.

It is not at all an 'accident' that Pasolini shifted repeatedly from one genre to another—painting, poetry, criticism, short stories, novels, feature films, reportage-investigations (for example, *Comizi d'Amore*, 1964), theatre, poetry (again)—while at another level engaging in continued provocation and masochism. Within any one genre, such as cinema, other genres often play a role: painting and music in *The Gospel According to St Matthew*; Orson Welles (dubbed by the novelist Giorgio Bassani) reads a Pasolini poem in *La Ricotta* (episode in *RoGoPaG*, 1962; re-released as *Laviamoci il Cervello*); Domenico Modugno, the pop singer ('Volare'), sings a Pasolini song in *Che Cosa sono le Nuvole?* (episode in *Capriccio all'*

Italiana, 1966); Pasolini himself plays a painter in *Il Decamerone* (*The Decameron*, 1970). Within the poetry and novels there is a constant attempt to handle the overflowing contradictions of the Italian language (cf. the Friulian poetry with the Roman novels). At other levels, the burden of the language problem (viz., that there is no 'standard' Italian) led him into theory (linguistics) and, in the cinema, towards silent movies (the central part of *Edipo Re* [*Oedipus Rex*, 1967], and much of both *Porcile* [*Pigsty*, 1969] and *Medea*, 1970). Within the cinema, he oscillated from the style of *La Ricotta* to that of *Che Cosa sono le Nuvole?* And in relation to this vast range of style and matter, he dabbled in Marxism without ever committing himself to it as a scientific discipline. As Franco Fortini, the Italian critic (and former collaborator of Pasolini on the review *Officina*), has pointed out apropos of Pasolini's poetry: 'Everything Pasolini writes is based on antithesis and contradiction.' The labour of juggling with so many contradictions reveals itself in the recurrent use of oxymoron in Pasolini's poetry; later, he succeeded to some extent in evading contradiction through a quite different montage of visual elements in the cinema.

Pasolini started out as a poet. He did his university thesis on Giovanni Pascoli, a decadent, pre-industrial romantic and a populist. Pasolini's early poetry, written in Friulian dialect, is heavily influenced by Pascoli. But while Pascoli was writing before the First World War, in a world roughly comparable to that of, say, Wordsworth, Pasolini was writing during and immediately after the end of the Second World War—a time when populist romanticism of the Pascoli kind was an anachronistic and unsustainable luxury. Both Pasolini's Friulian poetry and much of his subsequent work (the poems in *La Meglio Gioventù* through *L'Usignuolo della Chiesa Cattolica* and on to *Le Ceneri di Gramsci*) give the impression of a desperate rearguard battle against the 'outside' world and in favour of increasingly unattainable and remote objectives: the peasantry, 'Christian Friuli', his mother, God, etc.

But while in Friuli Pasolini started to read the works of Antonio Gramsci, the great

Italian Marxist. Being a *pasticheur*, however, Pasolini interiorized primarily only one moment of Gramsci's thought—the 'national-popular'. For Pasolini, as for many others, this was a way, through literature and literary criticism (which he saw as going very closely together), to try to evade both class and ideological contradictions. The title of one of Pasolini's volumes, *Passione e Ideologia* (*Passion and Ideology*), sums up his whole outlook. Because Pasolini loves the peasantry, the peasantry automatically becomes the most important social group; or, if it cannot be forced into that position, the whole problem of the objective role of classes politically is simply evaded.

This unsynthesized position later expressed itself in the most lamentable manner in Pasolini's poem, *Il PCI ai Giovani!!* (*The Communist Party to the Young!!*), written at the height of the 1968 political upheavals. In this poem Pasolini condemns the Italian students, who had been savagely assaulted by the police, solely on the grounds of their class *origins*. Neither students nor police are analysed or assessed in their political roles; and, above all, neither group is allotted any possibility of change in the future. It is a vision of the world which is predetermined and profoundly a-political. It is most certainly not Marxist. Rather, Pasolini's argument could be described as a case of arrested dialectic.

His blurred and evasive 'vision' of class carries over immediately into an equally blurred vision of politics. What Pasolini did was to affiliate himself in a very general way with the left-cum-Marxist cultural world which is vaguely under the hegemony of the Italian Communist Party. This is quite different from being a Marxist. In most European countries, and in the U.S.A., Communist parties have tended to adopt an *exclusive* approach, demanding some kind of orthodoxy. In Italy, the Communist Party early on opted for an inclusive (or 'hegemonic') approach. To some extent this is the legacy of the Popular Front period, which started in the 1930s and continued through the war and the Resistance and on through the Cold War. Italy is the only country where this trajectory occurred. Gramscianism provided the ideological underpinning for a Popular Front policy both politically and culturally.

But this inclusive approach is also the product of the peculiar Italian cultural tradition where there is no lay culture to correspond to the liberalism of the Anglo-Saxon cultures. Apart from Marxist (and pseudo-Marxist) culture, there is little but Catholicism. The relationship between Pasolini (or Visconti, or even Fellini) and the PCI was one of great flexibility on both sides. The Party was delighted to have Pasolini or Visconti around, and demanded little of them. Pasolini could place an unorthodox text on linguistics in the Party weekly, *Rinascita*, and at the same time attack the Party (for example, in the 1968 poem attacking the students).

When Pasolini started directing films, in 1961, he had already worked on the scripts of some fifteen other movies for directors like Fellini and Bolognini. It was on the strength of his well-received and controversial Roman novels, *Ragazzi di Vita* and *Una Vita Violenta*, that he was first asked to work on scripts, and many of the films he worked on as a writer are set in much the same milieu as his novels. This is also true of his own first films as director, *Accattone* and *Mamma Roma*, which form a group with the two Roman novels as much as with his later films. It is especially misleading to see Pasolini's films apart from the rest of his work—a view frequently adopted outside Italy, because of the compartmentalization of culture in the field of criticism. This has been aggravated by the fact that Pasolini was Italian. When Alain Robbe-Grillet, for example, moved from novels to cinema, some attempt was made, even by Anglo-Saxon critics, to consider his work as a whole. This was rarely done in the case of Pasolini. As far as most of the English-speaking world is concerned, he effectively *started* with *Accattone*—whereas such a view produces an arbitrary rupturing of his *oeuvre*. *Accattone* follows on from *Una Vita Violenta* (*A Violent Life*), the biggest change being that the film is purged of the novel's explicit political element. While *Una Vita Violenta* deals with the process of politicization, the two Roman films merely denounce, without drawing any conclusions.

After *Mamma Roma*, Pasolini made a forty-minute film, *La Ricotta* (part of *RoGoPaG*), which is transitional between the works on the Roman subproletariat and *The Gospel According to St Matthew*. The main character is a member of the Roman sub-proletariat who dies while acting the good thief in the crucifixion sequence of a Cine-città spectacular (directed by Orson Welles). *La Ricotta* must be seen as emerging partly out of the feeble response to Pasolini's first two films, and particularly to *Mamma Roma*, which portrays a death on the *letto di conten-zione* (a 'punishment bed'), a medieval device used in Italian prisons. *La Ricotta* was originally envisaged as a full-length feature, but ultimately had to be cut to the length of a long 'sketch', and bears the marks of this compromise. Along with *Sopraluoghi in Pal-estina per 'Il Vangelo secondo Matteo'* (*Locations in Palestine for 'The Gospel According to St Matthew'*, 1964), in effect a letter on a marginal negative moment, it marks the transition from the Roman films to *The Gospel According to St Matthew*: *La Ricotta* is a film about filming the Gospel the wrong way; *Sopraluoghi in Palestina* is about rationalizing a decision not to shoot it in the wrong place.

After the Roman films, Pasolini was cast-ing around for new material. A Third World project, *Padre Selvaggio*, collapsed. Yet *The Gospel According to St Matthew* is set in the same world—the peasantry of a backward country. The film is a swing away from the class among which Pasolini was living, the Roman subproletariat (about whom he was also then still writing), back to the class predominant in Friuli, the peasantry. In style, it is a move away from the reverential style of *Accattone* and *Mamma Roma* to a more eclectic form, more typical of his middle period poetry and his novels.

The Gospel According to St Matthew demonstrates a striking imagination. But the film also makes a series of abject concessions to reactionary ideology. One way to see this is to compare it with Rossellini's *Francesco, Giullare di Dio*. Both films show an attempt at realism; they try to show how something which has been transmitted through an unreliable text and tradition might actually have happened. But while Rossellini tackles the problem head on, Pasolini approaches his text in a much more devious way, mixing the Rossellini approach (e.g., when Christ comes down from the mountain and shouts at the first peasants he sees) with a much more questionable method which accepts the Christological tradition, particularly in paint-ing and music. The end result is a Christ who is essentially the Christ of the contem-porary Catholic church, who occasionally does some odd things (a Christ no more 're-volutionary' than the Jesus of the Jesus freaks). This at a time of confused and con-fusing 'dialogue' between the Vatican and Italian communism. It is *not* a Marxist film about Christ (or Christianity). It is a reac-tionary film, which ultimately serves reaction-ary ideology and reactionary political forces. A Marxist film about Christ remains to be made (as does a Marxist film about Marx).

A few examples of Pasolini's concessions in *The Gospel According to St Matthew*. First, the figure of Christ: a decidedly soppy char-acter, only 'saved' by the harsh voice dubbed onto him in Italian—a typical Pasolini com-promise. Second, Judas: if Judas existed, he must have been a strange man; it is a pity to represent him as a patently and stereotyped *evil* character. How did he become a disciple of Christ? The ambiguity and contradiction of the character are obliterated. Third, Pasolini's decision to re-insert the sequence of the 'investiture' of Peter (the key issue in the Reformation); this was done at the request of the Catholic organization which helped with the making of the film.

The contradictions of the film, and of the 'realist' tradition as a whole, are best resumed by the Crucifixion sequence. A highly realist moment when the nails are driven in and Christ groans is immediately followed by an incredibly self-indulgent sequence of Christ's mother, who is in fact played by Pasolini's own mother Susanna, lolling around at the foot of the cross. This sequence also resumes, on film, several moments of Pasolini's poetry: the emphasis on exposure, as, for example, in the poem *La Crocefissione* (*The Crucifixion*) and the hopeless responsibility of motherhood in *Ballata della Madre di Stalin* (*Ballad of Stalin's Mother*). Interestingly, Pasolini chose to accent the visceral aspect of the whole sequence with particularly melodramatic music (music being, of course, the most im-mediately 'effective' instrument'. The realism and inventiveness of Rossellini's *Francesco, Giullare di Dio* are recurrently visible in

A scene from *Salò*: 'a coolly horrific exposé of the depths of degradation; a terminal film in every sense of the word'.

The Gospel According to St Matthew, but they are overwhelmed by sentimentalism within the film itself, and by concessions to the religious establishment outside.

In *The Hawks and the Sparrows* Pasolini tried to deal with two difficult subjects together: the Italian cinema after the death of neo-realism, and Italy as a whole after the *supposed* demise of Marxism. The section on neo-realism draws heavily on Rossellini for its content, and on Fellini (alas) for its style. The section on the crisis in Italian society is littered with references to Lukács, Pope Paul VI, Cuba, Togliatti and suchlike. In the first section, the references are mainly to cinema, but the trouble is that the quotation marks are invisible: there is no sign to indicate what is quotation and what is narrative (or criticism). The same criticism that has been forcefully made of Pasolini's poem on the students and the police can be made of *The Hawks and the Sparrows*: the irony is lost in the imprecision of quotation and comment. Much of the film looks like bad Fellini (about as bad as cinema can get). The section on modern Italy is similarly confused. Pasolini fails to produce any evidence that Marxism or Togliattianism is dead. He has not found a cinematic style to describe the processes in which (rightly) he is interested.

The surrealist style adopted for the two colour shorts, *La Terra vista dalla Luna* and *Che Cosa sono le Nuvole?* (which grew out of *The Hawks and the Sparrows* and the Totò–Ninetto Davoli couple), seemed to be the mode best suited to allowing Pasolini to resolve (tentatively) his vacillating approach to the problem of whether cinema is dream or reality. In *Oedipus Rex* the two solutions are simply left open. There is no attempt at 'resolution'. The prologue is resolutely 'realist'. The central part, set in Morocco, is shot like a dream, and is virtually without dialogue. It is also the piece of Pasolini which most clearly reveals the influence on him of Japanese cinema (particularly Oedipus' fight with his father). The short film made at about the same time, *La Sequenza del Fiore di Carta* (episode in *Amore e Rabbia* [*Love and Anger*], 1969; also known as *Vangelo '70*), deals with much the same problem: the impossibility of tranquil ignorance (or innocence). But here the resolution is provided by God. Pasolini would seem to be

given to taking one step forward and two steps back.

Teorema (*Theorem*, 1968) returns to and resumes many of the earlier themes: modern Italian society and industrialization, sexuality and religion, surrealism and realism. Stylistically, it ranges from scenes wholly reminiscent of *Comizi d'Amore* (1964) to passages shot in the same location as *The Gospel According to St Matthew* (Massimo Girotti on the mountain). The project is simply stated: the modern industrial bourgeoisie has created a consumer society which it dominates and in which everything, including previously threatening factors such as Christianity, has been brought under control—everything, that is, except sexuality. Sex is the one factor which can still dislocate all members of the bourgeoisie. This is where the film connects with the enquiry which Pasolini carried out earlier into sex and sexual repression (*Comizi d'Amore*, a now rather inaccessible film). Interestingly, *Theorem* was Pasolini's first film about the bourgeoisie, a class he claimed to hate, and which he was apparently determined to throw off balance. But the bourgeoisie conjured up, while real enough, is sited in a void. The bourgeoisie is *a class*—yet Pasolini's treatment of class and class relations in the film is worse than unsatisfactory. The same problem recurs in *Pigsty*. The bourgeoisie is vigorously denounced (in one half of the film), but in characteristic Pasolini manner it is caricatured beyond the point of representation. The film, though, is a major extension of Pasolini's cinematic work into the realm of cannibalism and sexual relations with animals. Here, for the first time, Pasolini seemed ready to push out beyond the fringes he had explored in *Oedipus Rex* and *Theorem* and break through into the same sort of terrain as was later dealt with by David Cooper in his book *The Death of the Family*. In another way, *Pigsty* looked forward to the more relaxed Pasolini of *The Decameron*.

In between these two films, however, Pasolini veered back into the world of myth and mythology with *Medea* (1969), a rambling, amorphous poem around the (dubbed) person of Maria Callas. In no way was the film successful, except perhaps in the choice of scenery. There is a sense of groping exhaustion, perhaps reflecting a dead end in

Pasolini's mythical explorations. At any rate, for all its flaws and evasions, *The Decameron* showed a much more relaxed and humorous director than had hitherto appeared, with a surprisingly light touch in sexual matters. Pasolini suggested in interviews that he had by now reached the tranquillity of old age.

The Decameron was merely the first part of a trilogy, to be followed by *I Racconti di Canterbury* (*The Canterbury Tales*, 1971) and *Il Fiore delle Mille e una Notte* (*Arabian Nights*, 1974). Other possible schedules were enunciated and then abandoned (including films on St Paul, Calderón and Socrates).

Pasolini was indisputably one of the most gifted directors at work in Italy in the post-war period, but nearly all his work is flawed by self-indulgence, confusion and evasion. The sum always seems less than the parts.

That Pasolini was not an orthodox Marxist can scarcely be denied. And indeed, in films like *The Decameron, The Canterbury Tales* and *Arabian Nights*, his glorification of the peasantry of the pre-industrial era often reached heights of reactionary romanticization that surprised many of his admirers. But this was only one side of Pasolini; I cannot, however, agree with Stack in his opinion of *The Hawks and the Sparrows*. It seems to me that he is taking a far too literal approach to an essentially poetic film, and a film that in no essential way resembles those of Fellini, as Stack suggests.

Pigsty does indeed represent a major extension of Pasolini's work in the cinema; and it is the one film which prefigures Pasolini's *Salò, o le Centoventi giornate di Sodoma* (1975), his last film before he was murdered in 1975. *Salò* is one of the most profoundly depressing films I have ever seen, partly because of what we see and partly because of the gap between the author's avowed intentions and what the film tells us about the man himself. *Salò, or the 120 Days of Sodom* is, as the title suggests, a modern version of the Marquis de Sade's novel, set in the days of the Salò Fascist 'republic' of 1944. The reason for the choice of time and place, said Pasolini, was that the sadistic atrocities in the film were to be seen as an enormous metaphor for the Nazi-Fascist psychological dissociation which allowed them to perpetrate their crimes against humanity. But the film seems to go further than necessary

if its point is simply, as one French critic put it, 'a testament of rage and anger at the all-powerful of this world who have the power to treat men like things, like objects'. There are too many indications of complicity between the victims and their torturers. (In a famous essay Pasolini once wrote: 'It is always the victim's look that suggests the violence which will be done to him or her.') It seems to me that what the film expresses (independently of Pasolini's conscious intentions) is not only the power of the mighty to victimize the weak, but the desire of the weak to be victimized, their desire to be treated like objects. Far from being, as Pasolini claimed, 'nothing more than a cinematic transposition of Sade's novel', it seems to me that the film exhibits a fascination with being reduced to an object that went way beyond the demands of its ostensible subject matter. What we actually see and experience is not, in Eliot's useful phrase, objectively correlated to the purported theme. *Salò* is a disturbing experience because of its coolly horrific exposé of the depths of degradation and its all too complaisant acceptance of those depths. A masterpiece, as some claim? Perhaps, but also an agonized scream of despair; and, given the circumstances of Pasolini's death just after completing the film, a frighteningly prophetic work. A terminal film in every sense of the word.

Oswald Stack has edited an interview book, *Pasolini on Pasolini* (1969), and this remains the primary text on Pasolini, in spite of its date. Pasolini's own writings have not been widely translated, but a French edition of his essays, *L'Expérience Hérétique: Langue et Cinéma*, was published in Paris in 1976. In 1977, Paul Willemen edited a useful selection of texts by various writers, including Geoffrey Nowell-Smith and Roland Barthes, *Pier Paolo Pasolini*.

SAM PECKINPAH

Robin Wood

The value of Sam Peckinpah's work is still very much in question; its intensity is not. And art that expresses such energy and passion, such a commitment to personal impulse, commands, at least, respectful attention. *The Wild Bunch* (1969) and *Straw Dogs* (1971), whatever one's estimate of them, have that combination of candour and force which announces an artist who is not afraid of appearing ridiculous; those who profess to find them no more than ridiculous are perhaps nervously insulating themselves from the films' ferocious and contagious energy. At the same time, one may comment at the outset that it is a great pity that, in the eyes of the public and of most critics, Peckinpah's gentler and arguably finest films (I think especially of *The Ballad of Cable Hogue* [1970] and *Junior Bonner* [1972]) have been so overshadowed by the spectacular and explosive violence of the more notorious works—a violence that is certainly a major component of his artistic personality, but by no means the whole story.

Peckinpah's work situates him firmly within the great tradition of the American cinema. I mean by this rather more than that he has repeatedly returned to the Western genre, though that in itself is certainly of key significance. For all their radical differences of temperament and emphasis, Peckinpah (born in 1926) is the heir of Ford—an heir Ford would perhaps not have wished to acknowledge, but an heir none the less. Ford's work shows a consistent involvement with America both as a country and as an idea: his later films, most explicitly *The Man Who Shot Liberty Valance*, are evidence of a growing disillusionment with that idea. But Ford, rooted in those ideals of the American future looked forward to in his earlier work, could never quite make the transition from disillusionment to active rage and antagonism; even *Liberty Valance* is ultimately dominated by nostalgia.

The central values of Peckinpah's work can be seen as embodied in the myth of the 'Old West', with its emphasis on manhood and independence—the myth personified by Tom Doniphon (John Wayne) in *Liberty Valance*. To such a myth Peckinpah repeatedly returns—in *Ride the High Country* (U.K.: *Guns in the Afternoon*, 1962), in *The Wild Bunch*, in *Cable Hogue* and *Junior Bonner*—but he follows through the implications of such a commitment (clung to in the context of contemporary America) with a ruthlessness of which Ford (ultimately a more complex artist) was incapable.

Peckinpah's work to date witnesses the predicament of the artist who is vociferously anti-Establishment yet lacks any defined ideological alternative: it has the strengths and limitations which such a description suggests. It is doubtful, however, whether he could, or would wish to, be an American Godard: the sort of 'freedom' his work explicitly and implicitly extols is essentially primitive, even brutish, probably intractable in relation to the disciplines of a conscious social-political programme.

'Brutish' needs modification—especially when one thinks of the tenderness and sensitivity of *Cable Hogue* and *Junior Bonner*. The real strength of Peckinpah's work may lie in the relationship between that sensitivity and the primitive force endorsed by, especially, *Straw Dogs*. The essential point is that it is indeed a matter of relationship rather than contradiction: if there is a fundamental value in Peckinpah's work on which everything else is built, it is the sense of the holiness of impulse. *The Wild Bunch's* communally spontaneous decision to go back for Angel (and thus precipitate the cinema's most overwhelming holocaust); Dustin Hoffman's growing determination, in *Straw Dogs*, to defend a 'home' that doesn't really exist, succeeding only in destroying the illusion of it; *Junior Bonner's* purchase of the air ticket that will send his father to Australia; the delight with which Slim Pickens facilitates the escape of Steve McQueen and Ali MacGraw at the end of *The Getaway* (1972): all have their source in a common fundamental need. One can define that need as the urge to self-respect, or the sympathetic recognition of that urge in others; in all cases it is given an edge of desperation by our awareness that these characters have really nowhere to go, or that life won't be any different for them if they get there.

The violence of *The Wild Bunch* and *Straw Dogs* has provoked a deal of moral outrage, against which the films can be defended up to a point. The outrage arises from the spectator's difficulty in detaching himself—his sense of being implicated, and in more than negative ways (e.g., revulsion). The use of slow motion to depict acts of violence and their effects (it was not of course coined by Peckinpah, but goes back to *Bonnie and Clyde* and, ultimately, *The Seven Samurai*) has become a cliché of the modern cinema and one of its most annoying; yet, like

Steve McQueen in *Junior Bonner*: 'it is a great pity that Peckinpah's gentler and arguably finest films (*The Ballad of Cable Hogue* and *Junior Bonner*) have been so over-shadowed by the spectacular and explosive violence of the more notorious works'.

all such clichés, it can be assumed to have some authorization from popular response and popular demand. Peckinpah's defence of the slow motion in *The Wild Bunch*—that it conveys the sense of the protraction of time at moments of agony or horror—is not very convincing. Such an effect was achieved much more successfully (if no less artificially) by Eisenstein (in the Odessa Steps massacre of *Potemkin*) and Hitchcock (in *Marnie*'s horse-riding accident) by means of overlapping montage. Eisenstein and Hitchcock both play on the spectator's propensities for subjective involvement and identification, which is the secret of their success in these cases; the slaughter in *The Wild Bunch* has mostly the quality of spectacle. If audiences enjoy it, it can only be because they derive a certain half-horrified satisfaction from

watching (from the safety of their cinema seats) the effects of violence lingeringly displayed. The use of slow motion seems also, in subtly differing ways, to carry a sense of celebration: in *The Seven Samurai* it further emphasizes the film's strongly marked aspects of ritual; in *Bonnie and Clyde* it marks the point at which the protagonists die into the immortality of legend. In *The Wild Bunch* the slaughters become horrifying and exhilarating ballets of lingeringly convulsed bodies and suspended gushings of blood.

The equivocal attitude to violence suggested by this is fully confirmed by *Straw Dogs*. If one follows the film's narrative carefully, one finds that all the acts of violence perpetrated by the hero are logically motivated—he is forced into them step by step from the moment when he determines to earn and preserve his self-respect. Yet the effect of the violence is as much exhilarating as horrifying: when Dustin Hoffman swings the man-trap down over his adversary's head, most of us (unless we have deliberately rejected the film's hold on us) are in there swinging with him. This is what our 'moralistic' critics can't stand—the film's reminder that the violence is not in the action but in *them*. And, if one's moral position is the tenable one that violence is intrinsically wrong and must at all costs be held in check, then there is no doubt that *Straw Dogs* is an immoral film. Peckinpah sees life as, inevitably, a bloody struggle for survival—not just physical survival, but the survival of one's manhood. His films implicitly accept violence as a metaphysical fact, a condition of our existence, and go on from there at times equivocally to celebrate it, though the celebration is never simple or complacent, never free from an accompanying sense of horror.

The corollary of Peckinpah's commitment to impulse and spontaneity is the relative abeyance of reflection (*Pat Garrett and Billy the Kid* [1973] seems not so much meditative as tired and half-hearted, evidence of the slackness of Peckinpah's work when passion fails). It is the abeyance of critical awareness that makes possible the more unpleasant aspects of his films. With the emphasis on energy and 'maleness' goes the tendency Peckinpah seems to share with his heroes of reducing women to mere sexual objects. One doesn't know whether to blame actress, director or both for the entirely bland and uninteresting performance of Ali MacGraw in *The Getaway*, but it seems significant that the Peckinpah film in which the man–woman relationship is most central—both structurally and in terms of values—should have a yawning gap where its heart should be. The same fascination with 'maleness' also accounts for Peckinpah's inability to detach himself from the brutish and repulsive Rudy Butler in the same film: the presentation of his pathetic, humiliated victim's suicide as *funny* is in all Peckinpah's work to date the moment that is hardest to forgive.

That work is at its richest when such tendencies are most challenged or qualified. One might single out the complex, mutually

critical opposition of Charlton Heston and Richard Harris in the sadly mutilated *Major Dundee* (1965), or the Joel McCrea/Randolph Scott relationship of *Ride the High Country*. In *The Ballad of Cable Hogue*, Stella Stevens begins (seen through the eyes of the sex-starved protagonist) as a sexual object, and develops into much more: the film has a tenderness and delicacy not normally associated with Peckinpah but convincingly real, arising from a treatment of woman unique in his work.

Finally, *Junior Bonner*—both in themes and in quality—fully justifies my claim that Peckinpah is the true heir of Ford. Stylistically, the film, with its tense and nervous surface (one has the impression of more cutting than in any other Peckinpah movie), is very far from Ford. But its complex treatment of the tension between wandering and settling, and—exceptionally for Peckinpah—of the family, places it firmly in the tradition of Ford's Westerns. The film allows us to respond to its characters and situations in an unusually complex way. There is no question, here, of the reassertion of Fordian values: American civilization, and the family with it, is shown to be in an advanced state of disintegration. Yet the emotional pulls of family relationships are allowed their affirmative strength, the bleakness of the overall vision—the sense that no one has anywhere to go—being qualified throughout by a powerfully communicated generosity and human warmth. No director's work requires more careful discrimination, both within and between movies, but Peckinpah's positive achievement puts him securely in the forefront of American directors currently working.

Bring Me the Head of Alfredo Garcia (1974) and The Killer Elite (1976) were both rather coolly received by most critics: the *macho* sensibility has not been getting a good press lately. The first was condemned for its brutality, the second for its commercialism. Some have gone so far as to claim that Peckinpah has fallen into self-parody. *Cross of Iron* (1977) was dismissed, in the words of Russell Davies, as 'long, loud, male and nihilistic', and by *Variety* as 'pacifism, Peckinpah style, meaning mayhem is the message'. He is obviously going through a difficult phase; it will be interesting to see if

he can find a way out of the dead end into which he seems to have strayed.

See *Sam Peckinpah: Master of Violence* (1972) by Max Evans, as well as the relevant chapter in Jim Kitses' *Horizons West* (1969).

ARTHUR PENN

Robin Wood

Arthur Penn's is a cinema built on tensions and paradoxes. A gentle, sensitive, civilized man, he has made films notorious for their violence. His general orientation is towards author–director's cinema, the European art-movie, and he admits to idolizing Ingmar Bergman; yet his films are intensely American in subject-matter and usually rooted in the traditions of genre cinema, and he has only once directed from his own scenario (*Alice's Restaurant*, 1969, co-scripted with Venable Herndon, based on Arlo Guthrie's record and on factual material). He has worked in both theatre and television, and the style of his films can be partly described in terms of a tension between these two 'pulls': one thinks of him primarily as an actor's director, yet he talks of editing as the most important aspect of the cinema, the essential creative act, and shoots a great deal of material (either using several cameras or re-filming the same segment of action from different set-ups) from which he subsequently 'extracts' (his word) the film. The richness of his films arises, none the less, above all from the remarkably alive, responsive performances he elicits from his actors. On two occasions (*The Left-Handed Gun*, 1958, *The Chase*, 1966), the editing has been taken out of his hands; yet the films not only survive but impress as indisputably personal works. *The Chase*, which he himself partly rejects as 'a Hollywood film rather than a Penn film', remains arguably his best work to date, central to his preoccupations, consistently vivid in its realization.

Through all this one can trace a coherent psychological pattern: on the one hand a reliance on, and respect for, the instinctual (American cinema; the gravitation towards Westerns and gangster movies; the spontaneous, intuitive work with actors); on the other, a persistent yearning after intellectual control (European cinema; the desire to be total author; the conscious, objective decisions involved in editing). The oppositions are hardly as neat as this makes them appear: there is no reason, for example, why conscious intellectual decisions shouldn't play an important role in the direction of actors. Yet anyone who watches Penn direct is struck by the spontaneous, participatory nature of his involvement. He even at times mimes the action from behind the camera during shooting, out of view of the actors, as if to obtain the performances he wants by some kind of sympathetic magic.

This psychological pattern is reflected in the films, which consistently express in dramatic terms the struggle between spontaneous impulse and conscious control, the 'holiness' of the first (in Blake's sense: 'Everything that *lives* is holy') counterbalanced by the necessity for the second. Much of the quality of the films grows out of the interaction of these opposed drives—out of Penn's implicit acknowledgement of the validity of each, and the resulting sense of a dislocation or disharmony inherent in man's nature, in the human condition.

Made in 1958 when he was thirty-six years old, Penn's first film, *The Left-Handed Gun*, is centred on the struggle of Billy the Kid (Paul Newman) towards consciousness and self-awareness. His confused impulses of violence are complexly motivated, hence complexly evaluated, originating in a sense of moral outrage at a monstrous criminal act defended (indeed, instigated) by the law, escalating into a wilful and futile destruction. Against him are set two authority-figures, presented, if less inwardly, with great sympathy: Tunstall, the gentle pacifist father-substitute whose murder provokes Billy's career of destruction, and Pat Garrett, the sane, steady, settled defender of law and order. Penn's fourth film, *The Chase*, repeats this pattern, the values embodied in the spontaneous, instinctive Anna and Bubber Reeves (Jane Fonda and Robert Redford) set against the efforts at control of sheriff Calder (Marlon Brando).

Penn doesn't, as a rule, write his own scripts (though he admits to contributing, in various degrees, to all of them); on the other hand, he never accepts subjects unless he finds them congenial and feels he can make them his own by a process of assimilation and transmutation. He has associated himself repeatedly with William Gibson's play *The Miracle Worker*, producing it on stage and television and in 1962 directing the film version. It is easy to see why: the subject-matter offers marvellously intense and concentrated expression to Penn's preoccupations. The child Helen Keller (Patty Duke), unable to see, hear or speak, is a creature given over to uncontrolled, animal-like impulse. The education she receives from Annie Sullivan (Anne Bancroft) is essentially the process of transforming an animal into a human being. It is Annie who is both the centre of the film and a central Penn figure. Herself half-blind (a factual *datum* turned to expressive symbolic use), acting from personal psychological needs as much as from a dedication to her vocation, she comes as near as any character in Penn's films to reconciling the authority of conscious control with the vitality of instinctual drives.

Penn's work also needs to be seen in its social context of contemporary America, the desperation that is never far below the surface appearing to be the response of an alive and humanly engaged man to a society at once exploitative and disintegrating. The desperation and bewilderment are most explicit in Penn's least satisfactory film, *Mickey One* (1965)—significantly, a film made in complete freedom which Penn celebrated by indulging (and, one hopes, exorcizing) his desire to make a European 'art' movie. The film emerged as an unprofitable expression of confusion, a generalized statement of urban nightmare, suggesting by contrast how the apparent constraints of genre and popular narrative can act not only as necessary restraints but as positively enriching elements. Some of Penn's most brilliant and affecting set pieces, working within more clearly defined narrative contexts, disturbingly express his sense of disintegration, of the breakdown of all control, of things falling apart: the burning of the McSweens' home in *The Left-Handed Gun*; the climactic chaos of *The Chase*; the police siege, pursuit and death of Buck in *Bonnie and Clyde* (1967); the drift of the wedding celebrations of *Alice's Restaurant* into drugged apathy and disil-

lusionment; the Washita River massacre in *Little Big Man* (1970).

Despite the fact that Penn's choice of subjects has often been limited by commercial interests, and that several of his early films were adapted from plays or (in the case of *The Chase* and *Bonnie and Clyde*) made from scripts already in an advanced stage of elaboration before he took them on, Penn's work so far reveals a remarkably logical inner development. Only in *The Left-Handed Gun* is there a favourable portrayal of established society, and there it is a relatively primitive community (presided over paternally by Pat Garrett) which bears little resemblance to contemporary America. *Mickey One* portrays modern America in terms of complex, indefinable menace. In *The Chase*, society falls apart: the real climax of the film, and perhaps the most intense expression Penn has given us of the tragic, desperate side of his view of life comes when Calder, the film's one responsible and balanced adult, succumbs to the mindless violence of his environment by savagely beating the murderer of Bubber Reeves. In *Bonnie and Clyde* Penn moves the centre of the film outside society, which is presented as variously corrupt, limiting or ineffectual. The heroes are now the spontaneous, undisciplined, ultimately self-destructive outlaws; the authority-figure (Hamer, the Texas Ranger) is presented with marked hostility. The swing to the values of impulse is expressed stylistically in the richly inventive detail and irresistible *élan* that made the film Penn's first spectacular commercial success.

But Bonnie and Clyde offered Penn no possibility of any constructive alternative to the society they rejected: he presented them as unwitting folk heroes, as much products and victims of their society as outlaws, never achieving awareness of themselves or of the processes they were involved in. In his two subsequent films, *Alice's Restaurant* and *Little Big Man*, Penn has attempted, somewhat tentatively, to explore possible alternatives.

Alice's Restaurant, though sadly imperfect (the twenty minutes that recapitulate the narrative of the original Arlo Guthrie record rupture the tone and constitute a serious flaw), is perhaps Penn's most personal film.

Warren Beatty and Faye Dunaway in *Bonnie and Clyde*.

It is also his gentlest, taking its tone from the pacifist and largely passive hippies who populate it. Penn's interest gravitated to the community in the deconsecrated church in Stockbridge—to the attempt to found and develop a society of drop-outs. The film, predominantly elegiac, analyses the failure of the venture. The community is built on no firm or vital traditions, only on the vestiges of the tradition it has supposedly cast off. The one common bond—the belief in individual freedom—proves too negative to hold the group together. Significantly, the authority-figures of the film are much weakened, either actually dying (Woody Guthrie), or ineffectual (Ray, nominal head of the church community) or fatuous establishment figures (Officer Obie). The film, like its characters, lacks any vital or informing sense of direction: its movement is towards disintegration, and the personality of Arlo Guthrie, which Penn tries to invest with a certain affirmative potential, is too slight to counterbalance this movement.

The hippies of *Alice's Restaurant* become, essentially, the Cheyennes of *Little Big Man*. Here, white civilization is vigorously, if somewhat simplistically, ridiculed; the film is a moral fable whose positive values are embodied in the Cheyennes, the 'Human Beings', who preserve a kind of natural sanity, tolerance and goodwill in contrast to the psychopathic world of the whites. Penn partially fails, as Nicholas Ray partially failed with his Eskimos in *The Savage Innocents*, and for the same reasons: the presentation of the Cheyennes is confused and blurred by a divided impulse, the desire to re-create 'real' Indian culture partly conflicting with the desire to create an 'ideal' alternative to the white world.

Penn clearly wants to confront the tensions of his own society directly, but he has so far evaded such a confrontation. His problem is that of the artist who is antagonistic to his society yet is unable to elaborate any consistent or constructive ideology with which he might oppose it; he therefore centres his films on outlaws like Bonnie and Clyde or marginal groups too weak to affect the course of things, like the hippies of *Alice's Restaurant,* or he escapes into the indirectness of generalized parable, as in *Little Big Man.* The hiatuses in his work may suggest the increasing difficulties he has in affirming anything or even in offering confident statements. Yet he remains an immensely sympathetic figure, with a relatively small but vital body of work that demands recognition and respect.

Since *Little Big Man,* Penn has made only two films (unless one counts his episode *The Highest* in the Olympic Games film *Visions of Eight* [1973]): *Night Moves* (1975) and *The Missouri Breaks* (1976). Both films have their admirers, but neither marks any significant advance or development in Penn's chequered career. Indeed, Penn himself admits of *The Missouri Breaks* that 'there was a certain promise to that film—Jack Nicholson and Marlon Brando starring together, its "genre" Western nature—that it didn't fulfil. There was a lot of conjecture that somehow all the trouble was run up by Brando, but the choices were mutual.' Perhaps as a result of the relative failure of his last two films, Penn has announced that he is returning to the theatre for a while.

Robin Wood's monograph *Arthur Penn* was originally published in 1969. A revised updated version has appeared in French (1975).

LÉONCE PERRET

Noël Burch

The very few films currently available to the researcher from what may be regarded as Léonce Perret's most characteristic period (*c.* 1910–*c.* 1915; he made films well into the sound era, however) seem to indicate that within the system of representation common (and specific) to most French films of that period, his work constituted both the most intensive working of that system and the most extensive renewal of its incidental procedures along lines which (curiously) led now 'ahead' to the most sophisticated il-

lusionist codes of the future, now 'back' to that realm of 'pre-code freedom' which was the primitive cinema proper. In this sense he was one of those Janus figures of whom Edwin Porter was perhaps the most important and who played such a crucial role during that transitional decade (1903–13).

Perret (1880–1935) came to the cinema from a successful acting career on the stage (he had starred in the original cast of Sardou's *Madame Sans-Gêne* alongside the famous Réjane), joining the Gaumont troupe in 1907. He next went to Berlin to direct experimental talking pictures (!) and in 1909 returned to Gaumont where he began a series of comedies in which he himself played the main role under his own Christian name. The *Léonce* series, more comedy of manners than slapstick, was simply one of hundreds which had blossomed forth following the triumphs of Max Linder, André Deed and many others. From the surviving examples which I have been able to see, these films appear to have been wholly anonymous illustrations of the system of camera set-ups and editing which then prevailed in France, while Perret's screen *persona* is utterly without distinction.

However, the two feature-length melodramas from 1913 and 1914, *L'Enfant de Paris* and *Le Roman d'un Mousse,* attest to the remarkably rapid development of a very striking visual style (for which the cameraman Specht no doubt deserves much credit) in which the specifically compositional and dramaturgical possibilities offered by the prevailing modes were played out with a virtuosity unparalleled in France and unsurpassed anywhere in the world. Whether or not it was Perret who actually promoted the use of the exceptionally deep and handsomely appointed interiors which characterize these films—as opposed to the (economically over-determined?) 'shallowness' of those of Feuillade or even Jasset, whose work is perhaps most related to Perret's—the *mise en scène* of those interiors offers a singular combination of 'panoramic' depth held over from the primitive era proper and modern photographic techniques (Perret's films were among the first to make systematic use of back-lighting and appreciable variations in camera height). It is undoubtedly this combination which endows these films, for the

Jaque Catelain, Huguette Duflos and Georges Vaultier in a scene from one of the many 'lost' films of Perret, *Koenigsmark* (1924).

modern viewer, with a dramaturgical credibility at least equal to that of Griffith, however much their scenarios reflect the most ideologically weighted 'popular' literature of the late nineteenth century (as did those of nearly every film of the period, including the 'social' and 'naturalist' efforts of Bourgeois, Machin and Carré).

At the same time, Perret was also perhaps the first to introduce some of the more sophisticated editing procedures into the French system, and while his use of match-cuts was not so prolific as that of some of his American contemporaries, certain sequences display an astonishing mastery of editing and anticipate future and often remote developments of the illusionist system to an extent which fully justifies Georges Sadoul's claim that Perret was 'technically' in advance of Griffith. The sequence in *Le Roman d'un Mousse* in which the young heir is drugged by his villainous guardian and carried off over the ramparts of Saint Malô by a sea captain bribed by the guardian to shanghai him, constitutes a prophetic piece of 'durative' editing with constantly varied shot-angles which none the less 'carry continuity' to perfection; this is editing of a kind which, though probably inaugurated in England some ten years earlier, was not to be generally mastered for some years. Similarly, the serial *L'X Noir* (1915) contains one of the earliest French examples of a 90-degree direct match in an interior setting; and, elsewhere, a truly exceptional instance of ellipsis across a concertina cut (an adventuress starts to transform her appearance in a medium shot and in the immediately following close shot the elaborate disguise has been completed)—a procedure which, so far as I am aware, did not come into use at all for over forty years.

It is also principally in the only two Perret serials which, so far as I know, have survived (the other is *La Main de Fer*, 1911–12) that the director's startling departures from and/ or radicalizations of the prevailing system produce singularly beautiful, concrete instances of that historical bridge which may be said to link the 'pre-code freedom' of the primitive cinema with the vanguard cinematic practices of today. Also in *L'X Noir*, an action involving a descent along the face of a steep embankment and a departure in a rowing-boat is viewed through three circular vignettes successively appearing and vanishing at different points in a black frame: their disposition on the screen-surface indicates the successive stages of the character's trajectory (at the top, in the middle and at the bottom of the embankment) as he enters and exits from each in turn. This radical production of screen surface and of 'frame limit' clearly points to the procedures by which the vanguard practices of the 1920s and of the past two decades have at times fragmented a screen whose uniformity had become, certainly by the late 20s, an essential guarantee of illusionist continuity. It also points, of course, to the eye-catching pyrotechnics which the advertising film has derived from such critical departures, and this double descent is emblematic of what is no doubt a fundamental ambiguity implicit in what Georges Sadoul has correctly defined as Perret's *syntactical refinements*.

A less spectacular but perhaps more far-reaching example of Perret's strange propensity for 'prefiguring' the strategies of *deconstruction* as future cinema was to know them, is the protracted sequence in *L'X Noir* in which the frame is centred about a restaurant hat-rack and a doorway, into and from which a whole series of characters enter and exit, holding often only the briefest of conversations in the frame. This highly condensed (spatially and temporally) manifestation of *the shot as passing site* produced a sharply formalized *de-centring* effect premonitory of Warhol, Godard, etc.

It would be foolish to 'credit' Perret with an absolutely *original* role in the complex history of filmic practices: even the work of Méliès and Feuillade was over-determined by social, economic and cultural conjunctures to an extent and in a way that directors (Dreyer, Eisenstein, Vertov) who came after the watershed of *Caligari* were not. Nor can he be said to have contributed as decisively to the development of the codes as, say, Griffith, if only because Griffith was working within the framework of a national industry which was soon to deprive the French cinema of most of its economic and ideological ascendancy. However, it is important that his films, or as many of them as have actually survived, be made available for study (it would be particularly interesting to see some samples of his American work [*c.* 1920]) since they were clearly a variant of a 'national' mode of representation which was itself a singular moment in the development of what we continue to call, reductively to say the least, the 'language of cinema'.

Had it not been for the persistent championing of Perret by the late Henri Langlois, he would perhaps be a totally forgotten figure. As it is, very few of his films have been seen in recent decades, and these are only his French works. Contemporary critics, it is true, maintained that his American period was distinctly inferior; but contemporary critics have been known to be wrong. And Gloria Swanson maintains firmly that the *Madame Sans-Gêne* they made together was one of her best films—thanks to Perret's inspired direction. A screening of *L'Enfant de Paris* at the 1977 New York Film Festival proved that this work, at least, is still capable of fascinating a modern audience. A definitive judgement on Perret must await a retrospective screening of all his works that survive. But how many do?

Henri Fescourt's *La Foi et les Montagnes* (1959) contains much valuable information about Perret.

MAURICE PIALAT

David Wilson

Little known outside France, and with so far only three full-length films to his credit, Maurice Pialat (born 1925) has evoked comparison with Ermanno Olmi and Miloš Forman as a director whose films are anchored in the particular realities of the everyday. But where Olmi can be sentimental and Forman puckishly ironic, Pialat is discreet and restrained: he gets in close to his characters and situations but remains detached, so that what emerges often seems uncomfortably close to the audience's own experience. His style, at once intensely personal and self-effacing, is *pointilliste* (he was a painter before he turned, at a relatively late age, to full-time film-making), accumulating nuances of behaviour which may be separately insignificant but which together spell emotional crisis.

Each of Pialat's films hinges on a time of crisis—childhood, the break-up of a relationship, a death in the family—and in each case it is not so much the crisis itself as the characters' reactions to it on which the focus is turned. His first film, *L'Enfance Nue* (U.S.: *Me*, 1968), about a boy sliding into delinquency when he is boarded out with foster parents, inevitably invited comparison with Truffaut's *Les Quatre Cents Coups*. But although, like Truffaut, Pialat closely observed the secret, self-contained world of childhood, the real centre of the film was its rendering of the bemusement of the adults in the face of the apparent contradiction between the boy's response to their kindness and his delinquency. A key scene in this film was the death of an old woman, and death—in particular the way the process of dying excludes or distorts the emotional response of those affected by it—recurs as a dominant theme in Pialat's other two films. Metaphorically in *Nous ne Vieillirons pas Ensemble* (1972), where a couple (Jean Yanne and Marlène Jobert) destroy each other and whatever feeling exists between them in a constant round of separations and reconciliations; and as a numbing reality in *La Gueule Ouverte* (1974), which records in harrowing detail how a family copes with the discovery that the woman who has been its pivot and its very living strength is dying of cancer.

Life comes to terms with death in its own, often unattractive way, Pialat suggests; and the revelation is the more persuasive precisely because it is revealed in his films rather than stated. The style is naturalistic, the editing unobtrusive to the point of being elliptical. It is a method which seems perfectly suited to Pialat's concern to demonstrate that emotional crisis, far from being exceptional, is the banal norm.

Although Pialat, who is now fifty-three, has made only three feature films, he has worked extensively for television, and *La Maison des Bois*, made in 1971, was highly acclaimed. His next film after *La Gueule Ouverte* was announced as *Les Filles des Faubourg*, but the shooting has been long delayed. A pity, because Pialat seems to me to be one of the most important of the post-Nouvelle Vague directors.

LUPU PICK and CARL MAYER
Jean-André Fieschi

First and foremost, like Leopold Jessner's *Hintertreppe* (U.S.: *Backstairs*, 1921) and Murnau's *Der Letzte Mann* (*The Last Laugh*, 1924), the slow, heavy dramas of Lupu Pick—*Scherben* (U.S.: *Shattered*, 1921), *Sylvester* (*New Year's Eve*, 1924)—bear the stamp of Carl Mayer (1894–1944). To read a Mayer script is to be plunged straight into the dimensions of the drama: its rhythm, its scansion, its respiration. It is to read not a story but a score, complete with its themes, repetitions and tempi.

The stage is cleared for essentials. For Man, Woman, the Couple, the Mother, Death. For Drama. It is pointless to draw distinctions here between the 'realism' of the *Kammerspiel* and the 'metaphors' of Expressionism. For Mayer, the *Kammerspiel* is little more than a socialized and psychologized inflection of the Expressionist metaphysic. The spectres, *Doppelgängers*, vampires and other marionettes of fantasy are no longer personified but interiorized, as it were, through sudden instinctive drives in the characters, the infinitesimal suspension of a gesture, a numbness about the eyes, an almost surgical dissection of light and shadow, the disturbing unfamiliarity of everyday objects (a lantern, a plate, a jug, the fold of a curtain). To read Mayer is also to discover his intuitive feeling for camera movements, stressing a particular detail, sweeping through or spanning a scene, shaping the mass of dramatic material with often unpredictable stylistic drives.

To read Mayer ... It is in fact as a privileged reader of Carl Mayer that Lupu Pick (1886–1931) introduces himself in the preface he wrote in 1924 for the published script of *Sylvester*. 'I wanted to make the spectator share the feelings that this reading had aroused in me.' Pick emerges, however, less as a scrupulously faithful illustrator than as a man who, through his encounter with the imperious Mayer style, discovered his own personal style. The simplicity and the monumentality of *Scherben* and *Sylvester* (each shot is lingering, weighty), the extreme saturation of this omnipresent and rarefied dramaturgy in which silence seems occasioned less by the absence of a soundtrack than by the muted opacity of the characters themselves, bear witness to the great skill with which Lupu Pick allows one to read timeless tragedy in a trivial incident, and to flush out obsessions from their favourite hiding-place in the ordinary and everyday: the family.

Sombre, bowed by the weight of invisible burdens, these characters move like somnambulists on the brink of madness, murder, suicide. They might be inhabitants of a planet whose rarefied atmosphere imposes an exasperating deliberation of movement stifling any vitality, any cry, any speech. But one senses that an explosion is imminent; a final outburst will reveal that the system here is repressed violence. The modernity of Mayer, seconded by Lupu Pick's skill, lies in his management of perfectly controlled signs; in him this system of familial oppression found its modest, tyrannical master.

Translated by Tom Milne

Carl Mayer did indeed make an enormous contribution to the German cinema—he was the author of most of Murnau's scripts (including *Sunrise* and *Four Devils*). See the articles on The Cabinet of Dr Caligari and Murnau.

Three events seemed to contribute to the decline of Mayer's brilliant career: the death of Murnau, the coming to power of the Nazis, and the advent of sound. After 1930 he achieved relatively little: he died in England at the end of the war. See Lotte Eisner's *The Haunted Screen* (1969).

MARY PICKFORD, see p. 335

ROMAN POLANSKI, JERZY SKOLIMOWSKI AND THE POLISH ÉMIGRÉS

Mira and A. J. Liehm

In the mid-60s two Polish directors attracted international attention. Both talented and young, both overnight successes, they soon found Poland too small for them and they began to work abroad. Roman Polanski (born in Paris in 1933) and Jerzy Skolimowski (born in Warsaw in 1938) introduced a peculiarly Polish sensitivity into the French and English language cinemas. In spite of the obvious differences between them, they had several things in common. A sense of anxiety, a profound feeling for human fate in an alienated society, and common roots in the 'Polish destiny'—the unique historical experience of their country. The world of the absurd attracts them more than any other, but though their inspiration may come from the same sources as that of Beckett, Ionesco and Pinter, it differs from Western expressions of alienation in its basic realism. For Polish absurdity is based on the everyday experience of that nation, and it is a part of all its drives and efforts; it also reflects that rising pessimism which followed the enthusiasm of 1956.

Polanski had already concentrated on the burden of non-conformity in a conformist society in his experimental short *Dwaj Ludziez Szafa* (*Two Men and a Wardrobe*, 1958). He developed this theme in *Le Gros et le Maigre* (*The Fat and the Lean*, France, 1961) and *Ssaki* (*The Mammals*, 1962). The heroes of *Two Men and a Wardrobe* shared the same fate—pushing a wardrobe out of the sea (i.e. vainly striving for freedom in an unfree society). But in *The Mammals* their common burden—a sledge—finally turned them into rivals. The sea is frozen into an icy plain where only Death awaits the two former friends, seen by Polanski as two black spots on a white surface. For eleven minutes these spots move to and fro trying to enslave each other. It seems to be Polanski's belief that everyone has a chance to become either a master or a slave; the only

Knife in the Water, Polanski's first feature film, co-written with Skolimowski, 'was a sophisticated attack on two Polish generations'; in this sequence the generation gap seems about to be bridged by a knife.

question is who will be the first to exploit the other.

Noz w Wodzie (*Knife in the Water*, 1962), Polanski's most subtle film, was the last he made in Poland. Written with Skolimowski, it was a sophisticated attack on two Polish generations: an older one, living in the past, unable to deal with the present except in the most conformist way; and the younger generation, 'our cynical generation which still has romantic yearnings and at the same time longs for integration', as one of the characters in Skolimowski's *Bariera* (*Barrier*, 1966) puts it.

What else did Polanski and Skolimowski have in common? Perhaps it was their contempt for their contemporaries. These young Poles did not approve of the way the younger generation put all the blame for its predicament on its predecessors. Rather, they saw society as an entity, a self-contained and self-perpetuating circle. In the crucial scene of Skolimowski's *Rece do Gory* (*Hands*

Up, 1967; never released) a group of people, old and young, get on a train going to a never-stated destination. One car is filled with plaster, people roll in it, and one of them gets calcified. The implication is that these people are Poles who have evaded their moral duties. 'Even I was on the train,' says Skolimowski, accusing the whole of his generation, that generation of people in their thirties who live with their 'hands up'.

Actor, script-writer and director; a graduate of the National Film Academy at Lodz; collaborator of Andrzej Wajda and Andrzej Munk—Roman Polanski pursued his vision of people doomed to live in a vicious circle in all the films he made abroad. His heroes seldom catch a glimpse of hope and all of them are portrayed in extreme situations, with the 'civilized' veneer of human relations carefully stripped away. Evil has been Polanski's constant companion since his early childhood, which he spent—

his parents were deported to a concentration camp, and his mother died there—hiding in the ghetto. His nihilist aesthetic is mixed with that Polish despair rooted deep in Gothic horror. All nightmares come true, all hidden fears are real: 'This is not a dream, it is reality,' shouts Mia Farrow in *Rosemary's Baby* (1968).

Of all the films Polanski made during his early years abroad (*Repulsion*, 1965; *Cul-de-sac*, 1966; *Dance of the Vampires* [U.S.: *Dance of the Vampires*, or *Pardon Me, But Your Teeth Are in My Neck*], 1967; *Rosemary's Baby*), *Cul-de-sac* was the most accomplished. The hell its characters create is very real; so, governed by their unspoken conventions, are their actions and reactions. The plot, about a gangster taking over the household of a neurotic couple, differs from other stories of its kind both through its stoic

manner and the quasi-Dostoevskian relationship between the intruder and the victims. As in *Knife in the Water*, Polanski built up a system of tensions and counter-tensions rooted in the characters. In only one location, a house on Holy Island, and with only six actors, he created an ironic image of life on the brink of destruction.

In *Dance of the Vampires*, a splendidly executed example of its genre, he created a loving parody of the traditional vampire film, making good use of his experience of East European superstition. In this film, as in others, Polanski himself played one of the leading roles. Polanski, in fact, has always loved acting and made his debut at the age of fourteen in a small Polish theatre. When he was twenty-one, he acted in one of the most important Polish films of the time, Wajda's *Pokolenie* (*Generation*, 1954), and he ap-

Cathérine Deneuve in *Repulsion*, Polanski's first film to break through the language barrier.

peared in several of Wajda's later films before he left Poland.

Polanski has now become one of the most successful directors of our time. His capacity for the representation of evil is central to his work; it is also inimitable. In his first colour short *Gdy Spadaja Anioly* (*When Angels Fall*, 1959), the story of an old woman lavatory attendant who is 'visited' by her dead lover, he emphasized both the presence of death and its unity with life. In 1971, Polanski began shooting his version of *Macbeth* (1972). Again he emphasized the ordinariness of the story because, as he said after his wife Sharon Tate had been murdered, 'There is a lot of violence in the world; just look around.' So again he showed everything on the screen—all the murders, all the battle scenes which Shakespeare could only suggest. All his private world of horror, born many years ago in Poland, matched perfectly with Shakespeare's intentions.

Macbeth was followed by the tiresomely enigmatic *Che?* (*What?*, 1972) and then by his commercially most successful film *Chinatown* (1974), from an accomplished script by Robert Towne, and with fine performances from Jack Nicholson, John Huston and Faye Dunaway. This was followed by the much less successful (in every sense) *Le Locataire* (*The Tenant*, 1976), which was made in Paris and suffered from its silly, would-be Kafka-esque script and the usual problems of international film-making.

Always the angry young man of Polish cinema, Skolimowski became its greatest hope after Polanski's departure. During the 60s he was practically the only director whose films could stand comparison with the best work of Munk or Wadja. His work was rooted in the same visions, feelings and traditions as the Polish directors of the 50s. Since this is a world largely unknown to Westerners, their attempts to interpret this work through comparisons with directors like Resnais and Godard have always failed.

All three of Skolimowski's features shot in Poland—*Rysopis* (*Identification Marks: None*), his graduation film of 1964; *Walkower* (*Walkover*, 1965) and *Barrier* were conceived as metaphors of a dehumanized society. They were a series of visualized reflections linked by one idea: the confrontation between the attitudes and feelings of two generations. Skolimowski is fascinated by people with a rebellious streak and the tension between their desire to adapt to the existing structures and their refusal to surrender their individuality. As time went by, his heroes more and more often chose to adapt, and the director has in effect been arguing with them (and with himself) with an intensity which projects itself onto the audience.

Before graduating from the National Film Academy in Lodz in 1964, Skolimowski had studied anthropology, literature and art and had tried his luck as a boxer, actor and poet. In 1960 he collaborated on Wajda's *Niewinni Czarodzieje* (*Innocent Sorcerers*) and played one of the leading roles in it. Skolimowski's whole work is marked by his experience of Stalinism, which, in his view, persisted in Poland well into the 60s. Hence his fierce attack on dogmatic ideology and, in *Hands Up*, which he himself considers his best film, on all those who use their position in society to repress others. Skolimowski's statement about a country full of trains for unknown destinations, filled with Poles bound together by a collective tragedy, was clear and precise. Therefore, it could not help but displease those who felt directly concerned. After *Hands Up* was withdrawn from the 1967 Venice festival and banned, Skolimowski decided to work abroad, at least temporarily.

He had already made in Belgium a comedy called *Le Départ* (1967). In many ways similar to the films of Forman and Truffaut, it had as its hero a hairdresser's assistant (Jean-Pierre Léaud) who shared Skolimowski's passion for racing cars and boxing. As in *Barrier*, money and love are mutually exclusive, or at least so they seem at first; eventually love triumphs. In 1967, he collaborated on a Czech episode film called *Dialogue 20–40–60*. But in 1968 he tackled, for the first time, a big-budget production. *The Adventures of Gerard* (1970), starring Peter McEnery and based on stories by Arthur Conan Doyle, was a failure, or perhaps one should say an example of the difficulty in coping with unfamiliar material in an unfamiliar situation. But in *Deep End*, shot in 1970 in London and Munich, he hit his stride again. On the surface, this was a little thriller about a young boy—an attendant at a

Jean-Pierre Léaud as the hairdresser's assistant who shares Skolimowski's passion for racing cars and boxing in a scene from *Le Départ*, a film made in Belgium.

swimming pool—who figuratively goes off the deep end and murders the girl he is in love with. A mosaic of realistic scenes, the film's total effect was almost surrealist, and the theme of woman as a destructive element reappears with such incisiveness that, retroactively, it tells us much about the women characters in Skolimowski's previous films.

Skolimowski never fully broke off his relationship with Polish cinema, and in 1972 a feature film, *Poslizg* (*The Skid*), was shot there from a script written by him. But Skolimowski himself did not direct again for some years until he returned to England to make *The Shout* (1978).

Although originally working in another field and a member of an older generation, Walerian Borowczyk (born 1923) is closely linked with Polanski and Skolimowski. From 1957 when his *Byl Sobie Raz* (*Once Upon a Time*)—made in collaboration with Jan Lenica (born 1928)—won the Silver Lion at the Venice Short Film Festival, there has hardly been any international festival from which a Borowczyk film has been absent. Starting with micro-fantasies, often running for only three minutes, he progressively became one of the most incisive representatives of the cinema of dissent, with, as his chief target, man's desire to control others. Borowczyk has made over thirty animated shorts, using almost every kind of animation technique. He presents us with characters searching for something meaningful in the life of today, doomed to defeat and to an acceptance of existential absurdity.

Borowczyk's first film was made in 1946; it was called *August* and ran for five minutes. After a long gap, during which he took a degree in painting and graphic art (and, in

1953, won the Polish national prize for his graphic work), he decided to return to the cinema. In 1954, he made a film about Fernand Léger and, three years later, he made several experimental films with Jan Lenica. In 1958 he began to work for French television in its special research department. His most famous film of this period was *Dom* (*The House*, 1958), which was also his last Polish short. During the following years, he made many experiments in design and music and produced some of the best animated films of the 60s, such as *L'Encyclopédie de Grand'maman en 13 Volumes* (*Grandma's Encyclopaedia in 13 Volumes*, 1963) and *Renaissance* (1964).

Lenica left Poland at the same time as Borowczyk and he achieved international fame with his first film made in France: *Monsieur Tête* (co-directed with Henri Gruel, 1959). All of Lenica's later films are striking examples of an artist trying to overcome the gap between audiences and the most advanced artistic experimentation.

See also the entry on Borowczyk, which deals more fully with his career in France as director of live-action fiction films. One can consult Ivan Butler's *Roman Polanski* (1970) and the article on Skolimowski by Michael Walker in *Second Wave* (edited by Ian Cameron, London, 1970). There is also, in French, a monograph, *Roman Polanski* by Jacques Belmans (1971).

POLISH CINEMA SINCE THE WAR

Mira and A. J. Liehm

Polish cinema had to make a completely new start after 1945: production facilities had been almost totally destroyed and the film-makers dispersed. Nor were there any traditions to be renewed, as pre-war Polish films had been made almost exclusively for the home market. During the years following nationalization of the film industry, there were many difficulties to be overcome and by 1950 only seven features had been made. The first to gain international recognition was *Ostatni Etap* (*The Last Stage*, 1948), directed by Wanda Jakubowska (born 1907), which dealt with victims of Auschwitz, and *Ulica Graniczna* (*Border Street* or *That Others*

May Live, 1949), directed by Aleksander Ford (born 1907), an impressive evocation of life on the edge of the Warsaw ghetto.

Both Jacubowska and Ford had worked before the war, and both continued to make films, but while Jakubowska never made another film as interesting as *The Last Stage*, Ford (first Director General of the Polish State Film) remained one of Poland's leading directors for the next twenty years. In 1952, he evaded the pressures of Stalinist ideology by making *Mlodosc Chopina* (*The Youth of Chopin*); two years later his *Piatka z Ulicy Barskiej* (*Five Boys from Barska Street*) was one of the first Eastern European films which attempted to depict contemporary society in its true colours.

In 1954 two directors made their first films: Jerzy Kawalerowicz (born 1922) directed *Celuloza* (*A Night of Remembrance*) and *Pod Gwiazda Frygijska* (*Under the Phrygian Star*), a two-part film dealing with a pre-war working-class milieu, which showed great promise. The other new director was Andrzej Wajda (born 1926): his *Pokolenie* (*Generation*, 1955) was the first of many Polish films to deal with that lost generation, whose members were in their teens when the war broke out and who never really recovered from the tragedy of this particular 'Polish experience'.

Thus, after a period of rigid socialist realism, Polish cinema had made a new start. Its future development was influenced positively by the decentralization of production. The state remained the exclusive producer of films, but production was split into several groups, each headed by an experienced director and allowed considerable independence. This was one of the results of that political storm which led to the Polish October uprising in 1956 and which marked the end of Stalinism in Poland, temporarily at least.

So for a period of four years Polish film-makers had more creative freedom than had existed anywhere in Eastern Europe since 1945. The films that followed were seldom shown in the other Eastern European countries, whose authorities considered them pessimistic, individualist and unrepresentative. Only in the mid-60s were Czechoslovak and Hungarian audiences able to see the works of Wajda and Munk, while in the Soviet Union and the German Democratic Republic many of these films still remain unshown.

Andrzej Munk (1921–61) made his first film in 1955, *Blekitny Krzyz* (*Men of the Blue Cross*), and confirmed his exceptional talent with *Czlowiek na Torze* (*Man on the Tracks*, 1957), a powerful story about one of the many victims of the Stalinist era. The film was written by Jerzy Stefan Stawinski (born 1921), who also wrote many of the best films of that period: *Kanal* (1957), *Eroica* (1957) and *Zezowate Szczescie* (*Bad Luck*, 1960).

The great theme of the Polish cinema—the occupation and the resistance movement—was now shown in a new light. The war was no longer regarded as a heroic necessity, but as a supreme example of suffering made up of many individual tragedies which could never be wiped out by either a common faith or the victorious outcome of the war. (See, for example, Kawalerowicz's *Prawdziwy Koniec Wielkiej Wojny* [*The Real End of the Great War*], 1957). The Polish destiny, that of a nation eternally torn between two authoritarian countries, Germany and Russia, was now revived in all its complexity. These films were completely antithetical to all the 'war pictures' hitherto cherished by the official policy-makers of Eastern European countries. The most typical and symptomatic of these films was Wajda's *Popiol i Diament* (*Ashes and Diamonds*, 1958) in which the tragedy of a post-war Poland still torn by internal dissension was brought to life in all its ambiguity. The director did not condemn his hero for his crime—the murder of a Communist leader—but put both murderer and victim on the same level of guilt, suffering and innocence. Already, in *Kanal*, Wajda had not hesitated to shed new light on the national legend of the Warsaw uprising of 1944 and to show its participants as human beings destroyed by conflicting forces: the murderous tactics of the defeated Nazis and the all too cool political calculations of the victorious Soviets. The film's extreme honesty made it an unforgettable event in world cinema.

Even more controversial was Munk's *Eroica*, an ironic summing-up of the national mythology. The film is in two episodes: both of them dealing with the defeated Polish army and culminating in the birth of a new legend, a new hope—both predestined to a slow death.

1958 was an important year for the Polish cinema: it gathered fifteen awards at various international festivals. As well as the films already mentioned, one must add *Ostatnie Dzien Lata* (*The Last Day of Summer*, 1958), directed by Tadeusz Konwicki (born 1926) and Jan Laskowski (born 1928), a poetic study of a brief encounter between a man and a woman. Then there was Wojciech Has' *Petla* (*The Noose*, 1958), a despairing picture of the last hours in the life of an alcoholic; and, finally, Tadeusz Chmielewski's highly original comedy *Ewa Chce Spac* (*Eva Wants to Sleep*, 1958).

By the end of the 50s, a change of theme appeared necessary. The next step was obvious: the problems of contemporary life had now to be dealt with. But in Poland, as in Czechoslovakia and Hungary, the end of the 50s saw a considerable deterioration in the relations between artists and government; and the government eventually succeeded in silencing all dissenting voices. So the Polish boom stopped around 1960. After that there were very few noteworthy films among the yearly quota of twenty-five productions, and there were hardly any young people to follow the generation of the 50s. Wajda was the only director who continued to make films without any serious artistic compromises, but also without any great development. *Lotna* (1959), his first film in colour, turned back to the autumn of 1939 for its subject. *Niewinni Czarodzjieje* (*The Innocent Sorcerers*, 1960) was one of the very few films that tried to deal with contemporary problems without making concessions; however, Wajda was not able to make the film as freely as he had wanted and the finished work was severely criticized. The script was written in collaboration with Jerzy Skolimowski, who also played one of the leading roles, and their picture of Polish youth hiding their real feelings behind a wall of cynicism struck a sympathetic note with audiences all over the world. Wajda's next films were less successful: *Samson* (1961) was a rather empty story of a fugitive from the Warsaw ghetto, and *Sibirska Ledi Magbet* (*Siberian Lady Macbeth*, 1962; made in Yugoslavia) and *Gates to Paradise* (1967; a British—Yugoslav co-production) were not major works. *Wszystko na Sprzedaz* (*Everything for Sale*, 1968) was inspired by the tragic death of the great

Zbigniew Cybulski in Wajda's *The Innocent Sorcerers*; Skolimowski collaborated on the script and played a leading role . . . one of the very few Polish films that tries to treat contemporary problems without concessions.

Polish actor Zbigniew Cybulski, and in this film Wajda made his second attempt to concentrate on the psychology of his characters rather than on their social context. After a minor satirical comedy, *Polowanie na Muchy* (*Hunting Flies*, 1969), he went on to make *Krajobraz po Bitwie* (*Landscape After Battle*, 1970), based on a story by T. Borowski, an important Polish writer who committed suicide in 1959 at the age of twenty-nine. Borowski was one of the first Polish writers to be affected by the ambiguity of Polish behaviour during the war and the resistance. The film was to become the first of a series of important works based on Polish classics: in 1972 Wajda made *Wesele* (*Wedding*), after a play by Wyspianski, and in 1975 he directed *Ziemia Obiecana* (*Land of Promise*), from the novel by the Nobel Prizewinner Wladyslav Reymont.

Munk died in 1961 in a car accident,

shortly after having been strongly criticized for his brilliant satire *Bad Luck*, in which he dealt harshly with political and social conformity. *Pasazerka* (*The Passenger*), Munk's unfinished film, was completed in 1963 by Witold Lesiewicz, who cross-cut the finished footage in the concentration camp with stills from other sources, and achieved an extraordinary outline of a film which dealt with the individual responsibility for collective crimes.

In the 60s many directors turned towards historical super-productions. In 1960, Aleksander Ford made *Krzyzacy* (*Knights of the Teutonic Order*), a wide-screen, colour version of Sienkiewicz's classic novel. Six years later he emigrated to the West, and in 1971 he made, in Denmark, a rather pale film version of Solzhenitzyn's *First Circle* (*Den Første Kreds*).

Kawalerowicz made an adaptation of a Polish classic in his *Faraon* (*Pharaoh*, 1966),

Munk died in 1961 in a car accident. *The Passenger* was completed in 1963 by Witold Lesiewicz, who cross-cut the finished footage in the concentration camp with stills from other sources.

and Has made a rather extraordinary film from a no less extraordinary eighteenth-century Polish novel (written in French) called *Rekopis Znaleziony w Saragossie* (*The Saragossa Manuscript*, 1964). Ever since the beginning of their careers Kawalerowicz and Has had displayed widely differing interests. Kawalerowicz was something of an eclectic, attracted by existential problems; his best films were *Pociag* (*Night Train*, 1959) and *Matka Joanna od Anolow* (*Mother Joan of the Angels*, 1961), which attracted world-wide attention for his formal inventiveness, a vivid protest against a dogmatic system of ethics, and the profundity of his portrayal of his characters. After the rather pompous *Pharaoh*, Kawalerowicz did not work for four years. Then in 1969 he made a rather subtle film called *Gra* (*Play*), which depicted the relationship of a man and a woman trying to overcome a crisis in their marriage (as usual, his wife Lucyna Winnicka played the leading role). With the situation in Poland becoming more and more difficult, he was obliged to shoot his next film, *Maddalena* (1971), in Italy.

One of S. J. Lec's aphorisms says, 'The words that have not been used tell more about a period than those that have been misused,' and this observation holds true for Poland in the 60s. The small number of Polish films depicting contemporary life speaks for itself. There were some interesting films made, like Has' *Jak Byc Kochana* (*How To Be Loved*, 1963), and Konwicki's *Salto* (1965), but the most significant films were made by the soon-to-be-émigré directors Polanski and Skolimowski, for discussion of whose work see the entry above.

With the change of government and the aftermath of the workers' revolt in the northern Polish ports in 1970, the situation of the Polish cinema improved dramatically. Tadeusz Konwicki made his most accomplished film, *Jak Daleko Stad, Jak Blisko* (*How Far It Is and Yet How Near*, 1971), a work dealing with his generation's obsession with the tragedies of the recent past. Even more important perhaps was Janusz Majewski's *Dvoji Svet v Hotelu Pacifik* (*Hotel Pacific*, 1975), a film which portrayed both worlds of a large luxury hotel before the war—the life of the staff and that of the guests. Another promising new director was Andrzej Zulawski, whose first film *Trzecia Czesc Nocy (The Third Part of the Night*, 1971) was a deeply pessimistic, expressionist work. His next film, *Diabe (Devil*, 1971), was never released, so he went to France where he had a certain success with *L'Important, c'est d'Aimer* (1975). In 1976 he returned to Poland where he made an interesting science fiction film about the necessity of ideology, *Na Srebrnym Globie (At the Silver Globe)*. Marek Piwoski's interesting *Rejs (The Cruise*, 1970) was followed in 1976 by an exciting action film about gangsters and police provocation, *Przepraszam, Czy Tu Bija? (Foul Play*, or more literally, *Excuse Me, Do They Beat You Up Here?)*.

But beyond any doubt the most important new Polish director to appear since the generation of Wajda and Munk was Krzysztof Zanussi (born 1939). Indeed, many consider him to be the most interesting Polish director of any generation. For a consideration of his work see the separate article devoted to him.

One might also mention an early film by Has, *Pozegnania (Farewells*, 1958), which many remember fondly. For further reading, see Boleslaw Michalek's *The Cinema of Andrzej Wajda* (1973). Wajda's next films after *Land of Promise* were *Smuga Cienia (The Shadow Line*, 1976; a co-production with British television) and *Czlowiek z Marmaru (The Marble Man*, 1977). This latter film was almost immediately banned by the Polish authorities (though it has since been released).

ABRAHAM POLONSKY

Richard Corliss

Of all the Marxists who came to Hollywood, Abraham Polonsky (born 1910) was the most successful—single-minded, if you like—in setting the capitalist ogre within a gilded narrative frame. His scripts for his post-war trilogy on the profit motive—*Body and Soul* (1947), *Force of Evil* (1948), *I Can Get It for You Wholesale* (U.K.: *This Is My Affair*, 1951)—read like manifestos in the melodramatic form, and reveal characters utterly obsessed by money. As described by Roberts, the malignant, manipulative fight promoter in *Body and Soul*, life is just 'addition and subtraction; everything else is conversation'.

Body and Soul, directed by Robert Rossen, fits securely into Polonsky's very personal urban hellmouth, with its Brueghelesque, subway-at-rush-hour density, its stylized but fiercely realistic dialogue, and its cheeky characters who seem to carry both a chip and an albatross on their shoulders. But defining *Body and Soul*—and, to a diminishing extent, *Force of Evil* and *I Can Get It for You Wholesale*—are the spectral voices whispering through the tenements and boxing clubs, through the bookie joints and garment centres, like the whispering house in the film of D. H. Lawrence's story, *The Rocking Horse Winner*: 'There must be more money!'

Polonsky was one of the genuinely tragic victims of the Hollywood blacklist; *film noir*, and film, would have been richer in the 50s with his services. By 1968, when his name showed up as scriptwriter on the credits for Don Siegel's *Madigan*, cops-and-robbers movies had grown more acerbic, and Polonsky had possibly mellowed, to the point where the man and the genre could peacefully coexist. Whatever the degree of Polonsky's responsibility for the screenplay, *Madigan* does transcend Siegel's other exercises in urban paranoia precisely because of a complexity of characterization, and an ambiguity of motivations, that we associate with Polonsky's best work.

Tell Them Willie Boy Is Here (1969), which Polonsky wrote and directed, suffers from telegraphing its Message (Red Man, good; White Man, decadent bourgeois pig), but succeeds in transforming its renegade Indian hero into a smart 40s gangster, and Robert Blake into a pint-sized John Garfield. But with Hollywood a more cautious enclave than ever, the high rollers are unlikely to finance a renegade writer-director in his late-sixties, even if he *can* turn programmers into responsible art. Millions for *Jaws II*, but not a penny for Polonsky. There just *isn't* enough money.

For the record, Polonsky also directed in 1971 *Romance of a Horse Thief*, a film set on the Polish border in 1904 and thus a return to his ethnic roots. It was not very good. See also the article on Robert Rossen.

MICHAEL POWELL

John Russell Taylor

The process by which some film-makers become cult figures and others do not is deeply mysterious. On practically all counts, Michael Powell (born 1905) ought to be a cult figure, the object of passionate devotion for some, out-of-hand dismissal for others; but despite some stirrings of interest in France (where nearly all such cults are born) during 1970, he has never yet quite made it. The answer in his case may be that he is too eccentric to be accepted wholeheartedly as a British director by the British, and too significantly British to be accepted by the rest of the world as anything else.

He is British, above all, in his choice of his subject-matter and in his attitudes towards it; he is un-British, or at least far removed from the way the British traditionally see their artists, in the flamboyance of his artistic personality, his passion for pushing his films to extremes, his alarming, and withal rather splendid, disregard for good taste and fair play. His most famous and popular films, like *The Red Shoes* (1948) and *The Tales of Hoffmann* (1951), and earlier *The Thief of Bagdad* (1940), have been those in which the extravagances are rendered unalarming, legitimized, by appearing in a context of overt fantasy. But when the same qualities turn up without warning in apparently sober and naturalistic films, or at any rate in films based on subjects which we might expect to find treated soberly and naturalistically, then the problems come thick and fast—though more, it should be said, for critics than for the public at large: popular audiences have often found no difficulty in enjoying films which brought critics up short, hoist on their own principles.

Michael Powell's interests and aesthetic approaches have remained remarkably consistent throughout his career. It is perhaps significant, since he has been called 'the English Abel Gance', that he dates his interest in films from seeing the first number of *Picturegoer* in 1921 (when he was sixteen), with a picture of Ivy Close in *La Roue* on the cover. His first actual jobs in the cinema were as grip and later actor, assistant and general odd-job man on several Rex Ingram films,

starting with *Mare Nostrum* (1926), a spectacular, extravagant subject very much after his own heart. By 1931 he had got to direct some quota quickies, the first two of which, comedy thrillers called *Two Crowded Hours* (1931) and *Rynox* (1932), were unexpected critical and commercial successes. What principally impressed the critics in these and a number of subsequent films of the same type was the young man's individual eye for striking visual ways of telling a story; what chiefly impressed producers was his professionalism in bringing in his films on time and within their tiny budgets.

As a result of these modest but real successes, Powell was able in 1937 to use a subject of his own choosing, *The Edge of the World* (1938), a story made entirely on location in the Outer Hebrides with a cast of relative unknowns, inspired by the evacuation of St Kilda a few years earlier. The film was accepted at the time as a semi-documentary in the Flaherty model, but in retrospect the mystical aspects of the story, with its visions and premonitions, the romantic advocacy of traditional ways of life over material progress, the bold (sometimes even naïve) use of overt visual symbolism, mark it as a recognizable Powell film, obviously related to some of his later works, particularly *I Know Where I'm Going* (1945). At about this time Powell also made two rather Hitchcockian thrillers with Conrad Veidt, *The Spy in Black* (U.S.: *U-Boat 29*, 1939) and *Contraband* (U.S.: *Blackout*, 1940), and directed the major scenes of Alexander Korda's spectacular fairy story *The Thief of Bagdad*. *The Spy in Black* marked an important stage in Powell's career in that it was the first time he worked with the Hungarian writer Emeric Pressburger, with whom he was subsequently to share writer/producer/director credits on fifteen films.

Important though Pressburger undoubtedly was in the team, it was primarily as a writer: on the floor Powell was always in charge, and production chores were shared between them. Since they broke up after *Ill Met by Moonlight* (U.S.: *Night Ambush*, 1957), Pressburger has also made films separately, but both were negligible, while such later works of Powell's as *Luna de Miel* (U.K.: *Honeymoon*, 1958, released

Carl Boehm in the climactic scene from *Peeping Tom*: 'its photographer hero is devoted in true Sadist fashion to the creation and permanent recording of extreme emotional situations (specifically the realization of one's own imminent death) finding an immediate echo in the symbolist and decadent aesthetics of the Romantic Agony'.

1961), *Peeping Tom* (1960) and *The Queen's Guards* (1961) are completely consistent, stylistically and thematically, with the work they did together. *Honeymoon*, a slim tale of a dancer's private life which is made the excuse for a couple of big fantasy–ballet sequences, is clearly in the line of *The Red Shoes*, *The Tales of Hoffman* and *Oh . . . Rosalinda!* (1956). *Peeping Tom* is a rather sadistic drama of neurosis which continues themes from *A Canterbury Tale* (1944), *A Matter of Life and Death* (U.S.: *Stairway to Heaven*, 1946) and *Black Narcissus* (1947). And *The Queen's Guards* (not, in itself, one of Powell's happier works) is all of a piece with the meditations on patriotism and military necessity in films like *The Life and Death of Colonel Blimp* (U.S.: *Colonel Blimp*, 1943) and *The Battle of the River Plate* (U.S.: *Pursuit of the Graf Spee*, 1956).

Stylistically Powell is a master of colour and calculated visual extravagance. Sometimes, as in the drinking sequence of *The Small Back Room* (U.S.: *Hour of Glory*, 1949), his passion for expressionist fantasy gets the better of him, but as a rule it is kept under control and integrated into the film as a whole. Thematically Powell might be described as a philosophical Sadist, in rather the same sense that Buñuel is; but this is combined, rather bizarrely (and in a very British fashion), with something like High Tory politics and a sort of Celtic Twilight mysticism. In other words, Powell is a figure who seems to have strayed into the modern cinema out of the 1890s: one could imagine *The Red Shoes*, with its exclusivist view of the artist's dedication to his art (life for art's sake), or *Black Narcissus*, with its perverse equations of sexuality and ascetic religion, or *Peeping Tom*, with its photographer hero devoted in true Sadist fashion to the creation and permanent recording of extreme emotional situations (specifically, the realization of one's own imminent death), finding an immediate echo in the symbolist and decadent aesthetics of the Romantic Agony. Where they fit into the sober British cinema of the 40s and 50s is another matter. But fortunately, if films are good enough they don't need to fit.

Peeping Tom was the high-water mark in Powell's career. As Taylor points out, The Queen's Guard was not one of his happier works. Nor were its successors: Bluebeard's Castle (1964), They're a Weird Mob (1966), and Age of Consent (1969). There is a monograph by Kevin Gough-Yates, Michael Powell, published in Brussels in 1973.

OTTO PREMINGER

Jonathan Rosenbaum

Otto Preminger (born 1906) directed five films before *Laura* (1944)—one Austrian, four American—but since he disowns them, I haven't seen any of them, and no commentator to my knowledge has ever spoken well of them, we might as well begin with the (false) assumption that a *tabula rasa* preceded his early masterpiece.

False assumptions—and clean slates that tend to function like mirrors—are usually central to our experience of Preminger's work. His narrative lines are strewn with deceptive counter-paths, shifting viewpoints, and ambiguous characters who perpetually slip out of static categories and moral definitions, so that one can be backed out of a conventionally placid Hollywood mansion driveway by somebody and something called *Angel Face* (1952) (and embodied by Jean Simmons) only to be hurtled without warning over the edge of a cliff. As for *tabulae rasae*, there is Angel Face herself and her numerous weird sisters—among them Maggie McNamara in *The Moon Is Blue* (1953), Jean Seberg in *Saint Joan* (1957) and *Bonjour Tristesse* (1958), Eva Marie Saint in *Exodus* (1960) and, closer to the cradle, the almost invisible Bunny Lake in *Bunny Lake Is Missing* (1965) and Alexandra Hay in *Skidoo* (1968). There is even Jean Seberg, whose part

in *A Bout de Souffle*, Godard informs us, 'was a continuation of her role in *Bonjour Tristesse*. I could have taken the last shot of Preminger's film and started after dissolving to a title, "Three Years Later".' Or, to return to our starting point, there is Gene Tierney in *Whirlpool* (1949) and *Laura*.

Laura even *begins* with a false impression. After the credits the screen grows dark, and the voice of Waldo Lydecker (Clifton Webb) tells us, 'I shall never forget the weekend Laura died.' We go on to discover that a body whose face has been destroyed by a shotgun blast is discovered outside Laura's flat. Mark McPherson (Dana Andrews), a detective, sets out to learn who she was; haunted by her portrait and one of her favourite records, smelling her perfume and fingering her clothes, he fills the *tabula rasa* of her absence with a dream (we are implicitly invited to do the same), and then falls in love with the dream. At which point the real Laura, not dead at all, walks into the room.

At least four Lauras are created during the course of the film: one by Lydecker (he refers to her as his 'creation'); one by McPherson; a third by the audience, who follow Lydecker's narration and McPherson's investigation; and then a fourth by Gene Tierney as the lady herself, who enters the film to reconcile and confound all the other versions. But dreams have been generated by this time, and for the remainder of the film we see them being tested by and contrasted with their original stimulus, with gliding camera movements serving to reassemble and rearrange all the characters in relation to this central axis, a series of permutations which place everyone—including Laura—'on trial', in a kind of moral limbo. Even our own qualifications as 'impartial witnesses' are thrown into doubt by the shifting perspectives. Like the characters, we are prone to look at faces and invest portions of ourselves in them, to the extent that each important character becomes a different kind of mirror.

To some extent, all Preminger's films are enquiries, and if that is what makes them interesting, it is also what makes them problematic. (Some questions are more interesting than others.) A film-maker like Rossellini, Rouch or Preminger who chooses to pose questions rather than answer them is likely to encounter misunderstandings, particularly when these questions are placed within a fictional mode (e.g., Rossellini's *Viaggio in Italia*, Rouch's *Gare du Nord*, Preminger's *Whirlpool*), and even more so when, in Preminger's case, the plots pretend to resolve the questions which the style raises. Thus in *The Thirteenth Letter* (1951), for example, a remake of Clouzot's *Le Corbeau*, the search for the author of poison-pen letters in a small Canadian community so relentlessly places every character under suspicion that the dénouement proves to be anticlimactic, and wholly inadequate for releasing the anxiety which has been established.

As the least apparently autobiographical of all 'personal' Hollywood stylists, Preminger frequently mystifies the spectator who is looking for a fixed moral reference. When his camera starts to move, one feels that his characters are being not so much shown as observed, juxtaposed, interrogated; when it remains stationary, we might more readily confuse a specific statement or stance with Preminger's viewpoint, but then a subsequent shot or scene will usually come along to undermine that impression. The son of a public prosecutor and Attorney General of the Austrian Empire, Preminger grew up in Vienna watching trials—and later became a lawyer himself, after acting in several Max Reinhardt productions and directing a few plays—so it is hardly surprising that he should see most dramatic situations in the form of legal proceedings, where truths tend to be clearly relative rather than absolute.

The melodramas he directed between 1944 and 1952, which comprise the bulk of his most durable work, are largely a series of arabesques woven around obsessions and dangerous seductions. All of them were made for Fox (except *Angel Face*, which was made for RKO), and many of the same actors—Dana Andrews, Gene Tierney, Charles Bickford, Linda Darnell—reappear, like permutations in a recurring dream. Against their own better judgements and intentions, McPherson, in *Laura*, falls in love with a supposedly dead woman; Eric Stanton (Andrews), in *Fallen Angel* (1945), plans to marry June Mills (Alice Faye) for her money and then falls in love with her, while the waitress who inspired his scheme (Darnell) is murdered by an obsessive police inspector

(Bickford); Ann Sutton (Tierney), in *Whirlpool*, falls under the literally hypnotic influence of Dr Korvo (José Ferrer), and thereby becomes a murder suspect; a tough cop (Andrews) in *Where the Sidewalk Ends* (1950) accidentally kills a murder suspect, and then falls in love with his widow (Tierney); and Frank Jessup (Robert Mitchum) continues to trust the murderous Angel Face long enough to be destroyed by her.

The technical competence of these films varies considerably (the acting in *Laura*, for instance, is much more polished than that in *Whirlpool*); but Preminger's capacity for exploiting and exploring all their latent ambiguities remains fairly constant. During the same period he also directed two Lubitsch projects (*A Royal Scandal* [U.K.: *Czarina*], 1945; *That Lady in Ermine*, 1948) and a Lubitsch remake (*The Fan* [U.K.: *Lady Windermere's Fan*], 1949); he also made *Centennial Summer* (1946), an amiable version of Minnelli's *Meet Me in St Louis* and arguably Preminger's best musical; *Forever Amber* (1947; the first of his cautiously 'audacious' best-seller adaptations); and *Daisy Kenyon* (1947; a stately soap opera with some of the ambience of a *film noir*). And except for perhaps the first two or three, his interrogatory manner persists in all of these works. But the apogee of this period remains *Angel Face*, the last film Preminger directed before he became an independent producer, and certainly the most enigmatic and haunting of all the works after *Laura*. Jacques Rivette described Preminger's *mise en scène* on this occasion as 'the creation of a complex summary of characters and sets, a web of connections, an architecture of relations', and remarked that 'the relationships of characters create a closed circle of exchanges, where nothing solicits the spectator'.

The fascination and dangers of this approach—more than apparent in Rivette's own first feature, *Paris Nous Appartient*—are roughly equivalent: if every character and viewpoint represented is open to question, the spectator is virtually required to project his own fancies and biases into the narrative in order to make it coherent. And this becomes problematic as soon as Preminger begins to calculate these mirror-like 'open spaces' according to intricate commercial assessments of his audience, and uses his approach to ex-

Gene Tierney in *Whirlpool*: 'The melodramas Preminger directed between 1944 and 1952, which comprise the bulk of his most durable work, are largely a series of arabesques woven around obsessions and dangerous seductions . . . in *Whirlpool*, Gene Tierney falls under the literally hypnotic influence of Dr Korvo (José Ferrer) and thereby becomes a murder suspect.'

plore Big Subjects and promote parlour debates in which the intrigues serve an increasingly pedagogic—and occasionally even propagandistic—function.

Without denying the stylistic, psychological and narrative interest of such films as *The Court Martial of Billy Mitchell* (U.K.: *One Man Mutiny*, 1955), *Exodus*, *Advise and Consent* (1962), *The Cardinal* (1963), *In Harm's Way* (1965) and *Hurry Sundown* (1967), it must be acknowledged that on a thematic level—the level on which they are ostensibly presented—they rarely proceed beyond the intellectual level of *Reader's Digest*. And if most of the films in this period are accomplished in their overall designs and surface details—particularly their use of per-

iod décor and locations—their seriousness is usually compromised by the commercial safeguards round which they are structured. Admittedly, Preminger achieved notoriety when two of these films were condemned by the Legion of Decency; but now that the shock value of the words 'virgin' and 'pregnant' and the subject of heroin addiction has appreciably receded, *The Moon Is Blue* emerges as a flat, toneless and innocuous attempt at comedy, while the remaining interest of *The Man With the Golden Arm* (1955), a sleazy studio job, resides more in the imaginative use of music (e.g., a Shelly Manne drum solo to punctuate a 'cold turkey' withdrawal) and the relative funkiness of Frank Sinatra and Kim Novak than in the all too superficial exploration of its subject.

Advise and Consent has been praised as a bold exposition of the inner workings of the American government, a masterpiece of 'ambiguity and objectivity', and even as a revelation of Preminger 'as one of the cinema's great moralists'. But notwithstanding its strengths as entertainment (a cleanly articulated narrative following a large cast through a complicated plot; a fine neo-Wellesian performance by Franchot Tone as the President, and a showier one by Charles Laughton that deftly mixes with a more subtle rye; a lot of sensually grandiloquent tracks and cranes around Washington locations), the question remains how serious it actually is about its subject. When the Saul Bass credits conclude with the dome of the Capitol lifting to reveal Preminger's name, the limitations of the whole enterprise are already apparent.

The film is concerned not so much with politics or government as with public relations. According to its dramaturgy, the central issues involved in the appointment of Robert Leffingwell (Henry Fonda) as Secretary of State are his inconsequential fellow-traveller past and a homosexual episode in the past of the senator (Don Murray) investigating him. Neither of these facts is shown to have any political importance apart from these men's public reputations; but fundamentally the film is concerned with nothing else—it appears, in fact, that much labour was expended so that the audience wouldn't have to worry about the political issues at all. In the climactic speech—which, far from being 'objective', is clearly designed to impress us with its moral justice—Senator Munson (Walter Pidgeon) condemns the blackmailing Senator Van Ackerman (George Grizzard) by asserting, 'We tolerate just about anything here—fanaticism, prejudice, demagoguery—[. . .] but you've dishonoured us.' And this indeed is the stance of the entire film, which tolerates and even accommodates prejudice and demagoguery as long as it remains sufficiently theatrical (such as Laughton's juicy performance) but comes out squarely against blackmailing, nervous excitability and bad manners (Grizzard is cast as a pure villain from the moment he appears).

To complicate matters, Van Ackerman is shown as a pacifist while Laughton portrays a jingoist; as Penelope Houston has noted, 'The film is as well provided with checks and balances as the constitution.' But the net effect of all these 'counter-weights' is to convey only the *appearance* of objectivity, which contrives to make Preminger's hidden biases more subliminally persuasive. Equivalent strategies are to be found in projecting the Zionism of *Exodus* and the anti-Catholicism of *The Cardinal*: he will welcome antagonistic points of view within a single shot so that he can watch them co-exist, mingle, synthesize, or compete for supremacy, but he always makes sure that the overall 'composition' of these elements conveys a given slant, and the ostensible appeal to the spectator to 'use his own intelligence' is often a very clever means of directing and programming that intelligence. As Jean-André Fieschi has remarked of Tati's *Playtime*—a film, like many of Preminger's, largely concerned with crowds and multiple vantage points—'we are presented with wide avenues, all the better to guide us on to carefully illuminated footpaths'. The journey taken is implacably one from A to B, but we are given a choice of diverse routes by which we may traverse the distance.

Some of the films in Preminger's middle period escape some of the above strictures. *River of No Return* (1954), made to fulfil his Fox contract, benefits from an interesting performance by Marilyn Monroe and a pioneering use of CinemaScope which grants the viewer an unusual amount of liberty in spotting relevant actions and details; and the fact that it doesn't profess to take up a Significant Theme leaves Preminger relatively free to explore the characters for their own sake, as he did in the early melodramas. *Bonjour Tristesse*, despite its celebrated source and more opulent production values, is aided by a similar concentration of focus, as well as a striking juxtaposition of black and white with colour to reflect the tensions between a sombre present in a Parisian nightclub and a reckless past on the Riviera. Somewhat prophetically, Rivette noted at the time that the passage from *Angel Face* to this 1958 film traced a development from the sketch to the fresco, and in more ways than one *Bonjour Tristesse* represents—and its black-and-white/colour contrasts echo—a marriage between the funereal moods and modulations of *Angel Face* and some of the brassier show-manship of a one-ring circus like *Carmen Jones* (1954).

Anatomy of a Murder (1959), easily the most graceful and sustaining of the Preminger bestseller monoliths, is the only obvious instance in his work where the ambiguities unravelled in the style are supported by a deliberately unresolved ambiguity in the plot. Harking back to the thriller format of his better Fox films without the usual under-tow of neurotic anxiety, and dealing with the law (his pet subject) more centrally here than elsewhere in his work, he carries us through a murder trial without ever revealing whether the defendant is guilty or innocent, thereby encouraging the audience to become a separate jury, and focusing much of its attention on the legal procedures themselves. In the process, he establishes an evocative and credible portrait of a small town in Michigan, provokes a number of assured performances (from James Stewart, Lee Remick, Ben Gazzara, Arthur O'Connell, Kathryn Grant, George C. Scott and Joseph N. Welch) and, above all, imposes a lightness of touch that is apparent nowhere else in his work. (Oddly enough, despite its serious elements, *Anatomy of a Murder* comes much closer to working as a successful comedy than heavy-handed efforts like *The Moon Is Blue* and *Skidoo*.) Perhaps because of its uncharacter-istically loose and relaxed ambience—helped in no small measure by Sam Leavitt's photography and Duke Ellington's score—it endures as the least pretentious and most convincing of all Preminger's 'ambitious' works.

The relationship of the French word *procès* to the English word process highlights a preoccupation common to most of Preminger's films, which not only places characters 'on trial' but carefully charts the changes they go through in relation to various corporate and social entities. A standard criterion of implicit or explicit judgement for Preminger is social adaptability, and the typical villain or victim is usually identified by an obsessive personality that is unable to adapt and festers in isolation, frequently behind a deceptive mask: Dana Andrews and Clifton Webb in *Laura*, Linda Darnell in *Centennial*

Summer, José Ferrer and Gene Tierney in *Whirlpool*, Charles Boyer in *The Thirteenth Letter*, Jean Simmons in *Angel Face*, Eleanor Parker in *The Man with the Golden Arm*, Jean Seberg in *Bonjour Tristesse*, Ben Gazzara in *Anatomy of a Murder*, Sal Mineo in *Exodus*, George Grizzard and Don Murray in *Advise and Consent*, Kirk Douglas in *In Harm's Way* and Keir Dullea in *Bunny Lake Is Missing* all embody different versions and varying extremes of this malady, and it is scarcely accidental that virtually all the major acts of violence in these films—excepting only the massive battles in *Exodus* and *In Harm's Way*—can be traced back in some way to these characters' isolation or mal-adjustments.

One of the many peculiar aspects of Preminger's recent films—*Skidoo*; *Tell Me That You Love Me, Junie Moon* (1970); *Such Good Friends* (1972)—is that with few exceptions, all the central characters are viewed as alienated outsiders; it is no small irony that Carol Channing, in an extraordinarily grotesque performance, comes closer to being a balanced and flexible character than anyone else in *Skidoo*.

Much of the unpopularity (as well as the potential fascination) of these three films derives from the way that the theme of isolation vs. social cohesion becomes so shrill and ostentatious that all the latent perversities—what one might call the 'disturbing undertones'—implicit in the earlier works come screaming to the surface in a torrent of vulgarity, as if some restraining force which previously submerged, sublimated or localized these aberrations has finally broken loose to flood the screen. This is undoubtedly an over-simplification: storm warnings are already evident in the garish excesses of works at least as early as *That Lady in Ermine* and *Carmen Jones*; and the increasingly broad flourishes of *In Harm's Way*, *Bunny Lake Is Missing* and *Hurry Sundown* certainly begin to suggest a passage from fresco to comic strip. When Preminger wants to indicate the prissiness of Jere Torrey (Brandon De Wilde) in *In Harm's Way*, the gesture is so wide and sweeping that one could drive a truck through it; the delirious finale of *Bunny Lake Is Missing* registers like an effort to overreach all the rococo effects the film has already accumulated; while *Hurry Sundown* veers from Jane Fonda performing fellatio on an alto saxophone to liberal fantasies about blacks which contrive to cover the distance between Stepin Fetchit and Martin Luther King.

In *Skidoo*, alongside Preminger's efforts to bridge the generation gap by cramming stand-ins for Middle America (Jackie Gleason, Carol Channing, Mickey Rooney, etc.) and counter-culture (Alexandra Hay, John Philip Law) into the same shots, and putting Gleason through an acid trip, one finds an attempt to blend all sorts of irreconcilable Hollywood genres, or what Richard McGuinness has called 'comic books calcifications of them'. Both these attempts achieve a tacky (if appropriate) apotheosis in a Garbage Can Ballet rendered as an LSD vision of two prison guards, when Gleason and his hippy cellmate construct an escape balloon out of plastic food containers. *Tell Me That You Love Me, Junie Moon* saddles its three leads (Liza Minnelli, Ken Howard, Robert Moore) not only with crippling afflictions but with one sexual trauma apiece, each delineated in a lurid flashback; and *Such Good Friends* chronicles a wife's discovery of her husband's multiple infidelities—while he is dying because of medical incompetence—with such unrelenting excruciation that the failed comedy of *Skidoo* and the failed tragedy of *Tell Me That You Love Me, Junie Moon* seem to blend, like a multiplication of two minus numbers, into a very pungent and persuasive (if ungainly) compound of black comedy and bright tragedy.

The muted expressionist undertones of the Fox melodramas become blatant overtones in this late demonic trilogy, and such sequences as the acid trip in *Skidoo*, the flashbacks in *Tell Me That You Love Me, Junie Moon* and the stream of consciousness fantasies of *Such Good Friends* are unprecedented in his career, suggesting an arsenal of modish tactics that consistently miss the mark: aimed at a commercial target, each technique and 'topical' subject backfires, drawing attention more to Preminger's obsessions than to those of his characters. (Particularly striking is the strident flashback accorded to Liza Minnelli in *Tell Me That You Love Me, Junie Moon*, a suite of variations on the two sides of both her sexual nature and her acid-scarred face—reflected in the alternate use of Bach and dance music on the soundtrack and the angle/reverse-angle cutting—which comes across like an experimental student film made out of discarded Hollywood materials.) If the spirit of late Fritz Lang hovers over the grim ambiguities of the Fox melodramas, the ruling manner of the last films suggests the style and some of the preoccupations of yet another Viennese-born director, Stroheim; but it is an uncontrolled Stroheim run amok in the dishevelments and second thoughts of another age, a Stroheim with most of the ironies and fetishes intact but none of the restraint, and—camera movements apart—little of the grace or visual taste. And the enquiries that served to enrich the substance of the melodramas and disguise the superficialities of the big theme streamliners operate here as a cruel exposure, revealing the limitations of the material at every turn.

Perhaps it is as perverse as Preminger himself to prefer these late camp works to the Sunday supplements of his middle period. Yet for all their hysterical indigestibility, they are candidly (and sometimes painfully) personal works: what is lost in craftsmanship is gained in lucidity, even if this lucidity is often the expression of an ambivalence that borders on the schizophrenic. The last scene of *Such Good Friends*, when the heroine (Dyan Cannon) disappears with her two sons into Central Park, can be seen as the character's triumphant 'survival' of her ordeal if we listen to the soundtrack song, or as her ignoble defeat if we look closely at her face. Thus the ambiguity beginning in *Laura* ends in pure and simple contradiction: the blind viewer may say 'comedy', the deaf viewer may say 'tragedy', but the spectator condemned to see and hear will have to settle, like Preminger, for something else.

Preminger reached an all-time critical nadir with *Rosebud* (1975), and it is difficult to imagine in which direction he will go now. There is an (unauthorized) biography by Willi Frischauer called *Behind the Scenes* (1973), and one can also consult Gerald Pratley's *The Cinema of Otto Preminger* (1971). There are two monographs in French: Michel Mourlet's *Sur un Art Ignoré* (1965) and Jacques Lourcelles' *Otto Preminger* (1965). 1977 saw the publication of his autobiography, *Preminger*.

JACQUES PRÉVERT, see p. 189

VSEVOLOD PUDOVKIN

Vlada Petric

Since all significant directors of the Soviet *avant-garde* cinema conformed to the montage principle of film construction in developing their own various styles, it is often generalized that this principle is identical for all members of the so-called Soviet montage school. However, although their basic methods of editing are analogous, there are significant differences in the montage concepts of these film-makers, which are reflected in their theoretical writings as well as in their films. Therefore, an attempt to understand Pudovkin's work necessitates a comparison between his theoretical attitude towards the function of montage in both the silent and the sound film, and those of the other great Soviet film-makers: Kuleshov, Vertov, Eisenstein and Dovzhenko.

Lev Kuleshov, undoubtedly the father of the Soviet montage school, and perhaps of film semiology as well, was a formalist who proclaimed: 'The essence of cinema lies in the film's composition, i.e. in the exchange of the photographed pieces for the organization of impressions. What is most significant is not what is filmed in a specific shot, but how one shot replaces another on the screen, how they are structured in time sequence.' It was in Kuleshov's workshop from 1922 to 1924 that Pudovkin learned the specifics of film language, as well as participating as an actor in Kuleshov's earliest experimental feature films.

Dziga Vertov employed two divergent aesthetic attitudes, in his writings as well as in his films. One was concerned with the display of 'life as caught unawares by the camera' yet presented on the screen in a manner which reveals the film-maker's ideological standpoint. The second was manifested in Vertov's radical attempt to subvert the illusion of reality on the screen in order to create a 'more perfect and meaningful' cinematic vision which includes the most significant aspects of the objects and events filmed, viewed from the best-chosen angles and matched with each other by the move-ments occurring in them ('the theory of intervals', as Vertov called this method of editing).

Sergei Eisenstein's concept of montage was predominantly ideological in all its forms, i.e., conceived to convey the film-maker's socio-political message and to awaken the class-consciousness of the audience. This approach culminated in the theory of 'intellectual editing', exemplified in *October*, where the political message became the substantial content of the film and the montage structure was designed to fit it in the form of 'a conflict-juxtaposition of intellectual affects'.

In Alexander Dovzhenko's silent films the main function of montage was to present the story in an unconventional manner, and to enhance the emotional and psychological qualities of the characters. Dovzhenko's concept of montage was essentially emotional, in that it promoted the establishment of the appropriate mood, and proleptically associated events whose final impact largely depended on the montage structure of earlier or later sequences.

Vsevolod Pudovkin (1893–1953) consolidated these different concepts of montage in a more than merely mechanical synthesis, for his unifying imagination was capable of encompassing the anatomical unity of film and its literary basis as well; he perceived that the script itself is an equal component of the film's structure, which also has its own 'construction divided into a great number of separate pieces'; and therefore both film-maker and scriptwriter 'must take into account the basic property of the film—montage'.

In his famous 1926 book *Film Technique*, from which the above quotations have been taken, Pudovkin delineated his concept of montage as an interaction of many and various elements, including script, sound, music, colour and acting. Throughout his career Pudovkin contended that montage, as the highest form of editing, is 'the foundation of film art', and he consistently attempted to apply his view of it to the sound cinema, collaborating with Eisenstein in establishing the principle of asynchronism between image and sound, which was theoretically defined in their 1928 'Statement on the Sound Film'. In his large body of theoretical writings Pudovkin continued to expand his theory of montage by defining it in the context of dialectical thinking. With slight alterations, he reiterated this concept in a crucial essay, *On Montage*, written a few years before his death in 1953: 'Montage in my formulation does not mean a mere glueing together of a movie from shots; it also does not mean a substitution of this term for a rather poorly defined formal concept known as *composition*. I define montage as an all-inclusive revelation and explanation of the intrinsic inter-relationship between events in real life—a discovery which can be fully accomplished by the multiple possibilities of the film art.' In the same essay he affirmed that there exists 'a countless number of possibilities in connecting shots', but it is important to 'create an inner connection between the shots'. He particularly emphasized that, while montage is common to all the arts, 'if one follows a dialectical process of thinking, it appears that only cinema is capable of presenting a complete and immediate picture of life, by expressing it as a dialectical process of the greatest complexity, which requires that the method of dividing and joining various elements in a film's structure reaches its fullest and most perfect form'.

Being fully concerned with the narrative aspect of film art, Pudovkin relied on the elements of script and actors' performance in his work more than any other Soviet *avant-garde* director. But he was basically interested in discovering alternative modes of cinematic narrative. Hence he did not fully accept Kuleshov's principle of 'naturshchik', according to which the ultimate significance of an actor's face depends solely on the director's manipulation of close-ups; nor did he follow Eisenstein's concept of the type-casting of non-actors, whose close-ups are orchestrated in such a manner that their expressions assume a broader metaphorical signification. In a collection of essays entitled *Film Acting*, published in 1934, Pudovkin developed his own sophisticated theory of film acting, applying Stanislavsky's 'Method' to the cinema. Significantly, Pudovkin's final theoretical study was *The Actor's Art in Film and Stanislavsky's 'Method'* (1952), in which he restated his belief that Stanislavsky's system of psycho-emotional development and materialization of the actor's role is 'the most appropriate practical means for a realis-

tic actor in the narrative cinema'. At the end of the article he emphasized that 'the school of Stanislavsky, his method of working with actors, his concept of the director's creativity, and his attitude towards the goals of art in general, could not but deeply influence the realistic nature of cinematic art'.

It is necessary to note that the five major Soviet avant-garde directors, while individual *auteurs* in the truest sense of the word, at the same time developed extremely close working relationships with their various collaborators. Kuleshov worked closely with his students, including Pudovkin, Barnet and Khokhlova; Eisenstein depended on his cameraman Eduard Tisse, as well as on his first assistant Grigori Alexandrov; Vertov created some of his best films in co-operation with his brother Mikhail Kaufman, the cameraman, and his wife Yelisaveta Svilova, the editor; and Dovzhenko established a creative co-operation with his cameraman Danylo Demutzsky, and later with his wife, the actress Yulia Solntseva, who directed several of Dovzhenko's shooting scripts after his death. Similarly, Pudovkin established creative working relationships with his cameraman, Anatoli Golovnya, his scriptwriter, Nathan Zarkhi, and great actors like Vera Baranovskaya. Later he co-directed almost all his sound features with various 'minor' directors, and never failed to emphasize how important this creative co-operation was to him in the period in which his health was poor and he was ideologically criticized by the political authorities. One can say that the Soviet *avant-garde* film-makers were *auteurs* in the sense that they unified all their collaborators' talents within the bounds of their central montage concepts, and integrated all of their films' components into a unique cinematic structure according to their general aesthetic tendencies. Their final goal was not to suppress the imaginations of their collaborators, but, on the contrary, to inspire them to contribute their individual talents to a film's overall unity. Pudovkin, who provides the best example of such a creative collaboration between director and crew, wrote several articles on the problem of the relationships between the director and his assistants, co-directors, script-writer, cameraman, editor, composer and actors.

Mother: A. Christyakov as the 'impetuous belligerent father who spends all his wages on drink'.

As Kuleshov's student, Pudovkin's first practical experience in film production was as his collaborator on scripts and sets, and as an actor. His first independent films were 'mixtures' of the documentary and feature genres. *Shakmatnaia Goriatchka* (*Chess Fever*, 1925) is a short comedy which incorporates both documentary footage (from the international chess tournament in Moscow) and enacted scenes (in which the well-known directors Yakov Protazanov and Yuli Raizman appear as actors). *Mekhanika Golovnogo Mozga* (*The Mechanics of the Brain*, 1926), aimed at popularizing Pavlov's theories of conditioned reflexes, is a full-length film which even today can serve as a model of the educational–scientific genre. His first feature, *Mat'* (*Mother*, 1926), one of the most significant works of the silent era, was based on the novel by Maxim Gorky, adapted for the screen by N. Zarkhi and photographed by A. Golovnya.

From the very start of the preparation for this project Pudovkin worked closely with these two collaborators, so that the film's basic montage structure was developed co-operatively before the actual shooting began. Pudovkin acknowledged that the overall composition of *Mother* grew out of his and Zarkhi's work on the script. This can be best illustrated by an example from the film. Gorky, in the first chapter of his novel, mentions Pavel's father, Michael Vlasov, only briefly, describing him as an impetuous, belligerent man who spends all his wages on drink. For the film Pudovkin and Zarkhi invented a characteristic dramatic conflict between Michael and his wife, and executed it in a typical montage manner, expanding the actual duration of the *mise en scène* by first analysing the action into its constituent details and then joining them by montage into a dynamic sequence:

Title: Mother
Long Shot (exterior): The mother in the foreground hanging the laundry to dry on a rope above the kitchen table; reclining on a bed, Pavel is visible in the background; he then exits to the right.
Title: Son
Medium Shot (interior): Pavel asleep on the bed.
Title: Father

Long Shot (exterior): The father drunkenly passes through the gate into the garden and enters the house in the background.
Medium Shot (interior): The mother, leaning over the washtub, wrings out the laundry, then wipes her hands and rubs her forehead with her forearm.
Medium Long Shot (interior): The father opens the front door and pauses on the threshold.
Medium Shot: The mother straightens up and looks frame left.
Medium Long Shot: The father stands in the doorway, advances several paces, reaching for his coat which is draped across his left shoulder, and staggers off.
Medium Close-up: The father's torso, his eyes half-open.
Medium Shot: Pavel asleep on the bed.
Medium Close-up: The father's torso, his eyes focused straight ahead.
Close-up: The cuckoo clock on the wall, at first blurred, comes into focus.
Dissolve
Close-up: The flatiron suspended from the chain of the cuckoo clock.
Medium Shot: The mother glances over her left shoulder while leaning slightly forward.
Medium Long Shot: The father, standing in the doorway, walks forward (towards the camera).
Medium Close-up: The mother turns her head from full-face to profile.
Medium Shot: The father enters the shot from the right, comes up to the clock and unfastens the flatiron from its chain.
Close-up: The father's hand pushes the flatiron into his pocket.
Medium Shot: The father stands against the wall, arranging his pocket, then looks up.
Medium Shot: The mother looks off towards the left side of the frame.
Medium Shot: The father fumbles for a chair, brings it to the wall, climbs on to it and reaches for the clock.
Medium Shot: The mother goes round a curtain, rushing out of the frame to the right.
Medium Shot: The mother grabs the father by the legs while he is standing on the chair.
Medium Close-up: Pavel looks forward, towards the camera, raising his head from the pillow.

Close-up: The mother's hands grasp the father's legs.

Close-up (high angle): The mother's face and hands as she clings to the father's legs.

Close-up: The mother's hands grasping the father's legs.

Medium Close-up (low angle): The father's upper torso twisting from left to right while falling towards camera, his hands slipping from the clock.

Close-up: The father's boots slip off the stool from right to left.

Close-up: The wall clock twisting from right to left (the last two frames are blurred).

Medium Close-up: The father's torso collapsing on to the floor from right to left.

Close-up: Pieces of the wall clock scatter on the floor.

Medium Close-up: The father sits up on the floor.

Close-up: One of the clock's gears spins and finally comes to rest on the floor.

Medium Close-up: The father stares out of the frame to the left.

Medium Close-up: The father looks down to the right.

Close-up: The mother looks down to the right.

Close-up: Parts of the shattered clock lie about on the floor.

Medium Close-up: The father raises his head, his eyes roving to the left.

Medium Close-up: The mother raises her head and looks upwards (implicitly towards the spot on which the clock used to hang).

Medium Close-up: The father raises himself and partially exits through the top of the frame.

Medium Shot: The mother retreats to the background while the father enters frame in the foreground and approaches her, preparing to swing at her face.

Medium Shot: Pavel jumps out of bed, and hastily passes out of the frame to the left.

This shot-by-shot breakdown may be taken as a typical example of an analytical montage sequence which reveals the psychological relationships and emotional attitudes of the characters. The 'inner life' (Stanislavsky's term) of the actors is conveyed by the appropriate alternation of medium shots and close-ups of the actors' faces, their actions, and objects which play a symbolic role. The con-

flict is enhanced by means of cinematic language, so that the viewer does not feel any need for the interpolation of titles. The three titles at the beginning of the sequence, 'Mother', 'Son' and 'Father', are a thematic underscoring of the protagonists. But once the conflict starts, the psychological drama is built and communicated by purely visual means. Some of the shots, particularly the close-ups of the father and the mother fighting over the wall clock, are extremely short, between ten and fifteen feet long, and produce an effect of dynamic collision on the screen. Of course, the closing sequence in *Mother* is even more kinaesthetic, depicting the clash between the demonstrators and the soldiers, and including a paradigmatic associative montage segment in which shots of the May Day demonstrators running through the streets of Moscow are alternated with shots of huge blocks of ice in the river advancing irresistibly.

Symbolic objects play a particularly important role in Pudovkin's montage structures. The impact of these objects, like the dripping pipe in the scene in which the mother watches motionless over the dead body of her husband, is often intensified by photographing them in close-up. But they are no less effective when shown in medium and long shot to emphasize their multiplicity, like the black top hats of the businessmen standing in front of the stock exchange (photographed from a very high angle), which are contrasted with the faces of the dead soldiers scattered along the front-line trenches in *Konyets Sankt Peterburga* (*The End of St Petersburg*, 1927). Pudovkin believed that inanimate objects, shot from an appropriate angle and intrinsically related to the human characters in a film, could be as photogenic and contextually meaningful as human faces. He was among those directors who enthusiastically responded to Louis Delluc's book *Photogénie* (Paris, 1920), and in 1925 he wrote an essay with the same title expanding Delluc's basic definition of the photogenic impact of photographed human beings and objects. Not surprisingly, he tried to connect the notion of *photogenic* impact with montage, claiming that shooting angle and movement within the frame are essential for achieving a 'dynamic photogenic impact on the screen'.

The End of St Petersburg and *Potomok Chingis-Khana* (*Storm over Asia* or *The Heir to Genghis Khan*, 1928) are the most dynamic of Pudovkin's films, particularly in the sequences involving mass movement conceived as a rhythmic montage flow. As in the finale of *Mother*, in which the flowing water and blocks of ice assume a highly symbolic signification through montage interaction with shots of the demonstrators, in *Storm over Asia* the shots of the gusting wind and a sand storm—intercut with shots of the galloping Mongolian partisans—assume the same symbolic function within the closing segment of the film. As a rule, the endings of Pudovkin's silent films are composed as montage symphonies which culminate in visual crescendos. Of the nearly 2,000 shots in *Storm over Asia*, Pudovkin employed 471 (many no longer than a few frames) to compose the triumphant revolutionary ride of the partisans over the Mongolian plains, a sequence reminiscent of the finale of D. W. Griffith's *America*. Based on the conflict between movement in the frame and alternation of shots, this sequence is on a par with the best sequences of Pudovkin's own *Mother*, Eisenstein's *Battleship Potemkin*, Dovzhenko's *Arsenal* and Vertov's *The Man with the Movie Camera*.

In contrast to this dynamic style, the slow movement of images in Pudovkin's last silent film, *Prosto Shuchai* (*A Simple Case*, 1932), achieves a visual lyricism by retarding the flow of the photographed events. The screenplay (by Alexander Rzheshevsky, who also wrote the script for Eisenstein's unfinished *Bezhin Meadow*) exemplifies the theory of the 'emotional screenplay' which, by means of detailed descriptions and highly poetic indications of action and images, seeks to inspire the director's imagination through his emotional sensitivity. Immediately after the completion of *A Simple Case* Pudovkin formulated his most original theory, that of the 'close-up of time', claiming that it is possible and just as useful to focus the viewer's attention on the temporal evolution of an event by presenting it in slow motion as it is to underscore and isolate a detail in space by showing on the screen only a part of it in close-up. As a result of such a combined concentration of attention, the duration of the event is rhythmically and optically accentuated. *A Simple Case*, which was criticized as 'an overly abstract and pseudo-significant film', contains several sequences shot in slow motion which, by isolating details and juxtaposing them through parallel editing, have a genuinely poetic effect.

It is no wonder that such an impressionistic cinematic vision was severely criticized by the conventional reviewers. But Pudovkin believed in the poetic capacities of the film medium, and sought alternative forms in order to liberate narrative cinema from the linear continuity of the story-line. In the conclusion of his article on the function of slow motion in film, he predicted the future use (and misuse) of that device: 'A tremendous future lies open for the close-up of time, particularly in sound film, where the rhythm, specified and amplified by its interaction with sound, is extremely important.' In fact, Pudovkin had planned to shoot *A Simple Case* as a sound film, but because of technical circumstances could not realize his intention of achieving a contrapuntal sight and sound symphony on the screen.

The theory of sight and sound counterpoint is nowhere better exemplified than in Pudovkin's *Dezerter* (*Deserter*, 1933). In line with his contention that 'the first function of sound is to augment the potential expressiveness of the film's content', Pudovkin attempted to eschew the then current practice of treating sound in film 'as a pure accompaniment, advancing in inevitable and monotonous parallelism with the image', and in so doing created some of the most powerful sequences in post-synchronized cinema. In the particularly impressive May Day demonstration and dock sequences of *Deserter* he orchestrated sounds as he edited images, handling various sound tracks of different lengths and intensities in much the same way as a composer manipulates notes of music. Explaining this method at the end of his study *Film Technique*, he emphasized the constructivist interrelation of auditory and visual components: 'I recorded pieces of various music and sound of different volumes, transitions from bands to crowd noises, from "hurrahs" to the whirling propellers of aeroplanes, slogans from the radio and snatches of our songs. Just like long shots and close-ups in silent film. Then followed the task of editing the thousand metres of sound to create a hundred metres of rhythmical composition.' It is impossible to describe the impact of the interaction of the sound and visual components in *Deserter*; only in watching the film does one realize how its cinematic value can so far surpass the actual content of the story, and experience the way the movement within the frame and the juxtaposition of a complex soundtrack with a rhythmic visual montage together 'rise majestically to the level of an idea' (Barthélémy Amengual, *V. I. Pudovkin*).

Criticized for not being political enough in his art, Pudovkin turned after *Deserter* to a conventional narrative form, in accordance with the canons of Socialist Realism imposed on all Soviet film-makers throughout the period of Stalinist–Zhdanovist cultural politics (1930–53). Even so, in a decree issued by the Central Committee of the Communist Party on 2 September 1946, Pudovkin's *Amiral Nakhimov* (*Admiral Nakhimov*, 1946) was condemned, along with Eisenstein's *Ivan the Terrible, Part II* and Kozintsev and Trauberg's *Simple People*. The other two films had to wait a full twelve years to reach the general public, but Pudovkin's was allowed to be shown publicly a year after it was made.

Although not the equal of any of his silent masterpieces, Pudovkin's last film, *Vozraschenie Vasilicia Bortnikova* (*The Return of Vasili Bortnikov*, 1953), does contain some of the cinematic qualities present in his early works. Here, for the last time, Pudovkin manifested his impulse for experimentation in an attempt to apply the classic montage concept not only to sound, but to colour as well. This film is formally and ideologically significant, particularly in historical perspective, in that it marks the beginning in the Soviet cinema of a relatively unconstrained treatment of intimate human relationships, a topic which had previously been largely suppressed by Zhdanovist interference in the arts. It was officially presented at the 1953 Venice Film Festival, to which the Soviet Union had sent no films since 1948. In it, Pudovkin succeeded in blending aesthetically the private and intimate drama of a married couple with the theme of collectivism and the building of Socialism. He accomplished the fusion of the two elements by means of an appropriate montage pace, as well as through the symbolic use of colour in the sequences of the four passing seasons.

Of Pudovkin's other films, the most popular were his spectacular reconstructions of the lives of great historical personalities, such as *Admiral Nakhimov*, made in collaboration with Dimitri Vasiliev, as was *Zhukovsky* (1950). Mikhail Doller, Pudovkin's regular assistant director, became Pudovkin's co-director for the epic biographies *Pobeda* (*Victory*, 1938), *Minin i Pozharski* (*Minin and Pozharsky*, 1939) and *Suvorov* (1941). These epic biographical films demonstrate Pudovkin's unsuitability as a director of conventional narrative scripts whose meaning is dependent upon dialogue or pseudo-poetic commentary. However, although made under strict ideological control, they did achieve a minutely realistic depiction of period and characters. In their best moments, in which Pudovkin returned to his imaginative use of montage, they confirmed his innate talent for visual expression, as evidenced in the dynamic storm sequence in *Admiral Nakhimov*, executed in a classic montage style, and in the visually impressive battle sequences in *Suvorov* and *Volnya Rodini* (*In The Name of the Fatherland*, 1943). Perhaps the most expressive aspect of these films is the art of the veteran cameraman Anatoli Golovnya, which is most evident in his great sensitivity for shot-composition—particularly the highly dramatic alternation of light and dark so powerfully exemplified in *Minin and Pozharsky* (whose script was written by Viktor Shklovsky).

Undoubtedly, Pudovkin's sense of the epic genre was at its best when he used purely visual means of expression, or interrelated sight and sound according to constructivist principles. Since the necessary linearity of spoken dialogue ran counter to his visual dynamism, it proved to be a disastrous component in his sound movies. Aware of this conflict in his later epic films, Pudovkin designed *The Return of Vasili Bortnikov* with the visual elements predominant, saving it from the blatant 'literariness' against which he had long struggled.

Pudovkin was one of the most skilful visual story-tellers of the silent era, with a natural feeling for montage as the means of penetrating the psychological aspects of the narrative.

His montage structures possessed all the qualities of Griffith's visual style; indeed, he admitted that he had been significantly influenced by American films, although he never attempted to apply the power of montage to the sort of romantic melodrama so typical of Griffith's later features. As Anatoli Lunacharsky stated in 1928, Pudovkin's work was of 'epic breadth, convincing authenticity, with an intense and wide-ranging narrative structured in the manner of the great Tolstoy'. Expanding this judgement three decades later, Soviet film historian Nikolai Lebedev wrote that Pudovkin was 'the Tolstoy of Socialist Realism', a statement which Pudovkin's later films justified in an unfortunate way. But perhaps the best and most concise evaluation of Pudovkin's talent and his cinematic consciousness was one expressed by the French film historian Léon Moussinac in his famous comparison of the two Soviet *avant-garde* filmmakers: 'An Eisenstein film is like a cry, a Pudovkin film evokes a song.' Actually, Pudovkin's films *are* like great epic songs, but *visual* songs composed of motion picture images, accompanied by metaphoric, contrapuntal sound.

Pudovkin's principal writings are cited in the course of Petric's article (I would note simply that *Film Technique* and *Film Acting* were re-issued in London in 1958 and in New York in 1970); indeed, most current critical opinion would hold that he is more important as a theorist than as a director. His stock has fallen further than that of any 'great' director in recent years, and not without justice. See also Jay Leyda's *Kino* (1960) and the articles on Eisenstein, Kuleshov, Vertov and Dovzhenko.

NICHOLAS RAY

Jonathan Rosenbaum

Before the credit titles appear for *They Live By Night* (originally titled *The Twisted Road*, 1948), we see the film's two major characters, Bowie (Farley Granger) and Keechie (Cathy O'Donnell), kissing, while a subtitle introduces them in consecutive phrases, parsed out like the lines of a folk ballad: 'This boy ...' 'and this girl ...' 'were never properly introduced to the world we live in ...' Then behind the credits is shown a speeding car containing four men, filmed from the changing perspectives of a helicopter following its progress. As the credits end, we return to ground level in time to see and hear a tire blow out; the car swerves and jerks to a stop. The driver, who has been carrying three escaped convicts (Chicamaw, played by Howard da Silva, T-Dub [J. C. Flippen] and Bowie), is forced out of the car and—outside the camera's range—beaten; the sound of the first fist-blow coincides with a cut to Bowie's response as he watches the violence. Then we return to the viewpoint from the helicopter, which gradually descends as the convicts flee across an open field, approaching and passing a giant billboard.

The extraordinary beginning of Ray's first movie (he was born in 1911) prefigures not only the remainder of the film, but most of the major impulses in Ray's subsequent work. A romantic vision of the Couple is immediately juxtaposed with anarchic movement erupting into violence; desperate action is treated as a spectacular form of choreography. Each element is intensely articulated, yet 'distanced' into a sort of abstraction: the spatial–emotional continuity of the first shot set in relief by the underlining verbal montage that 'explains' it, the speeding car turned into creeping insect by the deterministic overhead angles which circumscribe its apparent freedom, and the violence displaced by the cut to Bowie, bringing us full circle back to the romantic hero already condemned in the opening shot—a circle of pain defining the limits of Ray's universe. And the exhilarating plasticity of the flight across the field, pivoted around the imposing billboard, fastens all three characters to the pop iconography of the society which surrounds and ultimately crushes them, the social recognition that moulds their identities and makes them 'real' at the same time that it signs their death warrants. (When Chicamaw later reads about their escape in a newspaper he remarks to Bowie, 'You're in luck, kid. You're travellin' with real people ...')

The second sequence begins with Bowie looking through the holes in a garden lattice like a caged animal while Keechie drives up

Farley Granger and Cathy O'Donnell as the doomed lovers in Ray's first film, *They Live by Night*: 'This boy and this girl were never properly introduced to the world we live in.'

in a car. A series of guarded exchanges initiates the defensive dialogues that invariably take place between Ray's couples before they strike a balance—a compromise between duel and duet that recurs with variations in the celebrated kitchen scenes of *In a Lonely Place* (1950) (Humphrey Bogart straightening out a grapefruit knife while he talks to Gloria Grahame) and *Johnny Guitar* (1954) (Sterling Hayden asking Joan Crawford to tell him lies, which she does in cadenced, ballad-like refrains), and comparable first encounters in *On Dangerous Ground* (1952), *Rebel Without a Cause* (1955), *Hot Blood* (1956), *Amère Victoire* (*Bitter Victory*, 1957) and *Party Girl* (1958). As their mutual suspicions begin to cool, and Bowie gets into the car, the sound of a passing train is faintly heard, a prefiguration of the much louder one that we will hear just before Bowie is shot in

the final scene. And after Bowie sits down next to Keechie, there is a cut to a shot framing them from the back of the car, where we see them through another mesh pattern, caged together at the very instant that they visually 'compose' a couple.

But if Ray seals the fate of his lovers from the start, this does not prevent him from participating in all the tremors of their awakening love. Although *They Live by Night* has frequently been compared to Fritz Lang's *You Only Live Once*, Lang's sympathetic detachment from his characters is quite different from Ray's passionate identification, an attitude that has much more in common with Murnau's late films. When Bowie and Keechie approach a sleazy marriage bureau, the camera moves alongside them, momentarily framing them between statues of Cupid and a victim of his arrow on the bureau's front lawn, then continues behind them as they move towards the front steps—a synchronized accompaniment recalling the couple's walk through the crowded city in *Sunrise*, when the camera enables us to follow them through the cross-currents of multiple tempos and directions by tracking along at a speed identical to theirs.

To etch out a framework of romantic futility and then to plunge into it without restraint is very characteristic of Ray. If we add to this tendency a strong empathy for adolescents, a particular flair for colour and CinemaScope, a visibly recurrent (but perpetually unfulfilled) desire to film a musical, a social conscience seeking to bear witness to the major problems of the time, and a taste for anarchic violence which alternately obscures, complicates and helps to illuminate these issues—culminating in grandiose fables, parables and pedagogical 'lessons' followed by a total break with commercial filmmaking and the gradual creation of a new aesthetic based on an increased degree of political commitment—we have arrived at a description not only of Ray's career, but of a considerable portion of Godard's.

Obviously one shouldn't push these parallels too far; but if we consider that Ray attracted more sustained enthusiasm among Godard and his colleagues at *Cahiers du Cinéma* than any other American director in the 50s, and was subsequently mentioned more often than any other director in Godard's films, it becomes clear that many of these relationships are far from coincidental. One suspects that what Ray represented for many of the younger *Cahiers* critics was the triumph of a very personal, autobiographical cinema forged into the studio styles of RKO, Republic, Paramount, Warners, Columbia, Fox and MGM; a restless, exploratory nature that tended to regard each project as an existential adventure and a foray of research into the background of a given topic (police brutality, juvenile delinquency, Gypsies, Chicago gangsters, Eskimos); a loner mentality epitomized in a line from *Johnny Guitar* ('I'm a stranger here myself'); a florid romantic imagination, dramatic intensity and visual bravado that could make *The Lusty Men* (1952) evidence of an obsession for abstraction equal to Bresson's (Rivette), *Johnny Guitar* 'the *Beauty and the Beast* of

Westerns' (Truffaut), *Rebel Without a Cause* and *Bigger Than Life* (1956) modern evocations of Greek tragedy (Rohmer), and *Bitter Victory* 'the most Goethean of films' (Godard).

Unlike Godard, however, Ray cannot be considered a major stylistic innovator, although it is worth noting that *They Live by Night* was probably the first feature film ever to use helicopter shots, and his particular appreciation of the horizontal line (derived, he says, from his early studies with Frank Lloyd Wright) made his compositional use of CinemaScope expressive and dramatically functional in a way that influenced many future directors, including Godard. (The same might be said of his symbolic use of primary colours.) But it is equally evident that in his choice of subjects as well as in his treatments of them, Ray was frequently ten years or more ahead of his time: consider his handling of youth culture in *Rebel Without a Cause*, drugs in *Bigger Than Life*, ecology in *Wind Across the Everglades* (1958) and anthropology in *Ombre Bianche* (*The Savage Innocents*, 1960). From this point of view, *King of Kings* (1961) is Ray's *Jesus Christ Superstar*, not only for its somewhat pop (and pop art) treatment of the Gospels *avant la lettre*, but more specifically because the flaming red garments and rebellious stances of its Jesus (Jeffrey Hunter) take us right back to James Dean in his leather jacket.

Paradoxically, it is the pop imagery of *Rebel Without a Cause* that makes the film appear somewhat dated today in relation to Kazan's *East of Eden*, a quasi-anachronistic work less bound to the *Zeitgeist* of any particular period. But the film has dated interestingly: if the manners and moods of mid-50s teenagers are captured with a comic-book flourish and heightened lyricism that now seem slightly surreal, this enables us to see that much more of the mythology of that time and culture. Yet for all the concreteness of its observations, *Rebel Without a Cause* is probably, after *Bitter Victory*, the most schematic and abstract of Ray's films. Jim (James Dean), Judy (Natalie Wood), Plato (Sal Mineo) and Buzz (Corey Allen) are carefully differentiated in their backgrounds in order to suggest a sociological cross-section, but at the same time they represent variations of the same dilemmas, and can even be called

Sterling Hayden and Joan Crawford in *Johnny Guitar*: 'Tell me lies . . .'

different facets of a single personality. The first shot in the film introduces us to Jim; the second and third shots link him to Judy and Plato in the police station, each counterpart unobtrusively providing a compositional 'balance' within the CinemaScope frame. (All three, significantly, are advised by a sympathetic police officer named Ray.) Later, in a moving scene on the edge of a precipice, Jim and Buzz suddenly become equals and friends before competing in a 'chickie-run' where the latter plunges to his death; Jim promptly assumes Buzz's role as Judy's boy-friend, and we realize that Buzz's death could just as easily have been Jim's, just as Plato's subsequent madness and death could also have been Jim's—indeed, the appearance and stances of Dean and Mineo recall separate aspects of Farley Granger in *They Live by Night*. In another sense, Jim's anger and imperiousness match his mother's; the two are

linked in an extraordinary subjective shot (later to be echoed in *Hot Blood* and *Wind Across the Everglades*) involving a 360-degree camera turn where he sees her upside-down, then right-side-up, descending a staircase; and Jim later assumes his father's role when he forms a nuclear family with Judy and Plato in a deserted mansion.

This semi-mystical sense of equality is central to Ray's work. The discovery of a moral equivalence between the supposedly antithetical natures of the antagonist heroes in *Bitter Victory* and *Wind Across the Everglades* provides the dramatic climax of both films. In *King of Kings*, the treatment of the Sermon on the Mount as a series of personal exchanges reflects the same preoccupation. (Robin Wood has suggested that in the same film, raising 'Barabbas to a prominence almost equal to that of Christ . . . making of him an alternative revolutionary instead of the traditional robber of the Bible, is, besides being highly characteristic of Ray thematically, above all an *architectural* decision, strengthening the linear narrative with a structure of parallels and oppositions'.) Between Ray's couples, we usually find a set of precise antitheses and balances: in *Party Girl*, the hero is lame and the heroine is a dancer; each is a 'prostitute'—he as a gangster's lawyer, she as a party girl—who reforms with the help of the other. It is worth remarking, however, that with the possible exceptions of Gloria Grahame in *In a Lonely Place* and Chana Eden in *Wind Across the Everglades*—both highly original and unjustly neglected performances—Ray's heroines seldom seem to have much identity apart from their relationships to men; in *Bigger Than Life*, the difficulty of Lou Avery (Barbara Rush) in standing out against her husband's crazed demands is one of the tragic levers in the plot.

Aside from its system of character equations, *Rebel Without a Cause* abounds in other abstract elements: the cramming of all the action into one improbable twenty-four-hour period; the link between the global annihilation in 'a burst of gas and fire' enacted in the planetarium, where the astronomer announces that 'the earth will not be missed', and the explosion of Buzz's car at the end of the 'chickie-run' (and the implicit fact that Buzz is subsequently not missed very much either); the arrival of Plato at Dawson High, with a sharp cut from the loud backfire of his motor scooter to the raising of an American flag; the curious recapitulation of references to animals (the toy monkey in the first shot and Jim's joke when handing Judy her compact—'You wanna see a monkey?'; the epithet 'chicken' and Jim's reply in the deserted house to Plato's 'Who's there?'—'Nobody, just us chickens'; Jim mooing at a reference to Taurus in the planetarium, then being taunted in the knife fight with Buzz like a torero's bull); the 'musical' stylization of the slow build-up to the knife fight outside the planetarium, with the actors posed and choreographed around Jim's car in a way that suggests a superior version of *West Side Story*.

Ray's occasional tendency to gravitate towards the style of musicals—a function of his colours, his somewhat theatrical manner of lighting sets, a penchant for viewing physical movement as spectacle, and a use of folk ballads along with other musical interludes—can be seen more distinctly in *Party Girl*, or in the opening scene at Vienna's saloon in *Johnny Guitar*, when Johnny introduces himself with a strum on his guitar and the Dancing Kid reciprocates by grabbing Emma and dancing her across the floor. But Ray's furthest step in this direction undoubtedly remains *Hot Blood*, an unevenly realized film which springs to vibrant life in all its 'musical' sequences: Cornel Wilde's defiant dance when he is refused employment as a dancing teacher (sarcastically flaunting the Gypsy stereotype that has been assigned to him), his 'whip dance' with Jane Russell, and the Gypsies' triumphant song that celebrates their marriage and later reconciliation.

Considering the stylistic traits touched upon so far—from romanticism to anarchistic violence, pop imagery to 'cosmic' abstraction, symmetry to choreography—we have clearly arrived at a complex of themes, procedures and attitudes which could legitimately be called larger than life, an impulse that manifests itself in details as fleeting as the word 'God' scrawled on the bark of a tree in *Johnny Guitar*, or as central as Richard Burton's dismissal of tenth-century Berber ruins in *Bitter Victory* as 'too modern for me'. It is a vision suggesting and requiring a large canvas.

Limitless aspiration combined with profound alienation is the condition suffered by the hero of *Bigger Than Life*—Ray's most powerful film, and in some respects his most important. And if his rendering of this anguish occupies a special place in his work, this is largely because it succeeds in attacking the roots of this condition rather than remaining on the level of its various symptoms. *In a Lonely Place*, containing many elements of an auto-critique, is an earlier foray into a similar sort of investigation: set in an extremely deglamorized Hollywood, it deals with the uncontrolled violence of a screenwriter (Humphrey Bogart) and its tragic consequences, his gradual alienation from everyone he feels closest to. *Bigger Than Life*, which concerns the effects of cortisone on a middle-class school-teacher, Ed Avery (James Mason), who has contracted a painful and incurable inflammation of the

Sal Mineo and James Dean in *Rebel Without a Cause*.

arteries—an objective correlative, perhaps, for Ray's own vision?—is less 'personal' in any autobiographical sense, but its implications are more universal. Its real subject is not the drug itself but what it reveals about Ed Avery; and beyond that, what Ed Avery reveals about the society he inhabits and—to a greater and lesser extent—emulates.

Bigger Than Life is a profoundly upsetting exposure of middle-class aspirations because it virtually defines madness—Avery's drug-induced psychosis—as taking these values seriously. Each emblem of the American Dream implicitly honoured by Avery in the opening scenes (his ideals of education, his respect for class and social status, his desire for his son to 'improve himself') is systematically turned on its head, converted from dream to nightmare, only by becoming more explicit in his behaviour. The dramatic function of his incurable disease and his taking of cortisone, carrying the respective promises of death and super-life, is to act on the slick magazine ads that he and his family try to inhabit in much the same way that the doctor's X-ray of his torso illuminates his terminal condition. An appearance of normality is subverted before our eyes, bit by bit, until it achieves the Gothic dimensions of a horror story that has always existed beneath the surface of his life.

Ray's departure for Europe and 'freedom' turned out to be disastrous on every level. He only made one film after *Fifty-Five Days at Peking* (1963), and even that (*We Can't Go Home Again*) is still not absolutely finished, although it was shown in an incomplete version at the Cannes Festival in 1973, on which occasion Rosenbaum dubbed it 'cinema at the end of its tether'. Ray died in 1979.

For further reading, see Colin McArthur's *Underworld USA* (1972) and, in French, François Truchaud's *Ray* (Paris, 1965).

SATYAJIT RAY

John Russell Taylor

When the film industry of yet another country hitherto unsung in film history comes to international attention, it is only natural that we should start out with mistaken, or at least grossly unbalanced ideas about it. It took some while after the first startling impact of Akira Kurosawa's films in the West for us to realize that he was not the be-all and end-all of Japanese cinema, but in fact just about the least Japanese of Japanese directors. Are we, then, likely to prove equally wrong about the Indian cinema if our ideas of it are based exclusively on the *Apu* trilogy and other works of Satyajit Ray, even though he is generally conceded to be the dominating figure in Indian cinema? On principle, one could say almost certainly.

The immediate and obvious answer about Ray, even without additional knowledge of what is going on elsewhere in the Indian cinema, is that one can never generalize from the work of great individuals. Ray is a great director, and *ipso facto* cannot be typical of anything, perhaps not even reliably of himself (it is the prerogative of all great artists to take us constantly by surprise). But it seems reasonable that he must have come from something and fit into some sort of context. And so he does. Not particularly a cinematic context: eighteen years after the appearance of *Pather Panchali* (1956), the first of the Apu trilogy, Ray is still a solitary figure, a unique talent in Indian cinema, and the Indian cinema, apart from a few directors like Mrinal Sen, has hardly moved on from the kind of nonsense he gently satirizes in the filmgoing sequence of *Apur Sansar* (*The World of Apu*, 1959), all trashy, theatrical, sentimental and fantasticated. But a literary and artistic context is very much there, to begin with in his own family, whose literary and artistic activities Marie Seton in her biography of Ray traces back exhaustively through fifteen generations. Without going into any such detail, it may be accepted readily that Satyajit Ray's background was highly literate and artistically sophisticated.

More important, no doubt, is the general cultural background. Ray is a Bengali, born in Calcutta in 1921, and all his films have been made in this minority language (spoken by some 20 million, however), a literary language far predating the now official language of India, Hindi, which is distilled from several dialects of the central plains. Ray's first films, the *Apu* trilogy, at once place him in a certain tradition, being based on a modern classic of Bengali literature, the semi-autobiographical novels by Bibhuti Bhusan Bannerjee; and a more personal kind of placing is implied by his much later filming of a famous children's book by his own grandfather, *Goopy Gyne Bagha Byne* (U.K.: *The Adventures of Goopy and Bagha*, 1968). More directly, the kind of cultural society from which the young Ray sprang can be observed in his film *Charulata* (U.K.: *The Lonely Wife*, 1964), set in the late nineteenth century, which shows something closely comparable to the cultural level and high-minded seriousness suggested in the works of Ibsen and Chekhov around the same period. If Ray seems in many ways the most Western of Oriental film-makers, it is because the traditions in which he was brought up are most closely analogous to those of Western life.

Not only the literary side of Bengali culture has been influential in Ray's career. He is a trained musician, who has composed music for all his own films since *Teen Kanya* (*Three Daughters*, 1961), as well as for James Ivory's film *Shakespeare Wallah* (1965). And his visual training has been no less far-reaching; indeed for some ten years before he made his first film he worked as a commercial artist in advertising, book illustration and design. As a writer he has not only written all his own scripts but also a number of critical articles, and worked on and off as a journalist, as well as more recently blossoming into an author of children's stories. And during his film-making career he has acquired other skills—ever since *Charulata*, for instance, he has been his own camera operator. This is not to say that he was necessarily first-rate in any of these other, specialized fields of activity. But an independent and proven ability in all these areas, as well as giving us some insight into the versatility of the man, has enabled him to exercise remarkably complete and detailed control over all aspects of his films—technicians such as the art director, cameraman and editor come much closer in his films than anywhere else, except perhaps in the films of Chaplin, to being pure executants of the director's ideas rather than contributors of their own creative personalities.

With all his separate interests and gifts, the cinema would seem to have been from the start the natural outlet which would best enable Ray to combine and fuse them all. But easier said than done. Ray began, by his own account, reading books on the cinema when he was still a teenager studying at Rabindranath Tagore's famous school at Santineketan. Shortly afterwards, as a young commercial artist of twenty-two, in 1943, he set seriously about trying to break into films. He came very close to doing so when an adaptation he had written of Tagore's story *Home and the World* was accepted for production. But Ray's ideas, which included such notions, deeply alien to the Indian cinema of that time, as shooting exteriors on natural locations and using non-professional actors, were found unacceptable by the producer and director.

In 1945, however, Ray was commissioned to illustrate a children's edition of *Pather Panchali*, and the idea of filming it began to germinate in his mind. In 1949 he had some brief but inspiring contact with Jean Renoir, who was shooting *The River* in India, and in 1950 he was sent to London for six months by the advertising agency for which he was working. There he 'saw all the film classics he could cram in' and began serious work on scripting *Pather Panchali*.

When I got back to India I set about raising the money and getting a crew together and finally we began. I had never worked in films before, my cameraman had never shot a film, my art director had worked on only one before and my editor had edited only two. Many of the actors were non-professional and the rest had no experience in the cinema. We had to feel our way tentatively, working only at weekends when we were free from our everyday jobs, and stopping for months at a time when the money gave out, until finally the government stepped in with the money to finish it.

The result was not, even then, very highly regarded in India, where there were various pressures and factions connected with the film's partial government sponsorship. The shooting took a long time, and the film, completed in 1955, did not appear until the beginning of 1956, when it seems to have achieved a measure of popular success, if little initial acclaim. None the less it was entered for the Cannes Festival that year and actually won a prize. This was something very new for the Indian cinema and established Ray as a name to be reckoned with at home. He was able on the strength of this success to go ahead with the sequel to *Pather Panchali*, *Aparajito* (*The Unvanquished*, 1957), which did even better by winning the grand prize at Venice in 1957. At the time he had no intention of turning the *Apu* films into a trilogy, but in 1959 he decided to complete the sequence with *Apur Sansar*, having meanwhile made two other, totally unconnected films.

The *Apu* trilogy is the work which first established Ray's fame, his style, and his approach to his subject matter. It therefore holds a crucial place in his career, and it calls for fairly detailed consideration for the light it throws on his work as a whole. It is difficult to believe that the three films were not conceived as one unified work—even though Ray tells us the notion of the trilogy came to him gradually. They are based on two books, the materials of which are symmetrically divided among the three films: the book *Pather Panchali* (literally, *Song of the Little Road*) takes us up to the half-way mark of the film *Aparajito*, when Apu and his mother return from the city to the country; the book *Aparajito* takes up the story a few years later, and tells of the later stages of Apu's education and something of his life as an adult. In reshaping the material in cinematic terms Ray has imposed a different sort of order, giving each section of his trilogy a dramatic centre and point of its own—unobtrusively he has found or invented a shape, or rather three shapes, from the much more loosely organized material of a *roman fleuve*.

As an adaptation of material from one medium to another, the *Apu* trilogy is a model—an outstanding example of creative rethinking. And the result is three films each of which can perfectly well stand on its own, and yet which gain immensely from being seen together, when the subtle lines of continuity, the recurrent yet constantly developing images and ideas can be properly appreciated. The first section, *Pather Panchali*, concerns the boy Apu's life in the village, with his whole family. For the second, *Aparajito*, Ray looked at the remainder of his source material and found in it, running through parts of the two novels, a unifying theme, that of the growing Apu's relationship, close but gradually detaching itself by force of education and circumstances, with his mother Sarbojaya—a theme which is naturally concluded with Sarbojaya's death some way into the second book. *Apur Sansar*, the third film, uses what is left of the literary material, the film being built round Apu's (unconscious) preparation for marriage, the marriage itself, and then the aftermath of his wife's death. Equally, *Apur Sansar* is unified by another theme, that of Apu's determination to be a writer, which is all bound up with his young manhood, and is finally put aside along with his immaturity.

The plot content of the films is in fact by Western standards very slight. They are built up from a succession of little incidents, at first glance linked together by no more than the and then . . . and then . . . and then . . . of a children's story. But to counteract the danger of shapelessness Ray devised a whole network of subtle pictorial and aural references to articulate his clear understanding of what each film is about. However wayward the detail may seem, it is controlled by a strict criterion of relevance, which we can always feel to be guiding things even if we are not from moment to moment consciously aware of precisely what it is.

The first, and in many ways the subtlest ensurer of consistency is the angle of regard Ray turns upon his characters and happenings. The first we see of Apu in the first film, apart from a glimpse of him as a baby, is as a shape sleeping beneath a blanket; then his sister shakes him and finds a way through his protective covering, and then we have a close-up of his closed eye, which promptly opens. One inference, which has been too readily drawn, is that Apu's is the eye we see through in the films, that we are seeing things from his point of view, as though this were a first-person narrative. But a moment's

consideration shows that this is not true, and that this particular shot indicates rather the reverse: seeing Apu's eye open to consciousness, we recognize immediately that we are seeing more than he does, spying on him as it were, observing him from the outside: we are at once conscious of our eye seeing his eye, and that the two are quite different things. This attitude is observed with absolute consistency throughout the trilogy: it remains firmly, if unobtrusively objective, using Apu, it is true, as a central figure but keeping him within a context which is observed by another, more analytic eye. In *Pather Panchali*, for instance, we may observe the child's wonder at new things—a theatrical troupe, a train—but we are not invited to share it, and the same is true of his reactions to the city at the beginning of *Aparajito*: we watch the child in his context, not the context through the child.

In other words, Apu is always a character in the films, not an enveloping consciousness. And therefore there is no danger of the filmmaker becoming lost in his creation. Which is as it should be, for Ray's theme is nearly always community, living together and finding ways of doing so without too far compromising the individual's individuality. We see Apu throughout as part of an evolving group, seeking solutions and finding answers. In *Pather Panchali* the group is largest, consisting as it does of his father Hari, an unsuccessful holy man; his mother Sarbojaya; his sister Durga, and Indra the aged aunt they look after as best they can. In *Aparajito* the group is reduced by deaths to just the two, Apu and Sarbojaya. In *Apur Sansar* Apu begins alone, and feeling the lack of a group to relate to, acquires a wife, Aparna, who gives a sort of stability to his life again (though perhaps at the expense of his own individuality, his writing); then he suffers a kind of breakdown when that relationship is removed by Aparna's death in childbirth, and finally finds himself again in the potentiality of a relationship with his young son. For Ray, Apu truly exists only in relation to others.

Given this unity of regard, each film is meticulously constructed to exemplify Ray's basic concept: if the comparison often made between *Pather Panchali* and Italian neorealism has any validity, it is not because of any rough documentary quality the Ray film may seem to have or its supposed concern with the underprivileged, but rather because Ray has something of the same cool endistancing quality that Rossellini has at his best (the side reminiscent at once of Brecht and Godard). Everything in Ray is demonstrated, externalized in some way. Which is not to say that his films lack richness or subtlety, but that their 'poetry' is of a Classical rather than a Romantic variety, depending on the exact management and constant redefinition of images so that they take on a complex of associations without ever losing their immediacy and propriety as literal statements of fact.

This can perhaps best be demonstrated by an examination of the two principal recurrent images in *Pather Panchali*, the train and the pond. I call them images rather than symbols because images are what they are, in the most literal sense of the term: things we see (or sometimes, with the train, merely hear), factual props in the life of the family. They do not 'symbolize' anything, in the sense in which the term is normally, if imprecisely used, to suggest some sort of exact equivalence between a concrete fact and an abstract idea. But gradually, by a process of accretion, each takes on a colouring of metaphor. The train moves, and suggests travel, progress; it is also a man-made machine, and therefore suggests the modern world at the limits (physical as well as mental) of the village, with its traditional forms of life. The pond is static, stagnant, a place to sit aimlessly by, a place to bury unmanageable, unwanted facts: it suggests the world of tradition from which Apu is destined to escape (by train, of course).

Much of the action in *Pather Panchali* is built on the alternation and elaboration of these two images. The train is first heard as a distant sound in the night while Apu is bending over his books, being taught to write by his father, the association thereby being directly established between the train and education, which is what will eventually separate Apu from his family background and make him part of the modern world. The pond is first importantly present shortly afterwards, when the aged Indra stays miserably by it as the children Apu and Durga run carelessly past on the way to new

experience—the travelling players at the village fair and, immediately following, direct confrontation with the physical reality of the train: the pond is clearly associated with the past, old age, passivity, resignation, in contrast with the children's carefree rush towards the future. But neither the train nor the pond is there just as a metaphysical trapping: Ray appreciates to the full the point once made by Pasolini that 'metaphor is an essentially linguistic and literary figure of speech which is difficult to render in the cinema except in extremely rare cases—for example if I wanted to represent happiness I could do it with birds flying in the sky . . . The cinema represents reality with reality; it is metonymic and not metaphoric. If I want to express you I express you through yourself, I couldn't use metaphors to express you.' So, it is the reality of the train, the reality of the pond which the cinema expresses: what associations they gather are something else again, and yet inexorably they gather them as the film progresses.

We may see how this comes about by a more detailed examination of the sequence in which Apu first actually sees the train. It is in fact quite elaborately intercut with another, parallel sequence, the death of Indra after she has been turned out of the family home. It is not the first time—the same thing had happened to her in the moments immediately before the play scene when she stood by the pond—for she is old and useless, and also humanly impossible to support, even in a family further from the borderline of starvation than Apu's. The play scene, the effect it has on Apu, is the main cause of the events which lead up to the first sight of the train; he quarrels with his sister Durga because he has appropriated some silver foil from her small box of childish treasures to make himself a crown in emulation of that worn by the principal actor in the drama he has seen acted. As a result of the quarrel (in which Sarbojaya automatically sides with her son), the children run off and rapidly begin to forget their disagreement in the open country. At this point, we come back to Indra, clearly ill and begging rather humbly to be taken back into the family home. Sarbojaya refuses. Then, out in the country, we see Durga and Apu reaching towards a reconciliation. Meanwhile, Indra begs for water and is told to get it herself, but Sarbojaya does finally make a gesture of assistance. That is all, though; she is adamant, and Indra is compelled to gather together her few belongings and hobble away for ever.

From here we cut back to the children, who have wandered further from the village than usual. The sequence begins with a shot of electric wires, and the distinctive hum of wires in the wind on the soundtrack. Then we see the wondering reaction of the children to a pylon, Durga's gesture of forgiveness towards Apu. Then Apu lost joyfully in grass higher than his head, appreciating to the full a strange new world of experience. And then, finally, the train—first as a moving puff of black smoke in the distance, then crossing the horizon, then, as the children run towards the embankment, approaching nearer and nearer until it fills the whole of the foreground, cutting off our view of Apu on the other side of the tracks, so that we can only catch sight of him in flashes between the passing wheels. The shape of the episode is rounded off by a shot of Apu and Durga, all differences forgotten, going home together, their discovery of Indra sitting alone in the woods, and the joking attempt to startle her which proves that she is dying as they run away to fetch help.

The opposition between youth and old age, death and the incursion of the modern world, poverty and progress, sounds simple and too schematic. But it does not affect the spectator that way. Though the juxtapositions sound like oppositions, in fact the effect is the reverse: they make us conscious of unity rather than diversity, the integration of the new experiences—the actors, the train, the grasses, death—into Apu's developing consciousness. This is achieved by the consistency of regard already mentioned, and by its most obvious physical manifestation in Ray's mastery of the long shot. Ray can also be, when necessary, a master of the meaningful close-up, but his characteristic method is to establish the physical and mental situation of his characters and places in relation to one another in long shots, often sustained while people and things move in and out of frame, or are followed around by the camera.

In the episode of the train and Indra's death there are two classic long shots—that in which Apu actually sees the train up close

for the first time, when he is physically integrated into the same field of vision as the train, but reduced to a flashing speck intermittently glimpsed beyond it (we are left again to divine his reactions; we are not shown them directly), and that in which the happy home-coming children are shown in the same panning shot as the dying Indra, physically related to her yet emotionally contrasted, as their singing continues on the soundtrack beyond our moment of realization that Indra is close to death. There is no comment by artificial and obtrusive emphasis—the comment is implied, absorbed into the form of the film.

Aparajito, the second film of the trilogy, seems to be generally considered the least satisfactory. Even many sympathetic critics feel that it is broken-backed and lacking in unity (especially since the period of time covered requires two different boy actors to play Apu), and that at best it makes formal sense only as a hinge between the two flanking films. I cannot agree with this—partly, I suppose, because by chance *Aparajito* was the first of the trilogy I saw, and I found then that it made perfect sense formally and intellectually taken by itself. What gives unity to it, despite its apparent break in the middle, when Apu and his mother return from Benares to the country and Apu grows several years into another actor, is the continuing theme of Apu's relations with Sarbojaya, and the tug between education and new experience on one hand and traditional ways of life on the other which coincides almost with that between his own individuality and the claims of his mother.

The form of the film is freer, more expansive than that of *Pather Panchali*. Again, the train provides the main linking image: the very opening shots of the film are from the train carrying Apu's family towards Benares. The first sequences evoke lightly and freely the life of the family in the city, particularly that of Apu, who relishes to the full the new experiences it brings him, his ability to wander almost at will through the strange and wonderful sights on the banks of the holy Ganges where his father works, and the train becomes reduced in importance to little more than one of the things Apu observes during his wanderings. Everything is necessarily disconnected, impressionistic.

The connecting link here is the decline, illness and eventual death of Hari, the father. This death is marked in the film by a shot of many pigeons suddenly taking wing, which has been interpreted as one of Ray's more obvious metaphors (the soul leaving the body). Curious that this very idea—birds flying free—should be that cited by Pasolini in the passage quoted as an obvious metaphor for happiness. What did Ray mean by it? Probably everything his commentators find and more. Like Ray's recurrent images, it is there for its suggestive power and its rich ambiguity, and it is remarkably successful, producing exactly the sense of release into a new dimension that the film at this point requires.

The rest of *Aparajito* concentrates directly on Apu's growing-away from his mother. Her decision to move back to the country may be read as an economic necessity, but it can also be seen as her first move in the battle to keep Apu, to enclose him in her own little world of quiet passivity, of withdrawal from the challenge of life. The first view of Apu in the new village is of him in the gateway of his grandfather's house, watching the train passing by in the distance, as though it has become as unattainable for him now as it ever was. The central section of the film, that in which Apu and Sarbojaya are shown virtually alone in the village while Apu is still a child, defines the grounds of the eventual, inevitable separation. Above all it is caused by education and Apu's desire, even need, for it. Sarbojaya is, both temperamentally and socially, fixed in the past: she cannot cope with the modern world and the city, and she mistrusts them. There may be some selfishness in her obstructiveness, but there is no malice, only fear that in his development Apu is sure to outstrip her.

The whole complex of emotions is nicely conveyed in a small scene near the centre of the film where Apu tries to give her some idea of astronomy, and her fascination with what he is saying because *he* is saying it, her natural motherly pride, is balanced by an obvious timidity, which drives her towards impatience with anything she does not understand, at already knowing less than her own child. A similar complex is evoked in the more important scene in which Apu tells her that he has been offered a scholarship to study in Calcutta. She is proud, but her first reaction is one of hurt—the immediate selfish one of 'who will look after me?' When Apu says he does not want to be just a holy man all his life (like his father), she at once picks up the implication and slaps him. But later her maternal feelings conquer, and she gives him her savings, telling him he can go. He accepts her sacrifice with an equanimity which is almost callous. And when he does leave he heads without a backward glance down the road towards the train—that same train which is quietly evoked on the soundtrack at the moment Apu first tells his mother of his wish to leave and his opportunity to do so.

The final section of the film is built on an alternation of scenes in Calcutta while Apu studies and scenes in the village during vacations. Apu seems at home in Calcutta, relishing his new friends, new learning; back in the village he views with boredom all the things that used to delight him as a child, and having delayed his arrival refuses to postpone his departure by even a day, to please his mother. Clearly she sees the situation as a struggle to keep him, and one which she has already lost. When the time comes to leave he goes, but relents at the last moment, deliberately misses his train and returns. But it is a sentimental gesture which does not alter the true situation. Once Apu is back in Calcutta they correspond, but she has cause to chide him for not writing more frequently, and we see her fading away visibly, getting weaker and weaker while he writes back evasively. The end of the film recapitulates various familiar motifs: Sarbojaya sitting pathetically under a great tree, as Indra sat among the bamboos to die in *Pather Panchali*; the sound of a train in the distance, with Sarbojaya hoping against hope that it will bring Apu back to her (the train, once a cause of fear and separation to her, now represents hope and the possibility of reunion); the props of village life—the barking dog, the house enclosure, the pond—as Apu returns at last, summoned by a letter telling him of his mother's illness. She is already dead when he arrives, and he makes an almost instant decision to return to his new life, to his examinations. The film ends with a decisive visual rejection of the old life, the old man standing at the door of the house enclosure as Apu walks off towards the train, Calcutta, and the freedom implied by the open sky of the very last shot, in which he is just a small silhouette at the bottom of the frame.

If the train and the railway seemed constantly recurrent in *Pather Panchali* and *Aparajito*, they are a dominant factor in *Apur Sansar*. Immediately after the credits train noises invade the soundtrack as we see where Apu lives in Calcutta after having had to leave school because of lack of funds. It is a garret by the railway tracks, and Apu is actually awakened by a particularly insistent whistle. He has entered the world of trains, with a vengeance. In certain ways he seems acclimatized to it, in other ways not. A sequence showing his ineffectual search for work and the receipt of a letter accepting one of his stories for magazine publication conveys the mixture of confidence and timidity, ambition and impracticality in his nature.

This sort of prologue leads into the central section of the film, when by a strange turn of events (at least to Western audiences) he marries a total stranger. He goes with his friend Pulu to the country to attend the wedding of Pulu's cousin (arranged, of course, like most Indian weddings even today). Her bridegroom turns out to be hopelessly insane, but according to custom and belief she will be forever cursed and unmarriageable if she does not marry someone on this day selected by astrological calculation. Apu's first reaction is 'But we are living in the twentieth century'; his second, as Pulu's best friend and accepting that it seems to be somehow meant, is to marry the girl himself. This may well seem arbitrary, though Indians tell us that such happenings are by no means unusual; but even here Ray prepares us for Apu's change of situation by bathing the country scenes immediately before the wedding in a sort of magical mysterious atmosphere so that we are ready to accept the marriage almost as a part of a dream the hero seems to be living at this time, in this place.

If dream it is, we, he and his bride are soon restored to reality when the film comes back to Calcutta. The bride's first reaction to Apu's home, the dirt, the noise and the strangeness, is tears, but before long the marriage, beautifully evoked in tiny details of casual intimacy and tenderness, comes to seem inevitable, the necessary complement of Apu's solitary life, for Ray can never stand to see his characters alone for too long—they live by interrelation. Thus when Aparna goes back to her village to bear their child and dies in separation from Apu, we understand his first violent reaction (he hits Aparna's brother, who brings the news) and then complete desolation. The death comes with the full weight of Ray's belief in the need for togetherness, and with the accumulated force of all those which have gone before: Indra's, Durga's, Hari's, Sarbojaya's. At this point the train plays its last important part in Apu's story: he nearly kills himself beneath it, succumbing to the forces in the world which he temporarily feels he cannot begin to understand or cope with.

Immediately before the news of Aparna's death is broken, we see Apu walking happily along the tracks towards his home, reading her last letter to him; he picks up a small child wandering dangerously near the track and returns it to a safer spot. After he has heard of his wife's death the effect is reversed. He is lying in a state of numbed lethargy, scarcely conscious of the kindly interfering of his neighbour. Then he gets up and looks at himself. As he does so, the clock stops ticking, and then we hear a train whistle. An inner emotional logic takes him immediately to the rails, where he stands waiting to jump beneath a train. But he does not die; instead a stray pig is run over, and its shriek brings him back to his senses. Images and associations from all the earlier scenes by the railway, right back to his first encounter with a train, are all capsulated here, and the effect has the sort of emotional intensity which has to be hardly won.

The rest of the film forms a sort of epilogue. For a while Apu wanders, and he rather histrionically burns the manuscript of his book at dawn on a mountain-top (his inability to get on with it had been the only blot on his otherwise perfect marriage). He takes a menial job in a mine. Finally, he determines to go to see his son before setting off abroad to make a new start. Here, in his son, is the prospect of togetherness, a new family situation, but Apu has deliberately rejected it. When he arrives, though, he finds that his son Kajal, though ready enough to call on his name as an abstract ally in his absence, is the one to reject him. But reconciliation is inevitable, and when Apu leaves at the last with Kajal on his shoulders, heading towards who knows what future, the effect is devoid of all sentimentality: in it human necessity and structural necessity are one, nature and art perfectly combined.

The *Apu* trilogy is unmistakably Ray's longest and most ambitious work; but it is an early work and for all its astonishing maturity and mastery it has weak points and fumblings, particularly in the third part—one has the feeling that Ray is more interested in Apu as a child and a youth than as a man. (Much the same is true of the most obviously comparable work of cinema, surprisingly not mentioned at all in the books on Ray by Marie Seton or Robin Wood, Mark Donskoi's *Maxim Gorky* trilogy, which could almost be the model for the *Apu* trilogy in Donskoi's use of recurrent images—the river instead of the train—his splendid use of an old actress—Massalitinova as compared with Chunibala as Indra in the Ray—and the rich ambiguity of his attitudes to old and new, sensitivity and ruthlessness, in the formation of a writer.) Nor does the trilogy by any means exhaust the range of Ray's interests, sympathies and abilities as a film-maker.

His next films (after the first two parts) were very different in subject matter and style, both from the trilogy and from each other. If the trilogy so far had helped to tag him as a rustic neo-realist concerned principally with the peasant classes, *Paras Pathar* (*The Philosopher's Stone*, 1957) took place entirely in the city, among the middle classes, and *Jalsaghar* (*The Music Room*, 1958) was the first of a series of films dealing with the Zamindar classes, the rich landlords of British India. Moreover, *Paras Pathar* was a satirical fantasy closest, if to any neo-realist film, to De Sica's *Miracle in Milan*. This miracle in Calcutta concerns a mild and harmless little clerk who suddenly finds himself possessed of the philosopher's stone and able to turn base metal into gold. The first part of the film manages to tread its tightrope of whimsical fantasy with considerable grace and precision—the first reactions of the poor Duttas to their new-found riches are very funny and believable enough to keep us in touch with reality despite the extravagance of

the point of departure. Particularly appealing is Dutta's drive round the city daydreaming of his forthcoming life as a rich man, and ending with him discovering in a scrap-iron dump the ideal materials to practise his new gifts on, two cannon balls. Later on, though, the comic tone is not kept up—the Duttas' situation becomes too seriously uncomfortable, and the satirical sidelights thrown on Calcutta bourgeois society are rather lacking in subtlety. All the same, *Paras Pathar* shows a gift for fantasy which Ray was not to exploit again until *Goopy Gyne Bagha Byne* in 1969, and has enough pleasures of its own to deserve an occasional airing.

Jalsaghar is a major work, and remains one of Ray's finest. It is curious that it should come immediately before the third part of the *Apu* trilogy, for while *Apur Sansar* is expansive, *Jalsaghar* is the most concentrated and restrained of Ray's films, a long, lyrical meditation on a single theme, the decline of an aristocratic family. The film is deliberately under-dramatized; the decline is a *fait accompli* from the first, and the whole story is told from the point of view of its principal victim (perhaps, too, its principal agent), an aged and solitary nobleman now near to death. Above all, this is an atmospheric piece, set in the mouldering remains of a once splendid country house on the edge of an empty, mournful estuary, almost the only sign of life apart from the few, slow remnants of the household being the one horse and the single elephant left to wander idly across the sandy flats.

Exactly why the family's fortunes have sunk so low we never learn; is it the excessive mourning and withdrawal from the world which follows the death of the hero's only son, or the natural extravagance and impracticality of a nature in which everything is subjugated to a love of music and the arts? It does not really matter; the entire film is a dying fall evoking a situation with the poet's sublime disregard for wordly whys and wherefores. Though there are one or two places, usually in action scenes, where this leads to perfunctory handling, in general *Jalsaghar* is one of Ray's most masterly films, exquisitely photographed and directed with a complete, unquestioning mastery of mood and tempo which matches the work of Jean Renoir at its best. Most wonderful of all, perhaps, are the two big sequences in the music-room itself, that leading up to the storm in which the hero's son is lost and that in which with a grand gesture he spends the last of his money on just one more crowning performance before he dies. In particular the first, with its long concentration on the mounting intensity of the Muslim singer's song, the physical signs of the rising storm in the shaking mirror and the swaying chandeliers, at first unnoticed by the rapt guests, the insect drowning in the Zamindar's glass of wine, and then the full fury of the storm, is unforgettable as a piece of musical, dramatic and visual construction. *Jalsaghar* is not the easiest of films, since it lacks the more accessible appeals to sentiment of the *Apu* trilogy, but for those willing to place themselves under its hypnotic spell it offers pleasures of unique delicacy.

The same cannot be said of *Devi* (U.K.: *The Goddess*), the film Ray made in 1960, immediately after *Apur Sansar*. Though some like it very much, it never seems to me to come over with quite the force and conviction that it should. Easy to feel, but hard to say why. The plot is both interesting in itself and exotic enough to acquire a bonus of Oriental glamour. A young wife is identified by her fanatical father-in-law as an embodiment of the goddess Kali, becomes more than half-convinced when an apparent miracle is performed through her agency, and is finally destroyed by the combined effects of her intellectual husband's scepticism, the religious pressures of the village, and the failure of a second miracle to materialize. It is, in fact, an unusually coherent, tightly knit plot, one of the best organized plots in Ray's *oeuvre*, and perhaps this is what is wrong with the film. Ray's is an expansive, rhapsodic talent, and it seems to blossom best when it has time to work by indirection, by the cumulative effect of recurrent images and delicate hints of character and motivation, and is least confined by a strict external form. *Devi* is more a matter of uncluttered story-telling than of atmosphere and the loving accumulation of detail. The story is, admittedly, quite well told, but somehow in the process much of the life of the film, the life which we normally expect of Ray's films, seems to have drained away. Of course, there are remarkable things in *Devi*, especially in

the hypnotic scenes of the religious ceremonies in which the unfortunate heroine is involved, and these introduce another element into our knowledge of Ray's range of effects: his ability to handle successfully a florid style with flashy camera-work and obtrusive editing effects. But by and large the film does not seem quite to live up to its ambitions, and it is interesting in Ray's progress mainly as marking a shift from a narrative to a more dramatic approach to film.

1961 was the centenary of Tagore's birth, and so it was only natural that Ray, once a pupil of Tagore's at Santineketan and the son of one of Tagore's closest friends, should make a film in tribute. In fact he made two, the documentary *Rabindranath Tagore* (1961), commissioned by the Indian government, and *Teen Kanya*, a three-episode film based on Tagore short stories, later shorn of one of its episodes and shown in the West as *Two Daughters*. Though a commissioned work, *Rabindranath Tagore* was also a labour of love. It traces Tagore's life partly by use of documents (paintings, photographs, books and manuscripts) and partly by reconstruction with live actors. On the whole it reflects Ray's technical skill and superior taste rather than his more personal gifts as a film-maker, but even so it is often fascinating, with its glimpses of mouldering architectural splendours and its revealing snapshots of the early years of this century. There are, however, three sequences worthy of Ray at his best and most individual: that in which the young Tagore, played by a boy with a radiantly expressive face, first starts to explore the world about him, which yields images as beautiful and astonishing as anything in the *Apu* trilogy; the passage evoking the onset of the rains, a frequent subject in Tagore's poetry; and the wordless demonstration of the evolution of Tagore's painting from early doodles in the margins of his writing to the highly sophisticated work of his seventies. For those sequences alone the film deserves an honourable place among Ray's works.

Teen Kanya is longer and more substantial, though its material is essentially slighter. In the original, the two primarily comic episodes, known as *Two Daughters*, were separated by another new venture for Ray, a ghost story called *Monihara*, which Ray felt would make the film, at nearly three hours, rather too long for non-Indian audiences. *Two Daughters* as it stands is one of Ray's most wholly delightful films, showing to the full his till then largely hidden gift for comedy. The first story, *The Postmaster*, is hardly more than an atmospheric sketch of the affection which springs up between a lonely young village postmaster, exiled from Calcutta, and his diminutive orphan house-keeper, but it is beautifully done, and the performance of the girl (Chandana Banerji), especially at the end, when the postmaster leaves without warning, is remarkable. The whole episode is built up with tiny touches of local colour and character, from the opening, when the rather stuffy but ostentatiously self-possessed postmaster is terrorized by a wild-looking lunatic in the outlandish remains of a soldier's uniform, only to be even more put out when a tiny orphan girl firmly drives his tormentor away. Later a friendship grows between them, with Ratan helping the postmaster to find his way around the unfamiliar village and its ways, while he teaches her to read and write. But if the theme of education seems to bring some scenes of *The Postmaster* close to *Pather Pan-chali*, the conclusion, when after a bout of malaria through which he is nursed by Ratan, the postmaster decides suddenly to return to the city, has a strange bitter-sweet quality. We feel, for all the comedy of the earlier sequences, that something sad is hap-pening, that probably Ratan, who came so near to developing into a mature woman ca-pable of coping with the modern world, may never do so now. The balance of comedy and sympathy in this slight, erratic tale of a brief contact between two very different people is perfectly managed.

The second story, *Samapti* (*The Con-clusion*), is a social comedy about an ill-judged marriage that works out in the end. Though the episode goes on too long, and the interludes of swift action are too brief to leaven effectively the hypnotic slowness of the rest, some of the individual scenes are very funny, particularly the hero's unfortun-ate visit to inspect the pudgy but do-mesticated bride his mother has picked out for him. He is an owlish law student, and he pigheadedly chooses instead to marry a tomboyish young woman, despite every-one's warnings, with nearly disastrous con-

sequences for both of them. The plot is spun fine, but never allowed to snap, the humorous observation of character is acute, and the part of the reluctant bride, a sort of Indian Baby Doll more interested in her pet squirrel than her husband, is made by direc-tor and actress at once funny, irritating and completely believable. In adapting a rather rambling story by Tagore, Ray has de-veloped the comedy so as to make it into a sort of Indian *Taming of the Shrew*, con-structed along much the same lines.

Like *The Postmaster*, it is a study in the maturing of a child-woman, though this time in absence rather than presence: Pagli plays the tomboy-child all through her wedding and wedding-night, shinning down a conven-ient tree to escape her sleeping husband and play with her squirrel instead, and it is only when he has gone, assuring her that she is still too immature for marriage but that he will be ready when she signifies she is ready, that she begins to develop and put aside child-ish things. The truce and happy ending are finally achieved by a compromise: she will not send for him and he will not come of his own accord, but he comes in answer to a transparently contrived summons to his mother's fictional sick-bed and then forgets his dignity far enough to go and look for his errant bride down by the river where they first met.

It is interesting to see Ray, even in this very light-weight context, constructing his drama on recurrent developing images in just the same way that he did the most serious sections of the Apu trilogy. In *Samapti* there are two of these: the mud flats on the river-bank where Apurba's romance with Pagli begins and ends, and the tree Pagli climbs down to escape from her wedding night and finally climbs back up again to signify her readiness for it.

The third episode, *Monihara*, is quite dif-ferent, and might well have created too strong a contrast of mood within *Teen Kanya* as a whole, being really a horror film. The story concerns a prosperous business man obsessed with his frigid wife who craves nothing but jewels, which he constantly buys her in a desperate attempt to gain some show of affection. One day his business is ruined, and his wife, fearing that he may want to sell her jewels, takes flight with a mysterious servant who has some sort of blackmailing hold on her. Whether he kills her or not, she vanishes, and reappears in ghostly form to claim the last gift her husband had brought her from the city. All of this is framed in the narration of a schoolteacher who may be mad or drugged, and directed towards a cloaked figure who at the end announces that he is the ghost of the husband and vanishes. Though this twist at the end is more comic than horrific, for the most part the film is horror taken straight, leading from a slow build-up to a spectacular set-piece of melodrama where the inanimate objects in the house seem to come malevolently alive to the terrified husband as he awaits his wife's ghostly return. The story remains an isolated essay in a genre alien to Ray, but within its confines done with surprising effectiveness.

Ray's two ensuing films, *Abhijan* (1962) and *Kanchenjunga* (1963), his first colour film, have had little showing in the West. This seems reasonable in the case of *Abhijan*, a picaresque adventure story centring on a taxi driver, his romantic and dramatic entanglements, which Ray apparently undertook to direct at the last minute and which has little to commend it apart from the interest of seeing him handle a subject much closer to the Indian commercial norm than any of his other films. But *Kanchenjunga* is a very different matter, one of Ray's subtlest and most personal films, and perhaps the most concentrated example of his preoccupation with interrelations within the family and the difficulties as well as the joys of togetherness. It is, incidentally, the first film based on an original story by Ray himself. Essentially it is a conversation piece. Its action strictly observes the unities, the film lasting exactly the 100 minutes that the action it represents takes. The script is, on one level, simple—merely eight members of a family drifting in and out of camera, talking often at random—with a couple of outsiders to influence the course of their meandering afternoon. But within this it is all very carefully and precisely patterned.

One element of the framework is a walk the younger daughter Monisha is taking with the unappealing but eligible Bannerjee, during which he is supposed to propose and she to accept him. Monisha and Bannerjee have their reflections (projections?) in the elder daughter Anima and her husband Shankar, who proved an unfortunate match and with whom she now constantly quarrels (while their little daughter looks anxiously on from a distance as she rides her pony round the hill in Darjeeling where the family is spending its afternoon). Do Anima and Shankar represent what Monisha and Bannerjee may become if she does not summon up the strength to resist her father's will? Possibly—at any rate, in the end, she rejects Bannerjee and seems to be looking instead towards the other outsider, the poor tutor Ashoke.

In one sense little happens; in another a great deal does. The drama here is much more interior than usual in Ray, and the surface is much more apparently literary: there is a lot of dialogue. But only apparently, for in this story the characters seldom say directly what they are thinking, or indeed anything particularly germane to the central issues of the drama, which are thought and fought out beyond, between and beneath the words they speak. Visually the film is cool and elegant, not over-stuffed with effects or even images apart from the main one, which is an image of absence, the mountain Kanchenjunga they cannot see till the end because it is cloaked in mist. Its final unveiling has been taken as a piece of naïve affirmation, as a monumental rebuke to the pettiness of these human entanglements. Actually, the presence or absence of the mountain has a not quite definable contribution to make to the edgy atmosphere of the afternoon, and its final appearance resolves nothing—the story is left, as Ray likes them, open-ended. We have seen the family, separate yet together; we have spent 100 minutes in the company of idiosyncratic, believable human beings and got to know something of them; and we come away with a Chekhovian sense of human fragility, human durability, and the mystery behind the simplest happenings.

Kanchenjunga is a high point in Ray's career; *Charulata*, which he made two years later in 1964, again using a story by Tagore, is another. In between comes *Mahanagar* (*The Big City*, 1963), which I do not find by any means so compelling, though it deals with a theme which obviously has special importance for Ray, since he dealt with it in *Apur Sansar* and was to do so again in *Pratidwandi* (*The Adversary*, 1970): the search for work in a big city. Clearly the film has considerable thematic importance in India, because it confronts the problem of whether wives should go out to work. It also, incidentally, raises the question of the Anglo-Indians and their status, poised between two cultures and completely accepted by neither. This said, though, much of the film strikes me as thin and summary in the staging, lacking the rich suggestivity and complexity of Ray's best work. What it says it states, and that is about all. Arati, the wife of an impoverished young bank clerk compelled to support his pernickety old ex-schoolteacher father and his younger sister, determines to go out to work to help support the family.

Despite her father-in-law's traditional resistance she persists and gets a job selling knitting machines. She is very successful and enjoys the work: she also becomes friendly with a fellow salesgirl, an Anglo-Indian called Edith. Her husband insists she quit, but relents just in time when his bank fails and he is out of work. Now idle, he develops unfounded suspicions about her fidelity and spies on her. Finally she discovers that Edith has been dismissed from the firm on a trumped-up accusation of immoral behaviour which she knows to be false, and herself resigns in angry sympathy, so that at the end of the film both husband and wife are out of work, if still determined to look on the bright side. Though there are some nice moments of sly social comedy in Arati's introduction to the sale of knitting machines, and the character of Edith is interesting on a purely informational level, the second half of the film has too large an accumulation of bare happenings, some of them decidedly melodramatic and all of them losing conviction by their number and succession. Ray seems out of his element in a plot-bound situation which does not leave his characters enough room to grow and develop by interaction. He does not seem creatively involved with much of *Mahanagar*, however much importance he may as a man attribute to the ideas and attitudes expressed in it.

Charulata, on the other hand, is by any standard one of Ray's masterpieces. Set in a moneyed and highly literate section of the Zamindar class in the 1870s, it is, to steal a phrase from the advertising campaign for a very different film, 'almost a love story', concerning the elusive, implicitly emotional relationship between the young wife of a newspaper proprietor and her husband's artistic cousin. The husband, Bhupati, is constantly preoccupied with the paper and with politics, and gets so excited about whether Gladstone or Disraeli will win the next British election that he never has time for Charulata. She naturally becomes more and more involved with her literary soulmate, Amal, now competing with him, now wheedling him, now brusquely rebuffing him. Things come to a head when Bhupati is defrauded by his brother-in-law and Amal begins to wonder guiltily if he too is committing a betrayal of faith, even though, as they say in Hollywood films, 'nothing has happened'.

The whole story is told in hints and sidelights; in fact, in a very real sense nothing does happen: it is all atmosphere and suggestion and unstated, even unconscious, emotional responses. *Jalsaghar* had already demonstrated, if demonstration were needed, how capable Ray was of dealing with a subject as sophisticated as this—and in *Charulata* he brings the whole battery of his talents to bear, with sometimes breathtaking results. The sheer visual beauty of the film is extraordinary and the more showy technical devices—fast tracking shots, zoom lenses—are used with exemplary discipline and discretion. The acting of the principals is here impeccable, catching exactly the William Morris-like fervour relieved with heavy playfulness which makes this stratum of Indian life seem, oddly, more English than England itself.

Charulata has its recurrent images, notably the ornate carved-wood Victorian bed in Charu's room where we first see her embroidering a gift for her husband, and near and around which a number of other key scenes take place. An apt choice: justified realistically in the sense that much of Charu's life is lived in her room, hence her bored sense of confinement and neglect by her fond but preoccupied husband; the bed also has strong sexual overtones which are, as is Ray's way with his images, just allowed to gather round it, and largely to be supplied by us, rather than being in any way directly insisted on. So the bed is an image for the drama as a whole, which is one of largely unrecognized sexuality. Charu and Amal drift into a friendly companionship, encouraged by Bhupati, with no notion of falling in love, or that they may be doing so. Charu's softening and unconcerned (because unrecognizing) abandonment to her new feelings is brilliantly conveyed in the famous garden scene where Charu swings higher and higher (another disguised sexual reference) while Amal reclines writing in the background under a tree, carrying out his part of their friendly literary competition. And again little is actually said—the growth of love, mainly Charu's for Amal, is shown in a number of tiny details—the song she hums and he takes up, the slippers she was embroidering for her husband and gives to Amal instead. Only when Charu steps out of the Victorian convention of reticence with her declaration of love for Amal does the situation become impossible. Amal leaves in shock and fear of his own feelings; Charu stays on, but her husband recognizes what has happened, leaves, and then comes back to an emotional stalemate, where everything is known between him and Charu but nothing can really be said.

Charulata, it is tempting to say, is Ray's most Western film—in discussing it one thinks at once of Ibsen or Strindberg (more in this case than of Chekov, who so often seems to offer close parallels to Ray's dramatic practice). But that is begging the question of whether most of Ray is not Western. Obviously there are things about his films, like their frequently very measured tempo (slowness, unsympathetic critics would say), which it is easiest to discuss as part of his Indianness. But apart from his subject matter it is hard to be sure that there is anything in his films which derives specifically from his Oriental background and heritage: he is very much a world film-maker, influenced more by Renoir, Donskoi, Welles (the swinging scene in *Charulata*, and the film's whole loving re-creation of its period milieu, has more than a hint of *The Magnificent Ambersons* about it) and even by the theories of Pudovkin, which were among his early reading, than by Indian cinema and its circumstances. There is nothing in his films which has to be related to anything but his own artistic development and taste as an individual; like any artist he is finally independent of his background, and whatever use he may chose to make of it is ultimately self-determined.

The films of 1965–67 may be taken as an interlude between *Charulata* and Ray's next major work, *Aranyer Din Ratri* (*Days and Nights in the Forest*, 1969). One of them, *Chiriakhana* (1967) I have not been able to see, but it would seem to be unimportant—a detective story started by Ray's assistants under his supervision and then completed (mainly for reasons of finance) by Ray himself: he does not consider it as one of his films. *Kaparush-o-Mahaparush* (1965) is deliberately slight but agreeable: the first story concerns a second meeting between young lovers, years later when she has married a decent bore after the lover ran out on her, and is mainly about how nothing happens because this time she chooses to stay with her husband; the second develops as a knockabout farce concerning the unmasking of a fake holy man by the relatives of one of his gullible followers—a genre for which on this showing Ray would seem to have little gift, whatever his talents in subtler comedy.

Nayak (1966) and *Goopy Gyne Bagha Byne* are both more substantial, but each in various ways is disappointing. *Nayak*, the second film from an original screenplay by Ray, is an evocation of the life and personality of a successful but dissatisfied film star during his train journey to Delhi. In the course of the journey he strikes up an acquaintance with a woman journalist, who at first sees this as an opportunity to get the materials for a saleable story, but eventually realizes that their relationship has become personal to the extent that it would not be ethical to use the information he has given her, and tears up her notes. He, for his part, is impelled to a sort of confession by a nagging sense that despite his evident success he is fundamentally mediocre and has not had the courage and the perseverance to make the most of what talent he has. Also by a dream which represents his fear of money—his fear of corruption by the money he has, his fear of not having it any more. There is another dream, this time about fear of death, and there are seven flashbacks which detail to us in bits and pieces the course of the star's early life. The film is efficiently enough made, but the imaginative pressure is low, and for

'The famous garden scene in *Charulata* where Charu (Madhibi Mukherjee) swings higher and higher (another disguised sexual reference) while Amal (Soumitro Chatterjee) reclines writing in the background under a tree.'

all its incidental touches of intelligent observation, *Nayak* seems to escape the sensational exposé genre only to fall rather too
far into the world of soap opera.

Goopy Gyne Bagha Byne (also known
simply as *Goopy and Bagha*) is another attempt on Ray's part at something new—or at
least something he had not ventured on since
Paras Pathar—fantasy. It is evident that
Goopy Gyne was a film Ray very much
wanted to make, and certainly one that he
had to fight·to make, considering its large
budget and spectacular resources compared
with his other films and the fact that it came
up at a time of crisis in the Bengali cinema.
But one cannot help wondering if the reasons
for Ray's determination and persistence
really had enough to do with strictly artistic
necessity; whether he was not perhaps
pushed too much by family feeling and by
love for his grandfather's book, on which the
film is based, without considering closely
enough how suited the material was to his
own temperament and skills as a film-maker.
There might also be another consideration in
play: as well as being a fantasy, *Goopy Gyne*
is a musical, with no fewer than eight full
musical numbers, and the opportunity it
offered Ray as a composer may well have
tipped the balance unduly in its favour.

At least we can say that *Goopy Gyne* was a
labour of love and no mere commercial chore
(though oddly enough, once completed, it
went on to be Ray's biggest box-office
success in India). One of the main pleasures
to be derived from it is a sense of relief and
relaxation—we feel that Ray is content to
have fun with his subject. It is a rambling
(too rambling) and picaresque tale of two
rather dopey musicians—Goopy the singer,
and Bagha the drummer—who, wandering
one day in the woods, encounter the King of
the Ghosts. He first terrorizes them (in a very
jolly dance sequence all shot in negative), and
then makes them the gift of three wishes and
a pair of magic slippers which will carry them
anywhere. A series of adventures separate
and reunite the two heroes, get them thrown
into prison and nearly executed, and enable
them finally, with the help of their magic, to
intervene in a war, avert the imminent battle,
and marry the daughters of two warring
kings, now peacefully reunited in friendship.

It would be easy, reversing the judgement

on *Charulata*, to say that *Goopy Gyne* is
Ray's most Indian film, and in a sense this
may be true—undoubtedly with its comedy
and romance and fantasy, its songs and
dances and spectacle, it is nearer than any of
Ray's other films to the sort of Indian cinema
best known in the West from *Aan, Savage
Princess*. Of course, it is immeasurably superior to its parallels, but a slight feeling
remains that it is disappointing from Ray—
less personal, less felt, less intensely realized
than even the lightest of his other works. It is
true, also, that purely technical limitation may
have something to do with this: a fantasy of
this kind has to be physically absolutely convincing, and suspension of disbelief is not
aided here by shaky back-projection and
travelling matte or obvious economies in sets,
costumes and spectacular highlights.

After these four films *Days and Nights in
the Forest* was a decided return to form, and
enforced some clear rethinking of attitudes
towards Ray which were beginning to become set in critics' minds. It has always
been easy, too easy, to pull out the conventional epithets for Ray's films. 'Measured',
we say, to suggest that they are slow, but are
obviously meant to be that way. 'Poetic'—for
Ray's approach to character and event is
clearly far from documentary, and his films
seem often to be built to music unheard as
well as to his own heard, and highly expressive, scores. 'Humane'—because his sympathy goes out to even the most unlikely
objects, realizing in practice that usually
somewhat unrealistic maxim that to understand all is to forgive all. But these ready
formulations leave the magic of his films
unexpressed. The very opening of *Days and
Nights in the Forest* is a perfect case in point.
A group of four somewhat ill-assorted
friends from Calcutta are out for a few days'
runaway holiday in the country. They joke
and mildly quarrel as they drive, the particular humorist of the party chattering on
about the forest and various failures of the
others to respond to the adventure of their
situation. Then without warning one of them
says 'look to your left', the camera moves, and
there, suddenly, flashing past the car window,
is the forest. The tempo slows, in comes the
music, and we go into the credits. Magical
is the word to describe the effect, got with
apparently the simplest, most naïve means.

There are many such moments in *Days and Nights in the Forest*. There are sections, particularly in the first half, which are rather too 'measured' for comfort, and the build to the appearance of the feminine interest is too long-drawn-out. But even this slight wearisomeness pays eventual dividends in that we really feel we have been living along with these people. There is, indeed, something Chekhovian about Ray's wayward, indirect means of character revelation. The scene in which nearly all the characters on a picnic agree to play an idiotic memory game is almost a perfect Chekhov scene, conceived in cinematic terms, with each revealing more and more of himself (or herself) by the ways he plays or refrains from playing. And the restrained climaxes to two of the three romantic elements in the story—abortive in one case, possibly pointing towards something further in the other—are among the best scenes even Ray has ever done.

In the wake of *Days and Nights in the Forest*, Ray embarked on another film in which the political theme, implicit in *Days and Nights in the Forest*, came to the fore. And by the time he came to make his next film after that, he became aware that what he had was a second trilogy, less closely knit than the *Apu* trilogy, but united by recurrent themes indicative of social change in modern India. In *The Adversary* we return to the theme and the world of the openings of *Apur Sansar* and of *Mahanagar*. The hero, Siddhartha, is compelled by his father's death (much as Apu was by his mother's) to give up his studies and look for a job. Like Subrata in *Mahanagar*, he has a family to support, a mother, sister and brother. But he cannot manage to get a job, because though like Apu he has intellectual qualifications he does not have the drive or the right contacts. So in practice the family is dependent on the earnings of his sister Sutapa, a modern young woman of considerable ambition and determination. Compared with her, Siddhartha is a curious mixture of the old and the new, like the adult Apu, being considered a fuddy-duddy conservative by his younger brother Tunu, who is caught up in student revolutionary politics. He is conservative even in his attitude to sex: his reaction to a proposed visit to a prostitute organized by one of his college friends is one of horror and

revulsion. A more settling and suitable romance with the daughter of an income tax inspector also comes to nothing when she becomes emotionally confused by the prospect of her widowed father's remarriage with her aunt. And Siddhartha cannot cope—he still cannot even get a job, and when he is about to have a crucial interview he gets so worked up against his prospective employers for their callousness that he turns on them, in circumstances somewhat similar to those which brought about Arati's resignation in *Mahanagar*, and refuses the job.

In the final sequences we see Siddhartha settled (like Apu at the mine) in a humble job selling medical supplies in a small town. He has achieved a sort of balance, but still cherishes ideas of returning to the city, reclaiming the girl he loves, and improving himself at last. In the following film, *Seemabaddha* (*Company Limited*, 1972), we see, as it were, the reverse side of the medal. Back in Calcutta, Ray shows us the new bourgeoisie functioning in a Westernized setting of big business. The central character, or at any rate the character who provides the film's moral centre, is a girl who comes to the city to visit her sister and brother-in-law. Like Siddhartha she is in a state of indecision about the future shape of her life, and the main reason she comes visiting is to renew contact with her brother-in-law, for whom she had strong feelings when she was in her teens, six or seven years before. It is a sort of sentimental journey, a journey to her own emotional past, and a checking-up: How has the young man she once had a crush on developed? What effects have life in the city, an executive job in big business, had on him? And by implication, is this a way of life she herself would wish to accept, or should she return to her revolutionary boy-friend in the country and contract out of this side of modern life?

She finds nothing very encouraging in the image of social success and urban glamour provided by her elder sister and the brother-in-law. At first they seem to have acclimatized well to the new way of life, but when a crisis comes at the man's office, as a result of faulty workmanship revealed in the factory where the electric fans he markets are made, he proves to be as obsessed with his career, with self-preservation, as any of his

Western peers. He is essentially the reasonably decent, reasonably honest middle-class man who is fine provided he is not pushed too far or cornered, but who is then willing to fight dirty and sacrifice anyone who gets in his way. He does so, and he succeeds: he ends up with his ambitions fulfilled (for the moment) with a directorship of his firm. So he is quite happy, but his sister-in-law much less so. She feels she cannot but reject his standards, his way of life—but whether that means that she feels enough for her revolutionary to go back and marry him, embrace his standards wholeheartedly, is another matter, and one on which we can feel no final certainty at the end of the film.

Company Limited is technically quite straightforward, after the elaborate structure of *The Adversary*, with its flashes forward and back, its adventures into negative in certain sequences and its instantaneous glimpses of potential action going on in its characters' heads. It is also a lot funnier, with much mordant humour in its observation of business ways and means, the contrasts of social life in Calcutta. It is rather as though the satire present within the fantasy of *Paras Pathar* has been transmuted by contrast with the realistic observation of, say *Mahanagar* to produce a satisfying new tone in Ray's work. The socio-political observation of the new trilogy is consistent in its humour and its underlying sadness—sadness rather than bitterness, for Ray does not seem to be the stuff of which revolutionaries are made. He observes human follies and failings, but remains sympathetic and understanding towards his characters—his sympathies can embrace the young executive in *Company Limited* as well as the idealistic sister-in-law, and one feels that the revolutionary boy-friend, if we ever saw him, would be no more likely to figure as an unequivocal all-round hero. Ray's is a world of complex humans, in which most people mean more or less well, and nobody gets to carry the banner of Ray's sympathy or the stigma of his total disapproval; it is a fallible, human world we can all recognize.

Satyajit Ray is a film-maker of world reputation, now at the height of his mature powers. He has lived through, and lived down, a number of pigeon-holing reputations. There was that of being an Indian film-maker, *the* Indian film-maker, as opposed to a film-maker *tout court*: with its implication that he was some sort of special case, requiring sympathy, tolerance, patronage, special standards of judgement. Then there was that of the Neo-Realist primitive, an instinctive artist whose first films just happened to come out right because of 'sincerity' and humane values, rather than because of any conscious art. Then there was that of the poetic symbolist, dependent on the manipulation of obvious (and often too obvious) visual metaphors for his effects. And all this time Ray has continued to make films in his own time, according to the dictates of his own artistic development and influenced as little as possible by critics or by commercial considerations.

Sometimes he may choose a deliberately simple, unadorned style, as in the *Postmaster* episode of *Teen Kanya*, when he feels that it matches the material, but in films like *Jalsaghar*, *Devi* and the *Monihira* episode of *Teen Kanya* his style can be as rich and highly wrought as any in the cinema today. Similarly the pace of his films may often be slow (and not only to Western viewers), but the slowness nearly always justifies itself as the only way of adequately exploring the material, and when he wants to, Ray can pick up pace with complete mastery and conviction, as in the swing episode of *Charulata*. Admittedly, in his constant experiment with new styles and materials some weak points have emerged—he is not at home with the staging of violent physical action, or of broad farce—but to balance this he has scored decisive successes in some unexpected genres, such as the horror film (*Monihara*), social comedy (*Samapti* and episodes of *Mahanagar* and *Days and Nights in the Forest*) and the highly sophisticated atmospheric conversation piece (*Kanchenjunga*). In spite of the critics, and in spite of commercial and political pressures at home, Ray goes on making films in his own fashion, with conscious and consciously developing art, on the principle that if they do not please him they are unlikely to please anyone else.

Ray's deepening interest in political subjects resulted in one of his best films, *Ashani Sanket (Distant Thunder*, 1973). Indeed, this seemed to mark a new phase in his career;

gone are the charms of *Days and Nights in the Forest*; the iron has entered into his soul and, after *The Adversary* and *Company Limited*, he has in *Distant Thunder* come to grips with the seemingly insuperable, alarmingly astronomical problems of India. The film is set in 1942; Singapore has just fallen. To remote Bengali villagers, it all seems far away, but soon the cost of rice begins to escalate. At first Ganga and his wife are not affected. He is a Brahmin, schoolteacher–priest–doctor all rolled into one. But he too is to suffer from the hoarding, the profiteering and the corrupt system. This raising of consciousness is masterfully counterpointed by the brilliance of colour and image which serve to intensify the contrast between the beauty of the setting and the (understated) horror of the situation.

The end-title flashes on the screen: in the 1943 famine, five million people died. Five million—who can feel anything for the death of five million? The number is beyond human sympathy; but because of the way Ray has led up to it, the statistic becomes overwhelmingly real.

Ray then made a second 'children's' film *Sonar Kella* (*The Golden Fortress*, 1975), which, if it did not scale the heights of *Distant Thunder*, was a great improvement on his earlier *Goopy Gyne*. In 1975, he returned to the 'political' film with *Jana-Aranya* (*The Middle-man*). Set in Calcutta, it tells the story of a young college graduate who can't find a job in spite of his diploma and qualifications. Breaking with his Brahmin tradition, he goes into the business of 'order-supply', a system of buying cheap and selling dear. But being a middle-man, he discovers, imposes a painful choice between morality and survival: from trafficking in goods, it is only a small step to trafficking in human beings—to, in fact, playing the pimp. Under Ray's piercing yet compassionate eyes, his characters darken with their loss of innocence. In its quiet urgency and emotional intensity, the film transcends its specific context: it is not only about India.

Ray's admirers often quarrel as to which are his best films: for example, I like *Devi* much more than Taylor does, and *Jalsaghar* a lot less. I also find *Mahanagar* much funnier than he seems to. I also found Ray's first film in Hindi something of a disappointment. *Shatranj ke Khiluri* (*The Chess Players*, 1977) is based on a short story about two men in nineteenth-century Lucknow who become so absorbed by chess that they

neglect their wives and families. This personal story is rhymed with the dethroning of the Maharajah of Lucknow by the British East India Company. He is too much the musician, too much the poet to resist successfully. At the same time, there is also a suggestion that the Maharajah is but a pawn in a larger chess game the British are playing out in India. On, admittedly, a single viewing, the two themes did not seem really to mesh or to illuminate each other. Perhaps the script was too slight for the weight Ray brought to bear on it.

But it matters little: Ray's *oeuvre* has grown over the years into one of the richest of any director, and in this respect, too, he resembles Renoir: there is something there for everyone.

The standard work on Ray is Marie Seton's *Portrait of a Director* (1972). See also Robin Wood's *The Apu Trilogy* (1972), a full-length study, and the chapter on Ray in John Russell Taylor's *Directors and Directions: Cinema for the Seventies* (1975).

CAROL REED and DAVID LEAN

John Russell Taylor

Though, even superficially, they are not very alike, Carol Reed and David Lean always seem to spring to mind together, no doubt mainly because of the post-war period of the British cinema when they were the presiding figures of a much discussed revival. Between *Brief Encounter* in 1945 and *The Third Man* in 1949 the films of Reed and Lean, though not by any means the only ones the patriotically minded British filmgoer could be proud of, were on every count the greatest glories. *Brief Encounter*, *Great Expectations* (1946), *Odd Man Out* (1947), *Oliver Twist* (1948), *The Fallen Idol* (1948), *The Third Man*: even today the films vibrate happily in the memory, and seen again help to restore confidence, sadly shaken by more recent offerings, in the outstanding talents of their makers.

Carol Reed was only two years David Lean's senior (they were born, respectively, in 1906 and 1908). But in films he managed a considerable seniority to Lean: nearly a decade separates Reed's first film as a director, *Midshipman Easy* (1935), from Lean's first solo work, *This Happy Breed* (1944).

James Mason in Reed's *Odd Man Out*: the film may have had its excesses, but Mason's performance was unforgettable.

And the intervening period was not filled, as it might well have been, largely by a succession of the 'quota quickies' which bedevilled the British cinema in the 30s. By luck or good judgement Reed managed to attract some notice right away, rarely made completely negligible films, and achieved an important success with *Bank Holiday* (U.S.: *Three on a Week-end*) in 1938. Inevitably the reasons often adduced at the time for approving of the film now seem a little shaky—its realism looks very studio-bound, its treatment of its working-class characters rather stiff and literary—but its vividness remains as a picture of England at a particular time, an evocation of a particular atmosphere. It has become a documentary almost in spite of itself.

As the war approached, Reed was engaged in rapid succession on two very different projects, a rough and lively picture of life in the provincial theatre, *A Girl Must Live*

(1939), and a suitably downbeat version of A. J. Cronin's glum best-seller about misery and disaster in the coal mines, *The Stars Look Down* (1939), which he followed with two stylish costume pieces, *Kipps* (1941) and *The Young Mr Pitt* (1942). After which, like just about everyone else, he plunged into war subjects with *The Way Ahead* (1944) and a feature-length documentary co-directed with Garson Kanin, *The True Glory* (1945). In all these films he demonstrated extraordinary technical skills, a special gift for handling actors (perhaps a legacy of his theatrical beginnings) and a distinct feeling for atmosphere. But it would have been hard to discover amid the great variety of his subjects and approaches to them anything which could be pinned down as a consistent, coherent Reed personality.

Meanwhile, Lean was working his way through the ranks from clapper-boy to newsreel editor to feature editor, and finally in

1942 to being the film technician who would show Noël Coward the ropes in his first, one-man-band of a film *In Which We Serve*. The success of this film, and Coward's approval of his co-director's work on it, led at once to three more assignments directing films written by Noël Coward, *This Happy Breed, Blithe Spirit* (1945) and *Brief Encounter*. It was the third of these which first suggested Lean as a force to be reckoned with on his own account. Coward's adaptation of his own one-act play opened it out boldly and effectively, but what made the film was the acting of Celia Johnson and Trevor Howard as the two decent, settled, happily married middle-class people who suddenly find themselves alarmingly, hopelessly in love, and Lean's stylish use of night streets, the comings and goings at the railway station where the couple's most highly charged meetings take place, and the pleasant, humdrum bustle of the little country town where the action is set—all to convey the very English notion of passion held firmly in control, but none the less real for that.

From contemporary romantic drama Lean turned in his next two films to Dickens and a more overtly romantic, picaresque style. *Oliver Twist*, despite many incidental delights, does not quite succeed—and indeed, how could it?—in imposing a satisfactory filmic shape on Dickens' expansive original; but *Great Expectations*, as well as being pictorially superb, manages to capture the essence of the book and hold the Gothick extravagances and the acute social comment in perfect balance. In *Brief Encounter* and *Great Expectations* the various elements fuse perfectly to capture with extraordinary vividness the tone of the times: a sort of bitter–sweet romanticism very different from the ebullient confidence of the years immediately after the First World War. Though, as his subsequent work has shown, Lean is a masterly technician without any very marked personal approach, in these years the man found his moment, and made films of an intensity (which touches even his less successful ones, like *The Passionate Friends* [U.S.: *One Woman's Story*, 1949] and *Madeleine* [1950]) that his later work has never been able to match.

The same, curiously enough, was true of Carol Reed, and for rather the same reasons.

His creative personality was always rather more marked and distinctive than Lean's—mainly on account of a certain melancholy undertow to even his jolliest works. So naturally he found himself most at home in these immediately post-war years, and made in succession three films which are his major claim to a place in film history: *Odd Man Out, The Fallen Idol* and *The Third Man*. All three are from stories by Roman Catholics of a somewhat fatalistic cast—F. L. Green for the first, Graham Greene for the other two—and all of them match their subjects with a grand, even at times flamboyant style. In *Odd Man Out* the style is not entirely under control: the more ambitious stylistic effects which punctuate the dying gunman's Calvary seem excrescent. But by the time Reed reaches *The Third Man* everything is perfectly integrated: the spectacular visual style, with its operatic lightings and strange angles, complements ideally the complex story of betrayal in divided, war-torn Vienna and the larger-than-life acting of most of the cast, particularly Orson Welles.

With the beginning of the 50s, the Festival of Britain and a certain degree of optimism in British life, both Reed and Lean found themselves rather less at home, and the kind of film they were specializing in rather less apt to the general mood. Reed turned again to period in *Outcast of the Islands* (1951), an uneven Conrad adaptation which yet contains some of his most powerful work, and then, after the relative failure of that, to pastiching himself in *The Man Between* (1953), which put the star of *Odd Man Out*, James Mason, in a *Third Man* situation, without matching either of the earlier films. Lean made a chilly but respectable drama about fliers and backroom boys, *The Sound Barrier* (U.S.: *Breaking the Sound Barrier*, 1952), and an elegant version of Harold Brighouse's North Country comedy *Hobson's Choice* (1954). Both, clearly, remained highly gifted film craftsmen, but anything approaching a personal style or personal brand of subject matter—which had seemed for the moment to be observable in their films—was gone.

The subsequent careers of both directors have included big box-office successes and films of some inherent interest, but nothing to match their work of the late 40s. Lean has indeed established himself as one of the big-

Jean Simmons, Martita Hunt and Anthony Wager in Lean's *Great Expectations*: 'as well as being pictorially superb, it manages to capture the essence of the book and hold the Gothick extravagances and the acute social comment in perfect balance'.

gest, most reliably money-making directors in the world with the succession of *The Bridge on the River Kwai* (1957), *Lawrence of Arabia* (1962), and *Doctor Zhivago* (1965), though of them all only *Lawrence of Arabia* offered anything really memorable in terms of visual treatment or writing (Robert Bolt), and by the time of *Ryan's Daughter* (1970) the whole machinery of making 'big pictures' appeared to have got out of hand and swamped all the individual talents connected with the film, Lean's as well as anyone else's. Reed was less spectacularly successful commercially, scoring his biggest box-office success with *Oliver!* (1968), a none too distinguished musical version of *Oliver Twist*, based on the Lionel Bart stage show. Of his other later films the most interesting is probably his return to collaboration with Graham Greene, *Our Man in Havana* (1960), which

moderates the melancholy with some pleasing wayward humour. But in the long run it can hardly be doubted that we shall look to *Brief Encounter* and *Great Expectations*, *The Third Man* and *Outcast of the Islands*, for the moments when the craftsmen which Lean and Reed have always been were most thoroughly subsumed into the artists they could be if the mood and the occasion were right.

Sir Carol Reed died in 1976. Of his two films after *Oliver!*, the less said the better. After the relative lack of success of *Ryan's Daughter*, Lean has been inactive since 1970. For further reading, see *The Cinema of David Lean* (1975) by Gerald Pratley and *David Lean and His Films* (1974) by Alain Silver and James Ursini.

KAREL REISZ

David Wilson

Karel Reisz was born in Czechoslovakia in 1926. One of the founders of Britain's Free Cinema movement in the late 50s, when he made the short films *Momma Don't Allow* (1955, co-directed with Tony Richardson) and *We Are the Lambeth Boys* (1959), Reisz graduated to feature films with *Saturday Night and Sunday Morning* (1960), which along with the first films of Lindsay Anderson, Tony Richardson and John Schlesinger came to be regarded as one of the key works of the British cinema's post-war renaissance. Less provocative than Anderson, less stylistically self-conscious than Richardson, Reisz shared with them an ambition to free the British cinema from its hidebound conservatism and unadventurous commercialism. Free Cinema set out to champion 'the significance of the everyday'. These were brave words, attuned to the mood of the time; but of the directors associated with the movement, Reisz, in his subsequent career, has seemed less concerned to send out social shock waves than to annotate, quietly and unfussily, the theme of personal identity.

This theme finds expression in his films as an exploration of the border-line between sanity and madness, the convention of reason and the unconventionally irrational. Some of his characters, like the hat-box murderer of *Night Must Fall* (1964), have teetered over the brink; others, like the antic schizophrenic in *Morgan—A Suitable Case for Treatment* (U.S.: *Morgan!*, 1966) and the dancer Isadora Duncan, have merely offended established notions of order and morality. If Reisz's style, generally plain and unadorned but occasionally (and particularly in *Isadora* [U.S.: *The Loves of Isadora*], 1969) giving way to flights of fancy, seems sometimes not quite to mesh with his material, it is probably more the fault of the material than of the director. His next film, *The Gambler* (1974), was made in America. It again gravitates round the theme of a man obsessed by the need to transgress the rules of reason, but is marred by a too literary script and a too literal-minded response to it.

Mention must be made of Reisz's enormously influential book, *The Technique of Film Editing* (1955). Roman Polanski, when asked what he had learned at the Polish National Film School at Lodz, replied that it had enabled him to see *Citizen Kane* many times and that it had introduced him to Reisz's book; and the book has influenced many other film-makers. I still think that Reisz remains potentially the most important British film-maker of his generation. Whether he will ever be able to achieve that potentiality is something else again; in any case, I think more highly of *The Gambler* than does Wilson.

JEAN RENOIR: to 1939

Richard Roud

Every man has his own Renoir; indeed, if Renoir is, as I believe, the greatest of all film-makers, one reason is that his *oeuvre* is so varied, rich and complex. There are two articles in this Dictionary: mine, which covers the period to *La Règle du Jeu* (*The Rules of the Game*, 1939), and the following one, which takes his career from 1939 on. But there could have been further sub-divisions. For a critic like Noël Burch the essential Renoir is the silent period, or more precisely *Nana* (1926). For me, it is the films from *La Chienne* (1931) to *La Règle du Jeu*. There are others who, although admiring the pre-war films, prefer the American period and the later French films of the 50s.

André Bazin and the *Cahiers du Cinéma* group tried hard—and with some success—to prove that there were no dividing lines, that Renoir's *oeuvre* was an integral whole. Others have found different dividing lines: 1936, 1938, 1939, 1950, etc., just as critics have divided Godard's work into different periods. By considering Renoir's pre-1940 films in isolation, I am not saying they are the only good ones, or even that they are very different in nature or quality from the others: I am simply saying that they are the ones that interest me most; therefore, *for me*, the best.

Born in 1894, Renoir was the son of the Impressionist painter Auguste Renoir. His interest in the cinema began at an early age (ten), but it was not until the First World War and the double revelation of Chaplin and *The Perils of Pauline* that he began to think about making films himself. After the war he nevertheless took up ceramics, only abandoning it in favour of the cinema in 1923. He began by producing and writing *Catherine, ou une Vie sans Joie* (1924), a vehicle for his wife, Catherine Hessling, whom he had married in 1919 (she had formerly been a model for his father). The film was directed by Albert Dieudonné. In 1924 Renoir directed his first film, *La Fille de l'Eau* (*The Whirlpool of Fate*, 1924): it is not a successful work, but it showed that he was already capable of capturing on the screen the atmosphere and beauty of landscape, and of suggesting that almost pagan reverence for nature which was to run through much of his work. On the other hand, there was already present in that first film the darker side of Renoir's persona: what we can call the Stroheim or Zola side. The sequence of the fire in *La Fille de l'Eau*, as Bazin remarked, already announces the Renoir of *Nana*, with 'that extraordinary demoniacal shot of Pierre Renoir's head in his pitchfork', and there are other touches of violence and cruelty in the film.

Nana, his next film, was directly influenced by Stroheim's *Foolish Wives*, which Renoir tells us he saw 'at least ten times'. Generally acclaimed his best silent film, its conjugation of Zola with Stroheim created a work which was unlike any other in the French cinema, although its affinity with certain German films was intensified by the presence of Werner Krauss in a leading role. Catherine Hessling played the lead again, and it would seem that one's reaction to the film is somewhat conditioned by one's feelings about Miss Hessling as an actress. I have always found her both touching and abominable, and her Nana something of a caricature of Zola's heroine. But the film is an extremely important one for many reasons.

For the first time, Renoir began to mix his genres, and the same mixture of comedy and tragedy, of the lyrical and the grotesque, that was to culminate in *La Règle du Jeu* thirteen years later is already present here. As Noël Burch points out, Renoir also began here his experiments with the opposition of off-screen space to screen space. 'More than half the shots . . . begin with someone entering the frame or end with someone exiting from it, or both, leaving several empty frames before or after each shot.' For a formalist critic like Burch, *Nana* is important because it marks the first *structural* use of off-screen space. Bazin, however, finds the film unsatisfying because the shots succeed each other with neither dramatic nor logical rigour.

La Chienne is an expression of the Stroheim–Zola side of Renoir: this is a city drama, and the softening effect of landscape is not allowed to intrude. Paradoxically, it is a very enjoyable film, even though there is nothing very pleasant about its subject—the downfall of a middle-aged man in love with a cold-hearted bitch. An amoral film in intention (Renoir announces this in a puppet prologue to the film), it has also been called a 'cold' film. Perhaps its 'coldness' is what has preserved it from the ravages of time. What has certainly contributed to keeping it alive is Renoir's sense of realism—not only visual but aural. This was the first sound film in France to be shot and recorded directly, in real locations—the noisy streets of Montmartre with its taxicabs and streetsingers.

Indeed, the use of sound was what was most commented on when the film appeared, particularly in the scenes which lead to the discovery of the murdered Lulu. Renoir fixes his camera on a streetsinger and the crowd gathers round him outside Lulu's house. When her lover goes upstairs, the camera simply rises vertically to the window of her flat, and then slowly descends. This simple movement is repeated later when the concierge leaves the crowd to go up and deliver the day's post. The song, which has gone on uninterruptedly, is only broken off when the concierge thrusts her head out of the window to report the murder. The narrative economy of the sequence (we know from this moment on that Dédé will be falsely accused of Lulu's murder), and the more abstract pleasure of the dialectical use of time and space, make this a great sequence. Dramatically it renders both the warmth of Renoir's response to the Montmartre setting and his objective view of his characters. But objectivity does not imply indifference: as one of his characters says in *La Règle du Jeu*: 'The terrible thing about this world is that everybody has his reasons.' And Renoir understands, and makes his spectators understand

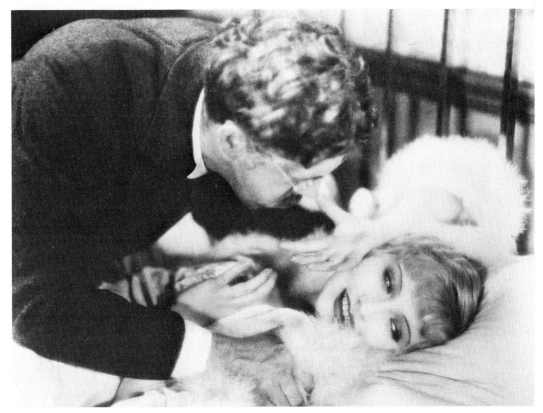

Michel Simon and Janie Marèze in the murder scene from *La Chienne*, an expression of the Stroheim/Zola side of Renoir.

and even empathize with Lulu and Dédé as well as with his hero. He neither sentimentalizes them nor sees them as types (the Pimp, the Tart, the Client): he does not, in fact, take sides. All are equally justified; all are equally guilty.

The following year, 1932, Renoir made two films: *La Nuit du Carrefour* and *Boudu Sauvé des Eaux* (*Boudu Saved from Drowning*). The first was an adaptation of a Georges Simenon thriller, and if the legend is true, the reason for the almost total incomprehensibility of its plot is that the editor of the film lost three cans of film at the end of the shooting and the film had to be edited without them. The film is none the less fascinating, not least for the performance of the director's brother, Pierre Renoir, as Maigret. The whole film takes place at a semi-deserted crossroads, and the soundtrack is replete with strange sounds of rifles going off, cars back-firing. The film has a *louche* atmosphere which comes as much from the locals from

the village as from the drug-smugglers. Not in the main line of Renoir's development, it has none the less been called (by Godard) the only great French thriller, the greatest French adventure film.

One is tempted to say that with *Boudu* Renoir turned the clock back to the rustling landscapes of *La Fille de l'Eau*. But that would not be strictly true, for the film is more of a synthesis of his impressionist tendencies and the naturalistic picture of Paris life he gave us in *La Chienne*. Part of the pleasure one gets now from *Boudu* comes from the simple joy of the reality of Paris in the summer, the parks, the *quais* of the Seine. These are pleasant in themselves but they also situate the story of the tramp Boudu in a definite time and place. The plot is schematic: Boudu the tramp is saved from drowning by a bookseller who tries to rehabilitate him. In return, Boudu carries on a brief but stunning affair with the bookseller's wife, and then becomes engaged to his mistress, who is also the maid. During the wedding ceremony, however, he gets fed up with it all, and disappears beneath the waters of the Marne. While everyone mourns his second drowning, Boudu picks himself out of the water a little further downstream, and a beautiful 360-degree pan expresses his joy at his regained freedom. His horizons once again unbounded, off he goes. The sense of place is further heightened by Renoir's use of depth of focus: there are many scenes shot from a point in one room in the bookseller's flat which stretch all the way across an air-shaft to another room in the flat: for once, one feels that this is a real apartment, and that it is inhabited by real people. Which is perhaps why Renoir's faithful evocation of a filmed time and place has dated less than, say, Carné's artistic stylization of Le Havre in the 1938 *Quai des Brumes*.

There may seem to be a contradiction in this insistence on reality and Renoir's impressionist treatment of landscape. Superficially one could say that in *Boudu*, as in *Partie de Campagne* (1936; released only in 1946 in a newly edited version) and *La Fille de l'Eau*, there are scenes which remind one of his father's paintings. But the influence of Auguste Renoir goes far beyond a similar taste for atmospheric Ile de France landscapes. We are all too apt to forget that in intention the Impressionists were *realists*. That is, Impressionism was an attempt to render reality more accurately. Renoir painted shadows blue because even though they *appear* black, they really *are* blue. And when Monet painted the Rouen Cathedral at different times of day, it was because he felt that a rendering of reality had to take into account that, because of the action of light, things change. The cathedral did not exist as an essence; it had no immutable form. It had to be shown as it was at a given moment: only thus could an existential impression of reality be achieved. And to do this, the painters were forced to leave their ateliers, just as Renoir left the studios. One of Auguste Renoir's most urgent artistic goals was to integrate figure with landscape: '*Je me bats avec mes figures jusqu'à ce qu'elles ne fassent plus qu'un avec le paysage qui leur sert de fond.*' (I fight with my figures until they merge with the landscape.) In his painting the figures are *in* their landscape, and in Jean Renoir's

films of this period his figures are in their milieu. This was important for him not only visually, but dramatically and even politically. Characters cannot be seen as entities apart from their environment; they must be seen *in* that environment.

This intention was already clear in *Boudu*; it was to become more strongly defined in *Toni* (1934). Before going on to *Toni*, however, one must not forget *Madame Bovary* (1934). Long considered one of Renoir's failures, and unseeable now except in a cut version, it has much to recommend it. There is the use of the Normandy landscape, and the contrast between that beauty and Emma's despair; and there is the acting of Valentine Tessier. A remarkable actress, she was none the less an odd choice for Emma; yet, as we will see with Nora Gregor, Renoir often managed to achieve extraordinary effects by casting against the grain.

Thanks to the understanding of Pagnol (see article above), Renoir undertook the filming of *Toni* in 1934. Following Pagnol's example in *Angèle*, Renoir abandoned the studios and filmed exclusively on the locations where his story of a *crime passionnel* among emigrant farm-workers took place. Some of the characters were interpreted by actors, others by the local inhabitants of Martigues in the Rhône delta. But even the professionals, with one or two exceptions, belonged to the social classes and nationalities of their roles. Renoir's ambition was that the audience should imagine that an invisible camera had filmed various phases of a conflict without the human beings involved ever noticing!

As in *La Chienne*, this triangle drama is never melodramatic because the girl Josepha is not the sluttish señorita, nor is Toni the good faithful working-man; even Albert is not played as the menace. *Toni* is superior to *Angèle* because its exterior realism is complemented by Renoir's psychological, social and dramatic realism. Then, too, the fluidity of his camerawork, his brilliant compositions in depth, his feeling for figures in a landscape, are much more impressive than anything Pagnol's occasionally clumsy style could achieve. Furthermore, perhaps because his father was a painter, Renoir was never tempted by the merely pictorial. His compositions never seem contrived or consciously beautiful. Because he had an instinctive understanding of painting, he was never tempted by the 'artistic' two-dimensional composition. 'To me,' said Renoir, 'the cinema is photography, and what is interesting is to photograph reality.' Reality was something you start from: there were no short-cuts to beauty.

Toni, together with *Le Crime de Monsieur Lange*, made the following year (1935), was a turning-point in Renoir's career. From here on, until *La Règle du Jeu*, his work was to be marked by an interest in social and political problems. This is not unconnected with the climate of the time: the Popular Front was emerging, and artists all over Europe, confronted with the flourishing of Nazism in Germany, were growing more political; in 1935, the Saar had voted for reunion with Germany, Hitler had re-established conscription, and Mussolini was actively intervening in Ethiopia. 1935 was also the year of the First International Congress of Writers for the Defence of Culture.

Le Crime de Monsieur Lange is something of a freak in Renoir's *oeuvre*, for it owes much to its scriptwriter, Jacques Prévert, and it is the only film of Renoir's of which this can be said. All Prévert's qualities are present in the script and dialogue: his verbal invention, his bite, and his sense of humour. But whereas in the Carné–Prévert collaborations Prévert's faults were intensified by that side of Carné which is also pretentious, literary and over-romantic, in *Le Crime de Monsieur Lange* Renoir's sense of reality compensates for Prévert's artificiality. And it is the explosion of the two opposed talents that makes the film so fascinatingly unique. In some ways, it can also be seen as a sketch for *La Règle du Jeu*, for it is both a study of personal relationships within a broad social context, and a spontaneous comedy which slowly begins to reveal an incipiently tragic sense of life. In its number and variety of camera movements, combined with Renoir's continued experiments in depth-of-field camerawork, it is something of a dry run for *La Règle du Jeu*. Here the movements of the camera are occasionally clumsy, but the famous shot in which Lange kills Batala is worthy of the Walpurgis Night sequence in the later film. Extensively analysed by Bazin, this shot and its effectiveness can be summed up as a combination of two factors. First, the fact that after Lange runs out of the building to pursue Batala, the camera suddenly leaves him and then describes a reverse 360-degree pan round the courtyard which works both dramatically and plastically. Dramatically it reminds us in the few seconds while we pan round the courtyard of the reason Lange has to kill Batala by evoking everything that has happened previously in this very courtyard (the film was originally to be titled *Sur la Cour*). Secondly, this shot is also a development of Renoir's experiments, going back to *Nana*, in the use of off-screen space. This conjugation of concentric *mise en scène* and depth of focus, as Bazin pointed out, would lead four years later to the brilliant effects of *La Règle du Jeu*.

One must not overlook the political aspects of the film, naïve as they may seem today, for they were an important element, not only of this film but of those that were to follow. Here the sentiments are simply liberal, with the co-operative as the solution to the class struggle. But Renoir's choice of Jules Berry as the wicked capitalist was somewhat self-defeating: to be sure, Batala is an ignoble individual, but Renoir was unable or unwilling to make Berry totally subdue his odious yet telling charm. As we shall see later, Renoir was often led by his actors, his raw material, into changing his original notions of what a film was to be about.

His next film, however, was commissioned by the Communist party itself. *La Vie est à Nous* (1936) was re-issued in the mid-70s, and it proved to be interesting in its less political aspects—the love story about the two poor students and the auction in the country. Otherwise mere agit-prop, it was less truly political than the other film he was to make that year, *Partie de Campagne*. This may sound like provocation; *Partie de Campagne* is generally thought of as Renoir's most lyrical, most idyllic work—and it is: the final scenes with Sylvia Bataille and Georges Darnoux are unforgettably poignant. But actually the reasons for the tragedy are political and economic. Henriette and Henri are not separated by metaphysical considerations; nor is she a Capulet and he a Montague. They are separated only by class barriers—a marriage between the two is unthinkable, and one of the most effective notes is that it is as unthinkable for *her* as it is for him. Their personal tragedy is that he is a particularly sensitive and gentle member of his class, and that she is a particularly beautiful and sensitive member of hers. But the class divisions exist, and this fact in no way diminishes the emotional power of the film.

Never completed, the film was released only after the war, when Joseph Kosma added a haunting score: although it runs for only forty minutes, it is one of Renoir's most beautiful works, not only for the rendering of the Ile de France landscapes, but also for the performances. Renoir's next film is also distinguished by its acting, but his adaptation of Gorky's *Lower Depths* (*Les Bas Fonds*, 1936) is, I think, a minor work. Louis Jouvet, Jean Gabin and Jany Holt all give remarkable performances, but the combination of Gorky and Renoir was not particularly fruitful. Perhaps if Renoir had gone whole hog and transposed the setting from Russia to France the film would have gained in verisimilitude.

In 1937 Renoir made *La Grande Illusion* (*Grand Illusion*), his most popular film. Of late, critical opinion has tended to underrate the film in order to boost *La Règle du Jeu*. But the fact that the latter is superior does not seem an adequate reason for downgrading an extraordinary achievement. In many ways, it is Renoir's most effective film—and also his most accessible. Its plot line is carefully worked out, and its theme is appealing. Once more we have an example of how the choice of the actors determined the final form of the film. Originally, the script was about three soldiers—the officer (Pierre Fresnay) and two ordinary Frenchmen, one of whom was to be played by Jean Gabin. But when his producers suggested he use von Stroheim, whom he had admired for years, in the small part of the German commander, Renoir was reluctant to have him in such a minor capacity. So he decided to build up the role, and this lucky stroke strengthened his film by adding a new element. No longer was it simply about three different classes of Frenchmen in a German prisoner-of-war camp: it was also to be a commentary on those class loyalties which cut across national frontiers. Furthermore, the original script did not include the Jew Rosenthal (Dalio); the third man was just another Frenchman. But by adding the idea of creed to the ideas of class and of nationality, Renoir significantly enriched the film.

In spite of the elevated nature of the subject matter, Renoir none the less indulged his penchant for the grotesque and for the breathtaking mixture of genres—taking us suddenly from the ridiculous to the sublime. The scene in which the 'Marseillaise' is sung during a prison camp show to celebrate a French victory was made much more effective by Renoir's insane inspiration of having an *English* soldier, in drag, as the one who leads the singing. All the exteriors were shot on location (in Alsace, the closest he could get to Germany at the time), and even some of the interiors were done there. As usual, this attention to realistic detail paid off.

La Grande Illusion was welcomed by the Left at the time as a committed film, and indeed the sacrifice by the aristocrat De Boieldieu (Fresnay) to save Maréchal (Gabin) was clearly not only an act of comradeship, but also an admission that the aristocracy as a class was condemned. Renoir's next film, *La Marseillaise* (1938), was commissioned by the C.G.T.—the congress of trade unions. It was begun as a co-operative venture, and shares were sold for two francs apiece to anyone who wanted to support 'the film of the union of the French nation against a minority of exploiters, the film of the rights of man and of the citizen'. It didn't quite work out that way. The film takes a series of moments beginning with the storming of the Bastille and ending with the flight of the royal family, and the thread that is supposed to bind the whole thing together is the story of a few Marseillais who march to Paris—singing all the way. In the late 60s the film was re-released in a more complete version than had previously been available, and many acclaimed it as one of Renoir's masterpieces. I wish I could agree. To me, it is often clumsy; the attempts at rendering the soldiers from Marseilles don't ring true; and the best scenes are those with the aristocrats—which doesn't help the general thrust of the film at all. Pierre Renoir as Louis XVI is truly touching; this wouldn't matter if the 'people' were equally so, but they are not. Once again everyone, for Renoir, has his reasons, but this attitude is not particularly suited to a film which is supposed to be about the triumph of the people over their aristo-cratic oppressors. Some find this basic am-bivalence a reason for liking the film—it *is* characteristic of its author, but it doesn't really work here. And I can't help feeling that Renoir was not cut out for the historical fresco: unlike Gance, he is too sensible; nor does he have a sufficiently developed sense of rhetoric to be able to ride roughshod over history in the magnificently loony way of Gance's *Napoléon*. His historical sense and his political convictions were simply not sufficiently rigorous to bring off 'The Film of the Revolution'.

He was much more at ease in his next project, a modernization of Zola's novel *La Bête Humaine* (1938). It should not be thought that Renoir was not interested in his subject matter, although it is true that he de-clared at the time that he couldn't have cared less about Zola, and that all he wanted to do was to play with trains. But what he meant, I think, was only that he was not very interested in Zola's notions of heredity. *La Bête Humaine* is part of the Rougon–Macquart series of novels, and its hero Jacques Lantier (Gabin) is supposed to pay for his alcoholic forbears who have tainted his blood. Such a determin-istic idea could not possibly interest Renoir, and the weakest scenes in the film are those when Gabin has to explain his fears of his heredity to the pale and uninteresting Flore (Blanchette Brunoy). Curiously, the 'pure' girl is as unconvincing here as she was in Carné's *Le Jour se Lève*.

In Renoir's version the story would have been the same had Gabin had an irreproach-able heredity. What interested him was the triangular relationship between the engine-driver Lantier, the station-master (Fernand Ledoux) and his young, minxish wife Séverine (Simone Simon). And it is really a three-way triangle, for a kind of masculine solidarity prevents Lantier from killing Séverine's husband as he had planned; ultimately, it is the wife who disposes of him. The documentary-like scenes on the Paris–Havre run have been (deservedly) much praised, but the film also contains one of Renoir's most unforgettable sequences: the railwaymen's ball. Renoir has always had a fondness for popular songs, and he knows how to use them to great dramatic effect—as in *La Chienne*, for example, where a song ac-companies the murder of Lulu, and in *Le Crime de Monsieur Lange*, where Florelle's singing '*Au jour, le jour*' is an important ele-ment of the film. But here, in the skimpily decorated room (cf. Olmi's improvised dance-halls), the old song '*Pauvre petit coeur de Ninon*' serves as an ironic yet pathetic counterpoint to the murder of Séverine's husband.

At the time of its British release, Graham Greene noted that the film's 'documentary' material, although well done, had been done before, if not so well. 'What is most deft is the way in which Renoir works the depot and a man's job into every scene—conversations on platforms, in washrooms and canteens. Views from the station-master's window over the steaming metal waste: the short, sharp lust worked out in a wooden plate-layer's shed among shunted trucks under the steaming rain.' And the film, despite its unevenness, triumphs because of the way in which the characters and their milieu are integrated.

The following year, 1939, saw the extraor-dinary adventure of *La Règle du Jeu*. Seldom, if ever, has a film had such a tortured genesis, a more disastrous initial career, and such a triumphant redemption. It is Renoir's most complex film—nine principal characters—and has as subject matter nothing less than the whole of French society—or at least middle-class society. If France were destroyed tomorrow and nothing remained but this film, the whole country and its civilization could be reconstructed from it. And not just the France of 1939 either—Renoir was origin-ally inspired by de Musset's *Les Caprices de Marianne*, and he carefully reread Marivaux before writing the script. It is France itself which the film explores, and this gives it its incredible richness, taking it beyond a mere portrait of the 30s.

But no matter how important a film's themes may be, how revolutionary its tech-nique, it stands or falls on its material qualities, and that means the performances, the direction of the actors—who are after all what we *see* and *hear* in the film: its raw material. And what Renoir did in this film was amazing. It is no secret, for example, that he chose Nora Gregor for the part of Christine because he had fallen in love with her, and only as he began to work on the film

Nora Gregor and Jean Renoir in *La Règle du Jeu*.

did he realize her inadequacies: her physical awkwardness, her difficulties with the French language. So he modified not only her role, but the others: Mila Parély's role as the mistress of Christine's husband was built up in compensation. What he was doing in fact was bringing the documentary method into fiction film-making. The resulting film is almost as much a documentary on the actors as it is a story. And then there is the role played in the film by Renoir himself. It is as though he included himself through a kind of scrupulous honesty: he could not exempt himself from his portrait of society; he did not wish to stand outside. And Renoir/ Octave serves as the standard against which reality and fiction can be measured. As in a Pirandello play, the two become ultimately confused; that would seem to be Renoir's point, even if he did not grasp it fully at the time.

Renoir is one of the cinema's most intuitive authors. It even seemed to people at the time that he did not always 'know' what he was doing. When the film had its catastrophic première, he was amazed at the reaction. But even though he may not have been intellectually aware of his audacity, the film was no accident. Everything in his career led up to it, just as everything since is a development of elements that are already present, however unconsciously or inarticulately, in this watershed film. But I cannot agree with a critic like Burch who maintains that Renoir chose his subject matter 'precisely for the interesting formal problems it raised'. True, the form and even the texture of the film derive, as Burch maintains, *directly* from the subject matter. But Renoir was no Paul Valéry—he was not the kind of artist who, like Valéry, created his most moving poem through a desire to try out ten-syllable lines instead of the usual French twelve-syllable line. 'The mad chases back and forth, the continual comings and goings of all sorts that bring the depth of field and off-screen space into play in a very complex way and constitute the essential formal devices of *La Règle du Jeu*, are merely the literal extension of the mistaken identities of lovers and the mutual meddlings of servants and masters in each other's worlds which provide the film with its content,' says Burch, and one can only agree. But to suggest that Renoir chose his subject matter because of the formal problems it raised is seriously to mistake Renoir's nature as an artist.

This is in no way meant as a denigration of Renoir. It just means that he is a different kind of film-maker from, say, Bresson. *Les Dames du Bois de Boulogne* is a more conscious work of art: everything has been planned, nothing left to chance. It is a more perfect film, but one which hardly needs the viewer to complete it. *La Règle du Jeu* is an 'open' work, and one from which no one was excluded, either in the making of it or in the experiencing of it now.

In that sense, *La Règle du Jeu* was very much ahead of its time, as indeed it was in other ways—like the way in which it brought absurdity into art. More than a decade before Samuel Beckett, Eugène Ionesco and the Theatre of the Absurd, Renoir made a film that was neither comedy nor tragedy, melodrama nor social realism, but, instead, an 'insane' combination of them all. The central point of the film, of course, is the Walpurgis Night sequence, the after-dinner entertainment where everything comes to a head, and which is like a Marx Brothers film scripted by a Feydeau who had suddenly acquired a tragic sense. And in this sequence Renoir's *mise en scène* reaches its apogee—not only, as Bazin pointed out, is it the most total expression of depth of field used to present the ambiguities of reality, but it is also one of the most astonishing combinations of lengthy shots to create that effect of vertiginous simultaneity which reinforces the theme of the film. The whole sequence is done, incredibly, in about fifty shots, and those fifty shots are, I think, more exciting, more meaningful, more 'cinematic' even than any number of Odessa Steps. And this, I believe, is because it was put together intuitively, because Renoir did *not* choose his subject matter because it presented 'interesting formal problems'. On the contrary, *La Règle du Jeu* is one of those rare examples of a film where content and form are truly co-existent. Writing about the film in 1954, Renoir said that while working on the script for the film, he was 'inspired with the notion of taking off, of getting completely away from naturalism'. Well, he did and he didn't. 'The film is an exact description of the bourgeoisie of our time,' said Renoir in 1938. Well, it is and it

isn't. What makes this film Renoir's masterpiece is that he was able to bring together in
one film both sides of his nature—both *La
Chienne* and *Boudu*, let's say—and because
the subject matter was such a total representation of himself, he was also able to find the
forms which would perfectly express the
content.

Ultimately, every great work of art is an
'exact description' not of the bourgeoisie or
of the working class, but of its creator, and
here Renoir himself stood at the crossroads
of history. He was not only Octave, but also
La Chesnaye and Jurieux, Christine and
Geneviève, Marceau and Schumacher; he
was also an example of the very society he
was condemning. He was weak, vacillating,
frivolous and opportunist, and therefore his
portrait was both faithful and profound.
Whatever the virtues of the films that were to
follow, it was too much to expect that they
could ever equal this one: how often can an
artist look steadily into the abyss and tell us
what he has seen?

**Seeing *Nana* again recently, I realized that I
was wrong about Hessling's performance:
she is so eccentrically extraordinary that the
question of whether she is good or bad is
immaterial. And the film, with all its
'coldness', looks even better today than it did
ten years ago. For the record, the films of
Renoir not discussed in my piece are: *Charleston* (1927); *Marquitta* (1927): *Tire au
Flanc*, a military farce (1928); *La Petite Marchande d'Allumettes* (1928); *Le Tournoi*
(1929); *Le Bled* (1929); *On Purge Bébé*, a film
of Feydeau's farce and Renoir's first sound
film (1931); and *Chotard et Cie* (1933), a
charming if minor work. For bibliographical information, see the next article,
Jean Renoir from 1939.**

JEAN RENOIR: from 1939

Tom Milne

On 7 July 1939, *La Règle du Jeu* (*Rules of the
Game*) opened in Paris. That summer, while
his masterpiece quietly agonized—derided by
both critics and public, cut from 113 minutes
down to 90, and finally banned as 'demor-
alizing'—Jean Renoir was in Rome working
on the script of a new film, *La Tosca*, to be
made for the Italian company Scalera Film.
When war broke out on 3 September, Renoir

abandoned the project, but was persuaded by
the French Ministry of Foreign Affairs to
return to Rome to undertake the film in the
interests of national propaganda. Filming
had only just begun when Italy entered the
war on 10 June 1940. Again Renoir left
Rome. By February 1941 he was in America,
and *La Tosca* had been completed by his assistant, Carl Koch.

It has been suggested that Renoir turned
to *La Tosca* as a safe bet after the *La Règle du
Jeu* fiasco. Certainly he seems to have been
thoroughly demoralized by the whole affair.
He allowed the excision of the scenes which
seemed to arouse the loudest jeers, only to
find that at the next screening audiences
jeered equally loudly at something else; he
seemed surprised at the passions aroused in a
society poised on the brink of disaster by a
film which was, after all, nothing else than a
mocking tribute to its decadence; and when
asked by René Clair after the first public
screening exactly what he had had in mind,
he could only say, 'I don't know, I don't
know any more.' *La Tosca*, therefore, may
have seemed a good idea not only because of
its built-in commercial possibilities, but
because it afforded an opportunity to efface
the memory of his *danse macabre* on the grave
of a dying society by paying magniloquent
tribute to the indomitability of the human
spirit in its proud fight for liberty. But there
is—or so it seems in retrospect—another
reason why Renoir should have chosen to
turn to opera.

The key to Renoir's work has always been
the tension between reality and fantasy, between life and the theatre. It is a subject to
which he has returned again and again,
sometimes directly and sometimes indirectly,
and which has become part of the Renoir
myth since *La Carrozza d'oro* (*The Golden
Coach*), which he made in 1952, turned
reality and fantasy inside out in a dazzling
display of illusionism to pose the question,
'Where does the theatre end and life begin?'
It seemed perfectly natural and logical, therefore, when he subsequently chose to explore
the legend of show business within an
enchanted evocation of the Paris of the
Moulin Rouge and the café-concerts in
French Cancan (1955); to turn the history of
General Boulanger's political intrigues into a
prancing ballet of love amid the military

manoeuvres and popular carnivals of Paris in the 1880s (*Eléna et les Hommes* [U.S.: *Paris Does Strange Things*, 1956]); to make an airy fairytale out of the theme of artificial insemination by setting it down in the ethereally sunny Provençal countryside of the Impressionists (*Le Déjeuner sur l'Herbe* [U.K.: *Lunch on the Grass*; U.S.: *Picnic on the Grass*, 1959]); or to experiment with multiple-camera television techniques in order to pay homage to one of his beloved actors by capturing a theatrical performance on film as richly and as three-dimensionally as possible (*Le Testament du Docteur Cordelier* [U.K.: *Experiment in Evil*, 1959, first shown 1961]).

However, there is also in these later films a note of serenity and resignation, of nostalgia for worlds lost but fondly preserved in memory, which is perhaps most openly and unequivocally expressed in *The River*. Made between 1949 and 1950 in India, *The River* (1951) was the film with which Renoir returned to the international scene after his war years in America when his films were either not seen or ignored in Europe; and with its tranquil vision of life as a river flowing on, barely disturbed by the ripples sent out by the human business of being born, growing up, falling in love and dying, it seemed to represent a complete break with the pre-war Renoir of *La Chienne* (1931), *Le Crime de Monsieur Lange* (1936), *La Grande Illusion* (1937) and *La Règle du Jeu*. Complete enough, at least, for most of Renoir's pre-war admirers to lament the passing of his talent, and for the publication of at least one book (*Jean Renoir*, edited by Bernard Chardère, Lyon, 1962) devoted to the proposition that a great director had degenerated, *circa* 1939, into an ageing babbler.

Actually, the proposition seems to be based not only on a misunderstanding of the later films, but on a misreading of the earlier ones as the work of a committed social critic. Renoir may have fathered neo-realism with *Toni* (1935), paid tribute to the Popular Front in *La Vie est à Nous* (1936), attacked war in *La Grande Illusion* and dissected social decadence in *La Règle du Jeu*; but underneath these films there lies a deeper, more personal note, more anarchic than social, which could still find regret for the comradeship of military life, regret for the elegance of the old aristocracy, regret even for the individual eccentricity that had to be suppressed for the common good. *Le Crime de Monsieur Lange* may be a bitter attack on industrial chicanery and profiteering, but what one carries away from the film is not so much Lange's dream of a co-operative publishing house, as his dream of the wild, fancy-free existence of Arizona Jim, the fictional hero whose adventures will bring co-operative comfort to all the ex-employees of the wicked publisher Monsieur Batala. If there is one moment in all Renoir's films from the 30s which might be said to contain the essence of Renoir, it is that exhilarating 360-degree pan which expresses the sense of liberation experienced by the tramp in *Boudu Sauvé des Eaux* (1932) when he finally escapes from civilization and finds himself penniless but free and on the open road. Twenty-two years later it is matched exactly—with the quiescence brought by age and experience—by the shot of Danglard, the ageing impresario of *French Cancan*, sitting quietly in the wings listening to the applause which means that his protégée has become a star and that he is now free to find a new protégée, to create a new star: to live, in other words, as his fancy and his instinct for freedom dictate.

Certainly Renoir changed. The impatient, crusading young film-maker became the serene and watchful artist of maturity, with some loss of attack perhaps, but an immense gain in wisdom. The change is partly in the natural order of things, perfectly expressed towards the end of his life by Renoir's own father, the painter Auguste: 'When you are young, you think everything is going to slip through your fingers. You run, and you miss the train. As you grow older, you learn that you have time, and that you can catch the next train. That doesn't mean that you should go to sleep. It is simply a question of being alert and not getting nervous.' Partly, though, it is the result of a subtle shift in his attitude to reality.

'To make films,' Renoir once said, 'may be one good way to discover bits of reality. I believe that one of the most important functions of the film-maker is the destruction of cliché. We are surrounded by cliché. We believe that life is what we are told. Not at all. Life is something very different. Life is a combination of what does exist and what you have in mind: this combination may bring a work of art, may bring one second of happiness, one thing being as important as the other.' This definition of the art of the film-maker applies equally well to both early and late Renoir—provided one makes the crucial readjustment of priorities between mind and matter.

In the 30s, Renoir was the exception who proved the rule of studio sets in French film-making. Almost invariably he preferred to work in natural surroundings wherever possible, setting what he had in mind—his stories and characters—against what exists. Without going so far as to suggest that Renoir's early subjects, in particular such social commitments as *La Vie est à Nous* and *La Marseillaise* (1938), were what he had been told (i.e., what was in the air amid the social solidarity of the Popular Front days), one can define the change in Renoir within his own terms. In the later films, one finds no trace of what he has been told: everything is drawn from his own experience. Furthermore, what exists is now his themes and characters, still richly and vividly individual, but drawn from—to use Wordsworth's phrase —the types and symbols of Eternity. They are, in other words, as much the stuff of archetypal experience as the characters of myth and fairytale. And what Renoir has in mind is now his settings, which become places of imagination as he tends more and more to re-create the past, using the studio instead of natural locations.

A good example is *French Cancan*, which takes place in an affectionately reconstructed Paris of the 1890s, teeming with rococo interiors, *bals musettes* and quaint little popular squares. The theme of the film is the legendary choice facing a young dancer on the brink of stardom: between a great love and a great career. As a matter of fact Nini, the can-can dancer, is faced in the best fairytale tradition with three choices of lover in addition to the stage: with security in the person of the baker's boy who wants to marry her, with passion in the impresario Danglard, and with romance in the adoring prince of a distant tiny kingdom. The first she disposes of in the pragmatic surroundings of the baker's shop; the second, equally pragmatically, in the wings of the theatre where she first hears the roar of the crowd; but the third, in a scene frequently misunderstood, she renounces, in a

little moonlit square as ethereally unreal as the Prince himself, his mournful declarations of undying love, or his earthly paradise of a kingdom which trades exclusively in diamonds and roses. As she sits with him on the tiny patch of studio grass, bathed in rosy moonlight from a cyclorama sky and watched over by a single unlikely tree, the film suddenly takes on an air of myth and magic, as though the legend of Cupid and Psyche were reborn again.

Circumstances may have had a good deal to do with this mutation in Renoir. At forty-six, he was no longer a young man when he arrived in America, and his attack was bound to have its edges smoothed sooner or later by age and experience. Moreover, in Hollywood he came up against a way of film-making which could see no point in going on location when everything could be done in the studio more conveniently and often more cheaply; and also against a determined insistence that, as a foreigner, he would be much more at home with foreign than with home-grown subjects. Twice during his Hollywood period Renoir managed to overcome both objections at once to make *Swamp Water* (1941) and *The Southerner* (1945), American subjects shot largely on location. Both films reveal a good deal of the old Renoir bite in the rough, warm humanity of their themes—the fight to clear an innocent man accused of murder in *Swamp Water*, and the fight against the land, the elements and human injustice in *The Southerner*—and more particularly in their response to landscapes in the lovely, mysterious swamplands of Georgia and the dry, cruel cottonfields of California (standing in for Texas). *The Southerner* was the only one of Renoir's American films to be well received critically when it was first released. Yet oddly enough it is not these semi-documentaries which stay in the mind as the most interesting work he did in America, so much as the totally unrealistic, studio-bound and often flawed work he did in *This Land Is Mine* (1943), *The Woman on the Beach* (1947) and, especially, *The Diary of a Chambermaid* (1946).

The Diary of a Chambermaid is a savage, quaintly fantastical adaptation of Octave Mirbeau's novel, translating it into a never-never France whose truth is not realistic but poetic. One does not, as in *La Règle du Jeu*, instantly recognize the social, historical and geographical accuracy of this country château whose aristocratic owners are locked in a grim *danse macabre* with themselves, their servants and their heritage. Yet *The Diary of a Chambermaid* is in effect *La Règle du Jeu* metamorphosed into the world of the imagination, having basically the same relationships, the same preoccupations, the same vision of social history, but seen this time through the painter's eye rather than the photographer's. In theory, the village sets are quaint France *à la* Hollywood. In practice, beautifully designed, lit and photographed by Eugene Lourié as art director and Lucien Andriot as cameraman, they have an impressionistic enchantment, nowhere more evident than in the scene where Celestine, in white dress and parasol, trysts with the tubercular Georges under the great oak in the middle of the village square. The scenes in the Lanlaire garden, too, have the same dreamy, sunlit beauty, so that one feels real regret when the Captain slashes furiously at the flowers or hurls stones into the neatly ranged rows of greenhouses. Even the family silver, eyed covetously by the evil butler as he unlocks the vaults where it lies in glittering, useless heaps, literally begging to be taken out and put into circulation, has a spellbinding quality about it. *The Diary of a Chambermaid* and *La Règle du Jeu* may be worlds apart in tone and style, separated by the yawning gulf between fantasy and reality, yet in their common attack on the inhibitions and degradations forced on humanity by a corrupt and meaningless social structure, the two films share an element of enchantment in which remembrance of things past illuminates the hope for a better world to come.

One should not forget that, for all its realism and social commitment, *La Règle du Jeu*, with its origins in the stylized comedies of manners of Marivaux and de Musset, is as highly formalized as a *commedia dell'arte* pantomime. Nor should one forget that it enshrines—undercutting its bitter social criticism—a strong element of nostalgia for the leisurely, aristocratic world it puts under the microscope. As Renoir commented years later: 'People thought that in writing *La Règle du Jeu* I was criticizing society, but not at all. I wish I could live in such a society— that would be wonderful ... What pushed me to make *La Règle du Jeu* was an ambition to treat a subject which would allow me to use the exterior forms of a French comedy of the eighteenth century. I was also a little bit influenced by Musset, but my ambition was to find again a certain elegance, a certain grace, a certain rhythm which is typical of the eighteenth century, French or English.'

It is this certain elegance, this grace, that one finds at the root of all Renoir's post-war films; and the first real intimation of its coming ascendancy over the old rough-and-ready social commitment comes in the opening sequence of *La Tosca*, which was all that Renoir actually shot of the film. As a huge gateway swings open and two horsemen gallop out to disappear into the night, the camera retires into the city, circling gracefully round a monument to pick the riders up as they proceed through the deserted streets, hovering by a fountain as they emerge into a square, then tracking gently along a statue-lined avenue as they arrive at Scarpia's palace. Here, as throughout the film, the baroque statuary of Rome is inextricably linked to the emotions of the film, working in much the same way as in Visconti's *Senso* to underline the authenticity, as well as the operatic extravagance, of the proud fight for liberty and the star-crossed love of Tosca and Cavaradossi which both end in execution at dawn.

After these opening shots, the temperature drops slightly as Carl Koch takes over; but the film has a unity of conception which suggests that Koch followed Renoir's treatment very closely. Human beings offset by architecture: the stone archways and lowering corridors of the castle where political prisoners await their sentence; the crenellated turrets and battlements of the roof glistening in the early morning mist where executions take place against a vast panorama of Rome; the imposing façade and lustrous interiors of the palace where Scarpia has his audience with the Queen, and where Tosca is seen hemmed in by the stripes of the carpet stretching along an endless corridor; the glittering church where Angelotti finds betrayal as well as shelter; the melancholy Gothic ruin which watches over Cavaradossi's country retreat. Emotions flutter vainly against immovable stone, punctuated by the endless, precise manoeuvrings of the firing-squad.

Paulette Goddard, Judith Anderson, Francis Lederer, and Irene Ryan in *Diary of a Chambermaid*: 'Even the family silver has a spellbinding quality.'

That Renoir's conception for the film was an entirely new departure for him is suggested not only by the opening sequence, but by the bravura crane shot which accompanies the aria '*Recondita armonia*' (sung off-screen) in the church sequence. Circling the church from the scaffolding where Cavaradossi is painting Angelotti's sister, it moves down to frame her kneeling in front of the chapel where her brother is hiding, then rises vertically once again to Cavaradossi watching from the scaffolding. Here the camera movement, operatic in itself, gathers up the three characters and their emotions into a perfect equivalent of the baroque lines of the church.

The Renoir of the 30s had always been considered the untutored genius of the French cinema. Of course he was nothing of the sort. Renoir could deploy brilliant technical invention as well as anybody, and better than most: the daringly simple vertical lift of the camera which discovers the murder of Lulu in *La Chienne*, for instance; or in *Le Crime de Monsieur Lange*, the way the camera watches from the courtyard as Lange leaves his office and descends the stairs, then suddenly turns its back on him to watch Batala, superbly confident that Lange must quickly reappear in frame to kill him; or the brilliant use of deep focus in both *Boudu Sauvé des Eaux* and *Madame Bovary* (1934) to evoke the cosy bourgeois comforts which stifle both Boudu and Emma Bovary. But in general during the 30s Renoir never bothered to adhere to formal structures; he preferred to improvise, to seize life on the wing, to trust to the rich, dense texture of actuality with which he could always clothe his actors. With *La Tosca*, however, the anarchic, *commedia dell'arte* freedom of action began to give way to formal control; and the path led through the operatic grandeurs of the baroque, where extravagance is reduced to order by firmness of line, to *The River*, in which Renoir encountered for the first time the one element required to complete his new serene, joyous and classically pure vision: colour. There followed the three golden master-pieces of the latter half of his career: *La Carrozza d'Oro, French Cancan* and *Eléna et les Hommes.*

Although not so designed, these three films in effect form a trilogy whose subject is love. In each of them, a woman is faced by a choice (broadly speaking, since there are infinite sub-divisions and variations) between the theatre and life; in each of them the setting is a historically imagined past, either eight-eenth-century Peru or France at the end of the nineteenth century; and in each of them colour is used to heighten the sense of an intense personal vision. Visually, in their rich, serene sensuousness, they are perfectly described by the words used by Renoir of his father (in *Renoir, My Father*): 'Renoir had succeeded in fulfilling the dreams of his whole life: "to create riches with modest means". From his palette, simplified to the last degree, and from the minute "drop-pings" of colour lost on its surface, issued a splendour of dazzling golds and purples, the glow of flesh filled with young and healthy blood, the magic of all-conquering light, and, towering above all these material elements, the serenity of a man approaching supreme knowledge. He now dominated Nature, which all his life he had served as a worship-per. In return she had finally taught him to see beyond surface appearances and, like her-self, to create a world out of almost nothing.'

Seeing beyond surface appearances, Jean Renoir creates in these three films a world of perfect harmony. Not our world as it is, but as it might be; not exactly an Eden, but a world reduced to its essentials. 'Birth, and copulation, and death/That's all the facts when you come to brass tacks,' says T. S. Eliot's *Sweeney Agonistes*; or, as Renoir would probably say, without euphemism but also without the note of puritan disgust, 'birth, and love, and death'. Beside these eternal facts of life, everything else is mere temporal disorder, and such sociological realities as war, poverty and crime play no part in his scheme of things. War rumbles intermittently through *Eléna et les Hommes*, but the blood is shed off-screen and what we see and hear are the parades and the popular

songs and the triumphal return of the plumed victor. Its side effects, too, are shown off-screen as the popular hero capitalizes on his military glory to further his political am-bitions; but on-screen, as one of the charac-ters neatly observes at the end, 'Dictatorship has no chance in a country where affairs of the heart are so important.'

This preoccupation with love in its com-monest definition—it's love that makes the world go round—could so easily be an im-possibly sentimental conception within an art form like the cinema which, even when it delves into fantasy, remains at least grounded in objective reality. In fact, it isn't sentimen-tal at all, because Renoir, echoing Shake-speare's 'All the world's a stage/And all the men and women merely players,' is fully aware that he is dealing with illusion. He is not creating art out of life, but life out of art.

Camilla (Anna Magnani), the actress her-oine of *La Carrozza d'Oro*, is faced with three choices. She can choose fidelity and domesticity with the soldier who longs for the simple life among the Peruvian Indians; she can choose passion with the fiery matador who is the darling of the crowds; or she can choose wealth and position with the Viceroy. Nini (Françoise Arnoul), the little dancer of *French Cancan*, is faced with an exactly similar choice between her baker's boy, her impresario and her prince. Camilla favours the Viceroy, who has placed himself entirely in her hands by making her a gift of the sym-bol of his power, the golden coach; Nini favours the impresario who has devoted his heart and soul to her creation. Ultimately, however, both women avoid the choice by choosing the theatre, where they will shine as stars. Yet in making this choice, Camilla and Nini affirm rather than deny the power of their loves.

For in each case the film ends with a mag-nificent *coup de théâtre*: *La Carrozza d'Oro* with the scene in which Camilla interrupts the ceremony where the Viceroy is to be deposed by driving up in the coach to an-nounce that she has presented it to the Church; *French Cancan* with the scene where Nini, after locking herself in her dress-ing-room and refusing to go on because Danglard insists that his need of her, and her need of him, will be over as soon as she becomes a star, finally erupts on to the stage

Anna Magnani in *The Golden Coach*: 'When Camilla renounces her desire by renouncing the golden coach, she is last seen taking her bow on stage, while among the crowd applauding her gesture are her three lovers.

at the centre of the cancan. Throughout each film, the golden coach or the cancan has gradually assumed autonomous existence as a symbol of an unattainable desire. When Camilla renounces her desire by renouncing the golden coach, she is last seen taking her bow on stage, while among the crowd applauding her gesture are her three lovers. When Nini renounces *her* desire by renouncing Danglard, she too is last seen on stage, while among the crowd applauding are her lovers. By their choices, Renoir suggests, Camilla and Nini have reconciled love and the theatre, have found love in the theatre, or maybe the theatre in love.

Actually, the equation is not so neatly balanced as I have suggested. Absent from Nini's final triumph is the Prince. Although Renoir fills the mathematical gap by producing a third lover (not Nini's but her rival's: the braggadocio Captain in love with the ageing dancer who would have taken Nini's

place had she failed to emerge from her dressing-room), and by providing each of the women with an adoring companion for the fadeout, one still feels that a loose end has been left dangling in the film's schema. The Prince remains a problem which will only be solved in *Eléna et les Hommes*, perhaps Renoir's most brilliant if not most perfect film (it was beset, among other things, by language difficulties with the international cast).

The Prince, with his unselfish devotion and undying love, his kingdom of diamonds and roses, his despairing attempt to kill himself rather than face life without Nini, and above all his touching little *mise en scène* of a night out with her to provide himself with some artificial memories, is exactly like the mysterious and mournful young heroes of Anouilh's *Pièces Roses* (or possibly *Noires*). Impossibly pure, impossibly sincere, impossibly—in a word—theatrical. Plot considerations apart, he could hardly be present in the flesh at Nini's theatrical triumph since he *is* the theatre. In *Eléna et les Hommes*, Renoir solves this problem by having two people, neither of them actors but both of them theatrical, act out a love affair which the theatre then shows them to be real.

Eléna et les Hommes might well be described as a joyous operetta of love's surprises, centering on the efforts of an impoverished Polish princess (Ingrid Bergman) to find herself a rich husband, and set in a Paris of ballad singers, military manoeuvres and popular street carnivals, with a country château where masters and servants frenziedly pursue their affairs in a frothy echo of *La Règle du Jeu*. Like Camilla and Nini, the Princess finds herself faced by three choices: the elderly but wealthy boot magnate, Martin Michaud; General Rollan, the glorious victor of war eager to further his political ambitions; and the latter's flamboyant but uncommitted friend, Henri de Chevincourt. Unlike Camilla and Nini, however, Eléna has a certain control over destiny. By the gift of her favourite flower, a marguerite, she jokingly insists that she can inspire men to fame and fortune; and she does, first a young composer, and then General Rollan, who leaps instantly to popular acclaim, from thence to power as Minister of War, and finally hovers on the brink of the *coup d'état* which will establish him as military dictator, while Eléna ponders her creation and wonders whether to accompany him on the final leap to fame. Dictatorship, of course, 'has no chance in a country where affairs of the heart are so important'; and Eléna finally discovers true love and Henri de Chevincourt, leaving the General to disappear alone into the night and find—one feels assured—obscurity.

Characteristically, Renoir made no great claims for the film. 'For a long time I had been dying to make something gay with Ingrid Bergman,' he explained in an interview, 'I wanted to see her laughing and smiling on the screen.' Commenting on the commercial and critical failure of the film, however, he added, 'I do not think the modern world is ready to hold intimate conversations with Venus.' For this, under the surface of gay and ribald *marivaudage*, is the subject of the film: the descent of Venus among men.

Eléna, with her enchanting smile and her mysterious marguerite, is the goddess incarnate. Immortal herself, she chooses General Rollan as the object of her inspiration, intending to render him immortal as the saviour of his country. But she has reckoned without Henri, who undermines the General's panache with his quiet devotion. In the last sequence, all three are besieged in a brothel from which Rollan must escape undetected if he is to be able to pull off his *coup d'état*. Henri suggests a way: he, Henri, wearing the General's uniform, will make love to Eléna in the window so that the watching populace will applaud their hero's amours while he, the General, makes his escape. The General consents, and leaves unnoticed in Henri's clothes with Eléna promising to follow. But as Eléna and Henri carry out the masquerade and kiss—framed as though by a proscenium arch in the window—Eléna is at last forced to accept the inevitable and acknowledge Henri's love. Eléna may be the goddess, the inspiration of love, but once again it is art which reveals the truth to the creator. Jean-Luc Godard summed up the film perfectly in a few typically cryptic yet perceptive lines: 'Through the most splendid of paradoxes, in fact, in *Eléna* the immortals seek to die. To be sure of living, one must be sure of loving; and to be sure of loving, one must be sure of dying. This is what Eléna discovers in the arms of her men . . .' It is also, one might add, what Renoir discovered in his career as a film-maker and enshrined in this trio of films flooded with intimations of mortality and recollections in tranquillity.

Renoir never again quite reached these Olympian peaks. After *Eléna et les Hommes*, he became interested in television techniques, and both *Le Testament du Docteur Cordelier* and *Le Déjeuner sur l'Herbe* experimented with the use of several cameras shooting simultaneously from different angles. In theory, the technique is perfectly suited to Renoir's temperament, since it allows him to give his actors three-dimensional coverage while leaving them greater freedom. In practice, however, it has proved a retrogressive step, since the graceful formality of his trilogy gives way to a certain ragged dishevelment. If several cameras are covering a single shot from all angles, there is less need to worry beforehand how it will look, how it will splice together with the rest of the film, how it will affect the overall rhythm.

Le Déjeuner sur l'Herbe is particularly attractive in that it is Renoir's most direct homage to his father, a hymn to nature shot partly on location on Auguste Renoir's former estate, Les Collettes. In scenes deliberately evocative of the Impressionists—a girl bathing in a pool, love-making under the trees, lunch on the grass—Jean Renoir dazzles one as completely as the Impressionists did with the tints of flesh, air, foliage and water. The vision, unfortunately, is too authentic. The landscape of the film is so much of the present—or of the past, depending on how one looks at it—that the creatures of the future he has imagined for it seem like fish out of water. Reversing the procedure used in his last three films, Renoir goes back to his 30s' approach: what exists here is the setting, and what he has in mind are the characters. And unlike the timeless characters in the trilogy, the professor of artificial insemination and his girl-guide leader are merely straw dummies representing an unacceptable, inhuman future, designed to prove that the eternal simplicities of nature (represented by the farmer's daughter played by Catherine Rouvel) still stand for life.

Le Testament du Docteur Cordelier, on the other hand, is a reworking of R. L. Stevenson's Jekyll and Hyde theme, which obviously attracted Renoir for two reasons. One was the chance to revisit the nihilistic tramp of *Boudu Sauvé des Eaux* and explore a darker facet of the joyous anarchy and freedom which come when the bonds of conventional morality are cast aside. The other was the chance to aid and abet a great actor (Jean-Louis Barrault) in a dual role which would give full scope to his talents as actor and mime. The focal point is therefore the moment when silver-haired, dignified Dr Cordelier turns into the shaggy, bestial Monsieur Opale, and rushes into the streets to explore his freedom, darting in on his victims for sudden, vicious attacks and insolently twirling his cane like a drum-majorette as he melts away in search of new targets for his sadism. Prancing, twitching, moving with the animal grace of a dancer, Barrault is magnificent, creating an extraordinary, chimerical figure whose intrusion into real Paris streets lends them a bizarre, unsettling air of menace. Yet at the same

time the technique of the film is its limitation. Certain scenes run on longer than planned because Barrault was enjoying inventing and Renoir was enjoying his invention; others, like the one where Opale tries to snatch a baby from its mother's arms, were improvised before real passers-by who were unaware of the camera. The result is a curious lack of balance in which the theme of the film is lost and one begins ultimately to feel Barrault's performance as an exercise in technique rather than as a characterization.

At first sight, Renoir's last two films seem both lightweight and recapitulatory, with *Le Caporal Epinglé* (U.K.: *The Vanishing Corporal*; U.S.: *The Elusive Corporal*, 1962) revisiting the subject of *La Grande Illusion* twenty-three years after, and *Le Petit Théâtre de Jean Renoir* (*The Little Theatre of Jean Renoir*, 1969) serving almost literally as a toy theatre souvenir packed with themes and characters borrowed from earlier films ranging through the silent *La Petite Marchande d'Allumettes* (1928) down to *Le Déjeuner sur l'Herbe*. In retrospect, however, they loom much larger, with *Le Petit Théâtre* in particular acquiring a testamentary quality—first adumbrated more tentatively in *Le Caporal Epinglé*—which confirms the Olympian intimations so prophetically detected by Godard in his review of *Eléna et les Hommes*.

Although *Le Caporal Epinglé* draws heavily on *La Grande Illusion* for its chronicle of a prisoner-of-war's determined efforts to escape from a German camp—even to the point of repeating the idyll with a German girl and the fears that the comradeship of the camp will not survive outside it—there is a radical difference between the two films. Where the Renoir of the 30s was preoccupied by the national and international social and cultural strata that aligned the prisoners and guards over and above their arbitrary present status as captives and captors, *Le Caporal Epinglé* is concerned more exclusively with the idea of escape, so that the film's motive force is that instinct for freedom which is never far from any Renoir film and which is here illuminated with a new clarity and purity. Until his friend Ballochet dies, virtually committing suicide in acknowledgement of his own weakness and cowardice, the Corporal's persistent attempts to escape are no more than a game of hide-and-seek, a round of happy improvisations designed to demonstrate his daring and doomed to failure because they spring from no inner need. But after Ballochet's quixotic gesture of affirmation in choosing to die to preserve the purity of his friendship, a subtle change comes over the Corporal; he is touched by the hand of grace, and like Fontaine in Bresson's *Un Condamné à Mort*, he wins the right to his freedom. Movingly, and with unequivocal simplicity, Renoir here resumes the message that is the legacy of his work: 'To be sure of living, one must be sure of loving; and to be sure of loving, one must be sure of dying.'

By the time he came to make *Le Petit Théâtre de Jean Renoir* in 1969, Renoir must have been more than half aware that this would be his last film, and it is quite consciously designed as a farewell to the cinema. Its three episodes take us chronologically through the main stages in his career, with *Le Dernier Réveillon* harking back to the naïve, fairytale artificiality and studio trickwork of his early silents, *La Cireuse Eléctrique* echoing the social concerns of the 30s, and *Le Roi d'Yvetot* slipping into the ideal world that never was of films like *French Cancan* and *Eléna et les Hommes*. The key to the film, however, is the little interlude placed as a homage to *La Belle Epoque* between the second and third episodes, and in which Jeanne Moreau, poised motionless in an exquisite black and yellow gown against a painted garden backcloth, sings 'Quand l'Amour meurt' (the song Dietrich sang in top hat and tails in *Morocco*). Hands and eyes hesitant and anxious, her slightly off-key rendition emblazoning the trembling heartache of the words, she conveys an ineffable sense of sadness and regret. With each episode celebrating the inescapable presence of old age and death, the song radiates a poignancy in which it is hard not to hear Renoir himself speaking: '*Lorsque tout est fini/Quand se meurt votre beau rêve/Pourquoi pleurer les jours enfuis?*' Typically for Renoir, however, the song he has chosen not only mourns the past but affirms the folly of regretting the loss of something that can never be recaptured.

And the exhilaration of *Le Petit Théâtre* is that, hand in hand with his intimations of death, Renoir offers his certainty of living and loving. Menaced with death by cold and

hunger, the two old tramps of *Le Dernier Réveillon* find freedom in their dream of love; society in *La Cireuse Electrique* may be being driven to madness and destruction by the encroachment of the machine, but children are still born, grow up and fall in love; and in *Le Roi d'Yvetot* above all, perfect love and friendship can still exist in the world that it is the artist's prerogative to create. *Le Petit Théâtre*, ultimately, is Renoir's statement of belief in the truth and the permanence of the vision he had in mind in his trio of masterpieces, *La Carrozza d'Oro*, *French Cancan* and *Eléna et les Hommes*.

There are two autobiographical works by Renoir, *Renoir, My Father* (1962) and *My Life and My Films* (1974). The best study of Renoir, and one of the best critical books on the cinema, is, I think, André Bazin's *Jean Renoir* (1973). Left unfinished at his untimely death, it was edited posthumously by François Truffaut. See also Leo Braudy's *Jean Renoir* (1972), Raymond Durgnat's *Jean Renoir* (1975) and Penelope Gilliatt's *Jean Renoir: Essays, Conversations, Reviews* (1975). Jean Renoir died in 1979.

ALAIN RESNAIS

Richard Roud

Of all the new French film-makers of the last twenty years, Resnais and Truffaut seem to have found the most universal acceptance. Right from the start, Alain Resnais (born 1922) has had his admirers, and there is a lack of controversy, a touching unanimity, about attitudes to his work. At the same time, much of what has been written about him is irrelevant. This article wishes to make several points. One is that defined by André Malraux, that art feeds upon itself just as much as it feeds on reality. And Alain Resnais has in fact stated a similar belief. His collaborator Robbe-Grillet said, in a published interview: 'I think that it is reality that directly nourishes the artist; if we are fascinated by art, it is only because we find there the things we already wanted to do solely under the impulsion of reality.' But Resnais agrees with Malraux: 'I think the desire to participate in the world of art exists very strongly.' Of course, it is not a question of direct imitation. I remember talking with Resnais about

Georges Franju's remake of Feuillade's *Judex*, and we both agreed that it proved you couldn't do the same thing again—you had to approach it from a different angle. Any slavish attempt to 'do' a Feuillade, said Resnais, was bound to result in failure.

The second point is that Resnais belongs to that first generation of film-makers brought up in the shadow of the Cinémathèque Française, the first generation for whom film history (the whole body of films since the beginning of the century) has meant something, has been important in their development. It is now no longer possible, as it was in the 20s and 30s, for a film-maker to start from scratch. The cinema has a past, and this has to be taken into account. Resnais is of the generation brought up on seeing films (unlike, say, Lang, Griffith, Murnau, etc.).

Thirdly, he has never worked alone, in a vacuum. The 'New Wave' movement may not have been as strong or as unified as we once thought, but Resnais has always been part of a small group of friends, the Left Bank Group, who have pursued common goals, although along different paths. The Left Bank refers, as I mentioned in the entry on Chris Marker, to the left bank of the Seine, but it is not so much an area as a state of mind. One which implies a high degree of involvement in literature and the plastic arts, a centre of the avant-garde and a cosmopolitan refuge since the turn of the century.

This 'leftish' political, artistic and social climate is what attracted Resnais, Marker and Agnès Varda to this neighbourhood. It is also reflected in their work. The writers with whom Resnais has chosen to collaborate are much more avant-garde than those used by the film-makers of the *Cahiers du Cinéma* group. Furthermore, all three directors share a passionate concern with political and social problems and a conviction that these problems have their place in the realm of art. In the past they have all worked quite closely together. Resnais and Marker co-directed a short; Resnais edited Agnès Varda's first film, *La Pointe courte*, which can be seen as the not very distant ancestor of *Hiroshima Mon Amour* (1959).

Of course, as Resnais himself once said, 'the most profound influences are perhaps the ones that have left no visible trace'. Like that of the musical score of *Lady in the Dark*

on his documentary *Toute la Mémoire du Monde* (1956). 'Music has a capital importance for me: often in a shooting script I start from an image around which develops a movement of other images which must connect with the first, like the elements of a musical composition. *Toute la Mémoire du Monde* even started from a few measures of a Kurt Weill musical comedy, *Lady in the Dark*—the circus music, to be exact. The result was a series of long tracking shots separated by some very brief static shots which seemed to me to correspond exactly to the baroque architecture of the National Library.' In a fashion that is characteristic of Resnais, the particular piece of music seems now to be lost, or at least not easily available; the recording from which he worked is now out of print (it wasn't, it would seem, the Gertrude Lawrence version, but the film soundtrack).

First and foremost, however, the major influence was Feuillade: 'Feuillade is my god. I had always been a fan of the Fantômas dime thriller novels, but when I finally saw the films at the Cinémathèque in 1944, I learned from him how the fantastic could be more easily and effectively created in a natural exterior than in a studio. Feuillade's cinema is very close to dreams and is therefore perhaps the most realistic kind of all, paradoxical as this may sound.' This attempt to find the fantastic that lies just below the surface of realism is one of the most important features of Resnais' films. *Muriel, Ou le Temps d'un Retour* (1963), for example, could not be more naturalistic in setting and plot; yet at the same time it could almost be described as science fiction in its premonitory implications.

Other older directors of the past who have influenced Resnais are Marcel L'Herbier and Jean Renoir. They couldn't be more different, one from the other, but each in his own way illuminates a different facet of Resnais' world. Renoir, of course, for the realistic side but, equally important, for the way in which he uses sound, since Resnais has always believed that in the cinema the soundtrack should be at least as important as the visuals. And this belief was confirmed for him by Renoir. After seeing *La Règle du Jeu* eight or nine times, Resnais finally took a tape-recorder with him and recorded the whole soundtrack—playing it over to himself at home, he realized just how well it stood up by itself. I have not tried the same experiment with Resnais' films, but I would not be surprised if the soundtracks alone could provide an experience which, though incomplete, would none the less be an autonomous and a rewarding one.

Marcel L'Herbier, a member of what is usually called the 'first French avant-garde', has for years been put down as dated and pretentious. And there is some truth in these accusations, or rather some of L'Herbier's films justify them. None the less, his belief in using important writers for his scenarios, and collaborating with important artists of his time (like Fernand Léger), is quite similar to Resnais' own views. Plastically, too, there are similarities in their approach to composition.

What made Resnais first decide that he wanted to become a film-maker was not a film about time or memory or any of the things people generally talk about when discussing Resnais. In fact it was a film about nothing at all except—movement. 'The first time that I had a strong, even a violent feeling that I wanted to make films was when I saw my first Ginger Rogers/Fred Astaire dance numbers. They had a kind of sensuality of movement which really took hold of me, and I decided then and there that I was going to try to make films which would have the same effect on people. I was going to try for the equivalent of that kind of exhilaration . . .'

He succeeded. One of the most brilliant examples of this is *Le Chant du Styrène* (1958)—or *The Styrene Song*. It is a sponsored film about the virtues of polystyrene. It appears that the company that commissioned the film thought that the French had a prejudice against plastics and wanted a film which would make them realize that plastics were in effect a 'noble' material, just as good as wood or metal.

The film is an opera without singing. Resnais originally wanted it actually to be a cantata, but the poet Raymond Queneau talked him into settling for formal rhymed verse couplets—alexandrines. The idea of using alexandrines was partly formal—Resnais said he felt vaguely that there was some kind of relationship between these long loping twelve-syllable lines and CinemaScope; furthermore their very formality appealed to his

sense of structure. But he was also convinced that the verse would make the subject easier to understand. And this turned out to be true. The company that had commissioned the film were not very happy with the commentary, so they prepared one themselves in prose. But then they discovered that somehow Resnais' version did at least vaguely leave the audience with *some* understanding of the chemical processes described; whereas their straight commentary left everyone in total confusion. So they went back to the original version.

One of the ways Resnais achieves this sense of exhilaration is by contravening a supposed law of film editing. Back in the 30s, or even before, it was promulgated by the industry that audiences must never be aware of the camera. So, whenever you cut from one shot to the next, you had to do it in a way that would seem natural and easy. And if you cut on a movement, or if you cut from a shot with camera movement, you must always keep the movement in the succeeding shot going in the *same direction as before*. Resnais, on the other hand, wants to make us aware, not of the camera, but of movement. And so he very often follows a shot which is moving from right to left by one that is going from left to right, or diagonally or vertically or whatever. And in so doing he succeeds in increasing the feeling of speed. In *this* film, movement was used (almost) for its own exciting sake. But Resnais has also used it for dramatic ends, as in *Hiroshima Mon Amour*—particularly the sequence in which Emmanuèle Riva tells the Japanese about her first love in Nevers. Probably every possible kind of movement was illustrated in that sequence, but the important thing is the way in which Resnais articulates the camera movements and the movements of the girl on the bicycle. Sometimes she is seen from above going downhill, at other times from below going up. Sometimes we pan with her over hill and dale; sometimes she disappears from sight while the camera movement continues. The slow, plaintive music acts in counterpoint to the allegro of the movements. Towards the end of the sequence the shots come faster and faster (that is, shorter and shorter) till the climax is reached: the couple making love.

This exhilarating sense of movement is

fundamental to all Resnais' films, and one can see it at work even in a film like *Muriel* where there are no tracking or dolly shots: the camera is always rooted to the ground—it can only pan or tilt on its axis. Even with such a technique, he achieves movement through the editing of the film. In the first reel of *Muriel* you can see that the beginning is almost entirely composed of brief shots: a hand, a doorknob, a kettle, a lamp. This expresses Hélène's nervousness and excitement at her impending meeting with an old lover. As she begins to become a bit calmer—while talking to her stepson about this lover, Alphonse—the speed of the editing slows down. Out on the street, however, the constant changes of movement give a feeling almost of syncopation.

The overlapping dialogue gives the sequence a forward impetus; as when Hélène, at the railway station, is asking anxiously about Alphonse, whom she has missed. We hear her talking, but we already see Alphonse and his 'niece' at a nearby café. At the end of that sequence Resnais translated the mood of growing anxiety as they approach Hélène's house by having the characters walking towards the camera very fast—almost walking into it.

Too much of the critical writing about Resnais has concentrated on his themes—time, memory, the past and the present. The time has now come to redress the balance. These themes are important, and yet from the way they have been written about, all Resnais' films might have been books or even essays. As a matter of fact, one sometimes gets the impression that the contributions of Resnais' scriptwriters—Marguerite Duras, Alain Robbe-Grillet, etc.—have taken precedence in some critics' minds over Resnais' own contributions.

The time has come to take a different line of approach, one which would try to grasp the essence of Resnais' films as films: why, for example, in spite of the differing personalities of his writers, all the Resnais films are recognizably by Resnais. This has little to do with time and memory. Rather, it has to do with structure and motifs. Just as anthropologists can break down a whole literature into a very limited set of motifs, so one can see throughout Resnais' work certain repeated elements. And by the way in which

Resnais uses them, by the way in which he constructs his films, structures them, one can perhaps come to grips with Resnais, the film-maker

Resnais' first three features, *Hiroshima Mon Amour*, *L'Année Dernière à Marienbad* (*Last Year in Marienbad*, 1961), and *Muriel* form a kind of whole: his next two films seem very much transitional works. What I want to concentrate on most are the *spatial* motifs in these first three films, for they are the most important in determining the structure of his work. To be sure, when one looks at the films one also notices all kinds of purely psychological motifs, which doubtless have their importance. For example, just as we have noticed that in Godard's films there are never (or hardly ever) any parent figures, so in Resnais' films there are no children. Now this could, I suppose, lead one to conjecture that for Godard the past is of no importance, and that the future does not interest Resnais. This would be going too far, and yet it is hard to avoid thinking that Resnais' well-known obsession with the past and memory is perhaps expressed concretely by his scarcely ever showing children in his films. You could also say that for neither of them is the family group of any importance; for the absence of parents in Godard and of children in Resnais comes down, after all, to the same thing.

And it is also true that Resnais' characters do not lead what might be called a settled existence. Hence his predilection for foreigners and hotel rooms: the French girl in the Hiroshima 'Hilton'; the Grand Hotel of Marienbad. Even in *Muriel*, Hélène seems only to be camping out: the apartment is not finished; doubtless it never will be.

Almost all his films have at least one actor whose native language is not French: Eiji Okada in *Hiroshima*, Giorgio Albertazzi in *Marienbad*, Ingrid Thulin in *La Guerre est Finie* (U.K.: *The War Is Over*, 1966). Even Delphine Seyrig, because of her combined Syrian and New York upbringing, speaks French with a slight hint of an accent in both *Marienbad* and *Muriel*. *Je t'aime, je t'aime* (1968) is the sole exception.

Now this is true of Godard, but in his case it is for almost purely formal reasons—he likes the way in which a foreign accent distorts, gives a new freshness to ordinary

Delphine Seyrig and Jean-Pierre Kérien in *Muriel*.

phrases. But in Resnais' case, the reasons are psychological. All his films deal with characters who are, so to speak, out of place, not at home in their own environment. They are all physically as well as psychologically displaced persons, as no doubt is Resnais himself. They are unsettled, their lives are taken up in a moment of change, of flux. And Resnais' films themselves are a torrent of changing images—unsettled, unsettling. But their movement is not always exhilarating; sometimes it is the movement of desperation. All the characters—particularly the women— are permanently hovering on the edge of hysteria.

This no doubt reflects something of Resnais' own personality, and therefore it is fascinating to see how he compensates for this unease. He does it through structure. And this is where we see that, in spite of the contributions of Duras, Robbe-Grillet, etc., Resnais is still very much the *author* of his films, at least in the sense that Henry James understood it. For James, authorship meant 'Composition, the arranging, the placing, the structuring of materials. Composition alone is positive beauty.' And by composition James meant architecture, which, with its emphasis on proportion and symmetry, is virtually analogous to composition. 'I have ever failed,' he said, 'to see how a coherent picture of anything is producible save by a complex of fine measurements.' Or, to use Resnais' own words, which are close to those of James: 'In a film, as in any work of art, it seems to me that everything has to be unified. A work can be very realistic in its details and yet rigorously formal in technique. Look at Cézanne's painting: Provence has never been more accurately rendered, the landscapes are sensitively precise. And, at the same time, it's an abstract composition, a play of lines and forms. The subject of the picture is the picture itself. Maybe I should call my method formalist realism (or realistic formalism), if those words mean anything. I feel I must never lose sight of the totality of a film because in order to communicate something, you must do it through forms.'

It is well known, I think, that Resnais has always insisted on his writers using a five-act structure for his scripts. Curiously enough, Henry James, too, used the act structure for his novels. Both of them obviously believe in

'the need for a general controlling form, a symmetrical arrangement'. In Resnais' case, the five-act structure, even though it may not always be immediately perceptible to the viewer, clarifies, intensifies, but above all controls the flux of imagery. But it is more complicated than that. In *Hiroshima Mon Amour*, for example, underlying this five-act structure, this time scheme, there is another which has to do with childhood in Nevers. It is in the middle of the Second Act that the first inkling of this important theme is introduced with the famous flash shot of the dead German's hand, which is evoked for the woman by seeing the hand of the Japanese on the bed. And then, gradually, we get more and more descriptions from the past, more and more scenes of Nevers which act in counterpoint to the basic five-act structure, which is concerned with the present alone.

In all Resnais' films there is this kind of secondary labyrinthine movement which snakes its way in and out of the top level, the primary structure. In *Hiroshima*, it is the dead German soldier slowly working his way into the actress's (and our) consciousness. In *Marienbad*, this parallel movement is provided by the sequences of the woman's bedroom which first begin to appear, briefly, half-way through the film, and then recur more and more often until the climax is reached. In *Muriel*, it is the figure of Ernest, the man from Paris, who arrives in Boulogne again at just about the film's half-way mark and keeps on putting in more and more appearances until in the penultimate sequence it is he who brings about the dénouement. But there is also Muriel—the Algerian girl whom we never see. In *La Guerre est Finie*, it is the phantom figure of Juan, whom we never see, but about whom the whole film is organized, who provides the dynamic movement to what might otherwise be the too static five-act form. Throughout Resnais' work, there is a constant interplay between the rigidities of the basic structure with other more dynamic elements.

Sometimes this is done quite consciously by Resnais: 'Occasionally, however, I like to break my formal composition: In *Hiroshima* the whole soundtrack is in the present tense —the Nevers scenes are silent—so I did once let the cry of the girl in Nevers be heard. In *La Guerre est Finie*, the camera always follows Diego except during one scene when he is asleep and Marianne is looking at him (maybe I do this to test the solidity of my construction).' Compare this with Henry James, who said: 'The perfection of form consists in the violation of form: the tension between the desire to impose rigid symmetries upon life and the acceptance of the disorder of experience.'

Resnais can, of course, afford to accept disorder, so strong are his basic symmetries. Or what James called the 'traceable lines', which make the divergent elements hang together. For example, all Resnais' films are built on triangular relationships. In *Hiroshima* it is the French actress, the Japanese architect and the German soldier. In *Marienbad*, it is the characters known as X, A and M: the husband, the wife, the lover. In *La Guerre est Finie* it is Diego, Marianne and Nadine. *Muriel*, Resnais' most complex film, is built on a series of interlocking triangles. There is Hélène, her lover de Smoke and her ex-lover Alphonse. But there is also Alphonse, his ex-mistress Hélène and his current mistress Françoise. And then there are Françoise, Alphonse and Hélène's son Bernard. He too has his triangle: himself, his girl-friend Marie-Do and Robert, his ex-buddy.

This triangular arrangement of the characters is interestingly paralleled in the triangular treatment of locations. In *Hiroshima* we have the hotel room and the towns of Hiroshima and Nevers. In *Marienbad*, there are the hotel's public rooms, the garden and the woman's bedroom. In *Muriel*, there are Hélène's house, Bernard's atelier and the town of Boulogne. In *La Guerre est Finie* the situation is largely the same: Paris, Marianne's apartment and Nadine's apartment.

Sometimes the use of these locations corresponds to the five-act divisions, but not invariably. Often, as with the labyrinthine movement of the fourth elements (Nevers, Ernest in *Muriel*, Juan in *La Guerre est Finie*), the movement from and to the room, the nest, adds its own formal pattern. The importance of the bedroom is not simply formal. With displaced characters such as those Resnais deals with, the room takes on great importance. In *Hiroshima*, for example, the room is all-important, and if we examine the

three times in the film when the heroine leaves or comes back to the room, we can see this quite clearly. We can also thereby gain some greater consciousness of the way in which Resnais' mind works. We have all been so preoccupied with the treatment of time in Resnais' films that we have failed to realize the essential importance of *space*: perhaps just because time is often one of the subjects of his films, space must provide the formal structure.

It is important to note also that all these rooms are upstairs. What more natural, perhaps. But some people do live on the ground floor. That upstairs is no accident is shown by the tremendous role played by staircases and elevators in Resnais' films. It is almost as if the descent into the street were some kind of memorable event: an event of crucial importance, the thing that separates the private life from the public life.

And of course it is, for almost all Resnais' films are concerned with the duality of the personal and the social, the affective and the political. Curious that the French phrase meaning to take up arms, to commit oneself politically, actively, is 'descendre dans la rue'—to go downstairs into the street. (Doubtless there are Freudian implications, too.) Often, too, it's not just upstairs and downstairs—there is sometimes a third place (like Bernard's atelier in *Muriel*, like Nadine's house in *La Guerre est Finie*, and the cellar in Nevers)—but again they never seem to be on the ground floor.

Let's examine the three sequences of arrival or departure in *Hiroshima*. The first occurs at the end of Act Two. After a night spent together, the French actress and the Japanese architect leave the hotel. He wants to see her again, even if only once more. She, on the other hand, tells him that she is leaving the next morning; that it's better for them to make a clean break now. But as they begin to walk slowly down the hotel corridor, she gives the first indication of her earlier long-forgotten love affair and its tragic consequences. The camera has been placidly preceding them down the corridor, but just as the words 'And then, too, I was once mad in Nevers' are spoken, she turns sharply in to the staircase. The camera pans quickly to follow her, and then there is the sharpest and fastest of cuts to a shot of a bus passing by

from right to left, which then reveals the façade of the hotel; we cut then to the couple
walking slowly towards us. So both her
distress at the evocation of her madness, and
her determination to break off the affair, are
translated by the extremely elliptical way in
which Resnais gets the couple out of the
hotel. It is all the more striking after the slow
ambling shuffle down the corridor, this cut
from them starting down the stairs to—not
even them coming out—but to a bus outside.
Thus, the sequence is a double kind of punctuation—the end of something (as she thinks)
and the beginning of the real exploration of
her past.

The next sequence comes at the end of Act
Four—following a day spent with the Japanese during which the story of her youth is
completed. Catharsis has in a sense taken
place, and they leave each other with the
words 'It is unlikely we shall ever meet again,
unless there is a war.' The actress decides to
go back to her hotel. But the ambivalence of
her feelings, her reluctance to go home, is
shown by the longish shot of her approaching
the hotel and in the slowness of her mounting
the staircase. She is no longer sure whether
she *wants* to return to her nest, to her life as it
was before. (A situation which, of course, is
very much paralleled in *Marienbad*, where
the subject is the heroine's reluctance to cut
loose.)

She walks slowly down the corridor towards her room, opens the door. We see her
from inside the room, but she can't bring
herself to go in. She walks on down the
corridor, beyond her room, goes from right
to left, and even goes out of the frame
altogether. Slowly, she makes her way back
to the room, goes in, and then to the washbasin. And then she is overcome by thoughts
of her 'impossible loves'—both the German
and the Japanese. She dries her eyes. Suddenly she has decided that she can no longer
stay in the room. She must go out, but
whether to find the architect or not is unclear. In any case, her determination is translated by a cut which is even more elliptical than
that of her first exit: we cut from her at the
washbasin to the staircase; but this time we see
both flights from below in a very deep shot of
her running down. We cut to the lobby and
she comes towards us. The camera pans to
follow her into the night. Into Hiroshima . . .

So not only has her exit been sharply contrasted with her entrance into the hotel, but
also in some degree with the first exit from
the hotel. That, too, was elliptical, but more
flatly so. There, we had a sharp business-like
cut from the top of the stairs to the outside—
the indifferent world (the bus passing). Here
we have an almost melodramatic shot of the
two flights of stairs seen sharply angled from
the lobby floor.

The third sequence of arrival or departure
comes just before the end of the film. During
the night she has wandered all over town—to
the railway station, where the architect finds
her; through the streets, finally ending up in
a hideously sinister nightclub where, in a
kind of parody of her first meeting with
the Japanese, another man tries to pick her
up. But the architect finds her there, too.
They sit, at separate tables, as the ghastly
dawn appears in the glass roof of the 'outdoor' nightclub. We cut to a view of the city
with smoke pouring from the chimneys, and
then in the most elliptical entrance of all, we
simply cut from the view of the city to the
woman already in her room, leaning against
the door as if trying either to barricade it, to
stop anyone from coming in, or perhaps even
to stop herself from going out. But when he
knocks she nevertheless opens the door.

These three scenes demonstrate the importance Resnais attaches to such entrances and
exits, placed crucially as they are at the important points in the film. Secondly, they
show the enormous variety of ways such
scenes are shot and edited. But even more
important, they demonstrate once more that
Resnais is very much the *author* of his films.

The substance of these three sequences
may have been written by Marguerite Duras,
but they have been given life by Resnais, and
more careful attention both to the motifs of
his films (which are consistent regardless of
who actually wrote the scripts), and also to
their structure, would lead to a much fuller
and deeper understanding of his contribution
to the cinema than any amount of discussion
of Bergson, time or memory.

One final word—an objection that is often
raised to any attempt at close analysis is: how
can the director expect an audience to pick
up these subtleties. And do they really exist?
There are several answers to this perfectly
reasonable question. One would be that it

doesn't matter if the audience doesn't perceive them directly—they will act on the audience in any case. But for the best answer, we must go back to Henry James: 'The artist,' James said, 'must combine and arrange, interpolate and eliminate: he must play the joiner with the most attentive skill and yet at the end of it all, he must effectually bury his tools and his sawdust and invest his elaborate skeleton with the smoothest and most polished integument.' If ever this dictum applied to a film-maker, it applies to Alain Resnais.

Je t'aime, je t'aime was the low-water mark of Resnais' career: a failure both critically and commercially, it was indeed difficult to defend. The reason for its failure can in part be attributed to Jacques Sternberg's script, which was too Resnaisian. What I mean is that the subject—a scientific experiment to attempt to make a man actually relive a moment of his life—was almost a parody of a Resnais theme.

Then, too, the choice of actors—Claude Rich and Olga Georges-Picot—was unfortunate. She was quite simply inadequate, while he did not have enough presence to carry the film. But parts of *Je t'aime, je t'aime* are magnificent, especially when the time machine goes wrong and we get a wildly unchronological view of the life of the hero, Claude Ridder, which none the less creates a convincing picture of the man: a splendid patchwork quilt in time.

The previous year, 1967, had seen Resnais' contribution to *Loin du Viêt-Nam* (*Far from Vietnam*), one of the best episodes in that uneven but important film. In his episode, Bernard Fresson portrays a man who finds it hard (as did Resnais himself) to come to grips with the conflict between the America he has loved—the America of comic strips, of Hollywood and Broadway, and the America now fighting a grotesque war in Vietnam.

After these two works, Resnais tried without success to set up several film projects, but not until 1974 did he make his next film, *Stavisky* ... Once again, as with *La Guerre est Finie*, the scriptwriter was Jorge Semprun. Not an ideal choice, I feel, because Resnais works best with scriptwriters who are on his own intellectual and artistic level. However, the film was far more successful than *La Guerre est Finie*, largely because of what Resnais added to the script. As I wrote

above, Resnais is very conscious of film history, and he tried to make *Stavisky* ... look as if it had been made in the 30s. Not entirely, of course; the film is in colour, if muted colour, but he refused to use zooms, or any camera movement that was not practised in the French films of the period. On the other hand, the music, always important in Resnais' films, was provided by Stephen Sondheim; and, without being a pastiche of the period, fitted well and was effective.

In fact, Sondheim's 'Death Waltz' motif summed up the film: it elegantly sounds the death knell of a civilization, the end of Biarritz-Bonheur; or to put it another way, it evokes the melancholy of the last days of frivolity before that war which began in 1936 and has yet to end. Stavisky, the swindler, the man who brought down a government, may have been the subject of the film, but it was the old Baron Raoul (played by Charles Boyer) who told us, in the words of Jean Giraudoux, what the film was really about: the dense fluidity of death. A phrase which also describes Resnais' camera style, and defines the film.

This is a film not about the politics of the Third Republic, but about death. The death of Stavisky and the death of an epoch. When it begins, Stavisky is already at that point in his career when he is beginning no longer to enjoy life. Resnais defines youth as that time when everything seems possible, and that is why his evocation of the period is much more than an exercise in Art-Deco nostalgia. Usually Resnais' camera movements are exhilarating; when he cuts on movement, as he so often does, the effect here is rather premonitory, menacing. When the camera, for example, moves down the façade of the Hotel Claridge and then cuts to an upward movement following the lift inside the hotel, it creates a sense of dread that is borne out all the way through the film.

As in his earlier films, a secondary plot weaves itself in and out of the story of the downfall of Stavisky: here it is the evocation of Trotsky's brief stay in France before he was expelled and sent off to Mexico—to his death, as it turned out. However, Resnais has not succeeded in integrating this second plot; it adds little, and one is always impatient to get back to the main story. For the second time in his career, Resnais used a 'star' in the main role: Jean-Paul Belmondo. Like Yves Montand in *La Guerre est Finie*, he's not bad, but I doubt that he was an ideal choice. In any event he is overshadowed by

Charles Boyer and Annie Duperey. For she, as Stavisky's wife Arlette, is in some ways as important as Stavisky. He tries hard to make money by any means, so that he can squander it on her: for his relations with her, like his gambling, are a way of exorcizing his fear of death.

Looking back on the film, one remembers moments with much greater precision than the film as a whole: the scene in Arlette's Biarritz hotel room filled with white flowers; the almost mortuary insistence on white throughout the film; the sequence in Père Lachaise cemetery when Stavisky goes to see the tomb of his father; his own death in the snowy outskirts of Chamonix.

Stavisky ... was a good film, but Resnais really got back into his stride, really recaptured the genius of the first three films, in 1977 with *Providence*. I mentioned earlier Resnais' predilection for having at least one foreigner in the cast of his films. Here the whole cast was foreign, for the film was made in English: it starred Dirk Bogarde, John Gielgud, Elaine Stritch, Ellen Burstyn and David Warner—an Anglo-American cast for a film that was shot in neither England nor America (except for a few location scenes in New England, without actors). The script was by the British playwright David Mercer. And yet in spite of this fundamental difference, the film showed Resnais back on the rails, back at the old stand. It was a film about psychologically displaced persons; it attempted and succeeded in finding the 'fantastic that lies just below the surface of realism and which is therefore more realistic'. It is not divided into five acts, but rather into three movements. Again it is an 'upstairs' film, with Gielgud in his bedroom; and, indeed, the hotel room in which we briefly see Elaine Stritch is provided with a staircase that appears and disappears. The house where Bogarde and Burstyn live defies architectural logic, like one of those puzzle paintings by Escher where staircases go up to lower floors, and one never quite knows where one is. And the plot is made up of a series of interlocking triangles. Clive Langham (Gielgud), his son Claud (Bogarde) and his daughter-in-law Sonia (Burstyn) make up one triangle. But there is another composed of Claud, Sonia and Claud's illegitimate half-brother (David Warner); and yet another, with Helen Wiener (Stritch), Clive and Claud Langham, for Stritch appears in the film as both Claud's mistress and his

mother, and therefore as Clive's dead wife Molly.

The first two-thirds of the film take place during a sleepless Chablis-sodden night when Clive, the dying novelist, is imagining a new novel in which his family will appear. Appear, however, as he sees them, which is to say with a more than jaundiced eye. The film (and Clive's villa) may be called Providence, but Clive is an author, not God. He is often surprised by what his characters do.

Too much has been made of the narrative device of *Providence*—the notion that we are seeing reality through the eyes of an author trying to write a novel. To my way of thinking, this is only a device, and the interest of the film does not lie in any light it may shed on the creative processes. The interchanging of characters that goes on in Clive Langham's mind is not only an expression of the way in which a novelist's mind is supposed to work. It is much more the expression of an important truth about human relationships. We do take on different roles, and these roles are usually derived from our family history. Long before Freud, Tin Pan Alley discovered that many men choose and act towards their wives as their fathers did towards their mothers: 'I want a girl/Just like the girl/That married dear old dad.' And many women towards their husbands as their mothers towards their fathers. More bizarrely, but just as frequently, psychoanalysts tell us, one can find oneself acting towards one's spouse as one acted towards one's mother or father; and one can even manipulate the spouse into acting towards oneself as one's parents did. So when Claud Langham begins to talk like his father Clive, when his mistress is played by the same actress who also 'plays' his dead mother, the film is about the way *all* our minds work.

Providence, even though taking place in an unnamed country (the film was shot in Belgium and France), is not without social and political content. From the very beginning, one of Resnais' labyrinthine sub-plots appears in brief but ever-longer flashes. We first see soldiers tracking down a dying man; there are helicopters hovering ominously overhead. Suddenly the import of these flashes becomes clearer when we see an image of people being herded into a stadium. 'These places are becoming almost *de rigueur* as fear symbols,' Clive laments petulantly, but these images, cliché or not, continue to appear. Gradually we come to

Ellen Burstyn in *Providence*, Resnais' finest film since *Muriel*.

realize that the film is *also* about a city that has been taken over by ... somebody. (Just as Clive's body has been taken over by disease, perhaps.) The climax of the 'novel' occurs when Claud and Sonia are rounded up by the police and they, too, are forced into the stadium. Then, a *coup de théâtre*—suddenly the night is over, and the screen is flooded with broad daylight. The disreputable old drunk, Clive Langham, is elegantly attired in white, and decorously seated in a wicker chair; on the lawn at the Villa Providence, he awaits the arrival of his children to celebrate his birthday. All is sunny, pastoral, idyllic—although there is a flash of Clive's wife dead in her bath, and another of an autopsy. Then his sons arrive: charming, friendly, ordinary, in fact. Everything we see seems to be a contradiction of what Clive had imagined. And yet ... some odd looks are exchanged from time to time, and some odd remarks are passed. Although the sun is high, the huge villa casts its shadow over the table where Clive is presiding over lunch. Then, after lunch, the family depart and the film is over. And most of the audience leaves the cinema

thinking that everything is all right, that the first two thirds of the film were only the sick imaginings of a dying man. But others are not quite so reassured.

Once again, time seems a less important element in the film than the unrealistic way in which Resnais juxtaposes things in space. Not just to achieve a nightmarish effect, but because Resnais feels that he can portray reality by defying the laws of realism. 'The perfection of form lies in the violation of form,' to repeat the Henry James quotation. And once more we find the tension between the desire to impose rigid symmetries upon life and the acceptance of the disorder of experience.

Without wishing to take any credit from David Mercer, this is Resnais' film. More than a film about an author trying to write a novel, more than a film about an old man passing judgement on his family, more than a film about a *Putsch* in some unnamed country with a very Chile-like stadium, this is a film about Resnais. Every frame, every movement, every cut expresses a human being. His heartbeat, his pulse-rate dictate the editing. It is a film about his fears of ageing, his political background, his views on society, on love, on family life.

I must add, finally, that the film was not appreciated by the great majority of American critics. They noticed some of the infelicities of Mercer's dialogue, but for the most part they objected to the very thing that was praised by the French press: the fact that the film is a calculated work of art. It is not spontaneous, it is not realistic, and it is complex. Whatever flaws may exist in the script, the film is Resnais' greatest since *Muriel,* and that means it is one of the great films of our time.

There are several books on Resnais in English: John Ward's *Alain Resnais, or the Theme of Time* (1968), *The Cinema of Alain Resnais* (1968) by Roy Armes, and, more recently, James Monaco's *Alain Resnais* (1978). Most of Resnais' scripts have been published in English.

LENI RIEFENSTAHL

John Russell Taylor

The coming to power of the Nazi party in Germany in 1933 precipitated the departure of many people working in the cinema, most notably Fritz Lang and G. W. Pabst. But it could hardly be said that the German cinema had been at the height of its power and reputation even before that: departures for more normal reasons had begun in the mid-20s, and the immense Hollywood success of Ernst Lubitsch had encouraged other notables, including F. W. Murnau, Paul Leni and E. A. Dupont, to make tracks in the same direction. And though some important films had been made in Germany at the beginning of the sound period, by and large the German cinema had not managed to retain the reputation and influence it had enjoyed in the early 20s; in many senses Hitler only speeded up a process already well under way before his arrival.

On the other hand, German cinema in the 30s was not quite such a barren waste as, for reasons of propaganda, it has usually been represented. At the time the products of German studios continued to be shown regularly abroad, and though some reservations were inevitably felt about the more overtly political and propagandist of them, the innocuous and often stylish entertainment films which made up most of the annual output were received with pleasure and enthusiasm which came to be discounted and forgotten only with the outbreak of the Second World War. It is only recently, in fact, that the charms of these films—starring Zarah Leander, Marika Rökk or, in the earlier years, Lilian Harvey; directed by Willi Forst, Veit Harlan or Douglas Sirk (then Detlef Sierck)—have begun to be rediscovered. Much the same complaints could be made against them as were made against the average Hollywood film of the time—that their intentions were hardly of the loftiest artistic variety, and so how could anything in the way of high artistic achievement be expected of them? (Which thought has, of course, not prevented the Hollywood entertainment film of the 30s from coming in for a lot of very serious consideration in the last few years.) But there remains one awkward figure in the cinema of Nazi Germany who refuses to be so easily dismissed: Leni Riefenstahl.

All things considered, Leni Riefenstahl must be one of the most unlikely figures ever to emerge as a major talent in the cinema. Born in 1902, she began her career with little idea other than to become a star—a natural enough desire in a beautiful young woman who had trained as a dancer and had some experience on stage before appearing in her first film, *Der Heilige Berg*, in which she played the female lead opposite Luis Trenker, in 1926. This was one of a series of open air dramas, set among the mountains and snows, in which the director, Arnold Fanck, specialized. And for the next few years it seemed that Leni Riefenstahl would specialize in them too—a glamorous athlete who looked good on skis and acted no worse but, for all one could tell to the contrary, no better than a dozen other young hopefuls of the German cinema. Even her most famous film as an actress, *Die Weisse Hölle von Pitz Palü (The White Hell of Pitz Palu,* 1929), which Pabst co-directed with Fanck, was no more than a particularly effective example of the mountain film genre; and an intriguing possibility that she might play Lola-Lola in Sternberg's *The Blue Angel* came to nothing. (Strange thought: is it possible that given a slightly different turn of events, Riefenstahl might have gone to Hollywood and become Dietrich?)

In 1932, however, her career assumed a new guise when she suddenly emerged as co-author (with the Hungarian film theorist Béla Bálazs) and director of a film in which she also starred, *Das Blaue Licht* (*The Blue Light*, 1932). At first sight this too could be written off as another variation on the theme of the mountain film. It concerns a young Italian girl of vaguely mystical tendencies who is the only person in a village capable of reaching a blue light which shines on top of a neighbouring mountain at full moon. It is in fact a cave of crystals to which there is only one secret route, but it is also, obviously, the Ideal, which Yunta alone can reach because she is pure of heart, while the others who try are destroyed. Finally a painter in love with Yunta accidentally discovers the secret route and reveals it, hoping thus to help Yunta and dispel the superstitious dread she inspires in the villagers. He is the realist who kills the dream, and Yunta dies as a result of his revelation, but her death benefits the lesser mortals who could not understand her or what she stood for while she lived.

Though this romantic and somewhat sentimental fantasy conformed in many respects to the norm of the mountain film, it goes much further than the vague back-to-nature yearnings of the genre in general by adopting a far more overtly symbolic attitude to its characters and insisting on the parable side of the story to the virtual exclusion of landscape and local colour. Indeed, Leni Riefenstahl has said that she would ideally have liked to make it entirely in a studio, where the sets and lighting could be strictly regulated and abstracted. But owing to restricted finances she had to shoot on actual locations, and was thereby compelled to find ways of manipulating nature in order to produce the desired formal, abstract quality. In so doing she made a film which looks backwards to the studio atmospherics, the much sought-after *Stimmung* of classic German silent cinema, as well as forward to her own mature achievements.

The precise politics by which she came to make her two major films in the Nazi era, *Triumph des Willens* (*Triumph of the Will*, 1935) and *Olympische Spiele 1936* (U.K.: *Olympiad, Festival of the Nations*; U.S.: *Olympia, Festival of the Nations*, 1936–38), remain obscure. In 1933 she had made her

last film merely as an actress, *S.O.S. Eisberg* (*S.O.S. Iceberg*), a spectacular German–American co-production, and had then, shortly after her return, been asked personally by Hitler to put together, quickly, a short on the 1933 Nazi party rally, *Sieg des Glaubens* (*Victory of the Faith*, 1933). It seems curious that such a job should be assigned to a woman, even if she did allegedly qualify as Hitler's ideal of Aryan womanhood, but it seems that Hitler admired *The Blue Light* and sensed in its creator just the right combination of technical skill and Germanic mysticism for his purposes, which were to mythologize rather than merely record the most dramatic moments of party ritual and ceremonial. In his belief in Leni Riefenstahl he stood alone, since Josef Goebbels, the Propaganda Minister, hated her and did all he could to put obstacles in her way—to such an extent that *Victory of the Faith* was underwritten by the party to an absolutely minimal degree, and *Triumph of the Will* was not party-financed at all, but set up as an independent production by Ufa films. Despite this, the support of the Führer was of course all-important, and ensured that even if other factions in the party gave her no more support than they had to, they at least did not dare to interfere; and on the organizational level she had all the co-operation she could wish, to the extent that much of the 1934 party rally, the subject of *Triumph of the Will*, was staged in large measure for the cameras, rather than the cameras having to be manoeuvred to accommodate the pre-ordained action.

The result can be seen, in one sense, as the most spectacular musical ever made. The torchlight processions, the parades the inspections, the dedications are like so many gigantic Busby Berkeley numbers, staged with seemingly limitless resources in Albert Speer's monumental architectural arrangements, the quintessence of the grandiose art-deco neo-classicism so beloved of the 30s. But that, needless to say, is only one way of looking at the film. It can also be seen both as a documentary and as a mythic fantasy. Documentary it certainly is, in the sense that it is a record of something that actually happened, in the same way as, say, Castleton Knight's film about the last British coronation, *A Queen Is Crowned*. The events them-

There is no still from *Triumph of the Will* that conveys the splendour of this terrifying masterpiece.

selves are not falsified, everything happened where and when and in the order that the film says it did. But at the same time Leni Riefenstahl's compositional skill and editing genius manage to transform the raw material of documentary into something quite different. As with *The Blue Light*, she regretted the need to shoot on location, and did everything possible to control and design the reality thrust upon her as if she were in a studio; so here everything is selected and manipulated to a larger, more mystical end. The very opening of the film, which appears to be (and indeed is) a factual account of Hitler's arrival in Nuremberg by air, becomes also an evocation of a god's descent to earth—from the endless vistas of clouds, seen from the god's-eye viewpoint of the plane, we pass to the plane's shadow moving majestically, inexorably over the sunlit city as those in the streets gaze up in rapturous expectation, and then finally move to the landing and descent of the Führer in a fashion which instantly transforms man into myth.

The rest of the film adopts the same approach. Constantly we lose all sense of perspective, are cut off from the basic realities by alternations of extreme long-shot and gigantic close-up; in the parades through the streets of Nuremberg the very perspectives are often misleading, making it impossible for us to judge distances correctly or assess relative proportions. The torchlit celebrations are turned into abstract patterns of sight and sound; and even the final series of speeches from the rostrum leading up to Hitler's own concluding address, where the naked propaganda content might threaten to overbalance the film and bore any but the fanatically converted, work because of the director's masterly control of rhythm and pacing, so that the tension grows and grows to the moment when Hitler himself takes the stand, aureoled like the saviour from the sky which he seemed to be in the opening sequence. Difficult though it may be for almost any contemporary spectator to divorce himself altogether from attitudes towards the materials out of which the film is made, even such committedly left-wing, dedicatedly anti-Nazi writers as Paul Rotha have had to admit that there was little or nothing Leni Riefenstahl did not know about film-making, that her mastery of editing was comparable with Eisenstein's, and that the film, whatever one's attitude towards its content, does transcend that content and compel one to judge it absolutely as a film.

The same is true—and the adaptation of attitude rather easier, for obvious reasons—in the case of *Olympia*, Leni Riefenstahl's official film record of the 1936 Olympic Games, held in Berlin. Again, the scope and mood of the film are monumental. If one compares it, for instance, with Ichikawa's film about the Tokyo Olympics, the difference is at once apparent. Ichikawa's attitude is one of humorous detachment: more than anything he finds these athletes funny, and provocative of his curiosity as human beings; and when he is, even a little unwillingly, forced into a sort of respect for them, as in the marathon, the effect is touching precisely because the respect is hard-won, and is accorded to the runners as human beings. Leni Riefenstahl, on the other hand, is nearly always mythologizing, monumental, heroic.

The film opens with a lyrically beautiful evocation of classical Greece, which moves into the string of runners bringing the lighted torch from Olympia, again seen in their heroic aspect, as almost superhuman, abstractly beautiful messengers from the gods. The second part of the film (which runs altogether 212 minutes) begins with a correspondingly evocative sequence, this time something which in other hands might have provided a human touch by showing us glimpses of the behind-the-scenes life of the athletes in the Olympic village, but instead keeps them always at a generalizing, impersonal distance—runners romantically glimpsed through the mists of dawn, or shadowily observed rippling heroic muscles

in the steamy half-light of the Turkish baths. There are, here and there, touches of humour in the film—notably in the horse-jumping sequences, where one is suddenly confronted with a less than heroic image of man on (but only just on) horse, hanging on for dear life. More characteristic, though, even if it carries the method of the film to extremes, is the high-diving sequence, in which the director gets so fascinated by the patterns the divers make in the air that finally all pretence of documentary is dropped and the episode ends with a succession of totally abstract shots of bodies turning, turning forever in the air, without visibly hitting the water at all.

The resources for *Olympia* were vaster even than those for *Triumph of the Will*—necessarily, since the action which constituted the film's basic material was hardly so controllable in this case. In consequence Leni Riefenstahl was left with miles of film, covering just about everything from every possible angle, at every possible speed. The film which eventually emerged is a masterpiece, first of all, of creative editing; but also, miraculously, considering the unpredictable circumstances in which the film of necessity had to be shot, Leni Riefenstahl managed to impose a personal angle of vision, an unmistakable look, on the total film. It is—as even those most unfavourably disposed to her will admit—a one-woman achievement, made by a director who kept every part of a vastly complicated piece of organization entirely under her own control and edited every inch of the film herself. And as such it remains a masterpiece undimmed by time, one of the cinema's supreme celebrations of the mystery, beauty and grandeur of the human body. The meaner, less heroic elements of the picture are rigorously excluded, but that is fair enough in a personal vision which does not falsify, but only selects.

After *Olympia*, Leni Riefenstahl's professional life suffered a series of misfortunes and setbacks. Exciting plans for a film of Heinrich von Kleist's tragedy *Penthesilea*, with the director herself playing the Amazon queen, had to be cancelled on the outbreak of war. Shooting on a pictorially beautiful, politically quite innocuous adaptation of Eugen D'Albert's opera *Tiefland*, again star-

Gold Medallist Hein of Germany throwing the hammer in *Olympia*.

ring Leni Riefenstahl, dragged on through-out the war, constantly interrupted, and by 1945 was barely completed, with the editing hardly begun. There followed the slow process of Leni Riefenstahl's official de-Nazification, then her litigation to get back the film materials, and *Tiefland* was only finally completed, edited and shown in 1954. Otherwise, despite a clean bill of political health given to her by the de-Nazification courts, the tag of 'Hitler's favourite film-maker' pursued her, adding to the prejudice that her being a woman naturally provoked, so that while the directors of far more politically objectionable Nazi films, like Veit Harlan, maker of the notorious *Jew Süss*, were happily reinstated and went busily back to work, she suffered continuing boycotts and protests, as a sort of solitary scapegoat for the cinematic sins of Nazi Germany.

No doubt her outstanding talent was the thing chiefly held against her—it is much easier to forgive and overlook a nonentity. In 1956 she began shooting *Schwarze Fracht* (*Black Freight*), a documentary about slave traffic in East Africa, but it had to be abandoned after a serious accident. In 1965 she began shooting *Nuba*, a colour documentary about the Nuba tribesmen of the Sudan; in 1977 it was still in the process of editing, after mishaps in the laboratory and various changes in the overall conception of how the material should be assembled. But at the age of seventy-five Leni Riefenstahl seems to have the energy and creative drive of someone half her age, and the determination to continue. No doubt *Nuba* will be finished and shown; maybe it will not even be her cinematic swan song. It is temptingly easy to deplore the many wasted years, the films that were planned but not made. But at least in *Triumph of the Will* and *Olympia* Leni Riefenstahl made two of the world's unassailable cinema masterpieces, and that in itself is more than enough to justify one lifetime's work.

Mention should be made of a colleague of Riefenstahl, Willy Zielke, who, after working with her, made in 1935 an extraordinary film called *Das Stahltier*. Nominally a commissioned film about the hundredth anniversary of the German railways, it was suppressed by Goebbels because it takes off from its theme into some weird empyrean heights where, through Zielke's brilliant editing, the locomotive, the 'steel animal', almost becomes a living character.

For further reading on Riefenstahl, see Siegfried Kracauer's *From Caligari to Hitler* (1947), David Stewart Hull's *Films in the Third Reich* (1969), Eric Barnouw's *Documentary* (1974) and Erwin Leiser's *Nazi Cinema* (1975). In recent years Riefenstahl has published two extraordinary books of her photographs of African tribes, but there is no sign of her still-forthcoming film *Nuba*. Two films not mentioned by Taylor are her 1935 *Tag der Freiheit* and *Unsere Wehrmacht*.

See also the articles on Dance in Film and Walt Disney [sic].

JACQUES RIVETTE

Jean-André Fieschi

The group, the theatre, the conspiracy

In so far as spotting motifs or threads is concerned, everything is already there in *Paris Nous Appartient* (*Paris Belongs to Us*, 1960). Everything, or at least the basic material (thematic, phantasmatic) subsequently recast in other registers, reworked on other stages: the later films.

In an improbable city—unrecognizable but familiar—in the attic rooms, the passage-ways, the back streets, the studios, the gardens, even on the rooftops, people pursue each other, tangentially meeting or melting away, as though haunted by phantoms of the imagination, with paranoia their inevitable lot. Obsession reigns: a clue or a proof, but of what? (a few guitar notes recorded on a lost or stolen tape)—or else a project, stubbornly maintained in the face of disaster: to stage Shakespeare, a demented play, and in make-shift circumstances, enmeshing a stopgap group of actors in this dementia. Over-wrought or obstinate, schemer or starveling, informer or exile, these characters seem to be both the playthings of some preposterous or terrifying cabal, and the inhabitants of a bad dream—the debris of calamitous History assuming the dimensions of nightmare—whose end they await (or precipitate): the meaning finally revealed. Excursions, encounters, interweavings, retracings: gradually the disorder unravels itself, until seemingly

Anna Karina as Suzanne Simonin in *La Religieuse*.

dispersed as in Shakespeare's *Pericles*, which serves as an inaccessible fable with its storms, its shipwrecks, its marvels, or as a mythical model. There is no centre to this drifting (no climax either, no thesis), which seems solely the pursuit of a delusion, its faint adumbration.

Here, the stages of a twin ceremonial are explored through forms (the cultural overhang from the 'classic' cinema reconsidered), and here put to the test, despite the semblance of a 'chronicle' (tracing a course rather in the manner of a weird game of snakes and ladders): an initiation rite unfolds with its trials and ordeals, bedecked with the flourishes of the penny-dreadful serial; and theatricality emerges as the quest, the essence at the secret heart—secret though tirelessly pursued, and tirelessly elusive—of any performance.

Should misgivings about incoherence or absurdity arise, the answer is that everything, here, must be taken on another level.

Group, theatre, conspiracy, everything is already there, except perhaps this: 'Time was, in a so-called classical tradition of cinema, when the preparation of a film meant first of all finding a good story, developing it, scripting it and writing dialogue; with that done, you found actors who suited the characters and then you shot it. This is something I've done twice, with *Paris Nous Appartient* and *La Religieuse* (1965), and I find the method totally unsatisfying, if only because it involves such boredom. What I have tried since— after many others, following the precedents of Rouch, Godard and so on—is to attempt to find, alone or in company (I always set out from the desire to make a film with particular actors), a generating principle which will then, as though on its own (I stress the "as though"), develop in an autonomous manner and engender a filmic product from which, afterwards, a film destined eventually for screening to audiences can be cut, or rather "produced" ' (Jacques Rivette).

The group, the theatre, madness

L'Amour Fou (1968) is where this transition, this metamorphosis takes place. Rouch, Godard and a handful of others shook the foundations of the temple, forced open some doors, indicated a few paths: Rouch's great fictional indirections (*Jaguar*) and Godard's fragmented narratives acted as a powerful stimulus to the appeal of free structures, unrestricted by the prevailing dramaturgic matrix (and the hierarchical system it imposed), whose end was in sight. The supremacy of the script as be-all and end-all of a film (formulated most explicitly by René Clair: 'My film is finished; all I have to do now is shoot it') tips the cinema heavily over into the area of illustration (telling a 'good', 'finely' acted story 'well'). The signifying convention is the rule (most of the time, unquestioned), presenting itself as *natural* rather than as the product of a culture, eternal rather than transient. It is fundamentally artificial, ideological through and through, however, subject to (and perpetuating) the illusion of transparency: the film being purely a transparent medium for a narrative, and the narrative purely a transparent medium for an idea or a message pre-existing its physical inscription (in bodies, compositions, lighting, movements, sounds, images).

To subvert this grid, dislocate this narrative code, radically alter means and effects, redistribute roles and functions: this, too, is the gamble of *L'Amour Fou*, its specific movement towards deconstruction/reconstruction, which is primarily to re(take) stock of the cinema in a quite literal sense.

The script: no *découpage* this time and no 'score', simply the thread of a plot. To wit, a sort of short story some thirty pages long, a hypothesis for the fiction to come, its minimal programme, its germ. No vestiges remain here of the 'two-column' cinema, with dialogue and soundtrack on one side, visual images on the other. There is, as a matter of fact, nothing but continuous prose, neither images nor sounds but situations potentially brought to a head as multiple narratives, indications of characters at crisis point, and again the theatre, the theatre as a stage—pure, stark, white (it is also a ring)—set for work: a place of exchange, of ritual, of drama or festivity (of sacrifice), of fantasy

embodied, of convulsion, of loss and profit, of sex, of gestures, of words (or of cries), of scansion. All this is not written, however, but literally played: revealing itself, filming itself, producing itself.

This stage divides itself into two. On it a group clears away some dead wood (from Racine, for example, this time): a company of actors, where the division of roles, sexes, powers comes into play. On it, a couple come apart, reach the end of their tether, a drama begins to fashion itself (attempts to fashion itself, stammering, skidding, reversing, seeking *its* form).

The film is the receptacle, the blank on which the conflict of forms, of forces, will appear. At the cost of a division; more than that, of a kind of free hand. For now it is *mise en scène* which places itself 'in the abyss', to use that figure described by Gide, then taken up and developed by Jean Ricardou:

> So let us look again at the celebrated passage from the *Journal* of 1893: 'I rather like it in a work of art when one finds its theme transposed to scale with the characters in this way. Nothing illuminates the theme more, or establishes the proportions of the whole more clearly. For instance in certain paintings by Memling or Quentin Metsys, a small mirror, dark and convex, reflects in its turn the interior of the scene where the painted scene is taking place. For instance (though a little differently), Velazquez' painting of *Las Meninas*. In literature, the play scene in *Hamlet*; and in a great many other plays too. In *Wilhelm Meister*, the puppet scenes or the festivity in the castle. In *The Fall of the House of Usher*, the story read to Roderick, etc.' Noting the analogy between this enclave and the enclosing of one blazon within another in heraldry, one may remember that Gide proposed to call it a placing in the heart-point, in the abyss.' (Jean Ricardou, *Le Nouveau Roman*, 1973.)

Which is to say that here, unlike Gianni Esposito in *Paris Nous Appartient*, an actor (Jean-Pierre Kalfon) does not ape the functions of a director but assumes them, takes them upon himself (it is his company that is involved, and his *Andromaque*); just as Petit Jules in Rouch's *Moi, un noir* assumed his

Bulle Ogier and Jean-Pierre Kalfron in *L'Amour Fou*, the turning-point in Rivette's career.

imaginary self, displayed it, offered it as a spectacle. So is *L'Amour Fou* then, as with Rouch, the documentation of this imagined self, its re-takeover? No. A second delegation of functions comes into play here: let this documentary take place, but taken over by another technique (a 16-mm Eclair), another eye, another director. So imagine a television crew covering the venture, obtrusive and omnipresent, recording rehearsals and interviews, whether footnotes at the bottom of the page or critical annotations in the margins. The upshot (at the rushes stage): two films in one, derived from the same contrivance, to be matched, articulated, edited together.

Hence the filming is no longer a transfer from the script, or the montage a transfer of the filming. On the contrary, a dialectic is set up between planning, filming and editing in which each phase, each stage, is a criticism (a critical transcending) of the previous one.

The montage: here *L'Amour Fou* is almost

a metaphor for the history of this particular form of scansion, a condensation of its successive stages:

So one might, very schematically, distinguish four moments: the invention of montage (Griffith, Eisenstein), its deviation (Pudovkin–Hollywood: elaboration of the techniques of propaganda cinema), the rejection of propaganda (a rejection loosely or closely allied to long takes, direct sound, amateur or auxiliary actors, non-linear narrative, heterogeneity of genres, elements or techniques, etc.), and finally, what we have been observing over the last ten years, the attempt to 'salvage', to re-inject into contemporary methods the spirit and the theory of the first period, though without rejecting the contribution made by the third, but rather trying to cultivate one through the other, to dialectize them and, in a sense, to *edit* them. (Jacques Rivette.)

The group, the theatre, madness, are now no longer objects but subjects: they reveal themselves during the course of the performance, but also they reveal the secret (tirelessly pursued through *Paris Nous Appartient*) at the heart of every performance.

The group: company or provisional family (clan). As one can see:

> Every group reproduces in its own way the mythical model of the Crusades or the quest for the Grail: its wish defines the holy land of which it is deprived and whose conquest it undertakes. (Didier Anzieu, *L'Illusion groupale* in *Nouvelle Revue de Psychanalyse* No. 4, 1971.)

Also:

> The group's imaginary space is the projection of the mother's fantasized body. (*Idem.*)

Group: actors, technicians, dream (a Utopia partially realized through the spectacle) of a lost unity, of an illusory community, a great, dismembered body in quest of an impossible and necessary suture; the spectacle (the film) is the evidence of this quest, of this impossibility, of this necessity.

Theatre: place, prize, hallucination. The wish and the fear that here, as in Mallarmé's poem, nothing will take place *but the place*.

Madness: excess itself is expressive here. Excess in acting (regression), excess in length (dilation: time overflows), excess of the wish (with its surrealist connotation, the title *L'Amour Fou* is to be understood as a general eroticizing of bodies, of observation, of fiction).

A director, according to Jean Renoir, ought to be able to 'play possum'. Far removed from the power fantasies and hypnotic overtures of a Mabuse (that caricature and definitive metaphor for the average film director), control is asserted here only through its semblance of withdrawal, of rejection. Another illusion, of course. The method can be clarified through music:

> Classical tonal thinking is based on a universe defined by gravitation and attraction; serial thinking, on a universe in perpetual expansion. (Pierre Boulez, *Série* in *Relevés d'Apprenti*.)

To which one might add as an echo a fragment from Rivette's own review of Kazan's *Splendor in the Grass*:

> Here the fragment, ineluctable, is a sign for the whole; the serial cell contains all the potentialities of the film; the inner melody can only be born of these broken fragments or dust particles. A stumbling, disruptive construction, in which the conflict between traditional dramatic elements and free structures—whose rigour is more veiled, their appearance one of improvisation—is the rejected image of the theme; a construction wich *seems* to be the work of time itself; a decisive step towards that fully atonal cinema adumbrated by all the great films of today.

It has been no secret since at least as far back as Epstein that the films described by film-makers are the films of their dreams. What Rivette says here of *Splendor in the Grass* is also a dream of a film in 1962 entirely in the mind, in limbo, perhaps even unthinkable. This was to become *L'Amour Fou* (much more than *Suzanne Simonin, La Religieuse de Denis Diderot*, with its musical *découpage* haunted by timbres, pitches, durations: by musical analogies). Consequence? Chance? Somewhere between the two, the film gathered itself, stirred, finally came into existence: the fruit of an impossible encounter between the two extremes of absolute control and absolute freedom (those two inaccessible and irreconcilable temptations). Infirm but incredible, *L'Amour Fou* may in its own way be halting, agonizing, cavalier and contorted, and also, even in its very weaknesses and indulgences, the first stage towards a new modernity, at least *ventured* if nct accomplished, a modernity aware of itself: both of its powers and of its insufficiencies. Of its folly, in fact.

Groups, theatre, conspiracy: excess

Jacques Rivette (born 1928) has made four feature films (or five if the last may be counted as double): *Paris Nous Appartient*, *La Religieuse*, *L'Amour Fou* and *Out I/Spectre* (1972). The first two, as we have seen, belong to the *classical* cinema: predominant are a dramaturgy pre-existing the filming, a written text, a planned shooting script. The films that follow radically modify the function and powers traditionally assigned to the film-maker: here the script is no longer a programme to be carried out, a score to be followed, but a sort of vast fictional trap, simultaneously rigorous and open, designed to orient the improvisation (by actors and technicians), to subject it to certain 'obligatory passages', or to abandon it to a free flow which will acquire its order, its scansion, its proportions only in the final montage, in an ultimate interplay between the inherent logic of the material filmed (its potentialities, its resistances) and the demands of a rational, critical organization. Critical in two ways: critical of the material filmed (concrete) and of the scheme (abstract) which provided the initial impulse. This attitude, with the principle pushed to its limits, resulted in the birth of a *film-fleuve* with *Out I* (1971), perhaps the longest in the history of the cinema: thirteen hours. But *Out I* is two films. A 'shorter' version exists, running for approximately four hours, which is not simply a digest of the full version (as was the case with the condensed version of *L'Amour Fou* disowned by Rivette), but a reorganization along new narrative lines, and with new preoccupations, of the completely transformed premises: it is another film, a splintered reflection of the first, illuminating, obfuscating, challenging it by suggesting other avenues or angles of approach for anyone who has seen both films, but also working perfectly as an autonomous experience. A case as systematic as this (two different films emerging from the same basic material) is unique.

Unique in length, unique in structure, *Out I* (the 'long' film) and *Spectre* (the 'short' one) offer a palpable experience of a vision irreducible to any other—as irreducible, on its 'narrative' ground, as those of Straub or Brakhage or Snow—the exploration of a sort of virginal fictional continent, a hallucinatingly gripping structural meditation, a 'voyage' into the space-time of a predatory, proliferating, multi-dimensional fable. To describe or to recapitulate (to reduce) it would be an impossible task here, even if only a structural description, a thematic analysis, or an account of its generative principle were attempted. Nothing can take the place of the 'trip' itself (the tangible experience undergone by the eyes, the ears, the whole

body, its excitement or its fatigue, the constant resurgence of the body through the film), no critical substitute, no commentary, no 'directions for use'. At best one might note the choice of generators, cautiously point out a guideline or two:

To begin with, *play* in all senses of the word was the only idea: the playing by the actors, the play between the characters, play in the sense that children play, and also play in the sense that there is play between the parts of an assemblage. This was the basic principle, implying a relative interdependence between the elements, and a relative distance maintained by the actors between themselves and the characters they were playing. (Jacques Rivette.)

What we are shown in this film is the infinite space *in the wings*. Two plays are being rehearsed (both by Aeschylus), rival, parallel, by two companies, two mentors: a man and a woman who used to live together. Exercises, rehearsals, psycho-dramas involving fictional characters and real actors, then critical discussions of these activities, are filmed integrally as they happen (in *Out I*; in *Spectre*, they are cut to the quick. Where *Out I* might frustrate through excessive length, *Spectre* can frustrate through being excessively elliptical). Other characters, other fictions are gradually injected between these seemingly 'documentary' blocks, first a few, then proliferating until they form an imaginary configuration where once again the conspiracy, the secret society perhaps, becomes both the source and the objective of frantic, obstinate, apparently logical (but paranoically logical) investigations in which a highly symmetrical pair of young people (a boy, a girl), more fictional than any work of fiction (Verne, Poe, Balzac or Kafka), more intrepid and much crazier than the heroes and heroines of the serials, are trapped and founder, or maybe even die.

In the wings of the theatre, in the wings of fiction or of conspiracy (conspiracy as a metaphor for all *mise en scène*, but with no Mabuse in evidence); all these spaces in the wings are presented as stages (not to mention corridors, cellars, garrets, the back rooms of shops) revealing the other scene as the only theatre, fostering dreams and phantoms. *Out I/Spectre* is not of course the first film

Dominique Labourier and Juliet Berto in *Céline et Julie Vont en Bateau*: 'Two girls meet in a Montmartre square; one a librarian, the other a magician.'

to attempt this. But it is certainly one of the most radical, one in which the great machinery of the imagination emits the most disturbing rays, casts out the most efficient net in which manipulators and creations, characters and structures, forms and spectators, are caught and interchange through the interplay of roles and dualities. Credit to an 'auteur' is warranted only by the final ordering of the material, decoding the illusion which then redoubles itself, leaving the spectre of actions and events, of adventures and ordeals, attributable equally to the pseudo-sleep of pseudo-sleepers and to the collective dream of waking dreamers. Nothing definitive should be said here, however: the tale is to continue soon on another stage and with other phantoms.

Translated by Michael Graham

Out I/Spectre remains, for me, Rivette's finest achievement to date; it remains etched on the mind like a bad dream. Its effect is not unlike that of the films of Feuillade or the paintings of Magritte: melodrama in a realistic setting, anguish on the boulevards, anxiety in cafés, terror in the repeated shot of the peripheral ring-road. A mind-blowing experience, in fact, but one which, instead of 'taking one out of this world', took one right smack *into* it. Or into a world which one only dimly realized was there—always there right beneath the everyday world.

It was followed by a lighter work: *Céline et Julie Vont en Bateau* (*Céline and Julie Go Boating*, 1974)—although it is impossible to translate the full implication of the title, which is more like Céline and Julie go 'on a ride', in the sense of being 'taken for a ride'. It's about two girls who meet in a Montmartre square: one a librarian, the other a magician. In the course of their friendship, they somehow get plugged into a drama that is going on in a suburban house, a drama which has been loosely adapted from an early Henry James story called *A Romance of Certain Old Clothes*. Mysteriously, the main film is intercut with this sombre drama about a widower, his daughter and the two women who look after the widower. As the film progresses, Céline and Julie (Juliet Berto and Dominique Labourier, respectively) actually become participants in the drama. It's impossible to explain how in realistic terms, but somehow it works: one believes.

After the relative light-heartedness of this film, Rivette returned in *Duelle* (1976) to more serious themes. *Duelle* in some ways resembles Cocteau's *Orphée*, a modern version of an old myth. But *Duelle* is a contemporary version of a non-existent myth about two goddesses (Bulle Ogier: sun goddess; Juliet Berto: moon goddess) who are allowed to spend only forty days a year on earth. The only way they can manage to stay here permanently is by getting hold of a huge diamond called the Fairy Godmother.

The hunt for the diamond and the struggle to possess it make up the pseudo-plot of the film. It's set in a thriller milieu—a dance hall called The Rumba, an aquarium, the Métro, a racetrack, the lobby of a grand hotel—and the playthings of the goddesses are dance-hall-girls, a night-porteress in a hotel. Bewildered pawns though they may be in this cosmic duel, one of them is ready to sacrifice herself by taking on both goddesses—and, satisfyingly, her sacrifice is rewarded.

Duelle was to be the first of four films, called collectively, after Nerval, *Les Filles du Feu*. But the lack of commercial success of *Duelle* was such that only one more of the series has been completed, and that film, *Noroît (Nor'West*, 1976), has been released only in Germany. As *Duelle* was a new version of the thriller, so *Noroît* was a new kind of pirate film, with Geraldine Chaplin and Bernadette Laffont as the two chief pirates. To me, it was much less interesting than *Duelle*, but then, I have never enjoyed pirate films of any kind. Nevertheless, I am sure that *Noroît* will some day achieve a wider release, just as I am sure that the other films will be made. As Fieschi concluded, 'nothing definitive should be said here, however: the tale is to continue soon on another stage and with other phantoms'.

For further reading, see the chapter on Rivette in James Monaco's *The New Wave* (1976) and *Rivette: Texts and Interviews* (1977), edited by Jonathan Rosenbaum.

GLAUBER ROCHA

Edgardo Cozarinsky

For international audiences of the middle 60s, Glauber Rocha coined and epitomized an image of Third World Cinema as aesthetically fascinating as it was intellectually challenging. For the first time, the confusing, contradictory reality of a continent whose historical and cultural development had not followed an accessible pattern for European or American intellectuals was not being explained away from their own point of view but staged by a haughtily foreign sensibility—such ready-made equations as Right-Wing, Tradition and Mysticism, against Left-Wing, Progress and Rationalism were dismissed with a shock of colourful violence in a body of work which thrilled the European intelligentsia by questioning their most enlightened assumptions. Rocha's influence should not be undervalued: his talent for the illuminating catchphrase ('the aesthetics of hunger'), his ability as a leader in cultural politics (which resulted in the shaping of Brazilian *cinema novo* as an instrumental model for Latin America and a powerful image for Europe and even the U.S.), assured him an early niche in film history, as well as the appointment, together with Bertolucci and Straub, as royal heir of the new cinema's *jeunesse dorée*, in Godard's *Le Gai Savoir*.

Rocha's films, impressive as they are, in the long run may appear to have played only a supporting role in this process. *Deus e o diabo na terra do sol* (U.K.: *Black God, White Devil*, 1964) and *Terra em transe* (1967) are the most interesting because they work with rural or urban surfaces, respectively, to uncover the mythical quality of an experience they plainly refuse to domesticate. *Antonio das Mortes* (1969) already looks self-conscious in its operatic and choreographic elaboration of mass rebellion and mystical-revolutionary violence: an intended festival audience can be read in each extravagant development. The exile films—*Der leone have sept cabeças* (U.K.: *The Lion Has Seven Heads*, 1970), *Cabezas cortadas* (1970) and *Claro* (1975), undervalued by the same critics who boosted Rocha's earlier achievements—carry to its logical extremes the work with film language and political folklore which the previous films attempted, and try to shape Rocha's Brazilian experience into an international Third World image.

Rocha has now returned to Brazil; what will come of this move remains to be seen. There is a study of his work by Michel Ciment in *Second Wave* (1970), edited by Ian Cameron; see also M. Estève's *Le Cinéma Novo Brésilien: Glauber Rocha* (1975).

ERIC ROHMER

Molly Haskell

Probably the most deliciously unexpected success of the late 60s, in terms both of the film-maker and of the film itself, was Eric Rohmer's *Ma Nuit Chez Maud* (U.K.: *My Night with Maud*; U.S.: *My Night at Maud's*, 1969), embedded as it was in a double irony: for the non-cognoscenti, it was a 'talky', highbrow film apparently destined for a coterie audience; for those who knew Rohmer, a donnish intellectual hiding behind a pseudonym to conceal his 'disreputable' profession from his bourgeois family, it was a star-studded, eminently accessible movie. Neither group, though, could have predicted the film's box-office success, particularly in America. It was considered too Catholic, too French—this tale, filmed in black and white, of a long winter's night in Clermont-Ferrand and an almost-affair between a conservative Catholic engineer (Jean-Louis Trintignant) with Pascalian principles, and a free-thinking young divorcée (Françoise Fabian) with less orthodox impulses.

But perhaps there was nothing really so surprising about the popularity of this film, voluptuously prim and dignified against the fragmented horizon of the 'liberated' 60s, or of its glowingly intelligent successor, *Le Genou de Claire* (*Claire's Knee*), released in 1970. For within the rarefied air of intellectual chamber drama, Rohmer was refurbishing such supposedly exhausted conventions as plot, with beginnings, middles and ends; romance; and words—heady, civilized discourse between men and women; all the babies of fiction that a nostalgic, non-McLuhanist public thought had been thrown out with the bathwater of antiquated plot machinery.

With the coolly contemplative *Six Contes Moraux* (Six Moral Tales), whose values and concerns were closer to the nineteenth-century novel than to the twentieth-century film (particularly films of the decade in which Rohmer chose to make his début), Rohmer established himself as a major new film-maker in a neo-classical tradition of one. But it was a tradition whose conservative implications—a kind of moral and social as well as aesthetic puritanism—would become more binding and onerous in *L'Amour, l'Après-Midi* (U.K.: *Love in the Afternoon*; U.S.: *Chloe in the Afternoon*, 1972), the final and most fastidious of the Six Moral Tales.

One of *Cahiers du Cinéma*'s first critics and latest-blossoming film-makers, Rohmer had toiled away from the early days of the magazine under his real name, Maurice Scherer (born 1920), adopting his pseudonym around 1955. (It was then that his major theoretical piece, *Celluloid and Marble*, on the relationship of film to the other arts, was being serialized in *Cahiers*.) His first feature film, *Le Signe du Lion* (U.K.: *The Sign of Leo*, 1959)—the story of an American expatriate on the downgrade in Paris—was a technically accomplished, uningratiating picture which had a small *succès d'estime* but no commercial career. Rohmer broke with *Cahiers* in 1963 over shifts in its *politique* (he continued to champion the American cinema when it was no longer 'correct' to do so), although he contributed a sketch to the *Cahiers*-omnibus film, *Paris vu par . . .* (*Six in Paris*, 1965). His item, *Place de l'Etoile*, is an ironic account of a bureaucrat forced to alter his route to work because he thinks he has killed a man.

In 1964 he began making documentaries for French television. Before, and in between, he set about, on a limited budget, making the Six Moral Tales. The basic pattern, a kind of Racinian formula of unrequited love minus the passion (A, who is committed to B, meets and is tempted by C but renounces her in favour of B), does not establish itself until the third tale. The first two, *La Boulangère de Monceau* (1962) and *La Carrière de Suzanne* (1963), were shot in 16 mm and never released theatrically. The third, *La Collectionneuse* (U.S.: *The Collector*, 1967), was actually written and meant to be shot fourth, but the unavailability of Trintignant at the time delayed the filming of *Ma Nuit Chez Maud* and reversed the order. *La Collectionneuse* falls naturally into third place, however, as a transitional film. Although they contain, in germ and with increasing complexity, the themes and preoccupations of the later films, the first three (particularly the first two) are really dry runs for the breathtakingly subtle and brilliantly cast and enacted amorous skirmishes of *Ma Nuit Chez Maud* and *Claire's Knee*.

In the first tale, a young man sets himself the task of seducing a girl who works in a bakery—and succeeds. In the second, a third person and dimension are introduced: a young man is unimpressed with a girl until he sees that she has won the attention of another man, whereupon his own interest is aroused. The perversity of human nature and the various subterfuges of desire—themes unifying all six tales—acquire greater complexity and malignancy in *La Collectionneuse*. In the idle ambience of St-Tropez, a handsome, humourless intellectual named Adrien (Patrick Bauchau) and a not-so-lovely but more likable painter (Daniel Pommereulle) are sharing a friend's villa with a girl (Haydée Politoff)—a bikini-wearing nymphette of silky, feline grace, the 'collector', who sleeps with a different boy each night with no more after-effect than a cat gets from a bowl of milk. The camera's analysis of her smooth bronze limbs as she walks along the beach introduces the note of eroticism that will be consistently and perversely contravened by the rest of the film, or rather, by the ethos of the film as it resides in the central character of Adrien. In that deftly reasoned (or rationalized?) fervour of renunciation that characterizes all Rohmer's protagonists, and becomes a fever of ecstasy with the hero of *L'Amour, l'Après-Midi*, Adrien refuses to be 'seduced' by the promiscuous girl, and saves himself for his sensible, winter-permanent love, the English girl seen briefly at the beginning of the film. Each protagonist has a similar 'commitment', and each commitment is similarly shadowy in relation to the woman who represents the present temptation, giving the rejection more importance and weight than the affirmation.

In thrall to the image of a blonde girl he has seen in church, and to whom he feels mystically bound by a congruence of faith and probability, the Trintignant character in *Ma Nuit Chez Maud* passes up intimacy with the vibrantly exciting Maud. As a diplomat spending the summer in Annecy (*Claire's Knee*), Jean-Claude Brialy toys with, then turns from Laura (Béatrice Romand), the precocious, vastly superior young teenager, to the blonde and inaccessible Claire (Laurence de Monaghan) and, when she becomes accessible, from her to his adult fiancée waiting in the wings. Bernard Verley's businessman (*L'Amour, l'Après-Midi*) fancies himself a dreamer and romantic and lover of women until a free spirit in the person of Chloë (Zouzou) presents herself, and he runs for his wife.

Risk is refused, both folly and passion circumvented. Morality, a function of character invoked to explain the workings of taste, place and circumstance, becomes even more ambiguous and relative as it seems to proceed so organically from the personality of the actor. Rohmer has an uncanny ability—implemented by long hours of conversation and taping with the cast before each picture—to phrase the dialogue in the actors' own words, indeed, to create the script out of their unique idiom and character. His protagonists are neither 'good' nor altogether sympathetic, and the implications of their decisions are clearer to us, their 'readers', than to themselves. Passionlessness is the one trait they all share, and their 'morality' is composed as much of self-delusion as of rectitude. And yet, to the extent that they are conceived within a classically inalterable, ethically binding universe, their choices are *moral*.

For Rohmer, love becomes both the trigger and the mirror of human behaviour, a vision dense with possibilities that is more often to be found in the novel than in film. Like the young men of Stendhal or Balzac, or the heroines of Jane Austen or Charlotte Brontë, Rohmer's protagonists define themselves, ethically and morally, by whom they choose to love and (even more important) *not* to love, by the romantic choices they make—prismatic choices in which place and time and a whole society are refracted. Rohmer makes no secret of his debts to a literary culture, both in his approach and in the heavily allusive content of his works. *L'Amour, l'Après-Midi* makes use not only of obvious classical references—*Daphnis and Chloe*, and the legendary Alexander (Frédéric's son); Diderot (Frédéric is reading the account of the 'noble savage' in *Le Voyage de Bougainville avec le Supplément de Diderot*)—by means of which Rohmer introduces the notion of anti-traditional, anti-bourgeois love only to reject it; it also suggests a thousand other sources and significations for the cultured French viewer. One critic has traced the untameable Chloë, the personification of liberty, to André Breton's *Nadja*, the queen of surrealism. And perhaps Frédéric himself suggests the overcivilized, culturally enervated Frédéric Moreau of Flaubert's *L'Education Sentimentale*.

And yet for all this, the films are no less 'cinematographic'. Cinema, Rohmer maintained (in *Celluloid and Marble*), stood alone in its unselfconsciousness among modern art forms as 'the last refuge of poetry'. The nature of the medium was such that metaphor, which had lost its natural roots in the other arts, could spring forth spontaneously in film. As a gesture that revealed, through the surface, the life of the spirit, metaphor depended on a connection between the material and immaterial worlds, on a sense of finality. With this sense of 'finality'—to be found in film, and in the work of Balzac, but absent from most twentieth-century thinking—a film-maker could preserve that which was denied to other artists: a 'classical optimism'.

Rohmer tried—with considerable success—to induce, with the rigorously 'closed' worlds of *La Collectionneuse* (the aggressive indolence of St-Tropez), *Ma Nuit Chez Maud* (the womb-like oasis in the winter desert of the provinces), *Claire's Knee* (the mixed ages and complex summer intimacies of Annecy's 'family' atmosphere), the sense of 'finality' he admired in Balzac. But to what degree did the 'classical optimism' follow naturally and to what degree was it the result of an imposed moral geometry?

In Rohmer's best films—*Ma Nuit Chez Maud* and *Claire's Knee*—there is, in the hero's final character equation, a delicate balance between gain and loss, between self-knowledge and self-delusion. But in *L'Amour, l'Après-Midi*, Frédéric's farcical escape from Chloë and fatuous reunion with his wife, and Rohmer's vindication of conjugal love (for the tearfully emotional reunion cannot be taken as anything less than a commitment on Rohmer's part—or as a contempt too artistically cynical to consider) represent a complete capitulation to bourgeois morality, a victory of blindness over (in)sight. Frédéric's self-deception, his commitment to the idea of an emotion, or a person, instead of to the person herself, is total. This oppressive conclusion to the moral tales, and the way Rohmer recalls the women of previous films through the narrow framework of Frédéric's fantasy life, suggests Rohmer has made a bargain with the devil: that for the privilege of retaining a 'classical optimism' and *mise en scène* he has paid with his soul. By an association which he makes inescapable, traditional aesthetic values become linked with reactionary social ones.

Frédéric, Rohmer's most antipathetic hero since Jess Hahn in *Le Signe du Lion*, is a 'goody-goody' in much the same way as Fanny in Jane Austen's *Mansfield Park*, and the film is unsatisfying for many of the same reasons. The judgement—in the terms with which Lionel Trilling brilliantly pinpointed the problem in the Austen work—is no longer dialectical, as it was in *Maud* and *Claire* (or *Emma* and *Sense and Sensibility*), granting persuasive authority and weight to the subversive characters, the ones who embody the impulse to liberation, but it is categorical, summarily rejecting the unfettered Chloë just as Fanny, in defending the values of Mansfield Park, repudiated the whole concept of theatre. Rohmer, through the bloodless Frédéric, goes beyond rejecting Chloë to humiliating her; Frédéric not only leaves her naked on a bed, but seems never *really* to have wanted her in the first place.

Of all the *Cahiers* critics-turned-directors who came under the influence of André Bazin (which is to say all of them), Rohmer is the one who most closely adheres, in his films, to the principles established by the master—but from instincts, classical and literary, which are entirely his own.

The child is father to the man, and the critic, in the *Cahiers* tradition, is father to the film-maker. As every critic gravitates towards the director, and the director's qualities,

Jean-Claude Brialy admiring Laurence de Monaghan's knee in *Le Genou de Claire*.

to which he himself responds, so Rohmer in his reviews of Hitchcock, Hawks, Welles and Mankiewicz reveals the moral and aesthetic, even *scientific*, predilections his own films will contain. He is nowhere perhaps so revealing of the values he himself will espouse as in his review of *The Quiet American*, particularly because in overpraising the virtues of this minor Mankiewicz film he betrays the emotionalism of a man defending the aesthetic members of his immediate family. In singling out (as Godard also had done) the director's use of 'words' and 'psychology' (both dirty words in the lexicon of the *politique des auteurs*), he labels the values that will be paramount in his own cinema.

'*Mise en scène?*' he asks rhetorically towards the end of his review. Then, directing himself to the 'purists', he asks for a looser definition of the term which would allow for a 'mixture of languages' and modes of adaptation, concluding with the question 'Would we ever have believed, for example, that our old friend *mise en scène* would one day be hiding beneath the mantle of a play on words?'

Earlier, in his plea for the word, Rohmer maintained that the cinema 'either distrusts words completely, or it cherishes them wholeheartedly. Above all, of course, it gives us things to see, but if it opens upon a world of brilliant talkers, it is important that they be as talkative as possible. To want to restrain their prolixity would be a grave betrayal of the realism fundamental to the cinematographic work.' And thus does Rohmer relate his own proclivity for words and cerebration, and his self-effacing classicism, to the principle of photographic realism—'*l'objectivité cinématographique*'—embraced by Bazin.

One might profitably compare the different demands made upon the same cinematographer, Nestor Almendros, by Rohmer and Truffaut (or, for that matter, the diametrically different voices with which both film-makers pay tribute to Balzac). Truffaut has Almendros climbing ladders and going through walls to obtain lyrically subjective images, while Almendros' set-ups for Rohmer, in a manner reminiscent of the invisible, functional style of Howard Hawks, disclose nothing that couldn't be seen by the eye of a man standing on the ground.

But the intense, physical immediacy of Rohmer's erogenous images—Maud's fur bedspread, Haydée's bronze body and (above all) Claire's knee—only emphasizes the psychological distance between the observed and the observer, between the man and the woman. To the extent that what aches to be touched goes untouched, Rohmer's style underlines, and luxuriates in, the voluptuousness of vain longing, and endorses the perverse preference of mankind (and cinema) for unattainable surfaces over knowable essences. In the ultimate rejection of the sensual there are intimations (borne out by Rohmer's affinity with Mankiewicz) of a certain contempt for the medium, a contempt that will probably always figure in the work of Rohmer but will be, at best, resolved in the paradox of attraction and repulsion. In the magnetic surface of Claire's knee, for example, harmlessly resting at eye level on the ladder, the rich ironies of Rohmer's artistic sensibility are transfixed in one of the most exquisite, self-revealing metaphors the cinema has ever produced.

In view of Molly Haskell's mention of a critic who traced the 'untameable Chloë, the personification of liberty, to André Breton's Nadja, the queen of surrealism', it is interesting that Rohmer made a short (which no one I know has seen) called *Nadja à Paris* (1964).

What Haskell calls Rohmer's 'ultimate rejection of the sensual' is perhaps true of the films she discusses. But since *L'Amour, l'Après-Midi*, Rohmer has made *Die Marquise von O . . . (The Marquise of O.,* 1976), in which, perhaps because it is not an original script, sensuality is very much to the fore. *The Marquise of O.* is an adaptation of a novella by Heinrich von Kleist; Rohmer, with a French crew, shot the film in Germany with German actors in German. Aided by cameraman Nestor Almendros, Rohmer has, without actual imitation, given us an image of Biedermeier Germany: neo-classical interiors and high-waisted gowns, the whole bathed in that unearthly light of painters like Caspar David Friedrichs. The actors, all drawn from Peter Stein's Theater an der Halleschen Ufer in Berlin, are superbly cast and directed.

The story is about a chaste widow who finds herself pregnant, with no idea of how she could have got that way. Although Roh-

mer keeps very closely to the Kleist text, the film comes out paradoxically as his most personal and perhaps most satisfying. Elegant and restrained, yet moving and warm, it can make one laugh and cry at the same time.

In 1978 Rohmer completed *Perceval le Gallois*. Like the *Marquise von O.* it is not an original script, and like that film it is not in French. Or rather, it is partly in Old French, for this is nothing less than an adaptation of the first half of Chrétien de Troyes' epic twelfth-century poem about Perceval the Welshman, the holy fool. Rohmer has remained relatively faithful to the original text in rhyming verse, and he has shot the film *entirely* in painted sets as stylized as a medieval miniature.

This may all sound like a scholarly exercise and one might think we are far from the world of the Six Moral Tales. Not so. After the first twenty minutes or so when one has to adjust to the language and the sets, the film takes off and by the end it has soared higher than any of Rohmer's previous films. Nor are we that far from the Moral Tales. Perceval, whom Rohmer describes as a medieval Buster Keaton, is also very much like the character played by Trintignant in *My Night at Maud's*; the adolescent girls who people the film are sisters to Claire, even if we are never allowed to see their knees.

The Perceval of Chrétien de Troyes has little to do with the Parsifal of Wagner; and Rohmer's film is far from resembling Bresson's *Lancelot du Lac*. The ostensible subject is still the quest for the H~ly Grail, but the film is open-ended. We last see Perceval going down the road in search of the Grail ... but he may already have found it. Because for Rohmer the quest for the Grail is less interesting than the way in which this quest moulds the character and behaviour of his hero.

Surprisingly little has been written about Rohmer; fortunately there is James Monaco's *The New Wave* (1976), which deals extensively and intelligently with Rohmer's films.

MIKHAIL ROMM

David Wilson

As with many of his contemporaries, Mikhail Romm's film-making career was largely determined by the vagaries of the Soviet political climate. And as with other Russian directors of his generation, there can only be speculation about how a civilized talent might have blossomed if Romm (1901–71) had not been obliged to hitch his star to the Stalinist heavy wagon. Achieved under constraints and shackled by committees, Romm's career is almost the archetype of the Russian cinema's decline, after the adventures and experiments of the 20s, into the Stalinist sterility of the 40s and 50s.

Romm's film-making début, following an apprenticeship as a script-writer, was *Pychka* (1934), an elegant, sophisticated version of Maupassant's *Boule de Suif*. This was one of the last silent films made in Russia, and the arrival of sound coincided with the ascendancy of socialist realism over the montage cinema of the post-revolutionary decade. Romm, not least, was obliged to toe the party line. *Trinadtsat* (*The Thirteen*, 1937) was an appropriately 'positive' drama of a desert patrol, owing something to John Ford's *Lost Patrol*. It was followed by the solemn hagiography of *Lenin v Oktyabre* (*Lenin in October*, 1937), which was made in record time for the twentieth anniversary of the Revolution, and *Lenin v 1918 Godov* (*Lenin in 1918*, 1939), films specifically designed to present Stalin as Lenin's natural heir. Even in such propagandist exercises, Romm's sense of style loosened some of the chains of ideological orthodoxy; and his *Tchelovek No 217* (*Person No. 217* or *Girl No. 217*, 1945), about Russian women in Nazi labour camps, is one of the less impersonal films made in Russia during the war.

Later films, like *Rousskyi Vopros* (*The Russian Question*, 1948) and *Sekretnaia Missia* (*Secret Mission*, 1950), had all the personality stamped out of them by the paralysing exigencies of Cold War propaganda. But the Russian cinema's tentative resurrection after 'the thaw' saw Romm, along with other veteran directors like Sergei Yutkevitch and Grigori Kozintsev, finding a new lease of life. His last two films—*Deviat Dnei Odnovo Goda* (*Nine Days of One Year*, 1962), a cool and open-ended look at the human face of science, and *Obyknovennyi Fachizm* (U.K.: *Ordinary Fascism*; U.S.: *Triumph of Violence*, 1965), an effectively discursive documentary enquiry into the psychology of fascism—impressively demonstrate what Romm might have achieved in a climate different from the long Stalinist winter.

For further reading, see Jay Leyda's *Kino* (1960) and *Cinema in Revolution* (1973) edited by Jean and Luda Schnitzer; there is also a monograph in French by René Prédal: *Romm* (1975).

ABRAM ROOM

Richard Roud

Abram Room (1894–1976) is one of those directors who is remembered for only one film; in his case it is *Tretya Meshchanskaya (Bed and Sofa)*, made in 1926, only two years after he began his career as a director. In fact, this is the only film by Room that most people have seen. Jay Leyda tells us, however, that its two predecessors, *Bukhta Smerti (Death Bay*, 1926) and *Predatel (Traitor*, 1926), were interesting works but in a different vein. *Bed and Sofa* is, as Leyda puts it, 'a masterpiece of intimate relations, intimately observed'. Even today, its viewpoint on the two-man, one-woman triangle seems fresh, even liberated; coming out of Soviet Russia in the 20s, it must have seemed revolutionary. Its plot is simple. A young couple live in a one-room flat. One night, the husband meets an old friend who has nowhere to sleep. Come back with me, he says, and you can have the sofa. The wife bitterly resents this intrusion, but the friend does his best to charm her—and succeeds. So much so, that when the husband has to leave town for a while, the inevitable occurs; when he returns he is offered . . . the sofa. The real originality of the film (scripted by Shklovsky) lies in what follows; far from opting for one man or the other when she discovers she is pregnant by one of them, she is so revolted by their *macho* selfishness that she leaves them both. Room's handling of the actors, and the affectionate accuracy of his observation, make what might have been a trivial anecdote into a charming and unforgettable film.

For further reading see Jay Leyda's *Kino* (1960).

FRANCESCO ROSI

Ted Perry

With few exceptions, Francesco Rosi's films have been based upon the lives of actual people—Salvatore Giuliano, Enrico Mattei, Lucky Luciano, Miguel Mateo Miguelin. The subject-matter is similarly drawn from actual situations—organized crime, war, real estate exploitation, bullfighting, the control of petroleum.

As a result Rosi's films are often praised because they deal in a forceful way with contemporary problems. Often they do, and often in an engaging manner. It is worth noting, however, that the formal structure of the films never quite matches the ideological problems. No matter how radical the ideas, no matter how complex and inaccessible the truth, the syntax or form of the film remains within conventional bounds. That does not mean Rosi's films are conventional, but rather that the aspirations of the thematic material are more radical than the cinematic form.

The strength of films such as *Salvatore Giuliano* (1961), *Le Mani sulla Città (Hands over the City*, 1963) and *Il Caso Mattei (The Mattei Affair*, 1972) is that they weave an intricate path between representation and fiction, between the imagined and the actual, the aesthetic and the documentary. The maintenance of this tension indicates that Rosi is not inclined to finish his films, in the sense of presenting them from a single, fixed viewpoint which leads to a clear and coherent statement. The dissection of a particular historical or present reality seems to be what attracts him and what generates his work. But he rarely reaches the kinds of conclusions which one expects from such a pathologist engaged in such an activity. Instead, the various events are viewed and presented from several aspects, leaving any final resolution and understanding, if they exist, to the spectator. The earlier films, such as *Salvatore Giuliano* and *Le Mani sulla Città*, accomplished this end with a rigorous compilation of facts, using only the simplest formal strategies. In more recent years, as in *Il Caso Mattei*, the cinematic style has become more bold, creating a more visually exciting if less effective tension between the aesthetic and the documentary.

Born in Naples in 1922, Rosi has been on a downward spiral for the past few years, or so it seems to me. *Uomini Contro* (1970) was dull, if worthy; *Lucky Luciano* (1973) was a disaster; and *Cadaveri Eccellenti* (*Illustrious Corpses*, 1976), though highly praised in Europe, seems to me unsatisfying: overstylized, relying too heavily on odd camera angles and distorting wide-angle lenses, it was elegant but empty. As Perry says, 'the aspirations of the thematic material are more radical than the cinematic form'.

There are indications, however, that inside the political Rosi, there is a comedy director struggling to get out. *C'Era una Volta* (*Cinderella, Italian Style*, 1967) is a much underrated film, made with style, charm and warmth. If only he would content himself with less ambitious projects like this one.

There is an excellent full-length study in French of Rosi's work, Michel Ciment's *Le Dossier Rosi* (1976).

ROBERTO ROSSELLINI

Robin Wood

Roberto Rossellini (1906–77) first achieved international repute as the founder and leading exponent of Italian neo-realism. The label is at best a half-truth, demanding various qualifications, but the issue here is complex. Alone of those major figures whose early development was rooted in the neo-realist movement, Rossellini remained faithful to certain of its aims and dogmas. By any definition, 'neo-realism' is scarcely relevant to the Antonioni of *L'Eclisse* or *Deserto Rosso*, to the Fellini of *Giulietta degli Spiriti* or *Satyricon*, let alone to the shameless commercialism of most of the later De Sica, or, for that matter, the subtler sellout of *The Garden of the Finzi-Continis*; but there is still something of the neo-realist impulse behind Rossellini's *India* (1958), or the subsequent historical reconstructions, from *Viva l'Italia!* (1960) to the TV film *Agostino di Ippona* (*Augustine of Hippo*, 1972). On the other hand, Rossellini didn't found neo-realism: that distinction must be accorded (if to any single figure) to Visconti (for *Ossessione*, 1942), with Renoir (particularly, but not exclusively, for *Toni*, 1934) as forerunner. Nor was Rossellini initially a neo-realist

(unless we interpret the term very loosely indeed): before *Roma, Città Aperta* (U.K.: *Rome, Open City*; U.S.: *Open City*, 1945), which most of us once assumed to be his first film, he made four features under the Fascist regime—of which I have been able to see only *La Nave Bianca* (1941), the earliest of the four.

With regard to this film, two questions seem pertinent: how just is it to describe it as a 'Fascist' film?; and how like and unlike Rossellini's subsequent movies does it prove to be? First, then, *La Nave Bianca* is a war movie made from the Italian viewpoint; it suggests that Italian sailors were largely likeable, Italian nurses humane and dedicated, and Italian hospital ships efficiently run. It is, in other words, no more (though no less) a 'Fascist' movie than most of its British and American counterparts of that period. Apart from the admittedly disconcerting Eisensteinian montage of low-angle shots of the guns of battleships with which it opens, it nowhere eulogizes power or right-through-might or the notion of the Superman (at least, it doesn't do so visually: the print I saw was unsubtitled).

Is there such a thing as a 'Fascist' style? A Fascist style would, I take it, by definition be dedicated to dominating and manipulating audience response, and would be characterized by 'dictatorial' set-ups and angles that force us to look at only those aspects or details that immediately suit the director's purpose and to respond only as he decrees. If this definition is accepted, it follows that the two most notable Fascist directors are (with the possible exception of Riefenstahl) Eisenstein and Hitchcock, and *La Nave Bianca* is a non-starter. In fact, the relationship of style to ideology is a far more intricate and complex one than any such description suggests.

La Nave Bianca seems to me in all senses an innocent film, the work of a man who not only hasn't grasped that he's working for the wrong side, but who hasn't yet perceived that the conditions in which human life is lived can be, and frequently are, appalling, that human suffering (whether physical, mental or emotional) is unbearable not only to experience but to contemplate. It is this innocence, primarily, that sets the film apart from Rossellini's later work, which is characteristically preoccupied either with suffering itself or with a transcendental reaching beyond it.

The melodramatic plot of *La Nave Bianca* (the beautiful nurse who tends the wounded sailor is in fact the idealized pen-friend he has never met) need surprise no one: Rossellini has shown no squeamishness about melodrama, and Ross Hunter himself might seriously have considered the plot-lines of the Rome episode of *Paisà* (U.S.: *Paisan*, 1946) or of *Europa 51* (U.S.: *No Greater Love*, 1952) (before rejecting them on grounds of insufficiently glamorous locale). It is a peculiarity of Rossellini's genius to wish repeatedly to fuse the 'truth' of melodrama with the 'truth' of documentary. What distinguishes *La Nave Bianca* (a film strongly tending to the documentary in its analysis of the mechanics of naval warfare and the care of the wounded) from the films that followed it within five years is its polished, unruffled style. Whether or not you regard Rossellini as a 'neo-realist' depends on how you define the term (and there are many definitions); what is clear is that the so-called 'neo-realist' style of *Rome, Open City, Paisà* and *Germania, Anno Zero* (*Germany Year Zero*, 1947), was a matter of personal necessity rather than of detached artistic principle, and the mark of his loss of innocence.

Let us admit that 'neo-realism' is little more than a convenient label, and the 'little more' a matter of only partly definable resonance rather than precise meaning. The term suggests some characteristics that are important to Rossellini but it by no means satisfactorily sums him up. Those characteristics can be listed thus: an interest in the social actualities of contemporary life; a consequent use of real locations rather than studio sets, a tendency to use 'real' people rather than professional actors; the attempt to capture, partly through these means, with as much immediacy as possible, the 'feel' of contemporary experience (the vagueness of my formula here is deliberate: a more precise one would be misleading); the adoption of the conventions of 'documentary realism', particularly of the kind of photography associated with newsreels.

Let us first be clear that this last is indeed a convention: in terms of the precise reproduc-

tion of what the world really looks like, there is no way in which drab or 'grainy' black-and-white photography can be argued to hold a monopoly on verisimilitude. (The depth-of-field Panavision colour photography of a Hollywood biblical epic might logically be held to have stronger claims; though that, of course, is a convention also.) That we are conditioned to accept (by a process of association) something approximating the look of newsreel as 'realistic' accounts partly for the immediate impact *Rome, Open City* and *Paisà* had when they first appeared, but it is also responsible for false assumptions and false expectations (Rossellini's reputation has never recovered from this initial international acclaim). The most pernicious of these has been the association of such a style with the 'objective' or 'impersonal'—the assumption that it either does or at least *should* confer objective validity on the subject matter to which it is applied. The more astute critics, even in the early days of Rossellini's reputation, were quick to point out that his plots were melodramatic, his use of his brother Renzo's music overtly dramatizing and manipulative, his attitudes often biased and occasionally (especially in *Germany Year Zero*) 'hysterical'. Their perception was accurate enough; their error was to take for granted that these were faults, because they conflicted with the spirit of (supposed) neo-realist theory.

It is difficult to envisage such a thing as perfectly objective reportage in the cinema. However determined the film-maker may be to neutralize his own personal intrusions, to turn his camera on the world in an attempt to capture 'reality', every positioning of that camera, every movement, every cut, will inevitably be a matter of choice reflecting personal viewpoint and personal bias. To adopt a particular style is automatically to express an ideology, a metaphysic. It is instructive to compare—as expressions of protest against 'man's inhumanity to man'— the last episode of *Paisà* (the rounding up and execution of partisans and American soldiers behind German lines in the Po valley) with the Odessa Steps sequence from *The Battleship Potemkin*. One might begin by contrasting the two directors' use of space and time. The Eisenstein sequence is a great poem made up of images connected more by association and deliberately created emotional effect than by spatial and temporal logic. It is impossible, even after repeated viewings, to work out where the various groups of people are in relation to each other; our sense of the actual length of the Steps is completely undermined, the soldiers seeming to march relentlessly on and on and never getting much further down; a mother whose child has been shot some distance above her is seen a few shots later going *down* the steps to retrieve its body. The editing is extremely fragmented (over 200 shots in ten minutes of film); the camera (once the slaughter has started) is fairly close to its subjects and in the great majority of shots static: we are not allowed the overall view that would restore our sense of spatial reality.

Rossellini, on the contrary, works in fairly long takes, almost entirely in long-shot, the camera in almost constant movement. When Rossellini 'cheats' on space—as in not letting us see the precise distance between the floating body of the dead partisan and the boat of the man trying to retrieve it, until, much to our surprise, there they are within the same frame—the effect is subtly disturbing, as if he were breaking the rules he has set himself (Eisenstein's rules are quite different). It is tempting to argue from this that where Eisenstein offers contrived, artificial 'effects' that force the spectator to respond in a certain precisely definable way, Rossellini leaves one free to contemplate at a distance, what one contemplates being 'reality'. Yet it is arguable that the emotional effect of the Po valley episode is at least as immediate and overwhelming as that of the Odessa Steps scene; and the spectator, supposedly left 'detached' by the 'objective' style, can scarcely be in doubt as to which side Rossellini is on, what his position is with regard to the action, and how he means us to react.

Against the famous shots of the runaway baby-carriage in *The Battleship Potemkin* one might set the brief scene in *Paisà* of the aftermath of the massacre at Maddalena's, a baby and a dog the only survivors, the scene consisting chiefly of a single tracking-shot accompanying the screaming baby as it totters in terrified bewilderment among the corpses. The feeling of the Rossellini seems to me by far the purer, the less suspect: I am worried throughout the Odessa Steps sequence by

a growing awareness of the enormous discrepancy between the emotional impact of the shots and the extremely calculated way in which they are set up, and I'm not sure that the insistent repetition of details—the close-ups of the soldiers' feet treading (with what looks like great deliberateness) on the dead child, for example—is free from sadistic relish. Yet for all Rossellini's use of long-shot, and the common (not always false) assumption of a correlation between camera distance and emotional distancing, the difference is not of lesser emotional impact. It seems truer to describe it in terms of different world-views. The Odessa Steps sequence (though the effect is qualified by one's sense of Eisenstein's complicated personal psychology) is protest rooted in assurance of right and its ultimate victory. The issues are clear-cut: the spectator is provoked to rage at monstrous injustice, but he knows the People will triumph in the end. Such assurance is inseparable from confidence as to what is the right effect to create, and sanctions the film's manipulativeness. The Rossellini of *Paisà* can offer no such assurance. The continual restless movement of the Po valley episode—lop-sided, seemingly random compositions, boats and men moving in and out of frame, the camera seldom still, disorderly groups scuttling about in long-shot—suggests total instability, the sense of a world where nothing is certain except ultimate desolation, physical and emotional, a world of random and casual cruelty in which men come and go, appear and die, scarcely knowing each other, unable to extend or receive any comfort.

The other episodes of *Paisà* (if one excepts the Fellini-dominated and quite undistinguished anecdote about American chaplains in a monastery) all take conventional romantic or novelettish motifs—American soldier tries to communicate with Sicilian peasant girl, black soldier befriends war orphan, prostitute finds chance to regain her purity, nurse risks life to join partisan-leader lover —and proceed to undermine all conventional expectations of how such plots should work out, leaving us in every case not only without complacency but without hope. The Naples episode can be taken as representative. The common account of it is that the black, exposed to the reality of the child's existence,

comes to realize that others are just as exploited and victimized as he is. In fact, the
implications go far beyond that. In a scene
consisting chiefly of a long, static take, the
drunken black and the boy sit on a heap of
rubble amid the ruins of the city trying to
communicate, the black fantasizing about the
riches and luxury of 'home' (i.e., America).
Suddenly, as he sobers, he realizes that 'I
don't want to go home . . . Home's an old
shack . . .,' and reacts to the realization by
collapsing into sleep. Our sense of an
intuitive human contact developing between
them finds intense expression in the child's
begging him not to sleep—'If you fall asleep,
I'll steal your boots.' It is impossible to
understand Rossellini if one cannot accept
the *simplest* effects of which the cinema is
capable. This moment—which depends in no
sense on 'cinematic' techniques, unless 'technique' means what one refrains from doing—
is among the most moving in the film; to
reject it as sentimental is merely to harden
one's heart. The child's desperate outburst of
honesty, prompted not by any principle but
by the tentative sense of fellowship triumph-
ing over the linguistic barrier, testifies to
Rossellini's belief in innate human goodness
and the possibility of its survival or re-
awakening in even the most desolate and
discouraging material circumstances.

The black falls asleep, the child steals the
boots. Later, recognizing the child, the soldier (in fact a military policeman) forces him
to return the boots, demanding to be taken to
his home. If 'home' for the black is an old
shack, for the child it is even less—a desolate,
squalid, over-populated underworld. The
black demands to see his parents; the boy
manages to convey that they were killed in
the Allied bombing. The man drops the
boots and flees—as much from guilt as compassion, for he is forced to recognize himself
as part of the war machine that has effectively ruined the child's life, even as he
recognizes his own under-privileged existence (his self-respect goes with his uniform)
as reflected in the child's.

This metaphysical awareness of the terribleness of existence—in which even kind and
good people are involved in processes with
appalling and uncontrollable consequences,
so that, for example, the massacre in the final
episode is provoked by the presence of the

American who offers ointment to protect the
baby against mosquitoes—is fundamental to
Rossellini's subsequent development. The
loss of 'home', the sense that everyone is a
displaced person, is central to this awareness:
apart from the monastery, the only settled
'home' in *Paisà* is Maddalena's, where the
whole family is ruthlessly butchered. The
'world' of *Paisà* will recur, but in a new perspective, in *Europa 51*. In the 'neo-realist'
period—a phase which has the characteristics
of a descent into hell—it culminates in the
extraordinary *Germany Year Zero*, the only
Rossellini film to centre on a child, and
dedicated to the memory of his own son.

Children (and babies—born and unborn)
are in fact of crucial importance in Rossellini's films from *Rome, Open City* through to
the Ingrid Bergman series. They represent
hope for the future, the possibility of new
growth and development, the possibility of
future health amid the terrible disorder of
the world. When Anna Magnani is shot
down in *Rome, Open City*, the moment gains
particular force from the fact that she is pregnant. At the end of that film, the children are
used as a poignant affirmation of hope: in the
last shot the camera pans with them, the city
in the background, as they leave the scene of
the priest's execution, and stops when St
Peter's is securely in the centre of the image.
But in *Paisà* the children, abandoned and
alone, are swallowed up in the universal
chaos: in the scenes involving children, the
pervasive desolation is most intensely expressed. Given the particular significance of
children in these films it follows that the
most terrible act imaginable is the *suicide* of a
child: an act that constitutes the climax of
Germany Year Zero and the starting-point of
Europa 51.

Germany Year Zero is a film of great and
obvious faults which its intensity renders
almost irrelevant. One can certainly feel that
the agonies are piled on with melodramatic
relentlessness; certain scenes, and certain
effects, could be accused of crudity, for
example the over-obvious irony of the juxtaposition of Berlin ruins with a gramophone
record of a Hitler speech about the inevitability of victory; one may well resent the facile
association (here and in *Rome, Open City*) of
Nazism with homosexuality. Yet it is one of
those works which is almost *beyond* art:

works so directly the product of a sense of horror, of the terribleness of things, that to ask them to behave decorously seems like callous impertinence, as if one demanded that a cry of pain be aesthetically satisfying. Rossellini's foreword tells us that the film represents neither a plea nor a charge, but a testimony.

The last half-hour of *Germany Year Zero* is among the very finest things Rossellini achieved. The child Edmund, prompted by the remarks of his Nazi schoolmaster about the survival of the fit and the necessary elimination of the weak, poisons his own sick father. From that point he becomes an outcast, existing in an insupportable isolation: it is the film's triumph that his abrupt, casual suicide seems at once inevitable and profoundly shocking. What makes the sequence of Edmund's movement towards suicide so poignant is the way Rossellini counterpoints this lost soul's progress to total isolation and despair with his discovery of himself as a child. The action that abandons him to nothingness also releases him from the adult responsibilities which have turned him prematurely into a wizened old man. For the first time in the film he begins to play—desultory, pathetic, solitary little games in the ruined streets, hopscotch around the dirt-marks, kicking some unidentifiable broken object. All his attempts at contact are rejected: the street-gang drive him off, finding him too underdeveloped and 'innocent' (the irony, that Edmund has committed a crime beside which their petty swindling is trivial, is unstressed); the pederast schoolmaster whose words provoked Edmund's crime rejects him with horror as a 'monster'; children playing football with a lump of rubble don't want him, and Edmund, accepting the implications of his own monstrousness, can't protest.

In the final sequence, in the tall ruined building from which Edmund abruptly throws himself, poignant details and suggestions accumulate. A broken gadget becomes a toy gun: after briefly playing with it, the boy presses it to his own head in a gesture that fuses casual play with underlying despair. On an upper storey of the building, he sees his shadow in a patch of sunlight, and 'shoots' it, a moment again juxtaposing strongly contrasting associations: sunshine and death, the

impulse to play and the impulse to suicide, innocence and guilt. The building is opposite what was once the child's home: he can see his father's coffin being taken out, his brother and sister in the street. Their proximity (they call his name) evokes the child's irrevocable loss of 'home' (the concept as well as the place). Just before he casts himself from the building, Edmund slides down a makeshift chute—even at the moment of ultimate despair, the child's healthy impulse towards play and normality continues to express itself.

Germany Year Zero, in its uncompromising bleakness and pessimism and in its extraordinarily depleted style, which eschews all but the plain, bare statement, suggests a possible future development to describe which one might evoke Samuel Beckett—though clearly Beckett's self-consciousness and obsessive formalism are quite alien to Rossellini. His actual development took in fact an opposite turn, but one that in retrospect is no less logical. After the plunge into hell represented by *Paisà* and *Germany Year Zero*, his insistent preoccupation is with salvation: in what it might consist, how it might be defined, how it might be achieved.

The achievement of holiness, or sainthood: provided one doesn't interpret the terms too narrowly, that could be seen as the unifying concern of Rossellini's entire career. In a remarkable number of films, in fact, the term 'sainthood' can be taken fairly literally. A synopsis suggests that it is applicable to *L'Uomo della Croce* (1943), one of the early 'Fascist'-period films. There is the priest's progress to martyrdom in *Rome, Open City*, and the repetition of the pattern 14 years later in *Il Generale della Rovere* (U.S.: *General Della Rovere*, 1959)—the progress, determined by circumstances acting upon his finest intincts, of an ordinary and distinctly unheroic man towards the assumption of an exemplary heroism. There are the films about actual saints: the St Francis film (*Francesco, Giullare di Dio* [U.S.: *Flowers of St Francis*], 1950) in the midst of the Bergman period; *Giovanna d'Arco al Rogo* (*Joan of Arc at the Stake*, 1954), with Bergman herself, after Arthur Honegger's opera-oratorio; *Atti degli Apostoli* (*The Acts of the Apostles*, 1968), a TV episode-film lasting in all over five hours; and, more recently, *Augustine of Hippo*. Related to these are the studies of exemplary historical figures, Garibaldi in *Viva l'Italia!* and the 1970 *Socrate* (*Socrates*).

But it would be wrong to limit this concern to its more literal manifestations. The Rossellinian concept of holiness is both mystical and practical: mystical, inescapably, because the concern is with inner spiritual movement and perception, with mysteries only partly susceptible to explanation; yet Rossellini's saints are invariably recognizable human beings—they are like ourselves, and we register their holiness as an extension of potentialities we intuitively understand and share. Its achievement is almost invariably linked with the confrontation of the fact of death, and with the acceptance of the 'otherness' of things: the human being becomes aware of his smallness in an infinite universe, which is infinite above all in its possibilities of 'being'. The moment of self-realization for Rossellini involves a simultaneous awareness of the strangeness and familiarity of things: everything is different, 'other', yet everything relates. Such an awareness dissolves the obstinacies of the personal ego, the self is released from its prison, the wholeness of the world is apprehended through the manifold otherness of creation. Through this experience, the individual reaches the joy of acceptance, and is transfigured. If Rossellini's St Francis is the key figure here, the experience which the films define is perceived as fundamentally human, and open to quite unsaintly individuals, like Karin in *Stromboli* (1950), a film that at every point—in its central relationship, in its treatment of nature, in its respect for primitive existence, in its overall movement towards the point where the heroine breaks out of the husk of self to find intuitive knowledge—demands comparison with the work of D. H. Lawrence. 'Religious' experience in Rossellini, central to his work, is never (as it is in Bresson) accessible only to Catholics (or indeed to Christians).

Stromboli, Europa 51 and *Viaggio in Italia* (U.K.: *Journey to Italy* or *The Lonely Woman*; U.S.: *Strangers*, 1954) seem to me the three greatest Rossellini movies I have seen. Before I attempt to define their qualities—to which the Rossellinian sense of mystery is central— the film that is an obvious candidate for Rossellini's worst, *Il Miracolo* (*The Miracle*, 1948, made between *Germany Year Zero* and the Bergman movies), offers itself most conveniently as a means of defining those qualities and that sense of mystery negatively, by contrast. The film's value for this purpose (it forms the second half of a two-part work called *L'Amore*, the first being *La Voce Umana*, a version of Cocteau's monologue *La Voix Humaine*) lies in its superficial resemblance to the works that were to follow: the peasant woman Nanina (Anna Magnani), pregnant, climbs a mountain to undergo a mystical experience (like Bergman in *Stromboli*); she is misunderstood, cast out and rebuked by her peers, yet believes herself in some sense singled out by God (like Bergman in *Europe 51*); as in the latter film, *The Miracle* preserves a certain ambiguity towards its central figure (saint or madwoman?).

The similarities are superficial, the differences fundamental. The essential nature of *The Miracle* is determined not by Rossellini but by two collaborators from whose influence he subsequently—and necessarily—freed himself: Anna Magnani and, especially, Fellini, author of the scenario. The film's ambiguities are of a very different order from those normally associated with Rossellini: they are inseparable from its pretentiousness and its characteristically Fellinian futility. For a start, there is the man Nanina takes for St Joseph and allows to impregnate her. His identity has occasioned some speculation. Filmographies refer to him non-committally as 'The Traveller'; Jose-Luis Guarner, in his monograph on Rossellini, calls him a 'tramp', which he certainly doesn't look like; another critic described him to me as a shepherd, though there is no sign of any sheep. For my part, I see no evidence that he *isn't* St Joseph (he never speaks, which could be taken as a sign of his mystery, as a cheap gimmick, or both). True, as played by Fellini himself ('Consider Phlebas, who was once handsome and tall as you'), he has a rather cynical smile; but perhaps he is thinking, 'Damned if I let the Lord get in first *this* time.' In any case, he is a totally alien character in Rossellini's world, where mystery is only perceived through the everyday, and is never synonymous with mere mysteriousness.

Then there is the peasant woman. We are

told that she is crazy, but we see little evidence of it—at least, she seems no crazier than most of Anna Magnani's creations. Although the film is so much (and so limitingly) a Magnani vehicle, there are uncanny moments when one feels the role was written (in anticipation, for this is six years before *La Strada*) for Giulietta Masina: the passionate would-be Madonna and the half-witted waif are not that far apart. Madwoman or female Christ-figure? Guarner tells us rather comically that it is 'not by chance' that 'certain images and gestures ... remind us consciously or unconsciously of Christ's passion': the Way of the Cross symbolism is laid on with a trowel. But the ambiguity is given no context in which it might be meaningfully interpreted. The point might be either 'The Madonna was really a crazy peasant woman' (which is cheap irony) or 'Any crazy peasant woman is really a Madonna' (which is cheap sentimentality); both, together with the mushy mystification resulting from the refusal to resolve our uncertainty, would be typical of Fellini. So is the great *show* of vitality (involving a lot of running around, scrambling about and carrying on), combined with the final sense of the futility and emptiness it covers up.

With the Bergman films we move into very different territory. For a start, although her performances here are among the greatest in the history of the cinema, Bergman never presumes to dominate the films to the extent that they dwindle around her into 'vehicles': if her performance in each case is central to the film's meaning, that meaning is never reducible to a matter of histrionic exhibition. Secondly, where *The Miracle* attempts a spurious timelessness and ends by existing in a vacuum, the Bergman films are very firmly rooted in the social realities with which Rossellini was earlier preoccupied: *Stromboli* and *Europa 51*, particularly, can be seen as explicitly carrying on from where *Paisà* and *Germany Year Zero* left off—from the confusion and despair of the aftermath of war. Edmund, unable ever to go home again, was Rossellini's ultimate displaced person; the action of *Stromboli* starts in a displaced persons' camp, and is concerned with the heroine's gradual discovery and acceptance of 'home'.

That these are great films is still a proposition far from general acceptance—though we have perhaps come some way from the universal ridicule that greeted *Stromboli* on its initial release. The obstacle to appreciation is absolutely inseparable from the films' quality, lying as it does in Rossellini's style and method. The problem can be partly defined through Ingrid Bergman's own reported comment (on her return to Hollywood after her association with Rossellini had ended) that it was nice to be back working with 'professionals'; or through George Sanders' evident unhappiness in *Journey to Italy*, his performance the film's one serious flaw. We are as far as possible here from the concept of the 'well-made film'. Rossellini worked with only loosely structured scenarios, inventing scenes and dialogue spontaneously: before Godard (on whom he was one of the decisive influences) his was the most resourceful and significant attempt in the fiction film to create film as a writer writes or a painter paints—to create directly, without the intervention of a script (even one written by the director himself).

Such an ambition in the cinema *necessarily* entails roughness, the possible equivalents for 'painting over' or the writer's revision being so restricted. It also demands a particular kind of acting and a particular kind of actor—a particular relationship between actor and role, actor and director. What is involved is a quite precise balance between acting and not-acting. That George Sanders was ill at ease with Rossellini's method—that he was looking for 'direction' in a sense in which the director was not prepared to offer it—is obvious throughout *Journey to Italy*, and it is totally fallacious to attempt to justify his performance in terms of the *character's* being ill at ease. Positively, one can see what Rossellini required by examining any of the Bergman performances. If one mentally juxtaposes them one realizes that the characterizations are quite distinct from film to film: her Catherine in *Journey to Italy*, very British for all the unexplained Swedish accent, would never try to seduce a priest to get her own way, as Karin does in *Stromboli*; and neither would be capable of achieving the saintliness of Irene in *Europa 51*.

Yet it is equally clear that these characters all relate closely to each other, and to the

Alexander Knox and Ingrid Bergman in *Europa 51* (U.S.: *No Greater Love*): 'one of the three greatest Rossellini films'.

actress herself, who is being asked to *be* as much as to act. Catherine's accent (the sort of thing that so bothers the literal-minded) is relevant here, a nice example of Rossellini's sense of artistic priorities. No one would claim it as an *asset* to the characterization, yet he was surely right in preferring that Bergman use her own voice and intonation unaffectedly, rather than lumbering her with an accent unnatural to her, which would have forced her into becoming an *actress*. In effect, he is encouraging her to draw spontaneously on her own responses, her own perceptions. None of the roles could be called autobiographical, yet each of them relates significantly to aspects of the actress' personal experience: like Karin, Bergman was (if voluntarily) a 'displaced person', like Catherine she had experienced the breakdown of a marriage, like Irene she can be presumed to have felt some guilt at her abeyance of responsibility to her children. To describe the films as 'documentaries on Ingrid Bergman' has considerable validity and force. The degree of characterization, of conscious 'acting', perhaps accounts, paradoxically, for the freedom with which the actress reveals herself, since it avoids the strain and *self*-consciousness of *cinéma-vérité*. The relationship here between 'acting' and 'being' might be felt to correspond in some way to the relationship between melodrama and documentary in Rossellini's films (most conspicuous in the 'novelettes' of *Paisà*): far from being incompatible, each enhances and enriches the other.

If it is legitimate to talk of 'improvisation' in Rossellini's films, it must be stressed that the improvisation is primarily the director's. Rossellini's neo-realism is allied only at the most superficial level to the Zavattini 'one-and-a-half-hours in the daily life of an ordinary woman' theoretical ideal. His movies are not behavioural studies, and the actors' performances are always strictly subordinated to the film's inner movement. If his art is faithful to certain neo-realist principles, it also transcends them. One can state the relationship thus: all art is poised somewhere between exploration and statement, and elements of both can be discerned in the work of any artist. It is a question of which is the dominant impulse; and one can see that Rossellini's art, though it certainly makes

statements, is primarily motivated by the drive to understand. This implies that Rossellini's camera is used primarily to record what is before it, without tricks and fakery, and with a minimum (though not an absence) of rhetoric; and that his work with actors, décor, landscape is a process of investigation rather than an expression of foregone conclusions. The central paradox of Rossellini's cinema is that, while he sees the function of the camera as necessarily restricted to photographing the actual, material world, he is of all film-makers the most rigorously and single-mindedly preoccupied with the spiritual and invisible. Nowhere is this paradox more vividly exemplified, nowhere are its seeming contradictions more successfully resolved, than in the Bergman films.

Rossellini himself has said (quoted by Guarner at the end of his book): 'I always try to remain impassive. I think that the surprising, extraordinary, moving thing about men is just that the great actions and achievements occur in the same way as the ordinary acts involved in living; it is with the same humility that I try to translate one into the other; there lies a source of dramatic interest.' The relevance of this to his work scarcely needs spelling out: the apparently casual 'miracle' at the end of *Journey to Italy* (the 'miracle' of the couple's reconciliation as much as the more literal one that precipitates it) expresses the spirit of it as surely as the intimacy (entirely free from impertinence or a sense of intrusion) with which Rossellini treats St Francis, St Augustine, Garibaldi or Louis XIV. The 'impassivity', however, is far from total: Rossellini is neither a purist nor a rigid theoretician. He is not averse, for example, to the overtly emotive close-up. His elemental use of light and darkness, sun and shadow, can verge on the Expressionistic. Towards the end of *Germany Year Zero*, Edmund steps out from shadow into sunlight as organ music bursts authoritatively from a church, and back into shadow when he rejects its summons; in *Europa 51*, during Irene's discussion with her Marxist friend, Bergman's face is at first in heavy shadow, but moves forward into the light as she speaks of the need for 'spiritual' (as opposed to merely material) regeneration; in the opening dialogue of *Angst* (Italian title: *La Paura* [*Fear*], 1954); as Bergman (again called

Irene) tries to break with her lover she is in the light, but sinks back into shadow as she succumbs to his persuasion to continue the affair.

Such moments of overt statement can be seen as intrusions of rhetoric into a style they define by contrast; though only the *Germany Year Zero* example is likely to strike us as contrived or over-emphatic. That style is easier to describe than to explain: long takes; a very mobile camera; a preponderance of long-shot; a general absence of 'subjective' camerawork; a general absence of 'striking', rhetorical angles. The description could cover the work of many directors; it takes on particular definition in relation to Rossellini's concerns. The camera movements are strictly functional, rather than dynamic and involving (as in Hitchcock) or expressive and decorative (as in Max Ophuls). The camera moves to record an action as clearly as possible, and to keep it as intact as possible. Rossellini is one of the pioneers of what the French call the *plan-séquence*—the organization within a single, mobile take of a scene which one would normally expect to see broken down into a number of brief shots. This practice in itself carries complex implications. First, it entails a rejection of the rhetorical or dramatic effects that can be achieved by cutting: effects of shock, or simple emphasis. Second, it demands the preservation of a certain distance between camera and actors, in order that a complex action can be 'composed' within the frame. Closely connected with this is the preservation of the relationship between characters and décor or landscape: scene after scene in the Bergman films is built on the impingement of setting or objects on the individual consciousness.

Above all, the necessity for Rossellini of the *plan-séquence* is determined by two interconnected metaphysical concerns: the sense of the *wholeness* of things, of a world where nothing exists in isolation but where every decision arises out of more or less mysterious interactions; and the sense of the mysterious paradox of freedom and determinism. It might be said that the Rossellinian *plan-séquence* not only *expresses* the latter but *embodies* it: the rapid organization of an action, under conditions of semi-improvisation, within a single long take, can be seen both as the result of spontaneous yet conscious decisions on the director's part and as determined by a complex network of factors—the overall movement of the action, the exigencies of décor and the restrictions on the camera's mobility, the logic of character-response and character-development, the accumulation of subconscious, psychologically determined impulses in the director himself.

This tension between freedom and determinism relates to another aspect of Rossellini's *mise en scène*, the tension between randomness and directedness. The camera-style of the Bergman films evokes again the sense of instability which was the keynote of their predecessors, but counterpoints it with something quite different. The scene in *Europa 51* in which Irene, adrift in the slums, watches the discovery of a drowned body, can stand as a representative example: the restless camera movements, continually reframing to include new background figures and exclude others, the fluctuating compositions and resulting sense of a world beyond the confines of the screen, suggest a chaotic, random, uncontrollable universe, the universe of the last episode of *Paisà*; yet the central focus is consistently on Irene, on the way in which her consciousness is formed and given direction by what she witnesses.

In Rossellini's historical films, and in certain of the post-Bergman fictional films such as *Era Notte a Roma* (*It Was Night in Rome*, 1960), the function of the *plan-séquence* is to analyse a complex but integrated action objectively and lucidly. In the Bergman films this function is complicated, and in certain respects deepened, by the presence of a central consciousness. The spectator's relationship to the characters Bergman plays is a complex one: the essential movement of the film takes place within the Bergman consciousness, and we both share and observe that movement. Apart from the scene in *Stromboli* where Antonio is taunted with cries of '*Cornuto!*' ('Cuckold'), the George Sanders sequences of *Journey to Italy*, and one brief scene in *Europa 51* where members of Irene's family discuss what should be done with her, we are allowed no experiences that lie outside the Bergman character's consciousness. Yet, though we become intimately involved in the movement and development of that consciousness, the films' method never becomes subjective. The camera distance imposed by Rossellini's technique, and the continually shifting perspective brought about by the movements of camera and actress within a single take, prevent simple identification and ensure that the main focus of our attention is on *her*.

Rossellini never explains, he merely *shows*, and we are left to extract what explanation we can from what is shown. More than with any other film-maker, the total effect of a Rossellini film depends on implication and accumulation—on our penetrating the appearance offered by the images to follow the inner movement that underlies it, and on the sense of apparently abrupt decisions that are in fact long prepared. One might instance the ending of *Stromboli*. We are made to share with Karin, very immediately, the experience of the volcano—which is the confrontation, simultaneously, of the power of nature, of God, and of the fact of death. The whole film, in retrospect, can be seen as the preparation of Karin for that experience. She returns (at least, as I understand the ending) to her 'prison'. But her return is voluntary, and for Rossellini imprisonment and freedom are spiritual states rather than physical facts. The paradox of physical imprisonment/ spiritual freedom is most fully and movingly stated at the end of *Europa 51*; and 'Il Generale della Rovere' will find *his* fulfilment and freedom in death. Or there is Catherine's response to Pompeii in *Journey to Italy*—her realization, confronted with the forms of the couple who were buried in the lava, that 'life is so short': a line that, alone, is merely banal, yet which, in its context, is among the most profound and moving in the whole of cinema.

It is useless to speculate on how Rossellini's work might have developed if his association with Bergman had continued; or on how far the decision to end that association was influenced by the failure of their films together to receive either critical or popular recognition. One guesses that the separation played its part in influencing Rossellini's subsequent gravitation to documentary; though the documentary impulse is implicit in his work from the outset. *Fear*, the last of the Bergman series, is about the break-up of a marriage through infidelity, suspicion and blackmail; it turns out that the husband himself has arranged the blackmail to force his wife to confess to him. The film has alternative endings, one with the marriage restored, one with Irene leaving her husband but renouncing suicide to live on for her children. The uncertainty seems symptomatic: the film is full of tenseness and pain, and is unlike its predecessors in that there is no convincing movement towards serenity, not even the ambiguous, paradoxical fulfilment-in-imprisonment of *Europa 51*. After it, there is a four-year gap in Rossellini's career, then his fictionalized documentary, *India*, a meditation on the concept of otherness.

La Nave Bianca, *Paisà*, *Germany Year Zero*, all have strong documentary tendencies. *Journey to Italy* can be seen simultaneously as a documentary on certain aspects of Italy and a documentary on Catherine/Bergman's responses to Italy. To divide Rossellini's films into categories is a fruitless procedure: he moved with ease from neorealist fiction to melodrama to documentary to historical reconstruction; the categories overlap, the lines of definition blur, each comes to look like the other. In this respect again Rossellini is a remarkably 'modern' director: one thinks of Godard, Makavejev, Straub, Herzog. His films, strongly personal without ever being introspective, are acts of exploration outwards from a defined centre of identity: it was logical to extend this examination of the exterior universe in both space and time, to make a film (one of his greatest) in, and about, India, and to reconstruct and analyse historically decisive actions or movements.

Rossellini's later work is partly characterized by his adoption (which also has its logic) of two technical facilities: the zoom lens, and television. The former, by supplying an alternative or accessory to camera movement, allowed him greater ease and fluency in organizing the *plan-séquence*, as one sees at once if one compares interior scenes in *Germany Year Zero* with interior scenes in *Era Notte a Roma*. It also greatly facilitated the filming of crowd or battle scenes without either fragmenting them or forfeiting the possibility of intimacy. Rossellini's use of the zoom is in fact entirely consistent: he never uses it for shock effects, or to communicate sensations. As Jim Hillier pointed out to me, in *Viva l'Italia!* Rossellini zooms out more often than in—starting a scene with a precise detail, then moving out to place that detail in the context of a whole action.

In his 60s films Rossellini used the zoom habitually, as a valid instrument of analysis. His zooms are never abrupt, but a zoom can never be entirely unobtrusive, and many object to it as a distraction, getting between audience and film. What may in some cases be a defect becomes with Rossellini a virtue. In the Bergman films his style balanced involvement with contemplation; in the later historical films—and in a film like *Era Notte a Roma*, where there is no dominant central consciousness other than the director's—contemplation takes precedence. Hence our awareness of the medium through which the action is presented—as long as that awareness is delicate and consistent, a matter of distance rather than distraction—is an asset. With the zoom lens, Rossellini has no need for contrived alienation effects.

The contemplative detachment given by the zoom lens, together with the historical distance of the subjects, gives such films as *Viva l'Italia!*, *La Prise de Pouvoir par Louis XIV* (*The Rise to Power of Louis XIV*, 1966) and *Augustine of Hippo* a serenity never to be confused with complacency or indifference. The serenity expresses itself in an increasing plastic beauty (*Augustine* is among the most beautiful films to look at in my experience) which has nothing of affectation or preciosity. The sense of ease and fluency in the later works is obviously connected with the adoption of television techniques and equipment, permitting further refinements in the swift and spontaneous organization of complex shots.

All of Rossellini's work is concerned ultimately with the effort to understand, and if his work can be called 'didactic', what it offers to teach is not so much a message as a method, a way of looking and considering and analysing. Our awareness of the medium in his later work is his means of directing *us*—of guiding our consciousness and our perceptions while keeping us detached from the action. One small illustration may help to bring these generalizations to a more precise focus. The scene of Fouquet's arrest in *The Rise to Power of Louis XIV* is a perfect example of the Rossellinian *plan-séquence*

with full benefit of zoom. We watch it from a high window: we can hear no dialogue, but the whole action—Fouquet's attempted departure, quite unaware of what is about to happen to him, the manoeuvre to separate him from his mistress, the business of escorting him to a carriage and leading him off—is analysed with perfect clarity. The continuity of the shot preserves the integrity of the action, the relation of this movement to that, our precise sense of where each character is in relation to the others. The poise and precision of effect, the Rossellinian contemplative serenity, are achieved partly through the shifts of focus, partly through the reframing which, starting from one beautifully organized composition, ends on another, but connects the two through the continuity of movement. We are detached from the action both physically (by the distance and the high angle) and intellectually (by our—at least—subconscious sense of the manipulation of the zoom). At the same time, our view of the action from above communicates something of Louis' sense of power and control, without identifying us with him.

Perhaps the most distinctive quality of Rossellini's historical films arises from his relationship to the figures he presents. One could say that he humanizes these without psychologizing. They are contemplated with interest and sympathy, from the outside. There is never any attempt to 'explain' them in psychological terms, and Rossellini characteristically chooses his actors more for their physical resemblance and presence than for their histrionic ability: Renzo Ricci is not asked to 'act' Garibaldi in *Viva l'Italia!*—not, at least, in any Stanislavskyan get-inside-his-skin-and-see-how-he-ticks sense. Rather, Rossellini *presents* Garibaldi as a figure in a carefully analysed historical context, a figure very much of flesh and blood—there is no heroic posturing, no tendency to stereotype or idealize conventionally—but a figure defined by the context rather than by 'inward' exploration. Like St Francis before him and St Augustine after, Garibaldi is at once a man of destiny and a man like ourselves: we are not awed by him, but we respect him as we might respect a distinguished acquaintance.

Finally, it should be stressed that, for all their apparent objectivity and detachment,

Rossellini's historical films remain as personal as any of his work. *The Rise to Power of Louis XIV* opens with a protracted sequence of immense concentration showing the death of Mazarin and analysing its political significance; yet its deepest function is to put before us, with much poignant counterpointing of acquired grandeur with the humiliating realities of physical decay, the fact of death itself and the way it calls into question the validity and meaning of all men's acts. At the end of the film Louis, having acquired absolute power through complex and idiosyncratic strategies, reads aloud, alone in his chambers, a maxim of La Rochefoucauld: 'Neither the sun nor death can be looked firmly in the face.' Louis, we know, is about to become *Le Roi Soleil*, and no one will be able to look him firmly in the face again; it is the achieved end of all his strategy. Yet, when he reads the maxim, he has just divested himself of the royal robes that are the expression of his grandeur and the royal wig that helps to conceal his shortness of stature: as an ordinary, not at all awe-inspiring mortal, a man like ourselves, he is faced with the ultimate fact of death and the question of the meaning and validity of all his life and actions, man and king, man and mask. *The Rise to Power of Louis XIV* is a film whose essential meaning is created by its last few seconds; a great film, and profoundly Rossellinian.

Rossellini's historical series, which also included *Blaise Pascal* (U.S.: *Pascal*, 1971), *L'Età di Cosimo de' Medici* (1973) and *Descartes* (1974), was interrupted in 1974 by a brief return to the fiction film with *Anno Uno* (*Year One*), which dealt unsatisfyingly and somewhat opportunistically with the beginnings of the De Gasperi regime in post-war Italy. The following year, however, he returned to his educational efforts with nothing less than *The Messiah*. With the exception, however, of *The Rise to Power of Louis XIV* and to a lesser extent *Blaise Pascal*, I find Rossellini's historical works something of a bore. I know that they were made for television and that he had to bear in mind that they would be seen by Sardinian peasants, but it is not only their oversimplification to which I object: it is also their lack of vitality. One of the most excruciating (not mentioned by Wood) was *L'Età del Ferro* (*The Iron Age*, 1964).

There is an important essay on early Rossellini by André Bazin in his *What Is Cinema?, Volume II* (1971). See also Jose-Luis Guarner's monograph *Roberto Rossellini* (1970) and *Sighting Rossellini, A Book of Texts*, edited by David Degener (1973).

Rossellini's last film, completed just before his death, was a fifty-minute documentary on the Centre Culturel Georges Pompidou in which his lack of sympathy for the 'Centre Beaubourg' as well as for much of contemporary art was painfully evident. His untimely death robbed us of what might have been a fascinating work—his next project was to have been a film on Karl Marx.

ROBERT ROSSEN

Edgardo Cozarinsky

Although Robert Rossen (1908–66) directed his first film in 1946, his career is rooted in the great days of action-packed, New Deal liberalism at Warners, where he scripted, among other films, *They Won't Forget* (1937) and *The Roaring Twenties* (1939). That ideological context is still apparent in his own early films. *Body and Soul* (1947) and *All the King's Men* (1949) show Rossen (like Losey, Polonsky or Richard Brooks, at the same time) trying to work out a new key for attitudes which the American post-war scene was fast rendering obsolete, but which still retained much of their intellectual relevance for them: those films seem to look back to a safer age of unambiguous moral choices and plain story-telling, against which the progress of John Garfield's boxer into money and corruption, and Robert Penn Warren's study of complicated personal and political allegiances are not allowed to display their potential complexity, not inferior to that of Welles' *Touch of Evil*. Rossen's hard-dying righteousness was a necessary element in *The Hustler* (1961), made more than a decade later, after his youthful political sympathies had left him hovering on the brink of the blacklist and pursuing with varying fortune a European career. A very rich depiction of involvement and power relationships which draws on *The Brave Bulls* (1951), the most personal and least script-bound film of his earlier period, *The Hustler* summed up and bade farewell to a whole formative tradition, dramatizing the gap between 30s and 60s, having Paul Newman do a retrospectively critical reappraisal of a Garfield-like part. Before his untimely death, Rossen made an exceptional if uncharacteristic last film—*Lilith* (1964), a story of *amour fou* which plays schizophrenia against bourgeois propriety, and lets Biblical symbolism stand for repressive culture. Constructed as a series of lyrical segments, the film's narrative is as violently opposed to the thoroughly composed set-ups and expressive dramaturgy of *Body and Soul* as it is to the brisk concatenation of informative episodes in *All the King's Men*. For a film-maker of irregular achievement, who always appeared more impressive than his work, *Lilith*, made in New York with Boris Kaufman as photographer, seemed to herald a freer, life-embracing (even if life-defeated, as in the story material) attitude: an unsolicited pathetic fallacy.

For further reading, see *The Films of Robert Rossen* by Alan Casty (1969). See also the article on Polonsky.

JEAN ROUCH

Jean-André Fieschi

A survey of Jean Rouch's career in films, which now covers over twenty-five years, from the first ethnological shorts to *Les Trois Conseils* (1976), suggests that what gives his work its novelty, elasticity and disruptive power lies chiefly in the discomfort it effects, using any means to attain its ends, resorting to different techniques, venturing into hitherto uncharted areas, mingling devices previously believed to be contradictory, and refusing to be confined by any established facts.

Truant ethnology, one is tempted to say of the African side of Rouch's work. A dunce directing (by comparison with the studious pupils: Rosi, Melville, Losey . . .) when he gets into more deliberately fictional areas: neglectful of the prescribed rules, and even rather priding himself on finding ways round them. Above all, though, contraband cinema, with Rouch ever ready to cross frontiers which he himself seems to have set up for himself. Hence the misunderstandings ac-

cumulated during his travels: unacceptable, this rather too whimsical ethnologist rather too fond of chasing butterflies; incongruous, this film-maker unacquainted with continuity, dramatic contruction, rounded characters.

What is exploded by Rouch's work (with the result that, rather as Boulez said of music after Debussy, the entire cinema now 'breathes' differently) is the whole system of statutory oppositions whereby, starting from the original Lumière-Méliès axis, categories were conceived of as documentary/fiction; style/improvisation; natural/artificial; etc.

Certainly there was a succession of tremors before Rouch (born 1917)—Vertov, Flaherty, Rossellini—clearly indicating the inanity of these traditional academic oppositions. But Rouch gave the extra turn of the screw that proved decisive. For a time, any real evaluation was avoided by falling back on the absurdly muddle-headed term *cinéma-vérité*, loosely borrowed from Dziga Vertov and his 'Kino-Pravda'. During the 60s, an interminable debate on the subject cluttered festivals, film magazines and conferences. Usually a suspect ideology of artlessness (the transparency of reality, intensified by the 'miracle' of direct sound and the myth of natural expression by the film-maker and his characters) took care of the problem of an artificiality as extreme as in any Hollywood movie though on a different level and achieved by different means. The rival schools weighed in with disputes in which everybody—Rossellini, Leacock, the Canadians—accused everybody else of cheating, laziness or illusionism. An undeniable fact today is that although Rouch took part in the debate, he did so without taking sides except as the spoilsport who exposed its inherent falseness.

'Anything could happen here': this phrase, spoken at the beginning of *Shanghai Gesture*, is a sort of 'open sesame' to Sternberg's aesthetic. It suggests a mental locus subject to substitutions, transformations, metamorphoses, marvels. If one wants to define the components of Rouch's work, one must look to Sternberg's narrative myths, Cocteau's poetic wonderland, the speculative flights of surrealism. Or to the story-teller spinning a yarn while wide-eyed children listen with bated breath: 'Listen, children, for goodness' sake.' This is how the tale begins of a lion hunt with bows and arrows, apparently in Africa but really in some strange country beyond 'the bush which is far further than far away, the land of nowhere'. After 'the mountains of the moon', the 'mountains of crystal' . . .

Each time a frontier must be crossed, or a mirror traversed, to reach that elsewhere or other world on which dreams and stories feed. Each film becomes an account of an initiation ceremony. Here the determining factors of the ethnologist's life—his wish, in fact—must be considered. Claude Lévi-Strauss (and Michel Leiris [in *L'Afrique Fantôme*]), is enlightening in this respect: 'The conditions of his life and work cut him off from his own group for long periods together; and he himself acquires a kind of chronic uprootedness from the sheer brutality of the environmental changes to which he is exposed. Never can he feel himself "at home" anywhere.' (Lévi-Strauss, *Tristes Tropiques*.)

In Rouch's early efforts, the camera, a supplementary tool in the ethnologist's equipment affording greater accuracy and flexibility, recorded rites and customs: those of the men who make rain, the millet people, the sorcerers of Wanzerbé. A tool recommended by Mauss, Leroi-Gourhan, Marcel Griaule, and even by pioneers like Dr Regnault as early as 1900. A 'scientific' tool capable, according to them, of avoiding or correcting undue subjectivity in the observer. And one not even indulging in selectivity.

So Rouch, in the early 50s, was recording rites, customs and techniques because 'If young ethnographers are well advised to favour rituals and techniques as subjects for filming, it is because rituals and techniques incorporate their own *mise en scène*.'

This kind of cinema, dependent upon the event, the moment, the place, is of course not *written*, not created. What is created, unexpectedly, as it unfolds within the framework of a scenario determined in advance but irrespective of the film-maker, is the cultural form of the ceremony recorded. The film-maker here is the *operator* (in Mallarmé's sense of control mechanism, distributor of signs, as well as in the strictly technical sense of cameraman): eye glued to the viewfinder, framing for the rectangle an elusive,

ephemeral performance—he himself being its first spectator—dependent not only on his cultural prejudices but on his reflexes, his speed, his patience, the very movements of his body which transmit slight tremors, jolts or stoppages to the camera. Movements by the camera, length of takes, variations in light, the grain of the film stock: usually nullified in 'scientific' films by the thesis which takes charge and the information that is offered, all the technical hazards through which matter is filtered and transformed (and which allow it to resist) are brought into the foreground for the first time in Rouch's work. On an equal footing, one might almost say, with the subject represented.

This discovery in practice of the *materiality* of the cinema itself was probably an important determining factor for Rouch: a materiality whereby the scientific statement of the evidence, slightly dislocated, becomes the fluctuating expression of an elusive subjectivity that is simultaneously present and withdrawn even as it is being formulated.

For instance, the group of short films presented under the collective title of *Les Fils de l'Eau* (1949–51, first shown 1958), and describing various aspects of the lives of tribesmen along the banks of the Niger: prayers for rain, the coming of the rain, the sowing and harvesting of millet, burial rites, circumcision, a hippopotamus hunt. Images apparently without frills, as though shot by any member of the crew who happened to be on hand, a commentary derived directly from the local dialect (in sentence structure, the incantatory manner, the repetition and variation of simple words), and tribal chants and music all combine to create the illusion—at times perfect—of a total absence of white men. A direct attempt to penetrate an alien mentality simply by describing faces, gestures and everyday objects.

But the voice which takes charge of these images, carrying them along and seeming to direct their flow as much as to submit to them, is the voice of Rouch. The captivating voice of the narrator, the story-teller, the barker who tells you in his own warm and persuasive way that we shall see what we shall see. A voice which mirrors the action rather than explaining or commenting on it, withdrawn from the images and 'charging' them.

Les hommes de la pluie: the earth is parched, the harvest threatened. Only magic practices can restore fertility. These practices are enumerated, described, demonstrated. And when the black sky opens in the final shots and the rain pours down inundating the dry and cracking earth, the expected miracle is literally realized, a relationship of cause and effect is established between the rite and its reward. The film thus seems to accept the miracle, even to stand as evidence of it. Hazy and disquieting, the washed-out, uneven colour, unlike any other (Godard wanted at one time to use it for *Les Carabiniers*: neither glowing Technicolor nor so-called 'natural' colour), accentuates the effect of strangeness.

To the illusion of the absence of white men is added the illusion of the absence of any manipulation in the filmed material (one never for a moment thinks of what might have been cut during editing; on the contrary, the impression one gets is that each scene is presented exactly as it was shot, breaking off only when the camera runs out of film or the observer out of interest), while at the same time an insistent presence—the voice—effects a displacement, suggesting that what we are watching comes unmistakably within the province of the fantasy film.

The fantastic element is in fact twofold; hence its particular effectiveness. Bound up with the 'elsewhere' made manifest, the quizzical otherness, so close and yet so far, there is the strangeness of what we see, defined as such solely by cultural differences; and there is the narrative method, unimpeachable in its logical sequence, introducing the fantastic along with an unfamiliar causality. And enhancing these powers, as is right and proper, there is every semblance of innocence, of simply stated fact: You see how it is . . .

Clearly this innocence derives from an ideology of immediacy, the intangible sense of actual experience, which Rouch claims as automatism, inspiration, even manifestation: 'What are these films, what outlandish name distinguishes them from the rest? Do they exist? I have no idea as yet, but I do know that there are certain very rare occasions when, without the aid of a single subtitle, the spectator suddenly understands an unknown tongue, takes part in strange ceremonies,

wanders in towns or through landscapes he has never seen but which he recognizes perfectly . . . Only the cinema can perform this miracle, though no particular aesthetic can reveal the mechanism, and no special technique can set it in motion: neither clever counterpointing in the cutting, nor the use of some stereophonic Cinerama process can create such wonders . . .'

And further on: 'It is as if there were no more cameras, no more sound recorders, no more photo-electric cells, none of the welter of accessories and technicians which comprise the great ritual of classic cinema. But the film-makers of today prefer not to venture into these dangerous paths; and only fools, madmen and children dare to push the forbidden buttons.'

This article (*Positif*, November, 1955) is a veritable mine, in that it is a fairly clear indication of how the scientific purpose was deflected in favour of the camera, at first only the instrument of revelation but suddenly given special licence. Look again at each of the assumptions and expressions in Rouch's chain of thought, so strikingly tinged with the tone of poetic revelation: privileged moment, communication without intermediaries, taking part in a ceremony, sense of recognition, miracle, wonders, dangerous paths, fools, madmen and children . . .

There is no point in using this manifesto to query the scientific basis of Rouch's approach, but it is clear that from the outset cinema and science acted for him as pretexts —or rather, generators—for each other. The relationship to be sought is therefore not primarily between a science (ethnological) and a given technique (in this case the technique of cinema, required to transmit this science through a specific medium), which is why film-makers and ethnologists get so little out of Rouch's work, a sort of double-agent cinema operating more broadly between science and fiction (of course Rouch's films can also be described, without too much play on words, as science-fiction).

Straddling techniques, straddling cultures, Rouch (ostensibly for pragmatic reasons) was to play increasingly systematically on this betwixt-and-between which he made the mainspring of a long, profoundly original, and extremely influential fictional cycle. Progressively, too, he complicated the game. At this point may be noted Rouch's relationship with his film-making predecessors: Vertov he praises as a director 'of films which beget films'; Flaherty is a 'Jack-of-all-trades, a man of action and a poet,' but above all 'a *metteur en scène*, one of the greatest'.

No matter how acute the sense of dislocation, his first films bearing witness to 'the marvellous African' still took a relatively classical reportage form. What is new about *Les Fils de l'Eau* and the cycle it inaugurates, by comparison with the indistinguishable mass of ethnological films, is the tone, the manifest presence of an aesthetic; and the difference between his footage and traditional factual reports, as projected on the screen, is above all a qualitative one: the information is there, but woven as it were into a texture which modifies, indeed transforms, its character and function. A takeover is effected on the discourse, a recognizable stamp placed on it, a scenic quality, the hand of a film-maker.

With *Les Maîtres Fous* (1955) comes a first, though still hesitant, edging towards more open forms, more disturbing structures: structures in which the disturbing element, the frontier crossed somewhere, is integral to their functioning. The film describes the great annual ceremony of the Hanka, or demons of power, in Ghana. Rouch is no longer simply recording a ritual, but making a more complex survey of an essentially cathartic collective practice, a sacrifice whose exceptional nature is clearly understood to be an assurance of social normality. As in every fantasy film, this 'normality' is established at the outset, and functions as the *alter ego* or double of the bloody sacred ceremony. The characters come from ordinary, everyday life, urban this time. There is nothing unusual about them at home or at work: labourers, waiters, workers. Then, during the ceremony (followed in detail, step by step), they become literally possessed, alienated, foaming, mixing the blood of dogs and the yolks of eggs, drunk on slaughtered animals, streaming with spittle, contorted. Afterwards, reclaimed by their (non-sacred) social context, they return to normal until the next sacrifice. This first reversal of everyday reality and the sacrificial ritual is suddenly punctuated by incongruous red and green images: the changing of the Horse Guards

against a lush prairie background.

Although the message is obvious in the ingenuous directness with which the supposed civilized and savage states are grafted to the same stem, and although an exercise like this basically reveals little but banalities, a powerful element of surprise nevertheless comes into play, less on the level of the discourse than on that of the film as fiction: a metaphorical disorientation, born of another space-time (of other narrative and cultural systems indicating the course of colonization) and imposing a second dislocation on the already disturbing dislocation which seemed to be the subject of the film. Here the reading system is geared down. The exploration of cinema as source material rich in possibilities other than simply transitive is succeeded by the exploration of cinema as structure (narrative, poetic, plastic, critical). A combinative is suggested between the basic data which the cinema (because of the nature of its relationship to reality) has brought into play since its very beginnings: reality and its characteristic resistance to let itself be inscribed within a frame, to submit to techniques which are inevitably constricting; and everything that the logic of concrete selection engenders as possibilities for new juxtapositions, and for modifying the raw material filmed (even when this is given data from the outset, already *mise en scène*, as in the case of the ritual or ceremony).

Rouch was to work on this given/ manipulation relationship, surveying its possibilities, charting hitherto unexplored junctures, so that his influence on the cinema then developing or searching for ways and means was probably greater than any other (on Godard, Rivette, and even, though one might not at first think so, on Straub).

One can see how the terms applied to elders like Vertov and Flaherty came to be revived in connection with his work.

What Rouch's practice of ethnographical cinema revealed was a corpus of repudiations rather similar, after due historical adjustment, to the one vented by Vertov in the euphoria of a new world requiring new forms: 'It was at the time when the outlines of the Kino-Eye movement were just beginning to take shape, when we had to decide whether we were going to follow in the footsteps of the art cinema and make products of cine-distillation like the entire fraternity of film-makers—an occupation both lucrative and sanctioned by law—or whether we were going to declare war on the art cinema and start to rebuild the cinema from scratch. Puppets or life? we asked the spectator . . .'

A corpus of repudiations equally concerned with actors and acting, text, décor, classical montage and methods of *découpage*, with what Bresson was to describe as caricature, and Straub as pornography. In this Rouch was to be one of the great gold-miners of the contemporary cinema. Taking a course directly opposed to Richard Leacock's counterfeit journalistic practice of supposed non-intervention, he worked on processes, interactions, mutual discovery between matter and method, film and discourse. Reality never offers itself as such to the innocent eye or virgin celluloid. What reality, anyway?

One might perhaps hazard that the movement of Rouch's work at this point is increasingly obviously directed towards the fictional, the imaginary already realized in the early films dealing with rituals, but progressively, differently encompassed and revealed; increasingly dependent upon a system of representation less direct than that of simple reportage, incorporating the element of fabrication proper to every system of representation, not to mention the discreet but central parts played by the observer who harvests the fiction and by the technical means which bring it to its completed theatrical form as the product of successive deposits deriving from various systems (the social and cultural system in which the original representation took place, the system into which it is received, the cultural and technical system through which it is transmitted). This is Rouch's cinema: the repository for a particularly complex network of transitions and displacements through which one arrives at a different and richer reading of the remark by Lévi-Strauss concerning the self-imposed exile of the ethnologist: 'Never can he feel himself "at home" anywhere.' Actually, this is the only sense in which Rouch can be described as an exotic film-maker. Exotic, undoubtedly; but only for the African aspect of his work?

Moi, un noir (1959) clearly states the question at issue in this dislocation: who, in other words, is 'speaking'? The film calling itself by this title? The film-maker ironically flaunting his difference? One of his characters? This time, at all events, it is a monologue we are invited to watch, to listen to; or rather, a tissue of monologues uniting into a single flow made up of a sum of differences. The characters: real (they exist, you might run into them in Abidjan, for instance), but also dual personalities, with behind them the mythical figures they themselves have chosen (Dorothy Lamour, or Eddie Constantine–Lemmy Caution–American federal agent, or Sugar Ray Robinson).

What Rouch then films, he is the first to attempt: not just behaviour, or dreams, or subjective themes, but the indissoluble amalgam binding them together. The film-maker's wish is to devote himself to the wish of his characters. To follow them step by step, along the basic lines of Zavattini's neo-realist principle, but with the sights set on what their speech reveals at least as much as on their behaviour. Embodying their disappointments, their daydreams, their desires. The war in Indo-China mimed by one; the liners another indicates in the harbour as he says he's knocked around the seven seas and had his fill of women; the monologue by the ladies' man; the brawl provoked with the Italian: unforgettable moments which reflect films the characters have seen, comic strips they have read, stories they have been told, and which they refashion with inimitable charm into a new narrative. Here all distinction between premeditation and improvisation seems to be abolished, *as though* a transparency between thought and representation were now possible.

Collective creation, improvisation, spontaneity, complicity: these are probably the prime means through which Rouch, the observer of rituals, crossed the line to become a creator of rituals in his own right.

Moi, un noir is undoubtedly a turning-point in Rouch's work. In the cinema, in fact. Telling us more about Treichville and its inhabitants than many a seemingly more 'objective' report. Telling us more, but above all, telling us differently.

In *Les Maîtres Fous*, the members of the sect themselves created the *mise en scène* for their collective delirium in which, decked out in the imaginary regalia of figures symbolizing colonialism (the governor, the general, the corporal, the engine-driver), they proceeded to enact an imaginary representation that is simultaneously 'wild' and 'ordered'. From *Moi, un noir* onwards, the camera assumes an entirely new function: no longer simply a recording device, it becomes a *provocateur*, a stimulant, precipitating situations, conflicts, expeditions that would otherwise never have taken place. It is no longer a matter of pretending that the camera isn't there, but of transforming its role by asserting its presence, by stressing the part it plays, by turning a technical obstacle into a pretext for revealing new and astonishing things. A matter of creating, through the very act of filming itself, an entirely new conception of the notion of the filmic event. First, with Rouch's camera either leading or tracking them, these inhabitants of Treichville played out what they had chosen to reveal of themselves before it. Then, after seeing themselves on the screen, they commented on the proceedings, reshaping or reorienting them. These successive operations engender a complex cultural object, opening the way to a virtually unexplored avenue: adventure films in which the adventure lies in the material and its discovery. An experimental cinema. A cinema, above all, in which the positions traditionally assigned to the director, technical crew and actors are reassigned and redefined. Film-maker/ camera operator (when he wasn't behind the camera, as in *Chronique d'un Eté* [*Chronicle of a Summer*, 1961] or *Les Veuves de Quinze Ans*, 1964—though *Gare du Nord*, 1965, is an exception—the result is a distinct loss, an atypical sense of embarrassment and awkwardness), actors/creators: the arrangement encourages improvisation on many levels. 'When I'm making a film, it takes a few minutes getting started, then I see the film taking shape in the viewfinder of my camèra, and I know at any given moment whether what I'm getting is any good or not. The constant tension is exhausting, but it's an excitement absolutely essential if one is to bring off this aleatory pursuit of the most effective images and sounds, without ever being certain until you're shooting the final sequences what the result will be . . . Oh, the number of unfinished films I've made because nothing happened—a ritual possession dance in which

nobody got possessed; because it grew dark; because I ran out of film . . .'

At this point, rather than a panorama of Rouch's work, the fundamental principle on which it is based should perhaps be described in some of its characteristics; characteristics, moreover, which interact on each other to a point where a veritable method—and an extremely coherent one—is discernible behind the flaunted empiricism of his technique.

A method which might equally well be described as a trap, or system of traps: for events, reports, fictions, metamorphoses. Because it is through the diversity of forms, figures and loci annexed by this technique in the course of its adventurous progress—even in its vagaries, its seesawing between techniques and cultures—that a genuine aesthetic is established, with its own laws and practices.

An aesthetic whose literary associations are obvious, and which appears to derive entirely from the surrealist principle of spontaneous juxtaposition. This meeting, like two chemical bodies acting upon each other, precipitates a new reality, irreducible to the simple sum of its parts. In literature, André Breton's *Nadja* and Louis Aragon's *Le Paysan de Paris* are key examples. But in Rouch's films the incidence of poetry is no longer simply transmitted but created, provoked by the camera.

Jaguar (1954–67, first shown 1971), for instance, records a hazardous quest, a succession of ordeals, a sort of odyssey collectively invented in the course of a methodical, delirious improvisation. Hardly surprising, then, that in what was originally intended to be a report on migration in Ghana, there was talk at one point during the creative euphoria of filming of introducing a dragon or some other monster. In the end the idea was not pursued, and here one undoubtedly has one of the keys to the enterprise: where to stop when documentary actuality is transgressed in favour of another, more complex reality in which the part played by the imaginary is no longer merely ornamental or subordinate, but genuinely basic? Where to stop, too, when the traditional dramatic time scale no longer applies? In other words, at what arbitrary moment should the experience be interrupted, according to what criteria should any particular episode be cut down or entirely excluded during the montage, when the whole richness of the experience lies precisely in the lack of any dramatic censorship, when the meaning lies as much in the erratic course of the narrative as in the content of individual scenes?

Thus we find films running for several hours (*Jaguar* and its sequel *Petit à Petit*, 1970), veritable modern serials as crammed with incident as *Les Vampires*, *The Perils of Pauline* or *The Daredevils of the Red Circle*. This radical renovation of cinematographic fiction, drawing on the very earliest sources, results in a change of direction for Rouch, a total reorientation from his original ethnographic position towards films of pure fiction, 'European' films, of which the best and most characteristic is probably his sketch in *Paris vu par . . .*, *Gare du Nord*.

To describe *Gare du Nord* as characteristic of Rouch's work, almost central to it, as I am tempted to do, may seem surprising: a Parisian film, a fiction film, a *directed* film, whereas Rouch's work seems to derive its charm and its disruptive power from the more exotic elements of ethnology, darkest Africa, improvisation, seeing how others live.

The fact is that with *Gare du Nord*, the questions 'What is Rouch the ethnologist after?' and 'What is Rouch the film-maker after?' receive answers which are perhaps less ambiguous and evasive than they seem. Depending upon whether one sees this film as an interlude, an exercise, a *tour de force*, or as an absolutely inevitable development (being already faintly adumbrated in the early films, and vividly present in the later ones), Rouch's *oeuvre* is defined either as eclectic, or as a unity of contradictions whose richness springs from the interaction of these contradictions. What is *Gare du Nord* saying through its incredibly precipitous little tragedy? What is being demonstrated? Who or what is speaking? Probably simply the fascination of the frontier, the breaking-point: the record of a dream, a utopia, a reality lost in—and by—the impulse which affirms it.

All the techniques of 'direct' filming are employed and pushed to extremes (synchronous sound, technical mobility, extended takes), but transposed: here the dialogue is

written, the locations preselected, the action determined. The enterprise of Hitchcock's *Rope* is renewed: to achieve a coincidence of real time with shooting time, reinforced by the illusion of a single twenty-minute take with the reel-change masked by a momentary darkness. 'As far as the dialogue and situations are concerned,' Rouch said, 'there is no question of improvisation, but for the director, crew and actors' performances the improvisation is total.' Emphatically fictional, *Gare du Nord* is a critical riposte to pseudo-'*cinéma-vérité*'. The prolixity, the digressions, the 'dossier' aspect are superseded by an astonishing effect of condensation.

In the film a young couple quarrel one morning in their apartment near the Gare du Nord. She reproaches him for his apathy, his lack of romance, his lack of ambition, and talks of Adventure, of Escape. He half-heartedly defends himself. Finally she says he is pitiful, slams the door, and goes down to the street, where she is nearly knocked down by a car. The driver gets out, runs after her to apologize, and offers her Adventure and Escape in precisely the terms she used herself. Then, just as they are crossing a bridge over the railway line, he faces her with a startling bargain: he has decided to kill himself, but if she will go with him, he won't do it. Otherwise, he will throw himself off the bridge. Falteringly, she refuses. Instantly, while she stands there, incredulous and shaken, he hurls himself over the bridge on to the railway line below.

This situation, revealed by a hyper-mobile camera hugging close to the tragedy that is evolving, with the experience lived by the characters coinciding exactly with the space–time unit carved out on the screen (Godard spoke of how 'seconds reinforce seconds; when they really pile up, they begin to be impressive'), imposes a dramatic texture reaching almost suffocating heights of intensity until the final fall (in more than one sense of the word) on the brink of a void (mental, physical) which is less a conclusion than what the film is all about.

Formal suspense and dramatic suspense are inextricably linked here in a synthesizing conception of technique. The constant modification of the frame, obedient to Nadine's wilful movements, subjected to the grainy uncertainty of a bluish light, assailed by

Nadine Ballot and Barbet Schroeder in Rouch's *Gare du Nord* episode from *Paris vu par . . .*
'Emphatically fictional, *Gare du Nord* is a critical riposte to pseudo-*cinéma-vérité* . . . to describe this
film as characteristic of Rouch's work, almost central to it, may seem surprising . . .'

waves of city sounds, defines a hallucinatory odyssey in which, momentarily, as she parts from her husband, the dream of 'elsewhere' is adumbrated before being suddenly, brutally transformed into the more radical parting of death, whereupon the frame opens out to efface the characters it had hitherto clung to so feverishly.

Surely it is impossible not to see here the affirmation of an aesthetic, with the ethnological 'elsewhere', assimilated into the imaginary space between three people, suddenly and retrospectively realizing its function? It was in *Gare du Nord* that the repeatedly shifting frontiers of adventure, dreams, illusion—and also of direct cinema and *mise en scène*—revealed themselves as the object of an itinerary which is only seemingly capricious, and which gambles on this capriciousness as its essence.

Since then, Rouch's quest has continued, multiform, ramified, accumulating a jumble of ethnological reports, psychodramas, mythologico-burlesque serials, fictions, experiences of every kind and condition which, more or less at the mercy of indefinable circumstances, may become films running twenty minutes or five hours, which may or may not reach the screen, but which are at all events 'films which beget films'—by Rouch and by other film-makers.

Translated by Tom Milne

I find Rouch's later films disappointing, but there is no denying his importance as one of the seminal directors of the 60s. For further reading, see Louis Marcorelles' *Living Cinema* (1973) and Eric Barnouw's *Documentary* (1974).

KEN RUSSELL

Robin Wood

The historical significance of Ken Russell's work has unhappily little to do with any positive qualities of intelligence or sensibility. His *oeuvre* provides a startling and at first sight very unexpected manifestation of the possibility of original and personal expression within a film industry that appears generally committed to the nondescript, the unadventurous, the pusillanimous.

This granted, it must be added that, on reflection, Russell's work offers less an antidote than a corollary: the concept of 'art' which his films express both thematically and stylistically is simply the other side of the coin of the British cinema's incorrigible middle-class respectability. The films offer endless titillation without ever becoming dangerously disturbing or genuinely subversive, their 'shocking' images, tricked out with the best Sunday-supplement garishness and a spurious but plausible artistic or intellectual pretext, constitute a sort of cultural pornography, both degraded and degrading.

The show of flamboyant and passionate Romantic creativity in Russell's films masks an apparently all-embracing hatred. If one looks at the presentation of positive values and positive relationships—love, for example—one finds only conventionality and mediocrity: the love story that might have given a perspective to the horrors of *The Devils* (1971) is difficult even to remember, and the Birkin–Ursula pastoral love scene of *Women in Love* (1969) irresistibly suggests a shampoo commercial. Russell's films about composers, resting generally on the facile and highly dubious paradox that great artists are contemptible human beings, suggest an animus against them, as if Russell resented their achievements or hoped somehow to validate his own 'art' by debasing theirs. At the same time, one always has the feeling that for Russell composers like Mahler and Tchaikovsky are basically pretexts for the effluence of his own fantasies, so that the loathing seems also directed inward, towards himself. The dangers of unchecked fantasizing are apparent in certain of the more pernicious aspects of his work: in *Mahler* (1974), for example, while the anti-Semitism seems quite unequivocal, the satire on Nazism which is presumably meant to balance it is expressive of an unpleasant fascination that half glorifies what is being ridiculed.

Above all, Russell hates the human body: its degradation might almost be regarded as his central theme, as it seems to provide many of his films with their creative élan. This explains why *The Devils*—less silly than *The Music Lovers* (1971), less obscene than *The Boy Friend* (1971)—is probably the most successful of his feature films: here, the human body is deformed, contorted, flung into heaped plague-pits, tortured, has its legs broken and its tongue pierced, and is finally burned at the stake: it is the film in which Russell goes all the way. It is also significant that his best work of all remains the TV film about the paralysed and syphilitic Delius, *Song of Summer* (1968).

After *Mahler*, came *Tommy* (1975), which has many claims to be Russell's most bearable film in years, precisely because its subject-matter (the Who rock opera) was well within Russell's intellectual grasp. His next film, *Valentino* (1977), starred Rudolf Nureyev. For further reading, see John Baxter's aptly titled *An Appalling Talent: Ken Russell* (1973).

ERNEST SCHOEDSACK and MERIAN COOPER

Elliott Stein

The two best-loved characters in world cinema are Charlie Chaplin and King Kong—the little tramp and the big ape. And in recent years, in the United States, Kong has had the edge. Kong has emerged in the last decades as one of our great culture heroes, an absorbed and central personage of the American mythos. If, to their shame, some encyclopedias of film pass over his three godfathers, Schoedsack, Cooper and O'Brien, Kong is everywhere.

In 1973, King Kong reappeared as a major leitmotiv in Thomas Pynchon's monumental novel *Gravity's Rainbow* (he was also a continuing hero of comic books and the subject of a poem in *Rolling Stone*); he incarnated the fantasies of Karel Reisz's lovely *Morgan*; he turns up in Schrafft's ads, in Ron-Rico rum ads; on tourist posters he is seen atop the Empire State Building ('Come to New York—a great place to hang around'); in a *New Yorker* cartoon, moving with the times, he crashes a cocktail party on the roof of the World Trade Center. During the 60s button-craze, one of the more popular, sported by young people from coast to coast, proclaimed: 'King Kong died for our sins'. He adorns shirts and ties, and on the cover of the September 1971 *Esquire*, Norman Mailer may be seen holding a very unliberated Germaine Greer in Fay Wray position. Kong's abiding popularity is all the more discom-

bobulating when it is considered that he was created over forty years ago, was only eighteen inches tall and spent much of his time on screen crushing and munching men, women and children. Beauty may have killed the beast, she has yet to bury him.

On Skull Island they say he is 6,000 years old, but ciné-palaeozoology traces Kong back half a century, to the siege of Polish-occupied Kiev, 1920, where two pugnacious American anti-Bolsheviks crossed paths for the first time.

Merian Coldwell Cooper was born in Jacksonville, Florida, in 1894. He was appointed to the Annapolis Naval Academy in 1911, but resigned during his graduating year in order to get his piece of the Great War. Passport difficulties prevented a trip to Europe, but Cooper was able to let off youthful steam by joining the Georgia National Guard, whose good neighbour policy then consisted of hunting down revolutionaries in Mexico. With America's declaration of war, he enlisted in the Army Air Corps and was sent to France. In 1918, his bomber was downed behind German lines. After the Armistice, when released from a German prison hospital, Cooper joined the Polish army and helped form the Kosciusko Squadron which resisted the Bolshevik invasion of 1920. He commanded the Squadron, developed new strafing and low-level bombing methods, and was shot down behind Russian lines in July 1920. After several months in a prison camp near Moscow, Captain Cooper escaped and found his way to the border. Later, the Poles erected a statue honouring the future director of *King Kong* (1933).

Ernest Schoedsack was born in Council Bluffs, Iowa, in 1893. At twelve, he ran away from home and headed for California. At seventeen, he was working on the Mack Sennett lot, employed as cameraman by Mal St Clair. In 1916, he enlisted in the photographic section of the Signal Corps and was sent to France, where he cranked footage on most of the major battles. After the Armistice, he remained in Europe as a freelance cameraman. When he first met Cooper in Kiev, Schoedsack was *en route* to Poland to cover the Russian–Polish hostilities.

Cooper returned home in 1921 and worked for a stretch on the *New York Times*. While studying map-making at the American Geo-

King Kong: He 'is everywhere'.

graphical Society, with an explorer's career in mind, Cooper became fascinated by reports of the extraordinary tribal migrations which were then still a yearly event in Persia. A film was in it: he spoke of the project to Schoedsack, and to Marguerite Harrison, a journalist (author of *Marooned in Moscow*) he had met in Poland. Mrs Harrison put up part of the money, the rest was borrowed from Cooper's family.

They travelled to Istanbul, then on to Persia for six months of daily life with the Bakhtiaris. During this tribe's annual migration to secure grazing for its flocks, the entire population forded rivers on goatskin rafts and crossed trailless mountains barefoot in the snow. The trio of Americans lived through this great adventure and got it in the can; Schoedsack and Cooper then left for Paris, where for lack of funds they developed and printed their footage themselves. They returned to New York to edit it.

Grass was first shown on the lecture circuit, with Cooper narrating. Jesse Lasky bought it for Paramount in 1925. The studio laid on a full publicity treatment: posters informed the public that 'Zukor and Lasky present *GRASS*—and *GRASS* is GREAT!' It was acclaimed by the press (Robert Sherwood: 'I have an idea this film will succeed in spite of its worth') and took in a good deal of money in large American cities.

Grass is rather great—no thanks to Paramount. Much of the credit must go to Schoedsack, whose camera captured some of the most remarkable and strikingly framed outdoor footage of the 20s. In later reels, the film becomes a fantastic covered-wagon epic (*sans* wagons), as lines of 50,000 people lead several hundred thousand animals, zigzagging the mountain snow, week after week. When, at last, the fertile plains are reached, *Grass* ends with the insert of a document signed by the American Consul, stating that

Schoedsack, Cooper and Mrs Harrison were the first foreigners to cross the Zardeh Kuh pass.

Unhappily, Terry Ramsaye, Paramount's title writer, churned out an endless string of inanities ('Gosh, it's another day!'). And since *Grass* is a collective odyssey, it never deals with families or individuals—the Bakhtiaris are seen from a distance like some race of rugged compulsive insects—the concentration on panoramic visions eventually fatigues. Quibbles aside, no balanced view of *Grass* will deny it a place of honour as a pure salient moment in the history of documentary cinema.

The next step for the Mutt and Jeff directors (Cooper was stocky and bald, 'Shorty' Schoedsack stood a muscular six foot four) was described in a Paramount press release: 'With *Grass* a tremendous success, Cooper and Schoedsack decided on a new venture. They would invade Siam, with Paramount's backing, and make a jungle picture.' Prior to D-day, Schoedsack went off on a holiday expedition to the Galapagos Islands where he met the future scenarist of *King Kong*, actress–explorer Ruth Rose—Mrs Schoedsack before long.

On arrival in Siam, S. and C. set out for the north and spent a few months getting the Laotian villagers used to *them* while they prepared their story-line: one family's struggle for survival in a hostile jungle where houses are built on stilts to keep tigers from the door.

Chang (1927) proved a sensation. Its background was as 'natural' as that in *Grass*, but for the average moviegoer it held the attractions of comedy relief, dramatic editing and a widescreen process named Magnascope, used during the climactic elephant stampede. As the changs (elephants) charged, a special projector lens was brought into play (at least in first-run theatres), the screen opened up and the image enlarged before spectators' eyes to three times its normal size. The use of Magnascope in *Chang* now seems an omen, in the light of the decisive role Cooper later played in the creation of Cinerama.

Chang was a critical success and the top-grossing film of the year. Cooper affirmed in 1966: 'It's still the best picture I ever made.' *Chang* was a trail-blazer, generating a cycle

which thrilled world audiences for a decade —*Trader Horn*, *King of the Jungle*, the MGM *Tarzan*s. Although it is usually lumped with *Grass* as one of Schoedsack and Cooper's two great 'documentaries', the films are worlds apart. *Grass* is a pure documentary, with no fabricated scenes. *Chang* contains no scenes *not* fabricated—or at least conceived or staged in advance, albeit in Siam, using natives as actors.

There are memorable sequences—a fine leopard hunt, the destruction of the family's house by the changs, the scene in which the villagers (who seem to have read *Macbeth*) advance in the water, disguised as trees, to sneak up on the herd, the exciting footage shot by Schoedsack from the bottom of a tiger pit as elephants cross overhead. The elephant footage became standard stock-shot material, used later in at least a dozen films. For a *Kong* addict, *Chang*'s indelible moment is a mother rescuing her baby from the stampede—an idea elaborated on by the directors six years later.

If *The Four Feathers* (1929) falls short of Zoltan Korda's superb 1939 version of A. E. W. Mason's imperialist classic, it is a giant step towards Schoedsack and Cooper's masterpiece. The credits just fall short of composing a *Kong* poster: David O. Selznick, associate producer; directed, produced and photographed by S. and C. (Ruth Rose along for location shooting); Fay Wray and Noble Johnson in the cast—only Willis O'Brien, master catalyst of the great collective dream a few years later, is missing.

Shot silent, during the transition-to-sound period, *The Four Feathers* was released with synchronized music and sound effects; in spite of the talkie craze, it proved a great hit—one of the last of the big silent films. As an adaptation of Mason's novel, this *Four Feathers* must be chalked up a failure, but viewed as a sort of *Beau Geste* with pachyderms, it more than holds its own.

Cooper invested most of his earnings from *Chang* and *Grass* in aviation stock. His business activities kept him in New York during the two years after the release of *The Four Feathers*. Schoedsack, meanwhile, was striking out on his own. The result was *Rango* (1931), shot in Sumatra. The simple story involves four characters, two apes and two humans, with a common enemy: tigers. *Rango* did not achieve the success of *Grass* and *Chang*. Its best reel was spliced into immortality in 1936 when Paramount buttressed Dorothy Lamour's début in *The Jungle Princess* by adding *Rango*'s monkey stampede.

How did *King Kong*, a risky, expensive venture, unlike anything ever attempted in sound films, get produced in the middle of the Depression by a studio itself in a shaky financial position? And whose baby was this monster? So many good fairies were bent over the giant gorilla's crib—*King Kong* is the anti-*auteur* classic par excellence—that versions differ, and problems of attribution have become entangled.

David O. Selznick resigned from Paramount in June 1931; later that year, David Sarnoff placed him in charge of production at RKO. Selznick brought back to Hollywood his old friend Cooper to assist him in evaluating ideas for films. One of the projects, *Creation*, conceived by Willis O'Brien, involved prehistoric animals.

Selznick's version is: 'As to *King Kong*, I would say I was simply executive producer. RKO, when I took it over, had a big investment in an animation process of Willis O'Brien's. I brought back into the business ... Merian Cooper and assigned him as one of his jobs a study of this animation process, and Cooper conceived the King Kong character idea. I had signed up and sent for Edgar Wallace and brought him to California, where unfortunately he died in consequence of getting pneumonia and refusing to have a doctor since he was a Christian Scientist. But while he was in California, I assigned him to work with Cooper on *King Kong*. I have never believed that Wallace contributed much to *King Kong*, but the circumstances of his death complicated the writing credits. The picture was really made primarily by Cooper and Ernest Schoedsack, under my guidance; and one of the biggest gambles I took at RKO was to squeeze money out of the budgets of other pictures for this venture.'

Cooper's giant gorilla story actually went back a few years, and did not involve animation. 'My original idea was to giantize the gorilla, personalize him, and then play him

against enlarged Komodo dragons. I was going to use real ones. I was going to try and take a couple of gorillas to the islands. I tried to make a deal with MGM and Paramount, but it was during the depression and nobody wanted to do it.'

When Cooper surveyed O'Brien's project at RKO in 1931, he realized that something approaching his original concept might be produced by means of animation at the studio, avoiding location expenses. RKO's New York executives were unconvinced. With Selznick's encouragement, Cooper and O'Brien went ahead with a test reel: Kong shaking the sailors off the log, Fay Wray up a tree as Kong battles with an allosaurus. Impressed with the tests, New York finally gave *Kong* the green light. Shooting started in spring 1932.

The film's world première engagement began on 2 March 1933, at the Radio City Music Hall and the New Roxy. Lobbies throughout the depressed United States were turned into circuses. Full-sized cannon guarded the entrances to cinemas, with signs assuring: 'This theatre is armed to defy King Kong!' Customers passed 30-foot wagons full of food: 'Just one breakfast for Kong!' and then walked by cages full of small monkeys on which signs read: 'We are the degenerate descendants of the mighty Kong!'

Put simply, *Kong* is the greatest adventure film ever made. It is also, and not incidentally, a supreme example of the manifold collaboration picture which attained perfection in the Hollywood studios during the 30s. Here, everyone knew his business and everything worked. *Kong* is therefore a puzzler for any hard-line *auteur*ist critic. During Schoedsack and Cooper's long, often parallel careers, it would seem that in Cooper were oddly united the talents of the good business man *and* the visionary; Cooper was the motor of conceptual force, with Schoedsack the stolid reliable technician. Their alliance resulted in a masterpiece only once—when O'Brien's singular genius was added to it in the service of a story in which they all had faith.

They did not work concurrently on *Kong*. Schoedsack is reported to have directed the opening reels in New York and those on board ship, Cooper the island footage and the concluding reels of Kong making mud pies of

New York. Cooper—animated and trick sequences; Schoedsack—dialogue scenes with actors. The great rehearsal scene, wherein Fay Wray, dressed in a medieval cloth of gold robe, is ordered by Robert Armstrong (as Carl Denham) to: 'Scream, Ann, scream for your life!' at some as yet unseen horror, is the finest moment of Schoedsack's directorial career.

Kong is a triumph of astute two-part construction. The slow, realistic opening in contemporary New York in the midst of the Depression (with dialogue in a vein similar to the wise-cracking survival brashness which marks the Cagney–Blondell pictures at Warners during the same period) and the tense uneventful sea voyage—these four straight Schoedsack reels with never a monster in sight come to a climax in that rehearsal scene, when Ann, dressed as 'Beauty', emits her premonitory primal scream. Then the fog rolls in, accompanied by Max Steiner's spooky arpeggios, and we arrive at Skull Island. No more joking now—the rest is one long nightmare, developing into an hysterical chase structure which mounts in intensity until The End.

More than forty years have gone by, but *Kong*'s special effects have never been equalled. Time, money, genius and love were all miraculously available at RKO in 1932, when O'Brien had complete control over a small crew of great matte artists who worked for over a year preparing fantasy effects. Unlike animated cartoons, his three-dimensional animation did not lend itself to assembly line methods in the Disney manner; it grew from the tremendously time-consuming work of a handful of men who followed the project from beginning to end. O'Brien's haunting Skull Island is marked by a credible visual unity reminiscent of Doré engravings—he created it partly through a costly and laborious technique involving the painting of fantastic atmospheric scenes on three separate planes of nine by twelve foot sheets of glass for each set-up.

Characters in great works of the imagination have been classically prone to break loose from their creators' intentions. Few of the millions who have thrilled to the film have wondered why its unconscious appeal is so strong. Why does this monster prompt such universal affection? Fay Wray and her young man, Bruce Cabot, are attractive, yet we do not love them: everyone falls for Kong, the savage innocent. As alienated as any Bergman or Antonioni heroine, he doesn't even have a friend to hear *his* side of the story. Visible sexual provocation is present (e.g., the incredible scene in which Kong peels Fay like a banana) but the film is cannier in planting wild seeds of conjecture in the back of the mind. How many children have been marked for life by reveries of what would happen if Ann Darrow had just shut up and relaxed? He is the only leading man in movie history to appear in scene after scene of frontal nudity with no visible means of procreation. Precisely for that reason, the most fantasized lump of anatomy in our time has been Kong's penis.

Kong and *The Most Dangerous Game* (U.K.: *The Hounds of Zaroff*, 1932) were sister films, started at about the same time. *Game*, produced by Cooper and directed by Schoedsack and Irving Pichel, was released first because of the long months required for *Kong*'s special effects. Both used parts of the same foggy hollow swamp sets constructed at RKO. A sprinty year for Fay Wray: Zaroff's hounds at her heels on Monday —then fleeing Kong on Tuesday—in the identical bog!

The Most Dangerous Game is based on Richard Connell's short story, essentially a taut two-character tale. The script adds a woman and some interesting erotic notions. Count Zaroff (Leslie Banks), a demented Russian whose one passion in life has been hunting animals, becomes bored with that sport and invents a new sensation: on a remote island, he provokes shipwrecks, wines and dines the battered survivors, then sets them loose in order to hunt them down as human prey. He seems impotent with women unless he has first tracked and killed their boyfriends. The construction is similar to that of *Kong*, but on a smaller scale: a slow build-up, then once tension has broken loose, one shock after another until the end. Miss Wray and Joel McCrea's flight through the jungle, pursued by the hounds—the camera pitching headlong after them into the foliage—is one of the best orchestrated chase sequences on film.

Long essays have been written in France (where the film enjoys a great reputation) on the character of Zaroff, 'the screen's finest example of the Sadean, Nietzschean super-man–villain', etc. Seen today, the film suffers from an unsatisfactory performance at dead centre. Zaroff, as played, lacks grandeur—a dangerous, yes, but doting and campy luna-tic, for Banks' performance is dreadfully theatrical.

Son of Kong (1933) directed by Schoedsack alone, was a hastily conceived cheap sequel to *King Kong*. The main attraction, Kong Jr, is a hopeless letdown. He mugs, gurgles, winks shamelessly at everyone in sight, and is far from the butchest of apes. Willis O'Brien created the special effects, but objected to the story. His lack of enthusiasm was visibly transmitted to his staff, who did, however, cook up a good earthquake. It is a very dumb film.

Cooper remained Selznick's executive as-sistant for two years. When Selznick left RKO in 1933 and moved over to MGM, Cooper was named vice-president in charge of production. Two of the most successful pictures made during his regime were *Little Women* (1933) and *Flying Down to Rio* (1933)—his creative involvement in both was extensive. It was Cooper who first set in motion the screen's best-loved dance team: he decided to use Fred Astaire in *Flying Down to Rio* in spite of advice that the dancer 'was not good looking'—and he selected Ginger Rogers as Astaire's partner. Cooper married actress Dorothy Jordan in May 1933.

In 1934, with the Depression in full force, Cooper announced plans to put seventeen films into immediate production. This meant an expenditure of $4 million and work for 3,500 people. One of them was John Ford, chosen by Cooper to direct *The Lost Patrol* (1934) and *The Informer* (1935). It marked the beginning of the great Ford–Cooper part-nership which would bring forth nine more films, among them several of Ford's finest.

Before leaving RKO, Cooper produced two 'spectaculars': *She* (1935) and *The Last Days of Pompeii* (1935). *She* reunited several of the Kong gang—screenplay by Ruth Rose, a thumping score by Max Steiner, Noble Johnson as the Amahagger chief. Even the colossal gate from *Kong* turned up again. In this film, it opens to reveal an art deco stair-case at the top of which She stands. Ran-dolph Scott has traversed Muscovy to find his dying uncle's old flame—and She (Helen Gahagan) is 500 years old. The actors, di-rected by Irving Pichel, do not sparkle; Miss Gahagan lacks glamour in the role of the merciless undying Queen admired by Jung. If this *She* is the best of the half-dozen filmed versions of Rider Haggard's tall story, the reasons are visual: frisky sacrificial dances, a whopping avalanche, leaps over chasms, and the oddly designed city beneath a glacier.

In *The Last Days of Pompeii* (directed by Schoedsack), Marcus (Preston Foster) is em-bittered when his wife and child are run over and killed by a nobleman's chariot. He decides that only money matters; he journeys to Judaea to amass riches as a horse-thief in the service of Pontius Pilate. On his return to Rome, he bodybuilds and soon rises to superstardom as a gladiator. By the time Vesuvius erupts (historically, a good thirty years ahead of schedule), Marcus is the rich-est man in Pompeii. But as the lava bubbles up and the buildings tumble down, he has a vision of Christ, and dies, realizing that money isn't everything. Although Jesus thickens the plot considerably, He is care-fully kept offscreen (the script even avoids using the word Christians, though they are all over the place) so that the picture would not vex the British censor and risk losing a pretty penny for RKO. Basil Rathbone as Pilate gives the performance of his career, washing his hands superbly. The final holocaust—one of Willis O'Brien's best—features the de-struction of the giant nude male statue be-tween whose legs the gladiators customarily entered the arena.

Merian Cooper was a leading force in the promotion of Technicolor in the film in-dustry. By 1932, Dr Herbert Kalmus had perfected his three-colour process, but money was scarce and no one cared to invest in a colour feature—'things are good enough in black and white'. In 1933, Cooper and John Hay Whitney formed Pioneer Pictures (releasing through RKO) to popularize colour productions. A short, *La Cucaracha*, was produced as a test of the new process; released in 1934, it made history. An even greater event was the first full-Technicolor feature, *Becky Sharp* (1935). Pioneer's goal was to 'colour the world'. When Selznick broke with MGM in 1935 to form his own company, Cooper aided him considerably by bringing in a large Whitney investment. Selznick reciprocated by taking over the operation of Pioneer, and Cooper was named vice-president of Selznick International.

Schoedsack moved to Columbia Pictures in 1937, where he made two exotic Jack Holt quickies. In 1940 he directed *Doctor Cyclops* for Paramount. Albert Dekker starred as Dr Thorkel, a mad scientist holed up in the mountains of Peru, who has discovered how to reduce people to 6-inch 'humanettes' by means of atomic rays. Thorkel is going blind and requires assistance; when his colleagues arrive, he picks their brains for a reel, then promptly shrinks them to mouse size. Dressed in pocket handkerchiefs, they hide in his lunch box. After some prancing about, Thorkel falls into a bottomless pit, the humanettes regain whatever full-size humanity they were possessed of to begin with, and return to Kansas City.

Dekker was an interesting actor, especially good in bizarre roles; he is in his element here. Schoedsack was often a careless director of actors; the rest of the cast are out of theirs. Not a good film, *Doctor Cyclops* is at best a two-finger exercise in the use of outsize furniture and trick photography. Its single inventive 'fun' shot is one of Dekker chasing a miniaturized horse through the grass with a butterfly net.

During the Second World War, Cooper was promoted to colonel and became first chief of staff for General Claire Chennault of 'Flying Tigers' fame. He participated in the 1942 air attacks on the Japanese and the New Guinea invasion and was a deputy chief of staff under General Douglas MacArthur. Later, he was named brigadier general in the Air Force reserve.

Schoedsack and Cooper worked together only once after the war. Their reduced collaboration was the consequence of eye damage suffered by Schoedsack while in the Air Force which had seriously impaired his vision. On Cooper's return to civilian life, he worked closely with John Ford, producing an impressive succession of Ford films: *The Fugitive* (1947), *Fort Apache* (1948), *Three Godfathers* (1948), *She Wore a Yellow Ribbon*

(1949), *Wagonmaster* (1950), *Rio Grande* (1950), *The Quiet Man* (1952), *The Sun Shines Bright* (1953) and *The Searchers* (1956).

S. and C.'s final collaboration was on *Mighty Joe Young* (1949), produced by Cooper, directed by Schoedsack, with Ruth Rose's script based on Cooper's original story. A trader's daughter in Africa finds a baby gorilla and raises him lovingly, lulling him to sleep at night with 'Beautiful Dreamer' played on a music box. She grows up to be Terry Moore; he grows up to be Mighty Joe Young, fifteen feet tall. They are both brought to Hollywood to perform in a nightclub by Max O'Hara (Robert Armstrong in the role of an updated Carl Denham character).

Mighty Joe Young was the first film since *Kong* in which the Kong family really hit its stride again. Pre-production and shooting took two years. Ray Harryhausen, working on his first big film, assisted O'Brien in designing Joe's armature. O'Brien's animations are masterfully integrated with the live action; the total effect may be less poetic than in *Kong* (this derives from the tongue in cheek script) but at moments the trick work surpasses that of *Kong*. The nightclub mayhem sequence is the finest composite trick action sequence in all cinema: a pride of lions breaks through its glass enclosure behind the bar to do battle with Joe—he hurls the lions—they skid on the tables—as the panicked customers flee. The orphanage fire scene is no less impressive. *Mighty Joe Young* was awarded the 1949 Oscar for special effects.

At the invitation of Mike Todd and Lowell Thomas, Merian Cooper agreed to supervise production of *This Is Cinerama* (1952), to direct some sequences and edit others. Cooper was awarded an honorary Oscar in 1952 'for his many innovations and contributions to the art of motion pictures'. His last public appearance was on 30 December 1971, when he delivered the eulogy at Max Steiner's funeral service. With a coincidental flourish worthy of an original story by Merian Coldwell Cooper, the two Carl Denhams died within a few hours of each other, in April 1973, and obituaries of Robert Armstrong and Merian Cooper, the *King Kong* pair, made headlines side by side.

The 1976 remake of *King Kong*, although of little interest in itself, did prompt the publishing of two books on the *real* Kong: *The Making of King Kong* by Orville Goldner and George E. Turner (1975) and *King Kong Story* (1976), an album put together by René Chateau. There is also the now unfindable special number of the French magazine *Midi-Minuit*, published in 1962.

MACK SENNETT

Jean-André Fieschi

'Bathing beauties frolicking on the sands, frenzied temptresses, tender lovers, crazy gags: he introduced a new element into the cinema which is neither comedy nor tragedy, but really the noblest form of cinema in terms of morality, love, poetry and freedom.' So wrote Robert Desnos in the newspaper *Le Soir* of 15 April 1927.

In fact, if one wants to be historical about it, this freedom Mack Sennett is credited with discovering made its first appearance in France and was developed there between 1905 and 1914. It is hard to believe the unremitting fantasy, the cruelty, the dream logic, the 'anything goes' atmosphere of Jean Durand's slapstick comedies (and to a lesser extent those of Louis Feuillade and Léonce Perret). Such a wealth of invention, which (like jazz) had its origins in a genuine popular culture, is unique in the cinema. Mack Sennett, the more truculent early Chaplin, the improbable W. C. Fields and the cartoons of Tex Avery give one a faint idea of what it was like. But with the bourgeois and petit bourgeois audiences fast swelling into a majority, the production concerns (bowing to a humanist viewpoint inherited from the nineteenth century) probably weren't too happy with so cavalier an attitude to the 'human person', such unusual emphasis on the body (and its excrements), or such joyous subversiveness. For Jean Durand there were no taboos. For Sennett, as we shall see, there were.

So it came from France, and Sennett was to acknowledge his debt, even more frankly than Chaplin acknowledged his to Max Linder: 'Now, I have been posing for many years as the inventor of slapstick motion-picture comedy and it is about time I confessed the

truth. It was those Frenchmen who invented slapstick and I imitated them. I never went as far as they did, because give a Frenchman a chance to be funny and he will go the limit—you know what I mean. But I stole my first ideas from the Pathés' (*King of Comedy*).

Be that as it may, among the old Hollywood tribes now on the road to extinction Sennett ranks after Ince and Griffith as one of the demi-gods, a founding father, a totem. They don't, we are told, make men like him any more. The custodian of lost secrets. The active participant in the golden age. There is a certain grain of truth in all this beyond the pious sentiments. If one considers the reality of this archaic image, beneath the assumed mantle of inventor one discovers an adventurous life, a sort of meeting on Mount Sinai (with D. W. Griffith figuring as God the Father), and a terrain fertilized by the new freedom of images to move faster than thought and ripe for any audacity.

Sennett was born in Canada of Irish descent in 1880. His admirer Theodore Dreiser was later to describe his involuntary blushing, his sidelong laughter, his mistaken enthusiasms. His biographers (Davide Turconi, for instance) note his original vocation to be an opera singer. The comedy of custard pies, pratfalls and chases, of perils and cross-purposes, making a mockery of drama through compression and acceleration, is not so very different from opera . . .

The tragedies seemed comic to him: 'I often thought how easy it would be, with the least bit more exaggeration—and they were exaggerated plenty as it was—to turn those old dramas into pure farce.' Exaggeration (compression and acceleration): the very principles of comic narrative. At around the same time, having established the principles on which dreams worked in 1900, Freud discovered that the principles governing laughter were exactly the same, though occurring in a social context which made the dream effect tolerable for everyone. The intolerable is of course an element constantly in play in slapstick: bodies are always threatened, abused, disabled, submerged, squashed, and so on. Terror, it has often been noted, is not very far away (the logic of the nightmare). We laugh at the things (dizzy heights, disasters) that would terrify us if we dreamed them alone at night.

Acceleration and compression can of course be seen constantly in action in the structure of these invariably exhilarating films. But in the material conditions of production in those days, in the division of labour and allotment of time, acceleration and compression were also the principles behind their very inspiration: often several films were made the same day, from bare outlines, under the 'Old Man's' supervision (he selected the crews and actors, wrote, edited and provided the motive force for the whole thing: like Ince in the dramatic field, he was not just a desk producer, but an organizer and a begetter of stories, part poet and part businessman, with a touch of the acrobat). So, in these very quickly made films, everything happens very quickly. As Eluard, Breton, Artaud and Desnos unerringly recognized, they are a sort of visual equivalent to automatic writing. The same is of course true of the serials of Perret, Feuillade and Gasnier, but in extended forms, expanded in time. To produce the effect of laughter (or terror) one must reach the unconscious, and to do this one must accelerate (or slow down in the extreme, extend). This acceleration creates a sort of dam against the course of daily life, on which slapstick feeds and which is made up of acts so familiar that they no longer contain any element of surprise. But Sennett tampers with the machinery, raising the tempo until surprise begins to blossom in layers: the conventional signs are scrambled, the real and the imaginary (like the ordinary and extraordinary) swap characteristics under the influence of a demonic fantasy which is the spectacle itself. Laughter explodes through the cracks as logical reality, pushed through the looking-glass (through the dream world), perpetually disintegrates.

Sennett enumerates the very principles of slapstick. These principles (again like those governing the serial; but then here we probably have the two most important specifically cinematographic forms right from the early days) are in fact baroque principles: repetition and continuity. It's like Leibnitz, prompts my girl-friend Tania, leaning over my old Underwood. And it is true that Leibnitz would have made Sennett laugh, if he had read him. Everything in his method, Tania continues, is the expression of everything through anamorphoses, repetitions, differactions: whether one cuts the continuous flux into infinite narratives or accelerates everyday life into a digest no sooner seen than gone, the result is 'ever and always the same thing, give or take a degree of perfection', as Harlequin, emperor of the moon, would say, precursor of slapstick and a philosophical hero embodying the truth according to Leibnitz in the *Essay on the Human Understanding*.

Although this undermining of time by reshaping, reducing or contracting its duration is concerned with creating surprise effects and tapping the unconscious, it is also a matter of collective effort. Yes, one would be missing the point if one tried to see Sennett as a 'film *auteur*'. 'A producer of laughs' was how he described himself. Producer, catalyst, company manager, animator of entertainments with deep and distant roots in the circus, the mountebanks, the magic lantern: the Bathing Beauties that Desnos spoke of (Sennett's trademark, along with the equally ritual Keystone Kops) clearly indicate where the film-maker in Sennett gave way to the master showman. He created and controlled the framework necessary in order to display these fantasies, supervised the themes, unearthed talent, defined 'characters' (almost all of whom slipped through his fingers, not the least being Chaplin, and each time the Old Man couldn't help feeling a little resentful, because all fathers are the same, and this one had a particularly developed sense of family).

The aspect of collective creation, the subjection of the group's imagination to the more or less despotic will of a master who is part awake and part asleep, the spontaneity and the improvisation, the element of mockery or deception: all this can be seen, rather more than nascent, in these supposedly archaic forms of cinema, and the old trunk has now sprouted 'modern' branches: Rouch and Rivette, among others. Thus the old cinematograph is reborn through sophisticated rereadings and rewritings of its own sources. In this sense there are no lost secrets—simply techniques which imperialist Hollywood had managed to suppress under a barrage of codes and standards after the coming of sound, and which remained there to be revived and reactivated.

Later on the cinema would be elevated to the rank of art. For the moment it was a

Marie Dressler in Mack Sennett's *Tillie's Punctured Romance*: waiting in the wings, in more ways than one, is Charlie Chaplin together with Mabel Normand.

popular entertainment, intended for the common herd, within the vital register of infallible performance and hazardous life from which it drew both its life-blood and its inspiration. Performances by actors who were also gag-men and stunt-men. The public might even get involved ultimately. Today it is invited to do so, as though entertainment could only regenerate itself by abrogating its own history so as to rediscover its sources. This is where Sennett once again becomes a magic name.

Mack Sennett made it his business to create types. To be distinctive and immediately identifiable ('Oh, look . . . Fatty!') was their primary function. The type is rigidly defined, geared to certain possibilities but also subjected to impossibilities. The clergyman, for instance, cannot be knocked about 'if he is young and smooth-shaven', in which case he becomes, according to Sennett, 'as immune as a blonde young lady' (*Motion Picture Classic*, November 1918). Similarly,

Shetland ponies must not be put into an undignified position. And while one could, of course, subject a pretty girl to a sudden drenching or have her fall in the mud, she must not be the target for a custard pie.

The type is defined in terms of the respect or disrespect his (or her) person must or must not inspire. Intrinsically, it doesn't mean young, blonde or smooth-shaven, clergyman or pretty girl; it means what you can throw a pie at, what you can (or cannot) tip into a pool of mud. In other words, the advantage of the type system is that it conjures up a distorted reflection of the social structure. The nightmare, in fact, takes place inside the class struggle (and the battle of the sexes). And the cops, whole bunches of them, endlessly pursue some unattainable fugitive. The cop, of course, is a perfect example of the type: 'The copper is fair game for pies, likewise any fat man.'

All this suggests a considerable degree of theorizing in Sennett, as well as a sound knowledge of the ideological market; and a respect for certain taboos is written into the rules of the game. The clergy, as we have seen. But there is an even more fundamental taboo. Mothers (as Griffith well knew, cf. *The Mother and the Law*) are untouchable. This was the lock to a still mythical America that couldn't be forced. 'No joke at the expense of a mother will raise laughs ... In slapstick, they can be used only to create emotion or atmosphere.' 'The father,' on the other hand, 'is one of our best targets.' You could do anything to him (except kill him). Slapstick comedy strips away the masks: disclosing everything that can be disclosed, stumbling only against the family structure of puritan pioneer America which was already becoming a relic of the past.

A rigorous production displays and dismantles reality. This involves expression and calculation. Expression: the composition of geometrical figures (Louis Delluc called Sennett a 'mathematician of the gag'). Calculation: implying the theory of probabilities. So Sennett, instead of quoting Leibnitz, quoted Gozzi, the eighteenth-century Italian playwright who demonstrated that all drama can be reduced to thirty-six possible situations. Similarly, 'there are only a handful of possible gags'. The scenario is simply their blender. For example, two detectives disguised as burglars capture each other, or a husband disguises himself as a burglar to frighten his wife, but she is visited by a real one. All gags are reducible to two, according to Sennett: 'the fall of dignity' and 'the mistaken identity'. The fall of dignity: exposure of the other side of the social and psychic coin. Mistaken identity: exposure of the repressed desire, for this is always when one hopes for the custard pie to fly, by mistake or misjudgement but in accordance with the secret desire. The strategy of the gags, in other words, is closely linked to the (unconscious) strategy of wish fulfilment.

In many ways, Sennett emerges as one of his own characters, an indefatigable foster-father to gags who was quite capable, we are told, of hiring a cameraman on the strength of some bizarre detail, some quiddity of reality. 'We hired him because he was moustachioed like a Grand Duke.' So the legend goes, anyhow, incorporating a good many other quaint or disconcerting facts. One must accept this legend for what it is: as just another Sennett production where the fiction greedily gobbled up and outgrew its own begetter. This was the order of the day in any case, because all around him legends were proliferating: upstream was Griffith's, and downstream the legend of the tramp, the unforgettable Little Fellow who was quarrelsome and rhapsodic by turns, and who had taken his first steps under the Old Man's promptings.

Translated by Tom Milne

A few biographical details: Sennett broke into films through a letter of recommendation to Marie Dressler (also a Canadian) given him by none other than Calvin Coolidge. She, in turn, introduced him to Griffith, for whom he played a few small parts. Then a director got sick, Sennett stepped in, and the rest, as they say, is history. Sennett finally gave up films in 1936, and spent the next fourteen years looking after the land he had inherited from his mother. He died in 1960.

Mack Sennett wrote his autobiography, which he called simply *King of Comedy* (1954). See also *Father Goose: The Story of Mack Sennett* by Gene Fowler (1934) and *Mack Sennett's Keystone: The Man, the Myth, and the Comedies* by Kalton C. Lahue (1971).

VINCENT SHERMAN

John Gillett

Vincent Sherman, who began his career as stage actor and scriptwriter, is one of those versatile American directors who produced his best work during a long period at one studio (Warners) without ever quite achieving a personal profile. One of his earliest films, *Saturday's Children* (1940), a working-class comedy romance, embodies a quietly civilized tone which was to appear again later, but he really made his mark with several Bette Davis vehicles—*Old Acquaintance* (1943), an intelligent theatrical adaptation which showed his skill with players, and *Mr Skeffington* (1944), a family saga full of enjoyable purple patches and sustained by a tight narrative line and by one of Claude Rains' best performances. *The Hard Way* (1942), with Ida Lupino, and *Nora Prentiss*

(1947), with a rejuvenated Ann Sheridan, stand high in the Warner roster of 'women's pictures', with the complicated plotting of the latter again controlled and transformed by Sherman's intelligent handling. *Adventures of Don Juan* (U.K.: *The New Adventures of Don Juan*, 1949) was a successful return to 30s' costume drama, with a good-natured performance by an ageing Errol Flynn and a feeling for decoration and colour suggesting that Sherman could also be a considerable visual stylist. His later work for other companies rarely gave him similar opportunities and, although well-made, the films seem rather inflated and anonymous by comparison. His British-made film, *The Hasty Heart* (1949), contains one of Richard Todd's earliest and best performances. In the 70s, he has made several large-scale TV-produced films.

Sherman was born in 1906. One might well ask, why an entry on Vincent Sherman, and none on Edmund Goulding? And there is no satisfactory answer—except that amidst the incredible riches of Hollywood cinema of the 30s and 40s, a line had to be drawn somewhere. But Goulding (1891–1959) was responsible for the first Garbo version of *Anna Karenina* (*Love*, 1928) and two of Bette Davis' better films: *Dark Victory* (1939) and *The Great Lie* (1941). And then there was that freakish *Nightmare Alley* (1947), in which Tyrone Power played a geek, a carnival man whose speciality is biting off the heads of live chickens.

DON SIEGEL

Robin Wood

Don Siegel's Charley Varrick is (as the film named after him insists a trifle ostentatiously) 'the last of the Independents'; the phrase neatly encapsulates the central theme of this director's work.

Invasion of the Body Snatchers (1956)—a film of which, to judge from interviews, Siegel is particularly (and justifiably) proud—is concerned with the take-over, by extra-terrestrial aliens, of the inhabitants of a small American town. The citizens are faithfully reproduced down to the smallest physical detail, but the resulting *Doppelgängers* (or 'pods', as the film calls them) lack all emotion: they point forward to a world of automata in which love, compassion, tenderness, generosity, friendship, no longer exist, a world of peace and rationality bought at the cost of all we regard as human. At last, only one man in the town—like Charley Varrick, the last of the independents—remains human, and he becomes a social outcast, a man on the run. In interviews, Siegel has spelt out both the allegorical content and his personal identification with it: within the movie industry, and especially on its business levels, he feels himself surrounded by 'pods'.

One needs, then, in order to define the value-structure of Siegel's work, some definition of what it means *not* to be a 'pod'. *Invasion of the Body Snatchers* itself unfortunately provides the least interesting and convincing definition: the emotion represented in the film by the love-relationship of Miles and Becky exists only on a level of cliché and overt (verbal) statement (the aliveness and spontaneity of the man/woman relationship in Howard Hawks' *The Thing*, a film with a very similar central theme, provides a useful touchstone here). The failure in *Body Snatchers* is significant: Miles and Becky are civilized people with roles and careers within established society, and Siegel isn't really very interested in them. The more Miles is forced out of society, the more alive he becomes, but it is the aliveness merely of desperation, and what sort of society it might lead to or be incorporated within is not clear. (Where, in terms of a future, is Charley Varrick going at the end of *his* movie?)

The 'pod' characters in Siegel's films are traditionally members of organizations, whether within or outside the law: cogs in big wheels. Those who escape being 'pods' belong to nothing; or (like Dancer in *The Line-up*, 1958, and the Clint Eastwood cops of *Coogan's Bluff*, 1968, and *Dirty Harry*, 1971) belong only nominally: too independent (or too neurotic) by nature to be safely contained within an orderly framework. Before he turned bank-robber, Charley Varrick was a freelance crop-duster, before that a stunt flyer: Siegel respects his background, but opens *Charley Varrick* (1973) at the point where he leaves it definitively behind in favour of crime.

If Siegel's heroes resist commitment to organizations, their personal commitments tend also to be short-lived. There is the

Mickey Rooney–Carolyn Jones relationship in *Baby Face Nelson* (1957); otherwise, the most obvious exception is Charley Varrick. Charley's commitment to his wife, and sense of loss at her death, are movingly done; yet, half-way through the film, Charley, Siegel and the audience have forgotten all about her. The later sequences where Charley makes love to Felicia Farr have warmth and tenderness, but there is no suggestion that the relationship is more than ephemeral. The fact that the man–woman relationships in *Madigan* (1968)—which remains, arguably, the best and richest film Siegel has directed, partly, but *only* partly, because of its atypical aspects—are so detailed and complex is perhaps to some degree attributable to Abraham Polonsky's share in the script.

In the last few years, Siegel (born 1912) has managed the difficult transition from the modest and at times humiliating role of employee–director at the mercy of studios and contracts to the point where *Charley Varrick* can bear the proud insignia, 'A Siegel Film'. The opportunities offered by greater freedom and control, larger budgets and long-er shooting schedules, have on the whole resulted, not in the kind of disastrous preten-tiousness for which the career of Jules Dassin provides the best (or rather the worst) example, but in the clearer emergence, stripped of their incidental encumbrances, of themes and attitudes discernible in the earlier work. Whether Siegel is making precisely the films he wants to make is debatable: the ex-traordinary assurance, and the thematic con-sistency, of his recent work assert that he is; *The Beguiled* (1971)—a cherished personal project—suggests a desire to move outside the genre with which he has become associated. Yet he continues to direct highly commercial crime-thrillers without any sense of superior-ity to his material or of compromised integrity.

The characters played by Clint Eastwood in *Coogan's Bluff* and *Dirty Harry* occupy a disquieting and equivocal position in the moral scheme of Siegel's work. They exhibit some of the characteristics of 'pods', totally without compassion, largely lacking all the finer emotions, regarding women as sexual objects and using them ruthlessly if it suits their purposes (as Coogan uses his antagon-ist's girl to get information). Yet Siegel clearly invites us to admire them—at least within the context of the worlds of their respective films. Their saving grace, in his eyes, would seem to be their resolute and uncompromising independence.

It is instructive to compare these charac-ters with the heroes of Howard Hawks, to whom they bear a superficial resemblance. One has the feeling with both directors that the protagonist's motive for action is only nominally the defence of society or of civilized interests, which exist in the films as little more than a pretext, but that they act in response to an inner need. For Hawks' heroes that need is self-respect, the central controlling moral value of his work. For Siegel's Eastwood heroes (and although the actor's charisma makes them special cases, they relate significantly to the others) the need is more complex, more obscure, and morally much more dubious. Their antagon-ists represent more grotesque, more 'acted out' projections of the dangerous and barely controllable forces that drive them; they obscurely recognize this, and are driven by a compulsion to destroy or suppress their op-posite numbers, to smash the reflection in the distorting mirror. For once a publicity slogan provided a really apt interpretative comment: 'Dirty Harry Callahan and the psychopath. Harry's the one with the badge.' At the beginning of *Coogan's Bluff*, Coogan tracks down and traps an Indian who has murdered his wife and broken out of the reservation. Nothing later in the film surpasses these scenes, whose intensity arises from the sense that Siegel (director, after all, of *Flaming Star*, 1960, perhaps the best American film centred on an Indian) could as well have made the Indian ('last of the Independents') his hero. The character is invested, within a few minutes, with impressive savage dignity. At the end of the film Coogan, the 'cowboy' from Arizona, defeats and recaptures his other assignment in a pursuit on motor-bikes: the two men, their interchangeability expressed through common skills and equal terms, leave the film appropriately hand-cuffed to one another.

The failings of these films—the feeling that the disturbing after-taste they leave is attribu-table to artistic shortcomings as much as to artistic success, a realized and controlled complexity—may not be directly Siegel's

Coogan's Bluff: 'The saving grace of the characters played by Clint Eastwood in *Coogan's Bluff* and *Dirty Harry* would seem to be, in Siegel's eyes, their resolute and uncompromising independence.'

fault, though one senses his compliance. Where Hawks in *Rio Bravo* very precisely 'places' the John Wayne character (in relation to Dean Martin, in relation to Angie Dickinson), counterbalancing his moral infallibility with a sense of limitations, subtly satirizing the Wayne *persona*, Siegel seems unable to control the charismatic force of Eastwood, so that, despite our sense of the moral ambiguities of the characters, it overrides the complexities inherent in the material. And Siegel, I think, must take the blame for the very contrived development of the Susan Clark character in *Coogan's Bluff*, potentially representing, as incarnated by this highly intelligent actress, the film's sharpest critical attitude to the Eastwood charisma, but insultingly manipulated to the point where she is reduced to silent worship as our sexual superman is borne aloft by helicopter.

In an interview in *Positif*, Siegel expressed dissatisfaction (not entirely convincing in terms of the quality and vitality of his achievement) at being type-cast as an 'action' director; he said that he would like to direct comedies. *The Beguiled*—an entirely personal choice of subject to which he was deeply committed—is certainly not that; but it may suggest the sort of film Siegel would make if he were free of those 'commercial' requirements by which even the most emancipated Hollywood directors tend to be circumscribed. While not necessarily his best film, it is important in indicating areas in which his range might be extended. It is—perhaps predictably—the one Siegel film which manifests ominous signs of the kind of intellectual/artistic pretentiousness that can afflict American directors who would secretly like to make 'art movies'—notably in the obvious and laboured symbolism of the injured and captive crow. It is, none the less, an impressive film, and less thematically atypical than may at first appear. It extends the notion of human life as still based essentially on the law of the jungle (which in Siegel's other films seems particularly associated with the city, *Coogan's Bluff*, for example, being pervaded by animal or hunting imagery), revealing the 'jungle' beneath the genteel graces of a seminary for young ladies at the time of the American Civil War. It plays on the fear of women (albeit exploited women) as predators, and above all on the fear of castration, interestingly complementing the insistence on assertive masculinity in other Siegel films.

The very limited values that Siegel's work embodies define him decisively as a minor artist; within those limitations, the intelligence and vitality of his work entitle him just as decisively to our esteem.

Mention should be made of the best of the early Siegel films, *Riot in Cell Block 11* (1954), as well as of his remake of *The Killers* (1964), and the more recent *Black Windmill* (1974), *The Shootist* (1976), and the less ambitious thriller *Telefon* (1977).

For further reading, see *Underworld USA* (1972) by Colin McArthur; Alan Lovell's 1975 pamphlet *Don Siegel: American Cinema*, and Vol. 4 of *The Hollywood Professionals* (1976), by Stuart Rosenthal and Judith Kass.

ROBERT SIODMAK

John Russell Taylor

Though Robert Siodmak (1900–73) had a long and productive career in the cinema, it is fair to say that all the films for which he will be remembered were made during one short period, in Hollywood between 1943 and 1949. During these years he established for himself a special corner in the 40s *film noir*, and made several prime examples which in their evocation of morbid atmosphere and in the sheer bravura of their staging have seldom if ever been surpassed. Siodmak came, like others of that period (Fritz Lang most notably among them) out of the German cinema by way of the French. His very first film, *Menschen am Sonntag* (1929), made in a somewhat vaguely defined collaboration with Edgar Ulmer, Billy Wilder and Fred Zinne-

mann, was a charming and long-famous essay in rosy location realism. After that there seems to have been nothing of note (his French films of the 30s were undistinguished) until he made *Son of Dracula* (1943) and that masterwork of camp cinema *Cobra Woman* (starring Maria Montez as twins, one good, one bad) in 1944. From those he went straight on to his first big critical success, *Phantom Lady* (1944), a classic *film noir* about a desperate search (through, inevitably, the rainwashed night streets of some Hollywood studio backlot) for a vital witness who, when found, proves to have gone mad. The film was full of bravura passages, yet the overall effect was haunting and gloomy. The same could be said of the films in the same genre which followed: *The Suspect* (1945), *The Strange Affair of Uncle Harry* (1945), his masterpiece *The Spiral Staircase* (1946) and *The Dark Mirror* (1946), in which Olivia De Havilland played twins, one good, one bad. Even when he became involved, with changing tastes, in the cycle of dramas shot on the street where it really happened, he managed nevertheless to drench them—films like *The Killers* (1946), *Criss Cross* (1949) and, best of all, *Cry of the City* (1948)—in a lot of Germanic *Stimmung*, with Expressionistic lighting, play of mists and mirrors, and deceiving appearances. Siodmak returned to Europe in 1951, and subsequently made some very jolly films, such as the Burt Lancaster burlesque *The Crimson Pirate* (1952), and one film about a sex killer in Nazi Germany, *Nachts wenn der Teufel kam* (U.S.: *The Devil Strikes at Night*, 1957), which recaptured much of the old feeling. But in the main he went back to being the competent jack-of-all-trades he had always been and the magic was gone.

Siodmak is likely to be remembered more for certain sequences than for films as a whole. Who can ever forget the scene in *Phantom Lady* with Ella Raines 'inspiring' Elisha Cook, Jr, as he beats his drums practically to smithereens? And the tough warden who calls out to Barbara Stanwyck: 'Judgement Day, Jordon!' in *The File on Thelma Jordon* (1949). Some of Siodmak's films are discussed in *Underworld USA* (1972) by Colin McArthur.

DOUGLAS SIRK

Jon Halliday

'There is a wonderful expression: seeing through a glass darkly. Everything, even life, is inevitably removed from you. You can't reach, or touch, the real. You just see reflections. If you try to grasp happiness itself your fingers only meet glass. It's hopeless.' (Douglas Sirk, talking to Jon Halliday, *Sirk on Sirk*, 1971). Born Hans Detlef Sierck in Hamburg of Danish parents in 1900, survivor of the Bavarian Soviet Republic of 1919, pupil of Erwin Panofsky, poet, painter and dramatist, Douglas Sirk spent some twenty years (1939–58) as the artist of an impossible America.

Before that, Sirk had had a highly successful career as a theatre director in Germany. By the age of twenty-nine he had been appointed head of the Leipzig city theatre, and had made a national name for himself with audacious productions of well over 100 plays, ranging from Calderón to Hofmannsthal, Grillparzer to Werfel. Caught by the advent of the Nazis in 1933, Sirk soon transferred to cinema; within three years he had become Ufa's most successful director and had created the country's biggest star, Zarah Leander. In late 1937 he was able to get out of Germany and, after working in France and Holland, he reached Hollywood towards the end of 1939.

During his first period in Hollywood (1939–48) Sirk was under contract most of the time to Columbia as a writer, but his most interesting work then was in his independent productions, particularly the three films starring George Sanders: *Summer Storm* (1944), *A Scandal in Paris* (1946) and *Lured* (later retitled *Personal Column*, 1947), not in his Columbia pictures. After a brief and unhappy return to Germany, Sirk went back to Hollywood in 1950 and directed some twenty films at Universal before abandoning America after the success of *Imitation of Life* (1959).

Like many of his own favourite writers, from Calderón to Henry James, Sirk was ahead of his time. As a stage director in Weimar Germany, he was nationally known. As a film director in Hollywood, he was virtually ignored by the 'serious' critics, and until fairly recently written off as a purely commercial director of melodramas. What the critics failed to note was that Sirk was all the time—in both Hitler's Germany and in Eisenhower's America—constructing 'secret' critiques of the society in which he was working. He himself in his interviews has made his position quite clear: in a society like Weimar Germany, with a large and active left-wing and a revolutionary culture which had mass support, an artist could (perhaps should) be explicit about the society in which he was working—thus his staging of plays like Bronnen's *Rheinische Rebellen* or Kaiser and Weill's *Silbersee*. In a society like early Nazi Germany (1934–37) or America of the 40s and 50s a degree of secrecy is necessary. It is in societies like these that the melodrama flourishes—for structural reasons. Both societies demand 'the play that pleases'. And the melodrama is itself the form which best allows a director to express his criticism of the society—thus for example, *Zu neuen Ufern* (*Life Begins Anew*, also known as *To New Shores*, 1937) and *La Habanera* (1937) in Germany; or *Summer Storm* and *Written on the Wind* (1956) in America.

Sirk has stated his particular interest in two elements: a certain type of character: 'the doubtful, the ambiguous, the uncertain'; and situations of what is conventionally known as 'social criticism'. In films like *Summer Storm* and *Written on the Wind* he was able to combine the two elements in a formula of his own liking, with, respectively, George Sanders and Robert Stack incarnating the doubtful, ambiguous and uncertain 'heroes' sliding inexorably downwards to their doom. In many other cases, particularly at Columbia, and in his earlier years at Universal before the big commercial success of *Magnificent Obsession* (1954), Sirk was not able to bend the stories or the characters to his own interests.

A full appreciation of Sirk's work in both Germany and America ought to define rather precisely the conditions of production: a simple comparison of, say, *Written on the Wind* (produced by Albert Zugsmith) with *Imitation of Life* (produced by Ross Hunter) marks the distance between, respectively, sympathetic and antipathetic conditions within the same studio, Universal. Yet even in the most adverse circumstances Sirk nearly always managed either to bend part of the film his way, or to introduce some Sirkian element, whether it be in lighting, dialogue, the use of colour, or music.

For of all the many-talented figures who moved from Europe to America, none had more skills than Sirk. A film like *Magnificent Obsession*, with an appalling plot, apparently far from Sirk's real concerns, shows him battling the very substance of the story with all the panoply at his disposal—light, colour and music, woven together by the work of his chosen cameraman, Russell Metty. *Magnificent Obsession* also shows Sirk's daring, his willingness to take on the most outrageous material and work on it with the deep irony which was one of the most important gifts he brought with him to Hollywood. This Euripidean irony was certainly one of the things which prevented him from being swept under by the Eisenhower–Hunter culture of the period. It was allied with two other formidable assets: first, a long grounding in classical drama, which was to help Sirk twist and transcend many a story like *Imitation of Life*. But even this classical training might not have been enough without Sirk's almost futuristic and surrealist imagination. *A Scandal in Paris* and *Written on the Wind* both reach right out beyond the normal boundaries of the American cinema into a world of craziness, deceit, mirror-images and doubt, a world which the society itself preferred not to know about at the time.

On the rare occasions when Sirk has met with appreciation, he has usually been praised as a 'stylist'. He certainly is a great stylist—indeed style was one of the things which he, like Max Ophuls, brought to America with him. But Sirk is more than a stylist, even in the widest sense of that word. He is also an acute observer, and presenter, of his age. Sirk is well aware that the past weighs like a nightmare on the brain of the living. But the present he shows is in many ways already the future. Whereas he sees the past as perhaps more distant than others see it (for example, *A Time to Love and a Time to Die*, 1958, or *Battle Hymn*, 1957), he sees the future as nearer than most imagine (*Imitation of Life* or *Written on the Wind* or *All That Heaven Allows*, 1955). This rare capacity to build the structures of history into even the most placid-looking film, like *All That Heaven Allows*, is one of the factors which set Sirk apart from the other German directors who moved to Hollywood (and even from a man with a great sense of history and drama like Rossellini). What Sirk was able to do was to *historicize* the American melodrama, to build into it the actual decay and disintegration of the society, unbeknownst to both complacent producers and complacent audiences. Hence his affinity to, and affection for, writers as far apart as Euripides and Chekhov—the latter the paradigm of the revolutionary writer who has remained a hero of the bourgeoisie.

Sirk's interest in doctors and medicine has frequently been remarked upon; and there is an insistent gallery of medical personnel treading their way through his films from *Der eingebildete Kranke* in 1934 to *Imitation of Life* in 1959, by way of *La Habanera*, *Thunder on the Hill* (U.K.: *Bonaventure*, 1951), *Magnificent Obsession*, *All That Heaven Allows* and *Written on the Wind*. But Sirk is interested in much more than just individual disease and breakdown. He is interested in the breakdown of societies. Thus *The Tarnished Angels* (1957, based on Faulkner's *Pylon*), set in the South during the Depression, is about a whole society at its nadir. In these conditions Sirkian elements of doubt, despair and escape are ready to hand—as they are, for example, in a situation like the Korean war, where Sirk dwells on another broken, vacillating flyer (*Battle Hymn*). In the apparently stable and prosperous America of the mid-50s, the elements of the breakdown are not immediately available in the same dramatic way—although, as Sirk foresaw, they are there for sure just below the surface: hence the construction of *Written on the Wind*, where infirmity is piled on infirmity, and alcohol, violence, sexual doubt and escape into the sky form the world of the rich.

But there is another facet to Sirk: away from the crumbling world of the America of the time, people could be affectionate and loving in a straightforward way. *Captain Lightfoot* (1955), set in Sirk's beloved Ireland, is a light-hearted, happy film about the revolutionary struggle against the British, even though terrible things keep happening almost all the way through the film. *Take Me to Town* (1953) is about an America of the

Death and Dorothy Malone in *Tarnished Angels*: 'based on Faulkner's *Pylon*, set in the South during the Depression, it is about a whole society at its nadir'.

past, long since disappeared, in which Sterling Hayden and Ann Sheridan can truly fall in love. And *A Time to Love and a Time to Die*, perhaps Sirk's most personal film, is an almost incredible challenge thrown in the face of death and destruction. In the ruins of the Germany in which he himself had lived, Sirk here built a wonderful love story of great simplicity. The two lovers, of course, are not allowed to keep their love. It is only an interlude before the time to die. But it is the very sense of death, the constant en-croachment of ruins, which gives so much power to the love story. Sirk, the master of hopelessness, is also the master of hope. But against fate, in which he certainly believes, nothing can be done.

Twenty years after his departure from Hollywood, after *Imitation of Life*, Douglas Sirk is emerging as the greatest portraitist of decaying and crumbling America, shot in glorious colour. Andrew Sarris prophesied years ago in *The American Cinema*: 'Time, if nothing else, will vindicate Douglas Sirk.'

The prophecy has already come true, and Douglas Sirk has taken his rightful place—on the screen, and among a new generation of *cinéphiles*.

For further reading, see *Sirk on Sirk* (1971), a series of interviews with Jon Halliday. There is also a special number of *Screen* magazine (London, September 1971) and a special issue of *Bright Lights* (Winter 1977–78) devoted to Sirk. See also the article on Stahl.

ALF SJÖBERG

Edgardo Cozarinsky

Alf Sjöberg's reputation has suffered from the hardships of both occasional recognition and enduring obscurity. *Hets* (U.K.: *Frenzy*; U.S.: *Torment*, 1944), bought by RKO after the 1946 Venice Film Festival, was shown throughout the world; *Fröken Julie* (*Miss Julie*, 1951), prizewinner at Cannes in 1951, also achieved a wide release. But these films are not isolated phenomena; they are, arguably, not even exceptional in a filmography where the undisputed masterpiece, *Karin Månsdotter* (1954), was killed by Swedish critics and public alike and remains almost unknown internationally.

Sjöberg's distinguished, uninterrupted work as a stage *metteur en scène* has always been the backbone of his creative personality. Since his formative period in the 20s, he has always kept in touch with the avant-garde— not only with the dramatists but with the political and aesthetic movements as well. This intellectual vivacity has not produced work of opportunist variety; on the contrary, it is amazing how obvious influences (as were Pabst and the Russian film-makers of the 20s on his early films, and the French existentialist writers of the 40s on his later ones) have always found their place in a national frame of reference. Most strikingly, Sjöberg's interest in topical issues and social history has not escaped from Sweden's so often self-decried provincialism—a certain lack of urgency, either an indulgent absorption in its own *Angst* or a purely well-wishing concern for social problems other than those faced by a welfare state.

Sjöberg (born 1903) co-directed his first film with Axel Lindblom at the very end of the silent period. *Den starkaste* (1929) opposes a typical *Kammerspiel* situation of jealousy and rivalry in a love triangle with an open sea and Arctic ice for scenery: a tension very appealing to his taste for built-in, if only theoretical, dialectics. Eleven years later, *Med livet som insats* (1940) can be considered a fresh departure in a different medium, not only as a sound film but also as a reaction against the too slick products of the Swedish 30s. Based on a Finnish story (made two years earlier as a Finnish film), set in an unspecified but recognizably Baltic country, dealing with resistance and tyranny in the guise of an adventure story, it struck its audiences as almost a foreign film. Not only because of the enduring Swedish tradition that equates political subject matter with foreign settings (from Molander's *En natt* of 1931 up to Johan Bergenstråhle's *Made in Sweden* of 1969); but also because its visual elaboration, eclectic and brilliant, looked unlike any Swedish film of the period.

The same is even more true of *Den blomstertid* (1940) and *Hem från Babylon* (1941), where novelettish material was turned inside out in search of ideological overtones, for the play of light and shadow as well as for narrative legerdemain. In *Den blomstertid* an island teacher sheds the nostalgia for her ghostly sailor lover and weds an earthbound teacher. In *Hem från Babylon*, an adventurer returns home after running for his life in war-torn China and a Paris full of exiles and spies, only to find his patient fiancée eager to embark on the same life of danger and excitement he is impatient to abandon. Both films deal with Bovary-like cases of self-delusion; both are ironical in espousing conventions of cheap fiction only to expose them, as it were, between quotation marks; both present Sweden as an island, diseased with the very neutrality that protects it. On a comparatively minor level, *Kungajakt* (1944), a very funny swashbuckler set during Gustaf III's reign, alludes to contemporary politics through its Fairbanks-like evocation of a beloved period of Swedish history.

The same subject-matter and treatment of those early films attain their highest degree of elaboration in *Resan bort* (1945). The film not only develops thinly related parallel actions (a triangle story with thriller elements on the one hand, and on the other a young Norwegian refugee, in love with a Swedish girl, trying to reach England and the RAF), but juggles freely with all the rhetorics alluded to—from Hitchcock's British spy films of the late 30s to Pabst's weakness for decadence and diagonal patterns of light inside a shot.

These highly original works were, for most Swedish critics of the time, little more than *exercices de style*. Though *Frenzy* was considered superior, it has not aged as well. In this story of young lovers terrorized by a sadistic teacher, Sjöberg's political abhorrence of Nazism and Ingmar Bergman's (his scriptwriter and assistant) conception of a universe ruled by Satan, clash uncomfortably. *Iris och löjtnantshjärta* (U.K.: *Iris*, 1946), a *Liebelei*-like love story between servant girl and aristocratic officer, seems much better now. The court of the evil rich, portrayed as Gothic figures, sets off a delicacy of feeling for the lovers that too seldom has graced a Sjöberg film.

By then Sjöberg had already made an early significant gesture to reconcile his awareness of the European intellectual climate with the Swedish tradition. *Himlaspelet* (U.K.: *The Road to Heaven*, 1942), based on a modern morality play by Rune Lindström, had its Everyman moving among biblical characters and episodes in the guise of Dalarna landscape and peasant folklore. The visual inspiration was the famous nineteenth-century naïve painters of that province, but also a classic of the Swedish silent period that had already re-created, though with less sophistication, their art— Sjöström's *Ingmarsönnerna* (1919). The morality of the play, however, is far from naïve: utterly sceptical, its underlying world image is an absurd and existentialist one, and in retrospect it is almost impossible not to read into the film the views that, at the time of its production, Camus and Sartre had not yet fully expounded.

Bara en mor (*Only a Mother*, 1949) is Sjöberg's greatest achievement in this direction. The story of a woman's life and of a social class (the *statarna*, itinerant field workers whose condition was abolished only in the 30s), the film chronicles several decades of personal and collective drama with great richness of episode and character, with that ample 'breath' of nineteenth-century realist fiction which was the model for Ivar-Lo Johansson's novel. Thanks to Eva Dahlbeck's strength and transparent beauty the mother figure emerges as one of Sjöberg's recurring archetypes—a life force that can endure physical pain as well as the shattering of her modest illusions. It is remarkable, though, that Sjöberg should have conveyed a sense of time passing, of people changing, of places abandoned and returned to, through a narrative that stresses the main character's submission to unmanageable forces to the point of enforcing a rigid continuity, an almost hypnotic chain of cause and effect between the film's episodes.

But then, as far as the dramatic mechanism is concerned, the naturalists' belief in hereditary or social conditioning may replace without too great strain the idea of Destiny. In *Miss Julie* Strindberg's single act explodes in all directions—memories of the characters' past, as well as their dreams, and even intimations of the future, are worked into an exacting structure of flashbacks (and even one flash-forward), where the past is always pressing upon the present. The camera pans or tracks away from the characters to find them in the same space as they were long before, and later goes back to them, again without cuts; occasionally, figures from the past walk by those of the present in the same static shot. This method (first explored in a sequence of *Bara en mor* and much commented on at the time of the film's release) reinforces, paradoxically, the tragic, almost Dionysiac drive towards destruction found in Strindberg's characters, and is not so cinematographic as it may seem at first glance: the simultaneity it employs is theatrical, in so far as it is based (and it stresses this fact) upon that unity of place which the cinema has always naturally ignored.

The closed perfection of *Miss Julie* was unfortunately absent from *Barabbas* (1953). The abstractions of Pär Lagerkvist's novel never acquired enough flesh on the screen to dress its allegorical bones. As an existentialist anti-hero, Barabbas himself was only a highly articulate contrivance, and the episodic construction of the film did not have, as in *Bara en mor*, a rich soil of realistic

Eva Dahlbeck and Åke Fridell in *Only a Mother*: Eva Dahlbeck's performance is one of the greatest in world cinema.

behaviour to sustain and make more meaningful its continuity of inevitable links in the
chain of fate. Sjöberg's best *trouvaille*, and a
characteristic one, was to cast Eva Dahlbeck
in three very brief roles—Barabbas' mother,
the Virgin Mary, and an anonymous passer-
by who pities the thief as he dies on his cross.
But *Barabbas*, after the international acclaim
for *Miss Julie* and the Nobel Prize for
Lagerkvist, had been devised as a prestige
venture for Sandrews, its producers, as well
as for the Swedish cinema itself. Its failure
was a painful one. Sjöberg's next film, also
ambitious and expensive, was an unmitigated
commercial disaster. It was, alas, also his best
film.

Karin Månsdotter consists of three starkly
distinct parts which retell the life of the low-
born concubine of Erik XIV. The first section recalls both Méliès and puppet-shows.
It opens in colour, with Karin presented
as a fairy-tale heroine, part Snow White,
part Cinderella, in brief scenes with painted
backdrops and between inserted titles. The
washed-out colours give way to sharp black
and white as the teenage farm girl realizes
that she is supposed to sleep with the King
but not to become Queen. The second section,
introduced as 'Some scenes from Strindberg's *Erik XIV*', is an exercise in larger-
than-life theatricality, a play of solitary
figures which cast enormous shadows on
imposing décors; though often compared to
Ivan the Terrible, the rhythm of its compositions and cutting is unmistakably Sjöberg's.
In it, Karin is a victim of political intrigue
and court manoeuvres which she cannot even
grasp. When the King is finally imprisoned
she is sent into exile with her children, and
the final section of the film takes the form of a
chronicle of her last years, reconstructed from
notes scribbled in the margins of the
Bibles in the different monasteries and
castles which were her prisons. As she em-
braces her children in the last shot and goes
off with them into the night, a guardsman
asks another who she is. 'The Queen' is the
curt answer, and Sjöberg's dramatic irony
becomes apparent—that Karin's childish
dreams have been mocked, but that each
humiliation has ennobled her on a moral
level.

The boldness of the film's structure (the
three parts are meant to clash dialectically)

works as a distancing device; its constant
criticism of the very notion of royalty, and
the realistic image it conveyed of Karin (a
'rags to riches' princess in traditional middle-
class piety), shocked the politically and aesthetically tame Swedish audiences of 1953.
(The same year, it is worth remarking, Bergman's defiant *Sawdust and Tinsel* [U.S.: *The
Naked Night*] also met with unqualified
rejection.)

After the obtuse reception dispensed to
Karin Månsdotter, Sjöberg seems to have
engaged, and failed, in various familiar directions. *Vildfåglar* (1955) is a doomed-love
story that doesn't come to life either in the
post-Expressionist territory of *Frenzy* or in
the carefully observed social milieu of *Iris*.
Its naturalistic Göteborg locations interfere
with its neurotic attempts at tragic grandeur,
and only a zigzag flashback concerning the
previous tenant of the lovers' studio is of
interest as narrative method and as a metaphor of the main characters' ill-fated struggle
against metaphysical evil. *Sista paret ut*
(1956), Sjöberg's second collaboration with
Bergman, eleven years after *Frenzy*, shows
an obvious effort towards a more simple
visual style. But Bergman exhausted his
script in a series of contrived verbal clashes
in the most tired convention of bourgeois
drama. Four years later, *Domaren* (1960),
from a play by Vilhelm Moberg, followed a
poet's progress towards madness in a society
where justice and wealth and psychiatry
defend ruthlessly coincident interests—a
striking conception that was smothered by a
high-flung allegorical treatment which never
achieved real greatness. The same proved
true of *Ön* (1966), where a Hamlet-like figure
wants to organize some islanders against a
government which threatens to expropriate
their land for nuclear experiments. Shreds
from Sjöberg's complete filmography (an
aristocratic but militant mother figure, fore-
boding family portraits and flashbacks in the
style of *Miss Julie*, an opposition of romantic
illusion and the didactic will that recalls *Den
blomstertid*, and so on) haunt the film, whose
pathetic shortcomings are those of its hero—an
evident passion and an incapability to make
himself heard and understood. A careful
recording of his own production of Strindberg's *Fadern* (U.K.: *The Father*, 1969) for
the Royal Dramatic Theatre, not without

naïve attempts at historicism (portraits of Schopenhauer, Bismarck and Nietzsche are used to put the play in an ideological context), is Sjöberg's most recent film.

Interrupted for almost a decade after its start in the last days of the silent cinema, overshadowed later by the emergence of Ingmar Bergman as the major Swedish film author, closed perhaps by *The Father*, Sjöberg's film work has been out of touch with any possible audience for too long now. But then, critics irritated by his over-elaborate compositions, his intricate patterns of lighting, his too brilliant editing, the tracking shots going to or coming from figures in movement, should see again so-called minor films (*Resan bort*, even *Hem från Babylon*) in the light of such an acclaimed modern film as *The Conformist* (1970). Bertolucci's ironical reworking of 30s rhetoric coincides almost constantly with Sjöberg's own treatment, even to the point of achieving an almost dreamlike continuity of brief sequences. It would not be too surprising if Sjöberg's *oeuvre*, confined for today's taste to outmoded keys of sensibility and intellectual commitment, turns out to be ripe for reappraisal.

It is perhaps worth reiterating that Sjöberg's films contain two of the greatest performances in the history of the cinema. One is well known—Anita Björk in *Miss Julie*; the other, even more remarkable, is not: Eva Dahlbeck in *Bara en mor*. For further reading on Sjöberg, there are Jean Béranger's *La Grande Aventure du Cinéma Suédois* (1960) and, in English, Peter Cowie's *Screen Series: Sweden 1 and 2* (1970).

VICTOR SJÖSTRÖM

Tom Milne

For a few years around the end of the First World War, the Swedish cinema nosed just ahead of Hollywood, qualitatively if not quantitatively, in a bid for pre-eminence on the world's screens. Although Mauritz Stiller played his part with films like *The Song of the Red Flower*, *Sir Arne's Treasure* and *Johan*, this supremacy was won chiefly on the strength of three films directed by Victor Sjöstrom (1879–1960): *Terje Vigen* (*A Man*

There Was, 1917), *Berg-Ejvind och Hans Hustru* (*The Outlaw and His Wife*, 1918) and *Körkarlen* (U.K.: *Thy Soul Shall Bear Witness*; U.S.: *The Stroke of Midnight*; now generally known as *The Phantom Carriage*, 1921). Critics raved about spiritual values, and Hollywood reached for its chequebook to lure Sjöström into a contract.

Like most cultural trends, the Swedish revolution was based partly on a misunderstanding, or rather an illusion inspired by unfamiliarity. Looking back at these films today, it is not difficult to see why they caused such a furore: apart from their technical mastery, the comparatively restrained acting and the luminous quality of the images (whether naturally or artificially lit), the ubiquitous presence of nature and natural forces among the *dramatis personae* gives them an epic breadth which must have seemed breathtakingly daring. 'The most beautiful film in the world,' Louis Delluc rhapsodized over *The Outlaw and His Wife*, hailing Sjöström as living proof that the cinema was an art and not merely a fairground attraction.

Seeking a focus for their enthusiasm, contemporary critics (subsequently followed by most historians) found it by seizing on the more exotic elements to define the work of Stiller and Sjöström as the expression of an essentially *national* temperament. Much play was made on the fact that *Terje Vigen* was based on a poem by Ibsen celebrating a nationalistic episode from the Napoleonic Wars, and on the powerful flavour of folklore and legend in both *The Outlaw and His Wife* and *The Phantom Carriage*. Yet these elements, important though they may have been in attracting attention, are marginal. The real importance of Sjöström's work was more accurately defined by another Scandinavian, Carl Dreyer, when he wrote in 1920 of the Swedish cinema in general and of Sjöström's *Klostret i Sendomir* (U.K.: *The Secret of the Monastery*, now known as *Monastery of Sendomir*, 1920) in particular, that these films demonstrated how suffering could take place as convincingly within the mind as under the more tangible threat of a revolver.

Since the interiorized suffering in all three Sjöström films takes the form of that self-flagellatory concern with sin and redemption peculiar to the romantic agony of Swedish Protestantism, one is to a certain extent flogging a dead horse in arguing against them as expressing a national temperament. But the point is that these three films are not altogether characteristic of Sjöström's work; and that, accepted by common consent as his masterpieces, they form a dubious yardstick against which his other films have been measured and found wanting. Absolutely typical in this respect is a book on Sjöström by René Jeanne and Charles Ford, published in France in 1963. After painting a depressing picture of Sjöström and his work as slow, sombre and impeccably sincere, they define his dominant theme as 'redemption by Nature, the purification of souls by vast natural phenomena, snow or fire'. Any film which does not fit into this preconception is dismissed as minor (*Tösen från Stormyrtorpet* [*The Woman He Chose*, now known as *The Girl from Stormycroft*, 1917]), a mistake (*Hans Nåds Testamente* [*His Lordship's Last Will*, 1919]), exotically alien (*The Monastery of Sendomir*), or inexplicably bizarre (*He Who Gets Slapped*, 1924). Faced with the charge that Sjöström had no sense of humour—increasingly prevalent in recent years as Stiller's comedies look increasingly airy and Sjöström's 'masterpieces' look increasingly earthbound—Jeanne and Ford respond simply by saying that he needed none.

Temperamentally, it may be true that Sjöström was humourless, though his brilliant comic performances in Stiller's two *Thomas Graal* films (1917–18) give one leave to doubt this. As a film-maker, however, there is no doubt that he could match Stiller touch for touch when he wanted to. Few films of the period could rival the airy grace with which *His Lordship's Last Will* opens. A shot of a stately mansion. Pan down to a shabby tramp sleeping in the sunshine outside the gates. Cut to a farm-labourer and a bevy of pigs happily blending their snores in the courtyard. Cut inside to a kitchen where the butler and his staff doze with their heads on the table while a cuckoo clock vainly chimes the hour. And finally, heralded by the title 'But the sleeping mansion also had its sleeping beauty; stealing upstairs, we find the bed-chamber', we discover the hero: an old gentleman in a vast nightcap and moustache-protector, also snoring happily in a large four-poster under a mosquito-net.

With a lazy wit oddly reminiscent of the Renoir of *Boudu Sauvé des Eaux*, Sjöström uses this opening sequence not only to establish an unusually precise picture of the geographical layout of the house, but to adumbrate his theme. Like Boudu, the ageing aristocrat, sadly contemplating his expanded waistline, receded hairline and sixty-fifth birthday ('That one should become so old and ugly before dying!' he mutters disgustedly in front of a mirror. 'Remove the image or I shall be sick'), has discovered the vanity of all human endeavour. Cheerfully letting his estate go to wrack and ruin, relying on his butler's well-filled snuffbox for the little pleasures he still enjoys ('Wish I could understand how you can afford such good stuff,' he mutters crossly), he has only one ambition left: to establish a state of such perfect indolence in his household that no sound of human or animal activity will disturb his long hours of hibernation in his comfortable bed. Aided by a performance of marvellous fantasy by Karl Mantzius—even in solving the unwelcome problem of his inheritance, the old man manages to confound self-seekers and let young love live happily ever after without actually doing anything about it—Sjöström scarcely puts a foot wrong in elaborating an exquisitely funny and touching comic fable out of this story of a sleeping beauty who stubbornly resists the world's efforts to free him from a self-imposed spell.

Delightful, but of no great consequence, *His Lordship's Last Will* is nevertheless important in that, being adapted from his own play by Hjalmar Bergman, who also scripted other films criticized for departing from the Sjöström canon like the superb *Mästerman* (1920) and *Vem Dömer?* (*Love's Crucible*, 1922), it makes one wonder to just what extent Sjöström was straitjacketed by his traditionally beneficial association with Selma Lagerlöf. That Lagerlöf's novels, with their simple narrative style, their conception of nature as an active force and their persistent return to the theme of man's dilemma between good and evil, struck an answering chord in Sjöström's temperament is beyond doubt. What *is* in doubt is whether this answering chord necessarily made for good films.

Karin Molander in *The Girl from Stormycroft*: 'a deceptively simple low-key film infused with a quiet lyrisicm', this little known film is one of Sjöström's finest.

Unquestionably it did so in his first Lagerlöf adaptation, *The Girl from Stormycroft*, a rustic drama about a peasant girl called Helga who becomes an outcast when she gives birth to an illegitimate baby, earns the respect of the community by refusing to let the father court eternal damnation (he is about to take a Bible oath denying his responsibility), and eventually wins the love of a nice young man by her selfless devotion. A deceptively simple, low-key film infused by a quiet lyricism which makes it a companion piece to Dreyer's *Bride of Glomdal*, *The Girl from Stormycroft* has its melodramatic flaws (the plot turns on the unlikely complication that the young man thinks he has committed murder while drunk) but still manages to astonish by its psychological accuracy and emotional subtlety.

In the opening sequence, for instance, walking down the road after being forced to take her case to court by her outraged father,

Helga is offered a lift by a young man who helps her into his carriage, looks at her more closely, and bursts out, 'Oh, are you the . . .?' She nods, and to his sympathetic amusement, insists on getting out to walk because, she says, she would never have accepted a lift if she hadn't thought he knew who she was. Perfectly establishing Helga's character —the sturdy peasant independence, but also the humility which makes her bow to public opinion—this encounter also foreshadows the complex reactions her predicament is to arouse in the community: respect from the judge and jurors for her Christian act in refusing to let her seducer perjure his soul; good-natured sympathy from the young man, who persuades his parents to take her on as a maid; greed from her parents, who see possibilities in this development; love from her new employers, who soon come to recognize her true worth; malicious speculation from the good bourgeois of the town; and growing sexual hostility from the young man's rich fiancée as she becomes increasingly aware of a threat she cannot combat. Vividly conjuring the community as a living organism rather than as a dramatic convenience, these ambivalent emotions are brought sharply into focus by a single gesture in the climactic scene just before the wedding when the young man, tormented by his imagined guilt, tells his fiancée he must go to the police in spite of her protests that she cannot possibly marry a branded criminal. As she listens to his tortured confession, her hand strays to her wedding crown, fiddles distractedly with the pin holding it, then flutters down again to her lap. The gesture, made almost of its own volition, suggests that her feelings are involved as well as her sense of the proprieties. Having hitherto viewed Helga purely from the standpoint of convention, she now begins to weigh her in the balance as an equal, to find her own love wanting, and to withdraw her claims in a moving last scene which becomes much more than the usual happy ending.

Full of delicate nuances and exquisitely underplayed by Greta Almroth, Lars Hanson and Karin Molander, *The Girl from Stormycroft* is very different from *The Outlaw and His Wife*, made just before but released just after it. Adapted from an Icelandic play about a man and woman outlawed by society and living out their frenzied passion unto death among the mountain glaciers, *The Outlaw and His Wife* is a tempestuous melodrama, vigorously but unsubtly acted by Sjöström himself and his third wife, Edith Erastoff, in which all the attention is lavished on the majestic, inimical landscapes. The result is monumental but hollow, and it was this monumentality that Sjöström unfortunately chose to emphasize in his next three Lagerlöf adaptations: the two-part *Ingmarsonerna* (*The Ingmarssons*, 1918–19), *Karin Ingmarsdotter* (U.K.: *God's Way*, now known as *Karin, Daughter of Ingmar*, 1920) and *The Phantom Carriage*.

Of this family saga following the sons and daughters of Ingmar through the generations, the first two parts are dedicated to social realism, the dignity of toil, peasant traditions, and they are aptly summed up by the opening scene of *Karin, Daughter of Ingmar*,

in which the camera rests tranquilly on a group of farm workers who pause in the fields as a church bell begins to ring. 'They were all still for as long as it takes to say the Lord's Prayer', a title explains as the camera patiently waits. Gauging his style to the peasant's measured tread, Sjöström systematically avoids cutting into movements or interrupting ruminations, letting the film move at what is assumed to be a rustic pace. The result, with son supplanting father in a vision of natural continuity, is slow, stolidly impressive, and more than somewhat tedious. Equally monumental but much less phlegmatic, *The Phantom Carriage* resorts to the sleight-of-hand used in *The Outlaw and His Wife*. Just as the fate of the outlawed lovers was lent a tragic grandeur by the landscapes, so the trivial sentimentality of the drunkard's salvation by a Salvation Army lass is screwed up to tragic implications far beyond its station by the atmosphere of supernatural awe.

Still held to be the masterworks by which Sjöström's reputation stands or falls, these films project an unappetizing image of him as a stolidly uninventive film-maker given either to overblown rhetoric or ponderous social realism, and always strictly functional in his *mise en scène*. Yet concurrently he was making films like *The Monastery of Sendomir*, where a lurid tale of marital deceit and revenge, adapted from a novel by Grillparzer, is turned into a superb chiaroscuro symphony as the betrayed husband and his vast Gothic castle sink simultaneously into the grip of dark despair. Shooting almost every scene so that the action is sinisterly framed by archways, crenellations or angled doorways, with mirrors reflecting suspicion and flickering candles the frailty of hope, Sjöström metamorphoses the castle from a place of secrets into a torture chamber. There is, in particular, a remarkable sequence where the Count, after pretending to leave on a journey, hurries back to catch his young wife *in flagrante*. But the lover manages to escape, glimpsed only as a silhouette in the moonlit courtyard, and the wife (a brilliantly contained performance by Tora Teje) brazens it out with such a display of cold disdain that the Count is routed. As he retires in confusion to his own chamber, his manservant plunges the castle into darkness by extin-

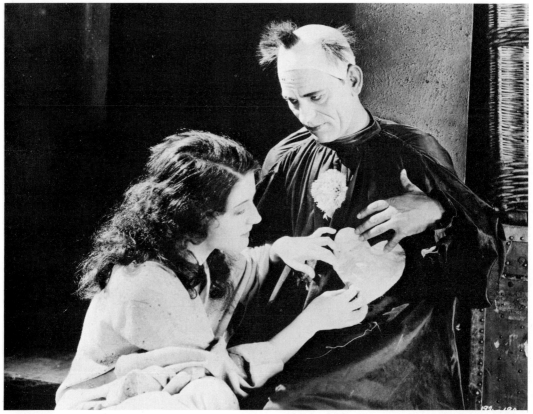

Norma Shearer pinning a heart on to the broken-hearted Lon Chaney in *He Who Gets Slapped*: 'the old gloom is replaced by a new grace'.

guishing the candles one by one, leaving the Count brooding over one last remaining candle until it slowly gutters out and there is only the moonlight to illuminate his tormented face. It is here, rather than in *The Outlaw and His Wife* or *The Phantom Carriage*, that Sjöström achieves the interior suffering noted by Dreyer.

Love's Crucible, another tale of marital betrayal, set in Renaissance Italy and photographed with a glowing opulence worthy of Sternberg, bears further witness to Sjöström's aesthetic preoccupations, with its images lovingly modelled on the Italian masters and the brilliant final sequence of the trial by fire marshalling superimpositions, rhythmic dissolves and a steadily tracking camera into a genuine *tour de force*. But perhaps the most interesting, and certainly the most neglected film from this period is *Mästerman*, scripted by Hjalmar Bergman from an original story about a grudging old money-

lender (magnificently played by Sjöström himself) who is feared by all until he is tamed by a spirited young girl who finds herself 'pledged' by her lover for a gambling debt. Walking a tightrope between comedy and pathos, so that one is never quite sure which is which as the old man falls in love with the girl, realizes that she still loves the young man who sold her into his hands, and gradually resigns himself to the generation gap, *Mästerman* is wonderfully funny and touching, and as subtly probing in its characterizations as *The Girl from Stormycroft*. The real originality of the film, however, lies in its use of written titles.

Hjalmar Bergman and Sjöström had already used very long and seemingly unnecessarily discursive titles for comic effect in *His Lordship's Last Will*; here, however, they are used to build a kind of creative dialogue between the spectator and the film. In the opening sequence, for instance, the

Lillian Gish in *The Wind*: 'a masterpiece, the film in which everything came miraculously together for Sjöström as both *auteur* and *metteur-en-scène* ... Illusions are literally swept away by the eternally raging wind, buried under the choking drifts of sand that creep into every crevice of the soul.'

pawnbroker is introduced as a stern, solitary man, hated and feared by all the townsfolk. Then the camera retreats with him into his sanctum, filled to a degree worthy of the Père Jules of *L'Atalante* with a bizarre collection of stuffed animals, dolls, skeletons and shawls. 'A treasure chamber where always the shutters were kept locked and many a strange thing was hidden', the title remarks, before going on to note that the pawnbroker was once a sea captain and—people say—a pirate and a slave-trader. What the title does not actually say but brings inescapably to the imagination, is that the real treasure hidden in this room is the old man's loneliness. The effect throughout is curiously prophetic of the off-screen narrative later developed by Bresson as a means to probe beneath the surface.

The awkward fact is that Sjöström tends to be a much more interesting film-maker in 'minor' works like *His Lordship's Last Will*,

The Monastery of Sendomir and *Mästerman*, where he is content simply to be a *metteur en scène*, than in the 'major' ones where he qualifies as a fully-fledged *auteur*. Perhaps this explains why he made three of his best films in Hollywood. There he was under no particular pressure to be 'Swedish' in the vein that had brought him international fame; and although *He Who Gets Slapped*, *The Scarlet Letter* (1927) and *The Wind* (1928) all deal with forms of extreme spiritual suffering, the old gloom is replaced by a new grace, as well as an awareness that the characters are more important than the message.

He Who Gets Slapped is particularly fascinating in that it is one of Sjöström's most daringly inventive films, a visually stunning adaptation of Leonid Andreyev's play about a scientist who laughs in hysterical disbelief when he realizes that his benefactor has stolen not only his research but also his wife, and who is frozen by that moment of shock into the fixation that only as a circus clown, an object of mockery and abuse, can he go on living. The moment, brilliantly enacted by Lon Chaney, is also brilliantly realized by Sjöström: as the scientist sinks down in despair at his cluttered desk, he accidentally knocks over a globe of the world that rolls away to become a ball spinning on the finger-tip of a grinning, white-faced clown, which in turn becomes a huge globe with a horde of tiny clowns clambering down invisible ropes to perch on its horizontal band, which, in a final metamorphosis, becomes a circus ring with a troupe of clowns watching a rehearsal.

In its acute masochism, expressionism blending neatly into the horror film ethos (the clown dies in the ring, to ecstatic applause from the audience, after exacting ghastly revenge on his tormentors by setting a lion on them), *He Who Gets Slapped* is *sui generis* in Sjöström's work. A blood brother here to the Tod Browning of *The Unknown*, Sjöström visualizes the clown's searing pain as a series of stark black and white contrasts radiating from the astonishing moment when, as he broods alone in the ring, the spotlight is switched out on him, leaving his chalk-white face as a tiny balloon suspended in a sea of darkness where it gradually vanishes, leaving emptiness. And Sjöström also turns the film into an echo of the clown's silent accusation with a superb final shot, when the troupe of clowns mourning for their comrade again become the tiny clowns perched on the spinning globe, this time facing the audience in unspoken reproach as they toss a miniature corpse out of the screen into our laps.

After the expressionistic sophistications of *He Who Gets Slapped*, Sjöström came back to more familiar territory with Nathaniel Hawthorne's sternly puritan Massachusetts in *The Scarlet Letter* and the starkness of the pioneers' prairie in *The Wind*. Fine as it is, and all the more effective in that Hawthorne's tale of darkness and despair is offset by idyllically sunlit settings, *The Scarlet Letter* remains a drastically truncated version of the novel in which the all too obvious gaps are precariously, though effectively, papered over by Lillian Gish's magnificent performance as Hester Prynne, the woman taken in adultery who is condemned to wear her shame publicly in the form of

a scarlet letter 'A' on her breast. *The Wind*, however, is a masterpiece pure and simple, the film in which everything came miraculously together for Sjöström as both *auteur* and *metteur en scène*.

'Man, puny but irresistible, encroaching forever on Nature's fortresses', a title announces. A desolate desert landscape. A train approaches. Dissolve to the interior of the train where Letty Mason (Lillian Gish), a fragile Southern belle, is on her way from Virginia to stay with her cousin on his Texas homestead. Outside the wind blows relentlessly, driving the dust and sand against the train windows in thick, choking clouds. Inside, cowering timidly, Letty flirtatiously accepts the attentions of a gallantly moustachioed gentleman (Montagu Love) as a welcome defence against the insistent threat of the wind.

Having thus effortlessly established the wind as a crucial metaphor, Sjöström proceeds to orchestrate the sexual theme with Letty's arrival at her cousin's starkly comfortless home. Shrinking from contact with the cheerfully unwashed and unshaven cowboys, daintily wiping her fingers on a wisp of handkerchief in hopeless protest against the all-encroaching sand filming the food and the dinner-table, Letty lives in constant fear of violation: of her cleanliness, of her sensibility, of herself. Attracting opposite to opposite, her timorous delicacy proves such an irresistible magnet—to her cousin, his children, the cowboys—that the cousin's wife quickly recognizes the threat and presents her with an ultimatum. Forced to settle for a marriage of convenience when the romantic stranger from the train hurriedly protests that he is already married, Letty chooses the more presentable of her two cowboy suitors.

What follows is credibly worked out on a realistic level: shutting herself away in a cocoon of distaste and treated with humble respect by her despised husband, Letty is raped by the stranger to whom she turns romantically for escape. Illusions are literally swept away by the eternally raging wind, buried under the choking drifts of sand that creep into every crevice of the soul. And in the magnificent final sequence where Letty watches in terror as the wind gradually erodes the grave to expose the dead hand of the stranger she accidentally killed and tried to bury, her hallucinated terror materializes in the form of a white stallion—the ghost of the North Wind that lives in the clouds, according to Indian legend, or more prosaically a stray from the wild herd being rounded up by her husband—that rides the dust-storm like a beautiful, haunting omen of doom. Here Sjöström blends fact and fantasy so completely that the West itself, viewed with blistering realism (the film was shot on location in the Mojave Desert), becomes a towering poetic image: *The Wind* is one of the few films ever really to have captured the mysterious essence of the pioneer spirit, of 'man, puny but irresistible, encroaching forever on Nature's fortresses'.

Sjöström actually made nine films in Hollywood between 1924 and 1930. The three that survive suggest that these may have been *anni mirabili* for him. So until the other six have been rediscovered and one can see how they fit into the pattern, the Sjöström story must necessarily be left incomplete and tentative. After leaving Hollywood, he directed only two more films, *Markurells i Wadköping* (*The Markurells of Wadkoping*, 1931) and *Under the Red Robe* (1937). Both are pleasant enough, but suggest that Sjöström may have abandoned directing because he was uncomfortable with the sound cinema: a speculation which his only sound film in Hollywood, *A Lady to Love* (1930), may or may not confirm.

Among the 'lost' Hollywood films is, amazingly, Sjöström's only film with Garbo, *The Divine Woman* (1928). What wouldn't one give to see that!

Milne mentions René Jeanne and Charles Ford's monograph (in French) *Victor Sjöström* (1963). There is also *Seastrom and Stiller: Two Swedish Directors in Silent American Films* (1969), by Hans Pensel. See also the article on Stiller and Peter Cowie's survey book *Screen Series: Sweden 1 and 2* (1970), and, in French, Jean Béranger's *La Grande Aventure du Cinéma Suédois* (1960).

Although Sjöström stopped directing films in 1937, he continued acting, most spectacularly in two Bergman films: *To Joy* (1949) and, of course, *Wild Strawberries* (1957).

JERZY SKOLIMOSKI, see p. 782

MICHAEL SNOW
Jonathan Rosenbaum

Within both the delimited confines of the 'structural film' (as such) and the cinema today as a whole, Michael Snow's films assume an importance so awesome in its ultimate implications that whole schools of contemporary film-making pale beside it. Treating the intermittent forward lurches of a zoom across a loft as both metaphor and practical agent for narrative penetration, *Wavelength* (1966–67) transforms and invests with fascination every perceptible element and object that can be discerned in its path, fusing art and science in pursuit of the purest kind of philosophical and phenomenological investigation. Its uncommon innovatory achievement—shared, to my knowledge, by only a few other masterworks of the past decade (*Deux ou Trois Choses que je sais d'elle*, *Playtime*, *La Région Centrale*, *Scenes from under Childhood*, *Out One/Spectre* and *Tom, Tom, the Piper's Son*, in their very separate ways)—is to redefine radically the *content* and *subject* of the screen image, proposing new relationships between spectator and screen which require substantially greater amounts of creative participation.

In *La Région Centrale* (or *The Central Region*, 1971), it cannot be denied that the form of participation required is unusually arduous, as it is for many in Rivette's *Out One/Spectre*: if the latter deserves the status of the *Finnegans Wake* of modern cinema—behavioural ambiguity assuming the role of verbal punning—*La Région Centrale* begs comparison with Gertrude Stein's *The Making of Americans* in its obsessed pursuit of endlessly circular linearity. As 'landscape painting', its first half-hour seems so exhaustive that one is left in suspension wondering where the remaining two and a half hours can go; by the end of the second hour, one can be so confounded by the camera's abandonment of any discernible centre of gravity—literally fearful of blindness now that the camera has broken free from the ordinary options and limits of the human gaze—that one is required to discover new modes of apprehending, learning to direct one's gaze with or against the camera's trajectory at different junctures. For such reasons—and not in spite of them—

La Région Centrale is to the adventure film what *Wavelength* is to the thriller.

See Sitney's article on American Avant-Garde Cinema, as well as his book *Visionary Cinema* (1974).

YULIA SOLNTSEVA

Jonathan Rosenbaum

Without access to the crucial evidence of *Michurin* (1948), Dovzhenko's only colour film, I cannot evaluate the plastic originality of his widow Yulia Solntseva's *Poema o Morye* (*Poem of the Sea*, 1958), *Povest' Plamennykh Let* (*The Flaming Years*, 1961) and *Zacharovannaya Desna* (*The Enchanted Desna*, 1965), all derived from posthumous Dovzhenko scripts. Nor can I claim any detailed textual understanding of them: the first and third were seen in unsubtitled prints, 70 mm and stereophonic, while the French-dubbed monaural version of *The Flaming Years* only persuaded me—along with the reactions of a Russian-speaking friend to *The Enchanted Desna*—that the more I understood of these films' Stalinist rhetoric, the more queasy I would become about enjoying their sheer sensual pleasures. As with Disney and Riefenstahl—whose relationship I have briefly explored in my article on Disney in this Dictionary—one can take unbridled delight in these films only by accepting wholeheartedly the mystifications that they perpetrate in relation to their subjects.

I should add that the only one of the three that I really care for is *The Enchanted Desna*. The best of *Poem of the Sea* seems reducible to static images of glowing artificiality, while the grey, heavy monumentality of *The Flaming Years* only takes flight in a dialogue between a delirious woman and an imposing male statue on a lovely Ukrainian hillside. It is an image that metaphorically might stand for the relationship Solntseva (born 1901) has consciously sought between herself and cinema: 'If Dovzhenko had lived, I would never have become a director. All that I do I consider as "propaganda, defence and illustration" of Dovzhenko.'

I once wrote that *The Enchanted Desna* was 'probably more exciting and beautiful than any Dovzhenko film since *Earth*', adding, 'If Solntseva's talent be treason, then let's make the most of it.' A subsequent look at Dovzhenko's *Ivan* immediately rid me of this foolish presumption, and I am no longer convinced that the wonders of *The Enchanted Desna* can or should be seen independently of Dovzhenko's genius. I only know that they fulfil the possibilities of *personal* wide-screen spectacle with a prodigiousness matched only by *Playtime* and *2001*, utilizing synchronous and non-synchronous multi-track sound with a nearly comparable inventiveness. The astonishing realization of a family's trip at night beside a lake, filtered through the presumed consciousness of Dovzhenko as a boy, is an experience of colour, texture and aural density combining to convey as enchanted a dream as the cinema has to offer; and other breathtaking moments—such as a field rapidly traversed by a camera as though by a plough—prove that the most spectacular cinematic means can be used with personal abandon and freedom.

Having made films of all the scripts that Dovzhenko left unfilmed at the time of his death, Madame Solntseva seems to have retired for good. Of course we will never know precisely who was responsible for the wonders of *The Enchanted Desna* (one of Godard's favourite films, surprisingly), and it doesn't really matter: the film is there. But how many other widows of great directors have been capable of making films as magnificent as Solntseva's trilogy?

SOVIET CINEMA SINCE THE WAR

David Robinson

As the Second World War ended, the Soviet cinema seemed full of optimism. It had triumphantly stood the test of wartime demands. The massive common effort of the nation had seemed to do away with all the stultifying bureaucracies, the narrow interpretations of a notion of 'socialist realism' of the immediate pre-war years. Late in 1944 an Artistic Council—composed entirely of creative people—had been set up to deal with production problems; and creative people too had been put at the head of the major studios: Sergei Vasiliev at Lenfilm, Grigori

Alexandrov (replacing Sergei Eisenstein) at Mosfilm; Igor Savchenko (replacing Sergei Yutkevitch) at the Children's Film Studios; Ptushko at the Animation Studios; and Sergei Gerassimov at the Documentary Studios, where he established a precedent by inviting prominent feature directors like Yuli Raisman and Yutkevitch to undertake factual subjects. In 1945 all the great classic Soviet directors—Lev Kuleshov, Eisenstein, Vsevolod Pudovkin, Alexander Dovzhenko and Dziga Vertov—were active, and all still comparatively young men. Even one great director prominent long before the Revolution, Yakov Protazanov, was still at work till the moment of his death in August 1945.

It seemed, however, a dark portent on the day in February 1946 when Eisenstein completed the cutting of the second part of his *Ivan the Terrible* trilogy. The same night, at a party to celebrate the award of a Stalin Prize to the first part, he collapsed while dancing, struck with the first of the heart attacks that were two years later to be fatal. While he was still ill, official criticism of the film and its 'negative' treatment of Russian history began, and was to result in Eisenstein's publication of a humiliating 'admission' of its 'errors'. This was only the beginning. In the autumn of 1946 the Central Committee of the Communist Party began a 'cleansing' of the cinema such as it had already initiated in literature, the theatre and music. Among the first targets were Pudovkin's biography *Amiral Nakhimov* (*Admiral Nakhimov*), which was only released (in 1946) after extensive revision; the second part of Leonid Lukov's *Bolshaya Zhizu* (*A Great Life*; not released until 1958) and Grigori Kozintsev and Leonid Trauberg's *Prostiye lyudi* (*Plain People*, also known as *Simple Folk*; released in a revised form in 1956). Eisenstein never recovered sufficiently to be able to take advantage of opportunities to revise the second part of his film or to begin the third; and *Ivan the Terrible, Part Two* also waited many years before it was shown either in the U.S.S.R. or elsewhere. The following year Yutkevitch's adaptation of the play *Lenin Chimes, Svet nad Rossiei* (*Light over Russia*; completed 1947), was suppressed; and Gerassimov's *Molodaya Gvardya* (*The Young Guard*, 1948) was ordered to be drastically revised to make clear that the organization of the Young Guard was not a spontaneous initiative on the part of a group of young people, but a result of the planning of 'the more experienced hands of the Communist Party'. Even a film which might have been supposed safe from this kind of political pressure, Dovzhenko's biography of the famous botanist *Michurin* (1948), fell into difficulties as a result of a scientific–ideological debate.

This extensive repression occurred at a time when production had fallen to a mere ten feature films a year (from a former peak of a hundred) as a result of Stalin's insistence on 'quality, not quantity'. For him 'quality' perhaps meant the screen metamorphoses of history which glorified an idealized image of the leader, clad always in luminous white. The star director of these films was the Georgian Mikhail Chiaureli, with *Klyatva* (*The Vow*, 1946; fragments of the film can be seen in Dusan Makavejev's *WR: Mysteries of the Organism*) and *Padeniye Berlin* (*The Fall of Berlin*, 1949), in both of which the Olympian, waxwork Stalin is played by Mikhail Gelovani. In Petrov's no less adulatory *Stalingradskaya Bitva* (*The Battle of Stalingrad*, 1950) Stalin is played by Alexei Diki. Other films no doubt equally acceptable to the authorities were the jolly, mendacious musicals of Grigori Alexandrov (*Vesna* [*Spring*], 1949) and Ivan Pyriev (*Kubanskie Kazaki* [*Kuban Cossacks*], 1950). A few honourable films slipped through the net: Donskoi's *Selskaya uchitelnitsa* (*The Village Teacher*, 1947), Alexander Zarkhi and Josef Heifets' *Volmya Zhizni* (*In the Name of Life*, 1947), Kozintsev's decent historical biography *Pirogov* (1947).

Films began to reflect the foreign policies of the Cold War era. By 1949 a virulent campaign against anything that smacked of 'cosmopolitanism' adversely affected many prominent careers. The early 50s also brought forth a whole cycle of violently anti-American subjects, to which many of the most distinguished directors lent their names: Alexandrov with *Vstrecha na Elbe* (*Meeting on the Elbe*, 1949), Mikhail Kalatozov with *Zagovov obrechyonnikh* (*Conspiracy of the Doomed*, 1950), Mikhail Romm with *Sekretnaya missiya* (*Secret Mission*, 1950), Abram Room with *Sud chesti*

(*Court of Honour*, 1949). As in the West, this was perhaps the unhappiest period of the post-war era.

In 1953 Stalin died; and in 1956 Khrushchev presented his famous Secret Report to the Twentieth Party Congress, in which he was obliged to point to the cinema as one of the most pernicious tools of Stalin's cult of personality. The reaction in the Soviet cinema following Stalin's death was inevitable and striking. In the final years of the Stalin era, reduced production and mistrust of untried hands in the industry had combined to keep down the output of young potential film directors from the Moscow Film School, VGIK. But now an enthusiastic new generation, with a sense of individual liberation, went into training. (In the same period, between Stalin's death and the Party Congress, three more of the great figures of Soviet cinematography had died: Pudovkin in 1953; Dziga Vertov, whose last years had been wasted as an ordinary newsreel editor, in 1954; Dovzhenko in 1956, just as he was preparing to shoot *Poema o morye* [*Poem of the Sea*; completed by Yulia Solntseva and released in 1958].)

Even before 1956, films celebrating more human attitudes began to make their appearance: Heifets' *Bolchaia semia* (*The Big Family*, 1954) and *Delo Rumyantseva* (*The Rumyantsev Case*, 1955) most notable among them. For the West, however, the first dramatic demonstration of a renewal in the Soviet cinema was the first film directed by Grigori Chukhrai, *Sorok pervyi* (*The Forty-first*, 1956). Although this was in fact a remake of a Protazanov film of 1927, it was startling in 1956 to see a Soviet film deal in terms of human sympathy with the story of the brief, doomed passion of a Red girl partisan and a White officer, her prisoner. The following year *Letyat zhuravili* (*The Cranes Are Flying*, 1957), a film by the veteran director Kalatozov, who had earned official displeasure as early as 1930 with his *Dzhim shvante* (*Salt for Svanetia*), used bravura effects without fear of 'formalism' (another sin which until now had been severely attacked), and told a story of the Second World War in realistic instead of heroic terms, admitting the presence of shirkers and black marketeers in wartime Russia. New, more human attitudes to the war,

showing ordinary people as heroes rather than the solitary Stalin, provided themes for other films of the 'renascence'. The actor Sergei Bondarchuk, who had made his screen début in *The Young Guard*, made his first film, *Sudba chelovieka* (*Destiny of a Man*, 1959); and Chukhrai enjoyed an even greater success with *Ballada o soldate* (*Ballad of a Soldier*, 1959).

Both in content and technique directors were finding their feet, trying out their new freedom. In 1961 Chukhrai's *Christoie nebo* (*Clear Sky*) broke further new ground by referring directly to the dark days and the relief (the 'clear sky') which came after the death of Stalin. For the first time for many years the values of Soviet films made them more acceptable in the West, and they began once more to reach an international audience. Among the new generation of directors were the Georgians Revez Chkheidze (*Chveni ezo* [*Our Yard*], 1957) and Tengiz Abuladze (*Magdalas lurja* [*Magdala's Donkey*], 1956); Lev Kulidjanov and Yakov Segel, who co-directed *Dom v kotorom ya zhivu* (*The House I Live In*, 1957); Alexander Alov and Vladimir Naumov, who collaborated on *Mir vodjaschemu* (*Peace to the Newcomer*, 1961); Andrei Tarkovsky, with his nervous, brilliant *Ivanovo detstvo* (*The Childhood of Ivan*, 1962); Andrei Michalkov-Konchalovsky (*Pervii Uchitel* [*The First Teacher*], 1965); and the Georgian-born, Kiev-based Sergei Paradjanov, who displayed an original, extravagant lyrical talent, as well as paying homage to Dovzhenko, in *Teni zabytykh predkov* (*Shadows of Our Forgotten Ancestors*, 1964).

The old FEKS Group made some of the best films of the period. Kozintsev followed a dazzling *Don Quixote* (1957; starring Eisenstein's Ivan, Nikolai Cherkassov) with two Shakespearian adaptations of keen intelligence and rich visual values: *Gamlet* (*Hamlet*, 1964) and *Korol Lir* (*King Lear*, 1970). Yutkevitch made a strange animated version of Mayakovsky's *Banya* (*The Bathhouse*, 1962); returned to the problems of re-creating Lenin's image on the screen with *Raskazyo Lenine* (*Stories about Lenin*, 1958) and *Lenin v Polshe* (*Lenin in Poland*, 1965); and in 1969 recalled the early experimental days with an elegant stylized examination of an episode in Chekhov's life, *Siuzhet dlya nebolshovo ras-*

skaza (*Subject for a Short Story* or *Lika, Chekhov's Love*). Josef Heifets' exquisite adaptation of Chekhov, *Dama s sobachkoi* (*The Lady with the Little Dog*, 1960), was, with its complete independence of all tradition, a one-film *nouvelle vague*.

With the second half of the 60s, however, the mood had changed. There were unmistakable signs of a new tightening of control. Films were shelved without explanation. As early as 1961, Marlen Khutsiev's attractive study of contemporary Soviet youth, *Mne dvadsat let* (*I Am Twenty*), ran into trouble and took three years to reach the screen. Other films either not released or held up for long periods were Alov and Naumov's adaptation of a satirical story by Dostoevsky, *A*

Bad Joke, and Mikhalkov-Konchalovsky's *Istoria Asi Klyachinoy, kotoraya lyubila, da nye vyshla zamuzh* (*Asya's Happiness*, 1966), which showed rural life realistically for once (Khrushchev himself had pointed to the tradition that had grown up since Stalinist days of portraying the hard life of the villages in deceptive rosy terms). The most notorious of the 'shelvings', however, was that of Tarkovsky's *Andrei Roublev* (1966), an imaginative reconstruction of the life and times of the great icon painter, which bears comparison with the best of Eisenstein's historical films. The painter is shown producing work of spiritual and humanist inspiration, against the background of a violent and bloody world. Perhaps Tarkovsky was too successful

A scene from Paradjanov's *Sayat Nova* (*The Colour of Pomegranates*), the greatest Soviet film since the war.

in his efforts to make history yield contemporary meaning. Release of the film was at first put off because the subject, it was claimed, was too 'dark' for the year of the fiftieth anniversary of the October Revolution. In the years that followed the authorities were neurotically reluctant to permit showings of the film. Finally, it was released generally, both at home and abroad.

There are not such wide differences between the film industries of East and West. The favoured films of this period were heavy, costly, pedestrian show-pieces like Igor Talankin's *Tchaichowsky* (1970). The leading 'official' Soviet director, however, was Sergei Bondarchuk, who made a vast four-part adaptation of *War and Peace* (*Voina i Mir*, 1965 and 1967), perhaps the most costly film ever made, a triumph of resources over talent with not the slightest trace of an inspiration such as fired *Andrei Roublev*. Its success, the reward of sheer display, brought Bondarchuk to direct an international production of comparable size and mediocrity in *Waterloo* (1969).

Yet despite the continuing output of films in official formulas, despite the revival of the old narrow notions of 'socialist realism' (even if the term itself was out of fashion), there were still new works to demonstrate that something in the Russian temperament could yet find in films a natural medium of expression. Five years after *Andrei Roublev*, Tarkovsky made another spectacle, an adaptation of Stanislaw Lem's science fiction novel *Solaris* (1972) which was at once monumental and subtle. Mikhalkov-Konchalovsky turned to Turgenev and Chekhov with original and gifted interpretations of *Dvorianskoe gnezdo* (*A Nest of Gentlefolk*, 1969) and *Dyadya Vanya* (*Uncle Vanya*, 1971). Paradjanov made a further visionary reconstruction of history in *Sayat nova* (*The Colour of Pomegranates*, 1974); and his cameraman Yuri Ilyenko revealed the combined influence of Paradjanov, Dovzhenko and Ukrainian folklore in his own first films, *On the Eve of Kupala Day* and *Byelala ptitsa s chernoi otmetinoi* (*White Bird with Black Markings*, 1971). Other directors who emerged in the 60s were Larissa Shepitko (*Zhoy* [*Heat*], 1966; *Krylya* [*Wings*], 1966; *Ti i ya* [*You and I*], 1971), and Elem Klimov with his satirical shorts and features *Dobro*

pozhalovat (*Welcome*, 1964) and *The Adventures of a Dentist*. The theme of *Welcome*, set in a Pioneer camp, has similarities with that of Alexei Saltykov's deceptively charming first feature *Drug moi, Kol'ka!* (*My Friend, Kolka*, 1961) which, showing a 'naughty' schoolboy, presented a defence of the youthful individualist. Saltykov subsequently directed *Predsedatyel* (*The Chairman*, 1964), a controversial picture of *kholkhov* life, but returned to history for the subjects of *Babe tsarstvo* (*The Women's Kingdom*, 1968) and *Direktor* (*The Director*, 1969). Gleb Panfilov promised much with his first two films, *Vognye broda net* (*No Ford in the Fire*, 1968) and *Nachalo* (*The Debut* or *The Beginning*, 1970); and Mikhail Bogin (*Zosya*, 1970), Vasili Shuksin (*Strannie liudi* [*Strange People*], 1970) and Vladimir Fetin (*The Don Story*, *Virineya*) are also hopefuls among the directors who made their first features at the end of the 60s.

Shepitko began her work in the Kirghiz Studios; Paradjanov and Ilyenko worked in the Ukraine; and the greatest evidence of vitality appears to come from these and other republic capitals, though their product is rarely exported outside the U.S.S.R. A group of young Uzbekh film-makers, for instance, received high praise in 1973; and the Georgian studios, with a long and established tradition, continue to produce interesting works—most notably in recent years the films of Georgii Danelia (*Ya shagayu po Moskviye* [*I Walk About Moscow*], 1964; *Tridstat tri* [*The Thirty-three*], 1965, a 'shelved' film; and *Ne goryuy* [*Cheer up!*], 1970). Nor should we forget another Georgian director, Georgi Shengelaya, whose lyrical *Pirosmani* (1971) magnificently captured all the charm of a late-nineteenth-century naïve Georgian painter. The continuing interest of the Soviet cinema is that, whatever the day brings, there is always a tomorrow.

Of all the post-war directors, the most important seems to me to be Paradjanov; unfortunately, only his first film has been seen in the West: *The Colour of Pomegranates* has been banned for export. Paradjanov himself was in prison for homosexuality and various other 'crimes'. In an attempt to raise support for the liberation of Paradjanov, a screening of a bootleg print

was arranged in Paris in 1977. Even in this cut (by twenty minutes), washed-out, 16-mm duplicate print, one could see that he is clearly one of the greatest directors alive. Totally original, and with an incredible eye for the telling image and plastic values, he surpasses in *The Colour of Pome-granates* his extraordinary first film. Late in 1977, Paradjanov was finally released from jail.

Tarkovsky has gone on working, and since *Solaris* he has made *Zerkalo* (*The Mirror*, 1975); its complex evocation of the author's life was admired by many, though not by me. Panfilov's next film, *Proshu slova* (*I Ask to Speak*, 1976), was released in the West and proved a worthy successor to *The Debut*. As in the earlier film, the leading actress is Panfilov's talented wife Inna Churikova. But this is a more ambitious and politically revealing film, and it augurs well for Panfilov's future.

See the articles on Donskoi, Kozintsev, Romm and Solntseva to complete this survey of Soviet cinema since the war. Books to be consulted include Jeanne Vron-skaya's *Young Soviet Film-Makers* (1972) and, in French, Jean and Luda Schnitzer's *Vingt Ans de Cinéma Soviétique* (1964).

JOHN M. STAHL

Andrew Sarris

Even the most systematic Hollywoodophiles of *Cahiers du Cinéma* during its vintage years were unable to provide much of a *dossier* on John M. Stahl, a middle-range director of impressive sobriety and intensity throughout a career ranging from 1914 to 1947. For American *auteur*ists, Stahl was a neglected pre-Sirkian figure whose career suddenly became illuminated (after his death in 1950) through an accident of film scholarship. Earlier, the French film historian Henri Agel had classified Stahl as a director of only one masterpiece: *Back Street* (1932). A sub-sequent recheck of Stahl's career for possible *auteur* analysis revealed a startling consis-tency from 1932 on. For the most part, Stahl, like Sternberg and Douglas Sirk, was involved with outrageously improbable story material. Indeed, the parallel with Sirk is inescapable inasmuch as they worked in dif-ferent decades on three of the same Universal projects—*Imitation of Life* (Stahl 1934/Sirk

1959); *Magnificent Obsession* (Stahl 1935/Sirk 1954); and *When Tomorrow Comes*, a 1939 Stahl production retitled *Interlude* for the 1957 Sirk version. The difference between Stahl and Sirk is very much the difference between the emotional social consciousness of the 30s and the stylistic self-consciousness of the 50s. Whereas Stahl's treatments are warmer, Sirk's are wittier. Stahl possessed the audacity of Sirk, but not the dark humour. Whereas Stahl was capable of a straight, reverent treatment of *The Keys of the Kingdom* (1944), Sirk transformed *The First Legion* (1951) into a devastating parody of the Jesuits.

In terms of post-Bazinian aesthetics, it is interesting to note that in *The Eve of St Mark* (1944), Stahl displayed a profound comprehension of the emotional implications of two-shots as opposed to cross-cutting. At times Stahl's conception of contrasts was as forceful as Sirk's. In *The Immortal Sergeant* (1943), for example, Henry Fonda thirsts in the desert with a mental image of Maureen O'Hara emerging dripping wet from a swim-ming pool. It is this kind of audacious effect which resonates through time when more discreet images have receded. And who can forget in this same vein the lurid spectacle of Gene Tierney (with lips blood-red) on horse-back as she spreads her father's ashes in *Leave Her to Heaven* (1946) or Margaret Sul-lavan's one last tryst with her forgetful lover on the second level of a duplex (*Only Yester-day*, 1933) or Irene Dunne's sombre farewell dinner with a hopelessly married Charles Boyer (*When Tomorrow Comes*) or Andrea Leeds with her *Letter of Introduction* (1938) to Adolphe Menjou? That many of these memor-able moments belong to what were once denigrated as women's pictures provides further explanation for Stahl's relative anony-mity in the more solemn critical histories.

John M. Stahl was born in 1886 in New York City. He made his acting début on the legitimate stage in 1909, and was appearing in movie bit parts as early as 1913. He worked as a director for a small independent company in New York in 1914. Soon after-wards he moved to Hollywood, where he worked for twelve years for L. B. Mayer, first at First National and then at Metro-Goldwyn Mayer, after First National was dissolved. For two years he was Vice-

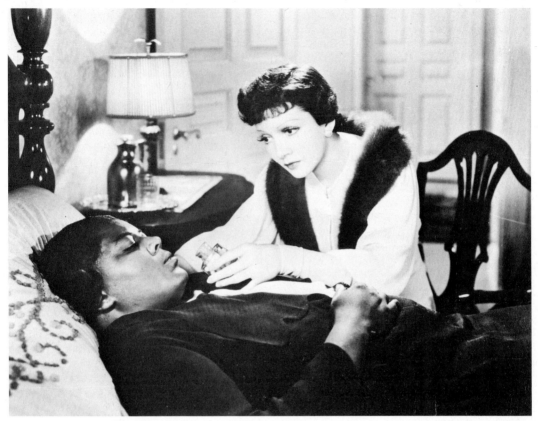

Louise Beavers and Claudette Colbert in *Imitation of Life*: 'words alone cannot convey the resonant vulnerability of Claudette Colbert's performance in *Imitation of Life*'.

President in charge of production at his company, Tiffany-Stahl. He was married to the former Mrs Roxana Wray.

In his early years as a director he was known for his almost semi-documentary pictures, closely tied to the day's headlines, and for the filming of outstanding contemporary novels. He was also known very early in his career as a woman's director. Towards the end of his life he was identified mainly with a series of romantic dramas. He was under contract at 20th Century-Fox when he died. He became annoyed with his reputation for a 'slow, measured tread' in the amount of time it took him to shoot a film, and insisted in a 1941 interview that he had never spent more than nine weeks in production. In a review of *Our Wife* (1941), a New York film critic claimed that though Stahl was known as a 'director of heavy, portentous dramas, full of meaning and serious thoughts' he had switched successfully on this occasion to

light comedy. In retrospect, however, *Our Wife* seems relatively strained as a comedy and, indeed, lacks the grace and charm of many of his 'heavy, portentous dramas'.

After ten years at Universal, Stahl decided to sign only one-film contracts in the manner of Frank Capra and Walter Wanger. Stahl made such a pact with Columbia, and another with United Artists, but cancelled the latter contract. He often cited the fact that he had brought in *When Tomorrow Comes* under budget. This kind of self-serving production story is often the last recourse of Hollywood directors accused justly or unjustly of extravagance, the very nebulous charge which served ultimately to wreck the careers of Griffith, Stroheim and Welles. Stahl's obituary in the New York *Herald Tribune* noted that the late director's greatest successes had been *Magnificent Obsession, Only Yesterday* and *Strictly Dishonorable* (1931).

A closer inspection of Stahl's career suggests an unusually complex pattern of pluses and minuses. Clearly on the debit side is his complicity with L. B. Mayer in adding a ludicrous 'love interest' sequence to Ernst Lubitsch's tastefully elliptical *The Student Prince* (1927), which starred Ramon Novarro and Norma Shearer. It seems that the literal-minded Mr Mayer felt that there was not enough boy–girl courtship in Lubitsch's relatively restrained (silent) treatment of the Sigmund Romberg operetta. Stahl dutifully directed Novarro and Shearer *à deux* in a tableau of reclining romance set in a field of garishly glowing flowers. (Two years earlier Mayer had influenced King Vidor in the direction of a fleshier treatment of *La Bohème*.)

Stahl's intrusion into a Lubitsch project is all the more egregious for its stylistic dissonance. Ironically, the offending footage in *The Student Prince* (overall, in any case, one of Lubitsch's least interesting silents) is thus far the only trace of Stahl's career to have survived from the silent era. Until very recently the spirit of historical (and feminist) revisionism was not strong enough to sanction the resurrection of films with titles such as *Wives of Men* (1918), *Her Code of Honor* (1919), *Suspicion* (1919), *A Woman Under Oath* (1919), *Women Men Forget* (1920), *Woman in His House* (1920), *The Child Thou Gavest Me* (1921), *Sowing the Wind* (1921), *The Song of Life* (1922), *One Clear Call* (1922), *Suspicious Wives* (1922), *The Wanters* (1923), *The Dangerous Age* (1923), *Husbands and Lovers* (1924), *Why Men Leave Home* (1924), *Fine Clothes* (1925), *Memory Lane* (1926), *The Gay Deceiver* (1926), *Lovers?* (1927), *In Old Kentucky* (1927). Also, the implications of Stahl's 'spelling out' sequence in *The Student Prince* tended to be especially incriminating during the long reign of Anglo-Russian montage theoreticians in most of the 'serious' film histories written in English. In the context of montage and ellipsis, Lubitsch served as an heroic ironist in contrast to such supposedly soppy and soapy single-take sentimentalists (and despised women's directors besides) as Frank Borzage, George Cukor, John Stahl, Edmund Goulding, Lowell Sherman, John Cromwell, William Seiter *et al.*

Hence, Borzage's direction of the Lubitsch-produced project *Desire* was criticized for lacking the lilt and snap of Lubitsch. More precisely, the film seemed to begin like Lubitsch (sardonic, twinkling) and end like Borzage (sombre, tortured). Similarly, Cukor's direction of *One Hour With You* from a Lubitsch plan failed to sparkle with Monsieur Ernst's witty asides and reaction shots. Indeed, the only critically fashionable attitude that a film-maker could take towards the bourgeoisie throughout the 30s was one of satirical derision. And the emotional problems of women were subsumed under the general heading of bourgeois self-indulgence. To make matters worse, the women's film, like the Western, was generally adapted from a culturally disreputable fictional genre, Fannie Hurst and Vicki Baum being the counterparts of Max Brand and Zane Grey. Yet, if the movie Western could claim a degree of aesthetic redemption through the grandeur of its natural landscapes and the kinetic energy of its heroic centaurs, the women's movie was no less deserving of admiration for the marvellously sculpted landscapes of an actress' face in luminously subjective close-up. Words alone cannot convey the grace and gallantry of Irene Dunne's performances in *Back Street*, *Magnificent Obsession* and *When Tomorrow Comes*, of Margaret Sullavan's portrayal in *Only Yesterday* and in Robert Stevenson's remake of *Back Street*, and of Claudette Colbert's resonant vulnerability in *Imitation of Life* as she reminded her grown-up daughter of the time long ago when the child-daughter had said with Proustian persistence, 'quack-quack, I want a quack-quack, I want a quack-quack' . . . fade out. The emotional effect of the 'quack-quack' is no accident; it is established by a lyrically lingering close-up of the rubber duck in the first scene of the movie.

As it happens, Bazinian anti-montage aesthetics has enabled us more to broaden our appreciation of the past than to anticipate the future. By shifting the analytical emphasis from what was left off the screen to what was left on, Bazin made it possible for film scholars of the 60s and 70s to re-evaluate many films which had hitherto been denigrated for their alleged lack of dynamism and dialectics. *Only Yesterday* is especially revelatory in this regard. What had seemed back in 1933 and through the next three decades to have been a disappointingly superficial and sentimental adaptation of Frederick Lewis Allen's witty memoir of American fads and foibles of the 20s re-emerged in retrospective screenings in the 70s as an astoundingly evocative film in the style and spirit of the early 30s. Scenes which had once seemed dull and turgid now seemed poignant and vibrant. Particularly affecting is Margaret Sullavan's desperate decision at a New Year's Eve party to renew her relation-ship with an old lover—her first—who has completely forgotten her. The succession of self-questioning expressions in Sullavan's fiercely passionate eyes foreshadows a similar dilemma for Joan Fontaine in Max Ophuls' sublime *Letter From an Unknown Woman.*

There are the remembered flaws also in *Only Yesterday*: the smug, pompous preen-ing of John Boles as the *homme fatal*, the mindless worship of child-cult (a spiritual disease especially endemic in the 30s), the too easy rhetoric of redemption, a foolishly writ-ten reunion scene between father and son on the contrived occasion of the mother's death, and a certain sketchiness around the edges of the secondary characterizations. By the same token, *Only Yesterday* seems to have im-proved with age through its behavioural beauties and incidental insights. For example, the comical informality of the courtship between Billie Burke and Reginald Denny seems to foreshadow the classical duet on the bongo drums between Binnie Barnes and Roland Young two years later in Leo McCarey's classic *Ruggles of Red Gap*. It was Stahl's misfortune also that the Dunne–Boyer romance in *When Tomorrow Comes* was eclipsed by McCarey's more inspiring and inspirational treatment of the two stars in *Love Affair*. None the less, *Only Yesterday* now seems strikingly prophetic, with its bril-liant vignette of Franklin Pangborn's slyly gay solicitude for his handsome young protégé and, above all, for the stirring por-traits of New Women projected by Margaret Sullavan and Billie Burke.

Imitation of Life, which seemed almost too painfully frank in its own time, now survives as a truer testament to that racism of Amer-ican life more ineradicable than most white Americans have ever cared to acknowledge. Again it is Stahl's extraordinary care and deliberation which is the key to his stylistic sincerity. That he had functioned on oc-casion in the Hollywood system as a producer and screenwriter indicates that he was far from being the lackey of L. B. Mayer which his unfortunate participation in the post-production tampering with *The Student Prince* would indicate. Instead, Stahl, like many of his underrated Hollywood col-leagues, possessed virtues as an artist and craftsman which are in short supply in the overly syncopated and overly satiric 70s. The emotional problems of women no longer seem as trivial and escapist as they once did, and the intensity of a director's gaze no lon-ger seems static and anti-cinematic. Thus, Stahl's cinema now seems ripe for re-evalua-tion.

See, obviously, the article on Douglas Sirk. David Thomson, in his *Biographical Dictionary of the Cinema*, concludes his piece on Stahl with the words: 'Any festival in search of a retrospective should keep him in mind.' I fully concur. It's high time Stahl was rediscovered; at his best he was better than Sirk.

JOSEF VON STERNBERG

Claude Ollier

Could the illusion of movement, an effect due to the persistence of fixed impressions on the retina, be at the source of our musing? On the interpretation of such a grandiose mi-rage through the projection of shadows in a dark room, Josef von Sternberg (1894–1969) based his ethics as a film-maker—an explorer of light.

Every light has a point where it is bright-est and a point toward which it wanders to lose itself completely. It must be intercep-ted to fulfil its mission, it cannot function in a void. Light can go straight, penetrate and turn back, be reflected and deflected, gathered and spread, bent as by a soap bubble, made to sparkle and be blocked. Where it is no more is blackness, and where it begins is the core of its brightness. The journey of rays from that central core to the outposts of blackness is the adven-ture of drama and light. (*Fun in a Chinese Laundry.*)

For Sternberg, light *is* matter, the only

matter whose existence he does not question. By virtue of it alone other matter has its being: all the objects in the world, animals and plants, landscapes and faces, are as if in a state of merely provisional existence: they lie unsuspected and unmaterialized until a shaft of light shines on them and proclaims them. Then they become mute and anonymous when its axis pivots away in a 'fade-out', or when its source is suppressed. There, from its far distant source, on to this collection of insignificant emblems, stored up like some great reserve of dramatic energy, the luminous mass strikes suddenly, revealing a network of lines, folding its brilliant or matte textures around the flesh of bodies or the colours of elements. Once the spotlight is turned off, the illusion of life and its memory fade away.

Withholding light, then, gives power over this phantasmagoria of the ephemeral, if not the key to it. Sternberg always claimed this power of control as the first attribute of a creator of films: whether he is mentioned in the credits as such or not, for each of his films he was his own cinematographer; in those films—and there are several—in which screenplay, actors and sets were forced upon him and which he directed in spite of everything because he feared that if he did not he would never have anything to direct again— in those films he could at least direct the photography, even though he might shoot the sky or the ceiling when what was otherwise in front of the camera was not even worth filming. He neither defended nor rejected these films; he simply 'practised scales' while waiting for something better. But he insisted that the *auteur* of a film had the same rights as the *auteur* of a poem or a painting. As with many other directors, his demands were rarely in harmony with those of the men who were backing the films.

Aside from its undeniable audacity, two qualities characterize his début as a director (*The Salvation Hunters*, 1925): a profound knowledge of material and technique, acquired through ten years doing all kinds of jobs in laboratories, warehouses and editing rooms; and a pronounced taste for experiment and research. And provided with very little money and whatever equipment and crew happened to be at hand, he began to film on the California coast in actual interior

and exterior locations, with little-known actors, a simple story of daily life. He completed it in record time, virtually improvising from beginning to end. It has been noted that these conditions are those in which, twenty years later, the so-called neo-realist cinema was formed in Italy.

To everyone's surprise *The Salvation Hunters* was a success. In terms of style nothing in American cinema at that period resembled it at all, with the exception of the films of Stroheim. Yet the characters, so much determined by *Stimmung*, the atmosphere of surroundings in which they live, so apparently imprisoned by the effects of the light which bathes them, might perhaps have been found in some Scandinavian film, and they turn up again—this time described as 'modern'—in the films of Antonioni.

Yet *The Salvation Hunters* from the outset is far from being based on any naturalistic or realistic aesthetic: no primordial function, descriptive or representative of a precise social milieu, is attributed to any object situated in the set nor to any miming or gesture of the actors. Miming, gestures, sets, objects are all rather material for the elaboration of a purely filmic milieu, abstracted from that socio-geographic reality from which, none the less, everything is taken: for Sternberg films a real boat, a real beach, and real walls under a real sky. All this will soon be handled differently. Still, the guiding principle is already present in this first effort, perfectly apparent: a tendency to abstraction.

In fact, Sternberg is as responsible for his film as he would be for a poem; he demands as much consideration for cinema, and the same status which society ordinarily allows to painting, architecture and music. And it must be recognized as part of this consideration that the filmic discourse is free to be specific, to establish itself at a distance from the world. If it is not a 'double' of the actual world, it is at least a world governed by laws other than those of imitation and representation, and certainly other than those of everyday causality. Implicit in a film director's activity is the conquest of the means necessary to attain this abstraction: such was Sternberg's goal, a goal not fully attained until 1930 with *Der Blaue Engel* (*The Blue Angel*). In the period preceding it, every opportunity for making a film was used by him to evaluate cinematic techniques and the possibilities of their combinations. It is unfortunate that neither *The Exquisite Sinner* (1926)—entirely remade by dissatisfied producers—nor *The Seagull* (1926)—made at Chaplin's behest, but which for some mysterious reason he chose never to screen publicly —can be seen. Thus, the next film in the chain is *Underworld* (1927), whose title curiously compresses both the notion of the world apart in the film and that of a descent. In what was the first gangster film and a model for a profilic genre, the world of the cinematographic image explored by Sternberg seems to obey several laws which might be formulated as follows: in the first place, everything which constitutes the image (furniture, faces, trees or articles of clothing) is plastically of equal importance and must be treated as a signifying value in the development of the idea. Secondly, a permanent bond unites the characters' actions and the décor in which they move, and which makes up a milieu privileged not in relation to social categories, but rather in relation to erotic ones. Finally, this bond can be manifest, and the image tends to be highly elaborate; or it can be discreet, and the image tends to be austere. The passage from one extreme to the other, notably through the process of long dissolves, becomes a dominant feature in Sternberg's aesthetic.

Already, in the following year, *The Last Command* (1928) brings the first large-scale scoring of these different instrumental voices. The film's screenplay, written by Sternberg himself, although suggested by Ernst Lubitsch, is indeed the only one of all those written or used by him which shows signs of a certain complexity. His circular Machiavellism is related to the most celebrated inventions of Borges, as it is based on the opposition of two worlds and on a reversal of the roles in which Chance casts the characters. A Russian general, commander in chief, and a young revolutionary meet on the first stage—that of History in 1917. The young man is an actor serving in the army. Captured, he is beaten and humiliated by this officer. His fiancée, an actress, seduces his tormentor, gains his confidence and betrays him when the revolution triumphs; but a little later, she helps him escape, aged, ravaged and abased. Ten years later, a Hollywood studio provides the second stage: the young revolutionary has become a film director. He is shooting a film about the war in Russia and the Revolution. He requires an extra for the role of the commander in chief. From among a number of photographs he chooses that of the real general who has ended up in the miserable ranks of extras. The two men meet once more under the spotlights. The one who at present directs verifies details of costume, make-up and military decorations. He who must now obey makes it a point of honour to play his role superbly, thus obliterating the shameful conclusion of the earlier conflict: a genuine death in front of the camera (both cameras) gives him his dignity once again.

The idea of the precarious nature of roles and their permutability recurs in most of Sternberg's later films. Here this idea is joined to that of the instability of scenes, of their successive interlocking or dislocation. This dislocation takes the form of degradation, a form which soon after became that of *Der Blaue Engel*. But *The Last Command* teaches still other lessons: it is the initial consecration of ambiguity as the fundamental trait of female character, a feature which was later to be more fully developed. Furthermore, this *mise en scène* of 'the irony of fate' brings with it a component of sadomasochism which generates scenes of unusual cruelty. Two feelings are equally present, pessimism and derision, and Sternberg's masterful direction of his actors (Emil Jannings, Evelyn Brent, William Powell) suggests them over and over again during the Russian episode. This episode is contained in a flashback occupying the whole central part of the film. There, the excuse of evoking the faraway, and the distortion of memory, provide him with the opportunity of curiously opposing the exotic expressionism of the Russian décor with the more sober settings in the studio, where a second camera comes into play and where everyone is seen in his final character, regardless of any previous historical role. Would it be reading too much into this admirable finale to make the following provisional conclusion? The truest dénouements are those which double the historic act, those which the brush, the pen or the camera rewrite. *The Saga of Anatahan* (1953) a quarter of a century later gives the final answer to this question, for Sternberg at least.

The three silent films made rapidly afterwards, *The Dragnet* (1928), *The Docks of New York* (1928) and *The Case of Lena Smith* (1929), seem more than anything else to consolidate what had already been acquired in *Underworld* and *The Last Command*. *Thunderbolt* (1929), which few people have seen, gave Sternberg the chance to explore the new material placed at his disposal: sound. His taste for manipulating cinematographic material, and for experiment as the primordial gesture of creation, disposed him favourably towards the microphone and the soundtrack. Unlike most film directors of the silent period, he enthusiastically hailed the invention of a mechanism for reproducing noise, music and words. For reproducing, but also combining, mixing and fusing it into a particular universe, parallel to the image, even independent of it. As regards the image, sound plays not the role of a complement or an illustration, but that of opposition, commentary and dialogue. Sternberg understood this immediately; from the outset he strove to employ sound in a way analogous to the way he had used images since his very first film. He rejected any realistic constraints, or slavery to pure and simple representation. The part played by sound in *Der Blaue Engel* is of prime importance, and its quality, which was the object of the director's constant attention despite rudimentary and inadequate equipment, remains among the best of the period.

Der Blaue Engel was the first sound film made in Germany. The sound not only provides a song which soon became famous, but an off-screen space as well, the cabaret stage, perceived from Lola-Lola's dressing room. It establishes relations between spaces as poles of action. Here again is the opposition of two worlds: the classroom and the cabaret; and the world of 'The Blue Angel' reveals itself objectively as what it appears to be in the eyes of Professor Unrath: a magical world, a world of difference ruled by magic laws, the world of temptation and desire with its prohibitions and transgressions. In brief, an *exotic* world. And now the path of abstraction, manifest already in the first *mise en scène*, and which before tended towards the

constitution of autonomous milieus heavily charged with eroticism, ends in an adult conception of Sternberg's aesthetic: that of a *universe apart*, totally artificial and abstract. This model, created in 1930 in *Der Blaue Engel*, will be reproduced in every one of the films for which Sternberg fully assumed responsibility.

Here in fact is realized that unstable dramatic situation in which possible roles will exchange their precariousness; here are conjugated the modes of degradation, of betrayal and abdication, in exact proportion as Woman's cosmic ambiguity becomes all pervading; here the subtlest web is woven, in which the characters are caught, in which they flail about in ritual gestures, semi-silent, 'for form's sake'. In such a universe, it is the truth of attitudes and glances which carries all the weight; the moments of a conflict more than a continuous narrative; the instant of release, that of response, the decisive shock and the behaviour which follows this shock more than its visual trace; whence proceeds the great number and the importance of ellipses—notably where aggressive gestures are concerned: the strangling of the prison guard in *Underworld* is the model example. It is as if the idea of an event counted more than the event itself. And so the idea of imprisonment, seduction, desire, of revolt and of submission, in brief, of all possible acts which a barely controlled instinct sets free, is more important than the detailed and exhaustive description of these acts.

This homogeneous universe, totalitarian and full to the brim, is the final product of a reduction of space, a universe in an advanced stage of spatial rarefaction and confinement. At first it seems as if one prison succeeds another, each more confining than the one before: the outside limits close in, the inside walls become more numerous and multiply, resulting in fragments, visual particles of extreme density, encumbered and cluttered with objects and obstacles, in shots filled to overflowing, saturated with things and glances trying to tie these things together, where everything filters through by osmosis, where all arises only to disappear by enchantment. These walls, in *Der Blaue Engel* and the films which follow, play a primordial role, for the material of which they are made makes their function extremely ambiguous; no doubt they divide, group and regroup, and isolate, but they are almost always movable or easily penetrable. They separate badly, divide badly, isolate badly: curtains, sliding doors, wall hangings, nets, more or less transparent, veils, screens, frills, lattice work, palms, feathers, shrubs and vines. These walls, which often work like Chinese boxes, are still imperfect and precarious: if there are prisons, their limits are never precisely stated ahead of time, nor are they definitively established: they may be contracted or extended. The exiguous areas to which Sternberg confines himself, and which he seems to enjoy, arise not from any need for confinement but rather from a desire to use these areas as laboratories where he is allowed to provoke, and study at leisure, such reactions as interest him—on a small scale, in small doses, all of it very concentrated. His universe is not so much restricted as *reduced*. If it is presented as having a closed periphery, it is merely because all exterior conditions must, for the duration of the experiment, remain unchanged. The closed and compact stage of Sternberg's films is only a reduced model of the best of all possible worlds as far as concerns the development of possibilities. The spatial limits do not imply that actions are possible only because one is cut off from the outside world, and that in a world which extends in all directions nothing like these actions could occur. On the contrary, these limits define the world as it is—lived, observed and judged, when censor mechanisms give way and taboos are overthrown, and man finds himself face to face with his desires. Existence may be no more than a prison, but inside this prison one is free, definitively so, to do whatever comes into one's head. Only fear holds us back; and the absolute evil is cowardice.

From the magic of Expressionism and *Kammerspiel* the 'laboratory' retains that which brings about the confrontation of two faces and two bodies, and the primal fashioning of a subtly sophisticated object well provided, regardless of what its inventor says, with finesse and sagacity.

The object soon ripens, becomes individual at the same time as it becomes ethereal, grows hard, and the spheres in which it turns grow abstract to the point of rarefaction, to the point of delirium. If the space of *Der Blaue Engel* has a good deal to do with Berlin, that of *Morocco* (1930) relates to the colonial world in which it is placed only through a bond of mythic connivance; *Dishonored* (1931) retains nothing more of Central Europe than the Front and the Frontier and the music which crosses them; the universe of *Shanghai Express* (1932) imposes an extremely oneiric concentrate of Asiatic exoticism. The American micro-spaces of *Blonde Venus* (1932) are like the sketched traces of typical places; the universe of *The Scarlet Empress* (1934) is a baroque and demented vision of Tsarist absolutism. Finally, the Spain of *The Devil Is a Woman* (1935) is a sublimation of the abundant Spanishness of painters and writers. (At this period only the world of *An American Tragedy* [1931] refers plausibly to that of the United States; but this 'realistic' film was more an exercise on an imposed theme than a creation claimed by its director.)

Whether it be geographical or historical, a narrative of fantasies or one of mythological tradition, the ideal exoticism of these films, shot with and around the most famous erotic fetish in cinematic history, carries to its extreme consequence that abstraction which was like an epigraph to *The Salvation Hunters*. From *Morocco* on, although the premises were perhaps already present in *Der Blaue Engel*, research is undertaken around the notion of the stereotype. Sternberg and Buñuel are perhaps the two film-makers to have most consciously and frankly used the stale and tabulated forms of that literature, theatre and iconography which is today described as 'for mass consumption'. Feuillade's art is another example of the sublimation, through the style of the *mise en scène*, of serialized novels of espionage and adventure, of mystery stories derived from the *roman noir* and from late nineteenth-century melodrama. But that which for Feuillade seems to proceed from a merely personal and 'natural' predilection, takes on for Buñuel and Sternberg such an entirely different appearance that it could hardly be said that either made wholly innocent use of these formulas. Buñuel's game with clichés is part of a dialectic of a relationship of the passions to social and ideological phenomena. Sternberg's, it could be said, short-circuits the social elements in order to put the passions in direct contact with ideology.

How stereotypes function for Sternberg must be looked at more closely. As an initial observation, it can be pointed out that these 'clichés' are to be found in every area of his films drawn from codes or language not specifically cinematic; this means, for instance, the story told by the screenplay, the dialogue, the set decoration and so forth. Here everything is strictly stereotyped in order to be brought as close as possible to the most commonly admitted givens on the subject. The signs provided correspond exactly to what is expected on the occasion. For example, there is not one line in *Morocco* whose content cannot be guessed before the character speaking it opens his mouth to say it, and nothing typically Spanish is missing from *The Devil Is a Woman*. Sternberg lavishes the most minute care in making up these signs, and he regards their placing in the film as of capital importance.

The first stage is the choice of story. Sternberg said and repeated that any story suited him, that the story was of no importance . . . He might have added 'so long as I choose it myself'. As a matter of fact each of the six films under discussion belongs to a clearly recognizable kind of popular literature: successively a novel of colonial adventure, a spy novel, a novel of the exotic East, a family melodrama, a historical serial and lastly a moral melodrama.

In the second stage, he carves scenes out of ultra-conventional material. It is here that the director begins 'to give himself away'. It should be considered that, in fact, the popular novel, more or less like the opera libretto, offers a condensation of dramatic and emotional features which have been inventoried long ago, rather like a series of events which have been catalogued. It follows that such a story—in which any sort of suspense concerning the succession of events has been eliminated—presents few problems in relation to reading the unfolding episodes. This relative facility authorizes any attempt at uncentring the plot, any of the displacements of accent which could be called 'transfers' of suspense. Rarely is interest or attention solicited for areas where, considering the type of plot, it would be expected.

This *uncentring* or skidding is most often effected by skimming over an important movement in the plot, or by carrying over one of these movements to a later one conventionally considered less significant. In other words, where a director would usually dwell at length, Sternberg skims, and he takes his time where skimming is more usual. An application of this principle is clearly seen in the construction of ellipses, which very often occur just where any other director would have shown events, and even emphasized them.

The third stage is the *mise en scène* strictly speaking: the disposition of actions in the décor and the composition of shots. Here again, by virtue of lighting, of the rhythm and intonation in the delivery of lines, of the direction of glances, of the intervention of characters in relation to objects, and especially by virtue of these gestures made in a constricted space, we find a transfer of interest whose strange result is to produce —amidst a conventional accumulation of events, a no less conventional exotic ambience—the rarest kind of event, the most unusual attitude, which the spectator none the less feels at the precise moment had to be revealed.

Thus there is here a truly filmic system, based on the disquieting and the surprising, arising out of a wholly artificial space organized by the director. This space is not only the product of the disposition of signs indexed according to original visual coordinates. Equally new are the sound coordinates, and those of the duration in which signs and gestures occur.

Returning to what has been said about Sternberg's conceptions of film sound, it should be observed that practically without any uncertainty, he succeeds in *Dishonored* in integrating different aural elements into a perfectly autonomous universe. The telegraph scene at the frontier outpost is exemplary in this way. Very few directors of this period understood the possibilities of the soundtrack to the point of creating what twenty years later would be commonly accepted: a veritable sound score, virtually independent from its anecdotal support. Only Fritz Lang showed from the outset (*M* in 1931; *Das Testament des Dr Mabuse* in 1932) such great concern with the discourse produced by sound, despite rudimentary conditions of recording, reproduction and mixing.

But the manner in which Sternberg plays with the duration of individual shots is also remarkably innovative and original. A certain slowness strikes the spectator in the films of this series—a slowness not merely to be explained by the filming of an exceptional creature: a moment *en trop* slips in between objects and the hands about to take them up, between the lips and the words they enunciate, between the moment when a gesture is completed and the moment when the image vanishes. An unusual duration insinuates itself between the successive stages of a movement, and sometimes the gesture seems no longer to belong solely to the person 'wearing' it, as if part of its trajectory occurred in an unknown land, as if it had escaped into a special zone of a different kind, abstracted from the conventional 'signifying' zone where it ought to have been confined by the event it is supposed to embellish. At such moments, the signs of passion are detached from the dramatic being and yield to another stage, one where a curious lack of division of gesture, word and emotion is current. This dramatic 'off screen' at the very inside of the screen, this unexpected spatial superfluity, this 'drift' of glances, gestures, carriage, accentuated quite beyond what is useful to an event's expression—it is this effect which seems more and more deliberately organized by the director of *Morocco* and *The Devil Is a Woman*, and which aims at a veritable *subversion of stereotypes*, a subversion arising from the inside of the frame, by elongation and distortion, and which explodes the outlines of the cliché and the system of representation which underlies it.

Thus, through a threefold decentring, interest is displaced from the plot to the sequence in itself, from the sequence to the event, from the event to the gesture, the instantaneous, the fragments of a phrase. Undermined and, as it were, submerged by the 'insignificant' essential which wells up from its centre to the edges of the frame, the image with its conventional configurations little by little goes to pieces. The structures of the typified world which it represents dissolve around the feminine effigy given as a model of the ephemeral, of the elusive, of the universally illusory. The *femme fatale*, emblem

of the nothingness which surrounds us, the woman without a shadow, traps in her gestures every subject constituted by the plot, absorbs them in her glance. The strangest of these films is *Blonde Venus*, where Sternberg re-presents the avatars of his favourite creature as if to suggest, in the very diversity of her successive manifestations, the permanence of a central irreducible radiance. He strives to the utmost to affirm this permanence through a series of surprises and misapprehensions. Sexual ambivalence, false unveilings and travesties, feathers—the bird woman—play a determining role in these poetics.

Of the seven films shot by Sternberg in the following eighteen years, the only two worthy of remark are the sumptuous and regrettably uncompleted *I Claudius* (1937), and the sophisticatedly charming *Shanghai Gesture* (1941), where Gene Tierney's 'Asian-like' mask prefigures that of Keiko in *The Saga of Anatahan*. Here in the clandestine casino, which should have been a brothel, a place open to violence and rape, is spoken the line which could serve as a motto for Sternberg's world: 'Here anything can happen, at any moment.' In 1953, after the project had run aground several times, Sternberg had the opportunity to make in Japan, with complete freedom, *The Saga of Anatahan*, which had been so close to his heart. This film was to be his last. I consider it to be one of the great masterpieces of talking pictures, the perfect work of convergence and achievement. Not only does the *auteur* masterfully control the keyboard of his techniques, but moreover, unexpectedly stepping back, he judges himself as a creator with an impassivity both attentive and free from pretence, if not from irony.

The Saga of Anatahan is at once a mimed legend, a plastic poem, an oratorio for eastern timbres with a western orchestra, chorus, and a speaker who directs the action rather than comments on it. The spectator is subjected to a completely modern test, situated as he is alternately at the centre and on the outside of a constantly revolving sphere, his vision now captured, now brusquely released, in the end more an interlocutor than a confidant in the dialogue between him and the *auteur* who reads his own prose aloud. All the components of the universe that we have attempted to retrace in

Charles Laughton and Flora Robson in the sumptuous 'epic that never was', the tragically uncompleted *I Claudius*.

its gradual construction are met with in this film, harmoniously integrated in their state of ultimate abstraction: the alternation between the austere and the over-elaborate, the precariousness of roles, the instability of scenes, the frenetic eroticization of a milieu apart, the fetishism of the décor and of the temporal flow, the condensation of emotional figures, the use of stereotypes on several levels, the progression of meaning through the exhaustive treatment of words and sound.

The process of spatial and temporal reduction is here particularly flagrant. A series of concentric circles is tightened from the beginning: a circle which is the Pacific (general theatre of war), another being the island where the shipwrecked characters are cast ashore (another, but derisory, theatre of war); a circle of the jungle (a homogeneous, abstract ambience), a circle of the hut on piles (a sanctuary presided over by the woman who 'animates' this space). And simultaneously, the object of the struggle is transformed in brief gliding movements: supplying food to Japanese posts in the archipelago; after the shipwreck, the symbolic defence of the island; repulsing the attack of a mythical invader; simple day-to-day survival; finally, after the discovery of the woman, a struggle against envy and jealousy. As a parallel the enemy changes. At the beginning it is the official American adversary; then the immemorial enemy of the Empire; then untamed nature and the couple of colonials living on the island; finally, once the man is eliminated, it is the woman who is the obstacle to peace. The adventure of these soldiers is known to be authentic. For seven years, isolated on Anatahan, they refused to believe that their Emperor had surrendered.

The material which Sternberg extracted from the story of one of these men condenses the events, allots the driving passions to about fifteen characters and installs a circulation of fetish objects readable on the strange map of Anatahan which Sternberg himself drew and coloured in. Thus twenty-two scenes communicate in an hour and a half of film the pulse of an adventure which might have lasted ten or twenty years (or no more than a few weeks), and one for which a synthetic jungle built on a sound stage provides the ideal location. Woven among overturned trees, zinc and papier mâché, a ballet of

races, leaps, stops, blows, cries and shrieks (these too synthetically re-created) composes a second, aerial system of relationships between duration and distance, perfectly in accord with the outrageous stylizations of creepers and palms; whence the logical choice of actors and dancers from the Kabuki theatre.

At the centre of this planetary microcosm, drawing back a curtain of sea shells, Keiko appears, the last stake in these struggles. Through a blinding narrowing of frontiers, an exemplary transfer—once again—from the field of history to that of eroticism. A man's life suddenly contracts from an overall view of the war to a close-up of a radiant face, childlike and mischievous. The signs of war are inverted, the weapons turned around: from the enemy, they are aimed at the friend, and then at oneself. Virtues practised the day before give way, while primitive exigencies arise and woman's typical role of submission is abolished. Woman, in fact, identified with life itself, becomes a cult object and an emblem of fatality. In reality, these men cast ashore on Anatahan remain there voluntarily. Their refusal to question their certainties coincides miraculously with the unconscious motive of their lethargy: the fatal dance for the possession of the female fetish. It is enough that Keiko leaves the island for them to consider returning to their homes, to their defeated country, the very thought of which they had censored.

But the chief novelty of *Anatahan* is the commentary on the action, by the *auteur* himself. The text which he reads is in fact more than just an element linking one scene to another, and more than just a commentary. It is a musical and signifying part of a poetic fresco for a screen in black and white. The English syllables are opposed to the very 'exotic' sonorities of the dialogue (which is never subtitled) and at the same time, the regularity of rhythm, the even detachment of the *auteur*'s intonation, contrasts with the aggressiveness of the actor's gestures and speech—'rough' to our ears—and with the vehemence of the music.

The principle consists of applying to the imaged representation the sound of a brief text which de-dramatizes, by immediate generalization, the subject-matter, which is neutralized by abstraction, and which in the same way disturbs the spectator's participation in the plot. Emotion no longer arises from the events themselves, but from the alternation of drawing near and moving back at the suggestion of the 'voice off', a coming and going based on the alternation of the struggle between violence (shown and lived) and calm (recited, earned by age and reflection), between madness and wisdom, between self-destruction and renewal and recovery. In its strict and distant course, this voice communicates over and over again the impression of a destined and inevitable development. The voice seems to summon a scene into being as often as to hold forth on its execution, seeming to solicit the *mise en scène* more than to criticize it. It organizes in fact the structure of the film, developing and pruning it, and in this way Sternberg seems to be considering his career as a *metteur en scène*.

Half-way along this itinerary, the *auteur* has inserted, between two very elaborate sequences, a rapid montage of newsreel material showing the mass repatriation of defeated Japanese soldiers: a brief, phantom-like, unreal eruption of the world in its historic context whose very appearance, through Sternberg's prodigious sophistication, has been forgotten. And unexpectedly it is the strangeness of this forgotten and suddenly revealed world which seizes us. This toppling over of worlds, of two rigorous, incompatible plastic elaborations, indicates that *Anatahan* functions in a profoundly original temporal mode, between the untemporal and the anachronistic, which is to say, between desire and eternity.

The final sequence provides an even more unsettling feeling, when an extraordinary exchange takes place between the two modes until then separate and independent. The flashbulbs of the reporters who have come to see the survivors at the airport blind the shining and frightened faces, not only of those who have finally returned to their homeland, but of their comrades who had perished on the island as well. And these are also the flashbulbs of the cinematographer, revealing the masks with which he had decked out his heroes. Creation and criticism rapidly exchange positions, the press correspondents, the first critics and investigators of the event, take up in some way where the film crew leaves off. In this reversal of perspectives, Sternberg provokes a brutal confrontation between two degrees of stylization and introduces the idea of a complete stylistic interlocking which can be traversed in two directions: from less to more abstract (the whole path of his work up to the finale of *Anatahan*) and from the most abstract to . . . the most concrete (and what would that be?). Here again, developed and enriched, is the supremely Borgesian oscillation upon which *The Last Command* was already based. But here the end is less a reconciliation than a new interrogation, an exploration.

The suspicion of the illusion of movement which was proposed at the outset as the centre of Sternberg's filmic activity glided successively towards the illusion of continuity, then towards that of representation and stereotypes (gestures, passions, dramas, tragedies) and finally to the illusion of worlds and their hypothetical hierarchy. The elementary questioning of the world through all its forms, performed by Sternberg through the systematic exploration of the powers of camera and microphone, is certainly related to the questions posed by a writer through the combinations of language and fiction. Courting and taming the ephemeral, this interrogation designates and sublimates it and so designates itself in every perishable image. The audacious, solitary and enigmatic work of Sternberg is part of a centuries-old tradition concerning the relationship of the work of art to the world, but the problems raised by such a conception are posed with the new tools of a new art and in so radical a way that their entire configuration is displaced. And is this imposing ideological relationship renewed as well? Recovered? Revivified by the light cast on it by the cinema? Or indeed, is it not Art, and that of Sternberg, which disappears in the grandiose finale of *Anatahan*, far away on the horizon?

Translated by Michael Graham

Claude Ollier is a distinguished novelist belonging to the school known as 'le nouveau roman'; so it is not surprising that his approach to Sternberg is quite different from the usual ones; he does not concentrate on the hot-house eroticism of Sternberg's films, nor on their camp splendours. (See Susan Sontag's definition of Camp in

Against Interpretation: 'The hallmark of camp is the spirit of extravagance. Camp is a woman walking around in a dress made of three million feathers ... Camp is the outrageous aestheticism of Sternberg's six American movies with Dietrich, all six, but especially the last, *The Devil Is a Woman*.')

What is astonishing, however, is that he never mentions the name of Marlene Dietrich. She is referred to obliquely as 'the most famous erotic fetish in cinematic history' or 'this exceptional creature', or 'his favourite creature'; but the name itself never appears. I imagine that Ollier has done this in reaction to the general tendency to confuse Dietrich with Sternberg, to ignore those films that he made without her.

But this cuts both ways: many writers seem to consider any films she made without him as being of no importance. This, too, is unfair, as a recent viewing of Curtis Bernhardt's *Die Frau nach der Mann sich sehnt* revealed. This film, made in 1929, is not only quite good in its own right, but also shows us that the Dietrich whom von Sternberg was supposed to have created *ex nihilo*, in *The Blue Angel*, was already a personality in her own right, and, as Bernhardt revealed in an interview, had her own ideas about the way she wanted to be photographed and about the lines she wanted to speak (or rather mouth, since this is a silent film).

This notion of a Dietrich totally the creation of Sternberg has been played up, not only by him, but also by her: she steadfastly maintains (and probably believes, by now) that *The Blue Angel* was her first film—which of course it was not. And *The Devil Is a Woman* was not her last film either. See the entry on Marlene Dietrich.

For further reading on Sternberg, see first of all his not always reliable autobiography, *Fun in a Chinese Laundry* (1965); see also Chapter 16 of Kevin Brownlow's *The Parade's Gone By* (1968), Herman G. Weinberg's *Josef von Sternberg* (1967) and Andrew Sarris' *The Films of Josef von Sternberg* (1966). There are many books on Dietrich: Charles Higham's *Marlene* (1977) and Charles Silver's *Marlene Dietrich* (1975) are the most recent; earlier works include *Marlene Dietrich, Image and Legend* by Richard Griffith (1959), *Dietrich* by Leslie Frewin (1955) and her own *Marlene Dietrich's ABC* (1962).

Finally, I should like to quote Andrew Sarris' superb encapsulated version of Sternberg's dramatic, as opposed to visual, world;

it, too, is important. 'His characters generally make their first entrance at a moment in their lives when there is no tomorrow. Knowingly or unknowingly, they have reached the end or the bottom, but they will struggle a short time longer, about ninety minutes of screen time, to discover the truth about themselves and those they love. Although there is much violence and death in Sternberg's world, there is relatively little action ... The paradox of violence without action is supplemented by the paradox of virtue without morality. There are no codes or systems in these dream worlds ... There persists an erroneous impression that the art of a *Morocco* or a *Shanghai Express* consists of the magnifying of trivialities. Yet there is nothing trivial about the size of Sternberg's emotions, and nothing disproportionate in the means employed to express them ... It is only when we look around at the allegedly significant cinema of Sternberg's contemporaries that we recognize the relative stature of a director who chose to write with a camera in the first person long before Alexandre Astruc's *camera-stylo* made such impious subjectivity fashionable and such personal poetry comprehensible.' (*The American Cinema*.)

GEORGE STEVENS

Edgardo Cozarinsky

Like Leo McCarey, George Stevens (1905–75) began by working with Hal Roach and Laurel and Hardy on two-reelers, where he acquired and perfected a sense of timing and comedy. But his sentimentality, unlike McCarey's, was softened by discretion and, in his later work, by a will to style of a kind that has become thoroughly unfashionable. Even Stevens' major films now seem confined to a tastefulness which precludes McCarey's emotionalism as well as his all-American brashness. Though his films of the 30s and early 40s are full of unassuming felicities (all of *Annie Oakley*, 1935; Katharine Hepburn as *Alice Adams*, 1935; the flashback structure of *Penny Serenade*, 1941), Stevens' best-known and most ambitious period begins after the war with *I Remember Mama* (1948), where a certain stylistic inflation is already noticeable.

Slow dissolves, intricate camera movements or long static shots, unconventional cuts: whatever the device, Stevens can be seen 'doing something' with every scene of his major films—the 1951 *A Place in the Sun* (where Dreiser's *An American Tragedy* is more diluted than in Sternberg's version of twenty years earlier), the 1953 *Shane* (where the archetypes of the Western are suffused into a nostalgic domesticity), the 1956 *Giant* (where Texas oil history and a convoluted family saga attain occasional grandeur). The issue is whether Stevens' approach is powerful or flexible or extravagant enough to absorb and digest such disparate materials into a self-sufficient manner, like Sternberg's or Ophuls'. Compared, for instance, with Douglas Sirk's handling at the same period of melodrama and the American scene, Stevens' approach looks obviously tame. Yet, a certain pervading charm still works in his less high-flown efforts— definitely lacking from the evangelic blockbuster *The Greatest Story Ever Told* (1965), it graces intermittently *The Only Game in Town* (1969), a doomed attempt to recapture the charm of the 30s.

Stevens also deserves to be remembered as the man who made the best of the Astaire-Rogers films, *Swing Time* (1936), and as the one who first brought together Spencer Tracy and Katharine Hepburn, in *Woman of the Year* (1942). For further reading, see Donald Richie's *George Stevens: An American Romantic* (1970).

MAURITZ STILLER

Richard Combs

Of the two great originals of the Swedish silent cinema, Mauritz Stiller seems the most eccentric and the least definable as an artistic personality. In Andrew Sarris' phrase, 'Seastrom [Sjöström] and Stiller stand at that odd confluence of Scandinavian air and sky later to give artistic life to Dreyer and Bergman,' and the two are commonly bracketed as dramatists with a peculiarly Swedish inclination for sombre passions and lowering landscapes. But as far as can be determined from the small portion of the work of both men that is still available, Stiller's output was the more varied and, in keeping with the dandyish figure which he apparently cut in person, his talents may have run closer than is usually allowed to the versatility and lightness of a genre stylist.

He was not in fact a native Swede, but was born in 1883 in Finland of Russian Jewish parentage; one of his earliest works in the style of the pastoral morality plays which now so much identify both himself and Sjöström was adapted from a Finnish source (*Sången om den eldröda blomman* [*Song of the Scarlet Flower*], 1919). And while very mindful of its landscapes (with different tints for different scenes, moods and seasons), the film is less interesting as a pantheistic celebration of nature in the Sjöström manner than for its treatment of the homeless, wandering hero, who recurs throughout Stiller's films. Stiller also came late to the kind of respectable literary adaptation which overtook the Swedish cinema during the First World War, when the dearth of foreign imports speeded the growth of a 'national' cinema, and the romantic and historical sagas of Selma Lagerlöf were gratefully absorbed by the industry in general and by Sjöström in particular. Stiller's first such adaptation was in 1919, when Sjöström turned over to him *Herr Arne's pengar* (U.K.: *Snows of Destiny*; U.S.: *Three Who Were Doomed*, also known as *Sir Arne's Treasure* and *The Treasure of Arne*). The bulk of Stiller's early output has been sternly summarized by one of his commentators as 'the most banal, thriller-type of magazine serial material', and a casual, cavalier attitude towards even his more prestigious sources is borne out by his subsequent disputes with Selma Lagerlöf over the free way he went about adapting her novels.

What survives of Stiller's films suggests at least one convenient division in his work: between the comedies and social satires (the most elaborate of which, *Erotikon* [U.K.: *Bonds That Chafe*, 1920], has frequently been cited as a precursor of Lubitsch) and the morally serious dramas of national life and historical circumstances. Where the two meet, in a way, is in a kind of ideal tragicomedy of human fallibility; in either genre Stiller was at his best when he could deal with the ambiguities and deceits of human behaviour in a supple and ironic form. Despite its fame in the anthologies, and Stiller's evident determination to make it the most sophisticated sex comedy of its day, *Erotikon* is really too calculated and lavish in its levity, with a grandiose opera being wheeled on at one point as a mocking aside on the charac-

ters' amorous shenanigans; for comic and
stylistic vivacity, the film loses out to the earlier Thomas Graal comedies. Similarly, the
last and most ambitious of Stiller's Lagerlöf
adaptations, *Gösta Berlings Saga* (U.K.: *The
Atonement of Gösta Berling*; U.S.: *The Legend
of Gösta Berling*, 1924), is too much at the
mercy of its ponderous set-piece construction to match the emotional intensity of *Sir
Arne's Treasure*, with the star-crossed love
affair of its treacherous hero and his erstwhile
victim, or of the extraordinary psychodrama
Gunnar Hedes saga (U.K.: *The Judgment*,
1923), which traces a spiritual regeneration
through a reconciliation of the hero's real
and fantasy life.

Stiller's most innovative work was
probably done in the comedies, which allowed his natural flamboyance free rein without resulting in the over-elaborate bravura of
the costume epics. *Thomas Graals bästa film*
(U.K.: *Wanted—a Film Actress*, or *Thomas
Graal's Best Film*, 1917), interweaves irreverent comedy about the film industry with a
delightfully complex mix of flashbacks and
fantasies that anticipates the experiments for
which Sjöström was to win so much praise
four years later with *The Phantom Carriage*.
Ironically enough, Stiller's greatest contribution to his medium is still likely to be connected with *The Atonement of Gösta Berling*
and his shaping of Greta Garbo for stardom
by tyrannizing her into losing 10 kilos for her
first film role.

Kärlek och journalistik (*Love and Journalism*, 1916) is one of the earliest of Stiller's
extant comedies, and one of the most successful. In some witty permutations of
deception and disguise, it works out its
'battle of the sexes' plot to a romantically
satisfactory conclusion. A famous Antarctic
explorer, Dr Eric Bloome (Richard Lund),
returning to his home town, is plagued by the
local newspaper, out for a scoop on his exploits. The first reporter despatched (a
woman, of very butch appearance, who
seems to be accidentally in disguise as a man)
returns with only a disgruntled account of
her brusque treatment by the family's old
nanny; the second, Hertha (Karin Molander), adopts more artful drag—clothing borrowed from her younger sister—and lands a
job as the Bloomes' maid. She finds the
material she needs for her story, while she

and the doctor in due course are mutually
smitten; but she is shown the door when she
is caught by the nanny rummaging through
his papers. The despondent explorer sets out
to find her, checking numerous schoolgirls
with the same name before he comes across
her, no longer dressed younger than her age,
in a chic restaurant; he takes her home to
delighted mama and startled nanny. What is
most striking about this brisk little farce is
how its adventurer-hero is so often left at a
disadvantage. Where the gloomy, haunted
heroes of his dramas clearly pre-empt the
stage, Stiller's comedies are largely ruled by
the reckless *joie de vivre* and scheming intelligence of his heroines. There is a moment in
Love and Journalism when Hertha, having
secured her entry to the Bloomes' home as
their maid, relaxes by herself in the evening,
lounging about nonchalantly in her pyjamas
with a cigarette. And Stiller reprises this sly
nod to a feminine free spirit in *Erotikon*,
when the eminently level-headed niece (and
the one faithful companion) of the cuckolded
professor of entomology similarly takes her
ease when her adulterous elders go out for
the evening.

Stiller employed Victor Sjöström, to unexpectedly vivacious effect, as the protagonist
of his two best comedies, *Thomas Graal's
Best Film* and *Thomas Graals bästa barn*
(*Thomas Graal's Best Child*, 1918). Both
revolve round the hero's various domestic
difficulties, but the first uses deft satire of the
movie business both as a framework for the
plot and as justification for the formal trickery with which it heaps up complications.
Graal is a writer for the 'AB Film Company',
and since ideas are coming slowly on his current assignment, he is being hounded by the
studio's manager (an early prototype of the
philistine producer), described as 'the enemy
of all authors . . . his only friend the waste
paper basket'. Partly to blame for Graal's
writing block is his infatuation with his
secretary Bessie (Karin Molander), the runaway daughter of a wealthy family. In an
introductory scene, Graal energetically per-
ambulates about the problem of keeping his
hands off his secretary while she types from
his fitful dictation; his romantic distraction is
barely disturbed when the script accidentally
catches fire. After a romantic tiff, Bessie
walks out, and the rest of the film becomes a

connecting tissue of flashbacks-cum-fantasies leading to their final reconciliation and engagement. Bessie's departure at least leaves Graal with a spark of inspiration, and he sets about a script that begins as a fanciful version of his courtship of Bessie, leading to a flash-back-within-the-fantasy as she relates her wretchedly poor and brutalizing family history, which gives way in turn to scenes—presumably taking place in the present—showing Bessie back in her cosseted nest, running coquettish rings round her bemused family. The Dickensian childhood turns out to be a story that Bessie has fed the gullible Graal, and it is the heroine's guile and thespian ambitions rather than the hero's more innocent narrative manipulations which bring them together again, with Bessie appearing at the studio and Graal finally turning performer himself, shouting his devotion to his lady on a balcony, while a crowd of curious onlookers gathers.

Conceived and played as a brisk collision of moods and whimsical invention, *Thomas Graal's Best Film* turns its flimsy premise into a triumphantly single-minded conceit. *Thomas Graal's Best Child* is longer, and although its set-pieces are wittily elaborated (Thomas Graal overdressing for his wedding, then having to undress in front of a shocked congregation in order to find the ring; he and his bride arguing on the way home whether their first child should be a boy or a girl, then huffily withdrawing to separate camps in their house, with much to-ing and fro-ing performed by the bewildered servants), the film is overextended and finally broken-backed. The wedding-day spat is settled in a neat elaboration of the street-scene finale of *Thomas Graal's Best Film*: Graal is forced to defend his wife's honour from the shouted flirtation of a drunken passer-by before an impromptu and noisily interfering public gallery. But the arrival of the child and the parental complications which follow make for a lame second act.

The success of these early comic sallies is due in some measure to their understatement as comedies of social manners. In their actor-ish delusions and disguises, the protagonists only mesh fleetingly with the society about them; and the milieux tilted at in, say, *Thomas Graal's Best Film* (the idle rich, the movie industry), seem made up of borderline caricatures, who serve in a way to 'place' the film but gain little purchase on it as they skitter through. When Stiller tackles social and sexual mores head on, as in the cross-section study of *Alexander den store* (*Alexander the Great*, 1917) or the 'daring' parody of marital infidelity in *Erotikon*, his touch goes heavy. *Alexander the Great* is a collection of skits on the state of love and courtship in petit bourgeois circles; its satire only really takes hold in the scenes of the most patently and absurdly arranged match of the piece—between the graceless (but penny-wise) daughter of the presiding matron of the Society for Combating Spiritual Need and an equally graceless, penniless but well-placed young lieutenant. The bold manner of *Erotikon* won it a degree of notoriety: faithless wife makes, not her husband, but her lover jealous when she seems to be casting her favours elsewhere; things are eventually sorted out, the wife stays with lover No. 1 and the husband, quite unexpectedly, is paired off with his perky young niece. But the risqué situations are too cutely prepared (the film opens with the unfortunate husband delivering a lecture on the bigamous habits of the 'Striver' beetle) and too padded in the production (the would-be lover takes the heroine for a spin, in one of the cinema's earliest aerial sequences; an exotic opera on Eastern infidelities makes the real lover squirm). Karin Molander frisks effectively as the niece, however, and is the film's one enlivening presence.

The weakness of Stiller's comic heroes, usually vis-à-vis their female counterparts, takes on more sinister tones in the dramas; the ebullient naïveté and harmless hamming of Thomas Graal becomes a darker tangle of deception in *Sir Arne's Treasure* and schizophrenic breakdown in *Gunnar Hedes saga*. Somewhere in between the two poles are the protagonists of the pastoral romances, the most stiffly moralistic of Stiller's films and a mode which he handled altogether more schematically than Sjöström. The narrative of *Song of the Scarlet Flower* is strong enough to withstand its division into chapters, complete with lessons pointed in the headings; what drives the film are its scenes of family strife and acrimonious confrontation. The hero is banished from his father's home when he refuses to abandon his affair with a ser-

Mary Johnson and Einar Hanson (left) in one of the most surrealistically beautiful sequences from *Gunnar Hedes Saga*. This film has a fair claim to being Stiller's one incontestable masterpiece; it traces a spiritual regeneration through a reconciliation of the hero's real and fantasy life.

vant girl, becomes a wanderer and freelance logging man, and is eventually scorned in his turn as a 'vagabond' by a wealthy patriarch whose daughter he shyly begins to court. Eventually the two lovers confront the old man, and when he insists that if his daughter leaves against his will she must go with no more than she had when she arrived, the girl calls his bluff by promptly beginning to strip. The wilfulness of such scenes ('You are your father's son—you don't care what you do, whether you build up or pull down,' laments the hero's mother at his stormy departure) startles into life these stolid figures in a country landscape, and hints at the perversity and tortured sensitivity that wreak havoc in the later dramas. *Johan* (1921) is more conventionally done, and despite the brisk action and flashback material that leaven this dour tale of a dissatisfied farmer's wife being whisked away by a romantic and unscrupulous stranger, Stiller seems unprofitably confined by a dramatic convention which allows the natural elements so large a part in the play of human passions.

An over-abundance of character and incident mars *Sir Arne's Treasure*, but the strange and ill-fated love affair at its centre holds this shaggy novelistic canvas together. Three Scottish mercenaries, fleeing cross-country after they and their comrades have been banished for conspiracy by the king of Sweden, try to reach the sanctuary of a waiting ship. Becoming like ravening wolves in their deprivation, they eventually light upon Sir Arne's fabled treasure, wiping out his entire household in the process. The single survivor, Elsalill (Mary Johnson), subsequently falls in love, unknowingly, with the youngest of the three, Sir Archie (Richard Lund), whose new affluence and elegant clothes have restored to him a degree of respectability—and a tortured conscience. Eventually a visitation from her murdered foster sister reveals the truth to Elsalill; she informs the authorities; then, aghast at the thought of what might happen to her lover, warns him. He unhesitatingly uses her as a shield when surrounded by guardsmen, and she is killed by a spear; Sir Archie then attempts to escape aboard the ship, pretending that the girl in his arms is still alive. With splendid formality in the closing shots, as the townspeople file across a sea of ice to collect

the dead Elsalill and the three guilty men, Stiller suggests an inexorable fate closing in on this tragically ambiguous affair between the ethereal girl, already (by virtue of her miraculous escape from death and her collusion with spirits) as much of the other world as of this, and her anguished lover, too much of this world to be more than tensely ambivalent in his affections.

Stiller's second adaptation from Selma Lagerlöf, *Gunnar Hedes Saga*, distills elements from much of his previous work, and has a fair claim to being the most personal of all his films and his one incontestable masterpiece. Like *Song of the Scarlet Flower*, and despite the spectacular sequences of the hero's spell as a reindeer herdsman (a sort of *Red River* of the frozen north), the drama is more acutely orchestrated indoors than out. Gunnar Hede (Einar Hanson), a dreamer with little interest in his parents' plans for him as a mining engineer, is eventually sent packing by his mother when he persists in his dalliance with a gypsy girl, Ingrid (Mary Johnson). Like the younger Stiller, this dissatisfied exile aspires to the despised calling of 'artiste'; himself a violinist, and once a struggling apprentice actor in the Finnish and Swedish theatre, Stiller anchors Gunnar's dreams in the image of his grandfather as a strolling fiddler and one-time adventurer who founded the family estate of Monkhyttan on his profits from reindeer herding.

When the gypsies arrive, Gunnar undertakes to improve Ingrid's violin playing (like other Stiller heroines, Ingrid turns out to be only an adopted daughter, as if the director needed to find some domestic, feminine correspondence with his footloose heroes). Gunnar's playing is applauded by the gypsies, who announce that he is an artist who could have the world at his feet, while commenting that Ingrid has little artistry and that it is useless to try to teach her. Soon after, Gunnar finds himself put out of the house, and decides to follow in his grandfather's footsteps by heading north after the reindeer herds. An accident leaves him in a dazed, hallucinating state, and he is returned to Monkhyttan, where he recognizes no one. In a poetically just parody of his parents' practical ambitions for him, he takes to collecting stones at the riverside, in the belief that they are valuable coins. In an echo of the gypsies' verdict on her own musical talents, Ingrid is told 'You shouldn't waste your time with Gunnar, he is incurable' as she tries to nurse him back to health. Finally, however, she repays Gunnar's favour ('Margareta,' he jokes in the earlier scene while taking the violin, 'she was a young girl who loved Faust and saved his soul with her love'), and wakes him from his trance by playing in the court-yard beneath his window. Gunnar thereupon discovers that the stones he has been collect-ing contain valuable minerals, sufficient to save the now impoverished Monkhyttan from being sold, and incidentally proving that he functions best as an engineer, no less than as an artist, when his imaginative facul-ties are allowed free play.

The psychological density and subtle at-mospheric control of *Gunnar Hedes Saga* is only fitfully evident in the subsequent *The Atonement of Gösta Berling*, Stiller's last Lagerlöf project, and his last film in Sweden before leaving for the United States at Louis B. Mayer's beckoning and on Sjöström's advice. A sprawling historical epic, *The Atonement of Gösta Berling* was originally made to be shown in two parts, but after the coming of sound they were shortened and amalgamated by Svensk Filmindustri and a music track added. But the interweaving of so many characters and plot threads seems inevitably to have reduced the film to a col-lection of illustrative tableaux, and in both the drama and the various comedy touches the acting is conspicuously broad; the tyro Miss Garbo is in fact the only element to register with any delicacy.

Stiller fared unhappily in America, finding both his projects and his working relation-ship with the studio uncongenial. Of the few films he made, at least two—*The Temptress* (1926), *The Street of Sin* (1928)—were par-tially directed by others (Fred Niblo and Josef von Sternberg, respectively). His health broken, he returned to Sweden, where he was attended by Sjöström at his death in 1928. The tragic irony is that, as the more endemically Swedish of the two, Sjöström should have made the more successful adap-tation to Hollywood. A cosmopolitan and bon vivant, Stiller celebrated the triumph of style—light, bright but wittily self-aware in its flaunting of roles—over the limiting cir-cumstances of time and place; he also became

the victim of his sense of the spiritual dangers as well as the challenges of exile.

See also the articles on Garbo and Sjöström. There is unfortunately no monograph in English on Stiller, but he is discussed in Peter Cowie's *Sweden 1 and 2* (1970). In French, see Jean Beranger's *La Grande Aventure du Cinéma Suédois* (1960) and the monograph *Stiller* by Bengt Idestam-Almquist collected in Vol. III of *Anthologie du Cinéma* (1975). Stiller, one of the truly great directors, has still to be rediscovered.

JEAN-MARIE STRAUB
Richard Roud

Perversely brilliant as the following essay by Jean-André Fieschi is, it is likely to make sense only to those who know the films of Jean-Marie Straub and Danièle Huillet. For the others (the overwhelming majority, alas), a few facts might be helpful. Straub was born in 1933 in Metz, capital of Lorraine. For the first seven years of his life, this was, of course, a French city; but in 1940 it was annexed by Germany, and for the next five years German was the only language taught at schools. So in many ways Straub is a director who belongs to both the French and the German schools, one who is imbued with French and German culture.

Straub studied film in Paris, and worked as an assistant to many directors, including Bresson and Rivette. It was there that he met Danièle Huillet, and it was there that he had his first personal confrontation with politics: the Algerian war. Straub was op-posed to this colonial war, and refused to do his military service. Instead, he left for Germany, accompanied by Danièle Huillet. His first film project was to be a film about Bach but it was hard to raise the necessary money; instead, he ended up making a short film based on Heinrich Böll's story *Bonn Diary: Machorka-Muff*. The film caused something of a scandal when it was shown at the Oberhausen short film festival, but Straub and Huillet were heartened by an encouraging letter from Karl-Heinz Stockhausen. The next film, *Nicht versöhnt*, caused an even greater scandal when it was shown at the Berlin Festival in 1965. Based on Böll's novel *Billiards at Half Past Nine*, it takes that kaleidoscopic novel about three generations in the life of a German family, told mostly in flashback, and quite simply explodes it. The whole novel is condensed into fifty-three minutes, and past and present are made to co-exist. Time is flattened out, generations are meaningfully confused—all in order to make, not a film about the advent of the Nazis, but one which would show that Nazism already existed before 1933 and continues still.

The film was badly received at Berlin because of Straub's minimal techniques, his use of ellipses, the 'peculiar' (i.e. Bressonian) way the dialogue was spoken, and perhaps also because the audience felt attacked by the film's message. It is a difficult film to follow because the flashbacks are 'unannounced'; characters are difficult to disentangle because of the three-generation spread. And yet there were those who found the film immediately compelling. As John Russell Taylor wrote, 'When I first saw the film, with no knowledge of the book, I still found it a totally fascinating experience. To begin with, an intuitive leap was necessary, and it is something one cannot decide to take, it must be forced on one . . . It is a classic example of the film-film, the film in which the medium is the message, which is "about" its own right to exist as a work of art . . . You have to take the film as a whole or not at all, but for those who can take it, it is one of the purest and most exalted experiences the cinema has to offer.'

The Straubs' next film was in fact easier to take: *The Chronicle of Anna Magdalena Bach* was a film of, not about, the music of Bach, and this already made it easier for audiences. Furthermore, it is, as Straub has said, a love story about Bach and his second wife; it is also a documentary on the actors and musicians (notably Gustav Leonhardt who plays, in both senses, Bach); and it is also a film with political and social aspects. The construction of the film is not unlike that of Bach's St Matthew Passion: the story-line of that work is almost entirely restricted to the recitatives of the Evangelist; but for the most part, it is the arias and choruses, the set-pieces which really provide the drama. And, since the Straubs have always believed firmly in the virtues of direct sound, we see the music we are hearing actually being performed. And because the performers are actually performing, the period reconstructions become totally convincing.

Fortunately, the Bach film enjoyed a certain degree of success; it brought the Straubs up from the underground. As a result, Straub's next film, *The Bridegroom, the Comedienne and the Pimp*, was made within a year. This short film is in some ways Straub's most extraordinary work. In its twenty-three minutes, it includes a ten-minute condensation of a play by Bruckner, a documentary on the street prostitutes of Munich, some texts by St John of the Cross and a love affair between an actress and a black American soldier which her pimp (played by Rainer Werner Fassbinder) unsuccessfully tries to break up. All these elements sound as if they had nothing to do with each other, but they do, for each acts as either catalyst or contrast, or sometimes both. It is also an expression of the triumph of love through sacrifice—as was Bresson's *Les Dames du Bois de Boulogne*.

The Straubs' next film was more controversial still. Commonly called *Othon* for convenience, and because that is the name of the Corneille play which has been filmed, its real title is a quotation from the play: 'Eyes do not want to be closed at all times, or perhaps Rome will permit herself one day to choose in her turn' (a rather republican statement for seventeenth-century Corneille, but it's there in the play).

The Straubs had meanwhile moved from Munich to Rome, where they still live. And it was on the terrace of the Palatine Hill, overlooking the Circus Maximus, that they filmed *Othon*, against a sound pattern of traffic noises, verses against Vespas.

Straub did not want to call the film *Othon* because Othon (or Otho, as he is known in English) is far from being the hero of the film: he is a political opportunist, and the opportunism of his court resulted in the decadence of the Roman empire. The film was shot entirely outdoors—to let air into the work. And the sights and sounds of contemporary Rome prevent one from losing oneself in the play; rather, they oblige us to think about the play and its connections with today. Further distancing is provided by the accents of the non-professional actors: with only two exceptions, none of them is French-born, so they speak with varying accents. On the other hand, the actors are all young, the same age as the characters they are playing, and this tends to increase our identification with them. Paradoxical? Not really; dialectical. The struggle of opposing techniques, opposing means of expression, can be likened to the mixture of several elements in a test-tube. The result can be an explosion, but a controlled one, and one which releases new energy.

Two years later Straub returned to Roman history with his *History Lessons*; based on a Brecht novel, *The Affairs of Mr Julius Caesar*, it is a demystification of Roman history which brings out the sordid economic and political realities behind Roman history as it is usually taught. The original Brecht text (or rather part of it) is read by a group of togaed people: a banker, a peasant, a lawyer, a writer. But these sections of Brecht are constantly counterpointed by long tracking-shots of a car making its way through the crowded streets of today's Rome.

At the same time, as if in preparation for *Moses und Aron* (*Moses and Aaron*, 1975), the Straubs made a short film called *Introduction to Arnold Schoenberg's Accompaniment to a Cinematographic Scene*. This piece of music (Opus 34) was written by Schoenberg in response to a music publisher's request for music to accompany (imaginary) silent films. Any kind of theme could be chosen; Schoenberg characteristically chose 'Threatening Danger, Anguish, Catastrophe', and the Straubs counterpoint this music with the reading of letters from Schoenberg to Kandinsky warning him of the rise of Nazism and explaining to him his fears of growing anti-Semitism in Germany.

Then, in 1975, came *Moses and Aaron*, a faithful version of Schoenberg's opera, and an original film in its own right. In it, the Straubs succeed in rendering visible not only the philosophical content of the work—the struggle between word (Moses) and image (Aaron)—but also its dramatic potential. The film was shot in Italy, but it was to be the Straubs' last film in German. It was followed in 1977 by *Fortini/Cani*, an adaptation of a work called *The Dogs of the Sinai* by Franco Fortini, a left-wing Italian-Jewish writer who examines his feelings, both as a Jew and as a radical, towards the Israeli–Palestinian conflict. To my way of thinking it is their least successful film, largely because the text by Fortini did not provide a sufficiently lyrical springboard to contrast dialectically with the dryness of the *mise en scène*. The original text is already too Straubian.

Finally, it must be said that the influence of Straub on contemporary cinema has been enormous. The films may not have had large audiences, but they have had a tremendous effect on other film-makers.

For further reading, there is my own *Straub* (1971), which is now somewhat out of date, but which does provide a close examination of the earlier works as well as the shooting script of *Not Reconciled*. More recently, the first issue of the British magazine *Enthusiasm* (December 1975) was entirely devoted to Straub and Huillet.

JEAN-MARIE STRAUB

Jean-André Fieschi

Films could be imagined in which real violence would, for once, speak. The white cloth stretched across the back of a black tunnel is usually open to the soporific, the complaisant, to misrepresentations and the circulation of the small change of fantasies. Once more cinema might become surprising, once more necessary.

Films could be imagined in which, at last, real Desire would speak. Francis Ponge in *Le Carnet du Bois des Pins* writes that during the war he lived in the south of France. He missed his library. So he undertook to write what he wished to read: to make writing the compensation for a simple but demanding desire.

One ought to be able to think that there is no other kind of writing, nor any other kind of pictures, or music, or films. In any event the nature of the mass of films is predictable: if they are indeed, like any social product, more or less diversified responses to a specific demand, the demand in question is a perverted one. In capitalist countries, cinema is indissolubly linked to Capital and to Ideology. Cinema sells dreams, the real disguised; fantasy, imaginary satisfaction; nostalgia, regression; sometimes it sells Utopia, always the Elsewhere.

A kind of cinema could be imagined which would sell nothing, just as Stravinsky said that music expresses nothing; a kind of cinema which would not consider the spectator as a customer, which would not lure him, nor seduce him, nor flatter nor despise him, would not rape him nor put him to sleep; a kind of cinema that would be the exact opposite of advertising. In 1974 on the walls of Paris could be seen a surprising series of posters. A man with a vague smile and a meaningful look addresses the passer-by, a possible customer, in the name of a well-known bank. And he speaks the truth: 'I'm interested in your money.'

A kind of cinema could be imagined which sells nothing; but which would not hold itself aloof. On the contrary, it would militate, and would neither ape anything nor exhibit itself, neither bargain nor repress. The viewer would at last be placed at a proper distance, neither ensnared in conniving proximity nor crushed by the exercise of an art which proclaims itself inaccessible.

This is only a dream. What free and alert spectator is being thought of, here and now, in Germany, Italy, France or the United States? Certainly not the bourgeois spectator. The bourgeoisie which by now is incapable of assuming its cultural past and whatever was or remains revolutionary in its culture, and all the more incapable of assuming the culture which lies ahead, incapable of thinking of it without fear; for the culture to come is its own tomb.

So then, what spectator? The man of the people, the worker, the peasant. But these people are excluded from culture by the reigning bourgeoisie, its State and its institutions. Yet it is to them that the culture of the past belongs. It is they who made it: they created wealth. It is to them that the culture of the future will belong. So this cinema could speak today to the man of tomorrow.

This is a dream, but a necessary dream, that of reappropriation. 'When one wishes to speak to the people, one must make oneself understood. But this is not a problem of form. The people do not understand only old forms. In making social causality clear Marx, Engels, Lenin continually employed new forms. Lenin not only said something different from Bismarck, he said it in a different way. In fact he did not bother himself about whether a form was old or new; he spoke in the form that was appropriate,' to quote from Brecht.

It could thus be imagined that beauty, violence and desire might be offered again, intact, to be discovered anew—the beauty, violence and desire present in the work which transforms music and texts; for instance, the music of Bach or the plays of Pierre Corneille, now the hunting reserves of specialists, professors and pedants. And might be offered in such a way as to be an insult to specialists and bad professors. In such a way that the music makes clear that it has not yet been heard, that these texts have

not yet been read. What would music and texts already heard and read be if not dust, cultural dust, museum pieces, savings bonds . . . What would music and texts be that did not resist, that would let themselves be tamed? And films?

This would be the stake: to speak to those who have neither heard nor read rather than to those who do it out of duty, through routine or idleness, and to say to them: 'Here, this too belongs to you, and is worth being read, heard or looked at; this violence is yours, and this desire.'

Why would this new cinema bother about the past? Why should revolutions, cultural or political, pose as guardians of a heritage?

'To guard a heritage in no way means remaining confined to that heritage' (Lenin). When resorting to the forms of the past, whether of Bach and Corneille, or Brecht or Schoenberg, the only nostalgia which can be read will be that—and it too will be violent— for a future for which these forms are still a summons.

Everything leads one to believe that in this different kind of cinema modesty will be taken for arrogance, purity for obsession, austerity for poverty, wealth for insolence.

Cinema designated as deviant, perverse, proud, perhaps even a little Jewish, and as such destined to the ghettos. It will be censured, or praised excessively, removed to a pedestal, if not to the corridor . . . in any case, it will not be accepted. Nor is there any need of a trial: the entire weight of dominant cinema by its mere existence condemns it to exile.

But if it were the other way round?

If instead it were this cinema, marginal and exiled which, by its very existence, won at great risk, questioned the existence of the entire mass of the dominant cinema?

If such a project could be formulated, would it not be the fruit of a rather comic and excessive ambition, perhaps even mystic or messianic?

Yet this cinema might not have an *auteur* (which is to say a person caught up in the fantasy of being a demiurge, referring to a rage for expression which is *only* personal). Who would speak then? Bach or Pierre Corneille only, or Brecht or Schoenberg?

One could imagine then that the word would be neither that of the *auteur*, nor that of his characters, nor that of the primary *auteur*, Bach or Brecht. Nor only that of the *auteur*, of his characters, etc.

That of the film perhaps: what circulates, in the film, between these words. *In* the film: but the film is not a receptacle or a filter. What circulates, transforms itself, generates itself *between* these words, their resistance and the resistance of the material—concrete materials: cameras and microphones and—less malleable—faces, bodies, ways of speaking. And more: light, wind, shadows . . .

And all this would be inscribed; or, as a cabinet-maker would say of his wood, or Freud of a dream, all this would *work*.

What would speak then would be a struggle, materially inscribed on this white surface at the end of a black tunnel; a conflict of forms, meaning and material. The film would be a documentary of this struggle.

This conflict would not be a spectacle. A side has to be taken, the struggle has to be joined; unless one could be satisfied with the worst, being a spectator—at a film: a shadow among shadows.

These films then would not be films, nor these spectators spectators? Would someone want to break the old machinery, or forbid the trip? These films would be actions. As Pierre Boulez said of Stravinsky, 'He simply acted.'

For instance, a man would be seen struggling with a text, its material nature: meter, scansion, sound and sense. At grips *with* a language, neither his own nor of his time, but strongly actualized by these distances, their effect of strangeness, at first disquieting and later curiously familiar. Slowly being burned by the sun—not spotlights—his lips cracking, his skin reddening. His voice, his rhythm, the way it carries, all subjected to the rivalry of the wind. This discourse would be caught in a tight network of other discourses, victorious over other resistances: fatigue, the sun, or again, the wind; or the murmur rising

Martha Ständner in *Not Reconciled*: 'I want to shoot the fat man on the white horse.'

Lilith Ungerer in *The Bridegroom, the Comedienne and the Pimp*: the final scene.

up from the town, its crowds or traffic; or yet again, the regular flow of a fountain.

And these discourses, these resistances, their fusion and clash; their web, tissue and texture would be inscribed in struggles for power, passions, interests, desires. Here could be read other forces, other struggles, other resistances: the fall of an Empire or impossible Love. In any case, history, that is, politics.

Brecht again (and for a long time to come): 'The dramatic aspect (the violence of confrontations) the passions (the degree of warmth), the surface covered by a character—none of this can be envisioned or conveyed separately from the functioning of society.'

A man could also be seen, for example, at grips with music or money. At grips with money and music (reality and desire). In any case with History, that is, again, Politics.

This cinema would show men at grips with what the cinema itself is at grips with: desire, work, money, politics. It would not show them the way a mirror does: that which already exists. But it would show the process itself: something existing, the trace of the struggle. Not only its lucidity but its spectre.

These beings at grips with work, with the sun, the wind, the text, desire, money, passions, fatigue, with history, would no longer be actors. But men, amateurs or officials, workers or idlers, peasants or writers, men and women, flesh and desire, confronting texts, materials, resistances and their own history. Struggling too, and naked in sun or rain. Here too the film would be a documentary.

It would no longer be a matter of telling *stories*, but of telling history: passion of all passions, narrative of all narratives.

So there would be History, men and women, and blocks—not scenes. Each film would be a game between blocks—of unequal duration—spaced far apart, where the spacing would play as well; where the spacing, its distance, the blank and the ellipse, the suppression of narrative articulations through which cinema ordinarily displays its infirmity—in short, the interval, as Vertov would have said, would be a figure. Where everything would be a sign: emptiness as well as fullness, words as well as silence, immobility as well as movement. Where the film would say that it was to be read, as reality is to be read so that it can be transformed. And there one would be, facing it as unarmed, or as armed, as in reality. Where what would be given to read, understand and transform would no longer be significations—fixed, arrested, dead—but relationships of material meanings.

Yet for all this the film would not be a pure metaphor or an aesthetic displacement of social relations: that would be too easy. And it would most vehemently repel the idea of passing for a model or for a giver of lessons.

But, instead, with its means, its aim, it would be the place of a transformation. Delivering no message but a sign, in its way, that the shock can begin, and here or by others be brought to its term.

At the most, the indication of this shock, the sign of the fissure, the euphoria of destruction (why not destroy? she says) which knows somewhere that it is the first stone. It is seen, which is already a great deal.

Cinema without filiation—without origins, one might be tempted to say; but such an affirmation no sooner risked than it would seem deceptive. Here too it is just the opposite: it is the business of works of rupture to reinvent their precursors. Have the films of Dreyer been seen—their violence, their desire, their aleatory and peremptory form?

These films, these acts, exist, fragile and insistent. They are these blocks of *amour fou*: *Machorka-Muff* (1963); *Nicht versöhnt oder es hilft nur Gewalt, wo Gewalt herrscht* (*Not Reconciled*, 1965); *Chronik der Anna Magdalena Bach* (*Chronicle of Anna Magdalena Bach*, 1968); *Der Bräutigam, die Komödiantin und der Zuhälter* (*The Bridegroom, the Comedienne and the Pimp*, 1968); *Les Yeux ne Veulent pas en Tout Temps se Fermer ou Peut-être qu'un Jour Rome se Permettra de Choisir à son Tour* (*Eyes Do Not Want to Close at All Times or Perhaps One Day Rome Will Permit Herself to Choose in Her Turn*, or *Othon*, 1970);

Geschichtsunterricht (*History Lessons*, 1972); *Einleitung zu Arnold Schoenbergs Begleitmusik zu einer Lichtspielscene* (*Introduction to Arnold Schoenberg's Accompaniment to a Cinematographic Scene*, 1972). They are signed by Jean-Marie Straub and Danièle Huillet.

Translated by Michael Graham

ERICH VON STROHEIM

Jonathan Rosenbaum

Two temptations present themselves to any modern reappraiser of Stroheim's work; one of them is fatal, the other all but impossible to act upon. The fatal temptation would be to concentrate on the offscreen image and legend of Stroheim (1885–1957) to the point of ignoring central facts about the films themselves: an approach which has unhappily characterized most critical work on Stroheim to date. On the other hand, one is tempted to look at nothing *but* the films—to suppress biography, anecdotes, newspaper reviews, reminiscences and everything else that isn't plainly visible on the screen. Submitting Stroheim's work to a purely formal analysis and strict textual reading of what is there—as opposed to what isn't, or might, or would or could or should have been there—may sound like an obvious and sensible project; but apparently no one has ever tried it, and there is some reason to doubt whether anyone ever will. (A purely ideological analysis may be just as unlikely: critics have dealt at length with Griffith, Chaplin and Ford from Marxist perspectives, but where does one go to find a Marxist analysis of *Greed* [1924]? Yet there may be no other fiction film in existence that has as much to say about the concrete effects of capital.) Over the past fifty-odd years, the legend of Stroheim has cast so distinctive a shadow over the commercial cinema in general and his own work in particular that the removal of that shadow would amount to nothing less than a total skin-graft. Above all, it would mean eliminating the grid through which his films were seen in their own time—a time that, in many crucial respects, remains our own.

From one point of view, Stroheim's films only dramatize problems of directorial control and intention that are relevant to most

Hollywood films. They dramatize these problems, however, in a particularly revealing way: we remember his best works (*Foolish Wives* [1921], *Greed*, *The Wedding March* [1928], *Queen Kelly* [1928]), not merely because of their power—which is considerable—but also because of their *will to power*, which is always even more considerable. We are constantly brought up against the problem of considering the films as indications and abbreviations of projected meta-films that were either reduced and re-edited by the studios or, in the case of *Queen Kelly*, never completed in any form.

It is central to Stroheim's reputation that he is valued today more for the unseen forty-two-reel version of *Greed* than for the ten-reel version that we do have. And if history and legend have conspired to install Stroheim as an exemplary figure in cinema—virtually the patron saint of all directors who have suffered at the hands of producers—it is precisely because of this discrepancy, the gap between the power and control that was sought and the amount that was visibly achieved.

How are we made aware of this discrepancy? Certainly we sense it almost as much in Stroheim's acting in the films of others as in his own projects—not simply because of all the dictatorial parts, from Prussian officers to assorted lunatics, but in the very style of his delivery, the very manner of his presence. Consider the sublime and all but hallucinatory tedium of his first role in a sound film, James Cruze's *The Great Gabbo* (1929), when he seems to speak each line at roughly half the speed of everyone else in the cast; here one can witness the will to power in a strictly temporal sense—the apparent desire to remain on the screen as long as possible—lending an intolerable tension and demonic mulishness to the part of the mad ventriloquist that go well beyond the melodramatic demands of the plot, as though he were pulling at his character like taffy to see how far it could stretch before breaking. In so far as a single performance can be compared to an entire film, it is likely that the duration of the original version of *Greed* was motivated along similar lines.

The opening credits of *Greed*, *The Merry Widow* (1925) and *The Wedding March* alert us to Stroheim's aspirations before anything else appears on the screen: the first two films are said to be 'personally directed by Erich von Stroheim', the third is labelled 'in its entirety an Erich von Stroheim creation'. But if accepting Stroheim's legend means submitting to a fiction—a supplement, in many cases, to the fictions that he filmed—denying it is tantamount to imposing another, alternate fiction. Bearing this in mind, an attempt will be made here to *isolate* his legend whenever possible, but not to dismantle it.

On the other hand, critical myths which interfere with any rigorous effort to see Stroheim's films as they are deserve to be abolished. A few of these are found in the brief article on Stroheim in Andrew Sarris' *The American Cinema*, where one encounters, along with some suggestive insights, the following debatable statements:

> ... Film-making, like life, is full of compromises and accommodations, but Stroheim seemed as intransigent on trivial issues as on major ones. What difference did it make, after all, if his royal troops wore the right underwear under their uniforms. Was not this realism carried to idiocy? [. . .] The mark of genius is an obsession with irrelevant detail.
>
> ... Perhaps the most remarkable aspect of Stroheim's style is its technical chastity. *The Wedding March*, made in 1928 when Murnau was at the peak of his influence, does not contain a single camera movement.

Two different notions of 'realism' are apparently being fused here, as frequently happens in discussions of Stroheim. It is important to distinguish between the verisimilitude of a film in relation to the spectator (whether what he sees looks 'true to life', etc.) and the verisimilitude that Stroheim often sought to achieve *on the sets and locations* of his films—in many cases, a different thing entirely. Whether or not he actually required extras in *Merry-Go-Round* (1923) or *The Wedding March* to wear monogrammed underwear—a newspaper legend whose veracity has never been established—this clearly has no bearing on what we see in the films; and if Stroheim's 'genius' has left a 'mark', this is surely to be found more in his visible and relevant details than in his invisible and irrelevant ones.

Stroheim's alleged inability to compromise

with producers is another offscreen matter, but one that has led to so much critical hyperbole over the years that a few adjustments are in order. One should recall that in the case of *Greed*, his most ambitious film, he was accommodating enough to reduce his own forty-two reels to twenty-four, then to ask Rex Ingram to pare this down to eighteen reels when MGM refused to consider handling even the second version. And his 'intransigence' in refusing to recognize the final ten-reel version was not so great that it prevented him from working again for the same studio immediately afterwards, on a film (*The Merry Widow*) whose history consisted of continual accommodations and compromises. Late in his career, Stroheim paraphrased a statement by Frank Norris: 'I never bargained . . . and I never took off my hat to convention nor fashion . . . and held it out for pennies . . . I have always told them the truth as I saw it.' That statements of this kind are still taken by many as the literal truth about Stroheim might be regarded as a tribute to the force of his films; but apart from the partial biographical distortions that this entails, it is a disservice to the films to treat them in so unambiguous a manner. Neither life nor Stroheim is quite that simple.

While it is correct that Stroheim tended to move his camera less often than Murnau and was less of a montage director than Griffith, it is misleading to conclude from this that he was 'technically chaste'. The cross-cutting between the fire and the approaching fire-truck in the last reel of *Foolish Wives* obviously owes a great deal to Griffith, and even in battered prints, the rhythmical control is sophisticated enough to suggest that Stroheim could make expressive use of montage when he wanted to without any technical handicap. Camera movement plays a significant role in all his work, even if he usually resorts to it so few times in a single film as to make each occurrence a privileged one. (Contrary to Sarris' claim, there are at least half a dozen camera movements in *The Wedding March*, and not one is gratuitous.) Nor does this constitute anything approaching the whole of his technical arsenal: blurred focus (generally to suggest tears in point-of-view shots assigned to heroines), superimpositions, various uses of colour (missing in contemporary prints), slow lap dissolves as

carefully calculated as Sternberg's, and above all, a masterful use of the iris and fade, are only a few of the techniques in his vocabulary. One never feels in his work, as one occasionally does in Chaplin's, that any of these devices is being appropriated from other directors like second-hand goods, despite the obvious debts to Griffith. A characteristic camera movement of Stroheim's is one offering a short narrative statement with a syntactical length roughly comparable to that of a short sentence, while the most important camera movements in Murnau's *Faust* and *Sunrise* are much closer to dense and labyrinthine paragraphs. (Ophuls' camera movements, by contrast, are more like run-on sentences *à la* Molly Bloom, while Buñuel generally continues the laconic, epigrammatic tradition of a Stroheim.) Even the frenzied cross-cutting in *Foolish Wives* has a manic, sightly zany pace to it suggesting Sennett almost as much as Griffith, although it doesn't really look like a strict imitation of either.

Some favourite devices, recurring frequently throughout Stroheim's work, are the long shot dissolving into a medium shot of the same character, the camera movement that turns a medium shot into a close-up, and the upward or downward pan taking in the whole body of an actor. Each represents a different way of taking a closer look at someone—the first usually introduces characters; the second permits an increasing concentration of dramatic focus and detail (like the extraordinary track up to the face of Dale Fuller, the exploited maid in *Foolish Wives*, where we are enabled to see revenge being hatched in her eyes); and the third is more in the nature of an inventory.

Eyes have an unusual authority in Stroheim's films, and what is frequently meant by his 'control of detail' is his uncanny gift for conveying information through an actor's eye movements. How someone looks and sees is always a central character trait, and the story of each film is partially told in glances.

A memorable example occurs in one of the privileged camera movements in *The Wedding March*, when Mitzi (Fay Wray), standing in a crowd, looks up at Prince Niki (Stroheim) mounted on a horse, and an

Boots Mallory and James Dunn, discovered by ZaSu Pitts in *Walking Down Broadway*.

upward pan gives us her exalted estimation of him. We can trace this shot all the way back to *Blind Husbands* (1919), Stroheim's first film, when Erich von Steuban (Stroheim) first encounters 'Silent Sepp', the local Tyrolian mountain guide. Each sizes up the other in a separate pan: Steuban looks at Sepp, a slow pan from feet to head; Sepp looks at Steuban, a slow pan from head to feet. The central metaphysical conceit of the plot is hung on these two camera movements; and, significantly, they are repeated in different but related contexts near the end. There is a slow pan all the way up the mountain— introduced as 'The Pinnacle' (Stroheim's own original title for *Blind Husbands*) on which the climactic struggle will take place— which Dr Armstrong (Sam de Grasse) and Steuban are about to ascend; and in the midst of this struggle, while Armstrong stands over Steuban, clutching him by the throat, a slow pan from Steuban down the mountain to the rescue party of soldiers and others, including Sepp, making their way up.

From top to bottom, from bottom to top: thematically and dramatically, all Stroheim's films refer to this basic pattern. *Blind Husbands* provides at best only a rough sketch of what is to follow, but the essential lines are already there. Sepp is the pinnacle, the higher aspiration, and also something of a dumb-ox innocent, earthy and inert, who prevents Steuban from seducing Mrs Armstrong (Francelia Billington) by appearing in the hotel corridor at just the right moment. (A cryptic monk appearing out of a rain storm in *Foolish Wives* functions identically.) Steuban is the depths, the lower aspiration, the grim, deadly and well-dressed seducer, full of bluff and pretension. In between stand the Armstrongs, an American couple, naïve without being simple or wise (like Sepp), adventurous without being irresponsible or pretentious (like Steuban)—two free-floating characters who are, by extension, ourselves: likeable zeros susceptible to the influences of a Sepp *or* a Steuban.

The spiritual and earthy aspects of Sepp are partially reflected in Mrs Armstrong, who looks to him for wisdom in their one scene together, when her husband and Steuban are on their way up the mountain. 'Are they in danger?' she asks, evidently believing in his clairvoyance, and he

responds without hesitation: 'Not if they've left their worldly troubles behind.' A crippled, retarded boy in the alpine hut appears to share some of this ESP.

All these characters represent archetypes traceable to the nineteenth-century novel. The credits indirectly acknowledge this heritage by claiming that the film is derived 'from the book *The Pinnacle* by Erich von Stroheim', a work that no visible research has ever uncovered—much like the book *Foolish Wives* that the heroine of *that* film is shown reading. If the 'realist' tag assigned to Stroheim often seems today like an outdated literary category—and one which might make Stroheim seem more outdated than he actually is—this is equally the case with his first literary models, Zola and Frank Norris. The fictional worlds of all three are so charged with metaphysical forces and intimations of fatality that the 'realism' they project is not one in which free will predominates; characters are usually doomed to be what they are by class and social position, heredity, mysterious turns of fate, or some malign combination of all three.

This is reflected in the countless images, symbols and icons of fate that appear in Stroheim's films, the hints and overt references to religious, occult and superstitious obsessions. There are the many crosses, churches and religious ceremonies that are not merely shown but *played up* in every film, and the religious overtones given to secular situations and characters (Steuban wooing Mrs Armstrong at the foot of a cross; ZaSu Pitts made to resemble a nun in the dentist's chair in *Greed*, the hospital bed in Stroheim's original ending of *Walking Down Broadway*, 1932); details such as Stroheim stroking a hunchback for luck in a casino (*Foolish Wives*), the hero of *Queen Kelly* proposing a wish when a wagon of new-mown hay passes, or later spilling salt and tossing some over his shoulder at the queen's banquet, immediately after their engagement is announced.

Steuban and the Armstrong couple can easily be seen as first drafts of Karamzin and the Hughes couple in *Foolish Wives*—an elaborate remake in many respects. *The Devil's Passkey* (1920), made during the interval between the two, is a lost film, but existing synopses indicate it to be another version of the same plot, which remained with Stroheim for years. But the distance traversed between Stroheim's first and third film is cosmic, even though only three years separate them. Vaguely sketched essences of character and locale become 'three-dimensional' embodiments—not merely ideas expressed, but ideas incarnated—and we leap from an apprentice work to something closely approximating a mature style.

Comparing the Italian and American prints of *Foolish Wives* in *Cahiers du Cinéma* No. 79, Jacques Rivette observed that they differ not only in length, order of sequences, and editing within scenes, but also in the fact that they don't always have identical 'takes' of the same shots. He offers the very plausible hypothesis that the longer Italian version corresponds much more closely to Stroheim's, while the American print is the version recut by Universal after the film's New York première. It seems quite possible that the remarkable close-up of Dale Fuller's story-telling eyes and the fire/fire-truck montage, as described here, never existed in the American version.

A particularly troubling problem with both versions is the absence of what must be considered the film's climactic sequences: the rape of Ventucci's half-witted daughter by Karamzin, which results in the murder of Karamzin by Ventucci (Cesare Gravina); and after Ventucci's depositing of Karamzin's body in a sewer (visible in both versions), the corpse shown at dawn in the midst of garbage floating out to sea; and Mrs Hughes giving premature birth to a child, which brings about a reconciliation with her husband. (These scenes are all indicated in Stroheim's synopsis. Some critics have described the rape as an uncompleted act, but the synopsis suggests otherwise: 'He violates her, but she is his last victim . . .')

Lacking these scenes, our understanding of Karamzin's function in the film remains incomplete. Unless we can see the contrast between his magisterial first appearance by the Mediterranean and his exit as 'rubbish' in the same setting, the trajectory of his scurrilous career is not fully articulated; and without the birth of the Hughes' child— apparently suggesting a quasi-mystical resurgence of life out of the ashes of corruption—

his death fails to achieve the proper resonance. But despite these and other regrettable lacunae, Karamzin remains Stroheim's most complex and fascinating character outside *Greed*, and provides the occasion for his definitive performance.

The differences between Steuban and Karamzin are so closely related to the differences between Stroheim's authority as a director in each film that it is difficult not to see both characters as partial autobiographical counterparts—a relationship which the name 'Erich von Steuban' already makes transparent. Karamzin displays all the low traits of Steuban, from vanity to cowardice, but two crucial characteristics are added: he is an impostor, and he is mainly out for money. Moreover, he is something of a professional con-man while Steuban is at best a promising novice in the arts of deception, too often a fumbler to convince us that he is truly malignant. Both characters are identified with an 'artistic' sensibility: one of Steuban's ploys with Mrs Armstrong is to play soulfully on the violin, while *Foolish Wives* invites us to relish Karamzin's more subtle methods of enticement, to delight in his grander fabrications.

To explore some of the implications of this view of Karamzin as a partial self-portrait, a few facts about Stroheim must be considered:

Karamzin as an impostor. When Orson Welles succinctly described Stroheim's art as 'Jewish baroque' in a 1958 interview in *L'Express*, he was anticipating a discovery that came to light in an article by Denis Marion two years later in *Sight and Sound*, over four years after Stroheim's death. Reproducing his birth certificate as partial evidence, Marion established that Stroheim was, in fact, Jewish—in background and upbringing, if not in subsequent practice—that the 'von' in his name was apparently a fabrication, and that neither his military experience nor his links with the Austrian aristocracy were as substantial as had generally been supposed. As one indication of the semi-permanence of Stroheim's legend, Thomas Quinn Curtiss virtually shrugs off the evidence of the birth certificate as follows: 'It remains inexplicable . . . that this should have escaped the scrutiny of the Nazis . . .; and it is also acknowledged that the Nazis were capable of forging such documents.' The general significance that this revelation has on Stroheim's work is certainly debatable, but it does offer the hint that were it not for all the partially self-imposed legends, Stroheim's impulse towards 'realism' and 'the truth' might not have been quite as strenuous as it was.

Karamzin and money. In an unpublished manuscript, Stroheim stated that '. . . R. H. Cochrane, vice-president of Universal and past master of publicity, got the great idea to call *Foolish Wives* the First Million Dollar Film (although the complete cost was only $730,000) in order to publicize the film and awaken the public's interest in it'. A sign was put up which spelled the director's name as '$troheim', listed the alleged cost of the production so far (a figure that was changed every week), and remained on display for 'one solid year'. As Stroheim points out, this naturally gave him the reputation of being 'the most expensive director in captivity'. Much of the money, of course, went towards 'exact' reproductions of Monte Carlo buildings like the Casino, the Hotel and the Café de Paris—a form of counterfeiting analogous in some ways to Karamzin's profession (distributing counterfeit money printed by Ventucci).

Karamzin as metteur en scène *and actor*. Accompanying Karamzin in his deceptions are 'Princess' Olga (Maude George) and 'Princess' Vera (Mae Busch), posing as his cousins, whom he instructs on how to 'act'. His manipulations of both Mr and Mrs Hughes and the servant girl—rich and poor alike—are clearly predicated not only on acting, but also on the kinds of illusions and staging that a film director makes use of; his monocle serves as a marvellous prop, but it also suggests a camera lens.

Something of a moralist despite himself, Stroheim loves to advise the spectator, not tell him what to do; he is much closer to Renoir or Rossellini than to Hitchcock or Fellini. The principal advice of *Foolish Wives* repeats that of *Blind Husbands*, but this time in italics: '*Watch out for him!*' We get it in our second glimpse of Karamzin, when he is aiming a gun at us, directly at the camera; the next shot confirms that he is only doing his morning target practice in a fancy bathrobe, but the image remains in our memory to

warn us—a disturbing reminder of Mrs Armstrong's dream in *Blind Husbands*, when Steuban's figure, set against a black backdrop, is pointing threateningly in the same direction, smiling and clenching a cigarette between his teeth. 'Watch out for him!' The Armstrongs and Hughes and a few unfortunate servant girls might have ignored the warning at first, but no one else did—least of all Stroheim's producers.

A classic instance of Stroheim as trickster: the episode of the armless ex-soldier. Already, in contrast to *Blind Husbands*, he is firmly establishing a very specific milieu and period in which to locate his story—Monte Carlo just after the War—where ex-soldiers on crutches and children playing soldiers (some of whom seem to mock and 'see through' Karamzin's postures) form an essential part of the background. But not realizing that the stolid man who neglects to pick up Mrs Hughes' gloves is armless, we assume that he's around merely to indicate the kind of courtesy that she's accustomed to receiving, and to provide Karamzin with an opportunity to display his own gallantry. The second time the man appears, exhibiting similar behaviour in an elevator, we might imagine him to represent some sort of running gag. Then, when we discover he is armless, we are brought up short, and moved to pity: a strong ironic point has been scored. But Stroheim refuses to stop there. As Mrs Hughes proceeds to fondle and caress one of the veteran's armless sleeves, pity quickly turns into disquieting morbidity, and what we have previously been led to ignore we are now obliged to dwell upon. In a brief instant that illuminates the rest of the film, comedy turns into tragedy and the tragedy becomes a fetish. It is a remarkable transformation of tone, created throughout by a series of false narrative expectations . . . If *Blind Husbands* squats somewhere uncomfortably between a 'symbolic' play and a cheap novella, *Foolish Wives* all but invents the novelistic cinema.

How does *Foolish Wives* resemble a nineteenth-century novel? By turning the spectacle of Griffith into an analysis of social and psychological textures—Monte Carlo was his *Intolerance* set—Stroheim asks us to move around in his frames and episodes in a way that grants us some of the freedom and leisure of a reader's experience. Griffith's suspense montage has enough Kuleshovian (and Pavlovian) effects to deny the spectator the opportunity to use much of his intelligence. This creates momentum, to be sure, but Stroheim usually sweeps the spectator along with a different kind of persuasion. Griffith either lulls or harasses you into the role of just plain folks; Stroheim starts with the assumption that you're witty, discerning, and twice as sophisticated as the fellow sitting next to you. Karamzin may be a sneak fooling that American ambassador and his wife with his phony credentials, but he doesn't fool us. We aren't saps like the maid, either, who gives all her money to Karamzin because she thinks he'll marry her, and allows him to deceive her (but not us) by letting water from a finger bowl drip from his fingers to simulate tears; we (but not she) can see him wipe his lips—almost unconsciously, as if by reflex—after he kisses her.

We hate him because he is evil; we love him because we know him: that's probably why we love to hate him. Stroheim loves to hate him too; it is something he is sharing with us as much as showing us. It is a very strange process: what the actor creates, the film-maker annihilates, and the portrait is as merciless as the character. He is confidential about what he shows us, like a novelist; he tell us the kind of things that are going on behind closed doors, when certain people are out of earshot. He wins our confidence by telling us secrets.

It was witty of Godard to suggest that Méliès made documentaries, and rewarding to look at Feuillade's films under that aspect; but Stroheim turned the fiction film into the documentary in a much more central and decisive way. He did this above all in *Greed*, and not so much through 'stripping away artifice' as by reformulating the nature that his artifice was to take.

This was not simply a matter of shooting *Greed* on location; more crucially, it was a direct confrontation with the challenge of adapting a literary work. *McTeague* is a work of fiction that impressed Stroheim and his contemporaries for its 'realism'; by attempting to arrive at an equivalent to this literary mode, Stroheim wound up having to deal exhaustively with all the essential problems inherent in adapting *any* fictional prose work.

There was certainly no film-maker before Stroheim who attacked these problems in quite so comprehensive a manner, and it is arguable whether there has been anyone else since. For this reason alone, *Greed* remains a laboratory experiment of the first importance —valuable for its failures as well as its successes, and comprising a virtual textbook on some of the formal issues that it raises.

When Stroheim filmed *Greed*, Kenneth Rexroth tells us in the Signet edition of Frank Norris' novel, 'he is said to have followed *McTeague* page by page, never missing a paragraph. We'll never know because the uncut *Greed*, greatest of all movies, is lost forever.' To understand the important aspects of Stroheim's adaptation, the first step is to dismiss hyperbole of this sort and work with the materials available: the novel, Stroheim's screenplay, the version of *Greed* that we *do* have, and the existing stills of scenes that were cut from the film.

The first thing that the published script tells us is that an enormous amount of material has been added to the novel, particularly in the opening scenes: about sixty pages —nearly one-fifth of the screenplay—pass before we reach McTeague eating his Sunday dinner at the car conductor's coffee joint, the subject of Norris' first sentence. Admittedly, much of this is devoted to expositions of characters and settings that Norris introduced at later points in the narrative; but in many cases, Stroheim's expansions on bare suggestions of Norris are considerable. Mac's life prior to his arrival in San Francisco is conveyed by Norris in a brief résumé of two paragraphs; in the script it takes up twenty-five pages. A brilliantly designed sequence that runs even longer, and is completely missing from the final version of the film, introduces us to all the major characters on a 'typical' Saturday afternoon that precedes the novel's opening.

Interestingly, this sequence is largely constructed around cross-cutting between characters whose interrelations in the plot have not yet become clarified—in the case of Mac and Trina, between characters who have not yet even met—so that the juxtapositions are unusually abstract, even from a thematic point of view. As an approach to narrative, which was already common in prose fiction but far from being a convention in cinema, this is probably the most 'advanced' and experimental departure in the script: apart from a few brief incidents of significance— Mac buying a canary, Maria Macapa first encountering Zerkow—nearly everything that takes place is descriptive and inconsequential as plot, and each character is linked into an overall pattern of significance that nothing in the story has yet justified. Harry Carr, one of the few people who saw *Greed* in its complete form, may have had this sequence partially in mind when he compared the film to *Les Misérables* and remarked that 'episodes come along that you think have no bearing on the story, then twelve or fourteen reels later, it hits you with a crash.'

Some other important elements in Stroheim's 'reading' of Norris involve degrees of emphasis and changes in viewpoint. It might be argued, for example, that Stroheim tends to show more generosity towards his characters than Norris does, on the basis of the following alterations (among others). The association of Mac with his canary—a trope clearly derived from Griffith— accentuates his gentleness. His brutal boast of killing a half-grown heifer, in Chapter 11, is omitted in the script. Norris notes that 'Neither Zerkow nor Maria was much affected by either the birth or the death of [their] little child,' while Stroheim makes much of Maria's grief over the child's death. Although Zerkow certainly remains a grotesque in the screenplay, all verbal references to him as a Jew—a pejorative term in the novel, used over half a dozen times—are missing. When Marcus renounces his claim on Trina to Mac at a Seal Rocks restaurant, the gesture is implicitly mocked and shown as hypocritical in the novel by Marcus' concurrent thoughts; omitting these thoughts, Stroheim makes the gesture somewhat more genuine in appearance, and it becomes touching: Marcus' finest moment. Most surprising of all, in relation to Stroheim's customary predilections, the script eliminates the most direct allusions in the novel to Trina's masochism, including a description of her conversations with Maria when both of them proudly show off their bruises, inflicted by Mac and Zerkow respectively.

Still other differences are circumstantial, e.g. most of the 'linear' catalogues of objects in the novel are rendered in the film as 'simultaneous' backdrops and settings; evidently out of respect both for 'realism' and for the capacities of his actors, Stroheim keeps certain violent or gory details from the novel offscreen (Trina vomiting, her dental operation, her eventual murder) or—in the case of Maria with her throat slit—shows them in silhouette. In Mac's penultimate encounter with Trina, when he begs for money at her window, the scene is virtually reshaped: Mac's gesture of throwing cherry stones at the window to attract Trina's attention is omitted, and the use of angle/reverse-angle expands the 'viewpoint' from that of Trina to a more objective treatment assimilating the viewpoints of both characters.

Undoubtedly the most problematical element in Stroheim's adaptation is its use of repeated symbolic motifs—shots of gold, greedy hands, animals and other emblems— which seem to be a direct misapplication of literary principles to cinematic structures. The recurrent image in *McTeague* of Mac's canary 'chittering in its little gilt prison'—a phrase repeated with slight variations in many contexts, before it appears as the final words in the novel—works symbolically and 'musically' because it is laced smoothly into the thread of the narrative, with no breaks in discourse or syntax. But in *Greed*, the repeated images have the disadvantage of interrupting the narrative, usually without adding any useful perspectives to it: they are like footnotes that mainly say '*Ibid*'. In their limited use in the film that we have and their *implied* use in the script, they tend to seem like dead wood clinging to the rest of the film.

Which brings us back to the 'realism', the documentary aspect of *Greed*. Clearly one of its most extraordinary aspects remains the unusual conviction of the performances, which is apparent even in the random instances offered by stills. Look at any frame enlargement from *Greed* showing ZaSu Pitts, Gibson Gowland or Jean Hersholt and one sees not a familiar actor 'playing a part' but a fully rounded character *existing*—existing, as it were, between shots and sequences as well as within them (or such is the illusion). How many films in the history of cinema would pass this elementary litmus test?

One recalls André Bazin's famous remark about Stroheim: 'In his films reality lays itself bare like a suspect confessing under the relentless examination of the commissioner of police. He has one simple rule for direction. Take a close look at the world, keep on doing so, and in the end it will lay bare for you all its cruelty and its ugliness. One could easily imagine as a matter of fact a film by Stroheim composed of a single shot as long-lasting and as close-up as you like.'

The spirit of documentary is no less present in Stroheim's introduction of outside chance elements into his fictions. This is not so much a matter of letting random accidents creep into the staged actions (as in Léonce Perret's 1913 *L'Enfant de Paris*, when a friendly dog wanders into a shot at the heels of an actor) as a sort of semi-organized psychodrama, exemplified in a scene missing from current prints of *Greed*: when Trina discovers Maria Macapa with her throat cut, she runs out of Zerkow's junk-house and hysterically reports the murder to the first people she sees. Stroheim shot this sequence with hidden cameras, and the responses came from passers-by who were not aware that a film was being made.

Greed stands at roughly the half-way point in Stroheim's fifteen-year career as a director, constituting both a caesura and a change of direction in his *oeuvre*. Four features precede it and four follow it, and beneath the continuity of certain undeniable stylistic and thematic traits, Stroheim's preoccupation with realism, his concern with narrative, and the nature of his ambition all undergo important transformations.

The first thing to be said about *The Merry Widow*, the film immediately following *Greed*, is that it represents a nearly total inversion of the former's approach: after filming his least compromised, most 'realistic' work, Stroheim promptly made a film that was his most compromised and least 'realistic'. At its best, *The Merry Widow* has a lightness of touch and grace of movement suggesting a pre-sound musical, with an idealized fairy-tale landscape (clearly established in the opening shots) that necessitates a very different kind of discourse. The most striking off-beat elements in this Hollywood dream-bubble—Prince Mirko (Roy D'Arcy) and Baron Sadoja (Tully Marshall)—figure in the overall scheme in a way that is analogous to the 'marginal notations' of irreverence that characterize most of Buñuel's films in the 50s: they offer ironic swipes at the conventional aspects of the material without ever seriously threatening the root assumptions of these conventions.

Prince Mirko is an obvious derivation of Erich von Steuban and Count Karamzin, but his role here is not as central: as a foil to the romantic figure of Prince Danilo (John Gilbert), he cannot wield the same kind of lethal authority. Similarly, the grotesque part of Baron Sadoja—a 'first draft', as it were, for the even more monstrous Jan Vooyheid, incarnated by Tully Marshall in *Queen Kelly*—is allowed to function as a grim commentary on the action and an intrusion on the central love story, but at no point is he really permitted to dominate the film.

Regarding *The Merry Widow* as a transitional work, one can perhaps best understand Mirko and Sadoja not as 'realistic' intrusions—they are anything but that!—but as rebellious counter-fantasies provoked by the more conventional fantasies embodied by Danilo and Sally O'Hara (Mae Murray). If the earlier films were an attempt to subvert Hollywood from an outsider's position—eliminating the characteristically romantic leads, and in the case of *Greed*, literally moving out of the studios to locations—*The Merry Widow* announces the counter-strategy of boring from within. This is rather like the approach Welles later adopted in *The Lady from Shanghai*, when, for example, there is a cut from a standard glamour pose of Rita Hayworth in a bathing suit to a close-up of a grotesque character (played by Glenn Anders) ogling her. There is more than one prefiguration of this procedure in *The Merry Widow*; the most celebrated instance occurs in the theatre, when Sadoja, Mirko and Danilo each look at the dancing heroine through opera glasses: the first concentrates on her feet, the second on her body, the third on her face.

Another noticeable shift in Stroheim's style is a somewhat different use of duration in relation to narrative. In *Foolish Wives* and *Greed*, duration was mainly a matter of the overall length and breadth of the films—the desire to assimilate some of the richness and freedom of the nineteenth-century novel that has already been discussed. But after *Greed*, despite Stroheim's continued interest in making long films, the novelistic aspect becomes less important, and the ritualistic, ceremonial aspects of duration gradually come to the fore—the obsessive desire to keep looking at something not in order to 'understand' or 'decode' it, but in order to become totally absorbed in it, transfixed by it; not to penetrate the surfaces of things, but to revel in these surfaces. The aggressiveness of Stroheim's camera eye ultimately leads to a kind of passivity. In the films after *Greed*, this change becomes much more explicit: the belligerent eye of the sceptic gradually turns into the passive eye of the *voyeur*.

This generalization tends to oversimplify a great deal of Stroheim's work, and probably shouldn't be taken as literally as it is stated above; but it does help to account for the peculiarly dreamlike elongations of actions and scenes in *The Merry Widow*, *The Wedding March* and *Queen Kelly*. A simple comparison might help to clarify the difference: when the camera slowly approaches Dale Fuller's face in *Foolish Wives* to reveal the revenge plans being formed in her eyes, the lingering effect has a purely narrative function, permitting us to watch a *process* more clearly than we could otherwise. But when the camera slowly tracks up to the face of Mae Murray in her wedding dress, and then recedes slightly to frame her entire figure as she proceeds to tear up the dress, we are being asked to concentrate on her primarily as an *object*: the 'process' at work is chiefly the camera movement itself. We can intuit that the character's visible distress leads to her act of violence, but the steps leading from A to B are implied more than chronicled: they are the scene's justification, but not its major focus.

Nor is it just a question of the relative lack of virtuosity in Mae Murray's performance. Gloria Swanson's performance in *Queen Kelly* is adept in its development and exposition of motives. But this is no longer the camera's primary subject: virtually all the characters in Stroheim's last silent films exist as essences, fixed points of reference—'static essentials', to borrow Pavese's phrase. That Stroheim intended to show Kelly undergoing a complete transformation—from innocent to prostitute to queen—must be acknowledged,

but the evidence of this change was not recorded on film; it is not until *Walking Down Broadway* that we find a visible (if partial) throwback to a 'narrative performance' in the part of ZaSu Pitts as Millie.

The Merry Widow announces a more static view of action and character; *The Wedding March* and *Queen Kelly*, both epics of slow motion, expand and sustain it. It is hardly accidental that religious and military ceremonies figure so importantly in these films—they, too, are 'static essentials'. The 'realistic' impulse goes through no less pronounced a change: the European countries of *The Merry Widow* and *Queen Kelly* are fantasy kingdoms, and even the celebrated accuracy of detail in the Vienna of *The Wedding March* is subject to fanciful additions and idealizations. 'I am through with black cats and sewers,' Stroheim is reported to have said while making the film. 'I am going to throw perfumed apple blossoms at the public until it chokes on them. If people won't look upon life as it is, we must give them a gilded version.'

And a gilded version is what *The Wedding March* supplies: even though the villain Schani (Matthew Betz), a pig-sty and a slaughter-house are all clearly intended to offset the apple blossoms, these supposedly 'realistic' elements are just as idealized as the romantic ones. Next to Stroheim's other villains, Schani is a crude cardboard cutout who is never allowed to expand beyond a few basic mannerisms (mainly spitting); and the other major characters—Prince Nicki (Stroheim), Mitzi (Fay Wray) and Cecelia (ZaSu Pitts)—are unusually simplistic creations for Stroheim.

One could be charitable (and many critics have been) by regarding the figures and themes of *The Wedding March* as mythic distillations of their counterparts in previous Stroheim films; or one can be less charitable and regard them as inert calcifications—rigid prototypes whose original *raison d'être* is lacking. *The Wedding March* is generally accorded a high place in the Stroheim canon, and it must be admitted that it has a magisterial, 'definitive' quality that is missing from most of his other work. But speaking from a minority viewpoint, it can be argued that a certain price had to be paid for this rather self-conscious classicism. Apart from rare scenes—like the remarkably subtle exchange of looks and gestures between Nicki and Mitzi during the Corpus Christi procession—the action, characters and symbolic motifs (e.g., the Iron Man) are so schematically laid out that they assume a certain thinness; investigation is consistently bypassed for the sake of a polished presentation.

Seen purely on its own terms, *The Wedding March* is undeniably an impressive work. Offering us spectacle more than drama, it is a stunning display of lavishness and an ironic commentary on a particular kind of royal decay lurking beneath it. It is only when we place the film alongside *Foolish Wives*, *Greed* and *Queen Kelly* that we can understand its limitations: what these films (and even the others, to lesser degrees) possess that *The Wedding March* lacks is an acute sense of *transgression*. And it is precisely this sense that makes *Queen Kelly*, for all its own limitations, a more pungent and exciting work: if *The Wedding March* converts many of the familiar Stroheim themes into a series of dry homilies and mottoes, all suitable for immediate framing, *Queen Kelly* converts many of these same themes into a species of delirium—a possessed work of hypnotic, almost hallucinatory intensity. In contrast to the icy elegance of *The Wedding March*, it breathes fire.

It is trashy, yes: but in the best sense, like 'Monk' Lewis' *Ambrosio* and William Faulkner's *Sanctuary*. And at certain moments it achieves an elegance of its own, an elegance recalling that of a Nathanael West or a Georges Bataille, in its stylistic control and continuity.

Which is not to praise *Queen Kelly* for its literary qualities: it has none, or at least no more than Stroheim's own novels such as *Paprika*. On the contrary, *Greed* and location work aside, it is the most 'cinematic' of his films, the one most alive to the medium's formal possibilities. The lighting is his most richly orchestrated, the camera moves about with an unprecedented freedom (assuming the hero's angle of vision, for instance, as it scans the doors in the convent for Kelly's room), and the use of duration has never been quite as operative as it becomes here.

It must be noted that the latter represents a formal decision imposed by fate and fortune as well as by Stroheim: the footage which we have is virtually unedited, and Lotte H. Eisner informs us that the scenes 'are stretched out a great deal longer than the director wished'. This calls to mind Truffaut's characterization of Welles as a filmmaker who shoots like an exhibitionist and cuts like a censor. *Queen Kelly* is Stroheim uncensored—which is to say, more kinky, because of the effect and implications of the durations, than he probably ever intended it to be.

The fireside seduction scene and the marriage of Kelly to Jan Vooyheid over the figurative and literal corpse of her aunt would probably seem more sentimental and less carnal if they were trimmed down to conventional lengths rather than unnaturally protracted. As they stand, these scenes tend to create an emotional detachment in the spectator by making the actors and settings into purely aesthetic objects, delectable or abhorrent surfaces arranged in such a way that the possibilities of identifying with them or sentimentalizing them are decreased. Considering the *increase* in sentimentality in all Stroheim's films after *Greed*, this is rather a throwback to the dryer, more 'scientific' style of his earlier period, but here it is exercised on a fictional world that is substantially more metaphysical and dreamlike, and less concerned with sociological and psychological matters. *Queen Kelly* is probably the closest thing in the Stroheim canon to an abstract work, a self-enclosed film that secretes its own laws. The sense of transgression that we experience in the previous films is always grounded in morality. Here it seems to come to life as a direct expression of the Id—as when Queen Regina (Seena Owen) beats Kelly with a whip across an enormous hall, down a grand flight of steps and out of the door and the palace—and morality mainly seems to figure in the action like the memory of a bad dream.

Unconsummated lust, a sustaining leitmotiv throughout Stroheim's work—a stalemated struggle reflected in the pull between the nineteenth- and twentieth-century aspects of his art—is finally stretched out into a slow-motion reverie, which is studied as if it were taking place under a microscope. Vooyheid is even seen as an insect, when he appears in the final marriage-and-death sequence comprising the recently discovered 'African' footage: a scarred praying mantis on crutches, with a cigar in his teeth or fist and various objects sticking out of his pockets like additional legs, and a tongue that moves over his lips like a feeler.

He and Kelly stand on opposite sides of the aunt's deathbed; a wedding veil is fashioned out of a bed awning by some local prostitutes. Intercut with close-ups of Kelly in tears are shots of the black priest—who, like her, is dressed in white—from her viewpoint, blurring (to suggest tears) and then turning into an image of Prince Wolfram in white robes; another blur, and the Prince is in a black uniform; still another blur, and we return to the black priest in white. When her aunt expires, Kelly throws herself down on the body; the priest kneels; and then Vooyheid, who is kneeling, slowly raises himself on his crutches until he is the only figure standing. As far as the silent cinema is concerned, this Manichean spectacle constitutes Stroheim's last rites: an arbitrary ending, perhaps—it was certainly not the one he had in mind for *Queen Kelly*—but an appropriately emblematic conclusion nevertheless. With the death of the aunt, we arrive at the imminent loss of innocence and the ascension to power of pure evil—a lurid ellipsis and a suspension of possibilities that were already rather explicit in *Blind Husbands*. But the 'message' is no longer, 'Watch out for him!' It has become, simply, 'Look at him!' And were it not for the somewhat problematical footnote provided by *Hello, Sister!* (1933), one might say that Stroheim's career as a director ends at roughly the same time that virtually all remaining pretence of free will vanishes from his imaginary kingdom.

Even in its mutilated, garbled and partially reshot form, *Hello, Sister!*, the release version of *Walking Down Broadway*, is recognizably Stroheim for a substantial part of its running time. The 'final shooting script' of *Walking Down Broadway*—dated 9/9/32, assigning story and continuity to Stroheim, and dialogue to Stroheim, Leonard Spiegelglass and Geraldine Nomis—helps us to understand some of the original intentions, but also suggests that even in its original state it would have been a minor Stroheim work. The absence of certain

audacities and eccentricities in the release version—which include Mac (Terrance Ray) on a dance floor '[holding] up his middle finger at Jimmy', jokes about Prohibition, and various things relating to Millie (such as her pet turtle Lady Godiva and her dialogue with Miss Platt, a middle-aged hunchback)—is somewhat offset by various banalities which are also missing. The ending of the film that we have is a standard Hollywood clincher, but it is hardly worse than the one prefigured in the script.

Much of the interest in *Hello, Sister!* today derives from the opportunity to see Stroheim recasting many of his most familiar procedures in the context of sound. The repetitious character trait that would have been expressed visually in *The Wedding March*—e.g., Schani spitting—is conveyed here in the dialogue: Mac uses the phrase 'Catch on?' nearly two dozen times in the script, much as Veronika (Françoise Lebrun) continually makes use of *'un maximum'* in the Jean Eustache film, *La Maman et La Putain*. Elsewhere the dialogue often becomes less functional and tends to distract from the visuals. The Southern and New York accents of Peggy (Boots Mallory) and Jimmy (James Dunn) are important aspects of the characters, but their narrative function is not controlled in the way that the actors' visual presences are. When Jimmy provokes Millie's sexual jealousy in a scene near the end by refusing her help ('You're all right, Millie—but you wouldn't understand'), the extraordinary expressiveness of ZaSu Pitts' reaction—the way her eyes flare up at his casual dismissal—is as striking as the close-up of Dale Fuller already alluded to in *Foolish Wives*. (The relationship doesn't stop there: both characters suffer from sexual rejection, and both take revenge by starting fires which provoke the grand finales of both films.) But Pitts' acting in this case becomes the *subtext* of the dialogue rather than vice versa, a classic instance of the way that sound films often teach spectators not to see; the mystery inherent in her character tends to be minimized by the 'explicating' power of the dialogue, and what might have been twice as powerful in a silent context can easily escape attention here.

To some degree, the dialogue in *Hello, Sister!* only makes more explicit some of the schematic simplifications of character and situation that are constants in Stroheim's work, negating some of the openness and the demands on the spectator's imagination imposed by silence. In every silent Stroheim film but *Greed*, the sound of English or American voices invading the continental kingdoms would surely have worked as an alienating factor. *Hello, Sister!*, which relates to *Greed* in many respects (Mac and Jimmy are derived from Mac and Marcus, and even a lottery figures comparably in the *Walking Down Broadway* script), is set in New York, and doesn't have to deal with this problem—indeed, the accents and inflections here are aids to verisimilitude—but at the same time, the screen is no longer quite the *tabula rasa* that it was, and the characteristic Stroheim stare (the trained concentration of the camera on his fictional world) recedes somewhat under the verbiage, which frees us partially from the responsibility of looking.

The major stylistic developments in Stroheim's career took place between *Blind Husbands* and *Foolish Wives*; one can speak of additional developments up to *Greed*, but after that one can principally refer only to certain simplifications and refinements. This is surely characteristic of Hollywood cinema in general, where Howard Hawks can devote a lifetime to refining *Fig Leaves* and *A Girl in Every Port*, and even a director as 'experimental' as Hitchcock is periodically forced to retreat to the formulas of earlier successes. In the case of a maverick like Stroheim, the miracle—apart from his remarkable early development—is not that he was not able to develop his style after *Greed*, but that he was able to make further films at all.

And in order to do so, he clearly had to pay a price. Whether or not future work in sound films would have led to other stylistic developments is impossible to determine; at best, all that *Hello, Sister!* suggests is the desire to accommodate his style to sound rather than to expand its basic options. Considering its relatively small budget, *Blind Husbands* can be seen as another sort of accommodation, and in a sense the evidence of the best in *Hello, Sister!* is comparable: it marks Stroheim as a promising director.

It should be explained that only the first part of *The Wedding March* is now extant.

Although made to be seen as one film, it was cut in two, and the second part, *The Honeymoon*, now lost, began with a 'digest' of the first part. So it is a little difficult to judge the work as it now stands. None the less, I would place it higher than Rosenbaum does in the Stroheim canon, if only for the performances of Fay Wray and ZaSu Pitts.

Although *Queen Kelly* was officially Stroheim's last film as a director, there were rumours that he did direct the big scene in Marcel Cravenne's *Danse de Mort* (1948), a version of the Strindberg play *Dance of Death* in which Stroheim and his wife Denise Vernac played the leads. It certainly looks that way, for this sequence rises above all the others.

Stroheim's career as an actor was quite prolific: *La Grande Illusion* (1937), of course, but also one pleasant French film of the period which his presence made pleasanter, Christian-Jacque's *Les Disparus de St Agil* (1938).

There are many books on von Stroheim: Thomas Quinn Curtis' *Von Stroheim* (1970), Herman G. Weinberg's *Stroheim: A Pictorial Record of His Nine Films* (1975), Jon Barna's *Erich von Stroheim* (1966) and Joel Finler's *Stroheim* (1967). There is also Weinberg's realization, in still form, of the complete *Greed* (1972) and *The Wedding March* (1975).

PRESTON STURGES

Penelope Houston

Preston Sturges (1898–1959) was once billed by his studio, Paramount, as the man who 'writes everything he directs'. The slightly breathless but unarguably exact description perhaps reflects its period. Sturges embarked on film direction at approximately the same time as Orson Welles, and the notion of the film-maker as a universal man (if only on a Hollywood scale) was in the air. Sturges, of course, enjoyed none of those special conditions allowed Welles by the terms of the famous unique RKO contract—privileges which, in any case, were soon to prove for Welles largely illusory. He had to talk Paramount into letting him direct, by offering them the script of *The Great McGinty* (U.K.: *Down Went McGinty*, 1940) for a nominal ten dollars provided that they would allow him to make it himself. But ironically it was Sturges, that *auteur* before the name if not before the fact, who succeeded in creating his own idiosyncratic, independent and obstreperous screen world, taking Hollywood and his audiences for the kind of ride that unseated Welles.

It was not to last. Sturges directed only twelve films, eight of them for Paramount during a period of extreme and resilient activity between 1940 and 1944. He 'wrote everything he directed'; and most of his scripts were originals. Three more films (the uncertain *Mad Wednesday* [originally released as *The Sin of Harold Diddlebock*, 1947] with Harold Lloyd; the fine, flawed *Unfaithfully Yours*, 1948, with Rex Harrison; and the noisy but lacklustre *Beautiful Blonde from Bashful Bend*, 1949, with Betty Grable) followed in the late 40s; the range of the casting perhaps suggests the film-maker's uncertainty about where to settle. There was a long silence, and then in the mid-50s came his last film, *Les Carnets du Major Thompson* (U.K.: *The Diary of Major Thompson*; U.S.: *The French They Are a Funny Race*), with Jack Buchanan as an ageing Englishman abroad. It was sadly, almost defiantly unfunny, as though the mainspring of Sturges' comic timing had snapped, or he had somehow lost contact with the sources of his own energy.

At the height of his career, Sturges was running on some high octane fuel of his own devising. Rumbustious, casual, noisy, intelligent, vibrating with surplus energy, his best films leap plot chasms of improbability and (in 40s terms) impropriety by sheer force of momentum and manic dynamism. Perhaps Sturges became bored with the exercise of his own sleight of hand, or dissatisfied with the self-imposed limits of his work and its ultimate disappointments; or perhaps he simply burnt out his talent. He was other things besides being a screen writer and director. He ran a restaurant; he was a passionate gadgeteer, credited with inventions as various as a library filing system and a vertical take-off aircraft (though how far these devices were taken up, and proved in practice to work, seems not to be a matter of public record). Like John Huston, he leaves an impression of having decided that life should be lived to the fullest. But where Huston has put many of his pleasures and jokes and enthusiasms into his films, Sturges' work

remains in some senses enigmatic, insulated behind a kind of detachment. If he borrowed some of the apparatus and opportunism of 30s fast-moving Hollywood comedy, it was in the darker climate of the 40s.

He learned his trade as a writer during the 30s, and his first original screenplay, for William K. Howard's *The Power and the Glory* (1933), was significantly not a comedy. The film holds a reputation as a kind of precursor to *Citizen Kane*—the somewhat stretched link being that Sturges' script also charts a story of disenchantment and failed promise through a structure of biographical flashbacks. (The studio, seemingly rather overawed, invented for this the word 'narratage', a coinage which happily did not survive.) He was a busy writer in a variety of genres; as Richard Corliss has summarized them in an article in *Cinema*: 'farce (*Hotel Haywire*, 1937), screwball comedy (*Easy Living*, 1937), historical spectacle (*If I Were King*, 1938), light-hearted romance (*Remember the Night*, 1940)'. Corliss also singles out *Diamond Jim* (1935, directed by Edward Sutherland) both as 'pure Sturges' and as a film which carried on the 'eerie portents of *Citizen Kane*'. But if Sturges was, and remained, a writer first and a director second, it was as a director that he gave his own scripts their unique tempo and momentum, and their paradoxical atmosphere of geniality and callousness, sophistication and raucousness, high comedy and underlying unease.

The paradoxes in Sturges' own career began early. He had a decidedly eccentric upbringing at the hands of a mother who sent him to school in Chicago dressed in a Greek tunic and later dragged him on resolutely cultural jaunts around Europe. When Preston was sixteen, she installed him as manager of the Deauville branch of her cosmetics business; and he is said to have rewarded her by devising a kissproof lipstick. The much-married mother (Sturges took the surname of one of his stepfathers, an amiable Chicago businessman) liked to claim descent from the d'Estes, and started her business, the Maison Desti, to market a face cream whose formula she had acquired from another husband, the son of the Turkish Court doctor. She was a friend of Isadora Duncan; and apparently it was she who lent Isadora the fatal scarf.

The pyjama game, I: Henry Fonda and Barbara Stanwyck in *The Lady Eve*.

James Agee, who wrote about Sturges' films with an apprehensive affection, and subjected the film-maker to a curious brand of sustained psychoanalysis in his *Nation* reviews, contended that in defence against his childhood Sturges developed 'a permanently incurable loathing for anything that stank of "culture" ' and 'an all but desperate respect and hunger for success which . . . again assumed the dimensions of a complex'. Of the films Agee wrote: 'They seem to me wonderfully, uncontrollably, almost proudly corrupt, vengeful, fearful of intactness and self-commitment . . . their mastering object, aside from success, seems to be to sail as steep into the wind as possible without for an instant incurring the disaster of becoming seriously, wholly acceptable as art. They seem . . . the elaborately counterpointed image of a neurosis.'

It is not too difficult to understand the nature of Agee's concern, even if it tended to find expression in a slightly nursemaidish insistence that Don't Care should somehow be *made* to care. Part of Sturges' wayward brilliance lay in an instinct for evasion and a battery of self-defensive tactics. He appears to have allowed a plot to handcuff him and tie him down; he seems to have reached the moment when he must reward Agee by turning serious. And then there's a great convulsion, and Houdini/Sturges is free again—free, and as a rule laughing, and perhaps betraying something in the act.

The last reels of Sturges' pictures consequently add up to a whole series of *volte-faces*, usually designed to reward the characters on their own terms. *The Palm Beach Story* (1942), for instance, is a romantic comedy about a wife (Claudette Colbert) on the run from her loving husband. On the train to Florida she encounters, by stepping firmly on his face, one of the most engaging characters Sturges ever invented. This is Hackensacker III (Rudy Vallee), a wistful, melancholy millionaire, whose generous impulses are always being curbed by some vestigial family instinct for keeping a watch on his small change. His days are spent in recording (but not adding up: that would be pointless) his tips and taxi-fares in a little notebook. While Miss Colbert looks greedily on, he gravely weighs up the merits of the fifty cent or the seventy-five cent breakfast. Peering out from behind the towering barricades of his money, he sadly notes, 'One of the tragedies of this life: that the men who are most in need of a beating are always enormous.' Sturges uses him cruelly. Hackensacker's serenading of the heroine, with full orchestra stationed in the garden, is the occasion for her romantic reconciliation with her husband. But the last sequence relents. Wife and husband produce an identical twin sister and brother (one for Hackensacker; one for his sister, Mary Astor), so that everyone gets what he thinks he wants.

What so exasperated Agee was Sturges' extension of this sprightly opportunism into less frivolous areas. The supremely equivocal ending of *Hail the Conquering Hero* (1944) is a case in point. Here, at the height of the war, Sturges had the temerity to question such things as mother love, the U.S. Marines and the respect paid by civilians to the combat veteran. The leading character is Woodrow Truesmith, son of a First World War hero, and brought up to venerate the Marines above all else. When he is discharged from the Corps because of hay fever, he is so scared of telling his mother that he takes a job in a shipyard and pretends to be on overseas service. Six Marines, one of them suffering from the most pronounced mother complex on record, befriend Woodrow and take him home. Hideously, they find that the town has arranged a hero's welcome, with four competing bands to greet him. Worse still, the solid citizens insist on drafting Woodrow as their candidate for mayor. His final confession brings the town baying after him like a lynch mob. But they only *look* like a lynch mob: in fact they love him more than ever, and deliriously acclaim their truthful mayor.

This ending has been interpreted as a really catastrophic sell-out, a sentimental triumph for Mother and the Marines. Or, equally validly, since the scenes are shot both with and against the grain of their content, it has been seen as an expression of a basic contempt. There is no pretence that a town which would elect poor, blundering Woodrow is anything but out of its mind; and consequently this is only a happy ending if you think it is. Woodrow certainly thinks so, and Sturges enjoys rewarding his heroes far beyond their just deserts, but up to the level of their dreams. His films fade out into a series of Cheshire cat grins. And maybe some of the grin is at the thought of the morning after: the moment, for instance, when the town wakes up to find it has landed itself with Woodrow.

Somewhat later, in *Unfaithfully Yours*, Sturges was still playing the same equivocal game. Rex Harrison in this darkling, pessimistic comedy plays an irascible orchestra conductor, English and epigrammatic, who decides on evidence which even Othello might have thought flimsy that his beloved wife is deceiving him. During an evening's concert, the moods of the music suggest assorted ways of dealing with the situation, from a devilishly cunning murder plot to noble forgiveness. In reality, later in the evening, all his plans become jumbled and all go farcically astray. Sturges, playing with and on the picture's changing moods, camouflages some essential frailties in the script with a beguiling attention to minor characters (Rudy Vallee again, as an even starchier example of the semi-fossilized millionaire; Edgar Kennedy as a melancholic, music-mad private eye). But again he has to end the picture; and his conductor, who has been allowed along the way to descend to the buffoonery of slapstick, emerges to a loving reconciliation. The wife's explanation is really almost as thin as the original damning 'evidence'. And perhaps that is Sturges' point. Othello wills his own jealousy. Subject him to the harassments of farce rather than those of melodrama, and he can decide that it's easier to trust his marriage. But nothing has really changed. The conclusion is rather less glib than Sturges, 'fearful of intactness', allows it to look.

Agee thought that Sturges' childhood had a lot to answer for. But if one follows him in this risky attempt to define an artist in terms of his upbringing, one might find other clues. Sturges was born in 1898, and his European exposure to hated 'culture' was acquired between about 1906 and 1914. It becomes tempting, in the light of these dates, to see it

The pyjama game, II: Veronica Lake and Joel McCrea in *Sullivan's Travels*.

all as one of those great Jamesian expeditions, innocence in search of the betrayal of experience. Take it back a little further in time and you have the perfect image: young Preston matched against the bored little boy in *Daisy Miller* who says so crossly, 'My father ain't in Europe; he's in a better place than Europe'—Schenectady, not Heaven.

In any case, several things seem to stand out from Sturges' films. Although only two of them (those starring Eddie Bracken) are actually set in the classic American small town, one's overriding impression is of this genial, comfortable, more than slightly ridiculous small town world. In *Sullivan's Travels* (1941), Sturges even made Hollywood look conspicuously more run down and homely than one usually sees it. Partly this may be due to his company of small part actors, who all seem to know each other so

well, and to make such allowances for each others' quirks, that they travel from film to film like a collection of indulgent, gossiping neighbours. But the Sturges town itself belongs to some period earlier than the 40s: it is like some childhood recollection brought hazily to life on the Paramount lot, as though in his ideas of America Sturges had somehow skipped a generation.

Paradoxically, it is this time-lag, this feeling that Griffith's idyllic Americana has somehow got cluttered up with juke-boxes, lunch-counters, 40s hair styles and Betty Hutton, that makes Sturges' films seem so dateless. Eddie Bracken, the tormented innocent of *Hail the Conquering Hero* and *The Miracle of Morgan's Creek* (1944), is more naïve than any 40s character has a right to be; but he is, in his wistful determination to do the right thing, very like someone out of a silent comedy. Even Sturges' language, with its mixture of slang, repetition, gibbering hesitations and entirely formal turns of speech, is quite timeless. Above all the racket of his films, voices can be heard talking in the relaxed, balanced aphorisms of classic English comedy. 'Let us be crooked but never common' is the motto of the con-man in *The Lady Eve* (1941). 'Chivalry is not only dead, it is decomposed,' laments Hackensacker III. 'Rich people, and theorists are usually rich people, think of poverty only in the negative,' says the butler of *Sullivan's Travels*. 'The poor know all about poverty, and only the morbid rich would find it glamorous.'

It is this timelessness which seems to give the films their free-wheeling assurance and conjuror's freedom of action. The links with reality are deliberately kept tenuous. Take, for instance, *The Miracle of Morgan's Creek*. The film's heroine, Gertrude Kockenlocker (Betty Hutton), is the volatile daughter of the local policeman, who contrives during one night to meet, marry, become pregnant by, and irrevocably mislay a soldier about whom she remembers only that his name may have been something like Ratsky-Watsky. (Only in a Sturges film could one find a family named Kockenlocker gravely debating whether someone else could possibly be called Ratsky-Watsky.) Norval Jones (Eddie Bracken), already pining for the military glory that eluded him in *Hail the Conquering Hero*, is summoned to the rescue. Dressed in a borrowed 1914 uniform, like some lunatic fugitive from Chaplin's *Shoulder Arms*, he gallantly sets out to provide Trudy with a marriage licence in the name of Ratsky-Watsky. Arrest; wild confusion, wonderfully absurd mock jail-break, with constable Kockenlocker (William Demarest) doing everything but order Norval out of his jail, and the incurably right-minded Norval refusing to see that he is being invited to escape. Then comes one of Sturges' more disconcerting sentimental interludes, with Kockenlocker banging crossly away at a Christmas tree star but pausing to remind Trudy, very seriously, of the stable in Bethlehem. And then the pandemonium of the ending, with Trudy producing sextuplets, bedlam in the hospital, and headlines ('Canada Protests', 'Hitler Demands Recount') flashing on and off.

The 'miracle' is frantic, absurd and actually rather touching, and it lets Sturges play his favourite game of flinging a film into such total chaos, as though all the characters were being swept off their feet by a tidal wave, that he can get away with practically anything. In *The Miracle of Morgan's Creek* he employs most, if not quite all, of his range of moods; and each of them, from tenderness to irascibility, the cantankerous comedy of small town humours to the ricocheting absurdity of farce, remains valid for precisely as long as it lasts on the screen. At the centre of it all, the film's anchor man, is the rock-solid figure of William Demarest, a gallant Puritan who doesn't see why his daughter should want to go out with soldiers, and who insists on standing no nonsense until nonsense overwhelms him.

By the end, nobody on or off screen is encouraged to remember that Norval is not the father of the sextuplets, and that the final masquerade is the most painfully ludicrous he has been asked to endure. This, too, is characteristic. If there is one consistent element running through Sturges' films, it is a view of life as some gigantic game of false pretences. In his first film, *The Great McGinty* (originally written seven years before he filmed it), the hero is a tramp (Brian Donlevy) who ingratiates himself with the boss of a political machine by voting some forty times, at two dollars a time, in a local election. Under the boss's patronage he finally achieves the Governor's mansion. Marriage to a charming prig, however, has undermined him, and it is the rogue's attempt to play the honest man that brings about his downfall. In *Christmas in July* (1940), a young clerk is tricked into believing that he has won $25,000 in a coffee company's slogan competition. (His terrible slogan—'If you can't sleep, it isn't the coffee, it's the bunk'—is repeated so insistently, and in so many contexts, that it acquires all the maddening force of an incantation.) This supposed success changes his life: he becomes the sort of man who wins $25,000. And the Sturges twist, after the trick has been revealed and he is left in the débris of his imaginary fortune, is that he wins the contest after all.

Right you are if *they* think you are: that seems the fairly explicit point of all these masquerades. A tramp becomes state governor; a booby is elected mayor; a girl's life changes (in *Easy Living*, one of the 30s scripts) when she acquires a fur coat and finds everyone expecting her to live up to it. Likeable buffoons are whirled into fantastic impostures, survive them in a state of quaking terror, and usually come out on top. But Sturges, unlike Capra, never uses his barnstorming finales as a means of suggesting that guileless virtue may defeat entrenched corruption. In his films, the victory is more likely to go to plain human silliness and gullibility; and that, presumably, is what a good liberal like James Agee couldn't stand. In one biting comment he called Sturges a coward, a snob and a cynic. But you can't accuse a man of lacking the courage of his convictions, when his main conviction would seem to have been that in this game of masquerade and false pretences anyone can win.

In an excellent article on Sturges (*Film Culture*, Fall 1962), Manny Farber and W. S. Poster comment that, 'The first impression one gets from a Sturges movie is that of the inside of a Ford assembly line smashed together and operating during a total war crisis.' This very American comparison comes in the context of an article which sees Sturges' work as 'an extreme embodiment of the American success dream' and analyses his suspect cynicism as 'the highly self-conscious philosophy of the hack'. It makes a useful antidote to Agee's reproaches and a more sophisticated approach to the problem of coping with Sturges' equivocations. As for the speed and confusion that make up the surface of a Sturges film, I would choose a more European comparison. To me the impression is rather of an old-fashioned coach business adapting itself in a flurry of urgent incompetence to the demands of the motor car, while a collection of cross-grained Dickensian minor characters stand grumbling in corners, convinced that no good will come of anything if they haven't personally approved it.

Never less than middle-aged, sometimes seeming almost dangerously advanced towards senility, the stalwarts of the Sturges stock company show a marvellous capacity to stand the pace. There is Raymond Walburn, the proud embodiment of inane gravity, forever rehearsing his acceptance speech as mayor, or realizing with horror that he has just given away $25,000 to a total stranger; little Jimmy Conlin, the tiny, spectacled old man, usually bouncing between two larger figures, like a Highland terrier warding off two German shepherds. Robert Greig, the butler frozen in eternal disapproval of his delinquent employers; Franklin Pangborn, of the despairing gestures and prim manner; Torben Meyer, glittering of eye and wild of accent; Georgia Caine, beaming mother or flirtatious widow.

Many of them turn up among the members of the Ale and Quail Club, that immortal group of ageing sportsmen encountered by Claudette Colbert in *The Palm Beach Story*. With timid gallantry, and a proper show of decorum on both sides, they buy her train ticket. But the excitement of the occasion overcomes them. Soon the sporting guns are out, chaos rages up and down the train as the howling dogs are released from the luggage van, a posse of Pullman attendants moves in with reproachful cries of 'Misdemeanour' (on such occasions Sturges' vocabulary could be matchlessly precise), and the great American clubmen, still shooting up the night, are abandoned in a railway siding. Their creator seems sorry to see them go; and his affection for these rich, battered relics, cast up on the further shores of middle age, is extended to almost all his minor characters. They are old and odd, spry and bumbling, firmly entrenched in their own concerns and—when not reduced to helpless speechlessness—given to a fierce articulateness. They form an American chorus, standing by while the hero falls, actually even more than metaphorically, over his own feet.

Sturges had an ingrained weakness for slapstick, perhaps in itself part of a feeling for a lost movie past. In *Unfaithfully Yours*, the urbane Rex Harrison lumbers about a wrecked hotel room, stepping solemnly through the bottoms of chairs. Most Sturges heroes have some difficulty in keeping their balance; and in *The Lady Eve*, that brilliant and guileful comedy in which Henry Fonda's placid love affair with a snake is interrupted by the appearance of Barbara Stanwyck, a cool card-sharp of the transatlantic liners, Fonda can hardly cross a room without bringing a waiter, a curtain or a plateful of food crashing to the ground. Fonda here is a younger Hackensacker, rich and prim and

The pyjama game, III: Joel McCrea and Claudette Colbert in *The Palm Beach Story*.

defencelessly conventional. In the company of the serpentine Miss Stanwyck, his physical and mental equilibrium are equally at risk. But in using actors like Fonda and Harrison, who lack the physical resilience of true clowns and become increasingly woe-begone in circumstances of slapstick, Sturges was showing his odd imperviousness—callousness, an enjoyment of indignity, or simply a stubborn devotion to the basic banana-skin joke.

The slapstick, while slowing the films down, perhaps finds a paradoxical justification in the speed that surrounds it. 'A Capra, Wilder or Wellman takes half a movie to get a plot to the point where the audience accepts it and it comes to cinematic life. Sturges often accomplishes as much in the first two minutes,' wrote Manny Farber in the article already quoted. He could even achieve it

before the movie starts at all, as in the action that goes on behind the credit titles of *The Palm Beach Story*. Here bride and groom hurtle in disarray towards the altar; a maid keeps fainting dead away at the telephone; and the effect is of action that could sustain the average comedy for a good half-hour compressed into two absurd, lightning minutes. Sturges wasn't a particularly inventive film-maker: he liked to keep a scene in medium two-shot, moving into close-up on key dialogue; his settings did their job, but they seldom strike the eye. But he knew everything about comic timing, and how to play a scene so that the impression is of unfaltering action, a flow of bustling, breathless movement which seems to be held just on the point where it threatens to break out of the frame. Sheer speed was one of his several defences: it left behind any need for consistency of attitude or steadiness of satirical gaze. There was one film, however, in which he was nearer than usual to coming out into the open: *Sullivan's Travels.*

It opens in Sturges' most allusive and involving style, with a fight between two men on the roof of a speeding train. Almost immediately, up comes an end title. We are in a Hollywood viewing theatre, watching the latest film of a comedy director making a more or less desperate effort to go straight; and the fight, as he angrily explains, is symbolic of Capital versus Labour. Sullivan (Joel McCrea) wants to film a novel called 'Brother, Where Art Thou?', while the studio bosses ask only for a repetition of 'Hey, Hey in the Hayloft' or 'Ants in Their Pants of 1939'. Goaded by their insistence that he doesn't know the meaning of poverty, Sullivan borrows a tramp outfit from the wardrobe department and takes to the road. Behind him, at a barely discreet distance, creeps a vast studio bus, with doctor, chef, secretary, bodyguard and publicity men, under orders to watch over the great director.

It is a wonderfully succinct opening, and it leads into a series of absurd adventures, as Sullivan tries vainly to break away from Hollywood. Running away from two over-kindly ladies whose liking for having a man about the house verges on the alarming, he gets a lift straight back to his starting point. Here he picks up Veronica Lake, coolest and quietest of the Sturges heroines, as a failed actress who can think of no greater present than an introduction to Lubitsch. 'There's nothing like a deep-dish movie for driving you out into the open,' she insists, as Sullivan tries to tell her that in a suffering world a director ought not to be making 'Ants in Their Pants of 1941'. Together they set off to sample poverty, first getting the butler to check with the booking-office where a tramp might properly be expected to board a freight train.

Slowly, Sturges begins to modulate the film's tone. The rich boy's search for the poor no longer seems quite so ludicrous; and it becomes something different when Sullivan is robbed in a freight yard, attacks a railway policeman and winds up in a Southern chain gang. Again, the point is one of identity—of who other people think you are.

Once Sullivan is recognized, he could have hit ten policemen and no one would keep him locked up. In the meantime, however, Sturges has put everything he knows (and a curious everything it is) into the theatrical, fanciful, maddening and effective staging of his key scene. As a treat, the convicts are taken to a film show in a black church hall, where the minister instructs his ragged congregation on their welcome to those 'less fortunate than we are'. Through the mists around the hall, the men advance to a grim rhythm of clanking chains. Inside, they and the blacks join in wild laughter at a Disney cartoon. Back in Hollywood, Sullivan confounds his bosses: he now knows that he wants to make people laugh.

As a comedy director's apologia, this is notably unconvincing—for the reason that any director who went into comedy with a sense of mission would probably make some terrible movies, and that Sturges' picture of the 'serious' alternative is ludicrous in 1941 or at any other time. And even at its face value, the scene of the laughing convicts has a kind of hysteria, a convulsive agony of mirth. Was Sturges here showing us the heart Agee suspected he didn't have? Or was he simply playing with an idea, and barnstorming it through when it got too hot to handle? Because Sturges was the great equivocator, we never quite trust him. He allows the moment to create its own logic; and is off again before we can pin him down.

In its details, *Sullivan's Travels* is beautifully organized: the gossiping studio staff, boxed up in their absurd bus; Sullivan's two butlers, so deeply shocked by the whole adventure; his terrible wife, laying flowers on his supposed grave with a gesture of frozen boredom; Jimmy Conlin, the trusty in the labour camp determined to get the recalcitrant Sullivan to the picture show— these are all among Sturges' best inventions. And the feeling of movement, of freight trains trundling through the night, makes this a very specifically American adventure.

When it came to the point, however, Sturges didn't know what to do with the poor. He sentimentalizes them, as Sullivan and the girl wander among the down-and-outs, and at the same time he is scared of them. He doesn't want to get too close; and so he falls back on mist, distance and roman-

tic music, with only the publicity cameraman, busily recording Sullivan's progress
from a vantage point in a tree, to hold the
film in contact with its satiric intention.
Faced with something extremely simple to
put across—the real thing, as opposed to Sullivan's hopelessly romanticized view of it—
his machinery of expression simply collapsed
under him.

It is an interesting collapse, because it
seems to reveal Sturges face to face with his
own limitations. His defences were built up
in depth, and his favourite approach was the
oblique and glancing one, with all the
retreats into burlesque left open. The world
of his comedy is self-contained and self-
protected, and he becomes ill at ease when
confronted with an idea to be followed
straight through, or a situation that can't be
resolved in an explosion of nervous energy.
Yet for a man who is supposed to have
thought only of success, he was extraordinarily preoccupied with the byways of failure,
with age and decay, and the wistful realization of their own uselessness that suddenly
assails his most sympathetic characters. His
films are sometimes nearly serious, and
usually wildly funny. They are sceptical and
distrustful of the foolishness and gullibility
of the many, while indulgently genial to
individual follies. Perhaps the key scene in a
Sturges movie is an earlier one in *Sullivan's
Travels*, where the director goes to another
rural picture show. There are the howling
babies, popcorn-chewing children, snoring
farmers, all the tired and apathetic and misty
faces. And among them the Hollywood aristocrat, dressed in a borrowed suit of clothes,
confronting the audience, the massive uncon-
cern of other people.

**For further reading, see *The Fabulous Life
and Times of Preston Sturges: An American Dreamer* (1973), by James Ursini.
Richard Corliss' *The Hollywood Screenwriters* (1972) contains a long article by
Andrew Sarris on Sturges as scriptwriter.
Finally there is the Manny Farber essay,
collected in *Negative Space* (1971), and the
Agee pieces in *Agee on Film*, Vol. I (1960).**

SWISS CINEMA

James Monaco

The history of Swiss film prior to 1965 is the
history of an art struggling to be born. The
first Swiss feature film, *Le Pauvre Village*, by
Jacques Béranger, dates from 1921. By that
time a tradition had already been established
which found a wealth of cinematic metaphor
in the scenic splendour of Swiss landscapes;
and location photography, often accompanied by a strong sense of documentary
realism, has marked the particular nature of
Swiss cinema.

During the 20s and 30s, production levels
were minimal, but the advent of the Second
World War gave a much-needed boost to the
Swiss film industry. The closing of the
borders to imports provided a strongly
motivated native audience for the first time,
and the presence of exiles, especially in
Zurich, gave a useful infusion of talent. During
the war, Swiss film production reached a
level of ten to fifteen features per year. But
when the war ended the exiles departed and
Zurich production retrenched, concentrating
on documentaries and industrial films.

During this twenty-five-year period several
film-makers established important reputations within the borders of Switzerland,
if not outside them. Charles-Georges Du-
vanel (born 1906) was one of the early
pioneers in documentary realism. Jean
Choux (1887–1946) began his career in 1925
with a French-influenced production, *La
Vocation d'André Carrel*, which starred a
then unknown actor named Michel Simon.
Leopold Lindtberg (born 1902, Vienna) is
probably the best known of the German
exiles who worked in Switzerland. His films,
including *Marie-Louise* (1944) and *Die Letzte
Chance* (*The Last Chance*, 1945, winner of
the *Palme d'or* at Cannes in 1947), were
among the first Swiss productions to achieve
international success. Hans Trommer (born
1904) and Valerian Schmidely (born 1909 in
St Petersburg) were responsible for *Romeo
und Julia auf dem Dorfe* (also known as
Roméo et Juliette au Village, 1941), long
considered the best Swiss fiction film of this
period.

The 50s and early 60s were gloomy years
for Swiss film, brightened only by the inter-

national success of *Heidi* (1952). Several factors combined to retard the development of a national cinema. The multilingual nature of Swiss culture meant that native audiences for French- or German-language Swiss films were so small as to be uneconomical, a fact reinforced by the dominance of American, French and German films in the Swiss market. While Swiss-Romand films might have found a market in France and elsewhere, the close cultural ties between France and the French-speaking part of Switzerland also meant that native talent could be siphoned off. (Michel Simon is the prime example.) The German-speaking majority, on the other hand, had the handicap of a strong dialect which made their films very much less attractive for export.

It was not until 1962, when the Swiss government passed a subsidy law which provided seed money for the Swiss film industry, that the situation significantly improved. (This plan was considerably augmented in 1970, a year which marked another quantum leap in Swiss film history.) Also important to the continued health of Swiss film has been the financial participation of Swiss television, SSR. In 1968 Alain Tanner (born 1929) and Claude Goretta (born 1929), who had known each other since their youth and who had had long apprenticeships, first in London (they co-directed the documentary short *Nice Time* in 1957), then in Geneva, where they each worked in television and documentaries and formed the *Groupe Cinq* together with Michel Soutter (born 1932), Jean-Louis Roy (born 1938) and Jean-Jacques Lagrange (born 1929). Not strictly a production company, *Groupe Cinq* gave the five directors a corporate identity with which to deal with SSR. The films they made under their agreement with the network mark the real beginning of the Swiss renaissance. Yves Gasser's production company, Citel Films, has also been an important haven for French-speaking Swiss filmmakers; in recent years co-production with French companies has proved a valuable source of capital.

Of the members of *Groupe Cinq*, Alain Tanner is by far the best known outside Switzerland. *Charles, Mort ou Vif* (Charles *Dead or Alive*, 1969) was the first Swiss film in twenty years to gain wide circulation

abroad. *La Salamandre* (1971) was the first native box-office success within the country. *Retour d'Afrique* (*Return from Africa*) followed in 1973, and the next year Tanner completed *Le Milieu du Monde*, generally regarded as the most successful of the Swiss 'New Wave' films until now. In each of these films Tanner was searching for a way to describe a *modus vivendi* which is profoundly Swiss but which is clearly relevant for non-Swiss people. Like Soutter and Goretta, Tanner uses landscape as a correlative for the spiritual states of his characters. In this sense his films are highly structural. In *Charles, Mort ou Vif* Charles, a middle-aged watch company executive, suddenly rejects his life, dropping out into an idyllic relationship with a sign painter and his mistress in the country. In *Retour d'Afrique* a young couple, Vincent and Françoise, decide to move to Algeria but are prevented from doing so. They remain in Geneva, but the city becomes their own private dark continent. In *Le Milieu du Monde* (co-scripted, like *La Salamandre*, by John Berger) Tanner constructs his most ambitious structural parable. Set in the great watershed between North and South Europe, the film describes a number of polarities in geographic terms: working class *v.* middle class, male *v.* female, politics *v.* existence. In addition, Tanner for the first time clearly develops a dialectic tension between the style of the film and its materials. The *mise en scène* is a strict, quasi-Brechtian set of long shots: 'a hundred little short films, each done in one take', according to Tanner. This approach was foreshadowed in *La Salamandre*, in which a fiction writer and a journalist confront the central character, Rosemonde, from differing perspectives. All Tanner's films have a political ground-base, but increasingly he sees the real politics of a film not in its subject matter but in the relationship it has with its audience. 'I felt very strongly,' he explains, 'that it was a little facile just to put good revolutionary phrases in the characters' mouths and be satisfied and maybe have a good laugh. So I then decided to shift the work of politics in a film, to put it in the *shape* of the film rather than the subject matter.' Looked at in this way, Tanner's cinema is reminiscent of Godard, if altogether more practical. *Le Milieu du Monde* is, in addition, a simple love story. But it is set in 'a time of normalization, where exchange is permitted and nothing changes'. Thus Tanner makes the Swiss experience serve more general purposes.

The films of Claude Goretta share Tanner's characteristic wit, but Goretta's sense of humour is shaggier. *L'Invitation* (*The Invitation*, 1972) is a mild-mannered, gently humorous essay in manners which gives us a garden party not unlike *The Exterminating Angel*. *Pas si Méchant que ça* (U.K.: *Not as Wicked as All That*; U.S.: *The Wonderful Crook*, 1975) tells the story of a pleasantly dumb young man who finds himself in control of the family furniture company with no sense whatsoever of how to run it at a profit. In order to pay his employees he takes to robbing banks and post offices. In the end he is caught, but the police allow him first to finish his role in a sketch he is performing for children: William Tell.

More intriguing perhaps than Goretta's quietly introspective tales are the disturbing, slightly surrealist essays of Michel Sout-

ter. In Soutter's films (*La Lune avec les dents*, 1966; *Haschisch*, 1968; *La Pomme*, 1969; *James ou pas*, 1970; *Les Arpenteurs*, 1972; *L'Escapade*, 1973) we are confronted with a mélange of half-told stories. Disparate characters encounter one another; each carries with him his own separate reality. Soutter is fascinated by the intersections of these various worlds. Behavioural patterns are seen as elements of a geography of the soul and compared directly with physical settings which often seem to have a stronger sense of themselves than the characters. Of special interest in this respect is *L'Escapade*, the most assured and carefully controlled of Soutter's films to date.

It should be noted that the Swiss film renaissance is not entirely a matter of directors. Actors (François Simon, Jean-Luc Bideau, Jacques Denis, Jean Champion, Michel Robin) and technicians (Renato Berta, Simon Edelstein, Joële van Effenterre) have made exceptional contributions to the films' success.

Miou-Miou in Alain Tanner's *Jonah Who Will Be 25 in the Year 2000*.

Isabelle Huppert and Yves Beneyton in Claude Goretta's *The Lacemaker*.

In German-speaking Switzerland the effects of the new, more productive financial arrangements have taken longer to be felt. The German Swiss director who has so far received most attention abroad, Daniel Schmid (born 1941), is ironically more closely associated with the Munich group, and his work is not representative of the Zurich scene. *Heute Nacht oder Nie* (*Tonight or Never*, 1972) and *La Paloma* (1974) align themselves with the hyper-kitsch aesthetic associated with the young German directors Schroeter and Fassbinder.

More in line with general developments in German-speaking Switzerland are the films of Peter von Gunten (born 1941) and Thomas Koerfer (born 1944). *Die Auslieferung* (1973) by von Gunten and *Der Tod des Flohzirkusdirektors* (*The Death of a Flea Circus Director*, 1973) and *Der Gehülfe* (*The Assistant*, 1976) by Koerfer have all been seen at festivals outside Switzerland. Like most of their German-speaking colleagues, these two directors spent long apprenticeships turning out short films and documentaries with a strong political basis, and their cinematic styles inevitably show this background as well as the generalized influence of Brecht. Also of interest among the Zurich group is Peter Ammann (born 1931), whose *Le Train Rouge* (*The Red Train*, 1973) manages to combine a documentary about Italian workers in Switzerland with a variety of versions of the William Tell legend; Markus Imhoof (born 1941), whose *Fluchtgefahr* has had some exposure abroad; Richard Dindo (born 1944), best known for his short, *Naive Maler in der Ostschweiz* (1973) and a feature, *Schweizer in Spanien* (1974); and Georg C. Radanowicz (born 1939), whose *Alfred R., ein Leben und ein Film* (1972) proved an interesting experiment.

Other Swiss-Romand directors who show promise include: Yvan Butler, a television reporter whose first feature was *La Fille au violoncelle* (*The Girl with the Cello*, 1973);

Claude Champion (born 1942), a documentarist best known for *Le Pays de mon corps* (1973); Simon Edelstein (born 1942), a cinematographer whose first film as a director was *Les Vilaines Manières* (1973); Bertrand van Effenterre (*Erica Minor*, 1973); Yves Yersin, *Die Letzten Heimposamenter* (*The Last Home Lace-makers*, 1973); Jean-Jacques Lagrange (born 1929), an original member of Groupe Cinq who has preferred to work in television; Jean-Louis Roy (born 1938), another original member of Groupe Cinq: *L'Inconnu de Shandigor* (1967), *Black-Out* (1970); and Jacques Sandoz (born 1942): *Stella da Falla* (1972).

Italian-speaking Switzerland is also represented in the renaissance: Bruno Soldini (born 1939) directed *Storia di Confine* (1972).

The most important recent event in the Swiss cinema has been Alain Tanner's *Jonas qui aura 25 ans en l'an 2,000* (*Jonah Who Will Be 25 in the Year 2000*, 1976), which many consider to be his finest film. It is a political comedy about eight people, including a teacher, a supermarket cashier, a farmer and a gambler; all veterans of '68, each of them has tried to find a solution to his dissatisfaction with society. For one of the women, Tantra is the answer (sex upside down fertilizes the brain); others go into ecology or consumerism. Tanner has so lovingly and vividly portrayed his characters that, as with early Renoir, one comes out of the cinema having made eight new friends. The script of this film, as of Tanner's best earlier work, was by John Berger: obviously they make a good combination.

The greatest *cause célèbre* has been Daniel Schmid's *Schatten der Engel* (*Shadows of Angels*, 1976). Co-scripted by R. W. Fassbinder, the film has even been ascribed to him. The controversy lay in the character of the 'rich Jew': many felt, quite wrongly to my mind, that this made the film anti-Semitic. It wasn't, but it wasn't a very good film either. Schmid laughingly referred to it as his first 'talkie', but in fact the script, with its endless dialogue, seemed too much for him to handle. It lacked all the mysterious, almost silent film enchantment of his earlier *La Paloma* and *Tonight or Never*.

There is a monograph by Freddy Buache, in French, on Schmid: *Portrait de Daniel Schmid en Magicien* (Lausanne, 1975). See also M. Boujut's *Le Milieu du Monde ou le Cinéma selon Tanner* (1974), and the same author's *L'Escapade ou le Cinéma selon Soutter* (1974). For a general survey, there is Freddy Buache's *Le Cinéma Suisse* (1974).

One should mention here, for the record, that Jean-Luc Godard was raised half-way between Lausanne and Geneva, in Nyon, Switzerland. One thinks of him as a French director, but his two first shorts were in fact made in Switzerland, and his second feature, *Le Petit Soldat*, is set in Geneva. In recent years, after leaving Paris, he shuttled between his new home in Grenoble and nearby Switzerland. And in 1977, he returned (for good?) to Switzerland.

1977 also saw the triumph of Claude Goretta with *La Dentellière*, which proved (for those who had not already been convinced by *Pas si Méchant que ça*) that he was much more than a director of good-natured little comedies. Starring Isabelle Huppert—and, in Goretta's hands, she proved herself a great actress—the film deals with the tragedy of a relationship between a bright young student (Yves Beneyton) and an inarticulate but sensitive and intelligent beauty parlour assistant. Like Chekhov, and like Ozu, Goretta treats here an 'everyday' tragedy delicately but forcefully, and gives moving expression to the 'tears of things'—*lacrimae rerum*, as the Romans called it, or *mono no aware* in the Japanese phrase.

JACQUES TATI

Jean-André Fieschi

The strange career of Jacques Tati (born 1908)—five films in almost twenty-five years—is original in two contexts: within that of French cinema, where only Vigo and Bresson can be compared to him, and within 'comic' cinema where his only antecedents, the white, moon-struck clowns (Keaton, Langdon, Laurel), only serve to reveal how much he differs from them, and how marginal and eccentric Tati's position is.

In truth, Tati's place is among the 'constructors', among those who above all were concerned with structural play, whose interest in structure imperatively commands each figurative element and assembles them in perfect constructions; where apparent, even clearly indicated, structure is not the skeleton of a formal discourse, but rather the discourse itself: similar to Fritz Lang in the early *Mabuse* or *Spione*, Bresson in *Pickpocket* and *Le procès de Jeanne d'Arc*, Antonioni in *Cronaca di un Amore*; today, certainly, to Jean-Marie Straub and Miklós Jancsó.

Such an enumeration, referring to otherwise irreconcilable aesthetics and ideologies, merely indicates that Tati belongs to a family of systematic film-makers, where every work is the sum of a series of strongly marked commitments, whether opposed to, or behind, or in advance of the dominant cinema of their contemporaries.

This relationship points to the most important paradox in his work: the list of other directors indicates a cerebral, restrained kind of cinema, one often accused of being abstruse or avant-garde. Whereas Tati seems, even at the cost of some favourable misunderstanding, to be the emblem of a kind of cinema which, if not really popular, is at least more innocent.

To bring forward some of Tati's own statements is no help at all. Not that he doesn't know what he is doing, or how good it is. In all his statements a kind of artisan's pride can be seen. Moreover he confesses both to being isolated and to being stubborn in the pursuit of his chosen ends. Dreyer and Sternberg similarly affirmed their marginality, the former with humility, the latter with pride. Similarly they produced minuscule arguments or sweeping generalizations, referring to banal or worn-out ideologies, always insufficient to deal with the power of their achievements—which doubtless they were not able to explain.

In Tati's case this ideology is all the more deceptive in as much as each time he articulates it, it represents the classic world vision of the *petite bourgeoisie française* (that of the films of René Clair), flattering and catering to the most suspicious sort of individualism, the most maudlin sentimentality, the little *bistrot*, the little dog, facile nostalgia, bewilderment when confronted with a modern world fundamentally not understood and with which such an ideology cannot cope, deprived as it seems to be of its symbolic attributes and references. But what Tati says, what his films say, cannot be flattened out into a simple and banalized discourse, bearing an unambiguous message highlighting a mildly zany character and a mere way of smiling.

To reduce thus *Les Vacances de M. Hulot* (*Monsieur Hulot's Holiday*, 1952), *Playtime*

(1967) and *Trafic* (*Traffic*, 1971) (three masterpieces among five films) to rather brief exercises in the line of a reactionary ideology, weakly critical, crystallizing a petit-bourgeois conscience baffled by the modern world, would be to see and understand nothing at all. Not that it is necessary to deny altogether the obsessive, programmatic presence of a kind of cheap, nostalgic music, sometimes even taking over altogether. *Mon Oncle* (*My Uncle*, 1958), for instance, thus lost all its edge to such a degree that it seems like a parody of its director's bad qualities. But the three films cited above—each in its own way —are such a new kind of cinema, so quietly audacious, so far removed from traditional dominant dramatic and plastic strategies that the only way one can see them merely in terms of Tati's humanistic presuppositions is either by refusing to look at them carefully or by distorting their essential nature.

In fact Tati achieves a totally original balance between tradition and innovation. The extreme linearity of the argument is traditional, belonging to the oldest burlesque traditions. This argument is often reduced to little more than a succession of moments, of blocks capable of supporting and permitting the specific variations which we call gags. The formal structure is also traditional (cf. Keaton again, Langdon, Laurel and Hardy) in its free, not to say relaxed appearance, yet so strongly restrictive, rigorous yet unforeseeable, logical yet surely arising from a logic more musical than literary.

Two enormous breaks divide these modest and vital works marking two turning points in contemporary cinema. *Monsieur Hulot's Holiday* which, together with *Le Journal d'un Curé de Campagne* (Bresson), *Ordet* (Dryer), *The Saga of Anatahan* (Sternberg) and *Cronaca di un Amore* (Antonioni), is one of the high points of 50s cinema. The other is *Playtime*, which almost fifteen years later occupies the same position, seemingly out of place, but in reality supreme.

Already in the achievement of *Monsieur Hulot's Holiday*, Tati's *tour de force* is evident, what critics called his style. The originality of construction was noticed: a succession of scenes which, in terms of duration, intensity, action or inaction, presence or absence of Hulot, are unequal. The novelty of his conception of sound was noticed. There was acclaim for a quality of laughter forgotten since the golden age of burlesque which Tati alone manages to reconstitute in his own way without resorting to parody. All this, by the way, has a real basis in truth, but it only partially accounts for what is interesting in the undertaking. It is perhaps André Bazin who best indicated the general orientation of Tati's procedure:

> Tati's comic spirit seems first of all to belong to Mack Sennett's burlesque logic from which Chaplin himself proceeds; yet it is subtly different. Burlesque, French as well as American, is based on the gag and the gag always supposes the exhaustion of a situation. Its most primitive form is the chase with its accumulation of catastrophes. Tati, on the other hand, depletes neither the characters nor the situations in which he places them. He himself seems unfinished; one might speak of his 'discretion of being . . .'

But all these elements as well as the unfinished quality, this kind of continuously suspended form calling for a continuously deferred resolution, dispense a strange aesthetic pleasure based on a certain disappointment of expectation. It only takes effect and weight in a highly sustained dialectic operating on the one hand between each sequence and the ensemble of the discourse in which it is inscribed; and on the other between each of the elements within the sequence itself. The particular tension which is present in the composition of each cell, and the play of the cells among themselves, a tension which generates a specific rhythm, is based on a complex system of relations and breaks running through the entire film like a thread, now evident, now concealed, a system which Hulot's character both reveals and sets in motion. He is its captive and its result. In other words, a Tati-film, or a Hulot-system, functions through a closely surveyed combination of a musical kind, between variable and fixed terms, themes and variations. Or again, and this is essential, it functions through the careful understanding of the very nature of the cinematographic material on which Tati works; that is, on the one hand, the fundamentally discontinuous character of cinematographic style (the cutting up of shots, sequences, the variability of ellipses,

etc.) and on the other, the disposition of these discontinuous elements in a syntagmatic chain: basing a 'continuous', 'linear', 'narrative' discourse on a succession of moments, shots and gestures literally '*découpés*' (edited/cut-out), taking this word as much in its cinematographic meaning (a cutting up of specific moments in time and space) as in its more common sense of the pastime indulged in by children (or Matisse) with scissors and coloured paper. A certain delineation of the world is thereby deconstructed before being reorganized in a wholly new way.

It may be asked, 'What film-maker doesn't do the same?' Yet montage in academic cinema is constantly concealed and dissolved in the most transparent possible style, dominated by angles and reverse-angles, etc., so that the fundamental discontinuity mentioned above tends to disappear into a continuity in which drama restricts style. For Tati, however, purged of its traditional attributes (rhetorical convention and clichés), it creates a new kind of space, as described by Noël Burch:

> Tati's genius consists in having extended to his films as a whole the organizational principles which for Sennett and his followers functioned only at the level of the individual gag. For Tati, a gag can be started in one sequence, completed in another, developed in a third, entirely repeated in a fourth, rejected in a fifth, etc. . . . This is just one of the means by which he reaches a formal unity through discontinuity of discourse, an unprecedented achievement in the history of what is called comic cinema.

Such a principle, generating purely formal suspense, produces its gratification by an oblique method which one might term a teasing technique: a pleasure (laughter, for example) is announced, virtually promised and perceived. Tati places the foundation of a gag as meticulously as Hitchcock lays the foundation of a dramatic resolution. All the signs converge towards an expectation which will often be disappointed by displacing its resolution. A scene from *Monsieur Hulot's Holiday* is here particularly explicit, especially as its parenthetic character in the story (in fact, it doesn't appear in certain prints of the film) makes the viewer wonder what the episode may mean. A very serious child buys two enormous ice-cream cones; then, holding one in each hand like an acrobat on a high wire, he undertakes the dangerous ascent of a stairway. The expected catastrophe does not occur during his climb but then he meets an obstacle: a door has to be opened, and the door-knob is above the child's head. With infinite caution he manages to get hold of the handle (he doesn't let go of his ice-cream; he turns it upside down, but without disaster) and at last opens the door. On the other side of the door, another child, sitting on a bench, is waiting for him, and takes one of the cones. Both begin to eat their ice-cream.

This episode, both perfectly 'round' and perfectly disappointing (the pleasure which it procures obviously resides in the disappointment itself), has no other function than to introduce into the film's development a sequence which plastically, dramatically and rhythmically plays the role of a breathing space in the structure of a work entirely based on the relationship, the modulation, of moments more or less weighted, of rhymes and reminders (visual and aural), of punctuation and growth.

That a perfect equilibrium could be based on a succession of partial disequilibriums is indeed one of the great lessons (formal, plastic and poetic) of burlesque cinema. Keaton especially, in films like *The General* and *The Navigator*, knew how to build unmatched edifices on such foundations. All the more so because, as has often been noticed, a genuine physical risk guaranteed the demonstration's acrobatic beauty. With Tati, the virtuosity of Hulot's character remains, but inclined to maladroitness, the uncompleted gesture; a certain hesitancy in his proceedings seeming always to look for its improbable justification. Langdon, with his moonish chastity, could be described together with Stan Laurel as one of the illustrious ancestors of Hulot.

But Tati is distinguished from such predecessors by what he uses as primary material, a certain realistic groundwork based on systematic observation. Next to Keaton and Langdon, essentially oneiric *cinéastes*, Tati seems altogether devoid of imagination, which is to say that nothing in his films seems to arise from any reliance on fantasy. On the contrary every element seems drawn from strict attention paid to gestures, attitude and behaviour offered by the show of everyday life. All this is not only recognizable as such by the spectator, but it often seems to him as if Tati had actually turned his camera on life itself.

This recognition is soon, however, joined by a perception of strangeness just as deep-seated; yet it would be hard to put one's finger on the exact moment of take-off. In Tati's work there are none of those brusque changes which fling a door open onto general delirium, culminating in paroxysm as in the Sennett tradition. Or if delirium occurs it is only through simple 'exaggeration' of the real: as the fireworks in *Hulot* or the destruction of the restaurant in *Playtime*. So, what is this strangeness?

> He sees problems where there are none, and finds them. He is capable of filming a beach scene simply to show that the children building a sandcastle drown the sound of the waves with their cries. He will also shoot a scene just because at that moment a window is opening in a house away in the background, and a window opening—well, that's funny. This is what interests Tati. Everything and nothing . . . Jacques Tati has a feeling for comedy because he has a feeling for strangeness. (Jean-Luc Godard—translated by Tom Milne in *Godard on Godard* [1972].)

And Tati himself:

> Comedy is the summit of logic. A gag is often a situation developed to its outside limits. Laughter is born of a certain fundamental absurdity. Some things are not funny of themselves but become so on being dissected. (Jacques Tati in *Les Lettres Françaises*, 24 October 1957.)

It is precisely through this 'dissection', and through accumulation, that the space thus established astonishes, seeming suddenly new, even though its elements, taken separately, are no more than banal. And here Tati is most inventive. At first rarefying anecdote, characters and décor almost to the point of abstraction, he then nourishes the development of his film almost to the saturation point so that a single viewing is inadequate for arriving at a real understanding

Jacques Tati wandering through the fearful future in *Playtime*.

of the resonance and repercussion of the signs employed.

Hence, remaining attached to the notion of genre is erroneous, so far does Tati push the idea of the unequal development of the gag to its utmost consequences. At times a gag loses all its funniness only to gain in pure strangeness, transformed into an effect of disorientation (while its material and model are based on an effect of recognition), into a mark of rupture. Yet the smallest effect is not without cause, suggested at least, before or after its apparition. But the gags are not placed in salient positions, as are the *bons mots* in boulevard theatre. Every remarkable idea seems clogged, every flash of wit annulled in a kind of imperturbable equalization. The spectator seems called upon to sort all this out by himself, to give each aspect its proper value. He is thus expected to remain very

alert. It is he who is ceaselessly required to tie together, and to relate, the disseminated terms of an extremely complex polyphony of gestures, noises and movements which without this effort would appear as a kind of cacophony. (*Traffic* in this way comes directly from *Monsieur Hulot's Holiday*, although it is more refined.)

If *Hulot* was already a film which required several viewings in order fully to enjoy its inventiveness, *Playtime*, as Noël Burch has written, is surely the only film which must be seen 'not only several times, but at different distances from the screen'. In fact, *Playtime* appears like an enormous test of variable perceptions. It is a test established by an impressive mass of interdependent commitments, based on a spectacular and novel logic which is like the extreme consequence of the lines of force which had hitherto dominated Tati's formal work. If it is a hazardous business to outline the hierarchy of these commitments, and to articulate which proceeds from which, it is easy at least to give a summary list of them and to show the principle of overlapping which orders them, starting from a simple matrix whose possibilities seem exhaustively explored: the wide screen. The frame is an immense receptacle of paths, trajectories, swarming masses, actions and interactions, an almost abstract and gigantic stage peopled with figures, colours, movements and rhythm, an area of a dissemination which could be called fortuitous if behind the appearance of chaos the law of its arrangement did not imperiously appear.

> I'd like to make a film—I'll not make a secret of it—without the character of Hulot. (Jacques Tati, interviewed by André Bazin and François Truffaut, *Cahiers du Cinéma*, No. 83.)

And almost ten years later:

> In *Playtime* Hulot isn't more important than the other characters. In a way, he's just in the ranks. I didn't want anyone to say, 'Tati's done this, Tati's done that.' No, not Tati, *Playtime*. Hulot's not a star any more, he doesn't draw a crowd. (Jacques Tati, *Cahiers du Cinéma*, No. 199.)

By losing his privileged position as a character, Hulot becomes what he was always tending towards: a simple function. There is no fixation, no deceptive reference in the midst of an immense, constantly changing space, delegating his silhouette to the double exits of invisible mirrors. Everything is played on *surfaces*, those of a blue-tinted metropolis, made from scratch, of steel and glass. To find a similar range for construction *ex nihilo*, for such total possession of a set, one has to go back to the great silent films—the magnificent décor of *Sunrise*, or Monte Carlo reconstructed lifesize on the California coast by Stroheim, his passion for detail carrying him so far as to have functioning house-bells in his casino. The surface of the screen, vertiginously peopled with a multiple choreography, disencumbered of psychology or anecdote and establishing a monumental plasticity for which the wide screen for the first time (and, excepting *2001: A Space Odyssey*, the only time) justifies itself otherwise than as a mere decorative outgrowth. 70 mm is thus explored for its real resources and possibilities. Sumptuous though it may be, the spectacular yields to the surveyed profusion of a calligraphy based on order and variation. The primordial comic cell, the gag, naturally obeys this order, and acquires renewed powers. The very notion of the gag is displaced, even more than in *Hulot*, and can hardly be reduced to a mere incitement to laughter. And here everything is a gag which participates in the meeting or clash between the idea of chance and the all-powerful and opposite idea of the programmed. A double idea which obsesses contemporary cinema (Rouch, Godard, Rivette, Straub, Jancsó . . .) and contemporary art in general (Cage, Stockhausen) and which Tati, in the most pragmatic and least theoretical way, conducts to a conclusion of awesome coherence.

As for the sound, it is the object of an equally novel treatment: a phrase suddenly becomes audible, as if by chance over an uninterrupted concert of whispers, onomatopoeia and noises; it is incongruous less through its meaning than through its relation to the ensemble of the sound continuum whence it emerged. There are no longer dialogues or informative enunciations: the aural universe is no longer the privileged support of meaning.

Innovating thus with dramaturgy, the frame, the function of character, the aural space, the very structure of the story, Tati merits his place among the most notable creators of cinematic forms today.

Translated by Michael Graham

I wish I could fully share Fieschi's views on Tati, but the disagreeable and to me totally unfunny Hulot seems to get in the way. There are two studies of Tati in English: Penelope Gilliatt's *Jacques Tati* (1976), and *The Films of Jacques Tati* (1977) by Brent Maddock.

LEOPOLDO TORRE NILSSON

Richard Roud

Leopoldo Torre Nilsson (1924–78) was the only Argentine director anyone knew in the years that followed his European début with the screening of *La Casa del Angel* (U.K.: *The House of the Angel*; U.S.: *End of Innocence*) at the Cannes Festival in 1957. This was not his first film; he had made several others, notably *Dias de Odio* (1954), based on a story called *Emma Zunz* by Jorge Luis Borges. But *The House of the Angel* was the first of a series of films which were to be scripted by Torre Nilsson's remarkable wife, Beatriz Guido. Her truly Gothic sensibility, combined with his Wellesian *mise en scène*, produced fascinating films like *El Secuestrador* (1958), *La Caida* (U.K.: *The Fall*, 1959), *Fin de Fiesta* (1960), *La Mano en la Trampa* (U.K.: *The Hand in the Trap*; U.S.: *Hand in the Trap*, 1961), *Piel de Verano* (*Summer Skin*, 1961) and *Homenaje a la Hora de la Siesta* (U.K.: *Four Women for One Hero*, 1962).

This baroque series culminated in two films: *La Terraza* (U.S.: *The Terrace*, 1963) and *El Ojo de la Cerradura* (*The Eavesdropper*, 1964). The first was both a picture of upper-class Argentinian youth and a free version of Sartre's *No Exit*. Five teenage couples take refuge on the roof garden of a block of flats and, for an afternoon and a night, create their own world, a parody of organized society in a decadent world. What made the film so extraordinary was the hallucinatory sensation created by those ten half-naked bodies, glistening with water, gliding in and out of the swimming-pool like our amphibious ancestors, evolving in ritual patterns high above an indifferent city. *The Eavesdropper*, which was filmed in English, starred Stathis Gialellis as a young Fascist terrorist obliged to hole up for a couple of weeks in a crumbling 1900-style Buenos Aires hotel largely inhabited by Spanish Republican refugees. A girl-friend (Janet Margolin), along for the ride, as it were, is at first totally enthralled by his physical charm. But as his paranoia begins to take over, so comes her realization of his true nature. The film was a kind of summing-up of Torre Nilsson's work, and a fusion of his two major themes: the denunciation of Argentinian fascism and a scathing examination of a self-destructive, claustrophobic world.

Since that date, alas, his films became less interesting, partly at least because he was obliged for economic reasons to choose subjects which did not really suit his talents —like the large-scale patriotic epic *Martin Fierro* (1968)—and partly because of the impossible political climate of his native land.

There is a monograph, in French, by Marcel Oms and others: *Torre Nilsson* (1962).

JACQUES TOURNEUR

Robin Wood

The Hollywood system is usually—and with considerable truth—regarded as restrictive and inimical to personal art; certainly it is unlikely that a Bergman or a Fellini would have found the freedom to develop within it. Yet the great complex of studios, stars, writers, genres, popular conventions, can also provide the means whereby a minor but distinctive voice that might go unheard amid the more assertive voices of a cinema of total authorship can find expression. Such a voice was that of Jacques Tourneur (1904–77). His films show little sign of the kind of original creative drive that must either assert itself in total independence or completely assimilate and transform the material it works with. Given a mediocre script (and he has had his fair share). Tourneur makes a mediocre movie, recognizably his (if at all) only by virtue of an externally applied camera style. His best movies belong as much to their genres as to their director. Yet it is possible to value Tourneur very highly indeed—to value certain qualities that in description can sound merely negative but which, given congenial circumstances, can quietly impose themselves as rare and positive virtues.

Tourneur is probably best known for his horror movies—the three he made for the producer Val Lewton in 1942 and 1943 (*Cat People*, 1942; *I Walked with a Zombie*, 1943; *The Leopard Man*, 1943) and the later, in certain respects very similar, *Night of the*

Dana Andrews receiving an unpleasant runic message at Stonehenge in *Night of the Demon*.

Demon, made in Britain in 1957. In an interview in *Positif*, Tourneur affirmed, with evident sincerity, the genuineness of his belief in the supernatural. It is this that gives his horror movies their particular quality: he consistently refuses to vulgarize the supernatural, consistently respects its mystery. Its manifestations are subtly, indirectly suggested. The crude process-shots of the avenging demon in *Night of the Demon*, added by the studio against Tourneur's wishes to give the film more obvious shock value, emphasize by contrast the reticence and delicacy of his treatment elsewhere. Scenes such as the cat-woman's nocturnal pursuit of Jane Randolph (*Cat People*), the walk to the voodoo meeting across moonlit canefields (*I Walked with a Zombie*), and

Dana Andrews' return through the woods from his visit to the necromancer (*Night of the Demon*) are in their economy and atmosphere models of their kind.

But Tourneur's reserve, and his respect for mystery, go much further. The camera style, which is the most distinctive feature of his heterogeneous *oeuvre*, has two chief characteristics, movement and distance. The fluid long takes that keep the characters in longshot within the shadowy environments, branches and foliage obtruding darkly in the foreground greatly enhance the haunting, sinister atmosphere of the suspense sequences; they also help to preserve the objectivity with which Tourneur customarily views his characters, and on which the ambiguities of the horror movies depend. Tourneur denies us identification with the nominally 'good' characters. In *Cat People* our sympathies are drawn much more to the sinister but pathetic Irena (Simone Simon), afraid she will turn into a panther if her sexuality is aroused, than to the decent but commonplace young Americans who are involved with her. In *I Walked with a Zombie* (one of Tourneur's finest films, and a minor classic), all our moral preconceptions are subtly undermined, all motivations prove ambiguous or suspect, and even the apparently immaculate heroine is not exempt from doubt. The shadowy nocturnal world of the film is more than 'atmosphere': it becomes the visual expression of Tourneur's sense of the mystery and ambiguity underlying all human action and interaction.

Besides his belief in the supernatural, Tourneur's own ambiguous relationship to America may partly account for the sensitivity and sympathy with which he renders the 'foreignness' of the worlds to which the Americans in these films are exposed. Son of Maurice Tourneur, who began his career in the silent cinema first in France, and then in America, but continued it (from 1927) in France and Germany, Jacques spent much of his childhood and youth in Europe, and made his first three films in France before settling in America in 1939. What Andrew Sarris calls his 'French gentility' seems in fact a combination of natural reticence and the detachment of the *déraciné*. The key to Tourneur's Westerns—*Canyon Passage* (1946), *Wichita* (1955), *Great Day in the Morning* (1956)—is the fact that he approaches the genre as an outsider.

It is instructive, in this connection, to compare *Canyon Passage* with Ford's *My Darling Clementine*. Both were made in the same year (1946); both are concerned with the development of early white civilization in the wilderness; both are built on a contrast between the settled life and the wandering life. A central sequence in *Clementine* depicts the dedication of a half-built skeletal church and the celebratory dance on the unroofed floor; in *Canyon Passage* there is an equally central sequence depicting the communal raising of a new cabin, a wedding and a dance. The difference is between commitment and detachment. Tourneur has us watch the people celebrating; Ford has us

imaginatively participate. From outside, we see the fire burning on the hearth of Tourneur's newly-raised cabin; we are not taken inside the door. As the marriage service is performed, his camera leads us impartially over various couples who typify contrasting attitudes to the notion of settling down. During the celebrations, our attention is transferred repeatedly from character to character, couple to couple, group to group: we are prevented from identifying with any, but are invited to consider and evaluate all. Wyatt Earp, the hero of *Clementine*, becomes committed to the defence of civilized order; the hero of *Canyon Passage* is committed chiefly to the preservation of his own independence. (Tourneur's own Wyatt Earp—Joel McCrea in *Wichita*—is notably more detached and objective in his stance than Ford's.) The only Indian in *Clementine* is a drunken ruffian whom Earp overpowers, briefly beats, and pushes in the direction of the reservation; the Indians of *Canyon Passage* materialize magically out of nature in the middle of the cabin-raising: Tourneur allows them the same mystery he elsewhere accords the supernatural, at once dangerous and attractive.

In several of Tourneur's best films there is a character who, one feels, is accorded a special status. He is always a minor character, more spectator than participant, detached, belonging to no one, but well-disposed, looking on perceptively and intelligently and acting decisively at crucial moments, when his participation is necessary: the deaf-and-dumb boy in *Out of the Past* (U.K.: *Build My Gallows High*, 1947), a *film noir* that is related interestingly, with its world of shadows and uncertainties, to horror fantasies; the mandolin-playing singer (Hoagy Carmichael) in *Canyon Passage*. These are perhaps the characters to whom Tourneur is closest. Related to them is Carrefour, the zombie of *I Walked with a Zombie*, one of Tourneur's most haunting characters, guardian of the crossroads, speechless intermediary between the shadowy otherworld and the world of consciousness, at once knowing and unknowing; the enigma at the heart of Tourneur's universe.

For further reading, see Joel Siegel's *Val Lewton: The Reality of Terror* (1972), as well as the special number of *Présence du*

Cinéma (1966) devoted to Tourneur and Dwan.

MAURICE TOURNEUR

Richard Koszarski

Of all the directors who flourished in the pre-1920 period, Maurice Tourneur certainly bore the most prepossessing artistic credentials. Born in Paris in 1876, by the turn of the century he had already completed a wide career in the visual arts as an illustrator of books and designer of posters and textiles, an interior decorator, and assistant to Rodin and Puvis de Chavannes. His theatre experience was gained with Réjane's company (for which he served as actor-manager on the 1901 world tour) and with Antoine at the Odéon. In 1912 he was persuaded to join French Eclair as a director, and two years later was sent by them to their American studio at Fort Lee, New Jersey. Here, in association with William Brady's World Films, he produced screen versions of Broadway successes. Tourneur raced through these films, releasing a new feature every other month during the years 1914–20; despite the haste, these were his most satisfying and successful years. Soon after his arrival in America he gathered round him a creative team which was to move with him from studio to studio during the turbulent years before 1920: Charles Maigne and Charles Whittaker were his chief scenarists, John van den Broek and Lucien Andriot his cameramen, and Ben Carré his gifted art director. By working closely with this unit, Tourneur was able to maintain a considerable degree of control over projects which would otherwise have turned hopelessly impersonal. When the unit dissolved around 1920, Tourneur found himself at a severe disadvantage, forced to work with inadequately developed screenplays and unfamiliar technicians.

Tourneur's pre-1920 American films (there were thirty-five) echo the standard theatrical fare of the period: sheer melodrama (*The Whip*, 1917), wistful romance (*The Wishing Ring*, 1914), storybook fantasy (*Poor Little Rich Girl*, 1917), and even the modern problem drama (*A Doll's House*, 1918, although with a somewhat altered ending).

While there are comic touches in his films, purely comic material did not attract Tourneur, who preferred more serious subjects. *The Blue Bird* and *Prunella* (both 1918) were his most important efforts, conscious attempts to find a cinematic equivalent of the work of Gordon Craig and the Moscow Arts Theatre. Their mixed critical reception (and commercial failure) soured Tourneur on further efforts to elevate the standards of film audiences, and he began to lose interest in his work, now made more difficult by the break-up of his production unit. After *The Last of the Mohicans* (1920), generally considered his finest film (co-directed by his assistant, Clarence Brown), Tourneur's career went inexorably downhill. As a freelance director he moved from studio to studio, but failed to find the proper dramatic framework to flesh out his by now excessively pictorial style. Films like *Lorna Doone* (1922) and *The Christian* (1923) clearly show his weaknesses outweighing his strengths. Signed by MGM to direct *The Mysterious Island* in 1926, he quarrelled with his 'producer' and walked off the film after months of preparation and two weeks of actual shooting. He returned to Europe and a not unsuccessful career, continuing much along the lines of his American work, with *Volpone* (1940) and *La Main du Diable* (*The Devil's Hand*, also known in the U.S. as *Carnival of Sinners*, 1943) among the high points. In 1948 he directed his last film, *L'Impasse des Deux Anges*. He died in Paris in 1961.

There is a monograph, in French, by Jean Mitry: *Maurice Tourneur* (1966); and there are some interesting comments on Tourneur in Kevin Brownlow's *The Parade's Gone By* (1968).

LEONID TRAUBERG,
see p. 554

FRANÇOIS TRUFFAUT

James Monaco

'Are films more important than life?' This is the central question of *La Nuit Américaine* (*Day for Night*, 1973), François Truffaut's film about film-making, a focal point of his twenty-year career as a director. As phrased by Alphonse, the young *cinéaste* and maniacal film buff played by Jean-Pierre Léaud, the question is a running gag in the film. But it is also a query which we might put in all seriousness to Truffaut, a man who has measured out his life in movies—his own and those of others. Having begun his career in film as a critic, he did not cease—once he became a film-maker—seeing and writing about other people's films. The title of the collection of criticism which he published in 1975, *Les Films de ma Vie*, echoes the title of his idol Jean Renoir's autobiography (*Ma Vie et mes Films*), alludes to Henry Miller's *Les Livres de ma Vie*, but, most important, strongly suggests that for Truffaut film and life are inextricably intertwined.

Born in Paris in 1932, Truffaut was immediately handed over to a wet-nurse and then sent to live with his grandmother until he was eight. When she died, his parents took him back, reluctantly. 'They weren't bad people,' he notes, 'just nervous and busy.' His experiences at school closely paralleled those of Antoine Doinel in *Les Quatre Cents Coups* (*The Four Hundred Blows*, 1959). He played truant often, finding some surcease at the movies or 'devouring Balzac' at the municipal library. When he was found out, he offered excuses as outrageous as those he later put in the mouth of Antoine, his cinematic *alter ego*.

By the age of ten Truffaut was a confirmed *cinéphile*. By fourteen he was pretty much on his own, holding for varying periods of time jobs as a messenger, shop assistant, storekeeper, clerk and welder. At fifteen he started his first film club, the 'Cercle Ciné-mane', whose very name confessed his manic obsession with cinema. Shortly afterwards his father tracked him down and turned him over to the police. He was sent to Villejuif, which he describes as 'half an insane asylum and half a house of correction'. Through the 'Cercle Cinémane', however, he had met André Bazin. Bazin and his wife Janine went to much trouble to get him released from Ville-juif, and Truffaut's natural parents 'rather easily gave up the rights that, by law, they had over me'.

Truffaut became an *habitué* of the Paris film clubs, eventually fell in love with a girl who ignored him (reflected in his episode in

L'Amour à Vingt Ans [*Love at Twenty*, 1962]), and in desperation joined the army. He had even less success in the military than he had had at school, went A.W.O.L. several times, and was finally discharged for 'instability of character'. (A brief allusion to his army career begins *Baisers Volés* [*Stolen Kisses*, 1968]). Here the parallel with Antoine Doinel ends. Unlike Antoine, François had had the good fortune to meet a surrogate father in André Bazin. The thirty-five-year-old film scholar encouraged the twenty-one-year-old ne'er-do-well to write. In the next few years, Truffaut produced nearly half a million words of film criticism, writing for a variety of publications including *Arts* and *Cahiers du Cinéma*, Bazin's 'own' magazine, and the most important film journal of the time.

It was in the pages of *Cahiers du Cinéma* that Truffaut developed *la politique des auteurs*, the most significant critical theory of the day. His colleagues in this endeavour were (among others) Jean-Luc Godard, Claude Chabrol, Eric Rohmer and Jacques Rivette, who with Truffaut later formed the nucleus of the New Wave. All five began making short films in the early and mid-50s. Truffaut's first effort was *Une Visite* (1955), shot in 16 mm in the apartment of his *Cahiers* colleague Jacques Doniol-Valcroze, starring Florence Doniol-Valcroze and photographed by Jacques Rivette. Alain Resnais spent a few hours one afternoon giving Truffaut ideas on how to edit his footage; Trauffaut lists him in the credits as editor.

Les Mistons (*The Mischief Makers*) followed in 1957. Played by Gérard Blain and Bernadette Lafont, this twenty-minute version of a short story by Maurice Pons captures succinctly the dilemma of childhood to which Truffaut later returned in *Les Quatre Cents Coups*, *L'Enfant Sauvage* (*The Wild Child*, 1969) and *L'Argent de Poche* (*Small Change*, 1976). 'Most films about childhood,' he has noted, 'make the adult serious and the child frivolous. Quite the other way around.' In the spring of 1958, Truffaut shot some footage of Jean-Claude Brialy and Caroline Dim, using the floods in the countryside near Paris as a background. He reached an impasse with the film and turned the footage over to Godard, who edited it, wrote a narration for it and called it (with typical irony) *Une Histoire d'Eau*.

In 1957 Truffaut had married Madeleine Morgenstern, daughter of an important producer. (They had two children before they were divorced in the 60s. They named the children Eva and Laura, after the films by Losey and Preminger.) By 1958 Truffaut had developed a reputation as an uncompromising and thoroughly demanding critic. He was described in *L'Express* as 'a hateful *enfant terrible* who puts his foot in his mouth with unbearable self-conceit'. Almost as a dare, his father-in-law suggested that, if Truffaut knew so much, he should make features himself. The result of this challenge was *Les Quatre Cents Coups*. In 1958 Truffaut the critic had been banned from the Cannes Festival; in 1959 he returned as a director, his film having been selected as an official French entry. He was chosen Best Director that year.

Les Quatre Cents Coups is the first of a series of four remarkable films which depict the stages of childhood, adolescence, young adulthood and marriage in the life of Antoine Doinel, played by an actor whom Truffaut discovered for *Les Quatre Cents Coups*, Jean-Pierre Léaud. Interestingly, Truffaut, who had championed the *auteur* theory as a critic, discovered once he began to make films that he was involved in an intense dialectic with his actors and that the films which emerged from these unusual artistic collaborations owed a great deal to the personality and intelligence of the players. The Doinel series is the most striking example. Léaud, whom Truffaut has called 'the most interesting actor of his generation' and who was only fourteen when Truffaut discovered him, has directly modified the course of this semi-autobiographical saga, softening and humanizing the image of Doinel which Truffaut had first conceived.

In the four films, *Les Quatre Cents Coups*, the *Antoine et Colette* episode in *L'Amour à Vingt Ans*, *Baisers Volés* and *Domicile Conjugal* (*Bed and Board*, 1970), Doinel is, respectively, 12, 18, 20 and 22 years old. When the films were made, Léaud was, respectively, 14, 18, 24 and 26. The series, taken as a whole, is not only an extended portrait of the *éducation sentimentale* of the character but also a fascinating reflection of the growth of an actor. Indeed, since Truffaut also was maturing as an artist during the twelve-year period in which the films were made, we can see significant changes in the styles of the various films. The first two are much more realistic in approach, the last two more aesthetically complex. In the films he made during the 60s between the episodes of the Doinel story, Truffaut was developing rather sophisticated aesthetic ideas, and this experience was reflected in the chapters of his quasi-autobiography.

Les Quatre Cents Coups deals with Antoine's love–hate relationship with his parents and his difficulties at school. Shot on location in the streets of Paris, it has a documentary quality to it. It ends with Antoine's momentary escape from the reform school. He is frozen in the last shot, on the beach, caught between his youth and the experience of the sea. *Antoine et Colette*, a half-hour contribution to the anthology film *L'Amour à Vingt Ans*, is, like its predecessor, shot in black and white. It picks up the story of Antoine as he first tries his wings, living alone, working in a record factory and, like Truffaut at this period in his life, in love with a girl who ignores him, finding himself getting along better with her parents than he does with her. We leave him at the close at home watching TV with these new-found parent-surrogates while Colette (Marie-France Pisier) is out on a date.

Baisers Volés begins as Antoine is kicked out of the army. Christine (Claude Jade) has replaced Colette in his affections, though she seems almost as immune to his awkward charms. He gets along well with her parents, too. Much of the film is devoted to a series of jobs which Antoine gets, keeps for a while, then loses with humorous aplomb. Central here is his position as an apprentice private investigator, in which guise he meets and falls dumbly in love with Fabienne Tabard (Delphine Seyrig), his first older woman. Time passes and Christine yields. They seal their marriage with buttered *biscottes* and heart-shaped bottle-openers the morning after. In the last scene they are left in the cold, bright March light of a Parisian park, the reality of marriage ahead of them.

If *Baisers Volés* seems almost too charming, that is partly a function of the way we read the film. During February and March 1968, while Truffaut was shooting the film, he was also deeply involved in the protests

Henri Serre, Jeanne Moreau and Oscar Werner in *Jules and Jim*, 'an undeniable masterpiece'.

which eventually saved the late Henri Langlois his position as head of the French Cinémathèque. The film opens with a shot of the closed Cinémathèque and is dedicated to Langlois. Unlike its relatively objective predecessors, *Baisers Volés* has an ironic depth to it: it is as much about Truffaut's filmic past as it is about his biographical past. In shape and execution it recalls a number of cinematic romances from the 30s and 40s and recreates the aura suggested by the 30s' Charles Trenet *chanson* which is its theme. The world of *Baisers Volés* is not charming but charmed: a past recalled and re-created through romantic images learned from films rather than life.

The fourth and final chapter of the Doinel saga, *Domicile Conjugal*, exhibits an even stronger cinematic irony. Antoine and Christine are married and live in a building with a courtyard full of colourful characters straight out of Renoir's *Le Crime de Monsieur Lange*. Antoine's jobs are even more absurd (he dyes

flowers at first, then operates a toylike model harbour for an American industrial firm). Christine is considerably matured (more so than her husband); she enjoys a budding career as a violinist (Antoine is quietly proud of her). The couple have a baby (he is named Alphonse, the name Léaud will take in *La Nuit Américaine*). Antoine is caught unprepared for this shock of adulthood, regresses into fantasy, and takes up with 'Une Femme Japonaise'. As he gains more self-confidence as an artist (a novelist rather than film-maker), as well as a husband, Antoine matures. The marital crisis is resolved, and at the close of the film Antoine and Christine are seen, almost in parody, as a typical bourgeois married couple.

While *Les Quatre Cents Coups* was a striking evocation of childhood in the 50s, *Domicile Conjugal* had very little indeed to do with life as it is lived in the 70s. Again, the structures of film have overtaken the patterns of life. If the last episode of the Doinel saga is to be understood at all, it must be seen as Antoine's ascension into cinema, into the fictional world of *Le Crime de Monsieur Lange* and 30s movies. In a sense, the question 'Is film more important than life?' is moot; for Truffaut the two are one.

Although Truffaut had been influenced in his development by a number of European film-makers (Renoir, Vigo, Ophuls, among others), his greatest interest had been in the American cinema: Hollywood. As a result, the theory of genres became increasingly important for him. He wanted, he said, to 'explode genres by combining them', and the dialectic between genre and *auteur* which becomes obvious in the latter Doinel films is central to most of his work in the 60s. In fact, he addressed himself to the task of confronting genres in his second film, *Tirez sur le Pianiste* (U.K.: *Shoot the Pianist*; U.S.: *Shoot the Piano Player*, 1960). As *Les Quatre Cents Coups* had been a product of both Truffaut's and Léaud's personalities, so this second film was driven by Truffaut's confrontation with Charles Aznavour (who plays Charlie Edouard), this time set not in a straight narrative like its predecessor but in the context of a very popular genre, *film noir*. 'I refused to be a prisoner of my first success,' Truffaut wrote. 'I discarded the temptation to renew that success by choosing another "big subject".'

Even in the context of an existential gangster film, Truffaut discovered correlations with his own situation. Charlie the piano-player, like Truffaut the film-maker, is torn between the opposing worlds of 'high' and 'popular' art. Like Truffaut, Charlie chooses the latter. It is here, too, that we begin to see a politics developing in Truffaut. It has nothing to do with great issues or high theory. It is a micropolitics that investigates the way men and women live together. It is muted and subtle, so subtle, in fact, that most critics of Truffaut choose to ignore it, treating its evidence simply as love stories. Yet from *Tirez sur le Pianiste* (which is essentially two stories: Léna's version of Charlie and Thérésa's) straight on to *L'Histoire d'Adèle H.* (*The Story of Adèle H.*, 1975), Truffaut has been intensely concerned with the way others see us and the profound effect this has on the way we see ourselves, a phenomenon which I take to be essentially political.

This is why doubles so often recur in Truffaut's *oeuvre*: Colette and Christine in the Doinel films, Jules and Jim versus Catherine, Linda/Clarisse in *Fahrenheit 451* (1966), Julie/Marion in *La Sirène du Mississippi* (*Mississippi Mermaid*, 1969), Anne and Muriel in *Les Deux Anglaises et le Continent* (U.K.: *Anne and Muriel*; U.S.: *Two English Girls*, 1971), as well as Charlie/Edouard. Sometimes embodied in one character, sometimes split between two, these bifurcated personalities offer Truffaut a chance to investigate the dynamics of human relationships, their micropolitics.

Truffaut's third film, *Jules et Jim* (*Jules and Jim*, 1962), was and is an undeniable masterpiece. Here, everything came together with extraordinary effect. Telling an historical story, Truffaut was able to indulge himself in some of the cinematic pleasures of that genre, at the same time speaking directly to the contemporary consciousness, for the triangle of Jules, Jim and Catherine, set in the 1910s and 20s, portrays a kind of relationship that is also characteristic of our time. Jules, Jim and Catherine struggle to define the boundaries of personal freedom in sexual relationships and they do so in such a way that we can see the roots of a new community taking hold, even as nineteenth-century social structures consume themselves in the First World War, the background against which the film is played. This sense of community, which is present in embryo here, was to become increasingly important for Truffaut in the films of the late 60s (*Domicile Conjugal*, *L'Enfant Sauvage*) and the mid-70s (*La Nuit Américaine*, *L'Argent de Poche*).

Almost as if in reaction to the huge commercial and critical success of *Jules et Jim*, Truffaut turned immediately to a series of restrained, introverted genre films which occupied him through most of the 60s. It was as if, having created two mature masterpieces, he backtracked to pursue an apprenticeship. The first of these, *La Peau Douce* (U.K.: *Silken Skin*; U.S.: *The Soft Skin*, 1964) is one of his most under-rated films, even today. It marked his return to film-making after having conducted the interviews with Alfred Hitchcock which led to his book *Le Cinéma selon Hitchcock* (1966). While *La*

Peau Douce has a subject which is far too European to be considered Hitchcockian, the *mise en scène* is almost as eloquent and assured. Whatever else one thinks of Truffaut's cinema, it is evident that as an *auteur*, a wielder of the camera-pen, he has few equals today. *La Peau Douce* is one of the prime examples of his command of cinematic language. It is about 'love in the city, instead of love in the country' (like *Jules et Jim*), he wrote, and it reveals the fractured sensibility of city life. It is a simple story of adultery and almost perfunctory revenge, but told in such a cinematic way that Hitchcock might be proud of his student. A collection of concrete images is edited together in a fluid, Resnais-like montage of detail shots and close-ups. The surface of life is beginning to break up: lights are switched on and off arhythmically, gears shift, lurching and grinding, camera shutters slice up time. Truffaut begins his contest with genres by succeeding in modernizing one of the oldest, finding a fluent cinematic vocabulary to tell what is, after all, a rather simple tale.

Fahrenheit 451 (1966), his attempt at science fiction, is more problematical. Visually, the film is stunning: Truffaut's first effort in colour. In the narrative, however, there are serious problems: it is theme-ridden. Ray Bradbury, the author of the novel on which it is based, willed to Truffaut some rather unsuccessful solutions to these problems. The 'book people' aren't set in a political context and as a result, most of the pleasures of the film are imagistic. 'Half the film is strictly visual,' Truffaut wrote in his diary of the film, later published, 'which makes me really happy. In almost all films, the footage of acted dialogue scenes tends to increase during shooting whereas the mute part diminishes . . .' The privileged, mute moments of *Fahrenheit 451*—the books aflame, the empty wallscreen, the narcissists on the monorail, the hollowness of the streets—these work well enough, but as Truffaut himself realized, they don't jell with the rest of the film.

La Mariée était en Noir (*The Bride Wore Black*, 1968), Truffaut's first attempt at pure Hitchcock, ironically reveals not what Truffaut has learned from the master, but what he hasn't. A revenge play characterized both by manic single-mindedness and a droll sense of

absurdity, it doesn't come alive for Truffaut. Reading between the lines, we can see where Hitchcock would have found real humour and, occasionally, terror. But in Truffaut's cautious hands these elements are muted. Jeanne Moreau as Julie Kohler is peculiarly stolid. The interest of the film lies in the way Truffaut has used it to experiment with narrative structure. He has taken the American novel by William Irish and rotated it 180 degrees. Whereas the novel is seen from the point of view of the detective, the film is seen from Julie's perspective. He has also dedramatized the action. Because we share the murderer's point of view, we are less interested in the mystery than we are in how she painstakingly goes about the job at hand (which is the revenge murder of five men). Finally, almost none of the dialogue deals with vengeance or murder; Truffaut concentrates it on the personal relationships. In a way his most ambitious genre film, *La Mariée était en Noir* is mainly of academic interest.

Truffaut shot *La Sirène du Mississippi* during the winter of 1968–69, only a half year after finishing *Baisers Volés*. The renewal of the Antoine Doinel story was salutary, for when Truffaut returned to genre films with *La Sirène* the result was his most complete success in the field: he had exploded genres by combining them. The film begins as a mystery, evolves into a Hitchcockian suspense chase and ends as a Truffaut love story. It has echoes of pre-war films like *The Blue Angel* and *Nana*, and it is also Truffaut's first 'star' film, with Jean-Paul Belmondo and Cathérine Deneuve at the height of their international popularity. The resonances of *La Sirène du Mississippi* are complex. Truffaut named the detective in the film Comolli, after an editor of *Cahiers du Cinéma*, because the real mystery of the film is cinematic: how can all these diverse elements be forged into a new cinema? *La Sirène* is a synthesis of the work Truffaut had been doing during the last six or eight years, rich with references to other films, styles and film-makers. There are allusions to Renoir, Hitchcock, Bogart, Doinel, *Pierrot le Fou*, *Tirez sur le Pianiste*, Nicholas Ray, Audiberti, Balzac, Cocteau.

Truffaut's previous genre efforts had been difficult for most audiences because of the intentional contrast between their traditional generic forms and the director's own cinematic idiom—realistic narrative. The stars of *La Sirène* allowed him to fuse these two opposite approaches; the presence of Belmondo and Deneuve on the wide screen in nearly every shot served as a focus of attention which gave the film unity. Although Truffaut never lost interest in this central conflict between the established forms of genres and the contrasting intentions of the *auteur*, with *La Sirène du Mississippi* he had effectively completed his self-appointed apprenticeship (ten years late) and gained a certain freedom.

He marked the occasion by himself taking the central role in his next film, *L'Enfant Sauvage*, one of his finest accomplishments. Truffaut plays Dr Itard, the teacher of the wild child, Victor of the Aveyron, because it occurred to him that the relationship between teacher and pupil was parallel to that between director and actor. The film is dedicated to Jean-Pierre Léaud, and just as Truffaut had learned much from the actor who gave life to his cinematic *alter ego*, so Itard, as Truffaut sees him, is involved in a relationship of equality with Victor. What gives the film special power (and has made it fascinating for children) is that once again Truffaut treats the child as a *person*, without any trace of condescension. He has balanced the elements of this mythic story: it is clear that the wild child enjoys a freedom from civilization of the sort many of us dream about; it is also clear that he would not long have survived in his 'natural' state. The poignancy of that dilemma lies near the heart of the film.

At the same time that *L'Enfant Sauvage*—black and white, 1 : 1.33 aspect ratio, heavily punctuated with irises—evokes an old genre (the scientific 'biopics' of the 30s), it nevertheless is addressed to us in direct and objective language. Narrated by Truffaut as Itard, the film often has the feeling more of a documentary or educational film than of a fiction feature. Above all else, Truffaut's cinematic 'tone of voice' has always been identifiable by its modesty (he often refers to himself simply as a *metteur en scène*). His films have a special reserve about them. He shoots his actors from a slightly greater distance than most directors, as if not to intrude. He seldom holds a shot for what

might be its natural period, preferring to cut away sooner, as if to avert his gaze. Because in *L'Enfant Sauvage* Truffaut is present as actor and narrator as well as director, this sense of restraint is redoubled.

L'Enfant Sauvage is a film about education, 'the leading out'. Victor has his own knowledge of the world, but he can't express it in Itard's language. As he learns that language, it changes the way he sees the world. The film deals with Victor's initiation through Itard into the civilized universe, so that he learns to sense and describe the world the way others do. At the same time, there is a strong moral dimension to Itard's programme. The climax of the film is Itard's test of Victor's own sense of justice, and to do this he must betray Victor, a final, painful irony.

Trauffaut made *Domicile Conjugal* only a few months after finishing *L'Enfant Sauvage*, and the perfunctoriness we sense in the last episode of the Doinel story is possibly the result of this hectic schedule. A year later, in the spring of 1971, Truffaut turned to another novel of Henri-Pierre Roché, the author of *Jules et Jim*, a project he had had in mind for a long time. *Les Deux Anglaises et le Continent* must be seen as a companion piece to that earlier film. Whereas *Jules et Jim* impresses by communicating a strong sense of the life force, *Les Deux Anglaises* is pervaded by an aura of death and decay. The almost maudlin sensitivity of Anne and Muriel is in direct contrast to the vitality of Catherine. The reserve of Claude Roc (Jean-Pierre Léaud in his first non-Doinel role for Truffaut) is another factor which increases our distance from the film. Stylistically, Truffaut further separates us from this story of neurotic, painful love by desaturating the colour so as to create the feeling of the two-colour process of the early 30s, a period into which this egregiously romantic film might have fitted very well. With the benefit of hindsight we can suggest that Truffaut gave us a much more forceful metaphor for sexual alienation in *Adèle H.* four years later; yet, difficult as it is, *Les Deux Anglaises* has its own attractions. Truffaut had been struggling with the text of Roché's novel for a good many years: part of the purpose of the high stylization of the film is to give us a sense of the complexity of this struggle with the text. Truffaut has noted that the Brontë sisters and Marcel Proust were very much in his mind during preparation and shooting. The film shares much of the introversion and rococo eroticism of those fictional worlds.

Exhausted after the difficult period of shooting on *Les Deux Anglaises*, Truffaut repaired to Nice to edit it. When he discovered the disused set of a Paris square (for *The Madwoman of Chaillot*) on the lot at the Studios Victorine, 'a desire which had been playing around vaguely in the back of my mind for many years suddenly became crystallized: I would shoot a film about shooting a film'. This was the spark of *La Nuit Américaine*, but first Truffaut had to shoot *Une Belle Fille comme Moi* (U.K.: *A Gorgeous Bird Like Me*; U.S.: *Such a Gorgeous Kid Like Me*, 1972). Like *Domicile Conjugal*, *Une Belle Fille* seems to have been shot perfunctorily, with impatience. Nevertheless, we can see what attracted Truffaut to this American novel. Camille Bliss (Bernadette Lafont) is not only an outrageous character, she is a woman. With the sole exception of *L'Enfant Sauvage* (and possibly *Les Quatre Cents Coups*), every one of Truffaut's sixteen films has exhibited his fascination with women's roles. Often, in the genre films, women are deceptively dangerous: Franca (Nelly Benedetti) in *La Peau Douce* blasts her husband with a shotgun; Julie Kohler efficiently disposes of five men; Julie/Marion in *La Sirène du Mississippi* lures Louis Mahé to potential destruction; Les Deux Anglaises weave a deathly web around Claude. *Une Belle Fille* offers for the first time a chance to treat this theme comically, but the comic elements are peculiarly American and, as so often before, the film is distanced by this clash between American and French concerns. The comedy is a bit too raucous and strident—and it doesn't quite come off.

Yet Camille is a wonderfully self-assured character. In *Une Belle Fille* Truffaut moves significantly closer to the woman's point of view and forecasts, comically, the maturity of sexual politics which is so gloriously revealed in *La Nuit Américaine*, one of his very best films.

Ostensibly, the purpose of *La Nuit Américaine* is to portray the Pirandellian ironies and the Hawksian pleasures of the job of making movies. It does this, certainly, but it does more as well. Setting himself up as the hard-of-hearing director Ferrand, the still centre of a storm of activity, Truffaut surrounds himself with a cast and crew that are mainly female. Alphonse (Léaud) is Ferrand's younger self; Alexandre (Jean-Pierre Aumont) may be in part a forecast of his older self. But the main interest and vitality lie with the women, an extraordinary group. The lead, if there is one, is Julie/Paméla (Jacqueline Bisset, another doubling), a beautiful and sensitive woman, but not a particularly strong actress. The strength lies elsewhere: with Séverine (Valentina Cortese), an ageing actress who fumbles her lines but who nevertheless (partly because she is Italian) is the most ebullient and open woman in all Truffaut. And with Stacey (Alexandra Stewart), an actress with a special sense of her own worth, who is pregnant, and who in the course of the film becomes a mother to cast and crew and is contrasted positively with Ferrand (who should be the 'father' of the group). And with Odile (Nike Arrighi) and Liliane (Dani), two tough young crew members who live their own lives, separate from the others. And especially with Joëlle (Nathalie Baye), who can say: 'I can see dropping a guy for a film, but I could never drop a film for a guy!' She can suggest off-hand to Bernard, the prop man, that they make love in the bushes and then react with humorous indifference when she inadvertently interrupts Bernard and Odile in bed a little while later. It is no accident that Truffaut has made Joëlle continuity assistant; we can take her as an homage to Suzanne Schiffman, who has been Truffaut's continuity assistant for so long, and who with Truffaut and Jean-Louis Richard wrote the script for *La Nuit Américaine*. The vitality of the women in the film might not impress us so much if it were not for the fact that there are not as many admirable roles for women in three years of American films these days as there are in Truffaut's homage to the sort of studio film-making which is dying out.

Looking very much like a film that might have been made in the American style in the 30s or 40s, with the quick, witty dialogue and insouciance of Howard Hawks and evincing the fascination with jobs that Truffaut sees in the work of Raoul Walsh, *La Nuit Améri-*

François Truffaut in his *La Chambre Verte*: through a glass darkly.

caine is Truffaut's most lively film since *Jules et Jim* and rightly deserves to be compared favourably with that earlier paean to the life force.

After finishing *La Nuit Américaine*, Truffaut took two years off from filming, during which time he edited several collections of André Bazin's criticism and a collection of his own criticism, produced a couple of films and prepared scripts for future projects. In the early months of 1975 he returned to the camera, shooting *L'Histoire d'Adèle H.* on location in Guernsey and Dakar. An extraordinarily intense portrait of the *amour fou* of the daughter of Victor Hugo, based on her recently decoded diaries, *Adèle H.* depends for much of its disturbing effect on the work of Isabelle Adjani, a brilliant young actress who was born at about the time Truffaut completed his first short film. As with Léaud, Truffaut uses an unusual acting talent and the resultant film is a collaboration between star and *auteur*. Adjani, on screen nearly every minute, is presented with two overriding objectives: Adèle is plainly mad (she spent her later years in an asylum) and the actress must communicate this, but subtly and positively; she must also somehow indicate the mythic dimensions of this true story—if *L'Histoire d'Adèle H.* were simply a portrait of insane love, it would not have half the impact it does. In truth, Adèle's situation was at least in part a response to the fame of her father and the attention he lavished on her then dead elder sister. It is also clear from the diaries that Adèle had at least a vague sense of her political position. When a man crosses half the world in search of a woman we consider it a great love story; when a woman does the same, we see her as mad.

Adèle H., a film of very dark colours and darker emotions, with a 30s soundtrack using music by the late Maurice Jaubert, is distanced in the same way that many of Truffaut's earlier films were. But it is also measurably more intense because it focuses so strongly on a single character; the other characters in the film are seen from Adèle's perspective, hardly more than shadows. *Adèle H.* is a distillation of Truffaut's major theme throughout the films that preceded it: his obsession with the manner in which human beings connect with one another, as often through pain as through love. Adèle is *une*

belle fille, and a bride wearing black, as well as a would-be *sirène du St Lawrence*. The conclusion we draw from her disturbing journey in search of Lieutenant Pinson is not dissimilar to the conclusion we drew from Antoine Doinel's comical adventures in the same vein: the sexual politics of love rest on elaborate (if often necessary) self-delusions.

Shortly after finishing *Adèle H.*, Truffaut shot *L'Argent de Poche*, a film in quite a different style. This story of a group of children allowed him to return once again, as he had done periodically in the past, to an analysis of that other central relationship in our lives, the one between adults and children. It is a film *for* children as well as *of* them, and so it re-creates the mythic, discontinuous, wondrous style of narrative that is characteristic of the best children's stories. At the same time, it sees children as very much a part of the more cruel adult universe: childhood is not easy, even if it is humorous.

Although François Truffaut has garnered his share of critical and popular attention during his twenty-year career as a film-maker, he has never quite been seen for what he is. It was a critical commonplace in the 60s (less true since *La Nuit Américaine*) that both reviewers and audiences were always vaguely disappointed with a new Truffaut film. They expected a great deal from the director of the two masterpieces *Les Quatre Cents Coups* and *Jules et Jim*. Partially this was a result of Truffaut's increasing stylistic reserve; most of his films speak very quietly indeed. More important, it was a matter of the highly sophisticated idiom he adopted, one which demanded that his audiences see his films as *he* did, set snugly in the context of fifty years of cinema history and quietly but directly reflecting the complexities of styles and approaches therein. This major element of Truffaut's work is often given lip-service, seldom discussed seriously.

When we have learned to deal with these twin aesthetic barriers, when we accept Truffaut's intentionally limited spectrum of concerns, then we may see him as a film-maker who has, quietly, expressed truths about sexual politics that rival those of Ingmar Bergman for their perspicacity, and who has moreover shown us with a precision and insight seldom matched in the history of cinema how generations of adults and children relate to and influence each other. Truffaut's greatest value as a film-maker lies here: in the intelligence he transmits to us of the way we—men and women, adults and children—manage, somehow, to live together.

After the highly successful *L'Argent de Poche*, Truffaut's next film was *L'Homme qui aimait les Femmes* (*The Man Who Loved Women*, 1977). If Truffaut's chief European influences had been, as Monaco points out, Renoir, Vigo and Ophuls, we have now to add a fourth name, that of Sacha Guitry, not only because of the form of the film—mostly narrated by its hero Bertrand Morane—but also because of the delivery of the actor Charles Denner, which is very reminiscent of the fluent, non-stop Guitry style.

In spite of the title, this is not a film about a Don Juan: Bertrand is, as Truffaut points out, simply a man who—like little Joey in Bruno Bettelheim's book *The Empty Fortress*—was not loved by his mother; and so his adult life is spent in the pursuit of women—all women. Often very funny—Nelly Bourgeaud as the respectable married woman who doesn't let her prudery get in the way of the most daring of amorous exploits—the film logically ends with Bertrand's death and the end of his frenzied attempts to possess every woman he catches sight of. The mixture of the comic and the serious is Truffaut's most successful since *Tirez sur le Pianiste*, and the performances—notably those of Brigitte Fossey and Geneviève Fontanel, as well as the already mentioned Nelly Bourgeaud and the incomparable Charles Denner—make the film one of his most satisfying works.

In 1978 Truffaut made a daring new departure with his *La Chambre Verte*, credited as 'based on themes by Henry James' but actually a fairly close adaptation of James' short story 'Altar of the Dead' with a notion or two from 'The Beast in the Jungle' thrown in. He plays the principal role himself, that of a bereaved widower (in the James story, the hero lost his fiancée, not his wife) who devotes himself to a cult of remembrance. The element that might have been borrowed from 'The Beast in the Jungle' is in fact vaguely present in 'Altar of the Dead': the possibility of there being some kind of romantic relationship between the hero and the woman who joins him in his attempt to keep the dead alive in their hearts and minds.

The film resembles *Deux Anglaises et le Continent*, but this is an even darker and more tragic film. Truffaut's performance is a real one (unlike the neutral one he gave in Spielberg's *Close Encounters of the Third Kind*): the only other major role is well done by Nathalie Baye. Of course, one could also compare this film with *Adèle H.*, in that both deal with an obsession with the impossible, but *La Chambre Verte* is less romantic, less distanced. It would seem that Truffaut is blessed with an infinite capacity for self-renewal, and that he will continue to surprise us.

Truffaut has been a prolific author himself: e.g. *Hitchcock* (1966), written in collaboration with Helen G. Scott; *Les Films de ma Vie* (1975; *The Films in My Life*, 1978), an anthology of his criticism. The scripts of many of his films have been published, and he has also edited several posthumous works of André Bazin.

There are several books on Truffaut: Don Allen's *Truffaut* (1974), C. G. Crisp's *François Truffaut* (1972) and Graham Petrie's *The Cinema of François Truffaut* (1970); see also the chapters on Truffaut in James Monaco's *The New Wave* (1977).

AGNÈS VARDA

Richard Roud

Agnès Varda (born 1928) came up the hard way. Starting as official photographer for Jean Vilar's Théâtre National Populaire, she somehow managed to finance a featurette in 1955, *La Pointe courte*, a co-operative production and one of the true ancestors of the *nouvelle vague*. It is concerned with the struggle of a small fishing village in the south of France against the economic domination of the big combines, as well as with the story of a young man from the village who has come home with his Parisian wife in a final attempt to sort out the failure of their marriage. The two stories are told side by side (as in Faulkner's *The Wild Palms*), and the two themes are never intermingled. It was up to the spectator to make the connections between the themes, to compare them, to contrast them. In spite of the brilliance of its conception and its astonishing visual beauty, the film was not entirely successful because of the inadequacy of its leading lady (Silvia Montfort). But the idea worked—so well that when Varda asked Resnais to help her edit the film, he was very reluctant to do so, precisely because she had succeeded in doing

Thérèse Liotard and Valérie Mairesse in *One Sings, the Other Doesn't.*

what he had been aiming at for a long time. (He finally gave in, however.)

After this first short feature, Varda turned to short films: *Du Côté de la Côte (The Riviera—Today's Eden,* 1958), an irreverent yet moving film about that most hackneyed of subjects, the French Riviera; *O Saisons O Châteaux* (1957), fashion models on parade at Chambord; and *Opéra Mouffe* (1958), a moving evocation of that Left Bank open-market street, la Rue Mouffetard, as seen through the eyes of a pregnant woman. (Varda herself was pregnant at the time.) Documentary is transformed into a visual commentary on love and death, birth and old age. And here lay the true originality of *Opéra Mouffe*—it achieved its ends through purely visual means. Realistic and fantastic, objective and subjective, social and personal, it confirmed that the maker of *La Pointe courte* was an original artist.

In her first feature, *Cléo de 5 à 7 (Cléo from 5 to 7,* 1962), she returned to the binary structure of *La Pointe courte,* and the film is again both objective and subjective—Cléo's odyssey from the Rue de Rivoli to the Salpêtrière Hospital, and her spiritual odyssey from ignorance to understanding. Cléo is a young singer who is suddenly faced with the possibility of death, and the film follows her for two hours, from her anguished visit to a fortune-teller to the hospital where she is to learn the results of a medical analysis. Follows her step by step: little is omitted, there are no ellipses. The streets and cafés of Paris, the taxis and the cinema, are seen as they really are and as they appear through the eyes of a woman who is tracked by death.

After the grimness of this first feature, Varda turned next in *Le Bonheur (Happiness,* 1965) to a world where all was at first Mozartian sweetness and light. At least on the surface. For this idyllic tale of a young carpenter and his wife is darkened by her inability to accept her husband's desire to add a third person to the idyll: he wants to keep his wife and have a mistress, too. The idea seems less shocking now than it did in its time, and indeed Jean-Claude Drouot and his wife who play the couple in the film are prefigurations of the flower people of the middle 60s. But the film, though widely popular, was rejected by many of those who had liked *Cléo from 5 to 7*: they thought Varda was selling out, or at the very least settling for the merely pretty. But in the light of later works like *Lion's Love* (1969) I think one can see that she was, quite bravely, trying to posit an alternative to the nuclear family; and because this idea was by and large unacceptable at the time, she felt obliged to sugar-coat it with ravishing photography and the music of Mozart.

Her next film was to be her least successful in the commercial sense: *Les Créatures* (1966). Again, she told two stories: the birth of a novel and the life of a couple culminating in the birth of their child. The other characters of the film, the islanders, are all worked into the novel. They are, in a sense, the pawns in a fascinating chess game which the hero plays on a life-sized board with the forces of evil and destruction. Is this fantastic game, in which the destinies of the characters are resolved, purely imaginary? In any case, the film seems to me to be a supremely intelligent *jeu d'esprit*; but the wit seemed to have been lost on many who saw it only as pretentiously intellectual, never realizing, as Henri Langlois put it, that *Les Créatures* was pure Méliès.

As a result of the film's failure at the box-office, Varda found it very difficult to put together another film in France. Her next film, *Lion's Love*, was made in America in 1969. The subject of the film is ostensibly an avant-garde woman director who has come to Hollywood to make a movie. But the fact that Varda chose Shirley Clarke (director of *The Connection* and *Portrait of Jason*) to play the director, Viva, and James Rado and Gerome Ragni (co-authors and stars of *Hair*) to play the friends who put her up, soon make us realize that the film's true subject is film-making itself, just as Pirandello's true subject was the theatre. And therefore, when Shirley Clarke is supposed to attempt suicide and

cannot go through with the scene, it is not at all surprising that Varda jumps in and acts the part herself. And when Viva complains (to camera) at the end of the film that her dream of being in a *real* movie has once more been frustrated, it is neither inappropriate nor startling. What did startle—even shock— American audiences was the confrontation between the four characters of the film and the assassination of Robert Kennedy. But like Varda's earlier films, *Lion's Love* is about that, too: the contrast and contradiction between public events and private viewing. On the one side, a tragic event reduced to a small image on the box; on the other, three people in a bed (Rado, Ragni and Viva form a *ménage à trois*) trying to care while having breakfast. Of course the news on the television is upsetting, but yes, you still go on eating breakfast. So perhaps the real subject of the film is not just film-making, but reality and illusion in the broadest sense, private faces and public places, a collage of America in the plague year of 1968.

Since then, Varda's career has gone through a difficult phase. Her episode for *Loin du Vietnam (Far from Vietnam*, 1967) was never used in the film although Chris Marker insisted on keeping her name on the credits. She then made a feature-length film for French television, *Nausicaa* (1970), which has never been seen. French TV refused to schedule it on the pretext that the film was too overtly against the Greece of the Colonels! This in spite of the fact that Varda had warned them that this story of a Greek woman was bound to have political elements in it. Indeed, they refused even to screen the film privately. After this blow Varda attempted to set up other films, and came close once or twice, but the films were never actually made. So she is at a difficult point in her career—ironically, considering the call for more women directors. But one cannot believe that a career which began so brilliantly and which continued to develop with promise can have come to such a premature end.

Varda's career did *not* come to a premature end. In 1977 she made one of her best films, *L'Une Chante, L'Autre pas (One Sings, the Other Doesn't)*. Feminist in inspiration, it is the story of two women whose lives become

inextricably intertwined. One (Valérie Mairesse, a great new discovery) liberates herself very early on; the other (Thérèse Liotard) takes a lot longer. This chronicle of parallel lives is both the story of a friendship and a dramatization of Simone de Beauvoir's phrase, 'One isn't born a woman; one becomes one.' Occasionally the film's ideological load threatens to swamp its dramatic impact, but Varda gets away with it by the skin of her teeth. And, cliché for cliché, a miss is as good as a mile. *L'Une Chante, L'Autre pas* came out only a month or so after Resnais' *Providence*, and six months before Chris Marker's *Le Fond de l'Air est Rouge*—thus marking an unexpected and highly satisfying return of the old 'Left Bank' group.

For the record, Varda made, for German television, an 80-minute documentary in 1975. Called *Daguerréotypes*, it was an investigation of the shop-keepers on the Rue Daguerre in Paris (where Varda has lived for many years). See also the articles on Marker and Resnais.

DZIGA VERTOV

Jean-André Fieschi

In 1916 Denis Arkadievitch Kaufman was writing: poems, essays, science fiction. Ten years earlier, as a schoolboy, he was already writing (poems, according to Sadoul); and he never ceased writing until his death in 1954: articles, projects, manifestos, journals. It was around 1916, too, that Denis Arkadievitch Kaufman (born 1896) chose a name for himself: Dziga Vertov. 'Dziga, derived from a Ukrainian word meaning a top, alludes to the wheel incessantly turning, perpetual motion. (It is also related to the word Tzigane, or gypsy.) Vertov is derived from the Russian word "vertet", meaning to turn, pivot, spin round' (Georges Sadoul). For us today, the name Dziga Vertov covers a body of texts (writings, films). These films and these writings do (and do not) tell the same story. They are the traces (films, writings) of a fierce and solitary struggle over the years to attempt to impose an idea (of cinema) that ultimately comes to look like an obsession.

The sentence of death pronounced by Vertov in 1919 against *all* pre-existing forms of cinema was never to be rescinded. Such determination to fight for his own conception

to the exclusion of all others is unique in itself. In the historical, political, social and cultural context in which it developed (the Soviet Union from immediately after the October Revolution to the eve of the Twentieth Party Congress), it is extremely specific—what we are confronted with here is Vertov's *wish*.

Dziga Vertov: over and above the texts bearing this signature (films, writings), the name denotes—more than any other contemporary, and that includes Eisenstein—an area of basic questions. An area in which this name serves less as a model than as a sort of fundamental reference point.

Let us return to chronological facts in order to sketch in some subsequent developments. It should be noted right away that in many respects these developments constitute our history. For Vertov's name cannot be related exclusively to the history of the cinema. What this name (this *oeuvre*) prophetically inaugurates is the articulation of methods of mass communication (then called the cinema) to politics, with (by intention, at least) a revolutionary—in other words, Marxist—purpose.

1916: Vertov, too, was a futurist. Intellectuals were making a clean sweep of the old world, which was showing cracks everywhere. An aeroplane propeller, said Marcel Duchamp, is more beautiful than the Winged Victory of Samothrace. Syntax, sounds and forms were torn apart. Nostalgia for the future was rampant among artistic groups and gatherings. The trappings of romanticism, symbolism and expressionism were banished to the prop room. The machine had arrived, seeming to vindicate the new poets because it worked, it drove, it flew.

It also recorded. In 1917 Vertov set up a 'sound laboratory'. The recording and editing of real sounds: sawmills, torrents, motors, words. Montage, in other words, had already arrived for him, as it had for Mayakovsky or Apollinaire as far as the written word was concerned. In other words, the mechanical means of reproduction permitted not only reproduction, but more particularly arrangement and manipulation.

First the word (the poems), then the sound. There remained the image. In 1918 Vertov became the compiler and chief editor of *Kinonedielia* (*Film Weekly*), the first series of newsreel programmes issued by the Soviet government. Vertov did not actually shoot these revolutionary newsreels, but organized, edited, titled and tinted them, imposing rhythms (first attempts at rapid montage, etc.).

Just imagine the overwhelming double shock: of history changing the face of Russia as never before, since the new world is already there, in the process of construction, while an old dream takes shape in the chaos; and of a nascent language, apparently freed from the old constraints, which enables one both to reflect the world and to reconstruct it, explain it, communicate its revolutionary exhilaration. Naturally Dziga Vertov at his editing table was intoxicated. For him, henceforth, cinema and revolution would be one. And indeed the cinema would be the revolutionary art *par excellence*.

In 1921, after the newsreels, came montage films including *Agitpoezd Vtsika* (*Agit-train 'Vtsik'*). 'This train, also known as *The Lenin Train*, was a mobile agit-prop unit that included a theatrical group, a cinema, cameramen, a small film laboratory and cutting-room, a library, political lectures, a printing press and so on. It travelled through the country from 22 April 1919 to 2 November 1921. The film describes the journey, incorporating footage taken by the unit's cameramen. Vertov had been on board during January and Feburary 1920. Over the same period, the steamer "Red Star" was navigating the Volga with the same equipment and purpose' (Georges Sadoul).

Yes, can one imagine that? When Lenin declared that the cinema was the most important of all the arts for the young Soviet republic, he was obviously not attempting to settle an aesthetic argument, and did not necessarily prefer films to dance or painting. On the contrary, what he had at once perceived was the political function behind the reproduction and dissemination of images in a vast land the majority of whose peoples were illiterate. Education, information, agitation. As Walter Benjamin later wrote: 'Earlier much futile thought had been devoted to the question of whether photography was an art. The primary question—whether the very invention of photography had not transformed the entire nature of art—was not raised' (*The Work of Art in the Age of Mechanical Reproduction*).

Dziga Vertov was probably the first of all those who created and organized images to understand this. What he saw was the political power of the new messages, making him historically the true founder of the audio-visual (and not only in the cinema either: the multimedia experience of the propaganda trains opened up a still virgin territory). But what Vertov also saw (and in these dizzy depths he was to be effectively engulfed) was the whole problematical question of the material itself: firmly anchored on the side of reality (political, historical) through his experience in newsreels and then with the propaganda trains, he was also aware of the magical mystery element in the shadow show. Henceforth, his utopian dream was to dismantle theatrical illusion by simultaneously producing (or trying to produce) an awareness of reality. Annette Michelson describes this process as a development (a discovery) transforming ... a Magician into an Epistemologist'. But it was on this very point that all the misunderstandings were to arise.

It was a time of aggressions, peremptory affirmations, repudiations. Listen to the voice of Vertov between 1922 and 1924, still untainted, even in its very excesses, by any interference:

We henceforth liberate the camera and make it work in a different direction, very different from copying. . . .

The scenario as produced by literary cuisine will disappear in the very near future. . . .

One of the principal accusations made against us is that we are inaccessible to the masses . . . If what the masses need is simple propaganda pamphlets, does it follow that they do not want serious articles by Engels and Lenin? You may have among you today a Lenin of the Russian cinema, and you do not let him work on the pretext that the results of his activities are new and incomprehensible. . . .

To see and to show reality, in the name of the world proletarian revolution, that is the elementary principle of the Kino-Eyes. . . .

Kino-Eye: opportunity to make the invisible visible, to lighten the darkness, to lay bare what is obscured, to make acting non-acting, to turn lies into truth. Kino-

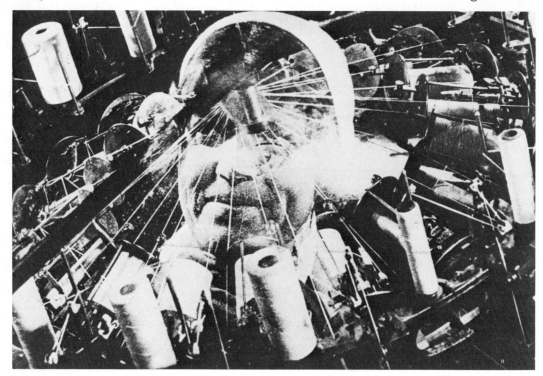

The birth, not of an experimental cinema, but of a *theoretical* cinema: *The Man with the Movie Camera.*

Eye, fusion of science and cinematographic activities, whose purpose is to hammer us with the communist decoding of reality; attempt to show the truth on the screen through *cinéma vérité.* . . .

Vertov never deviated from this messianic tone. He was truly the prophet, the guide, he who voices the truth; and the ingenuous linking of his name with Lenin's indicates clearly enough just how he thought of himself as sole harbinger of the future.

After the *Kino-Pravda (Film-Truth)* series, which appeared at roughly monthly intervals from 1922 to 1925, came *Kino-Glaz (Kino-Eye,* or *Life Seized on the Wing,* 1924). Working with his brother Mikhail Kaufman and his wife Yelisaveta Svilova, Vertov in a sense stripped his method down, fusing both his formal (or formalist, as they would be described) and 'political' preoccupations into a single discourse. It is clear that in his opinion he had succeeded.

In fact the *Kino-Eye* now looks like a rough draft for *Chelovek s Kinoapparatom*

(*The Man with the Movie Camera,* 1929). It contains an astonishing play (back and forth) between document (testimony, evidence) and reconstruction; or rather, a radical and progressive *task* of fictionalizing the documentary, to a degree where a genuine *dislocation* takes place, and one finds oneself far removed from the raw material. Figures of style are essayed here, various kinds of process shots, play with or by the camera, innovatory montage rhythms, intertitles that defuse subsequent scenes, frenzied accelerations, repetitions, variations, ellipses, building into a sort of catalogue of effects: the cinema-tool is evaluated in all its aspects and all its possibilities, with a sophistication and a trenchant audacity that still astonishes today, even after Brakhage, Ron Rice and, especially, Bruce Conner. For Vertov is experimenting less with technical devices—as L'Herbier often did at that time—than with a radically new *logic* in which space is restructured, and even time does not escape the manipulator's iconoclasm: for instance in the genuinely instructional scenes where the action is reversed so that bread becomes wheatgerm again, or an ox that has been butchered reconstitutes itself before our eyes. The effect is used to *demonstrate* rather than to amaze, as in Cocteau, although it also generates a certain childlike sense of wonderment. Between these two reverse-action sequences, moreover, Vertov introduces a rustic magician baffling a group of open-mouthed urchins with his tricks in some remote corner of central Asia. Like Abel Gance, Vertov was not afraid to weave metaphors: yes, this illusionist is the film-maker. But he was also governed, to the point of obsession, by a sort of moral impulse to expose the illusionistic element and its hallucinatory power (Brecht would find other means to impose the same strictures) by drawing attention to the technical processes of filming and the relevance to reality in the process of construction. Vertov saw himself as a *positive* illusionist.

The Man with the Movie Camera was the realization of this programme without any false pretexts. Now that contemporary polemics have quite literally passed the film by (about its formalism or otherwise, about the absurdity of the whole enterprise, about the usefulness of this sort of experiment, about the subjectivism—already violently denounced by Eisenstein in discussing *Kino-Eye*: 'From the reality around him Vertov takes what impresses *him*, and not what, by impressing the spectator, would enable him to harvest his psychism'), the film today is one of those that count the most in understanding the history of forms. But it was not a film that appealed to contemporaries busy with other concerns.

Dziga Vertov: 'The film *The Man with the Movie Camera* is not just a practical application, it is also a theoretical demonstration on the screen . . . The film is only the sum of the facts captured on celluloid; or if you like, not only the sum but the product, the "higher mathematics of facts". Each term and each factor is a tiny, individual document. The assembly of all these documents is calculated so that, on the one hand, only semantic concatenations of fragments which coincide with the visual concatenations are retained in the film, while on the other, these concatenations do not require the support of intertitles, and also so that the final sum of all these

concatenations emerges as an indissoluble organic whole' (1928).

Yes, what distinguishes *The Man with the Movie Camera* is the birth, not of an experimental cinema (what were Georges Méliès, Edwin Porter and Mack Sennett doing if not experimenting?), but of a *theoretical* cinema in the sense of what one might use today to describe the work of Paul Sharits or Michael Snow. But although it foreshadowed every language revolution and many an avant-garde to come, the rupture with prevailing forms of cinema, or even with Eisenstein the brother-enemy, was nevertheless not too radical.

(The antithesis of Vertov was of course not Eisenstein but Dovzhenko, the fabulous Dovzhenko who used his heritage, the common ideologico-mythological fund, as a springboard for creation, whereas Vertov, who had never really abandoned Proletkult leftist radicalism, dreamed of clean sweeps, a future free of all ties: 'Down with Russo-German psychological ciné-drama clogged by the perceptions and memories of childhood,' 1922.)

The Man with the Movie Camera was certainly an act of aggression, like the scalpel of *Un Chien andalou*, and therefore exposed Vertov to accusations of vandalism, or at best, buffoonery. What had been damaged? Quite simply the basic conception of what a film should be. It was an object difficult to pick up; then what use was it? Herein lies Vertov's delusion, a typically pedagogic one: he believed in the (immediate) utility of work like this. A necessary delusion: without it, where next?

Actually, the best thing one can do nowadays is to reintegrate these films into a film-historical context, where they fall retrospectively into place. In doing so, one also re-examines and retraces the theoretical breakthrough; and one discovers the numerous descendants (Ivens, Godard, Bruce Conner). But these films were not conceived as museum pieces. Whom were they meant for? Or had Vertov dreamed up some purely imaginary viewer?

For a long time it was held that there was an insuperable (and therefore misjudged) contradiction between Dziga Vertov's proclaimed allegiance to documentary (his belief in reality) and his 'formalism'. In one camp, *Simfonia Donbossa* (also known as *Entusiazm*,

Symphony of the Don Basin or *Enthusiasm*, 1930) and *Tri Pesni o Leninye* (*Three Songs of Lenin*, 1934); in the other, *The Man with the Movie Camera*. The implication here is that he packed away his toys in his playbox from time to time and got down to his commission to make a propaganda film. But this is to ignore Dziga Vertov's obsession, the very basis of his approach: to find new methods of representation worthy of the new man who was being born in the land of the Soviets, this new man who was throwing off the shackles of poverty, illiteracy and oppression. The Revolution was a sort of goddess. The same revolutionary fervour made Vertov sing of machines and harvests, rivers and flocks, in *Shestaya Chast Mira* (*A Sixth of the World*, 1926), and also dismantle the mechanisms of representation. He was the first to draw attention to the spectator: you, sitting in your seat in the cinema … His purpose was to eliminate all the characteristic features of the prevailing cinema, that 'ciné-poison'—the literary, psychological and metaphysical ballast—and to offer a new tool to the new man. That the new is born of the old and that the birth is sometimes difficult was something Vertov could not admit. It is to his mania (his persistence) that we owe these films, magnificent or aberrant, but invariably new.

What was Vertov's dream if not the obliteration of any gap between political and artistic avant-gardes? (Lenin's lack of enthusiasm for Mayakovsky, Vertov's principal identification figure, is well known.) How is it that for many film-makers and theorists today he has become the locus of a sort of paradise lost: a totemic figure of the revolutionary film-maker, in whom all contradictions between creativity and social utility, theoretical and practical tasks, formal concerns and 'message' are supposedly obliterated?

What the existence of his films and writings opens up is not an academic debate, but a problematic area which is still our own. The real folly lies in trying to imitate this prophetic pioneer (of television, the underground, militant cinema), when the principal lesson he left us was that one must invent.

As for the dream that a communist cinema might exist, that's another—and, truth to tell, a rather speculative—story. But Vertov

was able to conceive it in his time because a stupendous laboratory was in full operation: the laboratory of real history. It was there that the first distinct logic for the articulation of images and sounds was born, invented by a man so determined to be nobody's son that he would not use his father's name.

Translated by Tom Milne

For further reading, see Luda and Jean Schnitzer's *Cinema in Revolution* (1973), Jay Leyda's *Kino* (1960) and Georges Sadoul's monograph, in French: *Dziga Vertov* (1971). Vertov's own writings have been translated into French under the title *Articles, Journaux, Projets* (1972). See also Erik Barnouw's *Documentary* (1974).

KING VIDOR

Richard Combs

Family affairs have always been a reliable barometer of national affairs in the American cinema. The primacy of the family was one of Griffith's most distinctively Victorian articles of faith, evident not only in the strenuous parallelism of the private and the historical dramas of *Intolerance*, but in his Dickensian mode of social criticism. Orphans and foundlings, broken homes and irresponsible guardians were clear symptoms of social breakdown; in *Broken Blossoms*, the brutalizing of the heroine by her father is even set in the context of an East–West polarity of pacifism and violence, parental nurture and cruelty. For John Ford, the family is the bedrock of the pioneering experience, as immutable as the landscape of Monument Valley, until discordant strains begin to creep in with *Two Rode Together*, *The Searchers* and the unorthodox arrangements of *Seven Women*—which, but for its pastiche 30s style, fits well enough with latter-day assaults on the joys of living together by such as Peckinpah and Aldrich.

For King Vidor (born 1896) the family and the group experience are just as central, and as much a model for the growth of America itself, as they are for Ford. More thoroughly, perhaps, than anyone else, Vidor has worked through the fluctuating fortunes of the family—from optimistic affirmation and expansion to neurotic withdrawal and disintegration—as a way of measuring shifting versions of the American Dream. And while Vidor's contribution has been crucial, the very range of attitudes it has encompassed makes it difficult to define. The problem is partly the sheer size and diversity of his output, which refuses to be grouped round particular genres or subject-matter. The films of Vidor and Ford can be broadly linked as celebrations of growth; but lacking as consistent a background as the Westward expansion of civilization, and as clear a metaphor as the burgeoning township in *My Darling Clementine*, Vidor leaves one grappling with the indefinables of spiritual and emotional development. He has, on the other hand, generally avoided the ready-made mythology which merges Ford's heroes with his societies in simple communion; individual initiative and energy in Vidor are never quite so comfortably adjusted to any social order.

Even when he is working within traditional forms, Vidor's personal genres cut across a number of borders. His excursions out West, for instance, are as much concerned with man finding himself in his work, and in his society, as the direct confrontations of such problems in *The Crowd* (1928) and *Our Daily Bread* (U.K.: *The Miracle of Life*, 1934). Vidor's earliest 'man without a star' might be Zeke in *Hallelujah* (1929), who puts as much triumphant enthusiasm into his passing vocation as a spiritual troubadour as Dempsey (in *Man Without a Star*, 1955) does into his cap-and-bells performance on the banjo; Zeke eventually finds his way 'home', while Dempsey—after leaving his younger *alter ego* in the socializing care of a small-rancher family—continues his wandering, possibly across the Canadian frontier. The creeping urbanization of the West is partly played for laughs in *Man Without a Star* with the arrival of indoor plumbing down on the ranch; here and elsewhere, however, Vidor seems to welcome such development when it implies renewal, on various levels, for a stagnant community (*Duel in the Sun*, 1947; *Ruby Gentry*, 1953), and to regret it when it involves some psychic splitting of communities or individuals. In *Beyond the Forest* (1949), Rosa Moline dreams of escape from her rural home town to the big city, as Dempsey dreams of unending open spaces; both, finally, are deprived of all attachments

as their obsessions drive them to different kinds of destruction. Rosa dies by the side of the tracks leading to Chicago as a train thunders by, and Dempsey disappears into the landscape, almost wilfully transplanting himself to another time and place.

Stylistically as well, Vidor forges links between different subjects and different periods in his career. The expressionism that couples with the fierce melodramas through the late 40s and 50s survives from earlier contexts—the revivalist meeting in *Hallelujah*, during which Zeke is overwhelmed more by sexual than religious fervour, and the final purging of his misspent passion in a pursuit and duel through an eerie swamp (like the one where the two male antagonists of *Ruby Gentry* also come to a violent end). One of Vidor's most affecting moments of this kind occurs early in *The Crowd*—a deep, shadowy shot down a long staircase as John Sims fearfully walks up behind the ambulance men who have come for his dead father, with a dense gaggle of friends and neighbours waiting at the bottom. The preceding few minutes have, with Wellesian flair, covered the birth of young John (on 4 July 1900, 'America's 124th birthday'), presided over by an ebulliently proud father, a would-be sire-of-presidents ('There's a little man the world is going to hear from all right'). The disappearance of John's father so early in his life thus has the reverberation of a world crumbling. The significance of the moment—as John is thrust out into life with the inbred ambition to be 'somebody big' but abruptly deprived of his spiritual backing—has as recent an echo as Kubrick's *Barry Lyndon*, where the hero loses his father in the very first shot, and must subsequently struggle, on his own, to make it as a 'gentleman'.

One of the most profound of Vidor's films, *The Crowd* is about a baptism of fire, as fierce as any battle. At the age of twenty-one, John (James Murray) arrives in New York, more than confident that he can measure up to a stranger's gloomy prognostication of life in the big city ('You've got to be good in that town if you want to beat the crowd'). The lesson the city teaches him is that learning to live with the crowd is the more important and less soul-destroying endeavour; remarkably, the film brings him this far by blunting his arrogance sufficiently for him to accept his own limitations without negating his ambition or vitality. It is only a short distance from the cheery self-sufficiency of his ukelele-strumming and go-getting in the most deprived circumstances to the cheery self-delusion of his hopes to set the world on fire with his advertising jingles. Respecting the balance and proportion of the two, the film's energies flow in a gentle switchback—celebrating the one while lightly satirizing the other.

A vigorous ambivalence springs from Vidor's treatment of one or two central tensions. The excitement and the anonymity of the big city are orchestrated through a variety of moods, from ebullient optimism to ground-down despair. On John's arrival in New York, a montage of city bustle and thrusting skyscrapers gives way to a shot travelling up one building, in which our hero is indistinguishable amidst a sea of desk workers; later, in the washroom, John is irritated by his colleagues' jesting at his ambitions to get ahead ('You guys have been working here so long you all talk alike'); and after being persuaded by a friend to forget his studies for an evening at Coney Island, John waits for his blind date—his archetypal match, Mary (Eleanor Boardman)—outside a building where a stream of look-alike girls emerge to pair off with a succession of look-alike men. The most musical staging of these sequences is wound faster in the lightness and giddiness of the Coney Island excursion, which ends with the exhausted couples travelling home and John spotting the advertisement—offering the ideal home for the ideal couple—which prompts his marriage proposal to Mary.

This musical gaiety is subsequently replaced by more pessimistic variations on the theme: the 'ideal' home becomes a cramped tenement apartment, which John's own soaring ambition as an ad-man fails ever to change; the *joie de vivre* of the multitude of indistinguishable city folk becomes the threatening mean-mindedness of Mary's two brothers, identical in their black homburgs and bourgeois-capitalist satisfaction, who scorn John's failure to better himself; and further outings, such as a family picnic on the beach, are spoiled by feelings of bitterness and regret. The film returns at its end to something like the early buoyancy, though with the emotional undertow of lessons learned and painful adjustments made. Husband and wife are reconciled as they dance, faster and faster, to a record which he brings home after accepting the humbling job of sandwich-board man; and in the final shot, John and Mary are lost among the crowd as the camera pulls back from the spectators laughing uproariously at a stage show.

The strength of *The Crowd* is Vidor's (and his actors') ability to root the general implications of this tale of the common man (or of the common experiences of city man) in the particular history of one family. By comparison, the cross-section-of-life approach which Vidor employed a few years later in a sound film, *Street Scene* (1931), is cripplingly schematic. Determined to be as faithful as possible to the original play by Elmer Rice, Vidor was visually ingenious in coping with what was literally one street scene and the front of the tenement where his multifarious characters lived ('We would never repeat a camera set-up twice. If the setting couldn't change, the camera could'). But individuals remain ethnic and social stereotypes, and the interaction of the film's young lovers with this wittily observed but distinctly theatrical environment never achieves the necessary complexity of opposing ambitions and needs.

Some related reservations apply to *Our Daily Bread*, in which Vidor specifically took up the characters from *The Crowd*, John and Mary Sims (here Tom Keene and Karen Morley), and resolved the problems which the Depression had brought them by transferring them to the country, with the gift of a disused farm from a well-to-do uncle. Totally ignorant of country matters, the couple are helped by an old man—on his way to California after losing his own farm—and John is struck with the idea of starting an agricultural co-operative, in which all kinds of dispossessed craftsmen will find a home and just reward for their labours. Unfortunately, this utopian solution remains just that, with personal and social problems never really interacting, and so being resolved simply, one by one. Despite their poverty (which is presented jokingly, in terms of avoiding the rent collector and John having to exchange his fiddle for the chicken for Uncle's dinner), John and Mary

The revivalist meeting in *Hallelujah*: a fore-shadowing of the expressionism and the fierce melodramatics of the films of the late 40s and 50s.

at the outset are noticeably more harmonious than their namesakes in *The Crowd*, and basically remain so, despite the intervention of the city floozie who briefly lures John away when the farm project has begun to stagnate for want of proper irrigation. And just as this dramatic contrivance never really poses a threat to John's 'intimate' family, the larger community is never seriously threatened by internal differences. An early discussion about the possible forms of government for the commune is settled (after various kinds of socialism and democracy are rejected) in favour of John remaining sole leader; and the two most 'difficult' members of the group— the good-time girl and the surly ex-convict— finally serve a very sentimental function: she loses out in the limp romantic triangle, and provokes the hero's return, faith reaffirmed, to the commune; he surrenders himself to the police so the farmers can benefit from the reward money.

But the physical difficulties of the undertaking—more than the emotional or political problems which arise from them—are fully orchestrated by the film, literally so in the famous climax (the frantic digging of an irrigation canal to save the parched crops) in which Vidor employed his 'silent music' technique of synchronizing the action to a gradually accelerating metronome beat. Less spectacular are such symbolically sly and touching details as the cut from the young couple, settling down for their first night in the ramshackle farm and moving their pine-needle beds closer together, to John's spade striking awkwardly at the earth next morning.

Vidor seized the opportunity to make his musical staging audible as well as visible in his first sound film, *Hallelujah*, the story of a family in a Negro cotton-growing community. In order to secure MGM's backing, Vidor promised to deliver 'river baptisms, prayer meetings accompanied by spirituals, Negro preaching, banjo playing, dancing, the blues'; but the crude all-singing, all-dancing portrait which this list suggests is belied by the film's complex counterpointing of the communal fiestas (in the fields, at harvest time and, most intensely, in time of mourning) with the siren song that drives the tormented eldest son, Zeke (Daniel Haynes).

From the outset, a specifically sexual energy clearly merges in Zeke with the general physical exuberance of his friends and family, but it also shuts him out from the simple emotional contentment of this ideal agrarian family. During the harvest celebrations, Zeke attempts to steal a kiss from Missy Rose (Victoria Spivey), who has been brought up within the family almost as his sister and whom he is expected, one day, to marry (a hint of the incestuous tensions more divisive in later Vidor families: brother shoots sister's lover and is in turn shot by her in *Ruby Gentry*; two brothers compete for the half-breed daughter of their mother's old beau in *Duel in the Sun*). Refused the kiss, Zeke is subsequently bedazzled by a fast young city girl, Chick (Nina Mae McKinney), who indirectly causes a fight in which Zeke accidentally shoots his younger brother. Overwhelmed with guilt, he 'discovers' a vocation as an itinerant preacher—from which he is once more lured by his passion for Chick. She later betrays him with her old city-slicker lover, Hot Shot; pursuing the two to their destruction in a swamp (its infernal appearance amplified by Vidor's expressionistic tricks with sound), Zeke is released from his emotional thrall and, after an elliptically brief spell in prison, is free to return home.

What probably makes *Hallelujah* the strongest of all Vidor's pastoral idylls, his exploration of the roots of home and community, is its fierce sense of internal contradictions; of the individual energies that may or may not find themselves grounded in such a community. As a sublimation of unsatisfied drives, Zeke's conversion and fervour as a wandering revivalist minister are not treated as a 'false' solution—in fact, they seem to

flow naturally from the pantheistic awe invoked during the communal ecstasies of grief at his brother's funeral; nor does Vidor question Chick's new-found passion for Zeke after she hears one of his sermons. Zeke must travel to the end of his spiritual crisis before he can return, and his internal victory necessarily seems both more precarious and more hard-won than the arbitrary solutions to the crisis in *Our Daily Bread*. Vidor aptly complements his journey with a parallel cycle in Zeke's various jobs: from family farm to the uncertain 'converted' community of his religious devotees, to drudgery in a saw mill, and finally to rock-breaking in prison before his reinstatement to the farm.

Apart from the inspirational intensity of *Hallelujah*, and the shallow utopianism of *Our Daily Bread*, Vidor's arcadian explorations in the sound period include the more conventional romance of *The Stranger's Return* (1933), in which the heroine (Miriam Hopkins) returns from New York to the farm of her declining grandfather (Lionel Barrymore) and an extended family. Some tentative exercises during the silent period have usually been dismissed as indistinguishable Griffith derivations. Vidor's first feature, *The Turn in the Road* (1919), was built on an inspirational Christian Science theme (an original story by Vidor, its subject apparently harking back to his own family background). Produced, ironically enough, by a team of doctors turned producers, it was sufficiently successful to spawn a company, Brentwood Films, for which Vidor wrote and directed, with flagging inspiration and interest, three other films. Setting up his own studio (dubbed 'Vidor Village'), and intending to produce films which would 'reflect the writings of Booth Tarkington, Mark Twain and James Whitcomb Riley', Vidor first turned out *The Jack Knife Man* (1920), a tale of Mississippi boatmen which played on Griffith-like pathos; a later reviewer referred to it as 'the *Sunrise* of its day, a beautiful, artistically told little story of village and villagers'. The studio, however, soon folded, and with few exceptions until the end of the silent era Vidor was engaged on commissioned projects which he has recalled with little affection. *Happiness* (1924) is a delightful, light-hearted anticipation of *The Crowd* in its treatment of the struggles of ordinary city folk.

Pat O'Malley and Laurette Taylor in *Happiness*, 'a delightful light-hearted anticipation of *The Crowd* in its treatment of the struggles of ordinary city folk'.

In 1925, apparently after convincing Irving Thalberg that he was 'weary of making ephemeral films', Vidor initiated and shot *The Big Parade*, which he saw as 'the story of a young American who was neither overpatriotic nor a pacifist, but who went to war and reacted normally to all the things that happened to him'. It has been criticized for its failings as a realistic document of the horrors of war, and consequently as an ineffective anti-war statement; but *The Big Parade* records the impact of war on another level, as a series of small, discontinuous shocks, in which what the unformed, innocent hero, James Apperson (John Gilbert), experiences is not primarily brutalization and outrage but a greater involvement with life. His own family is metaphorically extended to include a French girl, with whom he falls in love, and her old grandfather; when his best friend disappears on the battle-field, Apperson's frantic search only turns up an unexpected substitute—a wounded German soldier, to whom he gives a cigarette.

In its loose, episodic style, reproducing the impact of events on a hero 'in whose hands does not lie the power to *create* the situations in which he finds himself but who nevertheless feels them emotionally', *The Big Parade* parallels *The Crowd* and the sadder-but-wiser John Sims who emerges from his battering by all the alienating forces of city life. Vidor has said as much ('Objectively life is like a battle, isn't it?'), and with the addition of *Our Daily Bread*, he foresaw 'a series of films depicting episodes in the lives of the average American man and woman'. The series seems to have got no further in the Hollywood mill; but production difficulties aside, it may not even have survived the onset of a certain disillusionment in Vidor himself. Made the same year as *Our Daily Bread*, *The Wedding Night* (1935) opposes the harsh, heartless urban world of writer Gary Cooper with the rustic community of Anna Sten—but steadily reveals among the country folk (albeit in an 'alien', Polish immigrant society) certain gross inequalities and brutalities (which eventually kill the heroine). By and large, in the late 30s, tales of renewal or optimistic accommodation within urban or rural settings give way to the more closed, bleak generic vision of Western subjects. Of the exceptions, *Stella Dallas* (1937) is the oft-told tragedy of the smalltown misadventuress, and *The Citadel* (1938), A. J. Cronin's story of Welsh coal miners, was made by Vidor in England.

As early as 1930, in *Billy the Kid*, Vidor's handling of a Western was noted for its violence, and for its picture of the mercenary interests inhabiting the bleached, uninviting landscape of New Mexico. (For all that he has been acclaimed as a poet of nature, Vidor's response to landscape seems always keyed to the human presence: the grey and scrubby vistas of *Our Daily Bread* indicate the effort required to make the land bear fruit; by contrast, the lush wilderness of *Northwest Passage*, 1940, is one of the greatest obstacles the Indian fighters have to overcome.) The culmination of this trend is that gloomy, introverted post-war trilogy —the super-Western, *Duel in the Sun*, the Southern Western, *Ruby Gentry*, and the backwoods *Madame Bovary*, *Beyond the Forest*.

Vidor's contribution to *Duel in the Sun* has always been in danger of getting lost in the legend of David O. Selznick, and the galaxy of collaborators (colour consultant Josef von Sternberg; uncredited director William Dieterle; numerous lighting cameramen and second-unit directors) assembled by the producer for this Western-look *Gone With the Wind*. But despite Vidor's reservations, and perhaps because Selznick's constant extensions of the material (especially his extravagant 'eroticizing' of Jennifer Jones) took the director further than he may have wanted to go into a style for which he was temperamentally quite suited, *Duel in the Sun* emerges as a delirious consummation of some recognizable Vidor moods and themes. The divergent, destructive energies of *Hallelujah*,

so usefully purged in the world at large before the hero is welcomed back into his family, here come home to roost: Texas land-baron Senator McCanless (Lionel Barrymore), though confined to a wheelchair, is still wrathfully protective of his empire against small homesteaders and the all-invading railroad. But the moral bankruptcy of his claim is sealed when one son, Lewt (Gregory Peck), doted on by his father for his scapegrace ways and ruthless self-assertion, comes to the Senator's defence (by derailing trains), while the temperate, fair-minded Jess (Joseph Cotten) is driven by his sympathies ('I'd like one McCanless to give something to this state and not just take from it') into the other camp.

But the film does not so much dramatize the struggle for a new world—Jess and the forces he represents are treated with a kind of neutral sympathy—as operationally celebrate the one that is dying. Hell-bent on destruction, Lewt meets his match in Pearl Chavez (Jennifer Jones), the half-breed daughter of Scott Chavez (Herbert Marshall). About to be hanged for killing Pearl's faithless Indian mother, Scott has consigned her to the safe-keeping of Senator McCanless' wife Lorabelle (Lillian Gish). With the shadow of the hangman's rope literally imposed on the opening sequence, events inevitably take on a fatalistic cast, especially given Pearl's suspicions of her 'bad blood'—confirmed by her failure to live up to the expectations of the idealistic Jess and her fierce attraction to Lewt. Eventually, the clash of these demon lovers seems to draw all the energies of the film, is nourished on the hot sultry style of the colour and imagery and, by its very intensity, cast a spell which transfixes all the epic forces of this most 'barbarous' vision of the 'civilizing' of the West. The whole pageant then dissolves—into the timeless world of the Indian legend, invoked at the beginning and end of the film, which tells of 'Squaw's Head Rock' and the 'lovers who found heaven and hell in its shadow'. *Ruby Gentry*, despite a similar range of unreconciled passion, and the mythic attraction/repulsion of its two guiding but frustrated spirits, remains wholly earthbound, and its conclusion is an untranscended bitterness and despair. The industrial processes of change are dramatically more

Patricia O'Neal and Gary Cooper in a typically demented scene from *The Fountainhead*, a film which 'might almost be a direct riposte to *The Crowd*, celebrating the triumph of Ayn Rand's proto-typical superman over the forces that would make him bow to the judgement of the mob'.

central than in *Duel in the Sun*, partly because Indian myth and Western lore have been replaced by what Vidor has called a more modern setting, closer to Tennessee Williams, where man is clearly responsible for the laxness and decay of his society, and partly because its hero, Boake Tackman (Charlton Heston), combines the élan and wilfulness of Lewt McCanless with a more positive philosophy ('A man and his work are the same thing') and ambition (he plans to resurrect both family and community by draining the marshland). His nemesis is Ruby Corey (Jennifer Jones), the girl from the distant end of the social scale whom he rejects for a wealthy match, and who takes her revenge (as the widow of businessman Jim Gentry) by flooding Boake's reclamation work. Finally reconciled with Ruby, Boake is shot by her brother Jewel and dies in the primal ooze to which his land is returning; Ruby retires to a death-in-life in brittle luxury.

Beyond the Forest is as tempestuous in mood, with a heroine, Rosa Moline (Bette Davis), who yearns to escape her claustrophobic small town for the big city, and consequently makes a fatal alliance with an industrialist. But a windily theatrical plot forces Rosa into an increasingly unsympathetic position, and so dilutes the reality of her restlessness. Vidor almost sidesteps into the background, finding in the small-town setting something akin to the rural havens he had left behind, and in Rosa's husband Lewis a *faute de mieux* hero (Joseph Cotten's stiff-backed humanitarian in *Duel in the Sun* become more sympathetic as a pragmatic country doctor).

But if this sequence of films runs gloomily counter to the progressive hopes of *Our Daily Bread*, centring more on the emotional complications which arose out of *Hallelujah*, Vidor continued through the 40s to respond to the options for industrial, technological man. As the vision became more exalted, however, from *An American Romance* (1944) to *The Fountainhead* (1949), the style became disconcertingly abstract. Returning Vidor to what he had always declared his favourite themes—'war, wheat and steel'—*An American Romance* is an inspirationalist essay on the latter subject, paralleling the industrial transformation of iron ore with the career and similar 'refining' of a young immigrant. Cut against Vidor's wishes, the film was a disappointment both artistically and commercially.

The Fountainhead might almost be a direct riposte to *The Crowd*, celebrating the triumph of Ayn Rand's prototypical *Übermensch*, visionary architect Howard Roark (Gary Cooper), over the forces that would make him bow to the judgement of the mob. Where *The Crowd* ends with the camera drawing back—resignedly but not bitterly—to absorb the hero with his fellows, *The Fountainhead* concludes with the camera rising (along with Roark's iron-willed lover and soul-mate) towards the architect, a solitary colossus atop the building which his uncompromising inspiration has reared.

The delirious phallic imagery of the shot is only tempered by the cold monumentality of the film's style—which lends a peculiar shock to all its erotic encounters, a kind of clinical hysteria. Vidor has applied a sweeping architectural vision, which not only is appropriate to his subject but renders the people part of the abstract geometry of the design. It converts the plot into some fairy-tale gloss on the film's concern with its craggy visuals, formal evidence of the thrust and drive of human nature. So 'epic' and sculpted a style may also have been the only sensible way Vidor could accommodate his own interest in the spiritual challenges of creativity—its blocks and frustrations and growth through opposition—to the inflammatory style and content of Ms Rand's script, which continually declaims against the grovelling mediocrity of the masses and their envious egalitarianism. It conflates and confuses so many political attitudes in its drive to exalt the Superman that the narrative result is a kind of *Wizard of Oz* nonsensicality.

On the outskirts of Vidor's *noir* trilogy, his last Western, *Man Without a Star*, looks back in many ways to the archetypal *Duel in the Sun*, in the clash between old-style expansionist ranchers and their smaller neighbours, and in the feuding affair of two kindred but irreconcilable egos—Dempsey (Kirk Douglas), the wandering cowboy who cares for nothing but his continued freedom of movement, and the lady ranch-owner (Jeanne Crain) who cares for nothing but her freedom to exploit fully what aggressive enterprise has given her. A more intimately scaled Western, however, *Man Without a Star* treats the contest of wills with only a half-hearted eroticism, and more adeptly defines its mutable but naggingly incomplete family relationships: at the beginning, Dempsey accepts the company of a young cowboy in whom he finds a substitute for his dead brother and a son for whom he is not quite willing to take responsibility. The theme, in fact, makes the film an interesting, though less satisfactory, replay of Vidor's *The Champ* (1931), about a down-and-out boxer (Wallace Beery) and his small son Dink (Jackie Cooper) scraping a living in Tijuana.

What characterizes both relationships is this precariousness of roles, which is treated with a certain ambivalent warmth in *The Champ*—father and son do enjoy a fraternity, even if Dink is not very very well looked after—but which is more dangerously unstable in *Man Without a Star*. There the mood is largely geared to the bitterness and self-disgust in Dempsey, who is amused to have a protégé but not pleased by what he sees of himself coming out in the boy. And the unreliability of both the older partners inevitably shapes events. The Champ's broken promises to give up drink and gambling, and to go back into training as a fighter, culminate in his taking on a match for which Dink realizes he is not prepared and which results in his death (after which Dink is absorbed by a more complete family, his mother—who had left the Champ some years before—and her new husband). In *Man Without a Star*, where Dempsey is the first to violate his own strictures on the Code of the

West (never turn your back in a fight; a cow-boy should never part with his saddle), the theme is neatly stated between his initial command to the boy—'Do like I do'—and his cheerfully ironic coda—'Don't do like I do, do like I say'—before he rides off, leaving the boy with the ranching family who have provided him with a home and a romantic tie.

But this last element is only indicated very perfunctorily, in comparison with *The Champ*, which maintains a consistent tension between the domestic life offered by Dink's mother (who is anxious to have her son back) and his insecure if colourful life with the Champ. That the alternatives in *Man Without â Star* are insufficiently dramatized may be due to the fact that it is very much Dempsey's (and Kirk Douglas') picture, dominated by the growling energy that Douglas can bring to the most negative heroes. But given the darkening tone of his post-war films, and perhaps even the erosion of his own sense of positive alternatives, it is tempting to see Vidor as more than half-assenting to Dempsey's notion of a world closing in behind him, and at the end moving with the hero beyond his country's border into his subsequent period of 'international' production.

As Raymond Durgnat has demonstrated, in his thoroughgoing account of Vidor's career in *Film Comment*, the two costume epics, *War and Peace* (1956) and *Solomon and Sheba* (1959), may not have taken him so far from his main concerns. There is in *War and Peace*, with its awesome historical perspectives figuring as just one more refracting surface in the moral growth and understanding of individual characters, something akin to *The Big Parade*, for which Vidor was criticized for dwelling so single-mindedly, in a story of global war, on the sentimental education of one doughboy. But the severance from American themes and subjects has left Vidor more dependent on the generic qualities of his material; the tone is often dismayingly flaccid, as though his native resources were atrophying for want of appropriate subjects or collaborators (a problem that perhaps goes back as far as *The Fountainhead*, though there the temperamental anomalies had more the effect of rousing contradictions). The rumours that Vidor has

since contemplated returning to material as simple, and directly inspirational, as *The Turn in the Road* are not too surprising—a career which has so fully played over the energizing challenges and painful checks of growth, and the corollaries of rebirth and regeneration, has perhaps quite naturally found itself once more at the beginning.

The pleasant exceptions to Vidor's 'commercial' movies of the 20s were *Wild Oranges* (1924), the delightful *Show People* (1928), and his version of *La Bohème* with Lillian Gish (1926). Nor should one forget, later, *Bird of Paradise* (1932) and the atypical but very funny *On Our Merry Way* (also known as *A Miracle Can Happen*, 1948).

The rumours Combs mentions about a return to 'inspirational' material are true. Indeed, the Christian Science aspect of *The Turn in the Road* resurfaced in Vidor's most recent film, a rather mawkish short, made privately, and scarcely ever shown: *Truth and Illusion: an Introduction to Metaphysics* (1974).

Vidor's autobiography is called *A Tree Is a Tree* (1953); his *King Vidor on Film Making* was published in 1972. More recently we have had John Baxter's *King Vidor* (1976), Raymond Durgnat's monumental two-part article on Vidor in *Film Comment* (July–August and September–October 1973), and an essay on him by Clive Denton in *The Hollywood Professionals*, Vol. 5 (1973).

JEAN VIGO

Gavin Millar

Few film-makers can have left such a profound mark on the cinema after such a short and commercially disastrous career. None of the three films by which Vigo (1905–34) is known, *A Propos de Nice* (1930), *Zéro de Conduite* (1933) and *L'Atalante* (1934), achieved any success at their first appearance. All were greeted by critics and distributors alike with coldness or hostility. *Zéro de Conduite* was banned by the French censors. Neither of the others received any extended form of public run at the time, except that *L'Atalante* was mutilated by the studio and released in a form that did no credit to Vigo, under the title *Le Chaland qui Passe*, the title of a popular song of the day which itself was incorporated into the soundtrack, replacing some of the original music. Even this was a box-office failure. On 5 October 1934, a few days after this version had finished its run at a public cinema, Vigo died at twenty-nine of the lung trouble from which he had suffered throughout his life. Despite this inauspicious career, Vigo and his films continued to grow in stature, and *L'Atalante* is one of the enduring master-pieces of the cinema.

The facts of Vigo's early life are of unusual significance. His father was Miguel Almer-eyda, who is customarily referred to as an 'anarchist'. But although Almereyda was closely associated with the publication *La Guerre Sociale*, which was broadly anarchist, he was also later associated with *Le Bonnet Rouge*, a socialist organ which had its sup-porters among the government. At any rate he was a notorious figure of the French left—at one time moving so far left as to form a tem-porary alliance with the extreme right, at others being accused of undermining the left by working with the government. His con-flicts with authority started in a small way —short terms of imprisonment for carrying an ineffectual bomb, taking part in illegal demonstrations and so on—and grew steadily more serious until, in 1917, he was accused of working to effect a dishonourable peace with Germany and was due to stand trial as a traitor. He was found strangled in his cell in prison before he could be brought to trial and it is almost certain that he was assassinated: it is not clear whether by order of people in high positions who were afraid of his possible revelations, or simply by the police, to whom he had been a lifelong enemy.

It is likely that he was innocent of the crimes with which the state would have charged him, and it was in an attempt to establish this and to rehabilitate his father that Jean Vigo spent his early adult years. His father became something of a remote hero for him. Remote not only because of his death when Vigo was only twelve, but equally because he had seen little of him in his childhood: partly because he was brought up by relatives or in boarding schools while his mother and father pursued their itinerant political careers (sometimes, in Almereyda's case, in prison), and latterly because his father installed Jean and his mother Emily in a separate establishment while he lived else-

where with his mistress. Nor were Jean and his mother particularly at ease with one another. But the young Vigo's real hatred was reserved for the boarding schools in which he had spent eight unhappy years, and, by extension, for the idea of authority which they represented.

In this latter opinion he was naturally much influenced by the example of his father. Almereyda's real name was Vigo, and he had arrived at his pseudonym, an anagram of 'y a (de) la merde', in a belief, which he shared with 'certain libertarian circles', as P. E. Salles Gomes, Vigo's biographer, puts it, 'in the revolutionary virtues of the "gros mot" and that, at the beginning of the cen-tury, was still one'. From an early age Vigo was anti-clerical, anti-militarist and anti-authority, especially when it was in uniform, and in an unreasonably aggressive way which was not typical of his character. The story is told that on the opening night of his film club in Nice the inspector sent to the premises by the Fire Service declared the building unsafe. Vigo surprised those who knew him as a quiet, reserved youth by his vociferous and disdainful hostility to the man in uniform.

A subversive social conscience and a scarcely examined hostility to entrenched power or privilege were the marks of his first essay in film-making, *A Propos de Nice*. This was a short documentary about Nice which swiftly resolved itself into an opposition be-tween rich and poor, between tourist Nice and the near-slums of the working-class quarter. The simple dialectical shape is echoed in the formal oppositions of the images: telegraph poles against 'telegraph pole' cypresses, a rich invalid being pushed in a wheelchair versus a poor street-sweeper and his cart. Neither the quality of the photography nor the originality of the shots was sufficient to disguise the fact that Vigo had hardly made a watertight political case. What is more interesting is to see how he had absorbed a variety of influences. Setting the carnival up against the cemetery recalls the Russian experiments in the discussion of ideas by montage and symbolism. Harping on the vanity of the beautiful, the ugliness of the rich and the mutilations of the poor recalls Stroheim. Expressionist sequences with actors were planned but not shot; several episodes recalling the French surrealist cinema of the 20s, and especially *Entr'acte*, were. One episode which looks derivative was actually the result of original thinking to overcome a purely administrative problem. Vigo had wanted to make a sequence illustrating the casino during its normal opening hours, and naturally he couldn't afford to hire a crowd and stage it. The same strictures applied to a scene at the railway station showing visitors arriving by train. In the end, Vigo neatly solved both problems by using a toy train and toy passengers, and having a croupier's rake swoop into frame and collect the passengers like so many lost chips. But in general the influences are more strongly felt than any personal and expressive statement Vigo was able to make with them. Since it was an apprentice work, that was only to be expected. With *Zéro de Conduite* Vigo was soon to produce a work which owed nothing to anyone else's cinema and was to prove profoundly influential.

Before that opportunity arose, he was offered a more routine assignment to make a simple, short documentary about a swimming champion, Taris, which would recount the facts of the man's life and give some elementary instruction in the sport. Vigo knew nothing about the subject and had quickly to inform himself. *Taris* (other titles: *Jean Taris, Champion de Natation*; *Taris, Roi de l'Eau*, 1931) was modestly successful and resulted in the offer of a similar documentary later, this time about a tennis star. Vigo was to spend valuable months of effort in the little time left to him in planning this short which, in the end, was cancelled. Meanwhile *Taris* brought him useful experience and in particular it brought him an image which was to prove an indispensable part of the beauty of *L'Atalante*. The shots of Taris swimming underwater so struck Vigo that he developed a similar image into a central motif of the later film.

Memories of earlier times and particular images of his childhood and adolescence form the substance of the first of his major films, *Zéro de Conduite*, despite the fact that he transmuted them into something very like a dream. The action takes place in a boy's boarding school in a dreary suburb of Paris, and the title itself refers to the habitual scold of the *surveillant* which Vigo remembered from his days at a school in Millau and later at Chartres. The three boys—Bruel, Caussat and Colin—were named after three of his best friends, and the fourth, Tabard, is, a little bit, Vigo himself. The intention was that the film should be a tightly documented account of the privations of life in such a barracks, with a slender plot involving a 'revolt' by the four heroes at the end. In the event, because of lack of time and money, the interruptions due to illness, etc., much of it was never shot. Other parts incorporated in the original have not survived. The result is that we have a strange, episodic, almost incoherent narrative whose wayward structure is as much accident as design. Furthermore it is still technically an apprentice work. There are elementary continuity and editing mistakes in the film and the sound quality is poor. Such is the strength of its internal logic, however, and the exultant lyricism of its mood that none of this matters.

The point of view is a child's—the children are all perfectly normal but the adults grow in degrees of caricature and fantasy as they ascend in authority. The principal of the college is a bearded dwarf, and he and his subordinates, in league with the state, the church and the military (representatives of which attend the final catastrophic *fête* when the revolt breaks out), are engaged in the fantasy pursuits of authority. They are oppressive, hypocritical, paranoid, mean, dishonest, perverted. They are intent, in other words, on erecting a hierarchical structure which depends for its stability on fear and subservience. It is the opposite of the boys' world, which Vigo presents as having no hierarchy, though it does have an aristocracy of charm or forcefulness of character: Tabard is feminine, beautiful and idealized; Caussat is attractively brusque, virile and resourceful. But it is a saving stroke of imagination that Vigo has made the adult world, in its way, equally idealized. The perversion, hypocrisy and meanness are on a childlike scale. The science teacher goes no further than to stroke Tabard's hair. Bec-de-Gaz, the *surveillant-général*, is a sneak-thief, but the limits of his crime are to rifle through the boys' papers for nude pictures and to steal their sweets when they are out of class. The college feeds its pupils perpetually on beans, but it does not starve or beat them. If Bec-de-Gaz is a sneak,

A scene from *Zéro de Conduite*.

then Huguet (Jean Dasté), the sympathetic young teacher, is a sport. He conceals the boys' plot from discovery, plays football in the playground, does imitations of Chaplin and stands on his hands. Indeed his moral affinity with the boys is conveyed purely in gesture and movement. Like Bec-de-Gaz, he rarely speaks. But where Bec-de-Gaz creeps and spies and sneaks and pounces as though he hated movement, as though too definitive a gesture would commit him, Huguet positively exults in it. At one point during a ball game in the playground he executes an extraordinary, high-kicking prance which brings him with a great swoop into a knot of struggling boys.

In contrast, the physical display by the firemen during the *fête* is a farcical model of regimented, pointless effort: one man swinging unimpressively on the parallel bars, another managing nothing very much on the horse. Against the dwarf principal who can barely lodge his bowler hat on the mantelpiece, the boys' triumphs therefore are physical. In a justly celebrated sequence they turn the severe box of their dormitory into a magical snow-flecked landscape, whirling the exploding feather pillows about their heads, 'crucifying' the sleeping *surveillant* Pète-Sec by tying him into his upended bed, turning cartwheels and, in slow motion, parading triumphantly through the long room, pressing their happy faces against a huge window. The 'revolt' itself, after this, is something of an anti-climax. The four heroes climb on to the roof, plant a black flag and bombard the dignitaries in the yard with books and chamber pots. Besides the antics of the unnimble stuffed shirts pinned below—some of them literally dummies—their careful progress towards the summit of the roof and towards liberty has all the force of a moral victory.

It is possible to analyse the film from many other aspects, not simply that of movement. Little attention has been paid to the dialogue, partly because there is so little of it, partly because it is so badly recorded. Whether for the latter reason or some other, Vigo developed a pattern of repetition (he uses it again with Père Jules in *L'Atalante*) which contributes centrally to the strange blend of realism and fantasy. The first night in the dormitory when Colin, Bruel and Caussat are made to stand for two hours beside the *surveillant*'s bed, Colin develops colic and pleads, unheard, to go to the lavatory. Although this was based on a real event in Vigo's school life, he has transmuted it strangely by turning the boys' pleas into an incantation: '*Monsieur, j'ai mal au ventre . . . Monsieur, il peut y aller . . . Oh j'ai mal au ventre . . . Monsieur, il a mal au ventre.*' Again, when Caussat plans a simple schoolboy revenge on Bec-de-Gaz, pouring glue where his pilfering fingers will dip, the collection of the glue-pots becomes a curiously intense rite. Caussat shuffles from desk to desk murmuring '*Passe-moi ton pot de colle . . . ton pot de colle . . . ton pot de colle . . .*' This heightened realism can nevertheless encompass moments of tenderness and sympathy based on character. Colin's mother —one of the few realistically and sympathetically drawn characters—is on the side of the boys, principally because she is also Mère Haricot, the cook, who knows how miserable their meals are. She can do nothing about it, apart from complain to Bec-de-Gaz, who takes no notice. The boys unfairly blame her, however, and when the beans are served yet again set up a howl of abuse against Mère Haricot which causes poor Colin to hang his head in pain. Seeing this, Caussat and Bruel bring the demonstration to a halt. It is one of the few hints, in a film filled with other virtues, of the tenderness which was to be the outstanding quality of Vigo's masterpiece.

There were other surprising advances to be seen in *L'Atalante*. *Zéro de Conduite*, for all its inspired idiosyncrasy, had nevertheless suffered from Vigo's own comparative technical inexperience. From the start of *L'Atalante*, Vigo is in full and relaxed control of the camera. The hero and heroine, Jean and Juliette (Jean Dasté and Dita Parlo), have just been married. He is the skipper of the barge 'L'Atalante', and the blissful couple walk in front of a gloomy procession from the church to the canal where the barge is moored. None of Jean's relatives is among the guests, only the old rogue Père Jules (Michel Simon), the mate, and a cabin boy (Louis Lefèvre), who scamper on ahead to prepare for the bride. The resentment among the guests is twofold: there is to be no banquet, and Juliette is being carried off by a stranger. With an

Dita Parlo in her wedding dress, 'clinging to the end of a boom which has swung her from the shore to the deck; the sexual symbolism is overt but not coarse': *L'Atalante*.

unsuspected confidence Vigo begins a long reverse tracking shot which moves diagonally on to the line along which the procession approaches, travels backwards with the couple and, letting them gradually catch up, pans contentedly with them, leaving the guests behind. From that moment on, it seems, Vigo's expertise will enable him to achieve any effect his intuition invents.

No description of shots or sequences can convey the unique flavour of what follows, any more than a plot synopsis would indicate the essential difference between the original mediocre romance that Vigo was offered and the film he made of it. 'La patronne', once on board, soon gets used to the rough life but longs nevertheless to 'arrive somewhere'. She spends her nights alone in her bed while Jean is at the wheel. Fascinated by Père Jules, she visits his cabin and is shown his treasures and souvenirs, collected in a lifetime of sailing round the world. Jean discovers them together and suspects her of flirting with the old man. They patch up their quarrel, though, once arrived in Paris at last, when Jean offers to take her out on the town. But Père Jules forestalls them by pretending to visit the doctor while they have to remain on board. The next day Jean makes up for it by taking Juliette to a dance hall where she is courted by a handsome, madcap pedlar whose witty fantasies contrast favourably with the sober but duller Jean. They quarrel again, she goes ashore to visit Paris on her own and he, in a fit of rage, sails without her. But without her he is distraught and as the weeks go by with no word of her, Père Jules has to cover up for Jean's neglect of the boat. Eventually, Père Jules sets out to look for Juliette in the streets of Le Havre, in defiance of Jean's instructions. By magic he finds her working in a miserable job in an amusement arcade. Jean and Juliette are reunited.

As in *Zéro de Conduite*, Vigo's acute sense of movement is what chiefly fills in the banal outlines of this story, as much as the richness of invention he brings to the characters. The boat moves all the time upon the water, and on the boat's deck the people move too, back and forth, with or against the current, with or against the direction in which they are travelling. The sense that Juliette is exchanging a fixed landlocked life for hazardous movement is announced in one extraordinary shot from the wedding scene. Taken from low down on the bank, it frames only empty sky when suddenly Juliette sweeps across it, clinging to the end of a boom which has swung her from the shore to the deck. The sexual symbolism is overt but not coarse, and it is deepened by what follows. Juliette, in her trailing white silk gown, roams bemusedly about the deck of the coal-black barge as it noses off into the dusk and mist. It is her first night on the water, and it is her wedding night. As in *Zéro de Conduite*, but more expressively, we seem to be present at some mute and intense rite.

The emotional weight of this first magical night upon the water carries the charge that will explode later in the film. Juliette has told Jean a superstitious story—the film is full of superstitions and coincidences—that when you plunge your head in water and open your eyes, you can see your loved one. The literal-minded Jean is enchanted by this tale and is forever doing it for fun to show Juliette how he loves her. But when Juliette truly disappears he jumps overboard to search for her in the waters of the canal. Remembering the image of Taris, Vigo photographs the face of the grief-stricken lover underwater, trailing bubbles, turning in hopeless despair this way and that. There is magic on board too. Père Jules has miraculously succeeded in getting an old phonograph to work again and it plays a haunting waltz. There then occurs a moment of inexplicable beauty which is one of the cinema's great triumphs. Père Jules and the boy decide that playing the phonograph to *le patron* might cheer him up. He has just climbed from the water where he has been searching for the image of Juliette. Proudly the boy, bearing the phonograph and its huge horn, like some precious gift, leads Jean and Père Jules along the whole length of the boat to the prow, where the camera awaits them. The waltz continues to sing out across the water. A long vista down the shining canal shows trees reflected on the surface and, in the distance, a factory chimney silently smoking. Jean stares, rapt, at the rebirth of the phonograph. As the waltz plays on, a remote and secret smile begins to steal across his face. There seems no question that he will find Juliette again.

In the event it is Père Jules who finds her, and he does it with the assistance of that magic which he takes for granted and which Jean, learning to look for Juliette in the water, not in fun now, but in earnest, has begun to accept too. It is the same magic that ensures that the good Huguet, having lost the file of boys he was supposed to be taking for a walk, will find them falling in behind him again at a crossroads some time later, without having known they were missing; the same magic which so arranges the tides that when the boy drops overboard the flowers to be presented to the bride a few minutes before she arrives, they are inexorably washed ashore at his feet again a few minutes later. Père Jules strays into an amusement arcade where gramophones relay popular songs at the drop of a coin. Wearing earphones, Juliette is listening sadly to *Le Chant des Mariniers*. Jules approaches and stands at her elbow, leaning towards her a little, unsurprised. Then, in one movement, he lifts her high in the air and carries her out over his shoulder. For that scene of recognition alone, for its tact and tenderness and gaiety, Vigo must join the ranks of the masters.

One must mention the enormous contribution to both *Zéro de Conduite* and *L'Atalante* made by Maurice Jaubert: his scores for these two films rank, I think, among the best music ever written for the cinema. Vigo thought so, too, and this was why he was so affected by the producer's replacement of Jaubert's music for *L'Atalante* by the contemporary pop song *Le Chaland qui Passe*. The prints shown today carry the original music.

For further reading, there is P. E. Salles Gomes' *Jean Vigo* (1957, English translation 1972), an exhaustive biography and analysis of Vigo's work and one of the best books about a director that has ever been written.

Clara Calamai (star of Visconti's earlier *Ossessione*) and Marcello Mastroianni in *White Nights*, a film 'which seemed to be the culmination of a move directly away from the theme and styles of neo-realism . . . but which possesses a unity of discourse and an absence of unwanted contradictions which is unique in Visconti's work'.

LUCHINO VISCONTI

Geoffrey Nowell-Smith

Luchino Visconti (1906–76) aristocrat and Marxist, realist, melodramatist, operatic producer and decorator *par excellence*, has been one of the most provocative and unapproachable figures in the post-war cinema. His early career took place under the shadow of neo-realism, but despite all claims to the contrary, his own included, Visconti was never integrally part of the movement. The heritage of neo-realism and the obligation to pay lip-service to a certain conception of social cinema pursued him throughout his career, so that his later films, in which he gives full rein to a taste for theatricality and spectacular *mise en scène*, are enriched by a thread of historical discourse of clear Marxist inspiration. At the same time the objective foundation on which he would like interpretation of his films to be based is frequently obscured by the intervention of a personal and subjective theme which is constantly hinted at but rarely expressed openly.

With an output of twelve feature films in thirty years, Visconti can hardly be called a prolific director. He has also at times had difficulties with censors and production companies, but basically he has continued to work in his own way, developing his chosen themes, isolated for the most part, except at the beginning of his career, from trends and fashions in the world outside. No single linear development can be discerned in his work. *Le Notti Bianche* (*White Nights*, 1957) seemed to be the culmination of a move directly away from the themes and styles of neo-realism, which his early work had prefigured or adopted. But with *Rocco e i Suoi Fratelli* (*Rocco and His Brothers*, 1960) he returned to questions dear to the classic tradition of social cinema. His subsequent work has been marked both by the recuperation of old themes and by the emergence of new ones, notably the exposition and defence of classic literature and the values of the humanist literary tradition crystallized around the exemplary figure of Thomas Mann. But his cinema remains founded on tensions, some explicit, some barely articulated, between conflicting values and conceptions of the world. It is this which gives his work its richness and also its continuing ability to exasperate and divide his critics.

His first film, *Ossessione*, made in 1942, is something of a *film maudit*. Mauled by the Fascist censorship, lost to view during the later stages of the war, then in trouble with the American occupying forces over a question of copyright, it was put together again in a more or less authentic version during the height of neo-realist enthusiasm, and was instantly hailed as the movement's first flower, a reputation it has taken some time to live down. *Ossessione* is certainly a realist film, at least to the extent that it mirrors some of the general aesthetic assumptions of the years in which it was made. But it would be more accurate to see the film as exposing a contradiction, often latent in neo-realist work, but rarely so openly brought to the fore, between a naturalistic camera style and a narrative content verging on melodrama. The camera style and the naturalistic use of locations were probably a legacy of Visconti's apprenticeship as assistant to Jean Renoir (*Partie de Campagne*, *Les Bas Fonds*) a few years previously; they are also features which will fade away as his own style matures. The melodramatic side, on the other hand, is something which will become increasingly dominant in later years, in *Senso* (*The Wanton Countess*, 1954), *Rocco and His Brothers*, *Vaghe Stelle dell'Orsa* (U.K.: *Of a Thousand Delights*; U.S.: *Sandra*, 1965) and even *Ludwig* (1973). Moreover it is the tension between this element and all the other contradictory aspects of his work which, in retrospective judgement, most clearly marks out the defining qualities not only of *Ossessione* but also of his later and greater films.

Ossessione is a film about the power of destructive passion. A young man, Gino, turns up one day at a country inn. He and Giovanna, the wife of the innkeeper, fall in love and decide to leave together, but she has second thoughts and returns to the inn. When the couple meet again by chance, in a nearby town, the husband, unaware of the affair, invites Gino back to the inn with them. Gino and Giovanna then murder the husband and try to settle down together. But life at the inn grows increasingly oppressive. Gino begins to suspect Giovanna of having used him as an instrument in order to get hold of the money on her husband's life insurance. Meanwhile the police are closing in. The couple attempt to escape, but Gino skids off the road and Giovanna is killed in the crash.

The plot and basic characterization here are taken from an American thriller, James M. Cain's *The Postman Always Rings Twice*, but the film is far from being a literal adaptation or transcription of the novel. The original story ends with the man being sentenced to death for the alleged murder of his mistress, which was an accident, after the guilty couple had already been tried and acquitted for the murder of the husband. Visconti eliminates this gratuitous allegory about the irony of justice and at the same time, in the course of Italianizing the setting, disengages the film stylistically from the punk rhetoric that marks the prose of the original. However, the adaptation takes over from the original story, and further develops, a number of central ideas such as the association of passion and guilt and the social nexus set up between money, sex and family. What is new, and for the future more significant, are the positive changes introduced by Visconti and his collaborators into the narrative structure. Two characters appear in the film who do not have direct equivalents in the novel. The first of these is a man known as 'the Spaniard', a strange vagrant being who befriends Gino after the first abortive elopement with Giovanna. The Spaniard's ideal is one of male companionship, with strong sexual overtones. He continues to shadow Gino even after the latter has settled down with Giovanna, and his presence at the very end carries a distinct implication that he may have been responsible for betraying the couple to the police. The second new character is a young dancer, Anita, with whom Gino spends an afternoon after learning about the insurance. Both these characters have similar roles to play: they represent for Gino alternatives—respectively friendship and easy-going sex—to the turbid passion of his relationship with Giovanna. Within the plot proper they are fitted into a cycle of actions each of which can be interpreted as involving an act of treachery or betrayal.

This idea of betrayal as a central motor of the action is important. It is a constant feature of Visconti's work, and there is a particularly strong link with *Senso* in the structure and sequence of the relationships formed, and betrayed, in the course of the film. There is however also a major difference between those two films, which lies in a feature which links *Ossessione* to Visconti's later work. This is its strong masculine bias. For it is only in the films of the 50s— *Bellissima* (1951), *Senso* and *White Nights*— that Visconti creates women characters with a real positive autonomy, other than the dubious capacity to corrupt and betray. Livia (Alida Valli) in *Senso* is indeed a traitor, but she is also the real focus of identification, political as well as personal, in a way neither Giovanna nor another equivalent character from a later work, Sophie in *La Caduta degli Dei* (*The Damned*, 1969), is ever allowed to be.

What is conspicuously lacking in *Ossessione* is a sense of historical and political perspective such as we find elsewhere in Visconti's work (and also, to be fair, in a lot of mediocre neo-realist productions). The gap is filled in *La Terra Trema* (1947), an epic film about the fishing community of Aci Trezza in Eastern Sicily. Again Visconti availed himself of a literary original, this time Giovanni Verga's classic novel *I Malavoglia*, but the story is treated even more liberally than in the case of *Ossessione*. Verga's novel is the history of the efforts of a family to survive and to remain united in the face of a dire struggle against the forces of nature. It is pervaded by a profound fatalism about the possibilities of human progress, at the individual or collective level. Visconti emphatically repudiates this pessimism. For him, the enemy of the fishermen, and of the Valastro family in particular, is not so much nature as society, and the key to their survival and even progress is symbolized not by the family home but by the boat which gives 'them an economic livelihood. The Valastro are in fact defeated—boat wrecked, mortgage foreclosed, family disgraced and dispersed. But hope comes out of the lessons of defeat. Young 'Ntoni, the hero, emerges from his experiences at the hands of the sea, the moneylenders and the Carabinieri saddened but with heightened consciousness, ready to fight again, and this time not individualistically, not alone.

The political scenario which Visconti derives from his Marxist rewriting of Verga is enriched at the level of *mise en scène* by a compact range of visual symbols which serve as bridges between two facets of the film's conceptual content. The central images of the film—the church, the harbour rocks, the wholesalers' scales—are apparently simple but on closer analysis prove to be uniformly ambivalent, expressive of the opacity of the fishermen's world and of the near impossibility of their obtaining a clear consciousness of its workings. Thus an oppressive institution (the church) provides the locale from which the storm-bell is rung and where the women wait anxiously for the boats to round the harbour. The rocks both threaten shipwreck and mark the limits of the protected haven. The scales are a measure not only of the size of the catch but of the rate of exploitation. The most dramatic scene of the film, and the richest in suggestive content, is when 'Ntoni and the other fishermen throw the scales into the sea. The embodiment of the relations of production is, so to speak, submerged in the means of production itself—the sea which is both the subject of the fishermen's wealth-producing labour and the bringer of death and destruction.

More than anything, it is the use of images for their dual aspects that makes *La Terra Trema*, despite the deficiencies of its scenario, on a visual and expressive level the most classically Marxist of all Visconti's films. This use of iconic and symbolic imagery is in fact very different from the procedures employed by the great Russian directors, notably Pudovkin, with whose work *La Terra Trema* has often been compared. But the care attached to formal composition and to a precise montage of signifying elements is reminiscent of Soviet work of both the silent and the early sound period. So too is the problem presented in the handling of verbal discourse. The expressiveness of the film is confined to the visual level and to the use of voices orchestrated as sound. The dialogues themselves give no support. Often improvised, they are spoken by the protagonists, the people of Aci Trezza themselves, in a dialect incomprehensible to most Italian audiences. They are therefore supplemented by a commentary, which both expounds the plot and emphasizes, rather didactically, the political significance of the action. It is a formalist solution to a problem posed, paradoxically, by the logic of the extreme form of realism adopted by Visconti for the style of the film. The problem, frankly, is not solved. But the attempted solution—a choreographic and operatic organization of the material— was to prove relevant to Visconti's subsequent concerns.

Ossessione and *La Terra Trema* merit detailed treatment because, although in some respects untypical of the mainstream of Visconti's work as it was to develop, each in different ways serves as an introduction both to the themes and to the problems with which he became increasingly concerned. In *Ossessióne* it is mainly a matter of thematic content, and to a lesser extent narrative structure. Many of the details for which the film is best remembered—the opening track of Gino waking up on the back of a lorry, or the local priest going out shooting with Giovanna's husband with a gun on his shoulder and cartridges slung around his cassock—are in fact quite without later parallels. Even the melodramatic treatment of human relations is present only in embryonic form. But *La Terra Trema* is packed with problems whose significance will appear gradually as Visconti's work progresses: those of the relationship between a highly politicized abstract scenario and its concrete realization in *mise en scène*, between individual drama and collective epic, and between operatics and realism as an expressive mode.

The film which most clearly picks up the political inheritance of *La Terra Trema* is *Rocco and His Brothers*. Made twelve years later, it can be seen almost as a sequel to the earlier film and as a substitute for its unfinished episodes. Again it is centred on a family, though this time not in Sicily, but among Southern immigrants in the North. Again, the price of progress is the destruction of the family. Aesthetically, the film has none of the uncompromising quality of its predecessor. It uses professional actors, Hollywood fashion, for their star quality rather than their realistic authenticity. It is also directed in such a way that the dramatic

Alida Valli, Rina Morelli and Farley Granger in *Senso*: '*Senso* is unashamedly expressionistic.
Everything in it is dramatized to the highest pitch.'

prevails over the epic dimension. The focal point of the drama is the struggle of two of the Pafundi brothers, Rocco (Alain Delon) and Simone (Renato Salvatore), for possession of the same woman (Annie Girardot), and that of the mother (Katina Paxinou) for control of the whole family. The secondary dimension, the journey of the family to Milan and the gradual liberation of its younger members from quasi-feudal servitude, is almost lost—except on those spectators who share the political and social conception that presided over the construction of the scenario and was then submerged in the overblown operatics of the finished film.

More than the unsuccessful resolution of the epic/dramatic, political/individual contrasts, what jars in *Rocco* is a sense of uncertainty. It is not, as some critics have maintained, that there is too little realism applied to the characters: if anything there is too much. But it is an unnecessary form of dramatized psychological realism, operating in a world of unrealistic make-believe. Without the guidance of a strong literary original, and without benefit of empathy with his proletarian subject, Visconti finds himself, basically, in the wrong mode. The characters act out their roles with a hopeless air of being miscast in the fiction that has been constructed around them. As the action escalates towards melodrama, it becomes clear that the melodrama is not intrinsic to the characters as filmically or dramatically conceived but is supposed, naïvely (and falsely), to emanate directly from real life.

This compromise with a Zavattinian concept of realism is even more marked in *Bellissima*, a film with Anna Magnani, scripted by Zavattini himself, which is perhaps the closest Visconti ever got to that typically Italian sub-genre, the naturalistic-picturesque. *Bellissima* is an agreeable film, with none of the delusions of epic grandeur that *Rocco* suffers from. It is Visconti at his lightest, and also in many ways at his best, for it shows that extraordinary sense of detail that is characteristic of all his work but which all too often elsewhere ceases to be detail and becomes over-emphatic symbolism. It is the story of a working-class woman who enters her child for a beauty contest in competition with the dolled-up progeny of the bourgeoisie, and who unexpectedly finds her ambitions realized but in the end decides to renounce them and return to normal life. It is full of telling criticisms of the world of Cinecittà and of the tyranny of producers and directors. If self-criticism was intended, it is remarkably light.

No compromise with Zavattinian realism is present in the two historical films which Visconti made about the Italian Risorgimento, *Senso* and *Il Gattopardo* (*The Leopard*, 1963). There is no question of either of these films being, even in part, a simple mirror of social conditions or of human feelings and behaviour. Both express a strongly worked-out conception, but they carry conviction not for their verisimilitude but for their coherence. *Senso* is unashamedly expressionistic. It makes no concessions to the everyday. Everything in it is dramatized to the highest pitch. Even the décors seem to vibrate with the passions of the human protagonists. *The Leopard* is more reflective, but the focus of the reflection is not observation but discourse, a discourse which, even more than in *Senso*, is that of the author speaking through his creation. It is this authorial presence behind the characters, not their incidental trueness to life, which gives the film such force as it retains even in the English language version, mangled beyond redemption in the studios and laboratories.

The discursive substance of both films operates at two levels, the personal and the historical. *La Terra Trema* had posited a revolutionary process which the history of subsequent years had not verified. Instead of revolution there was reaction. Why was this? In *Senso* and *The Leopard* Visconti brings historical reflection to bear upon this problem. What are the forces which have acted historically to suppress and defuse the revolutionary impulse and to strengthen the hand of conservatism and reaction? A large part of the answer lies in the phenomena of transformism and adaptation. In *Senso* Count Serpieri, Livia's husband, reaches an accommodation with Roberto, leader of the partisans. Meanwhile, on a national scale, Roberto and his group are being excluded from the political and military campaign to liberate Venice from the Austrians, which becomes an affair of the new ruling élite and its international allies. In *The Leopard* the Prince of Salina (Burt Lancaster) is shown as permitting his nephew Tancredi (Alain Delon) to join the Garibaldine forces and encouraging his marriage with Angelica (Claudia Cardinale), daughter of an uncouth plebeian snob, representative of the rising bourgeoisie. With Angelica absorbed into the aristocratic clan and Tancredi into the career bureaucracy of the new state, the Prince dies in the knowledge that his class, at the cost of certain sacrifices, will still survive.

Other aspects of Visconti's approach are less tied to history as such, and bring us closer to the heart of his personal themes. In *Senso*, as in *Ossessione*, the plot is unequivocally motivated by acts of betrayal, which are here personal and political at the same time. Livia's affair with the Austrian lieutenant Franz Mahler (Farley Granger) is not merely a marital infidelity but, more seriously, a betrayal of Roberto and the partisan cause. In *The Leopard* Tancredi's desertion of the Garibaldini in favour of integration with the Piedmontese is also a betrayal (though, in another sense, it is just a reversion to embedded class loyalties). Secondly, we should notice the introduction of the idea of decadence, as both an individual and a class characteristic. Though members of the ruling class are capable of reaching an accommodation with changes in the social order, they bring with them the cancerous negativity of their own decayed condition. The philistinism and cowardice of the new bourgeoisie are thus dubiously enriched by the corruption of the old cultured classes. Of all Visconti's characters only the Prince in *The Leopard* escapes this indictment—though the way in which he rises above it as an individual is through a pessimistic recognition of its overall truth.

This last point emerges even more clearly in Visconti's 'German' films, *The Damned* and *Ludwig*. In the former, the decadence of the old ruling class casts its shadow first over the *arriviste* Friedrich and then over the 'new order' inaugurated by the Nazis and the S.S. Nazism is therefore portrayed not only in terms of economic links with finance capital (a basic postulate of the Marxist analysis) but in its moral and ideological inheritance from sections of a capitalist bourgeoisie which is incapable of self-renewal but equally unwilling to surrender power, and which finally succeeds in transmitting only its increasingly unbridled corruption to its hideous successors, while all the other things for which it once stood are feebly abandoned. In *Ludwig* the issue is differently and more simply framed. Unlike the other films it does not show an accommodation being reached. On the one side stands the decadent 'mad king of Bavaria' with his retinue and artistic hangers-on: on the other the *bien-pensants* and philistines who eventually succeed in overthrowing him. The king's positive qualities are shown in the protection he offers to Wagner, the composer of a 'music of the future' paradoxically made dependent on patronage from the past order. His negative side (apart from his total political irresponsibility and incompetence) is most clearly expressed in his frivolous and egotistical exploitation of his actor friend Joseph Kainz, and also, more ambiguously, in his sexual proclivities. Rebelling against the obligation to subordinate his sex life to the perpetuation of his dynasty, he turns for enjoyment to an entourage of young male courtiers and servants. The relatively sympathetic portrayal of homosexuality at the personal and psychological level is offset by an implicit ideological condemnation of its sterility. As in *Morte a Venezia* (*Death in Venice*, 1971), homosexual love has two faces, a celebration of beauty and youth and an immanent destiny of barren narcissism, ageing and death.

Behind the individual issue of erotic choice stands, inevitably, the structural question of the family. Ludwig rejects the family, and thereby undermines one possible basis of his own power. But in practically all Visconti's other films the family plays a stronger role as a presence. Where it is present in this way, its destruction is necessary if progress is to take place. Conversely, its survival creates the possibility of conservation and transformism. This much has already been noted in passing in connection with *La Terra Trema*, *Rocco* and *The Leopard*. But the strongest statement of the thesis comes in one of Visconti's least appreciated films, *Vaghe Stelle dell'Orsa*, where the dynamic of family relations constitutes the central object of the film. Here the family is not destroyed by historical forces eroding it from the outside, but undermines itself from within. Though outside agencies precipitate the collapse, the locus of the action is strictly the family itself, in which latent tensions have exploded into open rupture and residual affection has regressed to its incestuous roots. The tendency of families, through the Oedipal mechanism, to reproduce and intensify their own pathological structures from generation to generation is here shown as having reached a point of no return. Any further movement can only result in destruction, which is indeed what happens. The father is dead, the mother in a mental home, the stepfather locked in permanent conflict with the children; the daughter Sandra (Claudia Cardinale) is fixated on her father's memory and the son Gianni (Jean Sorel) in love (not reciprocated) with his sister. Given this background, a reunion of the living members, plus Sandra's naïvely inquisitive American husband, to attend a memorial ceremony in honour of the father, provides a predictable occasion for a melodramatic dénouement. As the accumulation of past guilty secrets is laid bare and the tension mounts through a series of enforced confrontations, Gianni emerges as the sacrificial victim. But his eventual suicide, though the most drastic, is only one of a number of events whose cumulative result is the actual and symbolic death of the family as a structure.

An analysis of Visconti's treatment of the family could be developed further—to note, for example, the relative absence of fathers from his films. But it is necessary at this point to raise the question, briefly referred to above, of his personal involvement in his work. This is not out of any misplaced curiosity about his personal *life*, but because the standpoint of his *films* is full of apparent contradiction whose resolution hangs on this basic point. Thus there is an obvious contradiction in some of his films—*Senso*, *Rocco*, *The Leopard*—between a progressive schema on an historical scale and an involvement at the individual level with precisely those characters who oppose or are threatened by the progressive movement. Representatives of the new world, like Ciro in *Rocco and His Brothers* or Pietro, the young doctor who is a former admirer of Sandra's in *Vaghe Stelle*, are often singularly pallid and even pasteboard characters. Conversely, extreme decadents like Ludwig (Helmut Berger) or like Franz

in *Senso* receive close and sympathetic treatment, while perhaps the greatest sympathy of all is reserved for characters like the Prince (Burt Lancaster) in *The Leopard* or Aschenbach (Dirk Bogarde) in *Death in Venice*, the doomed representatives, in the one case, of the best aspects of a reactionary class, and in the other, of an untenable but heroic humanism with reactionary implications. This is the same opposition that we find in the treatment of the family, whose destruction, though necessary, is always tragic, or in that of homosexuality, which is seen at best as attractive but self-negating and at worst (as in *The Damned*) as integrally linked to barbarism and corruption. It is clear, furthermore, that the way the conflicts are articulated on the surface is not the same from film to film. It is rare to find two characters occupying exactly the same structural position in different films. Characters who conform to a structural pattern in one respect may diverge wildly in others. Thus a lucid historical self-consciousness is acquired at the end of *La Terra Trema* by 'Ntoni and at the end of *The Leopard* by a Prince—that is to say, in the one case by a young proletarian and in the other by an aged aristocrat. Equally the sexual role-casting may be variously distributed, with the later films in particular disrupting the patterns established in the earlier work.

To an extent this reflects simply the author's right to shape his material in different ways, to vary his patterns and indeed to change over a period of time. But in certain fundamental ways Visconti has not changed. The underlying contradictions remain the same and come together around the same nodal points, even though their particular forms of expression may vary. The source both of the contradictions and of their variations may be seen, not unduly speculatively, as stemming from Visconti's social position and his role as an artist in the contemporary Italian context. As a progressive artist, with a long-standing association with the Communist Party, he is committed to the destruction of the class from which he stems and to which he remains linked through family background and other social ties. But the complexities of Italian society and social ideology add further contradictions to that produced by his class origin and commitment. Thus, over questions of sexuality and the family, the position taken within his films may in some ways be more radical than that of the nominal progressives whose viewpoint is partially incorporated into his work. At the same time, the latent anti-feminism of many of his films (woman as *succubus* and as betrayer) is a throw-back to aspects of a Catholic ideology very little criticized by Italian progressive *milieux*, and criticized by Visconti himself, for whatever reason, least of all.

In the circumstances, it is not surprising if his films oscillate between a variety of viewpoints, on both class and sexual questions. These range from the orthodox Marxism of *La Terra Trema* to the barely qualified endorsement of the position of the Prince, both a member of a class and yet detached from it, in *The Leopard*; or from the malicious caricature of the Romy Schneider character in *Il Lavoro* (*The Job*) which Visconti made in 1962 for the episode film *Boccaccio '70*, to the extreme indulgence displayed to the same actress when she plays the Empress of Austria in *Ludwig*. Nor should we be surprised to find ambiguities within the same film, or in the treatment of a single theme, even such a staple favourite of Visconti as the defence of classical cultural values against vulgar modernity. Even less should we be surprised, on reflection, to find that it is the family which provides the clearest single focus for all the different aspects of the Viscontian problem. Private and public, individual and political, progressive and reactionary, abstract and concrete, all come together around this single question, whether it is the ostensible locus of the drama, as in *Vaghe Stelle*, or merely, as in *White Nights*, a significant haunting absence.

What is perhaps less obvious is the way the pattern of contradictions at the level of content is also reflected at the stylistic level. We have already mentioned the conflict, apparent in some of Visconti's films, between a highly politicized abstract scenario and a concretization in *mise en scène* which tends to negate the values of the initial schema. If Visconti were an entirely consistent and one-sided director, we might expect from his films an elaboration of the original values of the scenario expressed in the most appropriate seeming mode, which would be

realism. In fact, the finished film abuts, very often, not only in a counter-affirmation of antithetical values but in their affirmation not through realism but through melodrama. A tendency to emphasize and to dramatize is apparent throughout Visconti's work, and his theatrical and operatic productions are noted for their extremism, with an accumulation of 'realistic' detail being used for basically expressionistic purposes. In the films the process is slightly different, since the conflict is not between an original text—Verdi, Shakespeare, Pinter—and Viscontian *mise en scène*, but between two stages of activity each carried out by Visconti himself. The indulgence in sumptuous décor, the intensification of dramatic effect and the development of those aspects of the content which elude or contradict the progressive schema are part of one and the same process. But one cannot crudely identify the *mise en scène* with only the 'reactionary' side of Visconti's interests. It is in fact the vehicle for both sides, and functions precisely as an expression of conflict.

What happens is that the emphasis in the *mise en scène* (including under this head camera work, choice of settings and direction of actors) is always in favour of the physically present. And a comparison of the finished film with the original script shows most often a shift in balance in the course of filming from one set of elements on to another. What results is a loss of critical focus. The elements that are present are so obviously and obtrusively present, their power of attraction and repulsion is so overwhelming, the emotionality so intense, that the more nuanced discourse which attempts to situate and to a certain extent scale down the characters entirely disappears. Above all, the intensification of dramatic conflict leads to a presentation of problem situations as untenable. The characters and, through them, the author appear to be conspiring to represent the world as melodrama, as a site on which to fight out the eternal battles of passion and destiny.

Whether what Visconti puts into the film during shooting corresponds exactly to his deeply felt emotional involvement, while his scenarios are a mere expression of what he thinks he ought to be saying, is a useless and dangerous speculation. What is certain is that the net result is a loss of perspective. This loss matters least in those films whose original 'idea' is sketchiest and where the structures elaborated in the *mise en scène* do not enter into conflict with any pre-formed scheme. This is particularly clear in the case of *White Nights*, a minor film as far as its ostensible subject-matter is concerned but one of considerable richness and subtlety. *White Nights*, taken from a story by Dostoevsky, recounts the attempts of a lonely young man to woo a shy girl pathetically attached to the memory of a lover who, it seems, will never return. The structure of the film is given by a visual metaphor, that of the bridge over a canal which separates the world of his fantasies from that of hers. As a result of this metaphor, which so to speak feeds all the rest of the film, *White Nights* has both a unity as discourse and an absence of unwanted contradictions which are unique in Visconti's work.

Conversely, the problem is most acute when the idea being elaborated already has a form of discourse attached to it, which Visconti is not prepared to abandon as he did in the case of the Dostoevsky story. In films in which the conflict is between two aspects of Visconti's own approach the problem is contained. But where he attempts literal adaptations of literary classics, the result is apt to be totally devoid of any centre of meaning. This happens both with his treatment of Camus' *L'Etranger* in the film *Lo Straniero* (*The Stranger*, 1967) and again with his film of Thomas Mann's *Death in Venice*. In each case we are dealing with texts which not only present a schema of ideas but have a very distinct stylistic quality. Whereas in his early free adaptations Visconti was quite happy to modify or contradict the sense of the original, whether as given in its content or in its style, here he shows a quite embarrassing degree of nominal respect for his authors, while combining this with a total indifference to what they are really saying and an equal inability to recast their prose discourse as film discourse in order to make his own statement. There are moments in *The Stranger* when Visconti appears to be deliberately going against Camus and attempting to show something of the reality of colonial Algiers, in order perhaps to suggest to the spectator that the metaphysically mystified

consciousness of the hero has material roots. At other times he seems to go along with Camus and to suggest with filmic means some of the things also implied in the original prose. But for the most part the film is both solemnly literal in its approach to the text and blind to its most crucial aspects. Silences are made into a cacophony of noise; absences are filled out with the presence of something, generally something which has no reason to be there.

The case of *Death in Venice* is even more unfortunate. Mann has for a long time been a favourite author of Visconti's, and aspects of Mann's cultural concerns have found their way into several of his films, from *Rocco* onwards. But the transcription of Mann's complex and tightly constructed novella into a full-scale costume drama proved an equal abuse of the original and of the talents of the adapter. The loss of much of the complexity of Mann's text has no compensating gain. Although there are certain images in the film which crystallize the sense of ageing, of failure and of solitude which define the central character, Visconti's Aschenbach falls far short of the original, who was both representative of the values of a certain culture and presented by Mann as a very full and tragically representative figure. It is clear that Visconti would like to identify himself, perhaps very strongly, with what Mann was saying. Unfortunately these are not things which lend themselves to decorative elaboration and operatic dramatization. Visconti's strength is shown when he can use his decorative and operatic talents either for a totally original construction or on the foundations of a basically realistic historical narrative. It is by this strength that he should and will be remembered.

Luchino Visconti died in 1976. His penultimate film, *Gruppo di Famiglia in un Interno* (*Conversation Piece*, 1975), was a justification of Nowell-Smith's statement that 'Visconti's strength is shown when he can use his decorative and operatic talents for a totally original construction.'

The Italian title of the film—*Family Group in an Interior*—was more exact than the English one. The whole film did take place in an interior—or rather in two interiors: the flat of the Professor (Burt Lancaster) and the floor above, which he is

persuaded to rent to a Marchese (Sylvana Mangano) so that her kept lover (Helmut Berger) can have a Roman *pied-à-terre*. The professor lives alone with his housekeeper, his memories and his collections. Suddenly, there erupts into his well-ordered life all the horrors of the 70s—the New Rich Marchese, married to a Fascist industrialist, her *louche* lover, her nubile daughter. Their vulgar vitality pains him, but it also fascinates him. And although he is 'not interested in people who lose control of themselves' he is also not a little intrigued by this unholy *ménage*. By the end of the film, the professor has accepted them: they *could* have been the family he never had. Life may have passed him by, but at the last moment he has had a chance to give himself to someone.

The film had its weaknesses (Berger, in particular, was unbelievable as a veteran of the '68 barricades), but Visconti's genius for handling actors, for moving his camera and for creating atmosphere made it his best film in years. And his vicious portrait of the Marchese was a brilliant creation: horrible though she is, her vitality brings the professor back to life, with all its emotional demands. If Berger is a little too much the 'angel of death' (as in *Death in Venice*), she, paradoxically, speaks up for life.

Unfortunately, the English language version of the film was not as good as it should have been, and therefore the film's success was limited largely to Italy and France. Visconti's last film, *L'Innocente* (*The Intruder*, 1976), based on a D'Annunzio novel, was not well received except in the U.S. Sadly, it was not a major work, largely, I think, because of the casting (which was imposed on Visconti). Laura Antonelli is extremely beautiful, but she doesn't have that glow which would vitalize this heavy-breathing story of a betrayed wife who, deciding that what's sauce for the gander will also be sauce for the goose, comes spectacularly to grief. (What the younger Alida Valli could have done with such a part!) And Gian-Carlo Giannini, doing his best to make us forget that he is a comic actor, tries hard for the tortured Byronic look and only succeeds in appearing constipated. The film was indeed gorgeous to look at, but when the wallpaper upstages the actors, a film is in trouble.

Nowell-Smith has written a full-length study: *Visconti* (1973). In French there was an excellent number of *Premier Plan* (No. 17, 1961) devoted to Visconti, with articles by Giulio Cesare Castello, Roland Barthes, Alain Tanner and Karel Reisz.

RAOUL WALSH

Edgardo Cozarinsky

The career of Raoul Walsh (born 1887) and the history of Hollywood are so closely linked that they illuminate each other eloquently and dramatically. This connection, far from unique, is shared by directors like Allan Dwan, King Vidor, John Ford and Henry King. They all entered film-making in the early 1910s, turning out two-reelers at breakneck pace. After the Gold Rush, Hollywood stood in American life as the last outpost of the frontier myth, not yet absorbed into the ideology of glamour; and from then on these men kept continuously active until around 1960, with ups and downs that reflected their own, and the industry's, variable capacity for keeping up with the times.

Walsh's career, though, provides an exceptional instance of enriching interplay between personal legend and professional work. Already in 1913 he went to Mexico to shoot background footage and action scenes for *The Life of Villa*, a film Griffith was to direct for Mutual. The company had signed an exclusive contract with Pancho Villa, who agreed to supply information and supervision, and when Griffith, already engaged on *The Birth of a Nation*, passed the project to Christy Cabanne, not only was Walsh's footage incorporated, but he was also Villa's personal choice to play the Mexican leader as a young man. His next part was as John Wilkes Booth in *The Birth of a Nation* (1915). In 1923, after shooting on location *Lost and Found in a South Sea Island*, he recalls getting so drunk during the farewell party in Tahiti that his advances to a native girl led him to allow her family to connect his nostrils by perforation. (He is still able to demonstrate this, passing a thread from side to side.) Finally, the famous black patch over his right eye was earned in 1929, while shooting *In Old Arizona*. For a long time, Walsh's lean, muscular figure was an icon for the man of adventure his films were about. The raucous sailor he portrayed in *Sadie Thompson* (1928, with Gloria Swanson in the title role) is just one in the long gallery of lusty, loud servicemen in his films.

Walsh worked for most of the big companies in Hollywood, and there are recogniz-

James Cagney, Robert Osterloh, Edmond O'Brien, and G. Pat Collins in *White Heat*: 'this may well be the simplest and strongest of Walsh's films'.

able cycles in his work, depending on the stars, writers and technicians which those companies had under contract, as well as on changing approaches to subject-matter. If it is possible to consider Walsh a personality, it is not out of any diehard *auteur* theory. A craftsman, given the material and the instruments to work on it, cannot possibly prevent his attitudes, as well as his occasional indifference, from leaving their imprint. Those same companies, in their own interest, were quick to recognize what best suited the talents under contract. In Walsh's case this meant action films, whether war films, Westerns, gangster movies, seafaring sagas or the fast-paced comedies that look like developments of the frequent comic relief interludes in those same action films.

Walsh's consistent imprint is a way of dealing with subject-matter only through the action, and with action only through film lan-

guage. He is on record as saying that 'there are not five different ways of showing a man entering a room'. Any first-term pupil of a film school knows there are innumerable ways of showing a scrap of action, but the classical attitude, and talent, is to make the chosen one look as if it had been the only one possible. Walsh's famous reluctance to have a shot where nothing happens, or to let it stay on the screen longer than is needed to get across what the film needs to advance, is the empirical basis for a theory of the classical Hollywood film. In this respect his films are much more revealing than those of more 'personal' directors. Devoid of the sentimentality and conscious traditionalism of John Ford, and of the scepticism and intellectual astringency of Howard Hawks, Walsh works in a perfect balance between the romantic notion of the author as creator and the once prevalent highbrow prejudice of the Hollywood director as a well-oiled cog in the machine.

Though Walsh has directed at least a dozen extraordinary films, even in his least-known work there is an element of gusto that today seems inestimable. Elliott Stein has pointed out the sharp parody of the interior monologue from *Strange Interlude* (the intel-lectual film of the period) in *Me and My Gal* (1932). A shoestring-budget, sixty-four-min-ute quickie of the next year, *Sailor's Luck*, is more resourceful than many better-known comedies of the 30s, brilliantly tying up, in ever-mounting comic action, characters and situations. Even something so seemingly im-practicable as a Lily Pons vehicle turns out to be a crazy farce—*Hitting a New High* (1937), where the *prima donna* sings on treetops as an African 'bird girl', and a lion, which nobody suspects of being untamed, paces leisurely about a white art-deco hotel suite. At a time when Hollywood was delivering fresh enter-tainment every week, these films may have seemed run of the mill. Today they not only look more watchable than the more expen-sive, 'serious' product of the period, they are also endowed with an unfailing inven-tiveness, as remarkable as it is unprepossess-ing. Though *The Thief of Bagdad* (1924), *What Price Glory?* (1926), *Sadie Thompson* and *In Old Arizona* were 'big' films, Walsh kept turning out 'small' ones all through the 20s.

In retrospect, his period of almost ex-clusive attachment to Warners (1939–51, with two exceptions among twenty-six films) seems to have brought out much of his best. The precise staging and cutting of action, the laconic characterization, the unfailing sense of narrative in most of these films stand out clearly if compared with the standard Warner product of the period. *The Roaring Twenties* (1939) is not a mythical gangster film, like *Scarface*, *Little Caesar* or *Public Enemy*, but a very realistic portrait, in social and economic terms, of the period after the First World War. *High Sierra* (1941) bridges the gap be-tween the 30s gangster film and the 40s *film noir* with a story where criminal violence and sexual passion further each other in an un-relenting crescendo. Such melodramas as *They Drive by Night* (U.K.: *Road to Frisco*, 1940) and *The Man I Love* (1946), stories of doomed passion, are remarkable for an inten-

sity that derives not from a stylization as radical as Sternberg's, but from refining the understated codes of social intercourse through the style of the actors and the obvious devices of the scripts. *Gentleman Jim* (1942) is the most elegant variation on an idea of gallantry that Walsh embodied in Errol Flynn (something he could not achieve in his earlier brief association with Douglas Fairbanks Sr, and was only to recapture in the 50s, in his late encounter with Clark Gable). *Objective, Burma!* (1945) is almost a text book example of the war action film—factually all false, yet eliciting the fullest suspension of disbelief as it develops on the screen with a logic of physical action, a balance of tension and relaxation that has never been equalled. Even when psycho-analysis hit Hollywood, *Pursued* (1947) stayed free of pedantry in spite of the many Greek tragedy overtones in its Niven–Busch script; and *White Heat* (1949), though presenting a weird Oedipal relationship (Cagney weeping on Margaret Wycherley's lap), may well be the simplest and strongest of Walsh's films—the gangster anti-hero finally blows himself up yelling 'Look, Ma! Top of the world!' *Color-ado Territory* (1949) moves the *High Sierra* story to a typical Western setting and ends giving full rein to Walsh's taste for romantic tragedy: the final sequence is a *Liebestod* less hysterical than King Vidor's in *Duel in the Sun* but equally impressive. Even in the middle 50s, among the wide screens and garish colours that were inescapable at Fox, the wry humour and sexual frankness of *The Revolt of Mamie Stover* (1956) were the same as in Walsh's modest quickies of the 30s.

The risk of enumeration is apparent. The personality of Walsh is that of an *oeuvre*, and it is difficult not to find, even in his less dis-tinguished work, bursts of humour, imagina-tion and sheer film sense that beggar descrip-tion. Even more than Westerns or gangster films, war films provided Walsh with a propitious setting. In this, more than in any other aspect, his serene disregard for any critical revision of traditional attitudes is vis-ible, and describes an eloquent curve from *What Price Glory?* to his last but one film, the obscure *Marines, Let's Go* (1961).

The early adaptation of a successful play by Lawrence Stallings and Maxwell Anderson, coming in the wake of King Vidor's hit *The Big Parade* (1925), *What Price Glory?* almost did away with the irony of the stage original, simply through a dominating concern for the enjoyment of men in action, be it battles or tavern brawls. The 'war is hell' attitude was voiced in titles, in between the more exciting war action (Walsh is one of the few directors in whose films battles can be followed; the sense and legibility of tactical moves and development are never sacrificed to hectic 'visual' devices) and the barracks humour.

After the extreme formal severity of *Objective, Burma!*, and the looser pattern of his contemporary sabotage and spy thrillers at Warners, it is telling that both *Battle Cry* (1955, script by Leon Uris from his novel) and *The Naked and the Dead* (1958, the Norman Mailer novel, adapted by the Sanders brothers) do not look very different in Walsh's treatment, in spite of the distance in literary ambition between the original best-sellers. The best sequences in both films are the tavern rough-houses, where the excitement of soldiers in their time off and the repressed eroticism seem to explode in exact but unassuming accord with the wide-screen format, the pan shots and the editing.

Marines, Let's Go, a very minor film by any standard, would have been ignored or dismissed without great fuss a few years earlier. Instead, when the blacklisted men were coming back and the blockbusters were using them, when censorship was cracking up quickly and loudly, the *New York Times* found it 'no credit to anyone' and deplored its 'hollow and exasperating tribute to American fighting men in Korea'; the *New York Herald Tribune* thought it was 'tasteless . . . truly offensive' and said that 'Raoul Walsh should be ashamed of himself'; while *Variety* delivered the death blow—'dated, corny, juvenile and predictable'. These comments, if anything, mirror the broadening gap between the sensibility and attitudes of the men who established the industry and the needs of that industry to survive in a fast-changing social context. Though Walsh's last film, *A Distant Trumpet* (1964), is excellent, it is possible that he too could say, as William Wellman did to Peter Bogdanovich some time later, that he 'no longer knew how to make a film'.

For further reading, see Walsh's autobiography *Each Man in His Time: The Life Story of a Director* (1974). There are also two monographs on his work, one edited by Phil Hardy, *Raoul Walsh* (1974), and one by Kingsley Canham in *The Hollywood Professionals*, Vol. I (1973).

ORSON WELLES

Penelope Houston

Scott Fitzgerald once wrote that there are no second acts in American lives. It was a pronouncement curiously beside the point of Fitzgerald's own life (what, after all, is *Tender Is the Night* but the novel of an almost unendurable second act?); but it has always seemed almost excessively appropriate to the film-making career of George Orson Welles. The Wellesian first act remains unchallenged: the most dazzling, explosive and sheerly overpowering beginning in cinema history, a heavyweight arrival comparable in bravura and wallop to Cassius Clay's first victory over Sonny Liston. The Wellesian third act is now in progress: quieter, deeper, more slow-running and subdued, coloured with the regrets and dispassionate ruminations of advancing years. But the second act is the underdeveloped territory, the middle ground between prodigy and patriarch which should perhaps have yielded the richest harvest. Welles has described himself as 'frustrated'; and in the light of the perpetual motion of his creative life, this might sound like a not uncharacteristic exaggeration. But to write about Welles is to encounter frustration: the critic finds herself speculatively circling that unfilled gap at the centre.

Welles' *Histoire Immortelle* (*The Immortal Story*, 1968) has been likened to such films as Dreyer's *Gertrud*, Ford's *Seven Women*, Renoir's *Le Caporal Epinglé*; works whose qualities—the serenities and certainties, but also the fitful discontents—are reflections of their makers' age. The comparison has seemed apt; yet the shock is to realize that there should be no comparison, that Welles in his fifties had somehow caught up with the masters of a previous generation, and that we are ranking among the sages a film-maker actually of an age with such decidedly unpatriarchal figures as Losey or Antonioni. But

Welles' Mr Clay in *The Immortal Story*, and his almost grandfatherly Falstaff in *Campanadas a Medianoche* (U.K.: *Chimes at Midnight*; U.S.: *Falstaff*, 1966), are characters immemorially experienced, old as time. There is something disconcerting about an artist's assumption of patriarchal trappings before his years properly entitle him to them; and it is part of the massive Wellesian paradox that if his great, late films of the 60s suggest an artist rushing to embrace the certainties of age, his films of the 40s glitter spectacularly with the quite other certainty of their youth. The uncertain years come in between.

Welles, of course, was by no means a youth when in 1941 he made *Citizen Kane*. A twenty-five year-old film-maker (he was born in 1915) would have seemed no prodigy in 1920, or again in 1970, and it was only in its own middle years that Hollywood seemed to become peculiarly the province of the middle-aged. Having begun his career younger than anyone else, playing Shakespearian tragic roles in the nursery, acting and producing professionally while still in his teens, moving on in his very early twenties to the conquest of radio, Welles arrived in Hollywood as the Alexander of show-business, with only one world still left to conquer. The *War of the Worlds* broadcast (1938), which sent New Yorkers running to the hills from the imagined Martian invasion, had been the crowning sensation. Ironically, *War of the Worlds* was in effect a fluke, and in its substance apparently by no means the most striking of his radio productions; but it set the Welles legend in a particular, inescapable atmosphere of shock and suspense. He was believed to be capable of anything; and a kind of superstitious fear of the artist as magician has perhaps haunted him ever since.

Before coming to Hollywood, Welles had experimented briefly with film. A four-minute fragment dating from 1934, *The Hearts of Age*, has been unearthed and is described in Joseph McBride's book *Orson Welles*. In 1938 a forty-minute film, *Too Much Johnson*, was made to accompany a Mercury Theatre production. Stills survive, showing such Mercury stalwarts as John Houseman and Joseph Cotten, but the only print has apparently gone for ever, destroyed in a fire in 1970 at Welles' Madrid home. In

any case, these were fragments of buried juvenilia. It was as the infant impresario, and the man who had made life sensationally surrender to art, that Welles descended on a Hollywood no doubt expectant of outrage, and as suspicious as though they thought he had brought the Martians with him.

Hollywood had had ten years to recover from the invasion of theatre talent at the end of the 20s, and by 1940 it was a clannish town of professionals much involved in their own union and status conflicts. The Mercury Theatre entourage Welles brought with him came out of another world. Scott Fitzgerald's little satiric squib 'Pat Hobby and Orson Welles', written in the year before *Citizen Kane*, probably packed some ingrained suspicions into the dire warning which Pat Hobby, the shifty, calloused old screenwriter, gives the producer, Mr Marcus. 'I wouldn't be surprised if Orson Welles is the biggest menace that's come to Hollywood for years. He gets a hundred and fifty grand a picture, and I wouldn't be surprised if he was so radical that you had to have all new equipment and start all over again like you did with sound in 1928.' 'Oh, my God!' groans Mr Marcus.

To establish himself as an American film-maker in the context of the 40s, Welles had to impose this damaging reputation for unruly genius on a community of Mr Marcuses. His failure provides part, if by no means all, of the explanation for the missing second act in the Wellesian drama. But it's seldom asked what could conceivably have happened if Welles, in the 40s, had succeeded. In the excessively conformist Hollywood of the 50s, with its docile acquiescence in the blacklist, its querulous alarms about television's inroads into its audience and its general air of strained respectability, there could in any case hardly have been room for Welles. *Citizen Kane* was made just in time; if Welles had delayed his trip to Hollywood by as much as three or four years, it might never have been made at all.

By the nature of things, large elements of derring-do and sheer bravado must have entered into the making of Welles' first feature. And if so many of the normal artistic laws had not seemingly been suspended on behalf of *Citizen Kane*, this should now be working powerfully against the film. Nothing wears out quicker than the determination of yesterday to *épater les bourgeois*. But although the stylistic innovations of *Citizen Kane*—the overlapping dialogue, Gregg Toland's deep-focus camerawork, the heavy chiaroscuro and looming distortions, those round-the-corner, crick-of-the-neck angles that so exasperated conventional critics, the oblique and devious yet extraordinarily rapid narrative—have long since passed into cliché, one always re-encounters them in the film itself with the same astounding (and by this time astounded) exhilaration. Built mysteriously into the fabric of *Citizen Kane* is the excitement of its making. And this might seem a point too obvious to be worth stressing, except that it's hard to think of any other single work which has managed a similar retention of urgency. *A Bout de Souffle*, for instance, once seemed to reflect similar tensions, the sense that the cinema's box of tricks had been thrown open to someone ready to make it work for him in a wholly new way. But to re-see Godard's film is not to re-experience this feeling: it has moved into screen history, while *Citizen Kane* remains bafflingly outside time.

The story the film tells ought to be a melancholy one: the betrayal of hope and promise and love and brilliance, the disillusionment of cold, creeping age and of power misused, Charles Foster Kane's progress from the buccaneering adventure of running a newspaper to the petrified gloom of the marble halls of Xanadu. And the film wraps the disillusioning story of Kane within a framework of futility, as the enquiring reporter realizes that the heart of his story will forever elude him, that even the power of the press ('power without responsibility, the harlot's prerogative', of course) must finally retreat before the 'No Trespassing' sign. Even Rosebud, the last witness, the sled burning among the wanton debris of Kane's Xanadu, is only a clue and not an answer. It points to no more than the most significant of many turning points; and Welles (who has himself deprecatingly called the burning sled 'rather dollar-book Freud') has too high a sense of human potential to see a man's life as pivoting entirely on a single symbol, however evocative, of childhood despair and the lost opportunities of innocence.

But of course *Citizen Kane* never begins to feel like a depressing film: it is too dispassionate about its characters, too alert in its curiosity, too romantically buoyed up on its sense of possibility. The strongest comparison, it has always seemed to me, is with *The Great Gatsby*, Scott Fitzgerald's novel from the other side of the depressed 30s. About Gatsby, as about Kane, hangs the fascination of the insoluble mystery. In both cases, the works are powered by a strong romantic appetite, an American baroque style, a feeling not so much for the shattered reality as for the promise of the receding dream. '. . . He had come a long way to this blue lawn, and his dream must have seemed so close that he could hardly fail to grasp it. He did not know that it was already behind him, somewhere back in that vast obscurity beyond the city, where the dark fields of the republic rolled on under the night . . . It eluded us then, but that's no matter—tomorrow we will run faster, stretch out our arms farther . . . And one fine morning—'. For Kane, too, the future is lost in the past, lost in the 'dark fields of the republic'. Charles Foster Kane and Jay Gatsby, dreamers of the American dream, are the creations of artists who must have shared in the dream on their own account —whose experiences had entitled them to believe that they were touched by a kind of magic, and who could afford a certain luxuriant fatalism on behalf of their characters. Disillusionment, itself often a romantic condition, is the other side of that 'heightened sense of the possibilities of life' which Fitzgerald defined in Gatsby, and which Welles gave to the man who thought it would be 'fun to run a newspaper'.

How much, though, did Welles 'create' *Citizen Kane*? The perennial and fruitless argument was given another twist in 1971 by Pauline Kael's *New Yorker* articles 'Raising Kane' (later published in *The Citizen Kane Book*), which set out to rehabilitate the forgotten man of the film, Welles' credited co-scriptwriter Herman Mankiewicz. Even at that distance in time, Miss Kael's articles produced some ferocious reactions, and the question of *Citizen Kane*'s precise authorship (as a script, not as a film) can still arouse passions. But there remain two points worth stressing. Whatever the exact circumstances of its writing, and in whatever proportions the Welles and Mankiewicz texts were blended in the final shooting script, the *Citizen Kane* script was a product of considerable speed. In effect, *Citizen Kane* was made because Welles' first, cherished Hollywood project, an adaptation of Conrad's *Heart of Darkness*, couldn't get off the ground. A second notion, for an adaptation of Nicholas Blake's thriller *The Smiler with the Knife*, also collapsed. *Citizen Kane* was a solution to the growing problem of what Welles' first Hollywood film was to be: the film's etched sharpness is a product of energy, not of deliberation. And secondly, though the *Citizen Kane* script is a beautiful, adroit piece of screenwriting, the script is not the picture—nor, in itself, particularly innovatory. Other scripts, such as Preston Sturges' *The Power and the Glory*, had taken a man's life apart in flashback; other scripts from the same period were at once as shrewd and knowing and as romantically regretful. Arguments about exactly how the script came into existence remain irrelevant beside the hardly disputed question of who created the *film*. *Citizen Kane* on the screen is the product of a mind grandiose and wilful, flamboyant and haunted, a mind fascinated with the chiaroscuro of morality and the devious defeats of hope: the mind of Orson Welles.

Most intriguingly the film attracted a critique from Jorge Luis Borges, who was then reviewing movies for the Argentine magazine *Sur*. Borges pounced magnificently, laying down an almost Wellesian dogma: 'In one of the tales of Chesterton . . . the hero observes that nothing is more frightening than a centreless labyrinth. This film is just that labyrinth.' He ended his review, however, on a note almost as fascinatingly wrong as the Chesterton reference is right: 'I dare predict . . . that *Citizen Kane* will endure in the same way certain films of Griffith or Pudovkin endure: no one denies their historical value but no one sees them again. It suffers from grossness, pedantry, dullness. It is not intelligent . . .'

If *Citizen Kane* is unintelligent, then there can have been few intelligent films. But it is part of the film's prismatic nature that it responds at least adequately to so many different descriptions. Borges can see it as a maze without a centre, an image one might say of pointless power; and Miss Kael, more brusquely and brashly, can describe it as 'the biggest newspaper picture of them all'. Script attribution aside, Miss Kael did Wellesian criticism a service by her emphasis on the whole journalistic side of *Citizen Kane*— not merely the Hearstian lore, but the contrast between the new men of the news magazines, with their Luce talk and their mouse-like burrowings in the cause of research, and the old swashbucklers of the yellow press ('You provide the prose poems; I'll provide the war'). One of the themes running most constantly through Welles' career is a fascination with the mechanics and morality of power—the dying splendours of the Ambersons, the mad, megalomaniac spider's web in which O'Hara, the sailor in *The Lady from Shanghai* (1948), is trapped, the mysterious resources of Mr Arkadin, the power of the sheriff's badge in *Touch of Evil* (1958), of kingship in *Chimes at Midnight*, of faceless bureaucracy in *The Trial* (1962; made in France as *Le Procès*), of age and money in *The Immortal Story*. One of the problems for a modern artist concerned with power must always be the veracity of the setting, the finding of a stage on which the consuming exercise of will can be acted out. And in *Citizen Kane*, whether the journalistic detail derived from Welles or Mankiewicz, the imperial longings of William Randolph Hearst set this scale. Welles' Mr Arkadin is a shadowy machinator, and the quest for his life is the pursuit of a self-deluding fantasy. It is because Kane's treasure-house of Xanadu is built four-square on the foundations of Hearst's San Simeon that the film's architecture encompasses its own extravagance. Like one of Vanbrugh's great houses, *Citizen Kane* remains functional even in its excesses.

'I owe it to my ignorance. If this word seems inadequate to you, replace it with innocence,' Welles himself has said of *Citizen Kane*. And François Truffaut wrote of *The Magnificent Ambersons* (1942) that it was 'made in violent contrast to *Citizen Kane*, almost as if by another film-maker who detested the first and wanted to give him a lesson in modesty'. *The Magnificent Ambersons* is actually neither so different from *Citizen Kane* nor so modest; but it develops a side of Welles which was to remain to some extent dormant in his films until he came, a quarter of a century later, to *Chimes at Mid-*

night. He described the latter film as 'a lament for Merrie England'; and Welles is as aware as anyone that 'Merrie England' has no time or place, existed in no exact historical context. In the same way, *The Magnificent Ambersons* is a lament for a dying dream, something more intangible, and therefore perhaps more potent, than the betrayal of bright hope in *Citizen Kane*.

The Ambersons, Booth Tarkington's proud, decayed American aristocrats, bow down before the motor car and the new city; George Amberson Minafer (Tim Holt), the arrogant, selfish, hopelessly spoilt son of the house, defends it to the death (not his own death, but his mother's) against the loving inroads of Eugene Morgan (Joseph Cotten), the pioneer manufacturer of the horseless carriage who is by nature a new man with old manners. At the outset, as he had done in *Citizen Kane* and was to do so often in later films, Welles in effect adumbrates his theme: we are to see the comeuppance, as one old party in the street puts it, of the last of the Ambersons. And this use of the chorus of town bystanders and gossips, and Welles' fondness for spoken narrative, is another reminder of how much he had learned from radio—the only major film-maker, possibly, who came to movies essentially via radio, who had mastered the speed and suggestivity of sound before linking it to pictures. In his early films, the images had to keep up with the finesse of the sound transitions; and although by comparison with *Citizen Kane*, *The Magnificent Ambersons* is a still, quiet, reflective film, the suppleness of its use of sound gives the director the framework on which visual atmosphere can be overlaid.

The Magnificent Ambersons is the romantic high water mark of Welles' career, using the illusionist's art (which in *Touch of Evil*, for instance, he was to turn to the conjuring up of nightmare) to suggest a lost Eden of happiness and innocence and splendour. The ball sequence, 'the last of the great long-remembered dances', is a scene of dazzling exhilaration; but the lights are going out in the Amberson mansion, and the exuberance and wilfulness of the occasion are overtaken by that characteristic Wellesian regret for last things. The snow sequence (that same snow young Charlie Kane had been dragged away from) similarly owes its charm and vitality to

its evanescence. Remove the intimations of destiny, and the Ambersons would be merely a snobbish little clan clinging to empty aristocratic illusions. Welles' achievement is in lending them his own romanticism, at the same time keeping a due, dispassionate distance; protecting Agnes Moorehead's loving, spiteful, pitiful Aunt Fanny while seeing her wholly for what she is; bridging the gap, one might say, between the homely, silly, small-town word 'comeuppance' and the despairing darkening of the Ambersons' fortunes.

Romance tempered by irony has always been one of the most powerful Wellesian moods: he is almost incapable, either in his own person as an actor or in his films, of scaling down or miniaturizing. One reason for the failure of *The Stranger* (1946), the thriller in which Welles plays a Nazi who has gone to ground (and to seed) in backwoods New England, was that Welles simply could not assume the necessary camouflage: rejecting disguise, his Nazi insists on playing superman on Main Street. And one reason, perhaps, for the relative failure of his adaptation of Kafka's *The Trial* was his impatience with the sheer ordinariness of Joseph K. A Wellesian little man is a contradiction in terms. Rather, he turns the unexceptional house of the ultimately unexceptional Ambersons into a haunted palace, trailing greater glories than realistically belong to its inhabitants. Yet, always, he retains the saving sense of irony—the story-teller's answer to the perennial problem of angle and distance from his subject. In *The Magnificent Ambersons*, as in *Citizen Kane*, the irony is a function of the artist's omniscience: he knows the end before the beginning, he has set his scene in the past, and his characters are working their way along a predestined course. The true and tragic irony (one reason, no doubt, why Welles is so persistently drawn to Shakespeare) is the power to hold a dramatic moment in suspension because one knows what the outcome must be. Artists as romantically baroque as Welles, but lacking this ironic faculty, include both Losey and Visconti; and what one misses in *The Go-Between* and *Death in Venice*, those immaculate and fatalistic explorations of the Edwardian sunset, is the extra dimension of the ironic angle. Both Losey and Visconti

Tim Holt and Anne Baxter, Joseph Cotten and Dolores Costello in the ball sequence from *The Magnificent Ambersons*: 'the last of the great long-remembered dances is a scene of dazzling exhilaration; but the lights are going out in the Amberson mansion'.

keep plucking at the sleeves of their characters, nudging them into an awareness of what
lies in wait. Welles' story-telling style, in *The
Magnificent Ambersons* especially, is at once
more autocratic and more human.

In fact, Welles is profoundly a story-teller,
and it is not surprising that in *The Immortal
Story* he should finally have been drawn to
the work of another of the great, aristocratic tellers of tales: Isak Dinesen (Baroness
Blixen), the imperious Nordic sybil. Welles'
films, in the old-fashioned sense, tell stories;
they introduce the voice of the narrator, the
commentator, the gossip, the observers who
will describe the other characters to us, predict their destinies and finally stand guard
over their corpses. The reporters in *Citizen
Kane*, the townspeople in *The Magnificent
Ambersons*, play similar roles: they answer
Welles' wish to get the commentator into the
story. And in those arrogant early credits,
when the microphone swung round and the
voice purred 'My name is Orson Welles', the
story-teller himself was signing off—in, of
course, the style of radio.

There are, too, the stories within the films:
in *Lady from Shanghai*, for instance, the so
apposite anecdote about the cannibal sharks,
reddening the sea with their blood—or, indeed, the whole fascinating split mood of
this film, so that O'Hara (Welles) seems to be
not merely the victim of a lunatic and murderous conspiracy, but a typical Irish racon-
teur embroidering and philosophizing over a
good yarn. The most celebrated of all the
Wellesian anecdotes, however, is the fable
in *Mr Arkadin* (1955; U.K.: *Confidential
Report*) about the scorpion and the frog. The
scorpion asks the frog for a lift across the
river; the canny frog at first rejects such a
dangerous passenger, but is finally won over
by the scorpion's logical argument that he is
hardly likely to destroy himself along with
his carrier. Half-way across the frog feels the
fatal sting, and with its dying gasp seeks a
rational creature's explanation for this irrational act. 'I can't help it,' says the scorpion. 'It's my nature.'

Wellesian commentators, fascinated by the
kind of auto-destruct mechanism that seems
to have operated at various points in his career, of course seized on the parable. But it
has never been quite that simple. One could
almost as well argue that Welles is the frog,

the creature beguiled by the delusions of
reason, and that his movie-making existence
has been guided by simple principles which
circumstances have distorted and twisted
into ferocious paradox.

His career has been discussed in persistent
detail, by himself as well as by others; yet it's
still difficult to build up an objective picture
of what really went on in the years after
Citizen Kane, of how far Welles had become,
for instance, a highly symbolic counter (the
king as pawn) in the battles of the RKO
boardroom. It is always said that *Citizen
Kane* did poorly at the box-office because the
Hearst forces marshalled their considerable
power against it. Louella Parsons emerges as
the Joan of Arc of the yellow press, riding
into battle against a film which would otherwise have carried all before it. But *Citizen
Kane*, by its elliptical nature, seems hardly
the sort of film ever destined for a major box-
office triumph even if it had received an
ordinary release. And, given the element of
sheer cheek in its use of Hearstian reference,
it's hard to believe that the retaliatory reaction can have been entirely unexpected. If
RKO was really so taken aback at the film's
reception, it seems only further evidence
of Hollywood's innate capacity for self-
delusion.

In effect, RKO was soon to be in the
throes of one of those perennial Hollywood
battles between derring-do and safety first.
George Schaefer, who had brought Welles to
Hollywood with a contract allowing him
unprecedented control over his pictures, was
under heavy pressure. Eventually Charles
Koerner took over at the studio, and the victory for commerce was proclaimed in no
uncertain terms: 'Showmanship instead of
genius: a new deal at RKO.' (One is reminded of the endearing remark attributed
to Rita Hayworth at the time of her divorce
from Welles: 'I just can't stand that man's
genius.') Meanwhile, Welles himself had embarked on the extraordinary, doomed Latin
American venture, *It's All True* (1942), a
project which could be regarded as his *Que
Viva Mexico!* and which, like the Eisenstein
film, harboured any number of built-in possibilities for disaster.

This multi-part, mainly documentary film
was conceived as a contribution to the
United States' 'Good Neighbour' policy, and

was precisely the sort of chancy commitment that studios entered into in haste, on a wave of patriotic goodwill, and repented of more commercially and at leisure. Lines of communication were over-extended; wartime problems over transport and equipment were inevitable; above all, an exceptionally difficult undertaking was embarked on at speed, to get the film unit down to Rio in February 1942 in time for the Carnival which was to be one of the picture's themes. Richard Wilson, Welles' associate, has written that 'no script was possible until Welles had actually seen the Carnival'.

It's All True collapsed under a combination of circumstances originating less in Brazil than in the boardrooms in America. Welles was far from the scene of action when RKO, disconcerted at preview reactions to *The Magnificent Ambersons* (and no doubt using the picture as a tool in the company wars), re-edited the film, shortened it and re-shot the ending along mawkish lines never countenanced by the director. In Rio, to quote Richard Wilson, 'bills somehow weren't being paid for *It's All True*', and Welles had to fight for permission to keep shooting. And in July 1942, back in Hollywood, the Mercury production unit was ordered out of its offices—to make way, with appropriately preposterous Hollywood irony, for a Tarzan picture. Welles himself returned to America a month or so later, to find that *It's All True* was all over and that another 'lost' film had been added to screen history. Much of the footage does in fact still survive, in the Paramount library in California, where Charles Higham was able to view it while researching his book on Welles; some of it has vanished for ever, decomposing cans of celluloid junked in the Pacific.

Richard Wilson has pointed out the irony that 'Welles was approached to make a non-commercial picture, then was bitterly reproached for making a non-commercial picture'. And the whole melancholy episode, in so many ways a cautionary tale of movie-making attitudes, seems also crucially central to Welles' career. He had arrived in Hollywood on his terms, given a contract of dazzling promises; and he had been beaten on their terms. The contract had proved to be a licence allowing him one bite. He had been able to make what is still arguably the most

electrifying film in Hollywood's history; but he had been unable to save his more graceful, elegiac second picture; and his third film had been shot to pieces under him. He could now only placate Hollywood's gods by making a thoroughly commercial picture, and even if it had been within his temperament to do so (no Welles film has ever been a real commercial hit), they were now unlikely to give him the means. By a further ironic twist, Welles was to be increasingly in demand as an actor of outsize temperament as he ceased to be wanted by Hollywood as a director: behind a camera, he simply frightened them.

Even now, an American director out of favour with Hollywood has few alternative sources of backing; in the 40s, it really was Hollywood or nothing. Welles tried to mend some fences with *The Stranger*, and merely demonstrated that he lacked the artisan skills to lend plausibility to mediocrity. *The Lady from Shanghai*, a much better and essentially more enjoyable picture, was better in practically unhelpful ways. Like John Huston's later *Beat the Devil* it came somewhat before its time, allying masterfully eccentric characterization to a virtually incomprehensible corkscrew plot, at a time when audiences still expected to know what was going on on the screen. The story's machinations, and the final revelation of Rita Hayworth, the icy siren, as involved in them up to her pretty neck, are heavy with echoes of the corrupting fatalism of the 40s *film noir*. But *The Lady from Shanghai* lacks the hard-bitten, professional drive of *Double Indemnity* or the insolent allure of *The Big Sleep*. It is an exotic, rambling, moody film, slightly bemused like its Irish hero, a tall tale festooned with extravagances, like the final gunplay among the shattered distorting mirrors, a sailor's yarn in which the superb monsters played by Glenn Anders and Everett Sloane emerge like man-eaters from the depths. The baroque style, no longer preserving much sense of essential function, slips towards a beguiling but almost contemptuous excess, as though the whole film was for Welles a mocking, genial but slightly desperate venture into the fun-house.

But the ultimate irony was still held in reserve. Welles' last Hollywood film of the 40s—and the last film he was to make in America for almost a decade—was the bizarre quickie *Macbeth* (1948), shot in a brusque three weeks for Republic, a horse opera company capable of rising to occasional flights of resolute fantasy. In the circumstances, it was not surprising that the film had a certain wild-eyed quality—rugged, slaty, vaguely dripping sets, suggesting that the actors had just dropped tools at the coalface, eye-rolling performances from a cast generally much over-burdened by their roles, a lowering, dishevelled storminess of mood. In the theatre, Welles had staged a celebrated voodoo *Macbeth*; the screen attempt at a barbaric, Pictish *Macbeth*, a film of crags and crones, shaggy warriors and ferocious incantations, was fated by intractable circumstance. Welles had not come alone to Hollywood, but by the time of *Macbeth* he was struggling to mount a Mercury Theatre enterprise without the Mercury's actors to sustain it. The remarkable thing is the quantity of sheer power, melodramatic grandeur and intellectual feeling about the play that does come through. Welles has said of *Macbeth*: 'He was a detestable man until he became king, and then once he is crowned he is doomed; but once he is doomed, he becomes a great man.' That, at least, is in the film.

Macbeth was a demonstration of willpower in action: it took three weeks to make, and his next Shakespeare film, *Othello* (1952), took three years. In his book *Put Money in Thy Purse*, Welles' Iago, the late Michael MacLiammóir, chronicled the hazards and strains and derangements of a production protracted and interrupted beyond any normal endurance. Again, circumstances determined form: this was obviously not the *Othello* Welles would have made in more rational conditions, and if *Macbeth* was a rough sketch, *Othello* was a drawn-out dream. In place of the concentrated crescendo and steady pulse-beat of tragedy, the film is all improvised attack and rhetorical, visually verbose effect—not so much reading Shakespeare by flashes of lightning as watching Welles to an accompaniment of firecrackers. Brilliant devices, like the punishment cage in which Iago is left to moult like a dispossessed falcon, or the scenes of serpentine temptation between Iago and Othello, are cut off from coherence. In both Welles' first two Shakespeare films, he was exposed to all risks earlier held in check by the supporting strengths of his Mercury colleagues, forced into a perilous dependence on his own bravura. Welles was born with the power to astonish, and in some ways his film career could be read as a process of discovering how to curb that power, a journey away from effect.

Macbeth is a Wellesian role as Othello at that time was not. The hazards of ambition and the discovery of the demands and temptations of power has been one of the great Wellesian themes; but it is hard to believe in a Wellesian hero being deceived by a trick with a handkerchief. For Welles, essentially, belongs to the school of actors who do, rather than those to whom things are done, and the kind of masochism which comes so easily to Brando, and lurks not far beneath the surface with Olivier, enters much less into his make-up. When a Welles hero confronts a fatal destiny, his first reaction is likely to be enormous surprise; he does not think it could or would be so, because he knows his own capacity to rule the world around him. The cool racketeer Harry Lime in *The Third Man* (1949) is the most Wellesian creation he has ever played outside his own films (Welles, however, wrote his own dialogue): he is like a cat suddenly realizing that mice can bite, and he is made defenceless—as is Quinlan in *Touch of Evil*—by his own amazement at the ill-chosen agents of destiny. Iago, however, must be big enough to destroy Othello.

The mere execution of *Othello* has that element of heroic, obstinate resolution, irredeemably tinged by farce, which haunts so many Wellesian enterprises. Quixotic would of course be the adjective. And it is appropriate that among Welles' projects of this time should be his modern *Don Quixote*, begun during the middle 50s and still unshown. Given that Welles is not a masochist, he can hardly enjoy setting world records for the film longest in production, never quite abandoned, always defying completion. Given that *Don Quixote* is, in a sense, the story to which Welles *must* keep returning, the rich and enduring and inexhaustible source for the anarcho-aristocratic legends which fuel his own temperament, it could well seem impossible that he should ever really finish with this film. As with the tantalizing Borges story about the man who rewrites *Don Quixote*, there is too much of it in himself.

But Welles in the 50s seemed like other film-makers who had lost America without discovering Europe. The romance of *Citizen Kane* and *The Magnificent Ambersons* was partly, and powerfully, with the American past; cut off from that base, Welles seemed marooned and isolated. His problems in making any sort of film, anywhere, for anyone, were such that he was also in danger of becoming the prisoner of his own legend, treated like some baroque monument which has gone out of style, worth three stars in the guidebook, demanding a detour, but no longer essentially relevant. His mid-50s film *Mr Arkadin* in itself seemed an uncomfortably symbolic venture. The attractive plot idea, of a mysterious, omnipotent mogul who hires a seedy adventurer to enquire into his own dark past, with a view to obliterating its last dangerous traces, assembled the apparatus of the quest and the labyrinth, only to turn the parade of witnesses into a rococo charade. Mr Arkadin himself is a bloated power fantasy, master of disguise, mystery man for the sake of mystery, a creation out of display by disillusionment.

The unexpected thing, after this inflated rhetorical raree-show, is that Welles could possibly extract so much from the run-of-the-mill thriller he turned into *Touch of Evil*. *Mr Arkadin* has all the machinery; *Touch of Evil* has character, and Kane, Falstaff and Quinlan, in that order, perhaps make up the great triptych of Wellesian roles. The gross, greedy-eyed Quinlan, a huge walking hulk of corruption, is a kind of Falstaff run to seed—devious, wilful and larger not merely than life but than anyone else in the picture. Around him in this splenetic film, Welles assembled the vicious, grotesque, ornately malevolent inhabitants of the murderous little town which Quinlan rules by authority of his police badge. He shot the film, mainly by night, in the run-down Los Angeles suburb known as Venice; he packed Janet Leigh off to a mad motel to encounter a kind of foretaste of *Psycho*; he opened the film with the long, dark, justly celebrated tracking shot which follows a car towards an explosion; and ended it in darkness, as Quinlan, the vicious Cerberus of this outpost of Hades, is shot down by one of his own policemen. Out of the darkness comes Marlene Dietrich, to speak the kind of laconically

echoing epitaph Hemingway might have authorized: 'He was some kind of a man. What does it matter what you say about people?'

Touch of Evil restored Welles briefly to conditions of Hollywood professionalism, but was itself made almost by accident. Charlton Heston, who plays the upright investigator who brings about Quinlan's comeuppance, had been assigned to star, and accepted in the belief that Welles, who had in fact only been engaged as an actor, was to direct. Universal let him do so. And the fact that Welles accepted the none too promising assignment with such alacrity might be taken as an indication of his vast frustration. The film was not a commercial success; and to this day Welles has still not completed another picture in America. But it is a picture that has grown with the years, partly because the blackness and balefulness of its settings were in some ways a foretaste of an America to come; partly because it's a film that points both backwards and forwards in Welles' own career. Quinlan is not a remote fantasy megalomaniac like Arkadin. In the context of a small-town crime story swinging vertiginously towards nightmare, Welles again found a setting in which the exercise of power becomes both plausible and frightening, and in which he could look at the man described as 'a great detective but a lousy cop' from his own elaborately ironic moral viewpoint. Welles himself has taken a sterner attitude to Quinlan than some commentators on the film. 'It's a mistake to think I approve of Quinlan at all. To me he's hateful; there is no ambiguity in his character. He's more than a little ordinary cop, but that does not stop him being hateful.' The ambiguity is rather in the relation of the actor to the part, in the suggestions of flawed grandeur and intellectual power that make it impossible for Welles to play a wholly despicable character. Quinlan's awful charm is that he is right—however wrong his reasons. And, like Kane, he carries his past with him.

Welles' three films of the 60s in a sense contain the range of his post-*Citizen Kane* attitudes. All three could be said to be concerned with the workings of fate, justice and betrayal—and, as Graham Greene wrote in a very different context of Henry James, 'he could sit there ... and hear the footsteps of the traitors and their victims going endlessly by on the pavement'. *The Trial* follows *Touch of Evil* logically as an expression of Wellesian misanthropy and spleen. It ends with Joseph K., brought finally to his execution, flinging away his murderers' dynamite and with excessive symbolism setting off the all-destructive mushroom cloud. *Chimes at Midnight* is autumnal and philosophic, and at the same time the closest film in the Wellesian canon to *The Magnificent Ambersons*; and in *The Immortal Story* Welles is reverting to an even older role of story-teller— though, significantly, where Isak Dinesen's novella emphasizes the power of the story as an entity, the Wellesian version lays its stress on the withered authority of Mr Clay, the old Macao merchant who out of his disbelief in fiction decides to turn legend into fact.

The Trial is not a likeable film. It lacks Wellesian geniality, as it lacks the cool, logical apprehensions of Kafka; and stylistically it is in the most literal sense overblown, an expression of weary audacity, a film seemingly dominated by its décors. Welles shot much of it in a huge abandoned railway station in Paris, a place of cavernous spaces, a natural film studio. Joseph K. beats against doors of unnatural, dwarfing height, wanders through labyrinths (centreless, but not frightening) which loom like the last toppling strongholds of Expressionist décor. The film moves among its sets in a kind of echoing void, in which everything that happens to K. is dreamlike, but the way dreams are in the cinema rather than in life. Perhaps the termite toils of Kafka's Joseph K. are simply outside the scale of Welles' experience: the sheer shabbiness of the corridors of power, the form-stamping and the files, would never be the Wellesian way, just as Welles (who in the film plays the Advocate, and a multitude of voices) could never himself represent Kafka's querulous, clerkish victim. Like the frog in the fable, K. is looking for reason; and Welles gave him the mushroom cloud and the Expressionist ruins.

He has said that 'for me, Shakespeare is the staff of life': a comment which really comes into balance with such a film as *Chimes at Midnight*, at this particular juncture in his career. The fretfulness of *The Trial*, the grotesqueries of *Touch of Evil*, disappear; the air is clearer, and we see again what too much of his film-making career managed to lose, the essential magnanimity of Welles' creative process. In both his earlier Shakespeare films, the circumstances of production left him fighting to impose his personality on the play; in *Chimes at Midnight*, the interpretation of the story of Falstaff and Prince Hal is extremely Wellesian, but there is no imposition. The screen language is drawn out of the text, rather than laid on top of it; understanding is complete. And Welles' own Falstaff is the creation of an actor who has ripened and even softened into the part.

The whole film seems, in characteristic Wellesian style, to have been conceived backwards: everything is coloured by foreknowledge of the final crushing break between Falstaff and the young king, and by the intimations of the old man's mortality. Welles recognized that he lost the comedy of the part, because in his 'lament for Merrie England' he couldn't but see Falstaff as Shakespeare's 'great good man . . . His faults are so small and his virtues are so great, like bread, like wine'. Hal is a saturnine, calculating roisterer, Machiavelli's Prince in the making, testing himself in his games with Falstaff and gradually withdrawing towards his inheritance of the lonely crown. In the great battle scene, armoured knights are lowered by pulleys on to their chargers, to hack each other slowly to pieces in the mud. Falstaff and the tavern people stand for an older, simpler, more innocent world—a concept that can never be tested, a world that never existed, a dream of past time. The lost chimes at midnight join the Ambersons' 'great, long-remembered dances' and Falstaff, ageless as long as Hal gives him the opportunity to play at being young, dies of betrayal and is carried out in that immense, astonishing coffin.

Chimes at Midnight is founded on two great Wellesian themes: the nature and price of power, and the betrayal of possibility and friendship. Kane and his associates; George Amberson Minafer and his mother; the siren and the sailor in *The Lady from Shanghai*; Iago and Othello; Quinlan and the policeman who kills him; Hal and Falstaff; the betrayers and the betrayed move, locked together, through the films. But if this expresses their emotional force, their philosophical content has been blended with Welles' severe, almost autocratic morality. Unlike Stanley Kubrick, who has stylistically sometimes looked like Welles' closest heir, and who has achieved that total control over massive film-making resources which Welles has been denied since *Citizen Kane*, Welles has never seemed a film-maker for intellectual concepts or for ideas pushed to their limits in action. *Citizen Kane* probably covers a wider range of ideas than any other Welles picture, which could be taken as a clue to Herman Mankiewicz's contribution, and even there the vitality is in allusiveness and expression rather than in any particular depth of thought. Otherwise, Welles has never apparently felt the need for a plot or source material with a strong basis in intellectual logic. He has looked, rather, for characters who would reflect his philosophy—or perhaps more accurately he has required of his plots that they should express a philosophy rooted in character.

'Character', of course, must mean the character of Orson Welles himself—as it operates both behind and in front of the camera. At times he has deprecated the necessity to keep acting in his own films, arguing that circumstance rather than choice has forced it on him. Arguably, he is a self-conscious actor, fated or privileged to be instantly recognizable and constantly seeming to look for a kind of escape into make-up. Intellectually, he has claimed to distrust most of the characters he has played: 'I'm against the Faustian outlook, because I believe it is impossible for a man to be great unless he acknowledges something greater than himself. It can be the Law, it can be God, it can be Art, or any other idea, but it must be greater than man. I've played a whole line of egoists, and I detest egoism, the egoism of the Renaissance, the egoism of Faust, all of them ... If I had to choose, I'd always choose respect rather than egoism, responsibility rather than adventure. And that goes against my personality, which is that of the egotistical adventurer. I'm just cut out to follow in the footsteps of the Byronic adventurer, though I detest that kind of person in everything he does.' Morally, in true Byronic line, he has adopted the principle that 'I not only put forward the best possible arguments for my enemies being as they are, but I put into their mouths the best possible justifications I can find for their point of view'. It is

an attitude founded in chivalry—and in the arrogance of chivalry.

Welles has also said, with total justification, that he is among those actors who must play the king. It is not merely in physique but in temperament that he towers over any landscape he occupies—his only escape route being into conscious buffoonery, the bear allowing himself to play teddy bear. Before the cinema, he could have been one of the great actor managers, remoulding the classical repertory to his own scale; and even in the cinema, he has made his films facets of a continuing Wellesian drama. The heightened baroque style, modulating into tranquillity, proclaims the man; the area of the screen is an extension of his personality. And it is a personality which has been isolated in the cinema not merely geographically (since the early days, Welles has been effectively homeless as a film-maker) but temperamentally. His characteristic theme is that of a figure larger than the usual run of men, in the act of affronting his destiny. Themes which have preoccupied his contemporaries—alienation, the search for identity, non-communication—have simply passed him by. The king does not descend to the psychiatrist's couch or the fretful suburbs. 'I'm a man of the Middle Ages,' he has said, 'with certain implications due to the barbarity of America.' Possibly these are all other ways of saying that he is a great romantic.

Bernard Herrmann described *Citizen Kane* as 'a kind of dream autobiography' of Orson Welles. Hollywood sent him into exile, expelled him from Xanadu, played the role, one might say, of the person from Porlock. And it is perhaps because so much of his own work has been concerned with possibility and the receding dream that his film career tantalizingly suggests some great unfinished monument. It has been Welles' gift, and perhaps his curse, to be at once one of the most influential film-makers of the century, and the cinema's great anachronism.

'His film career tantalizingly suggests some great unfinished monument': yes, and there are at least two films which Welles has almost completed but which something stops him from finishing: *Don Quixote*, begun in 1959, and *The Deep*, as well as a number of aborted projects.
Since Miss Houston wrote this article,

Welles has brought out one film, variously
entitled *Fake* and *Fake?* and *F for Fake*
(1973). Although rapturously acclaimed by
some, it seemed to me very disappointing. It
was, in fact, something of a scissors and
paste job, with Welles using footage shot
by François Reichenbach of the late art
forger Elmyr de Hory to make some very
philistine points about the nature of the
work of art. I agree with Richard Corliss:
'With *Fake*, Welles is playing a cinematic
shell-game that reveals nothing but his con-
summate con artistry.' Corliss meant that
admiringly; I don't.

Welles' influence on the cinema, it should be
noted, began almost immediately; there was
no waiting period. A film like Sam Wood's
Kings Row, made only a year after *Citizen
Kane*, is much better than it ought to have
been because of the Welles influence on the
cameraman, James Wong Howe, the set
designer, William Cameron Menzies, and
even the composer, Erich Wolfgang Korn-
gold. The new Welles 'look'—depth of focus,
expressionistic angles, etc.—made a film
which, however trashy its origins, is still a
moving experience in 1978.

As befits 'one of the most influential film-
makers of the century', the Welles bibliography is large. First and foremost, I would
put André Bazin's *Orson Welles* (French
1950, English 1979) with its brilliant analysis of Welles' compositions in depth. There
are three other notable monographs on
Welles: *The Cinema of Orson Welles* (1961)
by Peter Bogdanovich, *The Films of Orson
Welles* (1970) by Charles Higham and *Orson
Welles* (1972) by Joseph McBride. See also
The Citizen Kane Book (1971) by Pauline
Kael, which includes the shooting script by
Herman Mankiewicz and Welles and the
cutting continuity of the finished film.

WILLIAM WELLMAN

Richard Combs

William Wellman's flamboyant personality
and rough and ready tactics on a set, his none
too gentle way of badgering an actor into giv-

Carole Lombard, Walter Connolly and Fredric March in a 'morning-after' scene from *Nothing Sacred*.

ing the performance he wanted, earned him the sobriquet 'Wild Bill'. Similarly, his deftness on screen with broad, colourful canvases, filled with vigorous action and peopled in the main by men (Wellman claimed to have preferred working with men because he disliked the fuss of make-up and hairdressing), sealed his election to the ranks of muscular *auteurs* like Raoul Walsh, a rung or two below Ford and Hawks. In fact, Wellman's movies might almost be divided along the same lines as Hawks': the full-blooded adventure yarns alternating with their natural opposite, the male-demeaning crazy comedies. But in Wellman's case, classification is confused by odd strains and troubling inconsistencies which have complicated his movies and diminished his standing as an individual stylist.

A deeply sardonic streak colours his work in any mode, and actually digs deeper than the emotional deadpan and casual way with violence in Hawks' films. Wellman (1896–1975) was always renowned for his violence: he persuaded Darryl Zanuck to produce *Public Enemy* (1931), a story which had been brought to Wellman by two Chicago druggists, by promising to make it more vicious than any other gangster movie; in *Yellow Sky* (1949), his way of establishing Gregory Peck as a villain to be reckoned with was to have him knock John Russell into a stream and then to kick his head, 'like a football', when he surfaced. His comedies *Roxie Hart* (1942) and *Nothing Sacred* (1937) offer blatantly opportunist heroines far more ruthless than the female sparring partners Hawks occasionally allowed to usurp the man's role; *A Star Is Born* (1937) is a satire on success in Hollywood, considerably rougher and more caustic than George Cukor's famous remake with Judy Garland; and *Night Nurse* (1931) pits Barbara Stanwyck and bootlegger Ben Lyon against villains (including Clark Gable) scheming to do away with two small children for the sake of their inheritance.

The latter film illustrates one difficulty in assessing Wellman, in that so much of his work for Warners in the 30s is virtually indistinguishable from that studio's whole cycle of journalistic exposés made in the same gritty, unvarnished style. His stylistic eclecticism elsewhere has brought him both praise and disfavour, his method ranging from multi-character, quasi-documentary paeans to the common soldier in *The Story of G. I. Joe* (1945) and *Battleground* (1949) to the bizarre coloration and allegorical intent of *Track of the Cat* (1954) and what Andrew Sarris has described as the fakery of 'painted backdrops treated like the natural vistas in a Ford Western' in *The Ox-Bow Incident* (1943; U.K.: *Strange Incident*). Wellman has been compared, on the one hand, to Griffith for the simplicity and lyricism of his treatment of a social order and its outcasts (particularly in the rural setting of films like *Beggars of Life*, 1928) and, on the other, to Stroheim for an inclination towards symbolism, edging close to expressionism in some of the effects by which he attempts to give an entirely subjective cast to the action. (In his adaptation of the Kipling story *The Light That Failed*, 1939, Wellman suggests the onset of author Dick Heldar's blindness in a scene in which full daylight turns gradually to night.)

Generally, Wellman's naturalism was at its simplest and most uncluttered in his treatment of 'public' subjects, his direct response to the humanity of his characters looking like a political statement in early films about the dispossessed during the Depression (*Beggars of Life*; *Wild Boys of the Road*, 1933) and like a kind of documentary reportage in his two films about the foot soldier in the Second World War. The public event which Wellman made most his own was the earlier conflict, 'my war, the First World War', and his sympathies were more for the combatants in the air. Wellman himself flew in the Lafayette Flying Corps, an offshoot of the Lafayette Escadrille, and his first resounding success as a silent film director was *Wings* (1927), a spectacular production for its aerial sequences and its climactic battle, tenuously held together on the ground by a tale of love and friendship, as were such later epics as a Wright brothers bio-pic, *Men with Wings* (1938). Wellman's last production, based on a story of his own, *C'est la Guerre*, about a flyer he had known, was so mishandled by Warner executives (the title was changed to *Lafayette Escadrille* [U.K.: *Hell Bent For Glory*, 1958], Tab Hunter was cast and a happy ending imposed) that the director retired out of disillusionment.

Away from the specific social arenas of

national endeavour or desperation, Wellman's style becomes more introverted, and his subjects tilted more interestingly towards allegory. With *Public Enemy*, for all its snug fit with the 'screaming headline' vogue of Warners' gangster movies, Wellman plays heavily on psychological tensions; but with his move to the timeless sphere of the Western, his interiorized style becomes more marked. *The Ox-Bow Incident*, *Yellow Sky* and *Track of the Cat* all evolve as struggles for power, with the family unit serving as metaphor for the instability and precariousness of any society. An anti-democratic slant is evident in the way *The Ox-Bow Incident* calls up fears of mob rule, and the corroding patriarchy and matriarchy of *Yellow Sky* and *Track of the Cat* respectively seem to suggest the inevitable corruption of any form of authority. The trouble with all three films is that Wellman's schematization of the conflict is too rigid to allow for much subtlety or interplay. *Track of the Cat* finally dwindles to a very thin abstraction, with its reduction of all colour to a black-and-white scheme and of the cat of the title to a wholly unseen, metaphorical threat.

The emphases of these films, with their scathing treatment of all socialized behaviour and their casting back of the individual on his own resources, also call into question the social concerns of earlier Wellman films. Describing his politics as 'kind of eccentric: I am a Republican sometimes and a Democrat at others', Wellman moved from *Wild Boys of the Road* to the strange political fable of *The President Vanishes* (1934), which concerns a Fascist-cum-Big-Business plot to overthrow the U.S. government and which was variously interpreted at the time as both a left-wing and a right-wing film; and eventually to the Red-baiting films (*The Iron Curtain*, 1948; *Blood Alley*, 1955) of the postwar years. His pragmatic, fundamentalist approach to both individuals and social issues recalls Ford without the veil of myth and nostalgic poetry. *Wild Boys of the Road* in some ways anticipates *The Grapes of Wrath*, and even Wellman, in the largely stodgy epic *Buffalo Bill* (1944), waxes wistful about the passing of the old West in a way which clearly mirrors Ford.

Far from being the 'recessive director' claimed by Sarris, 'one whose images tend to recede from the foreground to the background in the absence of a strong point of view', Wellman's failing seems to have been that of a director whose point of view (at least in his sound films) too often pushed forward at the expense of his images. In the restless shifts of his style and talent, he intersected (and occasionally trumped) some of the more honoured and solidly consistent of Hollywood directors, without ever establishing a medium of his own that was substantial enough to carry the several, and contradictory, messages of his lifetime.

It is difficult to disagree with Combs' assessment of Wellman's career: *The Ox-Bow Incident* indeed looks phoney today. However, his less pretentious works—*Nothing Sacred* and *A Star Is Born*—do stand up remarkably well. For further reading on Wellman, see his autobiography *A Short Time for Insanity* (1974), the interview with him in Richard Schickel's *The Men Who Made the Movies* (1975) and the chapter on him in Kevin Brownlow's *The Parade's Gone By* (1968).

WIM WENDERS

Jan Dawson

Of the talents to emerge under the collective rubric of the New German Cinema, the hardest to define has been that of Wim Wenders. Only in 1976, with his *Im Lauf der Zeit* (U.K.: *Kings of the Road*) winning him the International Critics' Prize at Cannes and breaking house records for a German film in Germany, did Wenders appear as anything more than an isolated and rather peripheral figure in the national cultural landscape.

It is easy to understand why Wenders' name has not been a household word outside the festival circuit. His films lack the flamboyance of Fassbinder's, the metaphysical ambition of Herzog's, the intellectual intensity of Kluge's: more significantly, they are also totally lacking in aggression. Their pacing and perspective, their vision of an incongruous universe in which the human characters are seldom the most interesting item on the screen, their emphasis on the language of gesture rather than on dialogue—all of these leave Wenders closer to Ozu than to

Rüdiger Vogler and Hanns Zischler in *Kings of the Road*.

the conventions of Hollywood narrative.

The films are frequently about absence (of women, of certainty, of history), and it's easy to understand the popular misconception that the films themselves are negative experiences. This is about 180 degrees from the truth. They're concerned with growth, with change; with the quest for human contacts. These processes involve a lot of journeys through a lot of cities, a lot of wrong movements and a lot of rock'n'roll. All the lonely people, finding out where they belong. Yet the conspicuous isolation of the introspective characters also masks the fact that the films are profoundly political: the fundamental questions of ideology and social values are presented, not in any conventional way, but —like the landscapes, characters and urban environment—materially, phenomenologically. Like his film and music criticism, his films reflect a purely descriptive approach. The paradox is that in the revelation of objects, landscapes and relationships with-

out any intrusive directorial presence, one recognizes Wenders' personal vision: the outward signs of a society in quest of both its roots and its future, of the point where object and subject might happily coalesce.

Born in 1945, Wenders himself was deflected from his ambition of becoming a priest by the twin revelations in his late teens of rock'n'roll music ('the first thing I appreciated that wasn't inherited') and of an illicit pinball-machine in the small Ruhr district town where he grew up. (Juke boxes and pinballs still provide his heroes with a large part of their physical and emotional contact.) His lapse from Catholicism was less a loss of faith than a gradual growing away from oppressive, dogmatic structures which he increasingly equated with both capitalism and fascism. Yet despite his mistrust of his country's past, and despite the imported emblems of his own rejection of it, he found something profoundly disturbing in the ease with which his countrymen repressed their own recent history and embraced the culture of their American occupiers. ('The need to forget twenty years created a hole, and we covered it with chewing gum. And Polaroid pictures.') Wenders saw this acceptance of American imperialism as essentially regressive. And his eccentric characters become representative of their generation by being, most noticeably in their emotional numbness, more regressive than most. As his films and his confidence evolve, they become increasingly people who are trying to find a way out of this impasse; to the point where Robert in *Kings of the Road* can formulate the problem: 'The Yanks have colonized our subconscious.'

His characters' growing optimism about the possibility of change closely mirrors Wenders' own. His first short films, made as a student at the Munich Film School, combined a descriptive approach with a terror of cutting, or of asserting a point of view. *Schauplätze* (1967) translates as 'Locations' and consisted of just that; *Same Player Shoots Again*, made the same year and named after the instructions on a pinball-machine, consisted of a single shot of a running man repeated five times (once for each ball!). Like *Silver City* (1968), a series of early-morning and late-night views from upper-storey windows, it was edited to repeated fragments of an old 78 record called 'Mood Music'. In *Alabama—2000 Light Years* (1969), Wenders' first film on 35 mm and his first collaboration with Robbie Müller, his cameraman ever since, the presence of a central character hardly added a psychological dimension. To a lesser extent, this was also true of Wenders' first full-length film, in which Hanns Zischler played a man newly released from prison who travelled from one wintry city to the next in an abortive attempt to achieve contact with his former friends. Here again, locomotion and music were shown as the only possible sources of emotional contact. The title was significant: *Summer in the City: Dedicated to the Kinks* (1970).

It was only in 1971, with *Die Angst des Tormanns beim Elfmeter* (U.K.: *The Goalkeeper's Fear of the Penalty*; U.S.: *The Goalie's Anxiety at the Penalty Kick*), based on the novel by Peter Handke, that a human character provided the centre of interest, albeit one unable to find in other people's lives a mean-

ingful connection with his environment. He was, however, the first of Wenders' characters to find his way to those deserted border towns which, literally observed, acquire a metaphysical resonance in *Alice in den Städten* (*Alice in the Cities*, 1974), where a journalist who has lost faith in words reluctantly accompanies a nine-year-old child on a search for her grandmother. The journalist was played by Rüdiger Vogler, with whom Wenders has now completed a trio of road movies: *Falsche Bewegung* (*Wrong Movement*, 1975), freely adapted by Peter Handke from Goethe's *Wilhelm Meisters Lehrjahre*; and *Kings of the Road*, in which Vogler plays an itinerant projector mechanic who lives in a pantechnicon well wired for sound.

In early 1977, Wenders completed (from his own screenplay) *Der Amerikanische Freund* (*The American Friend*), a film based loosely on Patricia Highsmith's novel *Ripley's Game*. An international co-production, it sounds as regressive a departure from his obsessive exploration of occupied Germany as his earlier film, made in Spain, of Hawthorne's *Scarlet Letter* (*Der Scharlachrote Buchstabe*, 1972). Perhaps *The American Friend*'s multi-national cast will help continue his achievement in using dialogue as form rather than content. And it may also be a sign of his own decolonization that he has changed the middle of the story. And the end. And the beginning.

Perhaps because of its 'thriller' construction, unorthodox as *The American Friend* may have been in other respects, it has turned out to be Wenders' greatest success—his 'break-through' film, at least in the United States and in France. Indeed, I think it may be his best film to date.

See also the articles on German Cinema since 1960, Herzog and Fassbinder.

MAE WEST

Carlos Clarens

With only eleven films to her credit, Mae West (born 1892) fully deserves an entry alongside Garbo as one of the most distinctive female icons of the 30s, as well as an *auteur* of unique stature. Unlike that more prolific superstar, West never required the services of a Stiller to discover and develop her screen self; it sprang fully-fledged from her own marcelled head and was honed down to the last insinuating inflection by years in vaudeville and the legitimate theatre. West wrote her own roles, supervised the *mise en scène* and regarded her leading men as straight men to her highly imitable innuendoes. In a period of art-deco heroines, vamps and molls, her hourglass robustness appeared as a healthy anachronism; whereas Garbo, in her romantic heyday, always seemed at the ready to sacrifice all for a man, West gave the impression of having shared a season or two in prison, or in a brothel, with her fellow performers, and regarded that as the best time of her life. Her homespun acceptance of a sexual and social reality usually skirted in American films outraged (in quick succession) Mary Pickford, Will H. Hays and the radio listeners of Middle America as the decade lapsed into repressive conformity. Forced to tone down her image as well as to purge her dialogue, West retreated to the safer (because harder to detect) subversions of Western parody in *My Little Chickadee* (1940), for all critical purposes the end of her career. It mattered little whether a Mae West vehicle was directed by a first-rate filmmaker such as Leo McCarey (*Belle of the Nineties*, 1934) or Raoul Walsh (*Klondike Annie*, 1936), by an honourable craftsman like Lowell Sherman (*She Done Him Wrong*, 1933) or Henry Hathaway (*Go West Young Man*, 1936), or by a nonentity such as A. Edward Sutherland (*Every Day's a Holiday*, 1937) or Gregory Ratoff (*The Heat's On* [U.K.: *Tropicana*], 1943). And it's useless to bemoan the fact that she was never directed by Hollywood's foremost directors of women, such as George Cukor or Gregory La Cava; these artists would have undoubtedly gilded a lily that was already made of the most genuine tinsel.

For the record, Miss West appeared in *Myra Breckenridge* in 1970, and then, at the age of eighty-five, she made the embarrassing *Sextette* (1977, director Ken Hughes). Too old is too old. *Goodness Had Nothing to Do with It* is the title of Mae West's autobiography (1956). There are also three other books that can be consulted: *The Wit and Wisdom of Mae West*, edited by Joseph

Weintraub (1967), *Mae West on Sex, Health and ESP* (1975) and *The Films of Mae West* (1976) by J. Tuska.

ROLAND WEST

Elliott Stein

Who thinks about Roland West these days? I do. He was one of America's supremely original visual stylists, the director of a series of stunning thrillers. The end of his career is shrouded in mystery—let's at least unshroud his reputation.

He was born in 1887; his first film was *Lost Souls* (1916), followed by *Deluxe Annie* (1918). *The Unknown Purple* (1924), with Henry B. Walthall (adapted from a play by West), is about a convict who invents a purple light which makes bodies invisible (thus pre-dating James Whale's *The Invisible Man* by a decade). *The Monster* (1925) stars Lon Chaney as Dr Ziska, a mad surgeon. Then came *The Bat* (1926) and in 1929, *Alibi* (U.K.: *The Perfect Alibi*). Though it is one of the most oppressive films ever made, *Alibi* was a success with critics and public. This may have had less to do with its very real merits than with the novelty of hearing guns fire. The *New York Times* review was headlined 'An Audible Thriller', and critic Mordaunt Hall was most impressed by the fact that West had 'even used whispers'. He found it 'by far the best of the gangster films'. Much of its brilliance can be traced to the close collaboration of West and his designer of genius, William Cameron Menzies, who had already served as art director on *The Bat*. The distorted sets, odd angles and restless camera make it West's most Germanic work. This claustrophobic little nightmare would be fully at home in a retrospective of the American avant-garde film.

After *Alibi* came *The Bat Whispers* (1930), a sound remake of *The Bat*, and it was a pictorial knock-out. The film was shot in 70 mm, and one should try to imagine what its restless, freakish stylization looked like in huge dimensions. There was only one more film to come, *Corsair* in 1931; after this visual treat, the rest was silence, and a breath of scandal. Thelma Todd, a good friend of West's, was found asphyxiated in her garage in 1935. No proof was ever adduced that

West had anything to do with her demise, but the affair apparently did not aid his career. He made no more films, married Lola Lane, and died twenty-one years after his last film, in 1952.

'The misty expressionism and delicate feelings of *Corsair* entitle the director to a place in film history,' wrote Andrew Sarris in *The American Cinema* (1968). '*Alibi* remains to be seen and saved from the limbo of legend.' Well, now it has been seen and it *is* good.

JAMES WHALE

John Russell Taylor

James Whale (1889–1957) is really not like anyone else in the cinema. One often says that, and then launches into some fairly close comparison. But Whale's background and career were so eccentric in relation to the kind of films he was making and where he was making them that it is difficult to find anyone comparable—least of all Tod Browning, with whom he is often arbitrarily bracketed because Whale made *Frankenstein* (1931) and Browning made *Dracula* for the

same studio in the same year. Whale at this time was a relative newcomer to Hollywood and for that matter to the cinema, having previously worked in his native Britain very successfully as a man of the theatre—actor, designer and ultimately director. It was his most famous and successful stage production, in 1928, of R. C. Sherriff's war play *Journey's End* which had brought him to America, first to stage the play in New York, then to Hollywood to film it. This first film appears to have been made in sequence: one can palpably sense the director working himself away from the heavily theatrical, overemphatic style of the early scenes towards the ease and fluency of the later ones, where the stage play, though transposed almost intact, gradually takes on a powerful cinematic life of its own.

But *Journey's End* (1930) gives little sense of one of Whale's most important attributes—his quirky gothic sense of humour. Little of that is visible, either, in his scenes of *Hell's Angels* (1930)—dialogue scenes in which one can at least appreciate his taste for strongly modelled effects of lighting and his skill at getting relaxed performances out of

Elsa Lanchester and Colin Clive in *The Bride of Frankenstein*.

his actors. With *Frankenstein* all is changed. The last vestiges of staginess have gone, and instead the film is put together with considerable flair and narrative sweep. The screenplay wisely dumps the philosophical formulations of Mary Shelley, and concentrates instead on action drama covering the fairly short period of time up to and after the creation of the Monster. But what is most extraordinary about the film is its tone. No *Angst* here, no Germanic *Stimmung*; instead considerable bravura play with the machinery of monster-making and a strong element of gallows humour in the depiction of the gothic trappings. Much of the film is coolly ironic: there is, for instance, the classic scene in which the Monster, wandering vaguely through the countryside, meets a little girl who is totally unafraid of him. They play by the edge of the water, and finally she throws her flowers into the lake and he, in all innocence, picks her up and throws her in after them. The whole sequence works with immaculate logic, like some sort of metaphysical conceit, and is horrific only at one remove, when one fully realizes what has happened, rather than by creating an atmosphere of horror to set our nerves a-jangle.

In essence, James Whale was an intellectual director, one who worked through his audience's intelligences, manipulating them with sophistication and wit in a way that few in Hollywood did at that time, and none working outside the specifically comic forms. In this he was a very European director, and perhaps one might say a very English director: the charm and cultivation and quirkiness are very apparently in an English tradition, the tradition of Jane Austen or, looked at another way, of Ronald Firbank. The Firbankian extravagance comes out even more in his next film, *The Old Dark House* (1932), a free version of J. B. Priestley's novel *Benighted*, which lands a motley group of travellers in a house where, as the old grandfather eventually remarks, 'Everyone's mad here except me—and sometimes I'm not so sure.' Pyromaniacs run loose and shocks are lurking round every corner, but the result, with its stunning expressionistic lighting and *outré* compositions, cannot really be taken, nor surely was it meant to be, as a horror film or even a thriller. It seems instead to be a joke that the director shares with a chosen few in

his audience, creating that feeling of complicity in shared experience which foreigners often find the most maddening thing about the snobbish, stand-offish English.

It would be difficult to say categorically whether *The Old Dark House* or *Bride of Frankenstein* (1935) is Whale's masterpiece. *Bride of Frankenstein* moves the tone of the Frankenstein cycle even further into bizarre comedy, played with perfect gravity by a crew of Whale's favourite actors—Colin Clive from *Journey's End* and *Frankenstein*, Boris Karloff from *Frankenstein* and *The Old Dark House*, Ernest Thesiger from *The Old Dark House*, and Elsa Lanchester as the Bride. (All English, it will be noticed, like most of the players in Whale's best films— clearly he felt most at home with actors of British stage background.) There are moments of wonderful oddity like the play of Ernest Thesiger, a quite incidental character, with his miniaturized humans; and the idea of doubling the roles of Mary Shelley in the prologue and the Bride herself is one of particular whimsical perversity. It is all very peculiar, and very personal. Between *The Old Dark House* and *Bride of Frankenstein*, incidentally, Whale had made his other major contribution to this weird horror-comedy genre of his own creation with *The Invisible Man* (1933), a subject where the possibilities for poker-faced comedy are very evident.

After *Bride of Frankenstein* Whale never went back to this form, nor perhaps did he want to. His version of *Showboat* in 1936, for years unseeable, proves on re-examination to be masterly, with some definitive performances (Helen Morgan, Paul Robeson) and an exquisite evocation of the period and the landscape, for the first time in Whale's work unmistakably American. It was probably his peak of commercial success and standing in Hollywood; indeed, his sudden demotion to much smaller-scale films, some of them scarcely more than B-features, is a mystery which some have attempted to solve with rumours of homosexual scandal. Be that as it may, *The Great Garrick* (1937) brought him back to the English theatre scene he knew so well and *Port of Seven Seas* (1938), an American remake of Pagnol's *Fanny*, has lasting charm. In 1941 he retired from film-making, to concentrate on painting, it was said, though he did do some minor theatre work in California and later in England.

In 1949 he was commissioned to make a forty-minute episode based on William Saroyan's drama about a lynching, *Hello Out There*, for a film produced by Huntington Hartford as a vehicle for his then wife Marjorie Steele. The film, which at times harks back visually to the chiaroscuro style of *Frankenstein*, was well received by preview audiences but apparently did not meet the producer's hopes for his star and was never released.

James Whale died in 1957, remembered, if at all, as the creator of *Frankenstein* and *Bride of Frankenstein*. But that, after all, is enough. Genuine originality in the cinema is such a rare thing that it deserves commemoration wherever it is found.

As one of the lucky few who has actually seen *Hello Out There*, I can testify that it wasn't bad at all. Two other films by Whale deserve mention: *Kiss Before the Mirror* (1933) and *One More River* (1934). Little has been written about Whale; see Carlos Clarens' *Horror Movies*. See also Stein's article on Tod Browning, even though, as Taylor says, Whale can't be compared with anyone.

Whale's long-lost version of *Waterloo Bridge* (1931) was finally rediscovered and shown at the Museum of Modern Art in 1977; alas, it turned out to be a bitter disappointment, with only a few redeeming touches.

BO WIDERBERG AND SWEDISH CINEMA SINCE 1960

Edgardo Cozarinsky

Any survey of Swedish film since 1960 is bound to acknowledge the influence of the Swedish Film Institute, Svenska Filminstitutet. Created in 1962, directed until 1969 by Harry Schein, it had a policy of production encouragement and quality awards that was responsible for the emergence, in 1963, of the first films by Sjöman, Widerberg and Donner. Between 1959 and 1962, with Bergman definitively established in the international limelight, the home product had reached its lowest point, as art or industry. The Institute is a typically Swedish institution, dependent on an enlightened Welfare State and a moderately affluent economy; if it did not bring about the most interesting European cinema of the decade, it is not only because talent cannot be produced out of the blue; the same conditions that make possible such an institution account for other features of the national climate—lack of conflict, a purely intellectual eagerness to take part in conflicts not directly experienced, a certain ingrained philistinism that shies away from the imaginative grasp of reality and favours 'responsible' social comment and 'progressive' politics. Acceptance breeds neutralization, in film-making as in most aspects of Swedish life.

Bo Widerberg's first feature, *Barnvagnen* (*The Pram* or *The Baby Carriage*, 1963), seemed to react against everything he had denounced as a critic in Swedish films—lack of feeling for the tone of daily experience, characters existing in a social vacuum. The story (an unwed mother chooses independence instead of either of her immature lovers) has been a recurring anecdote in Swedish films, but Widerberg, obviously influenced by Truffaut and early Godard, played it on off-guard gestures, silences, deliberately emptying his narrative of action, feeding it with minute observations of behaviour and poetic *trouvailles*. The same approach was used in *Kvarteret Korpen* (*Raven's End*, 1964), his next film, to depict proletarian life in Malmö around 1936. The period is suggested by cursory notations (men's caps, radio sets); the style of lighting is unmistakably post-Coutard, the resulting effect one of striking immediacy. Politics play an important part, but as in his later films Widerberg's approach is lyrical: the 1936 elections and a first love affair share the same irretrievable qualities of youth remembered. (Though Widerberg was only six at the time, milieu and characters are very autobiographical.)

Widerberg (born 1930) has declared that he would rather force the staging of any scene in order to use the natural sources of light; and in all his films there are awkward moments when people stay close to windows for just that reason. But the films at their best *are* about light as much as about their stories, the splendour of the captured moment being for Widerberg truer than any dramatic elaboration. Accordingly, his habit of freezing the last frame of his films is less a homage to

Thommy Berggren in *Raven's End*, Widerberg's second film and a depiction of proletarian life in Malmö around 1936.

Truffaut than a warning that any interruption in the flow of life is contrived. *Kärlek 65* (*Love '65*, 1965), is a personal variation on the theme of Fellini's *8½*, less derivative than self-indulgent. A few moments of revelation and some extraordinary images are small rewards for long stretches of fumbling and tentative finds. After a very minor comedy, *Heja Roland!* (*Thirty Times Your Money*, 1966), Widerberg achieved his first wide international success with *Elvira Madigan* (1967). This tragic story of the affair between a tightrope dancer and a high-born officer is based on a news item of the 1880s which had been the basis for songs and even a previous film. Though the lovers are there as early instances of drop-outs, and several contemporary readings effortlessly emerge, Widerberg's real concern is with the sensuous presence of cream and berry juice on lips and fingertips, with showing Elvira and

her Count chasing butterflies in slow motion to Mozart's music: this affirmation of beauty in the face of death carries, for him, the weight of a modest but combative ideological point.

Widerberg returned to working-class life and the 1930s in *Ådalen 31* (1969), a re-creation of events around the last strike in Swedish history in which workers were killed. The film belongs after May '68 as much as *Elvira* breathed the hippie mid-60s: the hungry, stubborn workers spend the summer days intoxicated with pride at their own resistance, dancing, playing games, making love. The film is Widerberg's most compact and best organized, though always faithful to his approach—the camera lingers on the beauty of a white sheet over a dead body, slowly invaded by a blood stain. *Joe Hill* (U.K.: *The Ballad of Joe Hill*, 1970) is less tightly assembled, but this chronicle about the Swedish immigrant who became an American union leader, who learnt to sing his agitation speeches and whose ashes were sent by mail to anarchists all over the world, is worthy of its dedication to the Massachusetts mill-girl strikers of 1912 who asked for 'bread and roses too'. Such a romantic, even sentimental approach to proletarian history may be out of fashion, but Widerberg's genuine talent is for pastoral. In his films socialism is the Golden Age to be reconquered, the doomed period of freedom allowed to his characters is a token of the possibility of paradise on earth.

Vilgot Sjöman (born 1924) was well known as a novelist and essayist when he came to film-making. His old friendship with Ingmar Bergman, and the fact that he followed (and wrote a book-length report on) the shooting of the master's *Winter Light*, may have suggested more influences than there really are in the suffocating *Kammerspiel* of his early films—stories about women like *Älskarinnan* (*The Mistress*, 1962) and *Klänningen* (*The Dress*, 1964), or *491* (1964), a Christian allegory on a good Samaritan who would not believe in evil. An opening of sorts came with *Syskonbädd 1782* (*My Sister My Love*, 1965), a free version of Ford's *'Tis Pity She's a Whore* transposed to the enlightened Sweden of Gustav III, where the incest becomes a defiance of divine order, and the final birth of a normal child stands for man's victory. But Sjöman's real break-through were the two films *Jag är nyfiken gul* (*I am Curious Yellow*, 1967) and *Jag är nyfiken blå* (*I Am Curious Blue*, 1968), yellow and blue being the two colours of the Swedish flag. They are a documentary on the political climate of Sweden in the mid-60s: the activist youth, the passive majority, statesmen, unionists, Yevtushenko and Martin Luther King all having their say; a fictional exposé of hardships in the practice of sexual freedom, from jealousy to scabies; and a film that shapes itself as it goes along, showing director, cast and crew occasionally stranded, dramatizing their relationship from rehearsals to editing, and becoming two films in order to include new points of view on the same action and issues. Consequently, they display Sjöman's independence from the closed, Bergman-inspired dramaturgy of his earlier films.

Any description of the *I Am Curious* films is bound to be more exciting than the films themselves. Though they raise all the theoretical problems and do most of the work on film language and rhetorics that the 'new cinema' of the period was busy with, they suffer from an insidious, pervading lifelessness. Sjöman's humour is mostly self-defensive; his cross-examination of his own assumptions strives after paradox but is basically of a kind with the heroine's ineffectual harassment of tanned, well-fed Swedish tourists coming back from Spain. Even the unprecedented sexual scenes, which contributed to the final collapse of censorship in the United States and assured the film a *succès de scandale*, are weakened by their own calculation—she may breathe on his pubic hair, but not a single erection is to be seen in the moments of supposedly hectic intercourse. (It must be noted that Sjöman believed firmly in shock tactics at the time— he had already included a girl raped by a large dog in *491* and a sudden menstruation in *The Dress*.)

Sjöman went from notoriety to obscurity. His next film, *Ni Ljuger* (*You're Lying*, 1970), a report on prison life, has been little seen, even in Sweden. *Lyckliga Skitar* (*Blushing Charlie*, 1970), a romantic comedy with political overtones, though less funny than intended, has considerable charm. Sjöman started late and may well develop late. His situation, so far, is unique in that it embodies a typically Swedish capacity for keeping up with the times but, as it were, from a short but paralysing distance.

Between 1962 and 1966, Jörn Donner (born in Finland in 1933) made one short film and four features in Sweden, but he never ceased to be an outsider. Both his documentary on jazz singer Monica Zetterlund, *Vittnesbörd om henne* (*Testimonies of Her*, 1963) and his first feature, *En söndag i september* (*A Sunday in September*, 1963), are formal experiments—the material is made eloquent by the defiantly non-narrative method of dealing with both fact and fiction. *Enfant terrible* of literature, politics and film criticism in his native Finland, Donner had a knack for being unpleasant to Sweden, and Sweden promptly reciprocated. His erotic comedy *Att älska* (*To Love*, 1964) is the most accessible of his films; *Här börjar äventyret* (*Adventure Starts Here*, 1965) perhaps the most daring—full of autobiographical motifs, this story of a Swedish businesswoman and a Finnish architect who hesitate to fall in love again, is a baffling essay on language barriers, on Finno-Swedish love–hate, on Hollywood glossy melodramas as models for personal relationships, and is also a homage to Douglas Sirk. It was abhorred or ignored. Donner struck back with *Tvärbalk* (*Rooftree*, 1967), his first film on alien material, a Sivar Arnér novel about a Hungarian Jewish war orphan who grows up a stranger amid smug Swedish affluence. In all these features, Donner worked with, and upon, Harriet Andersson, whether in naturalistic terms (*To Love*) or as a facsimile of a Hollywood star (*Adventure Starts Here*). After *Tvärbalk*, which he edited himself, he continued his career in Finland with some frankly commercial films, in most of which he acted as well. Though dismissed by Swedish critics, these films have shown an increasing flexibility of language, a perverse sense of humour and a capacity for social comedy most unusual in Scandinavia. In retrospect, his early work may be among the few Swedish films where the intelligence of the film-maker can be felt at work, as opposed to the numb intellectuality of a Vilgot Sjöman.

Passion, or any intensity of feeling, is so seldom projected by Scandinavian films that Mai Zetterling's first two features commanded attention to the sincere, if decorative, fury that animates them. Both *Älskande par* (*Loving Couples*, 1964; after episodes from one of Agnes von Krusenstjerna's *romans fleuves*) and *Nattlek* (*Night Games*, 1966; from Zetterling's own novel) are rather naïve in their relish for supposedly aristocratic depravity. But they are also unexpectedly professional in their handling of large casts and complex set-ups. Zetterling's best film is *Flickorna* (*The Girls*, 1968). Her outraged feminism sheds here the interior decoration and erotic oddities of her first films, achieving something close to a *conte philosophique*. Three actresses tour Sweden with a production of *Lysistrata* and are forced to come to terms with the meaning of Aristophanes' play in a Welfare State, and with their own attitudes to love, war and the theatre. These episodes are designed as didactic examples and, as such, have real bite.

Jan Troell (born 1931) has been hailed as a film-maker of classical stature, an heir to Sjöström. After his prize-winning short *Uppehåll i Myrlandet* (*Stopover in the Marshland*, 1965), he was launched by Svensk Filmindustri as the company's white hope with the 165-minute *Här har du ditt liv* (*Here Is Your Life*, 1966), based on Vilhelm Moberg's autobiography. Childhood in pre-1914 rural Sweden, amiable or frightening minor characters, the discovery of sex, work, death, the cinema, the growth of socialism, the literary vocation: the material of a *Bildungsroman* sprawls confidently, treated as a series of lyrical episodes, often brilliant but as a whole flabby. Troell does not try to cope with the tradition of social realism, to which this material belongs, or even to develop it in a new key. He is also his own director of photography, which accounts for a fastidiousness about visual textures, as elaborate in the 35-mm black and white of his first film as in the blown-up 16-mm black and white of the subsequent *Ole Dole Doff* (*Who Saw Him Die*, 1968), partly improvised in a Malmö school. Based on Troell's own experiences as a teacher, it is by far his most original work—a study of the relationship between a teacher's failure to banish authority in dealing with his pupils, and his tense, childless married life. It is badly served, however, by Per Oscarsson's histrionics in the leading role and by the nightmarish tone of the final part, which, unimpressive on its own, blurs many of the film's earlier insights.

Troell's most ambitious enterprise has been the two films *Utvandrarna* (*The Emigrants*, 1970) and *Nybyggarna* (*Unto a Good Land* or *The New Land*, 1970), based on Moberg's novels about Swedish emigrants to the United States. Three years in production, each over three hours long, the most expensive Swedish films ever made (and, fortunately for SF, the most successful, at least in Scandinavia), they continue the best traits as well as the limits of his first feature—overextended and diffuse, only occasionally intense, too pretty and too morose about their own prettiness. In a country where prepackaged radical politics set the tone, a conservative talent that dares speak its name may be welcome. But Troell invokes the ingredients of epic greatness without always showing the strength and tautness necessary to bring them off.

Kjell Grede's first film, *Hugo och Josefin* (*Hugo and Josefin*, 1967), was a deceptive children's film—a pre-pubescent summertime idyll, funny, moving, quietly mysterious. His next films (*Harry Munter* [*Gay Harry*, 1969]; *Klara Lust*, 1972) make clear that he aims at poetry, and that he has a personal way of dealing with recognizable Swedish properties—the brooding feeling for nature and its transient beauty, the lonely, frustrated figures from the 40s and 50s: all is there, but related in a new pattern. Facts and surfaces of social experience (American businessmen, international airports, low-rent apartments) do not really contrast with the fantasy life of the characters, but rather colour and are coloured by it. At his best, Grede (born 1936) can convey an enduring dream-like quality (a boy walking on stilts across a foggy lake) or a tender whimsicality (the family round a tub, bathing the grandmother in the garden); in the long run, though, the poetry achieved may be too quaint, too deliberate.

The most promising debut of the 60s was Jonas Cornell's *Puss och kram* (*Hugs and Kisses*, 1967), a comedy of social relationships with Pinter-ish overtones in its play with the reversal of allegiances and dependencies: dry, witty and with flashes of a very idiosyncratic fantasy. However, Cornell's subsequent *Som natt och dag* (*Like Night and Day*, 1969), which tried an equally formalized and sophisticated handling of drama, proved less successful; and his attempt at downright satire in *Grisjakten* (*The Pig Hunt*, 1970) was disappointing. Cornell's contribution was apparent in the script of *Jag älskar, du älskar* (*I Love, You Love*, 1968), the charming, tenuous first film by the critic Stig Björkman. On a much less intellectual level, the films of Hans Alfredson and Tage Danielsson (of the revue company AB Svenska Ord) are often pointed, as well as very funny, comments on the Swedish social scene (*Svenska bilder* [*Swedish Portraits*], 1964)— and they also achieve a successful transplant from American zany comedy (*Att angöra*

en brygga [*To Go Ashore*], 1965). Johan Bergenstråhle's first two films have tried to hit where it hurts—*Made in Sweden* (1969) deals with 'neutral' Swedish capital and its interference in the Third World, *Baltutlämningen* (*A Baltic Tragedy*, 1970) with the fate of those refugees from the Baltic countries whom Sweden returned to Russia in 1946. But both films also seem exhausted in the mere choice of subject-matter, their unpleasant truths coated in fashionable effects.

The prestige policy of the Swedish Film Institute made possible co-productions in which Swedish participation was only financial (Bresson's *Au hasard, Balthasar*) or with minimal Swedish elements, as was the case with films by Godard and Varda. At the same time, Sandrews invited Peter Watkins to shoot *Gladiatorerna* (*The Gladiators* or *The Peace Game*, 1969) in Sweden; and Susan Sontag made *Duett för kannibaler* (*Duet for Cannibals*, 1969) and *Broder Carl* (*Brother Carl*, 1971) there. This lively, adventurous climate was not all-pervading. The success of *I Am Curious* produced a series of shoddy and humourless exploitation products, as well as solemn 'sexual enlightenment' films. Some new directors appeared and vanished, others stayed—in a comparatively modish key, Jan Halldoff seems to aspire to Arne Mattsson's still unquestioned record for versatility. Perhaps the most interesting Swedish first film of recent times has been Lasse Forsberg's *Misshandlingen* (*Mistreatment* or *The Assault*, 1970). It confronts two forms of violence— the radical's exasperation at his inability to change society, and this same society's delimitation of reason and madness for its own protection. Shot as a straightforward account, the film is refreshing in its unromantic approach: the rebel is not a noble savage, the 'anti-psychiatry' stand does not imply a coven of Caligaris in the mental ward. The film shows, with precision and economy, that a social system conditions both those inside and those outside.

In 1977 Troell made Bang and Kjell Grede En Dares Försvarstal (Confessions of a Fool). One director Cozarinsky doesn't mention is Lars Magnus Lindgren, whose touching Käre John (Dear John, 1964) seems to have been something of a one-shot.

Widerberg has since made two features: *Fimpen (Stubby,* 1974) and *Mannen på Taket (The Man on the Roof,* 1976). I found both extremely disappointing, the first being an improbable one-liner about a boy of six who plays on the national Swedish soccer team and the second an adaptation of a well-known thriller that was anything but thrilling in film form. Jörn Donner went back to Finland, where he made *Mustaa Valkoisella (Black on White,* 1968), *69* (1969), *Anna* (1970), *Naisenkuvia (Portraits of Women,* 1970), *Perkele! Kuvia Suomesta (Piss Off! Images from Finland,* 1971) and *Hellyys* (also known as *Ömhet; Tenderness,* 1972). He has also made a Swedish version of *Hellyys* entitled *Baksmälla (Hangover,* 1973) and a documentary on Ingmar Bergman entitled *Tre Scener med Ingmar Bergman/ Ingmar Bergman in Maailma (Three Scenes with Ingmar Bergman,* 1976).

By and large, the Swedish renaissance of the 60s has ground to a halt; there are those who paradoxically claim that it is precisely the facilities offered by the creation of the Swedish Film Institute which are responsible for the birth *and* the death of the movement. It is difficult to say whether this is true, but the fact remains that the 70s have seen a progressive decline in that new Swedish cinema which began so well in the 60s. For further information, see *Film in Sweden: The New Directors* (1976) by Stig Björkman, and Peter Cowie's *Screen Series: Sweden I and II* (1970); and, in French, Jean Béranger's *Le Nouveau Cinéma Suédois 1958–68* (1968).

BILLY WILDER

Gavin Millar

It is a significant irony that, although Billy Wilder professes himself as nowhere more at home than in Hollywood, his way of life is reportedly far from typically Hollywood style, while, in *Sunset Boulevard* (1950) he has been responsible for making the shrewdest and coolest critique of it on film. Satirists too are without honour in any country they satirize, and Wilder has only been saved from recurrent damnation by the financial success of his films. The successes have been due in no small measure to his collaboration over many years with two scriptwriters: until 1950, Charles Brackett; subsequently, I. A. L. Diamond. But Wilder himself began as a scriptwriter. Born in Vienna in 1906, he was drawn to the attractively Bohemian Berlin of the 20s and there tried hard to break into the cinema by writing scripts. His first notable script credit was *Menschen am Sonntag* (1929), a film which also involved the talents of Robert Siodmak, Eugen Schüfftan, Edgar Ulmer and Fred Zinnemann. In 1933 Wilder prudently moved to Paris on the accession of Hitler and in the same year co-directed a feature, *Mauvaise Graine* (1933), with Alexander Esway, from his own story and screenplay. This effort recommended him to Hollywood, where he spent a number of lean years before beginning the collaboration at Paramount with Charles Brackett which in 1939 produced the script of *Ninotchka* for Lubitsch. In 1942 Wilder made his first feature film as director, *The Major and the Minor.* He has worked subsequently for several studios, and although he has never left Hollywood as his base, since 1959 he has had full, independent control of all his pictures.

It is reported that while in East Berlin at the beginning of shooting on his film *One, Two, Three* (1961) Wilder was praised by East Berliners for his severe criticism of the American capitalist system—as they saw it— in *The Apartment* (1960). It could only happen in New York, he was told. 'Yes,' he is said to have replied, 'it could never happen in Moscow. Nobody in Moscow has an apartment he can spare.' The report may not be up to the standard of his habitually corrosive dialogue, but it does illustrate Wilder's determination that there shall be no complacency unprodded, and no easy alignment for him, political or artistic, at the expense of hypocrisy. In a natural exile, this innate, bristling independence has made Wilder and his work frequently unpopular, but the same independence and wit are the qualities that have sustained the high standard of his satire. Throughout a long career he has worked in a great variety of genres, with the exception of the Western, and he has been equally unpredictable ideologically.

The Apartment, for instance, despite his retort, could well be seen as a sharp attack on a capitalist society which enshrines the ruthless pursuit of personal ambition. On the other hand, *One, Two, Three,* while not by any means an apology for the virtues of self-help, is no defence either of East German communism. The truth is that no one comes comfortably out of a Wilder picture. This refusal to betray sympathy or award moral marks has been reproved as coldness, bitterness, contempt for the audience, or, more generally, for humanity, and his critics have usually managed to indict Wilder at the same time on the grounds of bad taste. It is possible that Wilder's *saeva indignatio* is occasionally too frivolous to justify the affronts he offers. When Shirley MacLaine tries unsuccessfully to commit suicide in *The Apartment* and receives no sympathy either from her lover on the telephone or from the doctor, it is possible that Wilder runs the risk of appearing to share in the lack of feeling.

Broadly speaking, however, audiences have been more prepared to accept the harshness of this film than that of a later one like *Kiss Me, Stupid* (1964), where the theme of infidelity seemed to be cloaked with less dignity since it was not associated with any indictment of a corrupt system. Certainly Wilder had not suffered as much criticism of his 'bad taste' since the reception of *Ace in the Hole* (1951), thirteen years earlier. *Kiss Me, Stupid* tells the story of a singer on tour who is accidentally marooned for the night in a small town. The singer, Dino, needs a girl every night or he develops an apparently crippling 'headache'. He decides on the wife of the local music-teacher and amateur song-writer, Orville J. Spooner, but the latter, forewarned, substitutes the town's leading bar-girl, Polly the Pistol. Naturally a switch takes place, Dino gets Orville's wife, Orville gets Polly and also, much to his surprise, appears to have sold a song to TV. It will be seen that the theme is basically the same as in *The Apartment*, where the hero leases his apartment to his superiors for illicit liaisons and is rewarded with high-speed promotion. But where the earlier film was arguably aimed at a corrupt business—and therefore more impersonal—system, the later one appeared to be a sweeping condemnation of the American marriage and so to strike much nearer home. For much the same reasons, a year or two later, Jean-Luc Godard was forced by the censors to change the title of his film *La Femme Mariée* to the more specific *Une Femme Mariée*, thought to impugn less impertinently the honour of French womanhood.

It might be a justifiable criticism of Wilder to hold that he presents the worst about us with a rather unsavoury relish, but it is unusual for criticism of him to go that deeply into his motives. More often he is simply abused for having told the truth about an unpleasant area of human behaviour. So in the case of his celebrated early film *The Lost Weekend* (1945), the depressing story of an alcoholic, the public were initially shocked because no one had dealt with the subject so realistically before. For all its grimness it turned out to be a great critical and box-office success. It is difficult to know whether the outcry against *Kiss Me, Stupid* was a result of its telling home truths or of its flippancy of tone. Public opinion may have been more prepared to accept a tragedy about adultery and prostitution than a wry joke about them.

On the other hand, seriousness of tone has not always been a defence for Wilder. The trouble with *Ace in the Hole* arose despite, and indeed because of, the profound savagery of the piece. Kirk Douglas plays Chuck Tatum, a hard-up reporter needing a scoop. A man is trapped in a cave by a rock fall and Tatum delays the rescue operation deliberately in order to build up the suspense and importance of the story. The man dies. It wasn't only the press who felt that Wilder's tastes were too bleak and their profession too unfairly slandered. The public, the critics and the studio all felt that Wilder's revelation of human motives at their basest was unacceptable. This was also Wilder's first picture after the break-up with Charles Brackett, and the obvious inference was drawn that Brackett had been responsible for lending a humane softness to Wilder's misanthropy. But the corollary is that Wilder, who works always with script collaborators, is simply blown hither and thither by them. Neither of these assertions is provable and both are unlikely—Brackett, after all, scripted *The Lost Weekend*—and the most that can be said is that Wilder is sufficiently aware of the virtues of collaboration. If some distinction is to be made between *The Apartment* and *Kiss Me, Stupid,* the one for its savagery, the other for its flippancy, it cannot be attributed to the nature of the script collaboration, since Wilder worked with I. A. L. Diamond on both. On the other hand, the lightness of

'Ready, Mr DeMille!': Gloria Swanson in *Sunset Boulevard*.

touch in *The Seven Year Itch* (1955), for instance, ought perhaps to be attributed to the personality of the original playwright, George Axelrod, and although there are stories indicating that Wilder merely wanted to use the original as a springboard, the finished piece still bears a strong resemblance to Axelrod's own later work as a director (e.g. *The Secret Life of an American Wife*). The distinction is that in Axelrod's own film adultery does, in fact, take place, whereas in the Wilder picture it is simply threatened. But this is a mark of the change in fashion and public opinion over ten years, a reflection of what Axelrod knew he could get away with rather than what he wanted to write.

It's interesting to speculate on how much Wilder's occasional unpopularity and his ability to shock has been simply a matter of his being ahead of his time; of how much, indeed, he has helped to change public opinion rather than, as is often alleged, impose his own bad taste. Certainly the story of *The Seven Year Itch* offers endless opportunity for jokes in bad taste which Wilder on other occasions might have exploited. But the piece is unusually genial. Tom Ewell plays the husband whose wife is temporarily away from home and who becomes oppressed by the charms of a naïve blonde upstairs (Marilyn Monroe), who has little notion of the impact she makes. The closest the film gets to visual innuendo is an episode with a champagne bottle in which Tom Ewell gets his finger stuck. Subsequently the bottle produces its customary symbolic effervescence. Marilyn Monroe's most famous line is the revelation that she keeps her underwear in the icebox; and the pleasure of the film derives in large measure from such unconscious and mildly *risqué* exchanges.

The danger that Wilder most often courts springs as much from irreverence as from cynicism. It is an aesthetic problem rather than a moral one; it is that he has difficulty in sustaining the tone in any one genre. Accusations of bad taste arise most often when there has been a sudden change in tone —as when the hitherto comic character of Fran Kubelick (Shirley MacLaine) in *The Apartment* genuinely tries to commit suicide. For consistency of tone in both registers, serious and comic, Wilder's greatest successes have perhaps been *Double Indemnity* (1944)

and *Sunset Boulevard* on the one hand and *Some Like It Hot* (1959) on the other. *Double Indemnity* is a chillingly controlled story of an insurance crime. An insurance agent (Fred MacMurray) falls in love with an attractive married woman (Barbara Stanwyck), sells the husband a policy on his life and, in collaboration with the woman, murders him. There's a typical Wilder twist. They discover that they cannot collect the insurance. There is little tenderness between the lovers, moreover, since the insurance salesman finds out that the woman has been using him as a dupe. Their crime is discovered. If there is little reward for virtue in Wilder's universe, there is little reward for vice either. Chuck Tatum is stabbed to death. Joe Gillies, the unsuccessful scriptwriter of *Sunset Boulevard*, is not only the narrator of the film, he is also dead, just as Walter Neff, the insurance salesman, had been the narrator of his own crime in *Double Indemnity*. It is almost as though the characters are doomed from the start, and a cruel determination nips any human aspiration—even a criminal one—in the bud. The only alternative that Wilder occasionally manages is a descent into a saccharine and unconvincing resolution, engineered by a strange trick of fortune or a change in character. Thus the spineless and sycophantic C. C. Baxter (Jack Lemmon) in *The Apartment* suddenly determines to abandon ambition in favour of true love. Or the soft and easy-going loser of *The Fortune Cookie* (U.K.: *Meet Whiplash Willie*, 1966), Harry Hinkle (Jack Lemmon), although persuaded by his smart brother-in-law (Walter Matthau) to claim for monumental damages after a slight accident, actually turns out to be a moral winner in the end in a sudden assertion of character.

What holds Joe Gillies (William Holden) and the ageing ex-star Norma Desmond (Gloria Swanson) together in *Sunset Boulevard* is not love but mutual exploitation. She needs a young man around to sustain her illusions of unfaded beauty and stardom. He needs her financial cover while he tries to write. When she fears that Joe is leaving her, she kills him and goes mad. As a portrait of failure and the psychotic megalomania induced by changes of fortune, it makes a sobering picture. There are conflicting views about how representative of Holly-

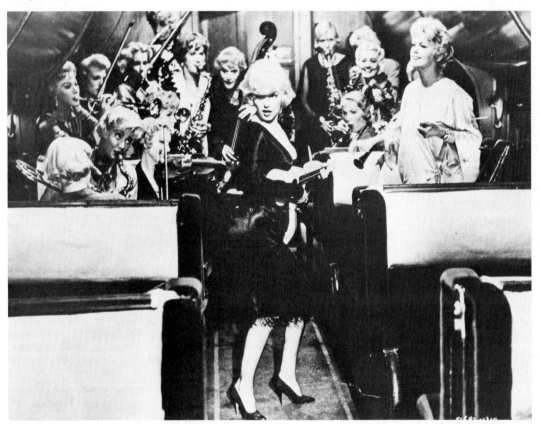

Marilyn Monroe (and, immediately behind her, Tony Curtis and Jack Lemmon in drag) in the 'Runnin' Wild' number from *Some Like It Hot*.

wood it is, but it is certainly imaginatively true about a central aspect of the dream factory's processing: that it attracts mediocre talents like Joe Gillies and squashes them by the hundred; and that it inflates real talents like Norma Desmond for a few years before exploding them and casting them aside. There is a certain grave elegance about the shape of the film, due largely to the strength of having taken opposite ends of the Hollywood spectrum—Joe and Norma—and joined them in a symbolic marriage of inconvenience. And there is a certain asperity about Wilder's implied reproof to the sensation-hungry audience which has spawned these creatures. That reproof—the charge of moral guilt laid on the audience—is at the heart of some of his best work, and it returns strongly in a more recent film, *The Private Life of Sherlock Holmes* (1970).

In the comic register, Wilder's most con-sistently brilliant piece of tightrope-walking has perhaps been *Some Like It Hot*, in which two male dance-band players (Jack Lemmon and Tony Curtis) smuggle themselves on to an all-girl band tour in order to escape retribution from the assassins of the St Valentine Day's Massacre which they happen to have witnessed. The ruse demands that the two men be in drag for large parts of the film, and it leads to predictable but comic encounters in the girls' sleeping-car. Once again Marilyn Monroe is the curvaceous *ingénue*, and Wilder has complicated her naïvety this time by adding, to her innate simplicity, an unawareness that her new admirers are male. Even the massacre is acceptably risible, such is the firmness of Wilder's control, and despite the dangers, he manages to keep the film from darkening at any point. Instead it rises steadily to a fine farcical climax in which a lecherous million-

aire, Joe E. Brown, elopes with the trans-
vestite Lemmon. To Lemmon's resigned confession that he is a man after all, the satisfied
Brown offers the memorable reply: 'Well,
nobody's perfect.'

And, to the charge that Wilder has only
contempt for his audience, it might be
returned that it is the business of the satirist
to confound expectations, and at his most
original Wilder plays strongly against our
stock responses. This has never been more
true than in *The Private Life of Sherlock
Holmes*. The very title suggests some scandalous revelation about a figure of great
moral dignity. At one point Watson asks
Holmes if it would not be too presumptuous
to enquire whether there have been any women in Holmes' life. Yes, answers Holmes, it
would be too presumptuous. The face that
Holmes turns to Watson is cold and private
and we, like Watson, are crushed. Wilder has
stirred our salacious curiosity and made us
feel ashamed, but also a little disappointed.
We are to be further disappointed in our heroic superman. Almost every decision that
Holmes makes is wrong, almost every conclusion, it transpires, is inaccurate. The
government, the state, the organization, in
the person of his brother Mycroft, who is
something important in Whitehall, was there
before him. It is Holmes now who is crushed
and who turns for comfort at last—answering
one question—to the glamorous woman spy
who is mysteriously involved. Alas, brother
Mycroft later reveals, she has paid the price
of her dangerous calling before a foreign firing squad. Holmes, his super-powers set at
naught, his first known romantic attachment
ended in tragedy, retires to 221b Baker Street
and his hypodermic needle.

Though it is as resolute as ever in con-
founding audience expectations, there is yet
something new in tone about the film. Beneath the witty and perverse surface there are
hints of a deeper feeling than usual. But
instead of sudden irruptions of tragedy above
an otherwise flippant surface, there seem
here to be darker currents running throughout the work, a subterranean sadness in the
very presence of Holmes which allows the
film to turn serious without an abrupt change
of direction. There is no lack of irreverence,
no lack of 'bad taste' jokes, no fear that Wilder is losing his cutting edge; but rather the

hope that he has struck a mode in which his
robust vulgarity and his passionate seriousness can co-exist.

Avanti! (1972) confirmed Millar's 'hope that
he has struck a mode in which his robust
vulgarity and his passionate seriousness can
co-exist'. For what could be more vulgar
than a comedy about two middle-aged people
who meet when each comes to claim the
corpse of a parent, only to discover that the
two loved ones had been lovers? This is
'meeting cute' with a vengeance. And yet
from this unpromising premise, Wilder
made one of his most moving films. The director himself characteristically claimed that
Avanti! was 'too mild, too mellow, too
gentle'; and maybe it was, in terms of box-
office, but only in those terms.

The Front Page (1974) did much better at
the box-office, but for those who had seen
either of the earlier versions (Milestone or
Hawks) this was a Front Page padded out to
novelette length. As always there were some
good performances, but one didn't feel that
Wilder's heart (yes, I am convinced he has
one) was in it.

Fedora (1978) was announced by Wilder as
his first serious picture since *Witness for the
Prosecution* and his first picture in Hollywood since *Sunset Boulevard*. Since it is also
about an ageing (ageless) Hollywood star, it
will inevitably be compared with *Sunset
Boulevard*, and, I fear, found wanting. What
is particularly wanting is one of the stars of
Witness for the Prosecution: Marlene Dietrich. The role of Fedora seems to have been
written for her, and it is unfortunate that
she was not able (or willing?) to play the
part. *Sunset Boulevard* succeeded because
one could easily believe Gloria Swanson had
been a great star. For one thing, she really
had been; for another, she has, as she constantly proclaimed, a face. Hildegard Kneff
does not. Furthermore, the very ingenious
'twist' in the story of the film is badly handled: it comes far too late in the film to do
any good. One sits there saying, my, that's
clever, but two-thirds of the film are over by
then, and the revelation doesn't work as well
as it would have had it come earlier. Still,
the film has its funny moments, like the one
in which the regal Fedora, on being told by a
young man she fancies that he usually takes
his dates out for a cheeseburger, replies
'And what, may I ask, is a cheeseburger?' It
is also a very handsome picture to look at
(photography by Gerry Fisher and sets by

Alexandre Trauner) and listen to (music by Miklos Rosza).

For further reading, see Axel Madsen's *Billy Wilder* (1968), Tom Wood's *The Bright Side of Billy Wilder, Primarily* (1970) and Maurice Zolotow's *Billy Wilder In Hollywood* (1977).

ROBERT WISE

John Russell Taylor

Robert Wise (born 1914) is almost the type of the stunningly capable Hollywood craftsman who can turn his hand successfully to almost any genre, do a thoroughly creditable job on it and make a long list of distinguished movies without ever really leaving, or perhaps trying to leave, much personal mark on any of them. For that reason he is never likely to be rediscovered by French intellectuals, or to get much serious attention from anyone else, except of course the moneymen, who are very properly respectful of his track record as a director of big moneymaking films. Ironically, the biggest moneymaker of them all, *The Sound of Music* (1965), was one of the films he least wanted to do and he had to be lured into with all sorts of financial blandishments. Despite which, it is extraordinarily successful in keeping at bay the worst possibilities of mawkish sentiment inherent in the subject, and is a film of real charm—the only one of the monster supermusicals of the 60s that is. More aesthetically successful, anyway, than the more pretentious *West Side Story* (1961), which he co-directed with the show's original stage deviser and director Jerome Robbins and which never quite makes up its mind whether it is going to be a neo-realist musical of social comment or a good old-fashioned Hollywood fantasy star vehicle.

Before Wise made his two big musicals he had been associated, in so far as he can be said to have specialized in anything, with horror films and rather savagely realistic dramas. He started out as an editor (most important credits on *Citizen Kane* and *The Magnificent Ambersons*) and graduated to direction under the banner of Val Lewton, horror king of the 40s, with *The Curse of the Cat People* (1944) and *The Body Snatcher* (1945), two superbly atmospheric pieces for which he

seems to have had a real fondness, especially since later on, when he had considerable freedom of action, he punctuated his superproductions with one modest return to the genre, *The Haunting* (1963). From the rest of his pre-*West Side Story* films, three detach themselves as having some extra quality: *The Set-Up* (1949), a really uncompromising boxing drama; *I Want to Live* (1958), the story of the conviction and execution of Barbara Graham (Susan Hayward), with its famous gas chamber finale; and *Odds Against Tomorrow* (1959), a rather meditative, downbeat film about a robbery, very stylishly shot in a frosty winter New York. Plus one cult science-fiction film which still looks pretty good, *The Day the Earth Stood Still* (1951). Since 1961 it has all been big productions (apart from *The Haunting*), more or less memorably carried through. *Star!* (1968), a biography of Gertrude Lawrence which was his follow-up vehicle for Julie Andrews after *The Sound of Music*, was a famous box-office disaster but contains some of his (and her) best work. *The Andromeda Strain* (1971) is a very superior piece of science fiction. And then there is *The Hindenburg* (1975), a contribution to the fashionable wave of disaster films. All very well, all very workmanlike. But it seems unlikely at this late stage that the real Robert Wise will ever stand up and be recognized.

It is curious to note that *Star!* was conceived on something like the same principle as *Citizen Kane*: beginning in a screening room looking at film clips and then going into flashback. I also think that *Star!* was much under-rated, probably because the serious critics can't stand Julie Andrews.

WILLIAM WYLER

Andrew Sarris

Although William Wyler's credits extend officially from 1926 to 1970, his period of pre-eminence was between 1936 (*Dodsworth*) and 1946 (*The Best Years of Our Lives*). Orson Welles has called Wyler, not inaptly, the great producer among directors; that is to say, the masterly selector of shots, the compleat angler of the most gripping camera angles. André Bazin hailed Wyler for liberating the cinema from montage with his long takes and deep-focus compositions, and the battle cry for a time (for both Bazin and his colleague Roger Leenhardt) was '*A bas Ford! Vive Wyler!*' Earlier, John Grierson had praised Wyler for his high-minded sobriety. A more conventional view of Wyler around Hollywood was that of the punctilious perfectionist, the scourge of stars, particularly in the more affluent period in which he was nicknamed 'Ninety-Take Wyler'. As compensation for some of the victims of Wyler's painstaking devotion to detail are the Oscars resting on the mantelpieces of Bette Davis (2), Walter Brennan (2), Audrey Hepburn, Olivia De Havilland, Greer Garson, Teresa Wright, Fay Bainter, Fredric March, Burl Ives, Charlton Heston, Barbra Streisand, and that agonizingly award-winning one-shot amputee, Harold Russell, who so traumatically tested the liberal conscience in *The Best Years of Our Lives*.

William Wyler was born in 1902 in Mulhouse, Alsace, then part of Germany. He received his education at Lausanne and the National Music Conservatory in Paris, where in 1920 he met 'Uncle' Carl Laemmle, head of Universal Pictures, and accepted a movie job in New York. After moving up to publicity director in the distribution end of the industry, he went to Hollywood, where he worked his way from prop boy to director of some fifty two-reel Westerns in 1926 and 1927. 'I made 'em in three days and for $2,000.' By 1928 he was promoted to five-reel Tom Mix vehicles and occasional 'Easterns'. He gradually built a minor reputation at Universal with *Hell's Heroes* (1930), a film which he took out of the studio vaults ten years later and re-edited to his own satisfaction; *A House Divided* (1932), a grim, Calvinistic picture patterned after Eugene O'Neill's *Desire Under the Elms*, with a memorable performance by Walter Huston writhing in

Walter Huston and Mary Astor in *Dodsworth*: you couldn't tell from this still, but this may well be Wyler's finest film.

Herbert Marshall and Bette Davis in *The Little Foxes*: a characteristic 'deep-focus' shot photographed by Gregg Toland.

Lon Chaneyish contortions as a crippled patriarch; *Counsellor-at-Law* (1933), highlighted by one of John Barrymore's best screen performances and one of the first cinematic intimations of melting-pot politics and anti-Semitic snobbery; and *The Good Fairy* (1935) starring Margaret Sullavan, who quarrelled with Wyler during the shooting, married him when the picture was completed and divorced him more than a year later.

With *These Three* in 1936, Wyler began a long and profitable association with producer Sam Goldwyn and cinematographer Gregg Toland. Critics became aware of a distinctive style in *Dodsworth*, *Come and Get It* (1936), which Wyler finished after director Howard Hawks left the project, *Dead End* (1937), *Wuthering Heights* (1939), *The Westerner* (1940) and *The Little Foxes* (1941), in addition to such gilded Bette Davis vehicles at Warners as *Jezebel* (1938) and *The Letter* (1940). In close collaboration with Toland, who traumatized the industry in 1941 with his photography for Welles' *Citizen Kane*,

Wyler developed an unusually deep focus for scenes, reducing cuts and close-ups to keep groups of characters within the frame for long periods without undue 'star' emphasis. This imposed a greater burden on actors to play a scene through in one long take rather than in a series of intercut sequences. Wyler explained his infrequent use of the close-up by citing films where the cutting 'didn't coincide with what I wanted to see. They'd hold on to a close-up so long I'd find myself trying to look around the corner for the other characters.'

During the Second World War Wyler served in the Army Air Force and went on several bombing missions to obtain footage for his acclaimed war documentary *The Memphis Belle* (1944). He also transcribed the exploits of fighter planes in the film *Thunderbolt* (1945). After *The Best Years of Our Lives* in 1946, Wyler's career followed an extremely eclectic pattern, from the warmed-over melodramatic theatricality of *The Heiress* (1949) and *Detective Story* (1951) to the drably

Dreiserian pathos of *Carrie* (1952); from the occasionally broad romantic comedy of *Roman Holiday* (1953) to the hyped-up domestic heroics of *The Desperate Hours* (1955); from the ponderously pacifist allegories of *Friendly Persuasion* (1956) and *The Big Country* (1958) to the overstuffed biblical epic *Ben Hur* (1959) and the unexpurgated remake of Lillian Hellman's latently lesbian *The Children's Hour* (U.K.: *The Loudest Whisper*, 1961), a quarter of a century after the censor had imposed heterosexuality on the 1936 version entitled *These Three*. Wyler redeemed his reputation somewhat with the expressively (if repressively) erotic *The Collector* (1965), a project with a cast of two (Terence Stamp and Samantha Eggar) for which his meticulous craftsmanship was ideally suited. It seems fitting that the French director Henri Verneuil should have lauded Wyler's art as 'the style without a style'. A less kindly critic once suggested: 'Subtract Toland from Welles, and you still have a mountain; subtract Toland from Wyler, and you have a molehill.' The polemics of *politiques* aside, there is surely more to be said about Wyler than that. Grierson, Bazin and Verneuil saw something up there on the screen, and it has to be faced—at the very least—as a personal style of sorts.

Even Wyler's directorial faults can be made to fit into the notion of a personal style. Hence, his lack of a light touch makes him gravitate most often to relatively serious jects where the comedy, if any, can be relegated to relief. But then again, his lack of spiritual depth seems to soften the harsh contours of morbid romances like *Jezebel* and *Wuthering Heights*.

Although William Wyler belongs to that category of director who began in the silent era, he seems (even more than Ford and Hawks) to have come into his own only at the dawn of the talkies. Hence, there is no mention of Wyler in the conventional film histories before *Hell's Heroes* in 1930. Basil Wright notes in his compendium of conventional wisdom, *The Long View*: 'In *Hell's Heroes*, a film of frank and frantic sentimentality by William Wyler, an effective *coup de cinéma* occurs when the sound of a church choir and congregation singing Christmas carols is suddenly switched off when the rough old villain staggers up the aisle carrying a baby he has brought across the desert at the cost of his own life. The audience is made to switch its identification from the church scene to the man himself at the point of death. It may sound a corny idea, but it was enormously effective.'

Until 1936 Wyler worked exclusively at Universal, and many of his films from this period remain obscure to this day. Still, from 1928 on, Wyler never made more than two movies a year, which indicates that a certain care (or procrastination) went into his most routine projects. Thus, Wyler was never as prolific as such legendary first-take speedsters as William Wellman, Michael Curtiz, Mervyn LeRoy and W. S. Van Dyke.

When Wyler left Universal for Sam Goldwyn in 1935, first to finish *Come and Get It* and then to do *Dodsworth* and *These Three*, a distinctive Wyler look emerged on the screen. At first it was considered simply a 'Goldwyn' look, and then, much later, a 'Toland' look. Whatever it was, it was a look that lasted for ten years until it reached its apotheosis in *The Best Years of Our Lives*. But it is unlikely that this look would have attracted much attention if it had not been coupled for the most part with a serious, high-minded, liberal concern with various social issues. As a producer, Goldwyn could be credited with an itch for 'significance', and he managed to recruit such writers as Lillian Hellman (*These Three*, *Dead End* [from the play by Sidney Kingsley], *The Little Foxes*), Sidney Howard (*Dodsworth*), Edna Ferber (*Come and Get It*), Robert Sherwood (*The Best Years of Our Lives*) and even Dorothy Parker for additional dialogue for *The Little Foxes*. What must be remembered is that the criticism of the sound film has seldom been able to appreciate stylistic achievements divorced from impressive 'themes'. Also, there was a carry-over effect when a director or producer changed pace with a divertissement after having done something 'important'. Thus, an aura persisted around such relatively frivolous Wyler enterprises as *The Letter*, *The Westerner*, *The Heiress* and *Roman Holiday* because of points previously scored with *The Little Foxes*, *Mrs Miniver* (1942) and *The Best Years of Our Lives*.

None the less, Wyler did achieve a special working relationship with Toland from their

In the foreground, Hoagy Carmichael, Harold Russell and Fredric March; way in the back (deep-focus *mise-en-scène* at its most extreme) Dana Andrews making a phone call: *The Best Years of Our Lives*.

first encounter on the set of *These Three*. As Wyler recalled this fateful and fruitful moment in film history (in *William Wyler* by Axel Madsen):

I was in the habit of saying, 'Put the camera here and shoot it with a forty milli-meter,' or 'Move the camera this way, or Light it this way.' Suddenly, Toland wanted to quit. I didn't understand why and he finally came to me to tell me he wasn't a man to be told every move. You just didn't tell Gregg what lens to use, you told him what mood you were after. When he photographed something, he wanted to go beyond lights and catch feelings. As we got to know each other, we evolved a smooth and beautiful relationship. We would discuss a picture from beginning to end, its overall 'feel' and then the style of each sequence. Toland was an artist.

The camera is a marvellous instrument. You have to use it with discipline. Any imaginative director who stages a scene or uses a set gets all kinds of ideas. That's great but you have to discipline yourself. Many cameramen's ideas of a good scene is when all the actors hit their cut marks. Soundmen like it when everything is very clear. This is where Toland was different.

His style of photography would vary just like my style of directing. In *Dead End*, we had a different style of photography than in *Wuthering Heights* or in *These Three*. Here, we were dealing with little girls' things. What was good was rather simple, attractive photography. In *Dead End*, we had flat, hard lights. We used open sun-arcs from behind the camera. We didn't try to make anybody look pretty. With Toland, I would re-hearse and show him a scene. Then, we would decide together how to photograph it. I would have certain ideas and he would contribute to them and together we would determine what was best.

One might say that Wyler made a virtue of eclecticism even in his professional relationship with Toland, but it isn't as simple as that. If Wyler has been penalized by the *auteur*ist critics, it is not because he lacks a personal style. Rather, it is because there is no thematic thread running from *Lazy Lightning* in 1926 to *The Liberation of L. B. Jones* in 1970. Wyler himself has never played the poetic personality game. More the captain of the team or the chairman of the board, he has none the less evolved into a recognizable stylist. From *The Letter* in 1940 to *Funny Girl* (1968), Wyler's *mise en scène* for a triangular sofa and suspended composition retains all its characteristic lines of force and tension. We can therefore deduce that from 1936 on, the very careful preparation of each Wyler project included stretching the screenplay to accommodate a scene in which two or more characters were suspended in the same frame of the film, but at a focal distance great enough to sustain a sombre mood of conflict and alienation.

The danger, as always, is that the Wyler–Toland collaboration can be overstressed as an example of the paradigmatic fallacy, that tendency in film criticism to select only those sequences which illustrate a stylistic thesis. During Wyler's best period (1936–46), he was in close rapport with many talented people in the film industry, particularly such players as Walter Huston, Ruth Chatterton and Mary Astor in *Dodsworth*, Bette Davis in her most prestigious films—*Jezebel*, *The Letter* and *The Little Foxes*—Laurence Olivier in *Wuthering Heights* and the talented all-star cast of *The Best Years of Our Lives*. He seemed in those years to be always on time, and no one noticed a certain coldness in his contemplative gaze, a certain fastidiousness in his manner—as if he could not bear to be too deeply involved with the feelings of his characters. Later, the coldness was unrelieved, and Wyler's career faltered during the death-throes of the studio system. He won the Grand Prix at Cannes in 1956 for the noble intentions of *Friendly Persuasion*, and he swept all the Academy Awards in 1959 for the chariot race in *Ben Hur*, but he was no longer on time with the *Zeitgeist*, and in the 60s it was an uphill struggle. But to the end his work was never shoddy, even when it was empty. In retrospect he belongs less with a Renoir or a Lubitsch as a personal director than with a Clair or a Mamoulian as an *objet d'art* director.

One could make out a case that Wyler was the American Carné, only instead of having a house scriptwriter (like Jacques Prévert) he had a house cameraman (Gregg Toland). In any case, both Carné and Wyler made some great films, and both were ten-year men.
The authorized biography, *William Wyler* (1973), is by Axel Madsen.

KRZYSZTOF ZANUSSI

James Monaco

Krzysztof Zanussi (born 1939) studied physics and philosophy before taking a degree from the Lodz film school, where his diploma film, *Smierc Prowincjala* (*Death of a Provincial*, 1966), won several international awards. He then shot several television films, of which the best known is his portrait of the composer Krzysztof Penderecki. With his first feature, *Struktura Krysztalu* (*The Structure of Crystals*, 1969), Zanussi embarked on a series of films notable both for their unusual setting—the scientific community—and for the way in which he uses the particular dilemmas of careers in science to investigate more general philosophical problems. *The Structure of Crystals* was a vector analysis of the divergent careers of two old friends, one of whom had successfully joined the scientific élite while the other had retreated to duty at a remote weather station. *Zycie Rodzinne* (*Family Life*, 1971), was an environmental experiment: a young technician is thrust back into the melancholic, almost Chekhovian world of his family which his training had allowed him to escape. His reactions to the now strange environment are instructive, if typical. *Za Ściana* (*Behind the Wall*, 1971), was a wry morality tale which described parallel geometries between professional politics on the one hand and personal, romantic emotions on the other. *Illuminacja* (*Illumination*, 1973), was an essay in moral and ethical theses couched in the form of a survey of the student days and early career of a young scientist, giving equal balance to his professional life (and the intellectual dilemmas it raises) and his private life (and the emotional problems it presents). Intercutting documentary scenes, *Illumination* is, so far, the most complete summary of Zanussi's complex intelligence. This intelligence, combined with the traditional humane realism of his films and their gritty and involving imagery, places his work in the vanguard of Eastern European cinema.

Zanussi made *Bilans Kwartalny* (*Quarterly Balance* [U.S.: *A Woman's Decision*], 1974) and *The Catamount Killing* in 1975, a straight genre film shot in Vermont with West German and English actors.

Zanussi's last two films were both disappointing; the first too unfocused, the second too unambitious. But in 1977 he returned to form in *Barwy Ochronne* (*Camouflage*), an incisive picture of the academic world. At a summer camp for scientists, a young man at the beginning of his career is confronted by an embittered and cynical older colleague. Their clash is all the more violent through Zanussi's characteristic use of understatement.

See the article on Polish Cinema since the War.

[*continued from p. iv, Volume One*]

Ceskoslovensky Filmexport: pp. 249, 251; RKO: pp. 258, 378–9, 476, 808, 911; Sud Pacific: p. 273; Soviexport: pp. 286–7, 324–5, 557, 559, 570, 802, 944, 1024; Palladium Productions: pp. 295, 306–7; Société des Films Armor: p. 330; Films Gaumont: pp. 352–3, 356–7, 495, 1040; International Film Seminars: p. 370; Forces et Voix de France: p. 387; Peter Darvill Assoc.: p. 390; August et Louis Lumière: p. 395; The Images Film Archive, Inc.: pp. 408–9; Transit Films: p. 422; Referat Audiovisuelle Medien: pp. 427, 430; Werner Herzog Filmproduktion: p. 435; Dino de Laurentiis Corps.: pp. 438–9, 526, 894–5; Artcraft: p. 456; Film Polski: pp. 464, 783, 789, 790; RTF: p. 472; Alfred Hitchcock, p. 504; Daiei Motion Picture Co. Ltd: pp. 519, 574, 578–9; Ambrosio-Caesare: p. 528; Samuel Goldwyn Productions: pp. 550, 1088, 1089, 1091; Hungarofilm: p. 535; Anthony Morris Ltd: p. 604; Grand National: p. 615; Cineromans Pathé: p. 626; National Film Finance Corps: p. 637; Decla-Bioscop: p. 642; Sofracima: p. 669; USIS: p. 680; OGC Prod.: p. 683; Scotia Barker: p. 685; UFA: p. 715; W. E. Bedford: p. 719; Titanus: p. 725; Carlton Film Export: p. 726; Elite Tonfilm Prod.: p. 729; Anatole Dauman: p. 742; Toho Co. Ltd: pp. 748–9; Gladiator Films: p. 759; GALA: p. 762; PEA Produzioni: pp. 768–9; ABC Films International: p. 773; EMI: p. 793; NTA: p. 810; R. D. Bansal Prod.: pp. 826–7; MOMA Film Stills Library: p. 837; Nouvelles Editions Françaises: pp. 842–3; Argos Films: pp. 738, 858–9; Action Films: pp. 865, 998, 999; Imperial War Museum: p. 868; Bundesarchive, Koblenz: p. 870; Société Nouvelle de Cinematographie: p. 872; Marceau Cocinor: p. 874; Fechner (Films) Christian: p. 877; Films du Losange: pp. 882–3, 908; Keystone Film Company: p. 919; Cinema International Corp.: pp. 925, 927; London Films: pp. 956–7; Specta: p. 1004; Les Films du Carosse: pp. 1012, 1017; Ciné Tamaris: p. 1020; Vides Cinematographica SpA: p. 1042; Lux: p. 1046; A. B. Europa Film: p. 1077; Mirisch Corp. of California: p. 1085. Pp. 209, 211 © *The Roy Export Company Establishment*. Stills of the films *Odd Man Out* (p. 830) and *Great Expectations* (p. 834) by courtesy of The Rank Organisation Ltd.

INDEX

Figures in **bold type** indicate illustrations

Index